Exceptional Lives

Special Education in Today's Schools

Fourth Edition

Rud Turnbull
University of Kansas

Ann Turnbull
University of Kansas

Marilyn Shank
University of Charleston

Sean J. Smith
University of Kansas

PEARSON

Merrill
Prentice Hall

Upper Saddle River, New Jersey
Columbus, Ohio

Library of Congress Cataloging in Publication Data

Exceptional lives : special education in today's schools / Rud Turnbull . . . [et al.].—4th ed.
  p. cm.
  Includes bibliographical references and indexes.
  ISBN 0-13-112600-8 (paper)
  1. Children with disabilities—Education—United States—Case studies. 2. Special
education—United States—Case studies. 3. Inclusive education—United States—Case
studies. I. Turnbull, Rud

LC4031.E87 2004
371.9'0973—dc21   2003041234

Vice President and Executive Publisher: Jeffery W. Johnston
Editor: Allyson P. Sharp
Development Editor: Heather Doyle Fraser
Editorial Assistant: Kathleen S. Burk
Production Editor: Sheryl Glicker Langner
Photo Coordinator: Valerie Schultz
Design Coordinator: Diane C. Lorenzo
Cover Designer: Ali Mohrman
Production Manager: Laura Messerly
Director of Marketing: Ann Castel Davis
Marketing Manager: Amy June
Marketing Coordinator: Tyra Poole

This book was set in Goudy by Carlisle Communications, Ltd. It was printed and bound by R. R.
Donnelley & Sons Company. The cover was printed by Phoenix Color Corp.

Photo Credits: Photo credits are on page 565.

Pearson Education Ltd.   Pearson Education Australia Pty. Limited
Pearson Education Singapore Pte. Ltd.   Pearson Education North Asia Ltd.
Pearson Education Canada, Ltd.   Pearson Educación de Mexico, S.A. de C.V.
Pearson Education—Japan   Pearson Education Malaysia Pte. Ltd.

10 9 8 7 6 5 4 3 2 1
ISBN: 0-13-112600-8

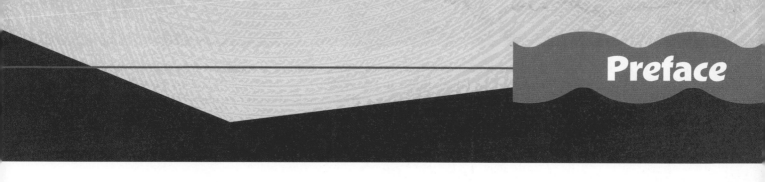

Our Vision

Consider two different lives, those of the children of three of the authors. Jay Turnbull is 35; that means he was one of the very first students to benefit from the federal special education law (enacted in 1975, when he was 8 years old). In those days, special education was in its infancy; the education he received was good enough—nothing great except occasionally and then largely because of a few exceptionally gifted teachers.

Nolan Smith is two. That means he is one of the many students who is now benefitting from a well-developed special education system that came into his life at the very beginning—not, as in Jay's case, when he was entering his ninth year of life. Unlike Jay, Nolan will benefit from new teaching techniques (universally designed learning), new models (inclusion and access to the general curriculum), new procedures (collaboration), and new understandings (about them and their peers from multicultural backgrounds). That is exactly how it should be: The new ways should replace the old if they provide more benefits. So much for looking back. Now, let's look forward.

Our vision defies specification. It is general, nothing more. One part of it is that what educators now regard as new will persist if it benefits students—all students, not just those with disabilities. Another part is that educators will continue to develop better ways to raise America's children. Yet another is that our country will finally face the realities of poverty and diversity and commit resources—not money alone, but also imagination and courage—to the students and families who are traditionally un- and under-served.

To the degree that this book makes it possible for educators to leave no child and family and teacher behind, fine. But there must be more. We educators must find better ways to educate children. And we must find the common ground and the new words to make it self-evident that we have not done enough for those who are, by one measure or another, "exceptional."

Only when "un" and "under" are purged from "served" and replaced with "well and rightly" will America's schools fulfill their promise: full citizenship for all students. That is what Jay sought and eventually received; that is what Nolan can almost take for granted, at least for now; and that is the birthright of all students and the obligation of all educators.

Our Book's Organization

Chapters 1 through 3 lay the foundation for the rest of our book. They tell a bit about history, quite a lot about the Individuals with Disabilities Education Act (IDEA), the law that Congress passed in 1975 and that it amended in 1997, and a great deal about today's schools. Most of all, they introduce you to our primary message: All teachers can educate students with disabilities, especially in the general curriculum, by using the principles of universal design, inclusion, collaboration, and multicultural responsiveness. We build on this foundation by describing in Chapters 4 through 16 how to educate students in special education—those who have disabilities (Chapters 4 though 6 and 8 through 16 are about students who have various kinds of disabilities) and those who have unusual gifts and talents (Chapter 7). When we write about the students with various kinds of exceptionalities, we use a "categorical" approach: Each chapter describes a different "category" or type of student—for example, Chapter 4 describes those with learning disabilities and Chapter 5 describes those with emotional or behavioral disorders.

Chapter Format

Chapters 4 through 16 have the same "flavor" and format. Their similar flavor comes from the four themes that we weave throughout each chapter: universal design, inclusion, collaboration, and multicultural responsiveness. Their similar format comes from the way we present our information. Each chapter follows this order:

▼ *Vignettes.*   We begin each chapter with a vignette, a short portrait of real students, real families, and real educators—the people in today's schools. These people represent a wide range of cultural, ethnic, linguistic, and socioeconomic groups, and they live in a wide variety of geographic locations.

▼ *Categorical Information.*   Next, we define the exceptionality, describe its characteristics, and identify its causes and prevalence. At the beginning of each chapter, you get a sharp picture of the exceptionality, framed in its most basic dimensions.

▼ *Evaluation Procedures.*   Now we take you into teachers' working environments. We explain how and why educators evaluate students (does the student described in the vignette have a disability or is the student unusually gifted?) and then how educators provide special education and related services. The process of evaluation is the same for all students with disabilities, no matter what the student's "category" is. This is because the Individuals with Disabilities Education Act sets out a standardized process. But the tools—the evaluation instruments—vary by category. We describe one for each category, one state-of-the-art way for determining whether a student is exceptional and, if so, the kind of education that schools should offer. Many of these evaluation tools, however, are suitable for students across various categories, as we often point out.

▼ *Assuring Progress in the General Curriculum.*   In the second half of each chapter, we address four major issues facing teachers in today's schools. Veteran users of this textbook will notice changes in this section that make the book more applied, more pragmatic, and more responsive to the realities of the inclusive classroom. First, we write about including students in the general curriculum in the most appropriate manner for the specific "category" being discussed. Second, we describe in practical terms how to plan universally designed learning by augmenting, altering, or adapting curriculum and instruction, and evaluation. Third, we write about collaboration and how it can make an exceptional student's education truly exceptional. Finally, we discuss how students' different ethnic, linguistic, and cultural backgrounds affect their education.

▼ *Learning from Others Who Teach Students with Exceptionalities.*   In the last section of each chapter, we illustrate how "best practice" programs provide inclusive, universally designed, and collaborative curriculum and instruction, in inclusive settings, at four different age-levels: early intervention and early childhood; elementary; middle and secondary; and transitional and post-secondary.

▼ *A Vision for the Future and Chapter Summary.* Having begun each chapter with a vignette describing the student today, we conclude our narrative by looking toward the student's future and imagining it as it can be if educators and schools do as we suggest. We end by summarizing the main points of the chapter.

Special Chapter Features

Real Students, Real Educators, Real Families, Real Issues

This is not a book of fiction. There are no imagined characters here. Every student, every teacher, every parent, every friend is real. To tell their stories serves a powerful didactic purpose: to describe, in their own words and through these snapshots of their lives, how special education benefits each and every one of them. These students, educators, family members, and friends show you what can happen—how exceptional lives can be made all the more exceptional—when you approach them on the basis of principles and state-of-the-art teaching techniques.

▼ *Chapter Vignettes* narrate the stories of these students and their families, friends, teachers, and other educators and service providers. We refer to these vignettes throughout each chapter to exemplify our key points and content.

▼ *My Voice* is a personal account or reflection about having a disability or talents and about how education affects the person's life; it further connects you to real people and helps you understand the impact you and others can make.

▼ *Making a Difference* describes how one person or a group of people has touched the lives of individuals with exceptionalities, often through their careers. These stories are samples of best practices and show how educators can overcome obstacles to appropriate education in the general curriculum.

Box 2–1

Making a Difference

Barbara Morgan: Forming the Forever Family

Some parents look forward to the empty nest. Barbara Morgan isn't among them. She's got four biological children: Ernie, 40; Mike, 39; Vicky, 38; and Becky, 35. She also has 15 grandchildren, four of whom are adopted. They all live near each other. To boot, in the past 3 years she's had 35 foster children in her home. She adopted three of them: Charity, 16, who has mild mental retardation; Heather, 10, who also has mild mental retardation; and Star, 7, who has severe mental retardation and is nonverbal. (You met Heather and Star in the opening pages of this chapter and have read about them throughout the chapter.) Consider, too, that Barbara is a single parent, and you get the idea that this remarkable woman has an abiding commitment to family.

Every day, Barbara Morgan brings Heather and Star to Luff Elementary School, parks her car, walks into the school building with them, and makes sure to greet the receptionist as many of her children's teachers as she can, catching them in the hallways or, when she has something she needs them to know, going to their classrooms and participating in problem solving.

Barbara is an alumna of Luff Elementary School. So are her four biological children. Thus, when it came to Heather's and Star's education, Barbara's instinct was toward Luff. The school district, however, placed both daughters in a school where the only students were those with disabilities. The girls' education seemed inadequate to Barbara; they were not making the kind of progress at school that they were making at home.

At home, Barbara had confronted and was solving the major challenges that her new daughters brought from their foster homes. Heather had tantrums when she was unable to have all the second and third helpings of food that she wanted; Barbara's response was to show her that there always would be plenty of food to eat, reducing her portions, teaching her to ask for seconds instead of grabbing for more food, and reassuring her that she can have food when she

does not scream. At Heather's first school, none of those techniques were put into place.

At Luff, the staff agreed to uses Barbara's techniques. The result: Heather no longer throws tantrums and screams, politely asks for seconds, and is content to have only first helpings if that is what Barbara has asked the cafeteria staff to provide. A greater result: Heather now is inc[...] lunchtime.

Star pre[...] came to Bar[...] ting, bangin[...] a bath, tota[...] (wrapped a[...] mouth); she [...] ally assaulte[...] a shaken ba[...] smiles, tear[...] with disabili[...] At Luff, [...] (Star's teach[...] class; Donn[...] gnette), wh[...] sign languag[...] taught Star [...] family!

When Ba[...] who, when [...] forever fami[...] will be there [...]

Wherever [...] ementary Sc[...] Barbara, He[...] family."

Box 4–1

My Voice

Rachel's Story: A College Graduate

This past Spring, Rachel—like thousands of other college and university students throughout the country—received her bachelor of arts degree from Mitchell College. Challenged by attention and learning issues throughout her life, Rachel succeeded through hard work, by using structured support, and by making the most of the modifications that had been put into place for her. Rachel's story is like that of many of her peers who are challenged with attention, organization, and time management skills because of a learning disability.

Rachel did well in school until the fifth grade. Attending a private school at the time, she began to notice difficulties in completing her schoolwork and staying on task. Her teachers noticed these difficulties as well and suggested that her parents have her tested.

Rachel and her parents discovered from these tests that she had attention deficit hyperactivity disorder as well as learning problems associated with memory and organization. The test results were a relief in that they helped to explain some of the challenges Rachel was having. She explains, "I was surrounded by all these bright friends that weren't having trouble with the assignments and the homework we had. I, on the other hand, was feeling pretty overwhelmed, and extra effort didn't seem to pay off." Finding out she had a disability didn't offer an immediate answer. Rachel's school was not prepared to meet the needs of students with disabilities, so her parents hired a tutor.

Amy became not just Rachel's tutor but also her advocate and friend. She began tutoring Rachel shortly after Rachel had been identified with attention and learning problems. Amy began by helping Rachel set up an organized and complete notebook. "Before Amy, my notes were all over the place, and I couldn't find what I needed half

the time. Amy helped with my studying but really helped empower me through organization." Amy also taught Rachel how to decide what was important to study, how to study, and how to prepare for tests and exams.

In the classroom, Rachel quickly realized her teachers were not prepared to accommodate her attention and learning needs. At times, some of her teachers were opposed to providing any accommodations for her needs. They seemed to say that if Rachel couldn't be successful on her own, that particular school wasn't the right one for her.

Fortunately, her advisor and Amy were able to advocate for her. Even with all of this support, however, Rachel continued to have problems; and by February of her junior year she was at risk of failing. It was then that her parents sent her to a private boarding school, where she repeated her junior year.

Rachel excelled in this small, supportive environment. Under the guidance of an academic advisor who advocated for her needs in the classroom while also working with her to establish these skills for her own independence, Rachel found the support she needed to remain on task and address some of her learning challenges. "I know most people hated the required study hall, but I loved it. We were all required to study, and this was so necessary for me." Rachel also received additional tutoring, which once again focused on empowering her as a learner. "We focused on learning strategies and memory techniques that I could use to learn the material and, more importantly, remember what I learned."

Rachel's professors also accommodated themselves to Rachel's learning needs. "They all offered me various ways to do my assignments. For instance, instead of papers, I was able to do a number of oral presentations. I got so good at the oral part that I joined debate team and drama club and performed in several plays."

Strategies and Tips for Special Education Teachers

The majority of students with disabilities can progress in the general education curriculum if educators will design programs and classrooms for individualized instruction; provide supplementary supports and services; collaborate with families, other professionals, and community agencies; and respond to the multicultural backgrounds of today's students. So, we offer several guides for general and special educators.

▼ *Into Practice* describes practical, step-by-step examples of how to use universal design, secure inclusion, practice collaboration, and respond to the multicultural nature of American schools.

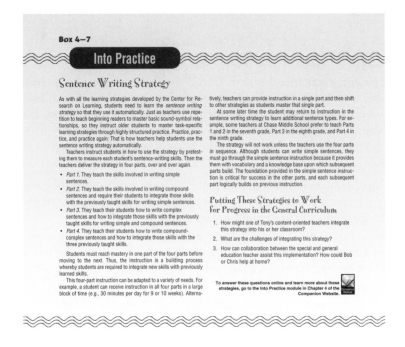

Box 4–7

Into Practice

Sentence Writing Strategy

As with all the learning strategies developed by the Center for Research on Learning, students need to learn the *sentence writing strategy* so that they use it automatically. Just as teachers use repetition to teach beginning readers to master basic sound-symbol relationships, so they instruct older students to master task-specific learning strategies through highly structured practice. Practice, practice, and practice again: That is how teachers help students use the sentence writing strategy automatically.

Teachers instruct students in how to use the strategy by pretesting them to measure each student's sentence-writing skills. Then the teachers deliver the strategy in four parts, over and over again.

- *Part 1.* They teach the skills involved in writing simple sentences.
- *Part 2.* They teach the skills involved in writing compound sentences and require their students to integrate those skills with the previously taught skills for writing simple sentences.
- *Part 3.* They teach their students how to write complex sentences and how to integrate those skills with the previously taught skills for writing simple and compound sentences.
- *Part 4.* They teach their students how to write compound-complex sentences and how to integrate those skills with the three previously taught skills.

Students must reach mastery in one part of the four parts before moving to the next. Thus, the instruction is a building process whereby students are required to integrate new skills with previously learned skills.

This four-part instruction can be adapted to a variety of needs. For example, a student can receive instruction in all four parts in a large block of time (e.g., 30 minutes per day for 9 or 10 weeks). Alternatively, teachers can provide instruction in a single part and then shift to other strategies as students master that single part.

At some later time the student may return to instruction in the sentence writing strategy to learn additional sentence types. For example, some teachers at Chase Middle School prefer to teach Parts 1 and 2 in the seventh grade, Part 3 in the eighth grade, and Part 4 in the ninth grade.

The strategy will not work unless the teachers use the four parts in sequence. Although students can write simple sentences, they must go through the simple sentence instruction because it provides them with vocabulary and a knowledge base upon which subsequent parts build. The foundation provided in the simple sentence instruction is critical for success in the other parts, and each subsequent part logically builds on previous instruction.

Putting These Strategies to Work for Progress in the General Curriculum

1. How might one of Tony's content-oriented teachers integrate this strategy into his or her classroom?
2. What are the challenges of integrating this strategy?
3. How can collaboration between the special and general education teacher assist this implementation? How could Bob or Chris help at home?

To answer these questions online and learn more about these strategies, go to the Into Practice module in Chapter 4 of the Companion Website.

▼ *Inclusion Tips* provide helpful advice and strategies for including students in the general curriculum. We address student behaviors, social interactions, educational performance and classroom attitudes in relation to what teachers may see in the classroom, what they may be tempted to do, other responses, and best practices for including the student's peers in the process.

Inclusion Tips

Box 5–3

	What You Might See	What You Might Be Tempted to Do	Alternate Responses	Ways to Include Peers in the Process
Behavior	The student refuses to follow directions and uses inappropriate language.	Respond in anger and send him out of the classroom. Place him in "time-out" for extended periods of time.	Building on his strengths and interests, try an approach based on catching him being good. Also try contingency contracting.	Use peer mediation as well as group contingencies.
Social interactions	He fights with other students and is always on the defensive.	Separate him from other students to prevent fights.	Give him time to calm down. Then teach appropriate social skills using modeling, videos, and social skills programs.	Pair him with different students who can model and help him practice social skills and responses.
Educational performance	He is rarely on task and appears to have an inability to learn.	Give poor grades and require him to remain until all work is done.	Develop a curriculum based on student interests and a motivational reward system for completed tasks.	Use peer tutoring and also find a buddy willing to be a friend and helpful tutor.
Classroom attitudes	He is depressed or sad all the time and does not speak or interact with others.	Discipline him for nonparticipation, and instruct him to cheer up.	Recognize the warning signs. Refer him for help. Collaborate with the school counselor.	Have different students daily write something good about him, and then verbally present it to him.

▼ *Technology Tips* highlight a technology teachers can use in the classroom (or one that supports classroom instruction) to help meet the educational needs of students with disabilities. The technology featured can be anything from a software program to an assistive or adaptive technology, or even specific educational websites.

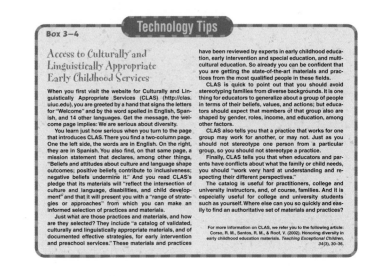

Technology Tips

Box 3–4

Access to Culturally and Linguistically Appropriate Early Childhood Services

When you first visit the website for Culturally and Linguistically Appropriate Services (CLAS) (http://clas.uiuc.edu), you are greeted by a hand that signs the letters for "Welcome" and by the word spelled in English, Spanish, and 14 other languages. Get the message, the welcome page implies: We are serious about diversity.

You learn just how serious when you turn to the page that introduces CLAS. There you find a two-column page. One the left side, the words are in English. On the right, they are in Spanish. You also find, on that same page, a mission statement that declares, among other things, "Beliefs and attitudes about culture and language shape outcomes; positive beliefs contribute to inclusiveness; negative beliefs undermine it." And you read CLAS's pledge that its materials will "reflect the intersection of culture and language, disabilities, and child development" and that it will present you with a "range of strategies or approaches" from which you can make an informed selection of practices and materials.

Just what are those practices and materials, and how are they selected? They include "a catalog of validated, culturally and linguistically appropriate materials, and of documented effective strategies, for early intervention and preschool services." These materials and practices

have been reviewed by experts in early childhood education, early intervention and special education, and multicultural education. So already you can be confident that you are getting the state-of-the-art materials and practices from the most qualified people in these fields.

CLAS is quick to point out that you should avoid stereotyping families from diverse backgrounds. It is one thing for educators to generalize about a group of people in terms of their beliefs, values, and actions; but educators should expect that members of that group also are shaped by gender, roles, income, and education, among other factors.

CLAS also tells you that a practice that works for one group may work for another, or may not. Just as you should not stereotype one person from a particular group, so you should not stereotype a practice.

Finally, CLAS tells you that when educators and parents have conflicts about what the family or child needs, you should "work very hard at understanding and respecting their different perspectives."

The catalog is useful for practitioners, college and university instructors, and, of course, families. And it is especially useful for college and university students such as yourself. Where else can you so quickly and easily find an authoritative set of materials and practices?

For more information on CLAS, we refer you to the following article: Corso, R. M., Santos, R. M., & Roof, V. (2002). Honoring diversity in early childhood education materials. *Teaching Exceptional Children*, 34(3), 30–36.

▼ *Collaboration Tips* describe how collaborative partnerships, processes, and strategies can help in achieving an appropriate education in inclusive settings.

Collaboration Tips

Box 3–3

Involving Community Agencies

The three students whom we feature in this chapter—Ronda, Donald, and Luisa—represent different multicultural characteristics and different challenges to collaboration. Let's just consider two of them, starting with Ronda.

Ronda's mother, Debra, is a single parent; Ronda's two older siblings live away from home. Debra works full time at Tulane University Law School and is a well-educated, articulate, and intelligent person whose expectations and ambitions for her children, especially for Ronda, are high: advanced university degrees for all three, especially for Ronda, with a dissertation on systemic reforms in special education ("The data will include all the papers and reports about her that I am saving for her," says Debra). Yet for Debra to attend all of the many meetings that the school has called has required her to miss 17 hours of work in the most recent school year, when Ronda began to benefit from school. And when the school called Debra before this year to "come get Ronda; she's uncontrollable," Debra had to respond or risk having Ronda placed into the custody of the school safety officer and the juvenile justice system.

Now let's consider Luisa. There are two fundamental challenges to collaboration, both arising from her diversity characteristics of being Latino and non-English speaking and her parents' undocumented status. How can the school communicate with her and her family (except, improperly, through her brother) when the school system as a whole does not hire Spanish-English speakers? And how can the school collaborate with her parents when it is an ally of the Immigration and Naturalization Service in identifying and reporting undocumented immigrants and therefore is properly regarded as hostile territory by her parents?

The answers come from restructuring the school system:

• *Flex time for educators and parents to meet.* Give the teachers some release time so they can meet parents after the usual hours of work—say, in the early evenings

• *Flex place for the meetings.* One option might be Catholic Charities, where Carolyn and Graziella work.

• *Employment of Spanish-English speakers.* As full-time or part-time staff or consultants, they will be trusted by the immigrant members of the community, as Graziella is.

• *Commitment to making a difference in students' lives.* Schools should seek out resources outside of the school system, such as Pyramid Parent Training Center and the many universities in New Orleans that operate teacher-training programs.

Restructuring the curriculum through universal design for learning makes progress in the general curriculum possible; so, too, restructuring the administrative systems makes collaboration possible, especially with families whose diversity consists of more than a student's exceptionality.

Putting These Tips to Work for Progress in the General Curriculum

1. What are the challenges?
2. What can the team do?
3. What are the results?

To answer these questions online and learn more about these ideas and concepts, go to the Collaboration Tips module in Chapter 3 of the Companion Website.

Including All Students

We provide educators with information and strategies for making curriculum, instruction, and assessment available to all students, regardless of their ability, behavioral differences, learning style, and cultural differences.

▼ *Planning Universally Designed Learning* tells how teachers can augment, alter, or adapt curriculum, instruction, and evaluation to assure all students' progress in the general curriculum.

▼ *Multicultural Considerations* prepares teachers to consider students' diverse backgrounds (their language, gender, ethnicity, race, socioeconomic status, geography, and exceptionality/ability) when planning curriculum, instruction, and evaluation and when collaborating with families and other service providers.

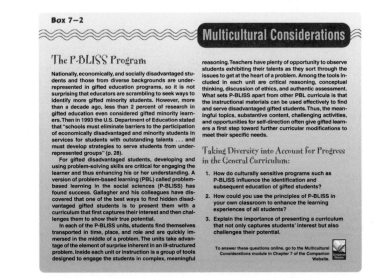

Supplements

Inclusive Classrooms: Video Cases on CD-ROM

Following examples of good teaching is one means of becoming an effective teacher. Simply reading and researching is not generally enough. But, witnessing meaningful teaching firsthand, observing best practice, and reflecting on the actions, decisions, and artistry behind good teaching can bring you farther along on your journey toward becoming a better teacher yourself. The CD-ROM and activity guide accompanying this text allow you to observe, reflect on, and learn from master teachers in their classrooms.

Purpose of the CD

This CD provides immediate access to living classroom examples of teaching and learning strategies for inclusion. These examples are video clips, grouped by topic and classroom, which give the pre-service teacher a good picture of what inclusion looks like in preschool, elementary school, and a secondary school classroom and a middle school collaboration/team meeting.

Each of the four cases contains 9 video clips that show expert teachers engaging all of their students—including those with learning disabilities, attention deficit disorders, and mild/moderate disabilities—in the classroom community and in learning. In addition, we have comments from the master teachers and experts in the field who have observed the classrooms, the most current and up-to-date research and literature on the topic, and reflections from students in the classroom (when appropriate).

To learn more about the functionality of the CD and how to build your own custom video case studies using the video clips on the CD, please see the guide that accompanies this text.

Companion Website. The companion website, located at http://www.prenhall.com/turnbull, is a valuable resource for both the professor and the student.

▼ *For the Professor—"Faculty Resources"*: The Faculty Resources section is a passcode-protected area of the companion website for professors only. Each chapter contains annotated topical *Lectures* and *PowerPoint Slides* that a professor can download and customize. In addition, the online version of the *Instructor's Manual* is available; so are *Presentation*

Outlines for each chapter. The *CW Activities—Instructor's Key* provides instructional guidance for incorporating the Companion Website activities for students into teaching, and the Standards Connection Matrix ties chapter topics and related projects and artifacts to the CEC Professional Standards and the PRAXIS™ Standards. The companion website also features a *Syllabus Builder* that enables instructors to create and customize syllabi online. To obtain a passcode to enter the Faculty Resources, a professor should contact the local Prentice Hall sales representative or call faculty services at 1-800-526-0485.

▼ *For the Student:* The companion website helps you—the student—gauge your understanding of chapter content through the use of overviews, supplementary chapter information, artifacts, and activities relating to the cases/vignettes discussed in the chapter, and interactive self-assessments. It also provides web links mentioned in the text, a variety of other online resources (such as IEP forms and collaboration charts, an electronic glossary, children's literature and video resource lists, and streaming video), and web-based Project Opportunities and Video for reflection and problem solving. Finally, through the Standards Connection Matrix, you can see the connections from chapter topics and related projects or artifacts to the CEC Professional Standards and the PRAXIS™ Standards.

ABC News Video Library—Exceptional Lives, Exceptional Issues. These are video segments from recent ABC News programs. Each segment highlights people living exceptional lives and the issues they face; each segment is sure to spark lively and reflective class discussions. You will find an annotated list of the videos in the Instructor's Manual. The list will help you connect chapter content to specific video segments.

Instructor's Manual. The Instructor's Manual includes brief chapter overviews and outlines, instructional goals, and pre/post instructional questions for students. In addition, activities and materials to support instruction include Internet-based activities and discussion starters to use in class. A case study in-class activity and case study analysis expand upon the cases/vignettes in each chapter and offer suggestions to enhance a student's understanding of chapter content. Each chapter also has a presentation outline that ties all of the ancillary components together in a cohesive package. To allow for more flexibility in instruction and provide opportunities for authentic learning and assessment, the Instructor's Manual also lists ideas for artifact or project opportunities for students, and relevant books and videos. At the end of each chapter, the Standards Connection Matrix aligns the CEC Professional Standards and PRAXIS Standards to chapter topics and related projects or artifacts. A comprehensive matrix aligning the CEC Professional Standards, PRAXIS™ Standards, and INTASC Principles is available in the appendix.

PowerPoint Slides/Transparency Masters. These visual aids display, summarize, and help explain core information presented in each chapter. You can download them from our companion website and use the downloads as PowerPoint slide presentations or print them onto acetates and use them as transparencies for overhead projectors.

Test Bank. Students learn better when they are held accountable for what they have learned. That is why we have developed a bank of over 50 test questions per chapter in a variety of formats (including true-false, multiple choice, short answer, and essay) that match the issues, questions, and projects we set out in each chapter. The test bank is available in hard copy and electronic formats.

Student Study Guide. A Student Study Guide helps students understand, analyze, and evaluate the chapter concepts and prepare for in-class lectures and presentations. Each chapter in the Student Study Guide includes the chapter overview; guiding questions of the chapter; key terms; and case reflections with a collaboration connection, diversity link, focus on inclusion, and universal design application. Project opportunities encourage authentic, concrete learning experiences and spot checks help students measure their comprehension of chapter content. Resources available on the Companion Website are in the Student Study Guide, and the Standards Connection Matrix aligns the CEC Professional Standards and PRAXIS™ Standards to chapter topics and related projects or artifacts. A comprehensive matrix aligning the CEC Professional Standards, PRAXIS™ Standards, and INTASC Principles is available in the appendix of the textbook.

Acknowledgments

This book is the product of collaboration. That's true in several senses. First, our book focuses on collaboration in schools and models that very trait. Second, it is collaborative in the sense that people with disabilities, their families, and many professionals opened their lives to us, allowing us to bring them to the center stage of each chapter, where, as actors in a play, they inspire, inform, and personalize our concepts, lessons, and approaches. We wish to thank those people who inspired and encouraged our writing. Third, our book is the product of a collaboration of professionals serving various roles—as authors, editors, and producers.

There is one person who, beyond all others, has inspired Ann and Rud Turnbull. Unable to write a single word of text, he nonetheless is an indispensable source of our knowledge, our greatest teacher, and the focal point of all of our work: "JT" Thank you, Jay Turnbull.

Because Amy and Kate Turnbull, JT's younger sisters, have taught us so much about the possibilities of inclusion and the reality about and hope for families, we also honor them with this text and our gratitude.

Marilyn Shank expresses appreciation to her father, Joe Shank, for his ongoing encouragement and wisdom. Other family members, including Tom and Kathy Shank, Wade and Jennifer Wilkes, Matthew Shank, Elsie Borsch, and Betty Slater, also supported her efforts. In addition, Rud and Ann Turnbull—her co-authors, mentors, and friends—have inspired her to emphasize proactive, strength-based interventions in her teaching and writing. Finally, she thanks all of her former and current students for teaching her more than she could ever hope to teach them.

Sean Smith is an author and the father of the young boy—Nolan—featured in the vignette in Chapter 1. He is also the creator and co-producer of our book's Companion Website. You will be able to follow Nolan, his sister Bridget, his brother JJ, and his mother Kris for many years to come; this book will chronicle his life in general and special education, now and in the future. To young Nolan, may all of the knowledge and wisdom that all of us have be given.

For Sean, his wife Kris was an integral part of the writing process. Her belief in his ability and her continuous support and flexibility allowed for Sean to plug away as he wrote his chapters. His family, especially his sister Sheila and his parents Mary Ellen and Robert Smith, were also central supporters, offering encouragement and insight. Finally, his children, Nolan, Bridget, and JJ, are the center of his life and his greatest teachers.

We would also like to give our sincerest thanks to Jody Britten at Ball State University for all of her hard work on the Student Study Guide, Instructor's Manual, and Test Bank, and for her collaboration with Sean Smith on the Companion Website. Her innovation, creativity, and knowledge of the field have enhanced these products, making them more useful for students and professors and tying them directly to the content and themes covered in the fourth edition.

Behind every writing team are the editorial and production staffers who ensure that authors' references and grammar are accurate, their spelling correct, their permissions secured, and their manuscripts ready to go into production. First and foremost, Lois Weldon never once flinched as we piled manuscript upon manuscript onto her already loaded-down desk. In addition to her technical expertise in preparing the manuscript and its various illustrations and figures, Lois always did whatever was necessary to help us meet deadlines and to accomplish what seemed like insurmountable tasks. Lois is our reliable ally in every way, and we express our heartfelt appreciate to her. Amber Olson assisted us in organizing references and provided much needed and appreciated backup for Lois. With their superb senses of humor, indomitable strength and stamina, and never failing tolerance of authors' multiple, frequently repetitive, and overlapping demands, Lois and Amber aided in the preparation of seemingly endless drafts of chapters, kept our work product and even our offices and lives organized, and helped design illustrative features that appear throughout.

At Merrill/Prentice Hall, our publisher, we have had the benefit of an effective, tolerant, and loyal team. When we approached delinquency in timelines or textual accuracy and fluency, they were admonishing; when we went astray of our goals and concepts, they were redirecting. In all matters, they were consummate professionals. Our executive editor is Allyson Sharp—and she's as sharp as her last name suggests. Our development editor is Heather Doyle Fraser; in her, we have a person whose cheerfulness, cordiality, and careful attention to detail are supplemented by her and her husband's sleuthing out of vignette subjects for some of the chapters. Jeff Johnston, vice president and executive publisher, continues to support us in every possible way; Sheryl Langner, our production editor, never once loses her calm and humorous demeanor, even when the deadlines loom and the hitherto-unattended details threaten to swamp us all. We were glad to welcome back, as our copy editor, the conscientious Dawn Potter, who worked with us on the first edition of this book. Each of these good colleagues deserve much of the credit.

A collective expression of gratitude is inefficient, so a few more words are in order. Ann Davis initially conceived the idea of a focus on the real lives of today's students; Ann's extensive and informed perspective about publishing and about special education helped shape the first and second editions' content, tone, and design—in a word, she made this book possible by soliciting us to write it and by helping us make it more readable and durable in the marketplace. Her contributions continue in her role as director of marketing.

Here at Beach Center on Disability, The University of Kansas, we had help with the first edition from Martha Blue-Banning, Dan Boudah, Mary Morningstar, Mike Ruef, and Vicki Turbiville, all former students and now proud possessors of their doctorates. We also benefitted immensely from the editorial eagle-eye of Ben Furnish, who, while earning his doctorate in theatre, was both our editor and a published scholar and editor at another university. Thanks to all!

Our colleagues at other universities have contributed mightily. Jane Wegner and Evette Edmiston at the speech-language clinic at The University of Kansas wrote Chapter 14 on communications disorders. Barbara Schirmer at Miami University in Oxford, Ohio, wrote Chapter 15 on hearing impairments, and Sandy Lewis at Florida State University wrote Chapter 16 on visual impairments. To each and every one of them: the simple phrase, "we are greatly indebted," seems hardly enough, but we hope it suffices; your knowledge is powerful, your ability to convey it is remarkable, and your ability to model one of this book's features, namely, the power of collaboration, is exemplary.

Others played their important roles. The families, students, and professionals in each vignette were unfailingly generous. They helped us bridge the geographical gaps between us; we know a few of them face to face, but we do not know many of the others in the same way. Yet, each has become an indispensable part of the whole. It is as though each of them, sensing that they will make a difference to you, the reader, tacitly agreed to become members of a larger, extended community—the community of families, students, and exceptionalities affected by disability and giftedness, and the community who, though so affected, nonetheless persevere and teach us.

Similarly, many professionals have contributed to the fourth edition. For their considerate reviews, we thank Vance Austin, Hofstra University; Karen B. Cole, Northern Illinois University; Susan Gregory, Montana State University, Billings; Philip L. Gunter, Valdosta State University; Helen Hamond, University of Texas, El Paso; Joy McGhee, University of Mississippi; Darra Pace, Hofstra University; and Georgine Steinmiller, Henderson State University.

Educator Learning Center:
An Invaluable Online Resource

Merrill Education and the Association for Supervision and Curriculum Development (ASCD) invite you to take advantage of a new online resource, one that provides access to the top research and proven strategies associated with ASCD and Merrill—the Educator Learning Center. At **www.EducatorLearningCenter.com** you will find resources that will enhance your students' understanding of course topics and of current educational issues, in addition to being invaluable for further research.

How the Educator Learning Center will help your students become better teachers

With the combined resources of Merrill Education and ASCD, you and your students will find a wealth of tools and materials to better prepare them for the classroom.

Research

▼ More than 600 articles from the ASCD journal *Educational Leadership* discuss everyday issues faced by practicing teachers.

▼ A direct link on the site to Research Navigator™ gives students access to many of the leading education journals, as well as extensive content detailing the research process.

▼ Excerpts from Merrill Education texts give your students insights on important topics of instructional methods, diverse populations, assessment, classroom management, technology, and refining classroom practice.

Classroom Practice

▼ Hundreds of lesson plans and teaching strategies are categorized by content area and age range.

▼ Case studies and classroom video footage provide virtual field experience for student reflection.

▼ Computer simulations and other electronic tools keep your students abreast of today's classroom and current technologies.

Look into the value of Educator Learning Center yourself

Preview the value of this educational environment by visiting **www.EducatorLearningCenter.com** and click on "Demo." For a free 4-month subscription to the Educator Learning Center in conjunction with this text, simply contact your Merrill/Prentice Hall sales representative.

Brief Contents

Chapter 1
Overview of Today's Special Education   2

Chapter 2
Ensuring Progress in the General Curriculum: Universal Design and Inclusion   42

Chapter 3
Ensuring Progress in the General Curriculum: Collaboration and Multicultural Responsiveness   78

Chapter 4
Learning Disabilities   102

Chapter 5
Emotional or Behavioral Disorders   130

Chapter 6
Attention-Deficit/Hyperactivity Disorder   162

Chapter 7
Giftedness   194

Chapter 8
Mental Retardation   224

Chapter 9
Severe and Multiple Disabilities   254

Chapter 10
Autism   282

Chapter 11
Other Health Impairments   310

Chapter 12
Physical Disabilities   342

Chapter 13
Traumatic Brain Injury   372

Chapter 14
Communication Disorders   398

Chapter 15
Hearing Loss   424

Chapter 16
Visual Impairments   456

Appendix: Understanding the Standards/Topics Alignment Matrix   487

Glossary   509

References   519

Name Index   543

Subject Index   553

Chapter 1

Overview of Today's Special Education   2

Who Is Nolan Smith?   2

Profile of Special Education Students and Personnel in Today's Schools   4

Who Are the Students?   4

What Are the Socioeconomic Characteristics of Students with Exceptionalities?   9

What Are the Racial/Ethnic Trends Related to Students with Exceptionalities?   11

Who Are the Special Education Personnel?   15

The Law and Special Education   15

Two Types of Discrimination   15

Two Revolutionary Judicial Decisions   16

Introduction to IDEA: Progress but Problems   17

Special Education and Students' Eligibility   17

IDEA: Six Principles   19

Zero Reject   20

Nondiscriminatory Evaluation   21

Appropriate Education   22

Least Restrictive Environments   28

Procedural Due Process   31

Parent-Student Participation   32

Bringing the Six Principles Together   32

Federal Funding of the Individuals with Disabilities Education Act   32

Other Federal Laws: Entitlements and Antidiscrimination   34

Entitlements and Other Services   34

Prohibiting Discrimination   34

Section 504 and ADA Coverage   35

IDEA, Section 504, and ADA: Overlapping Purposes   36

Special Education Outcomes   36

What Are the Long-Term Results for Students with Disabilities and to What Extent Are the Results Influenced by Diversity Factors?   36

A Vision for the Future   38

What Would You Recommend?   39

Summary   39

Chapter 2

Ensuring Progress in the General Curriculum: Universal Design and Inclusion   42

Who Are Heather and Star Morgan?   42

What Does Progressing in the General Curriculum Mean?   44

What Is the Background of Standards-Based Reform?   44

What Are Content and Performance Standards?   45

What Is the General Curriculum?   46

What Are the Accountability Issues?   48

Why Is It Important for Students to Progress in the General Curriculum?   53

How Does Universal Design for Learning Enable Students with Exceptionalities to Progress in the General Curriculum?   54

What Is Universal Design for Learning?   54

How Does Universal Design for Learning Enable Students with Exceptionalities to Progress in the General Curriculum?   61

How Does Inclusion Enable Students to Progress in the General Curriculum?   61

What Are Placement Trends for Students with Exceptionalities?   61

What Issues Are Associated with Placement in Residential/Home/Hospital Settings?   64

What Issues Are Associated with Placement in Special Schools?   65

What Issues Are Associated with Placement in Specialized Settings Within Typical Schools?   65

What Is Inclusion and What Are Its Four Key Characteristics?   65

What Are Educator, Parent, and Student Perspectives on Inclusion?   68

What Student Outcomes Are Associated with Inclusion?   72

How Does Inclusion Enable Students to Progress in the General Curriculum?   73

A Vision for the Future   74

What Would You Recommend?   75

Summary   75

Chapter 3

Ensuring Progress in the General Curriculum: Collaboration and Multicultural Responsiveness   78

Who Are Ronda Taylor, Donald Harness, and Luisa Rodriquez?   78

How Does Collaboration Enable Students to Progress in the General Curriculum?   80

What Is Collaboration and Why Is It So Highly Valued?   80

Who Are the People Involved in Collaboration and What Are Their Roles?   81

What Are State-of-the-Art Collaborative Approaches?   88

What Is the Process of Creating Collaborative Teams?   90

How Does Multicultural Responsiveness Enable Students to Progress in the General Curriculum?   92

What Is Culture and How Does It Affect Students' Progress in the General Curriculum?   92

How Can You Establish Reliable Alliances with Students and Families from Diverse Backgrounds?   94

How Can You Enable Students to Broaden Their Menu of Response Options?   95

How Can You Collaborate to Promote Cultural Mediation?   96

How Does Responsiveness to Multicultural Considerations Enable Students to Progress in the General Curriculum?   98

A Vision for Ronda's, Donald's, and Luisa's Future   98

What Would You Recommend?   100

Summary   100

Chapter 4

Learning Disabilities   102

Who Is Tony Lavender?   102

How Do You Recognize Students with Learning Disabilities?   104

Defining Learning Disabilities   104

Describing the Characteristics   106

Behavioral, Social, and Emotional Characteristics   109

Identifying the Causes   109

Identifying the Prevalence   110

How Do You Evaluate Students with Learning Disabilities?   110

Determining the Presence   111

Determining the Nature and Extent of General and Special Education and Related Services   113

How Do You Assure Progress in the General Curriculum?   114

Including Students   114

Planning Universally Designed Learning   114

Collaborating to Meet Students' Needs   120

What Can You Learn from Others Who Teach Students with Learning Disabilities?   121

Learning for the Early Childhood Years: Embedded Learning Opportunities in Nashville, Tennessee   121

Learning for the Elementary Years: Maple Elementary School, Springfield, Oregon   123

Learning for the Middle and Secondary Years: Chase Middle School, Topeka, Kansas   125

Learning for the Transitional and Postsecondary Years: Mitchell College's Learning Resource Center, New London, Connecticut   126

A Vision for Tony's Future   128

What Would You Recommend?   128

Summary   128

Chapter 5

Emotional or Behavioral Disorders   130

Who Is Matthew Ackinclose?   130

How Do You Recognize Students with Emotional or Behavioral Disorders?   132

Defining Emotional or Behavioral Disorders   132

Describing the Characteristics   133

Identifying the Causes   140

Identifying the Prevalence   142

How Do You Evaluate Students with Emotional or Behavioral Disorders?   144

Determining the Presence   144

Determining the Nature and Extent of General and Special Education and Related Services   146

How Do You Assure Progress in the General Curriculum?   147

Including Students   147

Planning Universally Designed Learning   149

Collaborating to Meet Students' Needs   150

What Can You Learn from Others Who Teach Students with Emotional or Behavioral Disorders?   154

Learning for the Early Childhood Years: Johns Hopkins University Prevention Intervention Research Center   154

Learning for the Elementary Years: LaGrange (Illinois) Department of Special Education   158

Learning for the Middle and Secondary Years: Frank Lloyd Wright Middle School   159

Learning for the Transitional and Postsecondary Years: Canada's YouthNet/Reseau Ado   159

A Vision for Matthew's Future   160

What Would You Recommend?   161

Summary   161

Chapter 6

Attention-Deficit/Hyperactivity Disorder   162

Who Is Kelsey Blankenship?   162

How Do You Recognize Students with Attention-Deficit/Hyperactivity Disorder?   164

Defining Attention-Deficit/Hyperactivity Disorder   164

Describing the Characteristics   165

Positive Traits Associated with Attention-Deficit/Hyperactivity Disorder   169

Identifying the Causes   171

Identifying the Prevalence   175

How Do You Evaluate Students with Attention-Deficit/Hyperactivity Disorder?   176

Determining the Presence   176

Determining the Nature and Extent of General and Special Education and Related Services   179

How Do You Assure Progress in the General Curriculum?   180

Including Students   180

Planning Universally Designed Learning   183

Collaborating to Meet Students' Needs   186

What Can You Learn from Others Who Teach Students with Attention-Deficit/Hyperactivity Disorder?   188

Learning for the Early Childhood Years: Multidisciplinary Diagnostic and Training Program   189

Learning for the Elementary Years: Take Charge!   189

Learning for the Middle and Secondary Years: Lehigh University's Consulting Center for Adolescents with Attention-Deficit Disorders   190

Learning for the Transitional and Postsecondary Years: *Peterson's Colleges with Programs for Students with Learning Disabilities or Attention Deficit Disorders*   191

A Vision for Kelsey's Future   191

What Would You Recommend?   191

Summary   192

Chapter 7

Giftedness   194

Who Is Briana Hoskins?   194

How Do You Recognize Students Who Are Gifted?   196

Defining Giftedness   196

Describing the Characteristics   198

Identifying the Origins   202

Identifying the Prevalence   203

How Do You Evaluate Students Who Are Gifted?   204

Determining the Presence   204

Determining the Nature and Extent of General and Special Education   208

How Do You Assure Progress in the General Curriculum?   209

Including Students   209

Planning Universally Designed Learning   210

Collaborating to Meet Students' Needs   215

What Can You Learn from Others Who Teach Gifted Students?   215

Learning for the Early Childhood Years: Montgomery Knolls Elementary School, Silver Spring, Maryland   215

Learning for the Elementary Years: Blue Valley School District, Kansas   217

Learning for the Middle and Secondary Years: Central Middle School, Grandview, Missouri   220

Learning for the Transitional and Postsecondary Years: *College Planning for Gifted Students*   221

A Vision for Briana's Future 222
   What Would You Recommend? 222
Summary 222

Chapter 8

Mental Retardation 224

Who Is Tory Woodard? 224
How Do You Recognize Students with Mental Retardation? 226
   Defining Mental Retardation 226
   Describing the Characteristics 227
   Identifying the Causes 230
   Identifying the Prevalence 234
How Do You Evaluate Students with Mental Retardation? 235
   Determining the Presence 235
   Determining the Nature and Extent of General and Special Education and Related Services 235
How Do You Assure Progress in the General Curriculum? 237
   Including Students 237
   Planning Universally Designed Learning 239
   Collaborating to Meet Students' Needs 245
What Can You Learn from Others Who Teach Students with Mental Retardation? 247
   Learning for the Early Childhood Years: Granville County Child Development Center, Oxford, North Carolina 247
   Learning for the Elementary Years: Teachers and Researchers in Kansas and Texas 248
   Learning for the Middle and Secondary Years: Teaching in the Natural Environment 250
   Learning for the Transitional and Postsecondary Years: Project TASSEL, Shelby, North Carolina 250
A Vision for Tory's Future 252
   What Would You Recommend? 252
Summary 252

Chapter 9

Severe and Multiple Disabilities 254

Who Is Joshua Spoor? 254
How Do You Recognize Students with Severe and Multiple Disabilities? 256
   Defining Severe and Multiple Disabilities 256

Describing the Characteristics 257
Identifying the Causes 260
Identifying the Prevalence 261
How Do You Evaluate Students with Severe and Multiple Disabilities? 262
   Determining the Presence 264
   Determining the Nature and Extent of General and Special Education and Related Services 264
How Do You Assure Progress in the General Curriculum? 265
   Including Students 265
   Planning Universally Designed Learning 268
   Collaborating to Meet Students' Needs 272
What Can You Learn from Others Who Teach Students with Severe and Multiple Disabilities? 274
   Learning for the Early Childhood Years: Circle of Inclusion 274
   Learning for the Elementary Years: Johnson City, New York, Central District 276
   Learning for the Middle and Secondary Years: Whittier High School, Los Angeles 277
   Learning for the Transitional and Postsecondary Years: Asbury College, Wilmore, Kentucky 278
A Vision for Joshua's Future 279
   What Would You Recommend? 280
Summary 280

Chapter 10

Autism 282

Who Is Jeremy Jones? 282
How Do You Recognize Students with Autism? 284
   Defining Autism 284
   Describing the Characteristics 284
   Identifying the Causes 289
   Identifying the Prevalence 289
How Do You Evaluate Students with Autism? 289
   Determining the Presence 289
   Determining the Nature and Extent of General and Special Education and Related Services 290
How Do You Assure Progress in the General Curriculum? 292
   Including Students 292
   Planning Universally Designed Learning 292
   Collaborating to Meet Students' Needs 297
What Can You Learn from Others Who Teach Students with Autism? 297

Learning for the Early Childhood Years: "Jump Start" in Exeter, New Hampshire   297

Learning for the Elementary Years: Tiffany Park, Seattle, Washington   300

Learning for the Middle and Secondary Years: Central Middle School, Kansas City, Kansas   302

Learning for the Transitional and Postsecondary Years: Community Services for Autistic Adults and Children, Rockville, Maryland   302

A Vision for Jeremy's Future   306
   What Would You Recommend?   307

Summary   307

Chapter 11
Other Health Impairments   310

Who Is Kyle Edwards?   310

How Do You Recognize Students with Other Health Impairments?   312
   Defining Other Health Impairments   312
   Describing the Characteristics of Sickle Cell Disease   312
   Describing the Characteristics of Epilepsy   315
   Describing the Characteristics of Asthma   317
   Describing the Characteristics of Cancer   320
   Describing the Characteristics of Diabetes   322
   Describing the Characteristics of Human Immunodeficiency Virus   323
   Identifying the Causes   326
   Identifying the Prevalence   327

How Do You Evaluate Students with Other Health Impairments?   328
   Determining the Presence   328
   Determining the Nature and Extent of General and Special Education and Related Services   328

How Do You Assure Progress in the General Curriculum?   330
   Including Students   330
   Planning Universally Designed Learning   333
   Collaborating to Meet Students' Needs   336

What Can You Learn from Others Who Teach Students with Other Health Impairments?   337
   Learning for the Early Childhood Years: Kids on the Block   337
   Learning for the Elementary Years: Class Act   338
   Learning for the Middle and Secondary Years: Meeting the Challenge   338
   Learning for the Transitional and Postsecondary Years: HIV University   339

A Vision for Kyle's Future   340
   What Would You Recommend?   340

Summary   340

Chapter 12
Physical Disabilities   342

Who Is Rommel Nanasca?   342

How Do You Recognize Students with Physical Disabilities?   344
   Defining Physical Disabilities   344
   Describing the Characteristics   344
   Identifying the Prevalence   349
   Preventing Physical Disabilities   350

How Do You Evaluate Students with Physical Disabilities?   350
   Determining the Presence   350
   Determining the Nature and Extent of General and Special Education and Related Services   350

How Do You Assure Progress in the General Curriculum?   353
   Including Students   353
   Planning Universally Designed Learning   354
   Collaborating to Meet Students' Needs   360

What Can You Learn from Others Who Teach Students with Physical Disabilities?   363
   Learning for the Early Childhood Years: Self-Determination Through Technology   363
   Learning for the Elementary Years: In the Gym with Assistive Technology   364
   Learning for the Middle and Secondary Years: Centers for Independent Living   366
   Learning for the Transitional and Postsecondary Years: Self-Determination in Higher Education   367

A Vision for Rommel's Future   369
   What Would You Recommend?   370

Summary   370

Chapter 13
Traumatic Brain Injury   372

Who Is Jarris Garner?   372

How Do You Recognize Students with Traumatic Brain Injury?   374
   Defining Traumatic Brain Injury   374
   Identifying the Types of Traumatic Brain Injury   374

Describing the Characteristics   375

Identifying the Causes   380

Identifying the Prevalence   381

How Do You Evaluate Students with Traumatic Brain Injury?   382

Determining the Presence   382

Determining the Nature and Extent of General and Special Education and Related Services   384

How Do You Assure Progress in the General Curriculum?   385

Including Students   385

Planning Universally Designed Learning   385

Collaborating to Meet Students' Needs   388

What Can You Learn from Others Who Teach Students with Traumatic Brain Injury?   390

Learning for the Early Childhood Years: The Children's Place, Kansas City, Missouri   390

Learning for the Middle and Secondary Years: Shawnee Mission West, Shawnee Mission, Kansas   393

Learning for the Transitional and Postsecondary Years: Pepperdine University, Malibu, California   394

A Vision for Jarris's Future   396

What Would You Recommend?   396

Summary   397

Chapter 14

Communication Disorders   398

Who Is George Wedge?   398

How Do You Recognize Students with Communication Disorders?   400

Defining Communication Disorders   400

Describing the Characteristics   403

Identifying the Causes   410

Identifying the Prevalence   410

How Do You Evaluate Students with Communication Disorders?   411

Determining the Presence   411

Determining the Nature and Extent of General and Special Education and Related Services   414

How Do You Assure Progress in the General Curriculum?   414

Including Students   414

Planning Universally Designed Learning   415

Collaborating to Meet Students' Needs   418

What Can You Learn from Others Who Teach Students with Communication Disorders?   419

Learning for the Early Childhood Years: Jessamine Early Learning Village in Jessamine County, Kentucky   419

Learning for the Elementary Years: Quail Run Elementary School, Lawrence, Kansas   420

Learning for the Middle and Secondary Years: Collaborative Language Literacy Laboratory, Galvez Middle School, Galvez, Louisiana   421

Learning for the Transitional and Postsecondary Years: Work and Community   422

A Vision for George's Future   422

What Would You Recommend?   422

Summary   422

Chapter 15

Hearing Loss   424

Who Is Amala Brown?   424

How Do You Recognize Students with Hearing Loss?   426

Defining Hearing Loss   426

Describing the Characteristics   427

Identifying the Causes   432

Identifying the Prevalence   433

How Do You Evaluate Students with Hearing Loss?   433

Determining the Presence   433

Determining the Nature and Extent of General and Special Education and Related Services   439

How Do You Assure Progress in the General Curriculum?   439

Including Students   439

Planning Universally Designed Learning   440

Collaborating to Meet Students' Needs   446

What Can You Learn from Others Who Teach Students with Hearing Loss?   450

Learning for the Early Childhood Years: Dallas Regional Day School   450

Learning for the Elementary Years: Northwest Regional Program, Oregon   451

Learning for the Middle and Secondary Years: Utah Extension Services   451

Learning for the Transitional and Postsecondary Years: Kent State University, Ohio   452

A Vision for Amala's Future   453

What Would You Recommend?   453

Summary   453

Chapter 16

Visual Impairments   456

Who Is Elexis Gillette?   456

How Do You Recognize Students with Visual Impairments?   458

Defining Visual Impairments   458

Describing the Characteristics   459

Identifying the Causes   462

Identifying the Prevalence   463

How Do You Evaluate Students with Visual Impairments?   463

Determining the Presence   463

Determining the Nature and Extent of General and Special Education and Related Services   466

How Do You Assure Progress in the General Curriculum?   468

Including Students   468

Planning Universally Designed Learning   469

Collaborating to Meet Students' Needs   479

What Can You Learn from Others Who Teach Students with Visual Impairments?   481

Learning for the Early Childhood Years: Blind Babies Foundation, San Francisco   481

Learning for the Elementary Years: Lawrence, Kansas   481

Learning for the Middle and Secondary Years: Tallahassee, Florida   483

Learning for the Transitional and Postsecondary Years: Living Skills Center, San Pablo, California   483

A Vision for Elexis's Future   485

What Would You Recommend?   485

Summary   485

Appendix: Understanding the Standards/Topic Alignment Matrix   487

Glossary   509

References   519

Name Index   543

Subject Index   553

Photo Credits   565

Note: Every effort has been made to provide accurate and current Internet information in this book. However, the Internet and information posted on it are constantly changing, and it is inevitable that some of the Internet addresses listed in this textbook will change.

Special Features

≈ My Voice ≈

Labeling   8
Stel Goes to Graduate School   9
The Power of Great Expectations and Visions   73
Cultural Mediation with Ursula and D. J. Markey   99
Rachel's Story: A College Graduate   106
Chris Fraser   171
Lights in the Fog: Living in a Twice-Exceptional Family   209
Sweet Alice Harris and Parents of Watts, Los Angeles   245
Race for a Miracle   261
Temple Grandin: Diagnosed as Having Autism as a Child   288
Ann Bessell Speaks Out on Educating Children with Chronic Illness   321
My Son Sam   351
Seth's Story   376
Elizabeth Smith   411
Barbara Schirmer: My Grandmother's Story   435
Robyn Brown's Supportive and Collaborative Friends   449
Tom and Kris Kiel   470

≈ Making a Difference ≈

What Don't You Understand About No?   16
Parent Training and Information in Kansas   29
Danny Wins His Lawsuit   31
Barbara Morgan: Forming the Forever Family   71
Creating a Learning Community   90
Parents as Teachers   120
Pawsitive Living   138
The Federation of Families for Children's Mental Health   142
An AD/HD Science Project   174
The University of Virginia's Summer Enrichment Program   202
The Surgeon General Speaks Out   233
We Weren't Ready, but We Started Anyway   269
"TAC-ing" for Students with Autism   299

Jonathan Bessell Writes to President and Mrs. Clinton   331
Judi Rogers Says, "This Can Be Done"   368
Beth Urbanczyk   392
Rhonda Friedlander   402
Famous Individuals Who Were Deaf   445
Ginny Chinn: Collaboration Is the Key   448
Donna McNear   462

≈ Into Practice ≈

Aligning Content Standards and Performance Standards for Students with Diverse Abilities   50
School Reform Through Student-Teacher Collaboration   83
Sentence Writing Strategy   127
Activities for Teaching Conflict Resolution   151
Accommodations for Attention-Deficit/Hyperactivity Disorder   181
Autonomous Learner Model   218
The Self-Determined Model of Instruction   242
Students Who Are Deaf-Blind Can Learn to Communicate   259
Highlights of Jeremy's Positive Behavior Support Plan for Inappropriate Verbal Disruptions (Talk-Outs)   304
Keeping the Emphasis on Education   335
Physical and Occupational Therapy in General Education Classrooms   355
Mnemonics for Solving Problems   395
Graphic Organizer Modifications   419
Conversational Scenarios   444
Promoting Travel in Schools   478

≈ Technology Tips ≈

Flexible Digital Textbooks   55
Access to Culturally and Linguistically Appropriate Early Childhood Services   95

Evaluating Educational Software for Students with Learning Disabilities   124

Tools for Success   152

Captain's Log and *Play Attention*   185

WebQuests   212

Visual Assistant: The See-It, Hear-It, Do-It Handheld Portable Prompter   228

Using Assistive Technology for Partial Participation in Recreation   271

Multimedia Social Stories   298

The STARBRIGHT® Foundation   313

Virtual Reality for Wheelchair Drivers   358

Personal Data Assistants   388

Assistive Technology for Students with Communication Disorders   418

Schoolhouse Palace   451

Assistive Technology for Students with Visual Impairments   475

Inclusion Tips

Ensuring Progress in the General Curriculum: Universal Design and Inclusion   74

Ensuring Progress in the General Curriculum: Collaboration and Multicultural Responsiveness   97

Learning Disabilities   117

Emotional or Behavioral Disabilities   148

Attention-Deficit/Hyperactivity Disorder   184

Giftedness   211

Mental Retardation   239

Severe and Multiple Disabilities   267

Autism   293

Other Health Impairments   332

Physical Disabilities   354

Traumatic Brain Injury   386

Communication Disorders   416

Hearing Loss   440

Visual Impairments   471

Collaboration Tips

Involving Community Agencies

The Power of 2: A Medium for Information and Collaboration   122

Collaborating with Class   188

Professional-to-Professional Collaboration   216

School Without Walls: Education for and with the Community   246

It's a Win-Win Proposition   273

Reading Peter Rabbit   301

Helping Others Grieve   337

Team Rommel   362

Starting with and Keeping a Team   389

General-Use Laboratory   421

A Three-Pronged Approach   447

Collaborating for Inclusion in Extracurricular Activities   480

Multicultural Considerations

National Association for Educational Progress: Math, Reading, and Civics Results   53

Adapted Posture of Cultural Reciprocity   96

Ecobehavioral Analysis Approach   118

SO Prepared for Citizenship   155

The Circle of Courage   156

Cultural Issues in Diagnosing AD/HD   179

The P-BLISS Program   205

Poverty, Race, and Classification   234

MAPs: When East Meets West   266

When Cultures Clash over Discipline   296

Reach for Health Community Youth Service Learning Program   324

Enhancing the Cultural Responsiveness of AAC   361

TBI and the Subculture of Violence   391

Communicative Interactions   401

Bilingual/Bicultural Educational Programs   442

Strategies for Teaching Braille to ESL Students   474

Chapter 1

Who Is Nolan Smith?

"Hanging in and hanging out." That's about the sum and substance of Nolan Smith's week, and yet these two phrases tell almost all there is to tell about this young 2-year-old who has Down syndrome.

"Hanging in" refers to Nolan's ability to win over the many professionals who are part of his young life and to benefit from their teaching. He interacts with a slew of professionals, but let's start with those who are most often involved with him. And let's bear in mind that each has to collaborate with Nolan's other therapists and, most of all, his parents, Kris and Sean (a co-author of this book).

A speech therapist from The University of Kansas's speech-language-hearing clinic, Carla Jackson, comes to his house once a week. She teaches Nolan how to form words, which he has difficulty doing. He will utter sounds, even whole sentences, with emphases in all the right places; but he just can't seem to put his mouth and brain into sync with each other. His brain knows what he wants to say; his mouth won't cooperate. Amazingly, he understands approximately 200 words; but as good as his receptive language is, his expressive language requires therapy.

While working to develop that critical skill, Carla also teaches Nolan sign language. "Nolan, Mother, Dad, Bridget (Nolan's older sister, now 3 years old), JJ (his baby brother, now 6 months old), food, drink, swim, Barney the dinosaur, TV, music, sleep, happy, and sad" are some of the words he uses regularly. Of course, as Carla teaches Nolan, she also conducts a lesson for Kris and Bridget.

A physical therapist, Karen Ely, comes to Nolan's home once a week now. (She used to come more often, but his progress is so good that he no longer needs that level of intense intervention.) At the beginning, when Nolan was only a few months old, Karen's goal was to strengthen him and then teach him some very important "moves"—holding his head up when he was lying face down, rolling over onto his back and then onto his belly again, crawling, and cruising from place to place. Now her goals are to teach him to stand for longer periods of time, using his muscles instead of the specially designed supportive shoes he used to wear, and to walk—today with assistance but soon without it.

Once a month, an occupational therapist has a session with Nolan, teaching him how to handle important objects such as a spoon or fork, how to button and unbutton his clothes, and how to put on his socks.

Annually, Nolan, Kris, and Sean attend the Down Syndrome Clinic at Children's Mercy Hospital, just an hour's drive from their home in Lawrence, Kansas. There they learn about the many medical aspects of Down syndrome and identify those that apply to Nolan.

For example, they learn that infants and toddlers with Down syndrome sometimes have a problem with their hearts; the heart doesn't move the blood from one chamber to the other as efficiently as it should. That knowledge triggers a visit to radiology for a sonogram of Nolan's heart. For the time being, there is no need to act; another visit, however, may prompt them and the hospital's physicians to undertake heart surgery. The family also learns that infants and toddlers with Down syndrome sometimes have thyroid problems; an evaluation by an endocrinologist is in order. And they find out that children with Down syndrome often have very weak neck muscles; so an X-ray of Nolan's neck might be necessary to inform Sean, Kris, and Nolan's professional team about his overall development.

Which brings us to the "hanging out" aspect of Nolan's life. He's a superstar in hanging out. His winsome smile, bright eyes, and eagerness to play with anyone at any time make it easy for him to participate in much of what his older sister Bridget does. Together, they have a busy life in Lawrence.

Each week, they attend the public library's story-time reading group; the arts center's music and movement classes; the "Mother's Day Out" and "Kids' Time In" programs at a local church; and daily swimming at the city pools, summer and winter, outside and inside. Accompanying him on these hang-out occasions are not only Kris but also, from time to time, two undergraduate students at The University of Kansas whom Sean has recruited to be part of the Smith household. Soon Briget will start her preschool education at the Raintree Montessori School, so, of course, Nolan already is on the list to attend when he reaches the magic age of 3.

"Hanging in" with the many therapists is Nolan's job, but it is his parents', too, because they are the main coordinators of this large team of early interventionists and often the advocates for Nolan's participation. Of course, they also are the long-range planners, the people who know that they must put their own resources—time, knowledge, energy, and money—into getting a life for themselves and for Nolan and Bridget and JJ. Just what kind of life will that be? If Sean and Kris have their way, their lives will be rich in quality, and Nolan's will be the kind of life that youngsters of his age but without his disability have.

Nolan's life will include education in inclusive classrooms, swimming (Sean was a varsity swimmer), and horseback riding

(Kris is an equestrian); Cub and then Boy Scouts; and eventually a real job for real wages in a real employment situation and a house of his own, where he lives with support.

By hanging in with the fact of disability and the many interventions that come Nolan's way and that have yet to become part of his life, and by hanging out in all the places where Bridget and the many children in his neighborhood go, Nolan demonstrates that, even though he has a disability, he is not unable.

Sean and Kris also demonstrate another aspect of life affected by disability: For all their knowledge and access to resources, they cannot go it alone. They have to create teams and even invite those team members to be part of their lives. Deliberately and out of love for Nolan, they have begun to "give Nolan away" to his community, to change not only his life but their own and the lives of all the people who will be privileged to be touched by Nolan, whether or not they have disabilities and are or are not in special education. As Sean, ever the special education professor, points out, quoting the federal law, "Special education is a service, not a place." So Nolan's place is where his sister goes and brother will go—into our schools, communities, and hearts.

What do you think?

1. **How might Nolan's early intervention prepare him to benefit from his preschool experience at Raintree Montessori School?**
2. **What will happen to Nolan's opportunities to hang out with children of his own age if he does not continue to receive speech therapy?**
3. **What skill is more important for Nolan to develop—speech or mobility? Or is it not desirable to set priorities?**

To respond to these questions online, participate in other activities, and learn more about Nolan Smith, go to the Cases module in Chapter 1 of the Companion Website. For more information visit our website at www.prenhall.com/turnbull

Profile of Special Education Students and Personnel in Today's Schools

Perhaps you have heard these lines written in 1624 by poet and minister John Donne: "never send to know for whom the *bell* tolls; It tolls for *thee*" (from *Devotions upon Emergent Occasions*, meditation 17).

Disability affects nearly 15 percent of all infants, toddlers, children, and adolescents; it eventually affects most of us as we age. For you, then, the disability bell could toll at least twice: once as you teach, and once as you age. For some of you, the bell peals more frequently because you have a family member or close friend with a disability or because you yourself have special needs.

When the bell tolls, it tolls not only for people with the disability but also for their families, friends, teachers, school administrators, and communities. That is why we recite stories about real families, real children, and real educators. But stories alone are not enough to introduce you to the field of special education; so we also review the most recent research data, combining the real-life personal face of exceptionality with evidence-based, best-practice approaches in special education. As we introduce you to special education and the families, children, and educators, we discuss four themes: universal design for learning, inclusion, collaboration, and responding to the multicultural diversity of students.

To learn more about the *Twenty-Third Annual Report to Congress on the Implementation of the Individuals with Disabilities Education Act* (U.S. Department of Education, 2001), go to the Web Links module in Chapter 1 of the Companion Website. There you will find a link to the website of the U.S. Office of Special Education and Rehabilitation Services, where you can find a copy of that report.

Who Are the Students?

To answer the question "Who are the students in special education?" we describe (1) the total number of students with disabilities, (2) the age groups of these students, (3) provision of gifted education, (4) the categories of disabilities, and (5) issues about labels and language.

Total Number of Students Served

In the 1999–2000 school year, almost 5.75 million students, ages 6 to 21, received some form of special education (U.S. Department of Education, 2001). Here's another way to think about that statistic: 11.4 percent of the schools' enrolled students received special education services that year. That percentage reflects a huge growth in special education. Although the population of students ages 6 through 21 grew only 12 percent from 1990–1999, the number of students in the same age range with disabilities grew by 30 percent (U.S. Department of Education, 2001).

In addition, almost 206,000 infants and toddlers (ages birth through 2), or 1.8 percent of U.S. infants and toddlers, received early intervention services similar to those that Nolan is receiv-

Danny Ramirez's transition plan was that he would work in animal care, as he is doing here. (See pages 30 and 31 for more about Danny.)

ing. And almost 590,000 preschool children (ages 3 through 5), or approximately 5 percent of the preschool population, received early childhood services (U.S. Department of Education, 2001); Nolan, too, will soon head to preschool. Clearly, he has benefited from inclusive special education.

Age Groups of Students Served

Figure 1–1 depicts the percentage of students served in the 1999–2000 school year, according to five age groups (0 to 2, 3 to 5, 6 to 11, 12 to 17, and 18 to 21 years). About 83 percent of the students were between the ages of 6 to 17. Approximately three times as many children, age 0 to 5 years, received special education services as did students age eighteen to twenty-one years.

Gender of Students

In the general education school population, males and females are enrolled in equal proportion; but more than two-thirds of all students receiving special education are male (U.S. Department of Education, 1998). Boys greatly outnumber girls in two categories: learning disabilities and emotional disturbance (Valdez, Williamson, & Wagner, 1990). The U.S. Department of Education (1998) suggests three possible reasons for gender-disproportionate representation throughout special education: (1) physiological/maturational differences—girls mature earlier than boys, (2) education bias—there are more female teachers than male teachers referring students to special education, and (3) assessment bias—the tests that determine who has a disability tend to select boys rather than girls.

Provision of Gifted Education

Special education also serves students who have unusual gifts and talents (see Chapter 7). Although these students are not included in the federal law related to students with disabilities, 33 states have legislation requiring services for gifted education (Landrum, Katsiyannis, & DeWaard, 1998).

Disability Categories

The U.S. Department of Education collects data from the states according to students' type or category of disability. Table 1–1 sets out the numbers and percentages of students associated with each category.

Slightly more than two-thirds of all students with disabilities are classified into two categories: specific learning disabilities (50.5 percent) and speech or language impairments (19.1 percent). These two categories, when combined with the categories of mental retardation (10.8 percent) and emotional disturbance (8.2 percent), account for 88 percent of all students with disabilities. Beginning in Chapter 4, you will meet students who have disabilities, just as you have been introduced to Nolan. You will read about their characteristics and the education they receive. But before you read about categories and characteristics, a word of caution is in order.

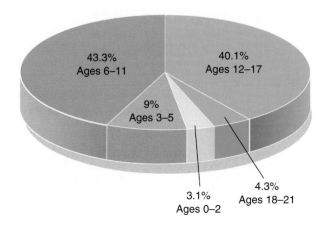

FIGURE 1–1
Percentage of students served by age groups in the 1999–2000 school year

Source: From U.S. Department of Education. (1999). To *Assure the Free Appropriate Public Education of All Children with Disabilities: Twenty-First Annual Report to Congress on the Implementation of the Individuals With Disabilities Education Act.* Washington, DC: Author.

TABLE 1–1

Categories of disabilities and corresponding numbers and percentages of students ages 6 to 21 served in the 1999–2000 school year

Disability	IDEA, Part B	
	Number	%
Specific learning disabilities	2,871,966	50.5
Speech or language impairments	1,089,964	19.0
Mental retardation	614,433	10.8
Emotional disturbance	470,111	8.2
Multiple disabilities	112,993	2.0
Hearing impairments	71,671	1.3
Orthopedic impairments	71,422	1.3
Other health impairments	254,110	4.5
Autism	65,424	1.1
Visual impairments	26,590	.46
Traumatic brain injury	13,874	.24
Developmental delay	19,304	.34
Deaf-blindness	1,845	.03

Source: From U.S. Department of Education. (1999). *To Assure the Free Appropriate Public Education of All Children with Disabilities: Twenty-First Annual Report to Congress on the Implementation of the Individuals with Disabilities Act* (p. A-2). Washington, DC: Author.

Labels and Language

How would you feel if you were known only by your disability and not according to your abilities? Devalued? Probably. Indeed, that is precisely how many families and special educators respond when a child with disabilities is labeled as a "disabled person" first and foremost. In Figure 1–2, you will find examples of how disability terms have changed over the years.

There is a great deal of controversy about labeling and about its consequences, which include classification in schools—specifically, classification into special education. Students can benefit if a label qualifies them to receive services because those services can outweigh the stigma that accompanies some labels (MacMillan & Meyers, 1979; Mesibov, Adams, & Klinger, 1997), even ones such as "nerd" (frequently applied to students with special talents and gifts; see Chapter 7). Indeed, some people with hearing and visual impairments (see Chapters 15 and 16) welcome the labels.

On the other hand, labeling can lead educators to regard a student as a broken person whom they must "fix" (Obiakor, 1999; Patton, 1998; Reschly, 1996). Labeling also can segregate students with disabilities from their classmates without disabilities (Kliewer & Biklin, 1996; Lipsky & Gartner, 1989). And even though the benefits of separate special education are supposed to outweigh the limitations of separation, they often do not, as we show later in this chapter (Adelman, 1996; Reynolds, 1991). Indeed, labeling can reflect biases against students' ethnic, linguistic, or cultural backgrounds (Obiakor, 1999; Patton, 1998).

Rather than debating the relative benefits and drawbacks of labels, some special educators are developing new classification systems. These emphasize students' instructional needs, not their labels, so teachers can provide students with appropriate education.

> The interest of many is in replacing current categories with a system that identifies special individual needs (1) only as such needs become relevant to providing an appropriate education and (2) through a process and terminology that have direct relevance to intervention and that minimize negative consequences. (Adelman, 1996, p. 99)

FIGURE 1–2
Terms reflecting social changes

Areas of Disability	Past	Present
Mental retardation	Idiots, feebleminded, cretin, mentally deficient, educably retarded or trainably retarded, morons, high level or low level	Mild, moderate, severe retardation and requiring intermittent, pervasive, extensive, and limited supports
Learning disabilities	Dyslexia, minimal cerebral dysfunction, specific learning disabilities, learning disabilities	Learning disabilities
Emotional disturbance	Unsocialized, dementia, emotionally disturbed, acting out, withdrawn	Emotional or behavioral disorders (EBD)
Attention deficit disorder (with or without hyperactivity)	Hyperactivity, specific learning disabilities	ADD (Attention Deficit Disorder without hyperactivity) or AD/HD (with hyperactivity) and combined
Head injuries	Strephosymbolia, brain crippled children, brain injured, closed head injury	Traumatic brain injury
Deafness	Deaf and dumb, deaf mute	Severely/profoundly hearing impaired
Persons with orthopedic disabilities	Crippled children, physically handicapped	Physical disabilities
Learning disability in reading	Dyslexia, minimal cerebral dysfunction, specific learning disabilities	Dyslexia
Autism	Childhood schizophrenia, children with refrigerator parents, Kanner's syndrome, autoid	Autism (high functioning or low functioning) or Autism spectrum

Source: From "The Ins and Outs of Special Education Terminology" by G. A. Vergason and M. L. Anderegg, 1997, *Teaching Exceptional Children, 29*(5), p. 36. Copyright 1997 by the Council for Exceptional Children. Reprinted with permission.

So we ask you to be cautious about using labels. Let Nolan be Nolan, not a youngster with a label. If you or other educators must use labels, avoid those that demean and stigmatize, for they almost always contribute to separation and devaluation in and outside of school (Goffman, 1963). Instead, use esteeming ones and emphasize your students' strengths. Figure 1–3 illustrates the impacts of labels, and Box 1–1 lets you hear from Nancy Ward, a national spokesperson for people with disabilities and thus a reliable source for knowing how people with disabilities often feel about labels. Read about Nancy and ask yourself if you use these labels to describe her— *"insightful," "good communicator," "assertive"*—instead of "retarded" or worse.

Because labels can affect teachers' and students' expectations, we hope that you will regard your students in terms of what they can do rather than what they cannot now do. Expect Nolan and others with disabilities to have or to develop (with the assistance of general and special educators, their peers, and their families) their inherent strengths and to make positive contributions to others and their communities. Expect them to be included in the same

To learn more about self-advocacy—students with disabilities speaking out to satisfy their own needs—go to the Web Links module in Chapter 1 of the Companion Website.

FIGURE 1–3
The impact of labels

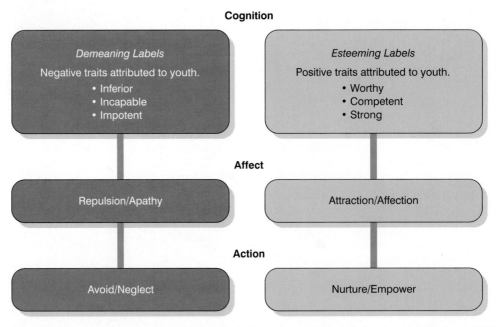

Source: From *Reclaiming Youth at Risk: Our Hope for the Future* (pp. 15–16) by L. K. Brendtro, M. Brokenleg, and S. Van Bockern, 1990. Bloomington, IN: National Educational Services. Copyright 1990 by National Educational Services. Reprinted with permission.

schools and many times in the same academic, extracurricular, and other school programs as their peers without disabilities; after all, that's Nolan's life—hanging out with children who do not have disabilities. Indeed, expect students with disabilities to have the same kinds of postsecondary experiences as you are having and as Stelios Gragoudas is having, as he explains in Box 1–2.

To show esteem for their students, most educators use "people-first" language. For example, instead of using phrases such as "the retarded" or "retarded children," they prefer "students with mental retardation." Even better, you might consider decreasing the use of labels. Why not just say "students"? Better yet, just "Nolan."

We use people-first language in this book to emphasize that disability does not supersede every other characteristic that a person might have.

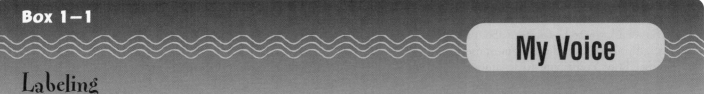

Box 1—1

My Voice

Labeling

I became a self-advocate ten years ago. Being a self-advocate is very important to me because my self-advocacy skills taught me how to see myself as a person because of all the labels placed on me. People used to make fun of me all the time.

It is real hard for me not to be upset by being called retarded or dummy, names like that. They would really hurt my feelings. It is real hard for me to deal with my feelings now. I have learned that getting mad does not do any good. I have learned to talk to people about how that makes me feel.

—Nancy Ward

Source: From *Self-Determination* by N. Ward, 1989, January. Paper presented at the National Conference on Self-determination. Arlington, VA.

Box 1—2

Stel Goes to Graduate School

Education has always been an important part of my life. My parents always stressed the importance of having the best education you possibly could obtain. It wasn't only learning that excited me; it was also being with other students, playing kickball, and making friends that enriched my educational experience.

I began my school career at the same time that P.L. 94-142 (better known today as IDEA) was passed. Therefore, educating students with disabilities was a new experience for my school district. The faculty did not know how to include students with disabilities into a program for students without disabilities. My teachers did the best they could by including me in all the instances they thought were appropriate. For the subjects that I needed extra help in, I went to a resource room where I could receive the extra assistance I needed. Thinking back, I liked that system. Even though I was out of my homeroom for a couple of hours a week, I still felt as if that room was my base. It was where all my friends were and where I could do exactly what all the other students were doing.

All that changed when I went to middle school and high school. It was as if my education took a 360-degree turn. When a student moves up to middle school, academics are the focal point of the educational experience. Therefore, my educational team had to answer a very important question: Could I keep up with the academic program that was offered at the middle school? My teachers were not too optimistic. They believed that even though I had fared well in elementary school, middle school was going to be too challenging for me. My parents, however, insisted that I be included in the general curriculum as much as possible. So my IEP called for me to be placed in the general curriculum for some of my subjects and in a resource room for the others.

This program was similar to my elementary school experience with one great distinction. In middle school, my base was not the place where I felt included. It was the place where I felt excluded. That base was my resource room, where I was excluded from most of the students who were in my academic classes. This did not allow me to form the kinds of friendships that I did in elementary school. I do not have many fond memories of that period of my educational career.

High school was a similar situation. Even though I had good grades in all of my academic classes, my teachers still recommended that academics should not be the focal point of my education and that I should focus on vocational goals. My parents did not agree with this plan. They always believed that I should be pushed to my limit.

The school agreed with hesitation and opted to place me in a collaborative program within the high school. I would be able to participate in the high school classes, and the collaborative would provide me with a tutor and other supports that I needed to succeed in high school. As I look back, the collaborative program was not all that bad. It provided me with additional services that I needed to succeed in my high school, such as speech therapy and adapted gym.

However, the same thing that had happened in middle school was happening all over again. Instead of feeling like a student at my high school, I felt like a guest. Even though I had my classes with students in the high school, when class was over, they would go in one direction and I would go back to the collaborative. Even though I was free to eat lunch with them, I chose not to because I felt like an outsider who was only a guest in the high school and I felt at home eating lunch with my fellow classmates in the collaborative program.

I always knew that I wanted to go to college. It was what everyone else in my class was thinking about, so I caught the bug as well. Once again, however, I met opposition from my special education teachers. The teachers from my high school classes were more supportive because they knew the work I had done in their classes and felt that I was ready for college-level academics.

The process of applying to school was very exciting. The experience of going to visit schools, meeting students with disabilities who were already in college, writing essays, and finding out how colleges supported people with disabilities was extremely informative.

It also provided me with a new idea of what it meant to be independent. To that point, independence to me meant going to the mall by myself or going on a trip with my friend instead of my family. In college, independence meant making sure I had all of the supports that I needed to live independently or talking with professors about accommodations that I needed in class. College gave me two things. It gave me the academic background that I needed to begin the career that I am still in today. Equally important, it gave me the skills I needed to live independently and to direct my own future.

I am still a student. I am working towards my doctoral degree in special education. Sometimes I think it would be amusing to go back to my high school and show some of my old teachers what I have accomplished since I started postsecondary education, but then I think it would be a better idea to focus my attention on improving special education and education as a whole so that every student with a disability can receive the most appropriate education alongside classmates without disabilities.

What Are the Socioeconomic Characteristics of Students with Exceptionalities?

The socioeconomic status of the students and their families profoundly affects students' educational needs. Two key aspects of socioeconomic status are family income and the level of family members' education.

Stelios Gradoudas is studying for his Ph.D. in special education while he also works at the Beach Center on Disability at The University of Kansas.

Family Income

Nearly one in five American children (19.9 percent) lives in poverty (Children's Defense Fund, 1999). Figure 1–4 highlights the devastating effects of poverty on children and their families. The poverty rate is even higher for children who have disabilities. Approximately two-thirds of youths with disabilities ages 12–17 are from households with an annual income of less than $25,000 (National Council on Disability, 2000). An analysis of a national data base of families who have children with and without disabilities revealed that (Fujiura & Yamaki, 2000):

Poverty affects children not just in areas such as food and shelter but also in the quality of their schools, as you will learn later in this chapter.

▼ The proportion of American children living in poverty has increased significantly in the past decade.

▼ The greatest concentration of poverty is found among single-parent households.

▼ Each of these trends is stronger in households where a child has a disability than in households where a child does not have a disability.

The interaction of urban living, poverty, and disability is especially distressing. For example, in 165 urban schools serving 140,000 students, more than 80 percent of the entire population lives in poverty (Gottlieb, Alter, Gottlieb, & Wishner, 1994). Within those 165 schools, approximately two-thirds of the children in the general education program were unable to read at grade level. These students "suffer the ravages of poverty" and its damaging effects on academic performance; they may not, in fact, have a disability as such (Gottlieb et al., 1994, p. 456).

To learn about the impact of poverty on children's development, go to the Web Links module in Chapter 1 of the Companion Website for a link to the Children's Defense Fund.

Family Education Level

Likewise, disability and a family's education level are related to each other. Seventy-eight percent of the heads of households who have children without disabilities have completed high school; by contrast, 59 percent of heads of households that have students with disabilities have completed high school (National Council on Disabilities, 2000). A family's education level can affect many aspects of a student's education, including the family's educational goals for their child, the family's capacity to assist with homework, its comfort in developing partnerships with educators, and its ability to support children to make educationally-related decisions (National Council on Disability, 2000).

FIGURE 1–4

Children's outcomes by family income

Outcome	Low-income children's higher risk
Health	
Death in childhood	1.5 to 3 times more likely
Stunted growth	2.7 times more likely
Iron deficiency as preschoolers	3 to 4 times more likely
Partly or completely deaf	1.5 to 2 times more likely
Partly or completely blind	1.2 to 1.8 times more likely
Serious physical or mental disability	about 2 times more likely
Fatal accidental injuries	2 to 3 times more likely
Pneumonia	1.6 times more likely
Education	
Average of IQ scores at age 5	9 test points lower
Average achievement scores for ages 3 and older	11 to 25 percentiles lower
Learning disabilities	1.3 times more likely
In special education	2 or 3 percentage points more likely
Below usual grade for child's age	2 percentage points more likely for each year of childhood spent in poverty
Dropping out between ages 16 and 24	2 times more likely than middle-income youths; 11 times more likely than wealthy youths.

Source: Sherman, A. (1997). *Poverty matters: The cost of child poverty in America.* Washington, DC: Children's Defense Fund.

What Are the Racial/Ethnic Trends Related to Students with Exceptionalities?

The current demographic composition of the United States is as follows (Deardorff & Hollmann, 1997):

▼ European American—73 percent

▼ African American—12 percent

▼ Latino (sometimes the term "Hispanic American" is a synonym for "Latino")—11 percent

▼ Asian American—3 percent

▼ Native American—1 percent

The terms that describe various racial/ethnic groups vary. Consistent with the recommendations of leading multicultural educators (Gollnick & Chinn, 2002), we usually use the terms identified in the previous list. We use other terms such as "black" and "white" only in quotation marks. We also only use the term "minority" in quotation marks.

Latinos are the fastest growing racial group in the United States and are predicted to have more members than African Americans by the year 2005 (National Research Council, 2001). Overall, the United States is expected to become far more diverse by the year 2050, with the European American population dropping from 73 percent to 53 percent of the total population (National Research Council, 2001). Because European Americans have a smaller percentage of children under the age of 17 than do the other racial/ethnic groups, the school-age population

Nearly half of all students in special education are from low-income families in urban areas.

is more diverse than the total U.S. population and will continue to be so (National Research Council, 2001).

National experts emphasize that "race and ethnicity continue to be salient predictors of well-being in American society" (National Research Council, 2001, p. 21). That statement certainly rings true, for race and ethnicity clearly are factors in the identification of students having a disability. Table 1–2 summarizes these recent trends of placement in special education for students from different racial/ethnic groups.

Table 1–2 also reveals that the greatest disproportionality affects African American students. From population statistics, one might expect that 14.5 percent of African American students would be identified as having a disability; however, 20.3 percent of African American students have an identified disability. The percentage of African American students who have been identified as having mental retardation is 34.2 percent, and the percentage identified as having emotional or behavioral disturbances is 27.3 percent.

What are racial/ethnic trends of students who are gifted? Ford (1998) cites data from a 1992 Office of Civil Rights Study that indicate that African American, Latino, and Native American students were underrepresented by 40 to 50 percent in gifted education. Alternatively, European American students were overrepresented by 17 percent and Asian American students by 43 percent. Three major factors are associated with the underrepresentation of students from African American, Latino, and Native American backgrounds (Ford, 1998):

▼ *Procedures for identifying students for gifted programs.* Teachers and parents tend to refer students from diverse backgrounds less frequently, and students from diverse backgrounds tend to be not as proficient in performing well on standardized tests as students from other backgrounds.

▼ *The practice known as tracking.* Educators place students from poor and diverse backgrounds in lower ability grouping and have lower expectations and provide fewer opportunities for them than for other students.

▼ *Students' own feelings.* They may feel isolated in gifted programs when the percentage of other students from diverse backgrounds in those programs is low.

TABLE 1–2
Percentage of Students Ages 6 through 21 Served by Disability and Race/Ethnicity in the 1998–1999 School Year

Disability	American Indian	Asian/Pacific Islander	Black (non-Hispanic)	Hispanic	White (non-Hispanic)
Specific learning disabilities	1.4	1.4	18.3	15.8	63.0
Speech and language impairments	1.2	2.4	16.5	11.6	68.3
Mental retardation	1.1	1.7	34.3	8.9	54.1
Emotional disturbance	1.1	1.0	26.4	9.8	61.6
Multiple disabilities	1.4	2.3	19.3	10.9	66.1
Hearing impairments	1.4	4.6	16.8	16.3	66.0
Orthopedic impairments	.8	3.0	14.6	14.4	67.2
Other health impairments	1.0	1.3	14.1	7.8	75.8
Visual impairments	1.3	3.0	14.8	11.4	69.5
Autism	.7	4.7	20.9	9.4	64.4
Deaf-blindness	1.8	11.3	11.5	12.1	63.3
Traumatic brain injury	1.6	2.3	15.9	10.0	70.2
Developmental delay	.5	1.1	33.7	4.0	60.8
All disabilities	1.3	1.7	20.2	13.2	63.6
Resident population	1.0	3.8	14.8	14.2	66.2

Source: U.S. Department of Education, Office of Special Education Programs, Data Analysis System (DANS).

The National Research Council (2002) recently issued a report about the disproportionate number of students from diverse backgrounds who receive special education services. The report answered four key questions. For each question, we summarize the data reported by the Council and supplement it with additional research findings.

First, "*Is there a reason to believe that there is currently a higher incidence of special needs or giftedness among some racial/ethnic groups? Specifically, are there biological and social or contextual contributors to early development that differ by race or ethnicity?*" The National Research Council (2002) answered with a definitive yes for the following reasons:

▼ Children from diverse backgrounds disproportionally are members of families with low incomes.

▼ Low income is associated with higher rates of exposure to dangerous toxins, poor nutrition, less stimulating home and child care environments, and lower birth weight.

▼ Given the higher accumulation of risk factors in children by race/ethnicity groups, it is not surprising that race/ethnicity differences are evident in school readiness at the kindergarten level.

You have already learned about the devastating impact of poverty on children's development. What factors contribute to African American students' having the most disproportionate placement in special education? One factor is that, for almost two decades, African Americans have been approximately 2½ times more likely than European Americans to experience poverty: "the higher disability rate commonly observed among minority children appears to be largely associated with the disproportionate representation of poor and single-parent households in the minority community" (Fujiura & Yamaki, 2000, p. 191).

Companion Website

To learn more about the National Research Council, go to the Web Links module in Chapter 1 of the Companion Website.

Second, "*Does schooling independently contribute to the incidence of special needs or giftedness among students in different racial/ethnic groups through the opportunities that it provides?*" The National Research Council (2002) concluded:

▼ Schools with more children from low income and racially/ethnically diverse backgrounds experience significant disadvantages as compared to schools with a higher concentration of children from middle- and upper-income backgrounds who are not characterized by racial and ethnic diversity, and these disadvantages are manifest in:
  • Lower per-student expenditures
  • Fewer advanced-level academic courses
  • Fewer experienced, well-trained teachers

Third, "*Does the current referral and assessment process reliably identify students with special needs and gifts? In particular, is there reason to believe that the current process is biased in terms of race or ethnicity?*" The National Research Council (2002) did not draw a definitive conclusion about those questions, although it pointed out that room for bias certainly exists in how referrals and assessment are handled. The Council was, however, clear on the subject of reliability of the referral and assessment processes:

▼ The referral process for special education is subjective and results in some students with significant learning problems not being properly referred.

▼ Major problems exist in the identification of students as having a learning disability or an emotional and behavioral disorder.

▼ Many students would benefit more from earlier identification so that special needs could be addressed as soon as possible.

Other recent research shows that both African American and Latino students are more likely to be referred to special education than are European American students (Hosp & Reschly, in press a).

For a very long time, educators have debated whether IQ testing is biased against students from culturally and linguistically diverse backgrounds. According to the National Research Council (2002), this debate has not been definitively resolved. The Council points out that many children from diverse backgrounds are not as familiar as their age-peers from other backgrounds with how to take a test and with the general educational norms and expectations; these two facts can contribute to lower scores.

Fourth, "*Is placement in special education a benefit or a risk? Does the outcome differ by race or ethnic group?*" The National Research Council (2002) reported that sufficient information is not available to answer these questions with confidence. The Council did, however, mention the following considerations:

▼ Some interventions developed for students with exceptionalities have been found to produce positive outcomes for students, but the extent to which these interventions are implemented is not known.

▼ Information is not available to determine whether students from diverse racial/ethnic backgrounds have the same opportunities to be exposed to quality interventions as students who do not experience diversity.

▼ Factors associated with high-quality intervention, such as teacher quality and parent advocacy, are less likely to occur in schools with a high concentration of students from poverty backgrounds.

The Council implored teachers to use evidence-based instruction—that is, instruction whose effectiveness has been documented through research—to promote achievement and appropriate behavior from the earliest years. Furthermore, no students should have to wait to fail in order to receive special services. As Figure 1–4 shows, it is important to support students who experience poverty beginning in their earliest years because these students have a lower chance of being successful in later years than their peers do.

Who Are Special Education Personnel?

If you are considering a career in special education, your job prospects are quite good. According to the most recent data from the U.S. Department of Education (2001), approximately 387,284 special education teachers were employed in 1998–1999 to teach students ages 6 through 21. But for the 1999–2000 school year, approximately 7,000 job openings existed for special education teachers (U.S. Department of Education, 2001). At least one special education teacher vacancy was present in almost 97 percent of school districts. Of these openings that occurred, more than 12,000 of the positions were left vacant or were filled by substitutes because fully certified special education teachers were not available.

Not all special education professionals are teachers. Remember Nolan and the early interventionists who work for him and his family? You will identify some of them in the following list of other personnel who provide special education services: school social workers, occupational therapists, physical therapists, recreation and therapeutic specialists, teacher aides, physical education teachers, supervisors/administrators, psychologists, diagnostic/evaluation staff, audiologists, work-study coordinators, vocational education teachers, counselors, rehabilitation counselors, interpreters, speech therapists, and professors such as Sean Smith, Nolan's father and co-author of this book. The number of certified nonteaching personnel in these roles during the 1999–2000 school year totaled 411,089. Teacher aides accounted for about 64 percent of these positions.

You know now that there is a shortage of both special education teachers and some related service professionals. What you may not know is how rewarding it can be to be a special educator. To get some sense of that reward, read Box 1–3, which tells the story of the 2002 Special Education Teacher of the Year.

To learn more about career opportunities in special education, go to the Web Links module in Chapter 1 of the Companion Website for a link to the Council for Exceptional Children.

The Law and Special Education

For more than 30 years now, the education of students with disabilities has been governed by a law that Congress enacted in 1975. That law is called the Individuals with Disabilities Education Act and is known as IDEA. Whatever role you play in American schools, you almost certainly will have to know something about this law, the rights it gives students, and the duties it imposes on schools. Let's begin with a bit of its history.

Two Types of Discrimination

During the early and middle decades of the 20th century, schools discriminated against students with disabilities in two significant ways (Turnbull, Turnbull, Stowe, & Wilcox, 2000). First, they completely excluded many students with disabilities. Or if they did admit students with disabilities, they did not always provide the students with an effective or appropriate education. Second, schools often classified students as having disabilities when they in fact did not have disabilities. Frequently, these students were members of culturally and linguistically diverse groups. In addition, schools sometimes labeled students with one kind of disability when the students really had other kinds of disabilities.

Beginning in the early 1970s, advocates for students with disabilities—primarily, their families, parent advocacy organizations, and civil rights lawyers—began to sue state and local school officials, claiming that exclusion and misclassification violated the students' rights to an equal education opportunity under the U.S. Constitution (Turnbull et al., 2000; Yell, 1998). Relying on the Supreme Court's decision in the school race-desegregation case (*Brown v. Board of Education*, 1954), they argued that, because *Brown* held that schools may not segregate by race, schools also may not segregate or otherwise discriminate by ability and disability. Students are students regardless of their race or disability.

Box 1–3

What Don't You Understand About No?

Each year, the Council for Exceptional Children, the nation's special educator professional association, selects a Teacher of the Year. In 2002, Kelli Kercheer, a high school teacher, took the prize. Why?

For starters, she won't take no for an answer. Some words are so simple that it is surprising that not everyone understands them. For example, IDEA applies to all students with disabilities. So what don't we understand about "all"? Likewise, what do we not understand about no? And where does yes fit in? After all, these are absolute words; they do not allow for equivocation. But when we start to jumble them up with each other, they can become complicated. That's when we turn to Kelli, who simplifies them for us.

Here's what she's heard. "No, your student with autism may not enroll in my keyboarding class; he'll make too much noise." "No, your student with a physical disability may not enroll in my Japanese language class." "No, your students with disabilities may not participate in the peer leadership group, the pep club, the choir, the diving team, or the school play."

It's best not to say no to Kelli. She's got strategies to turn no into yes. One is to create a peer-tutoring program in which students without disabilities learn about disabilities and how to react to the challenges they pose by interviewing students with disabilities, talking to people from different age groups about disabilities, and maintaining a journal about their own responses to disability and what they are learning. The upshot: The students don't just put themselves into the shoes of a person with a disability (to the extent possible) but they learn that students with and without disabilities have many of the same interests and talents.

From learning, Kelli goes to doing by pairing students with and without disabilities with each other at lunch and in extracurricular activities. From pairing comes friendship, and from friendship comes participation in the curriculum and the extracurricular activities of the school. Kelli's teaching, then, encompasses students with and students without disabilities. That's not enough, however: She has to change the attitudes and behaviors of general educators. The law requires inclusion; but until the teachers buy into the law, there will not be much inclusion. So step by step, Kelli and her special education students and their peers without disabilities begin to participate in the general curriculum.

For example, one student with autism stayed in the keyboarding class for a few minutes one week, for a longer time the next, and then full time thereafter. Likewise, a student with Down syndrome distributed the printed program at the school play one year; in the next year, the student had a speaking role in the play.

No can become yes. That may be one thing we do not understand about no. And yes can become "all." That's something else we may not understand about words. In the hands of a dream maker like Kelli, the teacher who expects much, not little, from students with disabilities, from those who do not have disabilities, and from her faculty peers, turning words around through action results in turning lives around through action. To make students' dreams come true means saying yes whenever someone says no. To make their dreams come true means saying all when some teachers say "some" or "one" student may participate.

Reversing expectations and abandoning negativity is what special education is all about; it's certainly what Kelli Kercher is all about. Now what about you? What will you be all about? Will you be a yes sayer and a dream maker like Kelli?

Two Revolutionary Judicial Decisions

The advocates' arguments proved to be very successful. In 1972, federal courts ordered the Commonwealth of Pennsylvania and the District of Columbia to (1) provide a free appropriate public education to all students with disabilities, (2) educate students with disabilities in the same schools and basically the same programs as students without disabilities, and (3) put into place certain procedural safeguards so that students with disabilities can challenge schools that do not live up to the courts' orders (*Mills v. Washington, DC, Board of Education*, 1972; *Pennsylvania Association for Retarded Citizens [PARC] v. Commonwealth of Pennsylvania*, 1972).

Within a short time, families began advocating in Congress for a federal law and federal money that would guarantee students' rights to an education and help states pay for special education. They were armed with these court orders and were supported by professionals, organized as the Council for Exceptional Children, and by governors and state legislators, who wanted the federal money to educate the students. The advocates were immensely successful.

Introduction to IDEA: Progress but Problems

In 1975, Congress enacted IDEA (then called the Education of All Handicapped Students Act, or Public Law (PL) 94–142).

In enacting the federal law in 1975, Congress intended to open up the schools to all students with disabilities and make sure that they had the chance to benefit from special education. Nowadays, the challenge is not to provide access only but to assure that the students really do *benefit*. In a word, educators and policymakers are determined to secure favorable results for students; they are focused on outcomes. Later in this chapter you will read about benefits and the results of special education, but now you need to know about the basic components of IDEA.

To learn more about IDEA, go to the Web Links module in Chapter 1 of the Companion Website and click on *www.ideapractices.org*.

Special Education and Students' Eligibility

Eligibility Based on Need

IDEA defines special education as specially designed instruction, at no cost to the child's parents, to meet the unique needs of a student with a disability (20 U.S.C., sec. 1401[25]). A student with a disability is one who has certain disabilities (which we identify later in the chapter) and who, because of the impairment, needs special education and related services (20 U.S.C., sec. 1401[3]). So special education is reserved for students who need it because of their impairments/disabilities and whose needs cannot be satisfied in general education.

Where Special Education Is Provided

Special education occurs in classrooms, students' homes (where Nolan receives his), hospitals and institutions, and other settings. So special education is provided wherever there are students with disabilities.

Components of Special Education

Special education is individualized to the student; that is the meaning of "to meet the unique needs" of the student. To meet a student's needs, it is usually necessary to provide more than individualized instruction by supplementing instruction with "related services"—namely, services that are necessary to assist the student to benefit from special education (20 U.S.C., sec. 1401[22]). Figure 1–5 identifies and defines related services. Nolan, of course, receives some of these already—speech therapy, physical therapy, and, less often, occupational therapy.

Categorical and Functional Approaches to Eligibility

As you just read, a student is eligible for special education and related services if the student has a disability and, because of the disability, needs specially designed instruction. Note the two-part standard for eligibility: (1) there is a *categorical* element—the student must have a disability; and (2) there is a *functional* element—the disability must cause the student to need specially designed instruction.

The Span of Special Education: Birth Through 21

Over the course of the years since it first enacted IDEA in 1975, Congress has expanded the group of students who have a right to special education. At first, the group consisted of students ages 6 to 18, but now it includes the very young (infants and toddlers from birth through age 2, such as Nolan), young children (ages 3 through 5), and older students (ages 6 through 21). Because the needs of and services provided to the very young (birth to 2) are so different from needs and services for older children (ages 3 through 21), IDEA is divided into two parts—Part B and Part C. (Part A sets out Congress's intent and national policy to provide a free appropriate public education to all students, ages birth through 21.)

Ages 3 Through 21 and Part B.
Part B benefits students ages 3 through 21 who have a disability and because of it need special education. As the preceding sentence says, and as you soon will read, Part B combines the categorical approach (that is, the categories of disabilities, the

FIGURE 1–5
Definitions of related services in IDEA

- **Audiology:** determining the range, nature, and degree of hearing loss and operating programs for treatment and prevention of hearing loss.
- **Counseling services:** counseling by social workers, psychologists, guidance counselors, and rehabilitation specialists.
- **Early identification:** identifying a disability as early as possible in a child's life.
- **Family training, counseling, and home visits:** assisting families to enhance their child's development (Part C only).
- **Health services:** enabling a child to benefit from other early intervention services (Part C only).
- **Medical services:** determining a child's medically related disability that results in the child's need for special education and related services.
- **Nursing services:** assessing health status, preventing health problems, and administering medications, treatments, and regimens prescribed by a licensed physician (Part C only).
- **Nutrition services:** conducting individual assessments to address the nutritional needs of children (Part C only).
- **Occupational therapy:** improving, developing, or restoring functions impaired or lost through illness, injury, or deprivation.
- **Orientation and mobility services:** assisting a student to get around within various environments.
- **Parent counseling and training:** providing parents with information about child development.
- **Physical therapy:** screening, referral, and service provision for therapy regarding bone and muscle capacity.
- **Psychological services:** administering and interpreting psychological and educational tests and other assessment procedures and managing a program of psychological services, including psychological counseling for children and parents.
- **Recreation and therapeutic recreation:** assessing leisure function, recreation programs in schools and community agencies, and leisure education.
- **Rehabilitative counseling services:** planning for career development, employment preparation, achieving independence, and integration in the workplace and community.
- **School health services:** attending to educationally related health needs through services provided by a school nurse.
- **Service coordination services:** assistance and services by a service coordinator to a child and family (Part C only).
- **Social work services in schools:** preparing a social or developmental history on a child, counseling groups and individuals, and mobilizing school and community resources.
- **Speech pathology and speech-language pathology:** diagnosing specific speech or language impairments and giving guidance regarding speech and language impairments.
- **Transportation and related costs:** providing travel to and from services and schools, travel in and around school buildings, and specialized equipment (e.g., special or adapted buses, lifts, and ramps).
- **Assistive technology and services:** acquiring and using devices and services to restore lost capacities or improve impaired capacities.

labels of disabilities) with the functional approach (the student cannot function in the general curriculum without assistance) to define which students qualify for special education. The IDEA categories for children ages 6 through 21 are the following (you will learn about these categories in Chapters 4 to 16):

▼ Specific learning disabilities (Chapter 4)

▼ Emotional disturbance (Chapter 5)

▼ Mental retardation (Chapter 8)

▼ Multiple disabilities (Chapter 9)

▼ Deaf-blindness (Chapter 9)

▼ Autism (Chapter 10)

▼ Other health impairments (Chapter 11)

▼ Orthopedic impairments (Chapter 12)

▼ Traumatic brain injury (Chapter 13)

▼ Speech or language impairments (Chapter 14)

▼ Hearing impairments (Chapter 15)

▼ Visual impairments (Chapter 16)

These same categories apply to children ages 3 to 9 (those in early childhood special education), but each state may provide special education to children who meet only the functional approach to disability—namely, those who

▼ Are experiencing developmental delays in one or more of the following areas: physical development, cognitive development, communication development, social or emotional development, or adaptive behavior, and development

▼ Because of these delays, need special education and related services

IDEA gives the states discretion whether to serve children ages 3 through 5 (early education). As of early 2002, all states do so.

Ages Birth Through 2 (Also Known As Zero to 3) and Part C. IDEA also gives the states discretion about whether to serve infants and toddlers such as Nolan. As of early 2002, all states were serving infants and toddlers under Part C.

Part C benefits any child under age 3 who (1) needs early intervention services because of developmental delays in one or more of the areas of cognitive development, physical development, social or emotional development, or adaptive development; or (2) has a diagnosed physical or mental condition that has a high probability of resulting in a developmental delay. Nolan meets the first definition. Part C does more than benefit the children who have identified delays. It also gives each state the option of serving at-risk infants and toddlers: those who would be at risk of experiencing a substantial developmental delay if they did not receive early intervention services. Note the difference: A child with a diagnosed condition that has a "high probability" of resulting in a developmental delay is not the same as a child who is "at risk" of having a delay.

IDEA: Six Principles

It is not enough for IDEA simply to identify the eligible students and to specify what services they have a right to receive. Because of the schools' past discrimination through exclusion and misclassification, IDEA also establishes six principles that govern students' education (Turnbull, et al., 2000). Figure 1–6 describes those six principles.

IDEA now grants educational rights to children with disabilities from birth through age 2 (Part C) as well as from ages 3 through 21 (Part B).

FIGURE 1–6
Six principles governing the education of students with disabilities

- **Zero reject:** A rule against excluding any student.
- **Nondiscriminatory evaluation:** A rule requiring schools to evaluate students fairly to determine if they have a disability and, if so, what kind and how extensive.
- **Appropriate education:** A rule requiring schools to provide individually tailored education for each student based on the evaluation and augmented by related services and supplementary aids and services.
- **Least restrictive environment:** A rule requiring schools to educate students with disabilities with students without disabilities to the maximum extent appropriate for the students with disabilities.
- **Procedural due process:** A rule providing safeguards for students against schools' actions, including a right to sue in court.
- **Parental and student participation:** A rule requiring schools to collaborate with parents and adolescent students in designing and carrying out special education programs.

Zero Reject

The zero-reject principle prohibits schools from excluding any student with a disability from a free appropriate public education. The purpose of the zero-reject principle is to ensure that all children and youth (ages 3 to 21), no matter how severe their disabilities, have an appropriate education provided free (at public expense). To carry out this purpose, the zero-reject rule applies to the state and all of its school districts and to private schools, state-operated programs such as schools for students with visual or hearing impairments, psychiatric hospitals, and institutions for people with other disabilities.

Educability

In essence, the zero-reject rule means what it says: *No* student may be excluded from an education because of a disability. To carry out the zero-reject rule, courts have ordered state and local education agencies to provide services to children who traditionally have been regarded as ineducable (not able to learn) because of the profound extent of their disabilities. The courts are saying that "all" means "all"—Congress was very clear that it intends IDEA to benefit all children with disabilities, no matter how disabled they are.

Expulsion and Discipline

There is a great deal of controversy about whether Congress intended schools to adhere to the zero-reject policy when it conflicts with another school policy—namely, zero tolerance of student misbehavior. May schools expel students with disabilities whose behavior violates school rules and even jeopardizes the health and safety of other students and faculty? Congress answered that question with a resounding no, but it also set out specific procedures that schools must follow when disciplining students. Let's review the basic rules.

In a nutshell, the school may not completely exclude the student from a free appropriate education if the behavior that got the student into trouble is a manifestation of his or her disability. This is the "no-cessation" rule.

To maintain the kind of good order that leads to learning, however, the school may suspend the student for up to 10 days in any school year. If the school wants to suspend the student for a longer period of time, or if the total number of separate days of suspension add up to 10 in any one school year, then the school is changing the student's placement and must follow specific procedures to do so. These are the "ten-day" and "change of placement" rules.

Before the school may change the student's placement, however, it must determine whether the student's behavior is a manifestation of the student's disability: Does the behavior occur because of the disability? If the student's IEP team finds that (1) the school failed to deliver the services called for by the IEP, (2) the student did not understand that his or her behavior was a violation of the school code, or (3) the student could not control his or her behavior, then the disability caused the student's behavior. This is the "manifestation determination" rule.

The IEP team may recommend a different placement if it finds that the behavior is a manifestation of disability or if it wants to remove the student for more than 10 days. That is because the team is changing or considering changing the student's placement. In either case, the IEP team must conduct a functional behavioral assessment of the student and develop a behavioral intervention plan to address the student's behavior. The team must consider whether to use positive behavioral interventions, supports, and strategies. This is the "SBA/BIP" rule.

In all of these cases, the student has a right to appeal the school's decision and to stay in his or her present program. This is the "stay-put" rule.

These rules do not apply if the student's behavior involves weapons or drugs or is likely to seriously injure others. In those circumstances, the school may immediately remove the student from his or her present placement and put the student into an interim alternative educational setting for a maximum of 45 days. The stay-put rule does not apply; school safety is more important than the student's rights. The student, however, retains the right to an appropriate program, to participate in the general curriculum, to appeal the decision, and to require the school to conduct a functional behavioral assessment and develop a behavioral intervention plan (including one that involves positive behavioral interventions, supports, and services). This is the "45-day" rule.

Nondiscriminatory Evaluation

The effect of the zero-reject rule is to guarantee all students with a disability access to school. Once in school, they are entitled to an unbiased evaluation of their educational strengths and needs.

You will learn about the education of students with severe and multiple disabilities in Chapter 9.

You will learn about positive behavioral interventions, supports, and strategies in Chapter 10. This approach involves conducting a functional behavioral assessment and developing a behavioral intervention plan.

Two Purposes

Nondiscriminatory evaluation has two purposes. The first is to determine whether a student has a disability. If the student does not have a disability, then he or she does not receive special education under IDEA or any further evaluation related to special education under IDEA. By contrast, if the evaluation reveals that the student has a disability, the evaluation process continues to accomplish its second purpose: to specify what kind of special education and related services the student will receive. This information is necessary to plan an appropriate education for the student.

Nondiscriminatory Evaluation Requirements

Because evaluation has such a significant impact on students and their families, IDEA surrounds the evaluation process with the procedural safeguards described in Figure 1–7. To (1) determine whether a student has a disability and (2) decide the nature of the special education and related services the student needs, educators typically follow a four-step process: screening, prereferral, referral, and nondiscriminatory evaluation procedures. The first three of these four steps are not required by IDEA but are put into place by educators as a matter of good practice or state or local policy. Picture these four steps as a funnel (see Figure 1–8).

▼ *Screening.* Administering tests to all students to identify which ones might need further testing to determine whether they qualify for special education.

▼ *Prereferral.* Providing immediate and necessary help to teachers who are experiencing challenges in teaching students to prevent the need for the student's referral for a full nondiscriminatory evaluation and possible placement in special education (Bahr, Fuchs, & Fuchs, 1999; Bahr, Whitten, Dieker, Kocarek, & Manson, 1999).

▼ *Referral.* Submitting a formal written request for a student to receive a full nondiscriminatory evaluation.

▼ *Nondiscriminatory evaluation.* Adhering to the full evaluation process that is described in Figure 1-7.

Once the evaluation team has determined that a student has a disability (or is gifted) and what kind of special education and related services the student needs, then educators must provide the student with that kind of education and those services. In short, the nondiscriminatory evaluation leads to, and is the very foundation of, the student's appropriate education.

The members of the evaluation team are also the members of the student's IEP team (see pp. 24 and 27). That way, the student's evaluation and program are synchronized with each other. The team members are the student's parents and the student (when appropriate and when the student reaches the age of majority, usually 18); at least one regular education teacher of the student; at least one special education teacher or provider involved with the student; a representative of the student's local educational agency who is qualified to provide or supervise special education and who knows about the general curriculum and the availability of resources; an individual who can interpret the instructional implications of the nondiscriminatory evaluation; and others at the request of the parents, student, or school.

Appropriate Education

Simply enrolling students (zero reject) and evaluating their strengths and needs (nondiscriminatory evaluation) do not ensure that their education will be appropriate and beneficial. That is why Congress has given each student in special education the right to an appropriate special education and related services.

The key to an appropriate special education is individualization. The plan for students ages 3 through 21 is called an **individualized education program (IEP).** The plan for students from birth through 2, such as Nolan and the Smith family, is called an **individualized family services plan (IFSP).** To guide you through the IDEA appropriate education requirements, we will discuss (1) the contents of IFSP/IEPs; (2) age-specific provisions, including early intervention and transitions to adulthood; (3) the participants who develop the IFSP/IEP; and (4) time lines.

In Chapters 4–16 you will learn about an evaluation process for identifying whether or not a student has a disability and for providing guidance on the nature of special education in related services that students need.

Figure 1–5 lists the related services.

Contents of IFSP/IEP

The IFSP describes the services that both the infant–toddler (Nolan) and the family (Sean, Kris, Bridget, and JJ) will receive. Like the IEP, the IFSP is based on the child's development and needs; it specifies outcomes for the child. Unlike the IEP, however, the IFSP also provides the option for families to identify their resources, priorities, and concerns related to enhancing their child's development. Furthermore, the IFSP must include outcomes and services for families so long as a family wants to achieve specific outcomes related to their child's development. Figure 1–9 sets out the contents of the IFSP.

The IEP is based on the student's evaluation, is developed by the same people who evaluated the student (and others as needed), and is outcome-oriented. IDEA specifies the content of each IEP, as shown in Figure 1–10. Taken as a whole, the IEP's content is the foundation for the student's appropriate education; it is the assurance that the student will benefit from special education and

FIGURE 1–7
Nondiscriminatory evaluation safeguards

The nondiscriminatory evaluation procedures and standards include the following:

Breadth of the Assessment

- Include more than one test, since no single procedure may be used as the sole basis of evaluation.
- Use a variety of assessment tools and strategies to gather relevant functional and developmental information for determining whether the student has a disability and the content of the IEP, including how the student can be involved in and progress in the general curriculum or in appropriate preschool activities.
- Assess the relative contribution of cognitive, behavioral, physical, or developmental factors.
- Assess in all areas related to the suspected disability, including health, vision, hearing, social and emotional status, general intelligence, academic performance, communicative status, and motor abilities.
- Assess specific areas of the student's educational need, identify all of the student's special education and related services needs, and do not rely on a single IQ score.
- Measure the extent to which the child who has limited English proficiency has a disability and needs special education rather than measure the child's English language skills.
- Use assessment tools and strategies that assist the team directly in determining that the student's educational needs are satisfied.

Assessment Procedures

- Are selected and administered so as not to be discriminatory on a racial or cultural basis
- Are validated for the specific purposes for which they are used (later in this chapter, you will be introduced to issues related to validation)
- Are selected and administered so as to best ensure that, when the assessment is administered to a student with sensory, manual, or speaking impairments, the results accurately reflect the student's aptitude or achievement level or whatever factors they purport to measure; must not reflect the student's sensory, manual, or speaking impairments unless the test or procedures themselves purport to measure skills in those areas
- Are administered in the student's native language or other mode of communication (e.g., braille or signing for students with visual or hearing impairments)
- Are administered by trained personnel in conformance with instructions by the producer of the tests or material
- Are accompanied by a review of existing evaluation data, including evaluations and information provided by parents, current classroom-based assessments and observations, and observations from teachers and related-services providers

(continued)

FIGURE 1–7
Continued

- Identify what additional data are needed to determine

  Whether the student has a disability or, in case of a reevaluation, whether the student continues to have such a disability

  The student's present levels of performance and educational needs

  Whether the student needs special education and related services, or in the case of a reevaluation, whether the student continues to need special education and related services

  Whether any additions or modifications to special education and related services are needed so the student can meet IEP annual goals and participate in the general curriculum

Timing of the Assessment

- Nondiscriminatory evaluation occurs before initial placement into or out of special education.

- Reevaluation occurs every three years or more frequently if conditions warrant or if requested by the student's parent or teacher.

Parental Notice and Consent

- Parents must be fully informed and provide written consent before each evaluation and reevaluation.

- Before any reevaluation, consent is required unless the school can demonstrate that it has taken reasonable measures to obtain consent and parents have failed to respond.

- Parents must receive a full explanation of all due process rights, a description of what the school proposes or refuses to do, each evaluation procedure that was used, and any other factors that influenced the decisions.

- Parent consent for evaluation is not parent consent for placement into or out of a special education program; separate consent is required for placement.

Interpretation of Assessment Information

- Draw upon and carefully consider a wide variety of information sources, including aptitude and achievement tests, teacher recommendations, physical status, social or cultural background, and adaptive behavior.

- Ensure interpretation by a group of persons consisting of educators and parents.

- Refuse to determine that the student has a disability if the determining factor is the student's lack of instruction in reading or math or limited English proficiency.

have real opportunities for equality of opportunity, full participation, independent living, and economic self-sufficiency (Turnbull & Turnbull, 2001; Yell, 1998).

In addition to the required content, IDEA also requires the IEP team—when developing each IEP, from the student's first to last IEP—to consider the following factors:

▼ The student's strengths

▼ The parents' concerns

▼ The results of all evaluations

▼ Special factors, namely,

- For students whose behavior impedes their own or others' learning, appropriate strategies, including positive behavioral interventions, strategies, and supports to address that behavior

- For students with limited English proficiency, their language needs as related to the IEP

FIGURE 1–8
Nondiscriminatory evaluation: A funneling process

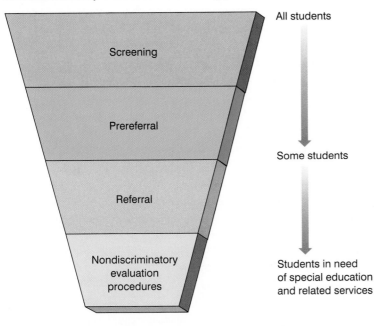

Screening

Prereferral

Referral

Nondiscriminatory evaluation procedures

All students

Some students

Students in need of special education and related services

FIGURE 1–9
Required content of an IFSP

The IFSP is a written statement for each infant or toddler, ages birth through 2, and the child's family. Whenever it is developed or revised, it must contain the following content:

- The infant or toddler's present levels of cognitive, physical, communication, social or emotional, and adaptive development, based on objective criteria

- The family's resources, priorities, and concerns related to enhancing their child's development

- The major outcomes for the infant or toddler and family and the criteria, procedures, and time lines for determining whether the outcomes are achieved and whether modifications of the outcomes or early intervention services are necessary

- The early intervention services to be provided to the infant or toddler and family and their frequency, intensity, and method of delivery

- The natural environments in which they will be provided and why they will not be provided in those environments if the plan so provides

- The dates for starting the services and how long they will last

- The family's service coordinator

- The infant's or toddler's transition plan (leaving early intervention and entering preschool or other appropriate services)

- For students who are blind or have visual impairments, the use of braille or other appropriate reading and writing media
- For students who are deaf or hard of hearing, their language and communication needs, opportunities for direct communications with peers and professionals in their own language and communication mode, academic level, and full range of needs
- For all students, whether assistive technology devices and services are appropriate

FIGURE 1-10
Required content of the IEP

The IEP is a written statement for each student, ages 3 to 21. Whenever it is developed or revised, it must contain the following:

- The student's present levels of educational performance, including
  - How the disability of a student (ages 6 through 21) affects his or her involvement and progress in the general curriculum, or
  - How the disability of a preschooler (ages 3 through 5) affects his or her participation in appropriate activities
- Measurable annual goals, including benchmarks, or short-term objectives, related to
  - Meeting needs resulting from the disability, in order to enable the student to be involved in and progress in the general curriculum
  - Meeting each of the student's other disability-related needs
- The special education and related services and supplementary aids and services that will be provided to the student or on the student's behalf, and the program modifications or supports for school personnel that will be provided so that the student
  - Can advance appropriately toward attaining the annual goals
  - Be involved in and progress through the general curriculum and participate in extracurricular and other nonacademic activities
  - Be educated and participate with other students with disabilities and with students who do not have disabilities in general education
- The extent, if any, to which the student will not participate with students who do not have disabilities in general education classes and in extracurricular and other nonacademic activities
- Any individual modifications in the administration of state- or district-wide assessments of student achievement so that the student can participate in those assessments; moreover, if the IEP determines that the student will not participate in a particular state or district-wide assessment or any part of an assessment, the IEP must state why that assessment is not appropriate for the student and how the student will be assessed
- The projected date for beginning the services and program modifications and the anticipated frequency, location, and duration of each
- Transition plans, including
  - Beginning at age 14 and each year thereafter, a statement of the student's needs that are related to transition services, including those that focus on the student's courses of study (e.g., the student's participation in advanced-placement courses or in a vocational education program)
  - Beginning at age 16 (or sooner, if the IEP team decides it is appropriate), a statement of needed transition services, including, when appropriate, a statement of the interagency responsibilities or any other needed links
  - Beginning at least one year before the student reaches the age of majority under state law (usually, at age 18), a statement that the student has been informed of those rights under IDEA that will transfer to the student from the parents when the student becomes of age
- How the student's progress toward annual goals will be measured and how the student's parents will be informed—at least as often as parents of students who do not have disabilities are informed—of the student's progress toward annual goals and the extent to which the progress is sufficient to enable the student to achieve the goals by the end of the school year

Participants Who Develop the IFSP/IEP

Because the nondiscriminatory evaluation lays the foundation for the student's individualized plan (IFSP or IEP), the IFSP/IEP teams consist of the same people who were on the evaluation team; but new members can be added to the teams as needed to develop a plan for an appropriate education for the particular student. Other people may be included in the IFSP or IEP conference. For example, a parent might wish to bring a friend who knows about the special education process. In addition, some of the student's friends can provide suggestions and support for inclusion (Turnbull & Turnbull, 2001). Figure 1–10 includes the members of the nondiscriminatory evaluation team; these same people are the members of the IEP team.

Educators are required to invite a student's parents to the IEP meeting and to arrange to hold the meeting so that parents will most likely be able to attend. If a parent does not want to participate in the IEP meeting, the school staff still must meet to develop an IEP because schools may not serve a student who does not have an IEP.

IDEA does not require schools to obtain parental consent to access the content of their child's IEP. If parents do consent, fine; if they do not, the schools may still implement the IEP, but the parent may challenge the IEP in a due process hearing (which we will discuss later). Remember, however, that IDEA does require notice to and consent from parents for every evaluation. IDEA also prohibits a school from placing a student into special education without first having an evaluation and IEP. Furthermore, IDEA provides that the school may not place the student out of special education (if the student has already been placed into special education) without a nondiscriminatory evaluation. A parent may challenge all placement decisions through the due process hearing.

Time Lines

IDEA requires an IFSP to be developed within 45 days after the child or family is referred for early intervention services. The IFSP must be reviewed with the family at 6-month intervals (or more often if a more frequent review is warranted) and thereafter annually.

IDEA requires an IEP to be developed for all students, ages 3 through 21, and to be in effect at the beginning of each school year. Also, the team must review and, if appropriate, revise the student's IEP at least once a year and more often if conditions warrant or if the student's parents or teacher request a review.

IFSP/IEP Conferences

IDEA does not have detailed requirements on the process that must be followed at IFSP/IEP conferences. Ideally, those conferences are conducted to help ensure collaborative decision making by all team members. Research on the IFSP/IEP, however, has generally reported that the traditional process has been more of a legal compliance—a paperwork process—than a problem-solving, dynamic process (Turnbull & Turnbull, 2001). To make the conference more collaborative, we recommend that you follow these nine components of the conference:

1. Preparing in advance
2. Connecting and getting started
3. Sharing visions, great expectations, and strengths
4. Reviewing formal evaluation and current levels of performance
5. Sharing resources, priorities, and concerns
6. Developing related goals and objectives (or outcomes)
7. Determining placement, supplementary aids/services, and related services
8. Addressing assessment modifications and special factors
9. Concluding the conference (Turnbull & Turnbull, 2001)

Mandatory review conferences have one principal reason: to determine whether the student's annual goals (IEP) or outcomes (IFSP) are being achieved. Accordingly, IDEA requires the IEP team to review it and revise it as appropriate to address five separate matters:

On the Companion Website, you will find suggestions for how you can effectively participate in each of these nine components of IFSP/IEP conferences.

At an IEP meeting, students may demonstrate their strengths, as this student is doing.

▼ Any lack of expected progress toward the student's annual goals and in the general curriculum (where appropriate)

▼ The results of any reevaluation

▼ Information about the student provided to or by the parents

▼ The student's anticipated needs

▼ Other matters related to the student's education (e.g., increasing inclusion in extracurricular activities)

If the team has any concerns about any of these five matters during the review conference, it is appropriate for the team to reevaluate the student, revise the IEP, reconsider the student's placement, or carry out all three of these actions.

Now that you have learned about appropriate education—IDEA requirements and the IFSP/IEP conference—you may wonder how parents of children with disabilities, who do not have the benefit of formal course work, learn all of this information to prepare them to be collaborative partners in the process. After all, IDEA authorizes parents to be collaborative educational decision makers; that is why IDEA also provides a training resource for them.

Pursuant to IDEA, Congress funds approximately 75 Parent Training and Information Centers. There is at least one in each state. Most centers are directed and staffed by parents of children with a disability; and under IDEA, the majority of board members must be parents of individuals with disabilities. The centers' mission is to provide information to parents to enable them to be effective educational decision makers as they, together with the schools, implement the six IDEA principles. Box 1–4 highlights how the Kansas Parent Training and Information Center accomplishes this mission in a very effective way.

Least Restrictive Environment

Once the schools have enrolled a student (the zero-reject principle), fairly evaluated the student (the nondiscriminatory evaluation principle), and provided an IFSP/IEP (the appropriate education principle), they must provide one more input into the student's education. That provision is education with students who do not have disabilities: the least restrictive environment

Box 1—4

Parent Training and Information in Kansas

Ask Connie Zienkewicz, director of Kansas' Parent Information and Training Center, Families Together, what is the most valuable service her organization provides families, and her answer, delivered without hesitation and with a great deal of certainty, is simple: *Getting them through the maze of education and community services.*

"We have families standing by who have the experience and expertise to help other families, one on one, in navigating the maze." Altogether, Families Together has 20 parents on its staff; each has a child with a disability. Each has experience with the schools or community providers, each has had training from experts. Each has encountered the usual problems facing families—problems about student behavior and school discipline, educational goals, least restrictive placement, transition to adult services, and community-based service provision.

Throughout the entire year, these parents operate out of four regional offices—those in Wichita, Topeka, Kansas City, and Garden City. During the school year, other families are available at regional offices (located in their homes) in Manhattan, Hays, Pratt, and Parsons.

Altogether, these four elements—statewide coverage, family experience, training from experts, and knowledge of local situations—create a network of communication among families. Need help with your child's school program? With your child's behavior? Finding an expert to treat an unusual medical condition? Finding a specialist in challenging behavior? Not a problem. Turn to the network. The network makes Families Together a force for change in Kansas.

But getting through the maze, says Connie, does not depend entirely on those four elements.

Beginning nearly 15 years ago, Families Together began to sponsor "enrichment weekends," times when families—parents, child with a disability, and brothers and sisters, uncles and aunts, grandparents and other family members—could get together to learn, problem solve, and just enjoy themselves. Two of those weekends occur each year.

But there are eight other occasions when families—usually the parents of the child with a disability—convene. These parent networking conferences are held regionally throughout a large, sparsely populated state. They involve training and information—lots of both.

And, most useful to the families, they provide opportunities for families to find others whose situations are like their own. There's the "eureka" factor, says Connie: "You mean to say that other families in Kansas have the same kinds of challenges we have? Eureka! We can learn from each other. We can support each other."

Two factors, then, help families in "getting through the maze." There's the information that Connie, her, staff, and various experts offer. And there's the family network—the reliable alliance with other Kansans, however far-flung they may be. It's not easy to negotiate the maze, but, in Kansas, it's not as hard as it could be, thanks to Families Together.

Source: From *Families, Professionals, and Exceptionality: Collaborating for Empowerment* (4th ed.) by A. P. Turnbull and H. R. Turnbull, 2001, Upper Saddle River, NJ: Merrill/Prentice Hall. Copyright © 2001. Reprinted with permission of Prentice Hall, Inc., Upper Saddle River, NJ.

(LRE) principle, formerly known as the mainstreaming or integration rule and now known as the inclusion principle. In early intervention, ages zero to 3, IDEA favors education in the student's "natural environment," which could be home or an out-of-home center. In all other education (students 3 through 21), IDEA favors education in the general curriculum (academic, extracurricular, and other school activities).

Reasons for the Rule

There are three basic reasons for the rule:

▼ There is a long history of segregating students with disabilities from students who do not have disabilities (20 U.S.C., sec. 1400 [c][2]).

▼ Students with disabilities will be more likely to have equal opportunity and to achieve the national policy goals of equality of opportunity, full participation, independent living, and economic self-sufficiency if they participate in the general curriculum to the maximum extent appropriate for them (20 U.S.C., sec. 1400 [c][1]); indeed, more than 20 years of research and experience have demonstrated that children with disabilities will have more effective education if they have access to the general curriculum to the maximum extent possible (20 U.S.C., sec. 1400 [c][5] [A]).

In Chapter 2 we will describe what is meant by having access to the general curriculum, and then you will learn more about how you can enable students in special education to have access to the general curriculum throughout the textbook.

Danny Ramirez is surrounded by his family (right to left)—his mother, Carmen; his father, Alfredo; his brother, Freddy; and his sisters, Itze and Claudia. Carmen and Alfredo successfully sued the El Paso, Texas, schools to have Danny included in the general education programs. Danny now works in animal care (see page 4).

▼ Students with disabilities should have the opportunity to associate with students without disabilities so that each can develop relationships with the other (Turnbull et al., 2000).

In Box 1–5, you can read about Carmen and Alfredo Ramirez and their son, Danny, who now is a high-school graduate profitably employed as an animal-care worker in Austin, Texas.

The Rule: A Presumption in Favor of Inclusion

Accordingly, IDEA creates a presumption in favor of educating students with disabilities with those who do not have disabilities. IDEA requires that (1) a school system must educate a student with a disability with students who do not have disabilities to the maximum extent appropriate for the student and (2) the school may not remove the student from the regular education environment unless, because of the nature or severity of the student's disability, the student cannot be educated there successfully (appropriately, in the sense that the student will benefit), even after the school provides **supplementary aids and support services** for the student (20 U.S.C., sec. 1412[a][5] and sec. 1413[a][1]).

Setting Aside the Presumption

The presumption in favor of inclusion can be set aside only if the student cannot benefit from being educated with students who do not have disabilities and only after the school has provided the student with supplementary aids and services. In that event, the student may be placed in a less typical, more specialized, less inclusive program.

The Continuum of Services

In Chapter 2 you will learn about each of these types of placements for students receiving special education.

Schools must offer a continuum, or range, of services from more to less typical and inclusive: that is, from less to more restrictive or separate. The most typical and inclusive setting is general education, followed by resource rooms, special classes, special schools, homebound services, and hospitals and institutions (also called residential or long-term care facilities) (20 U.S.C., sec. 1401[25]).

Box 1–5

Danny Wins His Lawsuit

When Danny Ramirez was born in the early 1980s, it was obvious to the physicians and nurses who delivered him that he had Down syndrome because he had the facial features characteristic of that condition. Thinking that they would spare his mother, Carmen, and father, Alfredo, some discomfort, they placed Danny in a nursery separate from all the other newborns in the El Paso, Texas, hospital where he was born. That was a mistake and the beginning of a crusade that culminated in a lawsuit.

The mistake was to separate Danny from other newborns, for Carmen and Alfredo, who were citizens of Mexico living legally in the United States, had already experienced discrimination based on the fact that they were not native-born and were Latino. They were not about to tolerate any more discrimination, based, this time, on disability. At their insistence, Danny soon was included in the same nursery as all other newborns; it took just a few hours for the hospital staff to recognize that they were engaged in a dispute with two determined parents and that, in the end, Danny's parents were right and would win: There was no medical reason to separate Danny from any other babies.

It was not long, however, before another public agency—the El Paso school system—repeated the same mistake as the hospital, placing Danny in a separate special education program, requiring him to be educated there, and insisting that he and his classmates should eat by themselves, apart from other students, in the school cafeteria. These two types of segregation were as unacceptable to Carmen and Alfredo as the separate nursery was. Segregation is segregation, no matter where it occurs; and there seemed to be no educational reason for the segregation, any more than there was a medical reason for it in the hospital.

Carmen, Alfredo, her brother (a lawyer admitted to practice in Texas), and a lawyer specializing in disability law sued the El Paso schools to have Danny included in academic, extracurricular, and other school activities, including mealtime. Having had a hearing before a due process hearing officer, a trial in federal court, and then a hearing on appeal in a federal court of appeals, they were vindicated at last by the court of appeals, when it ruled that the El Paso schools must provide Danny with education in an integrated setting.

The decision has been significant in many ways. It was one of the first under IDEA to interpret the law in favor of inclusion, so it benefited not only Danny but many other students because it was a precedent for other courts to follow. It laid the foundation for Danny to be integrated in academic programs throughout the rest of his school years. And it caused his inclusive education to be so appropriate for him that he is now employed in the job he wants: as an animal-care attendant.

Danny won his lawsuit, but he won a great deal more. He won the right and opportunity to have a life of his own choosing in mainstream society and to be as productive as he can be. That is an outcome that all students in special education should have. Talk about making a difference!

Nonacademic Inclusion

Schools also have to ensure that students with disabilities may participate in extracurricular and other general education activities such as meals, recess periods, and other services such as counseling, athletics, transportation, health services, recreational activities, special interest groups or clubs, and referrals to agencies that assist in employment and other aspects of life outside of school (20 U.S.C., sec. 1414[d][1][A][iii]).

In short, when providing academic, extracurricular, and other activities and services to students who do not have disabilities, schools must include students with disabilities to the maximum extent appropriate. That is because, as Congress said in 1997, special education is a "service for children rather than a place where they are sent" (20 U.S.C., sec. 1400 [c][5][c]). Box 1–5 tells about Danny's struggle.

Procedural Due Process

Schools do not always carry out IDEA's first four principles: zero reject, nondiscriminatory evaluation, appropriate education, and least restrictive environment. What's a parent to do? Or what if a school wants one type of special education, but a parent disagrees, perhaps to the detriment of the student? The answer lies in the due process principle, which basically seeks to make the schools and parents accountable to each other for carrying out the student's IDEA rights.

When parents and state or local educational agencies disagree, IDEA provides each with an opportunity to engage in a process of **mediation** (Mills & Duff-Mallans, 1999) and, if that is

To learn about the Consortium for Appropriate Dispute Resolution in Special Education and best practices for mediation and due process, go to the Web Links module in Chapter 1 of the Companion Website.

unsuccessful in resolving the dispute, to have a due process hearing. IDEA does not require mediation, and mediation may not be used to deny or delay the right to a due process hearing. But IDEA strongly encourages mediation and requires states to set up a process for it and to compel a parent who rejects mediation to receive counseling about the benefits of mediation.

A *due process hearing* is an administrative, quasi-judicial hearing similar to a mini-trial and is conducted before a person charged with making an objective decision who is called a due process hearing officer. At the hearing, the parents and schools are entitled to have lawyers, present evidence, and cross-examine each other's witnesses. In 1998 there were 3,315 hearings, yet 5,683,707 students were enrolled in special education. This means that only 0.0006 percent of students in special education had hearings.

Parent-Student Participation

Although due process hearings and other procedural safeguards can provide a system of checks and balances between schools and families, IDEA also offers another, less adversarial accountability technique: the parent-student participation principle. For example, parents are members of the teams that do the nondiscriminatory evaluations and IEPs; they have rights to receive notice before schools do anything about the student's right to a free appropriate public education; they have access to the student's records and can limit who can see those records; and they retain rights even when their children reach the age of majority. So the parent-student participation principle is a mechanism for shared decision-making.

Bringing the Six Principles Together

Now that you have learned about each of the six principles, how do they really work together to form a process of ensuring an appropriate education for students with disabilities? Figure 1–11 highlights the fact that the first four principles—zero reject, nondiscriminatory evaluation, appropriate education, and less restrictive environment—are the inputs into a student's education. The other two principles—procedural due process and parent-student participation—are accountability techniques, ways to make sure that the other four principles are implemented correctly. The figure identifies the principles, their purposes, and shows their relationships.

Federal Funding of the Individuals with Disabilities Education Act

As important as the six principles are, they would amount to nothing but rights on paper without money behind them. After all, rights run with revenues. Accordingly, Congress grants federal money to state and local educational agencies (school districts) to assist them in educating students ages birth to 21. The state and local agencies, however, must agree to comply with IDEA's principles, or else they will not receive the federal money.

The state and local agencies may not simply substitute the federal money for the funds that they themselves raise and spend on special education; they may not supplant state and local money with federal money. The federal money supplements state and local contributions.

There is no doubt about this fact: Special education is expensive. In the 1999–2000 school year (Chambers, Parrish, & Harr, 2002):

▼ $50 billion of federal, state, and local tax dollars were spent on special education services.

FIGURE 1–11
The relationships among the six principles of IDEA

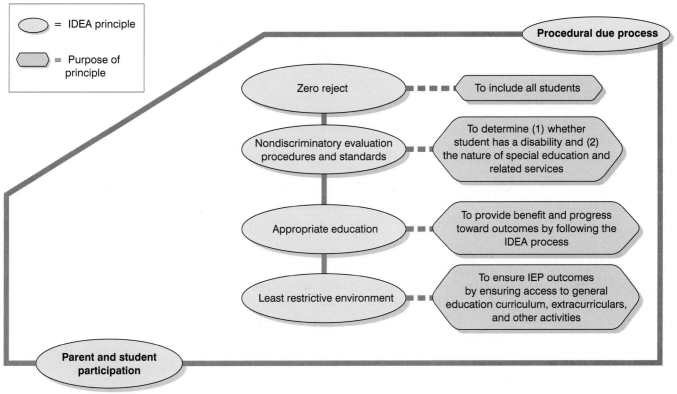

Legend

= IDEA principle

= Purpose of principle

Procedural due process

Zero reject

To include all students

Nondiscriminatory evaluation procedures and standards

To determine (1) whether student has a disability and (2) the nature of special education and related services

Appropriate education

To provide benefit and progress toward outcomes by following the IDEA process

Least restrictive environment

To ensure IEP outcomes by ensuring access to general education curriculum, extracurriculars, and other activities

Parent and student participation

The U.S. Department of Education has funded the Center for Special Education Finance to study fiscal policy issues related to the delivery of special education services. To learn more about special education fiscal information, go to the Web Links module in Chapter 1 of the Companion Website.

▼ To provide a combination of general and special education for students with disabilities, an average of $12,474 is spent for each student, or $5,918 more than the average spent for a student without disabilities.

▼ Federal funding for special education accounts for about 7.5 percent of all federal, state, and local special education expenses.

▼ It cost approximately $6.7 billion annually for all students with disabilities to go through the processes of referral, nondiscriminatory evaluation, and IEP development. That is a cost of $1,086 per special education student.

▼ From 1977–2000, special education spending increased by 30 percent. During this time the ratio of cost for special education students as compared to general education students has decreased from 2.17 to 1.90.

As states seek to make education more cost-efficient, will they sacrifice effectiveness? Will cost cutting be undertaken at the expense of appropriate services? And how can schools be made more accountable for producing the results that Congress wants—equality of opportunity, full participation, independent living, and economic self-sufficiency—in light of the fact that the demand for services may be larger than the resources available to meet the demand?

Those are good questions. But consider them in this light: Each state has taken upon itself, usually in its constitution, the obligation to educate all children, including those with disabilities. Thus, IDEA assists the states to do what they would have to do in any event—educate all children with disabilities. IDEA supplements state and local school budgets. The real question is this: Do the expenditures result in good outcomes for the students? Before we get to that question and its answers, let's consider a few other laws that apply to students with disabilities.

Other Federal Laws:
Entitlements and Antidiscrimination

As important as IDEA is, other federal laws affect special education and students in those programs. There are two types of these laws: (1) Some create an entitlement for students or authorize services for them, and (2) others prohibit students from being discriminated against because of their disabilities.

Entitlements and Other Services

Rehabilitation Act

If a person has a severe disability but, with rehabilitation, is able to work despite the disability, the person is entitled to two types of vocational rehabilitation services under the Rehabilitation Act. First, when people are 16 years old, they can receive work evaluations, financial aid so they can pursue job training, and job locator services, all from their state rehabilitation agency.

Second, persons with severe disabilities can enroll in the **supported employment** program. They work with the assistance of a **job coach,** whose duties include teaching the person with a disability how to do a job and then helping him or her do it independently. The supported worker must be paid at least the minimum wage, work at least 20 hours a week in a typical work setting, and be able, after 18 months of supported employment, to do the job alone without support.

Tech Act

The Technology-Related Assistance to Individuals with Disabilities Act of 1988, often called the Tech Act, authorizes federal funds to be granted to the states to help create statewide systems for delivering assistive technology devices and services to people with disabilities, including students with disabilities (Bryant & Seay, 1998; D. Smith, 1998). In Chapters 4 through 16, we describe how technology benefits students.

You will learn about the Tech Act in Chapter 12.

IDEA and the Rehabilitation Act create personal entitlements; they provide direct services to eligible people. By contrast, the Tech Act creates a statewide capacity to serve people with disabilities; instead of directly benefiting the people themselves, it helps the states meet the people's needs.

Prohibiting Discrimination

Education and rehabilitation are, of course, necessary to ameliorate the effects of a student's disability. But they are not sufficient by themselves to overcome the effects of the disability. IDEA, for example, does not prohibit public or private agencies from discriminating against the student on the basis of the student's disability. Yes, a student may receive special education; but that service might not create opportunities for the student to use the skills he or she has acquired through special education. Prejudice against people with disabilities may still foreclose opportunities for the student to show that, although he or she has a disability, the student is nonetheless still able.

How can society attack the prejudice? One answer is to use antidiscrimination laws like those that prohibit discrimination based on race or gender. The first such law, enacted in 1975 as an amendment to the Rehabilitation Act, is known as Section 504 (29 U.S.C., sec. 794) (deBettencourt, 2002; Smith & Patton, 1998). The second, enacted in 1990, is the Americans with Disabilities Act (ADA) (42 U.S.C. § § 12101–12213) (Turnbull & Turnbull, 2000; Yell, 1998). These are fundamentally similar laws. Section 504 of the Rehabilitation Act and ADA both basically provide that no otherwise qualified individual with a disability shall, solely by reason of his or her disability, be discriminated against in certain realms of American life. Figure 1–12 sets out the meaning of "person with a disability" under Section 504 and ADA. Both laws use basically the same definition.

Assistive technology replaces lost functions or enhances residual functions and consists of off-the-shelf, adapted, or specially made devices.

FIGURE 1–12

Definition of "person with a disability" in the Rehabilitation Act and ADA

Section 504 of the Rehabilitation Act and ADA define a person with a disability as one who

- Has a physical or mental impairment that substantially limits one or more of the major life activities of such individual (e.g., traumatic brain injury)

- Has a record of such an impairment (history of cancer that is now in remission)

- Is regarded as having such an impairment (a person who is especially creative but simultaneously is chronically "wired" or "high" may be regarded as having some emotional disturbances or attention deficit/hyperactivity disorders)

Note: A student who has HIV but is not so impaired that he or she needs special education is protected under Section 504 and ADA because the person meets the last two criteria: The person has a history of a disability, and others regard that person as having a disability. The same is true of a person who has attention deficit/hyperactivity disorder. See Chapters 11 and 6, respectively, for discussions of those conditions and the students' rights under IDEA, Section 504, and ADA.

Section 504 and ADA Coverage

Section 504 applies to any program or activity receiving federal financial assistance. Because state and local education agencies receive federal funds, they may not discriminate against students or other persons with disabilities on account of their disabilities. Clearly, Section 504 is limited in scope. What if an individual seeks employment from a company that does not receive any federal funds; or wants to participate in state and local government programs that are not federally aided; or wants to have access to telecommunications systems, such as closed captioning for people with hearing impairments? In none of those domains of life will the person receive any protection from Section 504. Instead, ADA comes to the rescue.

You will learn about 504 plans for students who meet the definition of disability under Section 504 but not under IDEA in Chapter 7 (gifted and talented).

ADA extends its civil rights/nondiscrimination protection to the following sectors of American life: private-sector employment, transportation, state and local government activities and programs, privately operated businesses that are open to the public ("public accommodations"), and telecommunications.

IDEA, Section 504, and ADA: Overlapping Purposes

Basically, IDEA and the Rehabilitation Act deal respectively with education and training for employment, while Section 504 and ADA make sure that the students can put their education and training to use through the IEP and its transition provisions. In short, the transition components of the IEP anticipate outcomes that are largely consistent with those that any student—whether one with a disability or not—typically will want: work, education, and opportunities to participate in the community. Those results cannot be achieved as long as there are barriers erected on the foundation of discrimination. These barriers—the deep roots of discrimination—are the targets of Section 504 and ADA.

Special Education Outcomes

What Are the Long-Term Results for Students with Disabilities and to What Extent Are Results Influenced by Diversity Factors?

After the schools started to implement IDEA in 1977 and until Congress reauthorized (reenacted) it 1997, the major federal criteria for evaluating special education were primarily numerical. The questions always were: How many more students are being served annually and in what types of placements are they served?

Now, however, federal and state policymakers and educators do more than count the number of students being served and tally their placements; today, the goal and the challenge facing special education is to improve the results for students. Congress reflected this goal in reauthorizing IDEA in 1997:

> Disability is a natural part of the human experience and in no way diminishes the right of individuals to participate in or contribute to society. Improving educational results for children with disabilities is an essential element of our national policy of ensuring equality of opportunity, full participation, independent living, and economic self-sufficiency for individuals with disabilities. (20 U.S.C., sec. 1400 [C][1])

The same task exists for general education: to improve the outcomes for students. Under the general education reform law that Congress enacted in 2002, entitled No Child Left Behind Act (NCLBA), Congress allots funds to the states, which in turn allot them to each of their school districts. As a condition of receiving the federal funds, each state and each of its school districts must set 5-year goals for improving the academic scores of all students, whether in general or special education, on standardized tests. If the students do not meet these goals by obtaining higher scores, the federal government will provide the districts with additional funds to meet the goals. If, however, they still do not meet these goals, the federal government will require the states to allot federal funds so that the parents of the children in the "failing" districts can attend any school of their choice, whether the school is inside or outside of the district and whether the school is a public school, a charter public school, or a private school, even one that is a parochial (religiously oriented) private school. No Child Left Behind Act, then, emphasizes that outcomes—measured by academic achievement—count for all students. For that reason, each student with a disability will take the state and district assessments—the tests of student achievement—unless the student's IEP team excuses the student because of the extent of the student's disability; in that case, the student takes an alternative assessment (see Chapter 2).

Now, let's return to IDEA and its outcomes. (The outcomes under NCLBA are not available yet because Congress just passed the law in 2002.) What did Congress mean when it spoke about equality of opportunity, full participation, independent living, and economic self-sufficiency as the national goals and thus the appropriate outcomes for students with disabilities? Here are the four terms and general definitions for each:

▼ *Equality of opportunity.* People with disabilities will have the same chances and opportunities in life as people without disabilities.

▼ *Full participation.* People with disabilities will have opportunities to be included in all aspects of their community and will be protected from any attempts by people to segregate them solely on the basis of their disability.

▼ *Independent living.* People with disabilities will have the opportunity to fully participate in decision making and to experience autonomy in making choices about how to live their lives.

▼ *Economic self-sufficiency.* People with disabilities will be provided with opportunities to engage fully in income-producing work or unpaid work that contributes to a household or community.

What is the evidence related to these outcomes? Unfortunately, research on results for students with disabilities does not provide definitive answers. A number of indicators, however, suggest that the desired results are still goals rather than outcomes.

One indicator of equality of opportunity is the extent to which students with disabilities are completing their high school education. The overall national dropout rate is approximately 12 percent (Kaufman, Kwon, Klein, & Chapman, 1999). Unfortunately, students with disabilities experience an even higher rate. For example, students with learning disabilities have a dropout rate of approximately 17 percent to 42 percent, and students with emotional or behavioral disabilities have a dropout rate in the range of 21 percent to 64 percent (National Center for Education Statistics, 1993, 1997, 1999). Only about 27 percent of all students with disabilities graduated with a high school diploma during each of the 3 years beginning in 1996 and ending in 1998 (National Council on Disability, 2000). From what you learned earlier in this chapter about the positive relationship of disability, poverty, and racial/ethnic diversity, you should not be surprised to learn that, across all categories of disabilities, males from diverse racial backgrounds (especially from urban communities and low-income homes) have the highest dropout rate (National Center for Education Statistics, 2000).

A second major indicator of the achievement of IDEA's goals relates to the area of postschool employment. Clearly, adults who are employed increase their chances for equal opportunity, full participation, independent living, and especially economic self-sufficiency. Although the employment rate for people without disabilities is 81 percent, the employment rate for individuals with disabilities is only 32 percent—a gap of 49 percentage points (National Organization on Disability, 2000). The employment rate for individuals with more severe disabilities is even lower: Only 19 percent of individuals with severe disabilities work either full or part time.

To what extent is diversity a factor in the employment of people with disabilities? Latino and African American individuals with severe disabilities are much less likely to be employed than are European American individuals with severe disabilities (National Council on Disability, 2000). Individuals with disabilities from low-income families are less likely to be employed after school than are individuals from higher-income families (Heal & Rusch, 1995, cited in Doren & Benz, 1998).

The final indicator of long-term results relates to the data on overall satisfaction with life. Approximately two-thirds of individuals without disabilities report that they are very satisfied with life in general, whereas approximately one-third of individuals with disabilities report the same satisfaction. People with very severe disabilities are much less satisfied with life in general than are people with somewhat severe, slight, or moderate disabilities (National Organization on Disability, 2000). Unfortunately, no comparable data are available on the impact of diversity factors on overall life satisfaction.

Like the student pictured here, who has both musical and technological capabilities, students with disabilities have many strengths. Their chances for graduation increase when educators play to their strengths.

To assess your knowledge of this chapter's contents, go to the Chapter Quiz module in Chapter 1 of the Companion Website.

For information on books, journals, and magazines, multimedia resources, and organizations related to special education, go to the Resources module in Chapter 1 of the Companion Website.

Here's the question that you have to answer for yourself and that we hope our book helps you answer: Given that there is a great deal of room for improvement in special education, what role will you play in making it possible for students with disabilities to make progress in the special and general curriculum so that their long-term results are as positive as possible?

A Vision for the Future

Let's look down the road about four years. Nolan is now 6 years old, and it's time for him to enroll in the first grade of his neighborhood school, Prairie Park Elementary. He finished his in-home infant-and-toddler program when he reached the age of 3, and he enrolled in Raintree Montessori School at age 3 and spent his third, fourth, and fifth years of life there. More than simply being at a school that includes students with disabilities in every aspect of its day, Nolan continued to receive at-home and in-clinic related services, with special attention to speech (speech therapy), mobility (physical therapy), and fine-motor skills (occupational therapy).

Imagine the first day of first grade—a school day reserved just for those in that class; the other students will begin their term the next day. Nolan, Sean, Kris, and Bridget all come to Prairie Park School. Whether at the school entrance, where hundreds of kids and their parents are visiting with each other, or in the school's hallways, where still others are finding their ways to their homerooms, Nolan is barely noticed. Sure, he's a bit smaller than some of the other first graders; and yes, it's a bit difficult for his teachers to make out every word he speaks. But he walks into school on his own; Sean, Kris, and Bridget follow close behind, but not too close—Nolan lets them know he's independent enough to get to his homeroom on his own, and Nolan and Kris scouted out the building each day for about a week before the first day of school. In his assigned seat, Nolan answers the roll call. "I'm here," he says, raising his hand, "and I'm happy to be here and I'm ready to work." A full sentence, right out of his own mouth. When asked about his summer, Nolan tells about swimming, horseback riding, and speech therapy. What Nolan demonstrates by walking and talking is that he has hung in there with his therapies; Sean and Kris have advocated for and then collaborated with the best programs and therapists available; the Raintree staff have been superb in providing the best education that any youngster could ever want; and Nolan's got his own gang of buddies, ready to advocate for him with any student or teacher who doesn't give him a fair shake. Hanging out produced that loyal following, just as hanging in produced benefits that will bear fruit for Nolan for the rest of his years in school.

What Would You Recommend?

1. If you were a member of Nolan's IEP team, what academic goals would you recommend for him? What social goals? What other goals? Which would be more important—the academic, the social, or the "other"? What "other" goals are likely to grab your attention?

2. Given that you know Sean is a professor of special education and that he is likely to be up to date on the best programs for Nolan, what will you do to be the best teacher you can be for Nolan? How will you relate to Sean and Kris? What resources will you want to have at your fingertips for Nolan's sake and for your own benefit as an effective teacher?

To respond to these questions online, participate in other activities, and learn more about Nolan Smith and progress in the general curriculum for students with disabilities, go to the Cases module in Chapter 1 of the Companion Website.

Summary

Profile of Special Education Students and Personnel in Today's Schools

▼ Just over 11 percent of all students, ages 6 to 21, have disabilities.

▼ About 1.8 percent of all children ages birth through 2 received infant-and-toddler early intervention services.

▼ Nearly 5 percent of all students ages 3 through 5 received early special education services.

▼ Most special education students are males.

▼ The federal law, IDEA, uses a categorical and functional approach to determine which students qualify for IDEA special education.

▼ Language sensitivity is important, and we recommend the use of people-first language.

▼ Family income makes a difference: The lower it is, the more likely it is that the child will have a disability.

▼ Family education also makes a difference: The lower it is, the more likely it is that the child will have a disability.

▼ The greatest disproportionality related to race and ethnicity is the higher-than-expected number of African American students in special education.

▼ African American, Latino, and Native American students are underrepresented in gifted education.

▼ Children from culturally and linguistically diverse backgrounds disproportionately are members of families with low incomes.

▼ Low income is highly associated with a number of risk factors that place students in jeopardy for achieving school success.

▼ The special education cadre consists of teachers and related service providers and administrators.

▼ There are teacher and related-service personnel shortages all across the United States.

The Law and Special Education

▼ One type was exclusion from school or ineffective education (functional exclusion).

▼ Another was discrimination by way of misclassification.

▼ The preludes to today's federal special education law were two court cases requiring schools to educate these students.

▼ The federal law, enacted in 1975, is the Individuals with Disabilities Education Act.

▼ There are 12 categories of disabilities for children ages 6 through 21.

▼ The law benefits infants and toddlers (Part C) and students ages 5 through 21 (Part B).

▼ The law uses the categorical and functional approaches to determine which students qualify for IDEA benefits.

IDEA: Six Principles

▼ IDEA has six principles that govern the entire special education enterprise.

▼ IDEA's six principles are

- *Zero reject:* a rule against inclusion
- *Nondiscriminatory evaluation:* a rule of fair assessments
- *Appropriate education:* a rule of individualized benefit
- *Least restrictive placement:* a presumption in favor of placement in general education programs
- *Procedural due process:* a rule of fair dealing and accountability
- *Parent and student participation:* a rule of shared decision making

Federal Funding of the Individuals with Disabilities Education Act

▼ Special education is a $50 billion enterprise.

▼ It is funded by federal, state, and local government funds.

▼ The cost of educating the average student with a disability is almost twice the cost of educating the average student who does not have a disability.

Other Federal Laws: Entitlements and Antidiscrimination

▼ The Rehabilitation Act provides for work training, especially supported employment.

▼ The Tech Act makes assistive technology available statewide in each state.

▼ The Rehabilitation Act, Section 504, and the Americans with Disabilities Act prohibit discrimination solely on the basis of disability in a wide range of services, both in and outside of school.

Special Education Outcomes

▼ The long-term results are poor in the areas of equal opportunity, full participation, independent living, and economic self-sufficiency.

▼ Among students from diverse populations, the results are poor compared to those for students from majority populations.

To find out how and where this chapter content connects to the CEC Professional Standards and the PRAXIS™ Standards, go to the Standards Connection module in Chapter 1 of the Companion Website. A comprehensive matrix aligning CEC professional standards, PRAXIS™ Standards, and INTASC principles to the entire text, is available in the Appendix and on the Companion Website.

Chapter 2

Who Are Heather and Star Morgan?

Travel with us to Independence, Missouri, birthplace of Harry S. Truman and home of Luff Elementary School. Enter the school on a local election day, passing the polling places—such an American activity, so symbolic of the full citizenship to which Luff's students aspire and toward which their teachers are guiding them.

Come into the third-grade classroom of Jean Ann Maloney. There you learn that the class includes Heather Morgan, who has mild mental retardation and has been adopted by Barbara Morgan.

You wonder, "How can a student with mild mental retardation be in a third-grade reading class?" You learn from Barbara that Heather is an avid reader. Today, she's in a group of four students; she accompanies her three peers in reading aloud from the same book they are using. Significantly, none of the other three students has a disability. It is clear that the school's administration and faculty have the same expectations for Heather as they have for the other students.

Now you go to a first-grade classroom. You learn about another student who has disabilities. She's Star Morgan. Like her sister Heather, she, too, has been adopted by Barbara. Barbara tells

you that Star has many more disabilities than Heather does. Using her hands to sign quotation marks, Barbara explains that Heather has "mild" mental retardation and Star has multiple disabilities, including "severe" mental retardation. In addition, Star does not speak; she can make sounds but not words.

All that aside, you notice aspects of Star that are quite unexpected. She's the student with the brightest eyes; they sparkle, hinting at capacities as yet untapped. She's also very shy except when she's leading her class by signing their favorite book, *Charles Tiger*. Leading the class? Yes, she's in front of her classmates, taking her unanticipated place with her teacher Donna Cummings and her paraprofessional Pam Eldridge. Her classmates speak the story and sign it simultaneously, following her lead.

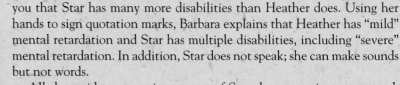

By leading, Star signifies that she has an extraordinary relationship with her classmates. It's one in which they learn from her; yes, she's teaching them to become bilingual and multicultural, to enter the culture of those who, like Star, cannot speak unless they sign or like those who have hearing impairments and cannot talk or hear except by signing. Diversity has a language of many tongues and hands.

One more stop is in order: the teacher's lounge. There Peggy Palser, Luff's principal, is meeting with Carrie Hamburg (K–3 special educator), Jackie Browning (4–5 special educator), Dana Pyle (curriculum and instruction specialist, all grades), and Rae Jean Aquero (school counselor, all grades). Jean Ann Maloney (Heather's teacher) and her paraprofessional, Jennifer Genochio, join them.

The topic of conversation is the *Missouri Assessment Program* (MAP), the annual mandatory assessment of student and school performance. MAP requires students to demonstrate higher-order skills. They will need prior information (vocabulary and grammar, addition and subtraction) to do well because MAP asks them to solve problems to demonstrate that they can apply what they have learned; MAP asks the students to "show me" (the state's motto) that they grasp the concepts.

Just how Heather will take MAP concerns Luff's faculty. They have the same concerns about Star, who will take the test in two years. Should Heather be required to take it in just the same way as her peers without disabilities do? Should Star? If not, what accommodations are reasonable? Should either of them be exempted and have the chance to demonstrate mastery through an alternative assessment? After all, just participating in general education is not enough. Progressing in it is the goal, and assessing their progress in such a way that they can truly demonstrate what they have learned is only fair. If these and all students are going to fully participate in the United States and be as economically self-sufficient as possible, schools such as Luff and states such as Missouri are obliged to reform

themselves: to teach content more effectively to all students. Otherwise, independence in Independence will escape far too many students. That's not an acceptable result.

So Luff's faculty and its principal are meeting. All of them are committed to educating and assessing all students, together—but not without accounting for individual differences.

It takes a large team to make an inclusive school, a team of collaborators committed to inclusion and to a universal, all-students approach to curriculum (what the students learn), instruction (how well the teachers teach), and assessment (how teachers know what students have learned). Just as the building is accessible to all students, so is the curriculum. Inclusion is more than a matter of simply being in a school. It involves being there in a significant way, as Star is. And universal design for learning (UDL) is more

than a matter of architecture. It's a matter of combining curriculum, instruction, and assessment for a single purpose: to reach acceptable outcomes for all students.

What do you think?

1. **How will Heather and later Star participate in the annual state assessment?**

2. **How can the curriculum be universally designed so that all students will be successful in general education?**

3. **What does research say about the success of teaching students such as Star and Heather in general education?**

To answer these questions online and learn more about Heather and Star Morgan, go to the Cases module in Chapter 2 of the Companion Website. For more information visit our website at www.prenhall.com/turnbull

Companion Website

As you learned in Chapter 1, the goal of this book is to prepare you as a future educator to enable students with exceptionalities to progress in the general curriculum. To accomplish that goal, we told you that we would ask you to concentrate on the book's four themes: universal design for learning, inclusion, collaboration, and responding to the multicultural diversity of students.

In this chapter, we address the goal of student progress in the general curriculum by focusing on the first two themes. You will learn the answers to these questions:

▼ What does progressing in the general curriculum mean?
▼ How does universal design for learning enable students to progress in the general curriculum?
▼ How does inclusion enable students to progress in the general curriculum?

In Chapter 3, we will focus on collaboration and multicultural responsiveness.

What Does Progressing in the General Curriculum Mean?

To understand the general education curriculum, you need to know about standards-based reform. In this section you will learn the answers to these questions:

▼ What is the background of standards-based reform?
▼ What are content and performance standards?
▼ What is the general curriculum?
▼ What are the accountability issues?
▼ Why is progress in the general curriculum important?

What Is the Background of Standards-Based Reform?

The background of standards-based reform lies in several historical facts. First, for many years state and local education agencies often did not have an explicit curriculum for all students. Typically, teachers chose materials, primarily textbooks, from which students could learn grade-level content; then the teachers instructed by focusing on the middle range of ability of the students in their classroom (Pugach & Warger, 2001; Wehmeyer, Lattin, & Agran, 2001). The result was that many students whose achievement was significantly below or above grade level did not have their educational needs met by this one-size-fits-all, middle-of-the-road curriculum.

Second, special and general education teachers have generally thought that students with disabilities should not be expected to participate in, much less master, the same curriculum offered to students without disabilities. For students with disabilities, the curriculum has developed from their IEPs (Pugach & Warger, 2001; Sands, Adams, & Stout, 1995). As you learned in Chapter 1, however, IDEA requires that a student's IEP be planned in a way that enables the student *to progress in the general curriculum*—that is, the same curriculum that students without disabilities receive.

Just what is that general curriculum, and how good is it? These and other questions underlie the standards-based reform movement. Here, too, history is a guide to the present.

Throughout the 1990s and continuing until the present, education leaders have asked their peers to raise standards for all students and to assess all students' progress to ensure that all of them are meeting those standards (American Federation of Teachers, 1999; National Research Council, 1993).

In 2001, Congress enacted a law that applies to all students (those with and without disabilities) and all schools. The name of the law is No Child Left Behind Act. Like its predecessor laws, No Child Left Behind Act seeks to overcome the low expectations that many special and general educators had for students with disabilities (Thurlow, 2000) and to buttress IDEA so that

We encourage you to reflect on what you learned in Chapter 1 about results for students with disabilities. How do you think that low expectations contributed to those results?

To learn about the standards recommended by national organizations, go to the Web Links module in Chapter 2 of the Companion Website.

Heather and Star can be included in the general education curriculum, with individualized supports. In a nutshell, No Child Left Behind Act adopts the following:

▼ The principle of accountability by requiring all states to carry out annual statewide reading and mathematics testing of all students in grades 3 through 8 and to set annual statewide progress objectives that all students in all grades must reach within the next 12 years (by 2013) and by requiring schools whose students do not meet those objectives to carry out improvements, corrective actions, and restructuring measures

▼ The principle of parent and student choice by requiring states to provide funds so that parents and students can leave failing schools and enroll in other public or private schools

▼ The principle of flexibility by allowing states, school districts, and schools to spend federal money (but not IDEA funds) in ways that they think most help their students meet the state achievement objectives

▼ The premise that reading is the beginning of all learning by increasing federal funds for reading instruction

There are two key points about No Child Left Behind Act. The first is that it requires the states to establish content and performance standards. The second is that these standards apply to students with disabilities.

What Are Content and Performance Standards?

Clearly, No Child Left Behind Act and its predecessors rest on the two principles of educational reform that a committee of the National Academy of Sciences stated when it set out the implications of standards-based reform for students with disabilities:

▼ All students should have access to challenging standards

▼ Policymakers and educators should be held publicly accountable for every student's performance (McDonnell, McLaughlin, & Morison, 1997, p. 9)

There are two types of standards for all students:

1. *Content standards*. These define the knowledge, skills, and understanding that students should attain in academic subjects.
2. *Performance standards*. These define the levels of achievement that students must meet to demonstrate their proficiency in the subjects.

Star Morgan leads her class as they read and she signs a book together.

To learn more about the content and performance standards in Missouri that pertain to Luff Elementary, go to the Web Links module in Chapter 2 of the Companion Website and link to the Missouri Department of Elementary and Secondary Education (www.dese. state.mo.us/standards).

So standards-based reform is a process that

▼ Establishes content and performance standards
▼ Develops and implements a general curriculum based on content standards
▼ Assesses student progress in meeting the general curriculum's performance standards

According to the most recent data, 49 states have adopted content standards, and 27 have developed performance standards (Giacobbe, Livers, Thayer-Smith, & Walther-Thomas, 2001).

What Is the General Curriculum?

Under IDEA, the general curriculum is "the same curriculum as for nondisabled children" (*Federal Register,* 1999, p. 12592). But what is the general curriculum for students without disabilities? Their curriculum emerges from the content and performance standards set by each state education agency for students at various grade levels. In Missouri, for example, the content and performance standards are set by the state board of education. Local education agencies are expected to adopt the state curriculum, and all teachers in each agency are expected to teach that curriculum. That's why, at Luff Elementary School, Heather and all other third graders will be tested to determine what progress in reading they have made. (First graders such as Star are exempt; *MAP* assessments begin at the third grade.) For example, Luff faculty teach language skills to all students through an approach called phonemic awareness. They infuse that approach into all grades. The approach benefits Heather and all other students; phonemic awareness is a universal approach to teaching and learning.

The faculty also cleverly integrates subjects, such as reading and mathematics. For example, they teach Heather the multiples of 2 and 3 by having her play with a manipulative multiplication chart consisting of windows that open two or three at a time ($2 \times 2 = 4$, $2 \times 3 = 6$) and then having her read about houses, windows, and numbers during her reading lessons. And because she likes to use a computer and has small-motor difficulties that make her handwriting very difficult to read, she has access to a computer program in which she can draw an animal and then write a story about the animal, using a spell-check program to correct her mistakes. For Heather,

Heather Morgan meets with her third-grade faculty, Jennifer Genochio and Jean Ann Maloney, to demonstrate her reading abilities.

learning to read, spell, do math, and use a computer are all part of her general curriculum, as they are for her third-grade classmates who do not have disabilities. The difference between them is in how she is taught (instruction) and how she shows what she has learned (assessment; for example, she recites her multiplication tables with Jennifer Genochi, her paraprofessional, while Mrs. Maloney requires the other students to work out story problems at the chalkboard or their tables).

Star's education consists of being in her homeroom most of the school week; but because she has greater educational needs than many students do, she leaves her homeroom for two highly specialized related-service interventions. One involves occupational therapy so that Star will learn her shapes, how to grasp a pencil, how to use it to form letters (especially the first letters of her first and last name), and how to fasten her clothes and tie her shoes in sequence: lace them up and then tie them. The other involves speech therapy because she has a small mouth, difficulty forming words, and, more problematic, an ability to speak but not to repeat what she says. She amazed her teachers by pointing to the school's Christmas tree and speaking the first words they ever heard from her: "Christmas tree." But she has never repeated that phrase or any others she has used ("backpack" and "high chair," for example), for reasons as yet unknown.

Does the standards-based reform movement achieve its goal of establishing the same general curriculum standards for all students, whether or not they have disabilities? Approximately half of the states require students to participate in the assessment process in terms of being accountable for the same math and reading content standards as are students without disabilities (Giacobbe et al., 2001). Is that a good result for students with disabilities? Those who favor the same standards offer two arguments (O'Neill, 2001; Thurlow, 2000):

▼ Comparable standards will result in higher expectations and higher achievement for students with disabilities.

▼ By being part of the standards process for assessment, students with disabilities will be part of the reform movement of education.

Opponents argue that the same standards approach puts students with disabilities at a distinct disadvantage relative to students without disabilities (Ford, Davern, & Schnorr, 2001; O'Neal, 2001):

▼ The same-standards approach can conflict with the individualized needs of the students as set out in their IEPs. For example, the focus on academics and passing the state and district assessments will deny students with disabilities adequate instruction in important areas such as vocational education and basic life skills.

▼ Students will be frustrated, discouraged, and drop out of school.

Standards-based reform does not need to mean that schools overlook students' individualized needs. At Luff Elementary School, Star gets plenty of instruction in academics *and* such matters as being safe in the community. She used to be a "runner," bolting from the playground whenever she had a chance. With the help of her mother, Barbara Morgan, the Luff faculty have put into place a program to reward her when she does not run. She also is being taught how to accept changes, even in routine matters such as class schedules; a calendar and advance notice of changes help. And she's learning how to be in the presence of a large number of students, as at school assemblies. Bit by bit, she's including herself in assemblies; if she becomes agitated, she can choose to leave them. These are community-living skills that will stand her in good stead as she progresses through school and then works and lives in Independence after graduating from school. So academics and highly functional training go hand in hand for Star.

Still, the needs and anticipated results for students with disabilities have been overlooked as states develop their curriculum standards. Approximately one-third of the state's special education directors have not been involved in creating academic content standards (Erickson, 1998). Also, only 17 percent of the states with standards have included individuals with disabilities or disability experts in developing the standards, and slightly less than one-fourth of the states mention students with disabilities in any of the core subject-area documents (Thurlow, Ysseldyke, Gutman, & Geenen, 1998).

Star Morgan follows another student in reading class, but all of the students are signing what they are reading.

What Are the Accountability Issues?

Overlooking the needs of students with disabilities is especially problematic given that state- and district-wide assessments impose accountability on educators and students to teach and master content and performance standards. These assessments measure each student's progress on the general curriculum's content and performance standards. Yet students with disabilities were not considered when the assessments were first developed and administered and when the results were first compiled and reported (Thurlow, 2000). Indeed, in the early 1990s, fewer than 10 percent of students with disabilities were included in the assessments of most states (Shriner & Thurlow, 1992), but by the late 1990s approximately two-thirds of all students with disabilities were participating in statewide assessments (Thurlow, 2000).

This progress is good because IDEA requires each student's IEP to state how the student will be involved and progress in the general curriculum, how each student's progress will be assessed, and how the state- and district-wide assessments will be modified for the student if modification is appropriate (as it will be for Star).

This means that the IEP team must consider any accommodations in the assessment process that the student might need to ensure that his or her achievement is fairly evaluated (Thurlow, Elliott, & Ysseldyke, 1998). Accommodations do not change the content of the assessment; rather, they result in one or more of the following changes (McDonnell, McLaughlin, & Morison, 1997; Thurlow, 2000):

▼ Changes in presentation (for example, changing the order for taking subtests)

▼ Changes in responding (for example, using a computer or dictating answers)

▼ Changes in timing (for example, having extended time or frequent breaks)

▼ Changes in setting (for example, taking the test in a quiet room or a small group away from the larger class)

Currently, all states that administer state-level assessments have written policies or guidelines concerning accommodations in assessments (Thurlow, House, Boys, Scott, & Ysseldyke, 2000). Under IDEA, a student who (according to the IEP team) cannot learn the same content as same-age peers who do not have disabilities may be exempt from the standard assessment. But IDEA still requires an assessment of the student's progress, although in an alternative manner. Most states are making progress in developing alternative assessments, although they need to do a great deal more in this area (Kleinert, Green, Hurte, Clayton, & Oetinger, 2002; Thompson, Quenemoen, Thurlow, & Ysseldyke, 2001).

Let's return to Heather, whom you met in the opening vignette, and learn how she is assessed. As a third grader, Heather must take the *MAP* assessments. Because she has mild mental retardation (as her mother explained) and because she is in the general curriculum and participates in the academic part with accommodations, Heather took the *MAP* assessment with modifications. She completed the test in a room away from her classmates and was allowed a longer time to finish it. She was allowed many breaks, and her teachers read the test to her and allowed her to dictate her answers. These are the same modifications that benefit her in her general education reading program; she is assessed as she is taught, all according to her IEP.

It is hard to know exactly what kind of assessments will be administered to Star when she reaches the third grade. Although it now appears that she has severe mental retardation, she is reading the same book as her first-grade peers who do not have cognitive disabilities. She may be able to stay at that level of reading, but then again she may not. If she cannot keep up the pace, she will undergo a reading assessment that is geared to her level. So a change in content is possible. Clearly, a change in her performance requirements is in order because she does not speak but uses only sign language. So she will demonstrate what she can do by signing her answers and perhaps by having a teacher sign the questions to her.

The process of aligning content and performance standards in a way that is fair for all students, including those with disabilities and from diverse backgrounds, is a daunting task. State departments of education vary in the comprehensiveness with which they have accomplished this alignment. The Kansas State Department of Education provides an excellent model for how content and performance standards are differentiated for students with disabilities. Box 2–1 provides an overview of the Kansas model and its application to students with diverse abilities.

One of the most controversial aspects of standards-based reform is high-stakes accountability (O'Neill, 2001; Thurlow, 2000). High-stakes accountability refers to decisions that are made on the basis of the results of the assessments. As of 1999, 26 states had implemented or were in the process of implementing high-stakes assessment consequences for students; and 40 states had implemented or were in the process of implementing them for educators.

For students, high-stakes accountability involves using assessment results to determine whether the student is eligible to progress through the grades, attend a magnet school, or even graduate and, if graduated, the type of diploma awarded. Although nearly half the states impose some form of student accountability (Thurlow, Nelson, Teelucksingh, & Draper, 2001), their policies vary widely (Guy, Shin, Lee, & Thurlow, 1999; O'Neill, 2001).

As of 2001, 18 states require students to pass the standards-based assessment to receive a high school diploma and six others were anticipating adding this requirement within the next several years (O'Neill, 2001). Denying a high school diploma is an extremely high-stakes result because a student who does not have a diploma is at a tremendous disadvantage in terms of employment and potential earnings. One research study reported that individuals who do not have a high school diploma or GED have wages that are 19 percent less per hour than those who do have one (O'Neill, 2001). Yet, reports from the early years of high-stakes testing indicate (O'Neill, 2001):

▼ In the early years of testing, a high number of students failed the tests, left high school without a diploma, and experienced the restrictions noted above.

▼ Some states raised their standards from minimal standards to college preparation standards, jeopardizing the graduation chances of students with some types of disabilities.

▼ There is a potential that data on the performance of students with disabilities will lead to higher expectations and higher achievement for these students.

The National Research Council (1999) has recommended that states apply high-stakes outcomes to students only after teachers change the curriculum and how they teach it so as to ensure that students have had full opportunity to master the skills. The Council also cautions teachers against "teaching the test." At Luff, teaching the test is out of bounds. There, the faculty are using methods of instruction that make the general curriculum accessible to both Heather and Star so that they will learn content standards from which test questions are drawn.

In Chapter 1 you learned that there is significant disproportionate placement of students from diverse racial and ethnic backgrounds in special education and that there have been disproportionate results for many students from diverse backgrounds in terms of educational outcomes. You also learned that many students from diverse backgrounds are disadvantaged in the processes of referral and eligibility for special education and for test taking. Do high-stakes assessments also

Box 2–1

Into Practice

Aligning Content Standards and Performance Standards for Students with Diverse Abilities

What Are Content Standards?

Like most states, Kansas assesses students to improve the effectiveness of instruction (how educators teach: educator accountability) and to determine how well students are mastering the state's curriculum (student accountability). Significantly, Kansas's assessments relate directly to the state's standards for the general curriculum. There are three elements in the standards, listed from the most general to the most specific:

- *Standards:* "a general statement of what a student should know and be able to do in academic subjects"
- *Benchmarks:* "a specific statement of what a student should be able to do"
- *Indicators:* "a statement of knowledge or skills that a student has demonstrated in order to meet a benchmark"

The following chart depicts Kansas's approach to aligning content and performance standards and to assessing students' proficiency in each standard. You will want to refer to this chart frequently as we explain it.

There are curricular standards in each of these four curriculum content areas: (1) reading and writing, (2) mathematics, (3) social studies, and (4) science. In the area of reading and writing, there are four standards:

- Demonstrate skill in reading a variety of materials for a variety of purposes
- Write effectively for a variety of audiences, purposes, and contexts
- Demonstrate knowledge of literature from a variety of cultures, genres, and time periods
- Demonstrate skills needed to read and respond to literature

Take the first standard: Students demonstrate skill in reading a variety of materials for a variety of purposes. That standard has three benchmarks; one is that "the proficient reader comprehends whole pieces of narrative, expository, persuasion, and technical writing." For

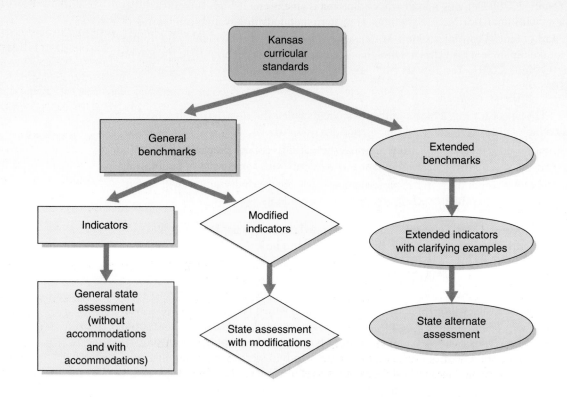

that benchmark for grades 1–4, there are six indicators, one being that the student understands the basic message of a text.

What Are Performance Standards?

Significantly, the state assessments—the students' performance standards—are based directly on the curriculum. That is what the chart depicts. How does the alignment between curriculum standards and assessment happen?

General Benchmarks and Indicators Without Accommodations

Let's begin with the typical student, Jane Doe, who has no disabilities at all. Jane takes a general assessment without any special considerations concerning how she participates. Significantly, many students with identified disabilities (who have active IEPs or "504 plans") also participate in the Kansas assessments at this level. Not all students who have disabilities are like Jane, however, in their participation. Some, such as Rafael, Ibrahim, and Jesse, may have a disability that requires a change in how they complete the state assessments. In Kansas, three additional levels are available on which a student with a disability may participate.

General Benchmarks and Indicators with Accommodations

Let's assume Rafael has a visual impairment requiring the assessment to be in large print or Braille and requiring him to respond by writing with a Braille typewriter. (You will learn about visual impairments in Chapter 16.) Let's also assume that he has been in the same classes as Jane but has used large-print books or a Brailled book and printer in class. Under the Kansas accommodations policy, Rafael may take the general assessment—the same one as Jane—with the same accommodations that he routinely uses in the course of his daily instruction so long as these accommodations are set out in his IEP. The content of his education is no different from Jane's, so the assessment should be no different except in how it is administered (just as his teachers instruct him differently from how they instruct Jane—they provide large-print or Brailled books for him). The accommodation does not change what is being assessed; it does not change the content and level of skill Rafael is expected to demonstrate. It does, however, change how he demonstrates what he knows. It is important to note that the majority of Kansas students with a disability complete the general state assessments with or without accommodations.

General Benchmarks but Modified Indicators with Accommodations

What about Ibrahim, who has autism and some cognitive limitations? (You will learn about autism in Chapter 10.) What about other students who do not have the same ability as Jane and Rafael? The same standards and benchmarks apply to Ibrahim as to Jane and Rafael. But the indicators are different; they are modified. For example, he still must demonstrate skill in reading a variety of materials for a variety of purposes (standard) and comprehend whole pieces of exposition, narration, persuasion, and technical writing (benchmark). However, one of the indicators—modified for him and some other students—is that he must "understand the basic message of the text." Ibrahim will be assessed to determine whether he satisfies this "modified indicator." But the way in which he is assessed will be different from how Jane or Rafael is assessed.

Extended Benchmarks, Extended Indicators, and Alternate Assessment

What about Jesse, who has significant mental retardation? (You will read about mental retardation in Chapter 8.) What about students such as those who have severe and multiple disabilities (see Chapter 9)? The same general education standards apply to him; but his curriculum, although it is substantially adjusted for his benefit, is still connected to the general education curriculum. How?

For Jesse and other students who need significant supports to progress in the general curriculum, reading is broadly defined to include "receptive communication." Receptive communication means that these students process messages through one or more of their senses. Similarly, writing is broadly defined to include "expressive communication." Expressive communication means that these students convey information graphically, orally, tactilely, by gestures, or by words.

For Jesse and other students who require significant supports in order to progress in the state's general education curriculum, the state department of education has added a fifth reading and writing standard: The student uses communication for the purposes of social interaction. By adding this fifth standard, the department has extended the standards for these students.

For example, the general benchmark is that the "proficient reader comprehends whole pieces of narration, exposition, persuasion, and technical writing." For Jesse, however, the benchmark is that he understands the concept of "sequencing." This benchmark extends the benchmark that is regularly applied to all other students except those requiring significant supports, as Jesse does.

Because Jesse's benchmarks and indicators have been extended to take into account his capacities, it follows that his assessment also differs. He takes the alternate assessment to demonstrate that he understands sequencing; he demonstrates that capacity by showing that he has learned to follow a visual schedule that depicts the order of activities that he is required to complete during the course of his usual school day.

To demonstrate that Jesse has learned sequencing and can follow a schedule, his IEP team develops an evidence file consisting of videotape segments, anecdotal notes, and photographs. Does Jesse get his drums when it is time for band? Does he report to the campus bus stop to go to his job training? The evidence that Jesse has mastered these sequencing skills are on videotapes, in the notes that his teachers and others make in his file, and in a photograph album that they maintain.

Aligning Content and Performance Standards with Assessments

Kansas educators have accomplished a difficult task and done it for all students. They have set curricular standards (content), performance standards (the student's level of performance), and assessments (vehicles for determining what students have mastered). The chart in this box shows how Kansas did the work of making sure that students with exceptionalities will progress in the general curriculum by having curricular standards developed for all of them, benefit from effective instruction, and demonstrate mastery. All students will master content, but some will have different content; all will have effective teachers; and all will demonstrate mastery, though some through different means and under different conditions.

Source: Adapted from Kansas State Department of Education. (2001). *Assessing diverse learners: Training-of-trainers manual* (rev. ed.), and from materials developed for the department by Dr. Susan Bashinksi, Beach Center on Disability, The University of Kansas, Lawrence.

disadvantage students from racially and ethnically diverse backgrounds? The data seem to say yes and are portrayed in the Box 2–2.

Students are not the only focus of high-stakes testing. Teachers stand to gain and lose too. Twenty-one states have established reward systems for educators, with approximately half of those states providing financial incentives such as a cash bonus of $5,000 for teachers in schools where students show an improvement rate of 20 percent or more (Giacobbe et al., 2001). In addition, some states provide rewards to students (for example, a $500 in-state college scholarship to students who perform at a satisfactory level in all areas being tested) and to high-performing schools (for example, a bonus that the school can use for purchasing additional resources).

Likewise, educators and schools who do not perform well can receive sanctions. These sanctions include loss of school accreditation and funding and a state administrative takeover of the school (Giacobbe et al., 2001). One result of these sanctions is that there is a trend for schools to exempt students with disabilities from testing in an effort to prevent a dip in their overall school scores. For example, Texas saw a 13 percent increase in the number of students with disabilities exempted from taking the test during the first year in which schools were held accountable for the scores of students with disabilities (O'Neill, 2001).

Although there are some grave concerns associated with high-stakes accountability for students, teachers, and schools, the intention and hope is that such accountability will enhance the quality of teaching and learning related to the general curriculum (Thurlow, 2000). Using the general curriculum is one way in which educators show they have great expectations for all of their students. That certainly is the case at Luff Elementary School.

High-stakes assessment can prevent some students with disabilities from graduating from high school, but it can also cause those who do graduate to be better prepared for adult life in college or at work.

Box 2–2

Multicultural Considerations

National Association for Educational Progress: Math, Reading, and Civics Results (percent)

Group	Math (1996)	Reading (1998)	Writing (1998)	Civics (1998)
All	61	74	84	70
White	73	73	90	80
Black	27	36	72	50
Hispanic	37	40	69	45
Asian/Pacific Islander	58	69	90	71
American Indian	50	47	73	49

Source: Thurlow, M. L., Nelson, J. R., Teelucksingh, E., & Draper, I. L. (2001). Multiculturalism and disability in a results-based educational system: Hazards and hopes for today's schools. In C. A. Utley & F. E. Obiakor (Eds.), *Special education, multicultural education, and school reform: Components of quality education for learners with mild disabilities* (pp. 155–172). Springfield, IL: Thomas.

Putting This Information to Work for Progress in the General Curriculum

1. What are the trends in terms of the results of these high-stakes assessments?

2. What are your reactions to the data in this box indicating that students from diverse backgrounds have significantly lower scores on standards-based assessment? What steps can be taken to ensure that all students have opportunities to progress in the general curriculum?

3. What can you as a teacher do in your classroom to make sure that all students, including those from diverse backgrounds, have individualized and appropriate instruction enabling them to progress in the general curriculum?

Why Is It Important for Students to Progress in the General Curriculum?

Why it is important for students with exceptionalities to progress in the general education curriculum, to be challenged by great expectations? Underlying high expectations is the value of full citizenship in the United States: To deny students the opportunity to benefit from the general curriculum may actually limit their education and postschool opportunities. Essentially, ensuring progress in the general curriculum safeguards them against second-class treatment and against being patronized because of their disability (Thurlow, 2000).

How do you provide standards-based education for all students? We will answer that question throughout all chapters in this book. We begin by describing how you can design curriculum, instruction, and evaluation to enable students with exceptionalities to progress in the general curriculum.

How Does Universal Design for Learning Enable Students with Exceptionalities to Progress in the General Curriculum?

In this section, you will learn the answers to the following questions:

▼ What is universal design for learning?
▼ How does universal design for learning enable students with exceptionalities to progress in the general curriculum?

What Is Universal Design for Learning?

Universal design originated as a concept in architecture. There, design seeks to ensure that buildings and public spaces are accessible to all people, including those who experience mobility impairments. Drawing from the success of designing buildings that are accessible to everyone from the outset, universal design for learning is a process for (1) considering the needs of all students in the classroom—including those with exceptionalities, linguistic diversities, and varied learning styles—from the *beginning* of the planning stage, and (2) designing curriculum, instruction, and evaluation with sufficient *flexibility* so that each student benefits (Hitchcock, Meyer, Rose, & Jackson, 2002; Pisha & Coyne, 2000).

Consider the implications of a universal design approach. Under the traditional approach in general education, teachers developed a curriculum and allowed students with disabilities accommodations such as extra time to complete an assignment or a reduced workload. By contrast, universal design for learning begins by assuming that students vary widely, even though they may all be in the same grade and same course, and is flexible in order to respond to a wide degree of student diversity from the very outset.

Exciting new possibilities are available for providing flexibility through the use of technology. In Box 2–3, you will read how technology is redesigning the format of textbooks to enable students who have difficulty reading to progress in the general curriculum.

Universal design can occur at many levels:

▼ At the state level when content and performance standards are developed and when students are assessed to determine how proficient they are with respect to the standards
▼ At the district or building level when comprehensive planning is carried out to ensure that all students have an opportunity to progress in the general curriculum
▼ At the classroom level when you as an educator ensure that teaching and learning occur for the students you serve

In the next section you will learn about how you can apply the principles of universal design to the curriculum, instruction, and evaluation of your students.

Universal Design of the Curriculum

To accomplish universal design of the curriculum, you will need to differentiate between (1) content you present and the students (including those with exceptionalities) to whom you present it and (2) the level of performance at which you expect each student to perform. As you already know, state departments of education have developed content and performance standards. In Box 2–1, you learned that the Kansas State Department of Education has created open-ended or universally designed standards that provide a wide range of flexibility in content and performance standards. In states that have incorporated universal design from the outset, the state guidelines will help you make differentiated decisions concerning content and performance standards for each of your students.

There are two major ways to add flexibility to the curriculum, as illustrated in Figure 2–1:

Previously you learned that teachers have typically aimed curriculum toward middle-of-the-road students.

To learn many applications of universal design to the field of education, go to the Web Links module in Chapter 2 of the Companion Website for a link to Universal Design Education Online (www.udeducation.org).

To learn more about the use of technology in universal design, go to the Web Links module in Chapter 2 of the Companion Website (www.cast.org).

Technology Tips

Box 2–3

Flexible Digital Textbooks

If you can't use your legs, then you can't climb stairs and thus can't get into many school buildings. That has been a fact of life for many students with disabilities; but it is a fact that is receding as old buildings are modified, new ones are built with ramps and elevators incorporated from the beginning, and electronic wheelchairs are built to climb stairs. Access to the buildings comes from the universal design of buildings (ramps and elevators) and from new technologies (motorized stair-climbing wheelchairs).

That's good progress, but what if a student can't read the books that her peers are reading? Maybe the student has a learning disability, a visual impairment, a short attention span because of hyperactivity, a mental retardation, or side effects of prescribed medication for physical or mental health reasons. How much progress can that student make in the general curriculum, even if she is in the same classroom with peers who do not have disabilities and is using the same textbooks? The answer has to be, "Not much."

The Center for Applied Special Technology (CAST) has developed a computer-based system for students who experience reading challenges with the general curriculum. There are four features of CAST's "Strategic Reader E-Textbook Project."

First, the students can use Microsoft's text-to-speech engine to have any electronic-text (e-text) read aloud to them. They will get the entire text, no watered-down version, word for word. What they would read is what they will hear.

Second, the students will receive supports for basic access to the text and for strategic learning. Because the layout of some textbooks is confusing, CAST will provide (1) a simplified and clarified presentation of the core content, with sidebars and graphics deleted and (2) an outline view of the key topics, prioritized, organized, and clustered so that the students will quickly see the text in first-, second-, and third-order headings in outline form.

Third, the students will benefit from supports on how to use the strategies (simplified text and outlines). They will be asked to read the outline before the text and be reminded to read the outline again before taking a test on the material. They also will be guided to websites that define terms or explain, in simple terms, the concepts of the text they have just read.

Finally, the students will be able to become more engaged with the text through techniques such as concept mapping or in-class presentations. For example, they can debate a proposition presented in the text ("A critical battle in the Vietnam War was a disaster for the North Vietnamese") by being guided into the text for facts to support their side of the debate.

CAST takes a text that traditionally has been accessible only in a book and converts the paper text to an electronic form and then builds in computer-based techniques for teaching the e-text. Imagine how much more success a student will have in mastering any text— even the one that presents the most difficult material at the highest level of secondary education—if they can just have access to it.

If you want to know more about what CAST does and what, in particular, it does to create e-texts (downloadable electronic texts from which to teach), CAST has made it easy for you by creating a central repository— a clearing house, so to speak—that lists some of the e-texts and hyperlink sites that are available to teachers and students. The CAST repository is called the Universal Learning Center and can be found at http://ulc.cast.org.

Putting These Tips to Work for Progress in the General Curriculum

1. What's the challenge?

2. What's the technology?

3. What do you do with it?

To answer these questions online and to learn more about this technology, go to the Technology module in Chapter 2 of the Companion Website.

Source: Adapted from Pisha, B., & Coyne, P. (2001, July/August). Smart from the start: The promise of universal design for learning. *Remedial and Special Education, 22*(4), 197–203; and O'Neill, L. M. (2001). The Universal Learning Center: Helping teachers and parents find accessible electronic learning materials for students with disabilities. *Exceptional Parent, 31*(9), 56–59.

FIGURE 2–1

Universal design for learning to ensure progress in the general curriculum: curriculum component

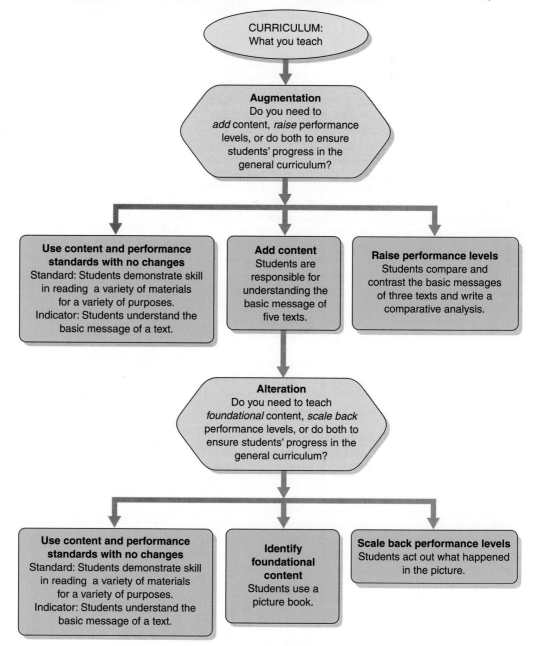

▼ *Augmentation*. The teacher adds content to the general curriculum and/or raises performance levels to meet students' particular needs (for example, content enrichment for students whose achievement is significantly above grade level).

▼ *Alteration*. The teacher teaches foundational content in the general curriculum and/or scales back performance levels (for example, a foundational curriculum for students whose achievement is significantly below grade level).

Star Morgan benefits from curriculum alteration when she is asked to learn the letter "t" in "treat" or "m" in "moon," but the other students are asked to learn that consonant and the vowels too. So the content area is still the alphabet and phonemic awareness, but the specific content objective is different.

Universal Design of Instruction

Universal design of instruction focuses on how to teach the curriculum so that teaching is consistent with each student's most effective way of learning. Instruction differentiates between how the content is presented and/or how the student responds.

Classrooms characterized by universal design incorporate two major ways of enhancing flexible instruction (Wehmeyer, Lattin, & Agran, 2001):

▼ *Augmentation.* The teacher teaches additional skills (for example, learning strategies that will increase the students' capacity to learn independently and to generalize their skills to new situations, mobility training for students who are blind, or bilingual education for students who do not speak English).

▼ *Adaptation.* The teacher changes how the content is presented during instruction (a student who is not able to read grade-level textbooks uses an audio version of the text), changes how the environment is arranged, provides environmental modifications (a student has a quiet space in which to work), and/or changes how the student is expected to respond (a student who is not able to write uses a computer).

Figure 2–2 provides an overview of a range of options for the teacher's presentation of the content and the students' response.

Universal design for instruction makes it possible for Heather and Star to participate in Luff Elementary School's general curriculum. In her third-grade class, Heather reads the same books as her

FIGURE 2–2

Adaptation options for presenting content, arranging the environment, and for modifying expectations for student response

1. **Adapt content presentation**
   - **Text.** Digital text (on a computer) can easily be transformed in size, shape, or color and can automatically be transformed into spoken speech.
   - **Audio.** Audio with captions provides flexible alternatives.
   - **Novelty and familiarity.** There are flexible options for the amount of repetition, familiarity, randomness, and surprise.
   - **Developmental and cultural interest.** Students contribute to the curriculum by adding their own images, sounds, words, and texts to what has already been developed.
2. **Provide environmental modifications**
   - **Seating.** The student is free from distractions and has access to peer tutors and special equipment. (This includes storage when students need to use particular technologies).
   - **Adapted work areas.** There are physical accommodations for students who need larger, smaller, or modified work areas due to their special needs.
3. **Adapt mode of student response**
   - **Writing.** On-screen scanning keyboards, enlarged keyboards, word prediction, and spell checkers can assist with writing tasks.
   - **Multimedia.** Multimedia presentations provide a response mode to those for whom speech is not a viable presentation method.
   - **Peer-assistance.** Students can provide oral responses to peers, who can write the information and turn it in.
   - **Oral reports.** Students can provide an oral report that can be accompanied by props and/or costumes.

Source: Adapted from *A Curriculum Every Student Can Use: Design Principles for Student Access* by R. Orkwis and K. McLane, 1988, Summer, Reston, VA: ERIC/OSEP Special Project, Council for Exceptional Children. Copyright 1998 by the Council for Exceptional Children. Adapted with permission. Go to the Web Links module in Chapter 2 of the Companion Website for a link to the full document.

FIGURE 2–3

Universal design for learning to ensure progress in general curriculum: Instruction component

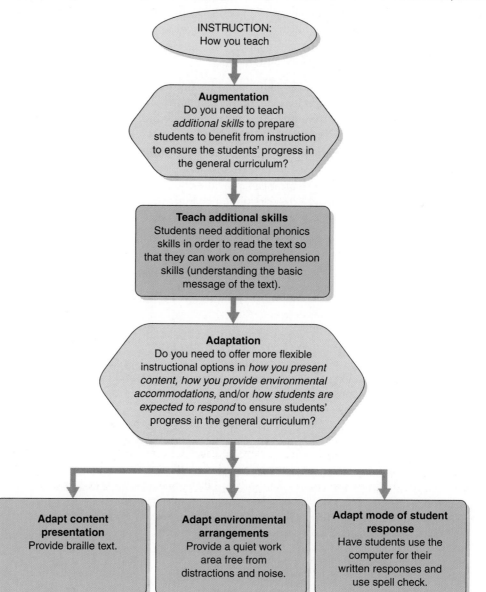

peers without disabilities do; she receives the same curriculum but with special assistance from paraprofessionals and special educators, who break the lessons into chunks, teach the separate parts, repeat the teaching time and again, require her to engage in more practice than other students do, and allow her to take more breaks than other students do (because she has a shorter attention span). In her first-grade class, Star also reads the same book as her peers; but she is pulled out of class for special instruction in reading, speech-language and sign-language instruction, and special assistance in behaving appropriately—for example, sitting quietly in school assemblies and not running away from the playground. It is remarkable that Star reads the same book, but bear in mind that she is in the first grade and has the benefit of a team of educators who sign and speak the words of the book to her and then model the sign for each word so that she can sign to her classmates. There is no doubt about the fact that Star receives a great deal more help than Heather does to participate in the general curriculum and probably always will; the extent of her mental capacities, her speech

FIGURE 2–4

Universal design for learning to ensure progress in general curriculum: Evaluation component

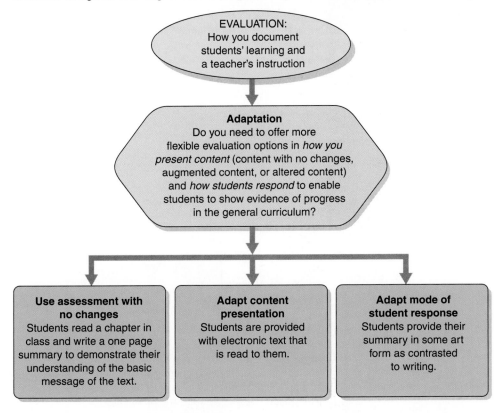

EVALUATION:
How you document
students' learning and
a teacher's instruction

Adaptation
Do you need to offer more
flexible evaluation options in *how you
present content* (content with no changes,
augmented content, or altered content)
and *how students respond* to enable
students to show evidence of progress
in the general curriculum?

**Use assessment with
no changes**
Students read a chapter in
class and write a one page
summary to demonstrate their
understanding of the basic
message of the text.

**Adapt content
presentation**
Students are provided
with electronic text that
is read to them.

**Adapt mode of
student response**
Students provide their
summary in some art
form as contrasted
to writing.

impairments, and her behavior make a huge difference. But also bear in mind that she is using some, if not all, of the same curriculum as her peers. Figure 2–3 illustrates the instruction component of universal design by using the same curriculum standard that you read about in Figure 2–2.

Universal Design of Evaluation

The third and last component of universal design is evaluation. Evaluation enables you to know how well you taught the student and how well the student learned what you taught. Like the curriculum and instruction components of universal design, evaluation also must be flexible so it can apply to all of your students (Rose, 2000; Wehmeyer, Lattin, & Agran, 2001).

> *Adaptation.* The teacher changes how the content is presented during evaluation (for example, Heather's teachers read some of the materials to her whereas other students have to read on their own) and/or changes how the student is expected to respond (for example, Star signs; Heather has a longer time for writing out her answers, or she can dictate them to her teachers).

Figure 2–4 shows how to make the evaluation process a flexible one in designing evaluation for the content indicator first introduced in Figure 2–1: "Student understands the basic message of a text."

Now that you have learned the three components of universal design for learning—curriculum, instruction, and evaluation—you should recognize that these three components are linked to each other. Figure 2–5 shows these links by its connecting arrows.

Effective teaching and learning involve making decisions about how the content (curriculum) will be delivered to students (instruction) and how students, teachers, and schools will be held accountable for the content and performance standards (evaluation).

In each of the
remaining chapters (Chapters
3–16), you will learn more
about universal design for
learning.

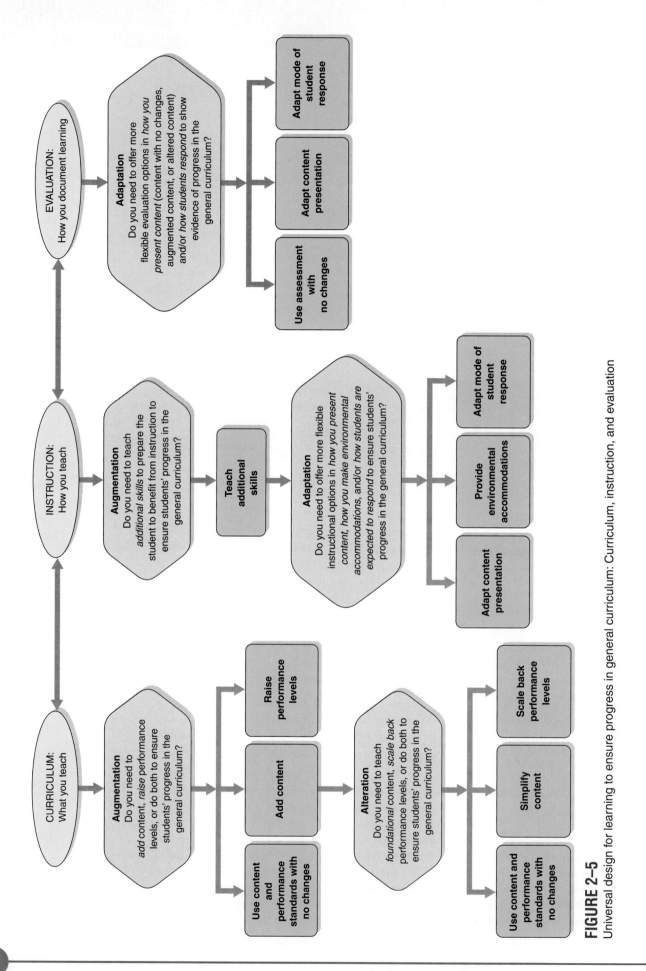

FIGURE 2–5
Universal design for learning to ensure progress in general curriculum: Curriculum, instruction, and evaluation

How Does Universal Design for Learning Enable Students with Exceptionalities to Progress in the General Curriculum?

If curriculum, instruction, and evaluation are flexible and tailored to the individual needs of all students in the classroom—those with and without exceptionalities—it becomes far more likely that students whose learning and behavior differ significantly from those of their same-age peers will still have opportunities to progress in the general curriculum. The fundamental contribution of universal design is to tailor teaching and learning to the needs of each student. It focuses on a student's strengths, takes the student's learning capacities into account, and offers each student a full opportunity to benefit from the general curriculum. Figure 2–6 summarizes the principles of universal design for learning (Wehmeyer, Lance, & Bashinski, 2001).

How Does Inclusion Enable Students to Progress in the General Curriculum?

You already know that progress in the general curriculum is one of IDEA's goals, and you know why that is an important goal for students. And you have just started to learn about one way to advance that goal: universal design for learning. There is still a second important way. It is called *inclusion*. We introduce you to this essential concept here and then elaborate on it in Chapters 4 through 16, where we set out information on how to teach students with exceptionalities. In this section, we answer the following questions:

▼ What are placement trends for students with exceptionalities?

▼ What is inclusion?

▼ What are educator, parent, and student perspectives on inclusion?

▼ What are student outcomes associated with inclusion?

▼ How does inclusion enable students to progress in the general curriculum?

What Are Placement Trends for Students with Exceptionalities?

The U.S. Department of Education annually reports to Congress on the percentage of students with disabilities who receive special education and related services in different educational settings. Figure 2–7 lists the Department's categories of educational placements and defines each placement (also called "environment").

What percentage of students with disabilities is educated in each of the six categories? How do you think the placement of students with disabilities has increased or decreased in each category over the past decade? Figure 2–8 answers these questions. There has been a progressive trend toward greater inclusion since the 1984–1985 school year, when the U.S. Department of Education first started collecting inclusion data. For example, in 1984–1985 about one-quarter of the students with disabilities received their education outside of the regular class less than 21 percent of the school day, but by 1988–1999 this percentage had increased to almost half (U.S. Department of Education, 2001).

One trend relates to the extent of placement in the general classroom. Clearly, fewer students with disabilities are served outside of the general classroom, and the amount of time they spend outside the classroom has decreased. In addition, the number of students in self-contained and separate facilities is gradually decreasing. The number of students in residential facilities and in homebound/hospital placements has remained at a low level over this entire time period.

FIGURE 2–6

Principles, rationale and criteria in applying universal design to curriculum, instruction, and evaluation

Principles/Rationale	Criteria
1. **Flexible use.** Curriculum, instruction, and evaluation should be designed from the outset for students with diverse abilities.	• Accommodates students with diverse abilities • Accommodates students who speak various languages • Does not stigmatize students • Benefits as many potential users as possible • Avoids inconveniencing students with any particular characteristics
2. **Simple and intuitive use.** Curriculum, instruction, and evaluation should be designed from the outset to be as easy to understand and use as possible.	• Is easy to use • Avoids unnecessary complexity • Provides clear directions and understandable examples • Breaks complex tasks into small steps
3. **Perceptible information.** Curriculum, instruction, and evaluation should be designed from the outset to be readily perceived regardless of environmental conditions or a user's sensory abilities.	• Communicates information to users independent of environmental conditions and/or users' sensory abilities • Highlights essential information • Breaks information into comprehensible chunks
4. **Tolerance for error.** Curriculum, instruction, and evaluation should be designed from the outset to minimize the likelihood of error and the negative consequences resulting from error.	• Avoids punishing students for mistakes • Provides ample time to respond • Provides immediate and thorough feedback • Monitors progress • Provides adequate practice time
5. **Reasonable physical, cognitive, and psychological efforts.** Curriculum, instruction, and evaluation should be designed from the outset to avoid making a user uncomfortable or fatigued.	• Presents information that can be completed in a reasonable timeframe • Avoids physically, cognitively, and/or psychologically exhausting the user
6. **Size and space for approach and use.** Curriculum, instruction, and evaluation should be designed from the outset to be used in a physically accessible manner.	• Requires reasonable amount of space • Incorporates accessible materials and learning activities

Source: Adapted from Wehmeyer, M. L., Lance, G. D., & Bashinski, S. (2002). Promoting access to the general curriculum for students with mental retardation: A multi-level model. *Education and Training in Mental Retardation and Developmental Disabilities, 37*(3), 223–234.

Another trend reveals that the percentage of students with disabilities in the different placement categories varies according to the age of students and their type of disability. More elementary students than secondary students are served in typical schools with peers who do not have disabilities. Students with milder disabilities (e.g., speech or language impairments and learning disabilities) are more likely to be in general education classrooms for the largest percentage of time compared with students with more significant cognitive disabilities (e.g., students with mental retardation or multiple disabilities).

FIGURE 2–7

Six placement categories designated by the U.S. Department of Education

Special education outside the regular class less than 21 percent of the day.
Unduplicated number of children and youth with disabilities receiving special education and related services outside the regular class for less than 21 percent of the school day.

Special education outside the regular class at least 21 percent of the day and no more than 60 percent of the day. Unduplicated number of children and youth with disabilities receiving special education and related services outside the regular class for at least 21 percent but no more than 60 percent of the school day.

Special education outside the regular class more than 60 percent of the day.
Unduplicated number of children and youth with disabilities receiving special education and related services outside the regular class for more than 60 percent of the school day.

Public separate facility. Unduplicated number of children and youth with disabilities receiving special education and related services for greater than 50 percent of the school day in public separate facilities.

Private separate facility. Unduplicated number of children and youth with disabilities receiving special education and related services for greater than 50 percent of the school day in private separate facilities.

Public residential facility. Unduplicated number of children and youth with disabilities receiving special education and related services for greater than 50 percent of the school day in public residential facilities.

Private residential facility. Unduplicated number of children and youth with disabilities receiving special education and related services for greater than 50 percent of the school day in private residential facilities.

Source: U.S. Department of Education, Office of Special Education. (1988). *OSEP IDEA, Part B data dictionary, 1988.* Washington, DC: Author.

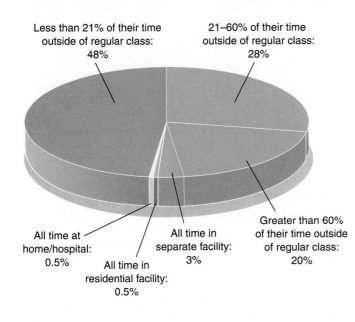

Less than 21% of their time outside of regular class: 48%

21–60% of their time outside of regular class: 28%

All time at home/hospital: 0.5%

All time in residential facility: 0.5%

All time in separate facility: 3%

Greater than 60% of their time outside of regular class: 20%

FIGURE 2–8

Percentage of students ages 6 through 21 in different education environments during the 1998–1999 school year

Source: From U.S. Department of Education. (2001). *To assure the free appropriate public education of all children with disabilities: Twenty-first annual report to Congress on the implementation of the Individuals With Disabilities Education Act.* Washington, DC: Author.

An institution for individuals with disabilities is at one far end of the continuum and is the most segregated placement.

TABLE 2–1

Percentage of students ages 6 through 21 with disabilities served in different educational environments according to racial/ethnic characteristics: 1989–1999

	American Indian/ Alaska Native	Asian/Pacific Islander	Black	Hispanic	White
Served outside of the regular class					
Less than 21 percent of the day	48.2	47.0	34.8	41.2	52.5
21–60 percent of the day	34.3	26.6	28.2	29.1	28.4
More than 60 percent of the day	14.6	22.2	31.5	26.1	15.3
Separate school	1.5	3.1	4.2	2.6	2.7
Residential facility	0.9	0.6	0.9	0.5	0.6
Home/hospital	0.4	0.5	0.5	0.6	0.5

Source: U.S. Department of Education, Office of Special Education Programs, Data Analysis System (DANS).

A disconcerting trend is the disproportionality in placement trends related to students characterized by racial and ethnic diversity. Table 2–1 provides placement trends related to race and ethnicity.

We now will briefly highlight issues associated with placement in residential/home/hospital settings, special schools, and specialized settings within typical schools. Then we will discuss the issues associated with inclusion in general education, particularly in academic programs and classrooms.

How do the trends that you detect in Table 2–1 relate to what you learned in Chapter 1 about the disproportionate representation of students from diverse racial and ethnic backgrounds being identified for special education services?

What Issues Are Associated with Placement in Residential/Home/Hospital Settings?

Settings that have a residential component—special schools that are not just day schools but provide 24-hour services, as well as hospitals and students' homes—are generally regarded as the most restrictive placements. Students who attend residential schools often do so because their local schools have not developed the capacity to provide universally designed learning for them. Thus, it is important to distinguish situations in which a student needs a more restrictive environment from those in which educators need to expand their skills.

Yet residential settings can also provide a critical mass of talented educators (except in homebound settings) and can benefit the students, some of whom may prefer to be with other students who have the same disabilities. Students with hearing impairments, visual impairments, and deaf-blindness are most likely to attend residential schools (U.S. Department of Education, 2000).

Students with physical disabilities, emotional disorders, and traumatic brain injury are most likely to be educated in a hospital or in their home (U.S. Department of Education, 2000). As illustrated in Figure 2–8, a low percentage of students are in these settings; this percentage has remained relatively stable over time.

What Issues Are Associated with Placement in Special Schools?

Separate schools typically congregate students with a certain type of disability and offer services related to the characteristics of that disability. Students with emotional or behavioral disorders are most likely to be educated in special schools; the next most likely are students with deaf-blindness and autism (U.S. Department of Education, 2000). Frequently, students with emotional disorders and autism are placed in special schools because of their problem behavior and because many teachers do not know how to address these behaviors.

What Issues Are Associated with Placement in Specialized Settings Within Typical Schools?

Specialized settings in many schools include the resource rooms and the special classes. As reflected in Figure 2–8, students who receive 21–60 percent of their education outside of the regular classroom typically are served in resource rooms. Resource rooms are staffed by special education teachers who work with students with disabilities for as little as one period or as many as several periods during the school day, depending upon the students' need for specially designed instruction. The students who are most likely to be served in resource rooms have learning disabilities and other health impairments (U.S. Department of Education, 2000). There are resource rooms at Luff Elementary because, as principal Peggy Palser notes, the reality is that full-time placement in general education classrooms does not benefit all students all the time.

The second type of specialized setting within typical schools is the special education classroom. Special classrooms usually are provided for students with more intense needs than those students served in resource rooms. Students with mental retardation, autism, multiple disabilities, and emotional disorders are most likely to be served in special classes (U.S. Department of Education, 2000). Traditionally, special education classrooms serve students with more significant disabilities and have a strong focus on functional skills such as career education and social behavior.

What Is Inclusion and What Are Its Four Key Characteristics?

Inclusion refers to students with disabilities learning in general education classes and having a sense of belonging in these classes. Inclusion has a long history in the field of special education. Figure 2–9 summarizes that history according to its four consecutive phases.

The student who is featured in Chapter 9 is Joshua Spoor, who attends a residential school. As you will learn in that chapter, Joshua has multiple disabilities, pervasive needs for support, and a family who has faced other challenges. He was placed in the residential school when his family was responding to the intensive needs of Joshua's mother, who had terminal cancer.

We discuss hospital and homebound services in Chapter 11, on physical disabilities.

In Star Morgan's first-grade classroom, all students become bilingual because all of them learn sign words.

FIGURE 2–9
Four consecutive phases of inclusion

1. **Mainstreaming:** an educational arrangement of returning students from special education classrooms to general education classrooms typically for nonacademic portions of the school day, such as art, music, and physical education (Grosenick & Reynolds, 1978; Turnbull & Schulz, 1979)

2. **Regular Education Initiative:** an attempt to reform general and special education by creating a unified system capable of meeting individual needs in general education classrooms (Gartner & Lipsky, 1987; Reynolds, Wang, & Walberg, 1987; Will, 1986)

3. **Inclusion through accommodations (instructional adaptations):** an additive approach to inclusion that assumes the only viable approach to including students with disabilities in general education classrooms is to add instructional adaptations to the predefined general education teaching and learning approaches (Pugach, 1995)

4. **Inclusion through restructuring:** a design to inclusion that recreates general and special education by merging resources to develop more flexible learning environments for all students and educators (McGregor & Vogelsberg, 1998; Pugach & Johnson, 2002; Sailor, 2002; Thousand, Villa, & Nevin, 2002)

Inclusion has four key characteristics:

▼ All students receive education in the home school they would have attended if they had no exceptionality.

▼ Consideration is given to placing students in classrooms according to the principle of natural proportions.

▼ Teaching and learning is restructured for all students so that special education supports exist within general education classes.

▼ School and general education placements are age- and grade-appropriate.

 While you are learning about these four key characteristics, we urge you to remember what you have already learned in Chapter 1 about IDEA's principle of least restrictive environment/ placement.

Home-School Placement

Under this principle, a student attends the same school he or she would have attended if they did not have an exceptionality. This is the same school that other children in the student's neighborhood attend. Heather and Star live in the Luff neighborhood and attend their neighborhood school; by attending Luff, not a separate school, they, like other students with a disability, contribute to a sense of a learning community (Hunt, Hirose-Hatae, Doering, Karasoff, & Goetz, 2000; Schnorr, 1997).

Principle of Natural Proportions

The principle of natural proportions holds that students with exceptionalities should be placed in schools and on classroom rosters in natural proportion to the occurrence of exceptionality within the general population (Brown, Udari-Solner, Frattura-Kampschroer, Davis, Van Deventer, Ahlgren, & Jorgensen, 1991). Roughly 9 percent of the general school population has disabilities. Rounding this off to 10 percent, the principle of natural proportions holds that, if a classroom has 30 students, not more than three of them should have disabilities. In a modification of this principle, Walther-Thomas and her colleagues (1999) suggest that not more than 20 percent of the total classroom should have disabilities. For a classroom of 30 students, this means six students. They also suggest that if some of the students have more severe disabilities and need extensive support, the overall number of students with disabilities in the class should be reduced.

Restructuring Teaching and Learning

Inclusion through restructuring involves general and special education educators, working jointly with related service providers, families, and students, to ensure that curriculum, instruction, and evaluation are universally designed in general education classrooms. Tremendous variability exists in how teachers provide special education supports within general education classrooms. Just consider the brief descriptions in Figure 2–9 of inclusion through add-on services and inclusion through restructured services. In state-of-the-art programs that are implementing inclusion through restructuring, the strengths and talents of educators with different types of training and capacities are pooled to provide individualized instruction within the general education classroom.

Age- and Grade-Appropriate Placements

Finally, inclusion favors educating all students in age- and grade-appropriate placements, just as Heather and Star spend most of their school days at Luff Elementary School with third and first graders, respectively.

These four principles are controversial. Indeed, two major issues are at the heart of the inclusion debate: (1) eliminating the continuum of placements and (2) increasing the amount of time students spend in the general education classroom.

Eliminating the Continuum. The concept of a continuum has been part of special education ever since Congress enacted IDEA in 1975. The continuum refers to services that range from the most typical and most inclusive settings to the most atypical and most segregated settings.

There was a time when accommodating students with disabilities in general education classrooms through supplementary aids and services was not even considered a viable option. That limited perspective caused Taylor (1988) to assert that students with disabilities were "caught in the continuum of services." Unfortunately, once slotted in more restrictive settings, few students ever left them for general education classroom settings.

The inclusion movement has tried to limit the need for more restrictive settings by creating a new partnership between special and general educators. This partnership seeks to provide individualized instruction to students in general education classrooms through a universally designed general curriculum (King-Sears, 2001). Inclusion now rests on the premise that it is not often appropriate or even necessary to remove some students from the general education classroom and to place them in a more specialized and restrictive setting to provide individualized and appropriate education.

To advance this premise, general and special educators collaborate to promote students' academic success, participation in extracurricular and other school activities, and sense of belonging (Voltz, Brazil, & Ford, 2001). Also common is the strategy of having separate spaces in schools that are used by many students for various purposes: resource centers, study labs, and break out rooms that enable students to meet together for cooperative learning groups, peer tutoring, and special group activities (Voltz et al., 2001). The approach of having separate space

You can learn state-of-art information about inclusion by going to the Web Links module in Chapter 3 of the Companion Website to link to the National Institute for Urban School Improvement (www.edc.org/urban/).

You will learn more about restructuring teaching and learning for the benefit of general and special education students later in this chapter in the section on collaboration.

that is used by many students contrasts with the approach of having specialized placements that are used by only those students with disabilities.

Increasing the Amount of Time Students Spend in General Education Classrooms. The second major issue at the heart of inclusion is related to age- and grade-appropriate placements and concerns the extent of time that a student spends in the general classroom. Inclusion proponents generally agree that placement in general education classrooms does not mean that the student never leaves those classrooms for special services. At Luff, the pullout model is rare. True, some students with disabilities use resource rooms some of the time; true, others leave their general education classrooms from time to time and for very specific instructional purposes. But consistent with the inclusion principle, the two special education teachers and the instruction specialist go into the general education classrooms to work with the general education teachers and their paraprofessionals. All of the Luff faculty regard Star and Heather as authentic members of their classes.

When special education supports are readily available within general education classrooms and universal design for learning has been fully implemented, students with disabilities will be more likely to perceive themselves as valued classroom members and will not need to leave the classroom as often to receive an appropriate education.

What Are Educator, Parent, and Student Perspectives on Inclusion?

In Chapter 3 you will learn about ways you can respond to students from culturally and linguistically diverse backgrounds to increase their opportunities to progress in the general curriculum.

The research on inclusion has some limitations. For example, most research studies do not describe the quality and quantity of inclusion; the extent of incorporating universal design in the curriculum, instruction, and assessment processes; and the extent to which students from culturally and linguistically diverse backgrounds have appropriate respect, support, and accommodations. Bear those limitations in mind as we highlight the perspectives of educators, parents, and students about inclusion.

Educators' Perspectives

Earlier, we noted that supporters of inclusion, including many educators, want to abandon the continuum of placements. They start with the assumption that students with exceptionalities, including those with very significant disabilities, can be educated in the general education classroom (progress in the general curriculum) with state-of-the-art support (Andrews et al., 2000; Sailor, 2002; Thousand et al., 2002; Wehmeyer, 2002). Not every educator agrees (Kauffman, 1995; Kavale & Forness, 2000; MacMillan, Gresham, & Forness, 1996; Zigmond et al., 1995). Indeed, there is a wide range of perspectives about the benefits and drawbacks of inclusion. Those who are hesitant about, or even are opposed to, inclusion fear that full-time general education placements may deny some students the benefit of intensive and individualized instruction (Andrews et al., 2000; MacMillan et al.,

The four principles of inclusion guide Luff Elementary School faculty and students when educating Star Morgan.

1996). Others adopt a middle-ground position, asserting that a wide range of placements is necessary to meet students' individual needs but that schools should try to include students in the general classroom and neighborhood schools. What are the specific concerns about inclusion?

Teachers often identify class size as one of the major obstacles to inclusion. Indeed, small class sizes in elementary grades often lead to improvement in student achievement, especially for students from culturally and linguistically diverse backgrounds (Finn & Achilles, 1999; Molnar, Smith, Zahorick, Palmer, & Ehrle, 1999). Reducing class size, however, is not an immediate solution, nor the only one; what also makes a big difference is a change in the way teachers teach (McCrea, 1996).

Many teachers and principals also report that special education resources have not been sufficiently infused into general education to ensure effective teaching (Barnett & Monda-Amaya, 1998; Boyer & Bandy, 1997; Fox & Ysseldyke, 1997; Minke, Bear, Deemer, & Griffin, 1996). It is true that inclusion requires educators to reallocate special education resources to general education settings so that individualized instruction in the general curriculum becomes feasible. Not all educators and schools have reallocated their resources.

A research synthesis summarized 28 studies conducted from 1958 to 1995 and summarized their implications for inclusion with respect to time, training, personnel, materials, class size, and severity of disability (Scruggs & Mastropieri, 1996). Figure 2–10 highlights the findings, which show that teachers believe they need more resources to make inclusion successful.

More recent research on teachers' perspectives has reported conflictual findings:

▼ Some studies indicate that general education teachers believe that they do not possess the necessary skills to teach students with disabilities and lack opportunities to collaborate with special education teachers (Schumm & Vaughn, 1995; Van Reusen, Shoho, & Barker, 2001).

▼ Alternatively, a national study of general education teachers reported that 87 percent reported feeling successful in teaching most students with disabilities to a moderate or great extent (Study of Personnel Needs in Special Education, 2002). Not surprisingly, having support to implement individualized instruction and having access to in-service training resulted in significantly more teachers feeling successful.

FIGURE 2–10
Implications from Scruggs and Mastropieri's (1996) research synthesis

- *Time*—Teachers report a need for one hour or more per day to plan for students with disabilities.
- *Training*—Teachers need systematic, intensive training, either as part of their certification programs, as intensive and well-planned in-services, or as an ongoing process with consultants.
- *Personnel resources*—Teachers report a need for additional personnel assistance to carry out mainstreaming objectives. This could include a half-time paraprofessional and daily contact with special education teachers.
- *Materials resources*—Teachers need adequate curriculum materials and other classroom equipment appropriate to the needs of students with disabilities.
- *Class size*—Teachers agree that their class size should be reduced, to fewer than twenty students, if students with disabilities are included.
- *Consideration of severity of disability*—Teachers are more willing to include students with mild disabilities than students with more severe disabilities, apparently because of teachers' perceived ability to carry on their teaching mission for the entire classroom. By implication, the more severe the disabilities represented in the inclusive setting, the more the previously mentioned sources of support would be needed.

Other research supports the importance of professional development and experience. The more well trained and experienced in providing universally designed learning a teacher is, the more the teacher will know how to practice inclusion and favor it (McLeskey, Waldron, So, Swanson, & Loveland, 2001; Soodak, Podell, & Lehman, 1998; Soodak et al., 2002). We hope you will begin to acquire some knowledge of those skills by reading this book and become advocates for inclusion and IDEA.

Parents' Perspectives

As a general rule, parents of students with disabilities appear to be more positive than educators about inclusion. Duhaney and Salend (2000) reached the following conclusions after reviewing 17 studies that reported the perspectives of parents of children with disabilities toward inclusion:

▼ Although there is a range of perspectives, the majority of parents appear to be positive about inclusive placements.

▼ Parents perceive that general education classrooms, as contrasted to more specialized settings, do a better job of (1) improving their child's self-concept, (2) enabling their child to have more appropriate role models and friendships, (3) making their child happier and more confident, (4) helping their child develop academically and (5) preparing their child for the real world.

▼ Parents have concerns related to the availability of qualified educators and individualized services, and they are frustrated about having to work hard to get the schools to provide inclusive programs.

Indeed, many parents report that they must be vigilant advocates for their children to have appropriate supports and services offered in inclusive programs (Erwin, Soodak, Winton, & Turnbull, 2001; Grove & Fisher, 1999). That's certainly part of Barbara Morgan's story, but it is not all of it, by any means, as you will learn by reading Box 2–4.

Parents of children with disabilities are not the only parents with a stake in education. Duhaney and Salend (2000) also summarized research on the perspectives of parents of children without disabilities toward inclusion. Similar to parents of children with disabilities, the majority of parents reported positive viewpoints.

▼ Parents of children without disabilities identified benefits for their own children such as greater sensitivity to the needs of other children, more helpfulness in meeting the needs of classmates with disabilities, and greater acceptance of diversity.

▼ They viewed inclusive classrooms as educationally effective for their children.

▼ They perceived that their children had fewer behavior problems, more friendships with peers with disabilities, and better self-concepts when they were in inclusive classrooms.

Students' Perspectives

Students' perspectives about inclusion and specialized placements are important; after all, the students are the people who are most affected by inclusion. A synthesis of eight research studies that examined the perceptions of students with learning disabilities revealed the following (Vaughn & Klingner, 1998):

▼ Students with learning disabilities vary in their perspectives about educational placements; they do not consistently prefer one placement over another.

▼ They believe that resource rooms provide useful help, a quiet place to work, and less difficult and more enjoyable instructional activities.

▼ They believe that inclusive settings provide more opportunities for making friends.

▼ Together with general education students, they favor having special education teachers who provide assistance to all students in general education classrooms rather than to only students with exceptionalities.

▼ They were unclear as to why they were identified for these services.

Box 2—4

Barbara Morgan: Forming the Forever Family

Some parents look forward to the empty nest. Barbara Morgan isn't among them. She's got four biological children: Ernie, 40; Mike, 39; Vicky, 38; and Becky, 35. She also has 15 grandchildren, four of whom are adopted. They all live near each other. To boot, in the past 3 years she's had 35 foster children in her home. She adopted three of them: Charity, 16, who has mild mental retardation; Heather, 10, who also has mild mental retardation; and Star, 7, who has severe mental retardation and is nonverbal. (You met Heather and Star in the opening pages of this chapter and have read about them throughout the chapter.) Consider, too, that Barbara is a single parent, and you get the idea that this remarkable woman has an abiding commitment to family.

Every day, Barbara Morgan brings Heather and Star to Luff Elementary School, parks her car, walks into the school building with them, and makes sure to greet the receptionist and as many of her children's teachers as she can, catching them in the hallways or, when she has something she needs them to know, going to their classrooms and participating in problem solving.

Barbara is an alumna of Luff Elementary School. So are her four biological children. Thus, when it came to Heather's and Star's education, Barbara's instinct was toward Luff. The school district, however, placed both daughters in a school where the only students were those with disabilities. The girls' education seemed inadequate to Barbara; they were not making the kind of progress at school that they were making at home.

At home, Barbara had confronted and was solving the major challenges that her new daughters brought from their foster homes. Heather had tantrums when she was unable to have all the second and third helpings of food that she wanted; Barbara's response was to show her that there always would be plenty of food to eat, reducing her portions, teaching her to ask for seconds instead of grabbing for more food, and reassuring her that she can have food when she

does not scream. At Heather's first school, none of those techniques were put into place.

At Luff, the staff agreed to uses Barbara's techniques. The result: Heather no longer throws tantrums and screams, politely asks for seconds, and is content to have only first helpings if that is what Barbara has asked the cafeteria staff to provide. A greater result: Heather now is included in the important socialization that occurs at lunchtime.

Star presented an altogether different challenge. When she first came to Barbara, she was, in Barbara's words, "wild, screaming, hitting, banging her head, not able to use the toilet, afraid of water and a bath, totally out of control." Star had been restrained with ropes (wrapped around her torso and legs) and duct tape (applied to her mouth); she had been submerged in bath water; she had been sexually assaulted; and she had suffered some brain damage from being a shaken baby. She never expressed any emotions other than fear: no smiles, tears, or giggles. Moreover, Barbara suspected that she was being sexually maltreated at the school attended only by students with disabilities.

At Luff, Barbara was "overwhelmed by joy." Donna Cummings (Star's teacher) and other staff members enrolled in a sign-language class; Donna's other ways of including Star (described in the vignette), which especially involved teaching other students to use sign language, have built on Barbara's own at-home signing and have taught Star that (in Barbara's words) "everyone is family"—good family!

When Barbara reflects on what she values, she quotes Heather, who, when asked what she wants most in life, said very simply, "A forever family." A forever family: one that will not hurt you, one that will be there whenever and wherever you need it.

Wherever you need it means at home and, significantly, at Luff Elementary School. There, the word *inclusion* has a deep meaning. As Barbara, Heather, and Star can attest, "inclusion" connotes "forever family."

▼ If they are from low-income families and generally are placed in self-contained classes more frequently than high-income students, they tend to have more negative views about both general and special education than do students from higher-income families.

▼ Young students with learning disabilities prefer to receive assistance within their general education class, whereas older students more frequently express positive views of resource rooms. Secondary-level students report a positive perspective toward resource rooms but feel stigmatized when they go there to receive help.

What about the perspectives of students without disabilities? As a general rule, they favor inclusion (Fisher, 1999; Fisher, Pumpian, & Sax, 1998; Klingner, Vaughn, Schumm, Cohen, & Forgan, 1998), for these reasons:

▼ Their rationale for inclusion was a commitment to human rights and a desire to help students with disabilities improve social skills and prepare for the real world, to assist peers in learning more tolerance, and to enable all students to benefit from educators' instructional adaptations.

▼ They expressed concerns because students with disabilities were teased, not given the same consequences for inappropriate behavior as their classmates without disabilities, and treated by some adults in the school in an attitudinally negative way.

▼ They suggested enhancing the positive attitudes of educators and ensuring that students with disabilities are more actively involved in school events.

What Student Outcomes Are Associated with Inclusion?

Two recent reports have comprehensively reviewed inclusion literature. The first review is a comprehensive analysis and synthesis of research on the efficacy of special education (Kavale & Forness, 1999). It focused on many variables related to special education, including placement. The authors concluded that placement in a special education class resulted in lower achievement for students who have lower cognitive ability: students with mental retardation and students whose IQs are between 75 and 90. Students identified as having learning disabilities (Chapter 4) or emotional and behavioral disorders (Chapter 5) generally tended to improve their performance when they were educated in a special class. The authors concluded: "Features of instruction are probably the major influence on outcomes, but these are not unique to setting. Setting is thus a macrovariable; the real question becomes one of examining what happens in that setting" (Kavale & Forness, 1999, p. 70).

Although it is undoubtedly true that what happens in a particular classroom or school affects the outcomes for students, it is also true that what school administrators and teachers expect and plan to happen, and what students themselves want to happen, profoundly influence student outcomes. That is one reason why the expectations of the faculty at Luff Elementary School are so important to Heather and Star and why those of their mother, Barbara Morgan, are also so important. In Box 2–5, you will learn that sometimes educators, parents, and students do not have the same outcomes in mind, but the outcomes can still include those that many educators expect of students without disabilities.

The second research synthesis focused mostly in the area of severe and multiple disabilities and reported a number of positive outcomes, including these (McGregor & Vogelsberg, 1998):

▼ With adequate support, students with disabilities demonstrate high levels of social interaction with typical peers in inclusive settings (Fryxell & Kennedy, 1995; Kennedy, Shukla, & Fryxell, 1997; McDonnell, Hardman, Hightower, & Kiefer-O'Donnell, 1991).

▼ The social competence, communication skills, and other developmental skills of the students with disabilities have improved in inclusive settings (Bennett, Deluca, & Bruns, 1997; Hunt, Staub, Alwell, & Goetz, 1994; McDougall & Brady, 1998).

▼ The presence of students with disabilities does not compromise the performance of typically developing students (Hollowood, Salisbury, Rainforth, & Palombaro, 1994; McDonnell, Thorson, McQuivey, & Kiefer-O'Donnell, 1997; O'Connor & Jenkins, 1996).

▼ Some evidence suggests that the costs of inclusive services over time are likely to be less than those of segregated forms of service delivery (in spite of the fact that startup costs may initially increase) (Halvorsen, Neary, Hunt, & Piuma, 1996; McLaughlin & Warren, 1994; Salisbury & Chambers, 1994).

After reviewing all this research on inclusion, one is left in a quandary. Some evidence documents many problems with inclusion, but some documents the success of inclusion—especially for students with severe and multiple disabilities.

Why have efforts in the area of severe and multiple disabilities led to more successful inclusion outcomes? There are a host of factors, but a significant one is that the literature regarding students with severe and multiple disabilities emphasizes restructured rather than additive instructional adaptations, curriculum modifications, and resources. Much of the research has been carried out in collaboration with educators, families, and students in an effort to enhance the

Box 2–5

The Power of Great Expectations and Visions

I had a learning disability throughout grades K–12, but in May 2002 I graduated with my first bachelor's of science degree (in geography) from Western Kentucky University in Bowling Green. I am going for two more degrees at WKU. One is the bachelor's of fine arts in graphic design and the other a bachelor's of arts in broadcasting. I will receive both degrees in May 2004. I never imagined so much success as I am now having in my life.

My teachers in high school believed it was impossible for me to attend a major university and graduate due to my severe learning disability. I was determined to succeed in life, though, and get a good college education despite what the test scores said, the Board of Education said to me, and my teachers said to me. It took a while for them to accept my goals in life and to support me. My high school teachers wanted me to just graduate with an associate's degree and never attend a university. I just wish they had pushed me more to my full potential in high school and had me reach for my dreams.

One of my goals has been to work for the Weather Channel as an on-camera meteorologist. I have had to abandon that goal because the math and physics required to be a meteorologist are just too hard for me and too challenging. But I am looking into attending the University of Hawaii—Manoa in the summer or fall of 2004 to get a bachelor's of science degree in global environmental science and to take other courses in geography and oceanography.

I am getting a lot of support from my professors, but accomplishing these degrees at Western Kentucky University has been extremely challenging. Still, I am getting through them all right with hard work and persistence. My learning disability was in math, which is a weak subject for me; so you can understand why being a meteorologist was beyond my reach, even with all the work I put in and all the support I received. But I can pursue other work in the area of the natural sciences, and that is what I will do at the University of Hawaii.

I also am getting support from the president of my university, the dean, the professors, and the advisors and alumni association. However, they don't know the entire story and all that I had to go through to get to this point in my life. I really can't believe my dreams of working in the natural sciences are coming true. That is why I would also like to help out in some way with kids who have learning disabilities.

—Chandra Beyerck, Western Kentucky University, Bowling Green

success of inclusion. Thus, it is likely that many of the research reports reflect extraordinary rather than ordinary settings. Even if the setting is extraordinary, it is good to be aware of what is possible when best practices are implemented. Some of these practices are set out, in very general terms, in Box 2–6.

The challenge for educators is not to discredit or diminish the extraordinary efforts but, consistent with IDEA and the research, to direct their efforts into transforming ordinary settings so that they, too, can match what is today regarded as extraordinary and tomorrow will be regarded as ordinary (Soodak et al., 2002). At Luff Elementary School, a team of dedicated administrators, special and general educators, and parents have converted the extraordinary into the ordinary. In Independence, they are working to make sure that all students, especially those with disabilities, learn how to be independent, self-sufficient adults to the maximum extent possible; and they are starting early.

In Chapters 4–16, you will also find "Inclusion Tips" boxes that provide suggestions tailored to the needs of students who have different types of exceptionalities.

How Does Inclusion Enable Students to Progress in the General Curriculum?

We hope the answer to this question is now obvious to you, given what you have already learned about standards-based reform, the general curriculum, universal design for learning, and the nature of inclusion. The general curriculum is more likely to be taught in general education classes than in any other setting: specialized settings in typical schools, special schools, and/or residential/home/hospital settings. When universal design for learning is implemented and when the four characteristics of inclusion are met—home/school placement, the principle of natural proportions, restructured teaching and learning, and age- and grade-appropriate placements—then students with exceptionalities can receive individualized and intensive instruction in general education classes.

Inclusion Tips

Box 2—6

	What You Might See	What You Might Be Tempted to Do	Alternate Responses	Ways to Include Peers in the Process
Behavior	The student shows an apparently poor attitude toward other students and does not easily cooperate with them during instructional activities.	Discipline the student for his poor behavior and separate him from the rest of the class.	Identify his strengths and work together on a list of positive things he can say when responding to other students during instructional activities.	Ask him to identify peers he would like to work with. Then work with this small group to practice verbal responses that would be helpful.
Social interactions	He has few friends and doesn't appear to want any.	Encourage him to take initiative toward others but also allow him to be by himself whenever he chooses.	Collaborate with the school counselor to plan ways to teach him specific social skills.	Work with identified peers to practice the specific social skills with him in and out of the classroom.
Educational performance	His work is acceptable, but he needs constant supervision.	Assign an aide to work with him and allow him to complete unfinished work at home.	Collaborate with the special education teacher to create step-by-step assignments that he can do on his own. Set up a reward system for each layer successfully completed without supervision.	Encourage him to work with his peers to monitor the layered assignments. Ask peers to work with him to construct a tracking system for class assignments.
Classroom attitudes	He never volunteers answers and is reluctant to participate in class activities.	Carefully choose activities that allow him to work alone.	Together with the special education teacher, work with him ahead of time on content to be covered and plan specific things for him to contribute.	Plan with peers positive contributions that each can make to upcoming class activities.

There are, however, two other ways for making it more likely that students with exceptionalities will progress in the general curriculum. These are *collaboration* and *multicultural responsiveness*. We will discuss them in Chapter 3 and then revisit them in each of the following chapters.

A Vision for the Future

If the education that Heather and Star are receiving at Luff Elementary School continues throughout their entire school careers, we can expect exactly what Barbara Morgan expects for her children when they are adults. Heather will be living on her own and working in Independence; she will have attained her own independence and be economically self-sufficient (at least in part). She will have friends in the community, as she does in school; she will have the same opportunities as her friends to participate in life in Independence; and she will fully participate and have equal opportunities there. Star, whose disabilities are more challenging than Heather's, will also be living and working in Independence but with a great deal more support. She probably will not live by herself; instead, she probably will be in a group home with three to five other adults or maybe in an apartment with a roommate who has a disability. In both settings, she will probably need support for the activities of daily living on a 24/7 basis; the support will be in areas of living such as dressing, preparing meals, going from home to work and back again, and participating in her community's recreation and leisure activities. But she also will have friends who will have disabilities and friends who will not have disabilities, so her support will come from paid, formal providers and from unpaid, informal sources.

But in order for Heather and Star to achieve those results, the kind of education they are receiving at Luff will have to continue. They will have access to the general curriculum; granted, some of the curriculum content will be altered, but the basic core of their education will be comparable to that of students without disabilities. And they will have to continue to receive their education with students who do not have disabilities; whatever is available in the classrooms, extracurricular activities, and other school activities for their peers who do not have disabilities will have to be available to them, sometimes with modifications and supports and sometimes not. Their elementary education lays the foundation for the rest of their education; more than that, it is the basis for their lives in Independence—really, for their own independence.

What Would You Recommend?

1. At Luff Elementary School, the principal, Peggy Palser, has a special education background. What difference do you think that made in her vision and knowledge concerning students with exceptionalities who are progressing in the general curriculum?
2. How do statewide assessments reflect high expectations for all students?
3. What steps need to be taken to ensure that universal design for learning is more fully implemented throughout general and special education?

Summary

What Does Progressing in the General Curriculum Mean?

▼ Standards-based reform has been developed because many schools did not have an explicit curriculum for students but followed a trend of having low expectations for students, particularly those with disabilities.

▼ Educators have been called upon to raise standards for all students and to assess all students' progress to ensure that all students are meeting those standards.

▼ Two types of standards include content standards (knowledge, skills, and understanding that students should attain an academic subject) and performance standards (levels of achievement that students must meet to demonstrate their proficiency in the subject).

▼ The general curriculum consists of the content and performance standards set by each state education agency for students at various grade levels.

▼ Almost all states have the same math and reading content standards for students with and without disabilities.

▼ High-stakes assessments involves holding students, schools, and teachers accountable for assessment scores on state tests.

▼ Each student's IEP team must consider whether a student needs modifications in the assessment process or if the student needs an alternative assessment.

▼ It is important for students with exceptionalities to progress in the general education curriculum to ensure that they are challenged by high standards.

How Does Universal Design for Learning Enable Students with Exceptionalities to Make Progress in the General Curriculum?

▼ Universal design for learning is a process for considering the needs of all students from the very beginning in designing curriculum, instruction, and evaluation to ensure that students benefit.

▼ Universal design for learning includes augmenting, altering, and adapting curriculum, instruction, and evaluation.

▼ Principles for universal design for learning focus on ensuring that it is flexible, easy to use, and convenient.

How Does Inclusion Enable Students to Progress in the General Curriculum?

▼ Over the past 10 years, there has been a progressive trend toward having more students with disabilities spend a greater percentage of time in general education classrooms.

▼ Aside from the general education classrooms, students with disabilities are served in residential/home/hospital settings, special schools, and specialized settings (resource rooms and special classes) within typical schools.

▼ There have been four phases of implementing inclusion: mainstreaming, the Regular Education Initiative, inclusion through adding accommodations, and inclusion through restructuring.

▼ Inclusion has four key characteristics:

- All students receive education in the school they would attend if they had no exceptionality.

- Consideration is given to placing students in classrooms according to the principle of natural proportions.

- Teaching and learning is restructured for all students so that special education supports exists within general education classes.

- School and general education placements are age- and grade-appropriate.

▼ The perspectives of educators vary concerning the appropriateness of inclusion.

▼ Teacher concerns include class size, infusion of special education resources into general education programs, having to modify job functions, and possessing necessary skills. Teachers who are better trained and more experienced tend to favor inclusion in contrast to teachers who are less well trained and less experienced.

▼ Parents of students with and without disabilities tend to be positive about inclusion.

▼ Students with learning disabilities reported several benefits of resource rooms: They provide help, offer a quiet place to work, and have less difficult and more enjoyable instructional activities. However, inclusive settings provide more opportunities for making friends. Students report feeling stigmatized when they leave the general education classroom to receive special help.

▼ Research varies on student outcomes of inclusion, with some research showing that placement in a special education class results in lower achievement for students who have lower cognitive ability. However, students with learning disabilities and emotional and behavioral disorders tend to improve performance in a special class.

▼ Positive outcomes related to social interaction, communication skills, and other developmental skills have been shown for students with severe disabilities who have been in state-of-the-art inclusive classrooms.

Council for Exceptional Children

PRAXIS

To find out how and where this chapter content connects to the CEC Professional Standards and the Praxis™ Standards, go to the Standards Connection module in Chapter 2 of the Companion Website. A comprehensive matrix aligning CEC Professional Standards, Praxis™ Standards, and INTASC principles to the entire text, is available in the Appendix and on the Companion Website.

~~~~~~

Chapter 3

Who Are Ronda Taylor, Donald Harness, and Luisa Rodriquez?

They call it the Big Easy. You know it as New Orleans. But life there is not so easy if you are Ronda Taylor, Donald Harness, or Luisa Rodriquez. Both Ronda and Donald are African Americans; Luisa is the daughter of two undocumented immigrants from Mexico but is a U.S. citizen, having been born here. (Because of her parents' fear about their undocumented status, they asked us to use a pseudonym rather than their daughter's real name. And we have done that.)

From the outset of her education, Ronda, now a 14-year-old student in the New Orleans public schools, and her mother, Debra Taylor, confronted a resistant school system. Despite a recommendation from her Roman Catholic preschool that Ronda be tested for special education placement before she enrolled in a public elementary school, the public school refused for 4 years to evaluate her for a disability. When the school finally evaluated her during her third-grade year, it denied her placement into special education, admitting she has speech-language disabilities but saying she also has to have strengths and that no strengths were apparent from her evaluation. Only at Debra's insistence did the school finally agree the next year to place her

into special education. Even then, the school varied her classifications: speech-language impairments, learning disabilities, emotional or behavioral disorders, and a condition related to autism known as Asperger's syndrome. Predictably, Ronda's placements and education were problematic. She repeated the third grade, was periodically suspended during her fourth-grade year because of her acting-out behaviors, was often physically restrained during her fifth-grade year by an uncertified teacher, and was placed with a novice sixth-grade teacher.

During none of these years did Ronda have a thorough reevaluation, although her behaviors were deteriorating annually; and during none of them did her evaluation connect to her teachers' curriculum. After Debra brought Pyramid Parent Training Center leaders to Ronda's IEP meeting in the sixth-grade year, the school finally agreed to a reevaluation and a new IEP; but even that agreement and IEP development required five meetings, the active participation of Pyramid Parent Training Center and nearly a

dozen other participants, and the insistence of the district's IDEA compliance officer. Ronda is now classified as having "other health impairments" (see Chapter 11) and learning disabilities; she is now taught by a certified teacher and is acquiring language, mathematics, and appropriate behavioral and social skills.

Donald Harness, who has autism, also faced the prospect of not benefiting from school, although he is in a suburban school district (unlike Ronda, who is in the inner-city of New Orleans). As his parents, Donald and Carolyn, tell it, the family faced the usual problems: uncertified teachers, educators' incapacity to address his acting-out behaviors, and a "standard operating procedure"— the district's recommendation that he take medication to correct those behaviors. When his parents and the leaders of Pyramid Parent Training Center attended Donald's IEP meeting in the 2000–2001 school year, the school faculty and administrators admitted they had tried everything they knew to do but were still unable to handle Donald's aggressive behaviors. Out of desperation and not wanting to invoke another standard operating procedure for its students (namely, referring Donald to the juvenile justice system at age 9), they agreed to apply the technique known as positive behavior support (see Chapter 10). The consequences have been remarkable: Donald is included in the general curriculum; is excelling in music, math, and computer education; has learned that he is responsible for his behavior; is behaving appropriately; for two years in a row has been voted "most improved" student; has won awards for his attendance; and has been selected as an outstanding member of his class.

Luisa Rodriquez and her parents face discrimination different from the kinds faced by Ronda and Donald and their parents. Neither of Luisa's parents has a green card—the certificate issued to immigrants so that they are legally admitted to and may stay in the United States. When her parents were laid off from work (there is a large underground of undocumented workers in New Orleans, who are paid in cash below the minimum wage), their only recourse was to seek help at Catholic

Charities of New Orleans. There, Graziella Seng listened to them describe their plight: no food, no way to pay the rent, and great reluctance to ask for public help because, if they are detected by public authorities, they will be returned to Mexico and Luisa's education will be interrupted. (Because she was born here, she is a citizen and has the same rights to education as other citizens, such as Ronda and Donald.) It is not exactly clear what her educational challenges are; she speaks only Spanish, and the school has simply refused to evaluate her for any disability, merely telling her parents that they

should take her to a doctor. Without money and not wanting to apply for public benefits, her parents could not take that advice; so Luisa, according to her younger brother, translating the school's communications to her parents, is failing in school. After earning the Rodriquez's trust by referring them to an organization that will provide them with free food for a month, Graziella will take up Luisa's school issues. In the meanwhile, however, Luisa lingers in limbo.

What do you think?

1. Where did the parents of Ronda, Donald, and Luisa find the greatest help? Inside or outside of the school systems?
2. Why were the school systems reluctant to classify Ronda and Donald into special education?
3. If few public agencies tolerate illegal immigrants, much less speak Spanish, how will Luisa receive any educational help?

For more information visit our website at
www.prenhall.com/turnbull

In Chapter 1, you learned about the educational and legal-policy foundations for student progress in the general curriculum. In Chapter 2, you learned about the general curriculum and why progress for students with exceptionalities is so highly valued. You also learned about two of this book's themes: universal design for learning and inclusion. These are not only themes but also powerful ways in which to enable students with exceptionalities to progress in the general curriculum.

In this chapter, you will learn about two additional themes of this book; they, too, relate to how you teach to ensure that students will progress in the general curriculum. These themes are *collaboration* and *multicultural responsiveness*. In this chapter, you will learn the answers to the following questions:

In this chapter, we lay the foundation for you to understand collaboration. In each of the chapters that follow, we give you specific collaboration tips.

▼ How does collaboration enable students to progress in the general curriculum?

▼ How does multicultural responsiveness enable students to progress in the general curriculum?

How Does Collaboration Enable Students to Progress in the General Curriculum?

In Chapter 2, you learned that inclusion through restructuring means that general and special educators merge their talents and resources in order to use universal design for learning to benefit all students. Collaboration is the approach that fosters this merger (Pugach & Johnson, 2002; Walther-Thomas, Korinek, McLaughlin, & Williams, 2000). Without collaboration, these educators will not be able to redesign the teaching-learning process so that all students—those with and without exceptionalities—will progress in the general curriculum. But collaboration also means that educators take advantage of resources outside of their school, just as families do. Sometimes an outsider's perspective breaks the log jams that can occur inside school systems; that's what happened when Ronda Taylor, Donald Harness, and Pyramid Parent Training Center teamed up and when their parents and the parent-advocacy center later collaborated with educators. In this section, you will learn the answers to these questions:

In the vignette, the last photograph on page 79 shows Carolyn Harness, Rud Turnbull, Ursula Markey, and Donald Harness.

▼ What is collaboration and why is it so highly valued?

▼ Who are the people involved in collaboration and what roles do they play?

▼ What are state-of-art collaborative approaches?

▼ What is the process for creating collaborative teams?

What Is Collaboration and Why Is It So Highly Valued?

Collaboration is a dynamic process in which educators, students, and families share their resources and strengths to solve problems in a creative and responsive way. Collaboration builds on the expertise, interests, and strengths of everyone involved in the educational process: students, parents such as Donald and Carolyn Harness and Debra Taylor, teachers, related-service providers, paraprofessionals, school staff, administrators, and community members such as Ursula Markey and D. J. Markey, the directors of Pyramid Parent Training Center. The ultimate goal of collaboration is to improve teaching and learning so that all students, including those with exceptionalities, can progress in the general curriculum. By acknowledging that each of these people can participate meaningfully in problem solving, collaboration creates opportunities for each of these people to solve problems jointly. It applies the adage that "all of us are smarter than one of us."

Historically, each general and special educator has had an explicit job description and has been expected to perform specified duties in an independent manner. Often, general and special education teachers worked in isolation from each other. That is still true. Because teachers typically spend 80 to 90 percent of their work day in direct student contact and sporadically use the

The quality of decisions is better when people with different resources and strengths collaborate.

planning periods, recesses, or lunch breaks to provide extra attention to students or to communicate with parents, they cannot capitalize upon each other's potentially valuable contributions (Hoerr, 1996). By contrast, collaboration enables problem-solving teams to work systemically on mutual challenges. It impels educators and others from outside the school (such as family members and child-family advocacy groups) to devise innovative solutions so that all students can progress in the general curriculum.

Who Are the People Involved in Collaboration and What Are Their Roles?

Students, families (such as those of Ronda, Donald, and Luisa), teachers, related-service providers, paraprofessionals, translators/interpreters, and administrators can be collaborators. So can other community resources. Remember the important role that Pyramid Parent Training Center and the Markeys played in helping to secure a positive outcome for Ronda and Donald? These are the community-resource collaborators.

Students

Students themselves, including those with exceptionalities, can be valuable members of collaboration teams. One reason for including them as collaborators is that a goal of special education is to foster student **self-determination** (Wehmeyer, 2002; Wehmeyer, Palmer, Agran, Mithang, & Martin, 2000). Self-determination refers to "acting as the primary causal agent in one's life and making choices and decisions regarding one's quality of life free from undo external influence or interference" (Wehmeyer, 1996, p. 24). Because self-determination fosters goal setting, problem solving, and self-advocacy, it can lead to independence, one of IDEA's four general outcome goals.

Contrary to the principle of self-determination, the majority of students in special education are not participating in the development of their IEPs (Johnson, Sharpe, & Sinclair, 1997). Why? Because teachers and parents are not sure how to enable students to participate in their IEP process and thereby in collaborative decision making. There are, however, strategies for preparing students and their parents for meaningful student involvement (Martin & Marshall, 1996; Van Reusen, 1998). These strategies primarily involve providing students with explicit

Later in the chapter you will learn more about the Markeys and how they enhance the quality of collaboration.

At an IEP meeting, students may demonstrate their strengths, as this student is doing as he uses assistive technology.

instruction in advance of their IEP conferences so the students can identify issues important to them and share that information with the other team members.

Students with and without exceptionalities can collaborate with each other in the general curriculum through peer tutoring and cooperative learning or by serving on school committees, advocating for classmates with special needs, and resolving conflicts through mediation (Thousand, Villa, & Nevin, 2002). Box 3–1 describes the process and benefits of involving students as collaborators to identify educational problems and create a more productive learning environment.

Parents

Parent–professional partnerships have been a major theme of special education best practices, and numerous approaches have been successfully implemented (Turnbull & Turnbull, 2001). One of the key features of successful parent-professional partnerships is a sense of equality between the parents and professionals.

There is no doubt about this fact: Equality is hard to achieve. Teachers may well believe that they know more than the students and the parents when it comes to the curriculum (what is taught), instruction (how it is taught), and evaluation (knowing how well the teaching and learning process achieve certain goals). But on other matters, students and parents may know a great deal: for example, about how a student's disabilities, strengths, or special gifts affect how the student learns. Equality does not mean that everyone has the same information. It does mean that everyone respects the fact that others bring certain knowledge to the collaborative process.

Too frequently, professionals interact with families in a way that connotes expert power (Turnbull & Turnbull, 2001); as a consequence, many parents may believe that they can contribute little to educational decision making. A "we–they" posture is particularly problematic, especially for parents who have low incomes or who are from a culture different from the educators' (Kalyanpur & Harry, 1999; Lynch & Hanson, 1998).

Some educators may believe that they know all there is to know about the student, the causes and manifestations of the student's exceptionality, and what to do about the student's education. They also may assume, simply because their students are from diverse backgrounds, that parents have little desire or ability to contribute to students' evaluations, IEPs, and placement decisions. Some teachers even assume that the parents do not truly care about their children.

As you learned in Chapter 1, IDEA gives parents the right to participate in decisions related to their children's evaluation, programs, and placement.

Box 3–1

Into Practice

School Reform Through Student-Teacher Collaboration

It's a rare teacher who will ask a student how to make the school better. Rarer still when the student has been classified as having an emotional and behavioral disorder. And rarest of all when a cluster of schools in the same district agrees to reform its schools by following the students' ideas.

But that is exactly what happened in an urban school district at the elementary, middle-, and upper-school levels. Teachers, along with students who were classified as having emotional and behavioral disorders, formed student advisory boards. These boards were led by students and gave advice to teachers and administrators.

The boards' first task was to ask the right questions, such as "What do students worry about most?" and "What kinds of problems do students have, and what solutions might work?" Those general questions led to more particular ones: "What kind of disciplinary procedures will help the students most?" and "What alternatives are there to suspension when students become angry?" All of the questions pointed to an ultimate one, phrased generally like this: "What kind of programs could teachers, parents, and students set up to help students get through school and learn?"

Across all of the schools and all grades, the major concern of the students was how they got along with—or, more precisely, did not get along well with—their peers. They were worried about bullying, fighting, and their reputations; they were worried about fitting in with their classmates.

They also were worried about how they got along with, or did not get along well with, their teachers. They worried about their reputations and about not being liked, about not being respected, about teachers talking about them behind their backs, about teachers who were inclined to embarrass them, and about counselors who would snitch on them.

Finally, they worried about their school work: about not being able to read, about being teased when they were pulled out of class for special education help, and about improving their grades.

Their solutions varied. At one elementary school, students and teachers launched a conflict mediation program to address their concerns about fighting. At another, they created a mentor program that involved students at an adjacent middle school who taught their buddies how to be cool and fit in without breaking school rules. At a middle school, they persuaded the administrators to create a composure room, where they could cool down when agitated. And at a senior high school, they created an in-school factory to make designer T-shirts, a good way to prove their work skills to prospective employers.

The results? The teachers were relieved to find that they did not have to be in total control of the school and its problems and solutions. The students learned to identify problems, propose solutions, and be responsible for themselves and their schools. And teachers and students alike learned how to collaborate with each other.

The problems they identified affect nearly every student in the United States; the solutions they devised may be good for their schools but not workable in other schools. That doesn't matter. The point is that these teachers and students together reformed their schools. Bit by bit, they chipped away at the challenges facing them. And they did it together.

What tips can you carry with you from this school district's experiences? Research suggests that three tips are basic:

- Treat students as people. Involve them in school governance. Treat them as though their opinions matter. Make their opinions matter.
- Appeal to students' sense of fairness. Assume they know the school codes of conduct. And then determine whether they think the codes are fair and are applied fairly.
- Offer training in self-determination and problem solving. Help students set their own goals. Let them have some choices in what courses they take or what activities they undertake.

Given this research and the experiences in these schools, here are a few other tips:

- Convene the meeting of the students in a comfortable, quiet place. Provide refreshments.
- Explain to the students and their parents that you are going to use their ideas as the basis for new programs at school.
- Treat the students and their parents as though they were adults and members of an important advisory board.
- Solicit all of their ideas. Don't judge the ideas; don't say, "Policy prohibits that"; don't be defensive. Remember, you are in the business of reforming your school.
- Record the ideas. Discuss the next steps. Reconvene to discuss progress in carrying out the ideas.
- Thank the students and their parents. Keep their faith by demonstrating good-faith action on your part.

Putting These Strategies to Work for Progress in the General Curriculum

1. What experiences have you had as a student at the elementary, secondary, or college level in which you had a chance to collaborate with educators to solve problems and promote your own success?

2. What is the likelihood that you will implement this approach as a teacher, and what particular tips do you want especially to remember?

3. What are the characteristics of those students whom you think are most likely to be invited to be collaborators and the characteristics of those students who are least likely to be invited? What can you do to ensure that all students have a chance to collaborate?

Source: Adapted from Bacon, E., & Bloom, L. (2000). Listening to student voices: How student advisory boards can help. *Teaching Exceptional Children, 32* (6), 38–43.

Those assumptions are usually mistaken: Debra Taylor is a well-educated professional whose employment at Tulane Law School gives her access to all Internet research capabilities and to a bevy of potentially interested and effective law professors. Carolyn Harness and Donald Harness are employed in administrative roles at Catholic Charities and the U.S. Postal Service, respectively. Moreover, both the Taylor and Harness families have access to Pyramid Parent Training Center. Likewise, Luisa Rodriquez has access to Graziella Seng at Catholic Charities and, through her, to other potential advocates. Not only is it bad education practice to make assumptions about parents and other family members, but the assumptions sometimes are simply wrong. And even if the assumptions are correct, parent advocacy centers such as Pyramid Parent Training Center, and other interested agencies such as Catholic Charities can and often do support parents to develop knowledge about a student's rights and about effective educational approaches that the schools may lack.

Successful collaboration (and the IDEA provisions) require professionals and parents to have more contacts with each other, enabling parents to share their important insights and goals. One reason for the IDEA provisions is that professionals who refuse to take parents' perspectives into account may well be providing an inappropriate education. They may overlook a student's strengths, not know what the student can do outside of school, not learn how to involve parents in following through on what the student is taught, and ignore the parents' preferences for certain types of teaching (e.g., total communication instead of signing in the case of a child who has a hearing impairment). This is not to say that all parents and their allies always have a full and accurate picture of their children's educational strengths or needs or that their preferences are always educationally defensible. It is, however, the case that IDEA makes it possible for children and teachers to benefit from parents' knowledge and perspectives (Turnbull & Turnbull, 2001; Turnbull, Turnbull, Stowe, & Wilcox, 2000).

In Chapter 1 you learned about the Parent Training and Information Centers, which are incredibly helpful resources in supporting parents to learn about IDEA requirements and to be educational decision makers.

Teachers

Many people mistakenly think special education requires instruction by a special education teacher in a special education classroom. On the contrary, almost all, if not all, teachers are or should be involved in teaching students with exceptionalities, consistent with IDEA's provisions related to IEP team membership and students' participation in the general curriculum.

Local schools have within them a natural and oftentimes untapped pool of "experts." These "experts" are the grade level teachers, school nurses, language arts and math teachers, guidance counselors, resource room teachers, vocational educators, physical education teachers, home economic teachers, and sign language teachers who make up the instructional staff of the school and who have expertise not only in their assigned teaching areas but in a wide range of other

Parents who have "walked the walk"—who have experience in special education—can be very effective teachers, mentors, and guides for parents whose children are newly eligible for special education. Here, parents gather to teach, learn, and support each other.

areas. Each teacher's unique skills and interests may be of value to another and a broader range of students than the subset of students assigned to his or her class. (Thousand et al., 1986)

Accordingly, especially given IDEA's emphasis on ensuring that students with exceptionalities will make progress in the general curriculum, the priority for special and general educators' collaboration should be on how they can jointly develop universally designed learning: curriculum, instruction, and assessment approaches that enable students with exceptionalities to progress in the general curriculum (Pugach & Warger, 2001; Walther-Thomas et al., 2000).

One barrier to collaboration is that many teachers lack scheduled opportunities during the school day, after school, or away from direct instructional responsibilities to plan how to collaborate with each other. Administrators can be very helpful to teachers in arranging for collaboration planning time, as you will learn later in the chapter.

Related-Service Providers

Related-service personnel are important members of collaboration teams because they provide instruction and other services for students with exceptionalities. In Chapter 1, you learned the definitions of related services (see Figure 1–5). Related-services personnel participate in evaluations; IEP meetings; assessments of student progress; and other conferences with parents, students, and professional peers.

Increasingly, related services (e.g., speech and language, physical therapy, occupational therapy) are being provided within the context of general education classrooms and in consultation with teachers and parents (Giangreco, Prelock, Reid, Dennis, & Edelman, 2000). In this way, related services are tied to student progress in the general curriculum. Also, by collaborating with related-services providers, teachers and families are increasingly able to incorporate aspects of the related services into their interactions with students.

Paraprofessionals

Paraprofessionals are important members of special education teams (Carroll, 2001; French, 2001; Giangreco, Edelman, Broer, & Doyle, 2001; Riggs & Mueller, 2001). Approximately 280,000 paraprofessionals provide special education supports and services to students with exceptionalities (ages 3 to 21) who are being served in general and special education classrooms (U.S. Department of Education, 1999). More than 3,300 paraprofessionals provide services to children from birth through age 2.

In Chapter 1, we asked you to pay particular attention to IDEA's goals and its six principles. Here, we emphasize that all educators have the duty to carry out IDEA and to do so in collaboration with each other.

Companion Website

To learn more about the related services of speech and language and physical therapy, go to the Web Links module in Chapter 3 of the Companion Website for a link to the American Speech and Hearing Association (www.asha.org) and the American Physical Therapy Association (www.apta.org).

Some educators and researchers have expressed concern about the role that certain paraprofessionals play in supporting students in general education classrooms. Although in many cases paraprofessionals have added appropriate and meaningful support for students with disabilities as well as their classmates, often the add-on paraprofessional model has resulted in the bubble effect: The student is educated in a protective bubble that a paraprofessional creates:

> During the years of our research, my colleagues and I saw students walking through hallways with clipboard-bearing adults "attached" to them or sitting apart in classrooms with an adult hovering over them showing them how to use books and papers unlike any others in the class. Often these "*Velcroed*" adults were easily identifiable as "special education" teachers because the students called them by their first names while using the more formal Ms. or Mr. to refer to the general education teacher. (Ferguson, 1995, p. 284)

A classmate described a "Velcroed" situation between a paraprofessional and a student with a disability:

> Whenever you try to talk to her you can't because her aides are there and they just help her say what she's trying to say and you want to hear it from her. They do it for her, and then they say, "Is that right?" It's like you're having a three-way conversation and [the aide] is the interpreter and it is not right that way. . . . It just doesn't work. (Martin, Jorgensen, & Klein, 1998, p. 157)

Appropriate collaborative roles for paraprofessionals include providing individualized instruction to groups of students with and without disabilities, facilitating friendships among students with and without disabilities, supporting peer tutors, using state-of-art technology, teaching in community settings, and assisting students with personal care (e.g., bathroom care and feeding). Significantly, most paraprofessionals provide direct instruction to students for at least three-quarters of the time they are on the job (Riggs & Mueller, 2001). That role certainly assists students to progress in the general curriculum. It also enables general educators and special educators to concentrate on other students—those with and without disabilities—and on their progress in the general curriculum.

Language Translators and Interpreters

Translators concentrate on communicating written materials, whereas interpreters concentrate on facilitating oral communication. Nevertheless, a study of 59 Chinese families, 58 of whom used Chinese as their primary language, revealed that 60 percent of the families reported that none of the professionals involved in the diagnosis of their child spoke Chinese: "It was hard for us to understand because we were confused. We did not know how to start or who to turn to. We felt alone and helpless" (Smith & Ryan, 1987, pp. 347–348). That is an unacceptable practice. So in Figure 3–1, you will learn best practices for collaborating with interpreters in meetings.

Because many schools have not incorporated translators and interpreters into their collaboration teams, they sometimes ask the children or family friends to interpret for parents. For example, Graziella Seng learned from a single interview with the parents of Luisa Rodriquez that Luisa's older brother translates when Luisa's parents and teachers meet. Luisa's father and mother both expressed concerns about that fact. Perhaps, they told Graziella, her brother does not tell the teachers everything that the parents say, or vice versa. Perhaps he is softening the messages; perhaps he is giving them different emphases; perhaps he is not fully understanding some of the language the educators are using. Perhaps the brother does not want to be a translator; he'd rather be just a brother and not be put into the position of translator and potential mediator.

Using children or family friends as interpreters is usually inappropriate, given the complexity of the information that needs to be shared and the issues associated with confidentiality and privacy. Having friends or family members interpret may result in confidential information being shared with people who normally would not have that information. And having children interpret for their parents places them in a role that can be extremely awkward for everyone. After all, it is the school's obligation under IDEA to make all information it shares with families accessible to families, even if that means providing translators. The parents should not have to take on the school's duty.

In Chapter 2, we introduced you to the principles of inclusion. What's the balance between a paraprofessional who is "Velcroed" to the student and a student who sometimes needs the paraprofessional's assistance?

FIGURE 3–1
Recommended practices for educators working with interpreters in meetings

Context	Recommended Practice
Before the meeting	• Have a list of interpreters available for families. • Encourage the family to choose an interpreter with whom they feel comfortable. • Discuss the importance of neutrality with the interpreter and other team members. • Encourage the interpreter and other team members to be self-reflective. • Provide the interpreter with written documents as advanced organizers. • Provide the interpreter with a glossary book of terms used in special education. • Support the interpreter's efforts in taking special education courses. • Discuss the duties and vital roles of interpreters and other team members.
During the meeting	• Create an informal atmosphere. • Avoid using professional jargon. • Use visual aids and concrete examples. • Avoid idiomatic words, slang, and metaphors that are difficult to translate. • Be aware of loan words (e.g., slang terms such as "cool"). • Use simple sentences. • Speak slowly and clearly. • Use consecutive interpretation. • Encourage the interpreter to take notes and ask questions. • Be sensitive to reactions shown by the interpreter to identify possible problems with interpretation. • Maintain eye contact with the family.
After the meeting	• Evaluate the meeting with the interpreter using the guidelines described in "Before the meeting" and "During the meeting." • Encourage the interpreter to ask questions to clarify issues about the meeting. • Identify problems that the interpreter may have encountered during the meeting. • Encourage the interpreter to advise you if you and other team members communicate with the family in a culturally inappropriate manner. • Brainstorm ways to address problems for future meetings.

The National Association of Secondary School Principals devoted an entire issue of their magazine, *Principal Leadership,* to inclusion. You can find a link to their website by going to the Web Links module in Chapter 3 of the Companion Website (www.nassp.org).

Administrators

Principals, superintendents, and directors of special education are indispensable collaborators because they have a great deal of power to arrange teaching schedules and professional development activities (in-service training) so that teachers can collaborate for inclusion. Administrators can promote collaboration when they assign duties to teachers and other staff, foster family–teacher partnerships, allocate money, and set the tone and direction of schools and entire school districts. The school reform movement has substantially increased administrators' influence within the school, across the school district, and within the community at large.

Administrative support has been identified as the most powerful predictor of general education teacher attitudes toward inclusive education (Villa, Thousand, Meyers, & Nevin, 1996). "In every successful inclusive schooling effort, there is at least one administrator who is recognized as providing support for implementing the vision of a school that welcomes, values, and supports the education of diverse learners" (Thousand, Rosenberg, Bishop, & Villa, 1997, p. 273).

A recent study focused on the leadership practices of building principals and the contexts that they help to create in order to promote a learning community for all students (Salisbury & McGregor, 2002). This study identified five building principals who were known for their exemplary work. All exemplified the following characteristics:

▼ *Self-directed risk takers*. They were involved in professional development and not afraid to try new approaches.

▼ *Invested in relationships*. They were collaborators who were willing to go the extra mile.

▼ *Accessible*. They were involved with teachers, staff, and students in addressing recurring, daily challenges.

▼ *Reflective*. They thought hard about the directions they wanted to take for themselves and for their schools and how they themselves and their colleagues should behave.

▼ *Collaborative*. They promoted time for collaborative teaming and shared their leadership with others.

▼ *Intentional*. They based their key decisions on the goals they had set and then persistently implemented those goals.

As we have indicated, one of the challenges to collaboration is to arrange teachers' schedules so they can find time to meet frequently and face to face and then to solve problems together. Figure 3–2 gives many practical suggestions about how to set aside time for collaboration.

You may recall Peggy Pulsar (Chapter 2), principal of Luff Elementary School. Her school was one of the five identified in this study. How do you think the successful inclusion of Heather and Star was facilitated because of her school's and her own exemplary work?

What Are State-of-the-Art Collaborative Approaches?

The current best practices emphasize restructuring and reallocating a school's resources so that educators, students, families, and community citizens (such as the staff of Parent Training and Information Centers and other similar organizations) can collaborate to promote teaching and learning for all students (Pugach & Johnson, 2002; Walther-Thomas et al., 2000). Consider how the elementary school featured in Box 3–2 used all of its resources to create a community of learning for all students. If you were a special education teacher in this school, how would this kind of collaborative approach enable you to support students to make progress in the general curriculum? Bear in mind that the responsibility for ensuring that students with exceptionalities make progress in the general curriculum does not rest on the shoulders of just one person. Clearly, in this exemplary approach, general and bilingual education teachers, the inclusion support teacher, paraprofessionals, parents of students with and without disabilities, students, and the principal combined their expertise, time, and energy toward the shared goals of teaching and learning for all students in the general curriculum.

Co-teaching is a model that embeds collaboration within general education classrooms and seems to increase the likelihood that students with disabilities will progress in the general curriculum. Co-teaching typically involves special and general education teachers working together to teach the general curriculum to students who vary widely in their strengths and unique learning needs (Bauwens & Hourcade, 1995; Walther-Thomas, 1997). Co-teachers collaborate to accomplish the following tasks (Walther-Thomas et al., 2000):

▼ Plan and teach together
▼ Develop instructional accommodations
▼ Monitor and evaluate student performance
▼ Communicate student progress to others

FIGURE 3–2
Arranging time for collaboration opportunities

Restructuring or rescheduling time
- Teach more minutes four days a week and use the time earned to have early release on one day.
- Trade in staff development days at the beginning or end of the school year and spread the time out throughout the year for planning time.
- Give teachers a common lunch period followed by a planning period for shared time daily. Provide a large group activity or small educational activities for kids after lunch. Have special electives and classes in the periods after lunch to free core classroom teachers.

Changing staffing patterns
- Bring in regular substitute teachers (the same teachers whenever possible) or specialist teachers once a week to take over the classes and free the regular teachers.
- Use other adults (administrators, volunteers, parents, instructional assistants) in the classroom to conduct an activity while teachers meet.
- Arrange field trips led by volunteers, regular substitute teachers, or elective teachers to enhance or augment the curriculum and to free time for planning.
- Hire physical education, art, and music specialists to provide 30 free minutes a day for classroom teachers. Or schedule music and physical education at the same time for all students in a grade so that there can be a grade-level meeting of teachers.
- Have a hobby period once a week. All adults in the school, including office staff, cafeteria workers, and instructional assistants, teach hobbies to students, freeing up teachers to meet. Parents or other community members could also be involved in a hobby period.
- Form a partnership with a university or local college that could provide films, TV lessons, and demonstrations using interactive teaching arrangements that enrich the curriculum. If university partners handle instruction and design follow-up activities, paraprofessionals can handle the monitoring.

Adding time to the school day or year
- Shorten the amount of classroom time each day, but add more days to the school year to cover state requirements. Use the extra time saved from each day.
- Extend the school day by starting earlier or finishing later. Have special classes in the early morning periods. Then required hours are completed in four and a half days. This provides a free half-day each week.
- Add meeting days to the school year. For example, one school built 21 pupil-free workdays into the calendar for the year.

Source: Adapted from National Institute for Urban Education. (2001). *On point . . . On time and how to get more of it.* Washington, DC: National Institute for Urban School Improvements (www.edc.org/urban).

At the school featured in Box 3–2, a special educator, a bilingual educator, and a general educator collaborated to teach language arts to students with and without disabilities, some of them native English speakers and others native Spanish speakers.

Does co-teaching work? Although there is limited research, the available data suggest that shared teaching has a positive impact on students' learning (Murawski & Swanson, 2001). In addition, parents of students both with and without disabilities have positive perspectives about co-teaching (Tichenor, Heins, Piechura-Couture, 2000). The majority of parents reported that their children liked having two teachers, many fun activities, and a broad range of projects in which they were involved. Parents of students with and without disabilities commented that they perceived increases in their children's academic achievement, self-esteem, and social skills as a result of co-teaching.

Later in this chapter, we will introduce you to multicultural considerations. Remember that in this exemplary school, educators used collaboration to address diversity considerations and progress in the general curriculum.

Box 3–2

Making a Difference

Creating a Learning Community

The United States may be a melting pot, but not all of its schools mix different kinds of children into the same pot. Or at least they don't often mix them deliberately.

But what if a school truly wants to exemplify the melting pot metaphor? What if it wants to create a single learning community for all of its children: those with and without disabilities, those from different cultures, and those who speak languages other than English? Such a school would do well to follow the lead of T. O. School in Berkeley, California.

There, a team consisting of the school principal, two bilingual education teachers, one general education teacher, the inclusion support teacher, and two parents (one of a child who is fully included despite the child's disabilities and one whose child does not have disabilities but is bilingual and enrolled in the school's English-as-second-language program) spearheaded a schoolwide effort to melt the separate programs into one. They were aided by a team of researchers from San Francisco State University.

They began by convening focus groups consisting of teachers (general, special, and bilingual) and parents (of general, special, and bilingual students). The focus groups revealed a consensus that the school is a community that embraces the cultural, language, and ability differences of the student body. By *community,* the teachers and parents meant that they all shared a sense of belonging to the school.

From that sense of shared ownership came action. Teachers communicated with each other about how to create classrooms that offered integrated activities and heterogeneous groups and cross-cultural and mixed-language contexts for instruction. The principal and other administrators made it easier for the teachers to break down the walls between their programs by providing them with times and places to collaborate, encouraging the teachers to seek resources to create collaborative practices, and acknowledging teachers' accomplishments. Parents supported the unified learning community by volunteering to work in the integrated classrooms. And the students enthusiastically worked with each other, developing greater feelings of competency and self-esteem, making new friends, and feeling that they were all learning and melting together.

The melting pot? It's more than a metaphor for our nation. It's a model for education.

Source: Adapted from Hunt, P., Hirose-Hatae, A., Doering, K., Karasoff, P., & Goetz, L. (2000). "Community" is what I think everyone is talking about. *Remedial and Special Education, 21*(5), 305–317.

There is some evidence, however, that general education teachers do more in the co-teaching arrangement than do special education teachers (Austin, 2001). That is because the subjects in which co-teaching has been most often practiced are those in which general educators are explicitly trained—namely, social studies, science, English/language arts, and math. Despite the allocation of teaching duties, the general education teachers asserted that co-teaching contributed to the academic success and social development of all of their students (Tichenor et al., 2000).

An emphasis on collaboration has become so commonplace, not only in education but across all fields, that it is easy to think it is being practiced when it really is not.

> The word collaboration is used indiscriminately in school settings. . . . But merely saying the word is not necessarily the same as carrying out the action. Collaboration requires commitment on the part of each individual to a shared goal, demands careful attention to communication skills, and obliges participants to maintain parity throughout their interaction. (Friend, 2000, pp. 1–2)

What Is the of Process of Creating Collaborative Teams?

For collaboration to work, a synergistic process is necessary: a process in which everyone's energy, creativity, and competence create "a whole that is greater than the sum of the parts" (Senge, 1990). Two of the country's leading experts in building collaborative teams assert that the following five elements are critically important in creating a collaborative process (Johnson & Johnson, 1997; Thousand & Villa, 1990, 2000, p. 258):

1. Face-to-face interaction among team members on a frequent basis
2. A mutual "we are all in this together" feeling of positive interdependence

Collaboration Tips

Box 3–3

Involving Community Agencies

The three students whom we feature in this chapter—Ronda, Donald, and Luisa—represent different multicultural characteristics and different challenges to collaboration. Let's just consider two of them, starting with Ronda.

Ronda's mother, Debra, is a single parent; Ronda's two older siblings live away from home. Debra works full time at Tulane University Law School and is a well-educated, articulate, and intelligent person whose expectations and ambitions for her children, especially for Ronda, are high: advanced university degrees for all three, especially for Ronda, with a dissertation on systemic reforms in special education ("The data will include all the papers and reports about her that I am saving for her," says Debra). Yet for Debra to attend all of the many meetings that the school has called has required her to miss 17 hours of work in the most recent school year, when Ronda began to benefit from school. And when the school called Debra before this year to "come get Ronda; she's uncontrollable," Debra had to respond or risk having Ronda placed into the custody of the school safety officer and the juvenile justice system.

Now let's consider Luisa. There are two fundamental challenges to collaboration, both arising from her diversity characteristics of being Latino and non-English speaking and her parents' undocumented status. How can the school communicate with her and her family (except, improperly, through her brother) when the school system as a whole does not hire Spanish-English speakers? And how can the school collaborate with her parents when it is an ally of the Immigration and Naturalization Service in identifying and reporting undocumented immigrants and therefore is properly regarded as hostile territory by her parents?

The answers come from restructuring the school system:

- *Flex time for educators and parents to meet.* Give the teachers some release time so they can meet parents after the usual hours of work—say, in the early evenings
- *Flex place for the meetings.* One option might be Catholic Charities, where Carolyn and Graziella work.
- *Employment of Spanish-English speakers.* As full-time or part-time staff or consultants, they will be trusted by the immigrant members of the community, as Graziella is.
- *Commitment to making a difference in students' lives.* Schools should seek out resources outside of the school system that can benefit students, such as Pyramid Parent Training Center and the many universities in New Orleans that operate teacher-training programs.

Restructuring the curriculum through universal design for learning makes progress in the general curriculum possible; so, too, restructuring the administrative systems makes collaboration possible, especially with families whose diversity consists of more than a student's exceptionality.

Putting These Tips to Work for Progress in the General Curriculum

1. What are the challenges?
2. What can the team do?
3. What are the results?

To answer these questions online and learn more about these ideas and concepts, go to the Collaboration Tips module in Chapter 3 of the Companion Website.

---

3. A focus on the development of small-group interpersonal skills in trust building, communication, leadership, creative problem solving, decision making, and conflict management

4. Regular assessments and discussion of the team's functioning in setting goals for improving relationships and effectively accomplishing tasks

5. Methods for holding one another accountable for agreed-on responsibilities and commitments

Box 3–3 suggests how you might collaborate with the parents of Rhonda and Luisa. In all of the remaining chapters of the book, we will include a Collaboration Tips box to demonstrate how you can collaborate so that students with exceptionalities can make progress in the general curriculum.

How Does Multicultural Responsiveness Enable Students to Progress in the General Curriculum?

Up to this point you have learned how universal design for learning, inclusion, and collaboration can make it possible for students with exceptionalities to progress in the general curriculum. You can also enable students' progress in the general curriculum by responding to their cultural diversity. As we pointed out in Chapter 1 (where we reviewed IDEA's findings of fact) and as the histories of Ronda Taylor, Donald Harness, and Luisa Rodriquez exemplify, students with specific characteristics are especially at risk for lack of success in the general education curriculum. These characteristics relate to their family's income; their family's education, ethnicity, and race; and the student's gender. These same characteristics are also associated with lower rates of high school graduation and adult employment (National Center for Education Statistics, 1993, 1997, 1999; National Council on Disability, 2000; National Organization on Disability, 2000). There is no doubt that educators face an especially challenging task: to ensure that students from diverse backgrounds have equal opportunities to progress in the general curriculum. To achieve that goal, you need to be especially sensitive and responsive to students' backgrounds. In this section, you will learn the answers to these questions:

Refer to Figure 1–2 to refresh your memory about the disproportionate representation of students from diverse backgrounds in special education.

▼ What is culture, and how does it affect students' progress in the general curriculum?
▼ How can you establish reliable alliances with students and families from diverse backgrounds?
▼ How can you enable students to broaden their menu of response options?
▼ How can you collaborate to promote cultural mediation?

What Is Culture and How Does It Affect Students' Progress in the General Curriculum?

Culture is the way in which each person is socialized from infancy forward to perceive and interpret what is happening and to determine the appropriate way to behave, initiate, and react

If you develop reliable alliances with the students and families you serve, it is more likely that you will have successful collaboration.

FIGURE 3–3
Cultural identity shaped through microcultural groups

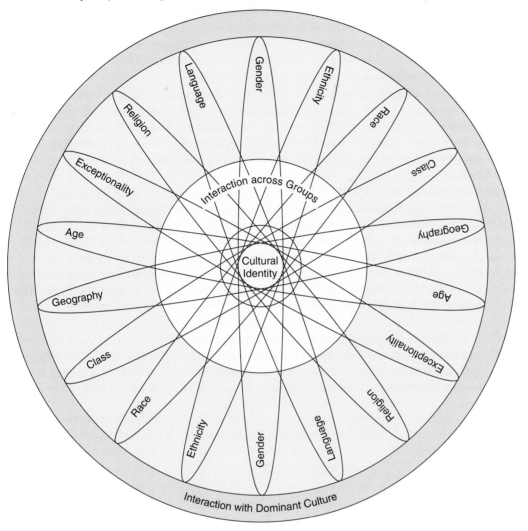

(Gollnick & Chinn, 2002). Culture influences our rituals (e.g., baptisms, bat and bar mitzvahs, marriages, and funerals); determines our language; shapes our emotions; and is the basis for how we determine what is right and wrong about ourselves, others, and society. When we apply this understanding of the effects of culture to classrooms, we begin to see that culture influences how eager or reticent children are to respond in class, interact with their peers, place priority on learning, follow directions, respond to teacher authority, and even determine what is humorous.

A student's culture consists of a broad range of characteristics, sometimes referred to as **microcultures** (Gollnick & Chinn, 2002). Figure 3–3 provides a visual illustration of some of the microcultures that merge to form one's overall culture.

Multicultural responsiveness means that a teacher and all colleagues in the education enterprise take into account a student's cultural background in planning universally designed learning. To infuse multiculturalism into all aspects of universally designed learning, you and your fellow teachers will have to be culturally competent. You will need to be able to do the following in order to achieve this cultural competence (McDiarmid, 1991):

▼ Gain insight into how education is perceived in your students' cultures, including issues such as the value of academic success, homework, school discipline, and teacher authority.

Luisa's parents, who have been employed for nearly a dozen years while in the United States, clearly have a work ethic, were reluctant to ask for help from Catholic Charities, and value her and her brother's success in school.

▼ Investigate students' prior experiences with the subject matter that you are teaching and seek to relate your instruction to what is familiar and relevant in their lives. Relevance to Luisa means having skills that will get her a job; so vocational training in work skills, including functional academics, are warranted.

▼ Identify the kind of skills and knowledge that is especially valued in your students' culture and seek ways to tie content standards to those priorities. Luisa's mother and father both work in service industries, he in restaurants and she in health care. These will be avenues that Luisa and her brother undoubtedly will explore, and their parents' experience can supplement the school's vocational and academic curriculum.

▼ Count on the strengths of students, their families, and their communities by incorporating these strengths into classroom instruction. Luisa's father came to the United States alone and then saved enough funds to make it possible for Luisa, her mother, and her brother to join him. Long-term planning, dedication to improving the family's economic position, hard work, and frugality—traits that Luisa's father clearly possesses—relate to subjects such as history (planning and the consequences of not planning) and economics and mathematics (family position, frugality, and the benefits of acquiring income and increasing it through savings and other investments).

▼ Encourage students to identify future goals and relate instruction to the goals that are especially relevant to them. Luisa will want to learn English so that she will be bilingual in a multilingual society and can teach her parents how to read and speak English, two prerequisites to their becoming more economically stable.

You have already learned how technology can enable students to progress in the general curriculum. Technology can also lead you to sources, such as the Early Childhood Research Institute on Culturally and Linguistically Appropriate Services, that can help you be culturally responsive. Read about this resource in Box 3–4.

We encourage you to learn more about the Council for Exceptional Children's Division for Culturally and Linguistically Diverse Exceptional Learners by going to the Web Links module in Chapter 3 of the Companion Website for a link (www.cec.sped.org/dv/ddel.html).

In each of the following chapters, we include a box on "Multicultural Considerations." Each of these features relates to a major theme of this book, and each helps you ensure students' progress in the general curriculum.

How Can You Establish Reliable Alliances with Students and Families from Diverse Backgrounds?

Good rapport between you and your students from diverse backgrounds and their parents is necessary for you to effectively educate students. But rapport is not sufficient. What is truly necessary is that you and they will establish a reliable alliance. What is the difference?

Rapport refers to a relationship characterized by harmony, conformity, accord, or affinity. People who have a sense of rapport usually feel comfortable with each other and are able to communicate candidly, honestly, and politely. Reliable alliances, however, go beyond rapport. A reliable alliance is characterized by a genuine and authentic relationship where both parties—you as an educator and the students and families you serve—know that you can rely on each other for emotional support and information (Turnbull & Turnbull, 2001).

To create a reliable alliance, two leading researchers in special education and multiculturalism, Maya Kalyanpur and Beth Harry (1999), suggest that teachers should adopt "a posture of cultural reciprocity" with parents. The guidelines in Box 3–5 will help you establish that cultural reciprocity. They will help you learn about each family's cultural priorities, share your own, and collaborate to ensure that students have equal opportunities to progress in the general curriculum. This same process can be used with students as you seek to get to know them, share your perspectives with them, and, in the process, establish a reliable alliance with them.

Technology Tips

Box 3-4

Access to Culturally and Linguistically Appropriate Early Childhood Services

When you first visit the website for Culturally and Linguistically Appropriate Services (CLAS) (http://clas.uiuc.edu), you are greeted by a hand that signs the letters for "Welcome" and by the word spelled in English, Spanish, and 14 other languages. Get the message, the welcome page implies: We are serious about diversity.

You learn just how serious when you turn to the page that introduces CLAS. There you find a two-column page. One the left side, the words are in English. On the right, they are in Spanish. You also find, on that same page, a mission statement that declares, among other things, "Beliefs and attitudes about culture and language shape outcomes; positive beliefs contribute to inclusiveness; negative beliefs undermine it." And you read CLAS's pledge that its materials will "reflect the intersection of culture and language, disabilities, and child development" and that it will present you with a "range of strategies or approaches" from which you can make an informed selection of practices and materials.

Just what are those practices and materials, and how are they selected? They include "a catalog of validated, culturally and linguistically appropriate materials, and of documented effective strategies, for early intervention and preschool services." These materials and practices have been reviewed by experts in early childhood education, early intervention and special education, and multicultural education. So already you can be confident that you are getting the state-of-the-art materials and practices from the most qualified people in these fields.

CLAS is quick to point out that you should avoid stereotyping families from diverse backgrounds. It is one thing for educators to generalize about a group of people in terms of their beliefs, values, and actions; but educators should expect that members of that group also are shaped by gender, roles, income, and education, among other factors.

CLAS also tells you that a practice that works for one group may work for another, or may not. Just as you should not stereotype one person from a particular group, so you should not stereotype a practice.

Finally, CLAS tells you that when educators and parents have conflicts about what the family or child needs, you should "work very hard at understanding and respecting their different perspectives."

The catalog is useful for practitioners, college and university instructors, and, of course, families. And it is especially useful for college and university students such as yourself. Where else can you so quickly and easily to find an authoritative set of materials and practices?

For more information on CLAS, we refer you to the following article: Corso, R. M., Santos, R. M., & Roof, V. (2002). Honoring diversity in early childhood education materials. *Teaching Exceptional Children, 34*(3), 30–36.

How Can You Enable Students to Broaden Their Menu of Response Options?

Let's suppose that you have students in your class who engage in behaviors or use expressions that differ from those typically used by your culture. One of your options is to encourage the students to conform to behaviors and language that are more characteristic of your culture. What message would that option send to the student, and how likely would success result from this approach? The message may well be that you do not value them and their families, and the result may be less than successful.

Another alternative is to broaden the students' menu of response options, helping them to practice other behaviors without also eliminating the behaviors that they culturally value. For example, you might tell students that learning alternatives to culturally rich slang might be valuable for them, given that slang may not be preferred by many employers who have jobs in which they may be interested. However, you might also explain that most of us speak differently at home and with our friends than we do at school or in the workplace. You might share examples of different culturally specific terms that have been often used in fiction, emphasizing its potency and rhythm, and encourage students to write stories using words and phrases from their culture.

We urge you to be open to differences and also to expand your own menu of response options. As you develop reliable alliances with students and families from diverse cultural backgrounds,

Box 3–5

Multicultural Considerations

Adapted Posture of Cultural Reciprocity

1. Learn about the family's strengths, needs, and expectations by listening to the "family story." Determine the family's priorities and preferences for their child's educational program: IEP, academic goals, placement, related services, extracurricular activities, and participation in other school activities. Try to understand and honor the family's cultural values and priorities to establish a reliable alliance with them.

2. Talk with the family about the assumptions that underlie their cultural values and priorities. Seek to find out about the reasons for their priorities and preferences.

3. As you reflect on their priorities and preferences, identify any disagreements or alternative perspectives that you or other professionals have associated with providing educational supports and services to the student and/or family. Identify the cultural values that are embedded in *your* underlying interpretation or in the interpretation of other professionals. Identify how the family's views differ from your own.

4. Respectfully acknowledge any cultural differences you have identified and share your perspectives on cultural values related to your and other professionals' assumptions.

5. Brainstorm and then determine how you can appropriately adapt your professional interpretations to the family's value system.

Putting These Considerations to Work for Progress in the General Curriculum

1. In what way is it helpful for you to know your own cultural values before collaborating with families from different cultures?

2. When you meet with a family from a culture other than your own, what aspects of the student's education should you discuss?

3. In what way can culture affect families' academic priorities?

Source: Adapted from Harry, B., & Kalyanpur, M. (1999). *Culture in special education.* Baltimore: Brookes.

---

you probably will have new insights and encounter new ways of receiving information and interpreting the world. You can expand your own menu by becoming comfortable with new ways of relating. In Box 3–6 you will learn how you might work with students to broaden their menu without squelching their preferred behavior. We also encourage you to recognize that some students and families from diverse backgrounds do not want to acculturate to the dominate culture. So although you might think it is valuable for someone else to expand her menu of response options, you will need to respect those who disagree with that approach.

How Can You Collaborate to Promote Cultural Mediation?

Cultural differences can create unfamiliar values, roles, expectations, and goals; each can be disconcerting to teachers, parents, and students who are trying to find common ground for collaboration to ensure students' progress in the general curriculum. Sometimes values, roles, expectations, and goals can cause conflict and warrant mediation of the conflict. Cultural mediation is especially helpful in promoting equal opportunity.

Ursula Markey and D. J. Markey are cultural mediators, supporting students with disabilities and their families in schools in New Orleans. In Box 3–7 you will learn about their values, roles, and mediation approaches. Wouldn't they be invaluable collaborators if you were a teacher in

Inclusion Tips

Box 3–6

	What You Might See	What You Might Be Tempted to Do	Alternate Responses	Ways to Include Peers in the Process
Behavior	He constantly moves around the classroom and resists staying in his seat.	Punish him by referring him to the office for in-school suspension.	Invite him to assist you with classroom tasks that require movement (collecting and returning papers, setting up art supplies).	Ask him to provide assistance to a classmate who has a mobility impairment, helping that student move around the room.
Social interactions	He will not make eye contact with the teacher or with the peers who are the classroom leaders.	Say to him, "Look at me when I am talking with you."	Establish a reliable alliance with him and ensure that he feels competent and confident in class.	Identify his strengths and arrange opportunities for him to provide peer tutoring to other students.
Educational performance	He does not complete class work because of being engaged in so many pre-work behaviors.	Give him an *F* for all papers that are not turned in on time.	Discuss with him the possibility of coming into the classroom 15 minutes early in the morning to take care of preferred pre-work behaviors.	Offer the same opportunity to other peers who need more time to complete their work.
Classroom attitudes	He uses slang, which intimidates classmates as well as yourself.	Make a hard-and-fast classroom rule that slang is not allowed.	Work with him to distinguish between slang that makes others comfortable and uncomfortable. Encourage him to think of ways to continue to use slang without intimidating others.	As part of multicultural education, have all the students share with the class a couple of slang terms that are rooted in their own culture and explain the meaning. Discuss others' reactions to each term.

the New Orleans schools? Haven't they been just that for Ronda Taylor and her mother, Debra, and for Donald Harness and his parents, Carolyn and Donald Harness? Wherever you teach, try to find mediators such as the Markeys; they can make your job easier and students' progress in the general curriculum success more likely.

The Markeys receive funding from the U.S. Department of Education to operate Pyramid Parent Training Center as a Community Parent Resource Center (CPRC). There are approximately 25 similar parent resource centers in communities characterized by a high concentration of cultural and linguistic diversity; each serves families who have children and youth with disabilities or limited English proficiency. The centers offer one-on-one assistance to families; distribute family-friendly materials on resources and special education information; advocate for the families and students; and engage in outreach to families, schools, and communities.

Companion Website

To learn more about the locations of and contact information for the Community Parent Resource Centers, go to the Web Links module in Chapter 3 of the Companion Website.

Ursula and DJ Markey provide training to families of children with disabilities on their children's rights under IDEA; in many cases, they also attend the IEP meetings of the students whose families they trained.

How Does Responsiveness to Multicultural Considerations Enable Students to Progress in the General Curriculum?

When you infuse multiculturalism into a universally designed general curriculum, establish reliable alliances with students and families from diverse backgrounds, enable students to broaden their menu of response options, and collaborate with cultural mediators, you provide a responsive context for students from culturally and linguistically diverse backgrounds to progress in the general curriculum. Throughout the rest of the book, you will learn strategies for providing universally designed instruction that can enable students from diverse cultures to make substantial progress in the general curriculum.

A Vision for Ronda's, Donald's, and Luisa's Future

Because their parents and allies (such as Pyramid Parent Training Center) have required the schools to cease practices that border on incompetent, illegal, or both and that reflect a failure to collaborate (such as long-term suspensions, untimely and inadequate evaluations, inappropriate IEPs, and denial of the benefit of state-of-the-art strategies such as positive behavior supports) and because the schools now comply with IDEA, apply state-of-the-art strategies, and collaborate with parents, Ronda Taylor and Donald Harness will exceed the norm (only 4 percent of the 12th-grade graduating class in the New Orleans schools consists of students with disabilities) by staying in school and graduating, moving into the work force, and living, with supports, in their communities. For them, the legacy of discrimination based on their ethnic/racial and presumed socioeconomic status cannot be denied; but it does not prevail because good education and good educators have made it a matter of the distant past for these two students.

Box 3–7

Cultural Mediation with Ursula and D. J. Markey

We are parents, and that's what makes all the difference for us and for the families with whom we work in New Orleans.

Our first son, Duane, was born with epilepsy and autism. We lost him in December 1999, when, at the age of 26, he had a seizure in his bedroom in our house. He died in our arms; for that fact, and for his life, we can only be grateful.

Our other son, Teiko, has some learning disabilities; but he is now launched into adulthood, having graduated from the New Orleans schools and now being enrolled in a postsecondary job-and-life-skills training program in Los Angeles.

We have said that our children have made all the difference in our lives, and that is true. But we also have been heavily involved, since the early 1960s, in the civil rights movement in New Orleans.

As African Americans, we see the disability rights and civil rights movements as one movement, with the disability rights movement being an extension of the civil rights movement.

In New Orleans, discrimination in education takes two forms. First, there's discrimination based on students' races. Second, there's discrimination based on the fact that they have disabilities.

We respond to discrimination by reaching out to the parents of the children, for far too often the parents lack the resources—time, money, and knowledge of the law and the best practices that could benefit their children—to combat discrimination and get an appropriate education for their children.

To reach out to parents and to mediate between them and the schools, we formed Pyramid Parent Training Program. We offer workshops, publish newsletters, refer parents to resources, and provide one-on-one assistance. We attend their children's IEP meetings. We also attend state and local school board meetings. By working on both the individual and the system levels, we mediate—that is, we serve as a go-between. Don't get us wrong: We advocate for the parents and their children, but we can't be successful advocates unless we also understand the school system and what drives it to do what it does.

You see, there is a cultural difference between the families and their children, on the one hand, and most professionals in the school system, on the other. The families and their children are from traditionally underserved or unserved segments of our population. They have experienced so much discrimination for such a long time in jobs, housing, access to medical care, and education that they begin to believe that their children are not entitled to an education that launches them to jobs, independent living, and community participation.

Many of the schools' professionals do not or no longer relate to these experiences. Some are white; all are educated and have been successful in the very system that employs them and that writes off their children.

And the families and schools have different agendas, too. The parents want their children to get an education that makes a difference in their lives. The schools have to serve as many students as possible with an insufficient amount of money and with the greatest efficiency possible. So the schools conserve resources and increase their efficiency by placing the emphasis on budgetary constraints rather than parent priorities.

With these two different cultures and agendas, the question we faced as parents and that other families face daily is this: How can we bridge the gaps between the cultures so that the students will get what IDEA promises? For us, the answer was to mediate between the cultures by telling the families, "You are not alone," and then proving it by helping them gain the knowledge and support they need. Whatever help we provide—we call it "leadership development"—we recognize that, within each parent, there is the power to be an effective advocate for his or her child. And we have to acknowledge the parallel: Within every educator there is the power to be an effective teacher of that child.

So cultural mediation consists of recognizing the potential in everyone to become part of a team that works for a child. Thus, team building is an essential part of our work that incorporates the recognition that cultural agendas may differ and that our job is to help both the families and the schools by raising the level of effective parent participation in the education process.

Louisa Rodriquez and her family also have secured a favorable outcome. An enlightened school board employed more staff to translate English-Spanish, launched a continuous program of professional development for all teachers to help them become more culturally competent, declined to participate in the immigrant sweeps that the Immigration and Naturalization Service has put into place in New Orleans's Latino community and in public service sectors such as the schools, and enrolled Luisa in English-as-a-second language and special education programs, acknowledging that she needs to learn English and that her health impairment qualifies her for special education. Moreover, there now is work for Luisa's parents and for her brother and herself, too. She has followed her mother into the health care industry and now works alongside her in elder-care programs sponsored by Catholic Charities, specializing in services to Latinos in New Orleans.

Pyramid Parent Training Center has been funded and refunded by public and private-sector grants and continues to advocate for students and families and collaborate with the public schools and other public agencies.

Yet the struggle continues for African American and Latino families in the Big Easy, as it does in other parts of the United States. It's not just an urban or southern issue; it's a national one that grows and grows as the population of the country and its schools changes. The work of responding to multicultural considerations, whether in the form of disability or in other forms, will not end; but the outcomes will be better for all concerned.

What Would You Recommend?

1. What approach would you take if you were in a school system in which quiet discrimination against students characterized by cultural and linguistic diversity were practiced? What strategies for working with the families would you adopt?
2. What experiences have you had in collaborating with professionals, and what strategies were used, or should have been used, to make those collaborations effective to produce the outcomes you wanted?
3. What experiences have you had in expanding your own menu of response options? What have you learned about cultures other than your own that you especially value?
4. How will those experiences affect you as a teacher?

Summary

How Does Collaboration Enable Students to Progress in the General Curriculum?

▼ Collaboration is a dynamic process in which educators, students, and families share their resources and strengths to solve problems in a creative and responsive way.

▼ Collaboration's ultimate goal is to improve teaching and learning and to enable all students, especially those with exceptionalities, to progress in the general curriculum.

▼ Students, families, teachers, related-service providers, paraprofessionals, translators/interpreters, and administrators are important contributors to the collaborative process.

▼ When students participate in collaboration, they are learning self-determination.

▼ It is good for parents and professionals to avoid a "we-they" approach to collaboration and for professionals not to exert their power and expertise over parents.

▼ Special and general education teachers, related-service providers, paraprofessionals, and administrators are expected to collaborate in teaching students with exceptionalities.

▼ Co-teaching involves planning and teaching together, developing instructional accommodations, monitoring and evaluating student performance, and communicating student performance to other educators and to families and students.

▼ There are five elements necessary to create collaboration teams: face-to-face interaction, a sense of "we are all in this together," trust and means for developing it, regular assessment of how the collaborators are working, and methods for holding each collaborator accountable.

How Does Responsiveness to Multicultural Considerations Enable Students to Progress in the General Curriculum?

▼ Culture is the way in which each person is socialized from infancy to perceive and interpret what is happening and to determine the appropriate way to behave, initiate, and react.

▼ Culture is made up of many microcultures, including ethnicity, race, class, geography, age, exceptionality, religion, and ability.

▼ Multicultural responsiveness is the approach of considering students' cultural backgrounds in planning universally designed instruction.

▼ A reliable alliance is characterized by a genuine and authentic relationship in which both parties rely on each other for emotional support and information. We encourage you to develop reliable alliances with all students and families, including those from diverse backgrounds.

▼ The posture of cultural reciprocity will assist you in developing reliable alliances.

▼ You can enable students to broaden their menu of response options by encouraging them to learn new behaviors or use different language without requiring them to eliminate the behaviors or language that they culturally value.

▼ You can broaden your own menu of response options by learning more about other cultures and valuing what you learn about them.

▼ Cultural mediators help educators, families, and students find common ground when collaborating to ensure progress in the general curriculum.

Council for Exceptional Children   PRAXIS

To find out how and where this chapter content connects to the CEC Professional Standards and the Praxis™ Standards, go to the Standards Connection module in Chapter 3 of the Companion Website. A comprehensive matrix aligning CEC Professional Standards, Praxis™ Standards, and INTASC principles to the entire text, is available in the Appendix and on the Companion Website.

Chapter 4

Who is Tony Lavender?

Working the room like Jay Leno, Tony Lavender, a shy sixth grader, serves as master of ceremonies for his school's annual talent show. As MC, he introduces the next event; but he is also quick to alter his personality and become a stand–up comedian. A young man with an exceptional vocabulary, Tony is often witty and has a knack for teasing without putting down an individual or offering negative sarcasm.

Tony might be quick with a joke and a performer, but he is also more comfortable watching television than interacting with a friend or his parents. That side of Tony reflects that he has a learning disability and has experienced more than his fair share of frustrations in school.

When he entered Susan Brumbley's special education classroom at Maple School in Springfield, Ohio, 7 years ago, Tony was desperate for help. "When I first met Tony, he didn't know his colors, his numbers, or days of the week," Mrs. Brumbley explains.

"He couldn't read the simplest of things," his father Bob adds. Using a thick, black marker,

Susan would write out a single letter on an 8½-by-11-inch piece of paper. Tony would stare blankly at it. In time, his teachers realized that Tony has a vision problem that contributed to his reading inability. But they still had to decide whether he also had a specific learning disability. To answer that question, they had to spend a great deal more time teaching Tony, step by laborious step, how to read.

Although his progress was glacial at times, Tony slowly began to understand letters, words, and sentences. What's more, he began to realize the keys to understanding those letters, words, and sentences; trust the woman he now called "Mrs. B"; and do his homework without quitting, no matter what.

What lies at the root of Tony's learning problem? That's a hard question to answer. His parents separated from one another when he was still young. As a toddler, he lived with his father. By the time Tony entered school, he had had limited exposure to reading and needed the intervention of someone like Susan to teach him how to read. Three years ago, at the end of the third grade, a breakthrough took place: "I knew something was going to happen, that he was going to blossom," Susan says. "He just had this desire, this with-it-ness, and then the light-bulb came on. He got it."

Tony's sudden ability to read did not occur in a vacuum. Susan is quick to praise Tony's father, Bob, and stepmother, Chris. "Both are devoted readers," she says.

"This has been a joint effort. Maple School has been wonderful," Bob adds. But Tony's progress has required him and his family to work just as hard at home as Susan and Tony have worked at school. Bob explains, "Tony loves television and would watch it morning, noon, and night if given the chance. We had to be strict and require at least 30 minutes of reading every night. If he missed a night, then he had to make up 60 minutes the next night." This structure required Tony to displace TV with reading. His favorite books are those in the *Harry Potter* series. "He has read every one," Bob adds.

Today Tony is about to complete his first year of middle school. Although he experienced a great deal of success with Susan in her separate special education classroom, this past year he was included in the general education classroom and has limited interaction with her and other special education teachers. Too good a reader for the special education reading group, Tony has struggled to fit into the large classroom. "His teachers this year can't say enough about Tony. They say he is the model student, always willing to help someone and always there with a smile. But this past year has been tough for him academically and socially," Bob explains.

Whether because of his past experiences or something else, Tony has a great fear of failure. If he realizes something will need concentration and extra work, he far too often shies away and is more than willing to retreat to the TV. "He doesn't want to put in the extra effort. I'm not sure if he is afraid or just frustrated from past failure," says Bob.

How can anyone explain the paradox of Tony the performer on stage and Tony the performer in class: the outgoing good guy and the shy, struggling student? How can anyone reconcile his success in learning to read with his fear of failure? These questions confront Tony, his family, and his teachers.

What do you think?

1. How would you build on Tony's performance personality and his apparent fearlessness to address any social skill and learning challenges he might have?

2. Do students like Tony—those with learning disabilities—share other characteristics besides academic challenges?

3. How would you support Tony to continue to be successfully included throughout middle school and high school?

To respond to these questions online, participate in other activities, and learn more about Tony Lavender and learning disabilities, go to the Cases module in Chapter 4 of the Companion Website.

Companion Website

How Do You Recognize Students with Learning Disabilities?

Defining Learning Disabilities

Ever since Sam Kirk first coined the term *learning disabilities* in 1963, legislators, parents, and professionals have debated about how to define the condition (Fletcher et al., 2001; Kavale & Forness, 2000). IDEA provides one definition, but even that one is controversial. Let's consider the IDEA definition first and an alternative one later.

IDEA defines (20 U.S.C., Sec. 1400) the term *specific learning disability* as a "disorder in one or more of the **basic psychological processes** involved in understanding or in using language, spoken or written, which disorder may manifest itself in imperfect ability to listen, think, speak, read, write, spell, or do mathematical calculations." This definition allows conditions such as perceptual disabilities, brain injury, minimal brain dysfunction, dyslexia, and developmental aphasia to qualify a student as having a specific learning disability.

Also under IDEA, however, a student cannot qualify in the learning disabilities category if the student's impairment is primarily the result of visual, hearing, or motor disabilities; mental retardation; emotional disturbance; or environmental, cultural, or economic disadvantage. Finally, if poor instruction is the primary cause of the learning problem, then IDEA clearly excludes the student from the category of learning disabilities.

Note that the definition has two special components: inclusionary criteria and exclusionary criteria. The inclusionary criteria are those related to listening, thinking, speaking, reading, writing, spelling, and calculating. The exclusionary criteria relate to impairments arising from other disabilities or from poor instruction.

As we said, the IDEA definition is controversial. Many professionals find fault with it and prefer the one adopted in 1988 by the National Joint Committee on Learning Disabilities (NJCLD), a coalition of professional and parent organizations. This definition identifies several important characteristics of a specific learning disability:

First, the condition is *heterogeneous*, or varied. If you were to observe 20 students with learning disabilities, you would find 20 different ways in which the condition manifests itself.

Second, students with learning disabilities *may* have associated social and behavioral difficulties, but under IDEA they may not qualify for services as having a specific learning disability primarily on the basis of these challenges alone. They must also have significant academic difficulty.

Third, learning disabilities occur *across the life span*. The disability is a lifelong condition.

Fourth, although the IDEA definition does not specifically mention cause, the NJCLD definition assumes that the cause is *intrinsic*, or inside, the student and is most likely the result of central nervous system dysfunction. Under the NJCLD definition, *extrinsic* causes for academic problems, such as poor instruction and cultural differences, can exist concomitantly with intrinsically caused learning disabilities; in other words, these other causes can exist at the same time as and along with learning disabilities.

Tony is an example of a student to whom the concept of concomitance applies. His vision impairment certainly has had an impact on his overall academic development. The question facing his teachers was whether his vision impairment contributed significantly to his academic difficulties or whether those difficulties resulted from specific learning disabilities. After thoroughly evaluating Tony, the team concluded that Tony has a learning disability and that his vision problem is not the primary cause of his academic difficulties. Now, just how does Tony's history exemplify what educators do in deciding whether a student has a specific learning disability?

Classification Criteria

Consistent with the IDEA and NJCLD definitions, most states and local school districts require students to meet three criteria for classification as having a learning disability (Mercer, Jordan, Allsopp, & Mercer, 1996):

To learn more about the NJCLD definition, go to the Web Links module in Chapter 4 of the Companion Website to link to NJCLD's website.

1. *Inclusionary criterion.* The student must demonstrate a **severe discrepancy** (a statistically significant difference) between perceived potential and actual achievement as measured by formal and informal assessments. For example, a student who scores high on the verbal section of an intelligence test but low on reading has a discrepancy.

2. *Exclusionary criterion.* The student's learning disability may not result primarily from a visual or hearing impairment, mental retardation, serious emotional disturbance, or cultural differences.

3. *Need criterion.* The student manifests a demonstrated need for special education services. Without specialized support, the student's disability will prevent him or her from learning.

It is difficult to distinguish students with learning disabilities from students who are low achievers for other reasons. But a distinction does exist (Fuchs, Fuchs, Mathes, Lipsey, & Roberts, 2001; Kavale, 2001). Students with learning disabilities generally perform better on intelligence tests than low achievers do. Low achievers, on the other hand, tend to score higher on achievement tests than those with learning disabilities do.

Intelligence Tests

Educators use two kinds of tests to determine whether a student has a disability. One is the intelligence test, the other a norm-referenced test. The intelligence test that most educators use is the Wechsler Intelligence Scale for Children—III/Revised (WISC III-R). This and other intelligence tests measure a sample of a student's performance on tasks related to reasoning, memory, learning, comprehension, and ability to learn academic skills; based on the student's performance, educators infer the student's intellectual capacity. IQ tests yield an intelligence quotient (IQ) that is a ratio of the student's mental age (MA) to his or her chronological age (CA): $IQ = MA \div CA \times 100$. So if a student has a mental age of 12 and a chronological age of 10, the student's IQ would compute at 12 divided by 10 times 100, which equals 120.

The bell-shaped curve in Figure 4–1 shows below-average, average, and above-average ranges of intelligence on the WISC-III. Note that 50 percent of the students at any particular age average an IQ below 100, and 50 percent average an IQ above 100. Most states identify students with IQs at or above 130 as gifted (Chapter 7) and students with IQs at or below 70 as having mental retardation if they also meet other criteria (Chapters 8 and 9).

To learn more about learning disabilities, go to the Web Links module in Chapter 4 of the Companion Website to link to LDOnline.

To learn more about IQ tests, especially why they are useful and why they are criticized as not useful, go to the Web Links module in Chapter 4 of the Companion Website.

FIGURE 4–1
Ranges of intelligence

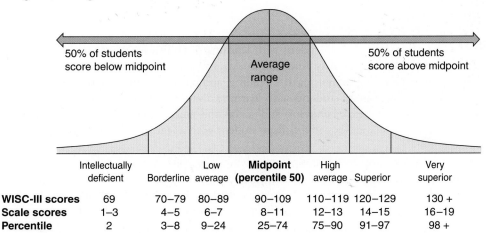

	Intellectually deficient	Borderline	Low average	**Midpoint (percentile 50)**	High average	Superior	Very superior
WISC-III scores	69	70–79	80–89	90–109	110–119	120–129	130 +
Scale scores	1–3	4–5	6–7	8–11	12–13	14–15	16–19
Percentile	2	3–8	9–24	25–74	75–90	91–97	98 +

Source. From *The WISC-III Companion* (p. 30) by S. Truch, 1993, Austin, TX: PRO-ED. Copyright 1993 by PRO-ED. Reprinted with permission.

Box 4–1

Rachel's Story: A College Graduate

This past Spring, Rachel—like thousands of other college and university students throughout the country—received her bachelor of arts degree from Mitchell College. Challenged by attention and learning issues throughout her life, Rachel succeeded through hard work, by using structured support, and by making the most of the modifications that had been put into place for her. Rachel's story is like that of many of her peers who are challenged with attention, organization, and time management skills because of a learning disability.

Rachel did well in school until the fifth grade. Attending a private school at the time, she began to notice difficulties in completing her schoolwork and staying on task. Her teachers noticed these difficulties as well and suggested that her parents have her tested.

Rachel and her parents discovered from these tests that she had attention deficit hyperactivity disorder as well as learning problems associated with memory and organization. The test results were a relief in that they helped to explain some of the challenges Rachel was having. She explains, "I was surrounded by all these bright friends that weren't having trouble with the assignments and the homework we had. I, on the other hand, was feeling pretty overwhelmed, and extra effort didn't seem to pay off." Finding out she had a disability didn't offer an immediate answer. Rachel's school was not prepared to meet the needs of students with disabilities, so her parents hired a tutor.

Amy became not just Rachel's tutor but also her advocate and friend. She began tutoring Rachel shortly after Rachel had been identified with attention and learning problems. Amy began by helping Rachel set up an organized and complete notebook. "Before Amy, my notes were all over the place, and I couldn't find what I needed half the time. Amy helped with my studying but really helped empower me through organization." Amy also taught Rachel how to decide what was important to study, how to study, and how to prepare for tests and exams.

In the classroom, Rachel quickly realized her teachers were not prepared to accommodate her attention and learning needs. At times, some of her teachers were opposed to providing any accommodations for her needs. They seemed to say that if Rachel couldn't be successful on her own, that particular school wasn't the right one for her.

Fortunately, her advisor and Amy were able to advocate for her. Even with all of this support, however, Rachel continued to have problems; and by February of her junior year she was at risk of failing. It was then that her parents sent her to a private boarding school, where she repeated her junior year.

Rachel excelled in this small, supportive environment. Under the guidance of an academic advisor who advocated for her needs in the classroom while also working with her to establish these skills for her own independence, Rachel found the support she needed to remain on task and address some of her learning challenges. "I know most people hated the required study hall, but I loved it. We were all required to study, and this was so necessary for me." Rachel also received additional tutoring, which once again focused on empowering her as a learner. "We focused a lot on learning strategies and memory techniques that I could use to learn the material and, more important, remember what I learned."

Rachel's professors also accommodated themselves to Rachel's learning needs. "They all offered me various ways to do my assignments. For instance, instead of papers, I was able to do a number of oral presentations. I got so good at the oral part that I joined debate team and drama club and performed in several plays."

Describing the Characteristics

There is no such thing as a typical student with learning disabilities. One student may exhibit strengths in math and nonverbal reasoning and weaknesses in receptive and expressive language skills. Another may be strong in motor skills, reading, and receptive language but weak in math and expressive language. But all students with learning disabilities face common challenges related to their learning abilities, behavior, and social and emotional skills. Box 4–1 describes some of the challenges facing Rachel, a college student with a learning disability and attention difficulties.

Individuals with learning disabilities commonly have average or above-average intelligence. Nevertheless, they almost always demonstrate low academic achievement in one or more areas. Learning disabilities are associated with at least six distinct characteristics: reading, written language, mathematics, memory, metacognition, and behavioral/social/emotional. Tony's strengths, for example, include good speaking skills and a willingness to perform for (but not easily) and interact with others; but Tony has had to work hard to overcome his challenges with reading.

Reading

Reading difficulties are one of the most significant problems experienced by children identified with learning disabilities. This is especially troublesome because reading is so important to individuals' performance in most academic domains and to their adjustment to most school activities (Chard & Kameenui, 2000; Fuchs et al., 2001). Evidence suggests that this problem is related to deficient language skills, especially phonological awareness (Coyne, Kame'enui, & Simmons, 2001). Students who lack skills in **phonological awareness** cannot recognize sound segments in spoken words (e.g., "push" has three sound segments, or *phonemes*: /p/ /u/ /sh/). Effective readers must use other skills, but phonological skills are especially important in learning to read.

Students with *reading disabilities* may exhibit word recognition errors. When asked to read orally, they may omit, insert, substitute, and/or reverse words. They also may have difficulty comprehending what they have read because they have limited ability to recall or discern basic facts, sequences, and/or themes. Likewise, they may lose their place while reading; read in a choppy, halting manner; or struggle to comprehend the text they are reading (National Reading Panel, 2000).

Severe reading problems are often referred to as *dyslexia* (Lerner, 2000), a term that distinguishes a person with severe reading problems from other readers who need remedial help. **Dyslexia** is a learning disability characterized by problems in expressive or receptive, oral, or written language. Individuals with dyslexia may have problems reading, spelling, writing, speaking, or listening.

Later in the chapter, you will learn how Direct Instruction helps students such as Tony develop effective reading skills.

Written Language

Students with learning problems, even those who read well, often have problems with written language (Graham, Harris, & Larsen, 2001). Their difficulties usually occur in the areas of handwriting, spelling, productivity, text structure, sentence structure, word usage, and composition. They may

▼ Feel overwhelmed by the idea of getting started
▼ Struggle to organize and use the mechanics of writing
▼ Struggle to develop their ideas fluently
▼ Often have difficulties spelling and constructing written products in a legible fashion
▼ Submit written work that is too brief

Handwriting problems are known as **dysgraphia,** a term that refers to a partial inability to remember how to make certain alphabet or arithmetic symbols in handwriting (Meese, 2001). Students' handwriting problems can arise from their lack of fine-motor coordination, failure to attend to task, inability to perceive and/or remember visual images accurately, or inadequate handwriting instruction in the classroom (Friend & Bursuck, 2002). Students with dysgraphia may learn much less from an assignment because they must focus on the mechanics of writing instead of on the content of their assignment.

Students may also have difficulty with spelling. Their common spelling errors include the addition of unneeded letters, the omission of needed letters, reversals of vowels, reversals of syllables, and the phonemic spelling of nonphonemic words.

Mathematics

As with students' reading disabilities, mathematical difficulties can range from mild to severe. A term commonly associated with math difficulties is **dyscalculia,** the lack of ability to perform mathematical functions (Price & Youe, 2000). Students' difficulties may include the following (Miller, Butler, & Lee, 1998):

▼ *Visual perception:* differentiating numbers or copying shapes
▼ *Memory:* recalling math facts
▼ *Motor functions:* writing numbers legibly or in small spaces
▼ *Language:* relating arithmetic terms to meaning or vocabulary

Instructional tools like computers can help students with disabilities write more easily.

▼ *Abstract reasoning:* solving word problems and making comparisons

▼ *Metacognition:* identifying, using, and monitoring the use of strategies to solve problems

Memory

Like many students with learning disabilities, Rachel (whom you met in Box 4–1) has difficulty with short- and long-term memory (Swanson, 2000). Rachel explains that her memory is "totally disorganized. I kind of remember hearing about the idea but have no recollection of its significance. Unless I remain focused and organized, I simply don't remember things."

Students who have difficulties with short-term memory cannot easily recall information shortly after it is presented to them. Students with long-term memory challenges cannot easily store information permanently for later recall. Research on short- and long-term memory has shown that students with learning disabilities (1) have poor strategies for memorizing information, (2) have insufficient metacognitive skills for recalling information, and (3) possess limited semantic memory capabilities (O'Shaughnessy & Swanson, 1998; Torgesen & Wagner, 1998). Together or separately, these limitations cause students' academic performance to be erratic. Let's consider only the challenge associated with metacognition.

Metacognition

When you study for a test on this chapter, how will you do it? You might review chapter headings, definitions, summaries, and class notes. Or you might use flashcards and/or memory devices, called **mnemonics,** such as acronyms for lists. You probably have found an approach to studying that works best for you. If so, you have good skills in the area of **metacognition.** That term refers to awareness of how you think and how you monitor your thinking (Swanson, 2001). Efficient learners take control and direct their own thinking process, but students with learning disabilities tend to lack these skills and have deficits in the following areas of metacognition (Gersten, 1998):

▼ Knowing a large number of strategies for acquiring, storing, and processing information

▼ Understanding when, where, and why these strategies are important

▼ Selecting and monitoring the use of these strategies wisely and reflectively

For instance, Rachel (see Box 4–1) has significant difficulty preparing for tests and related assignments. She explains, "I know I learn differently from my friends. It takes me much longer to learn a concept and remember it for a test or assignment. I know I need to organize and use strategies I've been taught, or otherwise I won't learn."

Later in the chapter, you will learn how learning strategies can assist students with organizing learning for enhanced memory. And in the chapter on traumatic brain injury, Chapter 14, you will learn about mnemonics.

Later in the chapter, you will learn about accommodations and modifications at the postsecondary level that help students succeed in college.

Behavioral, Social, and Emotional Characteristics

The processing problems that many students experience can also cause them to have difficulty understanding their own and other persons' social cues and behaving in socially acceptable ways. Add to this both their frustration that their ability to learn is not equal to their ability level and their difficulty in dealing with people who do not understand this poor performance, and you have students at risk for behavioral and social problems.

Research during the 1990s increased teachers' awareness of the behavioral, social, and emotional problems facing children with learning disabilities. Both Bender and Smith (1990) and Kavale and Forness (1996) have shown that children and adolescents with learning disabilities experience social problems, emotional difficulties, and conduct problems because of their deficits in social skills. In addition, children with learning disabilities are more likely to experience social rejection and low rates of social acceptance (Settle & Milich, 1999). Students who have social needs or social adjustment problems in school may need a teacher's direct intervention in a number of areas, including classroom conduct, interpersonal skills, and personal and psychological adjustment.

Interpersonal Skills

One problem for many students with learning disabilities is that they lack interpersonal skills. Unlike Tony, they are more likely to have fewer friends; to be rejected and neglected by their peers; and to be regarded by their teachers, parents, and peers as socially troubled. These challenges are caused by the students' lack of knowledge, inability to learn from appropriate modeling, inability to read social cues, and misinterpretation of the feelings of others.

Similarly, students with learning disabilities may know what to do, but they may not do what they know they should do. For example, impulsive students usually act before they think. Tony is fearless when it comes to performing in front of other children and even adults at a school function; but he continues to be shy, misinterpret social cues, and not know how to act in other social situations.

Motivation and Self-Concept

Individuals with learning disabilities are often frustrated after their many years of erratic and thwarted attempts at learning and mastering academic skills. Their chronic disappointment can cause them to have a generalized sense of diminished value and potential. These feelings may impair their ability to achieve academic success and their overall social and emotional development. Indeed, students' self-concepts are common problems (Lerner, 2000) and have been reported as early as grade 3 and remain stable through high school (Dev, 1998).

Moreover, these self-concepts can ultimately lead to the condition known as **learned helplessness** if teachers do not address these issues. Students with learned helplessness see limited relationships between their individual effort and their related success in school. When they do succeed, they attribute this success to luck; when they fail, they blame their failure on their lack of ability. If ignored, these students will continue to expect failure and will often give up when faced with an academic or social challenge.

Identifying the Causes

Neurological Causes

Throughout the history of the learning disabilities field, most researchers and educators believed that learning disabilities result from a **central nervous system dysfunction**—that is, from an underlying neurological problem (Hallahan & Mercer, 2001). New technologies have enhanced scientists' ability to assess brain activity more accurately. These technologies include magnetic resonance imaging (MRI), computerized axial tomographic (CAT) scans, and positron emission tomographic (PET) scans. Each technology has helped researchers understand more about the brain and how it functions, or does not function, when a student is trying to learn something.

To learn about social skill strategies, go to the Web Links module in Chapter 4 of the Companion Website for a link to Circle of Friends.

For example, the technique called functional magnetic resonance imaging (FMRI), reveals that students with and students without reading disabilities and dyslexia have significant differences in their brain activity and even in their brains' hemispheric structures (Shaywitz et al., 1998). Continued advances in these technologies should offer further definitive evidence of a neurological basis for students with learning disabilities. This growing evidence, however, still does not fully explain how individuals with learning disabilities acquire this neurological dysfunction.

Hereditary/Genetic Causes

As early as 1905, T. C. Thomas correlated a strong family history with "word blindness" (Light & Defries, 1995). Research on families continues to result in strong evidence that the tendency for severe reading disabilities is inherited. Similar evidence has been found in the area of speech and language disorders (Castles, Datta, Gayan, & Olson, 1999) and spelling disabilities.

Teratogenic/Pollutant Factors

There is solid evidence that pollutants and teratogens (aspects of the environment that cause developmental malformations in humans) cause learning disabilities. If a child ingests lead-based paint, the child's brain can be impaired; likewise, if a pregnant woman is exposed to lead from other sources, her fetus's brain also can be impaired. There also is clear evidence that, if a pregnant woman abuses alcohol or takes crack cocaine, she places her fetus's brain at great risk (Murphy-Brennan & Oei, 1999).

 When you read about mental retardation in Chapter 8, you will learn more about the effects of alcohol and drugs on a fetus.

Identifying the Prevalence

Specific learning disabilities continue to be the most prevalent of all disabilities. Approximately one-half of all students with disabilities served under IDEA have specific learning disabilities (U.S. Department of Education, 2001). This category also is rapidly expanding: Between the 1990–1991 school year and the 1999–2000 school year, the percentage of students ages 6 to 21 identified as having learning disabilities increased by 34 percent. And since 1975, the number of students identified with a learning disability has nearly tripled. Figure 4–2 illustrates how the prevalence of learning disabilities has increased relative to the two other highest-prevalence disability groups.

As you learned in Chapter 1, Asian/Pacific Islander, Hispanic students, and, to a lesser extent, white (non-Hispanic) students overall were underrepresented in special education; but African American students are overrepresented in all disability categories. To learn more about meeting the needs of students with learning disabilities from diverse backgrounds, please review Box 4–2.

This dramatic increase alarms certain professionals, causing some to fear that students are being overidentified with learning disabilities. By contrast, still others believe that the increased prevalence is reasonable, considering the newness of the field (Fuchs et al., 2001).

Researchers and educators have argued about the reasons for this dramatic increase. Some think better research since the 1980s has expanded educators' understanding of underachievement in reading. Others argue that educators' increased awareness about learning styles and challenges has prompted teachers and parents to refer more and more children for learning disability assessments.

To learn about the LD Summit and to review the issues facing the field, go to the Web Links module in Chapter 4 of the Companion Website.

How Do You Evaluate Students with Learning Disabilities?

Earlier in this chapter, you read about the inclusionary and exclusionary criteria that IDEA adopts. These, however, are not the only criteria that determine whether a student has a specific learning disability. Perhaps because they do not want to include students in the LD category who do not really have a learning disability, many states have added another criterion to

FIGURE 4–2

Prevalence growth

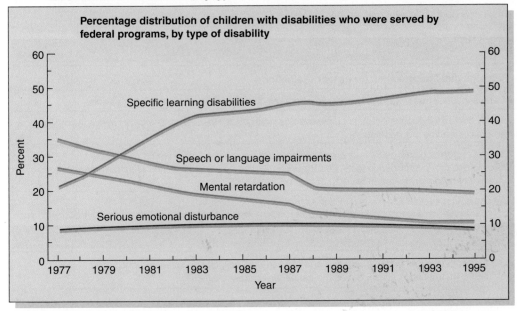

Children from birth to age 21 who were served by federally supported programs for students with disabilities, by type of disability: School years ending 1977–1995

Note: This analysis includes students who were served under Chapter 1 of the Education Consolidation and Improvement Act (ECIA) and Part B of the Individuals with Disabilities Education Act (IDEA). Data for 1995 are for children aged three to twenty-one.

Source: From U.S. Department of Education, Office of Special Education and Rehabilitative Services. (2001). *To assure the free appropriate public education of all children with disabilities: Twenty-third annual report to Congress on the implementation of the Individuals with Disabilities Education Act.* Washington, DC: Author; and National Center for Education Statistics. (2001). *Digest of Education Statistics.* Washington, DC: Author.

the two that IDEA sets out: The student must have a demonstrated discrepancy between perceived ability and actual achievement. This discrepancy is determined through a student's nondiscriminatory evaluation. In addition, the evaluation must demonstrate that a student has an educational need that is not, and presumably cannot be, met without special educational services.

Determining the Presence

Figure 4–3 shows the nondiscriminatory evaluation procedures for students with learning disabilities. Generally, students are referred for evaluation because, even after prereferral, they seem to have more ability than their academic performance in one or more subject areas indicates.

So a nondiscriminatory evaluation to determine whether a student has a specific learning disability must (1) adhere to the IDEA inclusionary and exclusionary criteria and (2) establish a discrepancy between the student's intellectual ability, as measured by an IQ test, and the student's achievement, as measured by a standardized achievement test.

In the field of learning disabilities, educators usually use the Wechsler Intelligence Scale for Children—III (WISC-III) (Psychological Corporation, 1999) to measure a student's cognitive abilities. This test has two scales: performance, which measures skills that relate closely to mathematics achievement; and verbal, which measures skills that relate closely to reading and written expression. When combined, performance and verbal scores yield a full-scale IQ score.

FIGURE 4–3

Evaluating whether or not a student has a learning disability

Nondiscriminatory Evaluation

Observation

Teacher and parents observe	Student appears frustrated with academic tasks and may have stopped trying.

Screening

Assessment measures	Findings that indicate need for further evaluation
Classroom work products	Work is inconsistent or generally poor. Teacher feels that student is capable of doing better.
Group intelligence tests	Usually the tests indicate average or above-average intelligence. However, tests may not reveal true ability because of reading requirements.
Group achievement tests	Student performs below peers in one or more areas or scores lower than would be expected according to group intelligence tests. Performance may not be a true reflection of achievement because of reading requirements.
Vision and hearing screening	Results do not explain academic difficulties.

Prereferral

Teacher implements suggestions from school-based team.	The student still experiences frustration and/or academic difficulty despite interventions. Ineffective instruction is eliminated as the cause for academic difficulty.

Referral

Nondiscriminatory evaluation procedures and standards

Assessment measures	Findings that suggest a learning disability
Individualized intelligence test	Student has average or above-average intelligence, so mental retardation is ruled out. Student may also have peaks and valleys in subtests. The multidisciplinary team makes sure that the test used is culturally fair for the student.
Individualized achievement test	A significant discrepancy (difference) exists between what the student is capable of learning (as measured by the intelligence test) and what the student has actually learned (as measured by the achievement test). The difference exists in one or more of the following areas: listening, thinking, reading, written language, mathematics. The team makes sure the test used is culturally fair for the student.
Behavior rating scale	The student's learning problems cannot be explained by the presence of emotional or behavioral problems.
Anecdotal records	The student's academic problems are not of short duration but have been apparent throughout time in school.
Curriculum-based assessment	The student is experiencing difficulty in one or more areas of the curriculum used by the local school district.
Direct observation	The student is experiencing difficulty and/or frustration in the classroom.
Ecological assessment	The student's environment does not cause the learning difficulty.
Portfolio assessment	The student's work is inconsistent and/or poor in specific subjects.

Nondiscriminatory multidisciplinary team determines that student has a learning disability and needs special education and related services.

Appropriate Education

By contrast, educators usually use the Wechsler Individualized Achievement Test (WIAT) (Psychological Corporation, 1992) to measure a student's achievement. This test reveals the student's academic skills in reading, written language, and mathematics.

To illustrate how educators determine whether or not a student has a severe discrepancy, let's consider the scores of a student named José; Figure 4–4 illustrates those scores. You will notice that José has peaks and valleys in his scores, suggesting the possibility of a severe discrepancy. (By comparison, students with mental retardation typically have flat profiles.) The first obvious discrepancy is a difference of 36 points (more than 2 standard deviations) between José's verbal and performance IQs. José also has a discrepancy of 2 standard deviations between his reading and mathematics scores, so some states would allow him to qualify for services based on this criterion alone.

In addition, José has an aptitude–achievement discrepancy between his full-scale IQ and his reading and written expression. So he does not qualify for special education services in mathematics based on his full-scale IQ. But if the state in which he lives allows educators to compare his verbal with his reading and written expression, he could qualify for services in reading but not written expression because of the discrepancy. And he could even qualify for services in mathematics when his math score is compared to his performance IQ, also because of the discrepancy.

Are you beginning to understand the need for more consistency in state definitions? Recently, some educators have advocated to abandon the discrepancy formula as the sole criterion for LD identification (Kavale, 2001).

Determining the Nature and Extent of General and Special Education and Related Services

There is still another problem with respect to evaluation to determine whether or not a student has a specific learning disability: Test items in typical standardized assessment measures (used during nondiscriminatory evaluation) generally do not reflect the content of a school's curriculum. That is why these tests, while useful for identifying students who have learning disabilities, are not useful for the purpose of developing IEPs (Erickson, Ysseldyke, & Thurlow, 1997).

Instead, educators often use a **curriculum-based assessment** to determine if a student has specific learning disabilities, develop IEPs, determine instructional effectiveness, and monitor ongoing student progress (Bauer & Shea, 1999). They can test all students in a particular school district, using the curriculum that all of them take in the general education track. They then can

FIGURE 4–4

José's nondiscriminatory evaluation scores

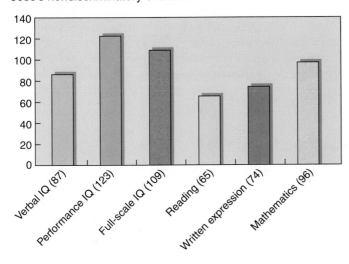

A thorough nondiscriminatory evaluation is critical to identifying specific disabilities and determining the educational needs of a child with a disability.

When we discuss elementary programs later in this chapter, we will describe how Mrs. Brumbley regularly collects data on Tony and his peers to ensure effective instruction.

determine the norm for all of those students—that is, the average range of scores. When they evaluate a particular student to decide whether or not the student has a specific learning disability, they compare the scores of the students as a group with the scores of the particular student. Figure 4–5 shows how this process works.

Curriculum-based assessment is criterion-referenced; that is, it is based on specific objectives from the students' curriculum. Students must receive a certain score for mastery (perhaps a 70 percent or better is a C). Teachers can administer the tests often and chart a student's progress; that approach helps the teacher know if the student is making progress and what to do to help the student make even more progress. Sometimes teachers find curriculum-based assessments in the manuals they use when they teach a certain course. Often, however, they must develop their own curriculum-based assessment instruments. When developing curriculum-based assessment, you will want to make sure that (1) the test items directly reflect the objectives emphasized in the curriculum, (2) the items are clearly stated, and (3) the time limit and level of mastery are reasonable.

How Do You Assure Progress in the General Curriculum?

Including Students

As illustrated in Figure 4–6 (page 116), students with learning disabilities have the highest rates of inclusion in general education classes when compared to students with other disabilities. Nevertheless, their inclusion cannot be effective unless educators use evidence-based strategies for instructing them. In this section, you will learn about one of those strategies.

Similarly, Box 4–2 (page 117) provides tips for increasing success for students with learning disabilities in the general education classroom.

Planning Universally Designed Learning

As you learned when reading about the characteristics of students with learning disabilities, two characteristics typically impede their progress in the general curriculum. These are their inabilities to read and to take charge of their own learning. Accordingly, effective teachers will instruct students on how to develop effective decoding and word recognition skills (to ensure that students have a good foundation for effective reading) and how to become active rather than passive learners. To teach these skills and active-learning habits, educators will augment their

FIGURE 4–5
Decision-making steps for identification of learning disabilities

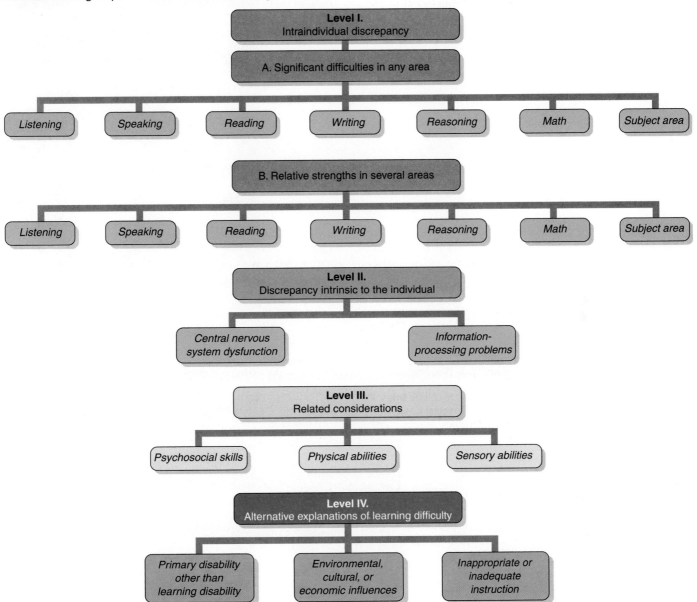

Source: From "An Operational Definition of Learning Disabilities Across the Age Span," in *Promoting Postsecondary Education for Students with Learning Disabilities: A Handbook for Practitioners* (pp. 74–75), by L. Brinckerhoff, S. Shaw, and J. McGuire, 1993, Austin, TX: PRO-ED. Copyright 1993 by PRO-ED. Adapted with permission.

instruction and curriculum with several strategies. We will discuss two of them: learning strategies and direct instruction (see Figure 4–7 on page 117).

Augmenting Instruction

One way to augment instruction for students with learning disabilities is to integrate **learning strategies** into teacher instruction and student learning. These strategies, developed by Don Deshler and his team of researchers at The University of Kansas Center for Research on Learning, help students with learning disabilities to learn independently and to generalize their skills and behaviors to new demands, especially those that become increasingly difficult to meet as the students progress from grade to grade (Deshler, 1998; Hock, Deshler, & Schumaker, 1999).

Learning strategies are perfectly suited to helping students meet the curricular goal of increasing their metacognitive skills—that is, the skills for learning how to learn that you read about previously in this chapter.

Effective teachers regularly take and chart student data, as this teacher is doing.

FIGURE 4–6

Educational placement of students with specific learning disabilities (1998–1999)

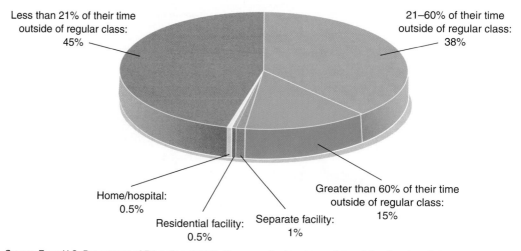

Less than 21% of their time outside of regular class: 45%

21–60% of their time outside of regular class: 38%

Home/hospital: 0.5%

Residential facility: 0.5%

Separate facility: 1%

Greater than 60% of their time outside of regular class: 15%

Source: From U.S. Department of Education. (2001). *To assure the free appropriate public education of all children with disabilities: Twenty-first annual report to Congress on the Implementation of the Individuals with Disabilities Education Act.* Washington, DC: Author.

Learning strategies work especially well for students who have learning disabilities in basic skill areas such as reading, language arts, writing, spelling, and math. Similarly, they are effective for specialized school tasks such as test-taking, paragraph writing, and lecture comprehension (Deshler, 1998). And they are effective in assisting students to comprehend content-oriented classes such as science and social studies.

The first step in using a learning strategy in any instructional area is to assess how well a student can perform a skill. The second step is to point out the benefit of using learning strategies:

Inclusion Tips

Box 4–2

	What You Might See	What You Might Be Tempted to Do	Alternate Responses	Ways to Include Peers in the Process
Behavior	She continually disrupts other students when she needs to be working independently on assignments.	Move her away from peers or put out of the class.	Check to be sure she understands and is able to do assignments. Develop a behavioral management plan to reinforce her on-task behavior.	Match her with a peer tutor when working on class assignments. Discuss with peers how to help her within the behavior management plan.
Social Interactions	She misinterprets social cues. She misinterprets facial gestures and/or verbal inflections.	Point out the misinterpretation and tell her how to do it "right."	Collaborate with the school counselor or resource teacher to plan ways to teach her needed social skills.	Establish a peer-partnership where the peer can practice specific social cues with her.
Educational Performance	Her work is inconsistent or generally poor.	Grade her down for poor or incomplete work.	Collaborate with special educators to teach her learning strategies. Provide extra time to complete.	Use age-appropriate materials with peer tutoring for reading assignments.
Classroom Attitudes	She easily gives up in areas of weakness to get out of work.	Excuse her from some assignments or reprimand her for her unwillingness to try.	Promote success with appropriate learning tasks that can be accomplished, and then provide her a strong reward system.	Give her opportunities to tutor others (peers or younger students) in areas of her success.

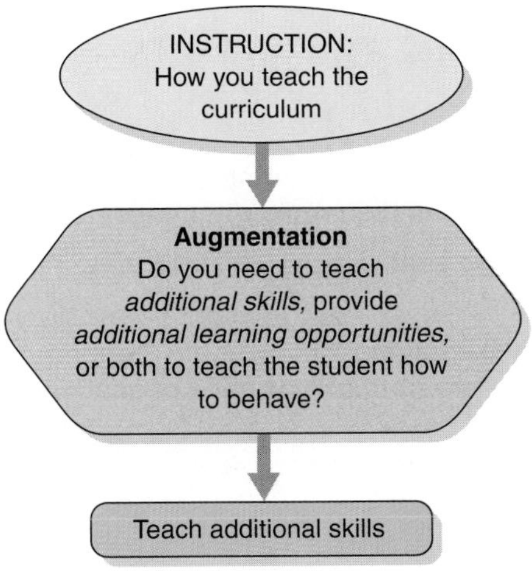

FIGURE 4–7
Instructional augmentation through learning strategies and direct instruction

INSTRUCTION: How you teach the curriculum

Augmentation
Do you need to teach *additional skills*, provide *additional learning opportunities*, or both to teach the student how to behave?

Teach additional skills

To learn about the work of the Center for Research on Learning at The University of Kansas, go to the Web Links module in Chapter 4 of the Companion Website.

namely, the student will ultimately learn how to learn on her own and succeed in and out of school. And the third step is to explain specifically what a student will be able to accomplish when she has learned the skill. Although it is not possible in this chapter to introduce you to all of the learning strategies, we can give you some examples.

Acquiring Information.   As you have read, students with learning disabilities have difficulty acquiring information; they do not have particularly strong metacognition skills. The *self-questioning strategy* is one of six strategies for acquiring information. The strategy requires students to create questions, predict answers to those questions, and search for the answers while they read a passage. Self-questioning is advantageous for four reasons:

▼ It requires students to actively interact with the material.

▼ It helps divide the passage into small, manageable units so the students can more easily acquire the information.

▼ It helps to promote intrinsic motivation for learning by having students identify their own reasons for reading a passage.

▼ It requires students to verbalize the information that they are learning, thereby enhancing their understanding and later recall of the information.

Even though the learning strategies are generally effective for many students, they may not be entirely effective for all. In particular, they may need to be modified or supplemented by other techniques, especially for students from diverse backgrounds, as Box 4–3 points out.

Box 4–3

Multicultural Considerations

Ecobehavioral Analysis Approach

Learning strategies can be effective tools but only if teachers directly relate them to their settings (schools and classrooms) and their students. To integrate the strategy into the general education middle or high school classroom, for example, teachers have to make them useful for all students, not simply the one identified with a learning disability. Similarly, to persuade a particular student to adopt a particular strategy, teachers have to make the strategy engaging to the student. This is especially true when students are from diverse backgrounds.

Over the past several years, researchers have identified two unique challenges in teaching students from diverse backgrounds: (1) designing a classroom in which teachers make instructional time challenging for students and (2) developing a classroom atmosphere of mutual understanding and accommodation. The questions for any general or special educator are "How do I design a classroom environment that will optimize learning? What are the most crucial instructional variables that are likely to affect student outcomes?"

These questions are important because there is evidence that the ecological arrangements of classrooms (that is, their physical attributes) and the delivery of instructional practices in classrooms (that is, how teachers deliver their course materials) can accelerate or decelerate students' academic progress and affect their overall rate of academic development. This is especially true for students from diverse backgrounds.

Taking Diversity into Account for Progress in the General Curriculum

1. How do you distinguish instructional practices that promote low as well as high rates of engagement?

2. What can you do to ensure engaging instruction for all students?

3. Do academic interventions that promote higher engagement also promote higher rates of academic growth? If so, why?

To answer these questions online, go to the Multicultural Considerations module in Chapter 4 of the Companion Website.

Storing and Remembering. Students with learning disabilities also have difficulty recalling what they have read or mastered earlier. To help them, teachers are instructing their students to use organizational strategies. The purpose of these strategies is to help students understand the direction they are taking when they are trying to learn and later recall information. Advanced organizers are especially helpful (Lenz, Alley, & Schumaker, 1987). The teacher basically "telegraphs" the content of a particular lesson using the following steps:

▼ Teachers instruct their students in how to listen for and use the advance organizer. For example, students must complete a worksheet as they listen to the teacher introduce each part.

▼ After using the worksheet, the teacher and students discuss the effectiveness of its use and how and when it might be used in various academic classes.

▼ Before presenting an advanced organizer, the teacher cues the students that it is going to be used.

One organizer is a *graphic organizer*. Sometimes referred to as *webs*, *maps*, or *concept diagrams*, graphic organizers assist students to (1) identify key concepts and subconcepts, (2) compare and contrast information, and (3) relate cause to effect (Friend & Bursuck, 2002; Woodward & Baxter, 1997). By enabling students to visualize information in an organized fashion, graphic organizers help them grasp key information. The styles of graphic organizers vary depending on concepts being taught and the maturity of the students. Generally, teachers and students brainstorm together to identify one or more effective models.

You will read more about learning strategies and their effects when we describe Chase Middle School.

Augmenting Curriculum

One way to augment the curriculum for students with learning disabilities is to use Direct Instruction (DI). The principles of DI (Engelmann, 1991) are as follows:

1. The student does not first learn something in a concrete singular sense and then generalize to some larger set.
2. Teachers can instruct generalizations explicitly and systematically by using examples that communicate a critical sameness among sets of examples.
3. Generalization represents efficiency.

The hallmark of DI is that it relies on a scripted lesson for a particular subject; the scripted lesson must have been tested and retested to ensure that students grasp the lesson the first time around. Thus, DI depends on the teacher's having a good curriculum in the first place (Tarver, 1999), and the scripted lesson is simply a time-tested way of teaching the content. Take a look at Box 4–4 to learn how a parent became a teacher and now uses DI for her students.

A variety of DI programs are available for teaching language, reading, spelling, writing, science, and mathematics, whether one on one, in small groups of students, or in larger groups of students, and whether in general or special education classes. Each program describes both the content and the procedures used to teach the information effectively. Increasingly, these programs are often accompanied by software-based applications to expand students' understanding.

Accordingly, each curriculum (subject content) provides (1) a carefully crafted sequence of tasks, (2) logical formats embedded in teacher-student communication that facilitate students' understanding of concepts and relationships, and (3) a careful arrangement of practice and ongoing assessments of learning.

For example, the *Reading Mastery* curriculum provides many examples of generalizations that students learn en route to becoming independent readers. An early lesson might have 3 minutes on pronouncing new sounds, 3 minutes on reading new sounds, 5 minutes on reading words "the slow way" (sounding them out), 5 minutes on reading old words "the fast way" (blending), and then 5 minutes of review. Later lessons work on many of the same strands, adding more concepts or addressing harder problems or examples. This organization holds students' attention and helps them retain knowledge from one day, week, and month to the next.

As the students progress through the curriculum, the teacher moves gradually from a teacher-guided to a student-guided format. The teacher's delivery techniques and classroom management procedures include rapid pacing, choral group responding mixed with individual turns, corrective

Box 4–4

Making a Difference

Parents as Teachers

Being the parent of a typically developing child has its rewards as well as challenges. A parent of a child with a disability has similar experiences, but at times the challenges can demand an unusual amount of attention and energy.

Mary can certainly attest to the "unusual attention and energy" part of being a parent. Her sons, Matt and Patrick, are both high school graduates and are both men with learning disabilities. Matt, age 26, is currently a police officer in Oregon, and Patrick, age 20, is a sophomore at Boise State University in Idaho.

Mary herself is co-director of A+ Adams & Associates, Inc., a private tutoring and assessment practice in Boise. Mary wasn't always the co-director; when her kids were young she was a stay-at-home mom. It wasn't until Matt had academic trouble in school that Mary started to think about altering her career path.

"Matt always struggled when it came to reading. We enrolled him in several remedial programs. The programs may have helped his self-esteem but they didn't help his reading." While in elementary school, Matt was found to have dyslexia. Concerned about the restrictive nature of the special education program at Matt's school, Mary worked hard to keep him in the general education classroom. She soon found out, however, that if Matt were to remain there, he would need help.

Mary hit the books and started to learn more about the various reading approaches that might help Matt. She met with reading specialists in the area and along the way met her present business partner, Jane. Jane shared with her the components of DI, and Mary began working with Matt and his younger brother. Patrick wasn't tested by the school, but Jane's assessment found him to have dyslexia as well. Not satisfied with the information she had, Mary decided to return to school, enrolling at Boise State University to get a master's degree in education with an emphasis in reading.

When Mary completed her degree, she went into business with Jane to offer support for children such as hers in the Boise community. DI remains at the heart of their practice as they work with identified and nonidentified children with learning disabilities. Their clients are varied, coming from public, parochial, and private schools in the area and ranging in age from 6 to 60.

Mary's work no longer focuses simply on the beginning reader. Instead, she now spends an equal amount of remedial work with high school students who are preparing for the ACT or SAT college entrance exams. Here, she employs a variety of learning strategies to assist with reading and test preparation. This is hard work, but Mary sees it as a calling. She is the parent of two young men with learning disabilities for a reason, and, with her skills, she hopes to make a difference.

To learn more about Direct Instruction, go to the Web Links module in Chapter 4 of the Companion Website.

feedback and reteaching, reinforcement, and review and practice. Frequent tests of students' proficiency help teachers determine students' levels of mastery, which of their skills need additional attention, and the quality of the teachers' instruction.

Because DI is intended for all students, lessons address different individual and cultural learning preferences, including visual, auditory, oral, and kinesthetic components. This comprehensive approach ensures that all children have a fair chance of being understood and becoming proficient. It also means that each child's knowledge is broader. For example, the main reading curriculum, *Reading Mastery*, combines instruction on decoding and comprehension, story reading, spelling, and writing.

Collaborating to Meet Students' Needs

Students with learning disabilities need teachers who will work together on their behalf (Robinson, 1999). Including parents such as Mary (see Box 4–4) as part of this cooperative interaction is critical as well. To work together effectively, teachers must have time together to plan, share information, and evaluate their instruction. Across the country, districts have modified class schedules to allow for district-wide planning. For example, adding 20 minutes to a school day makes it possible for teachers to have a half-day planning session (with early release for students) at least once every two weeks. During these planning days, teachers can

▼ Share information about particular students and determine areas of the students' difficulty

▼ Examine the cause of students' behavior

▼ Brainstorm possible solutions and interventions

▼ Select and implement an intervention

▼ Plan for subsequent evaluation and future implementation

Collaboration is more than an ideal and a goal; it also is a technique, and you will find tips on how to collaborate in Box 4–5.

To keep collaboration effective, general and special educators need to celebrate their achievements, reevaluate their collaborations, create ways to collaborate still more effectively, and monitor their collaborations. Many teachers neglect the important task of celebrating their accomplishments. For example, two teams at one elementary school met together for lunch once a month for the specific purpose of sharing successes. The positive focus of these meetings increased their motivation and encouraged new ideas for collaboration.

Similarly, team members need to take time to reevaluate their goals and make sure that their responsibilities are divided equitably (Friend & Bursuck, 2002). Feedback is also crucial for team success. A third party who occasionally observes team interactions can bring new insights.

What Can You Learn from Others Who Teach Students with Learning Disabilities?

Learning for the Early Childhood Years: Embedded Learning Opportunities in Nashville, Tennessee

For children from birth to age 3 who have or are at risk of having a learning disability or other disabilities, there is literally no substitute for early intervention. Recently, numerous early childhood special educators have recommended incorporating instruction into these children's daily activities by using a strategy called *embedded learning opportunities* (ELO) (Davis, Kilgo, & Gamel-McCormick, 1998).

This strategy gives children opportunities to "practice individual goals and objectives that are included within an activity or event in a manner that expands, modifies or adapts the activity/event while remaining meaningful and interesting to children" (Bricker, Pretti-Frontczak, & McComas, 1998, p. 13). While bathing, for example, children can learn skills to develop their communication (e.g., using words to label bath objects), cognitive (e.g., finding submerged objects), motor (e.g., picking up objects), and adaptive (e.g., washing hands and face) abilities. When teachers, caregivers, and therapists embed children's goals and objectives into the children's daily activities, they build on the children's interest and increase their motivation (Hemmeter & Grisham-Brown, 1997).

The ELO approach is a promising intervention strategy because it

▼ Provides children with lots of practice within the context of their daily activities and events

▼ Can be used in inclusive environments

▼ Capitalizes on a child's interest and motivation

▼ Is available to parents, teachers, therapists, and peers

▼ Is compatible with a wide range of curricular models (Bricker et al., 1998)

One example of an effective ELO program derives from a Nashville child-care program. The program enrolls 12 3- to 4-year-old children and provides them with a single lead teacher. Among the children are several who have learning disabilities, including Alex. Alex is 4 years old and has moderate delays in the areas of expressive language and speech; because he also has cerebral palsy, he has delays in his gross- and fine-motor and cognitive and social development. In his classroom, the children's daily activities include a large-group circle as an opening activity for the day and as a transition between outdoor play and lunch; time focused on dramatic play, preliteracy, and hands-on science and computer; outdoor play; lunch; and self-care and cleanup.

Using the ELO model, Alex's teacher created opportunities for him to place materials in centers (e.g., he placed a pitcher in the snack center). Then she added a task as a requirement for his center participation (e.g., he had to pour paints from one container to another in the art corner) and provided verbal prompts, models, and physical guidance during play (e.g., guided his pouring between containers during water-table play).

Box 4—5

Collaboration Tips

The Power of 2: A Medium for Information and Collaboration

It took only a few weeks, but Tony Lavender and his parents quickly learned that his middle school is not a simple extension of his elementary school. On paper he has merely moved from fifth grade to sixth and into a school with students in the seventh and eighth grades. But the change in reality is often dramatic for individuals with learning problems, as it was for Tony.

All too often, the challenge in middle school is to foster interaction and collaboration among content-oriented teachers. Mrs. Brumbley, Tony's advocate in elementary school, wasn't there to foster interaction between the special and general education teachers. Similarly, Tony's middle school didn't provide the supportive environment in which Tony had thrived. Instead, teachers worked independently and concentrated on their content-based subjects, offering minimal accommodations and modifications for students such as Tony. For students who could not succeed in this environment, separate pullout classes were available; but Tony's earlier successes negated his need for such intensive specialized support. Instead, as is the case in many middle and secondary environments throughout the country, Tony was caught between a general education classroom that didn't offer enough support and a special education environment that was too restrictive for his needs.

Can we fault Tony's teachers? Some might argue yes, but all too often these professionals lack the basic skills to meet the specific needs of individuals with disabilities. Their teacher preparation and related in-service activities often fail to develop instructional skills that allow them to offer effective modifications and accommodation for all students. Focus on content often leaves limited time for developing collaborative skills to meet the needs of diverse learners. Similarly, limited professional development opportunities generally focus on content-specific needs (i.e., teaching to state and national curriculum standards) rather than identifying ways to meet the learning and behavioral needs of students with disabilities. The outcome? Tony and his peers are left in need of critical instructional support.

How do we address this need? As we have already witnessed, one way to create positive outcomes is to provide middle and high school teachers with effective collaborative skills. Through collaboration, content-oriented teachers can use the expertise of special educators and related education professionals in their general education classrooms. What about the time factor and the limited professional development opportunities? A recent web-based tool called the Power of 2 helps teachers to address their information deficiencies in a flexible manner.

For example, let's consider "Sally," Tony's special education teacher this year. Over the past several years,

Sally has become frustrated with several of Tony's teachers. "John," his social studies teacher, has been an especially challenging individual to interact with. John has resisted changing what he does because he feels it would take away from the majority of students and limit the amount of content he needs to cover. Sally has heard about the Power of 2 and invites John to visit the site one day after school. Together, they type in the URL, http://www.powerof2.org, and watch as a brightly colored home page with a matrix that includes various descriptors appears. John immediately sees the "Resource" section and suggests further investigation.

Once there, they look at a list of resources organized under the headings "elementary," "middle," and "high school." Without much hesitation, John selects "middle school" and is pleased to find a list of instructional modifications organized under content topics as well as helpful links to check out.

Sally suggests they review how to modify essay tests when teaching American history. There they find a test modified by breaking multipart questions down to separate questions and using number cues to tell students how many answers are expected. Also, the example has simplified vocabulary, reduced the number of questions, and given definitions with the aim of having the student provide the terms. Sally and John continue their exploration, and John begins to recognize the accommodations he easily could put into place for Tony and his classmates without jeopardizing content.

Three hours later, Sally and John reluctantly abandon the computer. They have read and printed out four accommodation plans with adaptations for students with varying disabilities and some data collection forms. They find that they really like the descriptions of how the teachers define their roles and responsibilities in the cotaught classroom and how they handle coscheduling. They have enjoyed the video presentations of some classroom activities. In fact, John is impressed and interested in getting more how-to information on classwide peer tutoring.

Putting These Tips to Work for Progress in the General Curriculum

1. Who are the collaborators?

2. What are the challenges?

3. What can the team do?

4. What are the results?

To answer these questions online and learn more about these ideas and concepts, go to the Collaboration Tips module in Chapter 4 of the Companion Website.

In and of themselves, these activities do not guarantee that Alex or other children will make progress on their learning objectives, even when the activities are fun and engaging for them. Instead, teachers need to pair these learning opportunities with instruction that lets the children know what they need to do, how a correct response looks and feels, what the correct response is, and reassurance that a response will result in a positive outcome.

The ELO approach holds that teachable moments can be created and, when they are, need to be recognized and used to enhance the child's developmental progress. Thus, teachers use ELO instruction to provide fun, enjoyable, and interesting activities for young children.

What difference does all this make for children? A number of studies have examined the effects of embedding different intervention strategies and children's goals and objectives into their daily activities and routines (e.g., Sewell, Collins, & Hemmeter, 1998). The results of these studies show that instruction that is embedded in activities that are meaningful to the children can be an effective tool for addressing their needs.

Learning for the Elementary Years: Maple Elementary School, Springfield, Oregon

As you have learned, Direct Instruction can be an especially useful instructional intervention for students with learning disabilities. Just consider what happened when Tony's teacher, Susan Brumbley, decided to integrate it into her classroom instruction more than 12 years ago. When she started working at Maple Elementary School, "it was a **whole-language** school," explains Susan. "So I decided to break the mold and use DI materials, which ended up reintegrating kids into the regular classroom at a faster clip."

At a school where nearly 8 out of every 10 kids come from a family at or below the poverty level, altering students' reading abilities has been quite a challenge. Maple Elementary also has a population of students with significant turnover: Many enter and leave throughout the course of the academic year.

Under a **pullout model** that takes some students out of their homerooms and brings them to her special education resource room, students come to Susan for an hour at a time to learn to read. There, they are organized into groups and receive DI from her and her two paraprofessionals. While adhering to the principles of DI, Susan admits she has her own system for some things: "I often use more correction procedures than the program asks for. I keep data on every group and keep track of individual errors. This way I analyze where the breakdown occurs and see the pattern that exists. Then the next day I can reteach the skill in a 3-minute review or more if necessary."

Students need to know that hard work has its benefits; here a Reading Medal is awarded in a special ceremony.

Technology Tips

Box 4—6

Evaluating Educational Software for Students with Learning Disabilities

Never before have so many students with learning disabilities used computer software so often as in the early years of this century. Unfortunately, this doesn't necessarily equate to further learning because, too often, teachers and families do not consider students' specific educational needs and whether the software instruction truly meets those needs.

What Is the Technology?

It's the ability to categorize and evaluate software for its instructional benefit to students with disabilities. Fortunately, steps are being taken to consider ways of evaluating educational software for special education. Over the past decade, Higgins and Boone (2001) have developed a number of instruments to use when considering software applications. The flowchart on page 125 is a suggested path for the evaluation of education software for students with disabilities.

What Do You Do with It?

When seeking to use a software application to assist a student's learning, teachers and families should first consider whether the software meets the student's needs. They should access a free trial version of the software program by dialing the software company website (for download purposes) or by telephoning the

company directly to obtain a trial version. Next, they should review the application with specific purposes in mind, following the flowchart, and then decide whether to buy the software and use it as is or modify or supplement it.

Putting Software Evaluation to Work for Progress in the General Curriculum

1. Does the software application support the instruction conducted in the general education classroom?

2. Does the software application offer interactive multimedia components to capture and sustain the student's attention?

3. Is the software application flexible for the specific learning needs of an individual with learning disabilities? Does the application allow the teacher or parent to modify the program levels while also keeping track of the student's progress?

4. Does the software application help the student progress in the general curriculum?

To answer these questions online, review online software evaluation data bases, and learn more about software features that assist students with learning disabilities, go to the Technology Tips module in Chapter 4 of the Companion Website.

To see a brief video of Tony telling some of his favorite jokes, go to the Cases module in Chapter 4 of the Companion Website.

Susan also stresses that the success of her program involves a mandatory homework program. She regularly sends copies of the stories the students are reading to their parents and asks the parents to listen to their child read the stories, sign a form that proves they have done so, and make sure their son or daughter returns this signed sheet daily. This collaborative effort between school and home is successful because students now are reading in both places. On Fridays, she offers rewards to students who have successfully completed all homework over the course of the week.

Susan has also instituted an after-school reading program for students who need additional reading practice or help in writing, spelling, and mathematics. This voluntary program has flourished and further assists students to close the gap in their reading delays. Susan has been so successful that most of her students reenter their general education reading groups with abilities that exceed those of most low-achieving students. In fact, some students who were initially identified as having a learning disability are no longer in need of special education services at the time of their 3-year special education reevaluation.

Simply put, Tony and his peers have benefited tremendously from Susan's tireless efforts over the past 12 years at Maple Elementary. The key was not one person but a team at school and a team at home. Collaborating, these team members offered Tony and his class-

Box 4–6 (Cont.)

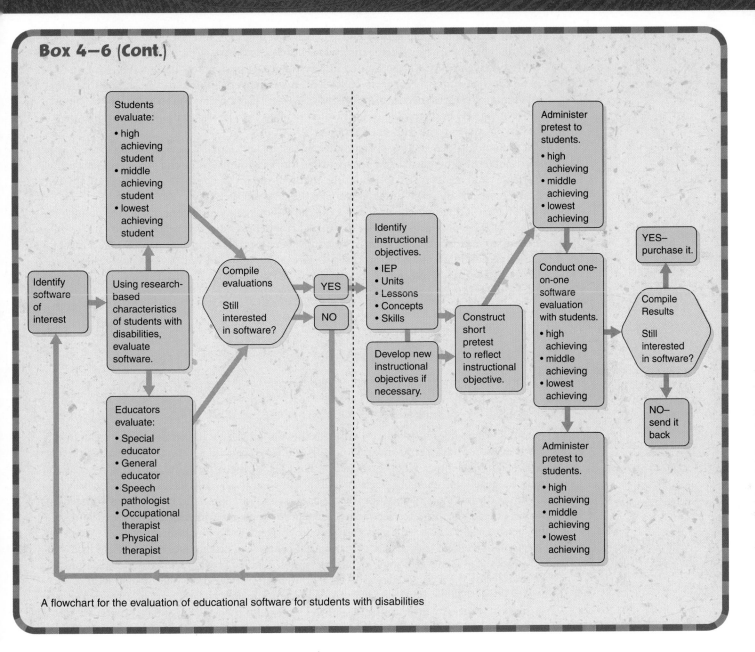

A flowchart for the evaluation of educational software for students with disabilities

mates the support, structure, and reinforcement he needed to succeed. More important, they have provided him with the tools to succeed in the general curriculum.

Among the tools available to teachers and students in all grades are various kinds of software. One of the challenges is to determine which kind is appropriate and which is not. Box 4–6 provides tips on how to evaluate software.

Learning for the Middle and Secondary Years: Chase Middle School, Topeka, Kansas

Incorporating learning strategies into the classroom takes time and effort. One school in Topeka, Kansas, has successfully incorporated an after-school program based on strategies and tutoring. The program at Chase Middle School, where 85 percent of the students are from economically disadvantaged families, has generated tremendous community interest, with many adults, from the community volunteering to be tutors. It also attracts the students: 100 of the 500 students at the school have applied for the limited number of spaces in the program.

The program currently supports 26 students a week, averaging 18 students a night. Students must commit to at least two tutoring sessions a week. Tutoring runs from 3 P.M. to 4 P.M. Monday through Thursday in the school library, which is a large, quiet space with plenty of tables for students and tutors to break into small groups.

"It's amazing to see 20 kids working with 10 adults and actually working," said Cheryl Kohr, lead tutor for the program. Cheryl is responsible for the administrative end of the program: scheduling tutors and students, troubleshooting, following up on student absences, selecting students for the program—all of the things that make the program successful.

"It's a multifaceted program," Cheryl explains. "You're teaching content. You're doing mentoring. You're becoming an advocate for the kid. You're teaching organization skills. You're helping them do their homework. You're teaching specific strategies. Sometimes you're just being there while a child works." The tutoring program employs a variety of the learning strategies created by the Center for Research on Learning at The University of Kansas. Box 4–7 illustrates one of these, the sentence writing strategy.

Learning for the Transitional and Postsecondary Years: Mitchell College's Learning Resource Center, New London, Connecticut

There is a simple rule that students with learning disabilities should follow as they head toward their transitional and postsecondary programs and need specialized services: the earlier, the better. Even in elementary school, teachers should begin discovering and encouraging students' strengths. Teachers should talk with students about what they would like to be and do when they grow up and what must happen for them to achieve their goals. And by arranging for students who are in secondary and postsecondary programs to have mentors who share career interests or who are successful adults with learning disabilities, teachers can help students realize that they, too, should have high expectations for themselves and lead productive and inclusive lives.

Despite the best efforts of some elementary and secondary programs, however, and despite the fact that during the past decade, colleges and universities have increased their support services for individuals with disabilities to assist them in their transition to and through two- or four-year institutions, students with learning disabilities struggle in their postsecondary programs.

Remember Rachel from Box 4–1? She began attending Mitchell College in the fall of 1997. The college is a traditional institution of higher education with two- and four-year degree programs and a well-earned reputation for supporting students with learning disabilities. The cornerstone of Mitchell's program to assist students to learn more effectively and efficiently is the Learning Resource Center (LRC), which is part of a college-wide Academic Success Center (ASC).

The LRC's staff is comprised of learning specialists who have specific training to work with students who have difficulties in reading, mathematics, writing, organization, and information processing. Students can access the LRC and its staff according to their level of needs.

For example, all students with disabilities can use *entitled support*, a basic level of support called Level 3. This system allows students to come and receive support at any time at the ASC or LRC. Support might include an ASC content tutor or a writing specialist.

More than that, the LRC provides learning specialists for students requiring more individualized attention. Students in Level 2, the *enhanced support* level, meet with an assigned learning specialist at least twice a week. The specialist helps the students acquire strategies to improve their study skills, retain what they have learned, and organize their learning tasks.

Comprehensive, or Level 1, support is available to students who need more targeted interventions. At this level, students meet with a learning specialist four times a week, developing effective study skills and organizational strategies, including how to use a graphic organizer or a Palm

Box 4-7

Into Practice

Sentence Writing Strategy

As with all the learning strategies developed by the Center for Research on Learning, students need to learn the *sentence writing strategy* so that they use it automatically. Just as teachers use repetition to teach beginning readers to master basic sound-symbol relationships, so they instruct older students to master task-specific learning strategies through highly structured practice. Practice, practice, and practice again: That is how teachers help students use the sentence writing strategy automatically.

Teachers instruct students in how to use the strategy by pretesting them to measure each student's sentence-writing skills. Then the teachers deliver the strategy in four parts, over and over again.

- *Part 1.* They teach the skills involved in writing simple sentences.
- *Part 2.* They teach the skills involved in writing compound sentences and require their students to integrate those skills with the previously taught skills for writing simple sentences.
- *Part 3.* They teach their students how to write complex sentences and how to integrate those skills with the previously taught skills for writing simple and compound sentences.
- *Part 4.* They teach their students how to write compound-complex sentences and how to integrate those skills with the three previously taught skills.

Students must reach mastery in one part of the four parts before moving to the next. Thus, the instruction is a building process whereby students are required to integrate new skills with previously learned skills.

This four-part instruction can be adapted to a variety of needs. For example, a student can receive instruction in all four parts in a large block of time (e.g., 30 minutes per day for 9 or 10 weeks). Alterna-

tively, teachers can provide instruction in a single part and then shift to other strategies as students master that single part.

At some later time the student may return to instruction in the sentence writing strategy to learn additional sentence types. For example, some teachers at Chase Middle School prefer to teach Parts 1 and 2 in the seventh grade, Part 3 in the eighth grade, and Part 4 in the ninth grade.

The strategy will not work unless the teachers use the four parts in sequence. Although students can write simple sentences, they must go through the simple sentence instruction because it provides them with vocabulary and a knowledge base upon which subsequent parts build. The foundation provided in the simple sentence instruction is critical for success in the other parts, and each subsequent part logically builds on previous instruction.

Putting These Strategies to Work for Progress in the General Curriculum

1. How might one of Tony's content-oriented teachers integrate this strategy into his or her classroom?

2. What are the challenges of integrating this strategy?

3. How can collaboration between the special and general education teacher assist this implementation? How could Bob or Chris help at home?

To answer these questions online and learn more about these strategies, go to the Into Practice module in Chapter 4 of the Companion Website.

Pilot. Some students also learn how to develop interpersonal and social skills because the absence of these skills complicates students' learning and overall development.

Another part of Mitchell's success involves an informed and uniquely trained faculty and campus community. Dr. Peter Troiano, an assistant dean and director of the Learning Resource Center, regularly informs college faculty and staff about the academic accommodations that students with disabilities need to succeed. While often focusing on new faculty during the fall of each academic year, Dr. Troiano also counsels veteran faculty who seek to update their skills in meeting the academic needs of their entire student body. Rachel has commented that her

To learn more about Mitchell College, go to the Web Links module in Chapter 4 of the Companion Website for a link to Mitchell's website.

success depends on faculty members who were willing and able to modify their instruction and assignments to meet her learning needs, thereby allowing her to focus on the content and to control her learning instead of relying on a learning specialist or the LRC for support.

A Vision for Tony's Future

Tony has been benefiting from excellent teaching during his entire school career. He is now a rising senior and has only one year left in public school. Just what his future is, no one knows. But his school career makes it bright. All of his teachers have consistently used the learning strategies approach. As he entered his adolescence, his academic challenges continued, but they were aggravated by the usual social and behavioral challenges that any student faces in those difficult years.

That is why he, his teachers, and his parents focused so much on developing his social skills. Among those skills were those that helped him overcome his shyness; make sure that his quick wit did not become biting and sarcastic; and assure that he has continued success as the school's master of ceremonies and as an actor and develop the self-confidence and the skills to confront the conflicts that will arise between him, his peers, and his parents and teachers. In everything that he, his family, and teachers did, whether in the realm of academics or social skills, they tried to find the answer to these questions: What lights Tony's fire? What makes his innate talents and goodness shine?

As they are for many peers his age, television and video games were a constant distraction for Tony and too often an escape from confronting his fears and ignoring his weaknesses. Tony, though, was no different from many of his classmates, so his involvement in many of the activities in his school became the means to an end. Those activities were theatrical: being an MC and a standup comedian and acting in school plays. They also included his participation on the school debate team. Is it too unrealistic to expect Tony to be the next Adam Sandler or David Letterman? The chances of that are slim, for those jobs are few and the competition intense. However, his chances of being a showman of one kind or another or of attending law school and becoming a trial lawyer are not at all slim. Building on his interests and strengths, and using research-based techniques for teaching, can make a huge difference in his life.

What Would You Recommend?

1. How would you plan Tony's transition from high school to college?
2. How would you support his success in reading to content comprehension in academic subject areas?
3. How would you help ensure that the successes of the resource room are continued in the general education classroom?
4. How would you further include Tony's parents in his academic success as part of a collaborative team as he transitions out of high school?

Summary

How Do You Recognize Students with Learning Disabilities?

▼ IDEA has inclusionary and exclusionary criteria for determining whether a student has a learning disability. There is controversy about the IDEA criteria; a group of professionals has recommended a different approach.

▼ Each state has criteria for identifying these students, which usually include three parts: a severe discrepancy between demonstrated ability and actual achievement, exclusion of other factors, and demonstrated need for special services.

▼ Students with learning disabilities are a heterogeneous population with varied learning, behavioral, and social characteristics.

- Students with learning disabilities often have difficulties with social skills; they have poor self-concepts and self-esteem. Years of frustration and failure can lead to the development of learned helplessness, when the individual looks externally for someone or something to complete the task or provide direction.
- Approximately 50 percent of all students with disabilities have learning disabilities.
- Research suggests that learning disabilities may be caused by central nervous system dysfunction that results in deficits in visual-spatial processing and phonological awareness.

How Do You Evaluate Students with Learning Disabilities?

- Nondiscriminatory evaluation includes the use of standardized intelligence and achievement tests to determine discrepancy.
- Curriculum-based assessment can be norm-referenced or criterion-referenced.

How Do You Assure Progress in the General Curriculum?

- Students with learning disabilities are the most likely group of students to be included in general education programs.
- Students with learning disabilities often require explicit instruction in a structured environment with augmented and adapted curricula. With the right support, students with learning disabilities can be successful in the general education curriculum without significant adaptations.
- Adapting the curriculum through learning strategies can teach students how to learn and thus empower them in school and life. Learning strategies should be incorporated across student instruction.

- Direct Instruction, an example of altering instruction, provides explicit structured instruction in a teacher-directed format for student learning.
- Collaboration can only be successful when all parties agree to dedicate time on a periodic basis. Finding time takes support from teachers and building leadership.

What Can You Learn from Others Who Teach Students with Learning Disabilities?

- A model of early intervention embeds learning activities in everyday activities, thus constantly teaching young children through the course of a normal day.
- Direct Instruction has been used for the past 12 years at Maple Elementary School in Springfield, Oregon, to teach reading skills to a diverse group of learners from poor economic and learning backgrounds.
- Effective writing skills can be successfully taught to middle and high school students using the sentence writing strategy.
- Colleges and universities are increasingly offering support services to assist students with learning disabilities to succeed in the postsecondary environment. Some of these accommodations include test accommodations, strategy instruction to help students develop learning tools, and anchored or problem-based learning to assist students in generalizing meaningful skills.

Council for Exceptional Children   PRAXIS

To find out how and where this chapter content connects to the CEC Professional Standards and the Praxis™ Standards, go to the Standards Connection module in Chapter 4 of the Companion Website. A comprehensive matrix aligning CEC Professional Standards, Praxis™ Standards, and INTASC principles to the entire text, is available in the Appendix and on the Companion Website.

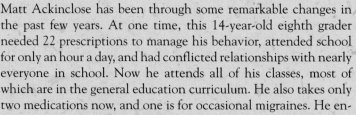

Chapter 5

Who Is Matthew Ackinclose?

Matt Ackinclose has been through some remarkable changes in the past few years. At one time, this 14-year-old eighth grader needed 22 prescriptions to manage his behavior, attended school for only an hour a day, and had conflicted relationships with nearly everyone in school. Now he attends all of his classes, most of which are in the general education curriculum. He also takes only two medications now, and one is for occasional migraines. He enjoys positive relationships with his school's administrators and faculty and with his peers. He is earning As and Bs in school and has a 99.5-percent average in his general education math class!

Matt's resiliency—his ability to overcome emotional and behavioral challenges—is a result of his determination and the supportive relationships he has with his mother, his therapist/social worker, and a special education teacher, among others. Those relationships and outcomes were hard to come by.

During Matt's early years, professionals routinely told his mother, Laura, to place him in a residential setting, but she refused. She knew in her heart that being separated from Matt was not the answer.

Matt's behavioral challenges began when he was just an infant. One day, when he was 7 months old, his face was bloody when his mother picked him up from daycare. Matt had banged his head on the crib and on the wall at the center repeatedly before a teacher could get to him. That was when Laura knew Matt needed help. She began a long search for someone: a psychologist, a physician, a teacher—anyone who could meet her son's needs.

In the meantime, Laura contrived new ways to keep Matt safe in his home environment. Unfortunately, one Halloween all of her precautionary measures failed. Matt got out of the house when some kids came to the door trick-or-treating. When Laura finally found him, he was standing in a nearby creek. She still remembers fearing that if she tried to get close to him, he would run, slip under the water, and drown or badly injure himself. At about this time he also threatened to kill Laura and himself; he was only 5 years old. Clearly, Matt was a boy in pain.

Instead of recognizing that Matt and Laura were struggling to overcome a serious disability, professionals criticized Laura's parenting. "They can make you feel like a war criminal!" Laura says of the treatment she received from teachers and other professionals who wanted to blame her for Matt's disability.

Laura saw the strengths in Matt that others were not willing to see: his intelligence, his persistence, his sensitivity. She was alone in her point of view until she made a fortuitous phone call one day six years ago to social worker Rebecca Hall.

Rebecca sensed that what Matt needed most was a caring relationship with someone he could trust, someone who would connect with him and believe in his potential,

someone who would not be intimidated by his words or behaviors, someone who would give him a sense of personal power by offering him choices, and someone who would work with him and not fight against him. She was determined to be that person.

Rather than focusing on Matt's deficits, Rebecca looked for his strengths. To Matt, she asked, "What do you do well? When do you feel successful?" She asked Laura about the times when Matt behaved in a way she liked. Then she worked with Matt and Laura to increase those positive behaviors. Rebecca taught Matt how much he had to offer others and also worked with him on problem-solving skills. She would ask, "What's the problem? What can be done to fix it? What would you be willing to do instead?"

Despite the fact that Matt's behaviors were improving, he and Laura still had difficulty finding a teacher who was willing to work with him until they found Charlotte Hott, a special education teacher. Charlotte's history with Matt began on a positive note when Rebecca placed a call to her and asked if Matt could enroll in her class. Charlotte replied without hesitation over the speaker phone, "I would love to have him!" Matt heard her response and realized that this teacher would care about him.

Charlotte welcomed Matt into her classroom. She built on the foundations of trust and strength-based interventions already in place, and she encouraged Matt and Laura through consistent, positive communication. Charlotte tailored her teaching approach to Matt's individual needs and realized, as Rebecca did, that a cooperative relationship with Matt was the key. "It's about respect," Charlotte says. "To get respect you must give respect."

When confronted by a tough lesson or a challenging social task, Matt frequently asked Charlotte, "Why are you doing this?"

"I always explained my reasons," Charlotte says. "I never said, 'Because I'm the teacher.'" She realized Matt was really asking if he could trust her.

Charlotte is the hub of a team consisting of Laura and Matt's general education teachers. Her role varies. For instance, Charlotte talked to Matt's physical education teacher and asked that he be allowed to participate in his school clothes rather than

shorts and a T-shirt. This simple accommodation has made it easier for him to participate fully. Although he does not require any accommodations in his math, science, and social studies classes, he sometimes has difficulty expressing himself in papers and reports in his language arts class, so Charlotte spends extra time with him to help him with these assignments.

"You can be trained to do this job," Charlotte says, "but you have to *want* to do this job. It has to be genuine with Matt." The results of this mutual respect are clear: Matt can better regulate his behavior, he takes fewer medications, he is making academic and social progress, he has improved self-esteem, and he and others know about his strengths.

Matt is ultimately responsible for the positive changes in his life; but he acknowledges that, because people care about him and teach him effectively, he wants to change and has learned how. These changes aren't going unnoticed. When Rebecca told Matt how excited she was that he was going to be featured in this textbook, Matt said, "Well, it's not like I won the principal's Pride Award or anything." What Matt didn't know at the time was that he would receive that award a few weeks later, an acknowledgment and a celebration of all of his hard work.

What do you think?

1. **Did you ever have a teacher who made a difference in your life? How did that teacher connect with you?**
2. **How do you think schools can create programs that are strength-based for students such as Matt?**

To answer these questions online and learn more about Matt Ackinclose and emotional and behavioral disorders, go to the Cases module in Chapter 5 of the Companion Website.

How Do You Recognize Students with Emotional or Behavioral Disorders?

Defining Emotional or Behavioral Disorders

Building on students' strengths rather than focusing on their problems and deficits has become an important theme in special education, social services, mental health, and juvenile corrections (Brendtro, Long, & Brown, 2000). Matt's teachers, his principal, his social worker, and his mother encouraged him to change by emphasizing his strengths. **Strength-based interventions** focus on developing **resiliency**—the ability to emerge as a highly functioning adult despite growing up in extremely stressful circumstances—through relationship building and by developing resiliency traits such as problem solving, conflict resolution, and communication skills. Identifying students with emotional and behavioral disorders—those most in need of strength-based interventions—is challenging because of "possible misinterpretation, stigma, and lack of a common understanding about the nature of these disorders" (Forness & Kavale, 2000, p. 264). Moreover, the IDEA (U.S. Department of Education, 1999) definition conflicts with a definition that many mental health professionals and educators rely on. Figure 5–1 compares the two definitions.

In Chapter 1 we discussed how labels can stigmatize. Which of the two definitions do you consider less stigmatizing?

FIGURE 5–1
Definitions of emotional and behavioral disorders

Individuals with Disabilities Education Act (1997)	Proposed Definition
(i) The term *emotional disturbance* refers to a condition exhibiting one or more of the following characteristics over a long time and to a marked degree that adversely affects a student's educational performance: (A) An inability to learn that cannot be explained by intellectual, sensory, or other health factors. (B) An inability to build or maintain satisfactory interpersonal relationships with peers and teachers. (C) Inappropriate types of behavior or feelings under normal circumstances. (D) A general pervasive mood of unhappiness or depression. (E) A tendency to develop physical symptoms or fears associated with personal or school problems. (ii) The term includes schizophrenia. The term does not apply to children who are socially maladjusted, unless it is determined that they have an emotional disturbance.	(i) The term *emotional or behavioral disorder* means a disability that is … (A) characterized by behavioral or emotional responses in school programs so different from appropriate age, cultural, or ethnic norms that the responses adversely affect educational performance, including academic, social, vocational, or personal skills; (B) more than a temporary, expected response to stressful events in the environment; (C) consistently exhibited in two different settings, at least one of which is school-related; and (D) unresponsive to direct intervention applied in general education, or the condition of a child such that general education interventions would be insufficient. (ii) The term includes such a disability that coexists with other disabilities. (iii) The term includes a schizophrenic disorder, an affective disorder, an anxiety disorder, or another sustained disorder of conduct or adjustment, affecting a child if the disorder affects educational performance as described in paragraph (A).

Source: 34 C.F.R., sec. 300.7 (c)(4); Forness, S. R. (2000). Emotional or behavioral disorders: Background and current status of the E/BD terminology and definition. *Behavioral Disorders, 25*(3), 266.

One major difference is that the IDEA definition excludes students with **social maladjustment,** a term that usually refers to students whose behavior (for example, gang membership) conflicts with society in general but is an adaptive, often peer-approved response to their environment (U.S. Department of Education, 1998). By excluding them, IDEA implies that such students choose to break societal rules but that students with IDEA-conforming emotional or behavioral disorders break those rules as a direct result of their disability (Costenbader & Buntaine, 1999). In other words, IDEA regards students with emotional or behavioral disorders as victims of their impairments but considers antisocial or socially maladjusted students as blameworthy and worthy to be controlled, contained, or punished.

Admittedly, the term *social maladjustment* is vague. Indeed, many students may be masking depression or other behavioral disorders behind their social maladjustment (Forness & Kavale, 2000). Students in gangs, for example, have "complex mental health needs requiring long-term, comprehensive, and collaborative services in the community" (Wood et al., 1997, p. 283). For these reasons, the non-IDEA definition includes students with "a sustained disorder of conduct or adjustment."

How can you recognize and intervene with students who are potentially violent? Go to the Web Links module in Chapter 5 of the Companion Website for helpful links on this important issue.

Describing the Characteristics

Too often, teachers of students with emotional or behavioral disorders in their classes focus on their deficits rather than their strengths. This was certainly true in Matt's case before Rebecca and Charlotte entered his life. Rebecca comments, "If kids are treated as damaged goods, they'll internalize that attitude." She uses a strength-based approach, not the "damaged goods" approach.

As Rebecca, Charlotte, Laura, and other important people in Matt's life began to focus on his positive qualities, he started to see himself in a new way. His many strengths are now emerging: sensitivity to the feelings of others, sense of humor, persistence, curiosity, athletic ability, and intelligence.

The emphasis on strength-based interventions stems from research on adults who exhibit resilience (Keogh, 2000). Professionals who use strength-based interventions focus on developing resiliency. They emphasize relationship building and focus on enhancing resilient characteristics such as self-awareness, motivation, sensitivity, problem-solving skills, curiosity, and perseverance (Mandleco & Perry, 2000; Stein, Fonagy, Berguson, & Wisman, 2000; Walker, 2002).

Strength-based practitioners believe "that children and their families have strengths, resources, and the ability to recover from adversities. . . . [They] maintain a holistic view when

Professionals debate whether or not students with social maladjustment should receive special education services. What is your opinion?

dealing with labels and confronted with deficit thinking. We see both the forest and the trees; we see both the problems and the strengths" (Laursen, 2000, pp. 70, 74).

Students with emotional or behavioral disorders are **heterogeneous**: Each one differs from the others, and each possesses unique strengths and needs. Also, some students do not receive services under IDEA because their emotional or behavioral disorders do not interfere with their educational progress. A student with a phobia of heights, for instance, may not need special education services or specially designed instruction. But a student who has a phobia of attending school would probably need special education services under IDEA.

Emotional Characteristics

The most commonly used psychiatric classification system is the *Diagnostic and Statistical Manual of Mental Disorders* (DSM-IV-TR) (American Psychiatric Association, 2000). Common conditions of childhood and adolescence that result in some children being classified as having emotional and behavioral disorders include (1) anxiety disorder, (2) mood disorder, (3) oppositional defiant disorder, (4) conduct disorders, and (5) schizophrenia.

Anxiety Disorder.   **Anxiety disorder** is the most common childhood disorder. Anxiety disorder is characterized by excessive fear, worry, or uneasiness and includes the following:

▼ **Phobia**: unrealistic, overwhelming fear of an object or situation.

▼ **Generalized anxiety disorder**: excessive, overwhelming worry not caused by any recent experience.

▼ **Panic disorder**: overwhelming panic attacks resulting in rapid heartbeat, dizziness, and/or other physical symptoms.

▼ **Obsessive-compulsive disorder**: *obsessions* manifesting as repetitive, persistent, and intrusive impulses, images, or thoughts (i.e., repetitive thoughts about death or illness) and/or *compulsions* manifesting as repetitive, stereotypical behaviors (i.e., handwashing or counting).

▼ **Eating disorder**: includes two major categories—*anorexia*, the deadliest of all psychiatric conditions (Verdon, 2000), an obsessive concern with losing weight and ultimately manifested by a refusal to eat; and *bulimia*, excessive eating followed by attempts to undo food intake by vomiting or taking laxatives.

▼ **Post-traumatic stress disorder**: flashbacks and other recurrent symptoms following exposure to an extremely distressing and dangerous event such as witnessing violence or a hurricane.

Anxiety disorders are associated with significant impairments in academic, social, and familial functioning (Langley, Bergman, & Piacentini, 2002; Saavedra & Silverman, 2002). Teachers need to understand that the behaviors of students with anxiety disorders are not willful, as one survivor of anorexia explains: "When other areas of my life felt out of control, there was always one thing I knew I could control. My weight and eating became the focus of my life, and all of my other troubles were forgotten—at least temporarily" (Sargent, 1999, p. 3).

Mood Disorder.   Mood disorder involves an extreme mood deviation in either a depressed or an elevated direction or sometimes in both directions at different times. **Depression** can occur at any age, including childhood. Students with major depression may experience changes in the following:

▼ *Emotion:* feeling sad and worthless, crying often, or looking tearful.

▼ *Motivation:* losing interest in play, friends, and schoolwork, resulting in a decline in grades.

▼ *Physical well-being:* eating or sleeping too much or too little, disregarding hygiene, making vague physical complaints.

▼ *Thoughts:* perhaps believing he or she is ugly and unable to do anything right and that life is hopeless.

You will find links to more information about these conditions in the Web Links module in Chapter 5 of the Companion Website.

Tragically, depression sometimes leads to suicide. Approximately 750,000 young people between the ages of 10 and 24 will attempt suicide this year; 5,000 will probably succeed (McIntosh & Guest, 2000). After accidents and homicides, suicide is the third leading cause of death in this age group (U.S. Department of Health and Human Services, 1995). Females are four times more likely to *attempt* suicide, but males are four times more likely to *commit* suicide (National Institute of Injury and Prevention, 1997). "Whenever an educator perceives a risk of suicide, he or she should treat it as an emergency" (Bostic, Rustuccia, & Schlozman, 2001, p. 93). Figure 5–2 will help you identify warning signs and provides intervention strategies to prevent suicides. Knowing your students as individuals is essential for recognizing risk factors and behavioral indications of depression and potential suicide (McIntosh & Guest, 2000).

A **bipolar disorder,** also referred to as *manic-depression,* occurs in children and adolescents as well as adults. Typically, a bipolar disorder begins in late adolescence or early adulthood (Miklowitz & Goldstein, 1997). Exaggerated mood swings characterize the condition. At times, the student experiences depression; at other times, the student experiences manic or excited phases with heightened levels of activity, ideas, and energy. Experiencing mania has been described as living life on fast-forward speed (Miklowitz & Goldstein, 1997).

Oppositional Defiant Disorder. Oppositional defiant disorder causes a pattern of negativistic, hostile, disobedient, and defiant behaviors (American Psychiatric Association, 2000). Symptoms include loss of temper, arguing with and defying adults, irritability, vindictiveness, swearing and using obscenities, blaming others for mistakes and misbehavior, and low self-esteem. The student may abuse drugs and alcohol. These behaviors seem to have a physiological basis (Hall, Williams, & Hall, 2000). Remember that Matt's behavioral issues became apparent in infancy. Students' symptoms may be exacerbated when they feel they have no control over a life situation such as divorce or a move (Hewitt, 1999). Appropriate interventions may prevent the student's oppositional-defiant disorder from escalating to the more serious level known as conduct disorder. One effective strategy teachers can use is *tagging,* telling a student, "I'd like to discuss this at a later time when both of us are calm," and ending the discussion, thus interrupting the oppositional cycle (Milne, Edwards, & Murchie, 2001, p. 24).

Rebecca and Charlotte have collaborated to work with Matt on his oppositional behaviors, and he is making excellent progress. Rebecca knew that she could not expect compliance without a relationship, that she could not force compliance but would have to gain his cooperation. Rebecca also emphasizes that you should tell students what you want them to do, not what you do not want them to do. Charlotte says teachers should give their students choices rather than engage them in power struggles. But when teachers provide a choice, they also need to clearly identify the consequences of the choices and follow through consistently with those consequences. Rebecca says that she applies the "relationship bank account" theory (Covey, 2000): If you've placed enough deposits in a student's account by praise, encouragement, and support, the relationship will remain solid when you need to make a withdrawal by providing consequences. You will find other ideas for encouraging compliance in Figure 5–3.

Conduct Disorder. Conduct disorder is a persistent pattern of antisocial behavior that significantly interferes with school, family, and social functioning (Sprague, 2000; Walker, Colvin, & Ramsay, 1995). Students with conduct disorders violate the basic rights of others or major age-appropriate societal norms or rules. The American Psychiatric Association (2000) has identified four categories of conduct disorders: (1) aggressive conduct, resulting in physical harm to people or animals; (2) nonaggressive conduct, causing property loss or damage; (3) deceitfulness or theft; and (4) serious rule violations. School truancy and running away are common examples of conduct disorder. Students with this condition exhibit little empathy for others. Their self-esteem is low or overly inflated.

In some states, conduct disorder is considered a social maladjustment rather than an emotional or behavioral disorder and is not included in the IDEA definition. The result is that students

For more helpful suggestions on encouraging compliance from students with oppositional defiant disorder, go to the Cases module in Chapter 5 of the Companion Website.

FIGURE 5–2
Suicide prevention

Warning signs (Kerns & Lieberman, 1993, p. 143)

1. Personality change: a gregarious child becomes withdrawn or a shy child becomes extremely outgoing.
2. Disregard for appearance: an adolescent who is normally scrupulous about how he looks suddenly begins to neglect his grooming, hygiene, and clothing.
3. Social withdrawal.
4. Giving away treasured possessions and putting affairs in order.
5. Preoccupation with death or morbid themes, including rock music, drawings, poems, and essays.
6. Overt or veiled suicide threats: "I won't be around much longer." "They'd be better off without me." "I wish I were dead."
7. Prior suicide attempts.
8. Acquisition of a means (ropes, guns, hoses).
9. Substance abuse.
10. School failure.
11. Sudden elevation of mood in a depressed child. This may mean the depressed child has found a "solution"—suicide.
12. Increased accidents or multiple physical complaints with no medical basis.

When a student has any of these symptoms, ask the following (McCoy, 1994):

- "It looks like you're feeling unhappy. Are you?"
- "Do you ever get the feeling that life isn't worth living?"
- "Do you sometimes feel like you don't want to live anymore?"
- "What have you thought about doing to end your life?"

If the student is not suicidal, you can say that you are glad because you care about her. You will not give her ideas. If the student is suicidal, she will probably be relieved that you cared enough to ask. If the student has a plan, do not leave her alone and immediately seek help.

What not to do (Oster & Montgomery, 1995)

- Do not be sworn to secrecy.
- Never leave a suicidal person alone.
- Do not appear shocked or alarmed.
- Do not try to be a therapist; just listen to concerns nonjudgmentally.
- Do not debate the morality of suicide; this can increase feelings of guilt and sadness.
- Do not point out that others have worse troubles; this leads to feelings of incompetence and being misunderstood.

Other strategies (McCoy, 1994)

- Take the student's comments seriously. "Take all symptoms of depression, all comments about death, all suicide threats or attempts seriously." Avoid dismissing these words or actions as manipulative or attention getting.
- Show that you care. Ask the student to share his feelings and listen supportively without judging or feeling a need to give easy advice. Help the student problem-solve alternative solutions. "What else could you do? How would that work?" Encourage the student to sign a contract that he will not hurt himself intentionally or by accident.
- Help the student regain a glimmer of hope. Emphasize that even serious depression is a temporary feeling; and if he will hang on, he will probably feel better in a week or so. Remind him that you will continue to be there for him.
- Find skilled help. The student may need crisis intervention and long-term counseling.

Source: Kerns, L. L., & Lieberman, A. B. (1993). *Helping your depressed child.* Rocklin, CA: Prima; McCoy, K. (1994). *Understanding your teenager's depression.* New York: Perigee; Oster, G. D., & Montgomery, S. S. (1995). *Helping your depressed teenager.* New York: Wiley.

FIGURE 5–3
Encouraging compliance from students with oppositional-defiant disorder

- *Avoid direct positive reinforcement.* Use of this technique can backfire with these students. Because they feel compelled to do the opposite of your request, especially in front of peers, when you praise them directly, publicly, and obviously, they may retaliate with the unwanted response (e.g., tearing up a paper you had praised).
- *Use indirect reinforcement.* To avoid public praise but still encourage the student for desired responses, the following techniques may be useful:
  - *Whisper.* Brief whispered encouragement without sustained eye contact allows a positive response. Comment on the product rather than your feelings about it.
  - *Leave notes.* Leave a brief message in a note on students' desks, mail it to them, or hand it to them as they leave the room.
  - *Provide rewards.* Concrete reinforcements can be used as long as you place stickers or marks on a chart without verbal comment. Give rewards without fanfare by simply placing them in their desks, or give them a note that tells them what they have earned. Avoid using response cost, a method that involves subtracting points or taking away rewards. This can backfire because students with this condition may view this as proof that they are not complying with what you want.
- *Avoid arguing.* Arguing can reinforce their oppositional position. Enforce the consequence and let it go.
- *Defer control.* Relabel who or what is in control. For instance, say, "The clock says it's time to go" rather than "it's time to go."
- *Provide choices.* By giving the students limited choices, the student retains a sense of control. If the student refuses to make a choice, you will need to make sure the consequence is clear.
- *Anticipate problems.* Prepare the student for difficult times or activities. By saying that you know this might be difficult, students can be placed in a double bind. This paradoxical approach may encourage them to prove it will not be difficult.
- *Allow them to release anger.* Physical activity can help these students dispel anger in a manageable way. Sports, working with clay, or even punching a pillow or tearing up an old magazine can be acceptable ways to release anger. Avoid emphasizing involvement in competitive sports until students have adequate control of their anger.
- *Outline consequences.* Having oppositional-defiant disorders does not excuse these students from taking responsibility for their behaviors. Provide students with a specific list of behaviors and consequences and enforce them consistently.
- *Offer therapy or counseling.* Make sure that the therapist or counselor you recommend is familiar with the needs of these students.

Source: From "Managing Children with Oppositional Behavior," by D. Knowlton, 1995, *Beyond Behavior, 6*(3), pp. 5–10. Copyright 1995 by the Council for Children with Behavior Disorders. Adapted with permission.

with conduct disorder may never receive needed interventions. Box 5–1 highlights a program that makes a difference in students' lives by teaching them empathy.

Schizophrenia. Schizophrenia is a disorder in which people typically have two or more of the following symptoms: hallucinations, withdrawal, delusions, inability to experience pleasure, loss of contact with reality, and disorganized speech (American Psychiatric Association, 2000). Although schizophrenia generally begins in late adolescence or early adulthood, some children have the condition. Childhood schizophrenia appears to result from greater genetic vulnerability (Kumra, Shaw, Merka, Nakayama, & Augustin, 2001).

Box 5–1

Pawsitive Living

The purpose of Pawsitive Living, a pet-assisted program for juvenile offenders in Birmingham, Alabama, is to "intervene in the locked-up hearts and minds of these children," according to Judge Sandra Storm (Hand-in-Paw, 2002). Animal abuse by children and adolescents, one of the DSM-IV-TR criteria for conduct disorder, can foreshadow violence against people (American Humane Society, n.d.). This documented link emphasizes the importance of taking animal abuse seriously and instilling compassion for animals, people, and the environment.

Juvenile offenders may be required to participate in Pawsitive Living, but many of them elect to continue in the program past their mandated sentences (Franklin, n.d., Hand-in-Paw, 2002). Pet partners—specially trained pets and their handlers, who volunteer their time—participate in the sessions, which are facilitated by trained mental health professionals. In the initial sessions, the teenagers build rapport through trust activities and learn about human-animal communication. Parents or guardians attend with their teenagers after the first three sessions. They learn anger management by role-playing scenarios such as "What would you do if your dog urinated on your favorite jacket?" The teens learn about appropriate and inappropriate

discipline as well as positive training methods. One way empathy is taught is by viewing the video *Charlie: The Dog Nobody Wanted*, which often triggers abandonment issues among the teens, many of whom come from foster care. They learn to recognize and reduce stress in themselves and animals and are given opportunities to groom pets. Pawsitive Living encourages tolerance by discussing dog breed stereotypes. Self-reflection exercises help them value their unique traits as well as those of others. In preparation for giving something back to the community, the teens learn about the special needs of children, the elderly, and people with disabilities. After receiving this training, the teens make nursing home visits with the Pet Partners. Teens who complete the program are invited back as mentors for the next group.

The young people keep journals throughout the program. One boy wrote that he confronted a man in his neighborhood who was abusing his dog (Hand-in-Paw, 2002). Another girl wrote, "I learned that animals have feelings like people" (Franklin, n.d., p. 1). In this program, not only the adults who organize Pawsitive Living make a difference but also the pets and even the teens, many of whom will have a more compassionate role in society.

Behavioral Characteristics

Students with emotional or behavioral disorders also have identifiable behavioral patterns that generally fall into one or both of two categories: *externalizing* or *internalizing* (Achenbach & Edelbrock, 1981; Gresham, Lane, MacMillan, & Bocian, 1999). Figure 5–4 offers a checklist of those behaviors.

Externalizing Behaviors. **Externalizing behaviors**—persistent aggressive, acting-out, and noncompliant behaviors—often characterize conduct and oppositional defiant disorders (Walker et al., 1995). Sometimes teachers do not recognize that teenagers and children who are depressed may exhibit externalizing, acting-out behaviors rather than the typical internalizing, withdrawal behavior more common in adults. Students with externalizing behaviors are more likely to exhibit **behavioral earthquakes**—high-intensity but low-frequency behavioral events such as setting fires, assaulting someone, or exhibiting cruelty—than their peers are (Gresham et al., 1999). Teachers tend to refer students with externalizing behavioral characteristics for special education services because they disrupt classrooms (Rubin, Chen, McDougall, Bowker, & McKinnon, 1995).

Like all other students, those with externalizing behaviors are subject to **zero tolerance** policies that allow educators to expel a student who exhibits violent behavior or brings drugs or weapons to school. IDEA provides that no student whose behavior is a manifestation of a disability may be expelled from school; the student's IEP team must make the **manifestation determination:** Did the behavior arise from the disability? Students can, however, be suspended for a short term (never more than a total of 10 days in any school year) or placed in a more restrictive setting. Farner (2002) argues that "correctly interpreting the characteristic behavior of children who are discouraged and developing strategies to meet their needs will be more effective than simply punishing and excluding students who are striving to have their basic needs met" (p. 19).

FIGURE 5–4

Internalizing and externalizing behaviors

Internalizing
- ❏ Exhibits sad affect, depression, and feelings of worthlessness
- ❏ Has auditory or visual hallucinations
- ❏ Cannot keep mind off certain thoughts, ideas, or situations
- ❏ Cannot keep self from engaging in repetitive and/or useless actions
- ❏ Suddenly cries, cries frequently, or displays totally unexpected and atypical affect for the situation
- ❏ Complains of severe headaches or other somatic problems (stomach aches, nausea, dizziness, vomiting) as a result of fear or anxiety
- ❏ Talks of killing self—reports suicidal thoughts and/or is preoccupied with death
- ❏ Shows decreased interest in activities that were previously of interest
- ❏ Is excessively teased, verbally or physically abused, neglected, and/or avoided by peers
- ❏ Has severely restricted activity levels
- ❏ Shows signs of physical, emotional, and/or sexual abuse
- ❏ Exhibits other specific behaviors such as withdrawal, avoidance of social interactions, and/or lack of personal care to an extent that prevents the development or maintenance of satisfactory personal relationships

Externalizing
- ❏ Displays recurring pattern of aggression toward objects or persons
- ❏ Argues excessively
- ❏ Forces the submission of others through physical and/or verbal means
- ❏ Is noncompliant with reasonable requests
- ❏ Exhibits persistent pattern of tantrums
- ❏ Exhibits persistent patterns of lying and/or stealing
- ❏ Frequently exhibits lack of self-control and acting-out behaviors
- ❏ Exhibits other specific behavior(s) that intrude(s) upon other people, staff, self, or the physical environment to an extent that prevents the development or maintenance of satisfactory interpersonal relationships

Source: Adapted from the University of Kentucky, Department of Special Education and Rehabilitation Counseling. (1997). *Behavior home page* (http://www.state.ky.us/agencies/behave/beesaman.html) Reprinted with permission.

To suspend or expel students is to deprive them of what they need most: an education in a caring environment.

Internalizing Behaviors. **Internalizing behaviors** include withdrawal, depression, anxiety, obsessions, and compulsions. Students with internalizing behaviors have poorer social skills and are less accepted than their peers are (Gresham et al., 1999). They tend to blend into the background to the point that teachers forget they are in the classroom. Because their behaviors are not as disruptive, they are less like to be identified for special education services. Educators sometimes assume that internalizing problems do not pose the long-term risks associated with externalizing problems. However, the level of social withdrawal of second-grade students predicted their low self-regard and loneliness when they were in ninth grade (Rubin et al., 1995).

Cognitive and Academic Characteristics

Students with emotional or behavioral disorders may be gifted or have mental retardation, but most have IQs in the low average range (Duncan, Forness, & Hartsough, 1995). Over half have

To learn more about IDEA's discipline policies, go to the Cases and Web Links modules in Chapter 5 of the Companion Website.

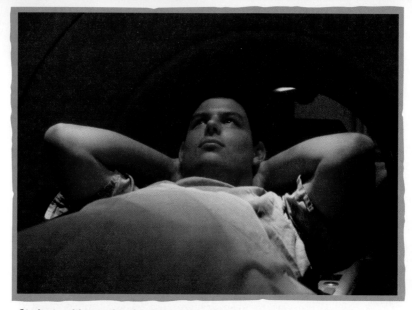

Students with emotional or behavioral disorders may also experience withdrawal or depression that reflect internalizing behaviors.

concurrent learning disabilities (Glassberg, Hooper, & Mattison, 1999). The relationship between academic and social behaviors seems to be reciprocal: Students who experience failure in one area also tend to experience failure in the other (Jolivette, 2000). Approximately 50 percent of students with emotional and behavioral disorders drop out of school (Wagner, 1995).

Most students with emotional or behavioral disorders (71 percent) have expressive and/or receptive language disorders (Benner, Nelson, & Epstein, 2002). Laura noticed Matt's language delay early; he began intervention for his speech problems at age 2. Many students with emotional or behavioral disorders do not know how to express their feelings with words, so they tend to act out their feelings instead. As Faber and Mazlish (1996) point out in *How to Talk So Kids Can Learn,* teachers can help students identify and express their feelings by active listening, which we discuss later in the chapter.

Identifying the Causes

Seldom can professionals determine with absolute confidence the causes of students' emotional or behavioral disorders (Sternberg & Grigorenko, 1999). Nonetheless, (1) several factors probably interact with each other to contribute to the presence of emotional or behavior disorders; (2) the decisions made about causes may be influenced by the evaluator's professional discipline, professional experiences, and beliefs about the causes of all human behavior; and (3) determining a cause is useful only if the information leads to effective interventions and preventions, not blaming (Kauffman, 2001). Researchers have examined two major categories of causes: biological and environmental.

Biological Causes

"There are far-reaching biological and physical influences on mental health and mental illness," according to the U.S. Surgeon General (2000, p. 52). Biological factors, however, do not exist in a vacuum but in a complex environmental context. Indeed, our current understanding of the causes takes into account the dynamic interplay between biological and environmental factors.

It is common knowledge that genetics influence children's physical characteristics. Only recently has it been clear that genetics also influence their behavioral characteristics, including anxiety disorders, depression, schizophrenia, oppositional defiant disorder, and conduct disorder

(Bassarath, 2001). The precise nature of the genetic transmission is still unknown; but as Hallowell (1996) has concluded, "All behavior and all personality are in some way genetically influenced, and to a greater degree than most of us take into account" (p. 62). Because biology often influences behavior, blaming parents for their child's behavior is not only unhelpful but also generally unjustified.

Environmental Stressors

Students who are exposed to trauma and maltreatment are more likely to experience emotional and behavioral disorders such as oppositional defiant disorder (Ford et al., 2000). Indeed, in the interaction of biological and environmental factors, frequent exposure to stressors can have adverse effects on the delicate balance of brain chemicals (Soulsman, 1994).

Stressful Living Conditions.   Although many families who live in poverty are emotionally healthy, the risk of a student developing emotional or behavioral disorders is more likely in impoverished circumstances than in abundant ones. A national longitudinal study of students with disabilities indicated that 38 percent of the youth with emotional or behavioral disorders came from households with an annual income of under $12,000 and another 32 percent came from households with an income of $12,000 to $24,999 (Fujiura & Yamaki, 2000). Further, 44 percent came from single-parent households. Low income and single-parent status are highly correlated (Fujiura & Yamaki, 2000).

Another issue relative to living conditions is foster care. Forming stable relationships with adults is important for developing resilience. Research suggests that children in volatile foster care placements are more likely to develop internalizing and externalizing behavior disorders than are those in more secure placements (Newton, Litronik, & Lansverk, 2000). Those with more initial externalizing behaviors were also more likely to experience placement changes, decreasing their likelihood of forming close attachments with adults.

The Federation of Families for Children's Mental Health, featured in Box 5–2, is a pioneer in advocating for comprehensive systems of care for families, particularly those from culturally and linguistically diverse backgrounds. By helping parents locate support services such as the wraparound services we describe later, the federation hopes to help reduce stressful living conditions that contribute to emotional and behavioral disorders.

Child Abuse.   Child abuse is an especially insidious type of violence. In a national survey, 556 teachers of students with emotional or behavioral disorders report that approximately 38 percent of their students have been abused physically or sexually, 41 percent have been neglected, and 51 percent have been abused emotionally; some have suffered more than one kind of maltreatment (Oseroff, Oseroff, Westling, & Gessner, 1999). Eighty-two percent of the teachers have reported evidence of their students' maltreatment, usually to school administrators but less often to a child abuse hotline run by state or local child protective service agencies. As a teacher, you are legally responsible to report suspected child abuse.

Students who have experienced abuse may display (1) poor self-image; (2) inability to depend on and trust others; (3) aggressive and destructive, sometimes illegal, behavior; (4) passive and withdrawn behavior, with fear of entering into new relationships or activities; (5) school failure; and (6) serious drug and alcohol abuse (American Federation of Teachers & AFL-CIO, 1996). Some, however, may conceal the abuse; they may even be popular, straight-A students. In Figure 5–5, you will find answers to common questions about child abuse.

School Factors

Students, especially boys, who experience peer rejection and aggression at school may be more likely to develop conduct disorders (Miller-Johnson, Coie, Maumary-Gremaud, Lochman, & Terry, 1999). Rebecca says that most of the issues that Matt discussed with her related to school problems. We have already addressed the importance of building positive relationships in developing resilience. Therefore, creating a strength-based classroom environment that encourages students to value all members may help prevent emotional and behavioral disorders. As a teacher, you have the power to help create this positive classroom climate.

The National Alliance for the Mentally Ill (NAMI) wants to improve people's mental health by "eradicating brain disorders." Go to the Web Links module in Chapter 5 of the Companion Website for a link to NAMI.

Go to the Web Links module in Chapter 5 of the Companion Website to link to the federation's website.

Box 5–2

Making a Difference

The Federation of Families for Children's Mental Health

Have you ever met a mother on a mission—the "won't take no for an answer" type? Now, put a dozen of them together for three days in February 1989 in Naomi Karp's basement, stir in a few furious fathers, add a couple of federal "advocrats" (bureaucrats on an advocacy mission), sprinkle liberally with some passionate professionals, and what do you get? The Federation of Families for Children's Mental Health.

Next, put it under the capable direction of Barbara Huff; export her from Kansas to Washington, DC; find a few federal dollars to launch the national office; organize a few state chapters; and watch the movement grow. For the federation, by the mid-1990s, was not just an organization. It was a movement. A special kind of movement.

What makes it special? Very simply, four traits; it is organized around principles and values. It welcomes both professionals and families alike. It is committed to working across racial, economic, and service delivery boundaries. And it is dedicated to the simple proposition that every child who has an emotional or behavioral disorder and that child's family will have appropriate and affordable services in his or her own community (Bryant-Comstock, Huff, & VanDenBerg, 1996).

Its message is straightforward: Children are children, first and foremost; their special needs are secondary.

- Families are not dysfunctional; systems are, and systems penalize families.
- Families are experts about their children; professionals and families should collaborate.
- Build on strengths; every child and every family has some.
- Support families where they live; resist out-of-home placements; push for inclusion in schools.
- Dare to dream and to hope.
- Take risks.
- Insist on full citizenship for children and families.
- Declare that it is just plain wrong for parents to have to give up legal and physical custody of their children in order to receive services from a state or its agencies.

And never, never quit. Against all odds, seek to change the odds. Gather about you the mothers on a mission. The furious fathers. The passionate professionals. The adventurous advocrats. And then watch it happen—the Federation Family, united and strong.

Source: Adapted from Huff, B. (1998). Federation Celebrates 10 Year Anniversary. In *Claiming Children*. Washington, DC: Federation of Families for Children's Mental Health, Spring, 1998.

Do you give and receive affection easily? Can you maintain a relaxed but firm atmosphere with students? Do you possess hope, optimism, empathy, quiet confidence, and joy as well as the ability to problem-solve effectively? Do you remain calm and act appropriately in a crisis? Are you willing to commit to children with emotional or behavioral disorders? Do you believe that they can be helped to change?

Research shows that these attributes help teachers work effectively with students who have emotional or behavioral disorders (Webber, Coleman, & Zionts, 1998). Although some of these teacher traits stem from temperament and experience, others can be learned and integrated by choice. One of those, the belief that teachers can help children with emotional or behavioral disorders, is the foundation of this chapter and is well exemplified in Matt's story.

Identifying the Prevalence

Approximately 1 percent of the school-age population (469,000 students) was served for emotional or behavioral disorders during the 1999–2000 school year (U.S. Department of Education, 2002). Some experts believe that a more accurate identification rate is 9 to 10 percent of the school population (Walker, Zeller, Close, Webber, & Grisham, 1999). Figure 5–6 summarizes some of the possible reasons for under-identification.

FIGURE 5–5
Questions and answers about child abuse

What is child abuse? Child abuse and neglect include acts or failures to act that result in an imminent risk of death, serious physical or emotional harm, sexual abuse, or exploitation by a parent or caretaker who is responsible for the child's welfare. This definition generally applies to a person under the age of 18.

How common is it? The National Clearinghouse on Child Abuse and Neglect (2002) reported that 879,000 children were identified as victims of abuse and neglect in 2000. Children who have disabilities are at a 1.7 times higher risk of abuse and neglect by their caregivers (families and professionals) than are children without disabilities.

How do I know if it is occurring? Physical indicators may include skin or bone injuries, evidence of neglect such as malnutrition, failure to meet medical needs, or lack of warm clothing in cold weather. Behavioral indicators may include a demonstration of sexual knowledge that is not developmentally or age appropriate.

What do I do if I think a child is being abused? Is this really my business? It *is* your business. The lasting effects of child abuse and neglect create barriers to learning. School professionals are in a unique position to identify when a child is being abused or neglected because they have contact with the child each day.

If you suspect that a child is being abused or neglected, it is your responsibility to report it to your state's child protection agency. Each state has an agency responsible for child protection, and every state legally mandates that educators report suspected child abuse or neglect. Most states have penalties for mandated reporters who fail to report suspected abuse or neglect. On the other side, all states provide immunity from civil or criminal penalty for mandated reporters who reported in good faith. Many school systems have their own policies concerning child abuse and neglect. These policies usually state their support for state reporting laws by requiring educators to report child abuse and neglect. They also may provide administrative penalties for not complying with the policies.

An easy way to find out your state's hotline number is to call 1-800-4-A-CHILD, which will direct you to your state's agency.

While it is your responsibility to report suspected abuse, it is not your responsibility to conduct your own investigation to determine if a child is being abused. Your child protection agency is trained to do that. No state requires that the person reporting has proof—only that the person suspects, has an uncomfortable feeling, or a reasonable cause to believe that abuse is occurring.

What kind of information will they want when I make a report? If you find that you need to make a child abuse or neglect report, you will want to have the following information ready when you make the call: the child's name, age, address, and telephone number; the parent's or other caretaker's name, address, and telephone number; the reason for your call.

What should I do when a student confides in me about abuse?

- Avoid promising the student you will not tell. You can say that you will inform the student about the nature or identity of the persons you may need to tell and why.

- Encourage the student to talk freely, and avoid judgmental comments.

- Take the student seriously. Psychiatrists have found that students who are listened to and understood at this time fare much better in therapy than do those who are not (American Academy of Child and Adolescent Psychiatry, 1997).

- Emphasize that the student did the right thing by telling.

- Tell the student that she is not at fault but avoid making derogatory comments about the abuser. The abuser may be someone the student cares for deeply, and such comments might cause the student to retract what was said.

- Promise that you will continue to be there for the student and will take steps to try to stop the abuse.

Source: National Clearinghouse on Child Abuse and Neglect. (2002, April). *National child abuse and neglect data system (NCANDS): Summary of key findings from calendar year 2000* (http://www.calib.com/nccanch/pubs/factsheets/canstats.cfm); American Academy of Child and Adolescent Psychiatry. (1997). *Child abuse: The hidden bruises* (http://www.aacap.org/publications/factsfam/chldabus2.htm).

FIGURE 5–6

Possible reasons for the underidentification of students with emotional or behavioral problems

Reason 1: reluctance to serve those students who have aversive conduct disorders. The view is that these students are willful troublemakers rather than students disabled by behavior.

Reason 2: federal constraints about disciplinary practices permitted for special education students. (Note: Districts are not permitted to expel students who are served by IDEA.)

Reason 3: significant costs associated with the education and treatment of these children and youth (residential programs, psychiatric services, and hospitalization).

Reason 4: insensitivity to disorders such as depression, anxiety, peer neglect and rejection, and affective disturbances.

Reason 5: the subjectivity involved in identification of emotional or behavioral disorders.

Reason 6: the label as stigma.

Source: From "Behavior Disorders and the Social Context of Regular Class Integration: A Conceptual Dilemma?" by H. M. Walker and M. Bullis, in *The Regular Education Initiative: Alternative Perspectives on Concepts, Issues, and Models* (pp. 78–79), edited by J. W. Lloyd, N. N. Singh, and A. C. Repp, 1991, Pacific Grove, CA: Brooks/Cole Publishing Co. Copyright © 1991 by Brooks/Cole Publishing Co. Adapted with permission of Wadsworth Publishing Co., Belmont, CA.

African American males are overrepresented in the category of emotional or behavioral disorders (U.S. Department of Education, 1998). The special education community faces three challenges in terms of this high identification rate: (1) unavailability of culturally appropriate assessment instruments, (2) concern about teacher expectations regarding appropriate behavior, and (3) building respectful family-professional partnerships that may prevent identification (Cartledge, Kea, & Ida, 2000; Townsend, 2000). Ethnically diverse groups are more likely to experience stressors such as "poverty, discrimination, violence, violent death, drug and alcohol abuse, and teenage pregnancy" that can contribute to mental health problems (Safren et al., 2000).

How Do You Evaluate Students with Emotional or Behavioral Disorders?

Determining the Presence

Along with direct observation, the checklist of internalizing and externalizing behaviors that we provided in Figure 5–4 will help you decide whether to refer a student for a nondiscriminatory evaluation. If a student exhibits these behaviors consistently and if the behaviors seem to interfere with the student's educational progress, you have good reasons to initiate the prereferral process; you may choose to bypass it and proceed to the referral process immediately if the student appears to be a danger to self or to others. Figure 5–7 describes the nondiscriminatory evaluation process.

The evaluation team usually asks teachers to evaluate the student's areas of difficulty and areas of strength. A student's strengths significantly affect the student's placement and likelihood of remaining at home (Oswald, Cohen, Best, Jenson, & Lyons, 2001). For that reason, teachers need to listen carefully to the life stories of their students, which often help identify strengths. "Their personal narratives help us detect exceptions to their problems . . . because it is often in

FIGURE 5–7
Evaluation of students with emotional and behavioral disorders

Nondiscriminatory Evaluation

Observation

Teacher and parents observe	Student has difficulty with appropriate social adjustments; may be unable to build and maintain satisfactory interpersonal relationships; may engage in aggressive behaviors; or may have a pervasive mood of unhappiness or depression. The student acts out or withdraws during classroom instruction and independent activities. Problematic behavior occurs in more than one setting.

Screening

Assessment measures	Findings that indicate need for further evaluation
Classroom work products	Student may require one-to-one assistance to stay on task. The student has difficulty following basic classroom behavioral expectations during instruction or assignments, resulting in incomplete or unsatisfactory work products.
Group intelligence tests	Most students perform in the low average to slow learner range. Performance may not accurately reflect ability because the emotional/behavioral disorder can prevent the student from staying on task.
Group achievement tests	Student performs below peers or scores lower than would be expected according to group intelligence tests. Performance may not be a true reflection of achievement because the student has difficulty staying on task as a result of the emotional/behavioral disorder.
Vision and hearing screening	Results do not explain behavior.

Prereferral

Teacher implements suggestions from school-based team.	The student is not responsive to reasonable adaptations of the curriculum and behavior management techniques.

Referral

Nondiscriminatory evaluation procedures and standards

Assessment measures	Findings that suggest emotional and behavioral disorders
Individualized intelligence test	Intelligence is usually, but not always, in the low average to slow learner range. The multidisciplinary team makes sure that the results do not reflect cultural difference rather than ability. The evaluator can sometimes detect emotional and behavioral disorders by performance on subtests of the intelligence measure and the student's behavior while taking the test.
Individualized achievement test	Usually, but not always, the student scores below average across academic areas in comparison to peers. The evaluator may notice acting-out or withdrawal behaviors that affect results.
Behavior rating scale	The student scores in the significant range on specific behavioral excesses or deficiencies when compared with others of the same culture and developmental stage.
Assessment measures of social skills, self-esteem, personality, and/or adjustment	Student's performance indicates significant difficulties in one or more areas according to the criteria established by test developers and in comparison with others of the same culture and developmental stage.
Anecdotal records	The student's challenging behaviors are not of short duration but have been apparent throughout time in school. Also, records indicate that behaviors have been observed in more than one setting and are adversely affecting educational progress.
Curriculum-based assessment	The student often is experiencing difficulty in one or more areas of the curriculum used by the local school district.
Direct observation	The student is experiencing difficulty relating to peers or adults and in adjusting to school or classroom structure or routine.

Nondiscriminatory evaluation team determines that the student has emotional or behavioral disorders and needs special education and related services.

Appropriate Education

these exceptions that possibilities for solution construction lie and the leverage to bounce back from life's hardships can be found" (Laursen, 2000, p. 70).

The *Behavioral and Emotional Rating Scale* (Epstein, 1999; Epstein & Sharma, 1998) provides another way to identify strengths in each of the following five domains (Rudolph & Epstein, 2000):

▼ *Interpersonal strength:* a child's ability to regulate his or her emotions and behaviors in social settings.
▼ *Family involvement:* the quality of family relationships.
▼ *Intrapersonal strength:* a child's perspective of his or her competence and accomplishments.
▼ *School functioning:* a child's success in school.
▼ *Affective strength:* ability to express feelings and accept affection.

This tool contains 52 items. Each is scored on a 4-point scale ranging from "not at all like the child" to "very much like the child."

Strength-based assessment has four assumptions:

1. Every child, regardless of his or her personal and family situation, has unique strengths.
2. Children are influenced and motivated by the way significant people in their lives respond to them.
3. Rather than viewing a child who does not demonstrate a strength as deficient, it is assumed that the child has not had the opportunities that are essential to learning, developing, and mastering the skill.
4. When treatment and service planning are based on strengths rather than deficits and pathologies, children and families are more likely to become involved in the therapeutic process and to use their strengths and resources. (Rudolph & Epstein, 2000, pp. 207–208)

Determining the Nature and Extent of General and Special Education and Related Services

Direct observation is a useful approach for teachers trying to determine a student's strengths and needs in the classroom as well as how successful their interventions are for that student. In this approach, the teacher or another rater watches and records the behavior of a single student or a group of students for a specified amount of time. The student might be engaging in a particular task, working on an assignment, playing during recess, or interacting with peers.

This kind of close observation requires teachers to do much more than simply look at the student. Raters use structured recording sheets to collect data and a set of codes for target behaviors (those that the IEP team wants to help the child strengthen or diminish). A target behavior—for example, talking out of turn (code=TT), getting out of seat (code=OS), raising hand (code=RH), saying thank you (TY)—must be *observable* (the behavior can be seen and identified) and *measurable* (the behavior can be tallied). Depending on the information needed, the teacher tallies the target behavior according to the following:

▼ **Frequency:** how often it occurs.
▼ **Duration:** how long it lasts.
▼ **Latency:** how long it takes for the behavior to begin once there is an opportunity.
▼ **Topography:** a description of motor behavior or physical movements.
▼ **Magnitude:** the intensity of the student's response.

For example, a teacher might code how long one student stays on task during a 15-minute period (duration) or how many times another talks out during math class (frequency). After collecting this information, the teacher implements an intervention. Direct observation after the intervention helps the teacher determine the intervention's effectiveness.

For access to a case study of Tijuane Philips, describing how her team identified and built on her strengths to help her overcome depression as well as aggressive and oppositional behavior, go to the Cases module in Chapter 5 of the Companion Website.

Direct observation is an essential component of *functional behavioral assessment*, an important tool for determining factors that trigger and maintain certain behaviors. You will learn how to use functional behavioral assessment in Chapter 10, which discusses autism.

How Do You Assure Progress in the General Curriculum?

Including Students

IDEA presumes that a student with emotional and behavioral disorders will be included in general classrooms unless the student's IEP team provides specific justification for placement elsewhere (Cheney & Muscott, 1996; Shapiro, Miller, Sawka, Gardill, & Handler, 1999). Inclusion, however, is occurring only very slowly (Sachs & Cheney, 2000). In the 10-year period from 1988–1989 to 1998–1999, the percentage of students with emotional or behavioral disorders who participated in general education for 80 percent or more of the day increased from 14 percent to only 26 percent (National Center for Educational Statistics, 2002). During that same period, the participation of students with learning disabilities increased from 20 percent to 45 percent. In Figure 5–8, you will find the percentage of students with emotional and behavioral disorders in each placement.

Approximately three times as many students with emotional or behavioral disorders as all other students with disabilities are served in residential settings, hospitals, or homes (U.S. Department of Education, 1998). Moreover, approximately 6,000 students with emotional or behavioral disorders are incarcerated in correctional facilities (U.S. Department of Education, 1999).

A lack of adequate support services is one barrier to inclusion. A solution is to wrap an array of necessary services around a student (Eber, 1996, 1997), just as Matt's mother, teachers, and therapist wrapped school and mental health services around him so he could move from homebound services to inclusion. Box 5–3 suggests some tips for inclusion.

One of the problems facing students and their families is the haphazard system through which state and local governments provide health, mental health, human services (e.g., conflict resolution or drug prevention), and education. The wraparound approach creates a whole coherent system, turning "haphazard" into "systematic."

The wraparound model is also a strength-based approach because it builds on the strengths of the student, the family, and the community. Similarly, the wraparound approach focuses on

For a link to the Council for Exceptional Children's special web focus *How to Manage Disruptive Behavior in Inclusive Classrooms,* go to the Web Links module in Chapter 5 of the Companion Website.

FIGURE 5–8

Percentage of students with emotional or behavioral disorders in educational placements

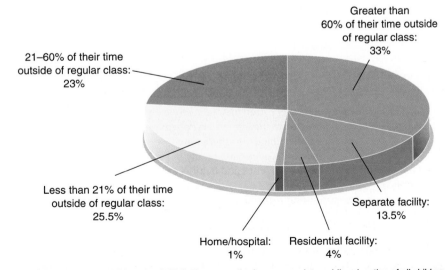

Source: From U.S. Department of Education (2001). *To assure the free appropriate public education of all children with disabilities: Twenty-first annual report to Congress on the implementation of the individuals with Disabilities Education Act,* Washington, DC: Author.

Inclusion Tips

Box 5—3

	What You Might See	What You Might Be Tempted to Do	Alternate Responses	Ways to Include Peers in the Process
Behavior	The student refuses to follow directions and uses inappropriate language.	Respond in anger and send him out of the classroom. Place him in "time-out" for extended periods of time.	Building on his strengths and interests, try an approach based on catching him being good. Also try contingency contracting.	Use peer mediation as well as group contingencies.
Social interactions	He fights with other students and is always on the defensive.	Separate him from other students to prevent fights.	Give him time to calm down. Then teach appropriate social skills using modeling, videos, and social skills programs.	Pair him with different students who can model and help him practice social skills and responses.
Educational performance	He is rarely on task and appears to have an inability to learn.	Give poor grades and require him to remain until all work is done.	Develop a curriculum based on student interests and a motivational reward system for completed tasks.	Use peer tutoring and also find a buddy willing to be a friend and helpful tutor.
Classroom attitudes	He is depressed or sad all the time and does not speak or interact with others.	Discipline him for nonparticipation, and instruct him to cheer up.	Recognize the warning signs. Refer him for help. Collaborate with the school counselor.	Have different students daily write something good about him, and then verbally present it to him.

problem solving and seeks solutions to the needs of the student and family. VanDenBerg and Grealish (cited in Pina & VanDenBerg, 1999, p. 30) recommend the following planning steps:

- Look at the student's and family's strengths, preferences, and culture.
- Develop a child-and-family team for support and planning and include the student and family on the team with professionals as appropriate.
- Have the team set goals for the student and family in prioritized life domain areas.
- Have the team determine the student's and family's needs underlying the goals (needs are not services!).
- Have the team develop strength-based and culturally competent options to meet the student's and family's needs and goals.
- Have the team develop a crisis plan or back-up plan.

As you have just read, a key element of the wraparound approach is the plan to solve existing or potential challenges. By having support services in general education and a detailed plan that was developed in part by a general educator, students are more likely to be successful in general education.

Companion Website

To learn more about the wraparound approach, go to the Web Links module in Chapter 5 of the Companion Website.

Planning Universally Designed Learning

An effective teacher will use a universally designed general classroom to meet the needs of students with emotional or behavioral disorders. This kind of classroom requires structure, predictable routines, positive and praise-oriented teacher-student interaction, and systematic and consistent teacher responses to student behavior (Smith, cited in Brownell & Walther-Thomas, 2001; Sutherland, Wehby, & Yoder, 2002; Wehby, Symons, & Canale, 1998). In addition, effective teachers encourage students to engage in self-management and conflict resolution.

Adapting Assessment: Self-Management

Self-management involves "actions an individual takes to change or maintain his or her own behavior" (DuPaul & Hoff, 1998, p. 291). Such actions can decrease disruptive behavior and maintain appropriate behaviors, even in the absence of a teacher (Peterson & Young, 1999). Rather than relying on external controls that a teacher applies to a classroom, the student practices at least two of the following: "goal setting, self-monitoring, self-instruction, self-assessment, self-determination, and self-administration of reinforcement" (Mitchem, 2001a, p. 76). The strategy, which is called *classwide, peer-assisted self-management* (Mitchem, 2001b), includes the following sub-strategies for teachers helping students learn to manage their own behavior. First, as a group, students learn the definition and rationale for self-management and decide how it can benefit them. Next, they learn the relationship among antecedents (the triggers of their behaviors), their specific behaviors, and the consequences of those behaviors. They also discuss how to respond appropriately and inappropriately to triggers and identify positive consequences for appropriate behaviors.

The teacher then reviews the school and classroom rules and two social skills: how to follow instructions and how to get the teacher's attention. Using an instruction given by the teacher as an antecedent, the students can identify appropriate and inappropriate responses and consequences for those responses.

The teacher instructs students on how to use a rating scale of "honors, satisfactory, needs improvement, and unsatisfactory" in terms of classroom expectations (e.g., following the teacher's directions). After asking students for the names of three students they would like to work with, the teacher pairs them and then groups them into two teams. The students practice rating their partner's behavior according to a scale on a card. Then, when cued, the students mark their and their partner's behavior and reflect on how their ratings compare with their partner's. Perfect matches earn bonus points. At the end of class, they report their partner's totals and then tally those with the totals of other members of their team. Both teams receive praise for their efforts, and the team with the highest points for the week becomes the winning team.

Augmenting Instruction: Conflict Resolution

Through conflict resolution instruction, students learn three important skills: effective communication, anger management, and taking another's perspective (Daunic, Smith, Robinson, Miller, & Landry, 2000). The benefits include "(a) providing students with a framework for resolving conflicts, (b) giving students an opportunity to assume responsibility for their behavior, (c) lowering teacher stress by reducing the number of student conflicts they have to handle, (d) increasing instructional time, and (e) helping students understand how cultural diversity can effect interpersonal communication and human interactions" (p. 95). Conflict resolution instruction is best infused into classes such as social studies or literature, in which conflicts between people and cultures can serve as examples (Daunic et al., 2000).

Students need to learn that conflicts can be gentle, tough, or solution-seeking (Addison & Westmoreland, 2000). When two students are friends and wish to continue to be friends, their conflict is gentle: They may prefer to yield or withdraw by avoiding, ignoring, or denying the conflict. In tough conflicts, one student verbally or physically threatens another. When seeking solutions, the students negotiate to find a consensus that satisfies both of them and preserves their friendship. Conflicts usually originate because of three major issues: (1) resources, (2) needs,

Previously in this chapter you learned about direct observation. How would you use direct observation in a self-management intervention?

The skills students learn about conflict resolution can help them resolve problems with their peers independently.

or (3) goals. Helping students identify the origins of the issues they face can help them resolve their conflicts peacefully.

Students also need to understand that anger is normal and provides important information; the person who is angry believes that a want or need is not being met. However, anger can be either constructive or destructive, and students need to discuss the differences.

Problem solving and successful decision making are important conflict resolution skills (Bullock & Foegen, 2002). Students need to identify the problem specifically, brainstorm and evaluate the pros and cons of solutions, decide which is the best solution, and make a plan to carry it out. In addition, they need to find solutions that will help both parties save face (Addison & Westmoreland, 2000). Students also benefit from learning to negotiate to make sure their needs are met, rather than backing down when conflict occurs. Box 5–4 provides you with other ideas for teaching conflict resolution. Box 5–5 tells you about Tools for Success, a software program that helps students increase their emotional intelligence through more effective conflict resolution, along with other skills.

Collaborating to Meet Students' Needs

Strength-based interventions emphasize the spirit of generosity: sharing gifts and talents with others. "Young people cannot develop a sense of their own value unless they have an opportunity to be of value to others" (Brendtro, Brokenleg, & VanBockern, cited in Panico, 1998, p. 37).

One of the most effective ways for students to serve others is through **service learning**, a method for students to develop newly acquired skills by active participation and structured reflection in organized opportunities to meet community needs (Muscott, 2000). Students who participate in service learning are less likely to exhibit rebellion or delinquency and more likely to cope effectively with life challenges (Laursen, 2000). Service learning creates collaborative partnerships for learning and can be as diverse as working with pets or participating in a community cleanup. Service learning can prepare students to make a living and allows people in the community to discover that students with emotional or behavioral disorders can contribute positively in a work environment.

Matt is fortunate to participate in a Work to Life program developed by Picaway Ross Vocational Center. Among other things, the service learning incorporated into this program helps prepare students for good citizenship. Currently, Matt is writing to a soldier to thank him for serving our country. Charlotte and Matt are baking cookies to send with the letter. In Box 5–6, we

For more information on and programs related to service learning, go to the Web Links module in Chapter 5 of the Companion Website.

Box 5—4

Into Practice

Activities for Teaching Conflict Resolution

Several strategies are helpful in resolving conflict (Addison & Westmoreland, 2000). The first is *active listening,* a nonjudgmental approach in which the listener paraphrases the content of what is said and reflects the feelings of the speaker: "I'm hearing you say that you are tired of having to do all this work and feel angry that I'm asking you to do it. Is that correct?" Another important strategy is *behavior examination:* learning to express feelings without aggression. Finally, students need to learn *tolerance:* accepting others' differences. Teaching students to resolve conflicts can be integrated into the everyday curriculum and does not have to be stressful. Addison and Westmoreland suggest the following games and activities.

Active Listening
Listening Mirror

Hold up a hand mirror and ask your students what they see. When they say they see themselves, explain that they see a reflection of themselves. Let the students discuss the difference. After telling the students that they are going to learn about another type of reflection, let them decorate a "hand mirror" made out of construction paper. Laminate the papers and provide the students with washable markers. Tell the students they are going to learn to listen to other people very carefully and make a reflection of their words. Have each student listen to a partner tell about something that happened to her in the last week and write down the partner's words. Have the partners trade roles and then share what they wrote. Ask them how they felt when in the roles of speaker and listener. Then discuss how being a listening mirror might help resolve conflicts.

Reflecting on Conversation

Divide students into groups of three: a facilitator and recorder, a listener, and a talker. At the facilitator's signal, the listener closes his or her eyes and the talker speaks on any subject. The listener needs to be aware of changes in voice patterns and tone as well as the content. After 3 to 5 minutes, the listener shares what the speaker has said and seems to feel and why. Have the students exchange roles until they have experienced each role.

Behavior Examination
Angry Shakes

You will need a blender, vanilla ice cream, milk, and strawberry-flavored drink. As you add ice cream to the blender, ask students to share how they would feel if a younger brother or sister borrowed their favorite CD without permission and lost it. Let them talk about what they would do. Add the strawberry drink and start the blender. Ask students what color the shake is now (pink). Explain that when they express anger inappropriately through yelling or hitting, they change the color of the conflict into violence. Pour out the shake, rinse the blender, and add more vanilla ice cream. Add milk and blend as you

talk about how the situation will stay calm if they talk quietly to the younger brother or sister about their feelings and help the sibling understand the importance of not borrowing without permission. Let the students sample the shakes as they talk about their own examples of conflict and whether the conflict was strawberry or vanilla.

Tolerance
Wizards and Frogs

Have the students discuss characters from J. K. Rowlings's *Harry Potter* series and note how Harry Potter's uncle, aunt, and cousin are not tolerant of his being a wizard. Playing the Peter, Paul, and Mary song "I'm in Love with a Big Blue Frog" can generate a discussion of intolerance for secondary students.

Problem Solving and Decision Making
Choose Your Own Ending

Read a story to students and stop at the point of conflict. Have the students brainstorm solutions that would provide a win-win solution.

Creative Negotiating
Harmony

Have the students role-play a scenario that is age appropriate. Elementary students might negotiate computer time with a sibling; secondary students might negotiate school cafeteria changes with the principal. Have them divide into groups of four to six members. Have half the members take one point of view and the other half the other person's point of view.

Putting These Strategies to Work for Progress in the General Curriculum

1. What other activities can you think of to help students learn these strategies?

2. Which strategies do you believe will be most challenging for students to learn? Why?

3. How do you handle conflict that occurs in the classroom? Are you an effective role model? What could you do to improve your own conflict resolution skills.

4. How could you help students apply these skills in everyday conflicts that occur in the classroom?

To answer these questions online and learn more about these strategies, go to the Into Practice module in Chapter 5 of the Companion Website.

Source: Adapted from Addison, M. M., & Westmoreland, D. A. (2000). Over the net: Encouraging win-win solutions through conflict resolution. *Reaching Today's Youth, 5*(1), 53–54.

Technology Tips

Box 5—5

Tools for Success

Emotional intelligence (EQ) is defined as "the ability to identify, experience, understand, and express human emotions in healthy and productive ways" (Oakwood Solutions, 2002, n.p). EQ, unlike IQ, can change; and improving EQ benefits health, education, relationships, and work, according to the creators of Tools for Success, computer software programs that guide students through the process of change. Based on a whole person model, Tools for Success includes three components: emotional intelligence programs, career exploration and assessment, and a functional literacy system. The focus is on "maintaining one's health by developing one's potential . . . by examining what is right and complete about people rather than what is wrong and incomplete" (Oakwood Solutions, 2002, n.p.).

The Personal Skills Map, designed to identify a student's EQ, is the core assessment tool of the program and measures self-esteem, interpersonal assertion, interpersonal awareness, empathy, drive strength/motivation, decision making, time management, sales orientation/leadership, commitment ethic, stress management, physical wellness, interpersonal aggression, interpersonal deference, and change orientation. The resulting profile can reveal traits such as low emotional support, personal abuse or burnout, systematically low self-esteem, and even dropout potential. After students complete and receive feedback on their profile, the program helps them "buy in" to change by (1) defining targeted skills, (2) showing how a lack of these skills interferes with successful living, (3) demonstrating how acquiring the skills improves personal performance, (4) listing steps to improve the skills, and (5) providing a personal contract for improvement of the targeted skills over a 21-day period.

The teacher then provides each student with skills training modules appropriate for his or her needs based on the personal skills map. The emotional intelligence profile specifically targets the skills identified in the personal skills map. The success profiler comprises a variety of systems: the change profile, the leadership profile, the learning profile, the sensitivity profile, the team pro-

file, and the violence prevention profile. Other available modules include the Anger Management Program, the Substance Abuse Prevention Program, and Conflict Resolution through Winning Colors.

The Conflict Resolution module helps students understand personal behavioral patterns related to the four parts of self: brown, or builder (leadership and decisiveness); green, or planner (planning new ways of doing things); blue, or relater (openness to others and expression of feelings); and red, or adventurer (excitement and action). After identifying personal behavior patterns, students learn to identify "what drives other people and how to better approach and work with these individuals," thus reducing conflict (Oakwood Solutions, LLC, 2002, n.p.).

Tools for Success is useful for general education classes because students with and without emotional and behavioral disorders can benefit from the program's skill diversity and individualized pace. The program also provides text-to-speech capabilities so that inefficient readers can use the program independently. An entire classroom could work through the software simultaneously in a computer lab.

Putting Tools for Success to Work for Progress in the General Education Curriculum:

1. After students have completed their Personal Skills Map, how could you generate a group discussion about what they have learned about themselves?

2. After students have completed Conflict Resolution through Winning Colors, how would you use their skills to resolve classroom conflicts?

3. How do you think you could benefit as a teacher from completing these modules?

To answer these questions online and learn more about these strategies, go to the Technology Tips module in Chapter 5 156of the Companion Website.

Source: Adapted from Oakwood Solutions. (2002). *Emotional intelligence demonstration programs: Education version.* Oshkosh, WI: Conover Company.

Service learning helps students with emotional or behavioral disorders develop positive character traits.

describe how a program called SO Prepared for Citizenship benefits elementary, secondary, and college students as well as the community. In Figure 5–9, you will find an assessment instrument for measuring student strengths that is used in SO Prepared.

Along with community collaboration for service learning, teachers must effectively collaborate with parents. At the beginning of this chapter, you learned how Matt's mother, Laura, who worked so hard to help her son, felt that she was being treated like a war criminal. As you discovered in the section on causes, researchers are beginning to discover genetic and physiological bases for emotional or behavioral disorders. Blaming parents may give teachers an excuse to give up on a child, but placing blame does nothing to solve problems. "One of the most important things I learned going through school," Charlotte says, "is 'always remember that parents believe that their child is a direct reflection of them.' So when you say, 'That kid's a bad kid,' they're thinking, 'I'm a bad parent.' That's why I always try to be upbeat. Communication comes down to this: It's daily; it's immediate; it's positive." A strength-based perspective carries over to the family, building on what members do right and providing supports for their needs as well as the student's.

Interventions for students with emotional or behavioral disorders are often necessarily intensive and multifaceted (Kauffman, 2000). In the Native American tradition, the circle of courage (see Box 5–7) with its four elements—belonging, mastery, independence, and generosity—is an example of a multifaceted intervention that is strength-based and promotes resilience.

The four research-based strategies you have learned about in this section tie closely to the four elements of the circle of courage. In the inclusion section we discussed wraparound, a model that helps both student and family to perceive ways of belonging. In the universal design section, you learned about teaching self-management to facilitate independence and conflict resolution to encourage a sense of mastery. Service learning, which we discussed in the collaboration section, promotes generosity. Enveloping Matt in the circle of courage allowed Rebecca, Charlotte, Laura, some of Matt's other teachers, and his principal to develop close relationships with him, resulting in positive changes in his life. Matt is becoming more resilient. In Figure 5–10, you will find other strategies to help you develop this type of relationship with your students.

FIGURE 5–9

SO Prepared for Citizenship: Citizen-Leader Evaluation Form

A PERSON OF CHARACTER * IS TRUSTWORTHY * ACTS RESPONSIBLY * IS FAIR AND JUST * IS CARING
* TREATS ALL PEOPLE WITH RESPECT * IS A GOOD CITIZEN

Student Citizen-Leader: _____ Date: _____

Adult Buddy: _____ Pod: _____

School: PMA or Dr. Crisp   Grade: _____ Teacher: _____

TODAY AT SO PREPARED, MY BUDDY: Please place a check for each behavior

Character Traits and Behaviors	Excellent	Good	Need Improvement	Not Applicable
Showed TRUSTWORTHINESS by 1. Telling the truth and keeping his/her word.				
Showed TRUSTWORTHINESS by 2. Not asking a friend to do something wrong.				
Showed RESPONSIBILITY by 3. Setting a good example for others.				
Showed RESPONSIBILITY by 4. Following directions.				
Showed FAIRNESS & JUSTICE by 5. Treating all people fairly.				
Showed FAIRNESS & JUSTICE by 6. Not taking more than their fair share.				
Showed CARING by 7. Helping others.				
Showed CARING by 8. Not being mean or insensitive to other people.				
Showed RESPECTFULNESS by 9. Being courteous and polite.				
Showed RESPECTFULNESS by 10. Not abusing, demeaning, or mistreating anyone.				
Showed GOOD CITIZENSHIP by 11. Playing by the rules.				
Showed GOOD CITIZENSHIP by 12. Doing his/her share of the activities.				

Please include any comments or examples of character on the back of this form.
Thank you for sharing your time to complete this form.

Source: From Muscott, H. (2001). Fostering learning, fun, and friendship among students with emotional and behavioral disorders and their peers: The SO (Service-Learning Opportunities) Prepared for Citizenship program. *Beyond Behavior, 10*(3), p. 40.

What Can You Learn from Others Who Teach Students with Emotional or Behavioral Disorders?

Learning for the Early Childhood Years: Johns Hopkins University Prevention Intervention Research Center

As early as first grade, learning problems predict depression, and aggression predicts "antisocial behavior, criminality, and early substance abuse" (Ialongo, Poduska, Werthamer, & Sheppard, 2001, p. 147). For these reasons, providing early intervention for learning and behavioral challenges is essential. Researchers at Johns Hopkins University in Baltimore, Maryland, created two

Collaboration Tips

Box 5—6

SO Prepared for Citizenship

How can students with emotional or behavioral disorders develop friendships with peers; learn important character, academic, and prevocational skills; establish resilience-building relationships with older teens and adults in the community; and develop a sense of significance, purpose, and accomplishment? Howard Muscott and his colleagues at Riviera College in Nashua, New Hampshire, hoped to accomplish these goals using an innovative service learning program: SO (service-learning opportunities) Prepared for Citizenship (Muscott, 2001).

In the planning stage, they identified community needs and decided how they could meet those needs. Teachers and administrators of local elementary and middle schools indicated that their most prevalent concerns were expanding character education beyond the school day to reduce incidents of cursing, bullying, and fighting and to increase compassion and cooperation. Both schools wanted students to develop citizenship through leadership training, team building, valuing of ethnic differences, collaboration, and civic responsibility. In addition, students needed to improve skills in math, science, reading, and art. When faculty at two local high schools and Riviera College were asked about their needs, the faculty said their students needed to develop "respect, responsibility, justice, trustworthiness, and caring" through "experiential learning opportunities and positive interactions among diverse ethnic groups" (p. 37). "These needs dovetailed beautifully with those of the elementary/middle schools," Howard Muscott says (p. 37). Service learning would meet the needs of all four schools. To assist with planning, development, and evaluation, a faculty member from the school and the college, student program coordinators, and sometimes curriculum coordinators and mentors formed planning and implementation assessment teams (PIATs) at the participating elementary and middle schools.

College students received academic credit for serving as curriculum coordinators. When they took a children's literature class, for example, they contracted with their professor to teach character traits using books. Riviera students, along with high school students, also served as mentors to a younger buddy. Mentors received five hours of instruction to prepare for three relational roles: "(1) effective caregivers who treat their younger students with respect and worth while helping them succeed at program activities, (2) moral models who demonstrate a high level of respect and responsibility in their interactions with others and discuss morally significant events, and (3) ethical mentors who provide direct instruction and guidance through explanation, storytelling, discussion, encouragement of positive behavior, and corrective feedback when students engage in behavior that is hurtful to themselves or others" (p. 38).

Although the program primarily targeted students with emotional or behavioral disorders, students with other disabilities, no disabilities, and giftedness also participated. Weekly sessions for character training at SO Prepared included opening circle, learning center time, and closing circle; and each taught four traits: (1) respect and diversity appreciation, (2) caring and compassion, (3) trustworthiness, and (4) fairness and justice. PIAT established collaborative learning teams at the elementary and middle school. Two or more buddy teams (a college or high school student paired with a younger student) formed partner teams for small group instruction. Larger teams called learning pods, usually consisting of two partner teams or eight people, allowed for group discussion and interaction.

Along with character education, SO Prepared allowed younger students and their mentors to participate in community activities to practice their skills. Students and faculty recommended projects to PIAT that met specific community needs: for example, local food drives or recycling projects.

In May, a three-hour celebration and awards ceremony recognized the accomplishments of students and was attended by community dignitaries as well as families and faculty. Awards reflected specific character traits, and consensus nominations from each pod were encouraged. Pre- and post-assessment of students using a behavior rating scale suggested that most students improved their behavior because of the program. Students, faculty, and parents rated the program favorably. One parent wrote, "My child has become more outgoing and seems to better enjoy the company of peers. She is more social and less shy. She is more confident. Thank you for giving my daughter the opportunity to learn through service" (p. 43).

Putting These Tips to Work for Progress in the General Curriculum

1. What are the challenges?

2. What can the team do?

3. What are the results?

To answer these questions online and learn more about these ideas and concepts, go to the Collaboration Tips module in Chapter 5 of the Companion Website.

Box 5—7

The Circle of Courage

Native American educator and researcher Martin Brokenleg and two colleagues identified four universal needs of children (Brendtro, Brokenleg, & Van Bockern, 1991). When these needs are not met, children can become discouraged and develop psychological and behavioral symptoms. Traditional Native American tribal culture sought to meet these needs. Brokenleg (1999) explains:

> Our research indicated that tribal cultures created environments that served to cultivate courage and responsibility in youth. Various tribes differed in many respects, but four common values appeared to exist in the precolonial histories of most tribal people. (pp. 194–195)

The number four is sacred to Native Americans, who view the individual as standing in a circle surrounded by four directions. These four life directions—*belonging, mastery, independence,* and *generosity*—form the Circle of Courage. This philosophy "is perhaps the most effective system of positive discipline ever developed. These approaches emerged from cultures where the central purpose of life was the education and empowerment of children" (Brendtro et al., 1991, p. 6). Modern psychology validates these universal needs for attachment, achievement, autonomy, and altruism (Brokenleg, 1999; Coopersmith, 1997; Dreikurs, 1998; Maslow, 1998). Brokenleg (1998) refers to these needs as a "human wellness code of immutable building blocks for the development of healthy personalities, families, and communities" (p. 195). Native American culture integrated opportunities to meet these needs in everyday life.

The Spirit of Belonging

In traditional Native American culture, all adults served as teachers for children. Children learned to view themselves as related to everyone with whom they had frequent contact. "The ultimate test of kinship was behavior, not blood; you belonged if you acted like you belonged" (Brendtro et al., 1991, p. 6).

The Spirit of Mastery

Precolonial Native American education emphasized cognitive, physical, social, and spiritual competence. Children learned cultural values through oral legends and

The spirit of belonging

The spirit of mastery

The spirit of independence

The spirit of generosity

ceremonies. Through these practices, children discovered that wisdom came from observing and listening to their elders. Games, creative play, and chores prepared them for adult responsibilities. Adults entrusted older children with the care of younger children. Native American children "were taught to generously acknowledge the achievements of others, but a person who received honor must always accept this without arrogance" (Brendtro et al., 1991, p. 8).

The Spirit of Independence

Social controls balanced autonomy in traditional Native culture. Children learned that dependence as demonstrated by value and respect of elders is essential for independence. The culture valued individual freedom; children learned self-management through modeling and guidance rather than through coercion, punishment, rewards, or an emphasis on obedience. Children were encouraged to "work things out in their own manner" (Brendtro et al., p. 8). Abraham Maslow (1998), well known for his hierarchy of human needs, more recently observed a toddler in the Blackfoot tribe. The child could not open a heavy door, despite repeated attempts. None of the adults helped him. After half an hour, the child finally managed to open the door. Then the adults praised his success.

The Spirit of Generosity

Giving was an important aspect of traditional Native ceremonies, and the highest virtues were generosity and unselfishness. Children learned to give without holding back. One child's grandmother asked him to give away his most precious possession, his puppy, so that he could become strong and courageous. "To accumulate property for its own sake was disgraceful" (Brendtro et al., 1991, p. 9). Children learned "to measure others by intrinsic worth rather than external appearance."

What happens when a child does not achieve these four values? "Discouragement is courage denied. When the Circle of Courage is broken, the lives of children are no longer in harmony and peace" (Brendtro et al., 1991, p. 10). The challenge for educators is to see the brokenness in these children and reclaim them by creating a classroom that embodies the core values of the Circle of Courage.

Putting These Ideas to Work for Progress in the General Curriculum

1. What significant people helped you develop the Circle of Courage? Was your Circle of Courage ever broken by someone?

2. As a teacher, how will you embody the core values of the Circle of Courage in your classroom?

To answer these questions online and learn more about these ideas and concepts, go to the Multicultural Considerations module in Chapter 5 of the Companion Website.

Source: Adapted from Brendtro, L. K., Brokenleg, M., & Van Bockern, S. (1991). The circle of courage. *Beyond Behavior, 2*(1), 5–12; Brokenleg, M. (1999). Native American perspectives on mastery. *Reclaiming Children and Youth, 7*(4), 194–196.

programs to provide interventions for poor achievement as well as aggressive and shy behavior. Referred to as the *classroom-centered intervention,* the first program combined mastery learning and a good behavior game. Along with this program, researchers developed the *family-school partnership intervention* to improve parent-teacher communication and parents' behavior management strategies. Three first-grade classes in each of nine schools participated: One class received classroom-centered intervention, the second received the family-school partnership intervention, and the third received no special intervention.

The classroom-centered intervention incorporated curriculum enhancements, specific behavior management strategies, and additional supports for students who were not performing adequately. The curriculum was enhanced with critical thinking, composition, listening, and comprehension skills. Students received behavioral interventions that included once-weekly class meetings to develop social problem-solving skills. They also played the good behavior game: The class was divided into three groups, and points were added for precisely defined appropriate behavior or taken away from a group when a member was shy or aggressive. Students could exchange points for tangible rewards. Gradually, material reinforcers were replaced with social reinforcers.

In the family-school partnership intervention, teachers and other school staff received seminar training in communicating with parents. Parents received weekly home learning and communication activities from teachers and behavior management training from a school psychologist/social worker teamed with the first-grade teacher. Each school also provided a voice mail system to allow parents to communicate easily with school personnel.

FIGURE 5-10

Seven habits of reclaiming relationships

	Behaviors	**Beliefs**
1. Trust	Doing what you say you are going to do	I'm accountable to the young persons I serve.
2. Attention	Putting the young person at the center	Children and youth are valuable and worthy of concern.
3. Empathy	Seeing the world through the young person's eyes	There are many versions of the same story.
4. Availability	Making time for children and youth a top priority	Young people are important and worth an investment of my time and energy.
5. Affirmation	Saying positive things to and about a young person and meaning it	Even troubled youth have positive qualities and constructive behaviors that can be acknowledged.
6. Respect	Giving young people a say in decisions that affect them	Feelings are valid, and young persons are the best experts on themselves.
7. Virtue	Holding young persons accountable for their behavior without blaming; being a role model	Children must learn self-discipline, and those who teach them must practice what they teach.

Source: Laursen, E. K. (2002). Seven habits of reclaiming relationships. *Reclaiming Children and Youth, 11*(1), 10–14.

The Johns Hopkins researchers knew that their interventions might increase short-term gains in academic achievement and appropriate behaviors, but they did not know whether these gains could be maintained. However, by the end of sixth grade, students in the classroom-centered intervention, when compared to students who received no intervention, were significantly less likely to receive a lifetime diagnosis of conduct disorder, to have been suspended, or to have or appear to need mental health intervention (Ialongo et al., 2001).

Although classroom-centered intervention resulted in the most significant changes, students in the family-school partnership program also improved compared to those children who received no treatment. The researchers speculate that combining the two interventions might result in even greater benefits for students. An exciting component of this research is that it reveals the difference that one school year can make in the life of a child.

Learning for the Elementary Years: LaGrange (Illinois) Department of Special Education

Beginning in 1993, the LaGrange (Illinois) Department of Special Education (LADSE), under the leadership of Dr. Lucille Eber, created a new type of program called the Emotional and Behavioral Disorder Network which took a wraparound approach to providing services. As you have learned, the wraparound approach responds to the haphazard human system that many students and families face by providing holistic support for the student and the family.

What services are wrapped around each child and his or her family? That depends on what they need. They may need behavioral support, in-home counseling, case management, or parent advocacy training. They may need money for clubs, sports, special lessons, or the basic necessities of life. Wraparound programs use funds already allocated to education, social services, and mental health agencies and redirect them to meet individual needs rather than place children into program slots.

Special education teachers function as wraparound facilitators, consultants, and co-teachers to help successfully include these students in general education classrooms. LADSE's parent partners element has led to lasting support networks and friendships among parents. Its buddy program recruits people ages 17 to 30 to be students' friends and provide social and recreational opportunities, along with academic assistance, for designated children. Here's what one parent says about the changes she's seen in her child: "My son faced long-term residential placement following two years of psychiatric hospitalization. Now I watch him from my door as he boards a bus every morning for a day school" (La Grange Area Department of Special Education, 1993).

This parent's experience generalizes to other families served by LADSE. Students using the wraparound services were less likely to receive self-contained placements and to require psychiatric placements. They also had improved academic outcomes (Goldman & Faw, 1999).

Learning for the Middle and Secondary Years: Frank Lloyd Wright Middle School, Milwaukee

In a society that emphasizes zero tolerance, Frank Lloyd Wright Middle School is a beacon of hope, existing to reclaim students rather than exclude them. The four bright lights of the circle of courage—generosity, belonging, independence, and mastery—shine throughout the school's curriculum, instruction, and extracurricular activities, increasing the likelihood that students with emotional or behavioral disorders experience inclusion.

Teachers at Frank Lloyd Wright Middle School believe "you can't teach 'em if you can't reach 'em" (Farner, 2002, p. 22). Students gain a sense of belonging by establishing close relationships in their "house," a group of 50–75 students who stay together for multiple periods with the same group of teachers. Teachers, including special education teachers, have the opportunity to know students personally, looping or remaining with the same group for two years, and "capitalize on student strengths to improve weaknesses" (p. 20).

Small groups of teachers have a common planning time to develop project-based learning. Students share real problems that concern them, and teachers integrate instruction into a variety of subjects around the student-generated themes, making sure that lessons and activities address state curriculum standards. The school has three benchmarks: Focus on success, use standards-based rubrics for comprehensive assessment, and make technology readily available to all students and staff (Farner, 2002). Learning also occurs in the community through volunteer work and service learning, allowing students to experience generosity.

The multipurpose period, which occurs at the end of each school day, facilitates mastery and a sense of independence. Adding this period resulted in higher test scores and more homework completion. During this flexible period, students receive individualized support from their house teachers, participate in applied arts with the teachers who have been assigned to their house that trimester, and have access to resources that they may not have at home. Rather than supervising the lunchroom or serving some other noninstructional role, teachers are assigned to the multipurpose period, giving them yet another opportunity to connect meaningfully with their students.

Wright Academy, a specialized school-within-the-school, allows students with the greatest needs to receive support from specially trained teachers while remaining connected to and participating actively with their peers. "The key to this Reclaiming school is the incredible dedication and shared vision of the staff. It is not the type of vision that is written down on a piece of paper and then put in a drawer or is mounted on a wall. This is a true vision that is evident in the daily interactions between community members" (Farner, 2002, p. 22).

For links to more information about some of these programs, go to the Web Links module in Chapter 5 of the Companion Website.

Learning for the Transitional and Postsecondary Years: Canada's YouthNet/Reseau Ado

How do you give a sense of belonging to a young person who is homeless? How do you help street-involved youth reconnect with the circle of courage when they often distrust mainstream mental health services? And if they manage to survive the streets, how can you help them overcome their lack of education and employment opportunities to become "healthy and productive adults" (O'Connor & MacDonald, 1999, p. 102)?

YouthNet/Reseau Ado, a Canadian program, serves two primary purposes: providing a support group for young people to discuss mental health issues and linking them with a safety net of youth-friendly mental health professionals. Support groups are co-facilitated by 20 to 30 year olds with graduate mental health training. (Young people who were surveyed identified this age group as old enough to have life experiences but young enough to relate to their concerns.) The groups destigmatize mental illness, promote good mental health, and provide early identification of mental health needs (O'Connor & MacDonald, 1999).

One group at a drop-in center, specifically designed for youth who were homeless or street-involved, included 17 members ranging in ages from 15 to 20, who met weekly for six months. Initially, attendance was high because many participants came for a meal and left after meetings. Facilitators enabled the group to decide to move to a new location, a community center that was not serving meals. The group also decided whether to be open (allowing new members to join each week) or closed (no new members). Initially, the nine members at the new location decided to be closed; but they later changed to open, only allowing their friends to join. Giving participants a sense of mastery through group ownership allowed a sense of belonging and coherence to develop by about the fourth week. At the beginning of each meeting, facilitators asked the young people to share the best and worst things that they had experienced since the last meeting. Some members reported that knowing the group would ask these questions caused them to plan activities such as going to the park or visiting friends rather than "begging, smoking marijuana, and killing time" all day. Another consistent element was a question of the day, such as "If a movie were made about your life, what would it be called and why?" or "Where do you see yourself in five years?"

During the last meeting, the participants—several of whom had left the streets and become productively employed—said that the program had benefited them by giving them an opportunity to talk in a nonjudgmental atmosphere, allowing them to hear the views and experiences of their peers, providing positive adult role models, allowing them to interact in a positive way with mental health professionals, and providing a source of stability in an otherwise chaotic lifestyle. (O'Connor & MacDonald, 1999). A strength-based paradigm is central to YouthNet/Reseau Ado: "This program does not view youth as patients but as experts in working with adults to design youth-friendly interventions" (p. 102).

A Vision for Matthew's Future

A strength-based approach emphasizes that students are potential victors, not victims (Laursen, 2000). Matt is an example of the power of that belief. Rebecca remembers fondly the first day that Matt called her to say he was too busy to see her. She knew then that Matt was beginning to stand on his own without her support. Next year, Matt will be in high school, his first experience away from Charlotte's support after several years in her class. She is beginning to prepare him for that transition. And Matt is still working on refining some of his social skills and developing a more positive relationship with his family. Rebecca believes that high school will be "Matt's chance to shine."

Beginning in his junior year, Matt will have a work placement through Picaway Ross Vocational Center, perhaps in auto mechanics. The program has a 95 percent post–high school job placement rate. Although Matt thinks he might be interested in auto mechanics, he also thinks he might become a professional golfer. Rebecca hopes he will try out for his school's golf team "to show himself off a little bit." Matt certainly has the intelligence to continue his education after high school, if he chooses. Several years ago, his prospects for the future were dismal; now his options seem limitless. Matt can have a productive, happy life, thanks to the caring of some important people in his life and his own determination.

When Rebecca and Charlotte talked to Matt about sharing his story in this textbook for teachers, he told them why he chose to do so—his vision for your future: "They need to know that you need to care and not give up. Keep trying."

What Would You Recommend?

1. If you were Matt's teacher, how would you prepare him for high school?
2. Matt's mother is a single parent. How would you provide support for her?
3. If you were on Matt's IEP committee, what goals and objectives would you want to see on his transition plan?

Summary

How Do You Recognize Students with Emotional or Behavioral Disorders?

▼ Students with emotional or behavioral disorders manifest emotional, behavioral, social, and/or academic characteristics that are chronic and severe and adversely interfere with their educational performance.

▼ The IDEA definition differs in several ways from that of the non-IDEA definition.

▼ Students may exhibit disorders including, but not limited to, anxiety disorder, mood disorder, oppositional defiant disorder, conduct disorder, or schizophrenia.

▼ Two broad categories of emotional or behavioral disorders include externalizing (aggressive, acting-out, noncompliant) behaviors and internalizing (withdrawn, depressed, anxious, obsessive, compulsive) behaviors.

▼ Although students with emotional or behavioral disorders experience social and academic challenges, it is important to maintain a strength-based perspective.

▼ The causes of emotional or behavioral disorders include biological causes, mainly genetics. The causes also include environmental causes, such as living conditions that lead to stress, poverty and single-parent households, lack of system supports, and child abuse.

▼ Prevalence estimates vary from 3 to 6 percent of all students. However, less than 1 percent are identified for IDEA benefits. Many of the identified students are from minority populations.

How Do You Evaluate Students with Emotional or Behavioral Disorders?

▼ The *Behavioral and Emotional Rating Scale*, an evaluation tool, identifies a student's emotional and behavioral strengths in five different domains.

▼ Professionals use direct observations of student behavior (systemically watching and recording observable and measurable student behavior).

How Do You Assure Progress in the General Curriculum?

▼ Students with emotional or behavioral disorders are less likely to be included in general education classrooms than are students with most other disabilities; however, programs such as the wraparound approach facilitate inclusion.

▼ Self-management and conflict resolution are two important skills for universally designed instruction.

▼ Service learning is an effective tool for community collaboration.

What Can You Learn from Others Who Teach Students with Emotional or Behavioral Disorders?

▼ The Johns Hopkins University Prevention Intervention Research Center established two first-grade programs, one focusing on curriculum and behavior, another on family-teacher communication, both showed reductions in emotional and behavioral disorders by the time students were sixth graders.

▼ The LaGrange Department of Special Education in Illinois uses a wraparound approach to provide students and families with comprehensive and integrated services.

▼ Frank Lloyd Wright Middle School incorporates the circle of courage as an alternative to zero tolerance.

▼ YouthNet/Reseau Ado links support groups and mental health services with young people who are homeless or street-involved.

Council for Exceptional Children **PRAXIS**

To find out how and where this chapter content connects to the CEC Professional Standards and the Praxis™ Standards, go to the Standards Connection module in Chapter 5 of the Companion Website. A comprehensive matrix aligning CEC Professional Standards, Praxis™ Standards, and INTASC principles to the entire text, is available in the Apendix and on the Companion Website.

Chapter 6

Who Is Kelsey Blankenship?

Imagine being 9 years old and acting in front of thousands of people. Kelsey Blankenship, a fourth grader from rural Ohio, performed twice to an audience of 6,000 in a Cincinnati competition, receiving a superior rating for both performances.

Superior acting abilities are remarkable for any child, but they are even more so for Kelsey. These performances represent a dramatic change in her because she has attention-deficit/hyperactivity disorder (AD/HD). According to her grandmother, Yvonne, a few years ago Kelsey would have "been all over the church" instead of learning her lines.

Kelsey's second-grade teacher, Barb Tootle, remembers those days well:

> You would always know where Kelsey was: There would always be some commotion. I would have students saying, "Kelsey did this to me; Kelsey did that to me." Kelsey never walked slowly through the classroom. It was more like pushing her way through. She would raise her hand, but she wouldn't have anything to say or would make something up.

But these days, Kelsey is a different child. Barb describes the change that occurred during second grade:

> Kelsey always came in with a smile. She would sharpen her pencil, hand in her homework, and do an activity that was on the board. She kept her hands to herself, not hitting people or taking their things; and she would pay attention. We would have good discussions, and Kelsey would be a part of them. She stayed on task. And her grades improved! She was happier.

Yvonne is also quick to comment on Kelsey's strengths, which are readily apparent now:

> One thing I like about her is her homework schedule. She does it immediately when she gets home. There's no fighting or fussing or anything. You wouldn't want a better kid. She'll do anything for you she can. She's a people person.

Kelsey still struggles with being patient and attentive. Now, however, Kelsey *has* friends and recently made the honor roll for the first time. She is focused enough to enjoy dramatics, art, music, cheerleading, and animals.

As her therapist, Chris Fraser, points out, the difference in Kelsey occurred primarily because Kelsey wanted to change and worked hard enough to make change happen. She

Attention-Deficit/Hyperactivity Disorder

was open to a treatment plan developed by her teacher, her therapist, and her psychiatrist as well as the two most important people on her team: Yvonne and Bill, the grandparents who adopted her. Kelsey calls them Mom and Dad.

Kelsey's journey toward change began when Barb Tootle contacted Yvonne. Yvonne remembers, "Kelsey was having problems in Mrs. Tootle's class, and I would always stop by and ask her how she was doing. Mrs. Tootle started talking about this AD/HD problem she thought Kelsey might have. So I talked to a couple of her other teachers, and they agreed we should check it out."

The evaluation confirmed that Kelsey has AD/HD. She and her parents began seeing Chris regularly. Chris helped the family interact in new ways. One difficult issue the family faced was homework; so Chris brought Kelsey's teacher, Barb, into one of the sessions. He recalls:

Kelsey's parents were getting frustrated because every night they were fighting her about sitting still and doing her homework. So Barb told them, "This is Kelsey's homework. She has to do it. And if she doesn't do it, she has to be accountable to me. Don't fight the war with her at home." Then we had Kelsey come in, and we explained, "Kelsey, this is your responsibility. If you don't get it done, that's okay. But you will face the consequences at school." That allowed her parents to back off. She started doing better because there was less parent-child conflict.

Chris also worked with Kelsey on problem solving. When some of the other students teased her about living with her grandparents, Chris encouraged Kelsey to think of ways to respond appropriately. Her creative, three-page list included "So?" "Whatever," and "I already knew that."

Yvonne and Bill work hard as a team to help Kelsey. Yvonne says, "Bill has been a big help. Sometimes I have a little temper, and he reminds me that she's just a little girl. We both help her with her homework. If there's something I don't understand, and Bill understands it, he'll help her."

Another important factor in Kelsey's change is medication. Her psychiatrist prescribed the stimulant Adderall. Yvonne says:

I was scared about the medication. I had heard all these things about what it causes you to do. Then I heard that, when they get older, they turn into addicts because they've been on all this medicine. I was scared to death to even put her on it. It was a hard decision to make.

Despite Yvonne's concerns, the change resulting from the medication was positive and dramatic. Barb remembers, "I can't tell you the total difference in the way she related to the other students in the classroom, on the playground, walking in the hallway and to the principal and the other teachers. Everyone noticed a difference."

Chris explains the key to making a multimodal treatment plan such as Kelsey's work: "Everybody needs to be pulled in. I think continuity is the most important part."

What do you think?

1. How might the outcome have been different for Kelsey if one member of her team had not agreed to collaborate?
2. What kinds of accommodations might Kelsey and other students who have AD/HD need in the classroom?

To respond to these questions online and learn more about Kelsey Blankenship and attention-deficit/hyperactivity disorder, go to the Cases module in Chapter 6 of the Companion Website.

How Do You Recognize Students with Attention-Deficit/Hyperactivity Disorder?

Because attention-deficit/hyperactivity disorder has received widespread media coverage in recent years, you may have already formed an opinion about this condition. When you hear the term **attention-deficit/hyperactivity disorder (AD/HD)**, do any of these thoughts cross your mind?

▼ People eventually outgrow AD/HD.

▼ AD/HD stems from a lack of will or any effort at self-control.

▼ AD/HD is caused by parents who don't discipline their children.

▼ AD/HD results from children watching too much television or playing too many video games.

▼ Dietary issues such as too much sugar cause AD/HD.

▼ AD/HD results from living in a fast-paced, stressful culture (Harman & Barkley, 2000).

All of those statements are misconceptions. Among the most insidious are the second and third, which assert that AD/HD is not an authentic, debilitating condition. Many who believe that AD/HD is not a genuine disability argue that the label was recently created to absolve parents and teachers from having any responsibility for a child's conflict with them and other adults (in Buonomano, 1999). However, AD/HD is not a new condition. In 1902, George Still, a London physician, identified a group of children with average or higher intelligence who exhibited difficulty with moral control, which he identified as an inability to obey adults and delay gratification. As early as 1937, a Rhode Island pediatrician discovered that administering stimulant medication to children with characteristics identified by Still resulted in a surprisingly calming effect (Bradley, 1937). According to Russell Barkley (2000), who is often referred to as the father of AD/HD because of his extensive research,

> The developmental-neurological nature of AD/HD directly contradicts our strongly held beliefs that self-control and free will are totally determined by the person and his or her upbringing. I believe that this contradiction is what underlies much of society's resistance to admitting [AD/HD] into the class of developmental disabilities for which we have great empathy and on behalf of which we make special allowances and rights.

Recent reports by the surgeon general (Department of Mental Health Services, 1999) and the National Institute of Mental Health (2000) also confirm that the condition is indeed neurological in nature. Because AD/HD has a biological basis, **multimodal treatment,** which often includes **psychotropic medication** (to help the students manage their perceptions, feelings, and behavior), together with educational, social, and behavioral intervention, is effective.

Defining Attention-Deficit/Hyperactivity Disorder

Attention-deficit/hyperactivity disorder is not a separate category under the Individuals with Disabilities Education Act (IDEA). However, IDEA does include students with AD/HD under the category *other health impairments* (see Chapter 11). A student with other health impairments

> has limited strength, vitality, or alertness, including a heightened alertness with respect to the educational environment, that:
>
> i. is due to chronic or acute health problems such as asthma, attention deficit disorder or attention deficit hyperactivity disorder, diabetes, epilepsy, a heart condition, hemophilia, lead poisoning, leukemia, nephritis, rheumatic fever, and sickle cell anemia; and
> ii. adversely affects a child's educational performance. (34 Code of Federal Regulations § 300.7 [c] [9])

You can find out more about CHADD, the largest AD/HD organization, as well as the surgeon general's and NIMH's viewpoints, by visiting the Web Links module in Chapter 6 of the Companion Website.

The criterion "heightened sense of alertness to the environment" allows students with AD/HD to be served under this category. Because, however, IDEA does not specifically define AD/HD, most professionals abide by the American Psychiatric Association's (APA) (2000) definition:

> The essential feature of Attention-Deficit/Hyperactivity Disorder is a persistent pattern of inattention and/or hyperactivity-impulsivity that is more frequently displayed and severe than is typically observed in individuals at a comparable level of development. (p. 85)

APA's limiting criteria of *frequency* and *severity* are important. Everyone is forgetful and absentminded at times, especially during periods of stress. Also, some people are simply more or less energetic than others. But unless those characteristics are chronic and severe and consistently interfere with the ability to function in everyday life, a person should not receive a diagnosis of AD/HD. For a student to receive IDEA services for AD/HD, academic functioning must be adversely affected.

To receive the APA diagnosis of AD/HD, the student must manifest the symptoms before the age of 7 and for at least 6 months. Additionally, the symptoms must be present in at least two settings. This criterion eliminates students who temporarily exhibit features of AD/HD because of environmental stressors.

You can learn more about the federal and DSM-IV-TR definitions of AD/HD by visiting the Web Links module in Chapter 6 of the Companion Website.

Describing the Characteristics

Not all students with AD/HD are **hyperactive** (exhibiting excessive, chronic energy and movement). In fact, some are **hypoactive,** which means they move and respond too slowly.

Figure 6–1 shows the APA diagnostic criteria for AD/HD. APA has identified three subtypes of AD/HD: predominantly inattentive type, predominantly hyperactive-impulsive type, and combined type. For that reason, the acronym *AD/HD* features a slash, indicating inclusion of all three subtypes: attention deficit disorder, hyperactivity disorder, or a combination.

Predominantly Inattentive Type

The first type of AD/HD, *predominantly inattentive type* (IN), describes students who have trouble paying attention in class and are forgetful and easily distracted. Sometimes authors refer to students with the inattentive type as having attention-deficit disorder (ADD).

Students with IN often appear lethargic, apathetic, or hypoactive. They tend to be internally rather than externally focused. Their minds may be hyperactive—thinking simultaneous thoughts, often with creative outcomes—despite the fact that their bodies may seem to move in slow motion.

Students with IN often seem to demonstrate problems with "recall or retrieval of words or concepts" (Barkley, 1998c, p. 8). Symptoms may appear later in these students (ages 8 to 12) than in students with other forms of AD/HD; and their prognosis (if identified) is generally better than for the other two types, perhaps because these students are more likely to cooperate with treatment.

Because students with IN usually are not as disruptive as students with hyperactivity-impulsivity, teachers may overlook them. Without a specific diagnosis and appropriate interventions, these students are at risk for long-term academic, social, and emotional difficulties (Solanto, 2002).

> Children with IN may appear [to be] underactive, sluggish, or daydreamers. . . . Instead of working on math problems, they might be gazing into space. When the teacher calls on them, they may have no idea what is being discussed. Since they don't absorb new information well or produce the same caliber of work as their classmates, children with IN may be mislabeled as "slow learners" or "learning disabled"—often on the basis of group-administered tests where they had difficulty concentrating. They often just quietly underachieve with no one fully aware of their potential. (p. 29)

Predominantly Hyperactive-Impulsive Type

The second type of AD/HD, *predominantly hyperactive-impulsive type* (HI), includes students who cannot seem to sit still, often talk excessively, and have difficulty playing quietly. They often challenge

FIGURE 6–1
Diagnostic criteria for AD/HD

A. Either (1) or (2)

(1) Six (or more) of the following symptoms of **inattention** have persisted for at least six months to a degree that is maladaptive and inconsistent with developmental level:

Inattention:

(a) Often fails to give close attention to details or makes mistakes in schoolwork, work, or other activities.
(b) Often has difficulty sustaining attention in tasks or play activities.
(c) Often does not seem to listen when spoken to directly.
(d) Often does not follow through on instructions and fails to finish schoolwork, chores, or duties in the workplace (not due to oppositional behavior or failure to understand instructions).
(e) Often has difficulty organizing tasks and activities.
(f) Often avoids, dislikes, or is reluctant to engage in tasks that require sustained mental effort (such as schoolwork or homework).
(g) Often loses things necessary for tasks or activities (e.g., toys, school assignments, pencils, books, or tools).
(h) Is often easily distracted by extraneous stimuli.
(i) Is often forgetful in daily activities.

(2) Six (or more) of the following symptoms of **hyperactivity-impulsivity** have persisted for at least six months to a degree that is maladaptive and inconsistent with developmental level:

Hyperactivity:

(a) Often fidgets with hands or feet or squirms in seat.
(b) Often leaves seat in classroom or in other situations in which remaining seated is expected.
(c) Often runs about or climbs excessively in situations in which it is inappropriate (in adolescents or adults, may be limited to subjective feelings of restlessness).
(d) Often has difficulty playing or engaging in leisure activities quietly.
(e) Is often "on the go" or often acts as if "driven by a motor."
(f) Often talks excessively.

Impulsivity:

(g) Often blurts out answers before questions have been completed.
(h) Often has difficulty awaiting turn.
(i) Often interrupts or intrudes on others (e.g., butts into conversations or games).

B. Some hyperactive-impulsive or inattentive symptoms that caused impairment were present before age 7 years.

C. Some impairment from the symptoms is present in two or more separate settings (e.g., at school [or work] and at home).

D. There must be clear evidence of clinically significant impairment in social, academic, or occupational functioning.

E. The symptoms do not occur exclusively during the course of a Pervasive Developmental Disorder, Schizophrenia, or other Psychotic Disorder, and are not better accounted for by another mental disorder (e.g., Mood Disorder, Anxiety Disorder, Dissociative Disorder, or a Personality Disorder).

Code based on type:

314.01 Attention-Deficit/Hyperactivity Disorder, Combined type: if both Criteria A1 and A2 are met for the past six months.

314.00 Attention-Deficit/Hyperactivity Disorder, Predominantly Inattentive Type: if Criterion A1 is met but Criterion A2 is not met for the past six months.

314.01 Attention-Deficit/Hyperactivity Disorder, Predominantly Hyperactive-Impulsive Type: if Criterion A2 is met but Criterion A1 is not met for past six months.

Source: Reprinted with permission from the *Diagnostic and Statistical Manual of Mental Disorders, Fourth Edition, Text Revision,* by the American Psychiatric Association, 2000, Washington, DC: American Psychiatric Association. Copyright 2000 by the American Psychiatric Association.

FIGURE 6–2
Differences between inattentive and hyperactive-impulsive types of AD/HD

Trait	Hyperactive-Impulsive Type	Inattentive Type
Decision making	Impulsive	Sluggish
Boundaries	Intrusive, rebellious	Honors boundaries, polite, obedient
Assertion	Bossy, irritating	Underassertive, overly polite, docile
Attention seeking	Shows off, egotistical, best at worst	Modest, shy, socially withdrawn
Popularity	Attracts new friends but doesn't bond	Bonds but doesn't attract
Most common diagnosis	Oppositional defiant, conduct disorder	Depression

Source: Reprinted with permission from John F. Taylor, Ph.D., Salem, OR. For more information, see his book *Helping Your Hyperactive ADD Child* (1997). Rockin, CA: Prima.

parents' child-rearing skills (Aust, 1994), having more difficulty with bedwetting, sleep problems, stubbornness, and temper tantrums than do children with IN or those without AD/HD. They also tend to be more accident prone, resulting in serious injuries and accidental poisonings.

Relatively few adolescents and adults with AD/HD classify as having only HI (Hynd, 1995). Most also have features of the inattentive type. Those who have primarily HI, however, can become workaholics who require limited rest. Despite being productive in their chosen occupations, they can frustrate those around them because of their tendency to be brutally frank, blurt out impulsive comments, and interrupt conversations. Figure 6–2 lists differences between the inattentive (IN) and hyperactive-impulsive types (HI). Students with the combined type may exhibit features of both.

Combined Type

The third classification—the *combined type* of AD/HD (CB)—describes students who have features of inattention *and* hyperactivity-impulsivity and is often referred to in the literature as ADHD (without the slash). As many as 85 percent of students with AD/HD fall into this category (Barkley, 1998b), including Kelsey. Her hyperactive-impulsive behaviors, including pushing, hitting, arguing, and raising her hand without knowing the answer, have diminished considerably. However, she still struggles with inattentive behaviors, including on-task and organizational issues.

Barkley (1996, 1998b, 2000) considers the IN type of AD/HD to be significantly different from the HI and CB types. His research suggests that those with IN may have a core problem in focused or **selective attention.** By contrast, those with HI or CB appear to have core problems with poor goal-directed persistence and interference control (inhibiting distraction) (Barkley, 1996, 1998b, 2000). What does this research suggest for the classroom? When you assign seatwork, your student with IN may have difficulty getting started on the task as well as setting priorities for completing the assignment. Your student with CB, on the other hand, may start immediately but find completing the task difficult because she is so easily distracted.

A Conceptual Model of Self-Regulation Characteristics

Most people can use the four **executive functions** of the brain that help organize and control behavior rather easily. These four functions of **behavioral inhibition** help them plan for the future (Barkley, 1998b). However, students with AD/HD often display deficits in these four areas, placing them at high risk for low self-esteem, conduct disorders, delinquency, poor grades, dropping out, employment problems, and interpersonal difficulties. AD/HD is a disability of performance

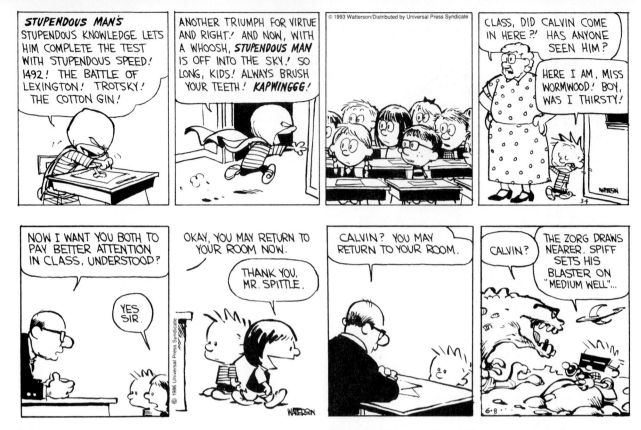

Calvin shows features of hyperactivity-impulsivity in the first cartoon. (By the way, he failed the test.) In the second, he exhibits characteristics of inattention.

rather than skill, according to Barkley (1998b). Students with AD/HD *know* what to do; the challenge is in *doing* what they know because of their deficits in behavioral inhibition. Knowing provides "little consolation to them, little influence over their behavior, and often much irritation to others" (p. 249).

The first executive function is *nonverbal working memory*, which allows students to retrieve auditory, visual, and other sensory images of the past. A deficit in this area can cause students to have difficulty learning from past experience. For example, Joshua, a student in your class, finds himself scolded and disciplined by in-school suspension (excluded from some aspects of school, although his IEP is still mostly carried out) for the same behavior that caused him to be disciplined two weeks ago. Was he sorry he committed the offense the first time? Yes. Does he dislike being scolded and disciplined? Yes. But he did not make the memory association about the potential consequences of his behavior when he committed a similar offense the second time.

Internalization of speech is also an important executive function. Most people talk to themselves, planning what they will do and say and recognizing when it is appropriate to speak their thoughts aloud. They also think about social rules when deciding their behaviors. Thinking aloud and blurting out comments is a common challenge for students with AD/HD, who may not recognize that doing so is socially inappropriate and irritates others.

The third executive function is *self-regulation of affect, motivation,* and *arousal*. Students with AD/HD who experience difficulty with this function lack "the drive, in the presence of external rewards, that fuels the individual's persistence in goal-directed actions" (Barkley, 1998c, p. 239). For example, assume that you are giving a test in your high school history class tomorrow.

Yoshi, a student with AD/HD in your class, needs the history credit to graduate. While at home preparing to do her homework, Yoshi's best friend calls her just as she has gotten her history book out of her backpack to study. The friend tells Yoshi about a party that "everybody is going to." Because she is more motivated by the immediate rewards of going to the party than the long-term rewards of passing history, Yoshi grabs her coat and heads to the party.

The fourth executive function is *reconstitution,* the skill of analyzing and synthesizing behaviors. In Chapter 4, we noted that many students with dyslexia have difficulty breaking words into individual sounds. Likewise, students with AD/HD have difficulty breaking their behaviors into steps or individual tasks. For example, Neveah has had two months to write a term paper for your English class. Rather than breaking the assignment down into individual tasks (e.g., gathering resources, reading the information and writing notecards, developing an outline, etc.) and sticking to a schedule to complete those tasks, Neveah suddenly remembers the day before the due date that she needs to write the report and frantically tries to throw something together at the last minute.

Along with distorted executive functions, students with AD/HD have a distorted *perception of time,* which Barkley (1998b) refers to as time myopia (nearsightedness). Tending to overestimate time intervals and underproduce them, people with AD/HD perceive that time moves more slowly than it does (CHADD, 1996a). They procrastinate, thinking they have more time than they do, and thus miss deadlines. Waiting is intolerable because time seems to pass so slowly. Students with AD/HD typically need coaching to develop consistent time management routines because, for them, the absence of time perception is like trying to read without sight.

In Figure 6–3, you will find a list of impairments in cognitive, language, adaptive functioning, motor development, emotion, school performance, and task performance as well as medical/health issues that are associated with AD/HD. Later in the chapter, we will discuss the implications of these impairments for instruction.

Positive Traits Associated with Attention-Deficit/Hyperactivity Disorder

In Chapter 5, we emphasized the importance of identifying students' strengths. Hallowell and Ratey (1995) emphasize that people with AD/HD have a variety of strengths.

> [They] are highly imaginative and intuitive. They have a "feel" for things, a way of seeing right to the heart of matters while others have to reason their way along methodically. This is the child who can't explain how he thought of the solution, or where the idea for the story came from, or why suddenly he produced a painting, or how he knew the shortcut to the answer, but all he can say is, he just knew it, he could feel it. This is the man or woman who makes million-dollar deals . . . and pulls them off the next day. This is the child, who, having been reprimanded for blurting something out, is then praised for having blurted out something brilliant. These are the children who learn and know and do and go by touch and feel. (p. 153)

The three defining characteristics of AD/HD—inattention, hyperactivity, and impulsivity—are "also key descriptors in the biographies of highly creative individuals" (Cramond, 1995). Kesley demonstrates creativity in her acting. Along with strengths in creativity, a surprising strength for students with AD/HD is their ability to *hyperfocus* (Hallowell & Ratey, 1995; Wells, Dahl, & Snyder, 2000). Novelty, interest, or the sudden awareness of a crisis related to an approaching deadline causes such individuals to lock onto a task, completely oblivious to everything else going on around them. Parents and teachers often wonder how children can have AD/HD when they can sit for hours, hyperfocused on a hobby. Many people with AD/HD are highly successful because of this skill, although their success may come at the cost of family, friends, and personal health. In Box 6–1, Kelsey's therapist, Chris Fraser, shares how characteristics of AD/HD have affected his life.

FIGURE 6–3

Summary of impairments likely to be associated with AD/HD

Cognitive

Mild deficits in intelligence (approximately 7–10 points)
Deficient academic achievement skills (range of 10–30 standard score points)
Learning disabilities: reading (8–39%), spelling (12–26%), math (12–33), and handwriting
    (common but unstudied)
Poor sense of time, inaccurate time estimation and reproduction
Decreased nonverbal and verbal working memory
Impaired planning ability
Reduced sensitivity to errors
Possible impairment in goal-directed behavioral creativity

Language

Delayed onset of language (up to 35% but not consistent)
Speech impairments (10–54%)
Excessive conversational speech (commonplace), reduced speech to confrontation
Poor organization and inefficient expression of ideas
Impaired verbal problem solving
Coexistence of central auditory processing disorder (minority but still uncertain)
Poor rule-governed behavior
Delayed internalization of speech ($\geq$ 30% delay)
Diminished development of moral reasoning

Adaptive functioning: 10–30 standard score points behind normal

Motor development

Delayed motor coordination (up to 52%)
More neurological "soft" signs related to motor coordination and overflow movements
Sluggish gross motor movements

Emotion

Poor self-regulation of emotion
Greater problems with frustration tolerance
Underreactive arousal system

School performance

Disruptive classroom behavior (commonplace)
Underperforming in school relative to ability (commonplace)
Academic tutoring (up to 56%)
Repeat a grade (30% or more)
Placed in one or more special education programs (30–40%)
School suspensions (up to 46%)
School expulsions (10–20%)
Failure to graduate high school (10–35%)

Task performance

Poor persistence of effort/motivation
Greater variability in responding
Decreased performance/productivity under delayed rewards
Greater problems when delays are imposed within the task and as they increase
    in duration
Decline in performance as reinforcement changes from being continuous to intermittent
Greater disruption when noncontingent consequences occur during the test

Medical/health risks

Greater proneness to accidental injuries (up to 57%)
Possible delay in growth during childhood
Difficulties surrounding sleeping (up to 30–60%)
Greater driving risks: vehicular crashes and speeding tickets

Source: From *Attention-Deficit Hyperactivity Disorder: A Handbook for Diagnosis and Treatment* (2nd ed.), by R. A. Barkley, 1998, New York: Guilford Press. Copyright 1998 by Guilford. Reprinted with permission.

Box 6—1

Chris Fraser

I've been waiting to have my voice heard for many years. I feel so happy and fortunate to be able to share what has been in my mind and heart regarding AD/HD. I have found that one of my life's greatest assets and greatest teachers has been growing up and living with attention-deficit disorder paired with a learning disability. Don't get me wrong: As you can imagine, I obviously haven't felt this way for the majority of my life. Rather, this has been a gradual realization that I have felt growing in my heart ever since I was a young child. Therefore, my personal perception of AD/HD is that describing it as a disorder is a matter of perspective.

As an adult, I work as a therapist in a community mental health center and share with children and their families an empowering and hopeful perspective about AD/HD: that it is a collection of adaptive mechanisms and temperament traits that are more suited to some societies and tasks than to others. I share this information because I wish I had been told this as a young child and because I came up with the concept on my own in high school. I can remember specifically a conversation with my friend Jawn, who was also struggling through the academic confines of traditional academia, in which we agreed that if we lived in a different time in the past, we would survive while most National Merit Scholars would perish. Since then, many publications and articles have been written about this very topic. As I began to discover these articles and research my findings in graduate school, I saw confirmation of a concept that I had already come up with and had used as a source of energy. I enjoy looking at AD/HD as an inherited set of skills, abilities, and personality tendencies that I can use to my benefit to be successful. For me, this has been a very healing and empowering way of looking at things.

I have a number of tips about how people with AD/HD can survive in a world that doesn't automatically accommodate some of our personality characteristics. I have developed these tips on my journey through academia and life as a person with AD/HD.

Tip 1: *Use your resources and advocate for your needs.* I was very sensitive about other people thinking I was not intelligent, and I didn't want to be seen as different in any way. Therefore, I was embarrassed to go to the resource room each day in elementary school, and in high school I didn't even use available resources. I didn't learn that it was okay and smart to use those resources until after I suffered my way through high school.

Tip 2: *Find your joy or bliss and follow it.* In college I found that, like other students with AD/HD, I have the ability to hyperfocus and excel in subjects I have a passion for. This acknowledgment of my strengths and interests gave meaning to the frustrations I endured in academia and gave me a sense of hope for the future.

Tip 3: *Work on acknowledging your growth areas and develop your own special ways of dealing with them.* In college I also found out that the real world was not going to accommodate to me, so I needed my own bag of tricks to survive in it. This was a difficult realization: I figured out how to deal with my growth areas through trial and error. I confess that I still am disorganized occasionally and that I still have difficulty managing time. But I deal with this growth area by making lists. I write things down before I forget them. I find that even if I don't refer back to the list, the process of writing things down helps me remember them better.

Tip 4: *Never give up on your dreams, and view your mistakes as learning opportunities rather than personal failures.* To this day, I am still developing my own tips for learning how to compensate for my growth areas and to use my capabilities as a person with AD/HD.

Overall, my family has made all the difference in the way I have learned to view my challenges. My father also grew up with AD/HD traits and at the end of high school was told that he was not college material. But he went on to get a bachelor's degree, a master's degree, and a doctorate in psychology. Hence, I grew up knowing that my father had experienced the same struggles I had. He ingrained in me the idea that I was capable of doing whatever I put my mind to. My mother was always a strong student and now works as a remedial reading and gifted teacher. Therefore, I was doubly fortunate because my parents had both personal experience and professional knowledge about AD/HD. I am also fortunate to have a wife who has special traits that compensate for my growth areas, with the result that I become more functional each year we spend together.

My journey as a person with AD/HD has involved continuous learning, struggle, toil, frustration, realization, and finally peace. Along the way I obtained a bachelor's degree in social work and sociology with a psychology minor and a master's degree in social work. But most important, by learning about how to help myself, I am now in a position to pass on this information and help others who live with AD/HD.

Identifying the Causes

Media speculation about the causes of AD/HD is rampant. You probably have heard some of these theories, which can be categorized into environmental and biological explanations.

Environmental Explanations

Before you learn about what causes AD/HD, it might be helpful for you to learn what does *not* cause AD/HD. Research has discounted many environmental explanations, including these popular myths: too much sugar, too little sugar, aspartame, food sensitivity, food additives/coloring, lack

Kelsey Blankenship's ADHD could easily be hidden below her winsome smile and newly acquired willingness and ability to attend to her homework and in-school behaviors, two talents that teachers have helped her develop.

of vitamins, television, video games, yeast, lightning, fluorescent lighting, and allergies (Baren, 1994; Barkley, 2000; Hoover & Milich, 1994). Research has also discounted poor parenting. Have you ever heard somebody say, "Why doesn't that parent just get control of that kid?" One study of parenting as a cause revealed that "the negative behavior of mothers [toward their child with AD/HD] seemed to be in response to the difficult behavior of these children and not the cause of it" (Barkley, 2000, p. 80).

Stress in a family or environment can temporarily cause symptoms of AD/HD. Have you ever stayed up all night to study for a test? If so, what was the next day like for you? The combination of stress and lack of sleep may have made you temporarily hyperactive. You were agitated; and when you tried to rest after the test, you could not. But these symptoms were temporary, subsiding when the stressful period ended. Stress may create the symptoms of AD/HD, but it does not create AD/HD.

Biological Explanations

Recent improvements in medical technology bring us closer to discovering biological explanations for AD/HD. These include pre-, peri-, and postnatal trauma and brain differences resulting from faulty genes.

Pre-, Peri-, and Postnatal Trauma.   As is true for students with severe and multiple disabilities (Chapter 9), certain **teratogens** (environmental substances that block normal fetus development) increase the likelihood that a child will develop AD/HD (Baren, 1994; Henderson, 1999, Zappitelli, Pinto, & Grizenko, 2001). *Prenatal* (before birth) teratogens include maternal smoking and alcohol or drug abuse, poor maternal nutrition, and the mother's exposure to chemical poisons. In addition, high blood pressure, age, and the emotional state of the mother as well as the length of her labor may be factors. If the mother has AD/HD, however, she is more likely to expose the fetus to these teratogens because people with AD/HD are more likely to participate in addictive behaviors, giving rise to the question of whether the condition is actually inherited (Lambert & Hartsough, 1998).

Peri- and *postnatal* trauma (during and after birth), such as brain injuries, infections, iron deficiency anemia, and exposure to chemical poisons, also increase the likelihood that a child will develop AD/HD (Baren, 1994; Schmidt, 1999; Zappitelli, Pinto, & Grizenko, 2001). Environmental

FIGURE 6–4
Areas of the brain and attention-deficit/hyperactivity disorder

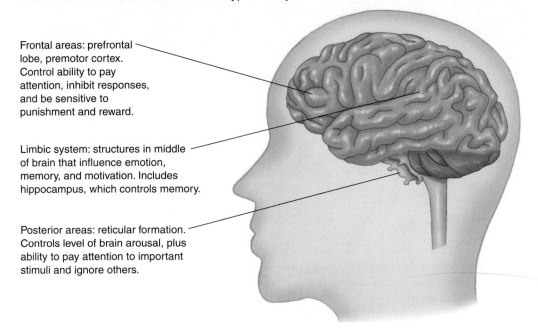

Frontal areas: prefrontal lobe, premotor cortex. Control ability to pay attention, inhibit responses, and be sensitive to punishment and reward.

Limbic system: structures in middle of brain that influence emotion, memory, and motivation. Includes hippocampus, which controls memory.

Posterior areas: reticular formation. Controls level of brain arousal, plus ability to pay attention to important stimuli and ignore others.

Source: From "The Human Brain," in *Teenagers with ADD: A Parent's Guide* (p. 12), by C. A. Z. Dendy, 1995, Bethesda, MD: Woodbine House. Copyright 1995 by Woodbine House. Reprinted with permission.

factors, however, account for only 20 to 30 percent of AD/HD in boys; the percentages are even less for girls (Barkley, 1998b). Because AD/HD exists on a continuum, severity of symptoms may be linked more to environmental factors than to the cause of AD/HD, which appears to be genetic (Zappitelli, Pinto, & Grizenko, 2001).

Brain Differences. For years, researchers have assumed that AD/HD is solely an attention disorder. Nevertheless, brain research is currently pointing to a different perspective (Barkley, 1998b). AD/HD appears to result from a failure in the brain circuitry underlying inhibition and self-control. As you can see in Figure 6–4, several areas of the brain may be involved in AD/HD.

Brain researchers have discovered that individuals with AD/HD do not have difficulty filtering out competing sensory inputs, as was previously thought. Instead, their difficulty stems from an inability to inhibit their impulses to that input. They also have difficulty preparing motor responses in anticipation of events and demonstrate insensitivity to corrective feedback. For example, a student in your class with AD/HD is unable to inhibit an inappropriate comment while you are teaching. Although the other students might think the comment silently, this student says what he thinks, much to the chagrin and/or amusement of those around him. Because he did not anticipate consequences, he is surprised to be reprimanded. He blurts another comment two minutes later, unable to learn from experience.

Recent research at the National Institute of Mental Health suggests possible involvement of "the prefrontal cortex, part of the cerebellum, and at least two of the clusters of nerve cells deep in the brain that are collectively known as the basal ganglia" (Barkley, 1998c, p. 69; see also Castellanos, 1997). Indeed, certain components of these areas, especially in the right hemisphere, are noticeably small in children with AD/HD, leading to a smaller overall brain volume in these children compared with the brains of children without AD/HD (American Academy of Neurology, 1999). This decreased size may help explain why a breakthrough study in the early 1990s found that the brains of participants with AD/HD did not convert glucose to energy on the right side as efficiently as did the brains of participants who did not have AD/HD (Friss, 1998; Mostofsky, cited in American Academy of Neurology, 1999).

We provide links to diagrams of the brain as well as to discussions on the causes of AD/HD in the Web Links module in Chapter 6 of the Companion Website.

Box 6–2

Making a Difference

An AD/HD Science Project

What new technology might provide an effective treatment for AD/HD? Ask the students from Salem High School in Salem, Oregon, who won the 1999 Toshiba/NSTA ExploraVision Award at the world's largest K–12 science competition. Of 13,000 students across the United States and Canada, the team won first place for "Defeating ADD Through Biosensing Technology." The students examined the "possibility of inserting a miniaturized microprocessor in the frontal lobe and connecting it to neighboring nerve cells through biotechnological techniques" (CHADD, 1999a, p. 2). Each student on the team received a $10,000 U.S. savings bond.

Although no one on the team has AD/HD, students said the struggles of friends and fellow classmates with AD/HD inspired their efforts. What are your thoughts about the potential development of this type of technology to help students overcome AD/HD?

Not only do these areas regulate attention, but they also help in "editing one's behavior, resisting distractions and developing an awareness of self and time" (Barkley, 1998a, p. 69). At least one of these components may also be involved in regulating motivation. These factors help explain why Kelsey and others with AD/HD find completing tasks on time challenging.

The different types of AD/HD may stem from different causes (Barkley, 1998a; Sonuga-Barke, 2002). Electroencephalograms (EEGs) indicate that students with the inattentive type (IN) are more likely to manifest disturbances in their early responses to sensory input. Those with the combined type (CB) demonstrate disturbances at a later stage of information processing (Barkley, 1998a). This difference may explain why those with IN find starting a task challenging, while those with the hyperactive-impulsive (HI) and CB types are distracted while trying to complete the task.

Recent research also suggests that the CB type may represent two distinct groups: those with poor inhibitory control associated with the prefrontal cortex and those with a motivational style characterized by inability to delay reward associated with the brain's reward circuits (Sonuga-Barke, 2002). The IN type may also fall into two groups, according to the results of an EEG study: In one group the cortex appears to be hypo-, or underaroused; in the other a maturational lag of the central nervous system occurs (Clarke, Barry, McCarthy, Selikowitz, & Brown, 2002).

Participants with AD/HD are more likely to use visual processing rather than memory and auditory processing areas of the brain when confronted with a mathematics task (Tannock & Martinussen, 2001). Their preference for visualization might suggest the importance of visualizing concepts for students with AD/HD when you are teaching them a new skill. In Box 6–2, you will learn how some high school students inventively use the information on AD/HD brain differences.

Genetics. Why do brain structures shrink in some children? Why do children with different types of AD/HD demonstrate brain differences? Why are some areas in the brain less active in some students with AD/HD? Genes seem to play a role, and different genes might be involved in the different types of AD/HD (Bierderman, cited in Friss, 1998).

Studies on twins and other research on families have provided clues that genes are somehow involved in the development of AD/HD (Smalley, 2000; Sohn, 2002; Tannock & Martinussen, 2001). Studies of monozygotic (identical) twins and dizygotic (fraternal) twins revealed that monozygotic twins have twice the concordance rate of AD/HD (60 to 80 percent of both twins receive the diagnosis) compared with dizygotic twins (only 20 to 30 percent receive the same diagnosis). This is the expected result for an inherited condition (Smalley, 2000). Researchers believe that 80 percent of attention, impulsivity, and hyperactivity differences between students with and without AD/HD have a genetic explanation (Tannock & Martinussen, 2001).

A genetic link suggests that AD/HD is not a pathological condition but instead a human trait. As a trait, AD/HD exists on a continuum; and society determines where the line for "abnormal" is drawn, just as it does with issues of "height, weight, intelligence, or reading ability" (Barkley,

As in Chris Fraser's family, AD/HD is often multigenerational, suggesting a genetic link. Enjoying a family ski trip, Chris Fraser, a Master's level Licensed Independent Social Worker, is pictured here with his father, J. Scott Fraser, a full professor at Wright State University.

2000, p. 74). Many of us have some characteristics of AD/HD, but those who receive the diagnosis represent the extreme on the continuum.

Identifying the Prevalence

Approximately 3 to 7 percent of school-age children have AD/HD (American Psychiatric Association, 2000). However, prevalence estimates vary widely because practitioners differ in their interpretations of criteria for diagnosing the condition, resulting in students being misdiagnosed or overlooked for needed diagnosis. Recently, the American Academy of Pediatrics (2000) established AD/HD clinical practice guidelines to help improve diagnosis and treatment. Identification of students with AD/HD is increasing dramatically. Several factors may explain the increase: heightened awareness, improved diagnostic practices, and societal changes that require more structure and concentration (Ingersoll, 1995). Probably every general classroom has at least one or two children with AD/HD (Barkley, 2000). The ratio of boys to girls is approximately 9 percent to 3 percent (American Academy of Pediatrics, 2000).

How does prevalence relate to the three subtypes of AD/HD? In the DSM-IV field trials (McBurnett, 1995), 55 percent of the children participating in the study were diagnosed with the combined type; 27 percent had the inattentive type; and 18 percent had the hyperactive-impulsive type. Younger children (4 to 6 years) formed most of the hyperactive-impulsive group (76 percent). The inattentive group contained the largest percentage of girls (27 percent). Girls who qualify for the combined type are likely to have more severe characteristics of inattention, impulsivity, and hyperactivity compared to boys (Nolan, Volpe, Gadow, & Sprafkin, 1999). The vast majority of students identified as having AD/HD are European American.

Approximately two-thirds of students with AD/HD have a co-existing condition (MTA Cooperative Group, 1999b). The overlap with emotional or behavioral disorders (Chapter 5), especially oppositional defiant disorder and conduct disorder, is seen mainly in children who have the combined type of AD/HD (Nolan et al., 1999). Prevalence rates range from 12 percent (learning disorders) to 35 percent (conduct disorders) (Agency for Health Care Policy and Research, 1999).

Many young children with AD/HD (approximately 50 percent) also have speech and language disorders (Chapter 14) (Goldstein, 1991). Students with complex partial seizures are more at risk for AD/HD (Medical Tribune, 1999). Furthermore, some students with mental retardation (Chapter 8) or autism (Chapter 10) have symptoms of AD/HD. To receive the additional diagnosis of AD/HD, however, the student must have symptoms that are excessive for his or her mental age rather than chronological age (American Psychiatric Association, 2000). Also, some students with AD/HD are gifted (see Chapter 7).

How Do You Evaluate Students with Attention-Deficit/Hyperactivity Disorder?

Determining the Presence

Initial diagnosis of AD/HD often involves a pediatrician, a psychologist, or a psychiatrist. In fact, the student may receive a diagnosis of AD/HD before starting school. For other students, as in Kelsey's case, a teacher suggests that a child receive a referral for evaluation. How do you talk to a parent about referring their child for AD/HD evaluation? Kelsey's therapist, Chris Fraser, has a suggestion:

> It's a very touchy subject with parents, and some of them take it as a personal assault on their family. I would take a very nonaccusatory manner. If I were a teacher, I would recommend saying, "You know, it's always good to rule things out. For example, you take them to the doctor and rule out that the child doesn't have measles by having tests. Your child seems to be showing some symptoms of AD/HD, but I'm not a doctor; I'm not a counselor or psychologist. There's a good chance that your child doesn't have AD/HD. But then we'll know one way or the other." It helps parents let their guard down and allows them to align with you instead of against you. If more people got that message, there would be a lot more compliance with going to a psychologist or psychiatrist.

Teachers should never suggest to parents that their child needs to be on medication or, conversely, should not take medication. Only a physician can make that determination. Teachers may tell parents that they may want to secure a medical evaluation because AD/HD is linked to a physiological condition.

Substantial research indicates the benefits of medication for many students with AD/HD (Moran, 1999; MTA Cooperative Group, 1999a, 1999b; Volkow et al., 2002). The National Institute of Mental Health's (NIMH) "Multimodal Treatment Study of Children with Attention Deficit Hyperactivity Disorder" (MTA), the longest and most thorough study yet completed on AD/HD (MTA Cooperative Group, 1999a, 1999b), concluded that medication alone is superior to behavioral therapy but that a combined approach adds to medication's effectiveness, sometimes even reducing the amount of medication needed. NIMH also emphasized that each student's treatment needs must be considered individually; some students will not tolerate medications well, but others may actually experience brain "maturation" as a result of medication (National Institute of Mental Health, 2002, p. 1).

After the student's parent(s) agrees to the referral for nondiscriminatory evaluation, the process described in Figure 6–5 begins. When a medical evaluation is warranted as part of the AD/HD evaluation, the school district is responsible for paying the physician. If you suspect that a student has AD/HD, you will want to keep a record of the characteristics (following the DSM-IV criteria) that you notice in the classroom.

You will find more information about using medication to treat AD/HD, including the NIMH study and specific medications and their side effects, on the Web Links module in Chapter 6 of the Companion Website.

You also learned about behavior rating scales in Chapter 5.

FIGURE 6–5

Evaluating whether or not a student has attention-deficit/hyperactivity disorder

Nondiscriminatory Evaluation

Observation

Teacher and parents observe	*Predominantly inattentive type*: Student makes careless mistakes, has difficulty sustaining attention, doesn't seem to be listening, fails to follow through on tasks, has difficulty organizing, often loses things, is easily distracted, or is forgetful. *Predominantly hyperactive-impulsive type*: Student is fidgety, leaves seat when expected to be seated, runs or climbs excessively or inappropriately, has difficulty playing quietly, talks excessively, blurts out answers or comments, has difficulty taking turns, or acts as if always on the go. *Combined type*: Characteristics of both are observed.

Screening

Assessment measures	Findings that indicate need for further evaluation
Classroom work products	Work is consistently or generally poor. Student has difficulty staying on task, so work may be incomplete or completed haphazardly.
Group intelligence tests	Tests may not reveal true ability because student has difficulty staying on task.
Group achievement tests	Performance may not be a true reflection of achievement because student has difficulty staying on task.
Medical screening	Physician or psychiatrist does not find physical condition that could cause inattention or hyperactivity-impulsivity. Medication may be prescribed.
Vision and hearing screening	Results do not explain academic difficulties.

Prereferral

Teacher implements suggestions from school-based team	The student still experiences frustration, inattention, or hyperactivity despite reasonable curricular and behavioral modifications.

Referral

Nondiscriminatory evaluation procedures and standards

Assessment measures	Findings that suggest AD/HD
Psychological evaluation	Psychiatrist or psychologist determines that student meets DSM-IV criteria for AD/HD.
Individualized intelligence tests	Student's intelligence may range from below average to gifted.
Individualized achievement tests	Performance on achievement tests may suggest that student's educational performance has been adversely affected by the condition.
Behavior rating scales or AD/HD-specific scales	The student scores in the significant range on measures of inattention or hyperactivity-impulsivity.
Teacher observation	The student's educational performance has been adversely affected by the condition. The behaviors have been present in more than one setting, were first observed before age 7, and have lasted for more than six months.
Curriculum-based assessment	The student may be experiencing difficulty in one or more areas of the curriculum used by the local school district because the behaviors have caused the student to miss important skills.
Direct observation	The student exhibits inattention or hyperactivity-impulsivity during the observation.

Nondiscriminatory evaluation team determines that student has attention-deficit/hyperactivity disorder and needs special education and related services.

Appropriate Education

You may also be asked to complete an attention-deficit or behavior rating scale to help with the evaluation process. Several of these scales reliably and validly assess AD/HD (Pineda, Ardilia, & Rosselli, 1999). Some behavior rating scales, such as the *ADHD Rating Scale—IV* (DuPaul, Power, Anastopoulos, & Reid, 1998), are specifically designed to identify AD/HD. Parents and teachers rate statements on a 4-point Likert scale ("never or rarely," "sometimes," "often," or "very often").

AD/HD seems to diminish IQ somewhat because of its effects on executive functions (Barkley, 2000). Some researchers have found that students with AD/HD perform better on some subtests than do peers without AD/HD, despite scoring more poorly on others (Pineda et al., 1999). The *Wechsler Intelligence Scale for Children* (WISC-III) (Wechsler, 1991) includes the Freedom from Distractibility Scale. Students who score poorly on this scale in relation to other scales may have AD/HD, so further assessment is warranted. Nevertheless, students who do not score significantly lower on this section may still have AD/HD (Anastapoulos, Spisto, & Maher, 1994). This finding means that schools should use more than one assessment measure to determine the presence of AD/HD.

Brain research is uncovering a potential method for clarifying the identification of students with AD/HD (Fischer, 2000). In this study, "the first to link medication to a change in brain activity" of students with AD/HD, 11 boys with identified AD/HD participated in a new diagnostic exam (Hagmann, 2000, p. 48). On a continuous performance test, which is a computer program used to assess attention, the boys pressed a space bar each time they saw a particular type of star flash on a computer screen—a boring, tedious task for those with AD/HD.

Six boys of the initial 11 fit the test's strict definition of AD/HD (Associated Press, 2000; Hagmann, 2000). Not only did the six boys pay attention less, move more, and show more impulsivity; but they also manifested corresponding brain differences on a new type of brain imaging. The more severe a boy's symptoms, the less active his brain was in an area called the *putamen*, which regulates attention and body movements. These 6 boys were also the only children of the initial 11 who responded to the medication Ritalin.

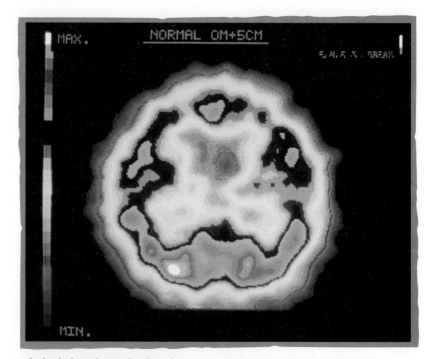

As brain imaging technology improves, students may be diagnosed with AD/HD by brain scans instead of by symptomatic behaviors.

Box 6–3

Multicultural Considerations

Cultural Issues in Diagnosing AD/HD

"Cultural, ethnic, and economic factors may result in either over-diagnosis or under-diagnosis" of AD/HD (Williams, Lerner, Wigal, & Swanson, 1995, p. 12). Limited access to medical services may prevent some students from being identified. Overdiagnosis can occur because some students have activity levels that are culturally appropriate but differ significantly from the majority culture of same-age peers.

Although certain behaviors seem to occur more frequently because of culture, it is important to remember that people vary widely within cultural groups, just as people with a particular disability vary widely. Assessment must consider cultural issues, but it also should take into account the student's individuality and the existence of subcultures.

Because they rely on subjective opinions of raters, the use of behavioral rating instruments can create problems in identification when the rater's cultural group varies from the student's. Thus, "It is important that educators be wary of the seductive quality of this pseudo-objectivity" (Reid, 1995, p. 559). One recent survey, for example, found that African American children were likely to be rated higher by European American compared to African American teachers on specific subscales of a popular behavior rating scale (Reid, Casat, Norton, Anastopoulos, & Temple, 2001). European American children, on the other hand, were likely to be rated

lower by European American teachers compared to African American teachers. Therefore, when assessing a student for AD/HD, it is important to make sure that at least one member of the team is a member of or has expertise in evaluating students from the student's cultural group (Council for Exceptional Children, 1992).

Instruments such as the *Child Behavior Checklist—Direct Observation Form,* a component of the *Achenbach System of Empirically Based Assessment* (Auchenbach, 2000), allow the evaluator to compare a student to control peers from the same cultural group and to observe the student in the same setting as peers.

Putting These Ideas to Work for Progress in the General Curriculum

1. When you begin teaching, how can you learn more about cultural differences to help you decide whether a student needs referral for AD/HD assessment?

2. Along with cultural references, how do you think stressful environmental conditions such as living in poverty might contribute to a misdiagnosis of AD/HD?

To answer these questions online and learn more about these ideas and concepts, go to the Multicultural Considerations module in Chapter 6 of the Companion Website.

Despite all the advances in evaluating students for AD/HD, students with cultural differences are at risk for over- or underdiagnosis of the condition. We address that issue in Box 6–3.

Determining the Nature and Extent of General and Special Education and Related Services

Under IDEA, the evaluation team must decide whether a student has AD/HD, the type of AD/HD the student has, the severity of the condition, its effect on the student's educational progress, and whether special education and related services are warranted in the category of other health impairments (Chapter 11). That duty is especially challenging when the student has AD/HD. One study found that only half of students who qualified as having AD/HD were receiving services (Bussing & Zima, 1998). "Girls were three times as likely as boys to have unmet service needs; minority status, low income, and health maintenance organization coverage also emerged as possible risk factors" (p. 880). Those students who have concomitant conditions such as learning disabilities and emotional or behavioral disorders may receive a dual diagnosis. For example, their IEPs may indicate a primary disability of learning disabilities and a secondary disability of other health impairments (AD/HD).

Not every student with AD/HD qualifies for IDEA services. Many students with AD/HD, especially when they begin a treatment regimen that includes medication, can function well in a general classroom, with accommodations. These accommodations might include extra time for tests or taking tests orally, a behavioral plan, a peer note taker, and/or a set time to leave the classroom for medication.

How can students be guaranteed needed accommodations if they do not need special education or related services? Section 504 of the Rehabilitation Act Amendments of 1973 and the Americans with Disabilities Act (ADA) prohibit discrimination against students with AD/HD or other disabilities if their disabilities substantially limit one or more of their major life activities (see Chapter 1).

To comply with these laws, states offer **504 plans.** A school team (typically, the student's teacher, the principal or principal's designee, and someone who is knowledgeable about the disability) decides what accommodations are necessary (Fossey, Hosie, & Zirkel, 1995). Parent and student participation is not mandated but is usually advisable. The team writes the accommodations into the plan. In Box 6–4, you will find a list of some accommodations for students with AD/HD on 504 plans (and IEPs).

If the student is not performing as expected even with a 504 plan, the team must determine whether the student needs special education and related services. At this point, IDEA comes into play and requires a nondiscriminatory evaluation that leads to an IEP.

On the Web Links module in Chapter 6 of the Companion Website, you will find links to various websites to help you understand and learn how to write these plans.

How Do You Assure Progress in the General Curriculum

Including Students

As you have already read, many students with AD/HD have seriously impaired social relationships (Barkley, 2000; Merrill & Beuter, 2001). For students with AD/HD to be effectively included in your classroom, they will need to experience positive relationships with their classmates. Problems with social relationships can lead to low self-esteem, depression, antisocial behavior, and loneliness (CHADD, 1996b). Whereas students with HI and CB types have more difficulty with aggressive behaviors that annoy peers, students with IN are more likely to withdraw, be overlooked by their peers, and be likely to have one close friend. Those with CB, in contrast, may make friends quickly yet have trouble keeping them. Students with AD/HD do not need a large number of friends to feel good about themselves. Often, one close friend will do. Box 6–5 gives you some inclusion tips.

CHADD (1996b) recommends the following steps to improve peer relationships: (1) Observe the student to determine effective, poor, and absent social behaviors; (2) focus on one or two behaviors for change; (3) directly coach, model, and role-play important behaviors; and (4) praise and reward the student for appropriate behaviors, capitalizing on his or her strengths (Roan, 1994).

Two behaviors seem to be especially important for students to learn in order to be accepted by their peers: group awareness and self-acceptance. Popular children take the time to find out what is going on in a group and match their behavior to the group (Roan, 1994). The three-page list that Kelsey and Chris created helped her to laugh at herself and not hide who she is.

Box 6—4

Into Practice

Accommodations for Attention-Deficit/Hyperactivity Disorder

Strategies for Teachers

Your students with AD/HD may or may not have an IEP. Some will have a 504 plan to help them succeed in the general education curriculum. Matching a student's strengths and needs to appropriate accommodations is essential. The following list provides helpful suggestions, but you will probably think of many other appropriate possibilities.

Inattention

- Seat the student in a quiet area.
- Seat the student near a good role model.
- Seat the student near a "study buddy."
- Increase the distance between desks.
- Allow extra time to complete assigned work.
- Shorten assignments or work periods to coincide with the student's span of attention; use a timer.
- Break long assignments into smaller parts so the student can see an end to her work.
- Assist the student in setting short-term goals.
- Give assignments one at a time to avoid work overload.
- Require fewer correct responses for a grade.
- Reduce the amount of homework.
- Instruct the student in self-monitoring by using cueing.
- Pair written instructions with oral instructions.
- Provide peer assistance in note taking.
- Give clear, concise instructions.
- Seek to involve the student in lesson presentation.
- Cue the student to stay on task, using a private signal.

Impulsiveness

- Ignore minor inappropriate behavior.
- Increase the immediacy of rewards and consequences.
- Use the time-out procedure for misbehavior.
- Supervise the student closely during transition times.
- Use prudent reprimands for misbehavior (e.g., avoid lecturing or criticism).
- Attend to positive behavior with compliments, etc.
- Acknowledge the positive behavior of nearby students.
- Seat the student near a role model or near the teacher.
- Set up a behavior contract.
- Instruct the student in self-monitoring of behavior (e.g., hand raising, calling out).

- Call on the student only when she raises her hand in an appropriate manner.
- Praise when she raises her hand to answer a question.

Motor Activity

- Allow the student to stand at times while working.
- Provide an opportunity for "seat breaks" (e.g., run errands, etc.).
- Provide a short break between assignments.
- Supervise the student closely during transition times.
- Remind the student to check over her work product if her performance is rushed and careless.
- Give the student extra time to complete tasks (especially for a student with slow motor tempo).

Mood

- Provide reassurance and encouragement.
- Frequently compliment positive behavior and work product.
- Speak softly in a nonthreatening manner if the student shows nervousness.
- Review instructions when giving new assignments to make sure the student compreherids directions.
- Look for opportunities for student to display leadership role in class.
- Meet frequently with parents to learn about student's interests and achievements outside of school.
- Send positive notes home.
- Make time to talk alone with the student.
- Encourage social interactions with classmates if the student is withdrawn or excessively shy.
- Reinforce frequently when signs of frustration are noticed.
- Look for signs of stress buildup, and provide encouragement or reduced workload to alleviate pressure and avoid a temper outburst.
- Spend more time talking to students who seem pent up or display anger easily.
- Provide brief training in anger control: Encourage the student to walk away; use calming strategies; instruct the student to tell a nearby adult if she is getting angry.

Academic Skills

- *If reading is weak:* Provide additional reading time; use previewing strategies; select text with less on a page; shorten the amount of required reading; avoid oral reading.

- *If oral expression is weak:* Accept all oral responses; substitute display for oral report; encourage the student to tell about new ideas or experiences; pick topics that are easy for the student to talk about.
- *If written language is weak:* Accept nonwritten forms for reports (e.g., displays, oral, projects); accept the use of typewriter, word processor, tape recorder; do not assign a large quantity of written work; test with multiple-choice or fill-in questions.
- *If math is weak:* Allow the use of a calculator; use graph paper to space numbers; provide additional math time; provide immediate correctness feedback and instruction via modeling of the correct computational procedure.

Organization Planning

- Ask for parental help in encouraging organization; provide organization rules.
- Encourage the student to have a notebook with dividers and folders for work.
- Provide the student with a homework assignment book.
- Supervise writing down of homework assignments.
- Send daily/weekly progress reports home.
- Regularly check desk and notebook for neatness; encourage neatness rather than penalize sloppiness.
- Allow the student to have an extra set of books at home.
- Give assignments one at a time.
- Assist the student in setting short-term goals.
- Do not penalize the student for poor handwriting if visual-motor defects are present.
- Encourage learning of keyboarding skills.
- Allow the student to tape-record assignments or homework.

Compliance

- Praise compliant behavior.
- Provide immediate feedback.
- Ignore minor misbehavior.
- Use teacher attention to reinforce positive behavior.
- Use prudent reprimands for misbehavior (e.g., avoid lecturing or criticism).
- Acknowledge positive behavior of a nearby student.
- Supervise the student closely during transition times.
- Seat the student near a teacher.
- Set up a behavior contract.

- Implement a classroom behavior management system.
- Instruct the student in self-monitoring of behavior.

Socialization

- Praise appropriate behavior.
- Monitor social interactions.
- Set up social behavior goals with the student, and implement a reward program.
- Prompt appropriate social behavior either verbally or with private signal.
- Encourage cooperative learning tasks with other students.
- Provide small-group social skills training.
- Praise the student frequently.
- Assign special responsibilities to student in the presence of peer group so others observe her in a positive light.

Putting These Strategies to Work for Progress in the General Curriculum

1. Can you think of at least one more accommodation in each area that is not on the list?

2. Sharise is a fifth grader with the combined type of AD/HD. She has difficulty staying on task and frequently blurts out comments and talks to others when she should be working. She has a wonderful sense of humor, so sometimes you have a hard time not laughing at her comments, inappropriately timed as they are. Which accommodations might be helpful for her?

3. Jonathan is a compassionate tenth grader with the inattentive type of AD/HD who is well liked by peers. He has difficulty getting to classes on time because he can't remember his locker combination. When he finally does get his locker open, everything spills onto the floor. He usually doesn't have the necessary supplies when he does make it to class. What accommodations would you recommend?

4. Miguel is a second grader with the combined type who tries hard in school and wants to please you. He also tries to make friends by doing whatever the other students suggest. He does not seem to realize that the other students are using him and are not really his friends. What accommodations might benefit Miguel?

To answer these questions online and learn more about these strategies, go to the Into Practice module in Chapter 6 of the Companion Website.

Source: List from Parker, H. C. (1996). Adapt: Accomodations help students with attention deficit disorders. *ADD Warehouse Articles on ADD* (http://www.addwarehouse.com). Adapted with permission.

Planning Universally Designed Learning

Augmenting Curriculum

Motivating students with AD/HD to attend to learning and then keeping them involved and interested can be challenging. (Of course, if students are innately interested in the topic, they sometimes hyperfocus on tasks; turning their focus elsewhere then becomes the challenge!) Students with all types of AD/HD have deficits with respect to motivation (Carlso, Booth, Shinn, & Canu, 2002). Students with CB seem more motivated by competitiveness and a desire to appear superior to others, while those with IN tend to be less uncooperative but more passive in their learning styles. Students with AD/HD are more likely than their peers to need external motivation, suggesting the need for developing a stimulating curriculum (Brim & Whitaker, 2000).

You may find it helpful to remember seven key words for increasing students' motivation to learn: relevance, novelty, variety, choices, activity, challenge, and feedback (Shank, 2002). When students cannot understand *relevance* (how the learning has some meaning for them personally), they are not as likely to attend to it. For students with AD/HD, who are not future-oriented, this relevance must take the form of learning something they can apply immediately to their lives. For example, "When you go to the store after school today and buy a cola, you want to know that the salesclerk is giving you the right change," is preferable to "When you grow up and buy groceries, you will need to know how much money to give to the clerk."

Novelty refers to presenting information that is new or presenting repeated information in a fresh way. Students must practice their spelling through repetition, but it will become novel using a *Wheel of Fortune* format.

Variety is also essential. One study found that students with AD/HD performed significantly better adding numbers on a computer when presented with a variety of screen colors, colored numbers, and movement effects than when viewing black numbers on a gray computer screen with no movement (Lee & Zentall, 2002).

Having *choices* also adds motivation. Contracting for grades gives students such as Kelsey an opportunity to demonstrate their learning through their strengths. At the beginning of each quarter, you can provide students with a three-page contract. The first page specifies what they will need to do to get a grade of A, B, C, or D in your class. You can list the percentages they need on tests and quizzes and the number of projects they need to do for each grade as well as the dates each will be due. List possible projects on the second page, making sure the projects address varied learning styles. Inform students that you will also consider their ideas for projects. Students return the third page to you. This page has lines for (1) the contracted grade, (2) the chosen projects and when they will be submitted, and (3) student and parent signatures.

Grade contracts allow all students, not just those with AD/HD, and their parents to know what is expected at the beginning of the quarter. This approach also accommodates workload according to ability. You can mail a copy of the contract home in the middle of the quarter, give a copy to students in class, and review it at parent conferences. This reminds parents and students of their commitment, which is necessary for many students but especially for those with AD/HD.

Activity is another motivational technique. Students with AD/HD may need to move in order to overcome their inattention (Brim & Whitaker, 2000). They need the freedom to structure their environment. You may not realize that the child with IN who is doodling may be concentrating better on your lecture than she is when she sits with her hands folded.

Some teachers might think that making accommodations for students with AD/HD means watering down their curriculum. Actually, the opposite is true. *Challenge* is critical for motivating students with AD/HD. Thus, not lessening the workload but changing the content is important. The content must be immediately stimulating, rewarding, and interesting.

Because students with AD/HD struggle with internal motivation, external motivators that provide immediate *feedback* are also crucial in keeping them motivated. Computer software can meet the need for motivational curriculum and immediate external reinforcement. Box 6–6 describes innovative computer programs to help students with AD/HD improve their executive functions.

Box 6–5

Inclusion Tips

	What You Might See	What You Might Be Tempted to Do	Alternate Responses	Ways to Include Peers in the Process
Behavior	*Inattentive type:* The student is inattentive, withdrawn, forgetful, a daydreamer, and/or lethargic. *Hyperactive-impulsive type:* He is restless, talkative, impulsive, and/or easily distracted. *Combined type:* Features of both.	*Inattentive type:* Overlook him. *Hyperactive-impulsive and combined types:* Be critical and punitive.	*Inattentive type:* Recognize his presence daily in a positive way. *Hyperactive-impulsive and combined types:* Catch him being good. Look for opportunities to praise. Work with parents on consistent behavior management plan.	Model acceptance and appreciation for him. Then peers are more likely to do the same.
Social interactions	*Inattentive type:* He withdraws from social situations. *Hyperactive-impulsive and combined types:* He bursts into social situations and may be gregarious or inappropriate and annoying.	*Inattentive type:* Call attention to his isolation in front of other students; try to force him to play. *Hyperactive-impulsive and combined types:* Pull him out of social situation for inappropriate behavior.	Role-play friendship skills. Help students discover their strengths, and encourage group participation in those activities. Start with small groups. Encourage membership in a support group for students with AD/HD.	For projects, pair him with another student who has similar interests and tends to be accepting. The initial goal is achieving one close friend.
Educational performance	Work is incomplete and/or sloppy. Homework is lost or forgotten. Materials are disorganized. He may experience success in areas of strength and interest.	Make punitive or sarcastic comments.	Teach students how to organize their materials. Help them find a coach. Break assignments into manageable parts.	Use peer tutors with him.
Classroom attitudes	His motivation is inconsistent or lacking.	Give up on him.	Use the five principles of relevance, novelty, variety, choices, and activity in your teaching.	Use cooperative learning activities that are based on the five principles.

Technology Tips

Box 6–6

Captain's Log and Play Attention

In one elementary school, Anishra, age 8, is playing a specially designed Bingo game on the computer. Todd, age 18, is playing the same game in his high school computer lab. Anishra and Todd share three features in common, along with AD/HD: They find the game enjoyable, stimulating, and age-appropriate.

Captain's Log (BrainTrain, 2000), a "complete mental gym," incorporates software that helps students and adults with AD/HD improve cognitive skills through exercises to enhance "attention, concentration, memory, eye-hand coordination, basic numeric concepts, and problem solving/reasoning skills" (p. 1). In addition, the game seeks to build self-esteem and self-control. Thirty-five games, arranged in five modules, make up *Captain's Log.*

Students wear a cool-looking helmet while using another cognitive skill builder, *Play Attention* (Play Attention, 2001). The program's purpose is to train students with AD/HD to focus and "enhance attention, visual tracking, time-on-task, data sequencing, and discriminatory processing" (p. 1).

The system actually processes brain output, allowing students to use only their mind to control the action on a video game. As their attention wavers, the game changes. For example, in an early game, students watch a bird flying across the computer screen. As their attention wavers, the bird begins to fall. They must refocus their attention to help the bird maintain its flight pattern. One student says, "I learned being focused and on task was the way to be. My grades went from *C*s and *D*s to *A*s and *B*s after using *Play Attention*."

You can use this software in your classroom to help students learn to focus their attention.

Putting Technology to Work for Progress in the General Education Curriculum

1. How can you help students generalize the skills they practice on the computer to attending to their seatwork?

2. How will you assess student progress from participating in these computer activities?

To answer these questions online, learn more about these strategies, and find links to these programs, go to the Technology Tips module in Chapter 6 of the Companion Website.

Despite their need for stimulating curricula, students with AD/HD also need freedom from competing distractions (Lee & Zentall, 2002). For example, although students with AD/HD may enjoy and perform well in a small cooperative learning group focused on a science experiment, they may experience agitation and loss of concentration when participating in one of five groups working on different science experiments in a small classroom. The effective classroom for students with AD/HD balances structure and flexibility.

Augmenting Instruction

Sometimes teachers lower their expectations for students with disabilities or provide help instead of teaching the skills the students need to manage their own life. To develop **self-efficacy**— belief in their personal capabilities and ability to achieve with effort—students need to understand their own strengths and needs. Knowing when to ask for help and developing organizational skills are essential self-efficacious tasks. For these reasons, teachers need to instruct students in the following (Bandura, cited in Eisenberger, Conti-D'Antonio, & Bertrando, 2000, p. 17):

- planning, organizing, and managing activities
- enlisting help and resources at appropriate times
- regulating personal motivation and sustaining involvement in activities
- applying metacognitive knowledge and strategies for task completion
- acquiring necessary knowledge and skills for managing the environment

Figure 6–6 shows how one student determined personal accommodations that fostered self-efficacy.

FIGURE 6-6

A student's accommodations identified by learning needs

Name Paul Jones	Date 9/12/03	Disability Auditory Processing/ADHD
My Academic Strengths	**Successful Strategies**	
Short-term Visual Memory	3-Fold Page, 2-Column Notes	
Verbal Reasoning	Study Partner, Stop and Think	
Visual Processing Speech (in gifted range)	Muscle Reading, Graphic Organizers	
My Learning Needs	**Successful Accommodations**	
Auditory Processing	Visual Format for Information, Directions	
Impulsive	Firm Limits and Boundaries—Avoid Verbal Debates	
Task Completion	School-Home Communication	
Attention and Concentration	Proximity, Goal Setting, and Reflection on Progress	

Source: From *Self-Efficacy: Raising the Bar for Students with Learning Needs,* by J. Eisenberger, M. Conti-D'Antonio, and R. Bertrando, 2000, Larchmont, NY: Eye on Education. Copyright 2000 by Eye on Education. Reprinted with permission.

See the Web Links module in Chapter 6 of the Companion Website for Links to sites about teaching self-efficacy.

Self-efficacy extends to self-management. For example, students who were taking medication and participated in a self-reinforcement program made more improvement in completing reading questions than did students who took medication only or participated in self-reinforcement only (Ajibola & Clement, 1995). For self-reinforcement, the students clicked a counter on their wrist each time they completed a reading question. They received a stamp in a payment book each day they met or exceeded their goal. When they received a specified number of stamps, they cashed in their payment books for a reward. Note that their reward was frequent (after each question) and external.

Collaborating to Meet Students' Needs

As a result of collaboration among her parents, teachers, and therapist, Kelsey has received appropriate accommodations. Students with AD/HD need to sense that all the important people in their life are working together for them. When you have students with AD/HD, you will need to work closely with the therapist, physician or psychiatrist, and the family. In some cases, you may need to help a student find a personal coach. Box 6–7 tells how one school district collaborated to meet students' needs.

Chris Fraser, Kelsey's therapist, suggests how teachers can best communicate with therapists or physicians:

You might want to keep track of the student's response to medication on a chart. We provide one for you in Chapter 6 of the Companion Website.

> It's worth it [for teachers] to make the effort with the doctor to see if she will talk to you. Whether it's by writing or the phone, an attempt needs to be made to communicate. Sometimes I ask teachers to leave me a voice message or an e-mail. Of course, the most important thing is confidentiality, and releases must be signed. You have to make sure before you leave a message that the therapist has password-protected, confidential voice mail and the same is true for e-mail.

One way you can collaborate to meet students' needs is by helping them to work with a coach or a professional organizer. A professional organizer may see clients one or a few times, helping them to find a way out of their clutter and developing an organizational system for

One of the challenges of students with ADHD is to develop friends. Here, Kelsey Blankenship and one of her friends show that this challenge can be overcome.

them. A coach, on the other hand, generally establishes a longer, more consistent relationship, helping a client focus on functional life issues. Coaching differs from therapy because the concentration is on goal setting and attainment rather than resolving emotional issues (Horan, 2000). Because students with AD/HD experience difficulty internalizing time, organizing, and working from internal motivation, finding a coach often fulfills the self-efficacious skill of "enlisting help and resources at appropriate times." According to one AD/HD coach, "Coaches help their clients create an individualized structure and a best-fit environment that compensates externally for what is weak internally" (Brown, cited in Horan, 1999, p. 13).

A coach can be a peer, a neighbor, or someone specially trained to perform that type of service, such as a professional organizer or someone who has been trained to coach people with AD/HD. Counselors such as Chris sometimes serve in this capacity. The crucial factor is the relationship the student builds with the coach. If the student perceives the coach as intrusive rather than supportive, another coach must be found. Hallowell and Ratey (1995) use the acronym HOPE to specify the questions a coach asks a student with AD/HD on a regular basis:

Help: What help do you need?

Obligations: What's coming up, and what are you doing to prepare?

Plans: What are your goals?

Encouragement: You are making progress!

By giving them compensatory strategies, coaching helps clients "behave the way they want to behave" (Horan, 1999, p. 13). "In a coach-client relationship, the client is responsible for doing the work: The coach's job is to support the client in her efforts."

The Web Links module in Chapter 6 of the Companion Website includes links to sites about coaches and professional organizers for people with AD/HD.

Collaboration Tips

Box 6–7

Collaborating with Class

How does a grossly underfunded school district meet the needs of students with AD/HD? In the Davis, Utah, County School District, collaboration helps (Harman, 2000). As you will recall from Chapter 1, students who qualify for IEPs under IDEA make their schools eligible for federal dollars, but students who have only Section 504 plans (under the Rehabilitation Act) do not draw in federal financial support. So how can a poor school district meet the needs of the Section 504 students?

Linda Smith and Linda Stover, who started a local chapter of Children and Adults with Attention Deficit Disorder (CHADD) in 1994, had already been collaborating with the director of student services, Katie Davis, by providing her with updated information on federal policy for serving students with AD/HD. Throughout the 1994–1995 school year, the three of them began educating school personnel and parents about the rights of students with AD/HD under Section 504. For example, they invited the school district superintendent and board members to a local CHADD meeting, and they secured the consent of local CHADD board members to serve as consultants to the school district.

By 1995, the district had a full-time director of Section 504 services, David Turner, who worked with CHADD parents to form Collaborative Learning Accommodation Services for Students, nicknamed "CLASS Act." CLASS Act consisted of 20 teachers. The group planned in-service meetings for teachers, parents, and administrators; obtained teaching materials and developed a budget; and developed an effective communication network. "The district wanted every teacher to know about CLASS Act," says Linda Sorensen, a member of the group (Harman, 2000, p. 27).

Each CLASS Act teacher was assigned to seven schools, and each offered in-service training at those schools. Sorensen says they told teachers they were bringing information on a new mandatory exercise program for teachers that involved running up stairs and on a track. After teachers learn about the real reason for the in-service, they are ready to hear that "'one size doesn't fit all' and to relate to the situation the kids [with AD/HD] are in" (Harman, 2000, p. 29).

CLASS Act teachers provide consultation services from in-house trainers, teachers, a nurse, a social worker, a parent representative, and a psychologist. They also provide training brochures for parents, teachers, and students. David Turner, director of 504 services, comments, "The 504 Plan should be a roadmap to help kids be successful in school. After all, teaching is about people helping people" (Harman, 2000, p. 29).

Putting These Tips to Work for Progress in the General Curriculum

1. What were the challenges?

2. What did the team do?

3. What were the results?

To answer these questions online and learn more about these ideas and concepts, go to the Collaboration Tips and Web Links modules in Chapter 6 of the Companion Website.

What Can You Learn from Others Who Teach Students with Attention-Deficit/Hyperactivity Disorder?

Professionals once believed that students with AD/HD outgrew the condition in adolescence. By contrast, current research suggests that up to 70 percent of the students continue to face AD/HD-related challenges as adults (Murphy, 1999). But a child who receives a diagnosis and a program beginning in preschool and continuing through the rest of her schooling will have tools to win the self-efficacy, academic, social, physical, and behavioral battles that people with AD/HD often face throughout life.

Learning for the Early Childhood Years: Multidisciplinary Diagnostic and Training Program

The University of Florida Multidisciplinary Diagnostic and Training Program (MDTP) promotes the inclusion of young children with AD/HD in their community programs (Travis, Diehl, Trickel, & Webb, 1999). Working jointly with the University's Colleges of Medicine and Education, the program increases the academic progress and social success of children in early intervention classes by using multimodal treatments. Initially, the children attend the MDTP-AD/HD diagnostic classroom to receive individualized interventions based on their learning characteristics. Then the students transition back to the general classroom with the ongoing support of AD/HD project teachers, who continue to collaborate with general educators and parents to maintain the positive effects of the initial training. The services include the following (Travis et al., 1999, p. 2):

- Comprehensive academic, behavioral, and medical evaluation at a multidisciplinary diagnostic clinic
- A data-based classroom that tracks the child's progress
- Educational interventions based on the child's learning characteristics
- A structured classroom environment with consistent routine and clear, concrete expectations and consequences
- Appropriate medication, if necessary, with systematic documentation of effects on academics and behavior
- Ongoing support for classroom teachers
- Follow-up of children transitioning into general education settings
- On-going research on children's attention to advance the understanding and treatment of attentional disorders

Many parents of young children with AD/HD worry that their children will lag academically and be socially rejected because of their disruptive and inattentive behaviors (Teeter, 1999). By providing early multimodal intervention, MDTP increases the likelihood that students with AD/HD will experience success throughout their school years.

Learning for the Elementary Years: Take Charge!

Founded by Mary Jane Beach, a therapist and educator who also has AD/HD, Take Charge! provides self-efficacy–related learning activities and support to help students enhance self-awareness and confidence, build routines, complete projects, improve communication skills, and prepare for inclusion. Take Charge! incorporates the motivational tools of relevance, novelty, variety, choices, activity, challenge, and feedback. The program, which is available for adolescents and adults as well, incorporates storytelling, puppets, and dramatic play for elementary-age children (Beach, Landenberger, & Beach, 1997).

Multisensory strategies help students focus and include the use of Take Charge! tools. For example, when students learn about values and life directions or choices, they examine a compass. North represents thinking and attitude, south represents feelings and emotions, east represents words and communication, and west represents action and change.

Collaboration is an important aspect of the program. Parents participate in Take Charge! In addition, students learn to work with a coach. Coaches receive 12 weeks of training to learn how to help students take charge of homework. Central to the coaching program are the 12 messages from students listed in Figure 6–7.

FIGURE 6–7
Student messages to coaches

- I want to succeed in school.
- Please help me figure out what I'm good at.
- Please figure out what will make it easier for me to learn.
- Please teach me the way I learn.
- Please help me care again.
- Please help me gain confidence.
- Please help me set reasonable goals.
- Please help me figure out the best routine for me, and help me schedule in time to plan and prepare.
- Please teach me how to calm down.
- Please tell me how to communicate with others.
- Please notice when I make progress.
- A chance to celebrate would be wonderful.

Source: From *Take Charge! Educational Coaching,* Lesson 1. © 2003 by Mary-Jane Beach. Bridges Associates, Inc.

Learning for the Middle and Secondary Years: Lehigh University's Consulting Center for Adolescents with Attention-Deficit Disorders

Current findings show that 80 percent of students with AD/HD continue to experience it into adolescence (CHADD, 2002b). Students with AD/HD are three times more likely to fail at least one grade and be suspended or expelled; approximately 35 percent drop out of school (Barkley, 2000).

The change-class, change-teacher aspects of secondary schools make communication among secondary teachers critical. Lehigh University's Consulting Center for Adolescents with Attention-Deficit Disorders (LU-CCADD) developed a program to help middle school teachers work more effectively with their students who have AD/HD (Shapiro, DuPaul, Bradley, & Bailey, 1996). The program has three components: in-service training, on-site consultation, and advanced knowledge dissemination and follow-up consultation.

Lehigh's first step was to provide school representatives with basic information about AD/HD through a two-day in-service training. The participants learned five important tasks for improving the self-efficacy of students with AD/HD: (1) school-based self-management strategies, (2) school-based behavior management skills for teachers, (3) home-based behavior management for parents, (4) medication monitoring and pharmacological interventions, and (5) social skills and problem-solving training.

Teams from each school developed action plans for students who experienced difficulties stemming from their AD/HD. One student, for example, had difficulty following directions, disturbed classmates, and was frequently off task. Working with all of the student's teachers, the team implemented one of the self-management programs members had learned about during the in-service training. They helped the student systematically judge his behavior against the behavior that teachers expected of him.

Parents received information during the program to help them understand policies that the district had developed and their children's rights under IDEA and Section 504. They were told how to contact the local CHADD organization.

Collaborative teams are a key factor in meeting the needs of adolescents. Programs such as LU-CCADD create self-efficacious secondary students with AD/HD and prevent them from getting lost in these larger settings.

Learning for the Transitional and Postsecondary Years: Peterson's Colleges with Programs for Students with Learning Disabilities or Attention Deficit Disorders

As many as 70 percent of children with AD/HD continue to have symptoms of inattention, impulsivity, and/or hyperactivity as adults (Murphy, 1999). In one study, young adults with either the combined or inattentive types of AD/HD, when compared to young adults without AD/HD, were less likely to graduate from college; more likely to have received special education services in high school; and more likely to experience substance abuse, psychological distress, and learning disorders (Murphy, Barkley, & Bush, 2002). These findings suggest that postsecondary students with AD/HD may need accommodations to allow them to achieve their potential. College campuses are required by the Americans with Disabilities Act to provide support services, such as alternative test-taking strategies, to help students succeed. The reference guide *Peterson's Colleges with Programs for Students with Learning Disabilities or Attention Deficit Disorders* (Mangrum & Strichart, 2000) describes colleges (also listed on a CD-ROM) that provide comprehensive programs designed specifically for students with special needs. The guide also includes helpful tools for deciding which college to attend.

Support services alone will usually not be enough to help a postsecondary student with AD/HD to meet the academic challenges. The student needs to possess self-efficacy skills. Vassar College, long noted for its high academic standards both in admissions decisions and in classroom expectations, admitted Andrew Batshaw, despite the fact that he has a learning disability and has been diagnosed as having AD/HD. And Andrew, who was diagnosed and began taking medication in elementary school, has succeeded, thanks in large part to the self-efficacy skills encouraged by his family and teachers. "I became comfortable with who I was," Andrew says. Being able to say those words is the foundation for self-efficacy.

While a junior at Vassar, Andrew was asked what he would tell a room full of high schoolers with AD/HD. His response? "Don't limit yourselves. If you apply yourselves and really want something, you will find you can do it. Look where you've come from, at what you've already succeeded in doing."

How does he recommend that teachers promote self-efficacy? "Don't limit your students. Understand that they have disabilities. Accommodate to them. But purge the word *can't. . . .* Don't limit their will to try everything."

To learn more about some of these programs, check the Web Links module in Chapter 6 of the Companion Website.

A Vision for Kelsey's Future

Kelsey dreams of being a veterinarian. She loves animals, and everyone on her team is supporting her dream to be a veterinarian. "I'd love to see her get good grades in school and get the opportunity to go on to college," Yvonne says.

"I want Kelsey to be happy," Barb adds. "I think she is now. And if she wants to be a vet, I hope she *is* a vet."

"First, small steps toward her goal begin today," says Chris. "Her work at school, volunteering at the pound, walking a dog—making it real for her. I would like her to learn to advocate for her needs, to blossom into a woman who is self-confident—who knows what she needs to be successful. I hope she learns how to articulate needs with teachers and professors and get better and better until she reaches her goal."

What Would You Recommend?

1. Kelsey will be starting middle school in a couple of years. How would you help prepare her for that transition?
2. What could you do if you were Kelsey's teacher this year to enrich her curriculum by capitalizing on her love for animals?

Summary

How Do You Recognize Students with Attention-Deficit/Hyperactivity Disorder?

▼ AD/HD is defined by criteria in the *Diagnostic and Statistical Manual of the American Psychiatric Association* (4th ed.) (DSM-IV) (American Psychiatric Association, 1994).

▼ Under IDEA, students with AD/HD are served under the "other health impairments" category.

▼ There are three types of AD/HD: (1) predominately inattentive type, (2) predominately hyperactive-impulsive type, and (3) combined type.

▼ Students with AD/HD appear to experience a developmental delay of inhibition, which affects their ability to separate facts from feelings, use self-directed speech, and break apart and recombine information.

▼ Students with AD/HD often experience associated positive characteristics, including creativity and a sense of humor.

▼ Prevalence estimates of AD/HD are 3 to 7 percent of the general population.

▼ Many myths about causes of AD/HD exist. Probable causes are more likely biological than environmental, and it is likely that more than one cause is responsible.

How Do You Evaluate Students with Attention-Deficit/Hyperactivity Disorder?

▼ Diagnosis of AD/HD by a psychologist, a psychiatrist, or a physician often occurs outside the school system. The person who makes the diagnosis becomes part of the evaluation team.

▼ Behavior rating scales designed specifically for AD/HD and continuous performance tests are often used during evaluation.

▼ Some students may falsely appear to have AD/HD to evaluators outside their culture.

▼ Students who have AD/HD that adversely affects their educational progress may receive an IEP as "other health impaired" if they need special education and related services.

▼ If the AD/HD does not adversely affect educational performance, the student receives a 504/ADA plan.

Appropriate accommodations for skill deficits are included in each plan.

How Do You Assure Progress in the General Curriculum?

▼ A multimodal approach to remediation, which may include medication, behavior management, coaching, education, counseling, and/or organizational training, is essential for students with AD/HD.

▼ Students with AD/HD benefit from a curriculum that incorporates relevance, novelty, variety, choice, activity, and challenge.

▼ For most students with AD/HD, the general classroom is the appropriate placement.

▼ Collaboration among professionals is important to provide the student with consistency and to monitor the effects of medication.

▼ Families sometimes get caught in a downward spiral of escalating discipline and negative behavior. It is important to provide support and resources to families who have a child with AD/HD. They need to learn to use positive and negative strategies based on the level of the student's behavior.

▼ Sometimes having one close friend can make a positive difference for a student with AD/HD.

What Can You Learn from Others Who Teach Students with Attention-Deficit/Hyperactivity Disorder?

▼ The University of Florida Multidisciplinary Diagnostic and Training Program (MDTP) promotes the inclusion of young children with AD/HD in their community programs by using multimodal treatments.

▼ *Take Charge!* provides self-efficacy–related learning activities and support to help students enhance self-awareness and confidence, build routines, complete projects, improve communication skills, and prepare for inclusion.

▼ Effective middle and secondary programs, such as those at Lehigh, concentrate on coordination of efforts for students with AD/HD across all teachers involved.

Giftedness

Briana meant an hour, round trip, in the car each day. Nevertheless, Deborah chose to enroll her daughter in this school because it would enable Briana to participate in an enrichment model that would challenge her academically and expand her educational opportunities.

Although the move to the new school offered academic benefits, it also created social challenges. At first, Briana's friends from her neighborhood asked her why she wasn't going to their school any more. Like Jamal in *Finding Forrester*, "Briana doesn't like to tell people where she is academically. She doesn't like to be seen as smart. Actually, she is often quite modest, which sets her apart from the norm," Deborah explains.

Not wanting to be seen as brainy, Briana began to remain inside the house more, preferring books to her old neighborhood friends. "It was a lot for a third grader to handle, being asked where she was and why she didn't go to school anymore," Deborah says.

Although Briana sometimes continues to prefer books to a social life, in general her social life is as busy as that of any other middle-school girl. Instead of neighborhood play, she spends a good portion of her social life practicing and performing with her church dance and choir group. Recently, the group was invited to perform at the University of Missouri at Kansas City and to attend training under the instruction of the Alvin Ailey dance troupe from New York City. These days, dance practice and performances across the Kansas City metropolitan area keep Briana and her mother quite busy.

In addition to her church group obligations, Briana also runs track. On most weekday afternoons, you'll find her running either for her middle school cross-country team or for her local Amateur Athletic Union track team. Briana started running during the summer after her fifth-grade year and is a "natural talent in the 400 and 200 meter," according to Deborah. "Every weekend we seem to be traveling to some city or another. She just missed qualifying for nationals last year but did qualify for regionals in the 400 meter." Briana's best time of 64 seconds in the 400 meter would make many a high school athlete take notice.

For Briana, running is serious business, as is the classroom. She is competitive and takes losing seriously. When she thinks she should have won, she often cries after a race. At the same time, she really cares for her other team members. According to her mother, "in cross-country events this year Briana was known to run beside a team member offering words of encouragement."

From all accounts, Briana is a well-rounded middle-school student; but her education has not been easy to provide. In the classroom, for example, it has been demanding to create learning situations that challenge her and encourage her talents. Briana often exceeds her teachers' expectations and demands; she challenges them to think beyond the borders of typical curricula and related assignments. Currently, the Program for Exceptionally Gifted Students (PEGS) is addressing many of her intellectual needs as a seventh grader. However, Deborah wonders whether transitioning to high school and the ninth grade (skipping the eighth grade) might be an appropriate plan for next year. Although Deborah and Briana's teachers are considering the social consequences, Deborah says, "Briana is tall for her age and is often mistaken for being older than she actually is. She has always been able to interact well with older children and adults." So the questions facing Briana, her family, and her teachers are the same ones that Forrester put to Jamal: "Where are you taking me? Where are you headed?"

How Do You Recognize Students Who Are Gifted?

Defining Giftedness

Many states have defined giftedness. Although their definitions vary, most are based on the federal definition as specified in the 1994 reauthorization of the Jacob K. Javits Gifted and Talented Students Education Act of 1988:

> The term "gifted and talented" when used in respect to students, children or youth means students, children or youth who give evidence of high performance capability in areas such as intellectual, creative, artistic, or leadership ability, or in specific academic fields, and who require service or activities not ordinarily provided by the school in order to fully develop such capabilities. (P. L. 103-382, Title XIV, 1988, p. 388)

In brief, this definition acknowledges that giftedness is worthy of federal attention, states that students meeting the definition require special services, describes areas and characteristics of giftedness, and establishes a standard for distributing federal funds to state and local education agencies.

Paradoxically, the definition and accompanying legislation do not require states to establish programs for students who are gifted and talented. This means that students who are talented and gifted are *not* guaranteed special services by federal legislation or laws. The choice of whether or not to provide service belongs to state or local education agencies. This right to choose marks a substantial difference between gifted education and special education for students with disabilities. By 1995, however, all 50 states had laws or regulations that recognized the needs of students who are gifted and talented (Passow & Rudnitski, 1995).

Review the discussion of disability legislation in Chapter 1, and you will recognize that giftedness is the only exceptionality discussed in this textbook that is not specifically covered under IDEA.

Some researchers have proposed conceptual models that explain the different factors involved in giftedness. For example, Renzulli (2000) developed and continues to examine the perspective that giftedness includes three factors essential for high-quality and creative productivity in any type of activity or endeavor. As shown in Figure 7–1, he proposed that an individual who produces new, original contributions in a field possesses the following characteristics: (1) above-average ability, (2) creativity (novel, useful, or unusual expressions within a domain), and (3) task commitment. This model stands the test of time and continues to help direct changes in how students such as Briana are served.

Sternberg and Zhang (1995) have also proposed a conceptual theory, termed the *pentagonal implicit theory.* Their model encompasses five criteria that a person must meet in order to be con-

FIGURE 7–1
Renzulli's graphic three-ring definition of giftedness

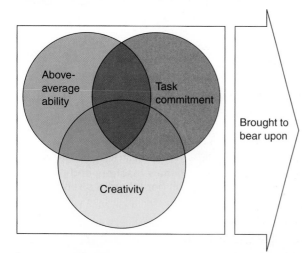

General performance areas

Mathematics • Visual Arts • Physical Sciences • Philosophy • Social Sciences • Law • Religion • Language Arts • Music • Life Sciences • Movement Arts

Specific performance areas

Cartooning • Astronomy • Public Opinion Polling • Jewelry Design • Map Making • Choreography • Biography • Film Making • Statistics • Local History • Electronics • Musical Composition • Landscape Architecture • Chemistry • Demography • Microphotography • City Planning • Pollution Control • Poetry • Fashion Design • Weaving • Play Writing • Advertising • Costume Design • Meteorology • Puppetry • Marketing • Game Design • Journalism • Electronic Music • Child Care • Consumer Protection • Cooking • Ornithology • Furniture Design • Navigation • Genealogy • Sculpture • Wildlife Management • Set Design • Agricultural Research • Animal Learning • Film Criticism • etc.

Source: From "What Makes Giftedness? Reexamining a Definition," by J. S. Renzulli, 1978, *Phi Delta Kappan, 60,* p. 184. Copyright 1978 by J. S. Renzulli. Reprinted with permission.

FIGURE 7–2

Pentagonal implicit theory: An adaptation of Sternberg and Zhang's (1995) five criteria

Criterion	Definition	How Determined	Example: Eight-Year-Old Piano Player
Excellence	Superior in some dimension or set of dimensions to peers.	Determined by an abundance in the dimension "relative to peers." The designation of excellence depends upon the skills of those against whom one is judged.	Plays the piano much better than other eight-year-olds with similar training.
Rarity	High level of an attribute that is rare relative to peers.	Determined by an abundance of an attribute only when an evaluation of that attribute is judged to be rare "relative to peers."	Playing is not only superior but rare compared to peers.
Productivity	The dimension(s) along which the indivdual is evaluated as superior must lead to or potentially lead to productivity.	For children, productivity is more often determined by potential products rather than actual products. But to earn the label *gifted* without qualification, a person must accomplish something.	Not only plays but writes music recognized as excellent by other musicians.
Demonstrability	The superiority of the individual on the dimension(s) that determine giftedness must be demonstrable through one or more tests that are valid assessments.	Determine by an assessment instrument that must have been validated.	Wins adult performing artists contest governed by official standards.
Value	Superior performance in a dimension that is valued for that person by his or her own society.	Determined by what is valuable in a specific culture, time, and/or place.	Is recognized by culture for superior performance—appears on television talk shows.

Source: Copyrighted material from *Gifted Child Quarterly* (GCQ) Vol. 39, No. 2, *What Do We Mean by "Giftedness"? A Pentagonal Implicit Theory,* by Robert J. Sternberg and Li-fang Zhang. Reprinted with permission from the National Association for Gifted Children, Washington, DC.

sidered gifted: (1) excellence, (2) rarity, (3) productivity, (4) demonstrability, and (5) value. Figure 7–2 defines the five criteria and how they are determined. The goal of this theory is to decide "what we value as gifted before embarking on a program of identification" (Sternberg & Zhang, 1995, p. 88) and to encourage us to "capture and systematize people's intuitions about what makes an individual gifted" (p. 89).

A definition (such as the two we have just described) that regards intelligence as multidimensional (spanning several domains of giftedness) and not unidimensional (based on scores alone) is referred to as **domain-specific giftedness,** an approach that has broad support (Gagne, 2003; Gardner, 1999). Domain-specific giftedness does not imply that giftedness operates in isolation. That is, a gifted mathematician may be equally gifted in art, leadership, and athletics. Some people exhibit more than one area of giftedness, whereas others excel in one area only.

Gardner proposed one such model (1983, 1993a, 1993b, 1999), which is different from the federal definition and includes physical and intuitive/intrapersonal giftedness. He describes eight specific intelligences found across cultures and societies. These **multiple intelligences** are musical, bodily-kinesthetic, linguistic, logical-mathematical, spatial, interpersonal, intrapersonal, and naturalistic. Figure 7–3 sets out Gardner's eight areas of potential giftedness and lists the typical characteristics and distinctive features common in gifted individuals.

Individuals who display a particular domain of giftedness, says Gardner, often show both expertise and creativity within that domain. **Expertise** pertains to the technical mastery of skills and knowledge within a domain. By contrast, creativity refers to unusual or unique expressions within a domain.

Finally, Gardner proposes that the term *genius* be reserved for "those persons or works that are not only expert and creative but that also assume a universal, or quasi-universal significance" (p. 52).

Another recent perspective on giftedness is that of **emotional intelligence.** Brain and behavioral researcher Daniel Goleman has described the factors at work when people of high IQ struggle to succeed while those of average IQ flourish (1995, 1998). Goleman's theory states that intelligence is not fixed at birth and that the qualities of self-awareness, impulse control, persistence, self-motivation, empathy, and social deftness can be nurtured and strengthened in any individual. According to Goleman, these factors contribute to a different way of being smart—one he terms emotional intelligence. Having high cognitive intelligence does not imply exemplary skills in any other area of life, and Goleman (1998) claims that it is emotional intelligence that shapes everything from personal success to physical well-being. His theory of intelligence, similar to Gardner's interpersonal and intrapersonal domains of giftedness, provides a broader explanation for how giftedness can be demonstrated.

Describing the Characteristics

Identifying the characteristics of all people who are gifted is complicated. However, special abilities often provide helpful clues to parents and general educators (those who most often identify students with exceptional abilities). Although the great diversity in giftedness means there is no typical gifted student, most who are gifted share some common traits. Building on the federal categories for giftedness, let's first examine characteristics common to individuals who are gifted:

1. General intellect
2. Specific academic aptitude
3. Creative productive thinking
4. Leadership ability
5. Visual and performing artistry

General Intellect

Students who demonstrate high general intellect are able to grasp concepts, generalize, analyze, or synthesize new ideas or products far more easily than can other students their age (Bloom, 1956; Clark, 1997). In addition, those students may indicate concern for issues or events relating to values, ethics, or justice at a young age.

Many students who are gifted have excellent memories and ask many questions. In preschool-age children, advanced vocabulary and extended periods of concentration are often typical. Further, it is not unusual for children who are gifted to process information both faster and more efficiently than other children do.

Specific Academic Aptitude

Students with exceptional ability may have an unusual aptitude in specific scholastic areas such as verbal or mathematical reasoning. Some, like Briana, read at a much earlier age than do the average student and many read independently and avidly.

Creative Productive Thinking

Students who are creative show many distinct characteristics. Compared to their peers, they may be more adventurous, independent, curious, spontaneous, flexible, sensitive, intuitive, and insightful. They may have little tolerance for boredom and may take risks more readily. They may

To learn more about exceptionally gifted individuals, go to the Web Links module in Chapter 7 of the Companion Website for a link to Michael Kearney's story.

Later in the chapter you will learn about ways to plan universally designed learning that will enable you to address these exceptionalities.

FIGURE 7-3

Potential areas of giftedness: An adaptation of Howard Gardner's eight areas of intelligence

Area	Gifted Person	Possible Characteristics of Giftedness	Early Indicators of Giftedness
Musical	Ella Fitzgerald Itzhak Perlman	Unusual awareness and sensitivity to pitch, rhythm, and timbre Ability may be apparent without musical training Uses music as a way of capturing feelings	Ability to sing or play instrument at an early age Ability to match and mimic segments of song Fascination with sounds
Bodily-kinesthetic	Michael Jordan Nadia Comenici	Ability can be seen before formal training Remarkable control of bodily movement Unusual poise	Skilled use of body Good sense of timing
Logical-mathematical	Albert Einsten Stephen Hawking	Loves dealing with abstraction Problem solving is remarkably rapid Solutions can be formulated before articulated: Aha! Ability to skillfully handle long chains of reasoning	Doesn't need hands-on methods to understand concepts Fascinated by and capable of making patterns Ability to figure things out without paper Loves to order and reorder objects
Linguistic	Virginia Woolf Maya Angelou	Remarkable ability to use words Prolific in linguistic output, even at a young age	Unusual ability in mimicking adult speech style and register Rapidity and skill of language mastery Unusual kinds of words first uttered
Spatial	Pablo Picasso Frank Lloyd Wright	Ability to conjure up mental imagery and then transform it Ability to recognize instances of the same element Ability to make transformations of one element into another	Intuitive knowledge of layout Able to see many perspectives Notices fine details, makes mental maps
Interpersonal	Martin Luther King, Jr. Madeleine Albright	Great capacity to notice and make distinctions among people: contrasts in moods, temperaments, motivations, and intentions Ability to read intention and desire of others in social interactions: not dependent on language	Able to pretend or play-act different roles of adults Easily senses the moods of others; often able to motivate, encourage, and help others
Intrapersonal	Sigmund Freud Ruth Westheimer ("Dr. Ruth")	Extensive knowledge of the internal aspects of a person Increased access to one's own feelings and emotions Mature sense of self	Sensitivity to feeling (sometimes overly sensitive) Unusual maturity in understanding of self
Naturalist	Rachel Carson John Audubon	Relates to the world around them In tune with the environment	Recognizes and differentiates among many types of an environmental item, such as different makes of cars Recognizes many different rocks, minerals, trees

The term "gifted" applies to many different traits, including those associated with extraordinary athletic abilities as evidenced by the Olympic Medalists on the USA women's soccer team.

also have a zany sense of humor and come up with more original ideas (Clark, 1997). When you consider these characteristics carefully, you may understand why some schools do not always encourage creativity. Yet such creativity has been linked with giftedness throughout history. For example, it is impossible to think of Einstein's creation of the theory of relativity without seeing characteristics of creativity: Independence, risk taking, originality, and intuitiveness surely were all part of the process (Karolyi, Ramos-Ford, & Gardner, 2003).

Leadership Ability

Students classified in the leadership category typically display well-developed social skills, empathy, ability to motivate others, ability to keep others united or on task, and effective communication skills (Sternberg, 2003). Gardner (1999) has recently explored the relationship among intelligence, creativity, and leadership. National political leaders, such as Mahatma Gandhi, fit into this category. Interestingly, Gandhi was not a good student. Yet with his peers, he took the role of peacemaker, becoming a moral arbiter. Years later, he displayed genius in his ability to lead.

Visual and Performing Arts

In the visual and performing arts, students show many of the traits associated with creativity, general intellect, and specific academic aptitude, including rapidity in mastering subject matter. In addition, they may have highly developed nonverbal communication skills; physical coordination; exceptional awareness of where they are in relation to other things and people; or specific skills in music, dance, mime, storytelling, drawing, or painting. For example, although Stravinsky was immersed in music as a child, he was not a musical prodigy (Gardner, 1993b). He had, however, a keen sense of sound and with his violin was able to imitate the unison singing of village women on their way home from work.

High-ability students with language, hearing, visual, physical, or learning disabilities may have a notable difficulty in one area but show specific academic aptitude in another area (Baldwin & Vialle, 1999). Taylor Smith and Morgan Jones are two fourth-grade friends who are both gifted in the visual and performing arts but struggle with dyslexia. Taylor is particularly gifted in singing and recently appeared at half-time with the Cleveland Browns football team. Morgan is a gifted dancer and appears in the *Nutcracker* with the Cleveland Ballet. Even so, their dyslexia means they cannot see words correctly and the process of reading is physically exhausting to them. They both attend Lawrence School in Broadview Heights, Ohio, a school that works with bright children who have learning disabilities to "enable them to return to the school of their choice armed with the ability to work to their potential and to succeed" (Hamilton, 1999).

To learn about exceptional individuals in the creative arts, go to the Web Links module in Chapter 7 of the Companion Website.

To learn more about gifted children with learning disabilities, go to the Web Links module in Chapter 7 of the Companion Website.

How would you describe Michael Jordan: gifted, prodigous, or genius?

Behavioral, Social, and Emotional Characteristics

Some of the characteristics of giftedness that we have just discussed are easy to identify, recognize, and confirm. Some students, however, are overlooked because their parents or teachers have preconceived notions about how students who are gifted should behave in class and at home. Some students who are gifted behave well, and some behave poorly (Seeley, 2003). In addition, some children who are gifted have a strong sense of humor or unquenchable curiosity that can sometimes be a distraction in class.

Participation and belonging are critical for all students. Students who are gifted sometimes find, however, that social and emotional factors often become obstacles because they may have interests or ways of thinking that differ from those of their peers who are less gifted academically. Typical problems experienced by gifted students include anxiety, heightened sensitivity, divergent thinking, excitability, perfectionism, and feelings of isolation (Davis & Rimm, 1998). Students who are "highly motivated, single-minded in the pursuit of their own goals, and very strong-willed" may appear rebellious and stubborn (Lovecky, 1992, p. 24). Some students who are gifted tend to try out scientific or conceptual world theories in unique or socially unacceptable ways (Leal, Kearney, & Kearney, 1995). As a result of being misunderstood, these students may feel different, alone, or isolated and in extreme cases may be unable to focus and even have adverse physical symptoms. Some students may find that a good antidote to these feelings is their participation in enrichment programs, such as the one that you will read about in Box 7–1.

There is growing concern about the number of students who are being misdiagnosed as having learning disabilities (Chapter 4) or attention-deficit/hyperactivity disorder (Chapter 6) when in

Box 7–1

The University of Virginia's Summer Enrichment Program

Who says all kids want to spend summer vacation at the beach? For JJ and his brothers and sisters, summer means the opportunity to explore new ideas and ponder unresolved issues at the University of Virginia's Summer Enrichment Program. Some students may delve into a facet of a single science or examine the mind of a Nobel laureate. Others may take seminars on topics, problems, or themes that relate to interactions among individuals or groups of people. For instance, a seminar may include the study of justice and injustice, examining how people feel about change, focusing on the effects of prejudice and stereotyping, or looking at the past to understand many current events. Still other participants may be interested in using the skills of artists or writers to explore the endless diversity of human culture. Architecture, anthropology, philosophy, foreign language, drama, writing, music, literature, and other art forms become the means, singly or in combination, through which students probe concepts and themes that have been important in the world over time. Some students, such as JJ's brother, produce a short movie and follow his UVA program with further study via a Smithsonian enrichment program.

What Made the Difference?

Similar to many comparable programs throughout the country, the UVA program is organized around two-week sessions in which the curriculum emphasizes extending a student's capabilities in problem solving, creativity, and critical examination and evaluation of content-rich fields of study. Working together in a learning community, gifted high school students do the following:

- Explore topics not generally available to them in the regular school year or study familiar topics from a new perspective and with greater abstraction or complexity
- Learn the significance of the subject studied and its global relationship to other fields of study
- Develop an understanding of the nature and purpose of the discipline they are studying and how a professional in that field might perform
- Become familiar with new materials in print or multimedia that provide high-level information pertinent to their field of study

Who Made the Difference?

For JJ it wasn't one individual but his fellow students, academic advisors, and the entire camp support staff. Living in a college dorm for two weeks was a critical part of the experience because it gave JJ and his peers a chance to talk about the day's events, share hobbies, and connect on other ideas and topics not often shared by friends and relatives at home. The academic advisors and camp staff were critical in designing the right environment to allow for the ongoing learning activities that create intellectual challenges.

To learn about gifted students with specific attention or learning disabilities as well as stories from individuals with these exceptionalities, go to the Web Links module in Chapter 7 of the Companion Website for a link to LD Online.

fact they are gifted (Silverman, 1998). Because many of the characteristics of giftedness are also associated with these other conditions, it is not always easy to recognize students' giftedness. Figure 7–4 depicts the differences between behaviors often identified as characteristics of both giftedness and AD/HD. Although students with these characteristics can be perfectionistic, easily distracted by external stimuli, unable to maintain attention, or have difficulty controlling their impulses, they also have a positive view of others, are sensitive, have a forgiving nature, and are able to produce work of significant quality when motivated and valued (Wallace, 1999/2000).

Identifying the Origins

Although most researchers today attribute giftedness to a combination of nature (genetic factors) and nurture (environmental factors), they disagree about the relative proportion of the two factors. Recent research seems to support the genetic perspective, suggesting that the brains of children who are gifted may be shaped and function differently from the brains of children in the normal range of intelligence (Henderson & Ebner, 1997). One study supporting this argument found that genetic differences account for about half of the IQ differences among individuals (Plomin & Price, 2003). Interestingly, verbal and spatial abilities are more likely to be inherited than are memory and speed of processing information.

There are proponents for both genetic and environmental causes. For example, Doman and Doman (1994) believe that environment has the greatest influence on intellect. On the other hand, Bruer's (1999) research states that it is an abuse of neuroscience to think that teachers and parents can inoculate children against later academic shortcomings. On a more moderate note,

FIGURE 7–4
Distinguishing between AD/HD and giftedness

Behaviors Associated with AD/HD (Barkley, 1990)	Behaviors Associated with Giftedness (Webb, 1993)
Poorly sustained attention in almost all situations	Poor attention, boredom, daydreaming in specific situations
Diminished persistence on tasks not having immediate consequences	Low tolerance of persistence on tasks that seem irrelevant
Impulsivity, poor delay of gratification	Judgment lags behind development of intellect
Impaired adherence to commands to regulate or inhibit behavior in social contexts	Intensity may lead to power struggles with authorities
More active, restless than normal children	High activity level; may need less sleep
Difficulty adhering to rules and regulations	Questions rules, customs, and traditions

Source: From *ADHD and Children Who Are Gifted* (ERIC Digest No. EDO-ED-93-5), by J. T. Webb and D. Latimer, 1993, Reston, VA: Council for Exceptional Children, ERIC Clearinghouse on Disabilities and Gifted Education.

Elkind (1981, 1987, 1988) points out the dangers of *hurried children*, those who are pressured to learn too much too soon.

Identifying the Prevalence

Finding and identifying students who are gifted are not always easy. Not only are their characteristics sometimes misleading, but there is also controversy over what giftedness is and how many students are gifted.

When IQ test scores are equated with giftedness, the top 2 or 3 percent of the general population is considered gifted (Piirto, 1999). Most schools use an IQ score of 125 to 130 as a baseline for identifying these students. IQ tests often record scores as high as 160, but scores of 180 to 200 have been estimated by other methods.

This means that the IQ of people in the gifted population ranges from 125 to 200 and that those at one end of the gifted spectrum may be very different from those at the other. However, most researchers today distinguish only two levels of giftedness: (1) gifted and (2) highly gifted, or genius. Figure 7–5 shows how IQ levels apply to these students.

A contrasting opinion—one that does not rely on IQ alone to determine giftedness—holds that there is a **talent pool** that includes the top 15–20 percent of students in general ability or specific performance areas, where an IQ of 115 is the lowest acceptable score. A talent pool allows more students to participate in gifted programs. This model (Renzulli & Reis, 1986), described as a *schoolwide enrichment model* (Renzulli, 2000), has recently been expanded in an effort to develop the talents of all students.

Given all these different ways to identify and serve students who are gifted, the best way to estimate the prevalence of giftedness in schools is to examine how many students receive gifted services. If your school chooses a 4.5 percent figure, then, of 350 students, about 16 students, or approximately one per classroom, would receive services. Under Renzulli and Reis's more inclusive talent pool approach, about 20 percent, or 70 students, would be served, with four or five students per classroom.

The 1998–1999 State of the States Gifted and Talented Education Report (Council of State Directors for Programs for the Gifted, 1999) revealed at what grade level services are typically provided. Of 43 states responding to the question, only 2 begin at the prekindergarten level, 18 begin in kindergarten, and 7 begin in first grade.

Later in the chapter you will learn about how the schoolwide enrichment model can augment instruction for gifted children.

To learn about the prevalence of gifted students, go to the Web Links module in Chapter 7 of the Companion Website for a link to specific data-based websites.

FIGURE 7–5
Normal curve and derived scores with application to the talented

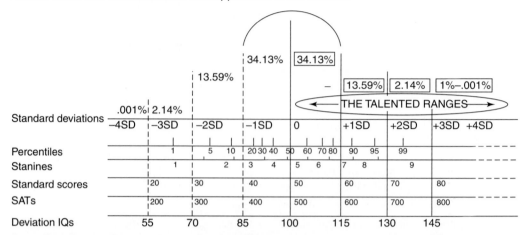

Standard deviations	–4SD	–3SD	–2SD	–1SD	0	+1SD	+2SD	+3SD +4SD
Percentiles		1	5 10	20 30 40	50 60 70 80	90 95	99	
Stanines		1		2	3 4	5 6	7 8	9
Standard scores	20	30		40	50	60	70	80
SATs	200	300		400	500	600	700	800
Deviation IQs	55	70		85	100	115	130	145

Source: From *Talented Children and Adults: Their Development and Education* (2nd ed., p. 106) by J. Piirto, 1999, Upper Saddle River, NJ: Merrill/Prentice Hall. Copyright 1999 by Prentice Hall. Reprinted with permission.

Briana Hoskins is one of those students who has exceptional talents in more than one young domain. Hers are in academics and, as pictured here, in dance.

How Do You Evaluate Students Who Are Gifted?

To identify and serve students who are gifted, educators undertake a thorough two-step diagnostic evaluation similar to the nondiscriminatory evaluation approach specified in IDEA for students with disabilities. First, educators determine the presence of giftedness. Then, they determine the nature and extent of special education services needed to challenge individuals and develop their talents.

Determining the Presence

Educators typically rely on formal means to identify giftedness. Three benefits result from formal assessment:

1. Schools obtain data to validate a student's placement.
2. A student is more likely to receive an appropriate education.
3. Meeting specific criteria will ensure federal funding of services.

Some problems are associated with testing for giftedness. For example, standardized tests have been criticized for demonstrating bias against students from culturally and linguistically diverse backgrounds, students from low socioeconomic groups, and students learning English as a second language (Castellano, 2003b). Indeed, students from these three groups are vastly underrepre-

Box 7–2

Multicultural Considerations

The P-BLISS Program

Nationally, economically, and socially disadvantaged students and those from diverse backgrounds are underrepresented in gifted education programs, so it is not surprising that educators are scrambling to seek ways to identify more gifted minority students. However, more than a decade ago, less than 2 percent of research in gifted education even considered gifted minority learners. Then in 1993 the U.S. Department of Education stated that "schools must eliminate barriers to the participation of economically disadvantaged and minority students in services for students with outstanding talents . . . and must develop strategies to serve students from underrepresented groups" (p. 28).

For gifted disadvantaged students, developing and using problem-solving skills are critical for engaging the learner and thus enhancing his or her understanding. A version of problem-based learning (PBL) called problem-based learning in the social sciences (P-BLISS) has found success. Gallagher and his colleagues have discovered that one of the best ways to find hidden disadvantaged gifted students is to present them with a curriculum that first captures their interest and then challenges them to show their true potential.

In each of the P-BLISS units, students find themselves transported in time, place, and role and are quickly immersed in the middle of a problem. The units take advantage of the element of surprise inherent in an ill-structured problem. Inside each unit or instruction is a group of tools designed to engage the students in complex, meaningful

reasoning. Teachers have plenty of opportunity to observe students exhibiting their talents as they sort through the issues to get at the heart of a problem. Among the tools included in each unit are critical reasoning, conceptual thinking, discussion of ethics, and authentic assessment. What sets P-BLISS apart from other PBL curricula is that the instructional materials can be used effectively to find and serve disadvantaged gifted students. Thus, the meaningful topics, substantive content, challenging activities, and opportunities for self-direction often give gifted learners a first step toward further curricular modifications to meet their specific needs.

Taking Diversity into Account for Progress in the General Curriculum:

1. How do culturally sensitive programs such as P-BLISS influence the identification and subsequent education of gifted students?

2. How could you use the principles of P-BLISS in your own classroom to enhance the learning experiences of all students?

3. Explain the importance of presenting a curriculum that not only captures students' interest but also challenges their potential.

To answer these questions online, go to the Multicultural Considerations module in Chapter 7 of the Companion Website.

---

sented in gifted programs, yet the current projections are that "minority students will soon represent more than one third of public school children" (Ford & Harris, 1999, p. 2). The risk of discriminating against students from diverse backgrounds exists but can be minimized by the innovative curriculum that you will read about in Box 7–2.

To ensure that assessments do not discriminate against students from diverse populations, researchers advocate using multiple means for determining the presence of giftedness (Dickson, 2003). Specifically, IQ and creativity test results may be balanced with a combination of other selection criteria, such as behavior rating scales, samples of artwork or creative writing, photographs of a previously completed science project, a videotape of an oral presentation, or other material from parents or teachers. These additional examples are called **documentation.** Figure 7–6 shows the standard process for evaluating students for the presence of giftedness.

We have already discussed intelligence testing in Chapter 4; in this chapter we will focus on two additional forms of assessment. First, we will look at a new alternative assessment developed to identify giftedness among students from diverse backgrounds, which is based on multiple domains of intelligence. Then we will examine creativity assessment as a means for determining whether or not a student is gifted or talented.

Please refer to Chapter 2 for a more extensive discussion of intelligence testing and how it impacts all students with exceptionalities.

FIGURE 7–6

Evaluating whether or not a student is gifted, using an IDEA-type of process

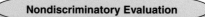

Nondiscriminatory Evaluation

Observation

Teacher and parents observe	Student may be bored with school or intensely interested in academic pursuits, has high vocabulary or specialized talents and interests, shows curiosity and frequently asks questions (especially *how* and *why*), is insightful, has novel ideas and approaches to tasks.

Screening

Assessment measures	Findings that indicate need for further evaluation
Classroom work products	Work is consistently superior in one or more academic areas or, in case of underachieving gifted, products are inconsistent, with only work of special interest being superior.
Group intelligence tests	Tests often indicate exceptional intelligence.
Group achievement tests	Student usually performs above average in one or more areas of achievement (cutoff for screening purposes is an IQ of 115).

Prereferral

Generally, prereferral is not used for students who may be evaluated as gifted.

Referral

Nondiscriminatory evaluation procedures and standards

Assessment measures	Findings that suggest giftedness
Individualized intelligence test	Student scores in the upper 2 to 3 percent of the population. Because of cultural biases of standardized IQ tests, students from minority backgrounds are considered if their IQs do not meet the cutoff but other indicators suggest giftedness.
Individualized achievement test	The student scores in the upper 2 to 3 percent in one or more areas of achievement.
Creativity assessment	The student demonstrates unusual creativity in work products as judged by experts or performs exceptionally well on tests designed to assess creativity. The student does not have to be academically gifted to qualify.
Checklists of gifted characteristics	These checklists are often completed by teachers, parents, peers, or others who know the student well. The student scores in the range that suggests giftedness as established by checklist developers.
Anecdotal records	The student's records suggest high ability in one or more areas.
Curriculum-based assessment	The student is performing at a level beyond peers in one or more areas of the curriculum used by the local school district.
Direct observation	The student may be a model student or could have behavior problems as a result of being bored with classwork. If the student is perfectionistic, anxiety might be observed. Observations should occur in other settings besides the school.
Visual and performing arts assessment	The student's performance in visual or performing arts is judged by individuals with expertise in the specific area. The student does not have to be academically gifted to qualify.
Leadership assessment	Peer nomination, parent nomination, and teacher nomination are generally used. However, self-nomination can also be a good predictor of leadership. Leadership in extracurricular activities is often an effective indicator. The student does not have to be academically gifted to qualify.
Case-study approach	Determination of student's giftedness is based on looking at all areas of assessment described above without adding special weight to one factor.

Nondiscriminatory evaluation team determines that student is gifted and needs special education.

Appropriate Education

Multiple Intelligences

Maker, Rogers, Nielson, and Bauerle (1994) developed the DISCOVER (*Discovering Intellectual Strengths and Capabilities through Observation while allowing for Varied Ethnic Responses*) assessment as an alternative assessment for identifying giftedness among students from diverse backgrounds. The rationale is that if these students typically score low on standardized IQ tests, educators need an instrument that more accurately taps into the students' abilities. The DISCOVER approach has been found valuable in general classrooms with a high proportion of Spanish-speaking or bilingual children (Castellano, 2003a).

A performance-based instrument, the DISCOVER assessment requires the student to undertake problem-solving tasks in six of Gardner's domains of intelligence: spatial, logical-mathematical, linguistic, bodily-kinesthetic, interpersonal, and intrapersonal. The tasks increase in complexity and openness as the assessment progresses.

The instrument draws on Maker's (1993) definition of giftedness as "the ability to solve the most complex problems in the most efficient, effective, or economical ways" (p. 71). A total of 82 behaviors and 68 characteristics of products (Maker, 1996) help assess which of the six intelligences are strongest in each child. During the process of evaluation (Seraphim, 1997), students work in small groups, while highly trained observers use standard observation sheets, pictures, and a video camera to note the students' problem-solving processes and products. Over a 2½-hour period, observers accept all products, give helpful clues when asked, adopt a nonjudgmental attitude, and rotate regularly to minimize bias.

Afterward, the observers collaborate to rate the students' strengths on a scale of 1 to 5, from "no strength observed" to "definite strength observed." Students with a superior problem-solver rating are those with definite ratings in two or more activities. These students are referred for placement in a program for gifted students or for further testing.

Creativity Assessment

The level of creativity of performers and artists is difficult to evaluate by using most tests of creativity, which measure its intellectual aspects only. Therefore, creative individuals are regarded as gifted primarily through consensus of knowledgeable evaluators. Nakamura and Csikszentmihalyi (2001) describe how creativity "does not happen inside people's heads, but in the interaction between a person's thoughts and a sociocultural context." Finding assessments that successfully bring these interactions together is a challenge.

Many tests successfully assess creativity (Fishkin, Cramond, & Olszewski-Kubilius, 2001), but divergent thinking tests are among the most popular techniques (Davis, 2003). For example, the Torrance tests of creative thinking (Torrance, 1966a, 1966b, 1990) assess two aspects of creativity. *Thinking Creatively with Words* (Torrance, 1966b) and *Thinking Creatively with Pictures* (Torrance, 1966a) are both untimed tests and may be administered individually or in groups.

Thinking Creatively with Words (focuses on the verbal, linguistic side of creativity from fourth grade through graduate school), asking students to complete seven verbal activities.

To see specific examples of instruments used to evaluate gifted students, go to the Web Links module in Chapter 7 of the Companion Website.

▼ Activity 1 asks the student to write out all the questions he or she can conceive about a simple picture.

▼ Activity 2 requires the student to list possible causes for the action shown in the picture.

▼ Activity 3 asks the student to list all the possible consequences of the action in the picture.

▼ Activity 4 changes the focus and examines a student's ability to improve a product by introducing another picture, such as a drawing of a stuffed animal. It then asks the student to list the cleverest, most interesting, and most unusual ways to change this toy to make it more fun to play with.

▼ Activity 5 examines a student's ideas about unusual uses of an ordinary object such as a button.

▼ Activity 6 asks the student to think of as many questions as possible about the ordinary object to lead to a variety of different answers and arouse interest and curiosity in others concerning the object.

▼ Activity 7 requires the student to accept an improbable situation such as imagining that people suddenly become invisible. It then asks the student to predict what would happen as a result of this situation. This activity focuses on the student's ability to predict outcomes and consequences.

Thinking Creatively with Pictures (evaluates a student's figural and spatial creativity from kindergarten through graduate school) determines a student's spatial abilities using pictures.

▼ Activity 1 presents a dark curved shape. The test asks the student to think of a picture or an object to draw that incorporates this shape. The test also asks the student to expand on the picture and to title it.

▼ Activity 2 asks the student to complete a number of pictures by adding lines to incomplete figures. The instructions ask the student to make things no one else will think of and to sequence and title the pictures to make an interesting story.

▼ Activity 3 gives the student 10 minutes to see how many objects or pictures can be made from a series of identical shapes, such as squares or triangles. The instructions again ask the student to sequence and title the objects or pictures.

Educators evaluate the test results using several criteria. For example, the verbal creativity tests are scored for fluency, originality, and flexibility according to the scoring guide that accompanies the test. In addition, there are specific guidelines with examples for evaluating student answers. Scores are then summarized, interpreted, and reported.

Determining the Nature and Extent of General and Special Education

After identifying a student as gifted, educators implement educational planning and regular evaluations based on the goals of the student's IEP. In most educational settings, the teacher evaluates a student's performance. With students who are gifted, the potential for placing some of the evaluation responsibility on the students themselves adds new possibilities to the evaluation process. For two areas of assessment, product measures and process measures, the student's responsibility for assessment is appropriate and can be integrated into the IEP goals.

Product Evaluation

Teachers commonly base academic assessment of students in both gifted and general education classrooms on a written product of the student's learning, often a test. The results from these tests help teachers track grades and learning. These approaches are restrictive because they do not provide the teachers or students with tools for understanding the process that the students use to learn.

Moreover, some students are rather complex because they have both exceedingly unusual gifts and talents as well as obvious disabilities; in other words, they have dual diagnoses that product measures/evaluation and process measures/evaluation do not fully address. To understand how a student can have both an unusual talent and a disability, read Box 7–3 and bear in mind that, if a student has a disability that interferes with progress in the general curriculum, then IDEA requires the schools to perform a full nondiscriminatory evaluation of the sort we discussed in Chapter 1.

Good teachers, however, use product measures not just for grades but also for students' benefit. These measures can help students who are gifted record their own progress and compete with themselves rather than with classmates. In addition, good teachers use product measures to assess the thoroughness of their teaching, looking for areas that need further or different instruction.

Process Evaluation

Educators should also evaluate the student's learning process (Andrade, 2000). Process evaluation happens when a teacher attempts to observe and learn from a student's comments or work.

Box 7–3

My Voice

Lights in the Fog: Living in a Twice-Exceptional Family

I had just entered my fourth-grade classroom, smiling oddly as I felt face upon face turn and steal a glance at me, the new kid. I felt my cheeks burning hot, like a freshly melded blacksmith's tool, but proceeded to my seat. It had been two weeks since the beginning of the school year, and one day since my decision to skip third grade after multiple hours of lethally monotonous work in the classroom.

My new teacher walked up to me. I remember the first conversation we had: "Ben, you know why you were moved up, don't you?" I looked at her vacantly. "Because I'm smart." "But why were you moved up instead of all the other kids in your previous class?"

In short, this discussion had me stumped. Though I raced mental fingers across the rough fabric of my well-baled tapestry of a brain, I could not, for the life of me, find out why I had moved up.

These days, however, it's next to impossible to avoid the reasons why I moved up, and why, even to this day, quick insights and a strange wit I carry in conversation garnish my life. These qualities are true with many a person with my malady. I have ADD, a disorder that feeds creativity and draws from analytical reasoning. I was also identified as a gifted learner, long before anyone suspected that I had ADD. The traits are intertwined for me. I can't stand to be bored, and I rarely think in straight lines.

My family has influenced me the most—intellectually as well as emotionally—more than any other group of people I've known. This idea makes obvious sense, but the fact that each member of my family is wildly smart yet saddled with a different disability makes my situation unique.

Blessed with a twice-exceptional family, I have gained a better sense of compassion as well as intelligence, as one cannot usually adorn themselves with the ability to understand, endure, and love wide ranges of both furious intellect and certain mental challenges at such an early stage in life as I have. By sharing my life with a twice-exceptional family, I have gained a keener perception of forbearance alongside a heightened appreciation of intellect in any given person I meet. For instance, my sister and I share a link between both our intellectual capabilities as well as our learning differences. While my beautiful eight-year-old genius of a sibling provides a home for sensory integration disorder—a condition that affects even the simple physical realms of writing, playing an instrument, or throwing a ball, a disability that differs drastically from my own ADD—we both stumble our way across the spectrum of organization and neatness. Though we both attempt to contain annoying habitual nuisance, it's extremely difficult to do so, and time and again, I grow closer to her as a brother when we clean together, do homework together, and get ready for school in the morning as a pair. In this way, our sibling relationship will forever reside in an unbreakable bond.

Likewise, though our types of brilliance differ quite a bit from each other—she's the poster analytical child, a squire to subjects in areas of math and science, and I more the creative type—we combine to create a fiercely passionate problem-solving team. Her critical reasoning is, at times, unmatched for someone her age, and my insights can add undercurrents to our simplest conversations.

Source: Cyr, B. (2000). Lights in the fog: Living in a twice-exceptional family. In K. Kay (Ed.), *Uniquely gifted: Identifying and meeting the needs of the twice-exceptional student.* Gilsum, NH: Avocus.

Teachers formalize "kid watching" when they take notes on the strengths and weaknesses their students demonstrate during problem-solving and learning activities. These notes are good resources during parent-teacher conferences.

Likewise, *reflective assessment* or *evaluation* (White & Frederiksen, 1998) involves teaching students to become aware of the process of their own learning. Reflective assessment results in students being able to actively monitor their own learning. Figure 7–7 shows how four areas of assessment work together on the student's behalf.

How Do You Assure Progress in the General Curriculum

Including Students

There are many effective teaching practices for working with students identified as gifted, depending on age level and area of ability. Box 7–4 provides tips that can be integrated with these practices to ensure success in the general education setting. There are also difficulties in selecting and

FIGURE 7–7
Focus points for assessment

	Product	**Process**
Teacher uses	*Written Tests/Projects* • Teacher's grade book • Report card • How student compares to other students	*Kid Watching: Teacher Portfolios* • Teacher's understanding of student • Teacher's instructional planning • Parent conferences
Student uses	*Written Tests/Projects* • Student understanding of what still needs to be learned • Review of material • How student compares to peers in the class	*Reflective Evaluation: Student Portfolios* • Active participation and responsibility in the assessment process • Development of self-monitoring strategies that use higher-order thinking skills

developing appropriate instruction. Understanding students' individual needs is critical to achieving the best match between a student's needs and the curriculum. Furthermore, using technology appropriately is both beneficial and challenging, as Box 7–5 makes clear.

Planning Universally Designed Learning

Gifted students' unique characteristics require that the depth of a teacher's content coverage should correlate to the aptitude and level of the students' sophistication. In addition, in order to address possible motivation, attention, and behavioral issues, good teachers should relate their instruction to their students' interests. Good teachers address their students' learning needs and related characteristics through universally designed learning.

Augmenting Curriculum

One way to augment general education instruction for students who are gifted is to enrich their instruction and related experiences, expanding their exposure to traditional curriculum. The term *enrichment* refers to curriculum as well as program delivery services. Enriched curriculum includes more varied educational experiences in an existing curriculum that has been modified or added to in some way (Renzulli, 1999b). These modifications or additions may be content or teaching strategies. The goal is to offer students curriculum that is greater in depth or breadth than what is generally provided.

Renzulli and his colleagues developed and implemented an *enrichment triad model* that has been used in hundreds of school districts across the country since the 1970s. Recent school reform efforts have led to an adjustment in this model, now referred to as the *schoolwide enrichment model* (SEM) (Renzulli & Reis, 2003). SEM's major goal is to promote challenging, high-end learning across a range of school types, levels, and demographic differences. This model attempts to create myriad services that can be integrated across the general education curriculum to assist all students, not just those with the gifted identification. In the end, the approach allows schools to develop a collaborative school culture that takes advantage of resources and ap-

Inclusion Tips

Box 7–4

	What You Might See	What You Might Be Tempted to Do	Alternate Responses	Ways to Include Peers in the Process
Behavior	The student might be the perfect student; or you might see the "know-it-all," the "put-down artist"; or she may ask so many questions that there is time for nothing else.	Tell her to be quiet and pay attention to her work.	Begin a dialogue journal. Ask her to write down her questions, using either paper, computer, or a tape recorder. Then research and discuss the answers together.	Have an all-class "Challenge Box," where students can write questions they think are difficult. Then allow the students who are gifted to work on these in small groups with their peers.
Social Interactions	She might be a leader who gets along well with everyone, or she might look like an "instigator" or a "manipulator" who cannot see another's point.	Keep her separated from other students to avoid potential problems.	Build on her leadership by using "Reciprocal Teaching," giving her responsibility for leading a class discussion of major concepts.	Have her work with small groups, teaching the other students to be the leaders in the "Reciprocal Teaching" activity.
Educational Performance	You might see academic aptitude in any area, or you might see the "dreamy doodler" or the student who can't change from one subject to another.	Discipline her for inattentiveness or give additional work to reinforce the lesson.	Ask her to design a better way to teach the content being covered.	Pair her with another student during these lessons, and allow them to take notes together on the topic being covered.
Classroom Attitudes	You might see attentive curiosity and creativity, or you might see the student who's into everything, the "stubborn mule," the "cut-up," and the one who can't leave anything alone.	Discipline her for her poor attitude. If it continues, you might be tempted to refer her for AD/HD testing.	Try giving her the opportunity to use the learning in areas of her own interest, working on individual projects with the teacher.	Continue the projects by allowing other students to join the group and test out her ideas.

propriate decision-making opportunities to create meaningful, high-level, and potentially creative opportunities for students (Renzulli, 1999a).

The original enrichment triad model was designed to encourage creative productivity on the part of students by exposing them to a variety of topics, areas of interest, and fields of study, and to teach them to apply advanced skills to self-selected areas of interest. To accomplish this, Renzulli included three types of enrichment (see Figure 7–8).

Type I enrichment exposes the learner to a wide variety of topics, disciplines, occupations, hobbies, persons, places, and events that ordinarily would not be included in the general education

Technology Tips

Box 7—5

WebQuests

Today, most schools and a growing number of homes have Internet connections. In classrooms all across the United States, teachers and students are integrating the content of World Wide Web pages into their daily instruction. To do just that is increasingly easy, for web applications and resources seem to proliferate overnight. At the same time, educators are often challenged by the amount of information available and how to apply specific resources as they teach.

What Is the Technology?

A WebQuest is an inquiry-oriented activity in which most or all of the information that students use derives from the web. WebQuests are designed to use students' time well; to focus on using information rather than looking for it; and to support students' thinking at the levels of analysis, synthesis, and evaluation. WebQuests are appealing because they provide structure and guidance for both students and teachers. The ideal of engaging higher-level thinking skills by making good use of limited computer access seems to resonate with many educators.

What Do We Do with It?

A WebQuest allows teachers and students to create activities around web-based resources. Instead of simply using a website, the teacher or student is directed through a quest in how to interact with the site(s), what activity to undertake, and how to evaluate success with the site(s). For example, a WebQuest begins with an introduction about the purpose of the quest. Next, the teacher assigns a task that focuses students on what they are going to do: specifically, the culminating performance or product that drives all the learning activities. Subsequently, an outline tells the student how he will accomplish the task. Using scaffolding (the process of building one skill on top of another and so on up through the skill levels), the student uses clear steps, resources, and tools for organizing information. Each WebQuest also includes an evaluation component that enumerates the specific criteria students must meet to satisfy performance and content standards. Finally, the WebQuest conclusion brings closure and encourages the student to reflect on his learning experience.

Putting WebQuests to Work for Progress in the General Curriculum:

1. How can a WebQuest be used to integrate home, school, and community activities?

2. Are WebQuests limited to only the gifted student, or does the technology offer application and potential advantages to individuals with disabilities as well?

3. How do current WebQuests help teachers engage the gifted learner as well as his or her peers? Also, does the technology lend itself to students of all age and grade levels and, if so, how?

To answer these questions online and learn more about these strategies, go to the Technology Tips module in Chapter 7 of the Companion Website.

To learn about how Briana's school implements the SEM process, go to the Web Links module in Chapter 7 of the Companion Website for a link to Briana's school website.

curriculum. For example, Type I experiences may involve community speakers, demonstrations, performances, multimedia presentations, or other illustrative formats.

Type II enrichment focuses on resources that promote creative thinking, problem-solving, and critical-thinking skills. This kind of enrichment consists of how-to-learn skills, including written, oral, and visual communication skills. Other Type II skills are specific to the student and can foster advanced instruction specific to the interest of the student.

If and when a student becomes interested in pursuing a self-selected area of interest and commits the time necessary for this endeavor, a Type III enrichment occurs. The goals of Type III include the following:

1. Providing opportunities for applying interests
2. Acquiring advanced-level understanding of the content and process that are used within particular disciplines
3. Developing authentic products
4. Developing self-directed learning skills
5. Empowering the individual to take control of his or her own learning through organization and feelings of accomplishment

FIGURE 7–8
Triad's three-ring approach

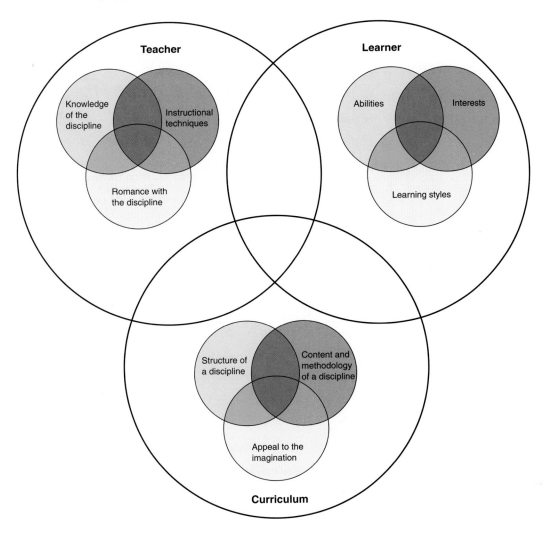

To further challenge the gifted student while providing challenging learning experiences for all students, SEM addresses additional needs and offers extended accommodations. SEM influences the general curriculum in three ways: (1) The curriculum is differentiated through compacting, textbook modification, and group jumping strategies; (2) traditional content is replaced by selected in-depth learning experiences; and (3) enrichment activities are introduced selectively into general curriculum activities.

The goals of SEM are to expand a continuum of special services that will challenge students and also infuse into the "general education program a broad range of activities for high-end learning that will: (a) challenge all students to perform at advanced levels, and (b) allow teachers to determine which students should be given extended opportunities, resources, and encouragement in particular areas where superior interest and performance are demonstrated" (see Figure 7–9) (Renzuli & Reis, 1997, p. 42).

Altering Curriculum

Altering the curriculum means teaching content that will enable students to apply critical thinking and problem-solving skills that are typically not addressed in the general education classroom. Problem-based learning (PBL) is a curriculum development and delivery system that recognizes the need to develop problem-solving skills as well as acquire knowledge and skills. PBL

FIGURE 7–9
Schoolwide enrichment model (SEM)

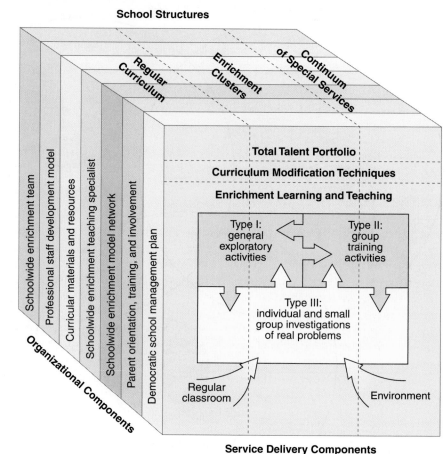

Source: From Colangelo, Nicholas & Gary Davis, *Handbook of Gifted Education*. Published by Allyn and Bacon, Boston, MA. Copyright © 2003 by Pearson Education. Reprinted/adapted by permission of the publisher.

uses real-world problems, not hypothetical case studies with neat, concluding outcomes. It is based on the belief that the process of struggling with actual problems forces students to learn both content and critical-thinking skills. Thus, problem-based learning has several distinct characteristics that make it a good choice when designing curriculum.

1. *The problems drive the curriculum.* The problems do not test skills; they assist in developing the skills.
2. *The problems are truly ill-structured.* There is never only one solution. As new information is gathered in a reiterative process, the perception of both problem and solution changes.
3. *Students solve the problems.* Teachers serve as coaches and facilitators.
4. *Students only receive guidelines for how to approach problems.* There are many different approaches to the problem.
5. *Assessment is authentic and performance-based.* Assessment is a seamless part and an end to the instruction.

PBL assists students in solving problems by continually encountering the type of ill-structured problems confronted by adults in the professional world. Thus, PBL seeks to develop learners who can

▼ Clearly define a problem
▼ Develop alternative hypotheses

▼ Find, evaluate, and use data from a variety of sources

▼ Alter hypotheses when given new information

▼ Develop clearly stated solutions that fit the problem

Collaborating to Meet Students' Needs

Delisle (1999) proposes three solutions for professionals, community members, and family members seeking to collaborate: flexibility, acceleration, and variety. Flexibility means that students should be allowed to move forward at their own pace after they have mastered a topic, learn from other experts in their area, and try lessons that require higher-level thinking. Acceleration refers to speeded-up learning: more content to be mastered in the same period of time as students who do not have special academic talents. And variety refers to different means for learning, including different instructional approaches and materials. Undoubtedly, these three solutions also require professionals to work closely with each other, as Box 7–6 points out.

Beyond school, communities can respond to the needs of students who are gifted. Historically, these students have found community outlets in extracurricular activities such as library reading programs, 4-H, Scouts, sports activities, community centers, and volunteer programs. Today, while traditional programs continue to be important and teachers can continue to encourage and facilitate them, new programs are becoming available as more businesses and universities are collaborating with schools, parents, and communities.

Mentorships are a good example of such collaboration. **Mentors** are people who know more than students do about a particular area and are willing to work with them on an individual basis. Typically, they are community experts who provide specialized knowledge and/or skills to expand students' talents in a particular area of study. When a novice and an expert are successfully paired, there is great potential for developing students' interest in trades and professions, interest that might otherwise be stunted or never explored (Herbert & Neumeister, 2000; Templin, Engemann, & Doran, 1999).

Teachers can help set up mentorships not only within the community but also within the school setting. Because they are individualized, mentorships can be an excellent opportunity for peer collaboration and integration across grade levels. Older students who are gifted in a particular area can become mentors for younger students who show aptitude in the same area. Within the business community, students who are gifted can learn problem-solving and critical-thinking skills necessary in successful businesses before encountering the realities of the business world. School projects can be built around developing business plans under the direction of community business leaders, thus preparing students to interact with the business world at a much earlier age.

What Can You Learn from Others Who Teach Gifted Students?

Learning for the Early Childhood Years: Montgomery Knolls Elementary School, Silver Spring, Maryland

Ironically, gifted programs are still rare for young children, which is when their giftedness is in its most formative stage. For example, Briana did not receive specialized support until the first grade. These students often lose their excitement and capacity for reflection and creative thinking as a result of schooling that fails to meet their educational needs (Hodge & Kemp, 2000). With the nation's educational focus moving more toward early readiness, some new and innovative programs are emerging that offer children opportunities to develop their gifts (Haensly, 1999).

Collaboration Tips

Box 7—6

Professional-to-Professional Collaboration

It may seem obvious that collaboration among general educators and gifted education teachers benefits students who are gifted. However, a study of professional development practices used in 1,231 school districts across the country showed that collaboration among gifted and general educators was rare (Westberg et al., 1998). Although gifted education specialists can provide professional development training to other faculty members within their school districts, they do not often do so. Research also reveals that collaborators often enter a collaborative alliance with different yet complementary sets of expectations for themselves and for students (Purcell & Leppien, 1998).

When general educators and gifted specialists work together on short-term and long-term curricular goals, then everyone benefits, teachers and students alike. Unfortunately, in some schools, students might attend a gifted program for a limited time and then return to the general education classroom for the remainder of the day, where they must make up all work they have missed. If the work covers new material that the student has not yet learned, then the makeup is appropriate. But often the return means that the students have to complete worksheets or assignments that are more like busywork than educational tools for developing strengths. A key person who can help in the implementation of inclusion in such situations is the gifted education specialist. This person can be the bridge between the general classroom setting and resources needed for serving students who are gifted.

Another way to assess what is best for the situation is through an alternative professional collaboration model called resource consultation. In this model, based on a collaborative problem-solving process (Ward & Landrum, 1994), shared responsibility among school personnel occurs at three levels:

- Level 1 primarily involves general education classroom teachers with team preparation and teaching of shared gifted students.
- Level 2 has the gifted education specialist and teachers share responsibility to provide the most appropriate education for the gifted.
- Level 3 involves instructional staff, counselors, school psychologists, administrators, and/or other support personnel.

In this model, each participant comes to realize the demands upon the abilities of others. Through school staff training and consultation, teachers and students all benefit.

It is also beneficial for a guidance counselor to be involved in the collaboration process for students who are gifted. Helping build professional collaboration and understanding of such students is a key factor in their success; this can be a guidance counselor's major contribution. Piirto (1999) discusses the many issues that these students may encounter. Anger, boredom, depression, introversion, meeting the expectations of others, peer relations, perfectionism, resilience, and underachievement are just a few. These are all important areas in which counseling can make a difference.

Putting These Tips to Work for Progress in the General Curriculum:

1. Who are the collaborators?
2. What are the challenges?
3. What can the team do?
4. What are the results?

To answer these questions online and learn more about these ideas and concepts, go to the Collaboration Tips module in Chapter 7 of the Companion Website.

Montgomery Knolls Elementary School in Silver Spring, Maryland, has such a program. This program helps identify and educate underserved children with gifts and talents, including children experiencing economic disadvantages, cultural diversity, language differences (primary language not English), and developmental delays indicating learning disabilities. Based on Gardner's (1999) model of different domains of intelligence, the program focuses on identifying and serving different types of giftedness and builds on the goal of ensuring that the instruction and content coverage correlate with students' aptitude, interests, and abilities.

Montgomery Knolls Early Childhood Gifted Model Program trains all faculty to look for different types of giftedness, plan activities specific to these areas, and then provide options for each child. Twice a year, teachers fill out a checklist on each child, identifying areas of strength.

Unusual musical talents sometimes co-exist with talents in mathematics or other academic disciplines requiring a high degree of conceptualization.

These young students benefit from the theme approach. They use their different gifts to express their own understanding of a unifying topic as well as to learn about other topics. This approach helps young students make abstract concepts concrete and real. For instance, during a study of dinosaurs, children with a strong spatial orientation wanted to know how big the dinosaurs were. To find out, they projected enlarged pictures onto the school wall to grasp the concept of size. By contrast, children with a linguistic orientation developed seven questions and then e-mailed them to a paleontologist, who answered their questions. Children with artistic talents used papier-mâché to make life-size features of the dinosaurs, and those with a musical ability wrote and sang songs about dinosaurs.

Dr. Waveline Starnes, initiator of the program, reports enthusiastic support from parents, teachers, and children: "There have been great benefits for teachers. The 'verbal veil' that had hidden the children's varying potentials has been removed, and teachers are looking for and seeing giftedness in all areas."

Learning for the Elementary Years: Blue Valley School District, Kansas

Most school districts initiate some sort of identification program and begin working with students during the elementary years. You may remember that Briana was identified during her first-grade year, and that by second grade was transferred to another school district to receive the specialized experience she required.

Blue Valley School District, a suburban district located in Johnson County, Kansas, is one example of a program that integrates features of enriching experiences and problem-based learning for students in grades 1 through 6.

Lucie Medbery and her colleagues adapt and implement SEM (schoolwide enrichment model) and have begun to integrate the autonomous learner model to better address the specific needs of the gifted child (see Box 7–7). Her program aims to expand the problem-based experiences that a student can complete individually or share with a group of learners. The results are promising, even with the youngest of her students, Graham.

A recent example of Lucie's efforts to facilitate group as well as problem-based learning involved simple household refrigerator magnets. "I brought in some refrigerator magnets one day

Box 7—7

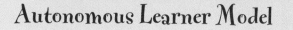

Into Practice

Autonomous Learner Model

Like problem-based learning, the autonomous learner model (ALM) seeks to develop independent, self-directed learners—not just those who are exceptionally smart but those who are "whole students" and are developed socially, emotionally, and cognitively. ALM features five dimensions in which a student receives a variety of supports and enrichment experiences. Each dimension consists of a number of areas that tie to specific learning objectives.

Orientation

- Understanding giftedness, talent, intelligence, and creativity
- Group building activities
- Personal development
- Program and school opportunities and responsibilities

Individual development

- Inter/Intrapersonal skills
- Learning skills
- Technology
- College and career involvement
- Organizational skills
- Productivity

Enrichment

- Explorations
- Investigations
- Cultural activities
- Service
- Adventure trips

Seminars

- Futuristic
- Problematic
- Controversial
- General interest
- Advanced knowledge

In-depth study

- Individuals project
- Group projects
- Mentorships
- Presentations
- Assessments

ALM's strength lies in its flexibility. As the teacher and student work together on various problem-based learning experiences, their role as lifelong learners adapt to and change with the requirements of the experience. Thus, depending on the instruction, the model allows for the changing of roles, as in the following patterns:

1. Teacher—student
2. Learner—facilitator
3. Teacher/facilitator—student learner
4. Learner/student—facilitator teacher

By changing roles, all students develop and appreciate their own strengths. A more important outcome of this model is that all students, specifically gifted learners, grow in self-esteem. By actively building autonomous learning opportunities into the curriculum, students have access to the development of skills that focus on their needs socially, emotionally, and cognitively at the transition stage of the curriculum. Thus, the teacher, by the very nature of his role as facilitator, can lead students away from being dependent to becoming independent learners/researchers.

An example of how well these principles can work appears in Lucie's youngest student, Graham. A third grader, he was identified as gifted and given an IEP in the second grade. Two or three times a week, Lucie pulls Graham out of his general education class to join several fourth- and fifth-grade students. During their time together Lucie "concentrates on pulling out the individual strengths noted in Graham's IEP." For example, Graham, who has a special interest in stars, is concentrating on constellations. Facilitating his learning, Lucie challenges him to learn more about constellations and to create a PowerPoint slide show on the constellations he researches. In addition, she assists further study by equipping him with a high-powered telescope to study star formations. At the same time, Lucie has introduced the Logo program to Graham, which offers problem-based activities that he can conduct autonomously from others.

However, Graham is not confined to independent work. Instead, Lucie sees the pullout program as an opportunity for students to spend time with their intellectual peers. Thus, she encourages them to pursue similar interests together as well as different interests independently. She notes, "They are all highly capable and often look to help each other as they expand their individual knowledge."

Putting These Strategies to Work for Progress in the General Curriculum

1. How might Lucie or one of her colleagues continue to build on and further integrate this strategy into his or her classroom?

2. What more do you need to know in order to implement this model?

3. How can collaboration between the gifted and general education teachers assist such implementation? How could parents and related resources help?

To answer these questions online and learn more about these strategies, go to the Into Practice module in Chapter 7 of the Companion Website.

and shared them with the group," she explains. "I asked them to investigate and problem-solve how these magnets are being used or what possible uses there are for magnets." Soon Graham and his peers were discussing magnetic resonance imaging (MRI). Next, they researched the technology and its various applications. "It was fascinating to watch and listen to the students move from magnets to MRIs. One student quoted Einstein's statement about the power of observation and related this quote or idea to what they were doing as a group," Lucie notes. To learn more, the group sought her help in identifying experts.

Lucie's group is also tracking the progress of a number of turtles that regularly visit the class with a local marine biologist. The biologist initially visited based on the interest of one student. This led to repeat visits with several turtles. Instead of simply marveling at the variety of turtles brought in for display, the students decided they wanted to track the growth and progress of the turtles. During each visit, students collect data on the growth of each turtle, changes in characteristics, and related information that they store in a Microsoft Excel document.

Lucie clearly sees herself as a facilitator as she seeks to create the appropriate environment in which individual or group problem-based learning can evolve. This may include finding research information or introducing technology applications that can help students learn. Lucie explains,

Magnet schools build on inherent strengths of students who are gifted, providing many opportunities for growth and challenge in a specific domain of talent.

"My role is to facilitate the learning experience, presenting problems for them to solve. I also feel it is my responsibility to help these students realize what it is to be gifted. That is why we like the autonomous learning model. It features problem-based learning but also stresses an understanding of what it is to be gifted, the characteristics one has as a gifted child, the issues that tend to come along with this exceptionality, as well as some of the skills one needs to fully develop (e.g., time management.)"

Learning for the Middle and Secondary Years: Central Middle School, Grandview, Missouri

As we have learned, gifted children need an enriched curriculum that can augment their learning and meet their instructional needs. So in many secondary programs students can select from special honor courses or advanced placement courses that offer enriching experiences and are substitutes for standard required coursework. Elective courses, taken in addition to the requirements for graduation, are also available, as are before and/or after-school electives, Saturday programs, seminars, and summer institutes.

Briana's middle school offers advanced courses as well as traditional courses extended through enrichment. The enrichment model at Central Middle School was developed around the Program for Exceptionally Gifted Students (PEGS) created and adopted across many school districts in the state of Missouri. The PEGS curriculum ensures mastery of the basic knowledge and skills contained in the Central School District curriculum. In addition, it provides an enhanced curriculum appropriate for exceptionally gifted students, based on the following principles:

1. Accelerated learning through curriculum compacting
2. Advanced training in critical and creative thinking, research, and content-related skills
3. Creative production as a result of a student's intense interest in a topic and a passion to solve real-world problems
4. Attention to the affective needs of exceptionally gifted students
5. Special mentorships for students
6. Mainstreaming for fine arts and physical education

For example, Central Middle School seventh graders recently studied the concept of scientific inquiry and method. Based on a state standard and part of a curriculum map designed for all seventh-grade science curricula, students in the general science curriculum explored this concept by baking cookies and altering various ingredients to measure the change in the cookies and related outcomes. Melinda Merrill, Briana's PEGS instructor, had Briana and her peers examine the concept of scientific inquiry and method by designing, conducting, and evaluating nine different experiments.

In one, PEGS participants examined the acidic makeup of a variety of liquids. For example, one day Melinda brought in various water samples: (1) simple tap water, (2) water from a local pond, and (3) water from a local stream. Melinda explains, "I provided the water samples; but Briana and the rest of the class were in charge of designing the experiment, figuring out the method of investigation, and ensuring that the experiment allowed them to successfully arrive at correct conclusions. We want them to develop their own skills in problem solving as we introduce the content. With the inquiry method, the skill was equally if not more important to learn than the actual content concerning the water and other parts of the experiment."

Upon completion of the lesson, both the PEGS and general science class completed the same science benchmark exam. "This examination is a state requirement and something that all students have to complete," explains Melinda. The required assessment does not limit the group, however, so Melinda conducts separate evaluations to expand student understanding and ability to apply beyond the classroom. She explains, "I regularly create problem-based games to test the students while also expanding their problem-solving applications. For the inquiry lesson, I adapted the game of Jeopardy to the design and method they created for the various experiments. The outcome was an engaging experience that made them think and have to quickly apply what they knew beyond classroom-based knowledge."

Not all of Briana's day is spent in the PEGS program; she receives much of her content-based courses with her age-appropriate peers. In these classes, Melinda works with Briana's teachers to create additional enriching experiences as well as problem-based exercises that go beyond the requirements of the class. For instance, in English Briana will participate with her peers in the study of theme and character development. Unlike her peers, who read at a fourth- to sixth-grade level, Briana reads at the 12th-grade level. Therefore, Melinda assists Briana in selecting a book that will enrich Briana's learning while maintaining the goals and objectives of the English curriculum. Melinda is also requiring her PEGS participants to read a science fiction book on either evolution or genetics. They are writing story lines based on the themes of the book and have attempted to tie some of this work back to the inquiry they are conducting in their science curriculum.

Melinda and her colleagues keep Briana engaged throughout the course of the day. Melinda, on her part, maintains an ability to enrich Briana and her peers through a PEGS statewide support network. Through this network, Melinda has access to peers who are addressing similar content and instructional needs.

Learning for the Transitional and Postsecondary Years: College Planning for Gifted Students

For a gifted student, planning for the right college or university requires a proactive approach that addresses the unique needs and talents of the individual. Indeed, according to Berger (1989), this planning or "learning about onself" is a 6-year process beginning as early as the seventh grade.

College Planning for Gifted Students (Berger, 1989) provides detailed information on how to plan for college. For example, during the seventh and eighth grades, students participate in guidance activities that emphasize self-awareness, time management, work/study skills, and an introduction to career awareness. In the 9th- and 10th-grade years, guidance activities continue to help students clarify their intellectual and social/emotional experiences, establish a sense of identity and direction, and set short- and long-term goals. Finally, by the 11th and 12th grades, guidance activities include arranging for mentor relationships and internships.

As gifted children are examining who they are, they also are learning about particular colleges and their respective programs. Learning about colleges is a two-step process. Step 1 involves collecting general information by reading, talking with people, and visiting colleges. Step 2 involves analyzing and evaluating information. Of course, the more students are attuned to their own needs, the more effective the research becomes.

Finally, gifted students are often drawn to selective colleges and universities that receive a significant number of applications for every freshman vacancy. Thus, as part of the planning process, students should thoroughly research what they need to do during the application process to enhance their chances of acceptance at a specific university. Recognizing that college planning is critical for all students, including the gifted student, more and more high school programs are developing cooperative programs with colleges and universities. These programs enable school students to get a jumpstart on the college experience by offering enriched or advanced-level courses designed to complete high school and/or curricular requirements. Usually in a joint program between a high school and a college, a gifted student is allowed to enroll in college courses while still in high school. In some secondary programs, these college courses are replacements for curricula requirements; in other settings, they constitute additions to an established high school curriculum. For most programs, registration in the college course results in the establishment of a college transcript, making credits applicable toward a college degree program. As a result, some gifted students begin their first year in a college or university program as a second-semester freshman or a sophomore, having completed a semester or two of college requirements during their secondary school experience.

On Chapter 7's Companion Website, you will find a link to learn more about *College Planning for Gifted Students.*

A Vision for Briana's Future

"Where are you taking me?" asked the author Forrester of his young protégé, Jamal. Forrester put the question to Jamal in the context of the boy's writing; he wanted Jamal to be crystal-clear about his message, so he took the reader to a certain conclusion.

Turn the question around and let Briana ask it to herself: "Where are you, my many gifts, taking me?" Assume that Briana has skipped a grade as she left elementary and entered middle school. That's a fair assumption, given that Briana moved from one school to another during her elementary school years. Assume further that she also developed even further her academic, athletic, and artistic skills. Picture her, like Jamal, in her last year of high school. "Where," she asks herself, "am I taking myself?"

For Briana and others who have multiple gifts, life after high school offers an abundance of opportunity. Already she has been besieged by college and university solicitations promising admission to the state university's honors programs, offering the benefits of the most select private colleges and universities, and asking her to come to summer sports camps. Dance and music conservatories have reminded her of the summer she spent in Kansas City with the Alvin Ailey dance troupe and of her ability to not only dance but to imagine a dance ensemble performing to, say, Duke Ellington's jazz symphony *Black and Tan Fantasy*. Like the colleges and universities, these conservatories plead, "Come spend the next four years of your life with me."

Like Jamal in the movie, Briana could not keep her gifts under wraps; and like him, she found ways to be socially accepted and remain emotionally and behaviorally balanced. Indeed, "Balanced Briana" has found a way to reach the golden mean, which the ancient Greeks advocated and which some may know in its Latin version: "mens sana in corpore sano," or "a healthy mind in a sound body."

Where, then, are her gifts taking her? A good question, but one that cannot be answered without also acknowledging that Briana's history in special education—with its flexibility, acceleration, and variety—are the keys to answering it. Wherever she goes after high school, she will seek and need flexibility in her academic and extracurricular activities, acceleration in all that she undertakes, and variety in the way in which she learns and indeed in what she does.

"Where are you taking me?"

"Anywhere your gifts lead, Briana; anywhere they lead."

What Would You Recommend?

1. To help Briana develop her present interests in singing, dance, and running to further balance her life?
2. To provide the best possible opportunities for Briana to build on her previous successes and make the best choices for the rest of her secondary school years?
3. To use Briana's strengths and abilities to further develop her as an entire individual outside of the PEGS program and other advanced curriculum classes?

Summary

How Do You Recognize Students Who Are Gifted?

▼ Students who are gifted and talented demonstrate unusual capabilities in intellectual, creative, academic, or leadership areas as well as in the performing and visual arts. These students require special services not ordinarily provided by the public schools or covered under IDEA.

▼ Recent changes in how educators define students who are gifted focus on the developmental nature of giftedness. This definition must include multiple domains of potential ability and not be determined solely by IQ.

- Students who are creative show many distinct characteristics; in comparison to their peers, they may be more adventurous, independent, curious, spontaneous, flexible, sensitive, intuitive, and insightful.
- Students who are gifted may demonstrate characteristics that look antisocial such as boredom, hyperactivity, or even insubordination. Educators who build on students' strengths help them to reach their potential.
- Many populations are vastly underrepresented in current gifted programs. For example, girls and students from ethnically diverse backgrounds often go undetected or have to work their way through successive levels of adverse circumstances.
- Most researchers today attribute giftedness to a combination of genetic and environmental factors, but they disagree about the proportions between the two factors.
- When IQ test scores are equated with giftedness, the top 2 or 3 percent of the general population is considered gifted. Using a talent pool that includes students with an IQ of a minimum of 115 means that 16 percent of students will be served.

How Do You Evaluate Students Who Are Gifted?

- To determine the presence of intellectual giftedness, students typically take IQ tests, achievement tests, and/or creativity tests such as the Torrance Tests of Creative Thinking.
- To ensure that assessments do not discriminate against students from minority populations, several types of measurement should be used.
- Once educators identify a student as gifted, educational planning and regular evaluations based on IEP goals are implemented. Including students in the evaluation process can be done with the use of instructional rubrics.
- Recent innovative evaluation procedures based on multiple domains of giftedness, such as the DISCOVER assessment, offer an alternative form of assessment for identifying and serving students who are gifted.

How Do You Assure Progress in the General Curriculum?

- Instructional goals that meet the needs of students who are gifted include (1) tailoring the pace of instruction to

students' pace of learning, (2) ensuring that the depth of content coverage correlates to students' aptitude and level of sophistication, and (3) relating instruction to students' interests.
- Teachers can meet the needs of students who are gifted through enrichment activities and a demanding and unusually fast-paced curriculum.
- Problem-based learning is a curriculum development and delivery system that recognizes the need to develop problem-solving skills as well as acquire necessary knowledge and skills.

What Can You Learn from Others Who Teach Gifted Students?

- Identifying preschool students with exceptional ability is difficult, but the current educational focus on early readiness is encouraging many new programs.
- Elementary programs that build on curricular goals, focus on students' interests, and ensure depth of content coverage are critical for student success and ongoing learning.
- The most common programs at the secondary level ensure depth of coverage with enriched curriculum meant to expand student's understanding of the content. Similarly, problem-based learning captures students' interests and challenges them to show their true potential.
- Planning for college needs to be a systematic process with steps beginning as early as seventh grade. With structure planning, gifted students can often get a jump start on the college experience by participating in enriched or advanced-level courses designed to complete high school and/or curricular requirements at the postsecondary level.

Chapter 8

Who Is Tory Woodard?

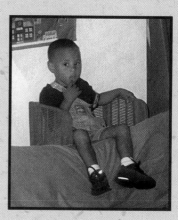

Think about this: Who are you? Let's be more specific. How do others describe you? The answer is "It depends." Who you are, at least in the eyes of others, depends so much on what your observable traits are, where you've been, what you have, where you are, where you're headed, and who and what is in your life.

Now, let's ask the same question about Tory Woodard. Who is he? We can define Tory by his observable traits. He is a young (3 years and 1 month old) African American boy. He lives in Butner, North Carolina, with his mother, Dierdre. He is surrounded by his maternal grandparents, Lonnie and Annie Woodard; by his uncle, Timothy Jiggetts, and Timothy's son (Tory's cousin), Andrewnika Hargrove; and by his aunt, Angela Jiggetts, and her daughter (Tory's cousin), Kelsi Ballard Jiggetts.

We can define Tory by where he's been. Born extremely prematurely (at 23½ weeks gestation), Tory was a patient at Duke University Hospital for the first six months of his life. There, he required mechanical ventilation for his first 63 days and overcame no less than five different and significant medical complications.

We can define him by what he has—namely, the ability to memorize songs, sing the alphabet song, count from 1 to 10, and comply with instructions. And we can define him by his needs: marked delays in cognitive, speech and language, and motor skills.

We can define him by where he is: a recently enrolled student at the Granville County Child Development Center in Oxford, North Carolina. We can define him by where he's headed: from the center to elementary school, with a bevy of intensive interventions that may very well blunt the effects of his present delays. And we can define him by who and what is in his life: a loving family, skilled and caring staff at the

a delay; but the absence of support may convert a delay to mental retardation. For Tory, we have reason to hope that the interventions and supports he now receives and the ways in which we respond to his strengths and needs will make all the difference. He may, indeed, continue to have a delay; and that delay may be so significant that Tory will meet the definition for having mental retardation. But that is by no means the end of the story for Tory: How effective his interventions are, and how his family, teachers, and peers respond to him—indeed, how we all respond to him—will make the difference for him and for us.

center, Duke Hospital, and, in time, the Granville County schools.

What we cannot do accurately for Tory is what you cannot do accurately for yourself. We cannot accurately define Tory by what he will become. There, we have far fewer hard facts on which to rely, but we have some. We know that he has had some growth spurts to compensate for his extreme prematurity. He has good adaptive skills—that is, he knows how to use his cognitive, speech and language, and motor skills to fit in with other students. He is benefiting from early intervention at the Child Development Center and is closely monitored at Duke, and he almost certainly will be able to benefit in the future by going to school with children his own age who do not have disabilities.

Significantly, his mother, Dierdre, and his teacher acknowledge that he has developmental delays; but Dierdre does not concede that he has mental retardation, and in that she might be correct. The reasons have a lot to do with what Tory gets (for early intervention is a form of remediation and prevention) and with how society defines mental retardation. As society defines the term today, *mental retardation* means that a person has significant intellectual and adaptive behavior delays. These delays may be part of Tory's life now but may not be part of his life in the future.

Bear this in mind: Tory is getting a lot of support, which may make all the difference for him, as it does for so many others who have lower intellectual and adaptive skills. And the nature and level of his support may mean that his delay will not result in retardation. Interventions and supports in his home, community, preschool, and later his school can make a delay simply

What do you think?

1. **How might Tory's strengths help him overcome some of his special needs?**

2. **Look into a crystal ball and see Tory in his first-grade classroom. What do you think first grade will be like for him?**

3. **What kinds of supports does Tory receive, and how might they prevent or (if not that) at least blunt the effects of any mental retardation he might experience?**

To respond to these questions online, participate in other activities, and learn more about Tory Woodard and mental retardation, go to the Cases module in Chapter 8 of the Companion Website.

How Do You Recognize Students with Mental Retardation?

Defining Mental Retardation

IDEA (U.S. Department of Education, 1997) defines mental retardation as "significantly subaverage general intellectual functioning existing concurrently with deficits in adaptive behavior and manifested during the developmental period that adversely affects a child's educational performance" (34 C.F.R., Sec. 300.7[b][5]). Likewise, the American Association on Mental Retardation (AAMR), the nation's oldest and largest professional association concerned with individuals who have mental retardation, defines it as follows: "Mental retardation is a disability characterized by significant limitations both in intellectual functioning and in adaptive behavior as expressed in conceptual, social, and practical adaptive skills. This disability originates before age 18" (AAMR, 2002). Figure 8–1 lists the five assumptions that are core to this definition of mental retardation.

We call your attention to items 4 and 5 in Figure 8–1. Each calls for supports to individuals with mental retardation to improve the likelihood of their successful functioning in every day environments. **Supports** refer to the services, resources, and personal assistance that improve the way in

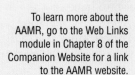

To learn more about the AAMR, go to the Web Links module in Chapter 8 of the Companion Website for a link to the AAMR website.

FIGURE 8–1

Assumptions regarding the definition of mental retardation and their applications to Tory

Five Assumptions	Applications to Tory
1. Limitations in present functioning must be considered within the context of community environments typical of the individual's age peers and culture.	This means that Tory's present functioning must be considered in light of the Granville County environments in which he participates, including home, neighborhood, church, and the Child Development Center.
2. Valid assessment considers cultural and linguistic diversity as well as differences in communication, sensory, motor, and behavioral factors.	This means that the assessment used with Tory must be valid for use with young children of African American heritage who have delays in their development.
3. Within an individual, limitations often coexist with strengths.	This means that Tory's limitations in development must not overshadow his coexisting strengths. What did you learn in the vignette about his strengths?
4. An important purpose of describing limitations is to develop a profile of needed supports.	This means that the purpose of assessing Tory to determine if he has mental retardation is to develop comprehensive supports that will enable him to increase his performance in all areas.
5. With appropriate personalized supports over a sustained period, the life functioning of the person with mental retardation generally will improve.	This means that Tory may not be considered to have mental retardation later in his life because of the strong early intervention that he is getting to enable him to overcome his delays.

Source: Adapted from American Association on Mental Retardation (AAMR). (2002). *Mental retardation: Definition, classification, and systems of supports.* Washington, DC: Author.

FIGURE 8–2
Definitions and examples of intensities of support

Intermittent

Supports on an "as-needed" basis. Characterized by episodic nature, person not always needing the support(s), or short-term supports needed during life-span transitions (e.g., job loss or an acute medical crisis). Intermittent supports may be high or low intensity when provided.

Limited

An intensity of supports characterized by consistency over time, time-limited but not of an intermittent nature, may require fewer staff members and less cost than more intense levels of support (e.g., time-limited employment training or transitional supports during the school to adult provided period).

Extensive

Supports characterized by regular involvement (e.g., daily) in at least some environments (such as work or home) and not time-limited (e.g., long-term support and long-term home living support).

Pervasive

Supports characterized by their constancy, high intensity; provided across environments; potential life-sustaining nature. Pervasive supports typically involve more staff members and intrusiveness than do extensive or time-limited supports.

Source: From *Mental Retardation: Definition, Classification, and Systems of Supports,* by R. Luckasson, D. L. Coulter, E. A. Polloway, S. Reiss, R. L. Schalock, M. E. Snell, D. M. Spitalnik, and J. A. Stark, 1992, Washington, DC: American Association on Mental Retardation. Copyright 1992 by the American Association on Mental Retardation. Reprinted with permission.

which a person functions—how he or she develops, learns, and lives (AAMR, 2002). Supports range from intermittent (provided from time to time) or pervasive (constant), as Figure 8–2 shows.

Whether a person such as Tory has mental retardation, then, is not a fixed conclusion. Instead, it depends in large part on how the person functions in the typical environments of daily life. Here, the supports that a person such as Tory receives in his daily life in his home community make a great difference. That's why early intervention, such as Tory's at the Granville County Child Development Center, is so important: Supports in the community make it possible for a person such as Tory to function more capably and to not be regarded as having mental retardation.

Describing the Characteristics

The three major characteristics of mental retardation are limitations in intellectual functioning, limitations in adaptive behavior, and, as AAMR points out, needs for supports.

Limitations in Intellectual Functioning

Intelligence refers to a student's general mental capability for solving problems, paying attention to relevant information, thinking abstractly, remembering important information and skills, learning from everyday experiences, and generalizing knowledge from one setting to another. It is measured by the intelligence tests that you have already learned about. A student is regarded as having mental retardation when she has an IQ score approximately two standard deviations below the mean.

Regardless of the precise IQ score, students with mental retardation typically have impairments in their intellectual functioning, including memory and generalization. They also may have decreased motivation as a result of repeated failures.

Memory. For many years, individuals with mental retardation have been thought to have impairments in memory, especially short-term memory (Ellis, 1970). **Short-term memory** is the

You learned about the bell-shaped distribution of intelligence in Chapter 4.

Later in the chapter you will learn about ways to plan universally designed learning that will enable you to address these impairments.

Technology Tips

Box 8–1

Visual Assistant: The See-It, Hear-It, Do-It Handheld Portable Prompter

Assume you are teaching three upper-school students with mental retardation to do the jobs they want to acquire in their communities. One student needs to learn how to set the tables in a restaurant or a senior citizens' home; another, to wash, dry, and fold laundry in a school or university athletic center; the third, to deliver the mail from a central mailroom to the offices of the judges and clerks of court in a county courthouse. Assume you have only one aide to assist you. How do you teach all three students, especially if they go off campus daily to learn in the places where they have to perform their duties?

One way to respond to that challenge is to use a Visual Assistant. This clever device, developed by Ablelink, Inc., of Colorado Springs, Colorado, is a "see-it, hear-it, do-it" device very similar to a Palm Pilot, another variety of handheld computer. It lets its users see a photograph of themselves doing one aspect of a job, then the next aspect, and the next, and so on. It also lets its users hear themselves or their teachers, job coaches, or employers prompt them about what to do during that aspect of the job and in the next steps as well. A simple icon on the screen cues the student. For example, an unfolded napkin appears on the screen, the student presses the napkin's image, and the computer shows the student folding the napkin and telling himself how to do that job. "See it" (the visual image), "hear it" (the spoken voice), "do it" (the job being done and then finished): These are the three components of the Visual Assistant.

The Visual Assistant is no larger than other commercially available handheld computers. And it is unobtru-sive, fitting into a purse, a fannypack, a backpack, or the pockets of cargo pants. As a teacher, you equip a student with a Visual Assistant, program it by using a Windows platform with touch-screen capabilities on your classroom's computer, and make sure that this particular assistive technology is written into your student's IEP as a related service.

Does it work? Yes, it enables students and young adults to do their jobs faster, and with fewer errors and prompts from teachers or coaches than if they were doing the same work under the same conditions without a teacher or coach (Davies, Stock, & Wehmeyer, 2002a, 2002b; Riffel, Wehmeyer, Turnbull, Lattimore, Davies, & Stock, 2002).

Does it increase teacher effectiveness? Yes, the teacher can work with more students in more and different community settings than if students did not have Visual Assistants.

And does it stigmatize the students in any way, making them stand out among other students or workers who do not have disabilities? No, because many students and workers use Palm Pilots, cell phones, tape recorders, or portable computers in many aspects of their everyday lives.

Putting These Strategies to Work for Progress in the General Curriculum

1. What is the challenge?
2. What is the technology?
3. What do you do with it?

To answer these questions online and learn more about these strategies, go to the Technology Tips module in Chapter 8 of the Companion Website.

mental ability to recall information that has been stored for a few seconds to a few hours, such as the step-by-step instructions teachers give their students.

More recently, researchers have reported that individuals with mental retardation can learn to use active strategies to improve their memory (Bray, Fletcher, & Turner, 1997). These strategies include learning to quietly repeat instructions to themselves and moving objects in a particular order as an aid to remembering a sequence of activities that have been told to them (Bray et al., 1997; Fletcher & Bray, 1995). Exciting new technologies can help students with mental retardation enhance their memory. One of those technologies is the handheld computer featured in Box 8–1.

Generalization. Generalization refers to the ability to transfer knowledge or behavior learned for doing one task to another task and to make that transfer across different settings or environments (Horner, Dunlap, & Koegel, 1988; Stokes & Baer, 1977). Individuals with mental retardation typically have difficulty generalizing the skills they have learned in school to their home and community settings, where there are different cues, expectations, people, and environmental arrangements (Bebko & McPherson, 1997; Langone, Clees, Oxford, Malone, & Ross, 1995). Why do they have this difficulty? Because their home and community settings often have greater complexity, more distractions, and more irrelevant stimuli than their classrooms do (Bebko & Luhaorg, 1998). In non-classroom settings, the cognitive demands on the students increase greatly, yet teachers value instruction in typical environments rather than simulated ones because those settings are where the students will have to function throughout their lives. To enable them to develop lifetime, real-life capacities, IDEA gives preference to the general education program as contrasted to separate programs.

Motivation. There is a great deal of research on the motivation of individuals with mental retardation (Switzky, 1997a, 1997b). The research consistently reveals that a student's low motivation often results from previous frequent failures. Low motivation leads to a problem-solving style that is called **outer-directedness**—distrusting one's own solutions and looking excessively to others for guidance. This is a special concern for students with mental retardation (Bybee & Ziegler, 1998) because outer-directedness can make them especially vulnerable to control by others. As you will learn later in this chapter, even very young students with mental retardation can benefit from instruction in how to be self-determined.

The program descriptions later in this chapter show how important it is for students to learn important life skills in community settings.

Limitations in Adaptive Behavior

In addition to significant limitations in intellectual functioning, mental retardation also means that a person has "significant limitations . . . in adaptive behavior as expressed in conceptual, social, and practical adaptive skills" (AAMR, 2002, p. 1). **Adaptive behavior** refers to the typical performance of individuals without disabilities in meeting environmental expectations (Demchak & Drinkwater, 1998; Widaman & McGrew, 1996). Adaptive behavior changes according to a person's age, cultural expectations, and environmental demands. That's why we defined Tory in the opening vignette in so many different ways, including some that depend almost entirely on the support he receives at home, in his community, and at the Child Development Center and what he will later receive in school.

To determine a student's adaptive behavior capacities, teachers and other professionals focus on the student's conceptual skills, social skills, and practical skills. A student may have a combination of strengths and needs in any or all of these areas (Greenspan, 1999; Thompson,

J.T.'s housemates encourage him to adopt an inner-directed approach to meeting his needs. He knows that he can choose to be on time for his morning bus and that by doing so he will be able to maintain his schedule at work.

McGrew, & Bruininks, 1999; Widaman & McGrew, 1996). Later in the chapter you will learn about the assessment process related to adaptive behavior. For now we will provide an overview of a representative adaptive behavior skill (self-determination) in the conceptual domain.

Self-determination refers to "acting as the primary causal agent in one's life and making choices and decisions regarding one's quality of life free from undue external influence or interference" (Wehmeyer, 1996, p. 24). Being a **causal agent** means that an individual is able to take action to cause things to happen in his or her life. Thus, self-determined people shape their future; they do not depend on random luck to cause good things to happen to them (Wehmeyer, Palmer, Agran, Mithaug, & Martin, 2000). Self-determination incorporates many skills, including choice making, decision making, problem solving, and goal setting (Wehmeyer, 2002).

Self-determination can make a huge difference in a student's life. Self-determined students are more likely to achieve more positive adult outcomes, such as earning more money per hour, than are peers who are less self-determined (Wehmeyer & Schwartz, 1997). They also are more likely to have a savings or checking account and to express a preference to live outside their family's home. Also, students at the secondary level who are self-determined are more likely than their less self-determined peers to join their teachers and families in making important decisions about their classes, curriculum, and extracurricular activities (Sands, Spencer, Gliner, & Swaim, 1999).

> Later in the chapter you will also learn about model programs in which students with mental retardation are provided with instruction that results in enhanced self-determination skills.

Identifying the Causes

There are two types of causes of mental retardation: those that refer to *timing* and those that refer to *type* (AAMR, 2002).

Causes by Timing

Timing refers to time of onset of the disability (see Figure 8–3):

▼ Prenatal (before birth)
▼ Perinatal (during the birth process)
▼ Postnatal (after birth)

Students with mental retardation, such as this student, are able to participate in their IEP meetings when they have appropriate supports to make their perspectives and preferences known.

FIGURE 8–3
Causes of mental retardation from timing factors

Prenatal	Perinatal	Postnatal
Chromosomal disorders	Prematurity	Head injuries
Metabolic disorders	Meningitis at birth	Lead intoxication
Maternal malnutrition	Head trauma at birth	Child abuse and neglect

A comprehensive study of a large number of school-age children with mental retardation revealed that 12 percent of them had a prenatal cause, 6 percent had a perinatal cause, and 4 percent had a postnatal cause. A probable cause could not be determined for 78 percent of the children (Yeargin-Allsopp, Murphy, Cordero, Decouflé, & Hollowell, 1997).

Causes by Type

There are four categories of causes that are categorized by type (AAMR, 2002, p. 126):

▼ Biomedical: factors that relate to biologic processes, such as genetic disorders or nutrition;

▼ Social: factors that relate to social and family interaction, such as stimulation and adult responsiveness;

▼ Behavioral: factors that relate to potentially causal behaviors, such as dangerous (injurious) activities or maternal substance abuse; and

▼ Educational: factors that relate to the availability of educational supports that promote mental development of adaptive skills.

Biomedical Causes. Biomedical causes develop within the individual. Typically, they originate early in a child's development and require extensive supports. A biomedical cause can be identified in about two-thirds of the children with mental retardation who require extensive and pervasive supports (Batshaw & Shapiro, 2002).

Chromosomal disorders are biomedical factors that occur at or soon after conception (in the prenatal period). When the egg and sperm unite during conception, they bring together genes from the mother and father. These genes determine the personal characteristics of the developing embryo and are found on threadlike structures called chromosomes. **Chromosomes** direct each cell's activity. Humans have 23 pairs of chromosomes in each cell, with one chromosome in each pair coming from the mother and one from the father. A chromosomal disorder occurs when a parent contributes either too much (an extra chromosome is added) or too little (all or part of a chromosome is missing) genetic material. Chromosomal disorders are the cause of mental retardation for approximately 30 percent of individuals who require extensive and pervasive support and for 4–8 percent of the individuals who need less intensive support (Murphy, Boyle, Schendel, Decouflé, & Yeargin-Allsopp, 1998).

Chromosomal disorders are verified through a procedure called **karyotyping,** which involves arranging the chromosomes under a microscope so that they can be counted and grouped according to size, shape, and pattern (Schonberg & Tifft, 2002).

Down syndrome, one of the most common chromosomal disorders, accounts for the largest number of cases of mental retardation in which extensive and pervasive supports are required. Down syndrome occurs when there is an extra 21st chromosome. Thus, an individual with Down syndrome has 47 individual chromosomes rather than 46.

Social/Behavioral/Educational Causes. We consider these three causes together because their boundaries often overlap, making it difficult to distinguish among them. The majority of

You will learn about the biomedical cause of chromosomal disorders in this chapter. In Chapter 9 you will learn about genetic abnormalities, and in Chapter 11 you will focus on environmental influences such as drugs and toxins.

In Chapter 1 you met Nolan Smith, who, as you will recall, has Down syndrome.

To learn more about Down syndrome, go to the Web Links module in Chapter 8 of the Companion Website.

To learn more about karyotyping, go to the Web Links module in Chapter 8 of the Companion Website.

individuals who have mental retardation experience adverse influences related to social, behavioral, and educational factors (Batshaw & Shapiro, 2002; Murphy et al., 1998).

▼ School-age children who are exposed to lead have a decrease of 2–6 points in mean IQ (Bellinger, Stiles, & Needleman, 1992; Dietrich, Berger, Succop, et al., 1993; Shilu, Baghurst, McMichael, et al., 1996).

▼ Head injuries caused by accidents, falls, and child abuse account for approximately half of the postnatal causes of mental retardation (CDC, 1991).

▼ Younger mothers with 12 years of education or less are more likely to have children with mental retardation than are other mothers (Chapman, Scott, & Mason, 2002).

In Chapter 1 you learned about the strong association between poverty and disability. Poverty is especially linked to mental retardation as distinguished from other disabilities (Duncan, Brooks-Gunn, & Klebanov, 1994; Feldman & Walton-Allen, 1997; Fujiura & Yamaki, 2000).

Although AAMR distinguishes among biomedical, social, behavioral, and educational factors, there is significant interaction among all four (Batshaw & Shapiro, 2002). A real-life example is perhaps the best way to better understand this interaction. Figure 8–4 tells Julie's story. Which causes of Julie's mental retardation can you identify? In what way did these causes interact?

FIGURE 8–4

Interaction of biomedical and psychosocial factors

Julie's Story

Julie was born prematurely, approximately two months early. Her mother was infected with HIV and had used cocaine through her pregnancy. Julie had difficulty breathing after birth and was on a ventilator for several weeks. On the third day of life, she had a severe intracranial hemorrhage with bleeding in several areas of her brain. After extended hospitalization, Julie was discharged to her mother's care. Tests revealed that she was not infected with HIV but that she did have brain damage. She developed seizures when she was about a year old and asthma shortly after that. Although she was referred for early intervention services, she never received these services consistently because of a long waiting list, disorganization in her mother's life, the lack of individualized supports to help her mother, and Julie's own frequent hospitalizations for seizures or asthma. An evaluation when she was three years old found that her intellectual functioning and adaptive behavior were at approximately the level of an eighteen-month-old child.

The causes for Julie's mental retardation include the following:

Factor	Biomedical	Social	Behavioral	Educational
Prematurity	X			
Intracranial hemorrhage	X			
Mother's HIV		X		
Lack of organization in the home		X		
Mother's drug use			X	
Lack of early intervention				X

Source: From "An Ecology of Prevention for the Future," by D. L. Coulter, 1992, *Mental Retardation*, December. Copyright 1992 by the American Association on Mental Retardation. Reprinted with permission.

Preventing Mental Retardation

Prevention efforts are classified into three types: primary, secondary, and tertiary (Baumeister, Kupstas, & Woodley-Zanthos, 1993). **Primary prevention** refers to an intervention that will prevent a disability from ever occurring. Examples of primary prevention include vaccines for the prevention of diseases such as rubella, educational programs that address the abuse of drugs by pregnant women, programs to reduce infant mortality, and prenatal testing.

Secondary prevention refers to intervention soon after detection of a biomedical or psychosocial problem and includes early intervention programs (such as Tory's at the Child Development Center), lead screening, phenylketonuria (PKU) screening (see Chapter 9), and medical control of seizure disorders. Early intervention is especially important, as you know from reading about Tory, in preventing the long-term effects of mental retardation. Indeed, the director of the National Institute of Child Health and Human Development, speaking about early intervention, concluded: "the more, the better; the sooner, the better; and the longer, the better. Such combinations will probably yield excellent results" (Alexander, 1998, p. 56).

Tertiary prevention refers to special education and vocational education for the purpose of reducing the long-term effects of a disability. Increasingly, there is an emphasis on tertiary prevention and health promotion through healthy lifestyles (Cohen, 2000). Box 8–2 describes the recent leadership of the Surgeon General on focusing the nation's attention on the importance of improving the health of persons with mental retardation, especially by promoting good health.

Box 8–2

Making a Difference

The Surgeon General Speaks Out

Have you ever tried paying close attention to one of your teachers or professors when you are feverish with the flu? When you've had a tooth pulled? When your sprained ankle is in an ice wrap? When you've been up all night with an upset stomach? When you are depressed because a close friend has just betrayed your confidence?

Physical and mental health influence everyone's ability to learn. That's one reason why Dr. David Satcher, the U.S. Surgeon General, recently issued *Closing the Gap: A National Blueprint to Improve the Health of Persons with Mental Retardation* (U.S. Public Health Service, 2001). In *Closing the Gap,* he and a national conference of health care providers, people with mental retardation, and their families conclude that people with mental retardation are less healthy and more likely to miss out on appropriate health care than are people who do not have mental retardation.

To address this disparity, *Closing the Gap* calls on health care providers, people with mental retardation, their families, and others, including educators, to implement six goals. Goal 1 seeks to integrate the promotion of good health into community environments, including schools; it asks educators to offer their students opportunities to learn about and practice healthy lifestyles by practicing self-care and wellness. Goal 2 seeks to have educators learn more about strategies to maintain good health and prevent bad health habits in their students. Goal 3 aims at involving people with mental retarda-

tion in their own health care—for example, by learning they should eat properly and exercise regularly. Goal 4 addresses the health care professions themselves, and Goal 5 deals with health care financing. Goal 6 focuses on how to integrate health care services into community programs, including schools.

Let's put these goals into a special and general education framework. Teachers can help implement Goal 1 by making sure their students brush their teeth after school lunches. They can help carry out Goal 2 by learning something about the special medical aspects of mental retardation and how, for example, diet and exercise can affect students' learning abilities. They can help with Goal 3 by suggesting to their students that self-determination means being responsible for your own good health. And they can help carry out Goal 6 by advocating for health care services as a related service for their students under IDEA.

The Surgeon General and everyone else at the conference wanted to make a difference. But they can't do it alone; they need the help of educators and others in the schools. The Surgeon General's challenge to educators is the same one he took upon himself: to speak out about the health care gap and to do something to carry out six national goals. The Surgeon General was ready to act. Are the schools? Are you? No one person can make all the difference, but many can together.

Box 8–3

Poverty, Race, and Classification

What are the trends in the identification of students with mental retardation?

- Between 1980 and 1994, African American students were overly identified as having mental retardation. During this 14-year period, the odds for African American students being overly represented declined from 3.2 to 2.3 (Oswald & Coutinho, 2001).

- African American students are more than twice as likely to be identified as having mental retardation than European American students are. African American students account for 17 percent of the general student population, but they account for 33 percent of the population of students identified as having mental retardation. European American students form 63 percent of the general student population and 54 percent of the population of students identified as having mental retardation (National Research Council, 2002).

What role does poverty play in the high incidence of mental retardation among African American students? Consider these findings:

- Poverty among African Americans is three times as high as poverty among European Americans is (Blank, 2001).

- A higher disability rate among children is associated with households characterized by poverty and single-parent status (Fujiura & Yamaki, 2000).

- Inner-city schools are disproportionately attended by African American students.

- Researchers have reported that more than 80 percent of the entire population of students in urban schools live in poverty (Gottlieb, Atler, Gottlieb, & Wishner, 1994).

- A vast difference exists in the human and material resources invested in students in poor versus wealthier school districts (Brantlinger & Roy-Campbell, 2001).

Taking Diversity into Account for Progress in the General Curriculum

1. How does poverty affect a student's intellectual functioning and adaptive behavior?

2. What criteria could you use to compare the quality standards of urban schools against schools in nonurban areas?

3. What are three steps that you could take as a teacher to ensure that African American students have equal opportunity to progress in the general curriculum?

To answer these questions online, go to the Multicultural Considerations module in Chapter 8 of the Companion Website.

Identifying the Prevalence

It is difficult to obtain an accurate prevalence rate for mental retardation. Reported rates are inconsistent and range from less than 1 percent up to 3 percent of the general population (Emerson, Hatton, Bromley, & Caine, 1998; MacMillan, Siperstein, Gresham, & Bocian, 1997). Perhaps most useful for educational purposes is the 0.96 percent rate reported in the U.S. Department of Education's (2001) *Twenty-Third Annual Report to Congress.* During the 1999–2000 school year, 614,433 students with mental retardation, ages 6 to 21, received special education services. Since 1990, the number of students with learning disabilities has increased at three times the rate of the number of students with mental retardation (U.S. Department of Education, 2001).

One of the most disturbing aspects of the data available on the prevalence of mental retardation relates to students who are African American, who are still disproportionately classified as having mental retardation (see Box 8–3). The box also contains data revealing that poverty, race, and classification into the category of mental retardation go hand in hand. The connection of these three factors is called **comorbidity.** Increasingly, educators are expected to collaborate not only among themselves but also across two or more other service systems, especially the family-support and child-welfare system and the neighborhood development initiative that you will read about later in the chapter.

How Do You Evaluate Students with Mental Retardation?

Determining the Presence

To determine whether a student has mental retardation, teachers assess the student's intellectual functioning and adaptive skills. They use assessments to identify the services and supports the student may need (Luckasson et al., 1992). The entire assessment process includes observation, screening, and nondiscriminatory evaluation (see Figure 8–5).

To meet the AAMR (2002) criteria for mental retardation, a student must experience significant limitations in both intellectual functioning and adaptive behavior as expressed in conceptual, social, and practical adaptive skills. We will focus here on the assessment of adaptive behavior—that is, whether or not the student has skills appropriate to his age and the environments typical of his community.

To measure adaptive skills, professionals use adaptive behavior scales that have been normed on individuals with and without disabilities. Unlike intelligence tests, which are given to the individual who is being assessed, most adaptive behavior scales are completed by interviewing a parent, a teacher, or another individual who is familiar with the student's daily activities (Gordon, Saklofske, & Hildebrand, 1998). Forty-nine states require an adaptive behavior assessment before a student can be identified as having mental retardation (Denning, Chamberlain, & Polloway, 2000).

The AAMR *Adaptive Behavior Scale—School Edition* (2nd ed.) (Lambert, Nihira, & Leland, 1993) is a commonly used measurement. The scale consists of two parts. Part 1 assesses personal independence in daily living and includes 9 behavior domains and 18 subdomains. Part 2 concentrates on social behaviors in 7 domains. The score for each domain is norm-referenced so that it is possible to compare the performance of the student who may have mental retardation with the performance of other students of the same age who do not. It is important to know that the domains of the AAMR *Adaptive Behavior Scale—School Edition* were developed before AAMR categorized adaptive behavior into the three general areas of conceptual, social, and practical. When the scale is revised, it most likely will conform to these three new areas.

Determining the Nature and Extent of General and Special Education and Related Services

A new measure for determining the nature and extent of special education and related services is the *Supports Intensity Scale* (Thompson et al., 2003). The scale is a standardized measure to determine just how much support a student needs. A professional interviewer collects information related to home living, community living, training/education, employment, health and safety, behavioral, social, and protection/advocacy needs. The information is collected according to each of the following three characteristics:

- ▼ *Frequency:* how often the student needs supports for each targeted activity.
- ▼ *Daily support time:* the amount of time that should be devoted to supporting the student during a typical day.
- ▼ *Type of support:* the nature of supports the student needs to engage in a particular activity.

These three criteria—frequency, duration, and intensity—reflect the student's needs and thus how teachers will respond to provide support for progress in the general curriculum.

Because measuring the intensity of supports is so new, most states continue to use the AAMR's 1983 classification system. That system categorizes mental retardation as existing at mild, moderate, severe, and profound levels (Denning et al., 2000). Figure 8–6 shows the 1983 AAMR classification system in the first two columns and the resulting special education classification terminology in the third column (MacMillan, 1982). Many school systems still maintain special classes for students with mental retardation according to this classification system, and today you

FIGURE 8–5

Evaluating Whether or not a student has mental retardation

Nondiscriminatory Evaluation

Observation

Medical personnel observe	The child does not attain appropriate developmental milestones or has characteristics of a particular syndrome associated with mental retardation.
Teacher and parents observe	If the student has not been identified as having mental retardation before entering school, the student, when placed in the general classroom, (1) does not learn as quickly as peers, (2) has difficulty retaining and generalizing learned skills, and (3) has more limitations in adaptive behaviors than peers.

Screening

Assessment measures	Findings that indicate need for further evaluation
Medical screening	A child may be identified through a physician's use of various tests as being at risk for mental retardation before starting school.
Classroom work products	A student who is not identified before starting school has difficulty in academic areas in the general classroom; reading comprehension and mathematical reasoning/application are limited.
Group intelligence tests	A group intelligence test is difficult because of the test's heavy reliance on reading skills. Intelligence score is below average.
Group achievement tests	The student performs significantly below peers.
Vision and hearing screening	Results do not explain academic difficulties.

Prereferral

Teacher implements suggestions from school-based team.	The student still performs poorly in academics or continues to manifest impairments in adaptive behavior despite interventions. (If the student's deficits in academics or adaptive behavior are obviously severe or if the child has been identified as having mental retardation before starting school, prereferral is omitted.)

Referral

If the child still performs poorly in academics or still manifests adaptive behavior challenges, the child is referred to a multidisciplinary team for a complete evaluation.

Nondiscriminatory evaluation procedures and standards

Assessment measures	Findings that suggest mental retardation
Individualized intelligence test	The student has significantly subaverage intellectual functioning (falls in bottom 2 to 3 percent of population) with IQ standard score of approximately 70 to 75 or below. The nondiscriminatory evaluation team makes sure the test is culturally fair for the student.
Adaptive behavior scales	The student scores significantly below average in two or more adaptive skill domains, indicating deficits in skill areas such as communication, home living, self-direction, and leisure.
Anecdotal records	The student's learning problems cannot be explained by cultural or linguistic difference.
Curriculum-based assessment	The student experiences difficulty in one or more areas of the curriculum used by the local school district.
Direct observation	The student experiences difficulty or frustration in the general classroom.

Nondiscriminatory evaluation team determines that student has mental retardation and needs special education and related services.

Appropriate Education

FIGURE 8–6
AAMR 1983 classification system

AAMR 1983 Classification	IQ Range	Educational Classification
Mild mental retardation	50–55 to 70	Educable mental retardation
Moderate mental retardation	35–40 to 50–55	Trainable mental retardation
Severe mental retardation	20–25 to 35–40	Severely/multiply handicapped
Profound mental retardation	Below 20 or 25	Severely/multiply handicapped

Source: From Grossman, H.J. (Ed.), (1993). *Classification in mental retardation.* Washington, DC: American Association on Mental Deficiency.

may still hear the term **EMR classroom.** As a general rule, that term refers to a classroom for students with mild mental retardation. *EMR* is an outdated abbreviation that stands for *educable mentally retarded.* Likewise, *educable students* is an outdated term that refers to students with mild mental retardation, and *trainable students* is an outdated term that refers to students with moderate mental retardation. Even the terms *mild, moderate, severe,* and *profound* have lost favor under the new definition of mental retardation. As you have already learned, the emphasis now is on the intensities of supports the student requires: intermittent, limited, extensive, or pervasive.

How Do You Assure Progress in the General Curriculum?

Including Students

To what extent are students with mental retardation included in general education classes? Figure 8–7 illustrates the percentage who were educated in the continuum of educational environments during the 1998–1999 school year. Students with mental retardation are more than twice as likely to spend more than 60 percent of the time outside of the general education classroom compared with the aggregate of all students with disabilities.

FIGURE 8–7
Educational placement of students with mental retardation (1998–1999)

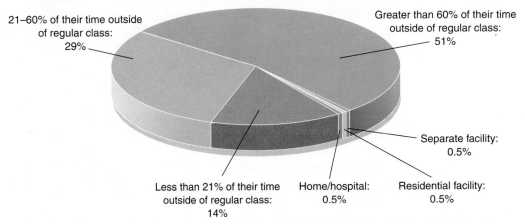

21–60% of their time outside of regular class: 29%

Greater than 60% of their time outside of regular class: 51%

Separate facility: 0.5%

Less than 21% of their time outside of regular class: 14%

Home/hospital: 0.5%

Residential facility: 0.5%

Source: From U.S. Department of Education. (2001). *To assure the free appropriate public education of all children with disabilities: Twenty-first annual report to Congress on the Implementation of the Individuals with Disabilities Education Act.* Washington, DC: Author.

These data show that teachers need to be well prepared to implement instruction, a point that the board of directors of the Council for Exceptional Children's Division on Mental Retardation and Developmental Disabilities reinforced:

> Preparation and training are essential to ensure the creation of schools that effectively include students with developmental disabilities. Such preparation and training must focus not just on students with developmental disabilities in the area of academic study and social skills but on all members of the education community. This preparation and training must include other students, parents, secretarial and custodial staff, bus drivers, professional support staff, teachers and administrators. (Smith & Hilton, 1997, p. 3)

Apparently, some teachers are doing a pretty good job because a synthesis of 36 studies on the academic and social progress of students with mental retardation in elementary through high school general education and special education classes shows the following (Freeman & Alkin, 2000):

▼ Students with mental retardation achieve high academic gains when they are more fully included in general education classes.

▼ Academic gains are more positive when there is a greater degree of inclusion.

▼ Students with mental retardation who were in general education classes full time were more socially competent and accepted than were students who were included in general education classes only part time or children who were on general education campuses but only shared recess time.

▼ The age/grade of the student appears to have more influence than extent of retardation in accounting for favorable inclusion outcomes. Students with mental retardation who are older experience more negative consequences from partial inclusion.

Another research study assessed high school students' attitudes toward individuals with mental retardation in 1987 and again in 1998 (Krajewski & Hyde, 2000). The researchers reported that students without disabilities have decreased their derogatory perspectives and increased their support of inclusion. They concluded: "Our results suggest that attitudes may be positively influenced by inclusion and that the longer inclusion is in place, the greater that influence" (p. 292).

Compared with the placement patterns a decade ago for students with mental retardation, placements now show a trend for students with mental retardation to spend more time in general education classes and less time in special education classes. Yet the percentage of students with mental retardation who have earned a diploma and/or certificate has decreased

Students with mental retardation make more academic and social progress and have better post-school outcomes when they go to school with their peers who do not have disabilities.

Inclusion Tips

Box 8–4

	What You Might See	What You Might Be Tempted to Do	Alternate Responses	Ways to Include Peers in the Process
Behavior	The student demonstrates potentially distracting behavior such as loud laughter.	Tell her to stop the behavior (laughter) and be quiet or leave the room.	Model your acceptance of her. Help her identify an alternative acceptable behavior, such as quiet laughter. Role-play the new behavior.	Teach peers to model and encourage quiet laughter.
Social interactions	She tries to hug a peer who does not want a hug.	Tell her that hugging is not appropriate behavior at school.	Give her an alternative: "Give me five" instead of hugging.	Give peers responsibility for helping to select and practice the alternatives with her.
Educational performance	She shows an apparent lack of interest and boredom with class activities.	Discipline her for lack of cooperation.	Maintain high expectations but modify the curriculum: same topic, different focus.	Establish a peer tutoring system within the class: different students help with different subjects.
Classroom attitudes	She demonstrates learned helplessness with new activities.	Let her be excused from the activity.	Give her many opportunities to do well on parts that she can successfully accomplish. Provide her with appropriate leadership opportunities.	Pair her with a partner who needs help in an area of her strength (e.g., music).

over the past decade, even as their inclusive placements have increased (Katsiyannis, Zhang, & Archawamety, 2002). Currently, causes for this finding are not clearly understood; but it is likely that state assessments have negatively affected the graduation rates for students with mental retardation. Box 8–4 provides tips for increasing the success of students with mental retardation.

Planning Universally Designed Learning

Previously in the chapter, you learned that students with mental retardation have limitations in intellectual functioning and that these limitations result in challenges associated with memory, generalization, and motivation. You also learned that these students have limitations in adaptive behavior in conceptual, social, and practical adaptive skill areas. We highlighted in particular an example of an adaptive skill in the conceptual domain (self-determination). We now tell how good teachers address these characteristics and associated learning challenges through universally designed learning. Universally designed learning can involve changes in what you teach (curriculum), how you teach (instruction), and how you document student learning (evaluation). We will focus on how you can *alter the curriculum* to teach functional skills and how you can *augment instruction* to teach students self-determination skills.

Altering the Curriculum

Altering the curriculum means teaching content that will enable students to learn relevant skills to function successfully in their community. Key functional academic content domains

State-of-art instruction includes typical community-based instruction, such as shopping and making change for the purchases.

[Best prac & funct. skills]

include applied money concepts, applied time concepts, community mobility and access, grooming and self-care, leisure activities, health and safety, and career education (Wehmeyer, 2002). Functional academic content prepares students for IDEA's long-term goals: equal opportunity, full participation, independent living, and economic self-sufficiency. Best practice includes teaching functional skills needed for daily community living and doing so in the settings in which those skills will be required (Kluth, 2000; Langone, Langone, & McLaughlin, 2000).

To what extent should functional skills be taught to students with mental retardation in classroom settings rather than typical community environments? The answer is that individuals with mental retardation are much more able to generalize their skills to typical community settings when their instruction occurs in those settings (Bates, Quvo, Miner, & Korabek, 2001). Further, teachers report that they see significant improvements in their students when relevant skills are taught in community settings (Agran, Snow, & Swaner, 1999; Langone et al., 2000). So the answer favors teaching functional skills in community-based instruction. Increasingly, educators are calling for more functional skills to be taught not only to students with mental retardation but also to students who are gifted (Hishinuma, 1994), students who are receiving bilingual education (Pasquier, 1994), and students in general education (Kesson & Oyler, 1999).

Figure 8–8 illustrates how you can start with the standards of the general education curriculum and then identify functional skills that can be taught within both school and community settings. Later in the chapter you will read about how middle and secondary schools have provided education in functional skills for students with mental retardation as well as for other students in general education classrooms.

Augmenting the Instruction

Augmented instruction involves teaching additional skills to prepare students to progress in the general curriculum. Bearing in mind that students with mental retardation face challenges related to *motivation* and *inner-/outer-directedness*, it is comforting to know that many of these students can acquire the skills of self-determination that many students without disabilities typically

FIGURE 8–8

Linking functional skills to general curriculum standards and instructional settings

	Functional Skills	Instruction in Inclusive Classrooms	Instruction in Community Settings
Social studies standard: understanding the geography of the interdependent world in which we live—local, national, and global.	• Locates addresses for leisure activities • Uses public transportation • Reaches a preferred setting	• Locates addresses for leisure activities on a city map	• Provides directions to a driver to locations for leisure activities
Mathematics standard: explaining and performing computation with whole numbers and money in a variety of situations.	• Uses money effectively to conduct transactions	• Assists the teacher in counting lunch money and reporting it to the office	• Uses money to make purchases at stores in the community related to hobbies and interests

Source: Adapted from Ford A., Davern, L., & Schnorr, R. (2001). Learners with significant disabilities: Curricular relevance in an era of standards-based reform. *Remedial and Special Education, 22*(4), 214–222.

[handwritten note: (teach problem-solving & self-regulating skills so students will become more self-determined]

demonstrate quite naturally and without augmented instruction (Algozzine, Browder, Karvonen, Test, & Wood, 2001). Wehmeyer and his colleagues have specified the key elements of self-determination (as you have already learned in this chapter) and developed a model process for teaching students to be more self-determining (Wehmeyer, 2001; Wehmeyer, Agran, & Hughes, 1998; Wehmeyer & Schwartz, 1997).

The self-determined learning model of instruction consists of three phases; each phase includes student questions, educational supports, and teacher objectives, as illustrated in Box 8–5 (Agran, Blanchard, & Wehmeyer, 2000; Wehmeyer et al., 2000; Wehmeyer, Agran, Palmer, Martin, & Mithaug, 2003). The goal of the model is to teach students to incorporate 12 problem-solving questions into one aspect of their own education and then to use the same approach in other aspects of their education as well as at home and in their communities.

Each of the three phases (What is my goal? What is my plan? What have I learned?) includes four questions that students learn to ask themselves. The purpose of each of the 12 questions is to help students learn to direct themselves (to be self-regulating) by using a problem-solving process. That process involves a means-ends, problem-solving sequence: Now that I know my goal (end), how can I achieve it (what will help, and what barriers are in the way)? The model also includes teacher objectives that the teacher can use to guide the students by explaining the meaning of the 12 questions. Sometimes the teacher will need to work with students to adapt the wording of each question so that it is easier for students to understand. Finally, a section on educational supports suggests strategies teachers can use to enable students to answer the questions.

Are students successful in accomplishing the goal of the model and incorporating 12 problem-solving questions to achieve a goal? Yes. In a study conducted by the model's authors, 55 percent of the students achieve their goal or exceeded it, while slightly more than 80 percent of the students made at least some progress toward their goal (Wehmeyer et al., 2000).

On the Companion Website, go to the Web Links module in Chapter 8 to find a link on self-determination curricula and how you can best evaluate them to select the one that will be most relevant for your students.

You will find a sample lesson from A teacher's guide to the self-determined learning model of instruction on the Web Links module in Chapter 8 of the Companion Website.

When you read the elementary school program later in this chapter, you will learn that self-determination can be taught to elementary-level students.

Box 8–5

Into Practice

The Self-Determined Model of Instruction

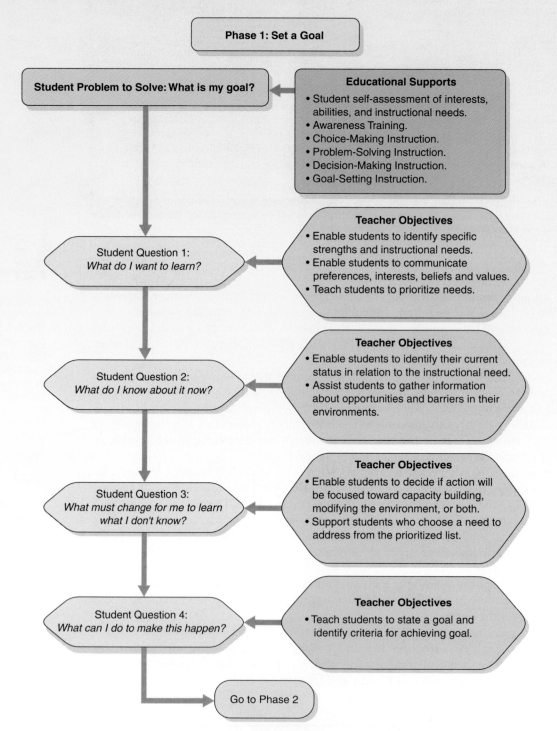

Phase 1: Set a Goal

Student Problem to Solve: What is my goal?

Educational Supports
- Student self-assessment of interests, abilities, and instructional needs.
- Awareness Training.
- Choice-Making Instruction.
- Problem-Solving Instruction.
- Decision-Making Instruction.
- Goal-Setting Instruction.

Student Question 1:
What do I want to learn?

Teacher Objectives
- Enable students to identify specific strengths and instructional needs.
- Enable students to communicate preferences, interests, beliefs and values.
- Teach students to prioritize needs.

Student Question 2:
What do I know about it now?

Teacher Objectives
- Enable students to identify their current status in relation to the instructional need.
- Assist students to gather information about opportunities and barriers in their environments.

Student Question 3:
What must change for me to learn what I don't know?

Teacher Objectives
- Enable students to decide if action will be focused toward capacity building, modifying the environment, or both.
- Support students who choose a need to address from the prioritized list.

Student Question 4:
What can I do to make this happen?

Teacher Objectives
- Teach students to state a goal and identify criteria for achieving goal.

Go to Phase 2

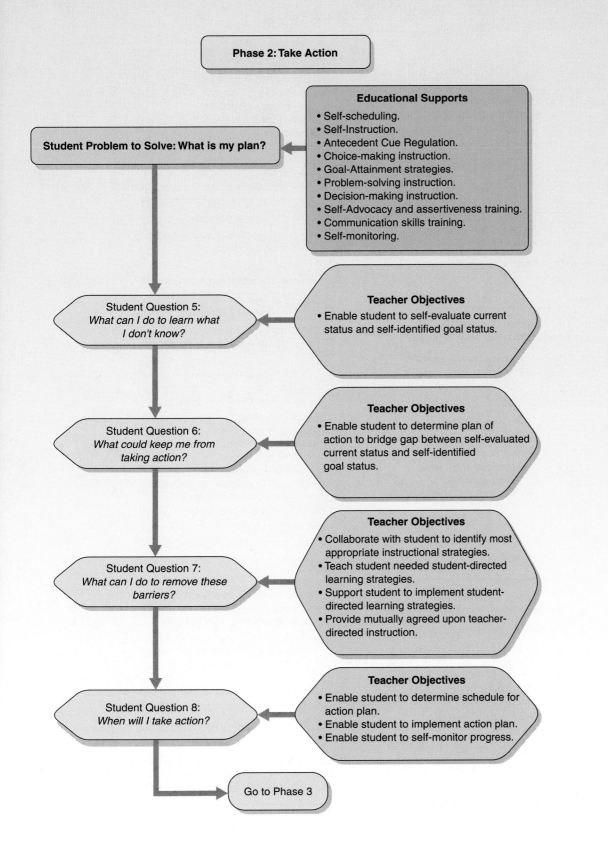

Phase 2: Take Action

Student Problem to Solve: What is my plan?

Educational Supports

- Self-scheduling.
- Self-Instruction.
- Antecedent Cue Regulation.
- Choice-making instruction.
- Goal-Attainment strategies.
- Problem-solving instruction.
- Decision-making instruction.
- Self-Advocacy and assertiveness training.
- Communication skills training.
- Self-monitoring.

Student Question 5:
What can I do to learn what I don't know?

Teacher Objectives

- Enable student to self-evaluate current status and self-identified goal status.

Student Question 6:
What could keep me from taking action?

Teacher Objectives

- Enable student to determine plan of action to bridge gap between self-evaluated current status and self-identified goal status.

Student Question 7:
What can I do to remove these barriers?

Teacher Objectives

- Collaborate with student to identify most appropriate instructional strategies.
- Teach student needed student-directed learning strategies.
- Support student to implement student-directed learning strategies.
- Provide mutually agreed upon teacher-directed instruction.

Student Question 8:
When will I take action?

Teacher Objectives

- Enable student to determine schedule for action plan.
- Enable student to implement action plan.
- Enable student to self-monitor progress.

Go to Phase 3

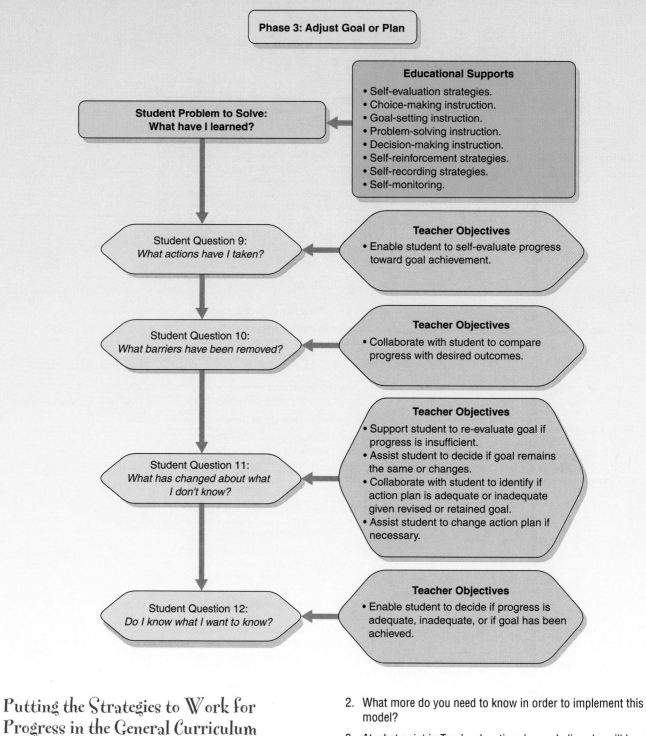

Phase 3: Adjust Goal or Plan

Student Problem to Solve:
What have I learned?

Educational Supports
• Self-evaluation strategies.
• Choice-making instruction.
• Goal-setting instruction.
• Problem-solving instruction.
• Decision-making instruction.
• Self-reinforcement strategies.
• Self-recording strategies.
• Self-monitoring.

Student Question 9:
What actions have I taken?

Teacher Objectives
• Enable student to self-evaluate progress toward goal achievement.

Student Question 10:
What barriers have been removed?

Teacher Objectives
• Collaborate with student to compare progress with desired outcomes.

Student Question 11:
What has changed about what I don't know?

Teacher Objectives
• Support student to re-evaluate goal if progress is insufficient.
• Assist student to decide if goal remains the same or changes.
• Collaborate with student to identify if action plan is adequate or inadequate given revised or retained goal.
• Assist student to change action plan if necessary.

Student Question 12:
Do I know what I want to know?

Teacher Objectives
• Enable student to decide if progress is adequate, inadequate, or if goal has been achieved.

Putting the Strategies to Work for Progress in the General Curriculum

1. What is a goal that you would like to achieve, and how can proceeding through these 12 questions help you achieve your goal?

2. What more do you need to know in order to implement this model?

3. At what point in Tory's education do you believe he will be able to benefit from this model?

To answer these questions online and learn more about these strategies, go to the Into Practice module in Chapter 8 of the Companion Website.

Source: Wehmeyer, M. L., Agran, M., Palmer, S. B., & Mithaug, D. (1999). *A teacher's guide to implementing the self-determined learning model of instruction (adolescent version).* Lawrence: The University of Kansas, Beach Center on Disability.

Collaborating to Meet Students' Needs

Collaboration in all phases of the education of students with mental retardation is critically important. One type of collaboration that many educators undertake is outside of the education system altogether, using family support programs. As you learned when we discussed the prevalence of mental retardation and especially as you read the data we reported in Box 8–3, African American students, particularly those whose families experience poverty, are disproportionately represented in the disability category of mental retardation. Their families can significantly benefit from family support that is provided to them in a culturally competent way.

A model of family support is Parents of Watts in Los Angeles, which is directed by Sweet Alice Harris. Parents of Watts reaches out to families in ways that make meaningful differences in their lives and encourages them to support their child's educational goals. Sweet Alice Harris describes her program in Box 8–6. If you were a teacher working with students who live in Watts or similar communities, how would collaborating with Harris and her staff or with their counterparts in other communities help you foster collaboration with families and achieve positive educational outcomes for students?

One of those outcomes is employment. Educators and prospective employers want students to acquire skills to work in the community. Box 8–7 describes the approach that a school district in Richardson, Texas, took to ensure successful employment outcomes for students with mental retardation.

Box 8–6

My Voice

Sweet Alice Harris and Parents of Watts, Los Angeles

I was a teenage parent at age 14, and homeless at 16. I understand what people in need go through, and I understand that they expect to hear "no" when they ask for assistance or support because "no" is all they've ever heard. Then someone says "yes" at last. Then something just comes alive in you and you put a smile on your face and you want to live. The hope is alive again. And when hope is alive you look at the whole world differently.

I started Parents of Watts (POW) in 1979 as an information group of volunteers. We worked out of my home addressing the basic needs of poor people of all races and cultures in our community. If they needed a place to sleep, we found them housing. If they needed food, we provided food.

We began our work during a time when ethnic tensions and violence between African American and Latino communities in Watts were becoming a serious problem. The Watts district of Los Angeles is home to 100,000 residents, of which 55% are African American and 40% are Latino. Both groups wanted better housing, education, jobs and recreation for themselves and their children. They wanted the same things—they just couldn't speak the same language, so they

would fight. Our goal was to introduce and support a dialogue between African Americans and Latinos toward developing a better understanding of each other's cultures and ways of solving problems.

We learned that one issue of concern that crossed cultural boundaries was the well-being of all the children in our community. So the children, all children, African American, Latino, and all children with special needs became the central point of discussion in our meetings. We began to identify priorities that would make our children's lives better, and gradually, as the word spread about what we were doing, our group began to reflect the true mix of cultures in our community. In seeking to improve conditions for all children, we somehow got past many of the misunderstandings and realized we were all parents who wanted the best for our children.

POW has grown to include 15 programs at six locations in the community. We have the support of other community resources such as clinics and schools in the area. We hope our program inspires other groups of parents to come together for the sake of a better future for their children.

How is it possible that this organization has become a major resource for families in our community (with 15 programs in 6 locations in Watts)? We just don't take "no" for an answer.

Source: Harris, S. A. (1998). Parents of Watts. In U. Markey (Ed.), Tapestry, II (pp. 12–13). New Orleans: Grassroots Consortium.

Collaboration Tips

Box 8–7

School Without Walls: Education for and with the Community

Let's test a pair of assumptions about teachers. First, teachers teach in classrooms, right? Wrong. Or at least wrong with respect to Debbie Wilkes in the Richardson, Texas, schools. Second, most collaboration happens among educators, right? Wrong. Or at least wrong when it comes to—yes, you guessed it—Debbie Wilkes.

For Debbie, now the special education supervisor in Richardson and a former classroom teacher in what was called the "mental retardation program," collaboration takes many different forms. First, she had to get rid of her self-contained classroom. Now she co-teaches with the general education faculty, finding out what they need to know to include students with mental retardation and showing them how to satisfy that need.

In addition, Debbie leaves the school grounds and becomes an active member of her community. With the support of the district's administrators, she attends the regular weekly or monthly meeting of eight different community and state organizations during her workdays. Especially when working with local business leaders, Debbie gives a single, consistent message: The schools are producing students who are ready to work; some do not have disabilities, and some do. At these meetings, she learns about market demand: how many employees the businesses need, what skills the employees have to have, and so on. Only then does she begin to advocate for the businesses to hire students. There's a second benefit to listening: Debbie takes that information back to the schools so the faculty can teach those skills. Collaboration is a circular activity; it includes many people inside a circle of learning and teaching.

Of course, the students and their parents are inside the circle. Debbie helps them think broadly about the kind of life they want to lead (dreams), be candid about their worries about their present and future lives (nightmares), and begin to take a series of logical steps that will help them fulfill their dreams (action steps). This kind of planning also takes place with the students' other teachers, family friends, and even, from time to time, the business leaders whom Debbie has cultivated through her membership in all those organizations. Debbie is quick to note that this kind of collaboration takes a lot of time. It doesn't happen in every IEP meeting, and it doesn't always happen in the school building, either.

Debbie has established a list serve that connects veteran parents (those whose children were her students many years ago and are still not living as full citizens in the community) with new parents (those whose children are just beginning to think about transition from school to work and independent living in the community). Debbie's list serve does double duty: It makes it possible for her to reach a large audience with a great deal of efficiency, and it helps her and the veteran parents share a powerful message with the new parents—namely, a good future lies ahead for those who plan ahead.

Debbie sums up her collaboration tips in a few well-chosen sentences. "It's all about connecting; it's all about community. If we want our students to be full citizens and participating and contributing members of their communities, we educators have to connect with our communities. If we don't, our students won't." So Debbie connects with general educators, school administrators, business leaders, parents, professional agencies, and parent-support organizations. She extends her circles of collaboration wider and wider, connecting herself and the circles so that her students will also be connected. "Collaboration means knowing what another person wants, how she is evaluated, and what will persuade her to work with you. You can't listen and learn if you're doing all the talking and teaching." Collaboration consists of listening, responding, and then asking—and making sure that the asking is inclusive, that it benefits all students, whether or not they have disabilities.

Putting Collaboration into the Context of Student Progress in the General Curriculum.

1. Who are the collaborators?

2. What are the challenges?

3. What can the collaborators do? What are the results?

To answer these questions online and learn more about these strategies, go to the Collaboration Tips module in Chapter 8 of the Companion Website.

What Can You Learn from Others Who Teach Students with Mental Retardation?

Learning for the Early Childhood Years: Granville County Child Development Center, Oxford, North Carolina

Previously in this chapter, you learned that early childhood education is one form of secondary prevention (Guralnick, 1997; Shonkoff & Phillips, 2000). For young children who have or are at risk of having mental retardation or other disabilities, there is literally no substitute for early education. For children, including Tory, at the Granville County Child Development Center in Oxford, North Carolina, the early childhood education they and their families receive makes a huge difference in their quality of life. It can prevent some disabilities from developing, it can blunt the effects of others, and it can enrich the lives of the children and their families.

The center has 12 children; 9 have disabilities or are at risk of having them. Some of these children live with their parents, some with their grandparents, and some with foster or adoptive parents. Some of the children are European American; some are African American. Some have parents who work, and some have parents who are unemployed—sometimes because they themselves have disabilities. Despite these differences, however, the children and families have at least two things in common.

First, the children with disabilities have been evaluated at one of North Carolina's many developmental evaluation centers, usually the one in nearby Durham. Their evaluations are interdisciplinary. Each child is assessed for medical, speech and language, hearing, vision, adaptive behavior, and intellectual capacity and needs. The strengths and needs of the child's families are also taken into account, and an individualized plan is developed.

Second, the center's program for each child has three parts.

▼ *Cognitive:* focusing on the child's ability to pay attention, to generalize learning to their homes and communities, and to become self-determined.

[handwritten note: Early childhood ed is form of secondary prevention- can prevent some disabilities from developing & enrich the lives of children & families]

Early intervention is a research-validated type of secondary prevention, as practiced in the Granville County, North Carolina, Child Development Center.

▼ *Adaptive:* focusing on areas such as communication, social skills, and self-care.

▼ *Supports:* focusing on supports for all students at the AAMR levels of intermittent to pervasive.

What about a functional curriculum based in the community and tied to everyday life? The answers are relatively simple and very appropriate for young children. The center itself is housed in several rooms in an African American Episcopal church in the heart of Oxford. It is supported by various religious and civic groups and by a multicounty mental health/developmental disabilities agency. When its walls need painting or its play equipment repaired, the families and the community respond. Its students regularly go downtown for various activities or just to show everyone there that "we are all in this together." And when they do go into town, they learn skills that will help them function in town. Indeed, what makes the Child Development Center a model is the nature and level of supports everyone provides and receives. Hear what Dierdre, Tory's mother, says about the supports: "I love to be at the Child Development Center, to just sit with the children and staff, learn what they do with my son, and carry that back to my home. I've got a good relationship with them. . . . I don't want him to leave the Child Development Center."

Learning for the Elementary Years: Teachers and Researchers in Kansas and Texas

You have already learned about the important adaptive behavior skill of self-determination and how to plan universally designed learning to augment instruction to teach self-determination skills. Many people may assume that self-determination skills cannot be mastered by students with mental retardation until they are in middle or secondary schools. Special education researchers at The University of Kansas and elementary school teachers in Texas and Kansas challenged the assumption that elementary school students with mental retardation and other disabilities do not want to be self-determined and cannot be taught to practice self-determination. They adapted and implemented the self-determined learning model of instruction for elementary students (Wehmeyer & Palmer, 2000).

The results were remarkable: Even the youngest of the students (ages 5–6) were able to set goals for themselves in partnership with their teachers and use the model to achieve those goals. As you learned in Box 8–5, there are three parts to the model: (1) 12 student questions, (2) teacher objectives, and (3) educational supports.

We encourage you to review Box 8–5.

For an elementary-age student, the 12 student questions have to be very simple and in words that the student selects. And they have to be meaningful and relevant; only then will the student use the model and thereby begin to learn to be more self-determined. An example of how to make the model simple and meaningful comes from research that the model's developers conducted in Texas and Kansas.

Analise, a third grader who has mental retardation, began the self-determination curriculum by saying what she likes to do at home and school and what she wants to learn. She likes to spell, but she wants to learn to write her own name and the names of her friends and to read. So the first part of Analise's self-determination goal is based on her interests and preferences. Because the curriculum is based on self-determination and self-evaluation, Analise has to answer these four questions:

▼ What do I want to learn?

Answer: I want to draw the symbol/icon that represents my name and the names of my friends, and to write my and their names.

▼ What do I know about that goal now?

Answer: I can draw the symbols/icons for my name and my friends'.

▼ What must change for me to learn what I do not know?

Answer: I need to learn to draw better.

▼ What can I do to make my learning happen?

Answer: I have to keep drawing and practicing.

Having set her goals, Analise now must decide on a plan to carry out her goals. Here, too, she must answer four more self-evaluation questions:

▼ What can I do to learn what I don't know?

Answer: I can learn to draw symbols/icons of my name and my friends'.

▼ What could keep me from taking that action?

Answer: Other children interrupt me, they erase my work, and I talk instead of working on drawing.

▼ What can I do to remove those barriers?

Answer: I write the symbols/icons and names again and again on paper.

▼ When will I take that action?

Answer: I will start tomorrow.

Finally, having set her goals and action plan, Analise has to answer four more self-evaluation questions about what she has learned:

▼ What actions have I taken?

Answer: I learned how to write.

▼ What barriers have been removed?

Answer: I found a quiet place to work.

▼ What has changed about what I don't know?

Answer: I starting writing, and it worked.

▼ Do I know what I want to know?

Answer: Yes, I can draw the symbols/icons of all of my friends, and I can write the names of some of them.

Of course, neither Analise nor other students in Texas and Kansas elementary schools acted alone. Relying on the teacher objectives that accompany the model, their teachers taught the students how to answer all 12 questions. For example, to teach Analise how to answer "What do I want to learn?" her teacher helped her identify her strengths and needs, identify and communicate her preferences, and recognize that she needs to make a plan to learn what she wants to learn. Most of the time, the teacher and the student will have a series of conversations about "what I want to learn" and the 11 other questions. In those conversations, the student begins to solve the problem herself, with the teacher as a guide but not the person who tells Analise what she needs to learn or what the other answers are. The educational supports identify strategies that the teacher can use to help teach Analise how to be self-determined. Those strategies can consist of choice making, communication-skills training, and self-monitoring techniques.

What are the results for the Texas and Kansas students and their teachers? Did they and the researchers at The University of Kansas successfully challenge the assumption that elementary-aged students, especially those with mental retardation, cannot learn to be self-determined? Yes, they did (Wehmeyer & Palmer, 2000). Second- and third-grade students with special needs, including some students with mental retardation, identified a broad range of problems, including their writing, learning not to disturb others, using correct punctuation, and finding a quiet place to study. Each student was successful in identifying a goal related to a priority need, discussing barriers to achieving the goal, and developing and implementing an option plan.

Is there any reason to doubt that young students with disabilities, just like young students who do not have disabilities, can learn to be self-determined? No. But it takes a change of attitude for the teachers. They have to want to teach self-determination; they have to want their students to start early to be their own persons.

Learning for the Middle and Secondary Years: Teaching in the Natural Environment

"Learn it where you'll need to do it." That's good advice for any student, especially ones who have mental retardation and for that reason are challenged to remember and generalize their education to the community and to adapt to community expectations.

"Teach it where you want your students to practice it." That, too, is good advice for teachers, especially those whose students have mental retardation and thus memory and generalization challenges.

The challenge comes in adapting these community-based instructional approaches to the goal of having students with and without disabilities learn side by side. If students with disabilities are in the community but not at school, how can they also be included in the general curriculum with students who do not have disabilities? Some schools have overcome that challenge (Kluth, 2000).

In Boring, Oregon, students with and without disabilities have the same work experiences on campus; they work side by side at jobs in the school's cafeteria, administrative offices, and custodial center. In the Flambeau School District in Tony, Wisconsin, students with and without disabilities work side by side but not on campus; instead, they go off campus and into the community to work together for as short a time as a day (shadowing a professional) or as long a time as two years to develop job-specific skills.

In Ferndale, Washington, students with and without disabilities researched how to construct an airplane. They used the Internet to research how planes fly (physics), are constructed (industrial engineering), and are financed (economics and mathematics). They then shopped for parts at the Boeing Company's nearby warehouse in nearby Seattle, built a model plane using those parts, and displayed the plane—the fruits of their joint community-based research—at a local air show. The students who did not have disabilities learned physics, engineering, and economics and mathematics. The students with mental retardation learned about the laws of nature (air, wind, height, depth), how to put parts together and to follow instructions when creating something, how to purchase goods, and how to use the Internet to ask questions and get answers.

From campus-based or off-campus work and research, it is an easy step to start service learning opportunities. In these, students with and without disabilities learn by contributing to local businesses or not-for-profit organizations, sharpening their work-related skills side by side with each other and with the adults who may well hire them.

Let's return to the question of whether schools can simultaneously offer community-based instruction and inclusive education. Can they? Of course, they can.

Learning for the Transitional and Postsecondary Years: Project TASSEL, Shelby, North Carolina

What makes it possible for a student with mental retardation to graduate from high school with a regular diploma and take a job in a large textile factory where he works for good pay and benefits and receives positive work evaluations? The answer lies in teaching functional skills in community settings, coupled with collaboration.

Shelby, North Carolina, is the seat of a largely rural county. Its school system consists of approximately 3,000 students in grades K–12, of whom approximately 250 have disabilities.

Project TASSEL is the system's transition program. It serves 120 students, ages 14 to 22. Most are 14 to 18 years old, and more than half have mental retardation. For students who choose the occupational curriculum (as distinguished from an academic curriculum), everything begins with collaboration when they enter the ninth grade (their first year in high school). That is when the Shelby schools create a school-level, community-referenced, interagency transition team for each student.

The teams consists of students, parents, teachers, vocational rehabilitation specialists, technical college administrators, and residential service providers. Each team focuses on a student's

Jerry Moss and other students who choose Project TASSEL's occupational curriculum have schools-without-walls experiences. At this industrial site, Jerry receives on-the-job training that supplements his classroom instruction.

strengths and needs, particularly in the adaptive skill areas of work, community use, and self-direction/self-determination.

The self-determination motto is simple and clear, one the students learn and practice with the help of school and community teams: "Nothing about me without me." Students, with support from their teams, identify future quality-of-life goals, especially those related to work. The self-determination curriculum is tied to everyday life experiences. In those scenarios, students simulate likely challenges in the community (you are sick and can't go to work, or your transportation has fallen through this morning) and then apply problem-solving skills that they would use in the community (what do you do, and whom do you call?). Over the course of their four years in high school, the students increasingly move off campus for their classes and instruction. That way, they learn skills that will generalize to the world of work; and they increase their adaptive skills, learning what it takes to adapt to and have a good quality of life in Shelby. By the end of their senior year, they must also have 360 class hours of competitive employment (work in an inclusive setting for at least the minimum wage, with or without a *job coach*—a person who shares the job with them and teaches them how to do it on their own or with only a little help).

All students benefit from the cooperation of 50 local businesses that provide contracts to the school's own factory, job-shadowing sites, paid community-based contracts, and individual job placements. This kind of school–industry collaboration means that, when a student graduates with a diploma in the occupational curriculum, local employers know the student is well prepared. You remember that one of the three elements of the definition of mental retardation refers to supports; now you see how the schools and community businesses collaborate to provide employment supports.

A Vision for Tory's Future

As we have already noted, it is difficult to foresee Tory's future. What we do know is that, at this moment in his young life, he has many things going for him:

▼ Solid evaluations from the Durham Developmental Evaluation Clinic
▼ Early childhood education and collaboration at the Granville County Child Development Center
▼ A devoted family in Dierdre, Lonnie and Andrew Woodard, Angela Jiggetts and Kelsi Ballard Jiggetts, and Timothy Jiggetts and Andrewnika Hargrove
▼ Strengths in various aspects of his life

Tory's future is promising if his present course continues. Imagine him 10 years from now, at age 13. He will be in middle school and will be pointed toward a high school and a transition program such as the one located in Shelby. And in due time, he, like other graduates of the Shelby program, will be working in Butner, his hometown—a real member, participating in real ways in his own community, a full citizen of North Carolina and the United States.

It's not a far-fetched vision. Indeed, it is the most realistic one. Everything is in place; everything favors it. Achieving it is up to Tory's teachers, other professionals, and family members. Indeed, it's up to future teachers such as you to move deliberately and powerfully toward that vision. None of us, including Tory, deserves any less.

What Would You Recommend?

1. Whom would you invite to Tory's first IEP meeting at the elementary school?
2. What actions would you suggest that Tory's family take to help him make and keep friends in his community?
3. Which of Tory's strengths seem to be his strongest, and what is the relevance of that strength to his access to the general curriculum in elementary school?

Summary

How Do You Recognize Students with Mental Retardation?

▼ Mental retardation is a disability characterized by significant limitations in both intellectual functioning and adaptive behavior as expressed in conceptual, social, and practical adaptive skills. This disability originates before age 18.

▼ The three main characteristics of mental retardation relate to limitations in intellectual functioning, limitations in adaptive behavior, and need for supports.

▼ The diagnosis of mental retardation requires an IQ score of 70 to 75 or below.

▼ Regarding intelligence, individuals with mental retardation have impairments in the learning process, including memory, generalization, and motivation.

- ▼ The three adaptive skill areas identified by AAMR include conceptual, social, and practical.
- ▼ The four levels of support identified by AAMR include intermittent, limited, extensive, and pervasive.
- ▼ Two ways to categorize causes of mental retardation include timing and type. Timing includes prenatal, perinatal, and postnatal. Type includes biomedical, social, behavioral, and educational.
- ▼ Mental retardation typically results from interactions among multiple causes.
- ▼ Prevention encompasses primary, secondary, and tertiary levels.
- ▼ Prevalence rates vary; fewer than 1 to 3 percent of the general population are people with mental retardation.
- ▼ A trend related to prevalence is the disproportionate number of African American students identified as having mental retardation.

How Do You Evaluate Students with Mental Retardation?

- ▼ AAMR proposes a comprehensive assessment that involves diagnosing mental retardation, classifying and describing the student's strengths and weaknesses as well as the need for supports, and developing a profile that includes intensities of needed supports.
- ▼ A measure frequently used to assess school-aged children's adaptive behavior is the AAMR *Adaptive Behavior Scale—School* (2nd ed.).
- ▼ The *Supports Intensity Scale* is a standardized measure of a student's level of support needs including exceptional medical and behavioral needs and supports related to eight types of activities.

How Do You Assure Progress in the General Curriculum?

- ▼ Students with mental retardation are one of the least likely groups of students to be included in general education programs.

- ▼ Research documents that students with mental retardation achieve higher academic and social gains when they are included in general education classes.
- ▼ Curriculum alteration can be achieved by teaching students functional skills and carrying out the instruction in community settings.
- ▼ Instructional augmentation can occur by teaching students self-determination skills through the self-determined learning model of instruction.
- ▼ Collaboration is especially important in promoting employment opportunities for students with mental retardation.

What Can You Learn from Others Who Teach Students with Mental Retardation?

- ▼ At the Granville County Child Development Center and in other early childhood intervention programs, the emphasis is on family-professional collaboration to provide intensive one-on-one and group instruction, especially in community settings.
- ▼ Self-determination skills can be successfully taught to elementary students by using the self-determined learning model of instruction.
- ▼ Students with and without disabilities can learn functional skills in school-based and community-based settings.
- ▼ Project TASSEL in Shelby, North Carolina, teaches functional skills and community settings, coupled with collaboration; and the result is that students are prepared for competitive employment.

Council for Exceptional Children   PRAXIS

To find out how and where this chapter content connects to the CEC Professional Standards and the Praxis™ Standards, go to the Standards Connection module in Chapter 8 of the Companion Website. A comprehensive matrix aligning CEC Professional Standards, Praxis™ Standards, and INTASC principles to the entire text, is available in the Appendix and on the Companion Website.

Chapter 9

Who Is Joshua Spoor?

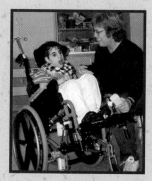

To say that Joshua Spoor, age 10 and in the fifth grade, is challenged is to put it mildly. Nearly every part of his body is affected by severe disabilities; that is why one way to describe him is to say that he has severe and multiple disabilities. Those alone, however, do not constitute the entire set of challenges facing this young boy. There is another, equally important and no less significant, challenge: Joshua lives outside his family's home. This fact requires the professionals at the residential center where he lives, his teachers in the school in the community where the center is based, and his father and new stepmother, who live in the same community, to create a triangle of collaboration for Joshua's inclusion in the local school. The root of these dual challenges is the condition that was diagnosed the moment after his birth.

Joshua was born with encephalocele, a rare disorder in which the newborn has an opening in the skull. The membranes that cover the brain and brain tissue come through this opening. The opening may be covered by skin and/or membrane of varying thickness. As is usual in individuals with encephalocele, Joshua has developmental delays, mental retardation, seizures, and significant visual impairments.

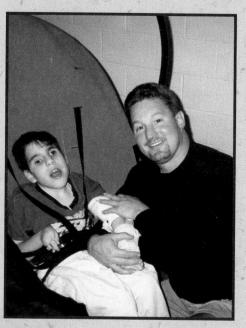

Joshua's early years were difficult. He often had seizures; some were mild, and others were more severe. It was common for Joshua to spend a couple of days in the hospital after one of these severe episodes. When Joshua was 3 years old, he went into the hospital after a seizure, developed an infection, and stayed longer than usual. He quit eating, and his health rapidly deteriorated. The doctors suspected that the surgically implanted shunt in his head was infected. Joshua was too ill at this point, however, to handle the trauma of another medical procedure. Because there was nothing medically to be done, Joshua's parents took him home after being told that he probably would die. How wrong everyone was!

Because Joshua, then age 4, needed 24-hour care and because his mother was ill with cancer, his parents reluctantly placed him in the Broome Developmental Center, a nearby residential facility. He still lives there, just a short walk from his father, Alan; his sister, Vanessa (8 years old); his brother, Ryan (6 years old); and Alan's new wife, Linda. (After Joshua's birth mother died, Alan remarried.)

Alan wanted a staff that would acknowledge Joshua's limitations but not stop there; he wanted them to focus on what might be possible. To his surprise, that meant enrolling Joshua at the local elementary and then the middle school in Johnson City, New York, where the Spoors live.

Alan's fears—that Joshua would be teased, or would not benefit from an inclusion-oriented school—proved unfounded. Instead, "Joshua has been welcomed. We have to give our kids away. That's the only way to change the world."

Severe and Multiple Disabilities

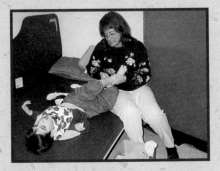

When Joshua was in the elementary school program, his classmates took turns reading to him, drawing pictures for him, writing notes to him, and helping him paint and color. With the assistance of an aide, Joshua spent at least half of each day in the general education classroom, leaving it for services such as physical, occupational, and vision therapy.

Now that he has entered C. Fred Johnson Middle School, Joshua receives more of his education in a self-contained classroom under the supervision of Ellen Starley, his teacher. Her biggest challenge is to have Joshua take a more active part in his learning and development by building on his strengths. Ellen and her colleagues work toward that goal through a complex and varied program. Joshua receives intensive, regular therapy: one hour a week of intensive physical therapy, two hours a week of adaptive physical education, one hour a week of occupational therapy, and a half-hour a week of visual stimulation. He gets the same interventions on a daily basis from Ellen or her aides, plus instruction in communication to turn his vocalizations into words and his gestures into signs.

Ellen says, "We're bombarding Joshua all the time, putting a lot of ourselves into his education. That's okay, but we need to help Joshua learn to be a more active learner." To do that and at the same time involve other students with him, Ellen includes Joshua with students who have fewer disabilities in classes on daily living skills. She makes sure that he eats lunch with his classmates, those with and without disabilities.

The many people involved in Joshua's life keep a correspondence notebook in Joshua's book bag. His peers sometimes write notes to him or draw pictures of what he and they are doing in school, using the notebook as a communication link between his family, the staff at the center, and school.

Joshua is a surprising youngster: He has survived the devastating effects of his birth disorder, the subsequent seizures and operations, the death of his mother, and a necessary out-of-home, community placement. You may well ask, "How has all this come about?" The answer has many parts:

- A school district, skilled teachers, and other professionals committed to inclusion
- Interactions with other students (both with and without disabilities)
- The continued devotion of his family

His father explains:

We're just about a half-mile from Joshua, so, even when the heavy snows come, we still visit him regularly. . . . It's an easy walk down the hill to the Center, and we all go together. After all, even though we give Joshua away to the school and Center, we haven't really given him away. He's still our son and brother, and always will be.

As you read this chapter, consider what you as a professional can do to promote educational opportunities that benefit students with severe and multiple disabilities.

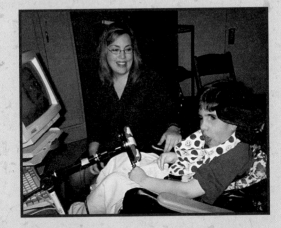

What do you think?

1. **If you were the principal at Joshua's middle school, what could you do to increase the opportunities for Joshua to share activities with peers who do not have disabilities?**
2. **How would you strengthen collaboration among those involved in Joshua's life?**
3. **What great expectations do you have for the lifestyle that Joshua can have as an adult?**

To respond to these questions online, participate in other activities, and learn more about Joshua Spoor and severe and multiple disabilities, go to the "Cases" module in Chapter 9 of the companion website.

How Do You Recognize Students with Severe and Multiple Disabilities?

Defining Severe and Multiple Disabilities

No single definition covers all the conditions associated with severe and multiple disabilities. Schools usually link the two areas (severe disabilities and multiple disabilities) into a single program for students who have extensive mental retardation and related disabilities, such as significant physical and language impairments. (Although some of these students may have average intelligence, their physical and language disabilities may mask it.)

IDEA regulations define multiple disabilities (but not severe disabilities) as follows:

Multiple disabilities means concomitant impairments (such as mental retardation–blindness, mental retardation–orthopedic impairment, etc.), the combination of which causes such severe educational problems that they cannot be accommodated in special education programs solely for one of the impairments. The term does not include deaf-blindness. (34 C.F.R., sec. 300 [b] [6])

Another IDEA regulation related to programs and services for students with severe disabilities defines severe disabilities as follows:

The term "children with severe disabilities" refers to children with disabilities who, because of the intensity of their physical, mental, or emotional problems, need highly specialized education, social, psychological, and medical services in order to maximize their full potential for useful and meaningful participation in society and for self-fulfillment. The term includes those children. . . . who have two or more serious disabilities such as deaf-blindness, mental retardation and blindness, and cerebral palsy and deafness. (34 C.F.R., sec. 315.4[d])

There are two characteristics common to these different definitions: The extent of support required by students across all adaptive skill areas is usually extensive or pervasive, and two or more disabilities typically occur simultaneously.

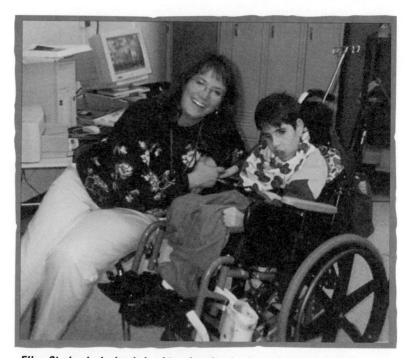

Ellen Starley is Joshua's lead teacher, but he depends as much on his related-services providers as on her to receive an appropriate education.

Describing the Characteristics

Just as it is difficult to find a single definition of severe and multiple disabilities, so it is difficult to accurately describe all characteristics of all people with those disabilities. In fact, "the differences among persons with [multiple] disabilities [may be] greater than the similarities" (Guess & Siegel-Causey, 1992). Nevertheless, five categories of characteristics help describe these students: intellectual functioning, adaptive skills, motor development, sensory functioning, and communication.

Intellectual Functioning

Most individuals with severe and multiple disabilities have significant impairments in intellectual functioning. As you have already learned, intellectual functioning is traditionally measured by an intelligence test. Yet for many persons with severe and multiple disabilities, traditional methods of intelligence testing are inappropriate (Brown & Snell, 2000). There are two reasons. First, students with severe disabilities typically are not included in the normative samples of standard intelligence tests, so the information generated from these tests is not useful in designing appropriate educational programs. Second, the students have not been exposed to some of the academic content on the test that is used to measure basic cognitive abilities. Nevertheless, academic skills are an indicator of intellectual functioning in these students.

Students with severe and multiple disabilities vary widely in their academic skills. Some develop functional academic skills such as how to count money, find items in a grocery store, and read road signs (Browder & Snell, 2000; Wolf & Hariott, 1997). Others have such extensive disabilities that their educational program may focus on learning to make eye contact, track objects with their eyes, and respond to stimuli around them (Guess, Roberts, & Rues, 2000).

Adaptive Skills

As you learned in Chapter 8, adaptive skills include conceptual, social, and practical competencies for functioning in community settings in an age-consistent way. Self-care skills are among the most important ones for inclusion in school and community.

The majority of individuals with severe and multiple disabilities can attain some level of independence in caring for their own needs (Farlow & Snell, 2000; Spooner & Wood, 1997). That is why parents give high priority to their children's self-care skills (Hamre-Nietupski, 1993) and why school programs typically include instruction in dressing, personal hygiene, toileting, feeding, and simple household chores. Joshua needs assistance with all of his self-care skills but is learning to feed himself by using his left hand, the lazy-Susan technology device that brings food to him, and its control switch.

Motor Development

Individuals with severe and multiple disabilities usually have a significant delay in motor development (Campbell, 2000). Their sensorimotor impairments often result in abnormal muscle tone. Some, such as Joshua, will have underdeveloped muscle tone; they often have difficulty sitting and moving from a sitting to a standing position. Like Joshua, their positioning is important (so he can use his left hand or activate his foot switch). Other students have increased muscle tension and extremely tight muscles. Too much tension can result in spasticity. Any abnormal muscle tone can interfere with a student's ability to perform functional tasks successfully, such as eating, dressing, using the bathroom, and playing with toys (Campbell, 2000). Despite their delayed motor development, many students with severe and multiple disabilities learn to walk with assistance.

Sensory Impairments

Hearing and vision impairments are common among individuals with severe and multiple disabilities (Utley, 1994). Indeed, two of every five students with severe and multiple disabilities typically have sensory impairments (Sobsey & Wolf-Schein, 1991). (Chapters 15 and 16 provide more information about hearing and vision impairments, respectively.)

To learn more about the characteristics and support needs of students who experience deaf-blindness, go to the Web Links module in Chapter 9 of the Companion Website.

You will learn about augmentative and alternative communication in Chapter 14 (communication disorders).

Although you might assume from the label "deaf-blind" that students with this classification have a total inability to hear or see, the fact of the matter is that students identified as deaf-blind have various combinations of vision and hearing impairments. Their impairments in *both* sensory modalities, however, are so severe that they need specially designed instruction tailored to their unique combination of disabilities (Engleman, Griffin, Griffin, & Maddox, 1999).

Nearly all students who are deaf-blind need to develop meaningful communication, including how to recognize and respond to tactile and gestural cues (Orelove & Sobesy, 1996). Box 9–1 provides practice suggestions for supporting students who are deaf-blind to develop communication.

Communication Skills

Communication challenges are not confined to students who are deaf-blind. Almost all students with severe and multiple disabilities experience communication challenges (Iacono, Carter, & Hook, 1998; Reichle, 1997).

Parents of young children with severe disabilities have reported a number of communication skills they want their children's educators to teach: asking for objects, objecting to the actions of others, maintaining conversational interaction, and drawing attention to pain or discomfort (Stephenson & Dowrick, 2000). Joshua's teacher, Ellen, is helping him use an electronic switch to signal his needs through an augmentative communication device or, in the future, through a computer (Beukelman & Mirenda, 1998; Siegel & Wetherby, 2000). The switch enables Joshua to signal that he needs to go to the toilet or is chilly; the augmentative communication device "speaks" his needs— "toilet" or "cold"— and thereby helps him communicate about discomfort instead of acting out to signal that he is uncomfortable or in pain.

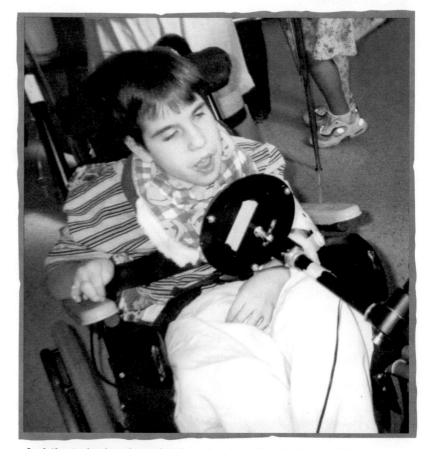

Assistive technology is a related service. It enables Joshua to attain more independence in his adaptive skills.

Box 9–1

Into Practice

Students Who Are Deaf-Blind Can Learn to Communicate

Imagine being unable to communicate. You can't hear what others are saying; no music enlivens your day. You can't speak, so you can't make your needs and desires known; and you certainly can't be self-determined without great difficulty.

Imagine being unable to see. You have no idea what your family or friends look like. Colors and shapes elude you. Even darkness and lightness have no meaning. You don't know when the day begins or ends.

If these are your impressions of students with deaf-blindness, you are only partially correct. Yes, some of these students have a total or near-total inability to hear and see. Many, however, have some residual sight; and many also have some residual hearing and can speak.

No matter how great their impairments, every one of these children has the same need: to communicate, to break through the walls of silence and sightlessness. And most of them do not learn primarily through their vision and hearing. That means they have to learn through other means.

As is the case with all other students with disabilities, their learning and your teaching begin with a nondiscriminatory and interdisciplinary evaluation and involve a team of professionals delivering general education, special education, and related services (typically, orientation and mobility training).

But can you include these students in the general curriculum or even in highly specialized programs? Some general guidelines are fairly obvious:

- Provide on-site (in-school, in-classroom) instruction for all staff and students who will work with the student.
- Use appropriate amplification devices and other assistive technology.
- Teach the student to use more than one device.
- Teach other people to communicate with the student in all of the ways in which the student communicates.

Other approaches expand on these four. One basic approach develops the student's receptive communication (ability to hear and see what you are saying and doing) and use his residual senses of hearing and vision:

- Maintain all interaction at students' eye level; they can use their residual sight and hearing more effectively when you accommodate them.
- Use touch cues to start or end your interaction with a student; a touch cue could be a simple one such as waving good-bye directly in front of the student's face (your hand movement and the wind it generates are good-bye signals) or some hand-over-hand cues (you and the student join hands and wave good-bye).

- Make sure other staff and students use only those communication techniques that the student understands; this reduces everyone's frustration and encourages communication.
- Adapt your communications to the student's pace; slow down and repeat yourself.
- Give your student lots of chances to communicate and make choices; reinforce communication and choice making.
- Change your classroom environment, reducing noises by putting up partitions to get smaller spaces (which make communication easier) and arranging chairs in a *U* shape or in a circle to encourage communication (the student can see and hear more easily when facing others).
- Keep your schedule consistent; the student will learn more if she knows that one event or activity always follows another.
- Use assistive technology, including low-tech devices such as communication boards or high-tech devices such as closed-circuit television, braille/print conversation technology, or voice-output devices (they "speak" to you).

Putting These Strategies to Work for Progress in the General Curriculum

1. Imagine yourself as an inclusion facilitator at the elementary level. A student who is deaf-blind enrolls in first grade. What steps would you take to ensure that this student has an opportunity to develop communication?

2. Imagine yourself as a general education math teacher at the middle school level. You have a student who is deaf-blind in your class. How might you universally design your math curriculum to ensure that the student is able to participate successfully in your class.

3. Specify a question that you have about students who are deaf-blind. Then go to the Web Links module in Chapter 9 of the Companion Website and connect with the website on deaf-blindness. Find the answer to your question on this website or link to others as necessary.

To answer these questions online and learn more about these strategies, go to the Into Practice module in Chapter 9 of the Companion Website.

Source: Adapted from Engleman, M. D., Griffin, H. C., Griffin, L. W., & Maddox, J. I. (1999). A teacher's guide to communicating with students with deaf-blindness. *TEACHING Exceptional Children, 31*(4), 68–73.

By using an augmentative communication board, students with communication limitations are able to "talk" with other people. This board consists of icons, words, and alphabet letters that the student touches to activate a sound or voice.

Identifying the Causes

It can be difficult to identify the exact cause or causes of severe and multiple disabilities. In fact, there is no single identifiable cause for these disabilities in an estimated 30 to 40 percent of all children born with them (Luckasson et al., 1992; McLaren & Bryson, 1987). The majority of known causes, however, relate to prenatal biomedical factors. In addition, complications during birth (perinatal causes) and after birth (postnatal causes) account for many of these disabilities. Genetic metabolic disorders occur prenatally and warrant your attention.

Genetic Metabolic Disorders

Abnormalities in a parent's genes can cause a disorder in a child's metabolism (Batshaw, 2002; Batshaw & Tuchman, 2002). They also can be the catalysts for parents and scientists to seek cures, as you will learn in Box 9–2.

Metabolism is important for body functions such as energy, growth, and waste disposal; the term itself refers to the chemical processes that break down toxins (poisons) and move nutrients through the bloodstream. The genetic metabolic abnormalities that are most frequently associated with severe and multiple disabilities cause a dysfunction in the production of necessary enzymes (Batshaw & Tuchman, 2002). Enzymes that have not been converted to a useful substance accumulate to toxic levels, thus damaging a fetus's physical and mental development.

One inherited metabolic genetic disease is *phenylketonuria (PKU)*. This disease is caused by the absence of an enzyme that is necessary to convert an essential amino acid to a different amino acid. Toxins are created in the central nervous system due to the absence of this enzyme conversion. It results in mental retardation if the newborn is not treated within the first few weeks of life.

PKU is carried through an autosomal recessive gene. This means that both parents must have a recessive gene; however, neither parent has PKU. When two adults who have a recessive gene (but likely do not know it) conceive a child, there is a one-in-four chance that the child will be affected by the disorder (Batshaw & Tuchman, 2002). A recessive gene might be passed on for generations before anyone develops the disorder; it may take that long for two recessive genes to meet.

Biomedical factors include chromosomal abnormalities, genetic metabolic disorders, developmental disorders of brain formation, and prenatal environmental influences.

To learn more about PKU, go the Web Links module in Chapter 9 of the Companion Website.

Box 9–2

Race for a Miracle

Brad and Vicki Margus are the parents of two sons, Quinn and Jarret, who have a rare genetic disease called *ataxia telangiectasia (AT),* which causes a gradual neurological deterioration. Babies born with AT appear normal in the first few years but then begin to wobble or sway as they move. By the time they reach adolescence, most must use wheelchairs; and by age 30, most die from cancer or infection. Since finding out about the diagnosis and grim prospects for Quinn and Jarrett, the Marguss family has thrown itself full time into finding a cure for the devastating disease. Brad and Vicki began a foundation, the AT Children's Project, with the goal of accelerating research toward finding a cure for AT.

Partially as a result of their persistent efforts to raise money and awareness for the fight against AT, amazing strides have been made in unlocking the secrets of this rare disease. For example in just the past few years, scientists have isolated the AT gene, administered experimental therapies to newborns with AT, developed mice carrying AT to help them understand how the disease works, and—most recently—located the source of the neurodegeneration that characterizes AT.

Vicki Margus explains why so many parents of children with disabilities are willing to take such risks and make such sacrifices. "Never in my wildest dreams could we know how much you could love someone until you have these children. And there's nothing that we wouldn't do for them."

To learn more about the Margus family's efforts to help science find a cure for *AT,* watch the accompanying ABC News video "Race for a Miracle" and go to the Web Links module in Chapter 9 of the Companion Website to link to the *AT* Children's Project homepage.

Currently, an international effort known as the Human Genome Project is constructing detailed genetic and physical maps of our 60,000–100,000 human genes. The project is jointly directed by the National Institutes of Health and the U.S. Department of Energy. The goal is to identify all of the genes in the human body by the year 2005. If scientists reach that goal, they will solve many mysteries related to healthy and unhealthy, able and disabled bodies and brains. This research has significant implications for understanding and preventing genetic disorders associated with severe and multiple disabilities (Moser, 2000).

Preventing Severe and Multiple Disabilities

Many factors can cause severe and multiple disabilities. Given the current level of medical technology, some, but not all, of these disabilities, are preventable. Advances in prenatal testing, such as **amniocentesis, chorionic villi sampling,** and **percutaneous umbilical blood sampling,** can help to identify and possibly prevent multiple disabilities through fetal therapy (Schonberg & Tifft, 2002). Figure 9–1 describes those tests. The ultimate goal of prenatal diagnosis is to identify and treat the developing child before or immediately after birth. Prenatal fetal therapy, such as in-utero surgery, is rapidly expanding.

Identifying the Prevalence

The U.S. Department of Education (2001) reported that 112,993 students ages 6 to 21 were served in 1999–2000 under IDEA's programs for students with *multiple* disabilities. This number represents 0.18 percent of all students in this age group who were served in IDEA programs. An additional 1,454 students ages 6 to 21 with deaf-blindness were served in schools during this same time. As you have already learned, IDEA does not identify *severe* disabilities as a separate category. Therefore, the U.S. Department of Education (2001) does not provide data on the number of students with *severe* disabilities served by schools.

To learn more about the Human Genome Project, go to the Web Links module in Chapter 9 of the Companion Website.

To learn more about and see photographs of amniocentesis, chorionic villi sampling, ultrasound, and other prenatal tests, go to the Web Links module in Chapter 9 of the Companion Website.

You will learn about fetal surgery for the purpose of prenatal diagnosis and treatment in Chapter 12, where we discuss spina bifida.

FIGURE 9–1
Prenatal tests

Amniocentesis

1. A needle is inserted through the mother's abdomen into her uterus and the amniotic sac.
2. Two tablespoons of fluid are withdrawn. The fluid is placed in sterile tubes for chromosome analysis.
3. Cells in the fluid are cultured, and then a karyotype (a way of arranging chromosomes for study) is completed that takes 7–14 days to get a result.

Chorionic villi sampling

1. A needle is inserted into the mother's abdomen or a catheter into the substance of the placenta but outside of the amniotic sac.
2. Suction is applied with a syringe, and 10–15 milliliters of tissue are aspirated into the syringe.
3. The tissue is grown in a culture, and a karyotype is made.

Percutaneous umbilical blood sampling

1. A needle is inserted through the mother's abdominal and uterine walls and into the umbilical vein.
2. Fetal blood is sampled.
3. A rapid karyotype can be conducted on the blood, which leads to a quicker result in situations in which a baby is showing signs of distress.

Each of these types of prenatal testing described in Figure 9–1 requires a needle to be inserted into the mother's body.

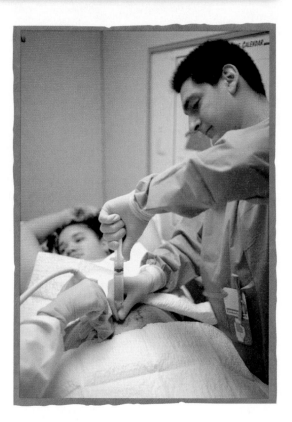

How Do You Evaluate Students with Severe and Multiple Disabilities

As you will recall from Chapter 1, IDEA's nondiscriminatory evaluation process determines whether the student has a disability and, if so, what the student's special education and related-service needs are. Figure 9–2 describes this process for students with severe and multiple disabilities.

FIGURE 9–2

Evaluating whether a student has severe and multiple disabilities

Nondiscriminatory Evaluation

Observation	
Physician/medical professional observes	The newborn may have noticeable disabilities associated with a syndrome or may have medical complications that are often associated with severe disabilities.
Parents observe	The child has difficulties nursing, sleeping, or attaining developmental milestones.

Medical screening	
Assessment measures	**Findings that indicate need for further evaluation**
Newborn screening measures such as the Apgar	Apgar scores are below 4, indicating possibility of severe disabilities.
Genetic evaluations	Evaluation leads to identification of a genetic cause.
Physical examinations	Medical procedures, including vision and hearing tests, blood work, metabolic tests, spinal tests, etc., reveal the presence of a disabling condition.

Prereferral
Prereferral is typically not used with this population because the severity of the disability indicates a need for special education and related services.

Referral
Children with severe and multiple disabilities should be referred by medical personnel or parents for early intervention during the infancy/preschool years. Many states have Child Find organizations to make sure these children receive services. The child is referred upon reaching school age.

Nondiscriminatory evaluation procedures and standards	
Assessment measures	**Findings that suggest severe and multiple disabilities**
Individualized intelligence test	The student scores at least two standard deviations below the mean (70 to 75 or lower), indicating that mental retardation exists. Most students with severe and multiple disabilities have IQ scores that are significantly below 70, indicating severe cognitive impairment.
Adaptive behavior scales	The student scores significantly below average in two or more areas of adaptive behaviors, indicating severe deficits in skills such as communication, daily living, socialization, gross- and fine-motor coordination, and behavior.
Profiles of intensity of needed support	The student rates in the extensive to pervasive level of support in most areas: communication, self-care, social skills, home living, community use, self-direction, health, and safety.

Nondiscriminatory evaluation team determines that student has severe and multiple disabilities and needs special education and related services.

Appropriate Education

FIGURE 9–3
The Apgar scoring system

	Points			Score			
				1 minute		5 minutes	
	0	**1**	**2**	**Michael**	**David**	**Michael**	**David**
Heart rate	Absent	Less than 100	More than 100	2	0	2	1
Respiratory effort	Absent	Slow, irregular	Normal respiration, crying	2	0	2	1
Muscle tone	Limp	Some flexion	Active motion	1	0	2	1
Gag reflex	No response	Grimace	Sneeze; cough	2	0	2	1
Color	Blue all over; pale	Blue extremities	Pink all over	1	0	2	1
			Totals	8	0	10	5

Source: From "The First Weeks of Life," by J. R. Evans, in *Children With Disabilities* (4th ed., pp. 93–114), edited by M. L. Batshaw, 1997, Baltimore, Paul H. Brookes Publishing Company. Copyright 1997 by Paul H. Brookes Publishing Company, P.O. Box 10624, Baltimore, MD 21285-0624. Reprinted with permission.

Determining the Presence

For the most part, children with severe and multiple disabilities are detected at birth through the use of the **Apgar test** (Evans, 1997). When using this test, the physician ranks the child on five physical traits (heart rate, respiratory effort, muscle tone, gag reflex, and skin color) at one minute and at five minutes after birth. The newborn receives a score of 0, 1, or 2 for each trait. Physicians assume that children with cumulative scores below 4 are more at risk for disabilities (Evans, 1997). Figure 9–3 shows examples of Apgar scores, showing that David is substantially more at risk than Michael for having disabilities.

Once an Apgar screening is complete, and assuming that the infant's Apgar score reveals potential complications, the next step is to conduct more precise and thorough testing to identify the nature of the disability, its possible causes, and the extent of the disabling conditions. This kind of diagnostic testing involves medical and physical examinations that are usually done over a period of several years to determine the extent of neurological impairments, sensory deficits, concurrent medical needs, and motor involvement (Batshaw & Shapiro, 1997; Heller, Alberto, Forney, & Schwartzman, 1996; Nickel, 2000).

Determining the Nature and Extent of General and Special Education and Related Services

It is increasingly usual for teachers to determine the nature and extent of special education and related services for students with severe and multiple disabilities by following a process called Making Action Plans (MAPs). MAPs customizes students' educational programs to their specific visions, strengths, and needs (Downing, 2002; Falvey, Forest, Pearpoint, & Rosenberg, 1997). This makes it an assessment strategy for advancing self-determination.

The MAPs process can involve the required members of multidisciplinary teams, including the student and parents, but also usually includes other family members (in addition to parents), peers of the student, and family friends. The facilitator may be any one of these in-

To learn more details about ratings on each of the five physical traits of the Apgar, go to the Web Links module in Chapter 9 of the Companion Website and link to www.cnn.com/HEALTH/indepth.health/infants/faqs/apgar.html#.

dividuals. The facilitator needs to ensure a positive brainstorming process to generate as many creative ideas as possible. The brainstorming generally follows eight key questions (Turnbull & Turnbull, 2001).

1. *What is MAPs?* At the beginning of the meeting, the facilitator explains the purpose of the process, the type of questions that will be asked, and the general ground rules for open-ended and creative problem solving. The facilitator especially tries to create an upbeat, energized, and relational ambience.

2. *What is your history or story?* Typically, the student and the student's family share background information, highlighting the triumphs and challenges that have been associated with living his life consistent with his visions, great expectations, strengths, and preferences.

3. *What are your dreams?* The student shares his great expectations for the future. Family members also share their great expectations and supplement what the student is saying if he cannot or chooses not to communicate with the group members. The key aspect of the MAPs process is to identify these great expectations as the basis for planning the customized school schedule and extracurricular activities.

4. *What are your nightmares?* Because students with exceptionalities and their families often have major fears that block their work toward great expectations, identifying their nightmares lets everyone know what those are so the team can put adequate supports into place. Some fears cannot be prevented, such as those about the progressive course of AIDS in a young child; but sharing them can help everyone know where the student will need support.

5. *Who are you?* The group will use as many adjectives as it takes to get behind the student's exceptionality label and describe the real or essential aspects of the student.

6. *What are your strengths, gifts, and talents?* Often teachers, friends, family members, and others can lose sight of the characteristics that the student can make the most of to achieve his dreams. So the MAPs meeting takes time to identify them.

7. *What do you need?* What will it take to make the student's and family's great expectations come true? What barriers stand in the way? Identifying these needs and barriers can serve as the basis for educational programming.

8. *What is the plan of action?* A plan of action includes the specific steps that need to happen to accomplish the great expectations. The plan of action can involve tasks, time lines, resources, and any other detailed information that will help the student realize his expectations.

As in all educational decisions, a family's cultural values affect members' great expectations and even their willingness to participate in the MAPs process. Box 9–3 points out some potential cultural clashes in how some Asian American families might regard the MAPs process.

How Do You Assure Progress in the General Curriculum?

Including Students

When Joshua Spoor was in elementary school, he was included in general education classes for more than half of his school day. Now that he is in middle school, including him in general education has become more challenging, even for the Johnson City school district, which has a history of inclusive education. Box 9–4 offers tips for educators who are responding to these challenges.

Box 9–3

Multicultural Considerations

MAPs: When East Meets West

What is the Challenge?

A challenge for special educators may arise when educators ask families from Vietnam, Korea, and China to engage in the process. Many features of the MAPs process reflect European American values, which may conflict with the cultural values of those families in several respects (Abery & McBride, 1998):

- Families operate on a hierarchical system within which elders, especially fathers, have a great deal of authority to make decisions and in which children are expected to be dutiful toward their families. In contrast, MAPs focuses on what the person (in this case, the child) with a disability wants.

- Families tend to assign more importance to the group (family) than to the individual. In contrast, MAPs values the preferences and desires of the individual and asserts that the group is the means for enabling the individual to accomplish his or her preferences.

- Families often defer to professionals and their knowledge. In contrast, MAPs asserts that everyone has worthwhile knowledge and expertise.

- Families often have a sense of pride in family (and shame related to disability) that may conflict with the use of an outside facilitator for MAPs.

- Families may tend to have a fatalistic view about disability ("it happened and we can't do anything about it") that may conflict with the MAPs expectation that the person with a disability will be self-determined and fully participate in his or her community.

What Can an Educator Do?

Given these cultural disagreements, what is an educator to do? These are the best rules of thumb:

- Explain MAPs and self-determination to families and offer them the choice of doing MAPs or not.

- Do not be alarmed if some (perhaps those who have been in the United States for a longer period of time and have a relatively high socioeconomic status) say yes and others (perhaps more recent immigrants who are still not economically established) say no.

- Show respect for a family's elders and other authority figures (father and mother), and do not be disappointed if the student does not participate much.

- Consider asking for permission to use a translator (if needed), preferably one that the family chooses. Language barriers can be great.

Self-determination is culturally grounded, and so is MAPs as a means for working toward it. Yet our country includes many cultures, some of which do not share your values and priorities. Because diversity is one of our country's strengths, educators should reinforce that diversity even if doing so means that MAPs is not appropriate for every student and family.

Putting These Ideas to Work for Progress in the General Curriculum

1. If you had dealt with a disability when you were growing up, do you believe your family would have been comfortable using the MAPs process? How does your answer relate to your family's cultural values?

2. Consider that you are a special education teacher and responsible for assessing an elementary student. You wonder if the student's family would be interested in using MAPs. Write a script of what you might say to the family to explain MAPs and ask them if they are interested in participating.

3. Consider the eight key questions of the MAPs process. How might those questions be adapted to take into account the cultural perspectives of diverse families?

To answer these questions online and learn more about these ideas and concepts, go to the Multicultural Considerations module in Chapter 9 of the Companion Website.

Source: Adapted from Bui, Y., & Turnbull, A. P. (in press). East meets west: Analysis of person-centered planning in the context of Asian American values. *Education and Training in Mental Retardation and Developmental Disabilities.*

Inclusion Tips

Box 9–4

	What You Might See	What You Might Be Tempted to Do	Alternate Responses	Ways to Include Peers in the Process
Behavior	She may have temper tantrums and hit herself or others.	Discipline and isolate her from the rest of the class.	Learn to identify cues that trigger positive behaviors. Reward appropriate behaviors.	Support the peers closest to her, and teach them to recognize and give cues that encourage positive behavior in a way that is respectful of her.
Social interactions	She is unable to communicate needs or wants using words.	Allow her to remain a class observer rather than a participant.	Use assistive technology to enable her to make her needs and wants known.	Teach peers to use the same assistive technology she uses so they can effectively communicate.
Educational performance	She is not able to read or write and her functional skills may be extremely limited.	Give up and let her color or do something quiet.	Create opportunities for her to participate in cooperative learning groups.	Arrange for peers to assist her with follow-through on task completion. Support them to be friends as well as peer tutors.
Classroom attitudes	She may appear bored or unresponsive and may sleep during class instruction.	Ignore her and focus on other, more attentive students.	Use times of alertness to give her choices of ways to respond and interact during instruction.	Pair her with buddies who can interact during class instruction based on her preferences.

Figure 9–4 reports the latest information available on the educational placements of students with severe and multiple disabilities. Leaders in the field have almost always advocated for inclusive education (Doyle, 2002; Kennedy & Fisher, 2001; Snell & Brown, 2000; Thousand, Villa, & Nevin, 2002). But advocacy alone does not assure inclusion. Research into evidence-based practices is also necessary. Note that a comprehensive synthesis of 19 research studies on the inclusion of students with severe disabilities identified five major themes related to successful inclusion with this group of students (Hunt & Goetz, 1997):

▼ Collaborating among teachers and parents at classroom, building, and systems levels
▼ Teaching new skills in general education classrooms (Giangreco, Dennis, Cloninger, Edelman, & Schattman, 1993; Hunt, Staub, Alwell, & Goetz, 1994)
▼ Promoting friendships in inclusive settings
▼ Facilitating positive outcomes for classmates without disabilities
▼ Adapting the students' curriculum

What are teachers' and parents' perspectives about inclusion for students with severe and multiple disabilities? A survey of secondary-school teachers' perspectives about the inclusion of students

FIGURE 9–4
Educational placement of students with multiple disabilities (1998–1999)

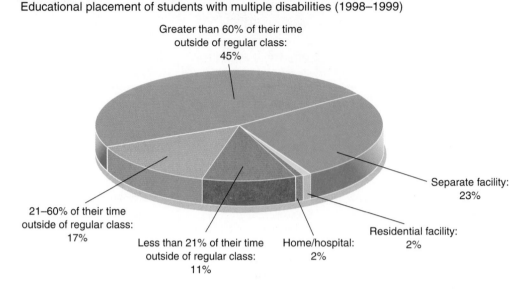

Source: From U.S. Department of Education. (2001). To assure the free appropriate education of all children with disabilities: Twenty-first report to Congress on the implementation of the Individuals with Disabilities Education Act. Washington, DC. Author.

with severe disabilities revealed that approximately three-fourths of the teachers either disagreed or were undecided about the appropriateness of having students with severe disabilities attend general education programs in their neighborhood schools (Smith, 2000). Eighty-three percent of the teachers reported that they lack sufficient training to teach students with severe and multiple disabilities.

Many parents agree with teachers that general educators are not well prepared to implement inclusion successfully (Palmer, Fuller, Arora, & Nelson, 2001). A survey of approximately 500 parents revealed that most parents believe that the nature of their child's disability is too severe and would overwhelm general education teachers. According to one parent, many parents are concerned about the mismatch between the child's needs in the general education curriculum, the lack of appropriate services, and peers' acceptance of their child. Parents reported that the primary benefit of inclusion is that their child has a greater chance to learn more academic and functional skills in general education classes because there are higher expectations in those classes than in special education classrooms.

Box 9–5 shares the perspective of an administrator who provided the leadership to assure inclusion for a student with a severe and multiple disability, knowing that all members of the multidisciplinary team had a great deal to learn in order to achieve success. Often you will hear educators lament that more time is needed for them to prepare for inclusion, but this administrator had the perspective that students cannot afford to wait and that educators must move ahead to learn the necessary skills even as they serve the students.

Planning Universally Designed Learning

Universally designed learning is especially important for students with moderate and severe disabilities because they require extensive and pervasive supports.

Adapting Instruction Through Partial Participation

One way to adapt instruction for students with severe and multiple disabilities is to be flexible about how and how much they participate. This flexibility is called **partial participation.**

The partial participation principle holds that students with severe and multiple disabilities should not be categorically denied all access to general education and other inclusive activities solely because of their intellectual, adaptive skill, motor, sensory, and/or communication im-

Box 9–5

Making a Difference

We Weren't Ready, but We Started Anyway

Over the past 10 years, administrators have been challenged to live our philosophy. In the early 1980s, we essentially predestined the way in which kids in special education were going to leave school. If a child with severe disabilities was bused from one community to another to be in a clustered program, we could pretty much guarantee that this situation would stay the same for the rest of that student's life. Then I realized what we had been asking parents to do. Would I, as a parent, be willing to have my child with or without a disability loaded onto a bus, driven past the school in the neighborhood where our family had chosen to live, to go to school somewhere else? But how do you go about changing the way we had done things in special education for 20 years? Well, in our case, we began with Lance.

In the spring, Lance's foster parents requested that Lance, who had severe disabilities, attend his home school in the fall. At the time, Lance was enrolled in a self-contained classroom in a clustered program in a community 30 miles away. Because we had been preparing for such requests philosophically, we really could not say no to

his parents. The change would be interesting, though, because this boy would attend a school that only students with mild disabilities had attended. How could we make this change?

We knew we needed a good idea about the IEP to be implemented in the fall. We needed to write down all the key activities that would take place. For example, someone would need to go into the school, explain to the staff what would be expected of them, and introduce them to Lance. When fall did come, school personnel met once a month with Lance's parents and service providers for 35–40 minutes to solve problems on the playground, in the hallway, or with a teacher who was frustrated in some way.

We were really lucky to have a great paraprofessional, good support from the principal, and constant support from Lance's parents. But the key person was Lance's teacher. She said, "Did I have enough training and enough information when I started? The answer was no. Would I ever have had enough information and training to start? The answer was no again."

As an administrator, I think her comment says an awful lot. It says, "Is there ever a right time to start? More important, can our students afford to wait for us to be ready?"

Source: Adapted from Kansas Department of Education. (2001). *Collective wisdom: An anthology of stories and best practices for educating students with severe disabilities and deaf-blindness* (p. 17). Topeka, KS: Author.

pairments (Snell & Brown, 2000). The principle rejects an all-or-none approach: Either students function independently in environments or not at all. Rather, it asserts that students with severe and multiple disabilities can participate, even if only partially, and indeed can often learn and complete a task if it is adapted to their strengths.

Partial participation is made possible through four types of instructional adaptations: adapting sequences through which a student learns, adapting rules, using personal assistance, and using materials and technology (Beukelman & Mirenda, 1998; Jorgensen, 1996; Kimm, Falvey, Bishop, & Rosenberg, 1995). We encourage you to reflect carefully on the four types of adaptations illustrated in Figure 9–5 to consider how each example enables a student to partially participate in a task. From what you know about Joshua and his educational program, which of these adaptations would enable him to partially participate in valued activities? Before you answer, read Box 9–6 and relate what you learn there to Joshua.

Adapting Instruction Through Peer Support

Peer tutoring involves pairing students one on one so that students who have already developed certain skills can help teach new skills to less well advanced students and also help those students practice skills they have already been taught. Peer tutoring is an effective instructional strategy across different areas of exceptionality. A comprehensive research synthesis of 35 studies between 1992 and 2000 with students with mild disabilities reported positive academic gains for students uniformly across the many different studies (Mastropieri, Spencer, Scruggs, & Talbott, 2000). These academic gains were primarily in areas of reading, spelling, and writing (including complex skills involving reading comprehension and written composition). The authors emphasized the increase in the number of studies that have included students with disabilities as tutors, not just as tutees. Overall, teachers reported that peer tutoring was an enjoyable classroom activity.

FIGURE 9–5

Examples of instructional adaptations

Student	Task	Adaptation
Adapting Skill Sequences		
Needs pureed food	Eating with peers in cafeteria	Pick up lunch tray early; prepare in classroom; take to cafeteria
Five-year-old student has ataxic cerebral palsy; has no mobility; unable to crawl	Being independently mobile in all events	Student may pass over crawling stage and learn to be mobile by walking
Fatigues extremely easily	Cleaning classroom	Clean one part of a classroom instead of cleaning whole classroom in one day
Has short attention span	Playing table games	Provide reinforcement throughout the game instead of just at the end
Has difficulty with balance	Using toilet independently	Sit on toilet, then remove pants
Is unable to maintain balance while bending and reaching	Picking up puzzle pieces from the classroom floor	Sit down on the floor, then pick up and put pieces into a box
Adapting Rules		
Has difficulty eating quickly	Eating with peers in cafeteria	Allow a longer lunch period for this student by starting earlier
Is unable to locate bus-stop landmarks	Riding the bus independently	Student asks bus driver to tell him or her when they are at the right stop
Has difficulty bending and maintaining balance	Sweeping floors	Sweeps dirt out the door instead of using a dustpan
Is unable to write name	Writing names on personal belongings	Write name with assistance or have a rubber stamp made
Cannot discriminate between written numbers	Doing math problems	Uses objects to count and solve math problems
Uses a wheelchair	Going to gym where there are stairs	Student goes around the gym to use a ramp
Uses crutches	Using school cafeteria	Ask peer to carry tray of food
Has limited cooking skills	Eating a complete meal	Have a team meal where each person prepares one course in a home economics class
Has poor fine motor skills	Using shop class appliances	Ask a friend or a teacher to plug in appliance
Has low reading ability	Reading directions for a group assignment	Peer reads all questions while student and peer take turns answering
Utilizing Personal Assistance		
Has poor fine motor skills	Turning book pages	Ask a friend to assist with turning pages
Uses a wheelchair	Riding in an elevator	Ask someone to push button for correct floor if button is out of reach
Materials and Devices		
Is unable to add or subtract amounts	Doing math assignment	Use calculator to add and subtract
Has low reading ability	Identifying home phone number	Use color-coded numbers
Uses a wheelchair	Cleaning classroom	Use long-handled brushes/sponges
Has difficulty matching colors	Dressing independently	Tag clothes that match with coded labels
Has poor fine motor skills	Playing table games	Use enlarged pieces and adapting switches
Has difficulty with balance	Walking to the classroom	Use a cane, handrails, or wheelchair

Source: From "Motor and Personal Care Skills," by C. H. Kimm, M. A. Falvey, K. D. Bishop, and R. L. Rosenberg, in *Inclusive and Heterogeneous Schooling: Assessment, Curriculum, and Instruction* (pp. 203–204), edited by M. A. Falvey, 1995, Baltimore: Paul H. Brookes Publishing Company, P.O. Box 10624, Baltimore, MD 21285-0624. Copyright 1995 by Paul H. Brookes Publishing Company. Reprinted with permission.

Technology Tips

Box 9–6

Using Assistive Technology for Partial Participation in Recreation

Assistive technology plays a large role in many IEP goals for students with severe and multiple disabilities, but let's focus on only one of them: participating in school recreation activities under the principle of partial participation.

As you know by now, a good teacher does not develop any program, much less one that uses assistive technology, without first fully evaluating a student. Nearly every assistive technology evaluation begins by determining how to overcome the three major barriers to the student's participation in school: (1) Is the student sufficiently alert to be able to learn, is he in a "shutdown" state? (2) Does the student have the ability to physically manipulate the assistive technology and other equipment or objects? (3) Does the student have social or behavioral challenges related to his use of technology? We have already discussed Joshua's physical abilities to use his switch, which is an assistive technology devices. Now, let's consider the arousal/shutdown barrier.

Many students with severe and multiple disabilities are very sensitive to sensory stimuli such as light, music, smells, and touch. One student's sensitivity can be positive: He likes bright lights and reaches for them. Another's can be negative: She closes her eyes, grimaces, cries, and tries to avoid the lights. There is no single response to lights or to other stimuli such as noise, smell, and touch. A team (the student's teacher, an occupational therapist, and a physical therapist) should assess what the student likes and dislikes, what stimuli are positive and negative. That assessment will tell them what kinds of assistive technology they may want to use and what kinds of opportunities exist for the student's peers without disabilities to support the student to use the technology.

If the team determines that the student likes light, then she could use a device that has bright flashing lights or a siren sound or both to signal the beginning or end of a quarter of a football game for which the student is the official timekeeper. The student is guided by a peer who does not have a disability about when to use the device. Similarly, the student could use balls or other play equipment that are lighted to participate with peers in throw-catch or other kinds of games. Or she can use playground equipment that is painted with bright contrasting colors, such as red, white, and blue steps on a slide or a bright orange seat on a swing.

If the team determines that the student likes sounds, then she can operate a boom box during a dance class or play catch-and-throw with a ball that has a bell or a beeper inside it. If the team determines that the student likes touch, then she can use a vibrating or textured ball for catch-and-throw.

There are many ways to get the student involved in outdoor recreation at the school. Wide paths with firm surfaces let her move easily to the playground. Swings with firm backs and seatbelts allow her to use the swingset. Sandboxes on elevated platforms at the height of a wheelchair open up that play area. Flotation devices such as life jackets and float suits keep the child above water in a school pool.

Many teachers might have the impression that students with severe and multiple disabilities simply cannot participate in school recreation, that they need specialized physical therapy. That impression may have been correct many years ago. It's absolutely wrong now. Assistive technology can make the principle of partial participation a reality for even the student who has the most pervasive needs for support.

Putting These Strategies to Work for Progress in the General Curriculum

1. What is the challenge?

2. What is the technology?

3. What do you do with it?

To answer these questions online and learn more about these strategies, go to the Technology Tips module in Chapter 9 of the Companion Website.

Source: Adapted from Gierach, J., Obukowicz, M., & Reed, P. (2000). Assistive technology for recreation, leisure, and activities of daily living. In P. Reed (Ed.), *Assessing students' needs for assistive technology: A resource manual for school district teams* (pp. 170–184). Oshkosh: Wisconsin Assistive Technology Initiative (www.wati.org).

Can peer tutoring, which has worked so effectively for students without disabilities and for those with mild disabilities, also be successful for students with severe and multiple disabilities? Although peer tutoring has not been applied as comprehensively with this group of students, research substantiates that peer tutoring is an evidence-based practice for providing universally designed instruction to students with severe and multiple disabilities.

- ▼ Peer tutors have successfully worked with middle school students in general education classrooms to teach them to self-record their performance on skills (Gilberts, Agran, Hughes, & Wehmeyer, 2001).
- ▼ A classwide peer tutoring program with middle school students with severe disabilities in inclusive classrooms resulted in increased rates of academic responding and reduced rates of problem behavior among students with disabilities (McDonnell, Mathot-Buckner, Thorson, & Fister, 2001).
- ▼ Peer tutoring was used among students with moderate and severe disabilities in inclusive classrooms to teach incidental information that helped to clarify the tasks they were asked to perform (Collins, Hendricks, Fetko, & Land, 2002).
- ▼ Peer tutoring embedded into cooperative learning groups enabled middle school students with severe disabilities to acquire functional academic skills (Wilson, 1999).

Box 9–7 highlights a successful and innovative high school program that uses a form of peer tutoring.

Although peer tutoring can benefit students with and without disabilities, we want to include a cautionary note: Overrelying on students for peer support might lead to relationships that tend to be one-way rather than reciprocal. Clearly, there is nothing wrong with help; friends often help each other. However, help is not and can never be the only basis for friendship. We must be careful not to overemphasize the helper-helpee aspect of a relationship. Unless help is reciprocal, the inherent inequity between tutor and tutee can distort the authenticity of a relationship (Van der Klift & Kunc, 1994).

Collaborating to Meet Students' Needs

To ensure that students with severe and multiple disabilities receive sufficiently intense instruction in general education classrooms, collaboration between general and special educators should have the following goals (McDonnell, 1998):

- ▼ Create a classroom structure to support the diverse learning styles and needs of all students.
- ▼ Use heterogeneous student groupings and rely on peer tutoring.
- ▼ Implement universally designed learning through partnerships with educators, family members, peers, and other volunteers.

Professional collaboration contributes to Joshua's middle school success. As you learned at the beginning of this chapter, Joshua receives intensive, regular, one-on-one services from therapists. And he gets similar interventions on a daily basis from his teacher, Ellen Starley, or her aides.

Not only professional collaboration but also student and family collaboration are important for Joshua. Ellen arranges for him to be read to and to play games with classmates who do not have disabilities during their free time. Ellen says, "Josh responds very well to people's voices. His father, brother, and sister make tapes, talking and singing to him, and he obviously responds happily. So I have made it easy for his classmates to do the same, using a vibrator at the foot of Joshua's wheelchair as a device he can push when he wants them to read to him or play games with him."

It's a Win-Win Proposition

Suppose you could, in a single program, accomplish several goals with one effort. For example, you effectively include students with severe and multiple disabilities into part of the general academic curriculum, remove them from their separate and self-contained classrooms for at least one class period a day to be in the general curriculum, help them learn functional academic and employment skills, and increase the number of genuine friendships they have with students who do not have disabilities. Would you be interested in adopting that program in your school? Probably.

What if that same program could simultaneously benefit students without disabilities in three or four different ways? Give them academic credit? Teach them how to be good citizens? Still interested? Definitely. After all, this is a win-win proposition for everyone.

The program is called Peer Buddies and is designed to promote social relationships among students with severe disabilities and their same-age peers without disabilities. In Nashville, Tennessee's, large urban school district, 9 of 11 comprehensive high schools paired 200 students with disabilities with 115 students who have no disabilities. The program was a great success. How do we know? A careful evaluation of the program tells us so (Hughes et al., 2001).

- Students without disabilities have positive attitudes about their peers with severe disabilities.
  - Students with severe disabilities are capable, far more so than many people think. They can "learn anything," "learn the basics," "learn to do many things."
  - They are not all that different from age peers who don't have disabilities. They "dress differently," "take longer to comprehend and learn," and "express themselves differently."
  - They have the same needs, desires, and feelings as their age peers without disabilities: "have fun," "play sports," "type on a computer." And they have the same challenges: "relationships, zits, changes."
- Students without disabilities personally benefited from being in the Peer Buddies program.
  - They learned about disability: It isn't a "setback; it's just an obstacle that takes a little longer to overcome."
  - They learned about relationships: "to open up and reach out," "to be more patient and deal with people better and cope with the quirks of their personalities."
  - They learned how to interact with people with disabilities, "to communicate" with them.
  - They experienced personal growth: They "learned to use [their] mind[s] in a completely different way" and "gained insight into [themselves] and sensitivity toward others."
- Students without disabilities provided benefits to students with disabilities.
  - They were academic tutors: they "helped with homework"; "taught reading, time telling, and identifying signs"; "helped . . . with math and spelling."
  - They participated in recreational and leisure activities together, promoted social integration in school, "helped [students with disabilities] make new friends" and "work on the job," and participated in community-based training.

All of these results are well and good. But did the program skew the relationships so that the helpers, simply by helping, were unable to also be friends? Not at all. None of the students without disabilities expressed any conflict or discomfort about being both a helper and a friend.

Here's the bonus: The students without disabilities received academic credit (½ semester) for this kind of service learning. To learn by serving others requires experiential learning—the chance to experience something valuable outside the classroom and to learn about yourself, others, and, indeed, about Americans and the United States.

That last item might sound a bit overly patriotic. But to learn that you, a student without a disability, is a peer, equal in many ways to a student with severe disabilities, is to learn some valuable lessons. Everyone can learn, and everyone can teach. Everyone is entitled to go to school and to be prepared to work. Everyone has something to contribute to others. And we are all in our schools and communities together. Civics lessons come in many ways; Peer Buddies is one of the better ones.

Putting These Tips to Work for Progress in the General Curriculum

1. Who are the collaborators?
2. What are the challenges?
3. What can a team of teachers, students with disabilities, and students without disabilities do?
4. What are the results?

To answer these questions online and learn more about these ideas and concepts, go to the Collaboration Tips module in Chapter 9 of the Companion Website.

Source: Adapted from Hughes, C., Copeland, S. R., Guth, C., Rung, L. L., Hwang, B., Kleeb, G., & Strong, M. (2001). General education students' perspectives on their involvement in a high school peer buddy program. *Education and Training in Mental Retardation and Developmental Disabilities, 36*(4), 343–356; Copeland, S. R., McCall, J., Williams, C. R., Guth, C., Carter, E. W., Fowler, S. E., Presley, J. A., & Hughes, C. (2002). High school peer buddies: It's a win-win situation. *Teaching Exceptional Children, 35*(1), 16–21.

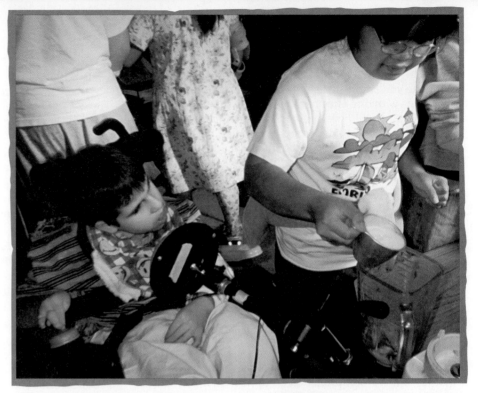

Even though Joshua does not receive most of his education with students who do not have disabilities, he is still a member of his school and benefits from his relationships with schoolmates who do not have disabilities; relationships and skill building go hand in hand.

What Can You Learn from Others Who Teach Students with Severe and Multiple Disabilities?

Learning for the Early Childhood Years: Circle of Inclusion

Some people have long believed that students with severe and multiple disabilities should only be in separate, special programs, those in which they have no typically developing peers. But research suggests a different conclusion. Researchers at The University of Kansas have developed and demonstrated a method for including infants, toddlers, and preschoolers with severe and multiple disabilities in typical programs (Thompson, Wegner, Wickham, & Ault, 1993; Thompson et al., 1991; Thompson, Wickham, Wegner, & Ault, 1996). Called the Circle of Inclusion, the program has been implemented in more than 20 preschool classrooms within 12 different early childhood programs (including two Head Start programs) and 10 K–3 programs. More than 600 typically developing children and 35 with severe and multiple disabilities have participated in the program.

What makes the Circle of Inclusion program effective? Not surprisingly, there are many factors:

▼ A value-based commitment to including children with significant disabilities in programs available to typically developing children, not a "fix-up-the-child" approach that requires the child to meet certain developmental milestones before being "rewarded" with an inclusive placement

▼ Friendships between young children with and without disabilities

▼ Collaboration among all parents and professionals

▼ Development of children's choice-making skills

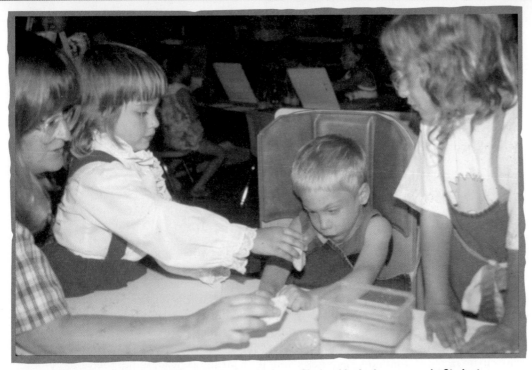

Raintree Montessori School in Lawrence, Kansas, takes a Circle of Inclusion approach. Students without disabilities "tutor" and thus learn from students with disabilities, such as this young boy.

▼ Use of the MAPs process

▼ Ongoing evaluation of how to make inclusion work

▼ Commitment to child-initiated, child-centered education grounded in developmentally appropriate practice

One of the original Circle of Inclusion programs took place at Raintree Montessori School's preschool in Lawrence, Kansas. There, students with disabilities, including students with severe and multiple disabilities, attend preschool and elementary grades with students who do not have disabilities. Indeed, enrollment places are reserved for children with identified disabilities, even though the school itself is so popular that it has long waiting lists of children without disabilities.

Raintree's students include Ginni, who has multiple disabilities. Nevertheless, she is an included student at Raintree. For example, her teacher, Pamela Shanks, incorporates partial participation and peer tutoring to make sure that Ginni participates at her level of skill with classmates who do not have disabilities.

How does Ginni communicate with her peers who do not have disabilities and even with her teachers, given that she has vision impairments and speech delays? She uses nonsymbolic language, commonly known as "body language." Not surprisingly, her peers without disabilities catch on quickly. There are, after all, many ways of communicating. Thus, she signals, "I'm afraid," or "You're in my space/face," by batting her eyes rapidly when her peers come too close to her. She turns her head away when she wants to say, "I've finished; go away, please." She raises her arm to point to objects or people she likes; and she even yawns deliberately to signal, "I'm bored with you or with what we are doing."

What do parents of children with disabilities think about Raintree? Annalise, the parent of one of those children, describes the school as "the best of both worlds. My son benefits from an inclusive setting and also has his entire special needs met. One boy [without a disability] has really taken my son under his wing. Having a wide age range in the class has been wonderful. The older children really look out for my son."

Companion
Website

To make a virtual visit to Raintree Montessori school, go to the Web Links module in Chapter 9 of the Companion Website.

The mother of Jordan, a typically developing student, points out that inclusion "increases his compassion" and notes that Jordan is learning to use sign language and regards his peers who use wheelchairs as "kids like him."

Do Circle of Inclusion programs really work? The resounding answer is yes. Ten years of research reveal that an inclusive program "offers a more desirable social and communicative environment for children with significant disabilities [than does a special education–only preschool] . . . and can match a high-quality special education program on environmental adaptations" (Thompson et al., 1996, p. 38). The students with severe and multiple disabilities learn to be part of the natural environment, just as IDEA's Part C requires.

Learning for the Elementary Years: Johnson City, New York, Central District

In the Johnson City, New York, Central District schools (where Joshua attends middle school and went to elementary school), two techniques contribute to an appropriate education with an emphasis on inclusion for students with severe and multiple disabilities. The first is collaborative problem solving (Salisbury, Evans, & Palombaro, 1997). Teachers were the first to learn to use collaborative problem solving; they then modeled it for their students. For example, Amy, a first grader, needs to spend 20 minutes each day in a prone standing device. This holds her in an upright position but keeps her from doing her desk work. How can she participate in class? Similarly, Rich has a double shunt in his head, so his doctor has prohibited him from participating in contact sports and baseball. How can gym classes be modified to include him?

The solutions to these problems came from a collaborative problem-solving process used by teachers and students alike (Salisbury et al., 1997). The process is fairly simple:

▼ Identify the problem.

▼ Generate possible solutions.

▼ Determine the feasibility of each solution.

▼ Choose a solution that maximizes inclusion.

▼ Evaluate the solution after it has been put into operation.

Engaging in problem solving with peers is a variation on peer tutoring: How can peers help find successful solutions?

Amy's classmates without disabilities suggested that she use the prone stander when all of the students are in the sharing-and-caring circle; they may be on a rug or sitting or standing in a circle, but Amy stands with them. Rich participates in gym as a helper; leads warmup activities; and gives "start/stop" directions that his physical therapist, physical education teacher, and peers have proposed and carried out.

As in the examples involving Amy and Rich, the students without disabilities called attention to situations in which their peers with disabilities were not participating with them; these challenges related to inclusion caused faculty and peers to engage in collaborative problem solving. The results were promising. Collaborative problem solving became a routine and then an integrated, normal process for the staff; it became intuitive. Increases in physical, social, and instructional inclusion occurred, in part because faculty and students themselves identified the problems and the solutions. The faculty came to value collaborative problem solving as a means to increase inclusion.

The second technique used in the Johnson City schools is called action research (Falvey, Eshilian, & Hibbard, 2000). **Action research** begins with teachers' data-based inquiry into problems and possible solutions. The inquiry is the basis for the teachers to implement solutions that they themselves propose. Although action research can be implemented in many different ways, the approach used in the Johnson City schools involves having a "critical friend"— not an employee of the school district—facilitate the action research process. In particular, this critical friend helps the staff collect data, analyze data, make sense of data, and act on it, all for the purposes of including particular students or making system-wide changes that enable all students with disabilities to be more included and more effectively educated (Salisbury, Wilson, Swartz,

Palombara, & Wassel, 1997). This approach involves the faculty: It's a bottom-up, not a top-down, approach. It assumes that the faculty know the problems they face and are ideally situated to design solutions. The results benefit the individual students; they also benefit the teachers, who now own the problem and its solution. Thus, they are committed to the change they institute.

Learning for the Middle and Secondary Years: Whittier High School, Los Angeles

As of the mid-1990s, Whittier High School in southeastern Los Angeles County served approximately 1,900 students in grades 9 through 12. Nearly three-quarters of the students were Hispanic/ Latino, about 18 percent had limited ability to speak English, and about 20 percent were from families who received welfare support (Eshilian et al., 2000; Falvey, Eshilian, & Hibbard, 2000; Thousand, Rosenberg, Bishop, & Villa, 1997).

Conscious that approximately 30 percent of its students dropped out before graduating and that only 10–15 percent of its graduates went to four-year colleges, and intent on implementing state-of-the-art inclusion, faculty members, staff, administration, parents, and community leaders adopted a mission statement that promotes academic excellence, respect for self and others, acceptance of the diversity of students' abilities and culture, involvement of all students in all aspects of the school, and a commitment that all students will reach their full potential. "All means all" at Whittier, including students with severe and multiple disabilities.

To improve the performance of students identified as having disabilities as well as those not performing at grade level academically but also not identified as having disabilities, students and faculty were divided into three teams at each grade level. Students remain in their team during their 9th and 10th-grade years. Each team consists of the following:

▼ Eight to 10 core curriculum/general education teachers certified in math, science, social studies, and English
▼ Two support teachers certified in special education
▼ An administrator
▼ A school counselor

The teams share a common preparation period, their classes are located near each other, all teachers are responsible for teaching all students, and the teams provide seven different levels of support for the students in each team. These levels of support enable the teams to individualize their instruction without having to pull out students from the classroom. The levels begin with total staff support (the most pervasive and extensive type, nearly a one-to-one approach), range through daily in-class staff support and team teaching (moderate levels of support), and end in consultation (the least amount of support).

This tiered approach relies on the talents of each teacher and on the talents of all of them together; and it benefits students who have received special education labels (including students with severe and multiple disabilities), students who have not qualified for special education services but are at risk of school failure, and students who have succeeded in traditional school systems. Whittier students do not carry special education labels; the support teachers are not called special education teachers; and the staff, by adopting this noncategorical approach, has discarded the idea that only specialists can work with students with disabilities.

The result of these many changes is that Whittier High School has developed a community of learners that supports all students. Does it actually work? Yes. José, a student with severe and multiple disabilities, uses a wheelchair; his friends makes sure he is wheeled from class to class each day. José works on recognizing numbers while most of his classmates study algebra. When it comes time for his math team to present its answer to an algebra problem, he writes the numbers (with help from his peers) on a poster using the lap tray attached to the front of his wheelchair as a desk.

Learning for Transitional and Postsecondary Years: Asbury College, Wilmore, Kentucky

Is it far-fetched to think that students with moderate and severe disabilities can attend college? You might think so, but you would be wrong. At least you would be if you were associated with Asbury College, a small liberal arts college in Wilmore, Kentucky, and with the Jessamine County Public Schools, located in the same county. Those two institutions have collaborated to ensure that, if they want to, high school students in their transition years can attend Asbury and receive high school credit through the College Connection Program (Hall, Kleinert, & Kearns, 2000).

The Jessamine schools have a longstanding commitment to educating students in inclusive settings, providing peer tutoring, and incorporating a functional curriculum. When the students and their parents shared through the MAPs process their great expectations of having postsecondary education and when they said they wanted the opportunity for friendships with college students who do not have disabilities, the students, their families, and their teachers turned, quite naturally, to Asbury because Asbury students have had their practicum experiences in the county schools and many of the college's graduates work in the school system.

For the seven students, ages 18 to 21, who began this unusual postsecondary program, the College Connection Program's orientation to the college was essential. It included excursions to the campus, meetings with college students, opportunities to exercise at the physical education center, and meetings with faculty and careful selection of classes. The classes included an introduction to social work, family studies, education technology, ecology, radio production, and various physical education/recreation classes. Their instruction was individualized through the joint efforts of teachers from the public schools and the college faculty.

The initial results were impressive. The high school students learned some necessary skills (for example, using the computer in the class on educational technology) and carried out various therapies (strength development and gross-motor skills in physical education). Just as important, they expanded their relationships with college students, participated in college-community events (e.g., students' annual Christmas caroling through town), increased their recreational opportunities (using the college's gym and attending its athletic events), had vocational training and even acquired for-pay jobs at the college, and learned age-appropriate "typical" communication and social skills.

Recent program expansion has taken the College Connection Program to a whole new level. The program has moved from a public school–based program that brought students to campus for various periods of time to a totally campus-based program. The school bus brings the students directly to campus, and their day begins and ends at Asbury.

Curriculum offerings have also greatly expanded. Spanish, children's literature, elementary math methods, theater, theater design and production, earth science, and psychology are a sampling of new course offerings. Students are also now expected to participate in service learning and community service projects, just like any other Asbury student.

The expansion in the academic arena has been a two-way street. The high school's special education teacher is an adjunct faculty member at Asbury and frequently lectures and team-teaches with college faculty in classes about exceptional learners and math methods. Campus job opportunities for Connection students also continue to expand and include work in the cafeteria, college post office, education curriculum laboratory, and athletic center. Students who complete the program often receive offers to continue in the competitive employment situation they held as students.

The creation of JAM (Jessamine/Asbury Mix) has provided a setting for interaction between Connection and college students in campus social life. Pizza parties, swimming, theater, concerts, athletic events, and some "just plain crazy" activities enrich Connection students' lives. Asbury students have learned that a major part of their education for life is knowing when and how to change their attitudes about others. That lesson is perhaps the most important one they will learn, for it will endure as the college students become community leaders, teachers, employers, and neighbors of people with disabilities.

Have the Jessamine schools and Asbury reached the end of the road? No, there is more to do. Just imagine students with severe disabilities living in the dorms, enjoying spring break, and even

When preparing students for transition, collaboration is important not only among professionals within the same educational setting but also between professionals in different educational settings in preparing students for transition.

On the companion website, you will find guidelines for how similar postsecondary programs can be set up with joint efforts between high schools and colleges.

Asbury College opens its doors and classes to students with severe disabilities.

sharing some of the college's international field placements. Recently, one Connection student accompanied a team of Asbury students on a spring break trip to a developing country. He participated in a humanitarian work project to rebuild a dilapidated school and worked at a children's home, where many of the children have disabilities.

Each success challenges participants to continue to dream. Those dreams are not far-fetched because the schools, the students with disabilities, the college students, the college faculty, and the entire community have learned that, without great expectations, nothing happens. But with great expectations, an inviting environment, and the right techniques, nothing is impossible.

A Vision for Joshua's Future

What does Joshua's future hold? The hardest times seem to be over: Joshua's health has improved, and he is surrounded by people who care about him: his parents, his brother and sister, a talented teacher, a host of professionals at C. Fred Johnson Middle School, and the professionals at the Broome Developmental Center.

But the past is a prologue. Moreover, as Alan says, "Anything Joshua does [since fighting his way back from his illness] is remarkable." So let us imagine Joshua a decade from now.

As a 20-year-old, he is in his last year at the Johnson City schools. He has mastered the control switch and now uses it to regulate his immediate environment. He turns the heat or air conditioning on or off and sets the degree of temperature that he wants. He remote-starts a small "jam box" to hear the voices of his family and the music he likes. His sister, Vanessa, has entered her freshman year at college; but she and Joshua communicate by e-mail: Joshua selects boilerplate paragraphs about himself and sends them to her, using the newest version of his switch. Ryan is a junior in high school, the same school that Joshua has been attending for several years. To no one's surprise, least of all Ryan's, Joshua is a well known and well liked member of the senior class. And come graduation day in June, Joshua will line up with his classmates, come across the stage of the high school, and receive his diploma from the superintendent.

By relying on innovative curriculum, methods of instruction, and assistive technology, Joshua's teachers, related-service providers, staff at the Broome Developmental Center, and father and stepmother have found work for him to do. Using computer software that Joshua "talks" to by remote-switch commands and that is programmed to accept his commands, Joshua actually places orders for the supplies his father needs to carry out his business as a carpentry contractor. Joshua's orders are relayed to a local wholesaler of wood and other supplies but not until Alan's business manager checks their accuracy. Even Alan's most far-fetched hopes for Joshua did not include this scenario: that Joshua would work for his dad after graduating from school. But as Alan has to remind himself, Joshua has always been a surprising son.

What Would You Recommend?

1. As Joshua learns at his own pace, how can his peers without disabilities support him while they receive their education at their own pace?
2. How would you coordinate his school-based team, developmental center team, and family for long-range planning and short-term, immediate communication?
3. How would you enable Joshua to participate in school leisure and recreation activities and learn to use his adapted assistive technology for employment purposes?

Summary

How Do You Recognize Students with Severe and Multiple Disabilities?

▼ The term *severe and multiple disabilities* defines a diverse group of people, and no single definition satisfies all occurrences. IDEA has two separate definitions, one for multiple disabilities and one for severe disabilities.

▼ Characteristics related to students with severe and multiple disabilities include impairments associated with intellectual functioning, adaptive skills, motor development, sensory functioning, health care needs, and communication.

▼ The prevalence data vary, but there are very few students with severe and multiple disabilities (0.18 percent of all students in the United States served under IDEA).

▼ Etiology is unknown in 40 percent of this population. The majority of known causes are prenatal biomedical factors, which include chromosomal abnormalities, genetic metabolic disorders, developmental disorders of brain formation, and environmental influences. In addition, complications during and after birth can account for severe and multiple disabilities.

▼ Some severe and multiple disabilities are preventable through medical technology, maternal education, genetic counseling, and fetal surgery.

How Do You Evaluate Students with Severe and Multiple Disabilities?

▼ Screening tests such as the Apgar are used by physicians to determine the type and extent of the disability. The evaluation process usually begins right after birth and may continue for several years.

▼ While controversial with this population, IQ tests and adaptive behavior scales are most often used to make classification decisions.

▼ Ecological assessments determine what functional skills a student needs to participate successfully in preferred environments.

How Do You Assure Progress in the General Curriculum?

▼ Almost half the students with severe and multiple disabilities are educated in separate classes; 30 percent are educated in separate schools, residential facilities, and home/hospitals; and another 25 percent are educated in general education classrooms/resource rooms.

▼ Research indicates that it is possible for students with severe and multiple disabilities to be successfully included in learning new skills in general education classrooms and experiencing successful friendships.

▼ Partial participation enables students with severe and multiple disabilities to participate to the extent that they are able to in classroom tasks by adapting skill sequences, adapting rules, using personal assistance, and using materials and technology.

▼ Peer tutoring has been used successfully in dyads and on a classwide basis to improve the achievement of students with severe and multiple disabilities.

What Can You Learn from Others Who Teach Students with Severe and Multiple Disabilities?

▼ More than 20 preschool programs have successfully included infants, toddlers, and preschoolers with severe and multiple disabilities through the Circle of Inclusion program.

▼ The Johnson City, New York, schools provide an excellent model of inclusion and collaboration through collaborative problem solving and action research.

▼ Whittier High School in Los Angeles made significant positive changes for students with disabilities part of a schoolwide improvement plan. Negative special education labels were removed, and all students were grouped heterogeneously.

▼ Students with severe and multiple disabilities can have inclusive opportunities on college campuses, as evidenced by the partnership between Asbury College and the Jessamine County public schools in Wilmore, Kentucky.

▼ Collaboration among professionals, families, and students is especially important in promoting the success of inclusion for students with severe and multiple disabilities.

Council for Exceptional Children   **PRAXIS**

To find out how and where this chapter content connects to the CEC Professional Standards and the Praxis™ Standards, go to the Standards Connection module in Chapter 9 of the Companion Website. A comprehensive matrix aligning CEC Professional Standards, Praxis™ Standards, and INTASC principles to the entire text, is available in the Appendix and on the Companion Website.

Chapter 10

Who Is Jeremy Jones?

The Kansas City metropolitan area consists of two cities—Kansas City, Kansas, and Kansas City, Missouri—that are divided by the wide Missouri River. Within this area live nearly a million people; most do not live in the two cities but in some twenty or so identifiable suburbs. A ring of interstate and state highways encircles greater Kansas City; and those highways and lesser boulevards, avenues, roads, streets, alleys, and lanes also transect the area. The interstates lead north to Des Moines; east to St. Louis and Washington, DC; south to Little Rock and Oklahoma City; west to Denver and Los Angeles; southwest to Houston; and southeast to Atlanta.

Jeremy Jones, age 13, knows his way around the entire Kansas City area and how to get from "KC" to any of those cities, or nearly anywhere else for that matter. With fierce determination and increasing energy, he spends some of this class time drawing accurate maps of the interstate and local highways and other thoroughfares. With confidence born of certain

knowledge, he asks, in a voice pitching lower with each month of adolescence, "Where were you born?" A teacher answers, "Topeka, Kansas." A speech therapist offers, "New Orleans." In a matter of seconds and with excitement that makes his hands shake (until he puts pencil to paper), he draws the map that will lead you there, city to city, interstates all the way. Between his cartographic excursions, he asks for simple school supplies: "Wal-Mart . . . Black Bic pens . . . Crayola supertips . . . markers . . . Papermate's Suspension pen . . . number 2 pencils . . . yellow pads . . . lined paper . . . three-ring notebooks . . . atlas of the USA."

Seemingly out of nowhere, he raises his right arm (his left hand holds fast to his pencil) and, upon being recognized by his teacher, exclaims: "Hands to self . . . don't touch others . . . not cool . . . no suspension, no discipline." Then, as if to make sure

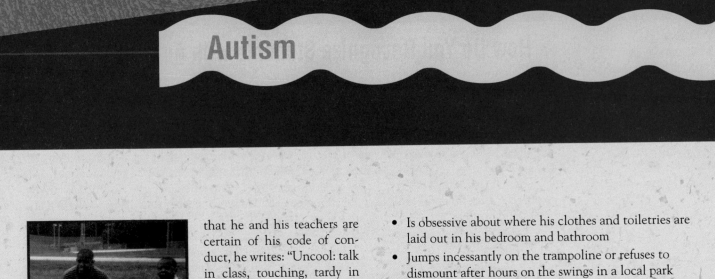

Autism

that he and his teachers are certain of his code of conduct, he writes: "Uncool: talk in class, touching, tardy in class, bad words."

What is surprising about Jeremy? Is it his skills in mapping? Yes, they are rather high for a boy who has autism and lives in the inner city of KC-Kansas. Are they at a level that makes him truly gifted? No, but they are considerable. Is it also remarkable that he will rehearse his social skills: Do not interrupt; raise your hand; wait to be called on; speak in a calm voice; keep your hands to yourself? No, because Jeremy and his teachers at Central Middle School, Kansas City, Kansas, together with a team of researchers at The University of Kansas, have been working on those skills, not just for Jeremy but also for all students at Central as part of an effort to ensure that schools are safe for everyone's learning. For Jeremy and other Central students, teachers applied a technique called *positive behavior support* on universal, group, and individual bases. By creating schoolwide commitment to positive behavior support and demonstrating that it helps all students, they have ensured that Jeremy—the only student with autism at Central—is included in and is progressing through the general curriculum.

At Mt. Calvary Baptist Church, where his mother, Joyce, sings in the choir and his father, Richard, teaches Sunday School, Jeremy sometimes joins the choir. His favorite music (gospel has replaced jazz) starts him grinning. Richard believes Jeremy is having one of his epiphany moments—a time when Jeremy obtains a religious knowledge that belies his limited intelligence.

Both at home and at school, when Jeremy's brain knows the word he wants to say but his mouth won't form it, Jeremy spells it out or simply claims victory over the intellectual challenge by declaring, "My brain is tired."

Is Jeremy over the hump of that mountain called autism? Hardly. He still

- Chews his pencils and pens
- Rocks powerfully on his family's furniture, testing its resiliency to the breaking point

- Is obsessive about where his clothes and toiletries are laid out in his bedroom and bathroom
- Jumps incessantly on the trampoline or refuses to dismount after hours on the swings in a local park
- Fixates on oscillating fans
- Surfs the TV in search of weather reports
- Remains aloof from his peers at school

His repertoire of behaviors is mixed—some problematic, others not. He still exhibits some aggression (breaking the fan or putting pencils through window screens) and self-injurious behavior (biting his hands and biting his fingernails until they seem to disappear entirely). He still insists on routines and predictability, a prisoner of the school calendar and of his immediate personal history. But he has a powerful long-term memory for people, their names and faces, and their places of birth; and he is a superb cartographer-to-be.

What do you think?

1. How would you support Jeremy so that he can continue to be successfully included throughout middle and high school?
2. Given Jeremy's strengths, what options might exist for enjoyable extracurricular activities and career development?
3. How might successful approaches in encouraging Jeremy's appropriate behavior at school also be useful as he participates in the church choir?

To respond to these questions online, participate in other activities, and learn more about Jeremy Jones and autism, go to the Cases module in Chapter 10 of the Companion Website.

How Do You Recognize Students with Autism?

Defining Autism

According to IDEA, autism is a developmental disability that significantly affects a student's verbal and nonverbal communication, social interaction, and education performance. It is generally evident before age 3. Autism's characteristics include engagement in repetitive activities and stereotyped movements, resistance to environmental change or changes in daily routines, and unusual responses to sensory experiences. Under IDEA, a student cannot be classified as having autism if the student's educational performance is adversely affected primarily by a serious emotional disturbance (34 C.F.R., Part 300, § 300.7[b] [1]).

Autism is a severe form of a broader group of disorders referred to as *pervasive developmental disorders* (Lord & Risi, 2000; Nickel, 2000; Tsai, 2000). As defined in the *Diagnostic and Statistical Manual of Mental Disorders*, pervasive developmental disorders include a cluster of five disorders that have their onset in childhood (American Psychiatric Association, 2000). These five disorders include Autistic Disorder, Rett's Disorder, Childhood Disintegrative Disorder, Asperger's Disorder, and Pervasive Developmental Disorder Not Otherwise Specified. Sometimes teachers use the term **autism spectrum disorder,** referring to some or all of these five disorders. That term, however, is not precisely defined in the *Diagnostic and Statistical Manual of Mental Disorders* (American Psychiatric Association, 2000).

In this chapter we will concentrate on **autism** because it has the highest prevalence of the five disorders and is the one you will encounter most frequently in school settings. We also will address some issues related to Asperger's Disorder, also known as Asperger Syndrome in the special education literature. Asperger Syndrome describes individuals with significant challenges in social and emotional functioning but without significant delays in language development or intellectual functioning (Klin, Volkmar, & Sparrow, 2000; Myles, Barnhill, Hagiwara, Griswold, & Simpson, 2001; Safran, 2002).

To learn more about Asperger Syndrome, go to the Web Links module in Chapter 10 of the Companion Website to link to Tony Atwood's information and support web page on Asperger Syndrome.

Describing the Characteristics

Autism is associated with seven distinct characteristics: (1) language development, (2) social development, (3) repetitive behavior, (4) problem behavior, (5) the need for environmental predictability, (6) sensory and movement disorders, and (7) intellectual functioning.

Language Development

Students with autism have a broad range of language abilities, ranging from no verbal communication to quite complex communication (Kjelgaard & Tager-Flusberg, 2001; Wetherby, Prizant, & Schuler, 2000). They usually have a number of language impairments. Two common ones are (1) delayed language and (2) echolalia.

Delayed Language. Although in the past it was expected that only about 50 percent of individuals with autism would eventually develop useful speech (Prizant, 1983), this expectation has proven to be low. Researchers now predict that as many as 85 to 90 percent of children with autism can learn verbal communication through state-of-the-art teaching and motivational approaches if they begin their education before age 5 (Koegel, 2000).

Children with autism often have limited communication skills. The quality of their communication often

▼ Focuses attention on one topic only

▼ Limits a communication topic to fewer than a couple of interactions

▼ Uses limited gestures to supplement their verbal skills

▼ Reverses pronouns (For example, the student may look at his teacher and say, "You want have a snack now," meaning that he, not the teacher, wants a snack.)

▼ Looks away from the speaker rather than maintains eye contact (Carpenter & Tomasello, 2000; National Research Council, 2001; Prizant, Schuler, Wetherby, & Rydell, 1997)

Echolalia.   **Echolalia** is a form of communication in which a student echoes other people's language by constantly repeating a portion of what he or she hears (Prizant, Wetherby, & Rydell, 2000). This type of communication tends to happen with almost all young children who are beginning to talk, whether they have autism or not; but usually it begins to disappear around the age of 3. Some people with autism, however, may have echolalia throughout their lives.

Echolalia is either immediate or delayed (Prizant & Rydell, 1984). Students who engage in immediate echolalia may repeat what they have just heard because they are unaware of an appropriate response. Delayed echolalia includes verbal repetitions that a student has previously heard during periods of time ranging from a few minutes previously to many years ago.

Some specialists have described echolalia as speech that is repeated in an automatic manner without having communicative intent (Howlin, 1982). Intervention procedures, based on this view, give children the command "Don't echo" to eliminate echolalia (Lovass, 1977).

Rather than subscribing to the traditional view that echolalia does not have communicative intent (Howlin, 1982), communication specialists increasingly believe that children and youth with autism may use echolalia to communicate a desire for the attention of their listener, to fill the silence in a communication exchange, to make a request, to indicate affirmation, to protest the actions of others, to provide information, or to accomplish any of those results (Prizant & Rydell, 1984; Rydell & Prizant, 1995).

Social Development

Atypical social development, characterized by delays in social interaction and social skills, is one hallmark of autism (National Research Council, 2001; Volkmar, Carter, Grossman, & Klin, 1997). The following four criteria are related to the social development of individuals with autism (American Psychiatric Association, 2000):

▼ Impaired use of nonverbal behavior

▼ Lack of peer relationships

▼ Failure to spontaneously share enjoyment, interests, and achievements with others

▼ Lack of reciprocity

One explanation for this kind of delayed social development seems to be that individuals with autism do not understand that their own beliefs, desires, and intentions may differ from those of others. This impairment is referred to as **theory of mind** (Perner, 1993; Twachtman-Cullen, 2000; Waterhouse & Fein, 1997). Impairments in a student's theory of mind often make it difficult for the student to form reciprocal relationships with others. For example, Jeremy has distressed many people by running up to them, touching them, or even hugging them. What he seeks is their friendship; what he provokes is their alarm, fear, or hostility. Only when the hugged person knows him well does he receive affection and friendship. What Jeremy knows is that he likes to be hugged; what he does not know is that others generally don't want to hug or be hugged, especially if they do not know him. Because he and his classmates simply do not have the same theory of mind, his social networks are smaller than he, his teachers, and his family want them to be. Research has produced a range of successful instructional strategies for supporting students to improve their social interaction (Hwang & Hughes, 2000; National Research Council, 2001; Rogers, 2000).

Social interaction is particularly problematic for students with Asperger Syndrome (Church, Alisanski, & Amanullah, 2000; Marks, Schrader, Longaker, & Levine, 2000; Myles et al., 2001). Social interaction problems include hyperactivity, atypical behavior as compared to the behavior of others, verbal aggression, withdrawal, and depression. Depression has been found to be a frequent problem for these students, and increased depression is associated with a tendency for students to blame negative events and social failures on their own ability and effort (Barnhill, 2001b; Barnhill & Myles, in press).

Later in the chapter, you will learn how two instructional strategies—positive behavior support and social stories—help students such as Jeremy develop appropriate social interactions.

Repetitive Behavior

Repetitive behavior involves inappropriate acts that include obsessions, tics, and perseveration. **Obsessions** are persistent thoughts, impulses, or images of a repetitive nature that create anxiety. **Tics** are involuntary, rapid movements that occur without warning. **Perseveration** includes verbalizations or behaviors that are repeated to an inappropriate extent. For instance, Jeremy is adamant about how his clothes and toilet articles are to be stored, and he perseverates about maps and Wal-Mart stores: "Do you know how to get to. . . .? Have you been to the Wal-Mart at Bannister Mall? To the Wal-Mart at Oakridge? To the Wal-Mart at . . . ?", adding the names of the innumerable shopping centers in the greater Kansas City area.

Repetitive acts involve repeated movements as well as repeated verbalization. Repeated movements include rocking back and forth, twirling objects, and/or waving fingers in front of the face. Jeremy's bouncing on a trampoline or dismounting from a swing only after hours of being on it are not so destructive as his constant jumping up and down on his bed, requiring his parents to replace the bed nearly every 6 months. For many years, professionals believed that these repetitive behaviors did not have any constructive purpose. Increasingly, however, researchers are discovering that repetitive behaviors are often attempts to communicate boredom and agitation or to regulate one's own level of awareness (Carr et al., 1994).

Nonetheless, these behaviors do interfere with students' ability to learn and often inhibit their successful inclusion in typical work, school, and community settings. Decreasing repetitive behaviors, however, is not sufficient; students also can benefit from learning more appropriate forms of communication, social skills, and leisure activities (Carr et al., 1994; Quill, 1995; Rogers, 2000; Weiss & Harris, 2001).

Problem Behavior

IDEA requires schools to consider using positive behavior support (which we discuss later in this chapter) when students have problem behavior that impedes their learning or the learning of others. Four categories of problem behavior in students with autism are self-injurious behavior, aggression, tantrums, and property destruction. We will focus on the first two.

Self-Injurious Behavior. Some individuals have self-injurious behavior, such as head banging, biting (for example, Jeremy bites his hand and his fingernails), or scratching (Mace & Mauk, 1999). These behaviors often persist into adulthood and create continuing demands for support from families and care providers (Ruble & Dalrymple, 1996). Individuals with severe self-injurious behaviors may permanently injure themselves; sometimes and usually for only a few

Regardless of Jeremy's autism, he still enjoys many leisure activities along with most students his age.

people, self-injurious behaviors are life-threatening. One of those life-threatening behaviors is called pica—eating nonedibles. For Jeremy, pica is manifested when he chews on pencils and swallows some of the wood splinters.

Aggression.   Aggressive behaviors are similar to self-injurious behaviors, but the behavior is directed toward others. Aggressive behaviors can be problematic in all settings. The principles of positive behavior support (which we describe later in this chapter) enable students to learn a wider repertoire of appropriate behaviors. Once they learn appropriate alternative behaviors, students often find it unnecessary to engage in aggressive behaviors.

Problem behaviors can serve a communicative function, enabling the student to obtain something positive, avoid or escape something unpleasant, increase or decrease sensory stimulation, or achieve two or more of these results (Carr & Durand, 1985). Some researchers have predicted that as many as 75 to 80 percent of problem behaviors may have a communicative function (Derby et al., 1992; Iwata et al., 1994). Given the functions that problem behavior serves, your role becomes one of teaching the student other ways to communicate these same intentions (Chandler & Dahlquist, 2002; Horner, Albin, Sprague, & Todd, 2000).

Later in the chapter, you will learn how to conduct a functional assessment to determine how a student's behavior is a form of communication.

Need for Environmental Predictability

Predictability and structure are important sources of security for many individuals with autism (Dalrymple, 1995; Lewis & Bodfish, 1998). When their predictability and structure are interrupted by events such as school vacations, overnight stays of friends or extended family, the celebration of holidays, a change in television schedules, or a move from one classroom to another, students often experience a high degree of anxiety. In addition, "things in their place" mean a great deal to some students. Most of us do not think much about whether the telephone is straight on a desk, whether the cosmetics are always in the same place on the bathroom counter, or whether a door is open or closed. These sorts of seemingly insignificant environmental patterns, however, disturb many students with autism to such a degree that the patterns impede their learning.

Various classroom supports can enable students to experience more predictability. The supports include schedules, routines, and strategies for accepting some change (Earles, Carlson, & Bock, 1998; McClannahan & Krantz, 1999). For example, students who do not read might use picture schedules to outline the schedule of the different activities or classroom periods they will have each day. Students who have higher cognitive abilities may find that both daily and weekly work schedules are helpful.

Later in the chapter, you will learn about social stories and how they can help students understand more about their schedules and routines.

Routines also enable students to understand when things will occur. For example, some students need to have activities that are almost always associated with the same time of day or the same day of the week. Because that kind of highly regular routine can create a problem when those times need to change, many students require instruction and support in learning to accept schedule changes. You might find it helpful to let students know in advance when there will be a change and when schedules and routines will return to the typical schedule. ("We will not have music this afternoon because there is a special school program. You will get to go to music again next Tuesday afternoon. You can look forward to having music and fun then.")

Sensory and Movement Disorders

Between 42 percent and 88 percent of children and youth with autism and Asperger Syndrome have sensory and movement disorders (Anzalone & Williamson, 2000; Dunn, Myles, & Orr, 2000; National Research Council, 2001). Some have under- or overresponsiveness to sensory stimuli, although more have overresponsiveness (National Research Council, 2001; Talay-Ongan & Wood, 2000). Temple Grandin (1997), who was identified as having autism as a child and then Asperger Syndrome as an adult, is now one of the most successful designers of livestock equipment in the world. In Box 10–1, she describes some typical problems with overresponsiveness to sensory stimuli as well as some practical solutions. Notably, individuals with Asperger Syndrome have more significant impairments in their responses to sensory stimuli than do individuals with autism (Rinner, 2000).

Movement disorders also are associated with autism (Dawson & Watling, 2000; Donnellan, 1999; National Research Council, 2001). Examples include abnormal posture; abnormal

To learn about Temple Grandin's livestock equipment designs, go to the Web Links module in Chapter 10 of the Companion Website for a link to her website.

Box 10–1

Temple Grandin: Diagnosed as Having Autism as a Child

- As an adult I find it difficult to determine exactly when I should break into a conversation. I cannot follow the rhythmic give and take of conversation. People have told me that I often interrupt, and I still have difficulty determining where the pauses are.

- Noise was a major problem for me. When I was confronted with loud or confusing noise, I could not modulate it. I either had to shut it all out and withdraw or let it all in like a freight train.

- I think a classroom should be quiet and free from distracting noises, such as a high-pitched vent fan. Some teachers have found that disturbing noises can be blocked out with headphones and music. When a child has to make a trip to a busy shopping center, a headset with a favorite tape can help make the trip more peaceful.

- I often misbehaved in church and screamed because my Sunday clothes felt different—scratchy petticoats drove me crazy; a feeling that would be insignificant to most people may feel like sand paper rubbing the skin raw to an autistic child. . . . Most people habituate to different types of clothes, but I keep feeling them for hours.

- Calming sensory activities immediately prior to school lessons or speech therapy may help to improve learning. These activities should be conducted as fun games.

- Abstract concepts such as getting along with people have to have a visual image. For example, my visual image for relationships with people was a sliding glass door. If you push it too hard it will break. To make the abstract concept more real, I would sometimes act it out—for example, by walking through a real sliding door.

- At puberty I was desperate for relief from the "nerves." . . . At my aunt's ranch, I observed that the cattle sometimes appeared to relax when they were held in the squeeze chute, a device for holding cattle for veterinary procedures. The animal is held tightly between two sides, which squeeze the body. After a horrible bout of the "nerves" I got in the squeeze chute. For about 45 minutes I was much calmer. I then built a squeeze-chute-like device which I could use to apply pressure (which I controlled). . . . I have made a successful career based on my fixation with cattle squeeze chutes. I have designed livestock handling systems for major ranches and meat companies all over the world. When I was in high school, many of my teachers and psychologists wanted to get rid of my fixation on cattle chutes. I am indebted to Mr. Carlock, my high school science teacher. He suggested that I read psychology journals and study so I could learn why the cattle chute had a relaxing effect. If my fixation had been taken away, I could have ended up in an institution. Do not confuse fixations with stereotyped behavior, such as hand flapping or rocking. A fixation is an interest in something external that should be diverted and used to motivate.

Note: From "Teaching Tips From a Recovered Autistic" by T. Grandin, 1988, *Focus on Autistic Behavior*, 3(1). Copyright 1988 by PRO-ED, Inc. Reprinted by permission.

To learn about the Autism National Committee and Advocacy Organization and explore the sensory and movement challenges of autism, go to the Web Links module in Chapter 10 of the Companion Website.

movements of the face, head, trunk, and limbs; abnormal eye movements; repeated gestures and mannerisms; and awkward gait (Leary & Hill, 1996). Motor clumsiness and disorders are also present in the majority of individuals who have Asperger Syndrome (Barnhill, 2001b). Movement disorders can be detected in infants as young as 4 to 6 months of age and sometimes they can be detected at birth (Teitelbaum, Teitelbaum, Nye, Fryman, & Maurer, 1998).

Intellectual Functioning

Autism occurs in children with all levels of intelligence, ranging from those who are gifted to those who have mental retardation. Approximately 20 percent of individuals with autism have normal intelligence, 30 percent have mild to moderate intellectual impairments (mental retardation), and 42 percent have severe to profound intellectual impairments (mental retardation)(Fombonne, 1999).

Individuals with Asperger Syndrome tend to have higher intellectual functioning than do individuals with autism (Volkmar, Klin, & Cohen, 1997). Their IQ scores tend to fall in the average range and to reveal a frequency distribution similar to that of the general population (Barnhill, Hagiwara, Myles, & Simpson, 2000).

Some people with autism also display the savant syndrome. **Savant syndrome** is an unusual condition in which individuals display extraordinary abilities in areas such as calendar calculating, musical ability, mathematical skills, memorization, and mechanical abilities (Kelly, Macaruso, & Sokol, 1997; Miller, 1999; Saloviita, Ruusila, & Ruusila, 2000). For example, a student with savant syndrome may be able to recite the baseball game scores and the batting averages of all games and players who have ever participated in the major leagues. A familiar example of savant ability is the betting calculations of Raymond in the movie *Rain Man*. But students' unusual ability in these areas also occurs in conjunction with low ability in most other areas (Cheatham, Smith, Rucker, Polloway, & Lewis, 1995; Nettelbeck & Young, 1996). It is not likely that Jeremy would be classified as having the savant syndrome, despite his cartography skills, because those skills are not terribly refined.

Identifying the Causes

Historical Perspective on Causes

When autism was diagnosed in the early 1940s, parents of children with autism were often regarded as intelligent people of high socioeconomic status who were also "cold." At that time, incredibly, mothers of children with autism became known as "refrigerator mothers."

By the 1970s, research established that autism is caused by brain or biochemical dysfunction before, during, or after birth and that it is totally unwarranted to blame parents. In 1977 the National Society for Autistic Children (now known as the Autism Society of America) asserted, "No known factors in the psychological environment of a child have been shown to cause autism." Today, parents are not seen as the cause of problems; they are seen as collaborators, as contributors to the solution of problems—a topic we will discuss later in this chapter.

Biomedical Causes

There is broad agreement that autism is caused by abnormalities in brain development, neurochemistry, and genetic factors (Akshoomoff, 2000; Towbin, Mauk, & Batshaw, 2002; Tsai, 2000). The current focus of biomedical research is on the normal and atypical development of the central nervous system and the genetic and biological influences that lead to autism. A particular focus is on how genes influence the formation of brain structures, including pathways and synapses that relate to behavioral regulation (Cohen & Volkmar, 1997). An international network of 10 collaborative research programs sponsored by the National Institutes of Health has been organized to identify subgroups within autism; to find causes for each; and to develop effective biological, behavioral, and/or alternative treatments (Bristol, McIlvane, & Alexander, 1998).

Identifying the Prevalence

The prevalence rate for autism is 7.5 children in every 10,000 (Fombonne, 2000). The prevalence of autism has increased over the past 15 years. Rates tend to be higher among students during elementary and secondary school years than in preschool years, probably because of more precise identification. Males outnumber females by approximately 4 to 1. During the 1998–1999 school year, the U.S. Department of Education (2000) reported that 53,561 students with autism were served by the schools. The prevalence rate for Asperger Syndrome is far less than autism's— 1.9 children in every 10,000 (National Research Council, 2001).

How Do You Evaluate Students with Autism?

Determining the Presence

Diagnosing autism is a complex process. Many children receive the initial diagnosis of autism from a physician or a nondiscriminatory evaluation team, typically during their early childhood

To learn about the many advocacy and public information activities of the Autism Society of America, go to the Web Links module in Chapter 10 of the Companion Website.

To learn about the international research program in autism, go to the Web Links module in Chapter 10 of the Companion Website for a link to the National Institute on Child Health and Human Development.

years. Evaluators usually administer some of the same tests given to students with mental retardation and students with severe and multiple disabilities. The criteria for determining whether a child has autism include speech and language (applied by 18 states), academic achievement (applied by 15 states), cognitive functioning (applied by 14 states), and medical physical status (applied by 14 states) (Conderman & Katsiyannis, 1996, p. 32). Figure 10–1 highlights the standard techniques used for observations, screening, and nondiscriminatory evaluation.

Various diagnostic tools can detect the presence of autism. One is the Autism Diagnostic Interview—Revised (Lord, 1997; Lord et al., 1997; Lord, Rutter, & Le Couteur, 1994). This semi-structured interview is administered by a professional to caregivers of children and adults suspected of having autism. The interview takes about 1½ hours and covers family characteristics, communication, social development and play, repetitive and restrictive behaviors, and general behavior problems. This tool differentiates between children and youth who have autism and those who have mental retardation.

Determining the Nature and Extent of General and Special Education and Related Services

In Chapter 12, you will learn about ecological assessment and why it benefits students with severe and multiple disabilities. Not surprisingly, ecological assessment is a valuable tool for students with autism. One especially useful ecological assessment is known as **functional assessment.** A functional assessment identifies specific relationships between a student's behaviors and the circumstances that trigger those behaviors, especially those that impede a student's ability to learn (Chandler & Dahlquist, 2002; Cunningham & O'Neill, 2000; Dunlap, Newton, Fox, Benito, & Vaughn, 2001; Schwartz, Boulware, McBride, & Sandall, 2001). Although functional assessment is helpful for many students, regardless of their specific category of exceptionality, it is particularly apt for students with autism.

You will use these basic steps when you conduct a functional assessment:

1. Describe as precisely as possible the nature of the behaviors that are impeding the student's learning or the learning of others.
2. Gather information from teachers, family members, the student, related service providers, and any other individuals who have extensive firsthand knowledge about the circumstances that are regularly associated with the occurrence and nonoccurrence of the problem behavior. Determine as specifically as possible the events that occur before, during, and after the student's appropriate and inappropriate behavior.
3. Determine why the student engages in the problem behavior. What is the student trying to accomplish through the problem behavior? What is the student

When we discuss middle and secondary school programs later in this chapter, we will describe Jeremy's functional assessment and link you to our Companion Website so you can study excerpts from his functional assessment and behavior intervention plan.

Although functional behavioral assessment is helpful for many students, it is particularly beneficial for students with autism. Here, teachers and a student discuss why a student behaves in ways that impede her education.

FIGURE 10–1
Evaluating whether a student has autism

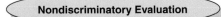

Nondiscriminatory Evaluation

Observation

Medical or psychological professionals and parents observe	Child is challenged by social conversations, does not play with others, is frequently unresponsive to voices, may exhibit echolalia or other unusual speech patterns, usually has language development delays, is disrupted by changes in daily routine, has difficulty sleeping, or engages in stereotypical behaviors.

Screening

Assessment measures	Findings that indicate need for further evaluation
Physical examinations	Physician notes that child is not reaching developmental milestones, especially in areas of social and language development. The child's physical health is usually normal. The physician may refer the child to a psychiatrist or psychologist for further evaluation.
Psychological evaluations	The child meets the *Diagnostic Standards Manual-IV* criteria for autism, including (1) qualitative impairment in social interaction, (2) qualitative impairment in communication, and (3) restricted repetitive and stereotyped patterns of behavior.

Prereferral

The student is usually identified before starting school. In rare circumstances in which the student is not identified before starting school, the severity of the disability may preclude the use of prereferral.

Referral

Children with autism should be referred by medical personnel or parents for early intervention during the infancy/preschool years. The child is referred upon reaching school age.

Nondiscriminatory evaluation procedures and standards

Assessment measures	Findings that suggest autism
Individualized intelligence test	Seventy-five percent of students with autism perform two or more standard deviations below the mean, indicating mental retardation. Others have average or even gifted intelligence. Evaluating intelligence is generally difficult because of challenging social and language behaviors.
Individualized achievement tests	Students with autism who have average or above-average intelligence may perform at an average or above-average level in one or more areas of achievement. Some individuals with autism have unusual giftedness in one or more areas. Students with autism typically have below-average intelligence.
Adaptive behavior scales	The student usually scores significantly below average in areas of adaptive behavior, indicating severe deficits in skills such as communication, daily living, socialization, gross- and fine-motor coordination, and socially appropriate behavior.
Autism-specific scales	The student's scores meet the criteria for identifying the student as having autism.
Direct observation	The student's self-initiated interactions with teacher and peers are limited. The student exhibits language delays and may use unusual speech patterns such as echolalia. The observer may notice that the student has difficulty in changes of routine and manifests stereotypical behaviors.
Anecdotal records	Records suggest that performance varies according to moods, energy level, extent and pile-up of environmental changes, and whether or not individual preferences are incorporated.

Nondiscriminatory evaluation team determines that student has autism and needs special education and related services.

Appropriate Education

Careful observation is especially important in conducting a functional behavioral assessment.

communicating? For example, does the student want to obtain something positive, avoid or escape something unpleasant, or increase or decrease sensory stimulation (Chandler & Dahlquist, 2002)?

4. Hypothesize the relationship between the problem behavior and the events occurring before, during, and after the behavior.

5. Incorporate the functional assessment information into the student's IEP. Focus on changing the environmental events and circumstances so that the student does not need to engage in problem behavior to accomplish his or her purpose.

6. Help the student develop alternative behaviors and new skills so that he or she can accomplish the same purpose in more socially acceptable ways.

How Do You Assure Progress in the General Curriculum?

Including Students

Relative to other students with disabilities, students with autism have one of the lowest rates of inclusion in general education classes. As illustrated in Figure 10–2, fewer than one-third of students with autism spend the majority of their time in general education classes (U.S. Department of Education, 2000). Yet effective educators can assure their progress in general curriculum. Box 10–2 provides you with suggestions for promoting the successful inclusion of students with autism.

Planning Universally Designed Learning

Two characteristics of students with autism that frequently create barriers to progressing in the general curriculum are students' problem behavior and their atypical social development. To

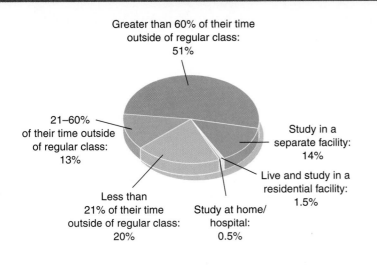

Greater than 60% of their time outside of regular class: 51%

21–60% of their time outside of regular class: 13%

Study in a separate facility: 14%

Live and study in a residential facility: 1.5%

Study at home/hospital: 0.5%

Less than 21% of their time outside of regular class: 20%

FIGURE 10–2

Educational placement of students with autism (1999-2000)

Source: Adapted from U.S. Department of Education. (2001). *To Assure the Free Appropriate Public Education of All Children with Disabilities: Twenty-first Annual Report to Congress on the Implementation of the Individuals with Disabilities Education Act.* Washington, DC: Author.

Inclusion Tips

Box 10–2

	What You Might See	What You Might Be Tempted to Do	Alternate Responses	Ways to Include Peers in the Process
Behavior	She often rocks back and forth over and over during class activities she's not interested in.	Ignore her behavior or tell her to stop.	Collaborate with the inclusion specialist. Suggest a preferred activity that builds on her strengths and interests.	Help peers to understand her behavior. Encourage and support their acceptance of her.
Social Interactions	She bites others who try to work with her and may repeat their language.	Isolate her from other students and discipline her behavior.	Collaborate with the inclusion specialist to establish a method of communication.	Pair her with students who understand her preferred communication method.
Educational Performance	She learns very slowly and needs a great deal of extra help to learn simple concepts	Expect less and make the requirements less structured.	Use visual images and music to teach abstract concepts.	Provide opportunities for peer tutoring with visual images and music.
Classroom Attitudes	She has an inability to focus and may become antagonistic during activities in which there is much noise or confusion.	Remove her from class activities to work alone.	Use social stories to help her predict activities and plan attitudes and responses for difficult situations.	Teach peers to write social stories that include all students. Have small groups, including the student, revise and work out different scenarios.

enable more progress, augmented instruction should focus on teaching students additional skills: (1) replacing problem behavior with appropriate behavior and (2) teaching students to use appropriate social skills.

Augmenting Curriculum and Instruction

One way to augment instruction for students with autism is to add positive behavior support. This technique is a proactive, problem-solving, and data-based approach to improving appropriate behavior and achieving important academic, social, and communication outcomes (Carr et al., 2001; Sugai et al., 2000). Thus, students are provided with additional skills aimed at replacing their problem behavior with appropriate behavior, which enables them to benefit much more effectively from the general education curriculum. In addition to focusing specifically on student skills, positive behavior has a broader focus of (1) rearranging school environments and (2) changing school systems to prevent students from having problem behavior in the first place. Because a student's problem behavior often resides in someone else's failure to provide individualized and comprehensive support (Turnbull & Ruef, 1996, 1997), positive behavior support seeks to create responsive environments that are personally tailored to the preferences, strengths, and needs of students who have problem behavior.

What does research say about the efficacy of positive behavior support? A review of more than 100 research articles published between 1985 and 1996 to investigate the behavioral outcomes for individuals with problem behavior (primarily individuals with mental retardation, autism, or both) who were part of this data base (Carr et al., 1999) concluded that

▼ Positive behavior support was successful in achieving at least an 80 percent reduction in problem behavior for approximately two-thirds of the behavioral outcomes that were studied in this research.

▼ Conducting a functional assessment substantially increases the success of positive behavior support.

▼ Positive behavior support is more effective when the focus is not just on the individual with problem behaviors but on all significant people (for example, helping teachers and families change their behavior to support the individual more effectively).

▼ Positive behavior support is more effective when teachers and families reorganize environments so that they are more conducive to supporting the student's success.

▼ Positive behavior support is just as effective with individuals who have pervasive needs for support as it is with individuals who have only intermittent support needs.

Positive behavior support is a good example of an intervention that was first developed to help students with more significant disabilities but that now has been applied to all students, even those who do not have disabilities (Sugai et al., 2000; Sugai & Lewis, 1999; Turnbull et al., 2002). Schoolwide positive behavior support includes three components: (1) universal support, (2) group support, and (3) individual support.

How do teachers use these three components? The answer comes from research data. Approximately 76 percent of students receive no more than one office discipline referral during a school year; these students do not have serious problem behavior and can benefit from universal support. Another 15 percent of students receive two to five office referrals; these students are at risk for having problem behavior and can benefit from group support. Finally, about 9 percent receive six or more office referrals; these students have intense problem behavior. Figure 10–3 illustrates the proportions of students whose behaviors vary from not problematic at all to intensely problematic. Typically, students with autism require individual support to learn appropriate behavior.

The primary goal of universal support is to create a positive learning context for all students. Educators carry out this goal by setting clear expectations for student behavior in all places and activities in a school (cafeteria, hallways, bathrooms, library, and playgrounds), making sure the students agree to those expectations, giving the students many opportunities to meet these expectations, and rewarding them when they do. Schools succeed in implementing universal support when they do the following:

To learn about the work of the National Center for Positive Behavioral Interventions and Support on schoolwide positive behavior support, go to the Web Links module in Chapter 10 of the Companion Website.

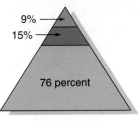

FIGURE 10–3
Percentages of students with, at risk for, and without serious problem behavior

9% →
15% →

76 percent

Typical Schools

▬ Students with chronic/intense problem behavior
▬ Students at risk for problem behavior
▬ Students without serious problem behavior

▼ *Clearly define behavioral expectations.* These expectations should be defined as simply, positively, and succinctly as possible.

▼ *Teach behavioral expectations.* Each expectation should be explicitly taught so that students know exactly what is expected of them.

▼ *Frequently acknowledge appropriate behaviors.* A rule of thumb is to have at least four times as many positive affirmations as negative sanctions.

▼ *Evaluate programs and make adaptations on an ongoing basis through a team approach.* The team should involve all stakeholders and should review data on behavioral incidences, attendance rates, detentions, and suspension rates and implement proactive strategies to ensure the decline of negative behavior and the increase of positive behavior.

▼ *Target support to address students who need more intense skill development and practice than is offered through universal support.* The targeted support might relate to particular behavior in the hallways or cafeteria, social skills, conflict resolution, and/or communication training.

Group support is the second component of positive behavior support (Hawken & Horner, 2001; Turnbull et al., 2002). Group support addresses problem behavior that is occurring with at least 10 to 15 students, each of whom has received universal support but has not yet learned appropriate behavior. Group support typically involves

▼ Observing the students individually and as a group

▼ Interviewing the ones who are having problem behaviors

▼ Developing hypotheses that deal with the behaviors of all of the members of the group

▼ Teaching the specific skills that all of the students need to eliminate their problem behaviors

Group support is often provided in those places where students have higher rates of problem behaviors, such as hallways, lunch rooms, and playgrounds.

The most intense level of positive behavior support is individual support—the type of support that Jeremy receives. Individual support is for students who are not able to sufficiently eliminate their problem behavior through universal and group support.

Individual support begins with a functional assessment, which is part of a nondiscriminatory evaluation, and then uses the assessment to develop the IEP. If a student has a behavior that impedes his or other students' learning, IDEA requires the student's IEP team to "consider, when appropriate, strategies including positive behavior interventions, strategies, and supports to address that behavior." That is why, for example, Jeremy's IEP team considered and then adopted positive behavior support to address his behaviors—namely, his touching, interrupting, talking in class, and tardiness to class. Note, then, that the functional assessment becomes the foundation for an IEP whose goals include reducing problem behavior, teaching appropriate behavior, maximizing positive outcomes such as communication and social skills, and thereby providing the student with access to the school's general curriculum. In adopting positive behavior support, however, Jeremy's team, and indeed his entire school, also decided to put into place a schoolwide positive behavior support approach (Turnbull et al., 2002).

You will read more about these three components on Jeremy and his schoolmates when we describe Central Middle School.

We want to caution you that not all parents adhere to the basic premise of positive behavior support, which is that students learn more effectively when they have positive consequences for their behavior and that punishment might lead them to suppress a behavior temporarily but does not teach them alternative appropriate behavior. Their perspective is represented in Box 10–3.

Augmenting Instruction

Students with autism and Asperger Syndrome often need additional instruction to learn how to interact appropriately with others in social situations—knowing what is cool and uncool behavior, understanding the perspectives of other people, and knowing the unwritten codes of conduct—what educators call the "hidden curriculum" (Myles & Simpson, 2001). Social stories are a good example of an augmented instructional strategy. Social stories are written by educators, parents, or students and describe social situations in terms of important social cues and appropriate responses to those cues. Social stories typically have four different sentence types:

- *Descriptive sentences* objectively define where a situation occurs, who is involved, what they are doing, and why.
- *Perspective sentences* describe a person's internal physical state or desire. Perspective sentences also frequently describe another person's thoughts, feelings, or beliefs, and motivations.
- *Directive sentences* directly define what is expected as a response, to a given cue or in a particular situation.

Box 10–3

Multicultural Considerations

When Cultures Clash over Discipline

Positive behavior support reflects certain cultural values. That is obvious if you consider just one word—the key word. *Positive* means that the ways of shaping a child's behavior should be positive. In other words, the ways of shaping a child's behavior should not be punishing.

Positive means that teachers and families will redesign children's physical environments, change the curriculum (what they teach children) and instruction (how they teach children), and deny the child any rewards for the child's problem behavior (for example, not give attention to the student in response to yelling and screaming).

Not punishing means that teachers and families will not use aversive techniques to change a child's behavior. For example, they will not inflict pain or tissue damage; they will not humiliate the child; and they will not deny the child the necessities of life (food, clothing, shelter, and health and educational care).

But what if a child's family has strong cultural beliefs about punishment? What if the family believes that to spare the rod is to spoil the child? Some families come from cultures in which punishment is not only acceptable but mandatory. These families may think of "using the rod" as loving and responsible discipline rather than punishment.

Positive behavior support clashes directly with the rod approach. It also conflicts with what some families and educators believe about discipline in light of their cultural values. We encourage you to work with your school principal and other school colleagues to inform parents about different approaches to problem behavior and then invite their input on how you and they can discipline children in a way that is consistent with research-based practices but does not violate family values.

Taking Diversity into Account for Progress in the General Curriculum

1. How do you distinguish positive behavioral support from punishment?

2. What can you do if a student's family believes in punishment but you and your colleagues practice positive behavioral support?

3. Does punishment advance or impede a student's participation in the general curriculum?

To answer these questions online, go to our Companion Website and the Multicultural Considerations module in Chapter 10.

- *Control sentences* are statements written by a student to identify strategies the student may use to recall the information in a social story, reassure him- or herself, or define his or her own responses. (Gray, 1998, pp. 178–179)

Several research studies have documented the effectiveness of social stories. One used social stories with three students, with a range of goals for each student. An elementary student with autism expanded her language (increasing her verbal greetings to others) and decreased her problem behavior (aggression and inappropriate touching) (Swaggart et al., 1995). Two young boys in the same study increased their social interaction (sharing and parallel play) while decreasing their aggressive behavior. In further research, social stories have been successful in decreasing problem behavior (tantrums) of students in school and home settings (Kuttler, Myles, & Carlson, 1998; Lorimer, Simpson, Myles, & Ganz, 2002).

Social stories can incorporate a wide range of creative approaches. A teacher in a resource room embedded social stories within a comic strip to enable a teenager with Asperger Syndrome to tune into the nuances of conversations with peers (Rogers & Myles, 2001). A music therapist composed original music, using the text of a social story as the lyrics (Brownell, 2000). He compared the effectiveness of (1) reading the social stories to students with (2) teaching the students to sing the story. The singing condition was significantly more effective for one of the four students involved in the research; the inappropriate behavior of the three other students decreased during the singing condition but not significantly. These results are promising in terms of adding a musical dimension to social stories.

In addition to music, you can use numerous other ways to incorporate media into social stories. Box 10–4 suggests an effective way to take advantage of technology in using social stories as an instructional strategy.

To watch music therapist Mike Brownell, go to the Video module in Chapter 10 of the Companion Website.

Collaborating to Meet Students' Needs

Collaboration is essential to address the complex needs of your students with autism (Ruble & Dalrymple, 2002). It is especially important to consider how to make instruction across school, home, and community settings as coherent as possible. Creating coherent instruction means having the key people in each of those environments collaborate with one another to plan and implement the curriculum and use the same methods of instruction. For example, you will find that positive behavior support is far more effective when teachers, parents, and community service providers are all responding to a student's problem behavior in similar ways. It is especially important to have a person on the evaluation and IEP team who has expertise in positive behavior support. This person might be a teacher, a school psychologist, a counselor, or a specialist from a local mental health center.

You learned previously about the sensory and movement disorders that frequently occur in students with autism and Asperger Syndrome. Collaboration among educators, occupational therapists, speech and language therapists, physical therapists, adaptive physical educators, and the students and their families results in an effective intervention because the related service providers specialize in knowledge related to sensory processing and motor development. Indeed, a recent national survey of occupational therapists indicated that occupational therapy is a frequent component of intervention programs for children with autism (Watling, Deitz, Kanny, & McLaughlin, 1999). The most frequent areas addressed by occupational therapists are sensory processing, coordination, and fine-motor skills. In Box 10–5, you can read how one new teacher and her allies collaborated to make a difference.

What Can You Learn from Others Who Teach Students with Autism?

Learning for the Early Childhood Years: "Jump Start" in Exeter, New Hampshire

Can autism be cured if met head on and early enough? Research has not yet answered that question affirmatively. But we do know that early intervention and education are critical to children

Technology Tips

Box 10–4

Multimedia Social Stories

You certainly remember your parents' or teachers' admonition, given to you as a child: Wash your hands before and after meals, after going to the bathroom, and at other important times. And you probably did what they asked—so often that it is now your habit, one you practice without even thinking about it.

But what if you are a young boy with autism who doesn't want to wash his hands? What if you resist "wash" instructions because you don't like the feel of soap (a sensory reason), want to escape from instructions, or want to get attention by not complying? The challenge is clear—to teach rudimentary, lifelong cleanliness habits. Would it help to have a social story that you can "see" and practice, using one of your favorite toys—a computer? The answer is yes.

What Is the Technology?

Researchers at The University of Kansas developed a social story about hand washing, using *HyperCard*™ software (Apple Computer, 1994). First, they developed the story; then they programmed it into the student's computer. The program consisted of a movie showing the student washing his hands, a synthesized computer voice telling the student what to do, and a navigational button that the student could use to key the computer to "tell" his story.

What Do You Do with It?

Together, the student's teachers and parents and the researcher repeatedly exposed the student to the programmed story; the student enjoyed using the computer and also learned every time he turned on his program what he should do about hand washing. The story helped the student learn that there are three settings in which he should wash his hands: before morning snack, before lunch, and after recess. The result: The student made impressive gains in each setting, and the teacher succeeded in combining the student's interest in computers with his need to learn a lifelong skill.

Putting Social Stories to Work for Progress in the General Curriculum

1. Are social stories effective interventions?

2. Is technology (here, a multimedia approach using computer and audio- and video-based instruction) effective? Why?

3. Is the technology readily available?

4. Does the teaching help the student progress in the general curriculum?

To answer these questions online and learn more about these strategies, go to the Technology Tips module in Chapter 10 of the Companion Website.

Source: Adapted from Hagiwara, T., & Myles, B. S. (1999). A multimedia social story intervention: Teaching skills to children with autism. *Focus on Autism and Other Developmental Disabilities, 14*(4), 82–95.

with autism and their families (Dawson & Osterling, 1997; Dunlap, 1999; Prizant & Rubin, 1999). Notably, "every study in the literature that has demonstrated significant changes in the general functioning of groups of children with autism in response to comprehensive treatment has involved children under the age of five years" (Rogers, 1998, p. 176). Different models have been developed for use in early intervention and preschool programs.

▼ Using **applied behavior analysis** that emphasizes assessment, programming, systemic reinforcement of appropriate behavior, and generalization of skills and behavior across settings (places) and people (Smith, 2001; Smith, Green, & Wynn, 2000)

▼ Deciding what areas of the child's behavior are the most important to improve (for example, motivation to initiate activities, self-management, or being responsive to multiple cues) and then using those improved behaviors as a catalyst for positive changes in other areas of the child's behavior (Koegel, Koegel, Harrower, & Carter, 1999; Koegel, Koegel, Shoshan, & McNerney, 1999)

▼ Using **incidental teaching** in natural environments such as the child's home, a child-care center, and the community (McGee, Morrier, & Daley, 1999)

Box 10–5

"TAC-ing" for Students with Autism

One day, you will be in the same position that Christine Lee found herself in—starting the first day of your teaching career. You are freshly out of a first-rate graduate-school program that certified you in early childhood special education, early childhood general education, and English as a Second Language; you have been trained in inclusive and multicultural education.

In your first job, you enter a state-of-the-art situation. You are employed by a large suburban school district that is headed by a progressive principal and loaded with financial and personnel resources, including every kind of specialist that any student might need and a longstanding and very active parent-volunteer program. You are assigned to teach six children with autism.

Each child has

- Actively involved parents and a special education advocate (most children will have actively involved parents, but most will not have another person who is specially employed to advocate for their special education rights)
- A different IEP because each displays learning and behavioral challenges that are quite different from his or her peers (that's typical)
- A need to access the general curriculum to the greatest extent possible (that, too, is typical)
- A need to be assessed for progress in the general curriculum through the state's standardized assessments (again, a typical situation)
- The right to be included in classrooms for peers without disabilities (a right for all students with disabilities)

You are facing the challenge to include these students in the general education program of a 600-student school, which, surprisingly, has never before experienced any students with autism. A typical profile of new teachers, schools, and students with autism? Pretty much so. An overwhelming task? Could be. After all, six children, each one different from the other despite sharing the same disability label; six different sets of educational strengths and needs; six different sets of parents and advocates; and a school that has never before enrolled any students with disabilities. This could be an overwhelming task, but for Christine it wasn't.

What made the difference? One answer lies in a single word. Training. Christine had been exposed to the newest strategies in special and general education—positive behavior support on both individual and group bases, assistive technologies for augmenting students' communication, and skills in working with students whose families are from culturally and linguistically diverse backgrounds. She also knew how to adapt the general education curriculum so that it fit her students' needs, using assistive technology and universal-design strategies.

Another answer also lies in a single word. Attitude. Christine was determined to succeed; so was her principal and her peers in special and general education.

Who made the difference? Not surprisingly, the answer lies not in a single person but in a single word and single approach. Collaboration. Call it teamwork among Christine, her mentor, her paraprofessional, and her principal. Christine knew she did not know enough to succeed on her own. Her mentor (an experienced teacher of students with autism who volunteered to be a mentor and then received special training and extra pay for taking on that role) knew about school culture and how to fit the autism program into the general education environment. Her paraprofessional, whom Christine herself hired, was a constant ally. And her principal brought to bear the full resources of the administration to support Christine, her mentor, and her paraprofessional.

Training. Attitude. Collaboration: To make a difference, any teacher, especially the new teacher that you will be, needs to be trained to teach in special and general education; to have a "will prevail" attitude concerning all aspects of the job and all people involved in it; to apply specific skills; and to collaborate, to reach out for and receive "knee-to-knee," "hand-over-hand," on-the-job support.

Source: Adapted from Boyer, L., & Lee, C. (2001, Summer). Converting challenge to success: Supporting a new teacher of students with autism. *Journal of Special Education, 35*(2), 75–83.

▼ Focusing on communication, sensory processing, motor planning, and shared affect with caregivers and peers (Greenspan & Wieder, 1999)

▼ Coupling positive behavior support with a strong emphasis on inclusion and family support (Dunlap, 1999; Fox, Dunlap, & Philbrick, 1997)

Glen Dunlap and Lise Fox, researchers at the University of South Florida, have developed an early childhood model program for children with autism called the Individual Support Program (ISP) (Dunlap & Fox, 1999; Dunlap et al., 2001; Fox, Benito, & Dunlap, 2002). Under the program, a behavior specialist, the child's family, and the child's teacher carry out a functional assessment of the child's problem behavior:

▼ What is the nature of the behavior?

▼ In what contexts does it occur or not occur?

▼ What are its antecedents and consequences?

▼ What are its communicative functions?

This collaborative assessment always assumes that problem behaviors are purposeful: The child uses them to communicate certain needs or desires and to get certain results.

Next, the specialist, the family, and the teacher decide how to change the environments in which the child uses these behaviors, the interactions that the family and others have with the child, and the child's own skills. They develop a plan to be used in all settings where the child will be (home, school and community) that addresses the following:

▼ Long-term supports for the child and family

▼ Strategies that the child and his or her family and teachers can use to extinguish the child's problem behavior

▼ Strategies to replace the problem behaviors with more appropriate behaviors

▼ Consequences that teach the child that more functional skills work better

In Box 10–6, you will read about Rosie Mack, a young child with autism, and how educators at the University of New Hampshire adapted ISP to create their own program, "Jump Start," collaborated with Rosie's family and teachers, and obtained amazing results in a very short time.

To learn more about "Jump Start," go to the Web Links module in Chapter 10 of the Companion Website for a link to the program.

Learning for the Elementary Years: Tiffany Park, Seattle, Washington

Among the many ways to instruct students with autism at the elementary level, positive behavior support can be especially useful. Just consider what happened when teachers at the Tiffany Park Elementary School in Seattle, Washington, collaborated with staff from the University of Washington and involved parents to deliver support to one student (individual support)(Family Connection Staff, DeVault, Krug, & Fake, 1996). Third grader Samantha ("Sam") Fake, like many students with autism, had problem behavior. As a result of effective support, she is now an honor student, writes poetry, uses a computer, and has friends of her own age who do not have disabilities. What happened to make this kind of difference?

Simply put, Sam benefited from positive behavior support. Her mother and father, her teachers, and specialists from the University of Washington first tried to learn why Sam fled her third-grade class, fought with faculty who tried to prevent her exit or to return her to class, and damaged school property during these episodes. To solve this puzzle, the team conducted a functional assessment, looking beyond Sam's behavior to find its purposes and its communicative intent. After directly observing and charting her behavior in different settings and under various circumstances (collectively, the settings and circumstances are known as **setting events**), they determined that her problem behavior was more apt to occur when setting events that seem to trigger impeding behaviors mounted up and snowballed. In short, Sam was overloaded and responded with inappropriate behavior.

They then identified what Sam likes, such as a consistent and predictable daily schedule; rewarding social interactions with others; and quiet, private spaces where she can calm down by herself. With the team's support, Sam learned new, more appropriate ways to influence her environments and interact with peers and to use individually contracted goal sheets to show that she had completed her academic work. For example, when Sam wanted to avoid a stressful situation at school, she would ask to leave class, go to a relaxation area, calm herself down, and then return to class. No adult would try to keep her in class or make a big deal about her leaving temporarily. Not only did Sam have choices and some control over her life, but she also had to change. So did her teachers.

Soon Sam and her team realized that it was more important for her to have a choice than to have the rewards. In time, the tangible rewards were simply phased out, but Sam's opportunities to choose were kept in place.

Collaboration Tips

Box 10–6

Reading Peter Rabbit

It took only 6 months, an amazingly short period, for Rosie Mack, age 3, to change dramatically—so dramatically that progress in the general curriculum was not just a phrase but a reality.

In a word, the challenge was to help Rosie behave in such a way that she could be included in a preschool with students who do not have disabilities. What stood in the way was Rosie's erratic behavior: She was alternatively hyperactive or withdrawn and sobbing. Rosie's behaviors were rather typical for a preschooler with autism. She needed to learn appropriate behavior (such as how to calm down), how to comply with safety instructions ("don't touch the hot stove") and other directions, and how to express her needs and choices other than by acting out ("tell me what you want, Rosie").

The collaborators consisted of Rosie's mother, Kathy; Kathy's parents, Lorraine and John Mack; Ann Dillon of the University of New Hampshire's "Jump Start" program (where positive behavior support is linked to family support and person-centered planning); Ann's graduate students; and the teachers and therapists in Rosie's early intervention program and elementary school.

Under Ann's direction but with Kathy's diligent participation, they began by conducting a functional assessment of Rosie's behavior; then they developed and carried out a plan for positive behavior support for Rosie. The plan included social stories (with graphic design by Kathy and photographs by Rosie's grandmother, Lorraine). At Ann's suggestion, Kathy or Ann's students read the stories to Rosie before she went to different places (for example, the preschool or the elementary school, a swimming pool, and a theater) or engaged in various activities (for example, being a patient at a dentist's or physician's office). The stories prepped her for what lay ahead, gave her a sense of predictability, and helped her be calm when places changed and people entered her life.

Again under Ann's guidance, the team engaged in family support. Following the guidance of Kathy, Lorraine, and John, they developed a shared vision for Rosie, which was for her to be included in general education and have friends—those who do and those who do not have disabilities. They also helped Kathy find child care, learn how to advocate for Rosie's inclusion in school and community, and meet some of Rosie's needs for strenuous physical activity. Grandfather John himself built Rosie's swing-gym set. Finally, the team worked with Rosie's teachers in the preschool and the elementary school to help them learn how to deliver positive behavior support to Rosie. And even though Ann herself pointed her team members in the right direction, seeming to lead, everyone participated equally in leading and following. As in the best collaborations, a teacher can jump-start the process, but everyone has to be a leader.

The results were remarkable. Rosie's problem behavior is a thing of the past. She progressed through the preschool and is now fully included, with support, in a typical first-grade classroom. She uses words and phrases to express her choices. If she doesn't know a word, she tells herself, "I will be okay," and uses hand signals, not acting-out behaviors, to communicate. She is fully included in her elementary school (with an aide), has friends who have and don't have disabilities, and has progressed from no literacy skills to knowing how to read and being a regular visitor to the community library. Rosie's favorite book is her well-worn copy of *The Tale of Peter Rabbit*.

As Kathy said, "We wouldn't be so much in control of our lives without Jump Start"; and as Ann said, "It's about the family and in turn about Rosie." So what do you learn from this example of collaboration?

Putting Collaboration into the Context of Student Progress in the General Curriculum

1. Who are the collaborators?

2. What are the challenges?

3. What can the team do? What are the results?

To answer these questions online and learn more about Rosie and "Jump Start", go to our Companion Website and find the module in Chapter 10, "Putting Collaboration into the Context of Student Progress in the General Curriculum."

Honor student Samantha Fake, second from right, shown here with three of her friends, has made remarkable academic progress and social progress because of positive behavioral support.

To see a brief video of Sam in her elementary classroom and samples of her functional assessment, go to the Video module in Chapter 10 on the Companion Website.

The key in all of this was the team's consistent restructuring of Sam's environments, their diligent data collection, their daily communication with each other, and their knowledge about what to do when Sam displayed those behaviors.

Sam's success is not so much a matter of fixing her as it is a result of helping her accommodate to the demands of an inclusive world and helping that world, and the people in it, accommodate to her.

Learning for the Middle and Secondary Years: Central Middle School, Kansas City, Kansas

Do you remember how Jeremy could map his teachers' route to anywhere, raised his hand to be acknowledged as the next speaker in class, and wrote that it is not cool to be tardy or swear? Jeremy's speech and language therapist assists him in developing social stories to guide his appropriate behavior. Jeremy keeps his social stories in a notebook and frequently reads them at home and school. He receives individual positive behavior support in his school. Just where did he learn his hand-raising routine and what is not cool? Read Box 10–7 to learn about Jeremy's individual positive behavior support.

Learning for the Transitional and Postsecondary Years: Community Services for Autistic Adults and Children, Rockville, Maryland

There is abundant evidence that adults with autism can lead lives characterized by independence, productivity, and inclusion, especially if they are involved with Community Services for Autistic Adults and Children (CSAAC), a Rockville, Maryland, nonprofit agency. CSAAC serves 93 adults in its vocational program (Smith, Belcher, & Jahrs, 1995) and 30 students in its

Like all other students at Central Middle School, Jeremy is expected to do homework, as he is about to do at his desk at home.

school program. They all prove their ability to make positive contributions and to be productive, tax-paying citizens. According to Karla Nabors, director of CSAAC's adult services, and Paul Livelli, director of CSAAC's Community School of Maryland, adults with autism are involved with CSAAC work at 55 different job sites. They are employed in areas such as the retail and distribution industry, the printing industry, the biotech industry, federal and county governments, and the food service industry. The employing companies and agencies range in size from very small (a few workers) to very large (more than 1,000 workers). Despite the fact that many of the workers at CSAAC were once institutionalized or inadequately educated, they average 30 hours of work each week; have held jobs for as long as 20 years or as short as a month; and earn from minimum wage to $11.75 per hour, some enjoying full employee benefits.

Most adults served by CSAAC work with co-workers without disabilities. Indeed, the longer they are employed, the more they associate with co-workers. Nabors and Livelli are certain that what stands in the way of these adults' inclusion is not their aggression, self-injury, or history of institutionalization. Instead, the barriers are their low levels of cognitive functioning and poor communication skills.

CSAAC's mission is to support individuals in achieving their personal goals and dreams with integrity and distinction. To put its mission into practice, CSAAC provides intensive support. The workers have job coaches who

▼ Teach the workers how to travel from home to work or transport the workers to their jobs

▼ Teach job responsibilities, work skills, social skills, and money management

▼ Oversee an individual's productivity, accuracy, and behavior on the job

▼ When necessary, prevent self-injury, aggression, or property destruction through the implementation of positive behavior support

CSAAC also provides comprehensive residential support so that adults with autism can live in condominiums, garden apartments, or townhouses where, as at work, they share the facilities (swimming pools, recreation areas, and laundry facilities) with their neighbors who do not have disabilities. There are 52 homes in the area and one beach house.

To learn more about CSAAC, go to the Web Links module in Chapter 10 of the Companion Website for a link to the CSAAC website.

Box 10–7

Into Practice

Highlights of Jeremy's Positive Behavior Support Plan for Inappropriate Verbal Disruptions (Talk-Outs)

Steps	Highlights
1. Description of target problem behavior	• Asks the teacher questions without first raising hand and being acknowledged during lessons • Asks the teacher repetitive questions (e.g., "Have I been bad?") • Uses loud voice and/or repeats person's name in a loud voice (e.g., "You mean, Ms. B.") • Makes out-of-context comments while other students are working quietly (e.g., "I don't like spiders. Spiders are unsanitary.")
2. Functional behavior assessment (FBA) findings	• Has difficulty when other peers whisper near him in class • Tends to begin to talk more loudly when he hears other students whisper • Appears to calm down when adults whisper and even tries to model or imitate the "whisper voice" • Imitates peers' appropriate verbal behaviors or in response to peers' imitation of his loud and excited talk • Talks out when teachers demonstrate anxious behaviors (e.g., shaking, cringing) or provide high levels of corrective feedback to students
3. Hypothesis statement developed	• Uses excessive and repetitive talk-out behaviors to get what he wants and to escape from frustrating or less preferred tasks, especially when he is told to wait for something he wants or is told that he cannot interact with a particular preferred person or object. • Uses talk-outs to get or obtain adult and/or peer attention • Uses talk-outs to reduce/alleviate stress, anxiety, or tension and/or to express his emotions, especially when his energy level is high and he needs to interact with peers and adults
4. Desired replacement behavior	• To work quietly in class and refrain from making out-of-context comments that disrupt the lesson • To raise his hand and wait to be acknowledged before calling out answers to questions and before talking out in class • To ignore peers' comments that taunt or mimic him • To engage in quiet self-talk to remind himself of the class rules about not talking out in class • To read and recopy social stories as a way of reinforcing positive behaviors in writing
5. IEP goals and objectives developed	Goal 3: Jeremy will improve his skills in language and communication. *Objective:* Jeremy will work quietly in class and refrain from making out-of-context comments that disrupt the class.

Objective: Jeremy will raise his hand and wait to be acknowledged before calling out answers to questions and/or talking out about things in class.

Objective: Jeremy will ignore and/or redirect himself by practicing quiet self-talk or reading social stories to himself in response to comments made by peers that taunt or mimic him.

Program guidelines were established using the FBA data to include

- *Prompting.* No more than one verbal or gestural/pointing prompt (redirection) per class

- *Criteria.* Nine of ten positive behavior opportunities; also, a decrease in target (problem) behaviors of 80 percent below baseline measures of inappropriate verbal disruptions (talk-outs) 4 of 5 days

- *Review and evaluation.* As measured by data collected

6. Create interventions based on FBA

Strategies to change setting events
- Schedule functional activities and build routines that offer opportunities for Jeremy to move around and burn energy, especially before times/activities that are predictable triggers for disruptive talk-outs, such as a class period that lasts longer than 50 minutes.

Strategies to change immediate antecedent events
- Offer more assistance—with minimal verbal interaction—when presenting new or difficult tasks or when working on assigned tasks at nonpreferred times of the day—e.g., fifth hour or late in the day when disruptive talk-outs are much more likely.

Strategies to teach new, desired replacement behaviors
- Teach Jeremy to self-monitor and self-manage talk-outs by using his social stories.

- Teach him how to appropriately terminate a nonpreferred task without talking out disruptively by showing him how to use an acceptable form of behavior that accomplishes the function "stop" or that protests/terminates acceptably an unwanted activity. (This communication form could be to raise or wiggle his hand, wait to be acknowledged, then say "Stop, please," or "Need to cool down now").

- Use gestural/physical, proximity prompts, but minimum verbal directions to get him going on one or more of the crisis management procedures.

Consequence strategies to strengthen existing, alternative, desired behaviors
- Continue to teach Jeremy to wait longer periods of time without getting undivided one-on-one adult attention by reducing proximity cues, giving nonverbal gestures (without eye contact) to wait, introducing social reinforcers frequently, and so on.

- Rehearse and role-play with Jeremy what to do when peers tease or mimic him, trying to get him to say silly things that just get him into trouble.

7. Crisis management/ emergency procedures

- Intervene physically between Jeremy and others to prevent injury or damage to property.

- Remove Jeremy from the situation/setting that is triggering the problem behavior to effectively manage and deescalate the crisis. Escort him down the hallway and prompt him to work appropriately to deescalate his agitation. (He can be taken into the counseling office and seated in one of the chairs to review social stories and work on self-management skills).

- Honor immediately either an independently initiated request by Jeremy to appropriately escape or a prompted request for a break or to terminate/suspend the activity.

8. Monitoring procedures for IEP team

- Use a frequency count of problem behavior occurrences on a daily basis using Jeremy's self-monitoring data and teacher-maintained data.

- Assess the percentage of times and situations where problem behavior is not used and alternative skills are practiced.

- Review data at a monthly meeting with the team (including his family).

Putting These Strategies to Work for Progress in the General Curriculum

Putting These Strategies to Work for Progress in the General Curriculum

1. How do the strategies discussed in this positive behavior support plan correspond to Jeremy's IEP goals and objectives?

2. What challenges do you foresee in integrating these strategies? How would you overcome these challenges?

3. How will collaboration between Jeremy's teachers and his parents and other family members assist in the implementation of his positive behavior support plan?

To answer these questions online and learn more about these strategies, go to the Into Practice module in Chapter 10 of the Companion Website.

Finally, all CSAAC staff facilitate interaction between the individuals with autism and co-workers and neighbors who do not have disabilities. In this way, CSAAC promotes inclusion and friendships, proving that interdependence—between individuals with autism, paid staff, and friends—is entirely possible.

By combining mission with technology, CSAAC demonstrates that people with autism can look forward to an enviable life after high school. To those who might be inclined to dismiss the outcomes of equality of opportunity, full participation, independent living, and economic self-sufficiency (IDEA's goals) as pipe dreams for individuals with autism, Nabors, Livelli, and their CSAAC colleagues have a single retort: "You're mistaken." And to those who regard the education of a student with autism as a prelude to a self-determined life, they have a single affirmation: "You're right on target." These days, for Nabors, Livelli, and others, there is no excuse for not knowing how to ensure that students with autism experience full citizenship; it's just a matter of mission, intent, diligence, and instructional support.

A Vision for Jeremy's Future

At the age of 13, soon to be 14, Jeremy has another 7 years of schooling ahead of him. Looking ahead and assuming that the positive behavior support that he has received at Central Middle School is continued when he enters Wyandotte High School and further assuming that his mother, Joyce, father Richard, and brothers and sisters follow the regimen that they have already begun, it is a safe bet that Jeremy will achieve the goals that IDEA sets for him and other students with disabilities.

He can fully participate in the life of Kansas City. At home, he's a "weather-news hound," accurate about which TV channels show what weather news when. Because the news about Central Middle School has been broadcast within the African American community (the news that the need for discipline is down and good behavior and learning are up), a celebrity weatherman, Bryan Busby, himself an African American, has taken an interest in Central. So it is not out of the question for Jeremy to be a production assistant for Busby.

How would Jeremy get to work, crossing the Missouri River from Kansas City, Kansas, to Kansas City, Missouri? Using the city's bus transportation system (remember, Jeremy knows Kansas City as few other people do) seems entirely feasible. Volunteering at Mt. Calvary Baptist Church can enrich him, just as it enriches his mother and father. Continuing education at Donnelly College, just a mile or so from where he lives, or at Kansas City Community College may be just the ticket to increasing his mapping skills. And hanging out with the young men and women who are part of the Central Avenue Betterment Association (the neighborhood Chamber of Commerce) seems quite likely. Indeed, as the word gets out that Central Middle School offers a good learning environment, especially for students whose behaviors otherwise would impede their and others' learning, it is certain that not only Jeremy but all other students will have community opportunities that otherwise would be out of their reach.

You see, it's not only Jeremy who benefits from positive behavior support and other state-of-the-art techniques; all students and their entire community do. What's good for one seems to be good for all. Special education's contributions—and the lessons of Jeremy Jones and his school and family—have a way of radiating across Kansas City, just as those interstate highways that he so loves to draw radiate throughout the entire metropolitan area. Are Jeremy's maps a metaphor for special education's impact? No doubt, they are.

What Do You Recommend?

1. To plan Jeremy's transition from the middle school to the high school?
2. To foster the relationship between Jeremy and the local celebrity weatherman, Bryan Busby?
3. To help ensure that Jeremy is not victimized by school or community violence?
4. To expand his network of friends to support him throughout his school and adult years?

Summary

How Do You Recognize Students with Autism?

▼ Autism is a developmental disability significantly affecting verbal and nonverbal communication and social interaction. It is generally evident before age 3 and adversely affects educational performance. Other characteristics include repetitive activities, stereotyped movements, behavioral challenges, need for environmental predictability, unusual responsiveness to sensory stimulation, and below-average intellectual functioning.

▼ Autism is part of a broader group of disorders called pervasive developmental disorders. Among the group is the disorder known as Asperger Syndrome.

▼ Two language impairments associated with autism are delayed language and echolalia.

▼ People with autism often have fewer and weaker social interactions with others than do people without disabilities.

▼ Stereotypical behaviors are inappropriate, repetitive acts that an individual frequently displays. These acts include obsessions, tics, and perseveration.

▼ Problem behavior faced by people with autism include self-injurious behavior and aggression.

▼ Predictability and structure are important sources of security for many individuals with autism.

▼ Sensory disorders often result in under- or overresponsiveness to sensory stimuli; movement disorders include abnormal posture, abnormal movements of various body parts, abnormal ocular movements, repeated gestures, and awkward gait.

▼ The majority of people with autism function intellectually as though they have mental retardation. Some, however, have the savant syndrome.

▼ Although parents have historically been seen as the cause of their child's autism, this viewpoint is totally unwarranted.

▼ Autism is caused by abnormalities in brain development, neurochemistry, and genetic factors; but the specific biological trigger is unknown at this time.

▼ The prevalence of autism is approximately 7.5 children per 10,000 children.

How Do You Evaluate Students with Autism?

▼ The Autism Diagnostic Interview—Revised is an assessment tool that is frequently used as part of the multidisciplinary process for evaluating students to determine whether they have autism.

▼ A functional assessment (which is one type of ecological assessment) identifies specific relationships between environmental events and a student's problem behavior. It leads to an individually tailored intervention plan aimed at helping students to function as successfully as possible.

How Do You Assure Progress in the General Curriculum?

▼ Students with autism who experience mental retardation typically require augmented and altered curricula. Students with autism who have normal intelligence and students with Asperger Syndrome can be successful in the general education curriculum without adaptations.

▼ Adapting the curriculum through positive behavioral support is an effective strategy for access to the general curriculum.

▼ Social stories, an example of an altered curriculum, describe social situations in terms of important social cues and appropriate responses to those cues.

▼ A model early intervention program, launched at the University of South Florida and adapted by staff at the University of New Hampshire, emphasizes family support, positive behavior support, communication, and community and preschool inclusion.

▼ Positive behavior support has been used at the Tiffany Park Elementary School in Seattle to promote model elementary school practices and to help students with autism get a better life within and outside of school.

▼ At Central Middle School in Kansas City, Kansas, schoolwide positive behavior support has resulted in a

significant improvement in appropriate behavior across the whole school as well as in successful inclusion for a student with autism.

▼ Community Services for Autistic Adults and Children (CSAAC) has demonstrated that adults with autism can live in typical homes and work in typical jobs when state-of-the-art training and supports are provided.

What Can You Learn from Others Who Teach Students with Autism?

▼ Early intervention and preschool programs use applied behavior analyses, incidental teaching, and family support.

▼ Elementary school programs use positive behavior support and give students choices about and control over many of their school activities.

▼ Middle and secondary school programs use schoolwide, small-group, or one-on-one positive behavior support.

▼ Transition and postsecondary programs focus on adults' cognitive functioning, communication skills, and positive behavior support.

Council for Exceptional Children — PRAXIS

To find out how and where this chapter content connects to the CEC Professional Standards and the Praxis™ Standards, go to the Standards Connection module in Chapter 10 of the Companion Website. A comprehensive matrix aligning CEC Professional Standards, Praxis™ Standards, and INTASC principles to the entire text, is available in the Appendix and on the Companion Website.

~~~~~~~~~~~~~~~~~~~~

Chapter 11

Who Is Kyle Edwards?

"I'm a superstar!" 10-year-old Kyle Edwards proclaims. "I've been on television, in the newspaper, and now I'm going to be in a textbook!" More than a poster child for sickle cell disease, Kyle has achieved superstar status because of his courage, compassion, determination, and wisdom.

Kyle is more like than unlike other boys his age. He enjoys riding his bike, playing basketball, and playing video games with his friends. He is, however, unlike most of his friends because his courageous battle with sickle cell disease involves episodes of excruciating pain that resulted in 10 hospitalizations during the last school year. According to Kyle, "it [is] a bad, shocking pain. It comes whenever it wants to. It feels like men with jackhammers banging on my bones. It feels like lightning going down or up my arm. Sometimes it hurts so bad you just jump when it comes."

Kyle lives with his grandmother, Dorothy, and his Aunt Tamisha (Tammy), who also has sickle cell disease. Dorothy explains how difficult it is to watch Kyle suffer during a pain episode: "A lot of times I go to the hospital, and I just break down because I know what he's going though. I know that he's in a lot of pain, and it's not going to stop. I have arthritis, and I know the pain that I have is nothing compared to the sickle cell pain."

"My auntie talked to me about how to help the pain," Kyle says. "If you are in a real bad pain crisis, then you should drink a lot of fluids or water. The fluids help the pain crisis, and that helps you not to cry. When you cry, you get a headache, and that just makes it worse."

Kyle also experiences other symptoms related to sickle cell disease that require specialized treatments and medications. He says, "I'm on more inhalers than my godbrother is, and he has asthma." Kyle has acute chest syndrome, a condition similar to pneumonia. "It's like you have fluid piling up in your chest. It feels like your chest is getting bigger, and it's hurting worse. You can't even touch it some of the times."

Kyle combines courage with compassion for other children with health impairments. His grandmother explains, "Kyle is religious. He met a little boy in the hospital who was in a lot of pain. He asked the parent if he could pray with the little boy because he knows that prayer changes things." Kyle's family receives good support from Nazaree Baptist Church. Kyle has two godmothers at the church; one is a preacher. His grandmother laughs. "That's why he's so spoiled—the people at my church and my family, and really just everyone he meets."

Kyle frequently shows compassion to other children in the hospital. "I can make friends fast," he says. "When I am in the hospital, there will be a kid who's never been in the hospital before, and I'll go in and say, 'I'm Kyle.' Then we just get to talking. I know how they feel because I've been in the hospital a lot.

It's not my first time, so I try to make them feel like the hospital's not all a bad place. Some people have a lot of bad feelings about the hospital, that they're going to get stuck and all that kind of stuff. I tell them, 'It's not all that bad 'cause once it's over, it's better.' "

Kyle is determined to lead a productive life despite sickle–cell related challenges. His Aunt Tammy is a good role model. She's studying to be an elementary school teacher at the University of Mobile. Tammy says, "A lot of times I felt that I could have used my sickle cell disease as a crutch, but I didn't. I guess I always wanted to be something in life and didn't want to depend on other people for what I needed. So I just had self-motivation. And having sickle cell will give me a better understanding of the daily lives of children in general. In my classroom, I won't think every student should come in motivated to learn on a daily basis. I'll be able to empathize with the students as far as having good days and bad days."

Kyle certainly shares his aunt's self-motivation and knows that school success is essential to achieving his dreams. Although he is absent from school frequently, he is determined to stay caught up with his work at the hospital. Kyle attends Class Act, elementary and secondary classrooms for children and teens at the University of South Alabama's Children's and

Women's Hospital. Staffed by teachers employed by Mobile County Public Schools, Class Act helps hospitalized students keep up with their classmates. Kyle's fourth-grade teacher faxes work to the hospital; and Anne Vella, his hospital teacher, helps him complete the assignments. After Kyle finishes his work, he practices his skills on one of the Class Act computers.

Kyle has wisdom beyond his 10 years: "My friends tell me I speak like I'm a preacher. I speak like I'm a 40-year-old. I was talking to a man at church, and he said we were having a good, long, adult conversation. And he learned more stuff about sickle cell than he already knew!"

What do you think?

1. How are Kyle's educational needs similar to and different from students with other health conditions?

2. How can teachers include Kyle and other students with health impairments in general education when they are frequently absent?

3. How can teachers effectively manage medications and health emergencies for Kyle and other students with health impairments?

To respond to these questions online, participate in other activities, and learn more about Kyle Edwards and other health impairments, go to the Cases module in Chapter 11 of the Companion Website.

How Do You Recognize Students with Other Health Impairments?

Ten to 30 percent of all students will experience a childhood chronic illness lasting three months or longer (Kliebenstein & Broome, 2000). Many will require classroom accommodations and/or special education services because of their condition. Kyle and other students who receive services under the IDEA's *other health impairments* category vary greatly. Some are born with the condition; others develop a health impairment during childhood or adolescence. Some have average ability; others with the same condition may be gifted or have mental retardation. Some have strong support from family and friends; others experience isolation. Some have a condition such as Kyle's that primarily affects people from specific ethnic groups; others have a condition that occurs across all populations. Some are incapacitated; others are rarely inconvenienced by their condition. Some have life-threatening conditions; others can anticipate a long and productive life. How, then, are these students similar? In Box 11–1, you can learn about the common issues, identified by the STARBRIGHT® Foundation, that confront these students.

Defining Other Health Impairments

The IDEA definition unifies these disparate conditions by defining students with **other health impairments** (OHI) as those "having limited strength, vitality or alertness, including a heightened alertness to environmental stimuli, that results in limited alertness with respect to the educational environment, that

1. is due to chronic or acute health problems such as asthma, attention deficit disorder or attention deficit hyperactivity disorder, diabetes, epilepsy, a heart condition, hemophilia, lead poisoning, leukemia, nephritis, rheumatic fever, and sickle cell anemia; and
2. adversely affects a child's educational performance." (34 C.F.R., sec. 300.7[c][9])

The word *other* distinguishes these conditions from severe and multiple disabilities (Chapter 9); physical disabilities, which are conditions that specifically result in musculoskeletal involvement (Chapter 12); and traumatic brain injuries (Chapter 13).

To be served under the OHI category, the student's health condition must limit *strength, vitality,* or *alertness* to such a degree that the student's educational progress is adversely affected. Kyle's pain episodes affect his strength and vitality as well as his alertness to his environment. Likewise, some students with cancer, because of their condition or treatments, may experience limitations in all three areas. By contrast, students with attention-deficit/hyperactivity disorder, including Kelsey, whom you met in Chapter 6, generally experience difficulty only with alertness.

Under IDEA, a student may have a chronic or an acute condition. A **chronic condition** develops slowly and has long-lasting symptoms. Students with diabetes, a chronic condition, experience lifelong medical needs. By contrast, an **acute condition** develops quickly with intense symptoms that last for a relatively short period of time. A student with pneumonia may need temporary homebound services; however, once she recovers from this acute condition, she no longer is entitled to special education. Although Kyle's sickle cell disease is chronic, the pain episodes themselves are acute because they develop quickly and subside suddenly.

More than 200 specific health impairments exist, and most are rare (Thies, 1999). Here, we focus on some of the more typical conditions: sickle cell disease, human immunodeficiency virus, cancer, asthma, epilepsy, and diabetes.

In Chapter 6, you learned that students with AD/HD also receive IDEA services under the Other Health Impairments category.

Describing the Characteristics of Sickle Cell Disease

Kyle is one of 80,000 Americans who have sickle cell disease, the most common inherited blood condition in the United States (WebMD Health, 1996–2002). He inherited two copies of the

Technology Tips

Box 11–1

The STARBRIGHT® Foundation

Green slime covers Morris, the game show host from Sickle Cell Slime-O-Rama, one of the many health care media programs created by the STARBRIGHT® Foundation. While playing the interactive computer game at the University of South Alabama's Children's and Women's Hospital, Kyle caused the balloons full of slime to drop on Morris by correctly answering questions about sickle cell disease.

Chaired by Steven Spielberg and General H. Norman Schwarzkopf, the STARBRIGHT Foundation projects "do more than entertain: they address the core issues that accompany illness—the pain, fear, loneliness, and depression that can be as damaging as the sickness itself" (STARBRIGHT Foundation, 2002a, p. All About Us). In fact, the Foundation identified numerous complex challenges facing children with health impairments (STARBRIGHT Foundation, 2002a, p. STARBRIGHT Healthcare Goals). The following are some of the more common issues:

- Loss of sense of control
- Lack of understanding about the condition
- Fear, worry, anxiety/stress, anger, guilt
- Change in family dynamics
- Experience of loss because of how life has changed
- Isolation
- Medical noncompliance
- Depression, withdrawal
- Boredom
- Loss of peer interactions
- Pain
- Decreased self-esteem
- Lack of feelings of normalcy
- Negative body image
- Impact on identity and social interactions, including those at school

To address these challenges, STARBRIGHT has developed various programs. Interactive CD-ROMs focus on topics such as asthma, diabetes, cystic fibrosis, sickle cell disease, kidney disease, and medical procedures. In the series Videos with Attitude™, adolescents talk candidly about the challenges of illness and strategies for coping, including topics such as communicating with doctors and going back to school. STARBRIGHT World™ is a private on-line network that creates a peer support community of children and adolescents living with serious illness across the United States. They meet and build relationships with others, who face similar challenges, via e-mail, monitored chats, and bulletin boards. STARBRIGHT World also helps them learn about their health care condition in kid-friendly terms and engages them in entertaining and educational activities such as writing and drawing contests and games. With parental consent, a child may receive e-mails from their teachers and classmates. Research conducted at hospitals across the country have shown benefits of STARBRIGHT's programs, including improved coping, a greater sense of responsibility for managing disease, increased sense of social support from peers, and increased willingness to return to the hospital or clinic for treatment.

You will find many of the STARBRIGHT Foundation's programs useful in your general education classroom as well as for your students who are hospitalized or homebound. You can order the interactive CD-ROMs, including Sickle Cell Slime-O-Rama and Videos with Attitude, to help peers understand the challenges faced by their classmates with health conditions. See the Foundation's website (http://www.starbright.org) for more information.

Putting STARBRIGHT to Work for Progress in the General Education Curriculum:

1. Explore the link to the STARBRIGHT Foundation in Chapter 11 of the companion website. Which projects could you use to include students with health impairments in your classroom?

2. How will you encourage students to share these projects to help classmates understand their condition?

3. Look again at the challenges the STARBRIGHT Foundation has identified for students with health impairments. Along with using some of these projects, what other strategies can you use in your classroom to help students meet the goals identified by the foundation?

To answer these questions online and learn more about these strategies, go to the Technology Tips module in Chapter 11 of the Companion Website.

Source: Adapted from STARBRIGHT Foundation. (2002). STARBRIGHT healthcare goals. In *STARBRIGHT Foundation* (http://www.starbright.org/about/goals.html).

Kyle enjoys playing Slime-O-Rama with his child life specialist Brenda White.

sickle cell gene: His mother had sickle cell disease, and his father has sickle cell trait. About 9 percent of African Americans have sickle cell trait, meaning that they carry one gene but have no symptoms. One in 500 African Americans and one in 1,000–1,400 Hispanic Americans are born with sickle cell disease (Nidus Information Services, 2001b).

Kyle and others who have two sickle cell genes often begin showing symptoms in the first year of life. Kyle's first symptoms were hand-foot syndrome: swelling of his hands and feet. Other symptoms include pain in the chest, abdomen, limbs, and joints. Nosebleeds; frequent upper respiratory infections; as well as heart, liver, and spleen enlargement can occur. Children may experience symptoms of anemia, including fatigue, irritability, and jaundice (Jakubik, 2000). Along with pain, adolescence may bring leg sores, gum disease, delayed puberty, and progressive anemia (American Academy of Pediatrics, 2002; WebMD Health, 1996–2002). Current treatment options have increased the typical lifespan from 20 years to more than 50 (DePaupe, Garrison-Kane, & Doelling, 2002).

The primary features of sickle cell disease are anemia and periodic pain. Not all of a student's **hemoglobin** (red blood cells that carry oxygen through the body) are normal. Long, sickle-shaped, stiff cells sometimes clog small blood vessels, preventing organs or tissues from receiving adequate oxygen. The results are severe pain, potential damage to organs and tissues, and sometimes strokes (American Medical Association, 1999). "Fever, respiratory discomfort, unusual malaise or changes in behavior, or discomfort or swelling in the abdomen or extremities" indicate a medical emergency and require quick response from teachers (Bonner, Schumacher, Gustafson, & Thompson, 1999, p. 190).

Many students with sickle cell disease are well adjusted and perform well in school, although they may be at risk for internalizing symptoms such as depression or anxiety (Barbarin & Whitten, 1994). Students who have overt strokes may have impairments in "global cognitive functioning, language abilities, visual-motor and visual-spatial processing and performance, sequential memory, and academic achievement." Those with "silent strokes" that are only revealed by magnetic resonance imaging may experience difficulty with "arithmetic, vocabulary, visual-motor speed, and coordination" (Bonner et al., 1999, p. 187).

Stressors such as extreme heat or cold, a poor diet, not enough liquids, and lack of sleep can trigger pain episodes in students with sickle cell disease (St. Jude's Children's Research Hospital, n.d.). Teachers need to make sure that the student has limited contact with others who have respiratory or other infections. They need to allow their students to drink fluids often, especially water and juices, to prevent and lessen the effects of pain episodes; permitting a student to keep bottled liquid in a cubbyhole or locker and drinking whenever necessary, even during class, is good practice. If the teacher keeps a cooler of water and paper cups in the back of the classroom, any student can have access to water when needed, reducing the awkwardness that a student with sickle cell might feel as the only student permitted to drink fluids in class. Drinking extra fluids and problems with water retention require these students to make frequent bathroom trips. Students with sickle cell need permission to do so unobtrusively. Additionally, some students with sickle cell have special dietary requirements and, like Kyle, may have to bring their lunches to school.

Teachers also need to be aware of students' sensitivity and unusual responses to heat and cold. Kyle says, "It could be real hot outside, and I could be cold. One time I wanted to wear a turtle neck, and my grandmother said, 'Kyle, it's too hot outside.' But I was cold. It can be rainy and cold, and I'll go outside in short sleeves."

Administering medication as soon as a pain episode starts can help reduce the intensity and length of a student's pain. Dorothy gives Kyle his medication immediately when he's at home. However, when he has a pain episode at school, she has to administer the medication after she picks him up, prolonging his pain. Kyle's school requires a note from the doctor listing specific times to administer medication, so "as needed" is not a sufficient guide for his school.

What can teachers do to help students with pain management? First, teachers need to observe students carefully for symptoms of pain. Especially as they enter their teens, students feel awkward about complaining or try to mask their pain, which can escalate quickly without treatment.

Teachers also need to consider the emotional aspects of dealing with pain. Kyle's hospital teacher, Anne Vella, emphasizes that "people experience more pain when they are left alone. And yet when students are in pain, they are often sent to the nurse's office to lie on a cot in a room by themselves." Kinesthetic approaches such as rocking or hugging, using imagery and comforting words, and providing distractions can help students cope with pain (Stephens, Barkey, & Hall, 1999).

Describing the Characteristics of Epilepsy

"I can do most anything," Jacob Empey says. "I'm just a normal kid, but I have seizures." What happens when a person has a seizure? Jacob explains: "Your body just goes out. Your brain makes your whole body and all your muscles start moving and wiggling."

Epilepsy is a condition characterized by **seizures:** temporary neurological abnormalities that result from unregulated electrical discharges in the brain, much like an electrical storm. If a person has seizures only once or temporarily, perhaps from a high fever or brain injury, he or she does not have epilepsy (Epilepsy Foundation of America, 2001, 2002). Most people associate epilepsy with convulsive seizures, but students can also have seizures that manifest as a brief period of unconsciousness or altered behavior that is sometimes misinterpreted as daydreaming (Nidus Information Services, 2001a; Cleveland Clinic Foundation, 1997).

Students can have two types of seizures: generalized or partial. **Generalized seizures** cause a loss of consciousness; the whole body is affected when the electrical discharge crosses the entire brain. **Tonic-clonic** seizures (once known as *grand mal*) and **absence seizures** (pronounced *ab-SAHNZ*) (formerly known as *petit mal*) are generalized seizures. A student who has a tonic-clonic seizure falls, loses consciousness, and has a **convulsion,** which is a sudden, involuntary contraction of a group of muscles. During an absence seizure, the student also loses consciousness but only for a brief period lasting from a few seconds to a half minute or so (Spiegel, Cutler, & Yetter, 1996). The student, teachers, and peers might not realize a seizure has taken place. Absence seizures can occur up to 140 times a day and severely affect learning. Before successful treatment, Jacob experienced absence as well as tonic-clonic seizures. Many times during the day, he momentarily missed what others were doing or saying.

During **partial seizures,** the electrical discharge is limited to one area of the brain. A **temporal lobe, or psychomotor, seizure** causes a student to appear to be in a dreamlike state (Epilepsy Foundation of America, 2001, 2002). The person, who afterward usually has no memory of what happened, makes random movements called **automatisms,** such as picking at clothes, repeating a sentence several times, or even running. A **focal motor seizure** causes the student to have sudden, jerky movements of one part of the body. The student who is having a **focal sensory seizure,** however, will see things and hear sounds that are not really occurring. **Myoclonic seizures** mostly affect infants and young children and cause them to look startled or in pain during the seizure.

FIGURE 11–1
First aid for seizures

Seizure Type	Characteristics	First Aid	Possibility of Injury
General Seizures			
Tonic-clonic	Uncontrolled jerking Loss of consciousness Disorientation Violent reactions Cessation of breathing Vomiting Loss of continence	Lay person on side. Move potentially dangerous or fragile objects. Place pillow under head. Never attempt to restrain or place anything in mouth.	Fairly high, due to bumping into objects during seizure
Tonic	Sudden stiffening of muscles Rigidity Falling to ground	Reassure individual. Provide place to lie down afterward. Stay calm.	Quite high, due to possibility of striking an object while falling
Atonic	Sudden loss of muscle tone resulting in a collapse on ground	Reassure individual. Provide a place to rest.	High, due to possibility of falling into object
Absence	Very brief interruption in consciousness Appearance of momentary déjà vu	Reassure individual following the event.	Fairly low
Partial Seizures			
Simple partial	Twitching movements Sensation of déjà vu	Reassure student.	Fairly low
Complex partial	Altered state of consciousness Psychomotor movements	Provide verbal reassurance during occurrence.	Fairly low unless there is increased physical activity

Seek medical attention immediately if . . .

There is no previous history of seizures, especially if the student is experiencing a tonic-clonic seizure.
Several tonic-clonic seizures follow one another in rapid succession.
A tonic-clonic seizure lasts for more than 2 to 3 minutes.
An injury occurs during the seizure.

Source: From "What Every Teacher Should Know About Epilepsy," by G. L. Spiegel, S. K. Cutler, and C. E. Yetter, 1996, *Intervention in School and Clinic, 32*(1), pp. 35, 36, and 37. Copyright 1996 by PRO-ED, Inc. Adapted and reprinted with permission.

Jacob's service dog, Hunter, senses Jacob's aura and alerts him. You can learn more about Jacob and Hunter in the Cases module in Chapter 11 of the Companion Website. You will also find important tips for including a service dog in your classroom in the Cases and Web Links modules.

Sometimes these children suddenly drop their heads forward and jerk their arms upward. Some students also experience an **aura,** an unusual sensation or visual disturbance that always occurs right before a seizure. Figure 11–1 lists appropriate first-aid measures for seizures.

Teachers need to identify and eliminate any environmental factors that seem to trigger a student's seizures. Extreme stress or fatigue as well as infectious diseases (especially if accompanied by fever) can trigger a seizure in some students. Additionally, bright lights and certain sounds or odors can trigger seizures. Perfume sometimes triggers seizures in Jacob.

Jacob's dog, Hunter, is more than a service dog, however important that role is. He also is Jacob's friend and an "included classmate" in Jacob's school.

Most children with epilepsy have average IQs, and those who have infrequent seizures seldom manifest learning difficulties resulting from their condition. Others, such as Jacob, who take certain medications or have frequent seizures, may be at risk for learning or behavioral challenges (Epilepsy Foundation of America, 2001, 2002). Age of onset, type, localization, and cause are also factors in determining the extent of these challenges (Tyler & Colson, 1994). Academic challenges often include math, reading, and tasks requiring memory. Boys tend to be more likely to have difficulty paying attention, and students with absence seizures are at risk for being misidentified as having attention-deficit/hyperactivity disorder (Agnew, Nystul, & Conner, 1998). Behavioral issues may stem from anxiety, low self-esteem, or overprotection by family and teachers. Debbie Broughton, Jacob's seventh-grade math teacher emphasizes, "Expect everything out of that child that you would for others. Try not to treat them differently or walk on pins and needles. They don't want to be singled out."

Classmates need factual information about seizures; otherwise, they might fear or tease the student (Epilepsy Foundation of America, 2001, 2002). Have students with epilepsy explain their condition, if they are comfortable doing so. Jacob and others find that such explanations can help them learn to handle their condition with confidence instead of embarrassment. Classmates also need to know first aid for seizures. Being able to respond to a seizure decreases their anxiety.

Describing the Characteristics of Asthma

Asthma, the most prevalent chronic illness of children and the leading cause of school absenteeism, accounts for almost 5 million school absences a year (American Academy of Allergy, Asthma, and Immunology, 1999; Simeonsson, 1995). The prevalence of asthma has become epidemic, increasing at an alarming rate in recent years, especially among African Americans and women (Dowling, 1997; National Heart, Blood, and Lung Institute, n.d.). From 1982 to 1994, childhood asthma increased by 72 percent (Malik & Hampton, 2002). By 2020, one in five families is expected to have a member with asthma (Pew Environmental Health Commission, 2000). Some students have only occasional symptoms. Others experience breathing difficulties almost daily. Symptoms may be mild, as when a student experiences occasional shortness of breath after a challenging football game; or they may be life-threatening, requiring emergency hospitalization.

"Contrary to popular belief, [a student with asthma] has no trouble inhaling; it's the exhaling they can't do properly" (Jacy Group, 1997–2000, p. 1). When a student has an episode (sometimes called an *attack* or *flare*), less air passes out of the lungs than the student has inhaled (*airway inflammation*), resulting in trapped air and excessive, thick, mucus formation (*airway constriction*). Because carbon dioxide triggers breathing, the trapped air causes the brain to continuously scream, "Breathe!" The lungs oblige (*airway hyperresponsiveness*), causing rapid, shallow breathing; and the cycle worsens.

The symptoms and severity of asthma vary widely from person to person and are generally classified as *mild intermittent* (two or fewer episodes per week), *mild persistent* (more than two but less than daily), *moderate persistent* (daily), or *severe persistent* (continual; interferes with physical activity) (National Heart, Lung, and Blood Institute, 1997). Although most students with asthma will have mild to moderate symptoms, asthma episodes can cause a medical emergency and, in rare cases (about 5,000 per year), lead to death (American Lung Association, 2002a; Malik & Hampton, 2002). European American children tend to experience less severe asthma than African American and Hispanic American children do, who have more emergency room visits and more difficulty participating in sports and exercise, attending school consistently, and obtaining good medical care (American Lung Association, 2002c). The mortality rate is also much higher among African Americans.

On average, teachers have two children with asthma in each classroom they teach (Getch & Neuharth-Pritchett, 1999). Basic preventions and treatments include taking medications, monitoring lung functioning, managing stress and exercise, controlling triggers, and managing episodes (National Heart, Lung, and Blood Institute, 1997). Students generally take two kinds of medications for asthma (National Heart, Lung, and Blood Association, n.d.): **Anti-inflammatories** help prevent asthma episodes from starting by reducing airway swelling, and **bronchodilators** stop asthma episodes after they've started by opening constricted airways (American Lung Association, 2002b). Students must take their medications as prescribed and as soon as they sense an episode coming. Some students, especially adolescents, might try to tough it out, especially if the school requires them to go to the office for their medication (Horner, 1999). Therefore, "students with asthma should be permitted to have inhaled medications in their possession for the treatment and the prevention of asthma symptoms when they are prescribed by that student's physician" (American Academy of Allergy, Asthma, and Immunology, 1999, p. 1). Any delay could cause a mild episode to become severe quickly.

Asthma symptoms and medications can adversely affect school performance. Lack of sleep and general malaise affect attention and concentration (Bender, 1999). Sometimes, medication may make students feel "hyper" (Thies, 1999). Steroids may cause depression, weepiness, anxiety, sleepiness, and weight gain.

Students with asthma will probably monitor their lung functioning by using a **peak flow meter.** To operate the device, a person with asthma simply exhales as hard as possible into the mouthpiece. The higher the reading, the better the lungs are working. Lower readings indicate that the airways are obstructed and the use of medications and/or avoiding allergens is warranted to prevent a flare. Physicians identify specific *green* (safe), *yellow* (caution), and *red* (danger) zones for each child. Parents use a peak flow meter to decide whether their children should miss school or have their medication adjusted (Helms, 2002).

Vigorous exercise (especially in cold air) frequently triggers asthma episodes, but moderate exercise improves breathing efficiency and overall health. Students will learn to recognize their own limits, and teachers should follow students' leads about their exercise regimen. Medications taken before exercising to prevent asthma episodes are now available.

No amount of stress causes an asthmatic episode unless the person already has hyperactive airways. "Emotions do not cause asthma, but can make asthma worse. Strong feelings can lead to changes in breathing patterns. Times of 'good' stress and 'bad' stress can cause problems for people with asthma" (National Jewish Center for Immunology and Respiratory Medicine, 2000, p. 1). Learning to express emotions and manage asthma effectively can minimize the effects of stress.

Relaxation techniques do not prevent episodes of impaired breathing, but they are useful for responding to episodes once they have begun. Deliberate self-calming activities help avoid the

An **action plan**, which we discuss later in the chapter, identifies needed responses to medical crises. An asthma action plan should identify the readings identified by the student's physician for *safe, caution,* and *danger*. Go to the Web Links module in Chapter 11 of the Companion Website for a link to an asthma action plan.

additional constriction of airways that often accompanies fear and panic. They are especially useful in the 10- to 15-minute interval before the medications take full effect.

Triggers do not cause asthma. The underlying asthma enables these agents to interfere with normal breathing. Common school triggers include dust and chalk dust; pollens and molds; strong scents such as perfumes, paint and chemical fumes; smoke; cold, hot, or smoggy air; exercise; laughing or crying too hard; upper respiratory infections; cockroach droppings; and classroom pets (Getch & Neuharth-Pritchett, 1999). Schools need to monitor their air quality carefully, and students may benefit from an air purifier in the classroom (DePaepe et al., 2002; National Environmental Health Association, 1995).

Managing episodes is an essential first-aid skill for teachers. Students with severe asthma *must* use medication as soon as they experience symptoms. Common symptoms requiring prompt attention include "(a) wheezing, (b) feeling tightness or pain in the chest, (c) coughing throughout the day, (d) difficult breathing and shortness of breath, and (e) little energy for active play" (American Lung Association, 2002a, p. 1). Teachers need to follow a student's action plan, speak reassuringly, and contact the school nurse or administrator and parents or guardians if the medicine does not seem to be working. When a student has a severe episode, he may hunch over with shoulders lifted, breathing only from the upper part of the chest and worsening his condition. If this happens, the teacher needs to gently ease the student into a fully prone or upright position or have the student rest his elbows on his knees to open up the chest as much as possible (American Lung Association, 2002a; Jacy Group, 1997–2000). In Figure 11–2, we list other symptoms requiring emergency treatment. Call paramedics immediately if these occur.

FIGURE 11–2
When to seek emergency care for asthma

- Symptoms worsen, even after the medication has had time to work (generally 5–10 minutes).
- The student cannot speak a sentence without pausing for breath, has difficulty walking, and/or stops playing and cannot start again.
- Chest and neck are pulled or sucked in with each breath.
- Peak flow rate lessens or does not improve after bronchodilator treatment or drops below 50 percent of the student's personal best.
- Lips and fingernails turn blue: Emergency care is needed immediately!
- A second wave occurs after an episode subsides; the student is uncomfortable and having trouble breathing but does not wheeze.

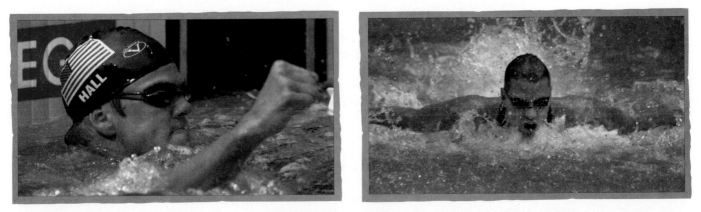

In the 2000 Summer Olympics, Gary Hall, Jr., who has diabetes, and Tom Dolan, who has asthma, did not let their health conditions stop them from winning gold medals for swimming. To learn more about these young men, go to the "Web Links" module in Chapter 11 of the Companion Website.

Middle school students in one study (Horner, 1999) emphasized that, although they wanted and needed support during their asthma episodes, they did not want to lose their independence. Some overpowering adults created feelings of helplessness. On the other hand, students' self-esteem was enhanced by adults who gave them affirmation and supported their independence. Talking to students ahead of time about their action plans and their suggestions for handling episodes gives them a sense of personal control.

Describing the Characteristics of Cancer

Cancer, a condition that causes the unrestrained growth of cells in body organs or tissues, is ruthlessly indiscriminate, attacking children and adults alike. In 2002, an estimated 9,100 children under age 15 were diagnosed with cancer; almost one-third of those had leukemia (American Cancer Society, 2002). Cancer is the primary cause of death by disease in children of this age group. Although an estimated 1,400 died from cancer that same year, mortality rates have declined 50 percent from the 1970s. Therapy advances have dramatically improved the prognosis of these children. The American Cancer Society projects that a child has a 72 to 92 percent likelihood of five-year survival, depending on the site of the cancer. The cure rate for childhood cancer is 60 percent, and one in 1,000 20- to 29-year-olds is a survivor of childhood malignancy (Kalwinsky, 2002).

"From the moment of diagnosis," writes Ann Bessell (2001b), the mother of a child with leukemia, "the lives of these children are irrevocably changed. For many, hospitalizations and medical procedures replace slumber parties, camping trips, and other childhood adventures" (p. 346).

A variety of treatments, including chemotherapy, surgery, radiation therapy, or a combination, are used to treat specific childhood cancers (American Cancer Society, 2002). Children often respond well to chemotherapy because several types specifically affect growing cells.

Unfortunately, the treatments for cancer generally cause side effects. Chemotherapy, for example, works indiscriminately on all rapidly dividing cells, including the intestinal lining (causing nausea) and hair follicles (resulting in baldness). In addition, the treatments often lower the student's white cell count, increasing the student's vulnerability to complications from such infections as chickenpox (Henderson, 1999; Tyler & Colson, 1994).

More than half the students with cancer have leukemia or brain tumors. These two cancers affect the central nervous system (CNS), potentially causing learning disabilities. Chemotherapy treatments for various cancers can also affect the CNS. Recent theories suggest that these students will not have the common type of learning disability that tends to be consistent over time. Instead, those who are affected will retain the skills that they had before treatment and lose some developmental skills later in life, often years afterward (Armstrong, Blumberg, & Toledano, 1999; Bessell, 2001b). Not all students, though, will have significant long-term effects.

Childhood leukemia survivors may develop nonverbal learning disabilities that affect their writing and concentration skills (Bessell, 2001a). These students will benefit from (1) removal of time constraints and writing requirements when possible, (2) handouts with preprinted assignments, (3) tape recorders for lectures and instructions, (4) dictating machines and word processors, and (5) calculators to avoid mechanical errors (Regan & Reeb, 1998). Despite children's potential for learning problems, one study found that those treated with chemotherapy do not significantly differ from those without cancer in social, emotional, and behavioral functioning (Noll et al., 1999). Teachers viewed them as more sociable and less aggressive, and peers believed they experienced greater social acceptance.

Ann Bessell's son Jonathan had difficulty receiving an appropriate education while undergoing treatments for leukemia. You can read more about that story in Box 11–2. Jonathan's experiences motivated Ann to pursue a Ph.D. in special education. She studied the psychosocial adjustment, quality of life, and school experiences of cancer survivors for her dissertation. The results indicate the importance of including students with cancer in general

Box 11–2

Ann Bessell Speaks Out on Educating Children with Chronic Illness

When a child is diagnosed with a chronic, life-threatening illness, it can be an overpowering experience for the entire family. Parents often find themselves in the role of advocate for their child, communicating the child's needs and protecting his or her rights. Nowhere is this more evident than within the context of the child's education. It is hard to believe that a family thrust into such a horrific vortex of medical and financial uncertainty must also fight for their child's schooling. However, such is the case for the many families faced with childhood cancer, AIDS, cystic fibrosis, muscular dystrophy, and other life-threatening pediatric medical problems.

When my son, Jonathan, was diagnosed at age 11 with lymphoma, a form of cancer, I focused on his medical treatment. . . . Throughout the many hospitalizations Jonathan endured, my husband Lee and I took turns sleeping at our son's bedside in the hospital and working when we could during the day. We continued our involvement with Little League baseball, participated in school activities, and supported each other. Together with his brothers, Ian and Paul, we were determined to maintain some semblance of normalcy for Jonathan.

However, we were astounded when Jonathan's first return to the classroom was tenuous at best. I requested that all his classmates be allowed to wear hats so Jonathan would not feel different, but it was denied because of school rules prohibiting hats. Jonathan was still very excited and determined to return to school, but soon began to experience the isolation of someone who was "different." There were whispers about his appearance, fears about the possibility of his disease being contagious, and parental concerns that close friendship with someone "dying" might be detrimental to their own children. Many families were supportive, but others disappeared. My family's strength was fostered by the belief that Jonathan was fighting for his life because death was not an option.

Rising to the challenge, Jonathan perceived these problems as opportunities to allay fears and educate others. He would explain his illness in great technical detail and quote optimistic statistics concerning his positive prognosis. When his friends told him they didn't know what to say or do, he said, "Just act normal and be my friend." His optimism never wavered, but he became upset and frustrated when no one seemed to care about his schoolwork. Teachers would not collect his homework or would avoid giving him class assignments. It appeared that the pervasive attitude was to minimize the importance of his education. A parent I met at the doctor's office shared with me [that] she was told, as we were, not to worry about school for her 6-year-old because, "It's only first grade. Worry about saving her life first, then concentrate on school."

What message is this sending to a child who has a chronic illness? Unfortunately, when children are excluded from school or not provided with educational opportunities, it may communicate that there are no expectations for them because death is probably imminent.

Education communicates society's cultural values and expectations for its children. Education within the school environment . . . is even more crucial as it provides children with the opportunity to learn, socialize with peers, experience success, and develop increased independence and control over their environment. It also provides a sense of normalcy.

Source: From Bessell, A. G. (2001b, September). Educating children with chronic illness. Exceptional Parent Magazine, 31(9), 44–45.

education with their same-age peers. Children who repeated a grade or were placed in special education as a result of their absenteeism, cancer-related effects, or other disabilities expressed that "school represented a scary place filled with the risk of failure" (Bessell, 2001a, p. 355). In Bessell's study, nearly 30 percent of the children with cancer had been retained in grade compared to 11 percent of the general population. "Getting held back was the worst thing that ever happened in school," one student confided (p. 356). Those children who received homebound services, which one child described as "the unbearable loneliness of being stuck at home and away from my friends," felt isolated and unready to return to school academically (p. 356). When homebound services are required, Ann Bessell recommends dual enrollment in home and school programs.

Most of the children in this study emphasized that the teacher is the key in creating an inclusive and successful school environment. "She always found a way to make me feel good and didn't treat me like I would break," one child said (Bessell, 2001b, p. 352). The highest-rated teachers were "understanding, aware of subtle changes, and willing to make modifications" (p. 352).

Describing the Characteristics of Diabetes

Approximately two out of every 1,000 young people under age 20 have diabetes (American Diabetes Association, 2001). Diabetes results when the pancreas stops producing or produces too little of the hormone insulin. This condition occurs in some people who are genetically predisposed and sometimes develops after a viral infection. When this happens, the cells do not absorb glucose; and unused sugar builds up in the blood. The kidneys try to filter out the excess sugar; therefore, to diagnose diabetes, doctors may test urine or blood to see if sugar is present (National Institute of Diabetes and Digestive and Kidney Diseases, 2002). A sign of poorly controlled diabetes is increased thirst, increased urination, and weight loss. Over time, increased glucose levels can damage the eyes, kidneys, nerves, or heart (American Diabetes Association, 2002).

Formerly called *juvenile diabetes,* Type 1 or insulin-dependent diabetes usually develops in individuals before age 35 and is most commonly diagnosed in young people between ages 10 and 16. Most who develop Type 1 diabetes are European American.

Students with diabetes may have symptoms of the flu before diagnosis (American Diabetes Association, 2002). Although some children and adolescents experience a "honeymoon" for a while after their diagnosis as the pancreas puts forth one last effort to regulate glucose, their condition eventually results in a complete or near-complete halt in the production of insulin. The onset is rapid; and without injections of insulin, students will become comatose and die (National Institute of Diabetes and Digestive and Kidney Disease, 2002). Type II diabetes (non–insulin-dependent diabetes) results in the body's inability to make enough or properly use insulin. Type II usually results from obesity and genetic factors and most often occurs in individuals over age 45. However, more children and adolescents are being diagnosed. Most are overweight and of African, Hispanic, or Native American descent (American Diabetes Association, 2002). Unfortunately, young people in their 20s who develop Type II diabetes as teens may face serious health complications, miscarriages, and even death.

The majority of students with diabetes do not consider themselves as having a disability or health impairment. What others think about their condition can be more troubling to them than the diabetes itself (Amer, 1999; Thies, 1999). Sometimes they try to hide their condition from teachers and peers, a dangerous decision if others do not know how to treat them during a blood sugar emergency. Creating a classroom atmosphere that encourages open discussion and acceptance is essential for students with diabetes. Although we provide some general information in this section, as with all students who have health impairments, you will need to learn the specific needs of your student and develop health care and action plans with parents at the beginning of the school year (Rosenthal-Maleck & Greenspan, 1999).

Two serious medical conditions can occur in the classroom if the student's diabetes is not under good control. If the student does not have enough insulin, he or she can develop **hyperglycemia** (too much sugar), which can cause **ketoacidosis.** If insulin is not administered, the student will fall into a diabetic coma. Symptoms suggesting ketoacidosis include hunger, fatigue, excessive urination, thirst, and blurred vision. Sometimes the person can appear to be drunk. The treatment is insulin. Stress, eating too many carbohydrates, illness, and forgetting to take insulin can all cause hyperglycemia.

At the opposite end of the spectrum is **hypoglycemia,** or not enough sugar. Increased physical activity, taking more insulin than needed, or not eating enough can cause a person to have too much insulin. Hypoglycemia occurs when too much insulin in the person's system causes the blood sugar level to drop dangerously low. Insulin shock or insulin reaction may occur before mealtimes, especially if the meal is delayed. Common symptoms include feeling dizzy, sweaty, shaky, or nervous and having headaches or blurred vision.

Teachers may be able to tell that a student is hypoglycemic sooner than the student can. Confusion, a symptom of low blood sugar, may cause her to be unaware and even disagree that she is low. A change in behavior often occurs. For example, the student might usually be outgoing; but when hypoglycemic, she becomes withdrawn or apathetic. The treatment is to give the student a sugar source such as some fruit juice, milk, or a soda (not sugar-free). Check with the student's parents to develop an action plan and to find out specifically what the student should take for

A sample 504 Plan for a student with diabetes, which includes an action plan, is available at the Web Links module in Chapter 11 of the Companion Website.

low blood glucose, when and how often to eat, and whether a special diet is required. If, however, the student begins to have convulsions or loses consciousness, it is important *not* to give any food or fluids. Instead, seek immediate medical attention from someone who can administer a shot of glucagon. Teachers who have a student with diabetes need to make sure they know who can administer glucagon in their school and, if possible, take this training themselves.

The only way to tell accurately if the student's blood sugar is too high or too low is by testing blood sugar. Normal blood sugar runs between 70 and 120 milligrams per deciliter, but students with diabetes may have blood sugar content goals outside that range. Teachers should help the student find a way to check blood sugar that is comfortable and unobtrusive. One student may prefer to check her blood sugar quietly at her seat; another might prefer to go outside the classroom or to the nurse's office. Let the child be in charge as much as possible.

Students with poor glucose control risk problems with information processing speed, visual spatial ability, and memory (Holmes, Fox, Cant, Lampert, & Greet, 1999). Lowered IQ is also a risk for some students, especially boys. In such cases, the student needs an academically- and health-focused nondiscriminatory evaluation.

Describing the Characteristics of Human Immunodeficiency Virus

Human immunodeficiency virus (HIV) gradually infects and eventually destroys T4 and other immune cells that protect the body from disease. As the virus progresses and the immune system weakens, a person with HIV is more susceptible to **opportunistic infections** such as some cancers, recurrent fungus infections (such as thrush, athlete's foot, or yeast infections), pneumonia, and tuberculosis. HIV is found in certain body fluids and can be spread through blood, semen, vaginal fluid, breast milk, and other fluids containing blood. HIV is passed from one person to another through sexual contact and blood-to-blood contact, including sharing needles or injection equipment (Centers for Disease Control, 2001).

HIV progresses through three distinct phases. In the first stage, the student is asymptomatic and feels healthy. Thanks to the increased effectiveness of drug therapies, students with HIV can remain asymptomatic for years. Several children born with the HIV virus have actually purged themselves of the virus ("Babies Who Beat AIDS," 1996). In 1999, a new combination of drugs simplified the treatment for HIV in children, and 48 weeks after beginning the treatment, the virus remained undetectable in many of the participants (Doctor's Guide, 1999). In the second phase, minor *symptoms such as fever and fatigue increase* as the immune system weakens. The final stage, **acquired immunodeficiency disease (AIDS),** occurs when a student has one or more opportunistic infections and a T4 count below 200. Symptoms often include seizures, memory lapses, impaired vision, blindness, severe weight loss, and, in children, loss of cognitive abilities.

The incidence of children being born with HIV has dramatically decreased (Avert.org, 2002). Women with HIV who take the drugs ZDV or AZT during pregnancy, labor, and delivery and give their babies AZT for six weeks after birth reduce the likelihood of their child being HIV positive by two-thirds (Centers for Disease Control, 1997). In addition, if the mothers have a cesarean section before labor begins, the rate of HIV transmission plummets to about 2 percent (Wilfert, 1998). Among adolescents, the major causes of HIV are sexual conduct and shared needles (Centers for Disease Control, 2002). More female than male teens contract HIV. A major concern is that teens may have a lackadaisical attitude about practicing safe sex because they falsely believe that HIV can be cured by the new drug therapies.

African Americans have the highest risk of HIV transmission: African American children are 17 times more likely to contract HIV than European Americans are. Although 15 percent of the adolescent population is African American, 64 percent of adolescent AIDS cases reported in 2000 were African American (Center for Disease Control, 2002). Hispanic Americans are the second-highest risk group. Schools need to develop programs to address the cultural issues affecting HIV transmission. You can read more about such a program in Box 11–3.

Box 11-3

Multicultural Considerations

Reach for Health Community Youth Service Learning Program

In Chapter 5, you learned about the benefits of service learning for students with emotional and behavioral disorders. The results of the Reach for Health Community Youth Service Learning Program in New York City suggest that service learning may also provide important health benefits for urban middle school students (O'Donnell et al., 1999).

African American and Hispanic American adolescents are at a disproportionately high risk for contracting HIV, as are teens in economically disadvantaged areas. In the two urban middle schools participating in the program, 99 percent of the students were African American or Hispanic American; and each school had a high-risk profile based on violence-related injuries, HIV and other sexually transmitted diseases, teen pregnancies, and below-grade standardized test scores. Sixty-eight general and special education classes participated. Some students participated in the Reach for Health classroom curriculum only; others participated in the Reach for Health classroom curriculum enhanced by service learning opportunities. These students had a three-hour-per-week placement at a nursing home, a neighborhood full-service health clinic, a day-care center, or a senior citizen center. Their tasks included reading to seniors; observing or assisting physicians and dentists; doing clerical work; and helping with meals, exercise, recreation, and arts and crafts. The students discussed their experiences in their health classes. Their curriculum focused on three health risks—alcohol use, violence, and sexual behaviors—that can result in HIV infection, other sexually transmitted diseases, and unintended pregnancy. Although the number of special education students was

relatively small, O'Donnell et al. (1999) found that the specially adapted Reach for Health curriculum seemed to reduce the high-risk sexual behaviors of this population. In addition, participation significantly increased the number of general education students who reported less recent sexual activity or more safe-sex practices. The authors concluded:

> Clearly, there may be additional potential benefits of service learning, including its potential contributions to students' academic achievement and their emotional and social well-being and to the development of civic pride and participation. Indeed, in addition to showing how students in urban schools can benefit from extending classroom learning to the community, an important outcome of our work is to show that by working collaboratively, teachers, school administrators, nursing faculty, college students, and staff at community health services can involve young adolescents in a program that makes a tangible difference in their lives. (p. 181)

Putting These Ideas to Work for Progress in the General Curriculum

1. What factors do you think contribute to the decrease in high-risk sexual behaviors among African American and Hispanic American students who participate in service learning?

2. How could you incorporate service learning in your health programs?

To answer these questions online and learn more about these ideas and concepts, go to the Multicultural Considerations module in Chapter 11 of the Companion Website.

In the past, some school districts barred students with HIV from attending school, despite IDEA's zero-reject principle (Turnbull & Turnbull, 2000). Current research discredits the unfounded fear that HIV is easily transmitted (Centers for Disease Control, 2001). Today, teachers face three major issues related to HIV in the classroom: (1) protecting confidentiality, (2) preventing the transmission of HIV, and (3) understanding how the condition can affect learning and behavior.

An initial concern for teachers is confidentiality. Families do not have to disclose that a student has HIV or any other condition. The parents may choose not to tell the child, although the American Academy of Pediatrics (1999) recommends that parents inform the child honestly. If family members choose to tell, they may do so only because of the strict medication regimen the student must follow at school. When that is the case, teachers and other school personnel must

FIGURE 11–3
Universal precautions

All school personnel and students should:
1. Use personal protective gear as a barrier when exposure to body fluids is possible. In school settings, personal protective gear includes water-impervious vinyl or latex gloves, disposable cloth towels, and wads of gauze or paper towels.

2. Remove personal protective gear correctly by not touching the contaminated side of the item and disposing of used personal protective gear and any contaminated materials in biohazard containers or biohazard labeled bags. Never re-use the gloves.

3. Wash hands and any contaminated body areas immediately with soap and water.

4. Seek medical attention for any significant exposure to blood of another person.

5. Clean surfaces and/or solid objects that may be contaminated. The hepatitis virus can survive at least a week in dried blood (National Safety Council, 1997). Surfaces and objects contaminated with saliva or blood should be cleaned thoroughly with soap and water and disinfected with household bleach diluted with water at a strength of 1:10 (National Safety Council, 1997). This solution has a 24-hour shelf life and must be mixed fresh for use each day. Keep contaminated objects or surfaces in contact with the bleach solution for at least 30 seconds and either allow to air dry or wipe with a disposable cloth.

6. Use pick-ups, a broom and dust pan, tweezers, or some other object to pick up sharp objects ("sharps"), such as broken glass. Dispose of sharps in a solid container marked with a biohazard label. Do not dispose of sharps in a soft, plastic garbage-bag type of container.

Teachers should:
1. Receive training in first aid and emergency care.

2. Use universal precautions for all first aid emergencies.

3. Keep a first-aid kit and a spill kit (including gloves, gauze, bandages/band aids, small jar of bleach, biohazard disposal bag/stickers) in the classroom or gymnasium at all times.

4. Have a fanny pack with gloves and bandages for playground duty or on field trips.

5. Use safety precautions when handling sharps.

6. Follow all precautions of the Occupational Safety and Health Administration (OSHA) and the specific Contagion Exposure Control Plan of their school (administrators should have copies of both).

Source: From "Educating Children and Youth to Prevent Contagious Disease" (Report No. EDO-SP-1999-8) (p. 3), S. J. Grosse, 1999, *ERIC Digest,* Washington, DC: ERIC Clearinghouse on Teaching and Teacher Education (ERIC Document Reproduction Service No. ED 437 368).

not share that the child is HIV positive without parental consent (Committee on Pediatric AIDS, 2000) or unless compelled to do so by law.

The second concern for teachers is to prevent the transmission of HIV in two ways. One way is to remember that "each classroom is a place to model, teach, and practice safe contagion prevention habits" (Grosse, 1999, p. 1). Teachers and their students need to use **universal precautions** to prevent the spread of HIV and other communicable conditions in school. You will find a list of these essential health precautions adapted for educators in Figure 11–3. The Centers for Disease Control (2001) states that HIV is not contracted through saliva, feces, nasal secretions, sweat, tears, urine, and vomit unless blood is visible. However, body fluids can also transmit other communicable diseases so teachers must use universal precautions with all students (Beverly, 1995; Grosse, 1999).

By the time they graduate from high school, 50 to 70 percent of teens are sexually active (Johnson, Johnson, & Jefferson-Aker, 2001). Therefore, another way in which teachers can help prevent the spread of HIV is by honestly informing students about the condition and how to prevent transmission. Teachers also need to help students strengthen interpersonal skills that will help them resist peer pressure. One study concluded that adolescents whose self-esteem was based on their peer interactions were significantly more likely to engage in sexual behaviors, increasing their likelihood of exposure to HIV, than were those whose self-esteem was based on home and school activities and relationships (Young, Denny, & Spear, 1999).

Peer-led instruction is a valuable tool in HIV education (Centers for Disease Control, 2002; Johnson et al., 2001). Adolescents can develop accurate booklets and videotapes for peer-led training sessions. Teachers of students with cognitive limitations will find Johnson et al.'s (2001) strategies for HIV instruction very helpful.

A third concern for teachers is that HIV can affect students' learning and behavior. Professionals once erroneously thought that cognitive impairments were common and severe in children with HIV. Actually, most children with HIV reach school age with unaffected cognitive functioning (Committee on Pediatric AIDS, 2000). But students may reach motor and mental developmental milestones later than expected because they do not grow or gain weight normally (Koop, 1998–2001). Medical intervention can help. Students with HIV can improve their language, sensory, and motor skills if they receive combination antiretroviral therapy (Averitt, 1998). As the virus progresses to AIDS, students may experience neurological conditions, resulting in difficulty walking, poor school performance, seizures, mental retardation, and cerebral palsy (Koop, 1998–2001).

The general classroom is the most appropriate placement for the majority of students with HIV (Committee on Pediatric AIDS, 2000; Prater & Serna, 1995). Teachers need to maintain a normal school environment for children with HIV. Sometimes, however, a student will need to receive educational services at home or in a school setting that allows for individualized instruction, perhaps because the student's behavior (e.g., biting) or medical condition (e.g., open sores) creates risks for other students. Homebound or special education placement may also be appropriate if the student's risk of contracting infections from other students is high due to immune deficiency or if the student's condition has caused academic limitations.

Identifying the Causes

The etiology, or cause, of specific health impairments varies. Most result from infections, genetic factors, and environmental influences. Sometimes the cause is unknown or is trauma-related, as when a child is severely burned.

Infections

Numerous diseases are caused by infections from some type of microorganism. Certainly, colds and flu do not typically result in students being identified as having a health impairment. Some infections, however, cause long-lasting consequences and can even lead to death. Even a common infection such as strep throat can result in rheumatic fever, a condition associated with heart problems if not treated. Other infection-caused conditions include HIV, tuberculosis, and some cancers. In addition, epilepsy can result from brain infections such as encephalitis and meningitis. Researchers believe diabetes can develop after a susceptible person experiences an infection (Epilepsy Foundation of America, 2001, 2002; American Diabetes Association, 2002).

Genetic Factors

Children born with abnormal genes for health impairments such as cystic fibrosis, hemophilia, or sickle cell disease will inherit the condition. The puzzle for geneticists has been locating the specific genes that cause these conditions. The Human Genome Project has required scientists to map the human genome, which contains 50,000–100,000 genes (Begley, 2000; National Reference Center for Bioethics Literature & the Joseph and Rose Kennedy Institute of Ethics,

2002). A draft of the completed human genome map brings science closer to solving many health-impairment mysteries.

A genetic component can also exist in the development of health impairments such as diabetes, asthma, epilepsy, and specific cancers. In these conditions, the abnormal gene apparently causes the individual to be predisposed to the condition; but the condition itself is not inevitable (Associated Press, 1999; P/S/L Consulting Group, 1997). Called **susceptibility genes,** these genes seem to work in conjunction with other currently unknown factors (e.g., environmental factors or infections) to cause a health impairment.

Environmental Influences

The environment can play a substantial role in a person's health. Environmental factors may worsen and even cause some health impairments. Conversely, a treatment regimen that includes avoiding environmental triggers can prevent death due to severe asthma. Doctors debate whether poor access to health care or air pollution might contribute to the deaths of students with asthma in inner cities (Podolsky, 1997). The environment affects other conditions as well. For example, in a year-long study of non-immune-suppressed children with HIV, multiple negative life events significantly increased the likelihood of their developing immune suppression (Howland et al., 2000).

Behavior-related precursors to chronic illness (e.g., smoking, inadequate exercise, poor eating habits) such as heart disease, diabetes, and cancer are rampant in American society. We have already mentioned that Type II diabetes, generally unheard of in past generations of children, is becoming more common because of childhood obesity. In addition, 60 percent of children ages 5 to 10 have at least one risk factor associated with cardiovascular disease (Wakefield, 2002).

Prenatal and Perinatal Influences

A mother's use of alcohol, drugs, or nicotine during pregnancy can increase the risk that her child will develop a health impairment. The substance or substances she uses are known as **teratogens**: environmental influences that prohibit normal growth development in the fetus. Other teratogens include exposure of the mother to infections, trauma, X-rays, or other radiation. A mother's use of alcohol, drugs, or tobacco, especially the use of two or more, greatly increases the risk that the child will have **fetal alcohol syndrome** with its accompanying cognitive and behavioral limitations (Cosden & Peerson, 1997; Jacobson & Jacobson, 1999), seizures, HIV, sudden infant death syndrome, asthma, hyperactivity, heart defects, or hearing or vision impairments (Carta et al., 1994; Crawford, 1997; DiFranza & Lew, 1996; Loftus & Block, 1996).

Postnatal Influences

Exposure to environmental agents after birth can also cause health impairments, including lead poisoning and some types of cancer. Lead poisoning is the most common environmental disease of childhood and can cause learning disabilities, decreased growth, hyperactivity, impaired hearing, and even brain damage (Centers for Disease Control, 1998; Commonwealth of Massachusetts, 2002). Lead poisoning is especially a hazard for young children under age 9 who live in buildings built before 1978 that contain lead paint.

Identifying the Prevalence

In the 1999–2000 school year, schools served 197,761 students (0.54 percent of the school-age population) ages 6 to 21 under IDEA as *other health impaired* (National Center for Education Statistics, 2001). This number represents a 351 percent increase from 1990–1991, largely resulting from the inclusion of students with attention-deficit/hyperactivity disorder (see Chapter 6) in this category. Although European Americans are proportionately underrepresented among students with disabilities, their highest representation is in the "other health impairments" category.

To learn more about the Human Genome Project and teratogens, discussed later in this section, go to the Web Links module in Chapter 11 of the Companion Website.

How Do You Evaluate Students with Other Health Impairments?

Generally, a physician identifies students as having health impairments. Students can receive 504 plans to accommodate their health needs in the classroom. However, if the student's condition appears to adversely affect educational progress, the teacher must refer the student for a nondiscriminatory evaluation.

Determining the Presence

The first step in determining whether a student qualifies as having a health impairment is a medical exam that includes a thorough medical history. Teachers need to document any symptoms that occur in the classroom.

After a physician makes a diagnosis, school personnel decide whether the student qualifies for special education and related services under the IDEA's *other health impairments* category and, if so, what services to provide. The evaluation team administers individualized intelligence tests, achievement batteries, and behavior rating/adaptive behavior scales for two reasons. First, the student's cognitive, academic, and behavioral functioning before the illness will affect her adjustment to the medical condition (Brown & DuPaul, 1999). Second, the evaluation serves as a baseline so the team can determine if the student's condition or treatments cause cognitive or behavioral changes. Moreover, because of these changes, the evaluation team may need to assess students with certain types of health impairments more frequently than students with other types of disabilities. Figure 11–4 explains the evaluation process for these students in more detail.

Determining the Nature and Extent of General and Special Education and Related Services

Do you find IEP, 504, health care, and action plans confusing? Go to the Web Links module in Chapter 11 of the Companion Website to find links to help you understand the differences.

Do you have adequate first aid and CPR training? In Chapter 11's "Web Links" module on the Companion Website, we provide a link to the American Red Cross, which offers this training throughout the United States.

Students are entitled to an IEP if their health condition limits their strength, vitality, or alertness and adversely affects their educational performance. However, students whose health impairments do not affect their educational performance usually need a 504 plan for health services and other accommodations (DePaepe et al., 2002). Close collaboration between school and medical personnel is necessary to meet the complex needs of these students. Whether the student needs an IEP or 504 plan, the school nurse is an important team member in decision making.

The student who has been hospitalized should have an IEP written before returning to school (Shields & Heron, 1995). The plan should state who will know about the student's condition and how this information will be provided (Kleiberstein & Broome, 2000). The team should schedule a reassessment every 12–18 months, sooner if treatment or condition progression can result in more rapid changes in the student's functioning (Armstrong et al., 1999).

The IEP also should include a **health care plan** that specifies procedures and standards for taking naps, receiving medications, and making up work missed during absences. It should also include an action plan for students who may have medical emergencies (Bruder, 1995; DePaepe et al., 2002). The health care plan should specify how personnel will be trained to follow the procedures in the action plan. At least two people at the school should be trained in emergency procedures to provide immediate care until the school nurse or emergency medical personnel arrive. Emergency medical kits should be fully stocked and readily available, and expiration dates should be periodically checked. All personnel need training in basic first aid, identifying and treating allergic reactions, and cardiopulmonary resuscitation (CPR) (DePaepe et al., 2002). The action plan should also include emergency phone numbers.

School health care services that the student needs are related services under IDEA (see Chapter 1) and may include skin, gastronomy, and respiratory care; catheterization; and medication delivery, among others. The services must not require a physician and can be administered

FIGURE 11–4

Nondiscriminatory evaluation of students with other health impairments

Nondiscriminatory Evaluation

Observation

Parent or teacher observes	Student may seem sluggish or have other symptoms that suggest illness. The parent takes the student for a medical examination.
Physician observes	During a routine physical or a physical resulting from symptoms, the physician determines reasons why the student needs further medical asssessment. Some health impairments are determined before or shortly after birth.

Medical screening

Assessment measures	Findings that indicate need for further evaluation
Battery of medical tests prescribed by physician and/or specialists	Results reveal that the student has a health impairment. A physician makes the diagnosis.

Prereferral

Prereferral may or may not be indicated, depending on the severity of the health impairment. Some students function well in the general classroom. A decision may be made at this point to serve the student with a 504 plan if accommodations are needed solely to monitor medications and/or to make sure that faculty knows what to do if the student has a medical emergency (e.g., hyperglycemia or hypoglycemia if the student is diabetic).

Referral

Students with health impairments that adversely affect their learning or behavior need to be referred for educational assessment.

Nondiscriminatory evaluation procedures and standards

Assessment measures	Findings
Medical history	Completed jointly by parents, medical, and school personnel, the history yields information needed to develop a health care plan.
Individualized intelligence test	The student's condition or treatment may contribute to a decrease in IQ from previous assessments.
Individualized achievement test	The student's medical condition and/or treatment regimen may affect achievement.
Behavior rating scales	The student may exhibit internalizing or externalizing behavior disorders resulting from the condition or the stress of treatment or environmental factors.
Curriculum-based assessment	The student is not mastering the curriculum in one or more areas as a result of the condition, treatment, and/or resulting absences.
Direct observation	The student may experience fatigue or other symptoms resulting from the condition or treatment, detrimentally affecting classroom progress.

Nondiscriminatory evaluation team determines that student has an other health impairment and needs special education and related services.

Appropriate Education

by school nurses or other trained personnel (DePaepe et al., 2002). School delivery of medication requires written parental permission and written authorization by a physician. How the medication will be stored and administered, including who will dispense the medication, are important components of the health care plan. The health care plan can also list goals for providing family support, including **respite care**—plans for giving family members an occasional and much needed break from caregiving. With parental permission, all school personnel who work with the student should receive a copy of and thoroughly understand the health care and action plans.

A transition-after-graduation plan is especially important for students with health impairments. A survey of these students revealed that more than one-third worried about getting a job, usually essential for health insurance. Yet only 6 percent had IEP plans that addressed postsecondary educational or vocational goals (Thies, 1999). Students such as Kyle who have sickle cell disease may be told, erroneously, that their pain episodes and need for frequent medications and blood transfusions will prevent them from getting a job. Indeed, ADA and Section 504 (see Chapter 1) provide for nondiscrimination. His Aunt Tammy is only one of many adults with sickle cell who are planning and achieving successful careers.

How Do You Assure Progress in the General Curriculum?

Including Students

The percentage of students with health impairments who spend 80 percent or more of their day in general education has increased from 30 percent in 1988–1989 to 44 percent in 1998–1999 (National Center for Education Statistics, 2002). Figure 11–5 illustrates the percentages of students in the continuum of services.

Receiving an appropriate education while in the hospital and at home is critical if students are to avoid retention, inappropriate special education placement, learned helplessness, or dropping out (Bessell, 2001b). Students with health impairments receive homebound services more often than students with any other type of disability. Kyle received homebound services for a while, but his grandmother decided that he needed to attend school with other students. As you

FIGURE 11–5

Placements of students with health impairments (1998–1999)

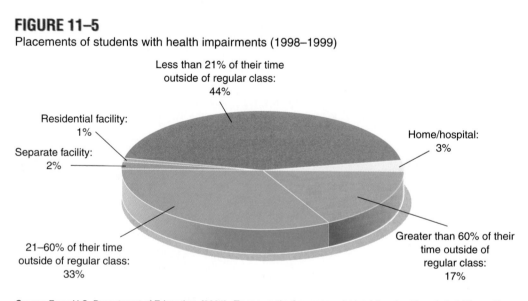

Less than 21% of their time outside of regular class: 44%

Residential facility: 1%

Separate facility: 2%

Home/hospital: 3%

21–60% of their time outside of regular class: 33%

Greater than 60% of their time outside of regular class: 17%

Source: From U.S. Department of Education. (2001). *To assure the free appropriate public education of all children with disabilities: Twenty-first annual report to Congress on the Implementation of the Individuals with Disabilities Education Act.* Washington, DC: Author.

have already read, students often feel isolated by homebound services (Bessell, 2001b). The Committee on School Health (2000) emphasizes that "homebound instruction is meant for acute or catastrophic health problems that confine a child or adolescent to home or hospital for a prolonged but defined period of time and is not intended to relieve the school or parent of the responsibility for providing education for the child in the least restrictive environment" (p. 1154). Parents, school administrators, teachers, and the primary care physician need to collaborate to consider how to address the standards and IEP objectives the student would achieve in school, the specific duration of the homebound services, and how to return the student to school as quickly and smoothly as possible. Receiving dual enrollment in homebound and school-based instruction allows the student to continue functioning as a classroom member (Bessell, 2001b).

Students with health impairments face special placement challenges because of frequent absences and hospitalizations. Jonathan Bessell, whose mother Ann shared her concerns about his educational needs earlier in this chapter, wrote to President Clinton because Florida refused to pay for a tutor when he received a bone marrow transplant in Massachusetts. Massachusetts refused to pay for a tutor because he was not a resident. You can read his letter in Box 11–4. Jonathan and his parents also filed a complaint with the Office of Civil Rights (OCR) and contacted county school board and state legislature members. OCR eventually compelled the local school district to reimburse his parents for the tutor they hired in Massachusetts. Jonathan lost his battle to cancer in 1994, but his determination to receive an education continues to make a difference. Ann Bessell (2001b) says, "I wanted Jonathan's message about school and education to be heard by others" (p. 46). Jonathan's parents and brothers continue to share his message at conferences and with organizations. In addition, they advocate for other parents in their efforts to receive accommodations and services for their children with health impairments.

Will discussing the health condition with the class benefit the student's inclusion? Parents generally feel that the school should be notified immediately after a student's diagnosis (Kliebenstein & Broome, 2000). However, parents of an adolescent who feels embarrassed about his or her condition also believe that they and their teenager should decide together about which key personnel and peers to tell.

Students with health impairments often feel powerless over their bodies (Fleitas, 2002). Discussing the condition without the student's knowledge or presence can add to that sense of powerlessness. Therefore, issues of confidentiality must be respected, and teachers need to ask the

Box 11–4

Making a Difference

Jonathan Bessell Writes to President and Mrs. Clinton

March 20, 1994

Dear Mr. President and Hilary,

I'm a 12 year old boy in 6th grade and I'm afraid I'll never get to graduate from elementary school. I've lived in Florida my whole life, but now I'm in Boston at Children's Hospital having a bone marrow transplant.

My problem is I'm being deprived an education because no one wants to pay for my tutor while I'm in the hospital. Florida says Massachusetts should pay for it, and Massachusetts says Florida should pay. I don't care who pays—I just want to graduate with my class. If I don't, I'll never get to be in the same class with all my friends.

I thought the government guaranteed all tax-paying citizens an education. My parents pays all kinds of taxes all the time, so I should get my tutor. Now I'm finding out that I have to be in the hospital for a long time, fighting for my life, and it will probably take just as long for all the lawyers to decide who should pay for the tutor. By the time that happens, I'll probably have to repeat 6th grade, and that's not fair!

It's not easy fighting cancer. People are always doing gross and disgusting staff to me, and this problem is making it even harder. I hope you can help me now when I need it.

Yours truly, Jonathan

Source: From Bessell, A. G. (2001, September). Educating children with chronic illness. *Exceptional Parent, 31* (9), 45.

Inclusion Tips

Box 11—5

	What You Might See	What You Might Be Tempted to Do	Alternate Responses	Ways to Include Peers in the Process
Behavior	The student may be absent a great deal with major health impairments.	Treat him as though he is not able to do the work.	Call or visit him during times of absence. Provide extra supports and help so he can complete needed work.	Set up a support system for when he is absent. Encourage peers to help him at home.
Social interactions	He may be self-conscious or embarrassed about his illness so that he withdraws from others.	Allow him to work alone, assuming he is merely low on energy or needs to be by himself.	Structure situations that encourage him to share his ideas and thoughts and allow others to recognize his strengths.	Building on his areas of academic strength, have him tutor peers as well as younger students.
Educational performance	With some illnesses, lack of strength and alertness hinder his capacity for full participation.	Call him down for not paying attention or excuse him from completing assignments.	Encourage him and offer extra help. Adjust assignments to create meaningful tasks.	Encourage peer interaction through cooperative learning.
Classroom attitudes	He may appear bored, confused, or overwhelmed by class activities when not feeling well.	Ignore his behavior or make an issue in front of the class.	Give him the benefit of the doubt. Check how he is feeling, then clarify, repeat instructions, or get needed help.	Have peers work with him to develop a cueing system that encourages him to signal when he is not feeling well.

student's permission before sharing health information. The most empowering strategy is for students to explain the condition to peers when they feel ready and in the manner that is most comfortable for them. We provide more recommendations for including students with health impairments in Box 11–5.

Another important facet of including students with health impairments is creating a safe classroom environment that not only addresses their medical needs but also their need for social safety, which includes helping them handle insensitivity. Teasing and bullying are serious issues for students with health impairments, especially because bullies and teasers often target students who seem vulnerable physically (Fleitas, 2002; McNamara & McNamara, 2000). Students who cry, get angry, or shrink away from teasers are more likely to experience victimization. In the *The Meanest Thing to Say* (Cosby, 1997), an effective book for helping students learn to handle insensitivity, Little Bill learns to stand up to a teaser by repeating the word "So?" after anything the teaser says. Helping the student problem-solve solutions to handle teasers is generally more effective than intervention from the teacher. In addition, students often model how teachers treat their classmates. For that reason, teachers must demonstrate value and respect for all students. Involving peers in planning for the student with health impairments during class meetings encourages them to view the student positively (Bloom, Perlmutter, & Burrell, 1999). Perhaps the most important tool for handling insensitivity is a good friend. Kyle says:

> My grandma has been taking care of me since my mama died when I was 2, and I really don't like people talking about her. When [a boy] was talking about my grandma, my friend named Michael said, "Stop picking on that boy. He's got sickle cell and you know that. You don't [need]

In Chapter 6, you learned how Kelsey and her therapist, Chris, created a three-page list of ideas for responding to teasing. This list empowered Kelsey to handle insensitivity confidently.

When his school refused to pay for a nurse to help Garrett Frye operate his wheelchair and oxygen machine and attend school (rather than be educated at home or in a hospital), he sued and won in the U.S. Supreme Court. The nurse's services are "related services" that enable him—and students like him who have physical disabilities and other health impairments—to be included in school and its general curriculum.

to fight him." And then when he still tried to fight me, Michael said, "Why not fight me instead?" So that made me feel . . . good that I have friends like that.

You will find other strategies for helping students handle insensitivity in Figure 11–6.

Planning Universally Designed Learning

When they return to school after an extended absence, students with health impairments make an important step toward regaining control of their lives and resuming pre-illness activities (Sullivan, Flumer, & Zigmond, 2001). The success of their school reentry depends largely on how teachers support their academic and emotional needs and compensate for their absences (Kliebenstein & Broome, 2000).

Adapting Instruction

The academic goals for students with health impairments should take into account their cognitive level or potential as well as physical condition or energy level (Wadsworth & Knight, 1999). Most students will have the same curriculum as their peers. But for the student whose absences are frequent, teachers need to ask three questions (Shank, 2002):

▼ What are the most important academic standards that the student needs to meet this year?

▼ How can I ensure that the student attains these standards in the most efficient way possible?

▼ How can I motivate the student to attain these standards?

When a history teacher asks the first question, she realizes that a student with cancer in her American history class does not need to memorize the dates of all the Civil War battles. Instead, she determines that the most important information is why the Civil War happened, when it took place, the major historical figures on both sides, the outcomes of some of the most significant battles, and the results of the war.

Second, the teacher strives for efficient standards mastery. She videotapes her lectures and provides extra credit to a student for peer tutoring. She cuts reading assignments to the information

Go to the Web Links module in Chapter 11 of the Companion Website for more ideas about helping students handle teasing and bullying.

FIGURE 11–6
Empowering victims to handle insensitivity

Supporting the victim of teasing

1. Get all the details from the student, allowing expression of feelings in preparation for problem solving.
2. Rehearse with the child making fun of the teasing:
   "So what?"
   "Can't you think of anything else to say?"
   "I heard that one in kindergarten."
   "That's so old it's from the stone age."
   "I fell off my dinosaur when I first heard that."
   "Tell me when you get to the funny part."
   "And your point is . . ."
3. Ask if the student used the technique and how it worked.

Supporting the victim of a fighter

1. Intervene with the fighter according to school policy.
2. Get all the details from the child.
3. Teach the student to avoid the fighter.
   a. Don't talk to him.
   b. Protect yourself by staying out of his reach.
   c. Play close to the yard monitor.
   d. Don't tease or make faces at him.
4. Ask if it worked.

Recognizing a student who is being bullied

1. School work begins to slide.
2. Shows less interest in school.
3. Has frequent headaches or stomachaches to keep from going to school.
4. Chooses an out-of-the-way route to go home.
5. Is missing books, money, or other belongings without a good explanation.
6. Begins stealing or requesting extra money.
7. Has unexplained injuries or torn clothing.

Neutralizing the bully

1. Get as much detail as possible from the victim.
2. The teacher takes charge. Not doing anything condones bullying.
3. Contact the parents.
4. Establish a consequence if the bully goes within 20 feet of the victim.

Source: Excerpted from *Good Friends Are Hard to Find,* by F. Frankel, 1996, Glendale, CA: Perspective Publishing (www.familyhelp.com). Copyright 1996 by Fred Frankel. Excerpted with permission.

that is most essential and allows the student to tape-record rather than write answers to handout questions.

Third, knowing that the student is fatigued from treatments and has been unable to participate in class activities related to the Civil War, the teacher seeks alternative methods to encourage motivation. During a visit to her public library, she checks out popular Civil War videotapes that address her academic standards and has the student watch the videos at home and tape-record his reactions to them. Because the student has access to a laptop at home, she asks him to search for some specific information about the Civil War on the Internet. When he returns to school, he shares some of this information with his classmates.

Although the teacher reduces the amount of work the student needs to complete, she maintains high expectations for his classroom involvement and learning. Kyle's fourth-grade teacher required him to complete an oral book report despite his frequent absences. Initially, Kyle resisted; but his

Box 11–6

Into Practice

Keeping the Emphasis on Education

As a teacher, you will want to learn about a student's condition, including future expectations or prognosis. Sources for obtaining this information include the student and the parents, medical personnel with the parents' consent, your local library, and the Internet. (The resources we provide in Chapter 11 of the companion website are a good place to start your search.) In addition, you will want to request help to facilitate school reentry when the student is ready to leave the hospital. Having an IEP or 504 plan in place before the student returns to school will make the transition easier. The hospital's teacher and/or child life specialist will provide essential information for reentry planning. Class activities involving the child can include the following (Bessell, 2001b, p. 46):

- Create a class unit about children with special needs.
- Write movie reviews or TV reviews to send.
- Send information about a new video or computer game, with secret codes.
- Share comic books and follow up with a call.
- Use e-mail to create buddy lists.
- Create a website/chat room/info-board.
- Make an audiotape or video.

- Schedule phone calls, visits, special events.
- Arrange for mail, [e-mail, and/or fax] deliveries every day, [including class assignments].

Putting These Strategies to Work for Progress in the General Curriculum

1. If Kyle Bessell were in your classroom next year, which of these strategies do you think would be most helpful for meeting his needs?

2. Which strategies do you believe will be most challenging to implement for him or other students? Why? How could you meet these challenges?

3. How could you incorporate some of these strategies to help students keep up academically?

To answer these questions online and learn more about these strategies, go to the Into Practice module in Chapter 11 of the Companion Website.

Source: Adapted from Bessell, A. G. (2001, September). Educating children with chronic illness. *Exceptional Parent Magazine, 31*(9), 46.

teacher maintained her high expectations, and Kyle discovered how much he enjoys public speaking. The report was good training for the work he does now as a poster child for sickle cell disease.

Kyle's hospital teacher Anne Vella emphasizes the importance of faxing assignments to the hospital or homebound teacher daily. Teachers can assign a classmate to keep track of handouts and assignments on days the student is absent so they are ready to send after school. Some teachers keep an assignment list for the next week that they distribute to all students on Friday or post to a website. Parents and students also appreciate receiving the school newsletter, phone calls, cards, and home or hospital visits when the student is absent to help them feel a part of the school community (Sullivan et al., 2001).

You will find suggestions from Ann Bessell in Box 11–6.

Adapting Evaluation

When teachers assess students with frequent absences, they need an efficient way to find out whether or not the students have mastered the essential standards for that school year (Shank,

2002). For example, if a test or a homework assignment has 50 math problems, the student may only need to complete 10 to demonstrate mastery. Some teachers resist reducing assignments because they perceive the practice as unfair to other students. However, "fair is giving students what they need, not treating them all the same" (Lavoie, n.d.). In fact, the student with the reduced assignment has a more challenging task. If that student misses one problem on the reduced math test, her grade is 90 percent. However, if the other students miss one problem, their grade is 98 percent.

Another evaluation adaptation is providing the student with alternative assessments such as portfolio or journaling projects that demonstrate learning while providing a legacy, as this English teacher did for a hospitalized student with leukemia:

> I told Bill that I would give him English credit for keeping a journal in a spiral notebook I provided. When I visited, we talked about what he had written. Some days, Bill wrote stories about riding his motorbike or going hunting with his father. On other days, he wrote about his cancer treatments and hospital experiences. The journal gave him opportunities to escape the hospital through fantasy and to deal honestly with his condition. He has since died, and I believe he also created a treasure for his family: a gift of himself.

Collaborating to Meet Students' Needs

Students with life-threatening illnesses present special collaborative challenges. They and their families need ongoing support from educators and others to help them cope. Research suggests that these parents value help in deciding on and achieving short-term goals for themselves and their children (Katz, 2002; Katz & Krulik, 1999; Perrin & Lewkowicz, 2000). The IEP conference is an appropriate time to plan realistic goals and the supports needed to achieve them.

In one study (Kliebenstein & Broome, 2000) a major concern expressed by teachers of students with health impairments was their lack of preparation for dealing with a student's death, a time when effective collaboration is especially critical. There is a cultural denial that children die (Hylton, Rushton, & Catlin, 2002): "The injustice and incomprehensibility of a child's death creates a denial and avoidance of death that is shared by both parents and professionals" (p. 57). Sometimes teachers act on this denial by convincing themselves that they are protecting classmates by not discussing the student's dying and death (Charkow, 1998; Sherman & Simonton, 2001). Lack of information can intensify peers' anxiety and cause them to create detrimental fantasies about what has happened (Perry, 2000; Sherman & Simonton, 2001). Further, "children and adolescents feel disenfranchised when their losses and their roles as grievers are not recognized, validated, and supported" (Corr, 1999, p. 443). All losses children experience should be grieved (McGlauflin, 1998).

When a student is dying, teachers must face their own grief as well as help students and families through the grief process (Milton, 1999). Asking for support from others is a healthy response to grief, and teachers who are grieving need to seek out trusted individuals who will allow them to express their pain openly and honestly (McGlauflin, 1998). Everyone grieves differently, especially children, who manifest complex emotions, including "anger, relief, despair, peace, guilt, numbness, agitation, and sorrow" (Naierman, 1997, p. 63). To help students and family members integrate a student's death into their lives, teachers must create a safe environment that respects grief as a normal, healthy response; honors all feelings; and provides nonjudgmental compassion (McGlauflin, 1998). In Box 11–7, we provide suggestions for collaborating with students and families to help them grieve.

Students with health impairments who spend a lot of time in the hospital, as Kyle does, frequently experience the death of peers, causing them and their families to face the child's mortality. Teachers can provide valuable support by writing sympathy notes, being sensitive to symptoms of depression, and taking time to listen. Kyle's mother died of sickle cell disease when he was 2 years old. In addition, he has lost two close friends, including a teenager who was a good friend to him in the hospital. "He would go into her room when she was sick," Dorothy recalls, "and they would both lie in the bed. She was 16 and was a really good friend. They are all like that—like a little family."

Kyle remembers when she died: "I couldn't do anything but cry. It's hard, but that still won't stop me from trying to make friends."

To learn more about helping yourself and others through the grief process, go to the Web Links module in Chapter 11 of the Companion Website.

Collaboration Tips

Box 11—7

Helping Others Grieve

When a student in your class is dying, the collaboration team is expansive and can include the student, parents, siblings, extended family members, medical personnel, classmates, school administration and staff, community members such as religious leaders, counselors, and yourself. Consider how one team worked through this transition (Cassini & Rogers, 1996).

The team consisted of fourth-grader Elyse Fardon, her parents, her sixth-grade brother Patrick, Elyse and Patrick's teachers, the principal, and a child life specialist from the hospital. When it became clear that Elyse would never be able to return to school, the team determined to do everything it could to help Elyse consider herself an included member of her fourth-grade class. Her parents sent pictures, so Elyse's classmates gradually saw the progression of her illness. Elyse's teacher took snapshots of the students and classroom activities for Elyse. The teacher also set aside a bulletin board in the classroom to display Elyse's work, helping other students realize that Elyse was still a contributing member of the class. The school gave Elyse a computer to use at home to complete assignments.

Once a week, the principal added to the school announcements that anyone who had a card, message, or drawing for Elyse should bring it to the office that day. The next day, the principal visited Elyse and delivered the gifts.

The team also realized that classmates needed accurate information about Elyse's condition. With parental permission, the child life specialist visited the school to answer students' questions and assure the children that Elyse's condition was not contagious. Her parents also gave permission for school personnel to contact Elyse's physician for updates on her condition.

Furthermore, the team realized the importance of addressing Patrick's needs. His teacher contacted the parents of Patrick's friends, asking them to volunteer to help Patrick attend after school activities and complete projects requiring adult supervision or library research.

When Elyse died, the school faculty avoided euphemisms such as "passed away" or "went to sleep forever." The principal read a prepared statement; and teachers talked with the students about what had happened, sharing their emotions openly. Together, they planned a memorial service for Elyse.

The team realized "that when the time span before the death is handled openly and respectfully, the mourning period following the death takes on the same disposition. When the death does occur, [the team] will be dealing with a deeply saddened group of classmates and faculty, rather than a frenetic, anxious crowd of teachers and fellow students" (Cassini & Rogers, 1996, p. 94).

Putting These Tips to Work for Progress in the General Curriculum

1. How can a hospitalized student still participate in school activities?

2. What support could you offer to classmates of a dying student?

To answer these questions online and learn more about these ideas and concepts, go to the Collaboration Tips module in Chapter 11 of the Companion Website.

What Can You Learn from Others Who Teach Students with Other Health Impairments?

Learning for the Early Childhood Years: Kids on the Block

How do you help preschoolers understand how health impairments affect some of their classmates? The terms associated with many of these conditions are difficult even for adults to understand. For inclusion to work during the preschool years, however, children must understand why Naomi has seizures, Manuel has no hair, and Sally can't eat candy bars. They also need to know why teasing and insensitivity are wrong.

Kids on the Block (KOB), has provided the answers to children since 1977. The program shares stories of children with health impairments through live puppet theater. The hand and rod puppets, which are as tall as a child, gesture while they move their mouths. The puppets seem so real that the children ask them questions after the presentation—and the puppets answer.

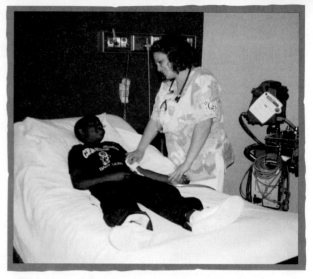

Kyle's nurse Karen Jackson and other staff at the University of South Alabama's Children's and Women's Hospital are not concerned only about Kyle's medical needs. They also want him to continue his education at the hospital.

To learn more about some of these programs, go to the Web Links module in Chapter 11 of the Companion Website.

In one KOB script, Scott, a puppet with asthma, takes karate lessons, much to the surprise of his friend Jason. Scott tells Jason he can do almost anything as long as he takes his medication. Scott also explains that he prefers words such as *episode* and *flare* instead of *attack,* which sounds scary, like something that cannot be controlled. A complete curriculum about sensitivity to differences is included with each script.

Learning for the Elementary Years: Class Act

Kyle is fortunate that he can attend Class Act at the University of South Alabama's Children's and Women's Hospital. The elementary and secondary teachers gather the students each weekday morning to attend the technology-equipped classrooms. Many young patients are surprised to learn that they will attend school! The hospital teacher contacts the student's school to let them know that the student should be counted as present and asks the school to fax the student's assignments. When the students complete their assignments, they can play educational games until they need to return to their rooms.

Anne Vella, who has a Ph.D. in special education and a master's degree in counseling, is the school's elementary teacher. She works for the Mobile County Public Schools, which allows the students' attendance to be counted when they attend Class Act. Her goal is to prevent student grade retention (students "held back") because of illness.

The hospital also employs Brenda White, a child life specialist. Brenda provides a different kind of education. She helps the students understand their medical condition and treatment procedures. Through play and talking, her goals are to reduce stress, anxiety, and fear of procedures. She also tries to keep life as normal as possible for the children.

Learning for the Middle and Secondary Years: Meeting the Challenge

The adolescent years are difficult for most students, with or without disabilities. A health impairment can adversely affect typical adolescent milestones: "achieving independence from family, formulating values and self-concept, and planning for the future" (Boice, 1998, p. 938). Teachers need to avoid overprotecting students with health impairments at any age but especially during adolescence, when students want to fit in instead of standing out (Sullivan et al., 2001). Providing fiction and nonfiction books about health impairments can sometimes help adolescents communicate their feelings about their illness (Hayes, 1999).

Meeting the Challenge (Kapp-Simon & Simon, 1991) is a program for encouraging adolescents to express their feelings about having health impairments and gaining a sense of control over their health and life. Meeting the Challenge teaches five categories of interpersonal skills: self-awareness, social imitation and conversational skills, assertion or direct communication, empathy or active listening, and conflict resolution and problem solving.

The program helps students identify maladaptive and adaptive reactions to specific situations. For example, students might be given a simulation experience of not being invited to a party that everyone else is attending. The facilitator asks students to think about common reactions to such an experience. Maladaptive reactions that students typically identify include "I look terrible," or "if I could just walk normally, I would have been invited." Other possible responses include bodily reactions such as getting a headache or a stomach ache. Students can also experience so much resentment and anger that they avoid talking to students who are going to the party. Or they might stay home from school on the day of the party.

The students then brainstorm adaptive reactions. They can tell themselves, "I'm not the only one who wasn't invited. Carl and Jamie weren't invited either, and they don't have anything wrong with them," or "Maybe I need to be friendlier." Students learn that they can minimize bodily reactions by relaxation techniques. They can also attempt to be friendlier and more outgoing at school.

Learning for the Transitional and Postsecondary Years: HIV University

The needs of individuals with health impairments during the postsecondary years include finding meaningful employment and leisure activities, knowing their legal rights and how to protect those rights, managing their condition to function as independently as possible, and addressing their own feelings about and others' reactions to their disabilities.

A higher percentage of young women than young men have HIV (Centers for Disease Control, 2000). One group wrote: "One of the hardest parts of living with HIV or AIDS is dealing with the anger and frustration of a disease that makes most of us feel powerless" (HIV University, 1995, p. 1). These women decided to take back that power by starting their own AIDS education school.

HIV University started with a question asked by women with HIV who wanted to live as fully as possible: "How can I channel my sadness, anger, and frustration in a positive direction so that it doesn't destroy me?" The women agreed on the foundational philosophy: The students own it. "It took a while for some people to get used to this idea," the women say. "Each time someone would ask a question (will we study 'X'?), whoever was facilitating the meeting would say, 'That's up to you to decide. It's your school'" (HIV University, 1995, p. 1).

As the women became acquainted, they started viewing themselves more as a family than a class. They had no models for their university, and that fact freed them from concerns about what others would think about how their school should be organized. The school developed programs that (1) provided emotional support; (2) eliminated barriers to participation (e.g., through on-site child care, transportation, and Spanish translation); (3) emphasized group problem solving to help women find solutions to particular challenges they faced; and (4) provided classes on relevant topics, such as anatomy and physiology, gynecology and sexually transmitted diseases, nutrition, treatment programs, monetary issues, self-advocacy, coping with grief and loss, and addiction. The women summarize what they have learned through their university:

> We hear a lot about empowerment in the AIDS movement, but you can't empower other people. Each of us can, however, offer the people we care about tools to empower themselves, and we can choose to claim responsibility for our own lives. (HIV University, 1995, p. 1)

A Vision for Kyle's Future

What does Dorothy dream of for her grandson's future? First, she says she hopes they will find a cure for sickle cell so he can live a normal, pain-free life. "I hope that he will graduate, go to college, and be a doctor" she says. "But Kyle doesn't want to be a doctor. He wants to be an artist because he's good at drawing."

Is that what Kyle wants? Well, among other things. We'll let Kyle share his vision for you in his own words:

"I want to be an athlete. I want to be the best athlete in the world. I want trophies from basketball, trophies from football, trophies from track because I like to run. Maybe I could be an illustrator or something in my free time. I like to do back flips and front flips. I want to go to the Olympics. I want to build a staircase to hold all my trophies.

"You know, I just thought about this. I could be a writer for kids' books. Because then I could make pop-up books.

"You know what I might do? I might just become a doctor and find a cure myself. I already know a lot about sickle cell. I might be a blood doctor that tells kids about sickle cell. I'll probably be the first person to find a real cure that really works. I'd probably win an award for that.

"And I thought maybe I could write about sickle cell and someday what I write might help find a cure."

What Would You Recommend?

1. In two years, Kyle will be going to middle school. If you were his middle school homeroom teacher, how would you help him manage his sickle cell at school?
2. What issues do you think will challenge Kyle more as he enters his teens? How would you help his family address those issues?

Summary

How Do You Recognize Students with Other Health Impairments?

▼ The conditions in this category vary widely in symptoms and prognosis.
▼ Students with health impairments have limitations in strength, vitality, or alertness. The condition can be chronic or acute.
▼ Health impairments include, among many others, sickle cell disease, HIV, cancer, asthma, juvenile diabetes, and epilepsy.
▼ Health impairments can be caused by infections, genetic factors, and environmental factors, including prenatal teratogens and postnatal influences.
▼ Schools served most students with other health impairments in the general classroom.

How Do You Evaluate Students with Other Health Impairments?

▼ Students may receive an IEP or 504 plan, contingent on whether their condition adversely affects educational performance, as well as health care and action plans. Teachers should frequently monitor the IEP of a student whose health may change often.

How Do You Assure Progress in the General Curriculum?

▼ Teachers need to help students learn to handle insensitivity.
▼ Teachers need to plan for school reentry and extended absences.

▼ When a student is dying, teachers should give themselves and other students permission to grieve.

What Can You Learn from Others Who Teach Students with Other Health Impairments?

▼ Kids on the Block uses puppets to instruct students about health impairments.

▼ Class Act at the University of South Alabama's Children's and Women's Hospital provides a way for hospitalized children to be counted as present at school.

▼ Meeting the Challenge teaches adolescents with health impairments to problem-solve.

▼ HIV University provides a place for women to learn about their condition and how to advocate for themselves.

Council for Exceptional Children

PRAXIS

To find out how and where this chapter content connects to the CEC Professional Standards and the Praxis™ Standards, go to the Standards Connection module in Chapter 11 of the Companion Website. A comprehensive matrix aligning CEC Professional Standards, Praxis™ Standards, and INTASC principles to the entire text, is available in the Appendix and on the Companion Website.

Chapter 12

Who Is Rommel Nanasca?

When Rommel (*roh-MELL*) Nanasca, now 18 years old, leaves home for school and his 12th-grade gifted and talented program each morning, he has already benefited from extraordinary care. His mother, Lorna, and her father and mother, who live with Lorna and Rommel, have lifted him from his bed and bathed him; he lacks the strength to do that for himself. One of them uses a special device—the **intermittent positive-pressure breathing (IPPB)** machine—to help Rommel breathe more easily because his lungs have become congested overnight. This technology helps him avoid colds and infections. The machine applies positive pressure to Rommel's chest, causing his lungs to exhale; he then inhales without their assistance. As one of the adults administers this treatment, another checks out the respirator from which he may have to receive oxygen.

They also have begun his day-long feeding process, using a jejunum tube (j-tube). The **jejunum** is the second portion of a person's small intestine. The j-tube has been surgically inserted into his intestines, and through it a special formula is dripped so he can receive his necessary nutrition. The reason that Rommel uses a j-tube is that he finds it too tiring to feed himself and to chew regular food. Family members also have slipped a T-shirt onto Rommel and strapped him into an armless vest of flexible plastic that supports his weakened upper body. The vest holds him erect and prevents further curvature of his spine (he has 90 percent scoliosis). Finally, they have lifted him into a wheelchair whose back and seat have been specially shaped to fit exactly and comfortably with his jacketed torso. It undoubtedly helps that Lorna is a nurse, that she has assistance (until 2000, when he died, Rommel's father, Romy, helped every day), and that Rommel is up for whatever comes his way . . . and a plethora of challenges have already been his lot in his extraordinary 18 years of life.

Rommel has spinal muscular atrophy. Respiratory distress is the primary complication of persons with that kind of atrophy. This is why he uses the IPPB machine to help his weakened chest muscles perform normal breathing functions.

Despite precautions and the good climate in the San Diego, California, area, Rommel has been hospitalized for pneumonia at least twice a year, every year, since he was a year old and until he was 14. Frighteningly, when pneumonia struck him in December 1996, he had

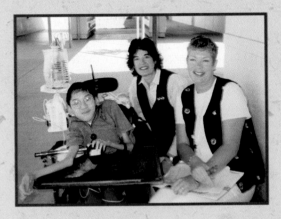

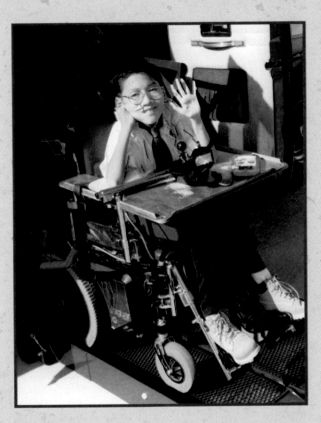

just survived a life-threatening episode at Twin Peaks Middle School, Poway, California. His breathing had become so labored that he was "coded," given immediate cardiopulmonary resuscitation, and rushed by ambulance to a local hospital.

The coding, emergency hospitalization, subsequent hospitalization on account of pneumonia a few weeks later, Rommel's dramatic loss of 10 pounds (to a weight of 44 pounds, 9 ounces), and the pure fatigue of chewing enough food to get adequate nutrition led his physicians, his parents, and Rommel himself to agree to the surgery to implant the j-tube so he can get his nutrition. These factors also led them and his school team to develop a regimen to maintain his health and prevent crises while enabling him to remain included in the general curriculum.

Lorna and her family face the challenges presented by spinal muscular atrophy in not just Rommel but also his younger brother, Ariel, age 12, who has the same condition but not to such an extensive degree. And they have to help Rommel's sister, 19-year-old Melanie, lead her very typical life as a freshman at University of California at San Diego. Fortunately, they have help from Lorna's three sisters and one brother, who live nearby.

Ask her how she lives in the face of these disabilities and with so many responsibilities, and Lorna replies, "Day by day, we do our best." Asked about the family, Rommel's occupational therapist agrees: "The Nanascas are unique. Theirs is a joyful home. They are upbeat despite their concerns. They go on with their lives. They make the best of everything." And if you ask Rommel himself, he'll tell you that the doctors and therapists are "just part of my life. I'm used to them."

What do you think?

1. How would you ensure collaboration among Rommel's family, educators, and health care providers?

2. How would you provide an appropriate education to Rommel and other students with physical disabilities if they have to stay home or are in the hospital?

3. How would you ensure that Rommel has access to his school and all of its extracurricular activities using his wheelchair and its apparatus?

To learn more about Rommel Nanasca and other students with physical disabilities, go to the Cases module in Chapter 12 of the Companion Website.

How Do You Recognize Students with Physical Disabilities?

Defining Physical Disabilities

IDEA and its regulations refer to physical disabilities as orthopedic impairments:

> "Orthopedic impairment" means a severe orthopedic impairment that adversely affects a child's educational performance. The term includes impairments caused by congenital anomaly (e.g., clubfoot, absence of some member, etc.), impairments caused by disease (e.g., poliomyelitis, bone tuberculosis, etc.), and impairments from other causes (e.g., cerebral palsy, amputations, and fractures or burns that cause contractures). (34 C.F.R., sec. 300.7 [b][7])

Although IDEA uses the term *orthopedic impairments*, educators typically use the term *physical disabilities* when referring to these same students. So there are two terms in use: the IDEA term and the educators' term. But special educators and special education agencies also sometimes refer to students with severe and multiple disabilities (see Chapter 9), other health impairments (see Chapter 11), or traumatic brain injury (see Chapter 13) as having physical disabilities. All of this different usage means that there is also an aggregate usage: The term *physical disabilities* typically refers to a large group of students who are quite different from each other. Because it is impossible for one chapter to cover all types of physical disabilities, we focus here on three different types: cerebral palsy, spina bifida, and spinal muscular atrophy (a form of muscular dystrophy). These three particular types will give you an overview of physical disabilities.

Describing the Characteristics

Cerebral Palsy

When Camille Durfee was still in high school, she gave a presentation at a special education conference. Using a custom-made communication device, Camille described herself:

> Hi, my name is Camille Durfee. . . . I am using a Liberator to communicate. . . . Give disabled people time to talk to you. I would like to be treated like a normal person. Look at me when you talk to me. Don't treat me like a baby. I like to listen to music and watch television. I also enjoy going to games and meeting new people. The hardest thing about being disabled is when my equipment breaks at the same time. I don't care if someone comes up and says, "Why are you in a wheelchair?" I have cerebral palsy.

What Is Cerebral Palsy?   *Cerebral* refers to the brain. *Palsy* describes the lack of muscle control that affects a person's ability to move and to maintain balance and posture. Thus, cerebral palsy is a disorder of movement or posture. These disorders occur because a person's brain cannot control his or her muscles (Bigge, Best, & Heller, 2001; Nickel, 2000). The impairment occurs in the brain's development (usually by 6 years of age), but the brain damage is nonprogressive (Dormans & Pellegrino, 1998). So neither Rommel, who has spinal muscular atrophy (a progressive, inherited disease), nor a 20-year-old who received a brain injury in an automobile accident can be diagnosed as having cerebral palsy.

There are four types of cerebral palsy; each refers to the person's movement patterns:

▼ **Spastic** involves tightness in one or more muscle groups and accounts for 70–80 percent of individuals with cerebral palsy.

▼ **Athetoid** involves abrupt, involuntary movements of the head, neck, face, and extremities, particularly the upper ones.

▼ **Ataxic** involves unsteadiness, lack of coordination and balance, and varying degrees of difficulty with standing and walking.

On the Companion Website, you will find information about United Cerebral Palsy Association, which is a national organization advancing independence, productivity, and full citizenship for people with cerebral palsy (www.ucpa.org).

Camille uses a device called a Liberator to help her communicate. Using a light sensor attached to her head, she activates this device, which displays her messages and also speaks them aloud.

FIGURE 12–1

Topographical classification system

A. *Monoplegia:* one limb
B. *Paraplegia:* legs only
C. *Hemiplegia:* one half of body
D. *Triplegia:* three limbs (usually two legs and one arm)
E. *Quadriplegia:* all four limbs
F. *Diplegia:* more affected in the legs than the arms
G. *Double Hemiplegia:* arms more involved than the legs

Source: From *Understanding Physical, Sensory, and Health Impairments: Characterizations and Educational Implications* (p. 95), by K. W. Heller, P. A. Alberto, P. E. Forney, and M. N. Schwartzman, 1996, Belmont, CA: Wadsworth. Copyright 1996 by Wadsworth Publishers. Reprinted with permission.

▼ **Mixed** combines spastic muscle tone and the involuntary movements of athethoid cerebral palsy.

In addition to characterizing cerebral palsy by the nature of a person's movement, professionals also refer to the part of the person's body that is affected. This is referred to as a **topographical classification system.** The specific body location of the movement impairment correlates with the location of the brain damage. Figure 12–1 describes the topographical classification system that evaluation teams often use.

What Causes Cerebral Palsy?   Cerebral palsy is caused by **prenatal** (e.g., infection or brain malformation before birth), **perinatal** (e.g., lack of oxygen or infection during birth), or **postnatal** (e.g., brain injury or meningitis after birth) factors (Bigge, Best, & Heller, 2001; Dormans & Pellegrino, 1998).

The severity of a person's cerebral palsy generally depends on the type and timing of the injury. For example, bleeding in the brain of very premature babies can cause extensive damage. Camille, however, experienced a normal birth and seemed physically sound. Only after she reached age 1 and had not developed normally did a brain scan show damage caused by a cyst. Although the brain damage left her without the capacity to speak or move anything but her head, little damage was done to the part of her brain that affects her intelligence.

What Other Conditions Are Associated with Cerebral Palsy? Many health and developmental problems may accompany cerebral palsy (Nickel, 2000). Because cerebral palsy results from brain damage, there is a significant relationship between cerebral palsy and mental retardation. Fifty to 70 percent of those with cerebral palsy also have mental retardation (Dormans & Pellegrino, 1998). It is important to remember, however, that some individuals with cerebral palsy have gifted intelligence.

Many people with cerebral palsy also have difficulty expressing themselves; they have articulation problems because they cannot coordinate their muscles around their mouth and throat. This is why Camille communicates with her teachers and peers using her eyes, facial gestures, and her Liberator.

Spina Bifida

You will learn more about the Liberator and other forms of assistive technology later in the chapter.

As a sixth grader in the Cullasaja Elementary School in Franklin, North Carolina, high in the Appalachian Mountains, Jimmy Chipman moves around school with the help of braces on his legs. When he is too tired to walk or when he and his peers have recess on the hilltop playground at school, he relies on his wheelchair to get to the playground. With the assistance of a physical therapist and an occupational therapist, he works to improve or maintain his strength. Being strong enables him to participate in some general education classes. Because he has missed so much time in school while hospitalized for five surgeries, however, he takes some of his academic work outside of the general curriculum. One aspect of his disability is especially problematic: Spina bifida, though it has affected him only from his knees down, has left him with **incontinence;** he is unable to control his bladder, bowels, or both. All that aside, Jimmy uses a computer easily and looks forward to attending the local community college.

What Is Spina Bifida? Spina bifida refers to a malformation of the spinal cord (Sandler, 1997). The spine is made up of separate bones called vertebrae, which normally cover and protect the spinal cord. In a person with spina bifida, the spinal column does not close completely and cover the spinal cord, usually resulting in a protrusion of the spinal cord, its coverings, or both. A saclike bulge may occur in any part of the person's spine, from neck to buttocks. The higher on the spinal column the defect appears, the more severe the person's loss of function. Typically, the defect occurs in the lower region and causes complete or partial paralysis of only the person's lower extremities and loss of skin sensation.

Spina bifida, which is not a progressive condition, has three common forms (see Figure 12–2):

▼ **Spina bifida occulta.** The spinal cord or its covering do not protrude and only a small portion of the vertebrae, usually in the low spine, is missing. (This is the mildest and most common form.)

▼ **Meningocele.** The covering of the spinal cord, but not the cord itself, actually protrudes through the opening created by the defect in the spine. (Although a more serious form, it usually does not cause a person to experience mobility impairments.)

▼ **Myelomeningocele.** The protrusion or sac contains not only the spinal cord's covering but also a portion of the spinal cord or nerve roots. (This is the most serious form, which results in varying degrees of leg weakness, inability to control bowels or bladder, and a variety of physical problems such as dislocated hips or club feet.)

Figure 12–3 shows that the spinal defect's location determines the degree to which mobility is affected. If the defect occurs at the thoracic vertebra T-12 or above, total paralysis of the legs results. The lumbar nerves move the leg muscles, and the sacral nerves control the foot muscles. As we have already noted, the lower the defect in the lumbar or sacral regions, the greater the ability to walk without braces and crutches.

FIGURE 12–2

Types of spina bifida

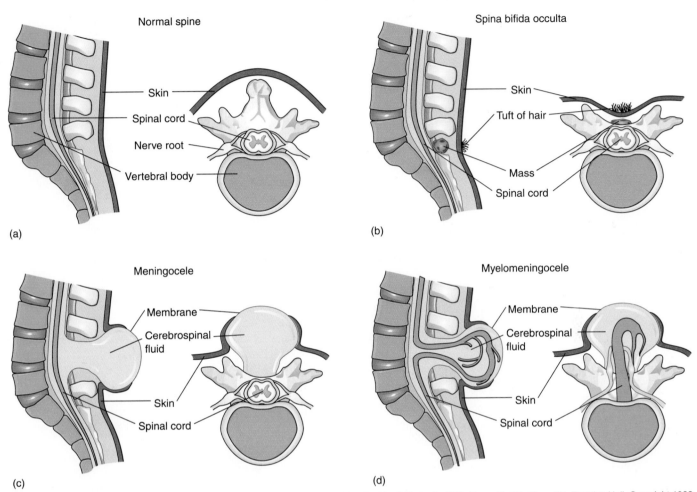

Normal spine

Skin
Spinal cord
Nerve root
Vertebral body

(a)

Spina bifida occulta

Skin
Tuft of hair
Mass
Spinal cord

(b)

Meningocele

Membrane
Cerebrospinal fluid
Skin
Spinal cord

(c)

Myelomeningocele

Membrane
Cerebrospinal fluid
Skin
Spinal cord

(d)

Source: From *Physical Disabilities and Health Impairments: An Introduction* (p. 118), edited by J. Umbreit, 1983, Upper Saddle River, NJ: Prentice Hall. Copyright 1983 by Prentice Hall. Reprinted with permission.

What Causes Spina Bifida? The exact causes of spina bifida are unknown, but the condition occurs during the very early days of pregnancy (Nickel, 2000). Parents do not carry any particular gene that specifically causes spina bifida, although their genes may interact with environmental factors (e.g., nutrition, medication, and exposure to high temperatures) to trigger the malformation in the developing embryo (Heller, Alberto, Forney, & Schwartzman, 1996; Nickel, 2000).

A woman who uses daily vitamin supplements containing folic acid reduces the risk that her baby will have neural tube defects such as spina bifida (Centers for Disease Control, 1992; Daly, Kirke, Malloy, Weir, & Scott, 1995). Folic acid is a B-vitamin that enables bodies to build healthy cells. Beginning in 1998, the federal Food and Drug Administration has required breads and enriched cereal grain products to be fortified with synthetic folic acid. Since then, there has been a 19 percent reduction in the number of cases of spina bifida and related conditions (Honein, Paulozzi, Mathews, Erickson, & Wong, 2001).

What Are Other Conditions Associated with Spina Bifida? Approximately 75 percent of children and youth with spina bifida have normal intelligence (Liptak, 1997), but some do have learning difficulties (Bigge et al., 2001).

On the companion website, you will find a link to the website of the Spina Bifida Association of America, where you can read stories from six parents who have children with spina bifida (www.sbaa.org/html/realstories/index.html).

FIGURE 12–3

Location of defect affects degree of mobility (T = thoracic, L = lumbar, S = sacrat)

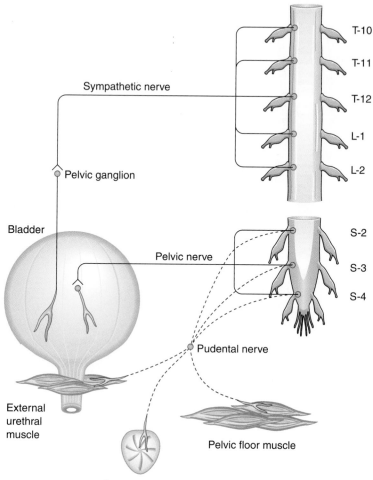

Source: From Bleck, E. E., & Nagel, D. A., *Physically Handicapped Children*. Copyright © 1982 by Allyn & Bacon. Reprinted by permission.

On the Companion Website, you will find a link to information on dietary sources of folic acid. How much folic acid is in your diet (www. spinabifidaaa.org/html/ sbaa_folic_ table.html)?

Myelomeningocele almost always occurs above the part of the spinal cord that controls the bladder and bowels (Liptak, 1997; Nickel, 2000). Constipation, bladder paralysis, urinary tract infections, and resulting incontinence are common. Kidney failure can also result. Many students (like Jimmy) can be taught the technique of **clean intermittent catheterization** and effective bowel management (Lutkenhoff & Oppenheimer, 1997). Working with a school nurse trained in these techniques, teachers can monitor students' self-management abilities (Heller, Forney, Alberto, Schwartzman, & Goeckel, 2000).

Muscular Dystrophy

As you learned when you first read about Rommel, he has spinal muscular atrophy, which is a form of muscular dystrophy.

What Is Muscular Dystrophy?   The term muscular dystrophy refers to a group of nine hereditary muscle-destroying disorders that vary in their inheritance pattern, their age of onset, the muscles initially attacked, and their rate of progression. The type of muscular dystrophy called Duchenne's disease affects one in every 3,500 males and is the most common form.

One of these nine muscle-destroying diseases is spinal muscular atrophy, which is characterized by muscle weakness and the wasting away of muscles (Heller et al., 1996). Instead of attacking the muscles themselves, as do many muscular dystrophies, spinal muscular atrophy attacks specialized nerve cells called **motor neurons,** which control the movement of voluntary muscles. Children and youth with spinal muscular atrophy usually have normal intelligence.

Rommel's mother, Lorna, is a nurse and noticed by the time he was 4 months old that he could not bear his own weight and had trouble sitting, even when supported. He was tested at 6 months and diagnosed at 9 months as having spinal muscular atrophy. Because he has no use of his legs, he has **paraplegia.**

What Causes Spinal Muscular Atrophy? Spinal muscular atrophy is an autosomal recessive disease; both parents must be carriers of the genes that cause this kind of atrophy. Parents who have been identified as carriers of the disease run a one-in-four risk of having children who have the disease and a one-in-two risk of having children who will carry the disease (Brooke, 1986). Although some neuromuscular diseases (such as Duchenne's muscular dystrophy) affect only boys, both males and females can develop spinal muscular atrophy.

What Other Conditions Are Associated with Spinal Muscular Atrophy? Typically, students also have skeletal problems such as **scoliosis** (a lateral curve of the spine). Rommel wears a body jacket during the day that supports his weakened upper torso and helps prevent scoliosis.

Many children with spinal muscular atrophy are prone to pneumonia and other respiratory problems (Bigge et al., 2001). You have already learned that Rommel is prone to respiratory infections. His propensity is caused by the gradual weakness in his abdominal muscles.

To learn more about catheterization, go to the Web Links module in Chapter 12 of the Companion Website for a link to the website of Children's Hospital Medical Center in Cincinnati.

Identifying the Prevalence

Because physical disabilities often occur in combination with other disabilities, it is hard to determine their prevalence. Nevertheless, the U.S. Department of Education (2001) reported that schools served 67,442 students, ages 6 to 21, who have physical disabilities during the 1999–2000 school year. This number represents 0.11 percent of all students receiving special education services.

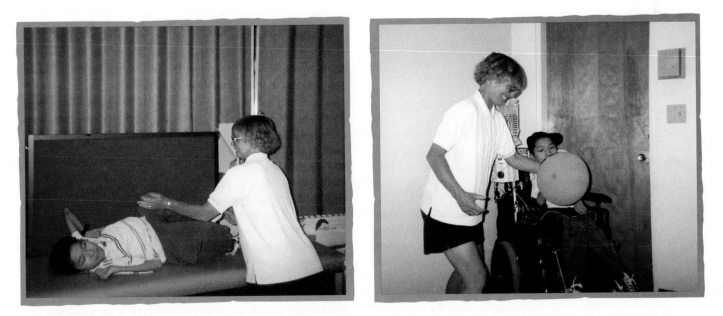

Rommel attends only general education classes, except for physical education, for which he receives special one-on-one instruction. His adaptive physical educator works with him on activities such as range-of-motion exercises and games to strengthen his respiratory capacity.

Preventing Physical Disabilities

There are many approaches to preventing physical disabilities. One state-of-the-art approach is fetal surgery on children with spina bifida. The surgery involves removing the uterus from the mother, draining the amniotic fluid from it, performing surgery on the fetus, and then replacing the fetus in the uterus and returning it to the mother (Bruner et al., 2000).

How Do You Evaluate Students with Physical Disabilities?

Determining the Presence

To be an eyewitness to a virtual fetal therapy surgery, go to the Web Links module in Chapter 12 of the Companion Website (www.fetalsurgeons.com/vspg 09.htm).

Two techniques—amniocentesis and ultrasonographic imaging of the fetus—assist physicians in diagnosing physical disabilities even before babies are born (Nickel, 2000; Schonberg & Tifft, 2002). Once a diagnosis occurs, families usually are given a choice of abortion, fetal surgery if that is possible given the particular diagnosis, or delivery of their baby, followed as soon as possible by surgery to close the baby's back lesions in order to decrease the severity of meningomyelocele side effects (Nickel, 2000). In Box 12–1, you will read about early detection, its benefits, the challenges it poses to parents, the stigma that can arise even before the birth of a child who has been detected to have a disability, and the effects of early intervention.

For many infants, however, a diagnosis does not occur until after they are born. An **Apgar screening** done immediately after birth may yield the first indication of a problem. An infant's poor response to the sucking reflex, convulsions, stiffness, or an unusual amount of irritability might indicate cerebral palsy. Initial screenings may also detect respiratory problems that are frequently associated with spinal muscular atrophy. Physicians become particularly alert if high-risk factors are involved during the pregnancy or delivery.

Many children with physical disabilities may have no problems at birth or in their newborn period. The initial diagnosis of children who appear normal at birth and later fail to develop normally varies according to either the age at which the child's developmental delay is noticed or the child's type of disability.

The evaluation team typically consists of the parents, the teachers, and professionals who represent different specialty areas including physicians, general and special educators, occupational and physical therapists, nurses, speech pathologists, psychologists, and adaptive physical education specialists. The exact makeup of the team depends on the student's age and known or assumed needs. Figure 12–4 illustrates the assessment process.

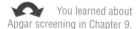

In Chapter 9 you learned about prenatal tests used during pregnancy to identify and increasingly prevent disabilities.

You learned about Apgar screening in Chapter 9.

Determining the Nature and Extent of General and Special Education and Related Services

Many students with physical disabilities need related services to assure accessibility to the school's physical environments, access to the general curriculum, and participation in extracurricular and other school activities. The student's evaluation determines the nature and extent of special education and related services. Occupational therapists are valuable members of the multidisciplinary evaluation team in documenting strengths and needs related to accessibility throughout all school environments (Barnes, Schoenfeld, & Pierson, 1997). Karen Boyd, Rommel's occupational therapist, visits him in all of his different environments (home, classroom, lunchroom, playground, library) to make careful observations. She also observes his movement patterns, looking for postures that he likes but that hamper or prevent him from using the joy stick to drive and steer his motorized wheelchair. She is concerned with how to place a lap tray across the arms of his chair in such a way that he can place his computer on the tray, have access

Box 12–1

My Son Sam

My name is Kim. I am twenty-seven years old. My son Sam was born in May 1992 with spina bifida.

I first found out there was possibly a problem with my pregnancy at fifteen weeks when I had the AFP (alpha-feto-protein) test done. . . . [One] day, my obstetrician called me at work and told me my AFP had come back slightly elevated. "My what? Is what? What does that mean? Is my baby going to be all right?" My heart jumped to my throat, could feel my pulse racing, I felt nauseous, and the tears started pouring. I had so many questions, and I was scared to death. I immediately made an appointment to have an ultrasound done in Chapel Hill. I then left work. I just had to!

Now came time for the ultrasound. Almost immediately the technician saw "something suspicious." Then the tears started flowing again. She went to get the doctor. Dr. Cheschier came in, looked at the ultrasound, and began explaining what she saw. I can't remember all that was said. I still couldn't believe this was happening to me.

After the ultrasound, Dr. Cheschier, Michael (my husband), and I went into her office and began discussing Sam's condition. The one good thing that came out of this day was that we found out that we were going to have a boy. From that day on the baby wasn't a fetus or an "it"; he was Sam.

For the next five months, my life revolved around doctor's appointments, gathering every bit of information I could find about spina bifida, working full-time, spending every moment I could with our daughter, buying a house, keeping my sanity, being optimistic, and keeping a smile on my face. I had meetings with all the specialists. I remember meeting with Dr. Sandler, asking him a thousand questions, and wishing he had a crystal ball so he could answer them. Will Sam be able to walk, to play sports, to go to the bathroom, to have girlfriends, to go to college, to get married, to have a family? No one knew the answers.

Then Sam was born May 6, 1992, at 10:00 A.M., in Chapel Hill. Sam weighed eight pounds, thirteen ounces, and was twenty inches long. He was beautiful!

Yes, he did have an opening in his spine, and he had to have surgery within the first few hours of his life. The operation went well. Sam was out of surgery in about three hours and went to the neonatal intensive care unit. I asked the doctors if Sam would be able to go home with me. Dr. Sandler said it was highly unlikely that a baby born with spina bifida would go home at the same time as the mother. Well, not only did Sam go home with me, he was in the NICU for only two days before he was moved to the regular nursery (although I kept him rooming in with me most of the time)!

Sam is now eighteen months old. He is walking, running, climbing, dancing, just like any other eighteen-month-old child. He did not develop hydrocephalus, and so he never had to have a shunt. Sam is unquestionably a miracle baby, and I know the chances of a child with spina bifida turning out to be this healthy are slim, but it happened.

Source: From *Living With Spina Bifida: A Guide for Families and Professionals* (pp. 6–8), by A. Sandler, 1997, Chapel Hill: University of North Carolina Press. Copyright 1997 by University of North Carolina Press. Reprinted with permission.

---

to his joy stick, and still be fed by the external pump for his j-tube and any oxygen that he may need. By taking a standard, off-the-shelf table, cutting it to fit Rommel and his chair, and putting a nonskid rubber pad under the computer, Karen makes it possible for Rommel to do all these things easily and safely.

Because incorrect positioning hampers a student's ability to perform activities well (Downing, 2002; Heller et al., 2000), Karen also observes how Rommel sits in his wheelchair. In addition, Karen observes how able he is to use both sides of his body in a coordinated manner. For students who use computers, bilateral skills may not be as important as they are for students who still use pencils, pens, and paper or scissors (holding the writing or cutting tool with one hand and the paper with another).

Karen takes an ecological inventory of Rommel's life at school and home. She examines the environments in which he is expected to function and then identifies the specific skills and activities he needs to participate successfully there (Bigge et al., 2001). Ecological inventories involve the following steps:

▼ Identifying the important environments in which students need and want to participate (Rommel participating within his home)

▼ Identifying the subenvironments within each larger environment (Rommel taking a bath in the bathroom)

FIGURE 12–4

Assessment process for determining the presence of physical disabilities

Nondiscriminatory Evaluation

Observation

Teacher and parents observe	The student has difficulty moving in an organized and efficient way; with fine-motor activities; with activities of daily living such as dressing; with postural control; and with speaking, comprehending, or organizing.
Physician observes	The child is not passing developmental milestones. Movement is better on one side of the body than the other. Muscle tone is too floppy or stiff. The child has problems with balance or coordination or has neurological signs that suggest a physical disability.

Medical screening

Assessment measures	Findings that indicate need for further evaluation
Developmental assessment	The child is not meeting developmental milestones or shows poor quality of movement on measures administered by physicians, physical therapists, occupational therapists, and psychologists.
Functional assessment	Activities of daily living are affected.

Prereferral

Prereferral is typically not used with these students because of the need to quickly identify physical disabilities. Also, most children with physical disabilities will be identified by a physician before starting school.

Referral

Students with physical disabilities who are identified before starting school should receive early intervention services and a nondiscriminatory evaluation upon entering school. Because some physical disabilities may develop after a student enters school, teachers should refer any student who seems to have significant difficulty with motor-related activities.

Nondiscriminatory evaluation procedures and standards

Assessment measures	Findings that suggest physical disabilities
Individualized intelligence test	Standardization may be violated because the student's physical disabilities interfere with the ability to perform some tasks. Therefore, results may not be an accurate reflection of ability. The student may be average, above average, or below average in intelligence.
Individualized achievement test	The student may be average, above average, or below average in specific areas of achievement. Standardization may need to be violated to accommodate the student's response style. Thus, results may not accurately reflect achievement.
Motor functioning tests	The student's differences in range of motion, motor patterns, gaits, and postures may present learning problems. Also, length and circumference of limbs, degree of muscle tone, or muscle strength may affect ability to learn specific skills.
Tests of perceptual functioning	The student is unable to or has difficulty in integrating visual/auditory input and motor output in skills such as cutting and carrying out verbal instructions in an organized manner.
Adaptive behavior scales	The student may have difficulty in self-care, household, community, and communication skills because of the physical disability.
Anecdotal records	Reports suggest that the student has functional deficits and requires extra time or assistance in mobility, self-help, positioning, and use of adaptive equipment.
Curriculum-based assessment	The student's physical disabilities may limit accuracy of any timed curriculum-based assessments.
Direct observation	The student is unable or has difficulty in organizing and completing work.

Nondiscriminatory evaluation team determines that student has a physical disability and needs special education and related services.

Appropriate Education

▼ Identifying the skills and capacities that students possess, the areas of skill that they might develop, and the supports available and necessary to assist them (identifying Rommel's strengths and needs and choosing the option of using a flat bed made of mesh that fits in his tub for use with his handheld shower)

▼ Monitoring to ensure that there is a group balance between a student's skills and supports (as Rommel's condition progresses so that he becomes weaker, current alternatives may need to be adapted)

Basing their actions on the results of ecological inventories at school, at home, and in the student's other environments, occupational therapists work collaboratively with other members of the student's multidisciplinary team to complete comprehensive assessments and use the results to develop the IEP.

How Do You Assure Progress in the General Curriculum?

Including Students

Figure 12–5 shows the school placement of students with physical disabilities during the 1998–1999 school year (U.S. Department of Education, 2001). Ninety-three percent of students with physical disabilities attend regular schools, as Rommel does. Approximately half are educated outside the general education classroom for less than 21 percent of their time (U.S. Department of Education, 1995).

Box 12–2 includes suggestions for how you can include students with physical disabilities in general education classrooms. Box 12–3 illustrates how the particular instructional approaches of occupational therapists and physical therapists can promote the success of inclusion for students with physical disabilities.

FIGURE 12–5
Educational placement of students with physical disabilities (1998–1999)

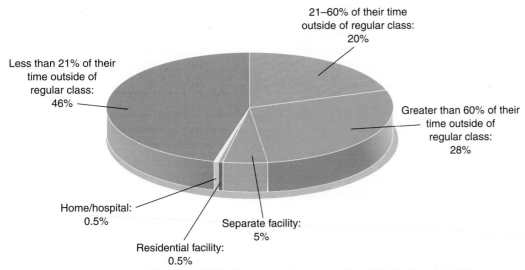

Source: From U.S. Department of Education. (2001). *To assure the free appropriate public education of all children with disabilities: Twenty-first annual report to Congress on the implementation of the Individuals with Disabilities Education Act.* Washington, DC: Author.

Inclusion Tips

Box 12–2

	What You Might See	What You Might Be Tempted to Do	Alternate Responses	Ways to Include Peers in the Process
Behavior	The student may have restricted movements, need special physical care, or use a wheelchair.	Allow her to be excused from many class activities or treat her as invisible.	Collaborate closely with the nurse, the aide, the inclusion specialist, and the physical therapist to strive for her full potential.	Encourage friends who can socialize as well as provide classroom support.
Social interactions	She may not be able to speak except with her eyes and gestures.	Avoid bringing her into situations with other students.	Use direct eye contact and AAC devices. Socialize with her, and treat her as other students.	Teach peers to use assistive devices. Provide many opportunities to use these in natural social interactions.
Educational performance	She may take more time to complete class assignments because of her physical limitations.	Grade her down for work not completed on time.	Provide her with extra time and help to complete work. Take advantage of available computer technology.	Provide a computer partner.
Classroom attitudes	Her attitude may be poor or resistant because she is not treated in a typical way.	Instruct her on appropriate ways to participate.	Get to know her and spend time with her discussing his interests and what she is experiencing daily.	Provide opportunities for cooperative learning activities consistent with her strengths and preferences.

Figure 2–5 in Chapter 2 illustrates universally designed learning related to curriculum, instruction, and evaluation.

Planning Universally Designed Learning

The majority of students with physical disabilities do not require adaptation in their curriculum (what you teach), but they often do require augmented and adapted instruction (how you teach) and evaluation (how you document learning). We will discuss two ways to adapt instruction and evaluation for students with physical disabilities: (1) adaptation for mobility impairments and (2) adaptation for communication impairments.

Adapting Instruction and Evaluation for Mobility Impairments

Assistive technology is a useful and common technique for adapting instruction and evaluation for students with physical disabilities who experience mobility impairments. The Technology-Related Assistance to Individuals with Disabilities Act of 1988 (the Tech Act that you read about in Chapter 1) authorizes the federal government to provide funds to states so they can create or improve statewide systems for delivering assistive technology devices and services. The Tech Act defines **assistive technology** as follows:

> Assistive technology means any item, piece of equipment or product system, whether acquired commercially off the shelf, modified, or customized, that is used to increase, maintain, or improve the functional capacities of a child with disabilities. (20 U.S.C. sec. 1401[1])

Assistive technology exists on a continuum:

▼ High-tech devices incorporate sophisticated electronics or computers.
▼ Medium-tech devices are moderately complicated mechanical devices (e.g., wheelchairs).

Box 12–3

Into Practice

Physical and Occupational Therapy in General Education Classrooms

Imagine for a moment that you are a general education teacher of third graders and that Maddie is enrolled in your classroom. Maddie has several challenges. For one thing, she has spastic quadriplegic cerebral palsy. She can't use her right arm for any purpose except to stabilize objects: It serves as a sort of wall because it is fixed into a half-cocked position. She can, however, use her left arm and hand. In addition, she uses a wheelchair throughout the school day because she cannot walk; and she also has a very weak back and poor posture. Finally, she has a learning disability. Ask yourself, "How can I include Maddie?"

The answer, as it is for Rommel, is that you ask for assistance from an occupational therapist and from a physical therapist. Although these therapists often work together, they bring different talents to the general classroom. The physical therapist is concerned with the student's sensory and gross-motor functions and particularly with the student's nervous and musculoskeletal systems. That means the physical therapist will assist the student to coordinate her body positions in order to complete certain tasks, learn how to move about in certain environments and overcome barriers in those environments (such as classrooms and playgrounds), and acquire and learn how to use mobility-facilitating equipment. By contrast, the occupational therapist is concerned with the student's fine-motor skills: manipulating small objects, handwriting, organizing to do certain tasks, orienting her body to certain spaces, and completing activities of daily living (such as dressing, bathing, and toileting). To carry out their duties, these therapists either work directly with the student, providing hands-on training; or they advise, consult, and monitor, providing indirect services. The following chart describes some of the ways in which these therapists can make it possible for you to teach Maddie in general education classrooms.

Physical Therapy

One	Two	Three
Maddie will receive instruction in maneuvering her wheelchair off the bus, over the school grounds, and into the classroom.	Maddie will work on postural control and stabilization of her upper body to improve use of her hands and head control for desktop work.	Maddie will work on postural control to improve her head, torso, and shoulder stability to allow her eyes and hands to move yet still attend to class activity. She will work on coordination of breathing during an activity to maintain her focus on the task.

Occupational Therapy

One	Two	Three
Maddie will work on organizational skills and efficiency during her routine.	The therapist will introduce a computer at her desk with adaptations. Maddie will work on fine-motor coordination and equipment use.	Maddie will work during class on attention to task-refocusing techniques.

Learning Outcomes

One	Two	Three
Maddie will independently complete her morning routine from exiting the school bus to storing her belongings and preparing for class.	Maddie will use a computer at her desk to complete 25 percent of her work independently.	Maddie will attend to the teacher and focus on the task at hand 70 percent of the time during classroom activities, requiring only minimal assistance 25 percent of the time to refocus her attention despite competing sounds, sights, or actions.

Putting These Strategies to Work for Progress in the General Curriculum

1. What is the distinction between occupational and physical therapists?

2. How can physical therapy and occupational therapy contribute to students' progress in the general curriculum?

3. Do related-service providers typically work alone? If not, what kinds of services and providers typically are involved with students with physical disabilities?

To answer these questions online and learn more about these strategies, go to the "Into Practice" module in Chapter 12 of the companion website.

Source: Adapted from Szabo, J. L. (2000). Maddie's story: Inclusion through physical and occupational therapy. *Teaching Exceptional Children, 33*(2), 26–32.

▼ Low-tech devices or items are less sophisticated and do not include mechanical parts (e.g., adapted spoon handles, Velcro fasteners).

"The technology involved may be as simple as Velcro or as complex as the computer chip" (Pellegrino, 2002, p. 461). Figure 12–6 highlights a broad range of assistive technology used in schools. We call your attention to the mobility category. In that category, you see five equipment options for students: scooters, walkers, crutches, bicycles, and wheelchairs. Many factors influence which device a student will use: the nature and extent of the student's disability; family and student preferences; funding; and judgments of the medical, rehabilitation, and other experts working with the student. Using adaptive equipment requires training and practice for students. For example, students need driving lessons in learning to use scooters or wheelchairs, especially power chairs. Virtual reality can be a stimulating medium for learning to drive a wheelchair, as you will read in Box 12–4.

Assistive technology devices also benefit students with mobility limitations in their hands and arms, making it possible for them to write (Heller, D'Andrea, & Forney, 1998). Among the tools are adapted writing tools such as the following (Bigge et al., 2001):

▼ Grips, foam material, or balls added to pencils or pens to enhance their grip
▼ Attachments, templates, splints, or weights that enable students to hold writing tools at the proper angle

In addition, assistive technology services (related to the devices themselves) make the devices useful to the student. These services include teaching the student to use a different body part to manipulate a writing tool such as a mouth or a head stick attached to a pencil.

Also, standard computers that present barriers to students with mobility limitations can be customized in many ways (Bigge et al., 2001):

▼ Having key guards (plastic grids that cover the keyboard with holes over each key) that enable students to not activate keys if their hands drag across the keyboard
▼ Having key locks that press keys such as control or shift while a second key is being pressed
▼ Arranging keyboards that enable more time-efficient use and less fatigue for people using a mouth/head stick or using one hand
▼ Using alternative input devices such as switches, voice recognition, and pointing devices

Adapting Instruction and Evaluation for Communication Impairments

Augmentative and alternative communication (AAC) refers to techniques and strategies used by students who are unable to communicate fully through natural speech and/or writing (Lloyd, Fuller, & Arvidson, 1997). The goal of AAC is to enable those students to experience all of the social, emotional, academic, recreational, and employment benefits that accrue from communication.

We have already briefly mentioned Camille's Liberator. It is a rectangular box, similar in size to a laptop computer, that sits at Camille's eye level and attaches to her motorized wheelchair by a tubular mounting device. The surface facing Camille is divided into a grid programmed with messages that she often uses. A symbol in each grid cell cues Camille to which word or phrase it contains. Cells also contain the letters, numbers, and many of the functions found on a standard computer keyboard. Once Camille has activated a particular cell by a light sensor attached to her head, the Liberator then displays the letter, number, word, or message and speaks it in a feminine voice. Without a doubt, Camille's Liberator makes a big difference in her life.

AAC devices have four key features: symbols, displays, selection options, and output modes (Burstein, Wright-Drechsel, & Wood, 1998).

Symbols Symbols represent meanings. Three forms of assistive technology use symbolic communication (Bigge et al., Heller, 2001):

▼ Nonelectronic devices, such as communication boards and communication notebooks (see Figure 12–7 for an example of a communication board)

To learn more about wheelchairs and scooters, go to the Web Links module in Chapter 12 of the Companion Website. There you can link to Wheelchair Net and Abledata.

To learn more about computer adaptations for students with mobility impairments, go to the Web Links module in Chapter 12 of the Companion Website for a link to Microsoft and Apple accessibility features (www.microsoft.com/enable and oscar.ctc.edu/access/resources/accessibility.html).

FIGURE 12–6
Common adaptive equipment for increasing functional mobility

Positioning

Bolsters/sand bags	Pillow-like objects used to support desired positions
Triangle/corner chairs	Provide three-sided support in upright position; can also be used with table
Bean bags	Allow comfortable positioning; adjust to individual
Wedges	Wedge-shaped foam pads used in prone position; allow work on head control, use of hands/arms
Car seats	Provide safety and appropriate positioning
Wheelchairs/inserts	Upright positioning and mobility inserts, individually designed and fitted
Prone boards	Standing positioning, allowing use of hands/arms

Mobility

Scooters	Used by young children from many positions
Walkers	Style varies with need
Crutches	Style varies with need
Bicycles (two or three wheels)	Can have adapted seats, handlebars, or pedals, as necessary
Wheelchairs (power and regular)	Standard: with specific equipment such as footrests, neckrests, headrests, side supports, and inserts Travel chairs: serve as both therapeutic chairs and car seats (rear wheels are collapsible)

Isolated Support

Braces	Plastic, fiberglass, or cloth; are removable support for scoliosis or joint strengthening; metal braces are being used less frequently
Splints	Used on hands, wrists, arms, knees, and ankles, for support or to help inhibit contractures

Activity-Oriented

Mercury switches	Devices worn on part of student's body where movement is desired; attached to radio or device that switches on when body part moves; other switches controlled by hands, feet, cheeks, voice, breath
Battery-operated devices	Toys, wheelchairs, communication systems adapted with special switches
Computer aids	Communication, leisure/recreation, calculators for shopping, and so forth
Toy modifications	Larger handles, switches, controls, adapted to be operated by different modalities (e.g., by voice)
Radio-controlled devices	Door openers, telephone answering machines, toys
Mobility devices	Battery-operated riding toys, power wheelchairs, scooters

Source: From "Motor and Personal Care Skills," by C. H. Kimm, M. A. Falvey, K. D. Bishop, and R. L. Rosenberg, in *Inclusive and Heterogeneous Schooling: Assessment, Curriculum, and Instruction* (p. 208), edited by M. A. Falvey, 1995, Baltimore, MD: Paul H. Brookes Publishing Company. Copyright 1995 by Paul H. Brookes Publishing Company, P. O. Box 10624, Baltimore, MD 21284-0624. Reprinted with permission.

Technology Tips

Box 12–4

Virtual Reality for Wheelchair Drivers

By now, nearly every student above the elementary grades knows that there is "real" reality and "virtual" reality. And nearly all students who are approaching or are at the age when they can drive legally live in both realities. They exist in the real reality that they do not yet have a driver's license. But they also exist in the virtual reality that comes when they imagine themselves driving, despite having a disability, and when, their imagination aside, they take a driver's ed course and confront, for the first time, a computer that puts them into harrowing driving conditions. What's all that got to do with technology? There are two relationships.

The first has to do with driver's ed and technology to adapt an automobile, especially the one used in driver's ed. The fact that the student has a physical disability does not necessarily mean he will never be able to drive. Automobiles can be adapted so that the accelerator and brake controls can be put at dashboard height and can be hand-operated. The ability of a student with a physical disability to navigate an adapted car may be as good as that of a student who does not have a physical disability, especially if the first student knows about mobility firsthand and is unafraid of any terrain or driving conditions that might arise. And that brings us to the second relationship of technology to these students' "reality."

Just how do students with physical disabilities acquire knowledge and confidence about terrains and mobility? Some acquire these attributes because they have learned to drive their chairs by participating in the virtual-reality mobility-training developed at Oregon Research Institute (ORI) www.ori.org/educationrr.htm#learningtodrive. There, researchers have developed a 3-D computer gaming technology that improves students' wheelchair driving/mobility skills and their non-virtual-reality mobility skills.

To access the Internet instruction, students log on to ORI's site (ori.org/~vr/projects/vrmobility.html). Once there, they find three quite different environments in which they have to use their chairs. "Sonora Springs" is a wide-open desert of hot sands; other than the desert itself, there are only a few huge rock formations. "Village Square" is a medieval village with an inn, stone pathways, geysers, a cave, and a large lake. "Riparian Ruins" is a long-abandoned city at the bottom of a large, now-dry lake. Half of the city is buried in silt; the other half protrudes invitingly.

The challenge for the students is to learn how to use their chairs in these three different environments. Sand, stone, and silt are barriers that test the students' mobility skills and creativity, putting their problem solving to the test. Conquer these environments, and the nonvirtual ones should not be too difficult.

To enter those virtual realities, the students need a computer with Windows 2000, a graphic accelerator card, some 3-D sound cards, and a good quality PC gaming joy stick.

When the challenges in the virtual reality are not as formidable as in real reality, students' participation in the school's physical environment is easier; indeed, physical participation is the linchpin for participation and progress in academic, extracurricular, and other general education programs. Moving toward a life of full participation and independence through technology is possible if the technology transports the students to a virtual reality and back again.

Putting These Strategies to Work for Progress in the General Curriculum

1. What is the challenge?
2. What is the technology?
3. What do you do with it?

To answer these questions online and learn more about these strategies, go to the Technology Tips module in Chapter 12 of the Companion Website.

▼ Dedicated communication devices that are specifically designed for communication, such as the Liberator

▼ Computer systems (not special devices)

Each of these forms of assistive technology enables students to communicate through symbols such as drawings, photographs, letters, words, or a combination of these symbols.

Displays   AAC devices have either fixed or dynamic displays. A fixed display offers an unchanging symbol arrangement. The pictures on the communication board in Figure 12–7 show

FIGURE 12–7
A communication board is an example of a fixed display

a fixed display; all of these pictures remain the same. By contrast, dynamic displays enable students to make choices by changing the display on the computer screen. Figure 12–8 features DynaVox 3100, which is one of the most powerful and flexible AAC devices available. DynaVox 3100 uses a touch-screen display that progresses (thus, is dynamic) through a natural process of forming and sending messages. The display has an extensive vocabulary of words. Students can have access to the words by touching the screen or using a mouse. The display also includes hundreds of preprogrammed communication pages for individuals of all ages and a word prediction dictionary of more than 128,000 word forms that enables individuals to create long messages quickly by offering a sequence of logical words. Because of its built-in infrared controls, DynaVox 3100 lets the student access and operate televisions, VCRs, computers, and other appliances; it can even provide an alarm system to remind students of schedule changes and to take their medicine. It also offers 10 different voices for voice outputs, including male and female, ranging from childhood through adulthood.

Selection Options   AAC devices typically offer two major types of selection options: scanning or direct selection. Scanning is suitable for the student who has extensive motor loss. Scanning involves pointing or using a cursor to scan an item at a time, a row of items, or a block of items. Many different options are available for scanning, and each can be tailored to the needs and preferences of a student (Glennen & DeCoste, 1997; Quist & Lloyd, 1997). The options include pointing without physical contact (such as eye gaze, light pointers, head-control mouth), touching/pressing, and speech recognition (a computer program understanding user vocalizations as a means of keyboard input) (Quist & Lloyd, 1997, p. 112).

Output   The fourth AAC feature is output. Output options are either intrinsic or extrinsic; intrinsic options are associated with low-tech options, and extrinsic ones are associated with high-tech options (Burstein et al., 1998). Intrinsic output occurs when, for example, a student points

To learn much more about DynaVox 3100, go to the Web Links module in Chapter 12 of the Companion Website for a link to the website of Sentient Systems Infrared Capability.

FIGURE 12–8
DynaVox 3100 is an example of a highly dynamic AAC system

Source: Courtesy of Sentient Systems Technology, Inc., Pittsburgh.

to the letters on a nonelectronic alphabet board and the student's communication partner (the person to whom the student is communicating) observes each letter and then puts the letters together to understand the message. Alternatively, extrinsic output uses voice (such as DynaVox 3100 and Liberator) or print as extrinsic output modes.

Rommel's school district provides him with a computer; and his occupational therapist, Karen Boyd, has adjusted its keys to their most sensitive setting. Rommel also has enjoyed using a computer graphic software program in a computer class. Because Rommel is so bright and relies on a computer for so much of his written work, he has been admitted to several upper-level courses, including a computer course.

AAC technology is evolving rapidly, and many new and exciting opportunities for communication are on the horizon for individuals with physical and communication disabilities. As with other educational decisions, there are some important multicultural issues to take into account when considering the most appropriate AAC options for students from culturally and linguistically diverse backgrounds. In Box 12–5 you will learn about tips for increasing cultural responsiveness and also read quotes from families from diverse backgrounds.

Collaborating to Meet Students' Needs

There is no better example of collaboration than that provided by the family and professionals who form "Team Rommel." Rommel is the team leader, knowing his health and health needs so well, being able to express them so articulately, having such a strong personality that he can set the general direction of his health and school services, and being so optimistic that his disposition attracts everyone to him. To fully appreciate how complex Rommel's needs are and how synchronous his team must be, read Box 12–6.

To read one of Rommel's science fiction stories, go to the Get to Know People with Physical Disabilities module in Chapter 12 of the Companion Website.

Companion Website

Box 12–5

Multicultural Considerations

Enhancing the Cultural Responsiveness of AAC

Research with families from African American, Hispanic, Chinese, Vietnamese, Navajo, and European American backgrounds has indicated that cultural values can influence decision making related to AAC (Kemp & Parette, 2000). This research reported a number of tips and also quotes from families from diverse backgrounds that enable us to hear their voices and gain their perspectives. We have included some of these tips and quotes in the following list.

1. **It's important to select symbols and photographs that represent the family's culture.**

   I think we also need to be very careful when we do use color. I found it very offensive when we had a demonstration of a board that used color and they used the color black for the symbol help. And there was the face of a black person in the front with the motion of a black person moving behind them and that to me was very stereotypical.

2. **The voices used on AAC machines should match the voice of the family's culture.**

   In the Latino culture, language is so tied with identity. It's just a part of who you are . . . even if you speak English fluently. If you have an accent or if most people around you have an accent and [you have] this voice who is supposed to represent . . . you [but] comes out in perfect English, [then that] is just not who you are.

3. **The color selection can be very important to some families such as Native American clans with particular color preferences.**

   And the grandmothers told me last year that they were really concerned about the colors too, 'cause they thought that certain colors were very important to their culture. They didn't see them well represented on the overlays.

4. **Stigma can be an important issue if people perceive that an AAC device draws unwanted attention to them.**

   I believe that most of the Chinese are afraid of losing face. Afraid of how people look at us; look at me. So they don't want to do anything that is different from others. So the AAC device just makes you stand out and makes you different and that's a stigma. So they have to deal with it—a resistance to AAC device first.

If you are interested in any of these options, or if you know teachers who might be, you or they may want to know that researchers at Southeast Missouri State University and University of Arkansas for Medical Sciences have developed a CD-ROM training tool, "Families, Cultures, and AAC," that introduces families and professionals to AAC through a bilingual text (English and Spanish). The CD-ROM has 1½ hours of video segments and includes 16 interactive games, a multimedia glossary, printable documents, and website links and is usable on either the Windows or the Macintosh platform. It can be obtained from Program Development Associates in Syracuse, New York (http://www.pdaffoc.com).

Putting These Ideas to Work for Progress in the General Curriculum

1. Are you aware of any AAC that seems to conflict with these tips concerning youths with children and families from diverse backgrounds? For example, does the AAC use colors or icons that may be offensive? Does it "speak" in a voice that is not at all like the voice and accents that families from diverse cultures use normally? If so, investigate whether the developer of the AAC has any adaptations that minimize these barriers to families' use of AAC.

2. What might you do if you find that families from diverse backgrounds decline to consider AAC?

3. What resources—such as books, videos, or CD-ROMs at school or other public libraries or information and demonstrations on the Internet—might families consult to learn about the advantages of AAC? (Make sure these resources are in the family's own language and do not perpetuate any racial/ethnic, linguistic, or cultural stereotypes.)

To answer these questions online and learn more about these ideas and concepts, go to the Multicultural Considerations module in Chapter 12 of the Companion Website.

Source: All quotations are from Program Development Associates, Syracuse, NY (http://www.pdaffoc.com).

Collaboration Tips

Box 12–6

Team Rommel

There is no single head of Team Rommel, unless it is Rommel. He is an expert on his own needs. It helps that he is highly self-determined. He himself was the final arbiter of whether he would have surgery to insert a j-tube into his small intestine so he could receive his food through the tube, and he is the person on whom everyone relies for direction about his needs.

Rommel is multiply challenged and needs assistance in many activities of daily living, such as bathing, putting on his back brace, using his breathing apparatus, suctioning secretions from his lungs, and using vehicles to go from home to school and back again. Add to his daily regimen the need to constantly check whether all of his regular and emergency equipment works (he carries an oxygen tank on the back of his wheelchair) and the requirements to enable him to make progress in the general curriculum, and it is obvious that Rommel is the center of a highly orchestrated and collaborative team.

So, Rommel cannot be the only member of his team. There is his mother, Lorna, a nurse herself; and her parents, who live with her and Rommel. They take care of his daily needs at home: bathing, dressing, using the breathing machine, feeding by mouth and by j-tube, and negotiating the maze of school, health care, and health insurance systems.

For his education, there is Kathy Schmitz, the school district resource nurse and certified health educator. More than anyone else, she sees the big picture and coordinates all of the other members of Rommel's team. Her attention is focused on two aspects of his life: his health and how to maintain it and prevent or respond to emergencies; and his academic progress, especially how accommodations to his disability should be made so he can achieve his maximum level of performance.

In the everyday routine of school, Becky Draper, Rommel's one-on-one nurse, provides all of the regular and emergency services that Rommel needs each day in school: suctioning secretions from his lungs, checking on his pulse and oxygen saturation, administering oxygen when he needs it, assuring that his j-tube/nutrition tube and pump are slow-dripping food into Rommel's gastrointestinal track, taking notes for him in class when he is too tired to do that, writing out the answers he dictates to the questions on examinations he is taking, and making sure that he knows what his assignments are and delivering them to him and then from him to his teachers when he is at home or in the hospital.

Robin Haupt, Rommel's physical therapist, and Karen Boyd, his occupational therapist, team up to design a special mold for Rommel's wheelchair, retrofit the arm rests of the chair so Rommel can reach the steering mechanisms more easily, and adapt the keyboard of his computer so he can use it more often and for longer periods of time without becoming fatigued. Robin also provides him with one-on-one physical education when he attends physical education class.

Within the school district, Rommel's teachers and school administrators, and even the school bus driver, know much about Rommel's limitations and how to accommodate to them. Giving him more time to complete his assignments, enabling Becky to attend all of his classes and take notes or write out his answers to questions, making accommodations in how he takes the state's student-progress assessment examinations, and assuring that he gets onto and off of the bus safely and that he is well seat-belted into the bus are all relatively simple accommodations that go a long way to making sure that Rommel participates in and progresses through the general curriculum.

Finally, Rommel's four physicians work with each other and with Rommel, Lorna, and the school team. There's the pediatrician responsible for Rommel's regular health care; an orthopedic specialist responsible for looking after Rommel's posture, especially his back; a surgeon who implanted and regularly checks Rommel's j-tube; and a pulmonary specialist who monitors Rommel's lung functioning.

To assure that Rommel progresses in the general curriculum, there has to be a large team of highly specialized experts. But that's not enough. Each expert, beginning with Rommel and his family and extending through all of the others, must recognize this essential fact: Each can contribute something, but no one person can contribute everything to the education and life of this remarkable young man.

Putting These Tips to Work for Progress in the General Curriculum

1. What are the challenges?

2. What can the team do?

3. What are the results?

To answer these questions online and learn more about these ideas and concepts, go to the Collaboration Tips module in Chapter 12 of the Companion Website.

What Can You Learn from Others Who Teach Students with Physical Disabilities?

Learning for the Early Childhood Years: Self-Determination Through Technology

In their very first years of education, students typically begin to learn to express their preferences and become self-determining, get along with others of their own age, and communicate effectively. What happens, however, when half of a group of preschoolers has no disabilities, the other half has cerebral palsy or other physical disabilities that impair their ability to communicate, and all are in the same program? How does a teacher accomplish these three goals? One part of the answer is that she uses assistive technology.

In Brockton, Massachusetts, Barbara Smith faced two challenges as a teacher (NCIP, 1998). Her first was to convert her classroom from an entirely self-contained one (for students with disabilities) into an inclusive one. She did just that, noting, "Integration is easily twice the work in terms of preparation, but when we consider the progress these kids have made, we could never go back." Her second was to offer a typical preschool curriculum to all of her students and to ensure that her students with disabilities would benefit from it, participate in it, and progress through the general curriculum.

For many years, Barbara had been using relatively simple low technology, such as communication boards and picture charts. With the assistance of Helen Vigra, the school district's computer specialist, Barbara began using computer-based tools to supplement these instructional tools. For example, a student who does not speak uses an electronic device that incorporates synthesized speech output. Another who has great difficulty using her hands uses a computer to access the same books that her peers are reading.

And then there is Sabrina, a 5-year-old who can neither speak nor point but who, through technology, can participate in the general curriculum. Sabrina uses two types of technology. One is low, and the other is high. She uses them together to indicate what she wants (self-determination), to read (acquire communication skills), and to speak and sing with her peers (communicate effectively). Thus, Sabrina uses assistive technology to progress in the general curriculum.

The wheelchair is a traditional form of assistive technology. Here, you see how it makes it possible for a student to participate in the general curriculum.

Sabrina's low-tech tool is an eye-gaze board. It is a simple Plexiglass frame that has Velcro tabs on it. After Barbara places six pictures of Sabrina's preferred activities onto the Velcro tabs and then arranges the board so it stands perpendicularly on Sabrina's wheelchair tray, Sabrina gazes at the picture that indicates what she wants to do. Barbara reads Sabrina's gaze, confirms that she and Sabrina are communicating accurately with each other, and then makes Sabrina's choice come true.

If, for example, Sabrina wants to read a book and has looked at the picture of the book, Barbara resorts to high tech. She makes sure that Sabrina is in front of a computer screen and then switches on a program that loads Sabrina's chosen book. The computer program brings the book to the screen and reads the story aloud while also highlighting the words. By hitting a switch on her tray, Sabrina can turn the book's page until she is finished reading. Then she hits another switch on her tray. That switch activates an electronic speech aid called SpeakEasy, which in turn says, "Come here, please," or emits any one of nearly a dozen other prerecorded messages that Sabrina will need throughout the day.

Obviously, the eye-gaze board and computer are useful when Sabrina is engaging in activities that she does alone, such as reading. But what if she is in a group activity, such as the sharing circle, and wants to let her teacher and peers know that, like them, she can identify the weather? Once again, technology assists her. Barbara places a clock in front of Sabrina; on the face of the clock are pictures of the weather. After Barbara turns the clock on, its hands begin to move around the dial. When they reach the weather picture that Sabrina believes describes today's weather, Sabrina hits a switch on her tray to stop the clock and declare to her peers, "This is today's weather." Likewise, when the students are singing "The Fish in the Sea Go Splash, Splash, Splash," Sabrina sings the "splash" part by activating the preprogrammed computer to "sing" the "splash" refrain.

To learn more about how technology supports preschool inclusion, go to the Web Links module in Chapter 12 of the Companion Website site. There you can link to Barbara's classroom and learn much more about her successful universally designed learning (www2.edc.org/NCIP/tour/Barbara-class.html).

Learning for the Elementary Years: In the Gym with Assistive Technology

Conjure your impression of Walden Pond, Massachusetts. You probably imagine a quiet, small pond with Ralph Waldo Emerson sitting beside it, thinking. That's one impression, a 19th-century version. The 21st-century version is quite different: John Passarini, a.k.a. the "Silver Fox" or "Mr. Wizard," rolls down the gentle slope of the hill to the pond, braking his tandem bike and guiding Ned, his sixth-grade student, who rides on the back seat.

John, the burly teacher, and Ned, a student with physical limitations, join other Wayland, Massachusetts, middle school students as all of them—repeat, *all*—complete their annual 18-mile round-trip hike to the pond at the beginning of each school year (Jurasek, 2000).

Is the 21st-century image out of sync with your impression of elementary school programs for students with physical disabilities? It should not be, for Passarini, a nationally honored teacher, uses state-of-the-art assistive technology to teach mobility, health, and even academics. Here's the difference about him: His classroom is the gym, and his certification is as both a physical education teacher and an adapted physical education teacher. He is that, but he is also an instructor of other skills and new attitudes.

In his class, each student with a disability has a buddy who does not have a disability. Together, they play such games as "The Blob and the Black Hole." The designated Blob (yes, it's Passarini himself) chases the space travelers (the students) with his "weapon," a foam boffer. To escape being "disappeared" from space, the students must flee (run) from the Blob; if he "makes contact" (tags them), or if they step onto a "black hole" (rubber mat), they disappear from space. They can find safety only by boarding a "space pod" (another rubber mat, differently colored to designate it as a safety zone) or by picking up the "space pellets" (foam balls) that Passarini has scattered throughout the gym and returning them to their own "space ship" (the home-free zone). All the while, students without and with disabilities help each other run, pick up balls, re-

Using hand-over-hand instruction, John Passarini coaches a student in lacrosse techniques so the student can join his peers without disabilities in catching and throwing and thereby receive the benefits of access to the general curriculum of physical education.

turn to safety, and shout out directions on how to avoid the Blob; and all the while, music from the movie *2001* blares in the background, Richard Strauss's *Also Sprach Zarathustra*.

What's going on? Obviously, there is exercise on the trek and in the gym; there is a curriculum on health and motor development. Equally obviously, there is the use of assistive technology (tandem bike, adaptive equipment, boffers, mats, and balls). Less obviously, there is inclusion, cooperative learning, peer tutoring, and the development of friendships that extend to other classrooms, to extracurricular activities, and to other school activities such as the trek to Walden Pond. In a nutshell, there is access to the general curriculum.

Even less obviously, there is a curriculum in self-esteem. Students with disabilities are learning to respect their own abilities, for they are players, too. And they are building on skills they learn in other classes, such as how to speak clearly when they call out to their buddies to throw or catch the space pellets before the Blob tags one of them and wins ownership of that valued property. Moreover, as the music plays (whether Wagner, children's music, rock and roll, country and western, or jazz), they are learning how to listen and how to move their bodies according to the music's tempo, rhythm, and volume.

It all sounds quite easy; but Passarini, like all good teachers working with students who have physical disabilities, is wise about the assistive technology. He selects equipment and devices with an eye toward inclusion, safety, and costs (so the technology can be used by any student). He also is systematic about his instruction. He provides minute, clear, and specific directions. He himself demonstrates what he wants the students to do, and then he taps various students to demonstrate the moves he wants all students to make.

Asked to describe his role, Passarini explains it directly. "When children believe that an adult enjoys being with them, and cares about their happiness, their minds and hearts open and the learning environment becomes productive." Given that special education is oriented toward the outcome of being a productive citizen, there is little doubt that John Passarini is developing just that, not only in his students with disabilities but also in his students who do not have disabilities. For him, inclusion leads to productivity. And it involves a whale of a lot of fun along the way.

Learning for the Middle and Secondary Years: Centers for Independent Living

Middle and secondary years are times for increasing autonomy for all students, including those with physical disabilities. But a survey of teenagers with physical disabilities reported that slightly more than half of the teenagers were unable to explain or discuss their disability, half of those taking medications did not know the names or the medications or the reason for taking them, and 90 percent were unable to describe their long-term therapeutic goals (Hostler, Gressard, Hassler, & Linden, 1989).

Yet students with physical disabilities need knowledge and skills related to their disability issues. That is why adults with disabilities have been successful in working with policymakers to develop Centers for Independent Living. These centers provide individual advocacy, peer counseling, information and referral, and training in independent living skills to individuals with disabilities; all of those services are provided by a staff comprised mostly of adults with disabilities. The independent living center staff also collaborates with schoolteachers and their students with physical disabilities and their families in developing the skills the students will need as adults.

In what ways can adults with disabilities make a difference in the lives of students with disabilities? To increase their self-determination, confidence, independent living skills, and community participation? To help them become more self-efficacious, where *self-efficacy* refers not to a person's skills but to one's own judgment of what one can do with the skills one has? The answer to each question is "absolutely." Adults with disabilities are experts because they themselves face roughly the same kinds of challenges as the students do (Powers, Sowers, & Stevens, 1995).

In a community of 100,000 in the Pacific Northwest, four students with cerebral palsy and one with spina bifida were paired with five adult mentors who have cerebral palsy, multiple sclerosis, muscular dystrophy, or rheumatoid arthritis. One student was 12 years old, another 15, another 18, and two were 19. Only one of the students had any cognitive limitation (mild mental retardation). Their mentors were professionals in fields other than education (mental health counselor and attorney), executives (office manager), and creative artists (dancer/musician and writer/college advisor). They ranged in age from 27 to 51. Each lived independently.

The students and their mentors engaged in two one-on-one activities per month over a six-month period (for a total of 12 activities) and attended three two-hour conferences on disability issues (for a total of six conferences). In the individual activities, the mentors helped the students learn how to handle challenging situations in the community. The situations involved improving accessibility, securing housing adaptations, managing personal care assistance, engaging in recreation and leisure activities, eating and drinking in public, riding the bus, finding jobs, and using public bathrooms. All of these activities enable the students to have more skills to live independently.

The mentors also contributed to the students' self-determination by suggesting how to solve the challenges to living independently, encouraging the students to ask questions about the challenges and even questions not related to the activity. The mentors shared information about past disability challenges and emphasized the importance of making one's own decisions, being responsible about taking risks, and never giving up.

When students who had mentors were compared with students (of the same age and with the same disability) who did not have mentors, the results of the mentoring program were remarkable. Those who had mentors showed marked improvement in their disability-related self-efficacy. They demonstrated more knowledge of strategies to meet challenges, and their parents regarded their children as more informed and self-confident. In addition, they began to participate in the community to a much greater degree than they did before they had mentors. They also initiated independent living skills that they had not tried before (such as getting a telephone with a speaker system, riding a bicycle, and advocating in school for greater disability accessibility). And they regarded their disabilities more positively and set higher postschool goals for themselves (such as going to college and living on their own). The mentors were sources of information and, more importantly, inspiration. It is as though they tell and show the students, "I've been there, I've been like you, and now you can be like me."

To learn more about independent living centers and the independent philosophy, go to the Web Links module in Chapter 12 of the Companion Website for a link to the National Council on Independent Living (www.ncil.org).

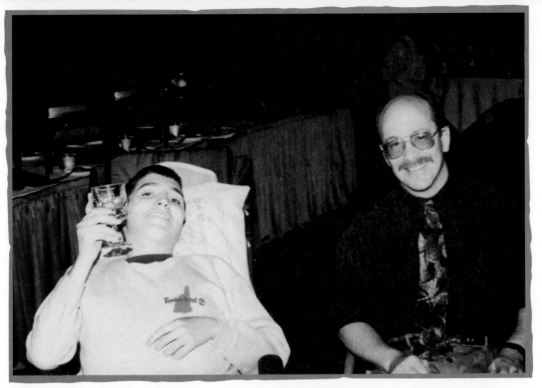

Students with physical disabilities can get information and inspiration from an adult mentor who also has a physical disability. (Photo courtesy of Laurie E. Powers, Oregon Health Sciences University.)

Learning for the Transitional and Postsecondary Years: Self-Determination in Higher Education

You will recall that IDEA's four goals are equal opportunity, full participation, independent living, and economic self-sufficiency. How do students with physical disabilities compare to those without disabilities on indicators related to these goals during the transitional and postsecondary years (Horn & Berktold, 1999)? Based on research conducted about students with physical disabilities who were in the eighth grade in 1988, by 1994, the following results were obtained:

▼ Seventy-five percent of students with physical disabilities received a high school diploma as compared to 84 percent of students without disabilities.

▼ Forty-five percent of students with physical disabilities attained a postsecondary degree or certificate as contrasted to just over 50 percent of students without a disability.

▼ Ten percent of students with physical disabilities were unemployed as compared to 4 percent of students without disabilities.

▼ Students with physical disabilities had an average starting salary of $23,345 as compared to $25,219 for students without disabilities.

In schools, junior colleges and technical institutes, and four-year colleges and universities at both the undergraduate and graduate level, people with physical disabilities and their teachers and professors are taking steps to improve these results and to achieve the four IDEA outcomes. One outcome, independent living, has several dimensions for students with physical disabilities. Of course, it means having postsecondary education. But it also includes, for many students, starting families of their own. Lest you think that students with physical disabilities cannot start their own families, read Box 12–7 and consider what Judi Rogers has accomplished and how she makes a difference not only for her own family but also for many other individuals with physical disabilities in preparing them for family life.

Box 12-7

Judi Rogers Says, "This Can Be Done"

"This can be done." Skeptical teenagers with a physical disability might say, "Yeah, right!" And their teacher may say, "Show me."

They are in a classroom in one of the schools in the San Francisco area, not a high-income suburban school but one of the truly low-income schools where a family of four earns, on average, $20,000 annually. The students are in their transition years from school to adulthood. They represent the Bay Area population: 44 percent Caucasian; 19 percent African American; 19 percent Hispanic; 9 percent Asian American, East Asian, or Pacific Islander; and 9 percent Arabic.

What are they skeptical about? Because the class is about health science (human sexuality), they question whether women with physical disabilities can have sexual relations, conceive children, carry a baby to term, and then raise a child. In a word, they wonder whether the most fundamental of life's events—those that people without disabilities take for granted—are accessible to people with cerebral palsy, spina bifida, muscular dystrophy, or any other condition that creates mobility and related physical barriers.

Judi Rogers has a simple answer to these skeptics. She wheels herself into their presence, her husband and teenage daughter with her. She doesn't have to declare, "Look, I have cerebral palsy, and here are my family members." That much is obvious. But she does say, "I am an occupational therapist, and I think I can help," or words to that effect. And she drops an interesting statistic somewhere early in her conversation: 10.9 percent of all families nationwide have one or more parents who have disabilities. Not so subtly, she is saying, "This can be done."

She opens a portfolio of photographs and letters that provide vivid evidence that literally thousands of women with physical disabilities in the San Francisco area have become mothers. The letters tell one story: I could not have imagined having my baby until I met Judi; and I could not have raised my baby without her advice, support, and innovative use of assistive technology. The photographs display the technology: portable bathtubs for babies on raised platforms; a modified Snugli that is easy for a mother to put on and take off of her baby; feeding equipment that a mother can hold easily; and a stroller that a mother in a wheelchair can use when she and her baby go for a walk.

Now Judi withdraws from the backpack attached to her chair several books, some by her and some by others but with chapters by her. She distributes them to the students and smiles knowingly as their skepticism visibly turns to fascination and then hope.

Questions, questions, and more questions—about obstetrical examinations, childbirth, nursing and feeding, and changing diapers and bathing; about just getting around an apartment, much less a city, with a baby in tow and a mother in a chair. Answers, answers, and more answers: Judi has been there and done that, or she knows mothers who have been there and done that and who are ready and willing to invite young women and their partners into a support groups.

With all the questions and answers, skepticism fades. Students start to talk about fulfilling their dreams of being a parent. Some start talking about their bodies, and that opens up another area for Judi to discuss: her own experiences with breast cancer and the training she provides to women with disabilities about that topic and about other health care issues. Judi knows all about surgery and chemotherapy; she even displays the wig she once wore. "Prettier with or without it?" she asks.

Humor couples with experience, both buttressed by fierce determination to live as independent and normal a life as possible, and melding into a role model for teachers and their students, for women and their partners of any age. Judi has woven together the disability and health care provider communities. Unintentionally, she has become a symbol and model for transforming pain and loss into creative drive and practical solutions.

As she wheels away, returning to her job at Through the Looking Glass (www.lookingglass.org), she says, "My lifetime of overcoming obstacles is a habit that's hard to break. You'll find that to be true for yourselves. Just remember, this can be done."

For many students, of course, the road to independence includes postsecondary education. Just how they manage to negotiate all of the challenges of that kind of an education is exemplified by a program at the University of California at San Diego (UCSD). It is a particularly good example because Rommel's sister, Melanie, attends UCSD and Rommel himself wants to enroll there when he graduates from high school. Those, however, are not the best reasons to use UCSD as an example of self-determined activism among students with physical disabilities. The best reason for selecting UCSD is that it has developed a highly effective peer mentoring program (Gimblett, 2000)

Under that program, upper-level undergraduate students and graduate students serve as mentors to lower-level undergraduates, transfer students, and new graduate students. They all recognize that students with disabilities often do not develop the social skills they need to succeed in college. Sometimes these students also are regarded by professors and other students as not being able to do the required academic work; indeed, they themselves may believe that they cannot do the job and may lack the motivation, much less the strategies, to succeed in colleges and universities.

Yet with help from their older peers, these new students often can do everything they need to do to earn their college and university degrees. Of course, peer mentoring alone does not suffice; assistive technology and a universally designed curriculum, delivered by accommodating professors, are also necessary. But peer mentoring helps.

At UCSD, for example, students with physical disabilities (as well as those with learning disabilities, AD/HD, vision and hearing impairments, and emotional challenges) help each other. They meet weekly to provide emotional support and information, discover what academic and social risks exist (for example, academic standards are high; and opportunities for drinking, drugs, and sexual liaisons are abundant), and develop strategies to meet and overcome the challenges and risks.

In those weekly sessions and in between-session telephone calls and e-mails that the mentors exchange with their underclass peers, the students discuss all sorts of issues. For example, they review time-management strategies. They identify the best accessible study locations and techniques for learning a particular subject matter; they tell each other what works for managing the stress of higher education and preparing for and taking examinations, for cultivating the interest of faculty advisors, and for communicating effectively in writing and orally. They talk about how to find and use extracurricular or off-campus activities and services and which of those activities and services are particularly helpful (or not helpful). They evaluate majors and career goals and share how to be effective self-advocates and disability activists.

Because peer mentoring at the university level usually is based on academic challenges, the mentors and mentees do not necessarily pair off with each other by reason of disability alone; mostly, they link up because they are in the same academic program. Thus, a student with a hearing impairment might mentor a student who uses a wheelchair so long as they have the same major. Indeed, the range of majors is broad, starting with anthropology and biology at one end of the alphabet and ending with sociology and theater at the other end.

The hub of all of this activity is the Office for Students with Disabilities. There, the program director, a computer-resource and fiscal management specialist, a testing and transportation specialist, and a real-time captionist are available to each student with a disability. They provide services to the students and to the academic departments, such as interpreter and real-time captioning services and reader and note-taker services; they also secure accommodations for students to take their examinations. They arrange for students to borrow assistive technology, and they repair or find repairs for that and student-owned equipment. They assist students in finding suitable housing and transportation and in securing services from the state's rehabilitation agency.

At UCSD, then, the combination of peer mentors and university staff in the Office for Students with Disabilities makes it entirely possible for students with physical disabilities—for students such as Rommel, who has services in his school that are comparable to some that he will get at UCSD—to achieve IDEA's goals: equal opportunity, full participation, independent living, and economic self-sufficiency.

A Vision for Rommel's Future

Rommel Nanasca and his family have had to adjust their vision as his physical disabilities change over time. For a while, it seemed that his life, much less his education, was in jeopardy. And then it seemed that his education would be limited because his body was limited. Now, with the use of medical and computer technology, there seem to be few limitations. There is practically nothing constant about his disabilities. Inexorably, they compel new visions and elicit new responses.

There are, however, constants in their life: Rommel's indomitable spirit and razor-sharp mind; Lorna and Romy's unending and loving commitment to Rommel, Ariel, and Melanie; Romy's sudden death; the support of Rommel's grandparents, uncles, and aunts; and the loyalty and competence of an extraordinary team of professionals.

Who would have thought that a boy with so many and such extensive physical challenges would have been able to attend school with students who do not have disabilities? To have planned for college? And to have written a fascinating science fiction story about the fear of death? It makes you wonder, doesn't it: What, if anything, does Rommel fear?

Rommel's father, Romy Nanasca, died in the summer of 2000. In this chapter, we honor his life, and we celebrate his family's continuing courage.

What Would You Recommend?

1. To ensure, through specific action steps, that Rommel's family and the school-based team continue to have positive collaboration?
2. To provide Rommel with interaction with his classmates if he needs to receive a good deal of his education at home?
3. To maximize opportunities for Rommel to experience an adolescence that is as typical as possible?

Summary

How Do You Recognize Students with Physical Disabilities?

▼ The term *physical disability* refers to a large group of students who, though quite different from each other, share the common challenge of mobility limitations.

▼ Cerebral palsy refers to a disorder of movement or posture occurring when the brain is in its early stages of development. The damage is not progressive or hereditary.

▼ Spina bifida is a malformation of the spinal cord. Its severity depends on both the extent of the malformation and its position on the spinal cord.

▼ Muscular dystrophy designates a group of nine hereditary, muscle-destroying disorders.

▼ Primary prevention of physical disabilities includes fetal surgery.

How Do You Evaluate Students with Physical Disabilities?

▼ Screening may take place before or directly after birth or later.

▼ An ecological assessment is conducted in a student's natural environments and leads to a plan for overcoming or compensating for the student's disability.

▼ Occupational and physical therapists play pivotal roles either directly or indirectly.

How Do You Assure Progress in the General Curriculum?

▼ Progress is assured by adaptations of instruction for mobility and communication reasons. Assistive technology is a technique for adaptation.

▼ Assistive technology for mobility includes devices that are low tech and those that are high tech.

▼ Assistive technology for communication includes augmentative and alternative communication (AAC).

▼ Collaboration usually involves professionals concerned with health, those concerned with education, and the student and family.

What Can You Learn from Others Who Teach Students with Physical Disabilities?

▼ A model early childhood program in Massachusetts uses computers as a form of assistive technology.

▼ Students in a middle school (also in Massachusetts) use off-the-shelf assistive technology in physical education classes.

▼ A program in the Pacific Northwest pairs adults and students who have disabilities with each other for "been-there/done-that" advice and counseling.

▼ At UCSD, peer mentoring helps students overcome the challenges of postsecondary education.

To find out how and where this chapter content connects to the CEC Professional Standards and the Praxis™ Standards, go to the Standards Connection module in Chapter 12 of the Companion Website. A comprehensive matrix aligning CEC Professional Standards, Praxis™ Standards, and INTASC principles to the entire text, is available in the Appendix and on the Companion Website.

Chapter 13

Who Is Jarris Garner?

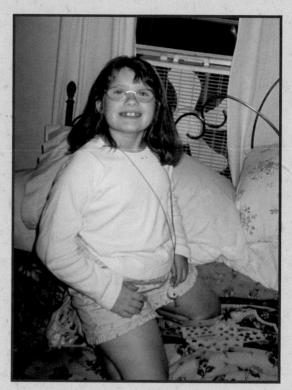

Imagine growing up with a brain injury. There are two aspects of that challenge. First, having a brain injury means having limitations in your ability to think and to imagine. Second, growing up with a brain injury can make development difficult and frustrating. Yet Jarris Garner has grown up with a brain injury and still has a vivid imagination and great expectations for a lifetime of success.

Jarris and her father and mother, Brent and Shawn, were involved in a very serious automobile accident when she was all of seven months old. So growing up with a brain injury is part of Jarris's life, all 10 years of it.

Both Jarris and Shawn were hospitalized after the accident. For six days following it, Jarris experienced multiple seizures. When her physicians finally were able to control her seizures, and after all of her external wounds were treated and healed, they discharged her, making only two recommendations to her parents. First, go to a quiet place. Second, be prepared for long periods of rehabilitation and uncertain outcomes because we cannot tell you precisely what the trajectory of Jarris's life will be.

The "quiet place" certainly could not be Jarris's home; she has two older brothers and an older sister. Grandmother's home, however, would work. So while Shawn recovered at her mother's, so did Jarris, with this difference: Shawn's mother devoted a great deal of attention to Jarris, playing and talking with her—all of which helped Jarris recover some of her lost physical and communication skills.

Grandmother's help was invaluable, but Jarris needed more. Shawn took a proactive approach, searching the Internet and local libraries for information about the effects of traumatic brain injury on infants and toddlers. What she learned was both alarming and hopeful. Alarming because so little research had been conducted on the effects of moderate to severe head injury to infants; more research had focused on toddlers and young children, but Jarris was just an infant when she was injured. Hopeful because Shawn learned that the Language Acquisition Program (LAP) at The University of Kansas would accept Jarris and work with her and her family on retrieving her language, boosting her communication skills, even teaching her how to use sign language, and preparing her for school.

LAP serves 36 children, ages 3 to 5: 18 in the morning and the same number in the afternoon. A third of the children are like Jarris in that they have significant language delays, a third speak English as a second language, and a third have no language challenges at all.

Instead of "feeling our way through the dark" as Jarris's physicians warned they would, Jarris, Shawn, Brent, and her brothers and sister have nearly "talked" their way out of the injury. That is because the LAP staff focused first and foremost on Jarris's language. They taught her how to use American Sign Language (ASL). In time and out of necessity, Shawn, Brent, and Jarris's brothers and sisters also have learned to use ASL; and her siblings expanded their knowledge by taking ASL as a second language while in high school.

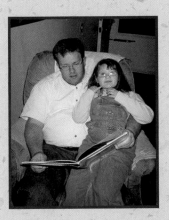

Teaching Jarris a different way to communicate was not, however, the only focus of the LAP intervention. By assuring that Jarris would be with children who do not have disabilities (but may not yet speak English), the LAP staff subtly taught her how to be part of a social community. She learned the social skills and appropriate behavior that she would have acquired naturally had she not been injured but that, in her and other children with traumatic brain injuries, are usually impaired as a result of the injury.

Now, at the age of 10, Jarris attends general education classes in her local school in Lawrence, Kansas. She is an avid football fan, although she will not play that sport and may have to be careful about participating in other contact sports so as not to reinjure herself. She is also a Walt Disney groupie: Not a single Disney movie escapes her rapt attention. Indeed, Disney movies not only entertain her but also spark her interest in acting. She reenacts the roles that Disney's heroines play, using her—yes, you guessed it—imagination.

So let's return to the challenge of imagining growing up with a brain injury. Imagine your parents being told that you and they are

starting a journey that few physicians can chart reliably. Imagine learning to speak by using signs and acquiring special ways to remember and behave in a world in which the greatest number of your peers do not understand you or your behavior because they have never had their brains bashed around in their heads.

And then imagine, as in a Disney movie, that there is a way out—a lap that you have to run once and then once again and then yet once again and so on, interminably. Could you run those laps? Jarris may not now be able to imagine what we ask you to imagine, but she has to run the laps. Who will run alongside her?

What do you think?

1. How would you support a child like Jarris who is reentering your general education classroom after rehabilitation from a brain injury?

2. How would you collaborate with rehabilitation staff and family members to ensure a successful transition?

3. Given Jarris's strengths, what types of activities could you provide to enhance her interaction with peers in her school and community?

4. How might Jarris's ability to communicate serve as an opportunity to teach other students and enhance their understanding of Jarris and other students with disabilities?

To respond to these questions online, participate in other activities, and learn more about Jarris Garner and traumatic brain injury, go to the Cases module in Chapter 13 of the Companion Website.

How Do You Recognize Students with Traumatic Brain Injury?

Defining Traumatic Brain Injury

Students with **traumatic brain injury** (TBI) have a brain injury caused by an external physical force. The regulations implementing IDEA define TBI as an *acquired injury* to the brain caused by an external physical force that adversely affects a child's educational performance and results in total or partial functional disability, psychosocial impairment, or both. Under IDEA, the term *TBI* applies to open or closed head injuries resulting in impairments in one or more of the following areas: cognition; language; memory; attention; reasoning; abstract thinking; judgment; problem solving; sensory, perceptual, and motor abilities; psychosocial behavior; physical functions; information processing; and speech. The key to this definition is the phrase *external physical force*. A common term for the effects of external physical force is **concussion,** meaning injury from a violent blow or impact. The term does not apply to brain injuries that are congenital or degenerative or that are induced by birth trauma (34 C.F.R., sec. 300.7[6][12]).

IDEA also does not cover students with two other types of brain injury. The first cause, **anoxia,** results when a person loses oxygen to the brain from an illness or an accident. A stroke, choking, or drowning are common causes of anoxia but do not derive from an external physical force. The second cause is a **congenital** brain injury—that is, one that is present at a baby's birth. Children with anoxia or congenital causes are included in the category "other health impairments" (see Chapter 11). Figure 13–1 illustrates the two types of brain injury.

Identifying the Types of Traumatic Brain Injury

Under IDEA, a student is eligible to receive services for a TBI for one of two types of head injuries: a closed head injury or an open head injury.

Closed Head Injury

A **closed head injury** results from the brain being whipped back and forth rapidly, causing it to rub against and bounce off the rough, jagged interior of the skull. Bleeding and swelling frequently result (Advisory Committee on TBI in Children, 2000). Figure 13–2 illustrates a common cause of head injury, an automobile accident.

This type of injury damages the neurofibers that are responsible for sending messages to all parts of the body. A closed head injury also places enormous stress on the *brain stem*, a relay

FIGURE 13–1

Types of brain injury: Continuum of possible brain injuries

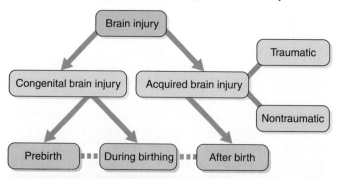

Source: From *Pediatric Traumatic Brain Injury: Proactive Interventions,* by J. L. Blosser and R. DePompei, 1994, San Diego, CA: Singular Press. Copyright 1994 by Singular Press. Reprinted with permission from Singular Publishing Group, Inc.

FIGURE 13–2

Closed head injury accident: When the head smashes into a car windshield, momentum throws the brain against the inside of the skull. Brain damage often occurs in the frontal lobes (A) at the point of impact; the temporal lobes (B) as they jam against the skull; and at the junction of the frontal and temporal lobes (C). Large veins above the ear (D) may also tear, causing a subdural hematoma.

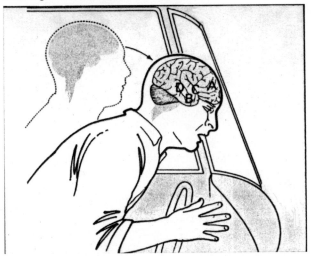

Source: From the U.S. Department of Health and Human Services. (1984). *Head injury: Hope through research.* Bethesda, MD: Author.

station for sensations going to the brain and signals going from the brain to the rest of the body. A closed head injury can affect a person physically, emotionally, and cognitively.

Even a mild closed head injury, sometimes called **postconcussional syndrome** or *mild TBI* (MTBI), can cause a serious and far-reaching impact on a person's ability to enjoy life and work and to earn a living. Whiplash, for example, with no striking of the head against an object or unconsciousness, may result in a mild head injury (Buyer, 1999).

Seth's story in Box 13–1 tells of a student with a "mild" head injury. He was 9 when he collided with a tree while sledding near his house. In the box, Linda McLaughlin, Seth's mother, talks about their experiences. Like Seth, many individuals who have been knocked unconscious immediately after an accident sometimes experience long-lasting symptoms. As many as 10 percent of those who sustain mild TBI experience symptoms that last for their entire lifetime (Tyler & Mira, 1999). Figure 13–3 lists some of the common symptoms.

Open Head Injury

An **open head injury** results from an insult to a specific area or focal point of the brain, such as might be caused by a gunshot wound or a blow to the head. Because different lobes or areas of the brain are responsible for specific functions, an open head injury generally affects only those functions controlled by the injured part of the brain. Figure 13–4 illustrates the six areas of the brain (including the brain stem) and their related functions.

Describing the Characteristics

Students with brain injury differ in onset, complexity, and recovery from students with other disabilities (Lash, 2000). But because their injuries may affect them in so many areas of their functioning, they can share characteristics with students who have learning disabilities (Chapter 4), emotional or behavioral disorders (Chapter 5), mental retardation (Chapter 8), health impairments (Chapter 11), physical disabilities (Chapter 12), or speech and language impairments (Chapter 14). Jarris, for instance, has a communication impairment.

To learn about the American Congress of Rehabilitation Medicine's definition for mild brain injury, go to the Web Links module in Chapter 13 of the Companion Website for a link to the congress's website.

Box 13–1

Seth's Story

Before the accident, most academic skills came easily to my 9-year-old son, Seth. But after his head injury, Seth's successful school performance changed dramatically. Following directions, being motivated to accomplish anything, and behaving appropriately in the classroom and with his peers were no longer second nature to him. His subsequent loss of self-esteem and his grief over what he could no longer do easily were extremely difficult for me to handle.

Seth's head injury was the result of his hitting a tree head on while sledding. Although Seth had been unconscious for five to six minutes, normal EEG readings and X rays did not prepare us to look for any residual brain damage. A few weeks after the accident, however, I ran into Seth's teacher at the grocery store. She asked me if I had noticed any changes in Seth's behavior at home. I told her that I thought Seth was beginning to show signs that he was entering puberty. It was several weeks later that Seth's teacher made a formal call to me to describe behavior changes at school that were totally unlike the Seth that either of us had known. But most important, the results of an Iowa Basic Skills Test shouted the alarm.

The achievement test had been given to all fourth graders in early March, six weeks after the accident. When compared with his second-grade results, Seth's achievement scores had dropped from the 99th percentile with a verbal IQ at the 87th percentile to barely the 50th percentiles in all achievement areas, with a verbal IQ percentile of 13.

On the basis of many different kinds of physical exams, a **neurologist** (a physician who specializes in the nervous system and its disorders) confirmed that Seth had indeed taken a blow to his head that had apparently caused some damage. The result is that Seth has difficulty using certain cognitive thinking abilities and often lacks motivation. His ability to read on a 12th-grade level was not affected. The neurologist told us that during the next 15 years Seth might reacquire many of his other previous abilities as well. Unfortunately, he will be finished with his formal schooling when that happens.

During Seth's fifth-grade year, he became very disruptive at school. His teacher reported that many mornings he would lie in front of the classroom door at school as classmates entered the room. And on other occasions he refused to participate in any classroom activities or discussions. He went from being one of the most popular students in the room to being jeered at by classmates. He often came home crying because old friends told him he was stupid. His grades fell from all *A*s to *C*s.

Seth's interpretation of the neurologist's exam was that his "brain was half dead." And for several months he was convinced that he could no longer do anything well. Actually, he did find things difficult. He no longer wrote using complex sentences; and to understand any mathematical concept, he had to have it presented with very concrete materials.

It has been several years now since the accident. Seth's wonderful ability to understand very subtle humor has returned. He practices much more appropriate behavior in school, and he is beginning to like himself again. He still doesn't do much unless he is told what, when, and how; but we love him just the same. And although I want people to be aware that Seth has a disability to overcome, I am quite protective in making sure that teachers and others relate their great expectations to Seth, affirming to him that he is whole and bright and has every reason to expect great things for himself.

Although students with brain injuries vary widely in their characteristics, they experience common physical, cognitive, linguistic, and behavioral changes (Lees-Haley, Fox, & Courtney, 2001). The number and magnitude of each student's changes will vary according to the site and extent of injury, the length of time the student was in a **coma** (an unconscious state), and the student's maturational stage at the time of the injury (Tyler & Mira, 1999). Figure 13–5 includes key points about the characteristics of brain injuries.

Physical Changes

The extent of students' physical changes can range from nonexistent (Seth), to moderate, to severe. Twenty percent of traumatic brain injuries cause students to experience seizures, but these often decrease or disappear with the passage of time (Hux, Marquardt, Skinner, & Bond, 1999). Sometimes the injury causes a temporary or permanent physical disability such as spasticity (uncontrolled contractions or spasms of the skeletal muscles) or paralysis (Swanson, 1999). The student may also experience growth-related problems, sleep disorders, or photosensitivity (ACTBIC, 2000).

More common than spasticity or paralysis are coordination problems, physical weakness, and fatigue. Students who were previously athletic find these changes to be especially frustrating. Fortunately, however, their coordination and physical strength usually improve as their brains

FIGURE 13–3
Symptoms of mild head injury

- Becomes restless or fussy
- Doesn't pay attention
- Forgets things
- Gets mixed up about time and places
- Takes longer to get things done
- Doesn't act the same
- Acts without thinking
- Becomes easily upset
- Loses his or her temper a lot
- Tires easily or needs extra sleep
- Doesn't see or hear as well
- Drops things or trips a lot
- Develops problems with words or sentences
- Has a harder time learning

Source: From *When Your Child Goes Home After Being Examined for Head Injury in an Emergency Department* by May Institute Center for Education and Neurorehabilitation, n.d., Randolph, MD: May Institute Center for Education and Neurorehabilitation. Copyright by May Institute Center for Education and Neurorehabilitation. Reprinted with permission.

FIGURE 13–4
Areas of the brain and related general functions

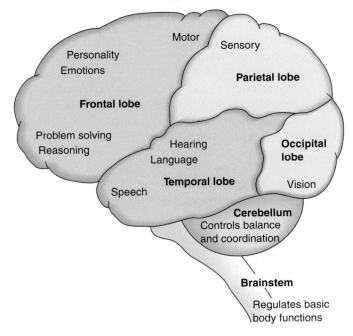

Source: From *Missouri Head Injury Guide for Survivors, Families, and Caregivers,* by Missouri Head Injury Foundation, 1991, Jefferson City, State of Missouri. Copyright 1991 by State of Missouri. Reprinted with permission.

FIGURE 13–5
Key points about brain injury characteristics

- Each student with [brain injury] has a unique pattern of abilities and deficits.
- Initial physical effects of injury often resolve quickly. Long-term cognitive, behavioral, and sensorimotor difficulties are often present.
- Memory, attention, and executive function difficulties are common.
- Slowed processing of information is common.
- Pre-injury skills may be preserved but are not predictive of new learning abilities.
- Psychological problems are complex and often the most debilitating.
- The relationships among cognitive, communication, social, behavioral, and physical difficulties have significant and complicating effects on the student's social success.

Source: From *Traumatic Brain Injury: A Guidebook for Educators,* by James DeLorenzo and Patricia Geary. State University of New York, 1995, Albany: New York State Department of Education, Office of Special Education Services. Copyright 1995 by New York State. Reprinted with permission.

You will learn more about Megan and her college experiences later in this chapter.

heal and they undergo rehabilitation, especially **occupational therapy** training to reacquire their fine-motor skills in order to function independently. Their fatigue often lingers, though; and if occupational therapy and other rehabilitation interventions are not brought to bear, their muscles may **atrophy,** resulting in lost or reduced muscle strength.

For example, before her accident, Megan Kohnke had been awarded a full scholarship to Pepperdine University because she was an exceptionally talented soccer player. After her accident, Megan had to be retaught everything, even how to walk and run, much less how to kick a soccer ball. Although she recovered to the point that she could practice with the Pepperdine University team and indeed started for Albertson College after transferring from Pepperdine between her sophomore and junior years, Megan will never be the player she was. She certainly will not "head" a soccer ball again.

Typically, students also experience headaches (Buyer, 1999). Almost one-third of students with TBI report headaches during the first year after the injury (Chapman, 1998). If your students have frequent headaches, you will need to make accommodations in their academic or other school schedules and assignments, give them opportunities to rest, and provide times and places for them to take their medications.

Some students with brain injury have vision or hearing impairments. Others may have perceptual impairments; often their vision and hearing are within normal limits with correction, but they have difficulty interpreting the information they receive through their senses. They also may experience adverse changes in their senses of taste, touch, and smell (Ponsford et al., 1999).

Cognitive Changes

The cognitive changes associated with TBI can be obvious or subtle but are almost always present. Your students may not be able to comprehend their lessons, solve problems, attend to their assignments, concentrate on their work, remember facts or events learned recently or longer ago, reason logically, process information easily and quickly, and otherwise display the same academic skills that they had before their accident (DePompei, 1999). They might also exhibit poor judgment and lack of foresight (Carney & Porter, 2001) and find it difficult to engage in planning and sequencing activities.

Linguistic Changes

Many students with brain injuries regain most of their speech and language facility, especially their expressive language (Blake & Fewster, 2001). But they may have long-term impairments with receptive and written language (Sohlberg, McLaughlin, Todis, Larsen, & Glang, 2001).

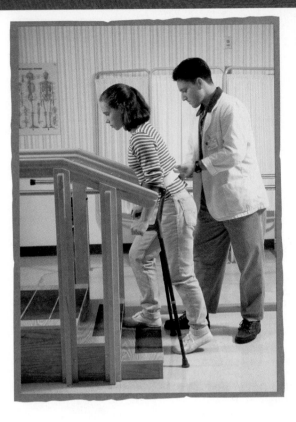

Individuals with traumatic brain injury may benefit from physical rehabilitation, which can help address fatigue, poor coordination, and other temporary or permanent physical injuries as a result of an accident.

They also may find it hard to learn new concepts (the ability to conceptualize) and new words (vocabulary building).

Sometimes students experience acquired childhood **aphasia** (an inability to use language appropriately) for a period of time after the injury (Feeney, Ylvisaker, Rosen, & Greene, 2001). More commonly, they may have difficulty finding the words they want to say or may speak slowly (Advisory Committee, 2000); and they may have problems understanding language (Appleton & Baldwin, 1998). Indeed, TBI can impair all aspects of a student's language (e.g., speaking and understanding, reading and writing) and persist even after the student appears to have recovered.

Because they have problems with understanding or using language, your students may revert to communicating in a more immature fashion, using phrases and gestures that would have been expected from a younger person (Swanson, 1999). For example, a few months after her accident, Megan and one of her friends were talking with each other when suddenly and unexpectedly Megan interrupted her friend and ordered her to get something. Her friend was startled by the outburst but followed Megan's direction. Megan didn't realize what she had done, but her behavior reflected a symptom of her injury. Similarly, any one of your students may find it difficult to socialize because she cannot perceive or interpret others' voice inflections or their nonverbal communication signals (Carney & Porter, 2001).

Typically, students with TBI also have difficulty understanding spoken language. Although the severity of their problem may vary, few of them escape without at least some degree of deficit in their higher-level comprehension. Their impairment can be compounded by their word-finding difficulties.

Later in the chapter, you will learn how mnemonics can help students such as Jarris and Megan develop memory techniques for their academic and social development.

Social, Behavioral, and Personality Changes

Students with TBI may begin to respond emotionally in ways that differ from or are more extreme than their preinjury responses. Their responses can include temper outbursts, euphoria, restlessness, irritability, anxiety, and fatigue. These behaviors may interfere with their self-esteem, school performance, friendships, community functioning, and family interactions (Ylvisaker et al., 2001).

Despite her difficulties with communication, Jarris has a full life and is able to enjoy her interactions with her siblings and other friends.

FIGURE 13–6
Causes of brain injury

```
              ┌──────────────────────┐
              │ Acquired brain injury │
              └──────────────────────┘
                 ↙               ↘
  ┌──────────────────────┐   ┌──────────────────────────┐
  │ Traumatic brain injury│   │ Nontraumatic brain injury │
  └──────────────────────┘   └──────────────────────────┘
            ↓                            ↓
```

Traumatic brain injury	Nontraumatic brain injury
Open: skull penetrated on direct impact	Anoxic injury Infections Stroke
Closed: skull or dural covering of brain not penetrated	Tumor Metabolic disorder Toxic substance ingested or inhaled

Source: From Pediatric Traumatic Brain Injury: Proactive Interventions, by J. L. Blosser and R. DePompei, 1994, San Diego, CA: Singular Press. Copyright 1994 by Singular Press. Reprinted with permission by Singular Publishing Group, Inc.

Between 15 and 25 percent of students with TBI struggle with depression (Tyler & Mira, 1999). Their depression may be associated with their low social status, which is caused by their poor social interaction, their inability to cope with teasing, or their social isolation, which arises from their inability to communicate appropriately with others. They may manifest depression through agitation and be at high risk for suicide.

Behaviorally, your students often experience an inability to initiate tasks; you sometimes may inappropriately perceive their inability as a lack of motivation or laziness. Students may also exhibit **disinhibition**—that is, poor self-monitoring skills (Ylvisaker et al., 2001).

Identifying the Causes

At we have already noted, the term *brain injury* under IDEA applies to acquired brain injuries. But the term also includes, although not under IDEA's definition, congenital or degenerative injuries or injuries that are induced by a birth trauma (Lea, 2001). Figure 13–6 illustrates the causes of brain injury.

There are three major causes of TBI (Buyer, 1999). Accidents are one major cause—typically motor vehicle, bicycle, or pedestrian-vehicle incidents (National Institute of Health, 1998)—and 28 percent of all accidents result in head injuries (LaForce & Martin-MacLeod, 2001). Indeed, motor vehicle accidents are the leading cause of TBI that requires the victim to be hospitalized (Centers for Disease Control, 2001). Both Jarris and Megan were involved in serious automobile accidents and were life-flighted to receive emergency assistance.

Falls are the second most frequent cause of TBI. The cause of children's falls vary but include falls from beds, chairs, tables, and even shopping carts (Centers for Disease Control, 2001).

Violence-related incidents are the third most frequent cause of TBI. These account for approximately 20 percent of all traumatic brain injuries and are the leading cause of TBI-related death (Centers for Disease Control, 2001). These incidents are almost equally divided into firearm and non-firearm assaults.

Within the category of violence-related incidents, child abuse accounts for the majority of infant head injuries (National Institutes of Health, 1998). Indeed, more than 80 percent of deaths from head trauma in children under age 2 are the result of nonaccidental trauma (Centers for Disease Control, 2000). Furthermore, more than three-fourths of children under age 3 who are physically abused suffer a TBI (Lees-Haley et al., 2001). A child who has **shaken-impact syndrome** is injured when the caretaker becomes angry or frustrated and shakes the child violently to try to make the child stop crying; the child dies in 10 to 25 percent of shaken-impact cases.

Sports and recreational injuries are the fourth major cause of TBI. Activities such as sledding (Seth's incident), diving, playing contact sports, or being hit by a ball cause 10 percent of traumatic brain injuries. Although these injuries account for only 3 percent of hospitalized persons with TBI, approximately 90 percent of all sports-related traumatic brain injuries are mild and may go unreported.

Identifying the Prevalence

TBI is a leading cause of death and disability among children and young adults (Centers for Disease Control, 2001). Each year, an estimated 1.5 million Americans suffer a TBI; 230,000 of them are hospitalized and survive, but 50,000 of them die and 80,000–90,000 have a long-term injury. Someone in the United States receives a head injury every 15 seconds; every five minutes, one person dies and another becomes permanently disabled (Centers for Disease Control, 2001). As a result of TBI, approximately 5.3 million Americans have a permanent TBI-related injury, one often not apparent to the casual observer. Indeed, TBI is called the *silent epidemic* because it is so widespread and unrecognized, unlike a broken leg (Centers for Disease Control, 2001).

Approximately 0.2 to 1 percent of the school-age population has sustained a recognized TBI (Tyler & Mira, 1999). As many as 3 percent of adolescents may have sustained a brain injury that is serious enough to cause them to have problems in school. A metropolitan school district will probably have about 75 students who sustain a TBI each year, while a small community may have three or four annually (U.S. Department of Education, 2002).

Males are more than twice as likely as females to experience TBI. The highest incidence of TBI is among persons 15 to 24 years of age and 75 years and older, with an additional peak in children ages 5 and younger. Alcohol is associated with half of all traumatic brain injuries, either in the person causing the injury or in the person with the injury.

In the 1999–2000 school year, 13,874 students received services under the IDEA category of TBI (U.S. Department of Education, 2002). This number represents a 6.9 percent increase, up from 12,976 students, from the previous year. Increases will probably continue as states develop and reevaluate their criteria for classifying these students. Identifying the prevalence of students with nontraumatic brain injuries is even more challenging because most are served under the categories of "severe and multiple disabilities" (Chapter 9) or "other health impairments" (Chapter 11).

To learn about the Life Flight Program that saved Megan's life, go to the Web Links module in Chapter 13 of the Companion Website for a link to the program's website.

To learn about what can be done to prevent childhood injuries caused by sports and recreation, go to the Web Links module in Chapter 13 of the Companion Website.

To gain full access to the reports and related data collected by the Centers for Disease Control, go to the Web Links module in Chapter 13 of the Companion Website.

How Do You Evaluate Students with Traumatic Brain Injury?

The evaluation of students with TBI needs to be comprehensive (across the student's physical, cognitive, emotional-behavioral, and developmental faculties) and ongoing because children change, just as Jarris, Seth, and Megan themselves changed after their injuries. Figure 13–7 illustrates the necessary steps that an evaluation team must take.

Determining the Presence

The comprehensive educational evaluation of students with TBI usually occurs simultaneously with extensive evaluations by medical and rehabilitation personnel, including physical and occupational therapists (Ylvisaker et al., 2002). Physicians often run a variety of tests to determine the location and severity of the student's injury. Computerized tomography (CT) or computerized axial tomography (CAT) scans offer doctors a picture of the student's brain and are useful in identifying large areas of bleeding or large contusions. Magnetic resonance imaging (MRI) can identify smaller and subtler brain anomalies or differences that a CT scan cannot provide. Another test for determining the location and severity of an injury to the brain is the positron emission tomography (PET) scan, which measures some of the energy-processing functions of the brain. It observes certain chemicals used by the brain, such as glucose. The PET scan tags these chemicals and examines the brain's ability to use them.

A comprehensive evaluation consists of both formal and informal measures, such as clinician and family observations. For example, within six weeks of her accident, Megan received an extensive neuropsychological evaluation as part of her rehabilitation program. The general areas of her evaluation included intellectual abilities, academics, memory, learning, visual-spatial skills, language, motor skills, executive functioning (planning and problem solving), personality, and psychological abilities.

Rehabilitation staff members conducted a series of informal assessments of Megan within the first several weeks of her accident. A **neuropsychologist** regularly asked her questions about society, such as the name of the president of the United States. At first, Megan couldn't recall his name but later did say, "It was the one who had lied."

Megan was also asked a series of questions to test her memory and ability to repeat and process information. For example, staff members gave her a sequence of numbers and asked her to repeat them. Like a sponge, Megan repeated an extensive sequence of numbers when asked. But she could not repeat numbers or information out of sequence.

A standardized IQ test was part of the neuropsychological battery to determine Megan's intellectual disabilities. Students such as Megan, who had a preinjury history of academic success, benefit from the IQ test because it yields a comparison of present and preinjury intelligence. Within five weeks of the accident, a neuropsychologist administered the Wechsler Intelligence Scale for Children—Revised (WISC-R) (Psychological Corporation, 1998) to Megan. Individuals such as Jarris, whose injury occurred early in life, benefit from the IQ test because it can identify what information the child is not acquiring at her present age level. Remember that brain injury causes a disruption in learning patterns and the inability to process new information.

Megan also received a neuropsychological assessment of her cognitive processing skills. The tests measured Megan's ability to attend, memorize, learn, perceive through her senses, use motor skills and language, problem-solve, and apply abstract reasoning. An example of a neuropsychological test is the Test of Problem Solving (TOPS) (LinguiSystems, 2000). The test determines how students such as Megan can explain inferences, determine causes of events, answer negative "why" questions, determine solutions, and avoid problems. Neuropsychological testing is also used for planning cognitive retraining for students with brain injuries. **Cognitive retraining** involves instruction to recapture the skills that the students lost as a result of their injury (i.e., processing information, communication, and socialization).

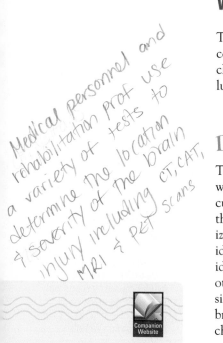

To review a full range of assessment components for a comprehensive evaluation, visit the Web Links module in Chapter 13 of the Companion Website.

When we discuss instructional augmentation later in the chapter, we will describe and share examples of mnemonics strategies and how they can help students with memory problems.

FIGURE 13–7

Nondiscriminatory assessment process for determining the presence of traumatic brain injury

Nondiscriminatory Evaluation

Observation

Parents observe	The student receives a head injury from an accident, fall, sports injury, or act of violence.
Physician observes	The student has an open or closed head injury caused by an external physical force. The student may be in a coma.
Teacher observes	In the case of a mild head injury that might not have been treated by a physician, the teacher observes changes in behavior, personality, social functioning, cognitive skills, language, or motor skills.

Medical screening

Assessment measures	Findings that indicate need for further evaluation
Coma scale	In instances of moderate to severe head injuries that induce comas, these scales provide some information about probable outcome.
Neurological exam	A neurologist examines the student for indications of brain injury.
Scanning instruments	EEGs, CAT scans, MRIs and other technology determine the extent of injury.

Prereferral

Prereferral typically is not used with these students because the severity of the disability indicates a need for special education or related services.

Referral

Students with moderate to severe traumatic brain injuries should be referred while still in rehabilitation. Teachers should refer students with mild head injuries if they notice any changes in behavior, motor, cognitive, or language skills.

Nondiscriminatory evaluation procedures and standards

Assessment measures	The findings that suggest traumatic brain injury
Individualized intelligence test	The student often shows extreme peaks and valleys on subtests and retains some skills but not others. Scores often look very different from scores received on tests taken before the injury.
Individualized achievement tests	The student usually has peaks and valleys in scores. The student often has holding skills in some areas while other skills are affected adversely by the injury.
Adaptive behavior scales	The student may have difficulty in social, self-care, household, and community skills as a result of the injury.
Cognitive processing tests	The student may have difficulty in areas of attention, memory, concentration, motivation, and perceptual integration.
Behavior, social skills, and personality measures	The student may demonstrate difficulty relating to others and behaving in socially appropriate ways. The student's personality may have changed from before the injury.
Anecdotal records	The student's cognitive, language, motor, and behavior skills appear to have changed from what was indicated in records before the accident.
Curriculum-based assessment	The student may have difficulty in areas of curriculum that were not problematic before the injury.
Direct observation	The student appears frustrated, has a limited attention span, fatigues easily, or lacks motivation to perform academic tasks. The student may have difficulty relating appropriately to others. Skills often improve rapidly, especially during the early postinjury stage.

Nondiscriminatory evaluation team determines that special education and related services are needed.

Appropriate Education

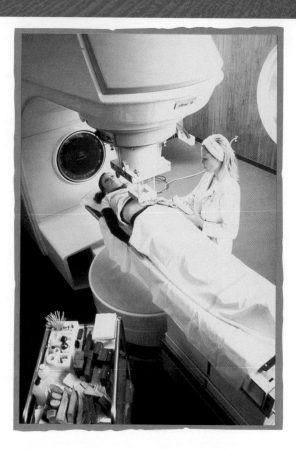

CAT scans, PET scans and MRIs can help doctors diagnose and treat patients.

Because a student usually makes neurological gains, ongoing assessment is the norm. Before her injury, Megan had scored above 130. Five weeks after her accident, she scored a 68 on this test; however, five months later, Megan improved her score to 108.

Determining the Nature and Extent of General and Special Education and Related Services

In Chapter 10 on autism, you learned about positive behavior supports, which can benefit students with TBI as well as those with autism or emotional or behavioral disorders (Chapter 5).

The primary goal for your students with TBI always should be to ensure their academic and social success (Sohlberg et al., 2001). This task, however, is not always easy. Because of the nature of students' injuries and their ongoing rehabilitation process, their IEPs need to be flexible and allow for continual adaptations as they progress and recover. Sometimes a student's IEP incorporates or is supplemented by a **personal intervention plan.** That plan focuses mainly on the causes of a student's behavior and what to do to improve it.

As is true for any IEP team, educators and parents need to make several critical decisions. For students with brain injuries, the team must ask and answer these questions (Ylvisaker, 1997):

1. What can the student do now?
2. What does the student need to do next?
3. Who will be responsible for the student's educational program?
4. How will the team determine if the educational program is working for the student?

To answer these questions, the team will do the following (Tyler & Mira, 1999):

▼ Obtain as much knowledge as possible about TBI, especially long-term outcomes
▼ Know the student's specific deficits
▼ Not equate the student's physical recovery with overall recovery

▼ Be clear about your behavioral and instructional expectations and do not assume that the student knows what you expect of him

▼ Not give your student major responsibility for making significant decisions about his education if he demonstrates deficits in judgment and reasoning because those deficits preclude him from fully understanding his own needs

How Do You Assure Progress in the General Curriculum?

Including Students

Educators can meet the needs of most students with TBI in the general education classroom if their students' IEPs identify appropriate curriculum outcomes (what the student will know and be able to do), instructional procedures and modifications (how teachers will instruct their students), assessment procedures (how teachers will know what their students learn), modifications to the classroom environment (such as seating), and support for educators (e.g., related services, supplementary aids and services, or paraprofessionals).

Box 13–2 provides tips for increasing success for students with traumatic brain injury in the general education classroom.

Planning Universally Designed Learning

Two characteristics of students with TBI frequently create barriers to their reentering and progressing in the general curriculum. These are their limitations in memory and their decreased ability to acquire and use new information.

Altering Curriculum and Instruction

Because students with TBI have difficulty with their memories, you should provide your students with strategies for storing and then remembering facts. A good strategy is called *mnemonics*. Mnemonics use poems, rhymes, jingles, or images that help students put facts into their memory banks and then help them retrieve those facts when they need them. For example, HOMES helps us remember the Great Lakes: Huron, Ontario, Michigan, Erie, and Superior. This mnemonic is an example of a first-letter acronym. It uses the first letter of each lake, in a common word, to prompt our memories.

"Fall backward, spring forward" helps us remember facts about daylight savings time changes. This mnemonic is an example of a movement that helps us remember to move the dials on our watches and clocks. We also use jingles: "M-I-double S-I-double S-I-double P-I" has a rhythm that helps us remember how to spell "Mississippi." A good teacher usually will use one of the following mnemonic techniques: the keyword method, the pegword method, or the letter-strategy method.

The keyword method works best when your students are not familiar with the information you are presenting to them. In the keyword method, your student forms mental pictures that relate new information in an unusual manner to known information. The keyword is often an acoustic reconstruction. That is, the student uses a "sound-alike" word to form the mental image. For example, to remember that an herbivore is an animal that eats plants, your student might picture animals in herds (the keyword), eating only plants (Mastropieri, Emerick, & Scruggs, 1988).

The pegword method uses rhyming proxies for numbers (one is bun, two is shoe, three is tree, etc.) to help your students remember numbered or ordered information. Pegwords are helpful when your student must remember ordered information or numbers associated with unfamiliar terms. To use this strategy, your student first learns a rhyming poem in which familiar concrete

Inclusion Tips

Box 13-2

	What You Might See	What You Might Be Tempted to Do	Alternate Responses	Ways to Include Peers in the Process
Behavior	The student may show behavior and personality changes, such as temper outbursts, anxiety, fatigue, or depression.	Respond with strong disapproval and discipline her new behavior.	Reward her positive behaviors. Provide predictable routines that encourage normal behavior patterns while teaching her new ways to respond within the school environment.	Give her time to work in natural settings with peers who will encourage appropriate behavior yet show acceptance during the relearning stage.
Social interactions	She may have forgotten social skills and experience social misunderstandings because of her new identity struggles.	Ignore her social difficulties and hope they go away.	Work with both the speech-pathologist and the school counselor to plan the best ways to use language and social skills in successful situations.	Allow friends with whom she feels secure to role-play social activities. Structure many opportunities for successful interactions. Use videotapes for self-evaluation.
Educational performance	Learning new information may be difficult for her, or it may take her much longer to process information	Require extra work in areas of difficulty rather than focus on holding skills and what she can accomplish.	Capitalize on what is familiar to retrieve and develop memory, organization, and cognitive processes. Prioritize the academic skills she needs to learn.	Have her brainstorm and work with her peers/friends to practice skills as well as to plan future projects and educational aspirations.
Classroom attitudes	She may appear easily distracted, have headaches, or show a lack of motivation during instruction.	Reprimand her apparent lack of participation. Discipline her or excuse her from class activities.	Allow her to take rest periods. Modify the amount and intensity of her assignments.	Pair her with a partner and friend who can help her focus and participate meaningfully during instruction.

objects are associated with something new. For example, to produce a visual image, substitute pegwords for the number that the student must remember. Then associate that number with a familiar object (e.g., one-bun; two-shoe; three-tree; and so on). Then, to produce the visual image, your student pictures the information in association with the familiar object. For instance, to remember that insects have six legs but spiders have eight, your students can create a picture of insects on *sticks* and another picture of a spider on a *gate*.

Letter strategies are a third type of mnemonics and include acronyms and acrostics. Acronyms are words whose individual letters can represent elements in lists of information; for example, HOMES represents the Great Lakes. Acrostics are sentences whose first letters represent new information that a student needs to remember, such as "My very educated mother just served us nine pizzas," to remember the nine planets in order (Mercury, Venus, Earth, Mars, etc.). However, most acronyms assume that your student will remember the name of something after retrieving the first letter of that object.

That is not often the case for students such as Jarris. If a student is unfamiliar with Lake Ontario, for example, remembering simply that the first letter is O is insufficient to prompt the student to recall the name Ontario. The student must practice the names of the individual lakes until they have become familiar.

If your students need to enhance an acronym or an acrostic, encourage them to create an image. Take, for example, the acronym FARM-B, which represents the five classes of vertebrate animals: fish, amphibian, reptile, mammal, and bird. To assist your students with these terms, ask them to visualize a farm with the examples of the five classes of vertebrate animals residing on the farm (Mastropieri & Scruggs, 2001).

Dozens of individual research studies demonstrate the effectiveness of mnemonic instruction for thousands of students; these studies include not only students with educational disabilities and other special needs but also typically achieving and gifted students. In these studies, students who have learned mnemonically have greatly outperformed students in a variety of comparison conditions (Scruggs & Mastropieri, 2000a, 2000b). In particular, mnemonic instruction appears superior to visual-spatial displays and/or direct instruction alone for enhancing students' memory.

Augmenting Curriculum and Instruction

Students with TBI may perform at or near their previous achievement levels on tests of old knowledge (e.g., seventh-grade–level achievement on a social studies test by a tenth-grade student who was injured at the end of seventh grade); however, there may be unpredictable knowledge gaps. Your students may be confused, frustrated or even unaware of these gaps because they expect their own abilities to remain unchanged after an injury. Your students' background knowledge is very important for their comprehension; indeed, the lack of adequate access to background knowledge may account for their comprehension failures and insufficient processing (Ylvisaker, 1998). So your students will benefit considerably from an extensive review of what they have been already exposed to before trying to learn new information.

Similarly, your students can benefit from modifications and accommodations. Modifications include establishing a balance between the student and the content, the materials, the environment, teacher expectations, and instructional and assessment procedures. If your students' capacities are not at the level necessary to meet your curricular or instructional demands (i.e., timed assignments to be completed independently with no cues or related support), they may fail. The challenge, then, is for you to modify your students' learning and testing situations so that they can be successful.

Accommodations in instruction affect how all students acquire new knowledge and put that knowledge into practice. Implementing small changes in your teaching methods or using alternative materials can greatly increase your students' learning. For example, you can provide notes, graphic organizers, and outlines for students to use while they present a lesson; highlight concepts; prepare the student for the idea; and repeat key parts of the material. Examples of material accommodations to improve access to effective instruction include the following:

1. *Alternate format to obtain information:* large print, simplified text
2. *Assistance with notetaking:* copy of notes, lecture outline, note taker
3. *Concrete objects, pictures, graphic, diagrams*
4. *Advance organizers or study guides*
5. *Adapted materials:* uncluttered format, fewer items, highlighted copy

You can also alter how your students practice and demonstrate what they are learning in assignments such as projects, worksheets, and homework or on in-class tests. These changes affect only how your students develop their skills and show they have learned, not what they must learn.

Accommodations for assignments and classroom assessments generally are the same. For instance, if one of your students needs a word processor for written work in class, he will probably need one for a written test. Accommodations of this type can also allow your student additional

You will read more about basic modifications and accommodations and their effects on Jarris and her schoolmates when we describe Centennial Elementary School later in this chapter.

Technology Tips

Box 13–3

Personal Data Assistants

The proliferation of Personal Data Assistants (PDAs) in today's society is astounding. While some people may prefer the traditional appointment book, many individuals with disabilities are enhancing their academic and work proficiency through the use of PDAs. Individuals with TBI who have challenges in organizing information or recalling specific appointments or important dates find the PDA to be essential for them to successfully participate in school or the workplace. The PDA can store information, offer automatic reminders, and present opportunities to share information that goes beyond the capabilities of the individual.

What Is the Technology?

PDAs (e.g., Palm Pilots) offer users the capacity to store, organize, and access information. Initially seen as an electronic calendar, today's versions allow the user to access the Internet, use most computing software, download entire novels, and access more than 100 wireless functions.

What Do We Do with It?

For the individual with TBI, the answer to this question seems to be endless. Today, a student might use a PDA to take class notes, beam assignments from his or her PDA to a teacher's PDA or vice versa, organize scheduled activities, or use it as a mobility tool to map out where she is now and where she is going. For individuals with more significant needs, software such as the Schedule Assistant (developed by AbleLink, Inc.) offers options that provide timed prompts during morning routines and keep track of bus schedules, appointments, work schedules, and so on. It also allows caregivers to record audio messages or reminders that will automatically activate at the prescribed time and day for the user to hear and then follow.

Putting PDAs to Work for Progress in the General Curriculum:

1. How else could a PDA be used in or out of the classroom for a student with TBI?

2. Is the PDA an effective device to assist students with TBI in organizing and reminding them of where they need to be, what they need to be doing, and similar life skill applications? Why or why not?

3. Are PDAs an accessible and cost-effective tool to consider for most students and their families? Is the technology used enough by the general population to ensure economical cost, regular updates, and easy access to maintenance if the product were to break?

To answer these questions online and learn more about these strategies, go to the Technology Tips module in Chapter 13 of the Companion Website.

To review effective modifications and accommodations, go to the Web Links module in Chapter 13 of the Companion Website for a link to the National Center of Educational Outcomes.

time to practice his new skills and apply recently acquired knowledge in real-world contexts. The accommodations change only how the student develops his abilities and shows what he has learned. Your expectations and standards for his performance remain the same. Box 13–3 sets out some tips for using technology to accommodate students.

You can also help your student address his time and schedule demands by modifying specific assignments or assessments. For example, you can reduce the required number of practice items you ask a student to complete, extend deadlines for assignments, or allow a temporary grade of "incomplete" for a complicated project.

Collaborating to Meet Students' Needs

Collaboration among professionals presents a variety of challenges. For instance, in addition to special and general education teachers and related school personnel, collaboration teams almost always include physicians, other health care providers, and rehabilitation professionals. Physicians and rehabilitation professionals can provide insight into a student's brain functioning and prognosis and can greatly assist educators in designing and carrying out a program of special education. Many rehabilitation centers realize the particular importance of the student's reentry to

Collaboration Tips

Box 13–4

Starting with and Keeping a Team

Because students with TBI must have a traumatic, external injury to their brains to quality under the IDEA category for TBI, they almost always have been patients before they become special education students. It really does not seem to matter what caused their injury; the cycle of typical student/patient/special education student is the norm.

Jarris and Megan were in automobile accidents, and Seth was in a sledding accident. Each was immediately taken to a hospital for his or her first treatment. Only after being a patient in a hospital were any of them released to rehabilitation. Even then, they continued in the role of patient. They became students again only after they returned to their schools, but they were not the same students they were before their accidents, and their programs were not the same either. They had moved from general to special education and then back again, but with support.

Collaboration among the various professionals and between them and the student's family can make all this movement back and forth—from one kind of person to another, from one kind of program to another—less traumatic for student and family. But collaboration is not always easy to achieve.

For one thing, physicians and other health care providers have a focus different from that of the other professionals. In some instances, they are intent on saving the student's life; that certainly was the case when Megan was life-flighted to a hospital and underwent several hours of brain surgery. If they are successful, they then focus on rehabilitation, itself a specialized field of medicine that involves not only physicians but also other professionals.

There are pulmonary therapists (to develop the student's lung and heart capacity), physical therapists (to develop the student's muscle strength and stamina), occupational therapists (to develop the student's ability to do the chores of daily living, such as brushing her teeth and tying her shoes), psychologists or cognitive retrainers (to help the student learn how to think again), and speech-language therapists (to help the student regain

the ability to communicate). Whether these professionals work in a hospital or rehabilitation center, they are trying to restore the student's ability to learn.

The educator, on the other hand, is trying to teach the student what he once knew and to move him to the next lesson, always increasing his cognitive abilities. The educator is also trying to help the student cope with behavioral and social challenges that invariably arise in school.

Finally, the student's family are experiencing their own grief; essentially, they have lost one child and now have a different one. Their goals may include all of the rehabilitation and educational goals of the professionals, but they also have to learn to integrate their child into their lives and family.

Collaboration, then, requires everyone to acknowledge that each has different specific goals, techniques, and talents. Of course, it helps for everyone on the team to identify the short-term goals and techniques needed to achieve those goals. More than that, however, it helps for everyone on the team to focus on the ultimate goal: to assure that the student recovers as much preinjury capacity as possible and learns to accommodate as effectively as possible to the challenges of postinjury limitations.

So collaboration consists of keeping the same long-term goal in mind, identifying the short-term goals and how they will help achieve the long-term goals, showing how one professional's techniques complement another's, and acknowledging that the different professionals bring different but equally valuable strategies to the collaborative effort, albeit at different times.

Putting Collaboration to Work for Progress in the General Curriculum

1. Who are the collaborators?

2. What are their challenges?

To answer these questions online, go to the Collaboration Tips module in Chapter 13 of the Companion Website.

school and employ a hospital-school liaison (sometimes referred to as a school reentry specialist) to improve collaboration. In Box 13–4, you will read about a model of collaboration that can help students with TBI and those with other disabilities as well.

Jarris's school has developed a core team to foster communication and collaboration among the various professionals involved in her growth and development. The participants are Jarris's regular and special education teacher, her parents, a speech pathologist, a physical therapist, an occupational therapist, and the school district's director of curriculum. Her core team meets monthly to discuss her ongoing development and to consider how to best address her learning needs.

Team members share their diverse perspectives when problem solving for Jarris's benefit. Rather than supporting her needs in isolation, the team has been able to propose solutions that members can implement and evaluate as a team and with the cooperation of her parents. For example, realizing that sign language is an effective augmentative communication for Jarris, Linda (her third-grade general education teacher) sought assistance in learning how to sign by inviting the district's deaf education teacher into the classroom to teach her and her students basic sign language.

What Can You Learn from Others Who Teach Students with Traumatic Brain Injury?

Learning for the Early Childhood Years: The Children's Place, Kansas City, Missouri

The preschool years are the age of rapid development; children quickly grow both physically and mentally. Although a child's injured brain may recover more rapidly during this period than at a later age, the child's brain injury may significantly hamper her ability to develop compensatory strategies. Jarris, for example, continues to have significant language development delays as a result of her accident and the subsequent seizures that occurred when she was 7 months old.

Traditional preschool programs generally do not serve the immediate and intense physical and mental needs of young children with TBI. That is why programs such as the Children's Place in Kansas City, Missouri, exist. The Children's Place is a nonprofit program dedicated to serving the developmental and behavioral needs of preschool children with challenges caused by their environment. As you have already learned, one of the leading causes of TBI, especially for children under the age of 3, is abuse. The Children's Place serves the needs of children who have been abused, including abuse that has resulted in TBI. For such children, the program often serves as a transition program from the rehabilitation center to a traditional Head Start or day-care facility. Children often spend several months or even years at the Children's Place.

At the Children's Place, a team of professionals ensures a holistic picture of the child. Team members include a social worker, an occupational and physical therapist, a speech pathologist, a psychologist, a psychiatrist, a dietician, the lead teacher, a teacher's aide, and the child's family members.

Team members work closely with the child's parents or other primary caregiver, always bearing in mind that there may be multicultural issues to address (see Box 13–5). Parents attend in-house training programs. There, staff members teach parents how to address their child's needs, offering role play as a method to illustrate how an intervention can be used in the home. In this practical, hands-on training program, parents model what they learn.

After the initial in-house training, a social worker visits the home to continue the child's program. This outreach training provides additional support in the home environment, where the parent and child need it most. In this setting, the family can more naturally interact with a supportive team member who will offer guidance and modeling. Staff member Margaret Comford explains, "Parent training is an integral feature of our program's success. Through the support of the team, parents are taught what they need to know to care for their child and develop the necessary skills to continue what we have started."

When a child arrives at the Children's Place, she is tested extensively to determine her current abilities and needs. The evaluation becomes the basis for an IEP that establishes immediate goals and objectives for the child. Every three months, the team reviews these goals and objectives to determine the child's ongoing needs.

Box 13–5

TBI and the Subculture of Violence

The statistics about TBI and violence are alarming (Centers for Disease Control, 2001). Firearms are the leading cause of death from TBI. Teenagers, especially males, are more likely to die from TBI than are any other people. Brain injury that kills boys and young men often results from shootings or motor vehicle crashes. African American citizens are at a much greater risk of dying from TBI that is related to firearms than are people of any other race. Teenagers and people over 75 are more likely than any other people to sustain TBI because of a motor vehicle crash or violence. Shootings cause less than 10 percent of all TBI yet are the leading cause of death-related TBI. And people who are involved in assaults in which firearms are not involved have a much greater chance of surviving TBI than do those who are involved in assaults in which firearms are involved.

These data tell us that multiculturalism and diversity are not matters of ethnicity, language, and place of origin alone. Instead, they tell us that there is a culture of violence in America. Fortunately, the culture is a "sub" one, relatively small but nonetheless exceedingly potent: The power of a weapon or a motor vehicle to destroy a life or damage a brain cannot be denied.

What can teachers do about one part of this subculture—the part that engenders a subculture of violence? Here, the challenge to a teacher is not how to assure that a student with TBI makes progress in the general curriculum. Instead, the challenge is to help prevent that student's placement into special education as a result of TBI; prevention means never having to face the challenge of reentering the general curriculum in the first place.

Talk about the danger of firearms. Ask students who have TBI as a result of deadly-weapon assaults to explain how the TBI affects them: What were their lives like before and after their injuries? Develop conflict-resolution programs that involve peers, adults, members of law enforcement agencies, staff from local emergency centers and rehabilitation facilities, and family members. Show films about TBI and its effects. Display the data about firearms, violence, and violent environments on classroom walls and bulletin boards. Do not single out any one race of students for special attention; violence is everywhere. Tell students about the zero tolerance policy of your school (see Chapter 1 and the special provisions about IDEA and discipline) and why zero tolerance of weapons makes good sense.

Taking the Diversity of a Subculture into Account for Participation in the General Curriculum

1. How can students who have experienced TBI as a result of violence at home, school, or elsewhere be effective teachers of their peers concerning the effects of violence and its relationship to TBI?

2. What roles might staff from hospital emergency rooms, rehabilitation centers, and law enforcement agencies play in instructing students about TBI and its effects?

3. What particular roles might special and general educators, respectively, play to support a student whose TBI is the result of violence when the student reenters the general curriculum?

To answer these questions online, go to the Multicultural Considerations module in Chapter 13 of the Companion Website.

Similarly, before the child begins or returns to a preschool program, the team tests her again and revisits her IEP to assist the staff at the program to which she is headed to develop an appropriate education program. Margaret Comford makes it clear that "we work with staff members at several local Head Start and preschool facilities to ensure what we've started can be continued at the next level. Many times, we'll go on site to train preschool staff on the program we designed for the child's needs. There, we'll demonstrate, if necessary, what we've done with the child and what we've found works." In Box 13–6, you will read about what one reentry specialist, Beth Urbanczyk, does.

A primary goal for students with TBI is to integrate them into a program with other students. Margaret Comford adds, "For many students with brain injuries at the preschool age, they need

Box 13—6

Making a Difference

Beth Urbanczyk

As a school entry and reentry specialist, I have the unique opportunity of working in the world of rehabilitation, early intervention, and education simultaneously. Infants, toddlers, and preschoolers present a unique challenge to rehabilitation and educational professionals. At issue is not only what the results of the injury will be for these children but when they will manifest themselves. The child's developing brain is injured; and as the brain continues to mature and develop, the eventual outcome is uncertain. The professionals involved therefore need to understand the functioning of the developing brain as well as the effects of a traumatic brain injury on a child.

These children have many transitions ahead of them. They need school reentry specialists to share information with the current program; this includes the injury and recovery process, functioning in previous settings, and plans for the future. If the initial entry into educational services is not carefully and thoughtfully planned, the future may be significantly compromised for these children.

What else do school entry and reentry specialists need to know? It is especially important to understand the systems that provide child services and the laws that guarantee children's rights to those services. Furthermore, I work with a variety of professionals across New York. Good communication skills (spoken and written) are essential in my occupation as I talk to these people and produce written documents that summarize our findings and plans.

These communication skills are also important when I work with families. Often, families are unfamiliar with early intervention and special education. I teach them how to advocate effectively for their children within those systems.

There is nothing more exciting than seeing a child you have worked with enter an early intervention program or preschool and succeed. I feel that the work I have done has made a difference in the lives of a number of children.

a chance to communicate with others. They need an opportunity to play in a supportive environment. We offer a supportive program where they can socialize and continue what began during their rehabilitation program."

Learning for the Elementary Years: Centennial Elementary School, Lawrence, Kansas

During the elementary years, connections in the brain, both between and within its hemispheres, become more efficient (Savage, 1997). Children build their basic academic, prosocial, and self-confidence skills during this period. Obviously, a brain injury can severely disrupt their skill development.

Jarris's injuries further complicated her educational needs as she entered the Lawrence, Kansas, public school system at Centennial Elementary School. The district's staff were unprepared to meet her diverse needs; however, through the hard work of her first-grade teacher, Linda Stidham, and the continued work of her core team, Jarris has begun to develop skills comparable to those of her grade-level peers.

Realizing that Jarris had significant learning needs in first grade, Linda sought to quickly develop a program that would accelerate Jarris's learning while meeting her immediate needs. In developing that program, Linda worked with special education and related support staff to create a program that served Jarris in her general education first-grade classroom for a majority of the day. A veteran teacher with more than 20 years of experience, Linda did not want to see Jarris continually pulled out of her classroom. Jarris already left for speech and physical therapy, and Linda wanted to prevent any further disruptions for Jarris. She explains:

I am not an advocate of pullout services or significant teaching in the resource room. I feel from extensive experience that the more you separate or point out a child's disability, the more they act differently. Yes, it is harder for teachers like myself to include students with disabilities because we are being asked to make sure students are achieving, especially on the state assessment. Unfortunately, many teachers see students with disabilities getting in the way of student learning and class achievement. I don't see students with disabilities as a distraction, but instead I see them as a child who needs an education and all the help I can provide.

From the first day of school, Linda made basic accommodations to create a structured learning environment for Jarris and her peers. For Jarris, this meant a daily review of the schedule and strict conformity to daily and weekly routines. If an early release or schoolwide function (such as a holiday concert or a guest speaker) altered this schedule, Linda and her peers prepared Jarris days in advance for this modified schedule. Linda explains:

> I quickly found that Jarris needed structure. So I organized the class to make certain everyone knew our daily schedule. This helped everyone but seems to have especially helped Jarris. If we change anything, I always let her know in advance and remind her regularly so that changes won't be a surprise.

This past year, Jarris completed her fourth-grade year in the general education setting. Still pulled out for speech and other related services, Jarris spends the majority of her school day in an environment that accommodates her specific needs along the highly structured lines that Linda began three years ago. Her father says, "Jarris is so outgoing. I don't know of anyone at that school, regardless of grade, that doesn't know her and doesn't like her. She walks down the hall waving at people and saying hi."

To further interact and communicate with Jarris, many of her peers have learned basic American Sign Language (ASL; see Chapter 14). A special education teacher also conducts workshops for school personnel and for those of Jarris's classmates who express an interest in TBI and in Jarris in particular.

Jarris's teacher, Susan, asks Jarris's peers to help meet her needs. For example, if Jarris has difficulty with an assignment, Susan organizes classwide peer tutoring groups. Susan always matches Jarris with a peer who has basic ASL skills. This way the entire class is engaged in a similar activity, and Jarris is supported in a specific matter to ensure interaction and learning. Shawna, Jarris's mother, says,

> Everything we do as a team focuses on accommodations and modifications for Jarris. We start with the simple and look for the more complex solutions when they are needed. For example, this summer she appeared in her summer camp play. Her limited communication skills prevented her from having a speaking part. This didn't stop her from having a funny role though. She had a hilarious scene as an old woman entering a hotel with her bags. The bellmen try to assist her and they can't lift her bags. Jarris, cane and all, smiles and easily lifts the bags and walks offstage. The crowd loved it, and she didn't need to remember a single line.

Promoting readjustments and preparing Jarris for new learning are now habits that her parents and teachers live by. Integrating accommodations that meet her needs while also coinciding with her general education peers will determine Jarris's ongoing success.

Learning for the Middle and Secondary Years: Shawnee Mission West, Shawnee Mission, Kansas

The long-term effects of frontal lobe injuries in children and adolescents require interventions to address students' present and anticipated future needs. Often at the middle and high school levels, they need to develop or refine their self-management, learning, thinking, and problem-solving abilities to succeed in the general curriculum.

For example, Paul, who was hit by an automobile when he was 9 years old, benefits from strategies, especially mnemonics, that recapture his preinjury learning and development. When Paul returned to his school with significant cognitive, language, physical, and behavioral issues, his teachers were not certain how to educate him. By the time he was 16, Paul was extremely difficult to manage. If he did not want to do something, he was quick to threaten to harm his teachers, paraeducators, or fellow students.

You may recall that, when we discussed positive behavioral supports in Chapter 10, we said that a functional behavioral assessment begins with an inquiry into why a student behaves in a certain way.

As he began his junior year, Paul was assigned a new resource teacher, Katie Williamson. Katie was new to the school and not familiar with Paul or his previous academic program. She quickly learned about his behavioral problems and how staff and students had dealt with Paul through avoidance. Katie also sought to understand the reasons for Paul's outburst. Katie began by trying to find out what Paul's "payoff" was. She explains, "The first question I always ask about a student's behavior is, What is the payoff? Why are they acting the way they are? For students with TBI, it usually comes down to what are they avoiding or what is frustrating them. If you don't address why they are doing it, then you can't stop the behavior when they do it."

To identify the reasons for Paul's behavior, Katie reviewed his daily schedule and activities. As a junior, he was included in many of the same academic classes as were his peers without disabilities. Although his cognitive functioning was significantly impaired, he spent a majority of the day in classes discussing academic subjects that were far above his ability and, more important, beyond his immediate needs. To get to these classes, Paul was required to walk from one end of the building to the other several times a day, a task that presented constant challenges to him because he could not remember how to go from one place in school to another.

After carefully observing Paul, Katie developed a plan to prevent his aggressive behavior and simultaneously enhance his functional abilities. Because Paul was not planning to attend college, Katie sought to develop skills that would help him live as an independent adult. Acknowledging Paul's memory limitations, Katie sought to address them through rhymes and mnemonics.

To address Paul's learning deficiency and to develop better social interaction with his age-appropriate peers, Katie created a number of social opportunities for him to interact with them in controlled situations. Katie explained, "Paul needed to interact with other students, so I would create positive opportunities. For example, I'd get some gum and give it to Paul, and we would walk the halls offering it to people. At first, his peers were surprised. They had only seen him as the aggressive kid; but when he offered them gum they were, 'like, thanks, man.'"

Katie also began to incorporate mnemonics that sought to enhance Paul's problem-solving ability. Box 13–7 illustrates some of these research-based mnemonics.

Learning for the Transitional and Postsecondary Years: Pepperdine University, Malibu, California

It can be challenging and even frightening for a student with TBI to transition from school to a college or university. To make this decision, students, their parents, and their high school faculty and IEP team members need to consider the student's academic strengths and weaknesses, acceptance of disability, level of independence, and stage of rehabilitation. They will want to identify postsecondary programs that are consistent with the student's abilities and needs (Bergland & Hoffbauer, 1996), and work with college and university student-support programs to specify how those programs will coordinate services and provide staff training.

Megan's near-fatal car accident happened just four days after she graduated from high school. A gifted student and soccer player, she had plans to attend Pepperdine University on a full athletic scholarship. After her intensive rehabilitation, Megan entered Pepperdine University a semester late. To prepare for her entry, Megan and her mother met with her rehabilitation team. Her neuropsychologist mapped out strategies and modifications that Megan would need to be successful.

Immediately after arriving at Pepperdine, Megan met with each professor and introduced herself and explained her disability. To illustrate her injury, she brought pictures of herself immediately after the accident, showing significant damage to her skull and featuring a bald Megan with a scar reaching from ear to ear. She wasn't seeking sympathy; rather, she used the pictures to show the professors what had happened to her. Since then, her hair had grown back and now covered the scar. But she wanted them to know that, even though she looked fine, she had significant challenges because of this injury. She also brought information about her high school grades and information about the rehabilitation she had recently completed. Megan explains,

To learn more about Megan and her experience with TBI, go to the Cases module in Chapter 13 of the Companion Website.

Box 13—7

Into Practice

Mnemonics for Solving Problems

A good mnemonic has several characteristics. First, it must solve a problem (i.e., it must make sense to people and their challenges). Without this connection, a student will not integrate the strategy into his learning. Second, the mnemonic should relate to the actual activity it is designed to address. Third, the mnemonic has a sing-song quality, like a rhyme, that helps the student connect the word to the sound. Fourth, the mnemonic implies activity and elicits a good mental image. Finally, mnemonics are simple and easy to rehearse and recall.

Often, students with TBI have a great deal of difficulty solving a problem in a logical way. They benefit from a step-by-step method for solving problems that can be applied in diverse environments and situations. Using rhyming verse and word mnemonics, Parente and his colleagues (Parente, Anderson-Parente, & Stapelton, 2001) developed a mnemonic called SOLVE. Each letter of the word SOLVE reminds the person of some important aspect of a problem-solving process. To start SOLVE, the student defines the problem and then creates and prioritizes possible solutions. Next, the student explains the option to a peer, teacher, parent or other interested party. This is critical because the act of verbalizing the problem and its possible solutions helps to clarify the solutions. Here is how SOLVE works:

Specify the problem—defines the problem
Organize your solution—keep several options in mind
Listen to advice—take others' advice
Vary your thinking—ask, "what makes the problem worse?"
Evaluate if your solution worked—read this verse again
    (Parente et al., 2001, p. 18)

The next step is for students to decide which of the several possible options would be the best solution. The DECIDE acronym teaches a rhyme that a student can follow to limit procrastination when thinking about a decision and to consider the decision from several possible viewpoints. DECIDE seeks to get the opinions of several different stakeholders so that the student will make more correct than incorrect decisions.

Do not procrastinate—decide to begin
Evaluate each option—choose those that are WIN-WIN
Create new options when the others won't do
Investigate existing policies—limit what you choose
Discuss the decision with others and listen to their advice
Evaluate your feelings—before acting, think twice.
    (Parente et al., 2001, p. 18).

Putting These Strategies to Work for Progress in the General Curriculum

1. How might one of Jarris's teachers integrate the SOLVE and DECIDE strategy into Jarris's education?

2. What are the challenges in integrating this strategy into a general education curriculum?

3. How can collaboration between the special and general education teacher assist its implementation? How could Brent or Shawna help at home?

To answer these questions online and learn more about these strategies, go to the Into Practice module in Chapter 13 of the Companion Website.

I wasn't looking for a handout but, instead, I wanted my professors to know what I had been through. I let them know that I was going to try extra hard, but without accommodations I wouldn't succeed. This wasn't easy for me. I used to be a very social person; but like most people who suffer from a TBI, I had lost confidence in myself and was uncomfortable talking with people, especially about me. However, I met with every professor and told them what my neurologist suggested and how I would need additional time to complete tests, I would need to tape every lecture, I would benefit from any type of handout that would further illustrate the lecture, and I would need the assistance of the writing center.

Megan's first semester at Pepperdine consisted of a number of other hurdles. One of the first involved being independent and attending to her basic needs. Unfortunately, simple activities such as selecting food at the cafeteria proved to be a challenge. Her mother explains,

> I went to Pepperdine with Megan and spent the first week with her. The first morning, we went over to the cafeteria, and I told Megan to get something to eat. I left to allow her the opportunity to make the appropriate selection. After a long time, she returned to the room not having eaten a thing. With all the choices, Megan didn't know how to make a selection. I quickly learned she needed direct instruction in how to select food items from the cafeteria if she was going to eat in this environment. So we went through the various lines and reviewed what a balanced meal would include and selected various items. This involved further demonstration and practice before Megan was comfortable and able to eat on her own.

When her classes began, Megan, armed with a tape recorder, recorded every lecture. At the end of the day, she returned home and transcribed these lectures by hand. Next, she reviewed her handwritten transcription and created another outline that would help her study. This was exceedingly time-consuming but necessary for Megan's learning needs. On test days, Megan was allowed to arrive early and begin the test 30–60 minutes ahead of the rest of her peers. As Megan explains, "I was the first person there and the last to leave for every one of my tests."

Megan's hard work and postsecondary accommodations have paid off. She successfully completed her undergraduate degree and is now completing her master's degree in speech pathology at Idaho State University in Boise, building on her experiences as an undergraduate and TBI survivor.

A Vision for Jarris's Future

Nearly nine years have elapsed since Jarris's injury; six since her entry into the LAP program, where she took her first steps on the journey to rejoining the world that she would have occupied except for her injury. Where is she now?

She has mastered ASL; her family has, too. Her teachers use some signs with her; and when she and they cannot communicate satisfactorily through signs to and from each other, Jarris's classmates lend a hand—literally! Her teachers have adopted universal design in their curriculum and instruction, giving Jarris access to the same opportunities to learn that her classmates without disabilities have. She still struggles to communicate and to master her academic subjects. But she has traveled a very long route and done it successfully, albeit with a great deal of support.

Brent and Shawna concur when asked about Jarris's future: "We want and expect Jarris to be able to choose what it is she wants to do and be able to pursue her dream just like anyone else. It's quite simple, actually. We believe Jarris has the potential, and we want to ensure that we do whatever is necessary for her to reach her potential."

So let's return to the initial challenge, the one we confronted when we first met Jarris. Can you imagine growing up with a brain injury? Ask that of Jarris, her family, and her teachers, and the answer will be, "Of course." The reason the answer comes so quickly and unanimously? History is prologue. The LAP was where Jarris's history began, and its end is not yet in sight.

What Would You Recommend?

1. To have Jarris included with her nondisabled peers to ensure inclusion as the curriculum becomes more academically challenging?
2. To further improve Jarris's language development? What assistive technology device would assist Jarris to further develop her language?
3. To advance Jarris's academic development by using social skills?
4. To enable Jarris to transition successfully into the middle school environment?

Summary

How Do You Recognize Students with Traumatic Brain Injuries?

▼ The IDEA definition of TBI includes acquired injuries to the brain caused by an external force but does not include brain injuries caused by anoxia, disease, or congenital brain injuries. This is a controversial exclusion.

▼ Closed head injuries and open head injuries are the two types of brain injuries included under the IDEA definition.

▼ Mild head injuries, called postconcussional syndrome, can adversely affect personal, academic, and social performance.

▼ TBI differs from other disabilities in onset, complexity, and prognosis.

▼ Students with TBI often experience physical, cognitive, linguistic, and social or behavioral changes.

▼ No generalizations can be made about prognosis based on the injury's mildness or severity.

▼ The three major causes of closed and open head injuries are automobile or bicycle accidents, falls, and violence.

▼ Called the *silent epidemic*, the effects of brain injury are widespread but often unrecognized.

How Do You Evaluate Students with Traumatic Brain Injury?

▼ Because the needs of students with TBI are diverse and rapidly changing, evaluation needs to be comprehensive and ongoing.

▼ The multidisciplinary team should evaluate the student in all areas of functioning, including cognitive processes, and work in association with medical staff to gain a thorough understanding of previous assessments.

▼ The IEP team should update the student's document frequently, probably every six to eight weeks initially, as the student might rapidly regain cognitive and physical abilities.

How Do You Assure Progress in the General Curriculum?

▼ Cognitive retraining is essential to any student with a brain injury. Similarly, structured teaching with accommodations and modifications offers the necessary program to meet the academic needs of the student.

▼ Traditional memory aids often do not work for students with traumatic brain injuries. Instead, parents and educators need to incorporate memory enhancers like mnemonics to further develop academic and social skills.

What Can You Learn from Others Who Teach Students with Traumatic Brain Injury?

▼ A model of early intervention, like the Children's Place, incorporates education with rehabilitation, thus constantly helping children improve through the course of a normal day.

▼ Accommodations and modifications do not need to be complex to be successful. Linda's and Joan's work at Centennial Elementary School have found that they need to be specific to the child but also focused on the entire classroom's growth.

▼ College or university may not be the next step for many individuals with more moderate to severe TBI. If it is a possibility, collaboration with the family, the student and the institution is necessary for the student to be successful.

Council for Exceptional Children   **PRAXIS**

To find out how and where this chapter content connects to the CEC Professional Standards and the Praxis™ Standards, go to the Standards Connection module in Chapter 13 of the Companion Website. A comprehensive matrix aligning CEC Professional Standards, Praxis™ Standards, and INTASC principles to the entire text, is available in the Appendix and on the Companion Website.

Chapter 14

Contributing writers
Jane R. Wegner and Evette Edmister, The University of Kansas

Who Is George Wedge?

You know that words have many meanings. Take the word "telegraph." It is a noun (a sent message), an adjective (as in "telegraph machine"), and a verb (to give advance warning). In the lives of George Wedge, age 7, and his parents, Linda and Phil, telegraphing has been a way of life, one that they experienced even before George was born.

Like many women, Linda underwent an ultrasound examination when she was pregnant. The results were alarming: Her unborn baby had a congenital malformation of his brain and surely would have a disability upon birth. What a telegraph! And what to do about it?

Step 1: Get help. Where? At the Douglas County, Kansas, Inter-Agency Coordinating Council for Infants and Toddlers (ICC). What kind of help? Information about their baby's speech-limiting condition, called Dandy Walker syndrome, and its likely effects. One potential effect was infant mortality. But even if the baby were to live, he might not walk, talk, or learn to read; and he might have a low IQ.

Step 2: Plan for early intervention, which is to say, don't give in and don't give up. As soon as George was born, Linda and Phil enrolled him in the county's early intervention program (through the ICC). Enrollment led him into a program for infants and toddlers at The University of Kansas's Sunnyside program (in a building on Sunnyside Avenue, of course). He began attending at the age of 3 months and graduated from it at the age of 3. Upon his graduation, George continued his education at the university's Hilltop Child Development Center, from which he graduated at the age of 6. George is now in kindergarten at Wakarusa Valley School in rural Douglas County.

Step 3: Provide intensive intervention, not just one but many: finger spelling and American Sign Language instruction, surgery to repair a cleft palate and to insert a feeding tube because George has difficulty swallowing, instruction on how to swallow and shape words, a hearing aid for his right ear, and an assistive technology device for augmentative communication (the Tablet Portable IMPACT from Enkidu Research).

Step 4: Assemble a team. Start with the ICC staff; add the Sunnyside and Hilltop staff. Augment with physicians. Corral George's brother, Roy, and other school-age boys and girls. Get instruction on helpful devices from the Capper Foundation in nearby Topeka. Include the teachers and related-service professionals. Give Phil's mother a role. Be sure Linda and Phil are the head coaches. And give the ball to George as often as he can carry it.

Step 5: Expect great results and celebrate them. Be grateful—more, be joyful—that George is alive. Applaud him and everyone on his team for the outcomes: his ability to form words and talk to those who know him well or pay close attention to him; his ability to use sign language and finger-spell; his mastery of his assistive

technology device; his progress through two programs that include children with and without disabilities in the same classrooms; his matriculation into and progress through kindergarten; his ability to walk, ride a horse, take classes at the local art center and museums; his developing talent as a chess player and his love of reading; and his ability to make friends and be the guy who helps them learn to use sign language, too.

Step 6: Prepare for and face the challenges of today and tomorrow. Acknowledge that George still needs to be taught how to swallow; that he still needs to learn how to shape words; that his teacher, Donna Sabata, is learning about communication disabilities but still wants to learn more; that his speech pathologist, JoLynn Alberston-Sears, has to teach not only George but also his classmates how to use sign language; and that his occupational therapist needs to adjust his hearing aids daily and occasionally repair his assistive technology devices.

Last step: Take a good hard look at George, Linda, Phil, and Roy Wedge. Reread the first telegraph that Linda and Phil received, the bad news one. Now send a different one, the good news one. Let it read as follows: "Past is prologue. Hard work

ahead. Nothing that you can't do. See you when George graduates from elementary, middle, and high school. Banking on him moving away for college or a satisfying job." Sign it "special educators and related-service providers." P.S.: "Speech pathology always available."

What do you think?

1. How are George's communication needs being met? What kinds of professionals are involved with him?

2. What needs to happen so that George's speech and language development will continue to improve? So that his social skills will continue to flourish?

3. How are his parents, teachers, and others collaborating to ensure his continued success?

To respond to these questions online, participate in other activities, and learn more about George Wedge and communication disorders, go to the Cases module in Chapter 14 of the Companion Website.

How Do You Recognize Students with Communication Disorders?

Defining Communication Disorders

Communication entails receiving, understanding, and expressing information, feelings, and ideas. It is so a natural part of our daily lives that most of us take our ability to communicate for granted. Most of us participate in many communicative interactions each day. For example, we talk with others face to face or on the phone; we e-mail a colleague or friend; we demonstrate social awareness by lowering our voices when we see a raised eyebrow combined with a frown; we wink at friends over private jokes.

Although we usually communicate through speech, we also communicate in many other ways. Some people communicate manually, using sign language and/or gestures. While speaking, others add nonlinguistic cues such as body posture, facial and vocal expression, gestures, eye contact, and head and body movements. Many speakers vary their voices by changing their pitch or rate of speaking. All of these skills make our communication more effective.

Most children come to school able to understand others and express themselves. Their communication abilities allow them to continue developing socially and take part in the lives of their classrooms. Indeed, communication and language include both the content and the medium through which learning occurs (Merritt & Culatta, 1998). Imagine the difficulties a student with a communication disorder might encounter with school scripts, social interactions, instructional discourse exchanges, acquisition of knowledge and language, and the development of literacy skills. Effective communication in school is a complicated process.

Speech and Language Disorders

Communication disorders relate to the components of the process affected: speech and/or language (ASHA, 2002; Stuart, 2002; Hulit & Howard, 2002). A **speech disorder** refers to difficulty producing sounds as well as disorders of voice quality or fluency of speech. A **language**

Communication involves speaking as well as a multitude of nonverbal behaviors such as facial expression, gestures, and head and body movements.

disorder is difficulty receiving, understanding, and formulating ideas and information. IDEA recognizes that both types of communication disorders can adversely affect a student's educational performance.

Speech disorders and language disorders are often associated with other disorders. Specifically, speech disorders are sometimes associated with **cleft palate or lip** (a condition in which a person has a split in the upper part of the oral cavity or the upper lip). George's speech difficulties are a result of his cleft palate, so he uses an augmentative and alternative communication (AAC) device called the Tablet to express himself more clearly. Language disorders are sometimes the primary feature through which other disorders are identified.

Cultural Diversity in Communication

Students from different cultural backgrounds may have language differences that affect their participation in the classroom. Although many individuals have a speech or language difference, they do not necessarily have a language or speech disorder. *Difference* does not always mean *disorder* (Battle, 1998). Box 14–1 Provides information relevant to classroom interactions and other cultural differences in communication.

Some students are bilingual, while others have dialectical differences. Every language contains a variety of forms, called dialects. A **dialect** is a language variation that a group of individuals use and that reflects their shared regional, social, or cultural/ethnic factors. For

To learn more about an organization that provides information, education, and support to families of children with communication disorders, go to the Web Links module in Chapter 14 of the Companion Website for a link to the Ontario Association for Families of Children with Communication Disorders home page.

Box 14–1

Multicultural Considerations

Communicative Interactions

Instructors need to remember that students come from varied cultural and linguistic backgrounds. Their interactions at school may be very different from those at home (Allington & Cunningham, 2002; Bunce, 2003; Giangreco, 2000). "Teachers need to be aware of possible causes of communication failure in the school environment in order to circumvent misunderstandings and to facilitate academic achievement and acceptance of the bilingual/bicultural child in the school system" (Bunce, 2003, p. 370).

Teachers can use cooperative group activities to foster multicultural relationships as well as role-playing and team-building exercises. The cultural influence and contributions of events and people within curricular content can highlight the value of diversity as well. Teachers can incorporate community activities and speakers that reflect differing cultures.

Students in the classroom need information about different cultural practices and reassurance that one cultural communicative practice is not better than the another. They are simply different; and these differences need to be respected, understood, and considered when people communicate (Bunce, 2003).

Some children may have a cultural difference combined with a speech and/or language disorder. Others may not have a speech and/or language impairment and do not need support services. However, in all cases teachers need to consider how instruction and assessments may need to be adapted and/or augmented in order to assist students' learning and participation.

Taking Diversity into Account for Progress in the General Curriculum:

1. Where in your school district can you learn more about communicative interactions of cultures other than your own?

2. How will you make your class aware of different communicative interactions?

3. How will you adapt and/or augment assessment and instruction to meet students' learning and participation needs?

To answer these questions online and learn more about these strategies, go to the Multicultural Considerations module in Chapter 14 of the Companion Website for a link to the Multicultural Pavilion website (http://www.edchange.org/multicultural/index.html).

Please review the discussion of multicultural responsiveness in Chapter 3, keeping communication in mind.

example, families with roots in Appalachia may "tote" rather than "carry" materials. Similarly, individuals in the southern United States may say that they are "fixin' " to do something rather than "going" to do something. Deaf individuals in California have a distinct technological sign for "computer" because Silicon Valley in California is the nation's center for computer technology.

Like language differences, speech differences occur across the United States. In the south, many individuals say "fahv" and "nahn" for "five and" "nine." Midwesterners may say that they want to "mayzure" something rather than "measure" it. Many Bostonians delete the *r* in the middle and at the ends of words, as do many southerners ("car" sounds like "kah" and "hurt" like "huht.") Because such speech differences result from geographic factors, a child who simply uses these variations should not for that reason alone be considered to have a communication disorder (Battle, 1996, 1998).

Although differences in dialects do not necessarily indicate communication disorders, a student with a dialectical difference may also exhibit a communication disorder. In Box 14–2, Rhonda Freidlander, a speech-language pathologist, tells how she works with families of children with communication disorders in the Salish and Kootenai tribes of the Flathead Nation, of which she is a member. To best serve tribal members with communication disorders, Rhonda must be able to distinguish characteristics that are based on dialects from true communication errors. She provides intervention services only to those individuals with communication disorders or impairments, not those with dialectical differences.

Box 14–2

Making a Difference

Rhonda Friedlander

Rhonda Friedlander, a member of the Confederated Salish and Kootenai tribes of the Flathead Nation, is a speech-language pathologist on the tribal reservation in northwestern Montana. Her caseload is drawn from the 6,700 tribal members who reside on the 1.2 million–acre reservation. A home visit for Rhonda often requires a 120-mile round trip. But that's not the least of it. She also has to take care not to let any of the families' livestock escape at the gate, and she usually has to meet the whole family—not only the nuclear family but also aunts, uncles, grandfathers, and, most important, grandmothers.

Talking about her work for her tribe's future, Rhonda notes that rates of communication disorders among Native Americans are much higher than the national average Because of many therapists' lack of cultural sensitivity, the remoteness of the reservations, low professional salaries, and high client caseloads, maintaining speech and language services for tribal populations is difficult.

Rhonda grew up on this reservation, so she understands the vocabulary variations of both Indian and non-Indian words and is able to respect a child's use of either vocabulary. She knows the cultural expectations of the children's language and experience. For example, tribal culture values listening and observing more than speaking and questioning.

The family is a critical component of Rhonda's program to improve children's speech and language skills. Traditionally, all learning is transmitted through the family members; children learn survival skills and daily living skills from aunts, uncles, and grandparents. And children also have the support of their community. So Rhonda's speech-language program involves both family and community support.

The tribal tradition of community support brings strong community backing for her efforts with the children. Other traditions also influence the way in which Rhonda provides speech and language services. For example, although the community supports her program, Rhonda herself rarely receives any praise or recognition. Individual contributions of one person are not valued above the contributions of another. Traditionally, all human beings are equal and are treated equally, regardless of accomplishment. Therefore, Rhonda provides services and relies on her personal awareness that she makes a positive contribution. She does not expect praise or recognition.

Rhonda believes that her program's success results from tribal support of her efforts and the support of individual families. The tribes support her program because they regard it as an effort to increase the likelihood for success for all tribal members. Families support Rhonda's efforts because they recognize her concern and respect for them and their children. When asked how she can provide such an exemplary program, Rhonda responds that it takes persistence, self-direction, and intrinsic motivation. But she adds that the full support of her tribe has been her greatest motivator.

FIGURE 14–1
Speech mechanism

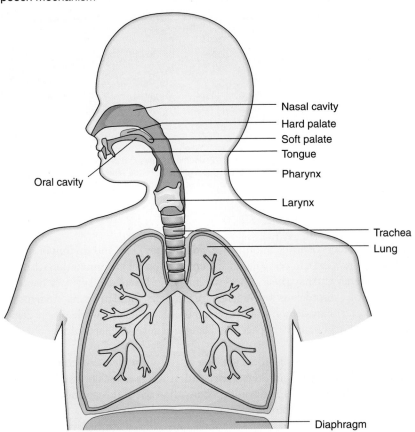

Describing the Characteristics

To become an effective communicator, a student must (1) master the many systems and rules that produce correct speech and language and (2) know and follow the language and speech rules of the different settings. For most children, the development of speech and language follows a typical and predictable pattern and time table. For others, it does not; these children may have a communication disorder.

Typical Speech Development

Speech is the oral expression of language. This expression occurs when a person produces sounds and syllables. A person forms sounds by varying the position of her lips, tongue, and lower jaw as the air passes through her larynx (voice box), pharynx (a space extending from the nasal cavities to the esophagus), mouth, and nose. The larynx sits on top of the trachea and contains the vocal folds (ligaments of the larynx); voice is produced here. As a person pushes air from her lungs, the muscles in her larynx moves her vocal folds, producing sounds. Figure 14–1 illustrates the speech mechanism.

Children quickly learn to produce speech sounds during their early years. By the age of 8, they have learned to produce nearly all the consonants and vowels that make up the words of the family's native language. Learning these sounds usually proceeds in a fairly consistent sequence, but there may be variation among children in the time of acquisition. Figure 14–2 illustrates the times at which 90 percent of English-speaking children have mastered the consonant sounds needed for speech.

FIGURE 14-2
Typical ages for mastery of consonant sounds

By age 3:	/p/, /m/, /h/, /n/, /w/
By age 4	/b/, /k/, /g/, /d/, /f/, /y/
By age 6:	/t/, /ng/, /r/, /l/, /s/
By age 7:	/ch/, /sh/, /j/, /th/ as in "think"
By age 8:	/s/, /z/, /v/, /th/ as in "that"
Even later:	/zh/ as in "measure"

Source: From "When Are Speech Sounds Learned?" by B. Sander, 1972, *Journal of Speech and Hearing Disorders, 37,* pp. 55–63. Copyright 1972 by the American Speech-Language-Hearing Association. Adapted with permission.

Speech Disorders

Speech disorders include disorders of articulation, voice, and fluency (rate and rhythm of speech). As you have learned, these disorders can occur alone, in combination, or in conjunction with other disorders. For example, students who have hearing losses (Chapter 15) or cerebral palsy (Chapter 12) often have articulation or voice disorders as well as language disorders. Similarly, some students with mental retardation (Chapter 8) may demonstrate no communication delays, while others demonstrate speech delays, language delays, or both speech and language delays (Chapter 15).

Articulation Disorders   Articulation disorders are one of the most frequent communication disorders in preschool and school-aged children. **Articulation** is a speaker's production of individual or sequenced sounds. An articulation disorder occurs when the child cannot correctly produce the various sounds and sound combinations of speech.

Articulation errors may be in the form of substitutions, omissions, additions, and distortions. Substitutions are common, as when a child substitutes *d* for the voiced *th* ("doze" for "those"), *t* for *k* ("tat" for "cat"), or *w* for *r* ("wabbit" for "rabbit").

Omissions occur when a child leaves a phoneme out of a word. Children often omit sounds from consonant pairs ("boo" for "blue," "cool" for "school") and from the ends of words ("ap" for "apple"). Additions occur when students place a vowel between two consonants, converting "tree" into "tahree."

Distortions are modifications of the production of a phoneme in a word; a listener gets the sense that the sound is being produced, but it sounds distorted. Common distortions, called lisps, occur when *s, z, sh,* and *ch* are mispronounced.

George substitutes, omits, and distorts speech sounds. His cleft palate prevented him from moving his tongue against his palate, so he is learning where to place his tongue to make particular speech sounds.

Articulation problems, like all communication disorders, vary. Many children have mild or moderate articulation disorders; their speech is understood by others yet contains sound production errors. Other children have serious articulation disorders, making it nearly impossible for others to understand them. When individuals have serious articulation disorders, they usually benefit from evaluation for an AAC device.

There are many reasons for you to refer a student with articulation problems to a speech-language pathologist. If a student's articulation problem negatively affects his interactions in your class or his educational performance, referral is in order. Likewise, if a child's sound production error makes his speech difficult or impossible to understand, referral is warranted. Furthermore, articulation problems resulting from neurological damage (e.g., cerebral palsy and stroke) typically require therapy. Therapy is also needed to assist students with clefts of the palate or lip if they cannot produce speech sounds or sound combinations correctly. Therapy may also be needed to help a student with a hearing loss who is experiencing difficulty in correctly producing speech sounds because he cannot hear the sounds clearly.

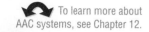
To learn more about AAC systems, see Chapter 12.

Apraxia of Speech.   Apraxia is a motor speech disorder that affects the way in which a student plans to produce speech. Apraxia can be acquired as the result of a stroke, a tumor, or a head injury. Apraxia can also be developmental. Students with apraxia have difficulty with the voluntary, purposeful movements of speech even though they have no paralysis or weakness of the muscles involved in speech. They have difficulty positioning the articulators and sequencing the sounds. A student with apraxia may be able to say the individual sounds required for speech in isolation or syllables but cannot produce them in longer words and sentences. She may be able to say sounds and words correctly when there is no pressure or request to do so but not when there is.

Some characteristics of apraxia are errors in production of vowels, inconsistent speech errors, more errors as words or sentences get longer, voicing errors (for example, *b* for *p* or *g* for *k*), and stress on the wrong syllables. These types of errors are not usually present in students who have traditional articulation disorders. Students with apraxia need frequent therapy that focuses on repetition, sound sequencing, and movement patterns (Caruso & Strand, 1999).

To learn more about apraxia, go to the Web Links module in Chapter 14 of the Companion Website to link to the Apraxia Kids website.

Voice Disorders.   Each person has a unique voice. This voice reflects the interactive relationship of pitch, duration, intensity, resonance, and vocal quality. Pitch is determined by the rate of vibration in the vocal folds; men tend to have lower-pitched voices than do women. Pitch is affected by the tension and size of the vocal folds, the health of the larynx, and the location of the larynx. Duration is the length of time any speech sound requires.

Intensity (loudness or softness) is based on the perception of the listener and is determined by the air pressure coming from the lungs through the vocal folds. Rarely do individuals believe that their voices are too loud. Rather, they may seek professional voice therapy because their voices are too soft.

Resonance, the perceived quality of someone's voice, is determined by the way in which the tone coming from the vocal folds is modified by the spaces of the throat, mouth, and nose. Individuals with an unrepaired cleft palate may experience resonance problems because the opening from the mouth to the nasal cavity may be too large or inappropriately shaped.

Sometimes students without a cleft palate have resonance problems; they may sound as if they have a cold or are holding their noses when speaking. This is called **hyponasality** because air cannot pass through the nose and comes through the mouth instead. Other students have a different trait, **hypernasality,** in which air is allowed to pass through the nasal cavity on sounds other than *m*, *n*, and *ng*. Speech therapy may be needed to teach these students appropriate ways to produce non-nasal sounds.

The quality of the voice is affected by problems of breath support or vocal fold functioning as well as resonance. You might have experienced short-term vocal quality problems after cheering at a football game. Repeated abuse of the vocal folds may cause **vocal nodules**, growths that result from the rubbing together of the vocal fold edges. When the folds cannot vibrate properly or come together completely, the sound of your voice will change temporarily until the vocal nodules heal. This short-term vocal quality problem usually heals because the vocal fold abuse is not constant. If, however, vocal nodules develop and persist, therapy may be needed to help a student learn to talk in a way that is less abusive to the vocal mechanisms. In most cases, nodules disappear after vocal rest and/or voice therapy. If vocal nodules are the result of an organic problem, therapy alone may not resolve them and surgery may be required (Pannbacker, 1999).

To learn more about the National Stuttering Association, go to the Web Links module in Chapter 14 of the Companion Website.

Fluency disorders.   Normal speech requires correct articulation, vocal quality, and fluency (rate and rhythm of speaking). Fluent speech is smooth, flows well, and appears effortless. **Fluency problems** are characterized by interruptions in the flow of speaking, such as atypical rate or rhythm as well as repetitions of sounds, syllables, words, and phrases.

All children and adults have difficulties with fluency on occasion. All individuals hesitate, repeat themselves, or use fillers such as "umm" at one time or another. Occasional dysfluency is not considered **stuttering**, which is frequent repetition and/or prolongation of words or sounds. Approximately 1 percent of the population (2 to 3 million Americans) stutter. More males than females stutter.

Typical Language Development

Children's language development is complex. It begins early and depends on biological preparation, successful nurturance, sensorimotor experiences, and linguistic experiences (McCormick, 2002a). Babies just 4 days old can distinguish one language from another (Cowley, 1997). By 3 weeks of age, infants with normal development communicate; specifically, they engage their caregivers in jointly referring to objects (e.g., infants look, and caregivers reply with, "Oh, do you see that?" or "You are looking at Mommy's face!"). They also engage caregivers with their deliberate, social smiles in the first weeks of life. By 2 to 3 months of age, infants coo (Schwartz & Miller, 1996). By 4 to 6 months, they produce universal speech sounds. Later that first year, babbling turns to vocal play in which babies string English sounds together, as in "ba, la, ba, la, ba." By their first birthdays, babies make sounds when spoken to, vary vocal pitch and intensity, and experiment with rhythm; they may even say their first words. They also start linking words to meaning at this time (Cowley, 1997; Wang & Baron, 1997). Within the next year, their spoken vocabularies increase to 200 to 300 words, and the 2-year-old's "no nap" may become the 3-year-old's "I don't want nap" (Cowley, 1997). Three-year-old toddlers understand simple questions and prepositions such as "in," "on," "under," and "up" and are able to follow two-step directions. The rapid development continues and by age four, preschoolers ask questions using "who," "what," "when," "where," "why," and "how" and have vocabularies of 1,000 to 1,500 words. By age 6, they use irregular verbs such as "be," "go," "run," and "swim" and can verbally share their feelings and thoughts. Figure 14–3 provides further information about normal language development for children ages birth through 6.

Although most of language development takes place in the preschool years, language development continues throughout the school years. This later development occurs in the areas of language structure, vocabulary, and language use. During the school years the language skills of reading and writing are also learned (Hulit & Howard, 2002). Though not as rapid as earlier language development, this later progression is equally important.

The five components of language that work together in our language system are phonology (sound system), morphology (word forms), syntax (word order and sentence structure), semantics (word and sentence meanings), and pragmatics (social use of language). Each dimension works together with the others, usually resulting in effective communication (ASHA, 1993).

Phonology.   The use of sounds to make meaningful syllables and words is called **phonology**. Phonology is a much broader concept than articulation. Phonology encompasses the rules and sequencing of individual speech sounds (called *phonemes*) and how they are produced, depending on their placement in a syllable or word. For example, consonants at the beginning of syllables or words (e.g., "tap") are produced slightly differently from those in the middle (e.g., "cattle") or at the end of syllables or words (e.g., "pat"). Phonological use requires correct pronunciation as well as awareness of sound differences as they signal change in meaning. In English, for instance, the word "bill" is different from "pill" by only one phoneme: *b*. By changing one phoneme, a speaker can produce a totally different word. Although English spelling has 26 letters, English speakers use them to produce 45 different sounds. For example, *th*, *sh*, *oy*, and *ou* are four completely different sounds that are represented in spelling as different combinations of two of the 26 letters (Owens, 2001).

Morphology.   **Morphology** is the system that governs the structure of words (ASHA, 1993). Phonemes have little meaning on their own, but some can be grouped into syllables or words that have meaning. The smallest meaningful unit of speech is called a *morpheme*. For instance, when *s* is added to "bill," the word becomes plural. Formerly having one morpheme, the word now has two: "bill" (a mouth structure or a written document) and "-s" (denoting plurality). Morphological rules allow speakers to add plurals, inflection, affixes, and past-tense markers to verbs. For example, correct use of morphological rules allows a child to change "swim" to "swimmed" and then, as the child matures, to "swam," an irregular past-tense verb. Understanding of morphological rules allows us to recognize meaning just by hearing it.

Syntax.   **Syntax** provides rules for putting together a series of words to form sentences (ASHA, 1993). Receptively, a child must be able to note the significance in the order of others' words (e.g., "I want that cookie" means that a cookie is desired by the speaker, whereas "Do I want that

FIGURE 14-3
Typical language development

Age	Developmental Milestones
Birth to 6 Months	Differentiated cry for emotions and needs such as hunger and pain Coos in response to familiar situations Laughs Responds to voices and other sounds differentially
6 to 12 Months	Listens to new words Understands own name and "No" Uses many sounds differentially and with inflection; babbles Imitates sound patterns and motor acts such as waving good-bye Responds to simple commands such as "come here," "give me _____" Recognizes the names of familiar people and objects
12 to 18 Months	Names familiar objects with single words Mixes jargon (speech sounds with inflection) with single words Uses speech socially to interact with others Recognizes more words and commands Has five- to fifty-word vocabulary Identifies one to three body parts (at eighteen months), such as "Where's your nose?" Points to pictures named in a book.
18 to 24 Months	Strings two or more words together Has 200–300 word vocabulary by twenty-four months Understands possessives Uses plurals No longer uses jargon by twenty-four months Uses simple adverbs and adjectives (big, nice, good) Uses some verbs Understands (but may ignore) simple directives Listens to caregiver's speech and imitates important parts
24 to 36 months	Understands objects by use, such as "what do we eat with?" Understands simple questions and pronouns Understands the prepositions *in, on, under, up,* and *down* Follows two-step directions Listens to stories Uses turn-taking in communicating with others Uses two-word and longer phrases Has vocabulary of 900–1,000 words Recounts events Asks simple questions

(continued)

FIGURE 14–3
Continued

Age	Developmental Milestones
36 to 48 months	Asks questions using *who, what, when, where,* and *how* Tells stories, both real and imaginary Understands most compound and complex sentences and uses some Can explain and describe events Vocabulary of 1,000–1,500 words Asks *why* questions Uses communication to engage playmates Uses verb contractions Has some articulation difficulties with /l/, /r/, /s/, /z/, /ch/, /sh/, /j/, /th/ Can complete verbal analogies, such as "Joe is a boy, Mary is a _____ "
4 to 5 Years	Uses the prepositions *in, on,* and *under* Understands *if, because, when,* and *why* Uses conjunctions and longer, more complex sentences Still makes some grammatical errors Can give first and last name, gender, and telephone number Uses past tense
5 to 6 Years	Has vocabulary of 2,500–2,800 words Responds to most complex sentences though sometimes confused Uses comparative adjectives (big, bigger, biggest) Uses irregular verbs (be, go, swim) Correctly uses articles *a* and *the* Tells familiar stories and imaginative tales Shares personal feelings and thoughts verbally Talks things out rather than always acts them out Can use the telephone Recognizes and tells jokes

Source: From *Early Language Intervention: An Introduction* (2nd ed.), edited by L. McCormick and R. L. Schiefelbush, 1990, Upper Saddle River, NJ: Merrill/Prentice Hall. Copyright 1990 by Merrill/Prentice Hall. Reprinted with permission.

cookie?" indicates a question in which the speaker is determining if he or she wants a cookie). Expressively, a child must be able to use word order appropriately (e.g., "I want a cookie" to indicate that a cookie is desired rather than "Cookie, I want"). Just as phonology provides the rules for putting together strings of phonemes to form words, syntax provides rules for putting together a series of words to construct sentences.

The first three dimensions of language—phonology, morphology, and syntax—all combine to determine the form of language—that is, what the language looks like. The next two dimensions of language—semantics and pragmatics—are more advanced dimensions of language, determining the content and social use of language (Bloom & Lahey, 1978).

Semantics. **Semantics** refers to the meaning of what is expressed. Semantic development has both receptive and expressive components. Children first learn to understand the meaning of words and then to verbally or manually use the words and sentences meaningfully. Children start out with a small number of words that represent a large number of objects in their environments (Mervis & Bertrand, 1997).

Pragmatics. The term **pragmatics** refers to the use of communication in contexts. Caregivers and infants use the rules of pragmatics in their interactions, and children learn to use social communication very early. After using smiles and simple verbalizations, children request objects, actions, or information; protest actions; comment on objects or actions; greet; and acknowledge comments. These skills allow children to use language socially to interact within their environments and with people in those environments more efficiently.

No one knows for sure just how the five dimensions of language come to work together so that children acquire useful language. Theories explaining how children acquire language abound (Loeb, 2002b). In the 1950s, Chomsky (1957) proposed that children are born ready to develop language skills because of an inborn language acquisition device. Later, behaviorists proposed that the ability to learn and use language is not inborn but happens as children imitate and practice. Today, researchers investigate the effects of a child's imitation, practice, and other social interactions on language development. Their research has been compiled into social interaction theories.

Social interaction theories emphasize that communication skills are learned through social interactions. These theories hold that language development is the outcome of a child's drive for attachment with his or her world; communication develops in order for the child to convey information about the environment to others. This means that how the child communicates is determined by the child's assessment of a listener's knowledge about the social context of the communication (McLean & Snyder-McLean, 1999).

The belief that social context and interaction within that context influence communicative choice is supported by philosopher Lev Vygotsky. Vygotsky (1978, 1987) suggests that children develop by supplementing their independent problem-solving abilities with adult guidance or peer collaboration. Children learn by doing, from interacting with their more experienced partners. Social interactionists agree with Vygotsky's premise that children learn language by interacting either with adults, who naturally have more experience, or with peers, who may have more or different experiences (Schneider & Watkins, 1996).

The social interaction theories show that the desire to communicate is the impetus for children to learn the rules and symbols of language. Some children, however, do not appear motivated to communicate. Having provided information concerning typical development and components of language, we turn our attention to language impairments that you might encounter in the classroom.

Characteristics of Language Impairments

Students may have language disorders that are receptive, expressive, or both. Their language impairment may be associated with another disability such as autism or mental retardation, or it may be a **specific language impairment**—not related to any physical or intellectual problems (Leonard, 1987; ASHA, 1980).

Phonology. Students with phonological disorders may be unable to discriminate differences in speech sounds or sound segments that signify differences in words. For example, to them the word "pen" may sound no different from "pin." Their inability to differentiate sounds as well as similar, rhyming syllables may cause them to experience reading and/or spelling difficulties (Apel & Swank, 1999; Lombardino, Riccio, Hynd, & Pinheiro, 1997). Phonological difficulties are common in children with language impairments and may affect reading (McCormick & Loeb, 2002).

Morphology. Children with morphological difficulties have problems using the structure of words to get or give information. They may make a variety of errors. For example, they may not use "–ed" to signal past tense as in "walked" or "–s" to signal plurality. When a child is unable to use morphological rules appropriately, the average length of her utterances is sometimes shorter than that expected for the child's age because plurals, verb markers, and affixes may be missing from her statements (McCormick & Loeb, 2002).

Incorrect morphology is associated with differences in dialects as well as with a variety of disabling conditions, including mental retardation (Chapter 8), autism (Chapter 10), hearing loss or deafness (Chapter 15), and expressive language delay. Incorrect use of morphology is also associated with specific language impairment.

Syntax. Syntactical errors are those involving word order, such as ordering words in a manner that does not convey meaning to the listeners ("Where one them park at?"); using immature structures for a given age or developmental level (e.g., a 3-year-old child using two-word utterances, such as "him sick"); misusing negatives (a 4-year-old child saying "Him no go"); or omitting structures (e.g., "He go now"). As with phonology and morphology, differences in syntax sometimes are associated with dialects.

Semantics. Children who experience difficulty using words singly or together in sentences may have semantic disorders. They may have difficulty with words with double meanings (e.g., "*break*" as a verb meaning "to rupture or ruin" or as a noun meaning "time off from"), abstract terms (e.g., "cooperate"), synonyms (e.g., "warm" and "tepid"), and idioms (e.g., "slip your coat on") (Johnson, Smith, & Box, 1997). Some students with semantic disorders may have problems with words that express time and space ("night," "tiny"); cause and effect (e.g., "push button, ball goes"); and inclusion versus exclusion (e.g., "all," "none").

Sometimes students with semantic language disorders rely on words with fairly nonspecific meanings (e.g., "thing," "one," "that") because of their limited knowledge of vocabulary. Specifically, these students find it much easier to say, "Give me that thing, please," than to try to remember a vocabulary word that is not part of their automatic language repertoires (e.g., "protractor," "scissors").

Pragmatics. Pragmatics focuses on the social use of language—the communication between a speaker and listener within a shared social environment. Pragmatic skills include using appropriate manners in varied situations, obtaining and maintaining eye contact, using appropriate body language, maintaining a topic, and taking turns in conversations.

Pragmatic disorders are reflected in many different ways. A student who talks for long periods of time and does not allow anyone else an opportunity to converse may be displaying signs of a pragmatic disorder. Similarly, a student whose comments are not related to the conversational topic or who asks questions but does not acknowledge the answers by responding to them may be exhibiting a pragmatic disorder (Miranda, McCabe, & Bliss, 1998). Students who have difficulty with pragmatics include those with autism (Chapter 10) and traumatic brain injury (Chapter 13).

Identifying the Causes

There are two types of speech and language disorders, each classified according to its cause: (1) organic disorders, those caused by an identifiable problem in the neuromuscular mechanism of the person; and (2) functional disorders, those with no identifiable organic or neurological cause.

The causes of organic disorders are numerous; they may originate in the nervous system, the muscular system, the chromosomes, or the formation of the speech mechanism. They may include hereditary malformations, prenatal injuries, toxic disturbances, tumors, traumas, seizures, infectious diseases, muscular diseases, and vascular impairments (Wang & Baron, 1997). Neuromuscular disabilities may result in difficulties with clear speech sound production. The speech disorder would then have an organic origin and be classified as an organic speech disorder.

A functional speech and/or language disorder is present when the cause of the impairment is unknown. In Box 14–3, Elizabeth Smith tells how her son Fred appears to have functional speech and language disorders; he exhibits articulation disorders and difficulty using plurals that are not definitely related to his seizures or attention-deficit/ hyperactivity disorder (Chapter 6).

Communication disorders can be classified further according to when the problem began. An impairment that occurs at or before birth is referred to as a congenital impairment. For instance, George, who was born with Dandy Walker syndrome, has a congenital organic speech impairment. A disorder that occurs well after birth is an acquired disorder. For example, a communication impairment may be present after a severe head injury (Chapter 13), which may then be described as an acquired organic speech and/or language impairment. A functional disorder may also be congenital or acquired.

Some causes have both organic and functional origins. In addition, portions of the communication disorder may have been present at birth, and other parts may have been acquired later in life.

Identifying the Prevalence

Of all the students receiving special education ranging in age from 6 to 21 years old, 19.2 percent receive speech and language services (U.S. Department of Education, 2001). Roughly 3 percent of these students have articulation disorders, 4 percent fluency disorders, 6 percent voice

The American Speech and Hearing Association (ASHA) provides detailed information regarding communication impairments and disorders. To learn more about ASHA, go to the Web Links module in Chapter 14 of the Companion Website.

The National Institute on Deafness and Other Communication Disorders (NIDCD) supports research on communication disorders and impairments. To learn more about NIDCD, go to the "Web Links" module in Chapter 14 of the companion website.

Box 14–3

My Voice

Elizabeth Smith

Fred Smith "amazes everybody," according to his mother, Elizabeth. "He's learning to read and likes being read to. Fred reading—that is a big step."

Why is learning to read a big step for Fred?

Fred, age 8, has both expressive and receptive language delays, attention-deficit/hyperactivity disorder (AD/HD), and a seizure disorder. He takes medication for his seizures and AD/HD. Elizabeth explains: "He has trouble expressing his thoughts and his feelings. This year, for the first time since he was 3, he is not receiving speech therapy. He comprehends what others say more quickly than before. We also agreed at his IEP meeting that he learns useful language when talking with his friends in his classes."

Her positive tone fades: "Still, though, Fred doesn't talk a lot. I have to ask him questions like 'Did you color at school today?' or 'Did you go to music?' to get him to start talking, and then he will usually tell me more about that particular activity. Also, I ask him what he is feeling or thinking and usually give him a word to use, like, 'Fred, are you feeling angry or are you tired?' Then he can usually tell me, using one of those words, how he is feeling."

At school, Fred receives his education in a special education classroom half of the day and in a general education second-grade classroom the other half of the day. Mary (Bo) McElmurray, his special education teacher, maintains close contact with his general education teacher, Marilyn Ammons, so that both can be actively involved in making sure that Fred does his best.

Bo notes, "His general education classroom teacher has worked very hard to provide modifications for him. For instance, she went over information from a social studies unit on symbols with Fred. However, even with the practice, he had a great deal of difficulty comprehending the information, so he couldn't tell me and his classmates in special

education much about it. Even with repeated review, he repeated words or phrases his teacher had said rather than sharing about it."

Although he is performing better than "even six months ago," Elizabeth continues to have concerns about Fred's social development. Fred does not have neighbors to play with "out in the country. But he has several kids he gets in trouble with at school," she adds, laughing:

Elizabeth concludes, "All of us have worked together to help Fred, and we all have benefited. That's what is special about special education—taking care to meet the needs of individual children."

Fred Smith and his special education teacher enjoy his successes as he discusses a positive day of social interactions with his friends in his general education classroom.

disorders, and 6.5 percent language disorders serious enough to qualify them for speech-language therapy as a related service under IDEA (U.S. Department of Education, 1996). Of all children and youth ages birth through 21, approximately 5 percent have a speech or language impairment serious enough to warrant special services (U.S. Department of Education, 1996). Of those being served, 49 percent had learning disabilities as a primary disability and a communication disorder as a secondary disability.

How Do you Evaluate Students with Communication Disorders?

Determining the Presence

The process of determining the presence of a communication disorder typically begins for school-age students with a screening or referral by teachers and/or family members. Figure 14–4 describes the evaluation process.

FIGURE 14–4
Assessment process for determining the presence of communication disorders

Nondiscriminatory Evaluation

Observation

Teacher and parents observe	The student has difficulty understanding and/or using language.
Physician observes	The student is not achieving developmental milestones related to communication skills.

Screening

Assessment measures	Findings that indicate need for further evaluation
Classroom work projects	The student may be hesitant to participate in verbal classroom work. Written classroom projects may reflect errors of verbal communication or, in some instances, be a preferred avenue of expression for the student.
Group intelligence tests	Tests do not differentiate the student from other students in many cases. Verbal portions of the tests may be affected by language deficits.
Group achievement tests	The student may perform below expectations from intelligence tests because of language (reading) requirements.
Vision and hearing screening	The student may have history of otitis media (middle-ear infections); hearing may be normal, or the student may have hearing loss. Limited vision may impact language skills.

Prereferral

Prereferral is typically not used with these students.

Referral

Students with significant language delays may be identified before starting school. These students should receive early intervention services and protection in evaluation procedures upon entering school. Because many speech and language disorders are not identified until a student enters school, teachers should refer any student who seems to have difficulty with speech or language.

Nondiscriminatory evaluation procedures and standards

Assessment measures	Findings that suggest speech and language disorders
Individualized intelligence test	The student may be average, above average, or below average in intelligence. However, this student, like some others, often scores lower on sections of the test requiring language skills.
Individualized achievement test	A strong connection exists between language skills and performance on achievement tests. Therefore, language-related subtest scores may be lower than scores on subtests such as mathematics that do not require language skills.
Speech and language tests (articulation/phonology, language sample, receptive language, expressive language)	The student performs significantly below average in one or more areas. Performance may vary according to mood, energy level, extent and pile-up of environmental changes and whether individual preferences are incorporated.
Oral-muscular functioning	In most instances, no problems are present.
Adaptive behavior scales	Tests may reveal that the student has significant difficulty in communication skills.
Anecdotal records, including medical history	The student may have genetic or medical factors that contribute to difficulties with speech or language. Moreover, students with other disabilities, including mental retardation, physical disabilities, hard of hearing or deafness, and learning disabilities, are at risk for having speech and language disorders.
Curriculum-based assessment	A language disorder may cause the student to perform below average in reading or written language.
Direct observation	The student may avoid oral tasks and/or appears confused during conversations. Others may have difficulty understanding the student's speech.

Nondiscriminatory evaluation team determines that student has a communication disorder and needs special education and related services.

Appropriate Education

The speech-language pathologist gathers information from school records, parent and teacher interviews, conversations with the student, in-school observations, standardized tests, curriculum-based assessments, and hearing and vision screenings. Formal methods of assessment are generally more quantitative in nature to determine whether the student varies from what is expected for her age. Informal assessment methods are more qualitative in nature and more apt to reflect the role of context and culture in the student's performance.

A speech assessment determines the presence of articulation, voice, or fluency problems. A standardized articulation test allows a speech-language pathologist to evaluate a student's abilities to produce speech sounds in single words and in sentences. Typically, younger students name pictures and older students read words or sentences while the speech-language pathologist listens, noting the phonemes in error and what the errors were. Test items include use of consonants in the initial, middle, and final positions (e.g., for p, students might name a "*p*ig," a "*zipp*er," and a "*cup*"). The speech pathologist compares the student's sound productions to what is expected for her age and analyzes the sound productions for patterns, usually doing the evaluation in a conversation or during classroom activities.

Voice evaluations include qualitative and quantitative measures. Qualitative measures include a written case history and interviews to obtain information about the onset and course of the problem, environmental factors that might affect vocal quality, and typical voice use (Verdolini, 2000), including pitch, intensity and nasality.

Fluency assessments include case history data and interviews with family members to determine their concerns, learn about the student's speech and language development, and obtain information about the onset and development of the student's dysfluency. The fluency assessment is based on a conversation with the student. The speech pathologist measures the amount of dysfluency as well as the type and duration of dysfluencies and speaking and notes associated speech and nonspeech behaviors such as eye blinking or head movements (Zebrowski, 2000).

Assessment of students for language disorders includes interviews, general language tests, tests that focus on specific components of language such as receptive or expressive vocabulary, language sampling and analysis, classroom observations, and curriculum-based assessments (Loeb,

Bilingual and bidialectical skills make this speech-language therapist especially effective, but note that she and her student also communicate by a semi-universal sign.

2002a). There are three areas to be assessed relative to language interactions in the classroom (Cirrin, 2000): (1) the student's ability to uses language effectively in speaking and listening tasks, (2) the teacher's language, and (3) the language requirements of the lessons and textbooks. This type of assessment helps define a child's language skills and identify other traits that were interfering with interactions with other children. For example, a preschooler does not participate in some activities or sit with other children because he wants to keep his hands clean and not be brushed or bumped into by them. With the assistance of an occupational therapist, he becomes able to tolerate a larger variety of tactile sensations and in turn has more opportunity to practice his speech and language skills with other children.

Sometimes a student will need specialized speech or language assessment, as when the student is bilingual or multilingual. The speech-language pathologist must be particularly skilled when assessing the communicative capabilities of students for whom English is not the primary language. Fair, unbiased evaluation is difficult for a student who is bilingual (one who uses two languages equally well), who is **bidialectal** (one who uses two variations of a language), or for whom language dominance (the primary language of the student) is not easily determined. To assess such a student, it is not sufficient to simply translate test items into the child's primary language. The speech-language pathologist must determine whether a bilingual student should be tested in his or her first language or in English. Then, the speech-language pathologist tests the student in the dominant language with appropriate diagnostic tools to determine whether a language disorder or disability exists. By determining a student's language strengths and preferences, using an appropriate assessment tool, the speech-language pathologist learns about the student's communicative abilities and needs and then can plan appropriate therapies. When standardized measures are used, they must be culturally sensitive.

Students who are nonverbal or use nonconventional means of communication require more descriptive than standardized assessment measures. Their communicative forms (conventional and nonconventional) and the functions these forms serve are documented during observations across environments and communication partners. For example, John looks at a friend's snack, then at his friend. He repeats this several times. When the friend gives John some of his snack, John smiles. John used eye gaze, or looking, to request his friend's snack.

Determining the Nature and Extent of General and Special Education and Related Services

To determine the nature and extent of general and special education and related services needed for a student with a communication impairment, the evaluation team needs to take a holistic view of the student's communication skills, observing his communication throughout a whole day and using ecological assessments (Chapter 9) to assess his skills across environments.

How Do You Assure Progress in the General Curriculum?

Including Students

Most students with speech and language impairments spend the majority of their day in the general education classroom (see Figure 14–5). According to the U.S. Department of Education, 88 percent of the children who receive speech and language services spend 21 percent or less of their time outside of the general education classroom for these services. The trend toward receiving services within the general educational classroom and spending more of the school day in the general educational classroom has been increasing since 1984 (U.S. Department of Education, 2001). That is so, in part, because effective teachers use some of the tips that you will find in Box 14–4.

FIGURE 14–5

Educational placement of students with speech or language impairments (1998–1999)

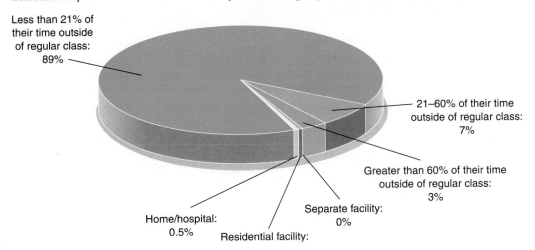

Less than 21% of
their time outside
of regular class:
89%

21–60% of their time
outside of regular class:
7%

Greater than 60% of their time
outside of regular class:
3%

Home/hospital:
0.5%

Separate facility:
0%

Residential facility:

Source: From U.S. Department of Education. (2001). *To assure the free appropriate public education of all children with disabilities: Twenty-first annual report to Congress on the implementation of the Individuals with Disabilities Education Act.* Washington, DC: Author.

Planning Universally Designed Learning

When planning universally designed learning for students with communication disorders, a teacher must answer two questions: How can I assure that my student understands what I am teaching, and how can I assure that my student can express what she knows?

Adapting Instruction

Students with communication disorders sometimes lack the language to express abstractions such as feelings, needs, or wants. You can, however, change classroom talk so that all of your students can be involved in classroom activities.

Try asking varied types of questions to encourage students' self-expression. You may want to ask real questions rather than those to which students already know the right response. For example, rather than asking, "What did we learn yesterday about the length of Christopher Columbus's voyage?" you might say, "Think of four things you learned yesterday about Christopher Columbus's voyage, and share them with a friend. Then we will write some of your favorites here on the board." Your approach allows students to generate many possible responses rather than one correct one. You also allow all students, including those with communication disorders, opportunities to experience success and take time to compose a message.

You also can help students by expanding their utterances, taking what a student has said verbally or with an AAC system and adding more information or creating a more complete phrase or sentence. For example, if a middle school student replies, "In there," when you ask where he left his homework assignment, you can expand his utterance by saying, "You said that you left the paper in the drawer. Great. That is where you were supposed to leave it." If the student is using an AAC device you can expand the utterance by using the device yourself. This provides the student with the expanded language as well as a model for more complex use of the device. Again, you are providing students with correct, more elaborate models, increasing the likelihood that they will produce more complete utterances themselves.

You also can augment or alter your classroom language by providing statements that explain a student's nonverbal behaviors. For example, if a student points to a cookie, you can respond by asking, "Oh, you want that cookie, don't you?" Your statement models for students what they might have said or wanted to say if they could have explained their wants and needs verbally. In future, they are more likely to interact verbally because you have provided them with models.

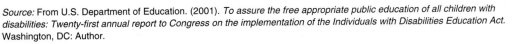 You learned about AAC devices in Chapter 12.

Inclusion Tips

Box 14-4

	What You Might See	What You Might Be Tempted to Do	Alternative Responses	Ways to Include Peers in the Process
Behavior	The student may have difficulty expressing her ideas in a large group.	Tell her to hurry up; the class is waiting. Do not allow her time to complete her idea, and move on to another student. Never call on her.	Provide a multiple-choice response option. Provide information in advance for preparation of rehearsed responses. Allow for small-group discussion and reporting.	Everyone in the group contributes. All students have alternate response options. All student contributions are recognized.
Social interactions	She may be alone during unstructured times.	Assume she is happy alone and let her be.	Demonstrate that you value her contributions. Provide a model and help her learn to interact with the students.	During unstructured periods, an adult (speech-language pathologist, paraprofessional, support staff, teacher, staff, member, etc.) helps facilitate interactions with indirect or naturalistic strategies.
Educational performance	She produces syntactically incomplete sentences verbally and in writing.	Constantly correct her with red pen or ignore her written difficulties. Assume the speech-language pathologist will remember the problem.	Provide visual and verbal models of complete sentences.	Allow for small-group interaction with assigned roles that rotate to every student.
Classroom attitudes	She may rely on the teacher as her sole support, expecting her to intercede with other students.	Tell her to go play with others. Assume the children will work it out on their own.	Teach all the students ways to interact and problem solve.	Provide opportunities for students to interact with one another independently.

You will want to respond positively to students' comments and utterances, showing them that their participation is valued and appreciated.

Students who have difficulty expressing themselves may need the opportunity to practice public verbalizations. For example, you could pose questions in advance so the student can practice her verbal response before answering in front of the class. Offering multiple-choice answers for questions may also be helpful.

FIGURE 14–6
Strategies for encouraging children's communicative development

- Talk about things that interest the child at least once a day.

- Follow the child's lead. Reply to the child's initiations and comments. Get excited with the child.

- Don't ask too many questions. If you must, use such questions as **how did/do, why,** and **what happened** that result in longer explanatory answers.

- Encourage the child to ask questions. Respond openly and honestly. If you don't want to answer a question, say so and explain why. ("I don't think I want to answer that question; it's very personal.")

- Use a pleasant tone of voice.

- Don't be judgmental or make fun of the child's language. If you are overly critical of the child's language or try to correct all errors, the child will stop talking to you.

- Allow enough time for the child to respond.

- Treat the child with courtesy by not interrupting when the child is talking.

- Include the child in discussions. Encourage participation and listen to the child's ideas.

- Be accepting of the child and the child's language. Hugs, acceptance, and compliments go a long way.

- Provide opportunities for the child to use language and to have that language help the child accomplish some goal.

Source: From *Language Disorders: A Functional Approach to Assessment and Intervention,* by R. E. Owens, Jr., 1991, Upper Saddle River, NJ: Merrill/Prentice Hall. Copyright 1991 by Merrill/Prentice Hall. Reprinted with permission.

Finally, remember that some students may need to use AAC systems to express thoughts and ideas. The systems may include sign language, gestures, facial expressions, line drawings, photographs, and/or voice output devices. Figure 14–6 provides you with further strategies for encouraging children's communication, and Box 14–5 explains AAC.

Augmenting Instruction

Some students with language impairments benefit from your repetition of the curriculum. For example, you can repeat what you have said or record yourself on an audiotape, allowing the student to listen to the information as many times as she needs. Try taping a story featured at preschoolers' group time and allowing the student to listen to the story repeatedly at home. Older students may find it helpful to tape lectures and review the tapes later at home.

Other students with language impairments benefit from the use of visual supports such as graphic organizers, photographs, line drawings, gestures, and/or sign language. Box 14–6 describes how graphic organizers help students organize information for writing, studying, or increased comprehension.

Some of your students will understand information better when you use photographs or line-drawn pictures. For example, if you ask your students to select a book from their reading level, read the book, draw a picture about the book, and then share the picture with a peer, consider using a photograph to illustrate each step of your direction. Point to the photo as you give your directions, and then post it where the whole class can see it. If you do not have a camera, use sign language or gestures together with verbal information.

Because some students with communication delays often experience poor or inappropriate social interactions (Asher & Gazelle, 1999; McLean & Snyder-McLean, 1999; Ostrosky, Drasgow, & Halle, 1999), they may require direct instruction in social skills. While assisting students with

The book *Map It Out: Visual Tools for Thinking, Organizing, and Communicating* and a website for Inspiration computer software provide more information about webbing and outlining. To learn more, go to the Resources and Web Links modules in Chapter 14 of the Companion Website.

Technology Tips

Box 14-5

Assistive Technology for Students with Communication Disorders

What Is the Technology?

Augmentative and alternative communication (AAC) systems are an integrated group of components that supplement the communication abilities of individuals who cannot meet their communication needs through gesturing, speaking, and/or writing. An AAC system may include an AAC device, which is a physical object that transmits or receives messages (e.g., communication books, communication/language boards, communication charts, or mechanical or electronic voice output equipment or computers).

An AAC device has two components: a symbol set and a means for selecting the symbols. A symbol is "a visual, auditory, and/or tactile representation of conventional concepts" (ASHA, 1991, p. 10). A symbol set could include gestures, photographs, manual sign sets/systems, pictographs (symbols that look like what they represent), ideographs (more abstract symbols), printed words, objects, partial objects, miniature objects, spoken words, braille, and/or textures.

What Do You Do with It?

Your students can use several means to select symbols on communication devices. A student can directly select his choices by looking at the desired symbol with his eyes, touching the symbol with his fingers, or moving a laser beam of light onto the symbol using a different part of his body (e.g., his head).

Another method of selection is scanning. Each symbol is presented or highlighted in small groups or one at a time in front of your student, who then signals when the desired symbol is presented or highlighted. The signal may consist of activating a switch, gesturing, changing her facial expression, vocalizing, and so on.

A third method for indicating symbol choice on an AAC device is encoding. Encoding involves giving multiple signals to indicate the location of the symbol or item to be selected. In this case, your student selects a numeral 1 and a numeral 3, for example, to indicate that she wants to communicate the 13th phrase of a list of 125 communication phrases.

Assistive technology is very important because it can offer individuals with communication impairments the opportunity and the capability to interact and converse with other people (Beukelman and Mirenda, 1998).

Putting These Strategies to Work for Progress in the General Curriculum

1. What are examples of ACC devices?
2. How do they assure progress in the general curriculum?

To answer these questions online and learn more about these strategies, go to the "Technology" module in Chapter 14 of the Companion Website.

To learn more about social stories, go to Chapter 14 of the Companion Website, find the Resources module, and look for Carol Gray's book.

 Refer to Chapter 10 for more information about social stories.

communication disorders to learn correct social skills, you can help all students learn to interact more appropriately by taking turns; paying attention to nonverbal communication such as frowns, smiles, and body language; and conversing socially rather than monopolizing a conversation (MacDonald & Rabidoux, 1997; Mirenda et al., 1998). Providing a social story explaining what will be happening the next day or during a particular event and your expectations for the student may also be helpful.

Collaborating to Meet Students' Needs.

Collaboration is critical when planning and providing services for individuals with communication disorders. Communication occurs throughout the day, so it is important that everyone who works with the student has a good understanding of how he best understands and/or expresses information. For instance, the lunchroom and recess staff may need to understand strategies to help a student initiate requests from others and take turns. Those staff members also could be an excellent resource for anecdotal information regarding progress toward the student's goals in a natural context with peers. Furthermore, collaboration may help lighten everyone's workload (Giangreco, 2000; Sandall & Schwartz, 2002).

Box 14—6

Into Practice

Graphic Organizer Modifications

Graphic organizers are tools that assist your students to comprehend and write more effectively (Cunningham & Allington, 1999). You must first determine which graphic organizer will best meet your desired curriculum outcome. For instance, you might choose a web design, a story map, a feature matrix, or data charts, to name a few.

Then consider how your students will participate. Some children find blank forms of the organizer beneficial. Others may indicate that writing or spelling is difficult, that decoding the words written on the organizer is difficult, or that restructuring opportunities are needed. Some students need to group information together and see the grouping to decide if the items go together or if they should be placed somewhere else.

You may need to adapt the organizers to allow all students access to them (Foley & Staples, 2000). You may need to provide concepts, facts, ideas, and/or events so the student can choose the information and then place it in the graphic organizer (Foley & Staples, 2000). Photographs, magazine pictures, commercial line drawings, written words, or any combination of visual symbols can represent the information to be placed in the organizer.

You should include information that both is and is not related to the concepts, facts, ideas, and/or events to assess your students' comprehension of the material (Foley & Staples, 2000). For example, if your goal in a second-grade classroom is to convey meaningful information in written form about science class, and the students' activity is to write what they have learned about frogs, then you could suggest that they first organize their thoughts using a web. You could provide a blank web with the main topic of frogs filled in for the students. You may then give photos or line drawings representing factual information about frogs learned in class. You may also include photos or line drawings representing information about other animals that are unrelated to the frogs. Your students then determine which information they should include in the web. They can place the pictures on the web and move them around as they determine if another grouping of information may work better. The students can then use the information to begin the writing process.

Putting These Strategies to Work for Progress in the General Curriculum:

1. What other adaptations could be made?

2. How can collaboration between the special and general education teachers help with the application of strategies?

3. How could materials be reused and organized to cut down on preparation time?

To answer these questions online and learn more about these strategies, go to the Into Practice module in Chapter 14 of the Companion Website.

What Can You Learn from Others Who Teach Students with Communication Disorders?

Learning for the Early Childhood Years: Jessamine Early Learning Village in Jessamine County, Kentucky

The Jessamine Early Learning Village is a unique learning environment for preschool and kindergarten children. It is a public school that serves all preschool and kindergarten children in Jessamine County. Six hundred children ages 3 through 6 are enrolled in the school. Some children have disabilities, some do not, and some are at risk of having them.

Assistive technology can be as simple and universal as a hand-held personal assistant, and even that device can be specially tailored for a designated user.

The staff consists of early childhood teachers, special education consultants, and related-services providers. There are three full-time and one half-time speech-language pathologists who provide services to all the children in the school, collaborating with teachers and other professionals in the classrooms. The speech-language pathologists collaborate with the teachers to plan the curriculum to accommodate students with communication disorders throughout the entire school day. For example, Shelley Nead, a speech-language pathologist, and her colleagues have begun an oral-motor program to help all students acquire appropriate movements and placements of the articulators for speech sound production. They believe that all children, including those with communication disorders, will benefit from the sensory-based experience with sounds. Shelley and her colleagues attribute the progress the children make in communication to the collaboration and the contextually based service delivery. Collaboration and inclusion are the keys to this successful program.

Learning for the Elementary Years: Quail Run Elementary School, Lawrence, Kansas

At Quail Run Elementary School, a school with 400 K–6 students, Nancy Averill, the speech-language pathologist, collaborates with general education teachers and resource teachers to develop strategies that are beneficial for all children in the classes. She provides most of her services in classrooms or during other school activities, such as recess or lunch, by facilitating social interactions and relationships. By integrating her intervention strategies into all classroom learning activities, Nancy helps her students participate in the general curriculum.

To find time for collaboration, Nancy, the grade-level teachers, and the resource teachers meet before the first day of each semester and after the early dismissal period on each Wednesday during the semester. When they meet, they review the school's monthly curriculum map, review students' progress, problem solve, and plan. Nancy regularly participates in language arts classes; she and the classroom teacher focus on phonemic awareness, spelling, vocabulary, and oral and written language. During math classes she works with small groups of students, emphasizing the vocabulary and language related to problem solving. Nancy also participates in science and social studies classes by working with small groups or individuals. The keys to the success of the collaboration and service delivery at Quail Run are the sharing of knowledge, the opportunity for collaboration time, and Nancy's responsive and flexible service delivery.

Learning for the Middle and Secondary Years: Collaborative Language Literacy Laboratory, Galvez Middle School, Galvez, Louisiana

Galvez Middle School is located in a rural parish in Louisiana. It is the home of 675 students in grades 5–8. The Language Literacy Laboratory was started in 2000 to replace the pullout model of delivery of speech-language services (Faucheux & Oetting, 2001) and to intervene in receptive and expressive language skills, math problem solving, reading comprehension, and written language skills.

The laboratory is a collaborative endeavor that supports and integrates with the general education curriculum through centers. The centers include a reading/visual center, a writing/manipulative center, a listening center, a computer center, and a role-play/game center. The focus of the laboratory is on skills needed in the classroom, and the content areas support the curriculum. You will read about how all these centers work together in Box 14–7.

The laboratory is directed by Susan Faucheux, the school's speech-language pathologist. She collaborates with three special education teachers, two teachers of students who are gifted and talented, a para-educator, and all of the general education teachers. Although the laboratory was initiated to serve students with communication disorders, it now serves approximately 45 students with communication disorders, 40 students at risk, and 30 students who are gifted and talented. The students who have been identified as gifted and talented assist in the laboratory. This program has documented changes in student grades, standardized test scores, promotion to high school, writing skills, and improved social skills (Faucheux & Oetting, 2001).

Collaboration Tips

Box 14–7

General-Use Laboratory

Collaboration is the key to a program such as the Language Literacy Laboratory at Galvez Middle School, says Susan Faucheux, the speech-language pathologist. The special education staff in the laboratory recognize collaboration as an ongoing process and have made sure that general education teachers recognize this as well. The special education staff attend general education grade-level meetings weekly. Their participation alerts them to what will be taught and how. The general education and special education teachers also share information through conferences, conversations, e-mails, mailboxes, workbaskets, and monitoring forms. The paraprofessionals and laboratory staff spend time in classrooms gathering information about the class, projects, tests, and papers so that the laboratory activities are relevant to the core curriculum content.

The Language Literacy Laboratory is a resource for all the students and teachers in the school rather than a special education program. Susan explains, "It is almost as if collaboration takes place on its own. It has become a normal event at our school." There is a sense of shared responsibility because the teachers and laboratory staff share knowledge and support each other's teaching practices and have the same goals for their students.

Putting Collaboration into the Context of Student Progress in the General Curriculum

1. Who are the collaborators?

2. What are the challenges?

3. What can the team do?

4. What are the results?

To answer these questions online and learn more about these strategies, go to the Collaboration Tips module in Chapter 14 of the Companion Website. You will also find a link to the circle of Inclusion website (http://www.circleofinclusion.org).

Learning for the Transitional and Postsecondary Years: Work and Community

A young adult who has completed his or her education typically will not require speech and/or language therapy. However, an individual with a communication disorder who has moderate mental retardation might require intervention on how to obtain and/or maintain a job or other basic life skills.

To benefit that person, the speech-language pathologist might role-play life skills such as interviewing, buying groceries, requesting items in a clothing store, or requesting services from a plumber. In the role play, the pathologist takes the role of the business person with whom the student is dealing. Often, the student enacts scenarios based on a job for which she is preparing (e.g., the student wishing to work as a child-care assistant might practice speaking with a parent). When individuals have the opportunity to practice new skills in therapy, they are more likely to use the communicative skills in real settings after they graduate.

If, however, role play alone is insufficient, therapy may occur in the natural setting such as the clothing or grocery store so that the individual with communication disorders can have positive experiences in that environment, increasing the likelihood for repeated success in that same environment with another individual.

A Vision for George's Future

Despite a tenuous beginning, George's future looks positive. Where will he be and what will he be doing when his education in the local school system is complete? His parents would like him to be in college. They would like him to have his own dreams and to achieve them. They want him to be self-determined. Perhaps he will pursue his interests in horses or computers. Professionals collaborating with George and his family expect him to successfully progress through the general education curriculum. Given his outgoing nature and good pragmatic skills, they expect him to have good friends and a wide social network. Communication will likely continue to be a focus for George's educational participation as the complexities of participation in the curriculum increase. Technology may become more important to George to compensate for his fine-motor and communication challenges. Assuming that collaboration and support continue as they have begun, George's future is full of possibilities.

What Do You Recommend?

1. To make sure that George's social and communicative needs are best met?
2. To ensure George's continued academic success?
3. To ensure that George has opportunities to pursue his interests?

Summary

How Do You Recognize Students with Communication Disorders?

▼ Communication disorders include both speech and language impairments.

▼ A speech disorder is an impairment of one's articulation of speech sounds, fluency, or voice.

▼ A language disorder reflects problems in receiving information; understanding it; and formulating a spoken, written, or symbolic response.

▼ Communication differences that are related to the culture of the individual are not considered impairments.

- Most speech disorders are articulation disorders. When mispronouncing, an individual may add, omit, substitute, or distort sounds.
- Voice impairments affect the quality of one's voice. Voice impairments may be noted in pitch, intensity, resonance, and vocal quality.
- Language is a shared system of rules and symbols for the exchange of information. It includes rules of phonology, morphology, syntax, semantics, and pragmatics.
- *Phonology* is the use of sounds to make meaningful words.
- *Morphology* governs the structure of words and the construction of word forms.
- *Syntax* provides rules for putting together a series of words to form sentences.
- *Semantics* refers to word meaning.
- *Pragmatics* refers to the social use of language.
- Five to 10 percent of the population has a communication disorder.
- Communication impairments can affect a student's academic, social, and emotional development.

How Do You Evaluate Students with Communication Disorders?

- The speech-language pathologist is the professional most likely to determine the presence and extent of a speech and/or language impairment.
- Assessments include the use of informal and formal measures. They should occur in settings comfortable and natural to the student.
- Analyses of an individual's conversation can provide information useful for determining a student's language development and use.

How Do You Assure Progress in the General Curriculum?

- Many students receive speech-language therapy while included in their general education classrooms, where they interact with their peers and teachers while improving their communication skills.
- The collaborative participation of students, their teachers, speech-language pathologists, and parents to enhance communicative development results in students' language objectives being targeted by these collaborators in many settings.
- Collaboration between the speech-language pathologist, general education classroom teacher, special education teacher, family, and the individual with a communication disorder is required so that the individual, no matter what age, will have opportunities to practice new skills with a variety of people in a variety of settings and situations.

What Can You Learn from Others Who Teach Students with Communication Disorders?

- Collaboration and inclusion are crucial to successful programs for students with communication disorders.
- Speech-language pathologists and teachers should collaborate to develop strategies that support the participation of all students, including those with communication disorders, in the general curriculum.
- Speech-language pathologists can provide services in many ways within a school, including working in the classroom with teachers.

Council for Exceptional Children   PRAXIS

To find out how and where this chapter content connects to the CEC Professional Standards and the Praxis™ Standards, go to the Standards Connection module in Chapter 14 of the Companion Website. A comprehensive matrix aligning CEC Professional Standards, Praxis™ Standards, and INTASC principles to the entire text, is available in the Appendix and on the Companion Website.

Chapter 15

Contributing writer
Barbara R. Schirmer, Miami University

Who Is Amala Brown?

Amala was 4 years old and had lived in an orphanage in India for less than a year when Robyn Brown adopted her and brought her back to live in Salem, Oregon. Before adopting Amala, Robyn had been a teacher of children who are deaf and a sign language interpreter for many years. That does not mean that life with Amala had no challenges. When she first came to Robyn's home, Amala would babble in what sounded like an Indian language and used just two gestures. She started preschool at Salem

Heights Elementary School, where Robyn teaches. Robyn's colleague, Eleni Boston, was Amala's first teacher. Many days Robyn could hear Amala in the room above her own. It took incredible self-control, and vast confidence in Eleni, for Robyn not to run upstairs to fix things.

During her elementary school years, Amala sometimes attended Salem Heights full time. At other times, she attended Oregon School for the Deaf for part of each day. After enrolling in middle school, however, she attended public school regularly, using a sign language interpreter and real-time captioning in general education classes, receiving services from a speech-language pathologist, and spending specific periods in the resource room with a teacher of the deaf for support with general curriculum subjects.

When Amala was in middle school, she tended to prefer friends who were deaf or hard of hearing. One reason for her reserve with hearing students was her personality; she is a naturally quiet and studious person. The other reason was the communication barrier. When asked about her friends today, Amala says that she has tons of friends. Some are hearing, and others are deaf or hard of hearing. She says that it is easy to make new friends who are deaf, but it is hard to make new friends who are hearing unless they know sign language. When asked how her friends would describe her, she says they would probably say that she is friendly, shy, soft-hearted, beautiful, honest, kind, and a hard worker.

As Amala moved through middle school and high school, she was challenged to keep pace with the general curriculum for two reasons: knowledge of concepts and proficiency in English. For Amala and other individuals who are deaf, incidental information is usually unavailable because they do not overhear the news on the television, other people's conversations (unless they are in sign language), and so on. Yet incidental information has a strong influence on a student's vocabulary and concept development. And despite her good English skills, Amala struggles to master English sentence structure in reading and writing.

One of Amala's strengths is her determination, particularly her desire to get a good education and start an independent life of her own. Independence is important to Amala, who has a text telephone (TT), a flashing alarm clock, a doorbell flasher, her own e-mail address, and even a barking dog to let her know that someone is at the door. She uses the telephone relay service to contact friends, the public library, and even to order pizza.

When she thinks about being deaf, Amala feels that everything is fine, although sometimes she would like to hear what hearing people are saying. She wants to tell other people who are deaf that it is okay to be deaf and that there is much more

opportunity for a person who is deaf than they may think. A person who is deaf can do everything that a hearing person can except hear.

Robyn wants future teachers to expect great outcomes from children and youth who are deaf or hard of hearing. Do not, Robyn warns, limit these students with a watered-down curriculum. Do provide them with daily opportunities to read and write. As a parent and a teacher of the deaf, Robyn wants future teachers to know that parents really do want a partnership with the schools. Also, she encourages teachers to see beyond school and into the child's life in college and the community. Finally, Robyn reminds teachers that children with a hearing loss are children first, with all of their own individuality, challenges, and blessings. Hearing loss is a piece of who they are, not the whole of their being. Amala wants to tell future teachers to be patient, set a goal, work on your weaknesses, and have courage.

What do you think?

1. How does Amala's hearing loss influence her educational and social opportunities?
2. What can Amala's teachers do to make certain that Amala has access to the concepts presented in the general education classes?
3. How can Amala's teachers and parent ensure that she has the opportunity to achieve her life goals?

To respond to these questions online, participate in other activities, and learn more about Amala Brown and hearing loss, go to the Cases module in Chapter 15 of the Companion Website.

How Do You Recognize Students with Hearing Loss?

Defining Hearing Loss

The Ear and Its Functions

To understand hearing loss, it is first essential to understand hearing. Hearing involves the gathering and interpreting of sounds. Each part of the ear serves a purpose in translating sound waves from the environment into meaningful information to the brain (Stach, 1998). As shown in Figure 15–1, the ear consists of three parts: the *outer*, the *middle*, and the *inner ear*. The middle ear links the air-filled outer ear with the fluid-filled inner ear.

Sound waves are vibrations in the air. Sound is measured in units that describe the *intensity* and *frequency* of these vibrations. Intensity refers to the pressure of a sound. An increase in sound wave pressure is perceived as an increase in loudness. The intensity of a sound is measure in *decibels* (dB), named in honor of Alexander Graham Bell. The decibel scale is based on ratios. Each 10 dB increment represents a tenfold increase in intensity. Therefore, a 20 dB sound is 100 times more intense than a sound at 10 dB, and so on.

Frequency refers to the number of vibrations that occur in one second. If a vibration makes 100 up-down movements in one second, its frequency is 100 cycles per second. An increase in the number of vibrations is perceived as a higher sound or a higher pitch. The frequency of a sound is measured in a unit called *hertz* (Hz). Pure tones consist of one frequency only. Speech and environmental sounds are complex tones and so encompass a range of frequencies. Figure 15–2 shows where everyday sounds occur. The frequency most important for hearing spoken language is generally considered to be 500–2,000 Hz.

Hearing is evaluated in terms of loudness and pitch. Results are charted on an **audiogram.** An audiogram charts pitch on the horizontal axis and loudness on the vertical axis. You can see in Figure 15–3 that the most commonly used terms to identify degree of hearing loss are *slight, mild,*

FIGURE 15–1
Diagram of ear

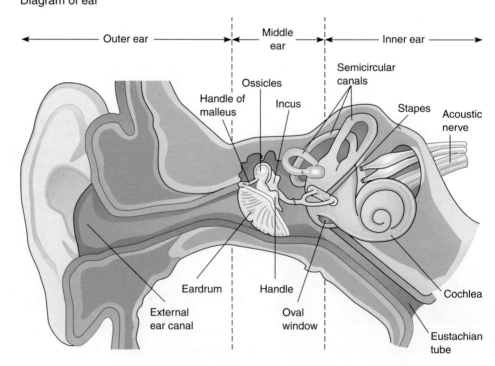

FIGURE 15–2

Frequency spectrum of familiar sounds

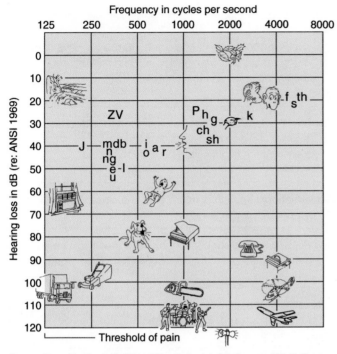

Frequency in cycles per second

Source: From *Hearing in Children* (5th ed.), by J. L. Northern and M. P. Downs, 2002, Philadelphia, Lippincott. Copyright 2002 by Lippincott Williams & Wilkins. Reprinted with permission.

moderate, moderate-severe, severe, and *profound.* When you look at Amala's audiogram (Figure 15–4), you see that she has a severe hearing loss at the very lowest frequency in her left ear and a profound loss at most of the frequencies in both of her ears.

Terminology

There is no consensus about how to refer to people who are deaf or hard of hearing. Some prefer the disability-first approach ("deaf person"); others prefer the people-first approach ("person who is deaf"). However, "person with hearing loss" is used infrequently because of the implication that the individual has suffered a *loss.* The term *Deaf* with an upper-case *D* refers to culturally Deaf people (Schirmer, 2001). By capitalizing Deaf, we recognize the social and cultural experiences of being deaf in a society in which the majority of individuals are hearing. Deafness is seen as a linguistic and ethnic minority culture.

In this book, we adopt a people-first approach. We also use the terms *deaf* and *hard of hearing* as they are used in the Council for Exceptional Children's (2002) performance-based standards for the preparation and licensure of special educators. We do not use the term *hearing impaired* because *impaired* implies a deficiency or pathology and carries a strong negative connotation. You will also notice that we use the terms *teacher of the deaf, school for the deaf, deaf education, Deaf culture,* and *Deaf community* because educators and individuals who are deaf consider these terms to be entirely appropriate and not stigmatizing.

Describing the Characteristics

Language and Communication

Learning language is the single greatest challenge for children who are deaf or hard of hearing. Unlike other children, children who are deaf acquire language largely through their eyes. This

The National Association of the Deaf represents deaf and hard of hearing Americans in areas including education, employment, health care, social services, and telecommunications. To learn more about the National Association of the Deaf, go to the Web Links module in Chapter 15 of the Companion Website.

FIGURE 15–3
Degrees of hearing loss

	125	250	500	1,000	2,000	4,000	8,000
0 10	(0–15 dB) *Normal*—There is no impact on communication.						
20	(16–25 dB) *Slight*—In noisy environments, faint speech is difficult to understand.						
30	(26–40 dB) *Mild*—Faint or distant speech is difficult to hear, even in quiet environments. Classroom discussions are challenging to follow.						
40 50	(41–55 dB) *Moderate*—Conversational speech is heard only at a close distance. Group activities in a classroom present a challenge.						
60	(56–70 dB) *Moderate-severe*—Only loud, clear conversational speech can be heard, and group situations present great difficulty. Speech is intelligible, though noticeably impaired.						
70 80	(71–90 dB) *Severe*—Conversational speech cannot be heard unless it is loud, even then, many words cannot be recognized. Environmental sounds can be detected, though not always identified. Speech is not always intelligible.						
90 100 110 120	(91+ dB) *Profound*—Conversational speech cannot be heard. Some loud environmental sounds may be heard. Speech is difficult to understand or may not be developed at all.						

is because the auditory information that they might be able to receive is incomplete and often distorted.

Individuals who are deaf or hard of hearing typically communicate in one of three ways: oral/aural, American Sign Language, or simultaneous communication.

Oral/Aural. Oral/aural communication is communication in spoken English through the use of speech, speech reading, residual hearing, and amplification of sound.

American Sign Language. American Sign Language (ASL) is a visual-gestural language (requiring the use of eyes and hands). ASL has a rule structure that is distinct from other languages, including English. In ASL, the shape, location, orientation, and movement of a signer's hands; the intensity of the signer's motions; the signer's facial expression; and the signer's body movement all communicate meaning. Because of the different rule structures for each language, it is not possible to sign ASL and speak English at the same time. ASL is considered to be the sign language of the Deaf community in the United States and Canada.

Finger spelling is generally used for spelling words and proper names that have no known sign. When finger spelling, the signer uses the manual alphabet to spell words letter by letter. A chart of the manual alphabet is shown in Figure 15–5.

Simultaneous Communication. **Simultaneous communication** involves the use of sign language (usually a manually coded English system or signs from ASL used in English word order), finger spelling, speech, speech reading, residual hearing, and amplification of sound. **Manually coded English** is a sign system that represents English through a visual-gestural modality and was

Postlingual Causes

A hearing loss that occurs after the child has developed spoken language is a *postlingual* **hearing loss.** Only 5 percent of children who are deaf or hard of hearing have postlingual hearing losses. The distinction between prelingual and postlingual is important educationally because the child with a postlingual hearing loss has an English language base for learning and communicating.

The most common causes of postlingual hearing losses are meningitis and otitis media. Other causes include side effects from medications, high fever, mumps, measles, infection, and trauma after birth. Unknown causes account for about 60 percent of children with postlingual hearing loss (Center for Assessment and Demographic Studies, 1998).

Meningitis. Meningitis is a bacterial or viral infection of the central nervous system that may extend to other organs, including the brain and the ear. Children whose deafness is caused by meningitis generally have profound hearing losses, and many of them exhibit difficulties in balance as well as other disabilities.

Otitis Media. Otitis media is an inflammation of the middle ear. It is the most common reason for visits to the doctor for children under age 6. Approximately 90 percent of children have at least one episode of otitis media by age 2, and approximately one-third of children under age 5 experience recurrent episodes (Bluestone & Klein, 2001; Schoem, 1997). Delays in speech or language development may result from inconsistent auditory input because of the ear infections and fluid in the middle ear. Medical treatment, including both antibiotics and surgical placement of tubes in the ear, is commonly indicated. If left untreated, otitis media can result in a buildup of fluid and a ruptured eardrum as well as other conditions that can cause permanent conductive hearing loss. Vaccinations against several of the most common types of pneumococcal bacteria causing otitis media have been developed.

Table 15–1 shows the changes in causes of hearing loss since 1982. As you can see, most causes are unknown. Robyn Brown, for example, does not know what caused Amala's hearing loss. In Box 15–1, Barbara Schirmer describes how her grandmother became deaf and the impact it had on her family.

Identifying the Prevalence

Approximately 22 million persons in the United States, or 8.6 percent of the population, have a hearing loss (National Center for Health Statistics, 2002). It is estimated that 1.3 percent of children under the age of 18 are deaf or hard of hearing, so hearing loss among children is a low-incidence disability.

Approximately 1.1 percent of all school-age children, ages 6 to 21, who received special education services during the 1996–1997 school year were served under the disability category of hearing impairment (National Center for Education Statistics, 2002). The prevalence of hearing loss is undoubtedly higher, given that some deaf and hard of hearing children are counted under one of the other disability categories. Approximately 22 percent of students who are deaf or hard of hearing have one additional disability, and 8 percent have two or more other disabilities (Gallaudet Research Institute, 2002).

The Gallaudet Research Institute gathers and analyzes data concerning the demographic and academic characteristics of deaf and hard of hearing populations, primarily to provide information needed by educators in the field. To learn more about the institute, go to the Web Links module in Chapter 15 of the Companion Website.

How Do You Evaluate Students with Hearing Loss?

Determining the Presence

The earlier a hearing loss is identified, the more quickly an educational program can be planned and carried out. Although the technology is available for identifying hearing loss virtually at birth, many go undetected during infancy. One reason is that a child's response to movement and

TABLE 15–1
Causes of hearing loss: Changes since 1982

Cause of Hearing Loss	1982–1983	1987–1988	1992–1993	2000–2001
Pregnancy Related				
Cytomegalovirus	NA	337	638	762
Heredity	6,390	6,063	6,324	8,380
Maternal rubella	9,001	2,438	992	365
Pregnancy complications	1,854	1,367	1,137	1,653
Prematurity	2,225	2,244	2,238	1,848
Rh incompatibility	792	2,74	179	125
Trauma at birth	1,350	1,151	1,176	559
Maternal substance abuse	NA	NA	NA	267
Medication taken by mother	NA	NA	NA	106
Postnatal disease or injury				
Meningitis	4,033	4,156	3,934	2,165
Otitis media	1,667	1,613	1,782	2,307
Medications taken by child	NA	NA	NA	549
Measles	419	174	132	NA
Mumps	126	48	22	NA
Infection	1,467	1,179	1,062	757
High fever	1,734	1,364	1,127	NA
Trauma after birth	438	317	340	371
Cytomegalovirus	NA	337	638	762
Other postnatal cause	NA	NA	NA	1,302
Cannot be determined	NA	NA	NA	21,106

*Measles and mumps were grouped with Infections in the 2000–2001 survey due to the small number reported.

Sources: 1982–83, 1987–88, and 1992–93 Annual Survey of Deaf and Hard of Hearing Impaired Children and Youth, Center for Assessment and Demographic Studies, Gallaudet Research Institute, Gallaudet University; *2000–2001 Regional and National Summary Report of Data from the 2000–2001 Annual Survey of Deaf and Hard of Hearing Children and Youth,* Gallaudet Research Institute.

The John Tracy Clinic provides parent-centered services to young children with a hearing loss and services to aid the professional community in understanding how to work with deaf children. To learn more about the John Tracy Clinic, go to the Web Links module in Chapter 15 of the Companion Website.

vibration may be mistaken for response to sound. A second reason is the lag time between parents' first suspicions of a hearing loss and diagnosis through testing as well as the lag time between diagnosis and educational intervention. Meadow-Orlans and colleagues (1997) found that, on average, parents suspect their children have a hearing loss at approximately 17 months, diagnosis is confirmed about five months later, and children wait an average of 10 months to begin speech and auditory development and 11 months to begin sign language instruction.

Infants can be assessed in two ways, and both types of assessments are screening procedures (Diefendorf, 1999). In a diagnostic auditory brain stem response test, the evaluator places sensors on the baby's head and in the ear, causes computer clicks to be sounded, and monitors the baby's response. In the otoacoustic immittance test, the evaluator places a microphone in the baby's ear canal and then measures the sounds that the hair cells in the cochlea make when they vibrate in response to external sounds.

As shown in Figure 15–6, infant hearing screening usually occurs at least twice during the first six months. Thereafter, the infant undergoes a behavioral audiological evaluation. This type of evaluation is also used for children who have not been screened as infants but whose parents suspect a hearing loss because the child is not responding to sounds, or is not babbling, talking, understanding others, engaging in vocal play, or singing.

Box 15—1

Barbara Schirmer: My Grandmother's Story

My grandmother, Frieda Steckler, became deaf in 1899. She had just come home from her first day of school in Galicia, Poland. Feeling sick, angry at her mother for working in the dry goods store, and wanting to stay away from the housekeeper, whom she disliked, she hid in a barrel. She could hear the rain pouring down. How long she was in the barrel, she doesn't know. Someone finally found her there, but by then she was burning up with fever. No one ever diagnosed the illness, but perhaps it was scarlet fever. When she recovered, however, her ability to hear was gone. Everyone said that the fever had burned out her hearing.

Frieda was just 6 years old. There were no schools in Galicia for a little deaf girl. But her grandfather, a rabbi, patiently taught her to read other people's lips when they talked Polish or Yiddish, the two languages Frieda knew before she became deaf. He taught her to read and write in Yiddish and to do arithmetic.

When Frieda was 14, her family moved to the United States. Her mother and father, Rose and Abraham, knew that it would be a challenge to get Frieda through customs on Ellis Island. If the U.S. officials found out that Frieda was deaf, her parents were sure that she would be sent back to Poland. They made arrangements with one of her aunts to take her in if the worst happened. But the official who interviewed Frieda at Ellis Island never knew she was deaf. He asked her a few questions in Polish; she watched his lips intently and responded appropriately.

But even after the family had settled in the United States, her parents worried that someone would report her to the authorities. They believed they were safe enough in the Jewish community of New York, where they lived. But if they sent her to school, someone might report her to the government. So Frieda never went to school. Her father taught her to sew and got her a job in a shirt factory making Gibson blouses. A few years later, she married Morris Schiller; and they had three sons and one daughter, Bella, my mother.

I spent a lot of time with my grandmother. Sometimes she babysat me. And for several years, my family lived with her and my grandfather. Even as a child, I knew that she was often angry at the world. I didn't know why but later realized that deafness wasn't her disability; it was her lack of education. And she knew it. She was so intelligent yet so limited. She never learned to read and write in English and never became a citizen of the United States. In the early years in New York, everyone in her community spoke Yiddish. But eventually hardly anyone outside of her family did. She was isolated and lonely.

In the year that I began my studies in deaf education at the University of Pittsburgh, my grandmother died. Surprisingly, I am the only one in my extended family who became a teacher of the deaf because many professionals in the field have deaf family members.

A few years ago, I was at a family gathering, and one of my cousins and I started talking about our grandmother. Robert told me that even though he didn't speak Yiddish, he and Grandma had some kind of special language that he's never been able to explain to anyone else. I did, too, I told him. And I had thought it was unique to my relationship with her. So although she had told my mother how sad it was for her that none of her grandchildren had learned Yiddish, we had each developed a special way to communicate with her.

My own teaching of deaf children and future teachers has been guided by the conviction that all children who are deaf are entitled to an education that enables them to communicate with the broader community, to integrate within society to whatever extent they wish, and to compete successfully in the work place.

A *behavioral audiological evaluation* is carried out by an **audiologist,** who is a professional trained to evaluate hearing, select and fit hearing aids, and evaluate assistive listening devices. These evaluations are called behavioral because the audiologist is drawing conclusions based on the child's behaviors during the testing situation. The audiologist uses an *audiometer,* which is an electronic device designed to generate pure tones at different levels of intensity and frequency. To the child, the sounds appear to range from very low to very high, very soft to loud.

The older child raises a finger each time a sound is heard and lowers it when the sound is no longer heard. Alternative assessments are available for young children and some older children with severe disabilities. Children younger than 6 months of age may suck more vigorously, blink, turn their head, or stop playing when they hear a sound. Children younger than age 3 can be trained to turn their head to a sound stimulus paired with a lighted toy. Children older than 2½ can be taught to perform a simple, distinct activity such as putting a peg in a board, putting a block into a cup, or picking up a toy when hearing a sound.

The audiologist presents sounds at levels of intensity from 0 to no higher than 120 dB and at frequencies from 125 to 8,000 Hz to determine the child's hearing threshold. A *threshold* is the

FIGURE 15–6
Infant hearing screening

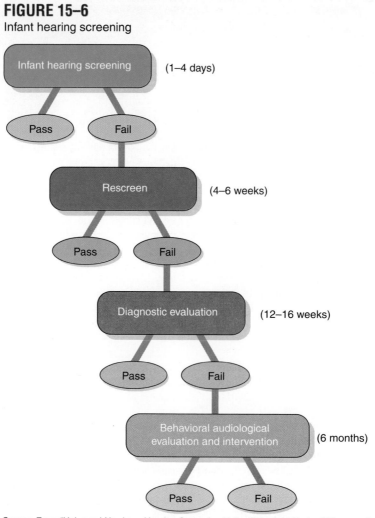

Source: From "Universal Newborn Hearing Screening Using Transient Evoked Otoacoustic Emissions: Results of the Rhode Island Hearing Assessment Project," by K. R. White, B. R. Vohr, and T. R. Behrens, 1993. *Seminars in Hearing, 14*(1), pp. 18–29. Copyright 1993 by Thieme Medical Publishers. Reprinted with permission.

level of sound so soft that it can be detected 50 percent of the time. The audiologist plots the child's threshold on an audiogram. Figure 15–4 shows Amala's most recent audiogram. Frequency is on the horizontal axis, and intensity is on the vertical axis. Often, audiologists use an X to represent the left ear and an O to represent the right ear. As you can see, in her left ear (her better ear), Amala cannot detect a sound at 500 Hz, which is a relatively low sound, until it is 85 dB loud, or as loud as barking dog. In contrast, a child with normal hearing would detect this same sound at a level between 0 and 10 dB. Amala also cannot detect a sound at 4,000 Hz, which is a relatively high sound, until it is 120 dB, or as loud as an airplane.

Hearing Aids

A **hearing aid** makes sounds louder but does not correct a hearing loss in the way that eye glasses or contacts correct a vision problem. A hearing aid is powered by a battery and operates by picking up sound, magnifying its energy, and delivering this amplified sound to the child's ear. It has a control switch to adjust volume and tone, and some aids have a digital programming feature that allows the user to adjust to different listening situations.

Audiologists retest the hearing of children with suspected or known hearing loss four times a year until age 3, twice a year until age 6, and annually after 6 years of age.

Cochlear Implants

A **cochlear implant** is an electronic device that compensates for the damaged or absent hair cells in the cochlea by stimulating the auditory nerve fibers. Unlike a hearing aid, a cochlear implant does not make sounds louder. Rather, it provides sound information by directly stimulating the functional auditory nerve fibers in the cochlea.

A cochlear implant has internal and external parts. The internal part is surgically implanted under the skin with electrodes inserted into the cochlea. The external part, worn like a hearing aid, consists of a microphone, a speech processor, and a transmitting coil.

Not every person with a hearing loss is a candidate for a cochlear implant, and the surgery carries risks. Cochlear implants have been particularly controversial for children because of the surgical risks, the potential discomfort, and the belief by many individuals in the Deaf community that deafness is not a disorder or disease that should be cured. Nonetheless, many individuals have benefited greatly from the implants.

Assistive Listening Devices

Hearing aids provide maximum benefit when the environment is relatively quiet, the acoustics are good, and the child is close to the speaker. In noisy environments, such as many classrooms, hearing aids do not work very well. Assistive listening devices can solve problems created by noise and distance.

Assistive listening devices that use FM radio frequencies are often referred to as FM systems. In educational programs, the teacher wears a wireless microphone, which enables both the teacher and the child to move about freely. In an FM system, the individual hearing aid will pick up sound only from the microphone, so activities such as group discussions can be cumbersome to carry out because the microphone must be passed from teacher to child or child to child.

Figure 15–7 illustrates the process for determining the presence of a hearing loss.

The assessment process for determining the presence of a hearing loss follows the procedure of nondiscriminatory evaluation that you learned about in Chapter 2.

FIGURE 15-7

Assessment process for determining the presence of a hearing loss

Nondiscriminatory Evaluation

Observation

Parents observe	In the early months, the behavior of deaf and hearing babies is similar. Parents may notice if the child does not respond to sound, babble, or engage in vocal play.
Physician observes	The baby does not show a startle reflex to loud noises. As the child matures, speech and language are delayed.
Teacher observes	If the child has not been identified before starting school, the teacher may observe communication misunderstandings, speech difficulties, and inattention.

Medical screening

Assessment measures	Findings that indicate need for further evaluation
Newborn screening	Most states require newborns to be screened for hearing loss.
Auditory brain stem response	Results may show inadequate or slow response to sounds.
Transient evoked otoacoustic immittance	Results may show that measurement of sound in the ear is lower than normal.
Behavioral audiological evaluation	The audiologist finds hearing thresholds higher than 15 dB.

Prereferral

Prereferral is typically not used with these students because of the need to identify hearing loss quickly .

Referral

Students who are deaf and hard of hearing and their families should receive early intervention as soon as the children are diagnosed. Children receive nondiscriminatory evaluation procedures as soon as they enter school. Some students with mild hearing loss may be referred.

Nondiscriminatory evaluation procedures and standards

Assessment measures	Findings
Audiological reassessment	Recent audiograms may indicate that the student's hearing loss has stabilized or is worsening. Testing for hearing aid function is a regular need.
Individualized intelligence test	The student's scores show a discrepancy between verbal and nonverbal measures. Nonverbal tests are considered the only reliable and valid measures of intelligence for this population.
Individualized achievement test	The student may score significantly lower than peers.
Speech and language evaluation	The student may have significant problems with receptive and expressive language. The student's speech is usually affected.
Adaptive behavior	The student may score below average in communication and possibly in other areas of adaptive behavior.
Anecdotal records	The student's records may indicate difficulty with reading, writing, or language arts.
Curriculum-based assessment	The student may be performing below peers in one or more areas of the curriculum because of reading and/or language difficulties.
Direct observation	The speech of students who are hard of hearing may be difficult to understand, and the student may misunderstand others.

Nondiscriminatory evaluation team determines that the student has a hearing loss and needs special education and related services.

Appropriate Education

Determining the Nature and Extent of General and Special Education and Related Services

The evaluation team must consider six major factors in determining the nature and extent of special education services for children who are deaf or hard of hearing. The first, communication, includes evaluation of the child's hearing loss (unaided, aided, and speech perception), spoken or sign language development, speech intelligibility, speech reading ability, and signing proficiency. The second is academic achievement as indicated by classroom performance and standardized tests. The other four factors are socialization, motivation, parent expectations and preference, and presence of any additional disability.

How Do You Assure Progress in the General Curriculum?

Including Students

Since the passage of the first version of IDEA in 1975, deaf education has stood somewhat apart from other areas of special education in terms of integration into the general curriculum. Whereas many educators, students, families, and advocates typically embraced the integration of all other children with disabilities in educational settings, professionals in the field deafness, parents of children who are deaf, and adults who are deaf held to the belief that the integration of children who are deaf with those who are hearing could not be assumed to be the best educational model. It should be noted, however, that inclusion has always been seen as most appropriate for students who are hard of hearing (as contrasted to those who are deaf). Box 15–2 provides suggestions for promoting the successful inclusion of students with hearing loss.

As you can see in Figure 15–8, 84 percent of students who are deaf or hard of hearing are being served in the public schools. Among those, almost half spend less than 21 percent of the time outside of the general education classroom.

FIGURE 15–8

Educational placement of students with hearing loss (1999–2000)

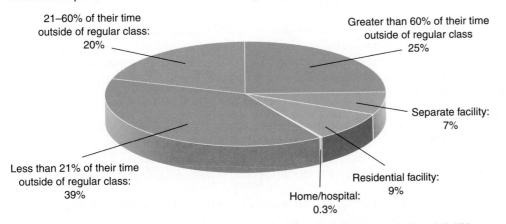

Source: From U.S. Department of Education. (2001). *To assure the free appropriate public education of all children with disabilities: twenty-third annual report to Congress on the implementation of the Individuals with Disabilities Education Act.* Washington, DC: Author.

Inclusion Tips

Box 15–2

	What You Might See	What You Might Be Tempted to Do	Alternate Responses	Ways to Include Peers in the Process
Behavior	The student might not participate in cooperative learning activities.	Tell him in front of the rest of the class to participate appropriately.	Be sure he understands the activity.	A buddy system may foster greater participation.
Social interactions	His speech may be difficult to understand, the other students may not know how to sign, and this may limit his ability to interact during small group discussions.	Randomly assign him to a group; assume the group will work out roles and participation.	Discuss the situation with the teacher of the deaf and the interpreter. The teacher of the deaf can work on making sure he is prepared for small-group discussions. The interpreter can encourage the other students follow the teacher's rules for turn taking.	Arrange instruction for peers to learn more sign language.
Educational performance	He may miss some things other students say and appear not to understand.	Tell him to ask his interpreter.	Ensure that the other students face him when they are talking. If the vocabulary in the cooperative learning activity is unfamiliar, provide a study guide.	Check the notes taken by the student note taker to be sure they are adequate. Arrange for peer tutoring of unfamiliar vocabulary.
Classroom attitudes	He may appear bored or inattentive because of not hearing all that is said or not watching the interpreter.	Discipline him for inattentiveness.	Be sure his hearing aids are working and that interpreting needs are being met during cooperative learning activities.	Group him with peers who are helpful and caring.

Planning Universally Designed Learning

Three characteristics of students who are deaf or hard of hearing that frequently create barriers to their progress in the general curriculum are their difficulty in acquiring English language skills, their difficulty in becoming proficient readers and writers, and the dual linguistic and cultural heritage for those who learn ASL and are members of both the Deaf community and the cultural community of hearing parents.

Altering Curriculum

Later in this chapter, you will learn about using conversation as an instructional strategy.

As you learned previously in the chapter, children who are deaf or hard of hearing typically communicate in one of three ways: oral/aural, ASL, or simultaneous communication. These three communication modes are used differentially to enable the child to learn either English or English and ASL.

Oral/Aural.   Oral/aural methods include instruction in spoken English; a curriculum in speech and aural habilitation; and the expectation that students will use speech, speech reading, and auditory skills for communication. Not all students benefit from speech instruction; indeed, as many students become older, their motivation for speech intervention often declines. The child's

Active engagement in reading is a crucial learning activity for children who are deaf or hard of hearing.

ability to read others' speech, sometimes called *lip reading* but more recently called **speech reading,** can be enhanced through training. However, since not all sounds are overtly formed on the lips, the child must fill in a substantial amount of missing information. The better the child's language, the better the chances of filling in syntactically and semantically correct information.

Speech-language pathologists are typically responsible for carrying out instruction in speech and aural habilitation. Because children who are deaf or hard of hearing do not hear speech or do not hear it without distortion, they can neither figure out how to produce speech nor monitor their own speech without assistance. They have difficulty producing individual speech sounds and problems with volume, pitch, and nasality. The speech-language pathologist helps them develop breath control, vocalization, voice patterns, and sound production.

It is useful for most students to use even their minimal residual hearing effectively. The speech-language pathologist works on simple awareness of sound, localization of sound, discrimination of sound differences, recognition of the sound, and, ultimately, comprehension of the speech being used by others.

Cued speech is a method of supplementing oral communication. Developed by Cornett (1967), cued speech employs a set of hand cues to distinguish between patterns of speech seen on the lips of the speaker. Cued speech has never been widely used in educational programs in the United States, although many parents strongly advocate its use (Calvert, 1986).

Bilingual/Bicultural.   Bilingual/bicultural methods include instruction in ASL, the expectation that the students will use ASL for communication, and the teaching of English through the written form with no or little use of spoken English. Most bilingual/bicultural programs in deaf education are based on English as a second language (ESL) models. ASL is introduced as the child's first language, and English is taught as the second language. Box 15–3 describes reasons for the development of bilingual/bicultural programs for students who are deaf.

Total Communication.   Total communication methods include instruction in simultaneous communication. The expectation is that students will use simultaneous communication for their academic and social discourse. Total communication methods also incorporate curriculum in speech and aural habilitation, and they sometimes include curriculum in ASL.

Total communication is an approach that has gone somewhat out of favor. One reason is that using every communication technique and mode available is unrealistic. Teachers typically emphasize speech and audition at the expense of sign language, or vice versa. And students attend more to one mode than to the other.

The Laurent Clerc National Deaf Education Center, Info to Go, provides information on topics dealing with deafness, hearing loss, and services and programs related to ages birth to 21. To learn more about the center, go to the Web Links module in Chapter 15 of the Companion Website.

Box 15—3

Multicultural Considerations

Bilingual/Bicultural Educational Programs

The interest in and advocacy for bilingual/bicultural programs grew dramatically during the 1990s. These programs emphasize the attainment of two languages, ASL and English, and two cultures, Deaf culture and hearing culture (that is, the culture of hearing parents).

There are several reasons why the ESL models that have been developed for children learning spoken languages have not been easily adapted to children learning one visual-gestural language and one spoken language. One reason is that ASL has no written form, and a written form of both languages appears to facilitate language acquisition of both languages. A second reason is that, except for children with parents who are deaf, children who are deaf are not likely to learn ASL as a first language from their parents, the individuals from whom almost all children learn their first language. Indeed, their parents

are often struggling to learn ASL themselves. A third reason is that some bilingual/bicultural programs introduce English through its written form only, and currently no research indicates that children who are deaf or hard of hearing can become proficient in English if exposed to only its written form.

Putting These Ideas to Work for Progress in the General Curriculum

1. What is the general education teacher's role in a bilingual/bicultural educational program?

2. How can hearing teachers help students who are deaf to learn ASL and English?

To answer these questions online and learn more about these ideas and concepts, go to the "Multicultural Considerations" module in Chapter 15 of the companion website.

A second reason is that total communication uses speech and sign language simultaneously; as you have already learned, it is not possible to speak and use ASL at the same time. Therefore, teachers use either manually coded English or pidgin sign language.

Many educators and members of the Deaf community are vociferous opponents of manually coded English sign systems because they believe that these systems are not languages at all but distortions of features of ASL. Researchers have found that most teachers using total communication methods actually use pidgin sign language, which is essentially an incomplete version of ASL and an incomplete version of English, providing none of the grammatical complexity of either language (Coryell & Holcomb, 1997; Hyde, Power, & Cliffe, 1992; Mayer & Lowenbraun, 1990; Woodward & Allen, 1993).

Augmenting Instruction

One way to augment instruction for children who are deaf or hard of hearing is through instructional conversations. Teachers use instructional conversations to enable students with hearing loss to develop language and literacy abilities and to employ their speech and residual hearing, when appropriate. In instructional conversations, the teacher uses conversational discourse during instruction rather than the question-answer routines that are more typical of classroom discourse. During question-answer routines, the teacher controls the dialogue, the child who is called on gives a brief answer, and the teacher's next question does not necessarily follow logically from the child's answer. The teacher controls the choice of topic, takes longer turns, monitors who takes turns and how long their turns are, and determines when the topic should be changed or terminated (Cazden, 1988; Stephens, 1988).

In instructional conversations, the teacher focuses on concepts and academic content while simultaneously addressing language goals through restating, clarifying, and extending what the child has expressed (Perez, 1996; Schirmer, 2000). These recastings of the child's language draw the child's attention to specific language features in ways similar to the conversational contexts of parent–child interaction that have been found to be the most conducive milieu for language

Why is conversation considered to be the ideal milieu for the language development of children who are deaf or hard of hearing?

development (Garton & Pratt, 1998; Snow, 1986). Instructional conversations parallel this ideal language-learning milieu of conversation.

The child who uses ASL will engage in a conversation in sign language with the teacher of the deaf or the sign language interpreter who is interpreting for the general education teacher. Box 15–4 illustrates an instructional conversation.

Augmenting Curriculum

Learning about **Deaf culture** is an important curricular goal for all students who are deaf or hard of hearing, regardless of educational setting, although many educators and members of the Deaf community argue that it is even more important in public school programs because children in these settings typically have relatively little contact with adults who are deaf or hard of hearing.

There are two goals of instruction about Deaf culture. The first is to help students develop an understanding of the culture of the Deaf community so they can participate with the community to whatever extent they wish. The second is to transmit the culture to the next generation of individuals who are deaf or hard of hearing.

Teaching strategies address the six components that form the nucleus of instruction about the Deaf community: (1) ASL; (2) political activism; (3) history and biography; (4) folklore; (5) clubs and organizations; and (6) theater, art, and literature. When teaching about ASL, teachers show the linguistic differences between ASL and English, explain how ASL developed as a language of the Deaf community, and engage students in conversation to demonstrate the conversational rules in ASL. In teaching about political movements and advocacy activities, teachers ask students to view captioned videos, read historical information, and discuss why and how movements get started and gain momentum. Students learn the history of the Deaf community through historical texts, biographies of individuals who made important contributions to society, and the personal accounts of guest presenters who are Deaf. Teachers bring students who are Deaf or hard of hearing to club functions and other activities that draw members of the Deaf community together. In class, students and teachers carry out some of the rituals and celebrations that teach about the values, behaviors, arts, customs, institutions, social forms, and knowledge that are characteristic of the Deaf community. Box 15–5 highlights several historically famous individuals who are (or were) deaf.

The National Theatre of the Deaf is a professional acting company made up of actors who are deaf and actors who are hearing. Together, they perform in a combination of sign language and spoken words. To learn more about the National Theatre of the Deaf, go to the Web Links module in Chapter 15 of the Companion Website.

Box 15–4

Into Practice

Conversational Scenarios

Conversational scenarios are one kind of instructional conversation. Originally developed by Stone (1988), the scenarios each include five essential elements:

1. The situation and topic are familiar to the student.
2. The teacher makes sure that the student understands the situation before beginning.
3. As the dialogue proceeds, there is a conversational need for the targeted language skill to arise.
4. The teacher does not tell the child what to say; rather, the situation and conversation bring about a need for use of the targeted skill.
5. The situation and conversation are carried to a logical conclusion.

Scenarios begin with the teacher setting the stage. The following is a scenario for a child who is learning how to initiate a conversation.

Teacher: Alison, let's pretend that you went to see a Cincinnati Reds game on Saturday. On Monday, you come to school and tell your friend, Jitendra, about it.

The teacher and child then role-play the scenario. But what happens when the child makes a mistake? The teacher intervenes only when the mistake relates to the specific skill targeted for the scenario. Errors involving other language skills can be noted by the teacher for future scenarios. But when the mistake is pertinent to the scenarios' objective, the teacher intervenes using one of four intervention strategies: teacher clarification, requesting clarification, role switching, and prompting. The language skill for the current scenario is "initiating a conversation," so the teacher intervenes only if the child makes a mistake related to this skill.

In the following scenario, the teacher intervenes by using *teacher clarification,* in which the teacher offers a statement that clarifies what the child has just expressed.

Alison (child):	Hi, Jitendra.
Jitendra (teacher):	Hi, Alison.
Alison:	They won 5 to 3.
Jitendra:	[Pauses, looks confused, then smiles] Oh, you mean, you went to a baseball game?
Alison:	Yes. I went to a baseball game. I saw the Cincinnati Reds. They won 5 to 3.

In the following scenario, the teacher intervenes by using *requesting clarification.* Here, the teacher makes a comment or looks at the child in a way that makes it obvious to the child that his or her utterance was not appropriate. The teacher then pauses, giving the child time to clarify it.

Alison (child):	Hi, Jitendra.
Jitendra (teacher):	Hi, Alison.
Alison:	They won 5 to 3.
Jitendra:	Excuse me? What did you say?
Alison:	I went to a baseball game. They won 5 to 3.
Jitendra:	Oh, you went to a baseball game. That's neat. Which teams did you see?

In the following scenario, the teacher intervenes by using *role switching,* in which the teacher switches roles so that the teacher can demonstrate the conversational skill. Child and teacher then switch back to their original roles.

Teacher:	Let's switch. I'll be Alison, and you be Jitendra.
Alison (teacher):	Hi, Jitendra.
Jitendra (child):	Hi, Alison.
Alison:	On Saturday, I went to a Cincinnati Reds game. They won 5 to 3.
Jitendra:	Neat.
Teacher:	Okay, let's switch back. You be yourself, and I'll be Jitendra.

In the following scenario, the teacher intervenes by *prompting,* stepping out of the role play and pointing out to the child the place in the conversation where the child is make a mistake.

Alison (child):	Hi, Jitendra.
Jitendra (teacher):	Hi, Alison.
Alison:	They won 5 to 3.
Teacher:	That was okay, but there's another way to start the conversation. Let's switch. I'll be you, and you be Todd.
Alison (teacher):	On Saturday, I went to a Cincinnati Reds game. They won 5 to 3.
Child:	I understand.
Teacher:	Great. Let's switch back. Remember about starting the conversation.

Teacher clarification and requesting clarification maintain the flow of the conversation and should be used first. Role switching and prompting obviously interrupt the conversational flow and should be used only when the other two strategies do not provide sufficient feedback for the child.

Putting These Strategies to Work for Progress in the General Curriculum

1. What opportunities for conversation can you make available in the classroom?

2. How can you use conversational scenarios with students who are deaf, hard of hearing, and hearing?

3. What might be the challenges in promoting conversation with children in early childhood, the elementary grades, middle school, and high school?

To answer these questions online and learn more about these strategies, go to the Into Practice module in Chapter 15 of the Companion Website.

Box 15—5

Making a Difference

Famous Individuals Who Were Deaf

An important part of any Deaf culture curriculum is information about the contributions of individuals who are deaf. In *Movers and Shakers: Deaf People Who Changed the World,* Cathryn Carroll and Susan M. Mather (1997) present a collection of stories about people who are or were deaf. The following are capsules of just a few of the 26 biographies in this book.

- Ludwig van Beethoven was born in 1770 and began to lose his hearing as a young man. When he could not hear well enough to perform, he continued to write music. The authors relate the story of Beethoven conducting his Ninth Symphony, the last he would write. That is the symphony that includes famous "Ode to Joy." When the music ended, a singer turned him around to face the audience, which was giving him a standing ovation that he did not hear.

- Francisco Goya was born in 1746 and began to lose his hearing while a student at Spain's Royal Academy of Fine Arts in 1786. In 1808, he painted one of his most famous work of art, *The Third of May,* which depicted a massacre in Madrid. By the late 1700s, Goya had learned a finger alphabet for communicating. One of the paintings he created soon after he lost his hearing is *Portrait of a Deaf Man.*

- William Hoy was born in 1862 and became deaf when he was 2 or 3 years old. After he graduated from the Ohio School for the Deaf, he was recruited to play for a baseball team in Oshkosh, Wisconsin. While playing in Oshkosh, he had difficulty following the ball/strike count when he was up at bat. His solution, the use of hand signals to represent balls and strikes, is still used in baseball today. Some historians credit umpires in the 1904–1905 season with creating these signals, but William "Dummy" Hoy first used them in 1891.

- Juliette "Daisy" Gordon Low was born in 1860 and became deaf when she was 19 years old as a result of an illness. In 1911, after a dinner with the founder of the Boy Scouts, she formed the first Girl Guides troop in England. One year later, she started a Girl Scout troop in the United States with the support of President Woodrow Wilson. She is credited with being the founder of the American Girl Scouts.

- Thomas Alva Edison was born in 1847. As a young child, he had many ear infections as well as scarlet fever. Consequently, he developed a hearing loss. His 1,000 patents include the lightbulb and phonograph, and he developed the first simple movies. Reportedly, he never used technology to improve his hearing because he felt that his hearing loss assisted his concentration.

Source: Movers and Shakers: Deaf People Who Changed the World, by C. Carroll and S. M. Mather, 1997, San Diego: DawnSignPress. Reproduced with permission.

Individuals who are deaf, hard of hearing, and hearing alike enjoy deaf theater and value the distinctive performances of actors who are deaf.

Collaborating to Meet Students' Needs

Special and general educators, speech-language pathologists, audiologists, interpreters, other professionals and paraprofessionals, family members, friends, and community members often join together to encourage language, academic, and social development. Given the increase in the number of students with hearing loss who are being served in general education classrooms, it is crucial for classroom teachers to be supported in their efforts to serve students who are deaf or hard of hearing. Box 15–6 illustrates how one child was able to be successful through the collaboration of his teachers, an interpreter, his parents, and a friend.

Ginny Chinn, Amala's seventh-grade teacher, believes that she was a much better teacher for Amala because of continuous collaboration with the resource room teacher, Amala's interpreters, and Amala's mother. Indeed, she is certain that she is a better teacher for all of her students because the strategies that she used to maximize Amala's inclusion were the same ones she used to maximize the inclusion of all students in instruction. Box 15–7 shares Ginny Chinn's perspective.

A partnership between educators and parents is crucial. Robyn has worked persistently, and sometimes tenaciously, with administrators and teachers to make sure that Amala receives the services she needs. She was able to get through some of the more difficult times with the support and collaboration of steadfast friends and colleagues, as she describes in Box 15–8.

A major barrier to collaboration for individuals who are deaf or hard of hearing is communication. Interpreters and technology, however, make access to communication easier.

Interpreters. **Interpreters** generally specialize in either community-based interpreting or educational interpreting. Through the Registry of Interpreters of the Deaf National Testing Services, interpreters seek certification as interpreters and transliterators. Interpretation involves interpreting between ASL and spoken English; and transliteration (representing or spelling in the characters of another language) involves transliterating between manually coded English sign systems and spoken English, both sign to voice and voice to sign.

A separate specialty is oral transliteration. The interpreter who uses this technique transliterates the spoken message from a person who hears to a person who is deaf or hard of hearing by

Collaboration Tips

Box 15–6

A Three-Pronged Approach

Ben, age 10, is having difficulty reading content material that is assigned for science and social studies by his fourth-grade teacher, Linda. The challenge is to provide Ben, who has a profound hearing loss, the support he needs to continue being included in general instruction for these subject areas. His difficulty with content reading material is characteristic of children who are deaf or hard of hearing because of the difficult vocabulary and complex sentence structures that are common in expository material.

As you have already learned, incidental information is largely unavailable because individuals who are deaf or hard of hearing do not overhear the enormous amount of information that is almost unconsciously absorbed by those with hearing. This incidental information has a strong influence on vocabulary and concept development. In addition, regardless of how effectively the child with hearing loss can comprehend complex concepts presented from teacher to student, reading about these concepts requires that the child be able to manipulate English sentences structures, which is a daunting task for the child who is not proficient in English.

The collaborators included Ben; Linda, his classroom teacher; Micah, his teacher of the deaf; Todd, Ben's friend, who is hearing; Taariq, his interpreter; and Ben's parents.

Linda taught several reading strategies to her class of 28 children, knowing that Ben was not the only child in the class who could benefit from improved ability to read content area material. Micah used these same strategies with Ben and several other students during small-group time in the resource room.

One strategy was semantic mapping for vocabulary development. Before reading, Linda chose a few words that represented new or complex concepts and that would be difficult to figure out from context alone. She put each word inside a circle and drew lines from the word. Then from each line, she drew a new circle. In each circle she wrote questions such as "What is it? What is it like? What are examples?" Taariq made sure that Ben had opportunities to contribute to the discussion by reminding Linda to pause between calling on children because the lag time between Linda's question and Taariq's interpreting meant that Ben was a few seconds behind the other children in "hearing" the question.

Linda also used the K-W-L approach: know, what, learn. Before reading, she asked the children to brainstorm what they knew about the topic. She wrote all their ideas on the computer, which was projected through an LCD projector, and then asked them to put their ideas into categories. After this group activity, she asked them to create individual questions regarding what they wanted to learn about the topic. She then assigned the text material for homework. Ben's parents made sure to dedicate a few minutes in the evening so that Ben could show them his questions and the answers he had found. The next day, Linda asked the children to discuss what they had learned. She focused their responses specifically on answering the questions they had written the previous day. She also drew their attention to similarities and differences between what they had previously known about the topic and what they had learned by reading the assignment.

A third strategy that Linda used was thematic organizers. For some text material, Linda created an outline or flow chart of major concepts and vocabulary the students would encounter in the material. She gave them the organizers before reading and asked them to pay attention to these concepts while they read. When they were comfortable with using thematic organizers, she left blanks for information that the children could fill in. Todd worked as Ben's study buddy, and they shared ideas about what to fill in for each blank. Todd often helped explain a concept in a way that was understandable to Ben.

Ben has been able to keep up with his fourth-grade peers in comprehending the content material assigned as homework. His teachers and parents realize, however, that as text material becomes more difficult, Ben will be increasingly challenged to be independent in reading material written at grade level. In the future, Ben's teachers may wish to find supplementary material written at his reading level.

Putting These Tips to Work for Progress in the General Curriculum

1. Who are the collaborators?

2. What are the challenges?

3. What can the team do?

4. What are the results?

To answer these questions online and learn more about these ideas and concepts, go to the Collaboration Tips module in Chapter 15 of the Companion Website.

Box 15—7

Ginny Chinn: Collaboration Is the Key

Working with the resource room teacher helped a lot because then I knew how strict I should be, how far I should push. The written materials helped, but talking with a teacher who had been through a teacher of the deaf program, who specialized in working with deaf students and knew the language—that, I think, is very beneficial. Without that contact, it would have been extremely hard. If Amala were a deaf girl put into my classroom without the support of the regional program for the deaf, it would have been a lot harder. I don't think I'd have served her quite as well. I don't think she'd have made as much progress in the classroom. That's a real key piece. The resource room and the classroom were working together. The kids knew that we were working together as a unit. This also included home and school. When the students know that all sides are working together, you can always get better results.

When I was asked to take a deaf student in to my class, my first thought was fear of the unknown, thinking that the interpreters would be listening to everything I said and perhaps judging my teaching, and I questioned whether I would be good enough. I was also a little nervous about how much I was going to have to modify what I was doing. But this was an ideal situation for me because I was at a point where I was ready for something new. I was very enthusiastic about having the kids integrated into my classroom and working with the resource room teacher.

Working as a team member, I learned to think more about how I gave information out to the students. I'd always tried not to have too much lecture, but I became even more particular about that. I tried to have a variety of activities so that the kids weren't inundated with a ton of information. I had things written out so that not all information was presented orally, and I was careful to avoid including information on an oral exam that might give away the answer when the interpreter signed or finger spelled it. I also tried to use more visuals so that all of the information wasn't just spoken. I was even more careful than before about checking for understanding. Reminding myself to be concerned about how the interpreters were getting the information out to the students was important because then they were able to do their job the best they could without being completely worn out.

I talked a lot with the interpreters, going over what we were doing and determining the best methods. I even tended to go over seating charts with them first. That's what made the team seem more like a team. It wasn't just the resource room teacher and myself; it was the interpreters, myself, the resource room teachers, and then, of course, the parents.

If I were to give advice to other teachers, I would tell them to make sure that you use all the resources available to you, find out what each other's roles are, respect what each person is doing as a professional, and use that. Take advantage of each other. Use others as a resource, respecting their expertise and their knowledge. I think that's one thing that made the program here successful and the kids in my classroom successful.

Frequent communication is essential to effective professional collaboration.

Box 15–8

My Voice

Robyn Brown's Supportive and Collaborative Friends

Two of my friends, Greg and Eileen, were incredibly supportive when the kids were young. They gave me a lot of perspective on raising kids. And they gave me a break. They would take the kids, spend time with them. We have a couple of other families with whom we trade off kids. Their kids come here, and my kids go there. It's been difficult sometimes to build a community of friends because some of the people I know, the teachers who sign, their kids don't sign. Or the kids who do sign, the parents don't sign.

And it's not like how it was growing up for me, and that's been hard. When I was growing up, our house was where all the baseball games were played. I'm sure I just kind of assumed that's how it was going to be when I was a mom, and it hasn't been that way because of the communication difficulties between the kids and the parents. But we do have a couple of families with hearing-impaired kids we spend time with. A few years ago, we went to Disneyland with a deaf woman and her kids. That was wonderful because everyone signed really well. We

just had a great time. The kids could be with me, they could be with her, they could be with the other kids, all without any interpreting. That was good. But those experiences don't happen very frequently.

When I talk with my friends who have hearing kids, I ask, "Is this a teenage thing, or is this a deafness thing?" That's one of my challenges, to realize what is typical behavior. My friend has a deaf daughter who's a young adult now. And that has been really helpful. I tell her, "Amala is making me crazy." And she'll say, "You know, when my daughter was that age. . . . " It's just so helpful for me to hear from other parents with deaf kids, and those with hearing kids, their experiences. Most of the time, it's just not that different.

One of the things that is different is providing Amala with an age-appropriate amount of freedom. Like many other deaf students in general education environments, she's older than most of her same-grade peers. The communication piece is a challenge, too. Plans change, emergencies happen, and although TTs have helped, she's not always near a text telephone. We are investigating the purchase of two-way e-mail devices. Maybe it will be a birthday gift: independence for her, peace of mind for me!

using speech and mouth movements. Oral transliterators typically work in settings in which the person with a hearing loss is at a distance from the speaker.

The educational interpreter's role is to facilitate communication and equalize learning opportunities in the classroom. The role of the interpreter in any setting is to aid in the process of communication.

Special Telephones. Telecommunication devices for the deaf were originally referred to as *TTYs*, for teletypes. The name was then changed to *TDDs*, for telecommunication devices for the deaf, and more recently to *TTs* for **text telephones**. Text telephones, which look like a computer keyboard with a cradle for the telephone handset, enable individuals to send a typed message over telephone lines to anyone else who has a TT.

With the implementation of the Americans with Disabilities Act, all states set up relay services to connect callers who use TTs to people who do not. Beginning October 1, 2002, *711* is the new three-digit number for access to all telecommunications relay services for calls from any telephone, anywhere in the United States. The relay operator, who has a TT, relays the message between the person using a TT and the person using a conventional phone. To facilitate access, many public places make TTs available as special pay phones.

Telephone amplifiers are used by individuals who are hard of hearing. Amplifiers can be built into phones or added to phones, and some phones are hearing-aid compatible.

Telecommunication companies have developed pagers that use a vibrating beeper to notify the customer who cannot hear the phone ringing that a message has been received. The keyboards of pagers and wireless phones can be used to send messages, bypassing the need to use voice.

Captioning and Real-Time Graphic Display. **Captioning** is the appearance of printed text that is designed to capture the dialogue and action of a television program, movie, newscast, sporting event, or advertisement. Most prerecorded programs and many live broadcasts are *closed captioned.* Since 1993, a federal law has required all new television sets with screens larger than

13 inches sold in the United States to be equipped with an internal decoder that can receive captions. The captions are typically scrolled across the bottom like a film with subtitles. To receive closed captions on an older television set, an external decoder must be attached.

Television shows, such as sports, news, and awards, are captioned as they occur. This is referred to as *real-time captioning*. The technology used in real-time captioning is also used in **real-time graphic display**. An individual trained as a stenotypist or court reporter types into a device with phonetic shorthand symbols. The device is connected to a computer that translates these codes into English, and the English is displayed on a screen. At lecture-type events, the screen is large enough for an audience to view. In classrooms, the screen is usually a computer screen.

The Internet. The Internet is a perfect medium for individuals who are deaf or hard of hearing. In addition to e-mail and the web, links between computers and telephone lines enable individuals who are deaf or hard of hearing to use computers as text telephones. With video capability, senders and receivers can see one another and read their messages. Box 15–9 describes a classroom project that involved pairs of students, deaf and hearing, in instructional conversations on the Internet.

Alerting Devices. Alerting devices use vibratory or visual signals to alert individuals with a hearing loss. Examples include vibrators connected to alarm clocks and the cribs of crying babies and flashing lights connected to smoke alarms, doorbells, and telephones. Some individuals who are deaf own hearing-ear dogs who alert their owners to important sounds in immediate the environment of the dog and owner.

What Can You Learn from Others Who Teach Students with Hearing Loss?

Learning for the Early Childhood Years: Dallas Regional Day School

The Dallas (Texas) Regional Day School Program for the Deaf provides services to more than 30 infants and toddlers from birth to age 3. The child's parent(s), educator of the deaf, and at least one other early childhood intervention professional develop the IFSP. The program is family-centered in that most families receive at least weekly home visits from a teacher of the deaf, who is called the parent advisor. The parent advisor listens to the parents, gathers continuous observational data, shares resources with the parents, and determines the topics that are appropriate as the parents are able to integrate new information and develop new skills. Parent advisors show parents how to encourage the development of language during daily routines and play that capitalize on the child's interests.

According to Karen Clark, education division head of the Callier Center for Communication Disorders at the University of Texas at Dallas, parents at this stage in their children's development have many questions about communication methodology. The parent advisors provide objective information about ASL, manually coded English, oral/aural methods, hearing aids, and cochlear implants. They also connect parents to other parents, adults who are deaf or hard of hearing, and professionals with expertise on topics of interest to the parents.

Audiological services are available through a contract with the Callier Center. Sign language classes occur weekly, including one class each week for families who speak Spanish. In the future, sign language classes may be offered conveniently to families via cable television.

The future holds many challenges for the Dallas program, including providing services to the greater numbers of children identified because of mandated statewide early hearing detection programs and the increased numbers of non–English-speaking families. But as Karen Clark says, "Our Dallas program looks forward to these challenges and to developing even better ways of meeting the needs of all families."

Earlier in the chapter, you learned about issues of cultural and linguistic diversity among families of children who are deaf or hard of hearing.

Technology Tips

Box 15—9

Schoolhouse Palace

Writing typically presents a tremendous challenge to children who are deaf. The Internet offers the opportunity for children to develop written language through written conversations, similar to the way that hearing children develop spoken language through spoken conversations.

E-mail discussions are one type of conversational format, but these types of conversations are asynchronous. The conversational partners do not "talk" in real time, and the nature of the dialogue is more like writing letters than having a conversation. Internet chat groups offer a forum that is more like a real conversation. However, chat rooms are not often educational in nature, and the participants are self-chosen. Indeed, many school districts do not allow students to engage in on line chats during school time because of the risks inherent in meeting unsavory individuals and having inappropriate discussions.

The Palace is a visual online community. Members upload the software and join one of the Palace chat rooms. There are actually a number of different Palaces. At Kent State University, Albert Ingram and Barbara Schirmer developed a Palace exclusively to provide a learning environment for children who are deaf to interact with teachers and peers, both deaf and hearing. They call it the Schoolhouse Palace.

In the Schoolhouse Palace, students are brought together for instructional conversations that are monitored by an online teacher. In one research study, Ingram and Schirmer brought together high school students from the Ohio School for the Deaf and Ravenna High School in Ravenna, Ohio. The students were divided into two-person teams. Each student had an avatar, which is a graphical representation, and could "dress up" the avatar with props. The conversation was visually represented within balloons above the avatars' heads, similar to a cartoon. The complete conversation scrolled along the side of the screen so the students and teacher could reread previous comments. Each pair was engaged in a cooperative learning activity on the topic of astronomy. In this study, the online teacher used an instructional strategy that encouraged the students to use descriptors in their written language. The conversations took place in a room called the "Bean Bag Room."

In future uses of the Schoolhouse Palace, on line teachers will encourage a range of written language features, depending on the IEP goals of individual students. The students will be able to design their own rooms. Groups of students will be able to go to different rooms and have concurrent conversations that do not interfere with one another. The teacher can visit each room, spending time with each group or pair.

Putting These Strategies to Work for Progress in the General Curriculum

The Internet offers wide-ranging opportunities for improving the written language of students who are deaf. If you are planning to use the Internet, you should ask the following questions:

1. Two challenges in using the Internet involve your students' keyboarding skills and your ability to monitor the on line chat environment. What other challenges can you foresee?

2. What skills do you and your students need to use the Internet?

3. How can you use the Internet to enhance learning?

To answer these questions online and learn more about these strategies, go to the Technology Tips module in Chapter 15 of the Companion Website.

Learning for the Elementary Years: Northwest Regional Program, Oregon

The Northwest Regional Program is one of eight regional programs in the state of Oregon serving students (ages birth to 21) who are deaf or hard of hearing. The state developed the regional program model for disabilities that it regarded as low incidence but having high impact—that is, few children who are fairly expensive to serve. The model allows several school districts to be served by one regional program. The Northwest Regional Program serves 20 districts, including small rural districts and large urban ones. In the school-age program (students ages 5 to 21), the majority of students with hearing loss attend neighborhood schools and receive some support services, depending on their needs. The Northwest Regional Program also offers self-contained classrooms. The configuration of each child's school day is distinct from every other child's, and the goal is inclusion. The teachers use whatever communication mode is appropriate for the students, and an ASL specialist goes into all of the classes to work with the teachers and students on ASL development. By the time students are in middle school, the self-contained classroom looks more like a resource room because of the amount of time students spend in general education classes.

Itinerant teachers of the deaf serve the students in their neighborhood schools. In addition, all of the students in the program—those in neighborhood schools and those in the self-contained classrooms—receive the support services of the audiology staff, a speech-language pathologist, a reading specialist, and a school psychologist, all of whom are trained to work with students who are deaf or hard of hearing.

According to Jill Bailey, the coordinator of the deaf and hard of hearing programs for the Northwest Regional Program, "Regardless of whether the students are in neighborhood schools or self-contained classrooms, the teachers work to make sure that what they teach is aligned with the state curriculum so that the students who are deaf and hard of hearing receive the same curriculum as all other students."

The conceptualization of a universally designed curriculum that you learned about in Chapter 2 is carried out in educational programs for children who are deaf or hard of hearing.

Learning for the Middle and Secondary Years: Utah Extension Services

The Utah Extension Consultant Division serves students with hearing loss throughout the state of Utah who are not served by the state residential school for the deaf or by the Salt Lake City program. According to Judy Parmelee, program specialist, the quality of education the students receive is judged largely by the extent to which they are able to succeed competitively within general education classrooms in the student's neighborhood school.

The program offers both oral/aural and total communication classrooms so that the methodology is appropriate for each student's language needs. Students who are in general education classes either part or full time receive three levels of consultation services from teachers of the deaf.

The first level involves the least intervention and provides assistance to the classroom teacher and other professional staff who work directly with the child. Among the strategies is the one you read about previously: instructional conversations.

The second level uses a consultation/collaboration model. In addition to consulting with the child's teacher and other professional staff, the consultant provides periodic direct intervention with the student, models teaching strategies in the classroom, and shares materials with the teacher. Language, reading, and writing are the central focus because the child's academic success is directly related to the development of language and literacy.

The third level is the most intense intervention and relies on a consultant/tutorial model. In addition to consulting with the child's teacher and other professional staff, the consultant works with the student on a set schedule and an ongoing basis, sometimes one on one and sometimes within the context of the general education classroom.

Learning for the Transitional and Postsecondary Years: Kent State University, Ohio

During the past few years, Kent State University in Kent, Ohio, has experienced unusual growth in the numbers of students who are deaf or hard of hearing. According to Anne Jannarone, director of the university program of assistance for students with disabilities, transition from high school into the university has been made easier as a result of the increased numbers of students with hearing loss because the students now have a small community of supportive peers.

The first step in determining a student's educational accommodations at Kent State is to review the student's last IEP, identifying the services the student received in high school. The student's counselor from the Office of Student Disability Services then meets with the student and assesses the types of adaptations the student will need. These depend on the courses the student will take and the student's communication mode. If the student will be using an interpreter, the student and interpreter meet ahead of time to discuss communication during class and exams. Some students also receive supplemental note taking by a classmate.

Real-time captioning is another service. Kent State uses a remote captioning service designed specifically for educational settings. The professor wears a lapel microphone that connects to a phone line, the captioner at a distant location hears the lecture from the phone and word-processes it, and the captioner's computer has a phone line that sends the information directly to the student's laptop computer. The student sees the professor's lecture across his or her laptop screen at almost the same time as the professor is talking, which is why the process is called *real-time captioning*. Anne Jannarone has found the service to be particularly beneficial to Kent State's deaf students who do not sign and cannot benefit from the services of an interpreter or who are in highly technical courses.

A Vision for Amala's Future

Amala will have many choices about her future when she graduates from high school. She can apply to any college, knowing that she will be judged on the merits of her past academic performance and not on the basis of her hearing abilities. She will be able to choose her social and recreational activities because they are the ones she enjoys, not because they are the only ones open to her. She can travel, and she can live wherever she would like. She can choose to pursue virtually any career. She will have the same mother-daughter joys and struggles with Robyn that all mothers and daughters have. And she can choose her own friends from among individuals who are hearing and individuals who are deaf or hard of hearing.

What Would You Recommend?

1. To provide a learning environment that is challenging yet supportive for Amala?
2. To help guide Amala's decisions about education and work after high school?
3. To facilitate Amala's communication with individuals at school, at work, and in the community who do not sign?

Summary

How Do You Recognize Students with Hearing Loss?

▼ Although hearing loss exists on a continuum, children are typically classified as deaf or hard of hearing.

▼ Intensity of sound is measured in decibels (dB), and frequency of sound is measured in hertz (Hz). Intensity is perceived as loudness, and frequency is perceived as pitch.

▼ Degree of hearing loss is commonly categorized as slight, mild, moderate, moderate–severe, severe, and profound.

▼ Communication modes used by individuals who are deaf or hard of hearing include oral/aural, American Sign

Language (ASL), and simultaneous communication in sign language and spoken English.

▼ Communication with parents, peers, and teachers plays a major role in the psychological, social, and emotional development of children with hearing loss.

▼ Achievement levels continue to be a primary concern, particularly among children from diverse racial, ethnic, and linguistic backgrounds.

▼ Conductive loss is caused by a problem in the outer or middle ear. Sensorineural loss is caused by a problem in the inner ear or along the nerve pathway to the brain stem.

▼ Prelingual hearing loss (at birth or before learning language) accounts for 95 percent of students who are deaf or hard of hearing; postlingual hearing loss (after learning language) accounts for 5 percent.

▼ Prevalence of hearing loss in children is estimated at 1.3 percent.

How Do You Evaluate Students with Hearing Loss?

▼ Infants can be assessed using an auditory brain stem response test or otoacoustic immittance test.

▼ Behavioral audiological evaluation is used beyond infancy. Hearing threshold levels are graphed on an audiogram.

▼ Hearing aids make sounds louder; but they do not restore normal hearing to the person, and they always involve some distortion of sounds.

▼ Cochlear implants provide sound information by directly stimulating the functional auditory nerve fibers in the cochlea; unlike hearing aids, cochlear implants do not make sounds louder.

▼ Assessment of language, hearing, speech, speech reading, signing, academic achievement, socialization, and motivation are essential for providing an appropriate education for students who are deaf or hard of hearing.

How Do You Assure Progress in the General Curriculum?

▼ Planning universally designed learning involves altering the curriculum through use of oral/aural communication in programs emphasizing speech skills, ASL in bilingual/bicultural programs, and simultaneous communication in total communication programs.

▼ Oral/aural methods are characterized by instruction in spoken English; curricular goals in speech and aural habilitation; and the expectation that students will use speech, speech reading, and auditory skills for communication.

▼ Bilingual/bicultural methods are characterized by instruction in ASL, classroom communication in ASL, and the teaching of English through the written form with no or little use of spoken English.

▼ Total communication methods are characterized by classroom communication in a manually coded English or pidgin sign language along with the simultaneous use of spoken English.

▼ Planning universally designed learning involves augmenting instruction to enhance language, reading, and writing development with strategies such as instructional conversations.

▼ Planning universally designed learning involves augmenting curriculum through teaching about Deaf culture and ASL.

▼ Collaboration is enhanced with communication access through interpreters, text telephones (TTs), telephone relay services, captioning, real-time graphic display, and the Internet.

What Can You Learn From Others Who Teach Students with Hearing Loss?

▼ Early intervention programs such as the one at Dallas Regional Day School involve family-centered practices that support parents in learning skills for communicating and interacting with their children.

▼ Elementary programs like Oregon's Northwest Regional Program serve diverse students within a range of educational placements from self-contained to general education classrooms.

▼ During the secondary school years, the priority in educational programs comparable to the Utah Extension Services is to maintain high academic standards and expectations for students who are deaf or hard of hearing.

▼ In colleges and universities like Kent State in Ohio, interpreters, note takers, and captioners provide access to information during class.

Council for Exceptional Children   **PRAXIS**

To find out how and where this chapter content connects to the CEC Professional Standards and the Praxis™ Standards, go to the Standards Connection module in Chapter 15 of the Companion Website. A comprehensive matrix aligning CEC Professional Standards, Praxis™ Standards, and INTASC principles to the entire text, is available in the Appendix and on the Companion Website.

Chapter 16

Contributed by
Sandra Lewis, Florida State University

Who Is Elexis Gillette?

Walking down the west wing of the mall, Elexis Gillette stops a passerby and asks for directions to the leather goods store, where he hopes to be able to buy his mother a birthday gift. He listens intently as the woman says, "Just down there a bit, after the food court." She tells him he can't miss it because it is "right across from the store with the big birdfeeders in the window." Although Elexis tries to ask for more specific information about where the store is, the stranger's response is confusing, and she leaves before he can ask her another question. He sighs, frustrated that it is such a challenge to find people who can give him clear directions, and waits for the sounds of someone else who might be able to clearly describe the information he needs.

Later Elexis brainstorms with his special education teachers, Brian Whitmer and Alexandra Carter, about how he could have handled the incident differently. They all agree that some people just can't give directions very well and that it's nearly impossible to tell which of the people passing you will take the time to give you the information you need in the way you need it. While not totally satisfied, Elexis does feel better knowing that even adults get frustrated when traveling. Like Elexis, both Brian and Alexandra are legally blind: They know from experience the hassles he faces.

Elexis, who is finishing his freshman year of high school, notes that one of his greatest challenges as a blind person is finding people who can clearly explain to him the world he can't see. "It seems as if no one thinks about what they're saying," he explains. It's a problem in algebra class; it's a problem in geography; it's a problem in the community: People with vision think and describe in visual terms. Because they don't experience the world primarily by its textures, sounds, and smells, as Elexis does, they have a hard time using information about textures, sounds, and smells to help him understand what he needs to know.

Other than this complaint, however, Elexis, who is blind from glaucoma, is usually satisfied with his life. He likes attending Athens Drive High School, in Raleigh, North Carolina, and is positive about his future. He knows that he has to work harder than people with vision do to achieve, but he has been fortunate to have many positive role models in his life: people who know that individuals with visual impairment and blindness can be successful. First, there's his mother, who also has glaucoma, who works full time and raises him as a single mother. "My vision teachers, they're cool. They have

regular lives, and they don't let their visual impairments stop them from doing what they like to do. Ms. Carter, she's even been skydiving."

Elexis knows that his success depends on his ability to be as responsible as possible for himself and his education. This philosophy of self-direction has been supported by the special education teachers he has had in school. Born with low vision, Elexis lost all of his vision in the third grade. His mother and his teachers didn't feel sorry for him but encouraged him to be involved in the activities of his peers. "My mother, because she's blind too, she knows all the tricks. I can't get anything by her."

Like many sighted people, Elexis, now 15, enjoys surfing the Internet, playing video games, and swimming. At school, he is on the wrestling team and plans to join the Model United Nations Club next year. With his competitive spirit and outgoing personality, Elexis has many friends at Athens Drive.

Elexis knows that he can't always do the same things that his sighted peers are doing. For example, when the rest of his physical education class was learning how to play badminton, he worked with Brian to learn the fundamentals of goalball, a game played by people who are blind and others who wear blindfolds. He likes this game and hopes to be on a goalball team during the summer at a sports camp for athletes with visual impairments.

Elexis also knows that there are some extra things to learn because he is blind. He regularly leaves school with his orientation and mobility instructor to learn how to travel safely using his cane. Obviously, he needs these skills more and more as he, like others his age, begins to spend more time with his friends and less time with his family.

When he's a junior, Elexis plans to attend the Cisco Systems computer training courses that are offered at Athens Drive. He will use the many specialized techniques his teachers have taught him to succeed with this course of study and hopes to leave school ready to begin a career in the computer field.

Elexis has had many positive influences that have provided direction so far in his life's journey. His mother has always been there for him. He attends school in a district that understands the kinds of supports he needs to succeed and willingly provides those supports. His teachers don't cut him any slack. Elexis is confident that even though he'll always have to deal with people who can't give directions very well, he has the personal, social, travel, and vocational skills to find his own way in the world.

What do you think?

1. How are the experiences of people who are blind, such as Elexis, different from the experiences of people who see?

2. In what kinds of activities can Elexis participate as an equal with his sighted peers?

3. What are the specialized services that Elexis has received in school, and who are the special professionals who have supported his education?

4. What can professionals do to ensure positive outcomes for all students who have visual impairments?

To answer these questions online and learn more about Elexis Gillette and other students with visual impairments, go to the Cases module in Chapter 16 of the Companion Website.

How Do You Recognize Students with Visual Impairments?

Defining Visual Impairment

When you think about visual impairments and blindness, you might imagine someone such as Elexis, who sees nothing at all and must use adaptive techniques for tasks that typically require vision, such as braille for reading or a cane to detect objects when traveling. It may surprise you to learn that most individuals with legal blindness have some usable vision and that most students who have visual impairments are print readers.

Two different definitions describe visual impairment. The legal definition of blindness is based on a clinical measurement of **visual acuity.** Acuity is determined by having the individual read the letters on a chart, each line of which is composed of letters written with a certain size of print. The ability to read the 20 line from a distance of 20 feet is typical, and a person who can read at that line is said to have 20/20 acuity. Individuals who can read only the top line from 20 feet, where the print size is 200 (the big E), when using both eyes and wearing their glasses, have 20/200 acuity; these people are **legally blind.** People are also legally blind if their **field of vision** (the area around them that they can visually detect when looking straight ahead) is less than 20 degrees (normal is 160 degrees), even if their visual acuity is normal. These individuals have **tunnel vision.** Figure 16–1 shows what people with various types of visual impairment might see.

The legal definition of blindness, as established by federal law in 1935 (Koestler, 1976), is an arbitrary clinical measure that is used to determine eligibility for special government allowances, such as an extra income tax deduction, specialized job training, and eligibility for certain support services such as the Talking Book Program. Many state, local, and private agencies also use legal blindness as their eligibility requirement. A person who is legally blind may have a great deal of useful vision: The legal definition of blindness is simply an eligibility standard; it does not provide meaningful information about the way in which a person experiences and learns about the world (Huebner, 2000).

How a person experiences and learns about the world is, however, at the core of the definition of visual impairment in the Individuals with Disabilities Education Act (IDEA). IDEA defines **visual disability (including blindness)** as "an impairment in vision that, even with correction, adversely affects a child's educational performance. The term includes both partial sight and blindness" (34 C.F.R., sec. 300.7[13]). Key to this definition is that the student has some kind of disorder of the visual system that interferes with learning.

FIGURE 16–1

An estimate of how a view appears for individuals with tunnel vision, macular degeneration, and reduced visual acuity

Source: Courtesy of the Jewish Guild for the Blind, New York.

Students with visual impairments represent a wide range of visual abilities. Educators classify these students by their ability to use their vision or their tendency or need to use tactile means for learning (Lewis & Allman, 2000b):

▼ **Low vision** describes individuals who can generally read print, although they may depend on optical aids, such as magnifying lenses, to see better. A few read both braille and print; all rely primarily on vision for learning. Individuals with low vision may or may not be legally blind.

▼ **Functionally blind** describes individuals who typically use braille for efficient reading and writing. They may rely on their ability to use functional vision for other tasks, such as moving through the environment or sorting items by color. Thus, they use their limited vision to supplement the combination of tactual and auditory learning methods.

▼ **Totally blind** describes those individuals who do not receive meaningful input through the visual sense. These individuals use tactual and auditory means to learn about their environment. They generally read braille.

You will learn more about braille later in this chapter.

These broad categories are only minimally useful. Every individual with visual impairment uses vision differently and in a way that is difficult to predict. When you teach these students, try to avoid the common errors of assuming that students who are functionally blind cannot see anything and that students with low vision are efficiently using that sense. Observe carefully how a student functions and then present instructional activities to maximize that student's learning.

Describing the Characteristics

The population of students with visual impairments is surprisingly heterogeneous. They differ from each other in how they learn and in their visual functioning, socioeconomic status, parenting style, cultural background, age of onset of visual impairment, the presence of concomitant disabilities, and innate cognitive abilities. Some are gifted or have special talents. A large number also have severe and multiple disabilities (Erin, 1996; Sacks, 1998). Yet each possesses an important characteristic in common, one that you have to consider when planning appropriate educational interventions: the limited ability to learn incidentally from the environment (Hatlen & Curry, 1987).

Almost from the moment they are born, children with good vision learn seemingly effortlessly through their visual sense. Their vision helps them organize, synthesize, and give meaning to their perceptions of the environment (Ferrell, 1996; Harrell, 1992; Lowenfeld, 1973). For example, a sighted baby spends hours looking at his or her hand before that hand becomes an efficient tool. A young child will drop a toy repeatedly, watching its path to the floor until he or she learns to understand *down*.

Think about the way in which a young child learns the concept of *table*. Even before she has a name for that object, she has observed a variety of tables in her environment: in the kitchen, living room, family room; at the homes of relatives and friends; at preschool. Tables are everywhere, and the sighted child begins to recognize that the things people call tables ("Put your cup on the table," or "Leave the magazine on the table," or "Go get Daddy's glasses off the table") have certain features in common. Soon she begins to perceive a relationship between the object and the word. Later, after more visual experiences, she will distinguish between desks, tables, counters, and other flat surfaces. No one ever really needs to teach this kind of conceptual information, for children learn it incidentally with little or no direct instruction.

Incidental learning is problematic in all visually impaired children (Ferrell, 1996; Hatlen & Curry, 1987; Scott, Jan, & Freeman, 1995). The child with limited visual access to her environment may find it necessary for her family and teachers to give her opportunities to explore carefully and completely, either visually at a close distance or through tactual means, every part of a variety of tables before she can acquire, organize, and then synthesize information about "tableness."

Incidental learning also affects how children come to perform skills. For example, most children need little training when they make toast for the first time. They have few problems with any of the steps involved in this rather complex task because they have observed adults make

Young children develop a "scheme" about tables through their experience with them. This incidental learning differs for a child who has always been visually impaired.

toast hundreds of times. Without hands-on instruction, children with visual impairments may not even be aware that a special machine is used in this task. Even youngsters with low vision, who may not see clearly at a distance of two or three feet, usually need special instruction and practice time to perform this and other tasks.

Because of the important role played by incidental learning for most individuals, the presence of a visual impairment has the potential to influence motor, language, cognitive, and social skills development. Generally, however, these influences are not long-lasting if the student receives appropriate interventions (Ferrell, 2000). Interventions must be designed to reduce the limitations imposed on an individual by a significant visual impairment, including (1) limitations in the range and variety of experiences, (2) limitations in the ability to get around, and (3) limitations in interactions with the environment.

Limitations in Range and Variety of Experiences

Vision allows a person to experience the world meaningfully and safely from a distance. Touch is an ineffective substitute for vision: Some objects are too big (skyscrapers, mountains), too small (ants, molecules), too fragile (snowflakes, moths), too dangerous (fire, boiling water), or too distant (the sun, the horizon) for their characteristics to be learned tactually (Lowenfeld, 1973). The other senses do not fully compensate for what can be learned visually: The song of a bird or the smell of baking bread may provide evidence that those objects are nearby but do not provide useful information about many of their properties. Individuals with visual impairment often have not shared the experiences of their peers with typical vision, so their knowledge of the world may be different.

Students with visual impairments also experience different social interactions because they cannot share common experiences with sighted friends. The student who has not seen the latest movie, played the newest video game, or taken driver's training may be at a disadvantage within the school culture. The potential for inadequate development of social skills and the related negative impact on self-esteem are serious concerns that may have a lifelong impact (Sacks & Silberman, 2000).

Similarly, their career development can be limited. While individuals with visual impairments are employed in a variety of occupations, many young adults struggle with determining an appropriate vocation because they are unaware of the jobs that people (with or without vision) perform (Wolffe, 1996).

Limitations in the Ability to Get Around

Individuals who are visually impaired are limited in their spontaneous ability to move safely in and through their environment. This restriction influences a child's early motor development

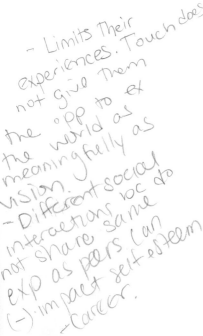

and exploration of the world; in turn, the same restriction affects the child's knowledge base and social development. The ability to move through the environment spontaneously probably is one area over which only moderate control can be exercised and is a continuing source of frustration for many adults (Corn & Sacks, 1994).

Individuals who have significant visual impairment are limited in their movement through space. This limitation directly affects their opportunities for experiences (Barraga & Erin, 2001). The child with impaired vision may not know what is interesting in the environment. Even if that child is aware of something to explore, he or she may not know how to negotiate the environment to get to the desired object. These children often become passive and in turn have fewer opportunities for intellectual and social stimulation.

Limitations in Interactions with the Environment

Knowledge about and control over the environment often are areas of concern for individuals with visual impairments. In some cases, their limited vision reduces their level of readily acquired information about their environment and their ability to act on that information. For instance, they cannot determine at a glance the source of a loud crash or a burning smell, so they cannot quickly determine an appropriate reaction. Similarly, they cannot adequately inform themselves about the effects of their actions on the people and things around them.

In young children, reduced vision correlates with poor motivation to move through the environment, manipulate toys, and initiate interactions (Fazzi, Kirk, Pearce, Pogrund, & Wolfe, 1992). Their tendency toward physical and social detachment (Wolffe, Sacks, & Thomas, 2000) and low motivation can have the long-lasting consequence of limiting their sense of competence and mastery. Individuals who have a poor sense of their ability to effect change in their lives are at risk for the development of poor self-esteem, poor academic achievement, and reduced language and social skills (Harrell, 1992).

The limitations in the range and variety of experiences, in the ability to get around, and in interactions with the environment influence how a student with a visual impairment experiences the world. Visual impairment can result in experiential and environmental deprivation.

Young children with impaired vision need opportunities to explore a variety of environments to develop a healthy sense of competency.

Box 16–1

Donna McNear

"To teach is to learn twice" is a quotation I've placed in my home, my notebook, and my office (J. Joubert, 1754–1824). As a teacher of children with visual impairments, I am continually traveling a path of learning. My work day is immersed in learning to create caring school communities and learning opportunities in which children can be successful.

As an itinerant teacher in seven rural school districts in east-central Minnesota, I begin my day in my car, traveling to see children in their home school districts. At the first school, I observe Chad, a preschool student with low vision, and assist the school staff in providing materials and arranging the classroom so he can easily see and participate in all activities.

I also stop at the high school to teach Tracy, who reads and writes in braille. I bring the worksheets the teachers have given me to put into braille and quickly visit with teachers between classes to answer questions and problem solve. Mr. Johnson, the science teacher, and I discuss the possibilities of providing tactual materials in a genetics unit. He comes up with a great idea and benefits from my support, approval, and encouragement. I meet with Tracy, who wants help learning new Nemeth code braille signs in the beginning algebra math unit and wants to review the route to the new girls' locker room for gym.

After an hour reviewing the information with Tracy, I travel to the next town and have lunch with the adapted physical education teacher. This gives us the opportunity to plan the physical education activities for Shannon, an eighth-grade student who is blind and is now working on swimming goals. After lunch I go to my office to make phone calls and have a meeting with the braillist, Connie. She wants to discuss the format for braille music.

On my way to the next town, I make a brief stop at Cory's house. He is 14 months old and has low vision. He just received glasses, and I spend a few minutes observing and assessing the difference his glasses make in how he uses his vision in daily activities at home. His parents also want to share new information from his ophthalmologist and ask a few questions.

My day ends with a mobility lesson with Annie, a high school student who is blind. I am also dually certified as an orientation and mobility specialist, which allows children in rural areas to receive needed training. We review the route to the post office so Annie can pick up a package.

Sharing a description of my day with my family at dinner, I remember a statement attributed to Lewis Mumford: "It is not what one does, but in a manifold sense what one realizes, that keeps existence from being vain and trivial." I do many things in a day for children, but what I realize about teaching and my students is what my work life is all about. I realize I am a mirror, a window, and a doorway for my students: a mirror to reflect positively who they are and their capabilities, talents, and dreams; a window to show them their opportunities, possibilities, choices, and other ways of being; and finally, a doorway for their future.

I have also realized my own mission in my work life: I see the meaning in my labor (beyond the reward of a check); I see my abilities recognized and valued; I view myself as a craftsperson, creating something of beauty and value; I have a job that is large enough for my spirit; and I feel I am leaving the world better than when I found it. Through my day-to-day teaching, I have learned love, fortitude, respectfulness, and humbleness. I have also learned to be delicate and to have passion for my time with children.

Later in this chapter, you will learn more about how teachers address educational needs related to the limitations we describe.

To learn about the structures of the eye, go to the Web Links module in Chapter 16 of the Companion Website.

Students with visual impairments, even those who have other disabilities, can learn; but because they receive unclear, incomplete, or no visual input, they require directed interventions to develop an understanding of the relationships between people and objects in their environment (Freeman, Goetz, Richards, & Groenveld, 1991). Visual impairment primarily affects *how* students learn skills but does not prevent the acquisition of skills when appropriate interventions are provided. In Box 16–1 you can read how one teacher views her role in providing interventions for students.

Identifying the Causes

As you can tell from Figure 16–2, seeing involves both the eye and brain. Damage to or malfunction of any part of a student's visual system can significantly impair how the student functions.

Damage to the structures involved in the visual process can be the result of an event that happens during the development of the embryo, can occur at or immediately after an infant's birth, or can result from an injury or disease that occurs at any time during a person's development. *Congenital* visual impairment occurs at birth or, in the case of blindness, before visual memories have been established. Elexis has a congenital visual impairment. That type of impairment can affect any child's earliest access to information and experiences. Students who acquire a vision loss af-

FIGURE 16–2
Visual pathway

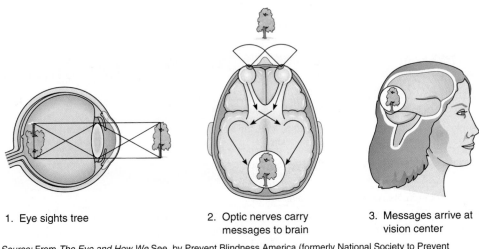

1. Eye sights tree

2. Optic nerves carry
   messages to brain

3. Messages arrive at
   vision center

Source: From *The Eye and How We* See, by Prevent Blindness America (formerly National Society to Prevent
Blindness), 1992, Schaumburg, IL: Prevent Blindness America. Copyright 1992 by Prevent Blindness America.
Reprinted with permission.

ter having normal vision have an **adventitious** visual impairment. That is, their impairment results
from an advent (e.g., loss of sight caused by a hereditary condition that has just manifested itself)
or an event (e.g., loss of sight caused by trauma). Although the educational needs of students with
adventitious and congenital visual impairments may be similar, even a short period of good vision
and concomitant typical development can enrich the student's understanding of self, others, and
the relationships among people, objects, and events in the environment (Scott et al., 1995).

Identifying the Prevalence

Because state and local educational agencies vary so widely in how they measure and report visual impairments, it is extremely difficult to count accurately the number of students with visual
impairments who are served in schools (Kirchner & Diament, 1999). The best estimates are that
approximately one to two students in 1,000 have a visual disorder that interferes with learning;
those children are eligible to receive special education services (Nelson & Dimitrova, 1993). Visual impairment accounts for about 0.04 percent of the total special education population (U.S.
Department of Education, 2001).

How Do You Evaluate Students
with Visual Impairments?

Determining the Presence

Like students with other disabilities, a student with visual impairment receives a nondiscriminatory evaluation (see Figure 16–3). Of course, evaluations of students with visual impairments
do have several highly specialized aspects.

Medical specialists usually determine the presence of a disorder of the child's visual system.
Physicians often detect a serious visual disorder when the child is very young or has just experienced a trauma. Their diagnosis generally is followed by a search for medical solutions to correct
vision. When no such correction is possible, referrals to the schools occur.

FIGURE 16–3
Assessment process for determining the presence of a visual impairment

Nondiscriminatory Evaluation

Observation

Parents observe	The child may not have any eye turn or may not respond to visual stimuli as expected.
Physician observes	The newborn or infant may have an identifiable visual disorder.
Teacher observes	The student squints or seems to be bothered by light, the student's eyes water or are red, the student holds books too close, or the student bumps into objects.

Medical screening

Assessment measures	Findings that indicate need for further evaluation
Ophthalmological	Medical procedures indicate the presence of a visual disorder or reduced visual functioning that cannot be improved to typical levels through surgery or medical intervention.
Functional vision evaluation	A visual disorder interferes with the student's ability to incidentally learn from the environment and the student's use of vision for performance of tasks.
Low vision specialist	A specialist evaluation indicates that visual functioning cannot be improved to typical levels through the use of lenses.
Vision screening in schools	For students with low vision who have not been identified before entering school, screening indicates the need for further evaluation.

Prereferral

Prereferral is typically not used with these students because the severity of the disability indicates a need for special education or related services.

Referral

Students with visual impairments should be referred by medical personnel or parents for early intervention during the infancy/preschool years. Many states have child-find organizations to make sure these students receive services. Children are referred for protection in evaluation procedures upon entering school. Teachers should refer any students with possible vision impairments for immediate evaluation.

Nondiscriminatory evaluation procedures and standards

Assessment measures	Findings that suggest need for special education services
Individualized intelligence test	Standardization may need to be violated because the student's visual impairment interferes with the ability to perform some tasks. Therefore, results may not be an accurate reflection of ability. Student may be average, above average, or below average in intelligence.
Individualized achievement tests	The student may not achieve in concept development and academic areas at levels of peers. Also, standardization of these tests, unless developed for students with visual impairments, may have to be violated because of the visual impairment. Results may not accurately reflect achievement.
Adaptive behavior scales	The student may have difficulty in self-care, household, and community skills because of vision and mobility problems.
Orientation and mobility evaluation	The student's ability to orient to the environment and to travel to desired locations may be limited.
Anecdotal records	The student may not participate in age-appropriate self-help, social, and recreational activities in home, community, or school.
Curriculum-based assessment	The student may not possess age-appropriate knowledge or skills in areas of communication, daily living, career awareness, sensory and fine motor, social, and self-advocacy.
Direct observation—learning media assessment	The student is unable to respond or has difficulty responding to print media without the use of magnification or alternative strategies, or the student cannot sustain reading in these texts for long periods of time.

Nondiscriminatory evaluation team determines that student has a vision impairment or blindness and needs special education and related services.

Appropriate Education

It is important for educators to know the cause of a student's visual impairment. Although a diagnosis of the cause, or **etiology,** may not provide accurate information about how much a student sees, this information is invaluable as educators plan the student's program (IEP). That is because an accurate diagnosis suggests typical characteristics associated with a particular eye condition, including probable lighting needs, a potential prognosis, and possible related medical disorders or learning problems.

Determining How a Student Uses Vision

Even given an accurate diagnosis and standard visual acuity measurements, it is impossible to predict exactly how a student with usable vision puts that vision to work to learn incidentally from the environment and to perform age-appropriate tasks. Educators, especially those who teach students with visual impairments, work with the student and her family to determine the effects of the disorder on the student's visual functioning when they conduct a functional vision assessment (FVA) (Anthony, 2000). While the results of an examination by an eye specialist are reported in clinical terms (such as 20/120), the results of an FVA are reported in language that informs educators and others in more concrete ways. For example, an FVA report might read, "The student can see three-inch-high printed letters at a distance of no more than five feet," or "The student can pick up a raisin on a white table when seen from six inches." Figure 16–4 shows part of an FVA designed for preschoolers.

Functional vision assessments describe how a student uses his vision in a variety of natural environments, such as under the fluorescent lights in a grocery store, on the playground in the glare of the midday sun, or in a dimly lit corridor leading to the school library. Appropriate FVAs also consider the different activities that occur in these environments. For example, a student at a grocery store may be able to see the products on the shelves but not be able to read the aisle labels that hang directly below the bright lights or the value of paper money at the checkout counter. Obviously, this kind of information is extremely valuable to the educators who work

FIGURE 16–4
Functional vision evaluation, prekindergarten level

Distant Vision
- Mimics teacher's facial expressions at _____ feet.
- Locates the drinking fountain at _____ feet.
- Recognizes own name, shapes, numbers at _____ feet.
- Identifies classmates at _____ feet.
- Locates personal possessions (lunchbox, jacket, backpack) in closet at _____ feet.
- Locates own cubby at _____ feet.
- Locates _____ of four dropped coins on a _____ (color) floor: quarter at _____ feet; nickel at _____ feet; dime at _____ feet; penny at _____ feet.
- Tracks and locates a _____ (size) moving ball at _____ feet.
- Avoids obstacles when moving round P.E. apparatus. Yes _____ No _____
- Visually detects and smoothly navigates contour changes in surfaces such as ramps and steps. Yes No

Near Vision
- Completes _____ (number of pieces) puzzle with head _____ inches from the board (describe how student performs task: e.g., trial and error, quickly, visually, tactually, etc.).
- Places pegs in a pegboard at _____ inches with head _____ inches from pegs (describe how student performs task).

Source: From *Functional Visual Evaluation,* by the Los Angeles Unified School District, 1990. Copyright 1990 by the Los Angeles Unified School District. Adapted with permission.

with the student because it helps them to understand and appreciate the student's particular needs and to design relevant instructional strategies (Bishop, 1996; Erin & Paul, 1996).

Most youngsters with usable vision need and benefit from periodic evaluations by a low vision specialist and an optometrist or ophthalmologist with special training in the evaluation of people with severe visual impairment and from the prescription of appropriate optical and nonoptical devices (Stiles & Knox, 1996; Wilkinson, 1996). Ideally, an FVA should occur before an examination by a low vision specialist so the teacher can share comprehensive information about the student's functioning. Of course, if the low vision specialist recommends optical aids or other devices, a follow-up FVA may be necessary to describe the student's functioning while using these devices.

Determining the Appropriate Reading Medium

For students such as Elexis, it is easy for teachers to determine how educational materials should be presented. Since he cannot see, braille clearly is the appropriate reading medium for him. Remember, however, that most students who are visually impaired have some usable vision; determining the appropriate learning medium for them is more complex.

Learning medium (plural *media*) is the term used to describe the options for the format of reading and literacy materials and may include braille, print, audiotapes, and access technology. Many children who can read print do so at such slow speeds or with such inefficiency that they also benefit from using braille. Teachers determine the appropriate reading media for students by conducting a learning media assessment (LMA) (Koenig & Holbrook, 1993). The LMA begins with a functional vision assessment but also includes additional considerations, such as the student's approaches (tactual or visual) to new situations or environments, the nature and stability of the eye condition, his visual stamina, and his motivation.

IDEA requires that members of the IEP team consider the use of braille or other appropriate reading and writing media for a student who is blind or visually impaired. Like a functional vision assessment, the LMA needs to be repeated at regular intervals to determine whether circumstances or the student's skills have changed and whether additional instruction in a different reading medium is necessary. Students who use both braille and print have the advantage of being able to choose the reading medium that works best for them under different conditions, such as when they are in a dimly lit restaurant or when reading assignments are long and eye fatigue is a problem.

Determining the Nature and Extent of General and Special Education and Related Services

The provision of special education services must be based on a student's specific needs as identified through a comprehensive assessment of the student's current level of functioning and knowledge in the following areas: academic skills and concept development, communication skills, sensorimotor skills, social/emotional skills, orientation and mobility skills, daily living skills, and career/vocational skills (Hazekamp & Huebner, 1989). Figure 16–5 sets out the skills that educators will evaluate in a comprehensive assessment.

Assessment is best accomplished by a team of individuals with previous and continuing experience with students with visual disabilities. In addition to those people who, under IDEA, must be members of the team, the team also should consist of an orientation and mobility specialist and a teacher of students with visual impairments. The outcome of a comprehensive assessment should be a description of the student's current level of functioning in all areas of potential need and the identification of skills to be addressed for that child to function optimally in current and future home, school, and community environments (Lewis & Russo, 1997; Pugh & Erin, 1999).

The list of people who must attend the IEP was described in Chapter 2.

Few teachers would consider it important to evaluate a straight-A high school student's ability to order a meal at a fast-food restaurant or to launder clothes, yet a student with a visual impairment who achieves at grade level may not function appropriately outside of the classroom. Many students with visual impairments lack these outside-of-school skills. Informal assessment techniques, including family and student interviews, the use of checklists, observation in natural

FIGURE 16–5
Potential unique needs of students with visual impairments

Concept Development and Academic Skills

- Development of concepts
- Determination of learning mode
- Academic support
- Listening skills
- Organization and study skills
- Reading charts, maps, graphs
- Use of reference materials

Social/Emotional Skills

- Knowledge of self
- Knowledge of human sexuality
- Knowledge of visual impairment
- Knowledge of others
- Development of interaction skills
- Development of social skills
- Lifelong recreation and leisure skills
- Self-advocacy skills

Orientation and Mobility Skills

- Development of body image
- Development of concrete environmental concepts
- Development of spatial concepts
- Development of directional concepts
- Understanding traffic and traffic control
- Trailing techniques
- Sighted guide techniques
- Use of vision for travel and orientation
- Development of orientation skills
- Use of long cane
- Independent travel in a variety of environments
- Public interaction skills

Communication Skills

- Handwriting
- Development of legal signature
- Use of braille writer
- Use of slate and stylus
- Use of word processors
- Use of adaptive equipment
- Note-taking skills

Sensory/Motor Skills

- Development of maximum use of vision
- Development of gross-motor skills
- Development of fine-motor skills
- Development of auditory skills
- Development of strength, stamina, and endurance in legs, arms, hands
- Identification of textures tactually and under foot
- Identification of kinesthetic sources
- Identification of olfactory sources

Daily Living Skills

- Personal hygiene
- Eating
- Dressing
- Clothing care
- Food preparation
- Housekeeping
- Basic home repair
- Money identification and management
- Use of telephone and information
- Use of desk tools
- Time and calendar
- Shopping skills
- Restaurant skills
- Community skills
- Knowledge and use of community services

Career and Vocational Skills

- Knowledge of relationship between work and play
- Understanding of value of work
- Knowledge of characteristics of valued workers
- Awareness of the variety of jobs people hold
- Awareness of jobs people with visual impairments often hold
- Awareness of jobs teenagers hold
- Job acquisition skills (want ads, résumés, applications, interviews)
- Typical job adaptations made by workers with visual impairments
- In-depth knowledge of a variety of jobs of interest
- Work experience
- Laws related to employment
- Management of readers, drivers

environments, and authentic and performance assessments, are the most valuable methods for determining the level of unique functioning of students with visual impairments.

When assessing a student's unique needs, educators should evaluate the age-appropriateness of a task from two perspectives. First, what are the student's peers doing? If Elexis's friends are at the stage of social development where hanging out at the mall is common, an assessment of Elexis's social skills should investigate this aspect of his functioning. Second, because sighted students are incidentally learning to perform some skills long before it is age-appropriate to expect mastery of these tasks, educators should evaluate a student's involvement in these tasks earlier than they would for sighted students. For example, while many students are not expected to launder their clothes independently until their late adolescence, educators should assess this task's component parts, such as scooping soap or sorting clothes by color, as soon as students with visual impairments mature.

Teachers also should avoid making assumptions about a student's previously learned information. For example, an 18-year-old woman with low vision, when tested to determine her knowledge of contraceptive devices, revealed that she was unaware that men's sexual organs differ from her own. Unfortunately, the teacher did not learn this fact until after the class had been discussing contraception for several days. Unaware of the role of incidental learning in learning about gender differences, she had assumed that all of her students, including her blind student, had acquired this knowledge.

Comprehensive assessments frequently include standardized and norm-referenced tests, which are often timed. An issue to consider about some tests is the additional time needed by students that can be directly related to their visual impairment. Taking tests often requires complex use of vision, such as frequent eye movements between the test booklet and the answer sheet or scanning of multiple-choice answers and stimulus paragraphs. Similarly, readers who use braille, who tend to have reading rates significantly below their peers with sight, and whose system of reading is not conducive to efficient scanning have difficulty with tests (Bradley-Johnson, 1994). Generally, students with visual impairments should be allowed at least time and a half to complete standardized tests (Spungin, 2002).

How Do You Assure Progress in the General Curriculum?

Including Students

As you have already read, blindness and low vision do not affect *what* a student can learn as much as they affect *how* a student learns. As a result, the majority of students with visual impairments attend public schools and spend at least part of the school day in the general education classroom (U.S. Department of Education, 2001). They are supported in these classrooms through the collaboration of teachers with special training in working with students with visual impairments. Students who have limited special needs receive support services from itinerant teachers, who travel from school to school to collaborate with general education teachers. Resource room teachers, who typically have a separate classroom in the school for private instruction, usually provide those students with more intensive educational needs with the support services necessary to achieve success in general education. Only students with the most intensive educational needs attend residential schools, where all of their teachers are specialists and all instruction is adapted to meet students' needs.

Educators of children with visual impairments have a long and proud history of including students with visual impairments in general education programs. The first inclusion program was established in Chicago more than a century ago, despite the fact that most students with visual impairments received educational services at residential schools at that time. In the 1950s, when there was a sudden increase in the number of premature babies with visual impairments, parents across the country demanded that local schools provide educational services for their children. Special teachers were trained and hired to meet this demand.

Accounts by individuals involved in this exciting and innovative time of local program development are filled with hopefulness and optimism for the future (American Foundation for the Blind, 1954, 1957; Hatlen, 1980–1981). Satisfied that the drawbacks associated with residential schools—removal from family and community—had been eliminated, families and educators were convinced that they had found the answer to educating all students with visual impairments through inclusion.

By the time the first wave of this new generation was graduating from high school, however, people began to express doubts about the efficacy of this model for all pupils. Although many students had achieved and were prepared to go to college or find adult employment, too many other graduates had very limited social and daily living skills (Hatlen, LeDuc, & Canter, 1975; Hoben & Lindstrom, 1980). Educators evaluated the needs of these graduates and the ways in which their school programs had failed them. They also evaluated more successful graduates. The result of these reviews was a resounding declaration of support for individualized services designed to meet identified needs, taking place in environments that facilitate learning for each particular student (Lewis & Allman, 2000a; Pugh & Erin, 1999; U.S. Department of Education, 2000). In Box 16–2, you can read about how one student's parents view her successful inclusion.

Planning Universally Designed Learning

As you learned in Chapter 2, the principles of universal design can be applied to the curriculum, to instruction, and to the evaluation of students and can involve alteration, augmentation, and adaptation. As valuable as the principles of universal design are, educators should be cautious about how they apply the principles to curriculum and instruction for students with visual impairments. That is because educators tend to underestimate these students' abilities and to provide too much support, leading to learned helplessness. In general, educators should expect these students to master the same content and meet the same performance standards as students with vision, even though the students with vision impairments may use adapted methods to access the curriculum and demonstrate these standards. In addition, because of the impact of visual impairment on students' basic knowledge of the world around them, their teachers should augment the curriculum with additional areas of instruction. You can read how teachers can promote success in general education through high expectations and meaningful interaction with peers in Box 16–3.

Adapting Instruction

To master the general academic curriculum, the one expected of all students, many students who are blind or have low vision require (1) adapted methods for accessing print, (2) instruction that is augmented by increased meaningful experiences, (3) opportunities to use assistive technology, and (4) provision of specialized instruction and materials.

Adapted Methods to Access to Print. Students with low vision access print primarily through the use of optical devices such as glasses, telescopes, and magnifying lenses. In some instances, they may read large-print books, though some researchers suggest that this practice does not lead to faster reading rates or more comfortable reading distances (Lussenhop & Corn, 2002). One of the advantages of magnification devices is that they allow the student access not only to materials provided in school but also to the printed materials that are available at home, at work, and in the community.

Students who do not learn as efficiently through their visual sense may access the academic curriculum through braille, a tactile method of reading. Like the print alphabet, braille is a code, a way of presenting spoken language in written form. As Figure 16–6 shows, there is one braille symbol for each of the 26 symbols (letters) of the English alphabet. The early publishers of braille developed numerous shortcuts for writing common words or letter combinations. These shortcuts are called braille contractions.

Because of the contractions, there is not a one-to-one correspondence between print and braille; so the level of difficulty in early reading books for print and braille readers is not the same.

Go to Chapter 16 of the Companion Website to read a statement about the placement of students with visual impairments that was signed by all the major organizations involved in the education of these students.

To learn more about braille, go to the Web Links module in Chapter 16 of the Companion Website.

(handwritten margin notes)
- I can have the same expectations
- augmentation b/c of know base
- adapt instr alternative options for accessing printed materials (large-print books, braille, AT)

Tom and Kris Kiel

As parents, we feel the responsibility of raising a healthy, happy, and productive child. When a visual disability affects your child, the pressures and responsibilities become even greater. We have found that the major resources available to us are our attitude and our sense of humor. We must not let ourselves focus on Tracy's blindness but on the whole child: Her blindness is just one small part of her whole being.

She is a sophomore in high school who is being included in our local school, and we realize how important it is to her to fit in with her peers. We have tried to challenge her in every aspect of her life, allowing her to explore and experience as much as possible. For example, when she wanted to know how high her house was, we put up the extension ladder and took her onto the roof. She now has a perception of how high it is. We feel that in order for her to fit in, she must have the ability to understand what is happening around her, even when she cannot see it. She must be able to perceive or sense

through what she hears and what she knows. Her life's experiences are the foundations that equip her to build bridges among her peers.

We as parents must use our own common sense and take command of our child's education. Each child is unique, and his or her learning style must be individualized to meet personal special needs. Tracy has attended our local public school since she was 4 years old. Our expectations for Tracy in school are that she will always be challenged. We have seen in her early school years how learning braille opened up her world and have watched the enjoyment she has found in her leisure reading. Assistive technology has also played an important role in Tracy's education. It has helped her to work more independently, thus becoming more self-sufficient.

Perhaps most important to us as parents has been the way in which attitude, life's experiences, and education can be woven together as the foundation for a happy and productive life. To laugh at life's experiences gives you the wisdom to build a brighter tomorrow.

To send a braille message to someone you know, go to http://www.hotbraille.com/ or the Web Links module in Chapter 16 of the Companion Website.

In Figure 16–7, you can compare a print passage with its braille translation. The number of braille contractions in this passage requires the braille reader to learn more difficult material much earlier, sometimes before all the print letters of the alphabet have been introduced to sighted students. Many new readers who are blind, such as Elexis, learn to read using *Patterns* (Caton, Pester, & Bradley, 1980), a special reading series that introduces the braille symbols in a logical manner. The specialist teachers of other students who are blind collaborate closely with the general education teacher to introduce the braille contractions, regardless of difficulty, in a way that allows the student to participate fully in the reading instruction offered in the general education classroom.

No curriculum exists for teaching literacy skills to students whose first language is not English (Milian, 2000). Teachers of students with visual impairments, teachers of English as a second language, and general education teachers must collaborate to create appropriate materials that enhance acquisition of language, reading, and braille skills. Box 16–4 presents some strategies for teaching braille to these students.

Even before reading instruction begins, students with visual impairments may not have had the same kind of exposure to letters and reading as their sighted peers have. Think of all of the opportunities that 3-year-old children with typical vision have to see letters, long before they are expected to read. Letters are everywhere: They appear on cereal boxes, on toys, on the newspaper or envelopes delivered daily to the house, on billboards, on street signs, on television, and in books. Even if these children are not learning the letter names, they see them and incidentally compare their outlines and shapes, establishing the background from which further learning occurs.

General education teachers of children with low vision need to make certain that students have opportunities to be exposed to letters and words that can be seen clearly. For preschoolers who are blind, two essential components of an early literacy program include systematically introducing braille and flooding the environment with incidental opportunities to find braille, such as with braille labels, storybooks, notes, and magazines.

Augmenting Instruction with Additional Meaningful Experiences. Often, students with visual impairments have difficulty understanding some of the ideas that their teachers are presenting because they have not directly experienced these concepts. They may need many

Inclusion Tips

Box 16–3

	What You Might See	What You Might Be Tempted to Do	Alternate Responses	Ways to Include Peers in the Process
Behavior	The student is a loner on the playground, choosing to play or walk alone.	Allow her to stay in class and read or do homework.	Teach her board or card games.	Once she has mastered the game, set up a game table during recess where anyone who wants to play can.
Social interactions	She doesn't say hello to peers in hallways or acknowledge peers' presence when entering room.	Assume she is stuck up and unfriendly.	Have the entire class prepare autobiographies, including life history, special interests, and photo or object identifiers for her and others to study.	Teach peers to say both her name and their own in greeting, as she may not be able to recognize them from their voices alone.
Educational performance	She is not learning new concepts or ideas as quickly as peers are and needs experiences with concrete materials.	Expect less from her or require her to practice difficult skills over and over.	Create meaningful situations where use of a concept or an idea is required by her in a variety of novel environments.	Have her act as a cross-age tutor to other students who benefit from use of concrete materials in learning.
Classroom attitudes	She might seem bored or uninterested during class demonstrations or teacher-directed activities.	Assume it is too difficult or simply ignore the inattention.	Make sure that she can "see" teacher's materials by having copies of printed/brailled materials at her desk during a lesson.	Have her and a peer help the teacher prepare lesson by getting out materials and preparing overheads and hands-on materials for class use.

additional experiences to make up for their lack of incidental learning. Universally designed instruction provides for these meaningful experiences and can benefit all students.

For example, early reading books designed for sighted children rely heavily on pictures to convey the meaning of the story. In addition, the pictures reveal to young readers information about the world that they may not have directly experienced. Not all new readers have been for a walk in a forest or have gone for a ride in a rowboat, but from pictures they can discern what the words in the story convey (Koenig & Farrenkopf, 1997). General educators of students with visual impairments must provide more experiential activities in their classrooms to assure that all students understand the text.

Older students with visual impairments also benefit from instruction that incorporates real experiences. Effective teachers use a tactual/kinesthetic approach to adapt instruction in some academic subject areas. Many of the concepts related to science, social studies, mathematics, art, and other subjects are especially appropriate for a tactual/kinesthetic approach. For example, when Elexis's science class studied germination, his teachers arranged for the entire class to use larger seeds so that Elexis could feel them easily. Instead of having him plant his seed in the dirt in a yogurt container, as his classmates did, Elexis planted his seed in water and checked daily for changes in how the seed felt and smelled. By using this method, he learned about root growth

— augmentation

FIGURE 16–6

English braille symbols

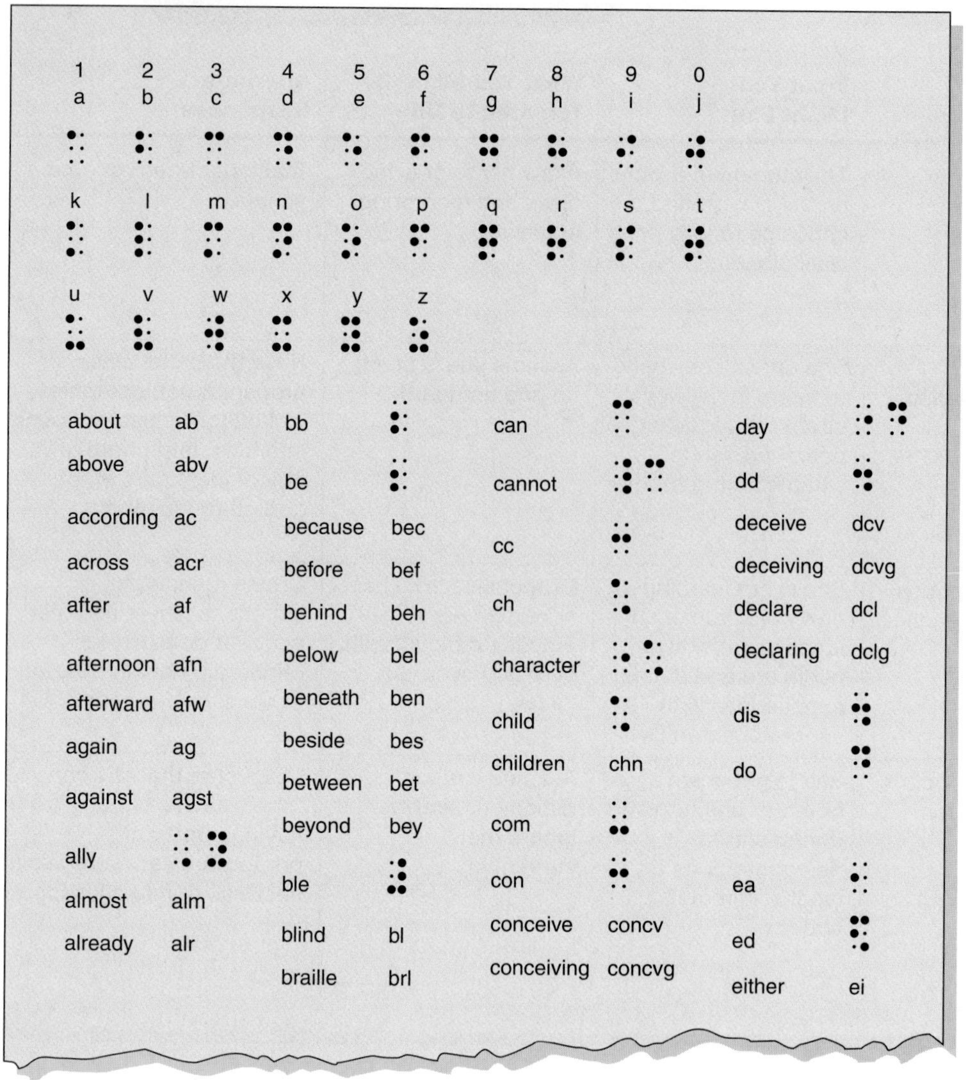

Source: Courtesy of Victor H. Hemphill.

(which had been presented through pictures in his science book) and also about seed germination and the growth of the leafy part of the plant.

Opportunities to Use Assistive Technology. As you have learned, students with visual impairments often require alternative methods to assure progress in the general education curriculum. Today, several types of devices make access to the curriculum much easier for people with visual impairment. Box 16–5 describes some of these technologies.

Some students, such as Elexis, use these technologies in combination. For example, when researching a paper, Elexis accesses the library's online card catalog with JAWS, which speaks the text on the monitor aloud to him. He takes notes about which books and articles to check out at the library on his Braille 'n Speak. Then, when he has the copies of the articles, he scans them with his optical character reader, which converts the print to an electronic form that he can either emboss in braille or read aloud using the computer's voice synthesizer. Using the braille translation software, Elexis prints out a copy of his paper in braille to proofread it before making the final print copy to turn in to his teacher.

FIGURE 16–7
Comparison of a passage in braille and print

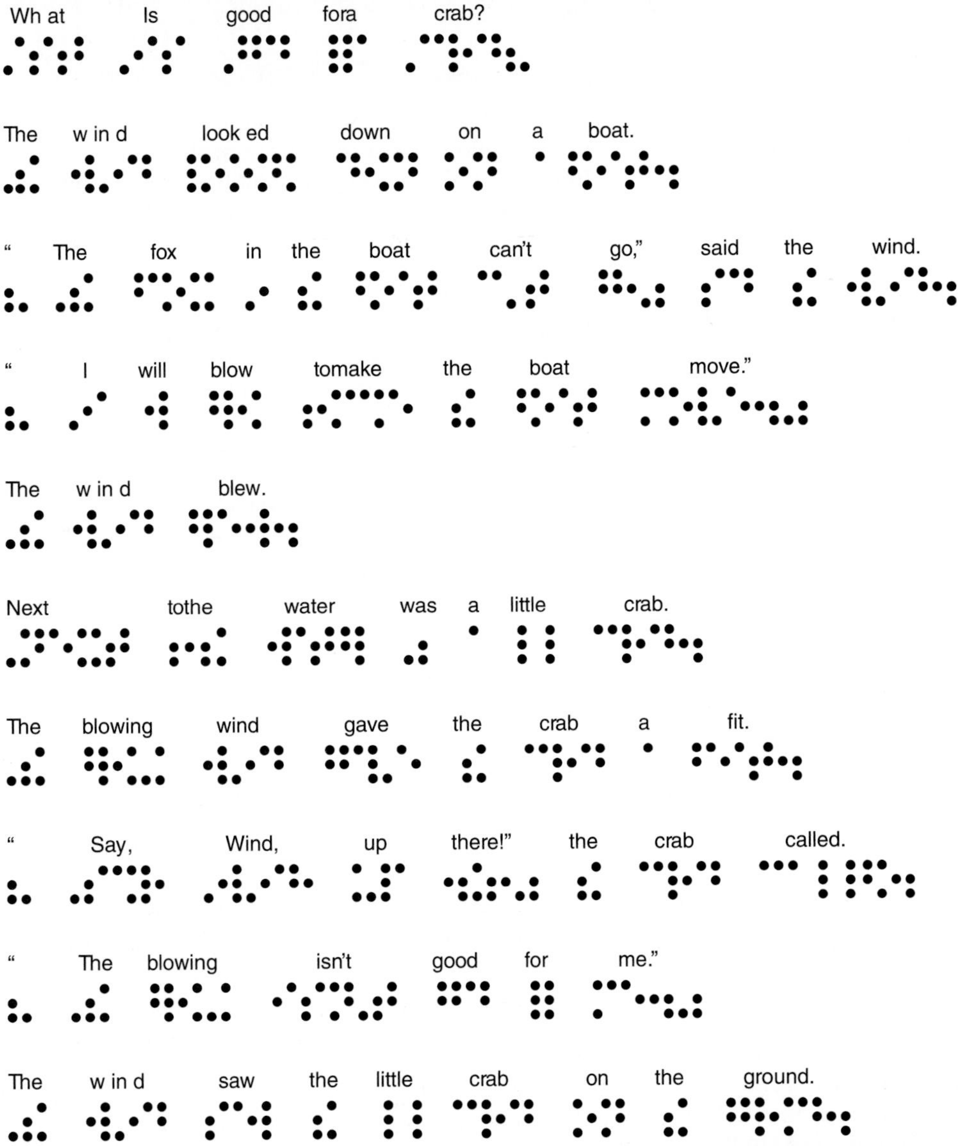

Wh at   Is   good   fora   crab?

The   w in d   look ed   down   on   a   boat.

"   The   fox   in   the   boat   can't   go,"   said   the   wind.

"   I   will   blow   tomake   the   boat   move."

The   w in d   blew.

Next   tothe   water   was   a   little   crab.

The   blowing   wind   gave   the   crab   a   fit.

"   Say,   Wind,   up   there!"   the   crab   called.

"   The   blowing   isn't   good   for   me."

The   w in d   saw   the   little   crab   on   the   ground.

Source: From "What is Good for a Crab" STORY CLOUDS, SCOTT, FORESMAN READING: AN AMERICAN TRADITION by Richard Allington et al. Copyright © 1987 by Scott, Foresman and Company. Reprinted by permission of Addison Wesley Educational Publishers Inc.

These technologies create the opportunity for students with significant visual impairments to access and participate in the general education curriculum—as long as it remains print-based. There is a dark side to the technological revolution, however, particularly for students who are blind. As teachers supplement more and more of the general education curriculum with graphics-based sources, such as dramatic interactive software programs, they make it less likely that the curriculum is accessible to students who cannot see the images on the screen. Already, vast areas of the Internet, because they are graphics-based, are not accessible to students with visual impairments. Even if these materials are presented with audio descriptions, they may be meaningless to the student who is blind simply because the student has limited experience with the object being described.

The challenge for classroom educators is to remain flexible in their use of curricular materials that are interesting and that can be meaningfully accessed by all students, including students

Box 16—4

Multicultural Considerations

Strategies for Teaching Braille to ESL Students

In General

1. Collaborate with ESL teacher, the orientation and mobility specialist, and others involved with the student's education to coordinate teachers' activities and to address jointly the student's language and visual needs.
2. Sequence language activities and structure lessons based on the school district's ESL curriculum.
3. Use real objects instead of visual examples.
4. Use thematic instruction whenever possible.

For Students in the Early-Production Stage of Developing English

1. Bring real objects that belong to the same category, such as fruits, to school. Make braille cards with words matching the objects. Assist the student to create first verbal and then written sentences using adjectives describing the objects (e.g., "The orange is bumpy.").
2. Create braille cards on which are written the names of classroom objects, such as door, desk, book, pencil sharpener, and so on. Read each noun, give the card to the student, and ask the student to place the card on the correct classroom item.
3. Read aloud to the student simple stories, poems, or rhymes that contain repeated phrases. Provide the student with a braille copy of material presented orally and ask her to move her fingers, held in the correct reading position, over phrases.

For Students in the Emergence-of-Speech Stage of Developing English

1. As the student to participate in an activity and then join the student to write a story about the activity on the brailler.

2. Provide the student with an audiotape and a braille version of an age-appropriate story. Encourage the student to read the braille while listening to the audiotape. Also, have the student write sentences or phrases about the story on the brailler.
3. Have the student participate in an activity of daily living or an orientation and mobility activity, audiotape the sequence of activities, and then write key words related to it on the brailler.

For Students at the Intermediate Fluency Level

1. Have the student create a book about an experience and share it with classmates.
2. Have the student keep a braille list of vocabulary words and a journal related to each of the content areas in which you provide instruction.
3. Create meaningful activities that require the student to speak, listen, read, write, and interact with others.

Putting These Ideas to Work for Progress in the General Curriculum

1. What are the special issues faced by students who are second language learners and who are also blind?
2. What is the role of collaboration when working with students who are second language learners and who read braille?

To answer these questions online and learn more about these ideas and concepts, go to the Multicultural Considerations module in Chapter 16 of the Companion Website.

Source: Adapted from Milian, M. (1997). Teaching braille reading and writing to students who speak English as a second language. In D. P. Wormsley & F. M. D'Andrea (Eds.), *Instructional strategies for braille literacy* (pp. 189–230). New York: AFB Press.

Technology Tips

Box 16–5

Assistive Technology for Students with Visual Impairments

Students with visual impairments often need to use a variety of technologies to access print materials and to create the products expected of all students engaged in the general curriculum. Some of the technologies used by these students include the following:

- *Optical character readers* (OCRs). Also known as scanners, these devices scan printed material and create a computer text file.

- *Screen readers.* Using synthesized speech, screen readers read the text that is displayed on a computer monitor as the user moves the cursor or inputs from the keyboard.

- *Braille embossers.* Connected to a computer and used in conjunction with braille translation software, braille embossers "print" a braille version of the text. Some braille embossers also print the ink-print translation on the same page.

- *Screen enlargement and navigation systems.* For students with low vision, screen enlargement software can increase the size of the characters on the screen, the cursors, and the menu and dialogue boxes. When the characters have been enlarged too much, it is easy to get lost within the document, so many screen enlargement programs also offer screen navigation systems.

- *Closed circuit televisions* (CCTVs). These devices can magnify any object placed on the viewing platform for viewing on a monitor.

- *Note-taking devices.* Several lightweight electronic note-taking devices are available that students use to take notes efficiently and then download them to a computer for study or to be printed or embossed as braille. Most of these devices have audio output; some also create braille on an electronic display.

Putting These Ideas to Work for Progress in the General Curriculum

1. What is the challenge?
2. What is the technology?
3. What do you do with it?

To answer these questions online and learn more about these strategies, go to the Technology Tips module in Chapter 16 of the Companion Website.

---

with visual impairments. Through universally designed instruction, teachers can make a dark future bright.

Provision of Specialized Instruction and Materials. Because of the complex or highly visual nature of some academic areas, such as mathematics, students with visual impairments may need specialized instruction to master the curriculum. In addition, many students need specialized instruction to master skills related to writing braille with a slate and stylus; use of the abacus for calculating; and development of listening, study, and organizational skills. For these purposes, special and general educators must collaborate to determine the best place for this instruction to occur. Sometimes it is more appropriate to provide initial instruction privately and then to practice emerging skills within the general education classroom.

A variety of adapted materials are available for use by students with visual impairments, including braille and large-print maps, measuring devices, graph paper, writing paper, calendars, flash cards, and geometric forms. A good source of adapted materials is the American Printing House for the Blind.

Augmenting Curriculum

As you have already read, students with visual impairments may have difficulty acquiring many of the functional life and social skills that students with adequate vision learn simply by watching parents, siblings, other adults, and peers. Effective teachers recognize how a visual impairment impedes sensorimotor development, orientation and mobility, recreation, social/emotional development, activities of daily living, and career education.

To visit the website of the American Printing House for the Blind, go to the Web Links module in Chapter 16 of the Companion Website.

Review the list of potential unique skills described in Figure 16–5.

All students with visual impairments benefit from an education that focuses on such daily living skills as taking care of their own living space.

You might ask yourself how instruction in these areas affects the student's progress in the general education curriculum. When children with visual impairments have had the same experiences as their sighted peers and when they are encouraged to be autonomous and allowed to make decisions for themselves, they are more interested and engaged in the content of the general curriculum and understand and appreciate it better. Mastery of these kinds of skills is critical to students' long-range educational and life outcomes. Students will need social, living, travel, and career skills to manage as competent adults and to apply the content and performance standards acquired in their general education programs. Typically, teachers need to expand three of the areas in the curriculum of students with visual impairments: daily living skills, orientation and mobility, and self-advocacy.

Daily Living Skills. Students with visual impairments require ongoing instruction in important skills of daily living, such as clothing management and kitchen skills. Generally, effective teaching strategies involve repeated visual or hand-over-hand kinesthetic demonstrations (or both), systematic instruction, gradual fading of assistance and prompts, and significant periods of practice (Koenig & Holbrook, 2000).

Often, people do not think to include a child with visual impairment in simple activities of daily living, probably because sighted children involve themselves in these activities through incidental learning. Involving the student in an activity and having high expectations that the skill can be acquired are critical factors in the acquisition of daily living skills. Because many adults think of people who are blind as helpless, they have low expectations for students with visual impairments to acquire typical skills. In addition, because adults may assume that students with low vision see more clearly than they do, the adults do not show these youngsters how to perform some of the activities that sighted children learn incidentally, such as buttoning a shirt, holding a spoon correctly, or making a bed. When these students do not spontaneously develop these skills, teachers may mistakenly think that the students also have additional cognitive disabilities and may reduce even more their expectations for students' achievement.

Low and inaccurate expectations of their abilities are students' worst enemies. Skilled teachers know to be constantly alert to what students are not doing for themselves. These teachers are prepared to challenge the subtle ways in which adults who are unfamiliar with the capabilities of students who are visually impaired lower expectations, promote their sense of inferiority, and decrease their self-motivation.

This young student who is blind works with an orientation and mobility specialist to learn how to move safely within his neighborhood before tackling the challenge of a busy city street.

Orientation and Mobility.   Orientation and mobility (O&M) skills, an IDEA-related service, are those that people with visual impairment use to know where they are in their environment and how to move around that environment safely. Unlike sighted students, students with visual impairments must learn to listen to the flow of traffic; react to changes of street and road surfaces; and use their vision, other senses, and perhaps a cane or other mobility device to detect objects in the environment and to help them know where they are.

The development of O&M skills begins in infancy and continues until the student can reach a destination safely by using a variety of techniques. Young children concentrate on developing body image, mastering spatial and positional concepts, learning the layout of their homes and schools, and developing environmental awareness. Older students focus on crossing streets safely and negotiating travel in increasingly complex situations, such as a town's business district or a shopping mall. Box 16–6 sets out some strategies for promoting travel in schools.

Even after a student acquires certain skills, it is sometimes necessary to use the services of an O&M specialist. For example, visually impaired adults who must orient themselves to new homes, neighborhoods, or work sites often contract with an O&M specialist to learn the layout of an area, landmarks, and the routes that they will use for orientation and travel.

Some blind adults learn how to travel with a dog guide. Primarily because of the responsibility associated with the care of these service animals, individuals under the age of 18 who still attend local schools rarely learn to use a dog guide; but children can be prepared to use guide dogs by learning to care for animals as pets (Young, 1997) and by becoming proficient at orientation skills, which are necessary for efficient traveling.

Self-Advocacy.   As adults, most people with visual impairments are required to explain their abilities and special needs to other people they meet: bus drivers, prospective employers, landlords, restaurant and hotel workers, and flight attendants. Sometimes these explanations are simple, such as asking a bus driver to call out the name of every bus stop; but sometimes they require

To learn more about dog guides, go to the Web Links module in Chapter 16 of the Companion Website.

Box 16—6

Into Practice

Promoting Travel in Schools

Students with visual impairments need to learn to travel independently in a variety of environments. An O&M specialist provides most of this instruction, but it is the responsibility of all adults who spend time with these students to reinforce the skills taught by the O&M specialists and to provide opportunities for students to practice what they are learning. General education teachers should discuss with the O&M specialist the O&M skills that their students are learning and ask how to reinforce or monitor these skills when the specialist is not present. Strategies for promoting travel in schools may need to incorporate both attitudinal and structural modifications.

Structural Modifications That Promote Travel

- Provide an organized classroom environment so that the student, once taught where materials and other key instructional items are located, can find them easily. Inform the student if classroom furniture or instructional items have been moved.
- Especially for new travelers, limit the number of obstacles along a route that might distract the student's concentration on technique, route, and destination.
- For older travelers, provide natural environments that pose challenging orientation and mobility problems.
- Keep hallways (floors and walls) clear where students use trailing techniques (move parallel to a wall with one hand extended in front along the wall to keep oriented and to follow a straight path).
- Place an identifying material at the level of a student's hand by the doors of classrooms and other important areas (library, lunchroom, office) so the student can identify these rooms.
- For young children, mark various areas of their classrooms with different textured floor coverings so that they can recognize these areas immediately when coming into contact with the texture.
- Mark stair treads, poles, and classroom doors with a contrasting color.
- Keep hall doors closed or all the way open to prevent injury.
- Provide a consistent storage area for students' canes, compasses, and other mobility devices.

Attitudinal Modifications That Promote Travel

- Allow even very young students to take your arm or hand when traveling together. Make it the student's responsibility to maintain the connection with you or any other guide.
- Don't allow children to hold hands when walking when that behavior is no longer age-appropriate for students with vision.
- Encourage the child who uses a cane to use the cane when traveling with friends. Too much reliance on a sighted guide in school can teach the child that his methods of getting around are inferior.
- Allow students who are blind or who have low vision to guide other students.
- Provide opportunities for students with visual impairments to run errands by themselves if such opportunities are offered to other students.
- When time permits, allow students who are lost to use their problem-solving skills to determine where they are and how to get back on their route.
- Tell the O&M specialist when you observe students using their skills correctly and independently and when you observe them having difficulty.
- Discuss with students the expectations that you have that they will be independent travelers as adults.

Putting These Strategies to Work for Progress in the General Curriculum

1. Which school personnel might need to be involved when planning the promotion of O&M skills for students with visual impairments?

2. What are some of the challenges involved in implementing these strategies at school?

3. What are the benefits to students with visual impairments when their educators promote independent travel?

To answer these questions online and learn more about these strategies, go to the Into Practice module in Chapter 16 of the Companion Website.

Source: Adapted from Griffin-Shirley, N., Trusty, S., & Rickard, R. (2000). Orientation and mobility. In A. J. Koenig & M.C. Holbrook (Eds.), *Foundations of education* (2nd ed.), Vol. 2: Instructional strategies for teaching children and youths with visual impairments (pp. 529–568). New York: AFB Press.

more detailed descriptions. For example, if Elexis goes to college, he may need to ask permission of each of his teachers to tape-record lectures, request personal copies of overhead transparencies, explain that it will be necessary to say aloud what they write on the board, and describe special accommodations that he needs (e.g., a reader or additional time during testing). Very likely, he will need to convince each of his professors that he can do the work for the class. In brief, he will have to be an effective self-advocate.

Elexis began his formal self-advocacy training when he entered seventh grade. At first, he simply listened as his resource room teacher explained his needs to his elementary and middle school teachers, but gradually he has become responsible for this task. He knows he can do this part of self-advocacy.

Elexis is less confident about his abilities in other new situations he will face as a young adult, such as advocating for his rights with landlords and, if he gets a dog guide, for access to public buildings, including concert halls and restaurants. His teachers are helping him to learn the laws (especially the Americans with Disabilities Act) and the communication techniques he can use to avoid confrontations (if possible) and to assert himself (as necessary). As part of Elexis's lessons in self-advocacy, his O&M teacher is introducing him to successful adults who are blind.

Collaborating to Meet Students' Needs

Meeting the academic, social, and functional life-skills needs of students with visual impairments frequently becomes a balancing act that demands considerable finesse and dexterity (Hatlen, 1996; Koenig & Holbrook, 2000; Pugh & Erin, 1999), prioritizing of goals, and creative problem solving.

Even within the academic area, achieving a balance becomes tricky. When Elexis was younger, he required at least twice as much time as his peers did to complete a typical math assignment, in part because the braille math code was unfamiliar to him. His teachers wanted to reduce the length of his assignments; but it was also obvious that, because of his lack of experience with numbers, he needed additional opportunities in order to achieve at the level of his classmates. The IEP team had to deal with his competing needs for more time to complete the assigned work and more experiences to understand it thoroughly.

Now at the high school level, Elexis still requires additional time to understand and complete assignments. He often spends more time each night doing homework than his classmates do. His IEP team struggles each year to work with him to determine when he will schedule instruction in orientation and mobility, career education alternatives, and skills needed to manage an apartment on his own. It would be easy to delay instruction of those skills to focus on the academic demands of high school, but the team members agree that Elexis needs to master them because they are essential to his success.

Creativity is the answer to many questions: creativity in scheduling, in instruction, in use of free time, and in collaboration among the many adults involved in each pupil's program. Critical to the success of this endeavor is that team members assume responsibility for the instruction and practice of newly learned skills whenever the natural opportunity to do so occurs. Each IEP team member also must believe that ultimate successful adult functioning depends on the student's attainment of skills in all of the curriculum areas—that no one area is more or less important than the others. It's a delicate balance.

In Box 16–7, you can read about the collaboration of general and special educators to meet the needs of a student who wanted to participate in his school's band.

Collaboration Tips

Box 16–7

Collaborating for Inclusion in Extracurricular Activities

Adults who are not familiar with the techniques used by individuals with visual impairments to accomplish tasks often have difficulty imagining that the students can participate al all. Often, effective problem solving to change attitudes and create practical answers requires both local and distant collaborators.

One such collaboration occurred when Ja'dine, a saxophone player in his school's orchestra, mentioned to his mother that he wanted to participate in the school's marching band. His mother's first thought was that Ja'dine was asking for too much—that, because of his blindness, he was going to be disappointed. She called Eloisa Ramirez, Ja'dine's special education teacher, and asked for her advice.

Eloisa was pleased that Ja'dine was interested in becoming involved in this extracurricular activity and wanted to support him. She recognized, though, that others at the school, like Ja'dine's mother, would have doubts about the wisdom of the idea. She talked with the school principal, who, though not entirely supportive of the idea, was willing to meet with the individuals most likely to be involved in implementing the plan.

In preparation for this meeting, Eloisa and Ja'dine made two lists. The first set out of the benefits he would experience as a member of the marching band. The second identified the adaptations that he might need. Before the meeting, Ja'dine practiced with Eloisa how he would present this information.

Attending the meeting were the orientation and mobility specialist, the marching band director, the principal, Eloisa, and, of course, Ja'dine and his mother. Ja'dine persuasively presented his case for being involved in the marching band. Having decided that he was committed to the work that would be required to make his idea a reality, the group then began examining how it might be accomplished. They identified two issues that had to be resolved. First, the principal was concerned that the district would use insurance liability as an excuse to prevent Ja'dine from marching. Eloisa offered to contact a state advocacy group of blind adults to get information that he could use to counter any arguments that the school district's insurance expert presented. This group even sent a representative to meet with district representatives.

The marching band director, who was uncertain how Ja'dine would be able stay in step, voiced the second concern. The O&M instructor suggested that there might be several ways in which Ja'dine could stay in formation with the rest of the band members. One strategy might be to use rigid poles to connect Ja'dine to the band members in front of and behind him. The band director wasn't too keen on this idea but agreed to allow the O&M specialist to attend band practice to work with him to identify other solutions.

During the summer, as the O&M specialist and the band director worked with Ja'dine and the other band members who were learning formations, other collaborators became involved. Eloisa had to contract with a faraway braillist who knew the braille music code and could emboss the needed braille sheet music. Ja'dine's peers in the band also became involved when his mother's work shift changed to early evenings and she was unable to get him to and from practice. Other band members had learned a lot about Ja'dine and his sense of humor as they practiced; they wanted to be with him and were more than willing to offer him rides.

At the first game of the season, Ja'dine proudly marched with his fellow band members. Watching from the stands were the team members who had helped to make this night possible. Farther away, but also smiling, were the advocate and the braillist. Indeed, success for students with visual impairments involves both distant and local collaboration.

Putting These Tips to Work for Progress in the General Curriculum

1. Who are the collaborators?

2. What are the challenges?

3. What can the team do?

4. What are the results?

To answer these questions online and learn more about these ideas and concepts, go to the Collaboration Tips module in Chapter 16 of the Companion Website.

What Can You Learn from Others Who Teach Students with Visual Impairments?

Learning for the Early Childhood Years: Blind Babies Foundation, San Francisco

Soon after Megan Smith was born, it became obvious that she was totally blind in one eye and had only minimal sight in her other eye. Within months after her birth, Megan and her family began to receive once-a-week visits from Lois Harrell, a specialist in the area of visual impairment employed by the Blind Babies Foundation (BBF) in San Francisco.

To achieve BBF's mission to provide services and programs that enable and empower families to meet the unique needs of infant and preschool children who are blind, Lois first helped Megan's mother, Beth, think like a blind person: to comprehend what the lack of sight meant for Megan's development. In that way, Beth could compensate for the lack of vision through stimulation of other sensory systems and facilitate Megan's development. For example, instead of brightly colored mobiles hanging above her baby's crib, Beth made mobiles of bells, rattles, and tactually interesting objects that Megan could reach. Lois also showed Beth how to teach Megan to rock and move her arms and legs, all preliminary to learning to crawl to reach a desired toy.

Early intervention programs such as BBF generally are home-based, although many successful programs also offer a center-based component where parents of infants go to observe preschool children with visual impairments and to meet the families of other youngsters who are blind or have low vision. The focus of early intervention in BBF and similar programs is to help parents understand the effects of visual impairment on learning and to present effective methods that reduce the impact of these effects on development. These programs emphasize strategies that enhance the child's acquisition of body image, language, early self-help skills, sensorimotor skills, concepts, gross- and fine-motor abilities, orientation, and early social interactions in home, school, and community environments where young children spend their time.

Preschool programs for children with visual impairments continue early intervention goals and provide many experiences that are the foundation for learning. Most of the activities are hands-on, meaningful, and related to real-life experiences. Students make their own snacks, wash their dishes, and find opportunities to change their clothes often, thereby practicing needed daily living skills. They collect tangible memories of their day and include them in braille or print experience stories that they dictate to their teachers. Teachers facilitate students' movement, meaningful language, exploration, and ability to control the environment to reduce the impact of visual impairment on development.

Many students with visual impairments are in heterogeneously grouped preschools and in preschools for children without disabilities. With the proper supports, these programs can be valuable learning environments for some children. It is easy to forget, however, that sighted children are acquiring many of the benefits of these programs through incidental learning, which is often unavailable to those with visual impairments. Although students with visual impairments participate, there is a potential that they will fall behind others in the class unless they get supplemental help.

Learning for the Elementary Years: Lawrence, Kansas

Mary Gordon has worked as a teacher of elementary-age students who have visual impairments throughout Kansas and Missouri for more than 20 years. Mary explains the purpose of her program: "When you can't see the chalkboard, and you can't see exactly where the rooms are, and you can't see this, and you can't see that, it takes twice as much energy to get through the day as it does for someone with sight. I provide instruction, materials, and support for students who may require many hours to master what a sighted child can learn through casual observation."

When her students are in music class, she presents braille sheet music. When they study geography, she provides maps with raised continents and tactilely different countries. When they are in science class, she describes the formaldehyde-soaked specimens as her students handle them. And when students seem exhausted, she is always ready with an encouraging word for the student and a teaching strategy for the general educators.

"My philosophy," says Mary, "has been to ensure my students the opportunity to learn everything their sighted peers do. Turning the philosophy into reality requires that every handout, map, graph, or other instructional device used in the regular class be transformed so that my students have access to everything their sighted classmates use."

Mary does one other thing: She teaches inclusion. "Each blind and visually impaired student should also become a real and integral part of his or her classroom. Since so much of our social interaction is visual, blind children must learn behaviors of sighted persons in order to obtain acceptance from their peers. To accomplish this, my students and I spend many hours practicing social skills that other students learn by observing. Learning to face the person to whom they are speaking, standing or sitting with appropriate postures, and eliminating mannerisms that might detract from their appearance are all imperative."

Elementary school is a key time for sighted children to develop a positive self-image, lay a solid foundation in academic and communication skills, and safely explore the world. For pupils with visual impairments, the focus of the educational program is the same as that for

A trip to the sculpture garden at the zoo provides a natural opportunity to encourage peer interactions.

students with vision; however, the techniques for accomplishing these goals may be different, requiring specialists to teach or reinforce concepts presented in class. In addition, and depending on the student's needs, the teacher emphasizes the development of career-awareness skills, additional self-help skills, social skills, knowledge of human sexuality, knowledge of one's visual impairment, and early advocacy skills. At the same time, the orientation and mobility specialist may be increasing the environments in which the youngster can travel knowledgeably and safely.

Learning for the Middle and Secondary Years: Tallahassee, Florida

Martin Vasquez's life has changed dramatically since entering middle school and being assigned to the itinerant program of Sandy Serventi, the teacher of students with visual impairments at Godby High School, in Tallahassee, Florida. While Martin was still in elementary school, Sandy conducted a comprehensive assessment of him and discovered that he could not make a sandwich or clean a sink. Because of his family's cultural attitude about the abilities of students labeled blind, he had not been expected to help with general household tasks; and because of his visual impairment, he had not learned how to perform these tasks incidentally. Sandy met several times at Martin's house with his mother and gradually persuaded her that Martin needed to learn to do more for himself at home—and that he needed a school program that focused on both his academic and nonacademic needs.

These days, Martin and Sandy usually work on transition skills. Although he initially spent two periods per day with her, their time together has been reduced to one hour per day. Today they are making a list of the utility services that he will need to contact when he moves into an apartment. Martin practices his note-taking skills as he contacts directory assistance to request the telephone numbers of the different utility companies and keys them into his electronic note taker. Later, he will retrieve the number and call to request information about having the utilities started.

On some days, Martin also works with his O&M specialist. Recently, they have been exploring apartment complexes close to the vocational school where Martin will enroll next year. Although Martin never needs to use his cane in the familiar environment of Godby High, in new areas it is critical to have the cane to detect unfamiliar stairs, curbs, cracks in the sidewalk, and other unexpected hazards. He will need to spend many long hours learning to negotiate safely the routes to use around the school's campus and to the grocery store, to the mall, and other community areas he will be using.

For students such as Martin, the middle and high school years are a time to catch up, to learn skills that students with good vision have been learning incidentally but that are not used until the teen years. Special teachers of these visually impaired students generally have to spend more time with them to meet their academic and disability-specific needs, while at the same time students are enrolled in general education classes to meet the school's academic graduation requirements. Sometimes they choose to delay their graduation in order to master all the skills they will need for successful, independent adult living.

Learning for Transitional and Postsecondary Years: Living Skills Center, San Pablo, California

Some students, such as Elexis, are well prepared for life after graduation. Their teachers and parents have taught them the academic, social, vocational, and life skills necessary for competent adult functioning. For other students, however, life after graduation is less certain. For these students, the Living Skills Center for the Visually Impaired, in San Pablo, California, offers a setting where participants learn the skills that enable them to choose their lifestyles, places of residence, leisure-time activities, and occupations. One participant is Erica Wildman, a student with significant low vision from San Diego, California.

Erica missed graduating with her class because, when her family moved to San Diego, some of her credits from her previous high school did not transfer. Although enrolled in school, Erica skipped school most of the semester. Her itinerant teacher, Rachel Sullivan, was concerned about Erica and met with her to discuss options for her future.

One option, of course, was to stay where she was and finish high school, a course of action that had not proved successful so far. Because she hadn't graduated yet and was between the ages of 18 and 21, however, Erica also had the opportunity to apply for enrollment at the California School for the Blind (CSB). With this option, she could attend general education classes for part of the day while learning skills related to successful adult living as a person with visual impairment at the residential school. A final option was the Living Skills Center.

At the Living Skills Center, Erica pays for and lives on her own in an apartment that she shares with another person with a visual impairment. In the same apartment building are seven other pairs of young adults with visual impairments in addition to other tenants. From her first day in the apartment, Erica was responsible for all of her needs and discovered for herself the gaps in her learning and experiences. But teachers are available who provide training in daily living skills, orientation and mobility, technology, vocational skills, and handling finances.

At the Living Skills Center, Erica focused initially on learning to shop for groceries at the store near the apartment and prepare her own food. Her first meals were pretty skimpy (and all cooked in the microwave oven), but gradually her skills in the kitchen improved. As her confidence increased, Erica made an appointment to see a vocational counselor, who spent several hours with Erica exploring her vocational interests and aptitude.

Erica decided her goals were to complete her GED and take courses in early childhood education at the local community college so that she could be licensed as a child-care worker. The vocational instructor at the Living Skills Center agreed to assist Erica in accomplishing these goals. Erica would continue to live in the apartment and would take advantage of the specialized instruction available to her at the Living Skills Center in technology, financial management, household management, and job-seeking skills.

Many schools for the blind have specialized apartment living programs for older students who have not graduated from high school. However, agencies such as the Living Skills Center, which serve young adults whose needs have not been met in school programs, are rare and increasingly necessary; it is not unusual for students who have low vision or are blind to need additional instruction in managing life independently after they leave high school. The philosophy of the Living Skills Center is particularly noteworthy in that it provides special services within the community and expects its clients to develop the skills to direct and manage their lives autonomously.

Transitional education includes training and job skills. Economic self-sufficiency is an obtainable goal for all people with visual impairments.

A Vision for Elexis's Future

If you were to meet Elexis today, you would notice his blindness, of course, but you would also notice that this young man has other interesting characteristics. He is someone you could talk to easily and who would put you at ease. If you spent much time with him, he would reveal his sense of humor and his devotion to his mother. You would learn that he is an athlete, an artist, and a person with plans for his future, although he is still not sure what he wants to do.

The future for Elexis is filled with countless interesting possibilities. Given his many skills and talents, his interests, his personality, and his positive attitude, few options for participation in vocational, family, and community endeavors will be closed to him. There is no doubt in Elexis's mind that he will graduate from college, work, and raise a family.

The vision for his future is bright today because his parents and teachers have focused on that bright vision since he was an infant. They have looked far enough into the future to see what skills he would need as an adult and have designed flexible educational programs to develop those skills. Recognizing that his blindness could prevent Elexis from easily discovering much about the world, they have provided him with the tools to be an active explorer and encouraged him to take the risks necessary to know himself, others, and the world around him.

He's someone you'd want to meet in your future.

What Would You Recommend?

1. To help Elexis's teachers understand his educational needs?
2. To parents of young children with visual impairments who want their children to grow up with attitudes and skills like those of Elexis?
3. To administrators of educational programs who want to design model programs for students with visual impairments?

Summary

How Do You Recognize Students with Visual Impairments?

▼ Legal blindness is defined as a central visual acuity of 20/200 or less in the better eye (with corrective lenses) or a central visual acuity of greater than 20/200 if the field of vision is less than 20 degrees. Legal blindness is a measurement that is used primarily to entitle people for government- or private-assistance programs.

▼ Within education, visual impairment, including blindness, is defined as an impairment in vision that adversely affects a student's educational performance.

▼ Students with visual impairments have a limited ability to learn incidentally from the environment and must be directly exposed to or taught much of what they need to know.

How Do You Evaluate Students with Visual Impairments?

▼ Ophthalmologists determine the presence of a visual disorder.

▼ Optometrists and low vision specialists determine if a visual disorder can be corrected through lenses or optical devices.

▼ A functional low vision evaluation determines how the student uses his or her vision in a variety of situations and places.

▼ A learning media assessment assists educators to determine the most efficient mode of reading and learning: braille, magnification, large print, and so on.

▼ Educators determine the effects of the visual impairment on the student's development of academic, communication, social/emotional, sensorimotor, orientation and mobility, daily living, and career/vocational skills. They use observations, parent and student interviews, and other informal testing procedures.

How Do You Assure Progress in the General Curriculum?

- ▼ Most students with visual impairments who do not have other disabilities are educated for most of the school day in general education classrooms. Special education services are provided by a teacher of the visually impaired who is assigned to that school either on a part-time or full-time basis.
- ▼ Professionals providing educational services to students with visual impairments support the full continuum of placement options and do not perceive any option as being more or less restrictive than others.
- ▼ Students learn through meaningful involvement in activities from beginning to end. Often they take a hands-on approach that maximizes the use of all senses. Through practice, they have increased opportunities to develop new skills.
- ▼ Professionals meet the academic and communication needs of students through the principles of universally designed instruction, particularly augmentation and adaptation.
- ▼ They meet the functional and life-skill needs of students to facilitate their eventual integration and full participation in adult society through curriculum augmentation. Instruction must focus on those skills acquired incidentally by sighted students through vision and those skills that are specific to students who are blind or have visual impairments.
- ▼ Professionals provide opportunities for students to develop competence, experience success, and acquire confidence in a variety of situations and circumstances.

What Can You Learn from Others Who Teach Students with Visual Impairments?

- ▼ In the early childhood years, the emphasis is on teaching sighted parents of infants and toddler with visual impairments to think like a nonsighted person; teaching the children to use hands-on, real-life skills (such as changing clothes and making snacks); and including the children in inclusive classrooms with support.
- ▼ In the elementary years, the emphasis is on teaching through tactile methods (braille, raised maps, handling specimens), practicing social skills that facilitate inclusion, and developing the student's orientation and mobility and self-advocacy skills.
- ▼ In the middle and secondary years, the emphasis is on transition from school to adulthood, from living at home with parents to living on one's own; on orientation and mobility training in the community (as distinguished from in the school and at home); and on mastering the content of state assessment tests.
- ▼ In the transitional and postsecondary years, the emphasis is on choosing lifestyles, places of residence, leisure-time activities, and work and on refining skills so that these choices can become realities.

Council for Exceptional Children **PRAXIS**

To find out how and where this chapter content connects to the CEC Professional Standards and the Praxis™ Standards, go to the Standards Connection module in Chapter 16 of the Companion Website. A comprehensive matrix aligning CEC Professional Standards, Praxis™ Standards, and INTASC principles to the entire text, is available in the Appendix and on the Companion Website.

Understanding the Standards/Topics Alignment Matrix

The matrix that follows is an "alignment" matrix. By that, we mean it aligns certain important strands of professional standards for special educators with the content of the chapters in this book.

There are three important strands of professional standards. Each one derives from a separate professional organization in special education, and each one also connects to today's best practices in special education.

One strand includes that standards of the Council for Exceptional Children, one of the leading advocacy and awareness agencies for individuals with disabilities (*www.cec.sped.org*).

A second strand includes the standards of Praxis™, the professional assessments for beginning teachers developed by Educational Testing Service (*www.ets.org*).

A third strand includes the Model Standards for Beginning Teacher Licensing and Development, developed by the Interstate New Teacher Assignment and Support Consortium. This is a collaboratively developed set of professional expectations for beginning teachers (*www.ccsso.org/intacst.html*).

The Council for Exceptional Children— Professional Standards

Established by the Council for Exceptional Children (CEC) these professional standards address ten critical areas of professionalism including foundations, development and characteristics of learners, individual learning differences, instructional strategies, learning environments and social interactions, communication, instructional planning, assessment, professional and ethical practice, and collaboration. As shown below each of these areas include an overview statement and more detailed measurable knowledge and skill statements. The knowledge and skills are limited to the CEC Common Core and do not include any standards from the CEC Area of Specialization Standards. The descriptions provided by CEC have been used verbatim.

Foundations

Special educators understand the field as an evolving and changing discipline based on philosophies, evidence-based principles and theories, relevant laws and policies, diverse and historical points of view, and human issues that have historically influenced and continue to influence the field of special education and the education and treatment of individuals with exceptional needs both in school and society. Special educators understand how these influence professional practice, including assessment, instructional planning, implementation, and program evaluation. Special educators understand how issues of human diversity can impact families, cultures, and schools, and how these complex human issues can interact with issues in the delivery of special education services. They understand the relationships of organizations of special education to the organizations and functions of schools, school systems, and other agencies. Special educators use this knowledge as a ground upon which to construct their own personal understandings and philosophies of special education. Knowledge and skills addressed in this standard include:

1. Models, theories, and philosophies that form the basis for special education practice.
2. Laws, policies, and ethical principles regarding behavior management planning and implementation.
3. Relationship of special education to the organization and function of educational agencies.
4. Rights and responsibilities of students, parents, teachers, and other professionals, and schools related to exceptional learning needs.
5. Issues in definition and identification of individuals with exceptional learning needs, including those from culturally and linguistically diverse backgrounds.

6. Issues, assurances and due process rights related to assessment, eligibility, and placement within a continuum of services.
7. Family systems and the role of families in the educational process.
8. Historical points of view and contribution of culturally diverse groups.
9. Impact of the dominant culture on shaping schools and the individuals who study and work in them.
10. Potential impact of differences in values, languages, and customs that can exist between the home and school.
11. Articulate personal philosophy of special education.

Development and Characteristics of Learners

Special educators know and demonstrate respect for their students first as unique human beings. Special educators understand the similarities and differences in human development and the characteristics between and among individuals with and without exceptional learning needs. Moreover, special educators understand how exceptional conditions can interact with the domains of human development and they use this knowledge to respond to the varying abilities and behaviors of individual's with ELN. Special educators understand how the experiences of individuals with ELN can impact families, as well as the individual's ability to learn, interact socially, and live as fulfilled contributing members of the community. Knowledge and skills addressed in this standard include:

1. Typical and atypical human growth and development.
2. Educational implications of characteristics of various exceptionalities.
3. Characteristics and effects of the cultural and environmental milieu of the individual with exceptional learning needs and the family.
4. Family systems and the role of families in supporting development.
5. Similarities and differences of individuals with and without exceptional learning needs.
6. Similarities and differences among individuals with exceptional learning needs.
7. Effects of various medications on individuals with exceptional learning needs.

Individual Learning Differences

Special educators understand the effects that an exceptional condition[2] can have on an individual's learning in school and throughout life. Special educators understand that the beliefs, traditions, and values across and within cultures can affect relationships among and between students, their families, and the school community. Moreover, special educators are active and resourceful in seeking to understand how primary language, culture, and familial backgrounds interact with the individual's exceptional condition to impact the individual's academic and social abilities, attitudes, values, interests, and career options. The understanding of these learning differences and their possible interactions provide the foundation upon which special educators individualize instruction to provide meaningful and challenging learning for individuals with ELN. Knowledge and skills addressed in this standard include:

1. Effects an exceptional condition(s) can have on an individual's life.
2. Impact of learners' academic and social abilities, attitudes, interests, and values on instruction and career development.
3. Variations in beliefs, traditions, and values across and within cultures and their effects on relationships among individuals with exceptional learning needs. Family, and schooling.
4. Cultural perspectives influencing the relationships among families, schools and communities as related to instruction.
5. Differing ways of learning of individuals with exceptional learning needs including those from culturally diverse backgrounds and strategies for addressing these differences.

Instructional Strategies

Special educators posses a repertoire of evidence-based instructional strategies to individualize instruction for individuals with ELN. Special educators select, adapt, and use these instructional strategies to promote challenging learning results in general and special curricula[3] and to appropriately modify learning environments for individuals with ELN. They enhance the learning of critical thinking, problem solving, and performance skills of individuals with ELN, and increase their self-awareness, self-management, self-control, self-reliance, and self-esteem. Moreover, special educators emphasize the development, maintenance, and generalization of knowledge and skills across environments, settings, and the lifespan. Knowledge and skills addressed in this standard include:

1. Use strategies to facilitate integration into various settings.
2. Teach individuals to use self-assessment, problem solving, and other cognitive strategies to meet their needs.
3. Select, adapt, and use instructional strategies and materials according to characteristics of the individual with exceptional learning needs.
4. Use strategies to facilitate maintenance and generalization of skills across learning environments.
5. Use procedures to increase the individual's self-awareness, self-management, self-control, self-reliance, and self-esteem.
6. Use strategies that promote successful transitions for individuals with exceptional learning needs.

Learning Environments and Social Interactions

Special educators actively create learning environments for individuals with ELN that foster cultural understanding, safety and emotional well being, positive social interactions, and active engagement of individuals with ELN. In addition, special educators foster environments in which diversity is valued and individuals are taught to live harmoniously and productively in a culturally diverse world. Special educators shape environments to encourage the independence, self-motivation, self-direction, personal empowerment, and self-advocacy of individuals with ELN. Special educators help their general education colleagues integrate individuals with ELN in regular environments and engage them in meaningful learning activities and interactions. Special educators use direct motivational and instructional interventions with individuals with ELN to teach them to respond effectively to current expectations. When necessary, special educators can safely intervene with individuals with ELN in crisis. Special educators coordinate all these efforts and provide guidance and direction to paraeducators and others, such as classroom volunteers and tutors. Knowledge and skills addressed in this standard include:

1. Demands of learning environments.
2. Basic classroom management theories and strategies for individuals with exceptional learning needs.
3. Effective management of teaching and learning.
4. Teacher attitudes and behaviors that influence behavior of individuals with exceptional learning needs.
5. Social skills needed for educational and other environments.
6. Strategies for crisis prevention and intervention.
7. Strategies for preparing individuals to live harmoniously and productively in a culturally diverse world.
8. Ways to create learning environments that allow individuals to retain and appreciate their own and each others' respective language and cultural heritage.
9. Ways specific cultures are negatively stereotyped.
10. Strategies used by diverse populations to cope with a legacy of former and continuing racism.
11. Create a safe, equitable, positive, and supportive learning environment in which diversities are valued.
12. Identify realistic expectations for personal and social behavior in various settings.
13. Identify supports needed for integration into various program placements.
14. Design learning environments that encourage active participation in individual and group activities.
15. Modify the learning environment to manage behaviors.
16. Use performance data and information from all stakeholders to make or suggest modifications in learning environments.
17. Establish and maintain rapport with individuals with and without exceptional learning needs.
18. Teach self-advocacy.
19. Create an environment that encourages self-advocacy and increased independence.
20. Use effective and varied behavior management strategies.
21. Use the least intensive behavior management strategy consistent with the needs of the individual with exceptional learning needs.
22. Design and manage daily routines.
23. Organize, develop, and sustain learning environments that support positive intracultural and intercultural experiences.
24. Mediate controversial intercultural issues among students within the learning environment in ways that enhance any culture, group, or person.
25. Structure, direct, and support the activities of paraeducators, volunteers, and tutors.
26. Use universal precautions.

Communication

Special educators understand typical and atypical language development and the ways in which exceptional conditions can interact with an individual's experience with and use of language. Special educators use individualized strategies to enhance language development and teach communication skills to individuals with ELN. Special educators are familiar with augmentative, alternative, and assistive technologies to support and enhance communication of individuals with exceptional needs. Special educators match their communication methods to an individual's language proficiency and cultural and linguistic differences. Special educators provide effective language models, and they use communication strategies and resources to facilitate understanding of subject matter for individuals with ELN whose primary language is not English. Knowledge and skills addressed in this standard include:

1. Effects of cultural and linguistic differences on growth and development.
2. Characteristics of one's own culture and use of language and the ways in which these can differ from other cultures and uses of languages.
3. Ways of behaving and communicating among cultures that can lead to misinterpretation and misunderstanding.
4. Augmentative and assistive communication strategies.
5. Use strategies to support and enhance communication skills of individuals with exceptional learning needs.
6. Use communication strategies and resources to facilitate understanding of subject matter for students whose primary language is not the dominant language.

Instructional Planning

Individualized decision-making and instruction is at the center of special education practice. Special educators develop long-range individualized instructional plans anchored in both general and special curricula. In addition, special educators systematically translate these individualized plans into carefully selected shorter-range goals and objectives taking into consideration an individual's abilities and needs, the learning environment, and a myriad of cultural and linguistic factors. Individualized instructional plans emphasize explicit modeling and efficient guided practice to assure acquisition and fluency through maintenance and generalization. Understanding of these factors as well as the implications of an individual's exceptional condition, guides the special educator's selection, adaptation, and creation of materials, and the use of powerful instructional variables. Instructional plans are modified based on ongoing analysis of the individual's learning progress. Moreover, special educators facilitate this instructional planning in a collaborative context including the individuals with exceptionalities, families, professional colleagues, and personnel from other agencies as appropriate. Special educators also develop a variety of individualized transition plans, such as transitions from preschool to elementary school and from secondary settings to a variety of postsecondary work and learning contexts. Special educators are comfortable using appropriate technologies to support instructional planning and individualized instruction. Knowledge and skills addressed in this standard include:

1. Theories and research that form the basis of curriculum development and instructional practice.
2. Scope and sequences of general and special curricula.
3. National, state or provincial, and local curricula standards.
4. Technology for planning and managing the teaching and learning environment.
5. Roles and responsibilities of the paraeducator related to instruction, intervention, and direct service.
6. Identify and prioritize areas of the general curriculum and accommodations for individuals with exceptional learning needs.
7. Develop and implement comprehensive, longitudinal individualized programs in collaboration with team members.
8. Involve the individual and family in setting instructional goals and monitoring progress.
9. Use functional assessments to develop intervention plans.
10. Use task analysis.
11. Sequence, implement, and evaluate individualized learning objectives.
12. Integrate affective, social, and life skills with academic curricula.
13. Develop and select instructional content, resources, and strategies that respond to cultural, linguistic, and gender differences.
14. Incorporate and implement instructional and assistive technology into the educational program.
15. Prepare lesson plans.
16. Prepare and organize materials to implement daily lesson plans.
17. Use instructional time effectively.
18. Make responsive adjustments to instruction based on continual observations.
19. Prepare individuals to exhibit self-enhancing behavior in response to societal attitudes and actions.

Assessment

Assessment is integral to the decision-making and teaching of special educators and special educators use multiple types of assessment information for a variety of educational decisions. Special educators use the results of assessments to help identify exceptional learning needs and to develop and implement individualized instructional programs, as well as to adjust instruction in response to ongoing learning progress. Special educators understand the legal policies and ethical principles of measurement and assessment related to referral, eligibility, program planning, instruction, and placement for individuals with ELN, including those from culturally and linguistically diverse backgrounds. Special educators understand measurement theory and practices for addressing issues of validity, reliability, norms, bias, and interpretation of assessment results. In addition, special educators understand the appropriate use and limitations of various types of assessments. Special educators collaborate with families and other colleagues to assure non-biased, meaningful assessments and decision-making. Special educators conduct formal and informal assessments of behavior, learning, achievement, and environments to design learning experiences that support the growth and development of individuals with ELN. Special educators use assessment information to identify supports and adaptations required for individuals with ELN to access the general curriculum and to participate in school, system, and statewide assessment programs. Special educators regularly monitor the progress of individuals with ELN in general and special curricula. Special educators use appropriate technologies to support their assessments. Knowledge and skills addressed in this standard include:

1. Basic terminology used in assessment.
2. Legal provisions and ethical principles regarding assessment of individuals.
3. Screening, pre-referral, referral, and classification procedures.
4. Use and limitations of assessment instruments.
5. National, state or provincial, and local accommodations and modifications.
6. Gather relevant background information.
7. Administer nonbiased formal and informal assessments.
8. Use technology to conduct assessments.
9. Develop or modify individualized assessment strategies.
10. Interpret information from formal and informal assessments.

11. Use assessment information in making eligibility, program, and placement decisions for individuals with exceptional learning needs, including those from culturally and/or linguistically diverse backgrounds.
12. Report assessment results to all stakeholders using effective communication skills.
13. Evaluate instruction and monitor progress of individuals with exceptional learning needs.
14. Create and maintain records.

Professional and Ethical Practice

Special educators are guided by the profession's ethical and professional practice standards. Special educators practice in multiple roles and complex situations across wide age and developmental ranges. Their practice requires ongoing attention to legal matters along with serious professional and ethical considerations. Special educators engage in professional activities and participate in learning communities that benefit individuals with ELN, their families, colleagues, and their own professional growth. Special educators view themselves as lifelong learners and regularly reflect on and adjust their practice. Special educators are aware of how their own and others attitudes, behaviors, and ways of communicating can influence their practice. Special educators understand that culture and language can interact with exceptionalities, and are sensitive to the many aspects of diversity of individuals with ELN and their families. Special educators actively plan and engage in activities that foster their professional growth and keep them current with evidence-based best practices. Special educators know their own limits of practice and practice within them. Knowledge and skills addressed in this standard include:

1. Personal cultural biases and differences that affect one's teaching.
2. Importance of the teacher serving as a model for individuals with exceptional learning needs.
3. Continuum of lifelong professional development.
4. Methods to remain current regarding research-validated practice.
5. Practice within the CEC Code of Ethics and other standards of the profession.
6. Uphold high standards of competence and integrity and exercise sound judgment in the practice of the professional.
7. Act ethically in advocating for appropriate services.
8. Conduct professional activities in compliance with applicable laws and policies.
9. Demonstrate commitment to developing the highest education and quality-of-life potential of individuals with exceptional learning needs.
10. Demonstrate sensitivity for the culture, language, religion, gender, disability, socio-economic status, and sexual orientation of individuals.

11. Practice within one's skill limit and obtain assistance as needed.
12. Use verbal, nonverbal, and written language effectively.
13. Conduct self-evaluation of instruction.
14. Access information on exceptionalities.
15. Reflect on one's practice to improve instruction and guide professional growth.
16. Engage in professional activities that benefit individuals with exceptional learning needs, their families, and one's colleagues.

Collaboration

Special educators routinely and effectively collaborate with families, other educators, related service providers, and personnel from community agencies in culturally responsive ways. This collaboration assures that the needs of individuals with ELN are addressed throughout schooling. Moreover, special educators embrace their special role as advocate for individuals with ELN. Special educators promote and advocate the learning and well being of individuals with ELN across a wide range of settings and a range of different learning experiences. Special educators are viewed as specialists by a myriad of people who actively seek their collaboration to effectively include and teach individuals with ELN. Special educators are a resource to their colleagues in understanding the laws and policies relevant to Individuals with ELN. Special educators use collaboration to facilitate the successful transitions of individuals with ELN across settings and services. Knowledge and skills addressed in this standard include:

1. Models and strategies of consultation and collaboration.
2. Roles of individuals with exceptional learning needs, families, and school and community personnel in planning of an individualized program.
3. Concerns of families of individuals with exceptional learning needs and strategies to help address these concerns.
4. Culturally responsive factors that promote effective communication and collaboration with individuals with exceptional learning needs, families, school personnel, and community members.
5. Maintain confidential communication about individuals with exceptional learning needs.
6. Collaborate with families and others in assessment of individuals with exceptional learning needs.
7. Foster respectful and beneficial relationships between families and professionals.
8. Assist individuals with exceptional learning needs and their families in becoming active participants in the educational team.
9. Plan and conduct collaborative conferences with individuals with exceptional learning needs and their families.

10. Collaborate with school personnel and community members in integrating individuals with exceptional learning needs into various settings.

11. Use group problem solving skills to develop, implement and evaluate collaborative activities.

12. Model techniques and coach others in the use of instructional methods and accommodations.

13. Communicate with school personnel about the characteristics and needs of individuals with exceptional learning needs.

14. Communicate effectively with families of individuals with exceptional learning needs from diverse backgrounds.

15. Observe, evaluate and provide feedback to paraeducators.

The PRAXIS Standards for Special Education*

Established by Educational Testing Services (ETS) these professional standards address three components of special education including understanding, delivery, and legal issues. Each standard is comprehensive, as shown below.

As discusses by ETS (ETS, 2003), the Special Education: Knowledge-Based Core Principles are attentive to understanding exceptionalities, legal and social issues, and delivery of services to students with disabilities. Each of these areas, as described by ETS, is detailed below.

Understanding Exceptionalities

1. Theories and principles of human development and learning, including research and theories related to human development; theories of learning; social and emotional development; language development; cognitive development; and physical development, including motor and sensory

2. Characteristics of students with disabilities, including medical/physical; educational; social; and psychological

3. Basic concepts in special education, including definitions of all major categories and specific disabilities; causation and prevention of disability; the nature of behaviors, including frequency, duration, intensity, and degrees of severity; and classification of students with disabilities, including classifications as represented in IDEA and labeling of students

Legal and Societal Issues

1. Federal laws and landmark legal cases related to special education.

2. Issues related to school, family, and/or community, such as teacher advocacy for students and families, including advocating for educational change and developing student self-advocacy; family participation and support systems; public attitudes toward individuals with disabilities; and cultural and community influences

Delivery of Services to Students with Disabilities

1. Conceptual approaches underlying the delivery of services to students with disabilities (for example, medical, psychodynamic, behavioral, cognitive, sociological, eclectic)

2. Professional roles and responsibilities of teachers of students with disabilities (for example, teacher as a collaborator with other teachers, parents, community groups, and outside agencies); teacher as a multidisciplinary team member; teacher's role in selecting appropriate environments and providing appropriate services to students; knowledge and use of professional literature, research (including classroom research), and professional organizations and associations; and reflecting on one's own teaching

3. Assessment, including how to modify, construct, or select and conduct nondiscriminatory and appropriate informal and formal assessment procedures; how to interpret standardized and specialized assessment results; how to use evaluation results for various purposes, including monitoring instruction and IEP/ITP development; and how to prepare written reports and communicate findings to others

4. Placement and program issues (including continuum of services; mainstreaming; integration; inclusion; least restrictive environment; non-categorical, categorical, and cross-categorical programs; related services; early intervention; community-based training; transition of students into and within special education placements; postschool transitions; and access to assistive technology)

5. Curriculum and instruction, including the IEP/ITP process; instructional development and implementation (for example, instructional activities, curricular materials, resources and equipment, working with classroom personnel, tutoring and the use of technology); teaching strategies and methods (for example, direct instruction, cooperative learning, diagnostic-prescriptive method); instructional format and components (for example, individualized instruction, small- and large-group instruction, modeling, drill and practice); and areas of instruction (such as academics, study and learning skills, social, self-care, and vocational skills)

6. Management of the learning environment, including behavior management (for example, behavior analysis—identification and definition of antecedents, target

*PRAXIS materials selected from The Praxis Series: Professional Assessments for Beginning Teachers. Reprinted by permission of Educational Testing Service, the copyright owner.

Disclaimer Permission to reprint PRAXIS materials does not constitute review of Endorsement by Educational Testing Service of this publication as a whole or of any other testing information it may contain.

behavior, and consequent events, data-gathering procedures, selecting and using behavioral interventions); classroom organization/management (for example, providing the appropriate physical-social environment for learning—expectations, rules, consequences, consistency, attitudes, lighting, seating, access, and strategies for positive interactions, transitions between lessons and activities); grouping of students; and effective and efficient documentation (such as parent/ teacher contacts and legal records)

The INTASC Standards for Teacher Education

The Interstate New Teacher Assessment and Support Consortium (INTASC) developed ten standards for beginning teachers. Used in many states for institutional review or teacher licensure, each standard includes relevant knowledge, dispositions, and performance indicators. As shown below these standards are attentive to curriculum, instruction, diversity, collaboration, and assessment among other critical themes.

Principle #1:

The teacher understands the central concepts, tools of inquiry, and structures of the discipline(s) he or she teaches and can create learning experiences that make these aspects of subject matter meaningful for students.

Knowledge

1. The teacher understands major concepts, assumptions, debates, processes of inquiry, and ways of knowing that are central to the discipline(s) s/he teaches.
2. The teacher understands how students' conceptual frameworks and their misconceptions for an area of knowledge can influence their learning.
3. The teacher can relate his/her disciplinary knowledge to other subject areas.

Dispositions

1. The teacher realizes that subject matter knowledge is not a fixed body of facts but is complex and ever-evolving. S/he seeks to keep abreast of new ideas and understandings in the field.
2. The teacher appreciates multiple perspectives and conveys to learners how knowledge is developed from the vantage point of the knower.
3. The teacher has enthusiasm for the discipline(s) s/he teaches and sees connections to everyday life.
4. The teacher is committed to continuous learning and engages in professional discourse about subject matter knowledge and children's learning of the discipline.

Performances

1. The teacher effectively uses multiple representations and explanations of disciplinary concepts that capture key ideas and link them to students' prior understandings.

2. The teacher can represent and use differing viewpoints, theories, "ways of knowing" and methods of inquiry in his/her teaching of subject matter concepts.
3. The teacher can evaluate teaching resources and curriculum materials for their comprehensiveness, accuracy, and usefulness for representing particular ideas and concepts.
4. The teacher engages students in generating knowledge and testing hypotheses according to the methods of inquiry and standards of evidence used in the discipline.
5. The teacher develops and uses curricula that encourage students to see, question, and interpret ideas from diverse perspectives.
6. The teacher can create interdisciplinary learning experiences that allow students to integrate knowledge, skills, and methods of inquiry from several subject areas.

Principle #2:

The teacher understands how children learn and develop, and can provide learning opportunities that support their intellectual, social and personal development.

Knowledge

1. The teacher understands how learning occurs—how students construct knowledge, acquire skills, and develop habits of mind—and knows how to use instructional strategies that promote student learning.
2. The teacher understands that students' physical, social, emotional, moral and cognitive development influence learning and knows how to address these factors when making instructional decisions.
3. The teacher is aware of expected developmental progressions and ranges of individual variation within each domain (physical, social, emotional, moral and cognitive), can identify levels of readiness in learning, and understands how development in any one domain may affect performance in others.

Dispositions

1. The teacher appreciates individual variation within each area of development, shows respect for the diverse talents of all learners, and is committed to help them develop self-confidence and competence.
2. The teacher is disposed to use students' strengths as a basis for growth, and their errors as an opportunity for learning.

Performances

1. The teacher assesses individual and group performance in order to design instruction that meets learners' current needs in each domain (cognitive, social, emotional, moral, and physical) and that leads to the next level of development.
2. The teacher stimulates student reflection on prior knowledge and links new ideas to already familiar ideas,

making connections to students' experiences, providing opportunities for active engagement, manipulation, and testing of ideas and materials, and encouraging students to assume responsibility for shaping their learning tasks.

3. The teacher accesses students' thinking and experiences as a basis for instructional activities by, for example, encouraging discussion, listening and responding to group interaction, and eliciting samples of student thinking orally and in writing.

Principle #3:

The teacher understands how students differ in their approaches to learning and creates instructional opportunities that are adapted to diverse learners.

Knowledge

1. The teacher understands and can identify differences in approaches to learning and performance, including different learning styles, multiple intelligences, and performance modes, and can design instruction that helps use students' strengths as the basis for growth.
2. The teacher knows about areas of exceptionality in learning—including learning disabilities, visual and perceptual difficulties, and special physical or mental challenges.
3. The teacher knows about the process of second language acquisition and about strategies to support the learning of students whose first language is not English.
4. The teacher understands how students' learning is influenced by individual experiences, talents, and prior learning, as well as language, culture, family and community values.
5. The teacher has a well-grounded framework for understanding cultural and community diversity and knows how to learn about and incorporate students' experiences, cultures, and community resources into instruction.

Dispositions

1. The teacher believes that all children can learn at high levels and persists in helping all children achieve success.
2. The teacher appreciates and values human diversity, shows respect for students' varied talents and perspectives, and is committed to the pursuit of "individually configured excellence."
3. The teacher respects students as individuals with differing personal and family backgrounds and various skills, talents, and interests.
4. The teacher is sensitive to community and cultural norms.
5. The teacher makes students feel valued for their potential as people, and helps them learn to value each other.

Performances

1. The teacher identifies and designs instruction appropriate to students' stages of development, learning styles, strengths, and needs.

2. The teacher uses teaching approaches that are sensitive to the multiple experiences of learners and that address different learning and performance modes.
3. The teacher makes appropriate provisions (in terms of time and circumstances for work, tasks assigned, communication and response modes) for individual students who have particular learning differences or needs.
4. The teacher can identify when and how to access appropriate services or resources to meet exceptional learning needs.
5. The teacher seeks to understand students' families, cultures, and communities, and uses this information as a basis for connecting instruction to students' experiences (e.g. drawing explicit connections between subject matter and community matters, making assignments that can be related to students' experiences and cultures).
6. The teacher brings multiple perspectives to the discussion of subject matter, including attention to students' personal, family, and community experiences and cultural norms.
7. The teacher creates a learning community in which individual differences are respected.

Principle #4:

The teacher understands and uses a variety of instructional strategies to encourage students' development of critical thinking, problem solving, and performance skills.

Knowledge

1. The teacher understands the cognitive processes associated with various kinds of learning (e.g. critical and creative thinking, problem structuring and problem solving, invention, memorization and recall) and how these processes can be stimulated.
2. The teacher understands principles and techniques, along with advantages and limitations, associated with various instructional strategies (e.g. cooperative learning, direct instruction, discovery learning, whole group discussion, independent study, interdisciplinary instruction).
3. The teacher knows how to enhance learning through the use of a wide variety of materials as well as human and technological resources (e.g. computers, audiovisual technologies, videotapes and discs, local experts, primary documents and artifacts, texts, reference books, literature, and other print resources).

Dispositions

1. The teacher values the development of students' critical thinking, independent problem solving, and performance capabilities.
2. The teacher values flexibility and reciprocity in the teaching process as necessary for adapting instruction to student responses, ideas, and needs.

Performances

1. The teacher carefully evaluates how to achieve learning goals, choosing alternative teaching strategies and materials to achieve different instructional purposes and to meet student needs (e.g. developmental stages, prior knowledge, learning styles, and interests).
2. The teacher uses multiple teaching and learning strategies to engage students in active learning opportunities that promote the development of critical thinking, problem solving, and performance capabilities and that help students assume responsibility for identifying and using learning resources.
3. The teacher constantly monitors and adjusts strategies in response to learner feedback.
4. The teacher varies his or her role in the instructional process (e.g. instructor, facilitator, coach, audience) in relation to the content and purposes of instruction and the needs of students.
5. The teacher develops a variety of clear, accurate presentations and representations of concepts, using alternative explanations to assist students' understanding and presenting diverse perspectives to encourage critical thinking.

Principle #5:

The teacher uses an understanding of individual and group motivation and behavior to create a learning environment that encourages positive social interaction, active engagement in learning, and self-motivation.

Knowledge

1. The teacher can use knowledge about human motivation and behavior drawn from the foundational sciences of psychology, anthropology, and sociology to develop strategies for organizing and supporting individual and group work.
2. The teacher understands how social groups function and influence people, and how people influence groups.
3. The teacher knows how to help people work productively and cooperatively with each other in complex social settings.
4. The teacher understands the principles of effective classroom management and can use a range of strategies to promote positive relationships, cooperation, and purposeful learning in the classroom.
5. The teacher recognizes factors and situations that are likely to promote or diminish intrinsic motivation, and knows how to help students become self-motivated.

Dispositions

1. The teacher takes responsibility for establishing a positive climate in the classroom and participates in maintaining such a climate in the school as a whole.

2. The teacher understands how participation supports commitment, and is committed to the expression and use of democratic values in the classroom.
3. The teacher values the role of students in promoting each other's learning and recognizes the importance of peer relationships in establishing a climate of learning.
4. The teacher recognizes the value of intrinsic motivation to students' life-long growth and learning.
5. The teacher is committed to the continuous development of individual students' abilities and considers how different motivational strategies are likely to encourage this development for each student.

Performances

1. The teacher creates a smoothly functioning learning community in which students assume responsibility for themselves and one another, participate in decision making, work collaboratively and independently, and engage in purposeful learning activities.
2. The teacher engages students in individual and cooperative learning activities that help them develop the motivation to achieve, by, for example, relating lessons to students' personal interests, allowing students to have choices in their learning, and leading students to ask questions and pursue problems that are meaningful to them.
3. The teacher organizes, allocates, and manages the resources of time, space, activities, and attention to provide active and equitable engagement of students in productive tasks.
4. The teacher maximizes the amount of class time spent in learning by creating expectations and processes for communication and behavior along with a physical setting conducive to classroom goals.
5. The teacher helps the group to develop shared values and expectations for student interactions, academic discussions, and individual and group responsibility that create a positive classroom climate of openness, mutual respect, support, and inquiry.
6. The teacher analyzes the classroom environment and makes decisions and adjustments to enhance social relationships, student motivation and engagement, and productive work.
7. The teacher organizes, prepares students for, and monitors independent and group work that allows for full and varied participation of all individuals.

Principle #6:

The teacher uses knowledge of effective verbal, nonverbal, and media communication techniques to foster active inquiry, collaboration, and supportive interaction in the classroom.

Knowledge

1. The teacher understands communication theory, language development, and the role of language in learning.

2. The teacher understands how cultural and gender differences can affect communication in the classroom.
3. The teacher recognizes the importance of nonverbal as well as verbal communication.
4. The teacher knows about and can use effective verbal, nonverbal, and media communication techniques.

Dispositions

1. The teacher recognizes the power of language for fostering self-expression, identity development, and learning.
2. The teacher values many ways in which people seek to communicate and encourages many modes of communication in the classroom.
3. The teacher is a thoughtful and responsive listener.
4. The teacher appreciates the cultural dimensions of communication, responds appropriately, and seeks to foster culturally sensitive communication by and among all students in the class.

Performances

1. The teacher models effective communication strategies in conveying ideas and information and in asking questions (e.g. monitoring the effects of messages, restating ideas and drawing connections, using visual, aural, and kinesthetic cues, being sensitive to nonverbal cues given and received).
2. The teacher supports and expands learner expression in speaking, writing, and other media.
3. The teacher knows how to ask questions and stimulate discussion in different ways for particular purposes, for example, probing for learner understanding, helping students articulate their ideas and thinking processes, promoting risk-taking and problem-solving, facilitating factual recall, encouraging convergent and divergent thinking, stimulating curiosity, helping students to question.
4. The teacher communicates in ways that demonstrate a sensitivity to cultural and gender differences (e.g. appropriate use of eye contact, interpretation of body language and verbal statements, acknowledgment of and responsiveness to different modes of communication and participation).
5. The teacher knows how to use a variety of media communication tools, including audio-visual aids and computers, to enrich learning opportunities.

Principle #7:

The teacher plans instruction based upon knowledge of subject matter, students, the community, and curriculum goals.

Knowledge

1. The teacher understands learning theory, subject matter, curriculum development, and student develop-

ment and knows how to use this knowledge in planning instruction to meet curriculum goals.
2. The teacher knows how to take contextual considerations (instructional materials, individual student interests, needs, and aptitudes, and community resources) into account in planning instruction that creates an effective bridge between curriculum goals and students' experiences.
3. The teacher knows when and how to adjust plans based on student responses and other contingencies.

Dispositions

1. The teacher values both long term and short term planning.
2. The teacher believes that plans must always be open to adjustment and revision based on student needs and changing circumstances.
3. The teacher values planning as a collegial activity.

Performances

1. As an individual and a member of a team, the teacher selects and creates learning experiences that are appropriate for curriculum goals, relevant to learners, and based upon principles of effective instruction (e.g. that activate students' prior knowledge, anticipate preconceptions, encourage exploration and problem-solving, and build new skills on those previously acquired).
2. The teacher plans for learning opportunities that recognize and address variation in learning styles and performance modes.
3. The teacher creates lessons and activities that operate at multiple levels to meet the developmental and individual needs of diverse learners and help each progress.
4. The teacher creates short-range and long-term plans that are linked to student needs and performance, and adapts the plans to ensure and capitalize on student progress and motivation.
5. The teacher responds to unanticipated sources of input, evaluates plans in relation to short- and long-range goals, and systematically adjusts plans to meet student needs and enhance learning.

Principle #8:

The teacher understands and uses formal and informal assessment strategies to evaluate and ensure the continuous intellectual, social and physical development of the learner.

Knowledge

1. The teacher understands the characteristics, uses, advantages, and limitations of different types of assessments (e.g. criterion-referenced and norm-referenced instruments, traditional standardized and performance-based tests, observation systems, and assessments of student work) for evaluating how students learn, what

they know and are able to do, and what kinds of experiences will support their further growth and development.

2. The teacher knows how to select, construct, and use assessment strategies and instruments appropriate to the learning outcomes being evaluated and to other diagnostic purposes.

3. The teacher understands measurement theory and assessment-related issues, such as validity, reliability, bias, and scoring concerns.

Dispositions

1. The teacher values ongoing assessment as essential to the instructional process and recognizes that many different assessment strategies, accurately and systematically used, are necessary for monitoring and promoting student learning.

2. The teacher is committed to using assessment to identify student strengths and promote student growth rather than to deny students access to learning opportunities.

Performances

1. The teacher appropriately uses a variety of formal and informal assessment techniques (e.g. observation, portfolios of student work, teacher-made tests, performance tasks, projects, student self-assessments, peer assessment, and standardized tests) to enhance her or his knowledge of learners, evaluate students' progress and performances, and modify teaching and learning strategies.

2. The teacher solicits and uses information about students' experiences, learning behavior, needs, and progress from parents, other colleagues, and the students themselves.

3. The teacher uses assessment strategies to involve learners in self-assessment activities, to help them become aware of their strengths and needs, and to encourage them to set personal goals for learning.

4. The teacher evaluates the effect of class activities on both individuals and the class as a whole, collecting information through observation of classroom interactions, questioning, and analysis of student work.

5. The teacher monitors his or her own teaching strategies and behavior in relation to student success, modifying plans and instructional approaches accordingly.

6. The teacher maintains useful records of student work and performance and can communicate student progress knowledgeably and responsibly, based on appropriate indicators, to students, parents, and other colleagues.

Principle #9:

The teacher is a reflective practitioner who continually evaluates the effects of his/her choices and actions on others (students, parents, and other professionals in the learning community) and who actively seeks out opportunities to grow professionally.

Knowledge

1. The teacher understands methods of inquiry that provide him/her with a variety of self-assessment and problem-solving strategies for reflecting on his/her practice, its influences on students' growth and learning, and the complex interactions between them.

2. The teacher is aware of major areas of research on teaching and of resources available for professional learning (e.g. professional literature, colleagues, professional associations, professional development activities).

Dispositions

1. The teacher values critical thinking and self-directed learning as habits of mind.

2. The teacher is committed to reflection, assessment, and learning as an ongoing process.

3. The teacher is willing to give and receive help.

4. The teacher is committed to seeking out, developing, and continually refining practices that address the individual needs of students.

5. The teacher recognizes his/her professional responsibility for engaging in and supporting appropriate professional practices for self and colleagues.

Performances

1. The teacher uses classroom observation, information about students, and research as sources for evaluating the outcomes of teaching and learning and as a basis for experimenting with, reflecting on, and revising practice.

2. The teacher seeks out professional literature, colleagues, and other resources to support his/her own development as a learner and a teacher.

3. The teacher draws upon professional colleagues within the school and other professional arenas as supports for reflection, problem-solving and new ideas, actively sharing experiences and seeking and giving feedback.

Principle #10:

The teacher fosters relationships with school colleagues, parents, and agencies in the larger community to support students' learning and well-being.

Knowledge

1. The teacher understands schools as organizations within the larger community context and understands the operations of the relevant aspects of the system(s) within which s/he works.

2. The teacher understands how factors in the students' environment outside of school (e.g. family circumstances, community environments, health and economic conditions) may influence students' life and learning.

3. The teacher understands and implements laws related to students' rights and teacher responsibilities (e.g. for equal education, appropriate education for handicapped students, confidentiality, privacy, appropriate treatment of students, reporting in situations related to possible child abuse).

Dispositions

1. The teacher values and appreciates the importance of all aspects of a child's experience.
2. The teacher is concerned about all aspects of a child's well-being (cognitive, emotional, social, and physical), and is alert to signs of difficulties.
3. The teacher is willing to consult with other adults regarding the education and well-being of his/her students.
4. The teacher respects the privacy of students and confidentiality of information.
5. The teacher is willing to work with other professionals to improve the overall learning environment for students.

Performance

1. The teacher participates in collegial activities designed to make the entire school a productive learning environment.
2. The teacher makes links with the learners' other environments on behalf of students, by consulting with parents, counselors, teachers of other classes and activities within the schools, and professionals in other community agencies.
3. The teacher can identify and use community resources to foster student learning.
4. The teacher establishes respectful and productive relationships with parents and guardians from diverse home and community situations, and seeks to develop cooperative partnerships in support of student learning and well being.
5. The teacher talks with and listens to the student, is sensitive and responsive to clues of distress, investigates situations, and seeks outside help as needed and appropriate to remedy problems.
6. The teacher acts as an advocate for students.

Standards/Topics Alignment Matrix

Chapter 1: Overview of Today's Special Education

CEC Standards	Chapter Topics
1	• Disproportionate representation. • Zero reject. • Expulsion and discipline. • Procedural due process. • Long-term results of special education. • Socioeconomic characteristics. • Family education level. • Racial and ethnic trends. • Appropriate education.
2	• Long-term results of special education.
3	• Instructional needs of students with disabilities. • Who are students with disabilities? • Long-term results of special education. • Family education level. • Racial and ethnic trends. • Appropriate education.
4	• Who are students with disabilities? • Instructional needs of students with disabilities.
5	• Who are students with disabilities? • Instructional needs of students with disabilities. • Expulsion and discipline. • Parent-Student Participation.
6	• Parent-Student Participation.
7	• Who are students with disabilities? • Instructional needs of students with disabilities.
8	• Who are students with disabilities? • Instructional needs of students with disabilities. • Nondiscriminatory evaluation. • Appropriate education.
9	• Disproportionate representation. • Special Education personnel. • Zero reject. • Expulsion and discipline. • Overlapping services to support students with disabilities. • Procedural due process. • Long-term results of special education. • Family education level. • Racial and ethnic trends.
10	• Appropriate education. • Special Education personnel. • Parent-Student Participation. • Overlapping services to support students with disabilities.

Praxis Standards	Chapter Topics
1	• Who are students with disabilities? • Instructional needs of students with disabilities. • Disproportionate representation.
2	• Discrimination. • Judicial decisions. • Individuals with Disabilities Education Act. • Principles of IDEA. • Rehabilitation services. • Section 504 and the ADA.
3	• Special education personnel. • Least restrictive environment. • Free appropriate public education.

INTASC Principles	Chapter Topics
1	• Who are students with disabilities? • Instructional needs of students with disabilities. • Disproportionate representation. • Special Education personnel.
2	• Who are students with disabilities? • Instructional needs of students with disabilities.
3	• Instructional needs of students with disabilities.
4	• Instructional needs of students with disabilities.
5	• Instructional needs of students with disabilities.
7	• Instructional needs of students with disabilities. • Characteristics of students with disabilities.
8	• Nondiscriminatory evaluation. • Appropriate education.
9	• Special Education personnel.
10	• Parent-Student Participation. • Overlapping services to support students with disabilities.

Chapter 2: Ensuring Progress in the General Curriculum: Universal Design and Inclusion

CEC Standards	Chapter Topics
1	• Standards-based reform. • Accountability issues. • Inclusion
2	• Universally designed curriculum, instruction, and evaluation. • Restructuring teaching and learning.
3	• Progressing in the general curriculum. • Inclusion • Restructuring teaching and learning. • Assessment accommodations.
4	• Progressing in the general curriculum. • Standards-based reform. • Universally designed curriculum, instruction, and evaluation.

	Chapter Topics
5	• Progressing in the general curriculum. • Accountability issues. • Universally designed curriculum, instruction, and evaluation.
6	• Parent responses to inclusion.
7	• Progressing in the general curriculum. • Universally designed curriculum, instruction, and evaluation. • Restructuring teaching and learning.
8	• Progressing in the general curriculum. • Standards-based reform. • Assessment accommodations. • Accountability issues. • Universally designed curriculum, instruction, and evaluation.
9	• Standards-based reform. • Accountability issues. • Inclusion • Parent responses to inclusion.
10	• Parent responses to inclusion.

Praxis Standards	Chapter Topics
1	• Progressing in the general curriculum. • Characteristics of inclusion.
2	• Standards-based reform. • Accountability issues.
3	• Universally designed curriculum, instruction, and evaluation.

INTASC Principles	Chapter Topics
1	• Universally designed curriculum, instruction, and evaluation.
3	• Universally designed curriculum, instruction, and evaluation.
4	• Universally designed curriculum, instruction, and evaluation.
7	• Accountability issues. • Assessment accommodations. • Progressing in the general curriculum.
8	• Accountability issues. • Assessment accommodations. • Progressing in the general curriculum. • Universally designed curriculum, instruction, and evaluation.
10	• Characteristics of inclusion.

Chapter 3: Ensuring Progress in the General Curriculum: Collaboration and Multicultural Responsiveness

CEC Standards	Chapter Topics
3	• Progressing in the general curriculum. • Multicultural responsiveness.
4	• Progressing in the general curriculum.
5	• Progressing in the general curriculum.
7	• Progressing in the general curriculum.
8	• Progressing in the general curriculum.
9	• Multicultural responsiveness.
10	• Collaboration to support student needs.

Praxis Standards	Chapter Topics
1	• Progressing in the general curriculum. • Multicultural responsiveness.
3	• Collaboration. • Related service providers.

INTASC Principles	Chapter Topics
1	• Progressing in the general curriculum. • Multicultural responsiveness.
2	• Multicultural responsiveness.
3	• Progressing in the general curriculum. • Multicultural responsiveness.
5	• Multicultural responsiveness.
7	• Collaboration. • Related service providers.
10	• Multicultural responsiveness.

Chapter 4: Learning Disabilities

CEC Standards	Chapter Topics
1	• Characteristics of learning disabilities. • Characteristics of specific learning disabilities as they relate to certain areas, as well as the behavioral, social, and emotional characteristics. • Augmenting curriculum and instruction.
2	• Characteristics of specific learning disabilities as they relate to certain areas, as well as the behavioral, social, and emotional characteristics. • Characteristics of learning disabilities.
3	• Curricular and instructional needs of students with learning disabilities. • Augmenting curriculum and instruction.

	• Collaborative relationships.
	• Characteristics of learning disabilities.
	• Specific instructional choices for students with learning disabilities.
	• Characteristics of specific learning disabilities as they relate to certain areas, as well as the behavioral, social, and emotional characteristics.
	• Identification of developmentally appropriate social goals.
4	• Specific instructional choices for students with learning disabilities.
	• Characteristics of specific learning disabilities as they relate to certain areas, as well as the behavioral, social, and emotional characteristics.
5	• Collaborative relationships.
	• Characteristics of learning disabilities.
	• Characteristics of specific learning disabilities as they relate to certain areas, as well as the behavioral, social, and emotional characteristics.
	• Identification of developmentally appropriate social goals.
7	• Collaborative relationships.
	• Specific instructional choices for students with learning disabilities.
	• Augmenting curriculum and instruction.
10	• Collaborative relationships.

Praxis Standards	Chapter Topics
1	• Characteristics of specific learning disabilities as they relate to certain areas, as well as the behavioral, social, and emotional characteristics.
	• Identification of developmentally appropriate social goals.

	• Relevant resources and materials that contribute to the literature base on instructional strategies.
3	• Collaborative relationships.
	• Collaboration to support instruction.
	• Specific instructional choices for students with learning disabilities.

INTASC Principles	Chapter Topics
1	• Identification of developmentally appropriate social goals.
2	• Characteristics of specific learning disabilities as they relate to certain areas, as well as the behavioral, social, and emotional characteristics.
3	• Characteristics of specific learning disabilities as they relate to certain areas, as well as the behavioral, social, and emotional characteristics.
	• Augmenting curriculum and instruction.
	• Relevant resources and materials that contribute to the literature base on instructional strategies.
4	• Relevant resources and materials that contribute to the literature base on instructional strategies.
5	• Characteristics of specific learning disabilities as they relate to certain areas, as well as the behavioral, social, and emotional characteristics.
	• Identification of developmentally appropriate social goals.
6	• Specific instructional choices for students with learning disabilities.
7	• Specific instructional choices for students with learning disabilities.
10	• Collaborative relationships.

Chapter 5: Emotional or Behavioral Disorders

CEC Standards	Chapter Topics
1	• Characteristics of emotional behavioral disorders.
	• Adapting instruction and assessment.
	• Environmental stressors.
	• Nature and extent of services.
	• Understanding causes.
2	• Internalizing and externalizing behaviors.
	• Characteristics of emotional behavioral disorders.
	• Nature and extent of services.
	• Developing resilience.
3	• Characteristics of emotional behavioral disorders.
	• Internalizing and externalizing behaviors.
4	• Adapting instruction and assessment.
5	• Developing resilience.
	• Collaborative relationships.
	• Internalizing and externalizing behaviors.
	• Environmental stressors.
7	• Adapting instruction and assessment.

8	• Adapting instruction and assessment.
9	• Environmental stressors.
	• Nature and extent of services.
	• Developing resilience.
	• Understanding causes.
10	• Collaborative relationships.

Praxis Standards	Chapter Topics
1	• Characteristics of emotional behavioral disorders.
	• Internalizing and externalizing behaviors.
	• Understanding causes.
2	• Manifestation determination.
3	• Collaboration.
	• Utilizing universal design for learning.
	• Cognitive and academic characteristics.

INTASC Principles	Chapter Topics
1	• Characteristics of emotional behavior disorders. • Adapting instruction and assessment.
2	• Characteristics of emotional behavior disorders. • Adapting instruction and assessment. • Cognitive and academic characteristics.
3	• Characteristics of emotional behavioral disorders. • Internalizing and externalizing behaviors. • Understanding causes.
4	• Characteristics of emotional behavior disorders. • Adapting instruction and assessment. • Cognitive and academic characteristics.
5	• Characteristics of emotional behavior disorders. • Adapting instruction and assessment.
7	• Collaboration. • Utilizing universal design for learning. • Cognitive and academic characteristics.
8	• Adapting instruction and assessment.
10	• Collaboration.

Chapter 6: Attention-Deficit/Hyperactivity Disorder

CEC Standards	Chapter Topics
1	• Characteristics of AD/HD. • Three types of AD/HD. • Positive traits of individuals with AD/HD. • Determining nature and extent of services. • Evaluation procedures.
2	• Characteristics of AD/HD. • Three types of AD/HD. • Positive traits of individuals with AD/HD. • Determining nature and extent of services.
3	• Characteristics of AD/HD. • Three types of AD/HD. • Positive traits of individuals with AD/HD. • Determining nature and extent of services.
5	• Positive traits of individuals with AD/HD. • Augmenting curriculum and instruction.
6	• Communicating new developments.
7	• Augmenting curriculum and instruction. • Determining nature and extent of services.
8	• Evaluation procedures.
9	• Evaluation procedures. • Communicating new developments.
10	• Collaboration. • Communicating new developments.

Praxis Standards	Chapter Topics
1	• Characteristics of AD/HD. • Three types of AD/HD.
2	• Coverage of AD/HD under IDEA.
3	• Collaboration. • Positive traits of individuals with AD/HD. • Augmenting curriculum and instruction.

INTASC Principles	Chapter Topics
1	• Augmenting curriculum and instruction.
2	• Augmenting curriculum and instruction.
3	• Characteristics of AD/HD. • Three types of AD/HD. • Augmenting curriculum and instruction.
5	• Characteristics of AD/HD. • Positive traits of individuals with AD/HD. • Augmenting curriculum and instruction.
10	• Collaboration.

Chapter 7: Giftedness

CEC Standards	Chapter Topics
1	• Characteristics of students who are gifted and talented. • Participating and belonging in the general education classroom. • Types of enrichment.
2	• Characteristics of students who are gifted and talented. • Types of enrichment.
3	• Characteristics of students who are gifted and talented. • Universally designed curriculum. • Types of enrichment. • Mentoring.
4	• Participating and belonging in the general education classroom.
5	• Participating and belonging in the general education classroom. • Behavioral, social, and emotional characteristics.
6	• Mentoring.
7	• Participating and belonging in the general education classroom. • Universally designed curriculum. • Mentoring.
10	• Collaboration. • Mentoring.

Praxis Standards	Chapter Topics
1	• Characteristics of students who are gifted and talented.

- Participating and belonging in the general education classroom.
- Behavioral, social, and emotional characteristics.

2
- How students who are gifted or talented are served under IDEA.

3
- Universally designed curriculum.
- Types of enrichment.

INTASC Principles	Chapter Topics
1	• Characteristics of students who are gifted and talented. • Participating and belonging in the general education classroom. • Behavioral, social, and emotional characteristics.
2	• Types of enrichment. • Behavioral, social, and emotional characteristics.

3
- Characteristics of students who are gifted and talented.
- Universally designed curriculum.

4
- Characteristics of students who are gifted and talented.
- Participating and belonging in the general education classroom.

5
- Participating and belonging in the general education classroom.

6
- Characteristics of students who are gifted and talented.
- Universally designed curriculum.

8
- Product or process evaluation.

9
- Collaboration.

10
- Collaboration.
- Mentoring.

Chapter 8: Mental Retardation

CEC Standards	Chapter Topics
1	• Intellectual functioning of students with mental retardation. • Understanding motivation. • Supports intensity scale. • Necessary supports.
2	• Intellectual functioning of students with mental retardation. • Understanding motivation. • Supports intensity scale. • Necessary supports.
3	• Intellectual functioning of students with mental retardation. • Academic and social progress. • Supports intensity scale.
5	• Academic and social progress. • Social and behavioral characteristics. • Necessary supports.
6	• Self-determined learning model. • Supports intensity scale.
7	• Self-determined learning model.
8	• Academic and social progress.
10	• Self-determined learning model.

- Supports intensity scale.
- Collaboration.

Praxis Standards	Chapter Topics
1	• Intellectual functioning of students with mental retardation. • Academic and social progress. • Social and behavioral characteristics.
2	• Identification of Mental Retardation by IDEA.
3	• Understanding motivation. • Self-determined learning model.

INTASC Principles	Chapter Topics
1	• Intellectual functioning of students with mental retardation. • Academic and social progress.
2	• Social and behavioral characteristics.
3	• Augmenting and adapting curriculum and instructional choices.
5	• Social and behavioral characteristics.
6	• Academic and social progress.
8	• Academic and social progress.

Chapter 9: Severe and Multiple Disabilities

CEC Standards	Chapter Topics
1	• Defining severe and multiple disabilities. • Extent of support. • Self-care skills.
2	• Defining severe and multiple disabilities. • Extent of support. • Intellectual functioning and academic skills.

- Promoting friendships.
- Self-care skills.
- Circle of inclusion.

3
- Defining severe and multiple disabilities.
- Extent of support.
- Intellectual functioning and academic skills.
- Circle of inclusion.

4
- Collaboration.
- Partnerships.

5	• Extent of support. • Promoting friendships. • Self-care skills. • Circle of inclusion.
6	• Communication skills. • Collaborative partnerships. • College connection program.
7	• Planning a universally designed learning environment. • College connection program. • Circle of inclusion.
8	• Extent of support. • Planning a universally designed learning environment. • College connection program.
9	• Planning a universally designed learning environment.
10	• Extent of support. • Communication skills. • Collaborative partnerships. • College connection program.

Praxis Standards	Chapter Topics
1	• Defining severe and multiple disabilities. • Intellectual functioning and academic skills.

Chapter 10: Autism

CEC Standards	Chapter Topics
1	• Characteristics of autism.
2	• Characteristics of autism. • Instructional decision making to insure progress in the general education curriculum for students with autism. • Evaluating students with autism. • Repetitive behavior. • Curricular and instructional needs of students with autism. • Post-secondary transition needs.
3	• Characteristics of autism. • Instructional decision making to insure progress in the general education curriculum for students with autism. • Curricular and instructional needs of students with autism. • Augmenting curriculum and instruction.
4	• Collaboration to meet student needs. • Curricular and instructional needs of students with autism. • Augmenting curriculum and instruction.
5	• Instructional decision making to insure progress in the general education curriculum for students with autism. • Repetitive behavior.

2	• Adaptive skills. • IDEA regulations. • Simultaneous disabilities.
3	• Planning a universally designed learning environment. • Partnerships and collaboration.

INTASC Principles	Chapter Topics
1	• Intellectual functioning and academic skills. • Adaptive skills.
2	• Intellectual functioning. • Peer tutoring.
3	• Adapting curriculum and instructional choices. • Planning a universally designed learning environment.
4	• Peer tutoring. • Class-wide peer tutoring.
5	• Peer tutoring. • Promoting friendships.
6	• Collaboration and partnering for success.
7	• Planning a universally designed learning environment. • MAPS process.
10	• Partnerships and collaboration.

6	• Environmental predictability. • Collaborative relationships. • Post-secondary transition needs.
7	• Instructional decision making to insure progress in the general education curriculum for students with autism. • Environmental predictability. • Curricular and instructional needs of students with autism. • Augmenting curriculum and instruction.
8	• Evaluating students with autism. • Curricular and instructional needs of students with autism.
9	• Evaluating students with autism.
10	• Collaborative relationships. • Post-secondary transition needs.

Praxis Standards	Chapter Topics
1	• Characteristics of autism. • Defining autism.
2	• Historical and biomedical causes.
3	• Collaborative relationships. • Collaboration to support instruction. • Specific instructional choices for students with autism.

INTASC Principles		Chapter Topics
1		• Progress in the general curriculum.
2		• Historical causes of autism.
3		• Augmenting curriculum.
5		• Social development. • Environmental predictability.
8		• Evaluating students with autism.
10		• Related services. • Collaboration to meet student needs.

Chapter 11: Other Health Impairments

CEC Standards		Chapter Topics
1		• Individuality of impairments. • Limitations of health conditions. • Environmental triggers of epilepsy. • Effects of cancer treatments on student behavior, functioning, and health. • Preventing students with other health impairments from dropping out of school. • Promoting school safety.
2		• Individuality of impairments. • Limitations of health conditions. • Social and emotional needs of students with other health impairments. • Environmental triggers of epilepsy. • Relaxation techniques. • Learning and behavior of students with HIV. • Sharing information regarding student health impairments with peers. • Effects of cancer treatments on student behavior, functioning, and health. • Creating an action plan for meeting the classroom needs of students with other health impairments. • Learned helplessness and students with other health impairments. • Promoting school safety.
3		• Individuality of impairments. • Augmenting curriculum and instruction. • Creating an action plan for meeting the classroom needs of students with other health impairments. • Learned helplessness and students with other health impairments.
4		• Sharing information regarding student health impairments with peers.
5		• Classroom needs of students with other health impairments. • Universally designed learning. • Social and emotional needs of students with other health impairments. • Environmental triggers of epilepsy. • Relaxation techniques. • Learning and behavior of students with HIV. • Sharing information regarding student health impairments with peers. • Social needs of students with other health impairments. • Learned helplessness and students with other health impairments.

		• Encouraging open discussions with students with other health impairments.
6		• Creating an action plan for meeting the classroom needs of students with other health impairments. • Encouraging open discussions with students with other health impairments. • Preventing students with other health impairments from dropping out of school.
7		• Universally designed learning. • Augmenting curriculum and instruction. • Encouraging open discussions with students with other health impairments. • Preventing students with other health impairments from dropping out of school.
8		• Augmenting curriculum and instruction.
9		• Limitations of health conditions. • Learning and behavior of students with HIV. • Sharing information regarding student health impairments with peers. • Preventing students with other health impairments from dropping out of school. • Promoting school safety.
10		• Classroom needs of students with other health impairments. • Creating an action plan for meeting the classroom needs of students with other health impairments. • Preventing students with other health impairments from dropping out of school.

Praxis Standards		Chapter Topics
1		• Individuality of impairments. • Universally designed learning.
2		• Definition of other health impairments. • Confidentiality in some other health impairments.
3		• Limitations of health conditions. • Collaboration to support instruction. • Specific instructional choices for students with autism.

INTASC Principles		Chapter Topics
1		• Progress in the general curriculum.
2		• Historical causes of autism. • Peer led discussions on HIV. • Progress in the general curriculum.
3		• Augmenting curriculum.
5		• Social development.

	• Environmental predictability.
7	• Progress in the general curriculum.
8	• Cognitive evaluation of students with other health impairments.

10	• Encouraging open discussions with students with other health impairments. • Peer led discussions on HIV. • Action planning for providing services.

Chapter 12: Physical Disabilities

CEC Standards	Chapter Topics
1	• Defining physical disabilities. • Causes of physical disabilities.
2	• Defining physical disabilities. • Causes of physical disabilities. • Different types and forms of physical disabilities.
3	• Defining physical disabilities. • Causes of physical disabilities. • Different types and forms of physical disabilities. • Collaborating to meet the needs of students with physical disabilities.
5	• Causes of physical disabilities. • Collaborating to meet the needs of students with physical disabilities.
8	• Evaluation of students with physical disabilities.
9	• Causes of physical disabilities.
10	• Collaborating to meet the needs of students with physical disabilities.

Praxis Standards	Chapter Topics
1	• Defining physical disabilities. • Causes of physical disabilities. • Conditions associated with physical disabilities.
2	• Understanding the presence of physical disabilities.
3	• Evaluation of students with physical disabilities. • Extent of services.

INTASC Principles	Chapter Topics
1	• Including students in the general education curriculum.
2	• Including students in the general education curriculum.
3	• Including students in the general education curriculum.
5	• Curricular adaptations and assistive technology.
8	• Evaluation of students with physical disabilities.
10	• Collaboration.

Chapter 13: Traumatic Brain Injury

CEC Standards	Chapter Topics
1	• Characteristics of traumatic brain injury. • Defining traumatic brain injury. • Types of traumatic brain injury. • Self-advocacy. • Understanding physical, cognitive, linguistic, and other changes.
2	• Characteristics of traumatic brain injury. • Defining traumatic brain injury. • Types of traumatic brain injury. • Self-advocacy. • Understanding physical, cognitive, linguistic, and other changes.
3	• Characteristics of traumatic brain injury. • Types of traumatic brain injury. • Providing supports to meet individual student needs. • Collaborating to meet the needs of students across environments. • Understanding physical, cognitive, linguistic, and other changes.
5	• Social, personality, and behavioral changes associated with traumatic brain injury. • Self-advocacy. • Providing supports to meet individual student needs.

	• Understanding physical, cognitive, linguistic, and other changes.
6	• Social, personality, and behavioral changes associated with traumatic brain injury. • Collaborating to meet the needs of students across environments.
7	• Self-advocacy. • Providing supports to meet individual student needs. • Understanding physical, cognitive, linguistic, and other changes.
8	• Evaluating students and determining the presence of a traumatic brain injury.
9	• Understanding physical, cognitive, linguistic, and other changes.
10	• Social, personality, and behavioral changes associated with traumatic brain injury. • Collaborating to meet the needs of students across environments.

Praxis Standards	Chapter Topics
1	• Characteristics of blindness and low vision. • Causes of blindness and low vision.
2	• Coverage of traumatic brain injury under the IDEA.
3	• Nature and extent of services. • Specialized instructional supports.

INTASC Principles	Chapter Topics
1	• Augmenting curriculum.
2	• Augmenting curriculum. • Understanding physical, cognitive, linguistic, and other changes.
3	• Specialized instructional supports.

4	• Processing and other changes associated with traumatic brain injury.
6	• Developing a universally designed learning environment.
8	• Evaluating students and determining the presence of a traumatic brain injury.
10	• Collaborating to meet the needs of students across environments.

Chapter 14: Communication Disorders

CEC Standards	Chapter Topics
1	• Characteristics of communication disorders. • Characteristics of language impairments. • Self-advocacy. • Functional communication disorders. • Organic communication disorders.
2	• Characteristics of communication disorders. • Defining speech and language disorders. • Characteristics of language impairments. • Self-advocacy. • Functional communication disorders. • Organic communication disorders.
3	• Characteristics of communication disorders. • Defining speech and language disorders. • Characteristics of language impairments. • Self-advocacy.
5	• Social interaction theories.
6	• Understanding cultural diversity in communication.
7	• Understanding cultural diversity in communication. • Characteristics of language impairments. • Self-advocacy.
10	• Understanding cultural diversity in communication. • Collaboration.

Praxis Standards	Chapter Topics
1	• Defining speech and language disorders. • Characteristics of language impairments.
2	• Communication disorders as defined by the IDEA. • Nature and extent of services.
3	• Assistive technology. • Specialized instructional materials.

INTASC Principles	Chapter Topics
1	• Understanding typical speech and language development. • Including students with non-disabled peers.
2	• Assistive technology. • Understanding limitations.
3	• Including students with communication disorders in the general education curriculum.
4	• Adapting instruction. • Using augmentative and alternative communication systems.
5	• Assistive communication systems and visual supports.
6	• Typical speech and language development.
8	• Evaluating students with communication disorders. • Bilingual evaluation.
10	• Collaboration.

Chapter 15: Hearing Loss

CEC Standards	Chapter Topics
1	• Defining hearing loss. • Understanding the process of hearing. • Meeting behavioral needs of students with hearing loss. • Providing related services to support students with hearing loss. • Peer and teacher training and support.
2	• Defining hearing loss. • Understanding the process of hearing. • Meeting behavioral needs of students with hearing loss. • Self-advocacy. • Transitionary services to support independence.

3	• Defining hearing loss. • Meeting behavioral needs of students with hearing loss.
4	• Importance of high expectations. • Collaborating to meet the needs of students with hearing loss.
5	• Importance of high expectations. • Understanding social needs of students with hearing loss. • Understanding multiple levels of support.
6	• Providing related services to support students with hearing loss. • Transitionary services to support independence.
7	• Importance of high expectations.

- Understanding social needs of students with hearing loss.
- Peer and teacher training and support.
- Understanding multiple levels of support.
- Self-advocacy.

9
- Understanding social needs of students with hearing loss.
- Providing related services to support students with hearing loss.
- Self-advocacy.

10
- Providing related services to support students with hearing loss.
- Peer and teacher training and support.
- Collaborating to meet the needs of students with hearing loss.
- Understanding multiple levels of support.
- Transitionary services to support independence.

Praxis Standards	Chapter Topics
1	• Characteristics of hearing loss. • Causes of hearing loss.

2
- Referral processes for students who are deaf or hard of hearing.
- Nature and extent of services.

3
- Assistive technology.
- Specialized instructional materials.

INTASC Principles	Chapter Topics
1	• Utilizing American Sign Language, fingerspelling, and other forms of communication. • Focus on communication.
2	• Assistive technology. • Understanding social needs.
3	• Augmenting curriculum and instruction.
5	• Real-time graphic display. • Using the Internet.
6	• Assistive technology.
8	• Evaluating students who have hearing loss. • Academic versus communication needs.
9	• Understanding the importance of high expectations.
10	• Psychological development. • Collaborating to meet the needs of students with hearing loss.

Chapter 16: Visual Impairments

CEC Standards	Chapter Topics
1	• Characteristics of blindness and low vision. • Legal definitions of blindness. • Defining visual impairments. • Limitations of students with blindness or low vision. • Self-advocacy. • Limitations in interactions. • Understanding limitations.
2	• Characteristics of blindness and low vision. • Legal definitions of blindness. • Limitations of students with blindness or low vision. • Orientation and mobility. • Self-advocacy. • Understanding limitations.
3	• Characteristics of blindness and low vision. • Limitations of students with blindness or low vision. • Orientation and mobility. • Self-advocacy.
4	• Self-advocacy.
5	• Self-advocacy. • Understanding limitations. • Limitations of students with blindness or low vision. • Limitations in interactions.
6	• Self-advocacy.
7	• Characteristics of blindness and low vision. • Limitations of students with blindness or low vision. • Self-advocacy.

8
- Self-advocacy.

9
- Legal definitions of blindness.
- Limitations of students with blindness or low vision.
- Limitations in interactions.
- Understanding limitations.

10
- Collaboration.

Praxis Standards	Chapter Topics
1	• Characteristics of blindness and low vision. • Causes of blindness and low vision.
2	• Legal definitions of blindness. • Nature and extent of services.
3	• Assistive technology. • Specialized instructional materials.

INTASC Principles	Chapter Topics
1	• Assistive technology. • Orientation and mobility.
2	• Assistive technology. • Understanding limitations.
3	• Understanding limitations.
5	• Self-advocacy.
6	• Assistive technology.
8	• Evaluating students who have visual impairments.
10	• Collaboration.

Glossary

This glossary contains terms that we have boldfaced in our text. It also contains other terms that you will want to know as you work in special education.

504 plans are created by a school-based team to provide accommodation accountability for students who have disabilities that do not adversely affect their educational progress.

Absence seizures are a type of generalized seizure that cause the person to lose consciousness only briefly.

Acquired brain injury includes injuries caused by internal as well as external forces.

Acquired immune deficiency syndrome (AIDS) is the final stage in the progression of HIV. The infected person has a T4 cell count less than 200 and one or more opportunistic infections.

Action plan coordinates a student's medical information and needs among family and medical and school staff. All participants receive a copy, and one copy is attached to the IEP.

Active listening consists of paraphrasing content and identifying feelings when listening to another person.

Acute condition refers to any health condition that is severe, requires immediate attention, and is short-lasting.

Adaptive behavior represents skill areas that are central to successful life functioning, such as communication, self-care, home living, and social skills.

Adventitious refers to an impairment that occurs after typical functioning has been established.

Albinism is a hereditary condition that often results in lack of pigmentation of the skin and parts of the eye, resulting in reduced visual acuity (low vision) and, usually, legal blindness.

American Sign Language (ASL) is the sign language of the Deaf community in the United States and Canada. It possesses all of the grammatical complexity of spoken languages.

Amniocentesis is a prenatal diagnostic procedure performed in the second trimester of pregnancy to determine if a fetus has a disability.

Anoxia is a condition in which the body receives no oxygen.

Anterior visual pathway comprises the parts of the eye that are located in front of the lens (i.e., pupil, iris, cornea, etc.).

Anti-inflammatories help prevent asthma attacks from starting.

Anxiety disorder is characterized by overwhelming fear, worry, and/or uneasiness. The condition includes phobia, generalized anxiety disorder, panic disorder, obsessive-compulsive disorder, and post-traumatic stress disorder.

Apgar screening is a method for determining the health of a newborn immediately in transition to life outside the womb. The screening occurs in the first minute after birth and again at the fifth minute after birth. It assesses, on a scale of 0 to 2, each of the following 5 attributes of the newborn: appearance (color), pulse (heartbeat), grimace (reflex), activity (muscle tone), and respiration (breathing). These 5 scores are added together so the infant receives a score of 1 to 10, where a score below 5 at 5 minutes after birth indicates that the infant is at risk for neurologic impairment.

Aphasia describes an injury to certain areas of the brain that results in problems with speaking or total loss of speech. Possible causes are traumatic brain injury, lack of oxygen, stroke, or an illness that causes brain swelling.

Applied behavior analysis is the systematic collection and graphing of data to ascertain a student's progress toward a specific objective.

Appropriate education is an IDEA principle that requires schools to provide an individualized educational program for students with disabilities that is appropriate to their educational strengths and needs.

Articulation is the speaker's production of individual or sequenced speech sounds.

Assessment refers to the specific instruments used to gather information and usually includes standardized and nonstandardized tests; the student's cumulative records and work products; and teacher and other observations of the student in the classroom, other school environments, and even outside the school.

Assistive technology refers to devices or services that restore, maintain, or replace lost bodily functions through the use of technology. The principles of engineering and ergonomics are applied to create devices that also are known as *adaptive equipment*.

Asymptomatic, or latency, stage occurs when a person has the HIV virus in his or her bloodstream but does not have outward symptoms of illness.

Ataxic cerebral palsy is a form of cerebral palsy in which a person has abnormal voluntary movement involving balance and the position of the trunk and limbs.

Athetoid cerebral palsy is a form of cerebral palsy in which a person has rapid, random, jerky movements and slow, writhing movements.

Atrophy is a wasting away of an organ or body tissue.

Attention-deficit/hyperactivity disorder (AD/HD) is characterized by symptoms of inattention, hyperactivity, and/or impulsivity that are developmentally inappropriate and are not the result of other conditions. Symptoms must have occurred before age 7 and exist in two or more settings. Students may be classified with one of three types: predominantly inattentive, predominantly hyperactive-impulsive, or combined.

Audiogram is a graph used to display the results of a hearing test. Intensity is plotted on the vertical axis and frequency on the horizontal axis.

Audiologist is a specialist who is trained to identify and evaluate hearing, select and evaluate hearing aids and assistive listening devices, and recommend habilitation.

Augmentative and alternative (AAC) devices allow a person with communication impairments to communicate through artificial means such as a word board, a computer, or a voice synthesizer.

Aura is an unusual sensation or visual disturbance that occurs right before a seizure.

Automatism refers to an automatic fine-motor movement that is part of an epileptic seizure.

Baseline data are data that show the nature, frequency, and/or intensity of a behavior or other observable phenomenon before you begin your intervention.

Basic psychological processes are the ability to interpret information received through auditory (oral), visual (sight), kinesthetic (motor), and tactile (touch) channels and to communicate information through those channels.

Behavioral earthquakes are high-intensity, low-frequency events such as setting fires, assaulting someone, or exhibiting cruelty that signal severe emotional or behavioral disorders.

Behavioral inhibition includes the ability to (a) delay personal gratification or reinforcement, (b) interrupt an ineffective response to replace it with a more effective behavior, and (c) continue with a desirable behavior despite interference. A lack of behavioral inhibition affects executive functions, self-control, and time perception.

Bell-shaped curve depicts the normal distribution of a characteristic (e.g., intelligence) in the general population.

Benefit standard refers to a U.S. Supreme Court interpretation of "appropriate education" requiring the education to benefit the student.

Bidialectal people have the ability to use two variations of a language, such as being equally fluent in black English and standard English.

Biomedical causes originate early in a child's development and require more extensive supports.

Bipolar disorder is characterized by extreme mood swings from depressive to manic phases.

Bronchodilators stop asthma episodes after they have started by opening constricted airways.

Captioning is the appearance of printed text scrolled across the screen of a television or computer monitor designed to capture the dialogue and action of a television program, movie, newscast, sporting event, or advertisement.

Cataract is a disorder of the eye that occurs when the lens of the eye becomes cloudy or opaque, usually resulting in low vision.

Causal agent means that an individual is able to take action to cause things to happen in his or her life.

Central nervous system dysfunction is a disorder in the messaging system of the brain and/or spinal cord.

Chorionic villi sampling is a prenatal diagnostic procedure performed in the first trimester of pregnancy to obtain fetal cells for genetic analysis.

Chromosomes direct each cell's activity and contain DNA and genes that determine a person's physical and mental condition.

Chronic condition refers to any health condition that develops slowly, is recurring, long-lasting, and almost always present.

Clean intermittent catheterization (CIC) refers to the procedure whereby a person or an attendant (a trained health aide) inserts a tube into the person's urethra to induce urination. It is "clean" because the procedure is done under sterile conditions, and it is intermittent because it is done "as needed" or on a regular schedule; the tube is not permanently placed in the person's urethra.

Cleft palate/lip describes a condition in which a person has a split in the upper part of the oral cavity or the upper lip.

Closed head injury results when the brain whips back and forth during an accident, causing it to bounce off the inside of the skull.

Cochlear implant is an electronic device that provides sound information by directly stimulating the functional auditory nerve fibers in the cochlea. The internal part is surgically implanted under the skin with electrodes inserted into the cochlea; the external part consists of a microphone, a speech processor, and a transmitting coil.

Cognitive retraining helps students regain perceptual processing, communication, behavioral, and social skills that were lost as a result of traumatic brain injury.

Collaboration describes an "interactive process" that "enables people with diverse expertise to generate creative solutions to mutually defined problems" (Idol, Paolucci-Whitcomp, & Nevin, 1986, in References, Chapter 14).

Colostomy is a surgical procedure that involves creating an opening into a person's abdomen so that bowel contents can be drained into a bag attached to the person's body.

Coma is a state of deep or prolonged unconsciousness usually caused by injury or illness.

Combined type of AD/HD includes characteristics of both the inattentive type and hyperactive-impulsive type of AD/HD.

Comorbidity refers to the simultaneous existence of two or more factors that jeopardize the health or well-being of an individual or family affected by disability.

Compensatory strategy training is a form of cognitive retraining that helps students who have traumatic brain injury to clarify, remember, organize, and express information.

Component training is a form of cognitive retraining that provides students who have traumatic brain injury with intensive and systematic training of specific cognitive skills such as memory, attention, organization, and perceptual processing.

Concomitance means occurring at the same time without causal relationship.

Concussion is a condition of impaired functioning of the brain as a result of a violent blow or impact.

Conduct disorder is characterized by acting out destructive feelings or impulses, which results in serious and repeated violations of society's rules and the rights of others.

Conductive hearing loss is hearing loss caused by a problem in the outer or middle ear.

Congenital refers to an impairment that is present from birth or from the time very near birth.

Contingency contract is a signed agreement between student and teacher that if the student performs in a certain way, the teacher will provide the student with a desired reinforcer.

Continuum of services is the concept that services for students with disabilities begin with the most typical and extend to the least typical, most segregated, as the students' disabilities become more and more severe.

Convulsions are sudden, involuntary contractions of a group of muscles.

Cortical visual impairment is the diagnosis given to a visual impairment that results from damage to the part of the brain responsible for reception of visual information from the eye and initial transmission of this information to the associative parts of the brain.

Creativity means unusual or unique expressions within a domain. Students who are creative may be more adventurous, independent, curious, spontaneous, flexible, sensitive, intuitive, and insightful than their peers. They also have more original ideas and may have a zany sense of humor.

Criterion-referenced tests determine whether a student has mastered a particular skill; thus, these tests compare a student to a standard of mastery.

Cross-categorical classes are those in which students with various kinds of disabilities are educated together. For example, students with mild mental retardation and learning disabilities may be in the same class, thus making it cross-categorical (the students cut across both categories).

Cued speech is a method of supplementing oral communication with a set of hand cues to distinguish between patterns of speech seen on the lips of the speaker.

Curriculum-based assessment is a test whose items reflect the content of the student's curriculum; the test may be norm-referenced or criterion-referenced.

Deaf culture refers to the pattern of beliefs, values, behaviors, arts, customs, institutions, social forms, and knowledge that are characteristic of the Deaf community.

Depression is a mood disorder characterized by protracted and unreasonable feelings of unhappiness.

Dialect is a regional variety of a language, such as when some-one speaks English using terms or pronunciations used only in that region.

Differential reinforcement of other behavior encourages appropriate behavior by reinforcing a positive behavior that is incompatible with the undesired behavior. The focus is on praising good behavior rather than punishing inappropriate behavior.

Differentiation refers to instruction or curriculum that has been modified from the standard curriculum in content, process, product, or effect to meet the needs of the students.

Direct observation is used to obtain specific information on a student's behavior by watching and recording to what degree, how often, or for what length of time a behavior does or does not occur.

Disinhibition refers to the removal of a constraining or limiting influence, as in the escape from higher cortical control in neurologic injury.

Documentation describes types of measurement used to determine giftedness.

Domain-specific giftedness describes giftedness that occurs in a specific area such as math, art, leadership, or athletics. This does not imply that giftedness operates in isolation but that some children have specific abilities that are not revealed by test scores alone. Researchers agree that within each domain or category there are varying degrees of giftedness, ranging from gifted and talented to the rare genius.

Duration means how long a behavior lasts.

Dyscalculia refers to a lack of ability to perform mathematical functions.

Dysgraphia refers to the partial inability to remember how to make certain alphabet or arithmetic symbols in handwriting.

Dyslexia is a disorder in recognizing and comprehending written words as a result of a developmental language impairment.

Early expressive language delay describes a significant delay in the development of expressive language that is apparent by age two.

Eating disorder is an obsessive concern with losing weight so that a person refuses to eat a proper diet, engages in binge eating followed by attempts to undo the food intake, and has issues of self-concept associated with obesity.

Ecological curriculum organizes knowledge and skills for students based on the task analysis of important skills they need to learn in order to function successfully in preferred environments.

Emotional intelligence includes qualities of self-awareness, impulse control, persistence, self-motivation, empathy, and social deftness.

Emotional or behavioral disorder is a chronic condition characterized by behavioral or emotional responses that differ from age, cultural, or ethnic norms to such a degree that educational performance is adversely affected.

EMR classroom refers to a classroom for students with mild mental retardation.

Etiology describes the cause or origin of a medical condition.

Evaluation refers to the interpretation of information secured through assessment.

Evaluation team is the IDEA term referring to the team responsible for administering a nondiscriminatory evaluation to determine if the student qualifies for special education.

Executive functions are not often publicly observable and have the common purpose of internalizing behavior to plan for change and the future. They include nonverbal working memory, internalization of speech, self-regulation of affect, motivation, and arousal and reconstitution.

Expertise means the technical mastery of skills and lore within a domain.

Expressive language disorders describe difficulties with expressing ideas, verbally, manually, or in other ways.

Externalizing behaviors are behavior disorders comprising aggressive, acting-out, and noncompliant behaviors.

Facilitative role means helping your colleagues develop a capacity to solve problems, engage in tasks, or deal independently with professional challenges.

Fetal alcohol syndrome results from the mother's alcohol use during pregnancy. The children often are small for gestational age, have facial deformities, and have congenital heart defects. Mild to moderate mental retardation is common.

Field of vision (visual field) is the entire area of which an individual is visually aware when that individual is directing his or her gaze straight ahead, typically 160 degrees.

Finger spelling refers to the hand configurations that represent the letters of the alphabet. Sometimes referred to as a *manual alphabet*, finger spelling is generally used for proper names and words with no known sign.

Fluency problems are difficulties with the accuracy and the rate with which speech is produced. Fluent speech is smooth, flows well, and is effortless.

Focal motor seizures are partial seizures that results in sudden, jerky movements of one part of the body.

Focal sensory seizures are a type of partial seizure that cause a person to see or hear things that are not there.

Fovea is the point on the retina of the eye where light rays are supposed to focus and that is responsible for the clearest visual acuity.

Frequency means how often a behavior occurs.

Frontal lobe is the frontal part of the brain; involved in planning, organizing, problem solving, selective attention, personality and a variety of higher cognitive functions.

Functional language problems are those difficulties associated with using language in everyday, real-life activities.

Functional retraining is a form of cognitive retraining that uses everyday curriculum and activities of a student with traumatic brain injury to teach cognitive skills.

Functionally blind is a term used to describe those individuals who can use their available vision to some limited degree (to sort color or to determine the presence of a light source) but who acquire information about the environment primarily through their auditory and tactual senses.

Generalization is the ability to apply what is learned in one setting to another.

Generalized anxiety disorder is an excessive, overwhelming worry not caused by any recent experience.

Generalized seizures cause a loss of consciousness. There are two types of generalized seizures: (1) A tonic-clonic seizure causes someone to fall and have a convulsion; (2) an absence seizure causes the person to lose consciousness only briefly.

Genius refers to persons or works that not only are expert and creative but also assume a universal, or quasi-universal, significance.

Gifted people have high performance capability in areas such as intellectual, creative, artistic, leadership, physical or intuitive/intrapersonal ability, or in specific academic fields.

Glaucoma is a medical condition that results from too much pressure within the eyeball. It can lead to tunnel vision and, ultimately, total blindness.

Grand mal seizure (See *tonic-clonic seizures*.)

Health care plans coordinate students' medical information and needs among family members and medical and school staff. All participants receive a copy, and one copy is attached to the IEP. An action plan is included when a student's condition could result in a health care emergency.

Hearing aid is an electroacoustic device designed to make sounds louder. Powered by a battery, hearing aids pick up sound, magnify its energy, and deliver the amplified sound.

Hemoglobin are red blood cells that carry oxygen through the body. Some hemoglobin are abnormal in students with sickle cell disease.

Heterogeneous refers to a diverse population of students.

Hyperactive refers to excessive, chronic energy and movement.

Hyperactivity-impulsivity as defined by DSM-IV-TR criteria for AD/HD, refers to a student who excessively fidgets, squirms, leaves seat, runs, climbs, talks, blurts out answers, displays impatience when forced to wait, and/or interrupts others.

Hyperglycemia occurs when a person has too much sugar in his or her bloodstream as a result of lack of insulin.

Hypernasality is a speech problem in which air is allowed to pass through a speaker's nasal cavity on sounds other than those for which air is supposed to pass through the nasal passage.

Hypoactive refers to a severe, chronic lack of energy and movement.

Hypoglycemia occurs when blood sugar is too low because of having too much insulin.

Hyponasality is a speech problem in which air cannot pass through a speaker's nose as it is supposed to and comes through the mouth instead. The speaker may sound as if the nose is being held.

Inattention as defined by DSM IV-TR criteria for AD/HD, refers to a student who daydreams, is disorganized, does not follow through with tasks, does not attend to details, loses things, and/or is often forgetful.

Inclusion is the term educators use to describe the goal of integrating students with disabilities into the same classrooms, community activities and resources, and home settings as students who do not have disabilities. Inclusion means no longer segregating students with disabilities into separate classrooms, schools, transportation, and living arrangements.

Incontinence means the inability to control one's bladder or bowels. Clean intermittent catheterization is a process whereby a tube is inserted into the urinary tract to allow elimination through the tube.

Individualized education program (IEP) is a written plan for serving students with disabilities ages 3 to 21.

Individualized family services plan (IFSP) is a written plan for providing services to infants and toddlers, ages zero to 3, and their families.

Instructional rubric is an evaluation tool based on two dimensions, specified instructional criteria and gradations of quality.

Integration is a synonym for inclusion. See the definition of inclusion.

Intermittent positive-pressure breathing (IPPB) machine is used outside a person's body and forces the lungs into an exhale function, facilitating breathing.

Internalizing behaviors are behavior disorders comprising social withdrawal, depression, anxiety, obsessions, and compulsions.

Interpreters are professionals who translate from one language to another. The role of a sign language interpreter is to aid in the process of communication between individuals using sign language and individuals using spoken English.

Jejunum is the second portion of a person's small intestine; a tube placed in it allows the person to receive nutrition through the tube.

Job coach is a person who supports an individual with a severe disability to be successful in supported employment by teaching the individual job skills and helping him or her perform the job.

Karyotyping involves arranging the chromosomes under a microscope so that they can be counted and grouped according to size, shape, and pattern.

Language disorders are problems in receiving, understanding, and formulating ideas and information.

Latency refers to how long it takes for the behavior to begin once there is an opportunity.

Learned helplessness refers to a condition in which individuals who have experienced repeated failure tend to expect failure.

Learning disabilities include disorders involved in understanding or in using spoken or written language that result in substantial difficulties in listening, speaking, reading, written expression, or mathematics. Other conditions such as emotional disturbance or sensory impairments may occur along with a learning disability but are not the primary cause of the learning disability.

Learning medium is a term used to describe the format(s) preferred by people who have visual impairments to access written materials and generally refers to print, large print, or braille.

Learning strategies are techniques, principles, or rules that help students to learn independently and to generalize what they learn.

Least restrictive environment is an IDEA principle that requires that students with disabilities be educated to the maximum extent appropriate with students who do not have a disability and that they be removed from regular education settings only when the nature or severity of their disability cannot be addressed with the use of supplementary aids and services.

Legal blindness is a term that refers to individuals whose central visual acuity, when measured in both eyes and when wearing corrective lenses, is 20/200 or whose visual field is no more than 20 degrees.

Low vision is experienced by individuals with a visual impairment who can use their vision as a primary channel for learning.

Macula is the thinnest area of the retina. Most of the nerve cells of the macula are responsible for vision in good light and provide a sense of detail and color.

Macular degeneration   is a type of visual disorder that results in the loss of function of the macula, the part of the eye responsible for detail and color vision.

Magnet schools   are schools that educate gifted and talented students by placing a strong instructional emphasis on one or two specific domains of talent.

Magnitude   means the intensity of the response.

Major depression   is characterized by excessive perceptions of sadness and worthlessness, with changes in emotion, motivation, physical well-being, and thoughts.

Manifestation determination   refers to the policy of making a decision on the consequences of a student's behavior based on whether the behavior was willful or the result of a disability.

Manually coded English   is any sign language system that represents English in a visual-gestural modality mechanism.

Mediation   is the process whereby both parties to a dispute agree to discuss and try to resolve their differences with the help of an independent third party. A *due process* hearing is like a trial, an adversarial process held before an impartial person called a *hearing officer*. The hearing is conducted like a trial, and the hearing officer is like a judge.

Meningocele   refers to the sac of membranes that covers the spinal cord. A person who has meningocele usually has no symptoms of spina bifida.

Mentor   is a person who knows more than a student does about a particular subject area and is willing to work with the student on an individual basis.

Metabolism   refers to the chemical processes that break down toxins (poisons) and move nutrients through the bloodstream.

Metacognition   is the ability to think about one's thinking or organize one's thoughts in a meaningful way.

Mild brain injury   is a traumatically induced physiological disruption of brain function, as manifested by at least one of the following: (a) any period of loss of consciousness, (b) any loss of memory for events immediately before or after the injury, and (c) any alteration in mental state at the time of the injury (e.g., feeling dazed, disoriented, or confused).

Milieu teaching   is an approach to language intervention in which the goal is to teach functional language in a natural environment.

Mixed cerebral palsy   refers to the condition in which a person with cerebral palsy has more than one type of cerebral palsy (different motor patterns) and no single form (pattern) is more dominant than any other.

Mnemonic   is a device such as a rhyme, formula, or acronym that is used to aid memory.

Moderate brain injury   is an injury that results in a Glasgow Coma Scale score of between 9 and 12 during the first 24 hours after injury.

Morphology   is the rule system that governs the structure of words.

Motor neurons   are the neurons that activate a person's muscle cells; a neuron is one of the conducting cells of the central nervous system. A neuron is "conducting" because it is the means through which various central nervous system activities occur (or are impaired).

Multilingualism   is the ability to use more than one language for communication.

Multimodal treatment   is the use of concurrent treatment approaches. For those with AD/HD, treatment may include as many as six components: medical management, education, coaching, counseling, organizational training, and behavior modification.

Multiple intelligences   describe different kinds of giftedness that are found across cultures and societies.

Myelomeningocele   also called meningomyelocele, occurs when the person's spinal cord is malformed, causing paralysis, sensory loss below the lesion of the spinal cord, hydrocephalus ("water on the brain"), and resulting mental retardation.

Myoclonic seizures   are a type of partial seizure that cause an infant or young child to look startled or in pain.

Myopia   is the medical term for near-sightedness, which results when light rays entering the eye focus in front of the retina.

Neonatal intensive care unit (NICU)   is a hospital facility for treating newborns with serious birth defects. It contains feeding, oxygen, and other life-support services.

Neurologist   is a physician who specializes in the nervous system and its disorders.

Neuropsychologist   is a psychologist who specializes in evaluating (testing) brain/behavior relationships, planning training programs to help individuals return to normal functioning, and recommending alternative cognitive and behavioral strategies to minimize the effects of the brain injury.

Nondiscriminatory evaluation   is an IDEA principle that requires schools to determine what each student's disability is and how it relates to the student's education. The evaluation must be carried out in a culturally responsive way.

Norm-referenced tests   compare a student with his or her age- or grade-level peers and have two purposes: to help to determine whether a student has an exceptionality and to assess various skills.

Obsessions   are persistent thoughts, impulses or images of a repetitive nature.

Obsessive-compulsive disorder   refers to obsessions manifesting as repetitive, persistent, and intrusive impulses, images, or thoughts, such as repetitive thoughts about death or illness and/or compulsions manifesting as repetitive, stereotypical behaviors such as handwashing or counting.

Occupational therapy   is the therapeutic program of self-care, work, and play activities to increase independent function, enhance development and prevent disability; may include the adaptation of a task or the environment to achieve maximum independence and to enhance the quality of life. The term *occupation*, as used in occupational therapy, refers to any activity engaged in for evaluating, specifying, and treating problems interfering with functional performance.

Open head injury results when a specific area or focal point of the brain is injured. A gunshot wound would cause an open head injury. The types of changes in personality or cognitive functioning depend on the area of the brain affected.

Opportunistic infections usually do not affect the general population but only those who have immune deficiency because of another illness. People with HIV are among those who are susceptible to opportunistic infections.

Optic nerve atrophy is a disorder of the optic nerve, the nerve that transmits visual information from the eye to the brain which often results in reduced visual acuity, or low vision.

Optic nerve hypoplasia is a disorder of the optic nerve that often is associated with midline or other brain abnormalities and that may result in varying degrees of visual impairment, including total blindness.

Organic language problems are difficulties in understanding or using language that are caused by a known problem in a person's neuromuscular mechanism.

Other health impairments include conditions that result in limited strength, vitality, or alertness, including a heightened alertness with respect to the educational environment, and that adversely affect a student's educational progress. Chronic and acute conditions are included, but conditions primarily affecting the musculoskeletal systems are not included.

Outer-directedness is a condition in which individuals distrust their own solutions and seek cues from others.

Panic disorder involves overwhelming panic attacks that result in rapid heartbeat, dizziness, and/or other physical symptoms.

Paraplegia refers to the impairment and limited use or no use of the arms.

Paraprofessional is a person who may have as much training as a teacher (although usually less) and who functions essentially like a teacher and works under a teacher's supervision.

Parent and student participation is an IDEA principle that ensures that parents and students have an opportunity to participate in joint decision-making with educators.

Partial participation is being flexible about how and how much students participate.

Partial seizures occur when electrical activity is limited to one area of the brain. There are three types of partial seizures: (1) Temporal lobe, or psychomotor, seizures cause a dreamlike state in which the person makes random movements called *automatisms*. (2) Focal sensory seizures cause the person to see or hear things that are not there. (3) Myoclonic seizures cause an infant or young child to look startled or in pain.

Peak flow meters measure the ability of students with asthma to push air out of their lungs.

Peer mediation is a problem-solving system of instruction in which students help each other resolve their conflicts.

Peer tutoring is the instruction of one student by another for the purposes of instructional and social support.

Percutaneous umbilical blood sampling is a prenatal diagnostic procedure for obtaining fetal blood for genetic testing.

Perinatal means at birth.

Personal intervention plan includes information on what triggers inappropriate behavior, the typical behaviors displayed by the student, the desired behaviors, goals for achieving the behaviors and supports the student needs to achieve the goals.

Phobia is an unrealistic, overwhelming fear of an object or situation.

Phonological awareness is a foundational reading skill in which a student recognizes sound segments in words presented orally.

Phonology is the use of sounds to make meaningful syllables and words.

Pidgin sign language refers to the use of signs from American Sign Language in English word order but without the grammatical complexity of either language.

Portfolio assessment is a technique for assembling exemplars of a student's work, such as homework, in-class tests, artwork, journal writing, and other evidence of the student's strengths and needs.

Positive behavioral support is a proactive, data-based approach to ensuring that students have needed skills and environmental supports.

Postconcussional syndrome refers to a mild closed head injury that may not show damage on medical tests but results in changes in personality or cognitive functioning.

Postlingual hearing loss is hearing loss that occurs after the child has acquired language.

Postnatal means after birth.

Post-traumatic stress disorder refers to flashbacks and other symptoms of resulting from a psychologically distressing event such as physical or sexual abuse, exposure to violence, or experiencing a natural disaster.

Pragmatics is the use of communication in social contexts.

Predominantly hyperactive-impulsive type of AD/HD is characterized by fidgeting, restlessness, difficulty engaging in quiet activities, excessive talking, driven personality, blurting out inappropriate comments, and/or the tendency to interrupt or intrude.

Predominantly inattentive type of AD/HD is characterized by daydreaming, careless work, inability to follow through, organizational difficulties, losing things, distractibility, hypoactivity, lethargy, and/or forgetfulness.

Prelingual hearing loss is hearing loss at birth or before the child has learned language.

Prenatal means before birth.

Prereferral occurs when a student's general education teacher asks others (educators and families) to help problem solve in order to identify instructional strategies to adequately address learning and behavioral challenges.

Primary prevention refers to an intervention that will prevent a disability from ever occurring. Examples include surgery on a fetus, the non-use of alcohol and drugs during a woman's pregnancy, and the provision of prenatal nutrition.

Procedural due process is an IDEA principle that provides a system of checks and balances with schools and parents in resolving differences that they have with each other.

Process definition refers to a U.S. Supreme Court interpretation of "appropriate education" as one that effectively implements IDEA's six principles.

Prodigy is a gifted individual who shows unusual promise in a specific task or domain.

Pseudo-ADD is a condition with characteristics of AD/HD resulting from living in a fast-paced society that emphasizes self-gratification.

Psychosocial disadvantage refers to conditions of individuals that develop from social and environmental influences.

Psychotropic medication is medication that alters perception, feelings, and/or behavior.

Pullout model is the term educators use to describe individualized educational support services (i.e., resource room) provided for a child with a disability outside the general education classroom by a special educator or another professional.

Quadriplegia refers to a weakness or paralysis of all four extremities—both arms and both legs.

Reading medium is a term used to describe the format(s) preferred by people who have visual impairments to access written materials and generally refers to print, large print, or braille.

Real-time graphic display synchronizes English on a screen with a speaker. An individual types into a device with phonetic shorthand symbols, the device is connected to a computer that translates these codes into English, and the English is displayed on a screen.

Receptive language disorders describe difficulties with receiving and understanding language.

Referral occurs when an educator or a parent submits a formal request for the student to be considered for a full and formal nondiscriminatory evaluation.

Related services means the services that are specified in IDEA that a student needs in order to benefit from special education.

Reliability refers to how consistently a test yields similar results across time and among raters.

Resiliency is the ability of some individuals who have grown up in extremely stressful, inconsistent, and/or abusive environments to emerge as highly functioning, successful adults.

Resonance describes the perceived quality of an individual's voice.

Respite care is the provision of planned activities in which the family can participate and/or babysitting services to allow family members to have a break from caregiving.

Retina is the innermost layer of nerve cells located at the back of the interior eyeball whose purpose is to convert light energy into electrical energy, which is then transmitted to the brain.

Retinitis pigmentosa is a visual disorder in which the retina is slowly destroyed, causing at first tunnel vision, and in some people, total blindness.

Retinopathy of prematurity is a type of visual disorder that is associated with premature exposure of the developing retina of the eye to oxygen, resulting in various levels of visual impairment.

Savant syndrome is a condition in which individuals typically display extraordinary abilities in areas such as calendar calculating, musical ability, mathematical skills, memorization, and mechanical abilities.

Schizophrenia is characterized by psychotic periods resulting in hallucinations, delusions, inability to experience pleasure, and loss of contact with reality.

Scoliosis is a lateral curve of the spine.

Screening is a routine test that helps school staff identify which students might need further testing to determine whether they qualify for special education.

Secondary prevention refers to intervention soon after detection of a biomedical or psychosocial problem and includes early intervention programs, lead screening, phenylketonuria (PKU) screening (see Chapter 9), and medical control of seizure disorders.

Seizures are temporary neurological abnormalities that result from unregulated electrical discharges in the brain, much like an electrical storm.

Selective attention refers to the ability to focus attention on a designated task.

Self-advocates protect their own interests. Advocates protect the interests of other people.

Self-determination refers to the ability of individuals to live their lives the way that they choose to live them, consistent with their own values, preferences, and abilities.

Self-efficacy is the use of performance attainment strategies that allow students to perceive themselves as having control over their environment.

Semantics is the meaning of what is expressed.

Sensorineural hearing loss is hearing loss caused by a problem in the inner ear or along the nerve pathway to the brain stem.

Service learning is a method for students to develop newly acquired skills by active participation and structured reflection in organized opportunities to meet community needs.

Severe brain injury produces at least 6 hours of coma and a Glasgow Coma Scale score of 8 or less within the first 24 hours after injury.

Severe discrepancy in this context is a statistically significant difference between ability and achievement as measured by standardized tests. Interpretation of *severe* *discrepancy* varies widely among states. A student may qualify as having learning disabilities in one state; but when she moves across the state line, she may no longer qualify. This lack of consistency in state definitions is a major concern for the field.

Shaken-impact syndrome refers to brain damage caused by someone who has vigorously shaken an infant for 5–20 seconds.

Short-term memory is the mental ability to recall information that has been stored for a few seconds to a few hours, such as the step-by-step instructions that teachers give their students.

Simultaneous communication is a method of communication that involves the use of sign language and spoken English.

Skull fracture is a break in the bony framework of the head that protects the brain.

Social interaction theories are theories proposed by researchers such as Lev Vygotsky that support the belief that language is learned through encounters with others.

Social maladjustment is an adaptive response to environmental conditions resulting in socialized aggression (e.g., gang-related behavior or juvenile delinquency).

Spastic cerebral palsy is a form of cerebral palsy in which a person's limbs are tight and inflexible. Spastic diplegia refers to tightness of the legs; spastic quadriplegia refers to tightness of the legs and arms and usually the trunk and muscles that control the person's mouth, tongue, and pharynx.

Spasticity is uncontrolled contractions or spasms of the skeletal muscles.

Special education means specially designed instruction, at no cost to the child's parents, to meet the unique needs of a student with a disability. Special education includes instruction in the classroom, home; hospitals and institutions, and other settings, and includes instruction in physical education.

Specific language impairment describes a language disorder with no identifiable cause in a person with apparent normal development in all other areas.

Speech disorders are disorders of articulation, voice, and/or fluency.

Speech reading is the ability of an individual with a hearing loss to read the speech of others through lip movements and facial cues only.

Spina bifida is a condition in which the person's vertebral arches (the connective tissue between one vertebra and another) are not completely closed; the person's spine is split—thus, spina (spine) bifida (split). Spina bifida is the most common form of neural tube defect.

Spina bifida occulta the most common form of spina bifida, is a condition in which the separation of the spinal arches is hidden—thus, occult, or hidden. The person has no visible abnormalities on his back, no sac or protruding spinal cord, or any symptoms of a split spinal cord. Spina bifida occulta is the most common form of spina bifida.

Strength-based interventions focus on relationship-building, enhancing resiliency traits the student already possesses, and instilling resiliency traits that are lacking.

Stress-induced agitation syndrome consists of characteristics of AD/HD resulting from the stress of living in poverty and potentially violent situations.

Stuttering is frequent repetition of words or speech sounds.

Subtyping is the practice of dividing students into small groups, based on common characteristics.

Supplementary aids and support services are those that are provided in general education classes or other education settings so that students with disabilities will be educated with students who do not have disabilities to the maximum extent appropriate for the students with disabilities.

Supported employment means the employment of a person with a disability for at least the minimum wage, working alongside other employees who do not have disabilities. The person is assisted by a job coach: a person who teaches the job and helps perform some of it.

Supportive role means caring and being there for your colleagues to share in times of need and in times of joy.

Supports refer to the services, resources, and personal assistance that improve the way in which a person functions: how he or she develops, learns, and lives.

Susceptibility genes work in conjunction with other currently unknown factors (e.g., environmental factors or infections) to cause a health impairment.

Symptomatic stage occurs when HIV reproduces more actively and the infected person begins to experience illnesses, including opportunistic infections.

Syntax is the set of rules for putting together words in sentences; grammar.

Syntax errors are those mistakes in using the rules that govern the arrangement of words in a language.

Talent pool describes the top 15 to 20 percent of students in general ability or specific performance areas.

Task analysis is a detailed specification of each of the skills or behaviors that are needed in order to participate in the activity.

Temporal lobe, or psychomotor, seizures are a type of partial seizure that cause a dreamlike state in which the person makes random movements called *automatisms*.

Teratogens are substances that can interfere with normal fetal development.

Tertiary prevention refers to special education and physical, occupational, or vocational training on a long-term basis for the purpose of reducing the effects of a present disability.

Text telephone (TT) is a telecommunications device that enables individuals to send a typed message over telephone lines to anyone else who has a TT.

Theory of mind is a concept that refers to impairments of individuals with autism associated with not understanding that their own beliefs, desires, and intentions may differ from those of others.

Tics are involuntary, rapid movements that occur without warning.

Tonic-clonic seizures are a type of generalized seizure that cause the person to fall, lose consciousness, or have a convulsion.

Topographical classification system ascribes a disability to the part of the brain that is affected.

Topography describes motor behavior or physical movements.

Totally blind is a term that describes those individuals who use their tactual and auditory senses to acquire information about their environment. These individuals do not receive meaningful input through the visual sense.

Tracheostomy is the surgical creation of an opening into a person's trachea (wind pipe). Into the opening is placed a tube that allows the person to breathe, almost always with the help of mechanical ventilation.

Traumatic brain injury is caused by an external physical force, resulting in impaired functioning in one or more areas. Educational performance is adversely affected. The injury may be open or closed.

Tunnel vision occurs when an individual's visual field is reduced significantly so that only a small area of central visual acuity remains. The affected individual has the impression of looking through a tunnel or tube and is unaware of objects to the left, right, top, or bottom.

Universal precautions are a list of necessary hygienic procedures to prevent the spread of communicable conditions.

Validity refers to how well the test measures what it says it measures.

Visual acuity is the term that describes the clarity with which a person sees. The visual acuity considered typical is 20/20.

Visual disability (including blindness) is defined by IDEA as an impairment in vision that, even with correction, adversely affects a child's educational performance.

Vocal nodules are small knots or lumps on the speech mechanism that result from the rubbing together of the vocal fold edges.

Whole language techniques are strategies and activities used for teaching language in its spoken and written forms that incorporate naturally occurring behaviors, such as speaking, writing, and reading, in learning to use language more effectively, correctly, and appropriately.

Zero reject is an IDEA principle that requires schools to enroll all students.

Zero tolerance is a policy of immediately expelling a student who exhibits violent behavior, carries a weapon, or uses drugs.

Chapter 1

Adelman, H. S. (1996). Appreciating the classification dilemma. In W. Stainback & S. Stainback (Eds.), *Controversial issues confronting special education: Divergent perspectives.* (2nd ed., pp. 96–111). Boston: Allyn & Bacon.

Bahr, M. W., Fuchs, D., & Fuchs, L. S. (1999). Mainstream assistance teams: A consultation-based approach to prereferral intervention. In S. Graham & K. Harris (Eds.), *Teachers working together: Enhancing the performance of students with special needs* (pp. 87–116). Cambridge, MA: Brookline Books.

Bahr, M. W., Whitten, E., Dieker, L., Kocarek, C. E., & Manson, D. (1999). A comparison of school-based teams: Implications for educational and legal reform. *Teaching Exceptional Children 66*(1), 67–83.

Brown v. Board of Education. (1954). *347 U.S. 483.*

Bryant, B., & Seay, P. C. (1998). The Technology-Related Assistance to Individuals with Disabilities Act: Relevance to individuals with learning disabilities and their advocates. *Journal of Learning Disabilities, 31*(1), 4–15.

Chambers, J. G., Parrish, T. B., & Harr, J. J. (2002). *What are we spending on special education services in the United States, 1999–2000?* Special Education Expenditure Project (02-01) (http://www.seep.org/Docs/AdyRptl.PDF).

Children's Defense, Fund. (1999). *The state of America's children yearbook.* Washington, DC: Children's Defense Fund.

Deardorff, K., & Hollman, F. (1997). *U.S. population estimates by age, sex, race, and Hispanic origin: 1990 to 1996.* Washington, DC: U.S. Government Printing Office.

deBettencourt, L. U. (2002). Understanding the differences between IDEA and Section 504. *Teaching Exceptional Children 34*(3), 16–23.

Doren, B., & Benz, M. R. (1998). Employment inequality revisited: Predictors of better employment outcomes for young women with disabilities in transition. *Journal of Special Education, 31,* 425–442.

Ford, D. (1998). The underrepresentation of minority students in gifted education: Problems and promises in recruitment and retention. *Journal of Special Education, 32*(1), 4–14.

Fujiura, G. T., & Yamaki, K. (2000). Trends in demography of childhood poverty and disability. *Exceptional Children, 66,* 187–199.

Goffman, E. (1963). *Behavior in public places: Notes on the social organization of gatherings.* Glencoe, IL: Free Press.

Gollnick, D. M., & Chinn, P. C. (2002). *Multicultral education in a pluralistic society* (6th ed.). Upper Saddle River, NJ: Merrill/Prentice Hall.

Gottlieb, J., Alter, M., Gottlieb, B. W., & Wishner, J. (1994). Special education in urban America: It's not justifiable for many. *Journal of Special Education, 27*(4), 453–465.

Heal, L. W., & Rusch, F. R. (1995). Predicting employment for students who leave special education high school programs. *Exceptional Children, (61),* 472–487.

Hosp, J. L., & Reschly, D. J. (in press a). Referral rates for intervention or assessment: A meta-analysis of racial differences. *Journal of Special Education.*

Hosp, J. L., & Reschly, D. J. (in press b). Regional differences in school psychology practice. *Journal of Special Education.*

Kaufman, P., Kwon, J. Y., Klein, S., & Chapman, C. D. (1999). *Dropout rates in the United States: 1998.* Washington, DC: U.S. Department of Education, Office of Educational Research and Improvement.

Kliewer, C., & Biklin, D. (1996). *Labeling: Who wants to be called retarded?* (2nd ed.). Boston: Allyn & Bacon.

Landrum, M. S., Katsiyannis, A., & DeWaard, J. (1998). A national survey of current legislative and policy trends in gifted education: Life after the National Excellence Report. *Journal for the Education of the Gifted, 21*(3), 352–371.

Lipsky, D. K., & Gartner, A. (1989). *Beyond special education: Quality for all.* Baltimore: Brookes.

MacMillan, D. L., & Meyers, C. E. (1979). *Educational labeling of handicapped learners. Review of research in education* (Vol. 7). Washington, DC: American Educational Research Association.

Mesibov, G. B., Adams, L. W., & Klinger, L. G. (1997). *Autism: Understanding the disorder.* New York, NY: Plenum.

Mills, G. E., & Duff-Mallams, K. (1999). A mediation strategy for special education disputes. *Intervention in School and Clinic, 35*(2), 87–92.

Mills, G. E., & Duff-Mallams, K. (2000). Special education mediation. *Teaching Exceptional Children, 31*(4), 72–78.

Mills v. Washington, DC, Board of Education. (1980). *348 F. Supp 866 (D.DC 1972); contempt proceedings, EHLR 551: 643 (D.DC 1980).*

National Center for Education Statistics. (1993). *Adult literacy in America.* Washington, DC: U.S. Department of Education, Office of Educational Research and Improvement.

National Center for Education Statistics. (1997). *Profiles of students with disabilities as identified in NELS: 88.* Washington, DC: U.S. Department of Education, Office of Educational Research and Improvement.

National Center for Education Statistics. (1999). *Digest of education statistics.* Washington, DC: U.S. Department of Education.

National Center for Education Statistics. (2000). *Dropout rates in the United States.* Washington, DC: U.S. Department of Education.

National Council on Disability. (2000). *Federal policy barriers to assistive technology.* Washington: Author.

National Organization on Disability. (2000). *Harris survey of Americans with disabilities.* (Study No. 12384). New York: Author.

National Research Council. (2001). *Educating children with autism.* Washington, DC: National Academy Press.

No Child Left Behind Act. (2002). P.L. 107-110.

Obiakor, F. E. (1999). Teacher expectations of minority exceptional learners: Impact on "accuracy" of self-concepts. *Exceptional Children, 66*(1), 39–53.

Patton, J. M. (1998). The disproportionate representation of African Americans in special education: Looking behind the curtain for understanding and solutions. *Journal of Special Education, 32*(1), 25–31.

Pennsylvania Association for Retarded Children (PARC) v. Commonwealth of Pennsylvania. (1971, 1972). *334 F. Supp. 1257, 343 F. Supp. 279.*

Reschly, D. J. (1996). Identification and assessment of students with disabilities. *Future in Children, 6*(1), 40–53.

Reynolds, M. C. (1991). *Classification and labeling.* In J. W. Lloyd, N. N. Singh, & A. C. Repp (Eds.). *The regular education initiative:*

Alternative Perspectives on concepts, issues, and models (pp. 29–42). Sycamore, IL: Sycamore.

Sherman, A. (1997). *Poverty matters: The cost of child poverty in America.* Washington, DC: Children's Defense Fund.

Smith, D. (1998). Assistive technology: Funding options and strategies. *Mental and Physical Disability Law Reporter, 22*(1), 115–123.

Titchkosky, T. (2001). Disability: A rose by any other name? "People first" language in Canadian society. *Canadian Review of Sociology and Anthropology, 38*(2), 125–140.

Turnbull, A. P., & Turnbull, H. R. (2001). *Families, professionals, and exceptionality: Collaborating for empowerment.* (4th ed.). Upper Saddle River, NJ: Merrill/Prentice Hall.

Turnbull, H. R., Turnbull, A. P., Stowe, M., & Wilcox, B. L. (2000). *Free appropriate education: The law and children with disabilities* (6th ed.). Denver: Love.

U.S. Department of Education. (1998). *To assure the free appropriate public education of all children with disabilities Twentieth annual report to Congress.* Washington DC: Author.

U.S. Department of Education. (2001). *To assure the free appropriate public education of all children with disabilities: Twenty-third annual report to Congress on the implementation of the Individuals with Disabilities Education Act.* Washington, DC: Author.

Valdez, K., Williamson, B., & Wagner, M. (1990). *The national longitudinal transition study of special education Students: Statistical almanac* (Vol. 1). Menlo Park, CA: SRI International.

Yell, M. (1998). *The law and special education.* Upper Saddle River, NJ: Merrill/Prentice Hall.

Chapter 2

American Federation of Teachers. (1999). *Making standards matter 1996: An annual fifty-state report on efforts to raise academic standards.* Washington, DC: Author.

Andrews, J. E., Carnine, D. W., Coutinho, M. J., Edgar, E. B., Forness, S. R., Fuchs, L. S., Jordan, D., Kauffman, J. M., Patton, J. M., Paul, J., Rosell, J., Rueda, E. S., Schiller, E., Skrtic, T. M., & Wong, J. (2000). Bridging the special education divide. *Remedial and Special Education, 21*(5), 258–260, 267.

Barnett, C., & Monda-Amaya, L. E. (1998). Principals' knowledge of and attitudes toward inclusion. *Remedial and Special Education, 19*(3), 181–192.

Bennett, T., DeLuca, D., & Bruns, D. (1997). Putting inclusion into practice: Perspectives of teachers and parents. *Exceptional Children, 64*(1), 115–131.

Boyer, W. A. R., & Bandy, H. (1997). Rural teachers' perceptions of the current state of inclusion: Knowledge, training, teaching practices, and adequacy of support systems. *Exceptionality, 7*(1), 1–18.

Brown, L., Udvari-Solner, A., Frattura-Kampschroer, Davis, L., Ahlgren, C., Van

Daventer, P., & Jorgensen, J. (1991). Integrated work: A rejection of segregated enclaves and mobile work crews. In L. H. Meyer, C. A. Peck, & L. Brown (Eds.), *Critical issues in the lives of people with severe disabilities* (pp. 219–228). Baltimore: Brookes.

Duhaney, L. M. G., & Salend, S. J. (2000). Parental perceptions of inclusive educational placements. *Remedial and Special Education, 21*(2), 121–128.

Erickson, R. (1998). *Accountability, standards, and assessment.* Washington, DC: Academy for Educational Development, Federal Resource Center.

Erwin, E., Soodak, L., Winton, P., & Turnbull, A. (2001). "I wish it wouldn't all depend upon me": Research on families and early childhood inclusion. In M. J. Guralnick (Ed.), *Early childhood inclusion: Focus on change* (pp. 127–158). Baltimore: Brookes.

Federal Register. (1999). Washington, DC: U.S. Government Printing Office.

Finn, J. D., & Achilles, C. M. (1999). Tennessee's class size study: Findings, implications, misconceptions. *Educational Evaluation and Policy Analysis, 21,* 97–109.

Fisher, D. (1999). According to their peers: Inclusion as high school students see it. *Mental Retardation, 37*(6), 458–467.

Fisher, D., Pumpian, I., & Sax, C. (1998). High school students' attitudes about and recommendations for their peers with significant disabilities. *Journal of the Association for Persons with Severe Handicaps, 23*(3), 272–280.

Ford, A., Davern, L., & Schnorr, R. (2001). Learners with significant disabilities: Curricular relevance in an era of standards-based reform. *Remedial and Special Education, 22*(4), 214–222.

Fox, N. E., & Ysseldyke, J. E. (1997). Implementing inclusion at the middle school level: Lessons for a negative example. *Exceptional Children, 64*(1), 81–98.

Fryxell, D., & Kennedy, C. H. (1995). Placement along the continuum of services and its impact on students' social relationships. *Journal of The Association for Persons with Severe Handicaps, 20,* 259–269.

Gartner, A., & Lipsky, D. K. (1987). Beyond special education: Toward a quality system for all students. *Harvard Educational Review, 57*(4), 367–395.

Giacobbe, A. C., Livers, A. F., Thayer-Smith, R., & Walther-Thomas, C. (2001). Raising the academic standards bar: What states are doing to measure the performance of students with disabilities. *Journal of Disability Policy Studies, 12*(1), 10–17.

Grosenick, J. K., & Reynolds, M. C. (1978). *Teacher education: Renegotiating roles for mainstreaming.* Minneapolis: National Support Systems Project.

Grove, K. A., & Fisher, D. (1999). Entrepreneurs of meaning: Parents and the process of inclusive education. *Remedial and Special Education, 20*(4), 208–215, 256.

Guy, B., Shin, H., Lee, S. Y. & Thurlow, M. L. (1999). *State graduation requirements for students with and without disabilities (Technical Report 24).* Minneapolis: University of Minnesota, National Center on Educational Outcomes.

Halvorsen, A., Neary, T., Hunt, P., & Piuma, C. (1996). *A model for evaluating the cost-effectiveness of inclusive and special classes.* Hayward, CA: California State University, PEERS Project.

High Stakes: Testing for Tracking, Promotion, and Graduation. (1999). Washington DC: National Academy Press.

Hitchcock, C., Meyer, A., Rose, D., & Jackson, R. (2002). Providing new access to the general curriculum: Universal design for learning. *Council for Exceptional Children 35*(2), 8–17.

Hollowood, T. M., Salisbury, C. L., Rainforth, B., & Palombaro, M. M. (1994). Use of instructional time in classrooms serving students with and without severe disabilities. *Exceptional Children, 61*(3), 242–253.

Hunt, P., & Hirose-Hatae, A., Doering, K., Karasoff, P., and Goetz, L. (2000). "Community" is what I think everyone is talking about. *Remedial and Special Education, 21*(5), 305–317.

Hunt, P., Staub, D., Alwell, M., & Goetz, L. (1994). Achievement by all students within the context of cooperative learning groups. *Journal of The Association for Persons with Severe Handicaps, 19*(4), 290–301.

Kauffman, J. M. (1995). How we might achieve the radical reform of special education. In J. M. Kauffman & D. P. Hallahan (Eds.), *The illusion of full inclusion* (pp. 193–211). Austin, TX: PRO-ED.

Kavale, K. A., & Forness, S. R. (1999). *Efficacy of special education and related services.* Washington, DC: American Association on Mental Retardation.

Kavale, K. A., & Forness, S. R. (2000). History, rhetoric, and reality: Analysis of the inclusion debade. *Remedial and Special Education, 21*(5), 279–296.

Kennedy, C. H., Shukla, S., & Fryxell, D. (1997). Comparing the effects of educational placements on the social relationships of intermediate school students with severe disabilities. *Journal of The Association for Persons with Severe Handicaps, 19*(4), 277–289.

King-Sears, M. E. (2001). Three steps for gaining access to the general education curriculum for learners with disabilities. *Intervention in School and Clinic, 37*(2), 67–76.

Kleinert, H., Green, P., Hurte, M., Clayton, J., & Oetinger, C. (2002). Creating and using meaningful alternate. *Teaching Exceptional Children 34*(4), 40–47.

Klingner, J. K., Vaughn, S., Schumm, J. S., Cohen, P., & Forgan, J. W. (1998). Inclusion or pull-out: Which do students prefer? *Journal of Learning Disabilities, 31*(2), 148–158.

MacMillan, D. L., Gresham, F. M., & Forness, S. R. (1996). Full inclusion: An empirical perspective. *Behavioral Disorders, 21*(2), 145–159.

McCrea, L. D. (1996). *A review of literature: Special education and class size*. Lansing: Michigan Department of Education.

McDonnell, J., Hardman, M., Hightower, J., & Kiefer-O'Donnell, R. (1991). Variables associated with in-school and after-school integration of secondary students with severe disabilities. *Education and Training in Mental Retardation, 26*, 243–257.

McDonnell, J., Thorson, N., McQuivey, C., & Kiefer-O'Donnell, R. (1997). Academic engaged time of students with low-incidence disabilities in general education classes. *Mental Retardation, 35*(1), 18–26.

McDonnell, L. M., McLaughlin, M. J., & Morison, P. (Eds.). (1997). *Educating one and all: Students with disabilities and standards-based reform*. Washington, DC: National Academy Press.

McDougall, D., & Brady, M. P. (1998). Initiating and fading self-management interventions to increase math fluency in general education classes. *Exceptional Children, 64*(2), 151–166.

McGregor, G., & Vogelsberg, R. T. (1998). *Inclusive schooling practices: Pedagogical and research foundations: A synthesis of the literature that informs best practices about inclusive schooling*. Pittsburgh: Allegheny University of the Health Sciences.

McLaughlin, M. W., & Warren, S. H. (1994). The costs of inclusion: Reallocating financial and human resources to include students with disabilities. *School Administrator, 51*, 8–18.

McLeskey, J., Waldron, N. L., So, T. H., Swanson, K., & Loveland, T. (2001). Perspectives of teachers toward inclusive school programs. *Teacher Education and Special Education, 24*(2), 108–115.

Minke, K. M., Bear, G. G., Deemer, S. A., & Griffin, S. M. (1996). Teachers' experiences with inclusive classrooms: Implications for special education reform. *Journal of Special Education, 30*, 152–186.

Molnar, A., Smith, P., Zahorik, J., Palmer, A., & Ehrle, K. (1999). Evaluating the SAGE program: A pilot program in targeted pupil-teacher reduction in Wisconsin. *Educational Evaluation and Policy Analysis, 21*(2), 165–177.

National Research Council. (1993). *National science education standards*. Washington, DC: National Committee on Science Education Standards and Assessment.

National Research Council. (1999). *High stakes: Testing for tracking, promotion, and graduation*. Washington, DC: National Academy Press.

O'Connor, R. E., & Jenkens, J. R. (1996). Cooperative learning as an inclusion strategy: A closer look. *Exceptionality, 6*(1), 29–51.

O'Neill, P. T. (2001). Special education and high stakes testing for high school graduation: An analysis of current law and policy. *Journal of Law and Education, 30*(2), 185–222.

Orfield, G. (1997). Going to work: Weak preparation, little help. In K. Wong (Ed.), *Advances in educational policy. Vol. 3: The Indiana youth opportunity study: A symposium*. Greenwich, CT: JAI.

Orkwis, R., & McLane, K. (1998, Fall). A curriculum every student can use: Design principles for student access. ERIC/OSEP Topical Brief, pp. 3–19.

Pisha, B., & Coyne, P. (2001). Smart from the start: The promise of universal design for learning. *Remedial and Special Education, 22*(4), 197–203.

Pugach, M. C. (1995). On the failure of the imagination in inclusive schools. *Journal of Special Education, 29*, 212–223.

Pugach, M. C., & Johnson, L. J. (2002). *Collaborative practitioners, collaborative schools* (2nd ed.). Denver: Love.

Pugach, M. C., & Warger, C. L. (2001). Curriculum matters: Raising expectations for students with disabilities. *Remedial and Special Education, 22*(4), 194–196, 213.

Reynolds, M. C., Wang, M. C., & Walberg, H. J. (1987). The necessary restructuring of special and general education. *Exceptional Children, 53*, 391–398.

Rose, D. (2000). Universal design for learning. *Journal of Special Education Technology, 15*(4), 47–51.

Sailor, W. (Ed.). (2002). *Building partnerships for learning, achievement, and accountability*. New York: Teachers College Press.

Salisbury, C., & Chambers, A. (1994). Instructional costs of inclusive schooling. *Journal of The Association for Persons with Severe Handicaps, 19*(3), 215–222.

Sands, D., Adams, L., & Stout, D. (1995). A statewide exploration of the nature and use of curriculum in special education. *Exceptional Children, 62*, 68–83.

Schnorr, R. F. (1997). From enrollment to membership: "Belonging" in middle and high school classes. *JASH, 22*(1), 1–15.

Schumm, J. S., & Vaughn, S. (1995). Getting ready for inclusion: Is the stage set? *Learning Disabilities Research and Practice, 10*, 169–179.

Scruggs, T. E., & Mastropieri, M. A. (1996). Teacher perceptions of mainstreaming/inclusion, 1958–1995: A research synthesis. *Exceptional Children, 63*, 59–74.

Shriner, J. G., & Thurlow, M. L. (1992). *Special education outcomes, 1991*. Minneapolis: University of Minnesota, National Center on Educational Outcomes.

Soodak, L. C., Erwin, E. J., Winton, P., Brotherson, M. J., Turnbull, A. P., Hanson, M. J., & Brault, L. M. (2002). Implementing inclusive early childhood education: A call for professional empowerment. *Topics in Early Childhood Special Education, 22*(2), 91–102.

Soodak, L. C., Podell, D. M., & Lehman, L. R. (1998). Teacher, student, and school attributes as predictors of teachers' responses to inclusion. *Journal of Special Education, 31*, 480–497.

Taylor, S. (1988). Caught in the continuum: A critical analysis of the principle of least restrictive environment. *Journal of the Association for Persons with Severe Handicaps, 13*(1), 41–53.

Thompson, S. J., Quenemoen, R. F., Thurlow, M. L., & Ysseldyke, J. E. (2001). *Alternate assessments for students with disabilities*. Reston, VA: Council for Exceptional Children.

Thousand, J. S., Villa, R. A., & Nevin, A. I. (Eds.). (2002). *Creativity and collaborative learning* (2nd ed.). Baltimore: Brookes.

Thurlow, M. L. (2000). Standards-based reform and students with disabilities: Reflections on a decade of change. *Focus on Exceptional Children, 33*(3), 1–16.

Thurlow, M. L., Elliott, J. L., & Ysseldyke, J. E. (1998). *Testing students with disabilities: Practical strategies for complying with district and state requirements*. Thousand Oaks, CA: Corwin.

Thurlow, M. L., House, A., Boys, C., Scott, D., & Ysseldyke, J. (2000). *State assessment policies on participation and accommodation for students with disabilities: 1999 update (Synthesis Report 33)*. Minneapolis: University of Minnesota, National Center on Educational Outcomes.

Thurlow, M. L., Nelson, J. R., Teelucksingh, E., & Draper, I. L. (2001). Multiculturalism and disability in a results-based educational system: Hazards and hopes for today's schools. In C. L. Utley & F. E. Obiakor (Eds.), *Special education, multicultural education, and school reform: Components of quality education for learners with mild disabilities* (pp. 155–172). Springfield, IL: Thomas.

Thurlow, M., Ysseldyke, J., Gutman, S., & Geenen, K. (1998). *An analysis of inclusion of students with disabilities in state standards documents (Technical Report 19)*. Minneapolis: University of Minnesota, National Center on Educational Outcomes.

Turnbull, A. P., & Schultz, J. B. (1979). *Mainstreaming handicapped students: A guide for the classroom teacher*. Boston: Allyn & Bacon.

U.S. Department of Education. (2000). *To assure the free appropriate public education of all children with disabilities: Twentieth annual report to Congress on the implementation of the Individuals with Disabilities Education Act*. Washington, DC: Author.

U.S. Department of Education. (2001). *To assure the free appropriate public education of all children with disabilities: Twenty-third annual report to Congress on the implementation of the Individuals with Disabilities Education Act*. Washington, DC: Author.

U.S. Office of Special Education Programs. (n.d.). *SPeNSE summary sheet: A high quality teacher for every classroom* (http://www.spense.org/SummaryReportserviceproviders.doc).

Van Reusen, A. K., Shoho, A. R., Barker, K. S. (2000). High school teacher attitudes toward inclusion. *High School Journal, 84*(2), 7–20.

Vaughn, S., & Klingner, J. (1998). Students' perceptions of inclusion and resource room settings. *Journal of Special Education, 32*(2), 79–88.

Voltz, D. L., Brazil, N., & Ford, A. (2001). What matters most in inclusive education: A practical guide for moving forward. *Intervention in School and Clinic, 37*(1), 23–30.

Walther-Thomas, C., Korinek, L., & McLaughlin, V. L. (1999). Collaboration to support students' success. *Focus on Exceptional Children, 32*(3), 1–18.

Wehmeyer, M. L., Lance, G. D., Bashinski, S. (2002). Promoting access to the general curriculum for students with mental retardation: A multi-level model. *Education and Training in Mental Retardation and Developmental Disabilities, 37*(3), 223–234.

Wehmeyer, M. L., Lattin, D., Agran, M. (2002). Achieving access to the general curriculum for students with mental retardation: A curriculum decision-making model. *Education and Training in Mental Retardation and Developmental Disabilities, 36*(4), 327–342.

Will, M. C. (1986). Educating children with learning problems: A shared responsibility. *Exceptional Children, 52,* 411–416.

Zigmond, N., Jenkins, J., Fuchs, L. S., Deno, S., Fuchs, D., Baker, J. N., Jenkins, L., & Couthino, M. (1995, March). Special education in restructured schools: Findings from three multi-year studies. *Phi Delta Kappan,* pp. 531–540.

Chapter 3

Austin, V. L. (2001). Teacher's beliefs about co-teaching. *Remedial and Special Education, 22*(4), 245–255.

Bacon, E., & Bloom, L. (2000). Listening to student voices: How student advisory boards can help. *Teaching Exceptional Children, 32*(6), 38–43.

Bauwens, J., & Hourcade, J. J. (1995). *Cooperative teaching: Rebuilding the schoolhouse for all students.* Austin: PRO-ED.

Carroll, D. (2001). Considering paraeducator training, roles, and responsibilities. *Council for Exceptional Children, 34*(2), 60–64.

Ferguson, D. L. (1995). The real challenge of inclusion: Confessions of a "rabid inclusionist." *Phi Delta Kappan, 77,* 281–287.

French, N. K. (2001). Supervising paraprofessionals: A survey of teacher practices. *Journal of Special Education, 35*(1), 41–53.

Friend, M. (2000). Myths and misunderstandings about professional collaboration. *Remedial and Special Education, 21*(3), 130–132.

Giangreco, B. F., Prelock, P. A., Reid, R. R., Dennis, R. E., & Edelman, S. W. (2000). Role of related services personnel in inclusive schools. In R. A. Villa & J. S. Thousand (Eds.), *Restructuring for caring and effective education: Piecing the puzzle* (pp. 360–388). Baltimore: Brookes.

Giangreco, M. F., Edelman, S. W., Broer, S. M., & Doyle, M. B. (2001). Paraprofessional support of students with disabilities: Literature from the past decade. *Exceptional Children, 68*(1), 45–63.

Gollnick, D. M., & Chinn, P. C. (2002). *Multicultural education in a pluralistic society* (6th ed.). Upper Saddle River, NJ: Merrill/Prentice Hall.

Harry, B., Kalyanpur, M., & Day, M. (1999). *Building cultural reciprocity with families.* Baltimore: Brookes.

Hoerr, T. R. (1996). Collegiality: A new way to define instructional leadership. *Phi Delta Kappan, 77,* 380–381.

Hunt, P., Hirose-Hatae, A., Doering, K., Karasoff, P., & Goetz, L. (2000). "Community" is what I think everyone is talking about. *Remedial and Special Education, 21*(5), 305–318.

Johnson, D. W., & Johnson, F. P. (1997). *Joining together: Group theory and skills* (6th ed.). Needham Heights, MA: Allyn & Bacon.

Johnson, D. R., Sharpe, M., & Sinclair, M. F. (1997). *State and local education efforts to implement the transition requirements of IDEA: Report on the national survey of the implementation of the IDEA transition requirements.* Minneapolis: University of Minnesota, Institute on Community Integration, National Transition Network.

Kalyanpur, M., & Harry, B. (1999). *Culture in special education: Building reciprocal family-professional relationship.* Baltimore: Brookes.

Lynch, E. W., & Hanson, M. J. (1998). *Developing cross-cultured competence: A guide for working with children and their families* (2nd ed.). Baltimore: Brookes.

Martin, J., Jorgensen, C. M., & Kelin, J. (1998). The promise of friendship for students with disabilities. In C. M. Jorgensen (Ed.), *Restructuring high schools for all students: Taking inclusion to the next level* (pp. 145–181). Baltimore: Brookes.

Martin, J. E., & Marshall, L. H. (1996). *ChoiceMaker: Infusing self-determination instruction into the IEP and transition process.* Baltimore: Brookes.

McDiarmid, G. W. (1991). What teachers need to know about cultural diversity: Restoring subject matter to the picture. In M. M. Kennedy (Ed.), *Teaching academic subjects to diverse learners* (pp. 257–269). New York: Teachers College Press.

Murawski, W. W., & Swanson, H. L. (2001). A meta-analysis of co-teaching research: Where are the data? *Remedial and Special Education, 22*(5), 258–267.

National Center for Education Statistics. (1993). *Adult literacy in America.* Washington, DC: U.S. Department of Education, Office of Educational Research and Improvement.

National Center for Education Statistics. (1997). *Profiles of students with disabilities as identified in NELS: 88.* Washington, DC: U.S. Department of Education, Office of Educational Research and Improvement.

National Center for Education Statistics. (1999). *Digest of education statistics.* Washington, DC: U.S. Department of Education.

National Council on Disability. (2000). *Federal policy barriers to assistive technology.* Washington, DC: Author.

National Organization on Disability. (2000). *Harris survey of Americans with disabilities.* (Study No. 12384). New York: Author.

Pugach, M. C., & Johnson, L. J. (2002). *Collaborative practitioners, collaborative schools* (2nd ed.). Denver: Love.

Pugach, M. C., & Warger, C. L. (2001). Curriculum matters: Raising expectations for students with disabilities. *Remedial and Special Education, 22*(4), 194–196, 213.

Riggs, C. G., & Mueller, P. H. (2001). Employment and utilization of paraeducators in inclusive settings. *Journal of Special Education, 35*(1), 54–62.

Salisbury, C. L., & McGregor, G. (2002). The administrative climate and context on inclusive elementary schools. *Exceptional Children, 68*(2), 259–274.

Senge, P. M. (1990). *The fifth discipline: The art and practice of the learning organization.* New York: Doubleday.

Smith, M. J., & Ryan, A. S. (1987). Chinese-American families of children with developmental disabilities: An exploratory study of reactions to service providers. *Mental Retardation, 25,* 345–350.

Thousand, J. S., Fox, T., Reid, R., Godek, J., Williams, W., & Fox, W. (1986). *The homecoming model: Educating students who present intensive challenges within regular education environments.* Burlington: University of Vermont, Center for Developmental Disabilities.

Thousand, J., Rosenberg, R. L., Bishop, K. D., & Villa, R. A. (1997). The evolution of secondary inclusion. *Remedial and Special Education, 18*(5), 270–284, 306.

Thousand, J. S., & Villa, R. A. (1990). Strategies for educating learners with severe handicaps within their local home schools and communities. *Focus on Exceptional Children, 23*(3), 1–25.

Thousand, J. S., & Villa, R. A. (2000). Collaborative teaming: A powerful tool in school restructuring. In R. A. Villa & J. S. Thousand (Eds.), *Restructuring for caring and effective education: Piecing the puzzle* (pp. 254–292). Baltimore: Brookes.

Thousand, J. S., Villa, R. A., & Nevin, A. I. (Eds.). (2002). *Creativity and collaborative learning* (2nd ed.). Baltimore: Brookes.

Tichenor, M. S., Heins, B., & Piechura-Couture, K. (2000). Parent perceptions of a co-taught inclusive classroom. *Education, 120*(3), 569–574.

Turnbull, A. P., & Turnbull, H. R. (2001). *Families, professionals, and exceptionality: Collaborating for empowerment* (4th ed.). Upper Saddle River, NJ: Merrill/Prentice Hall.

Turnbull, H. R., III, Turnbull, A. P., Stowe, M., & Wilcox, B. L. (2000). *Free appropriate public education: The law and children with disabilities* (6th ed.). Denver: Love.

U.S. Department of Education. (1999). *To assure the free appropriate public education of all children with disabilities.* Washington, DC: Author.

Van Reusen, A. K. (1998). *Self-advocacy strategy instruction: Enhancing student motivation, self-determination, and responsibility in the learning process.* Baltimore: Brookes.

Villa, R. A., Thousand, J. S., Meyers, H., & Nevin, A. I. (1996). Teacher and administrator perceptions of heterogeneous education. *Exceptional Children, 63*, 29–45.

Walther-Thomas, C. (1997). Co-teaching experiences: The benefits and problems that teachers and principals report over time. *Journal of Learning Disabilities, 30*, 395–407.

Walther-Thomas, C., Korinek, L., McLaughlin, V. L., & Williams, B. T. (2000). *Collaboration for inclusive education: Developing successful programs.* Boston: Allyn & Bacon.

Wehmeyer, M. L. (1996). Self-determination as an educational outcome: Why is it important to children, youth, and adults with disabilities? In D. J. Sands & M. L. Wehmeyer (Eds.), *Self-determination across the life span: Independence and choice for people with disabilities.* Baltimore: Brookes.

Wehmeyer, M. L., Palmer, S. B., Agran, M., Mithaug, D. E., & Martin, J. (2000). Promoting causal agency: The self-determined learning model of instruction. *Exceptional Children, 66*(4), 439–453.

Wehmeyer, M. L., Sands, D. J., Knowlton, H. E., & Kozleski, E. B. (2002). *Providing access to the general curriculum: Teaching students with mental retardation.* Baltimore: Brookes.

Chapter 4

Bauer, A. M., & Shea, T. M. (1999). *Inclusion 101: How to teach all learners.* Baltimore: Brookes.

Bender, W. N., & Smith, J. K. (1990). Classroom behavior of children and adolescents with learning disabilities: A meta-analysis. *Journal of Learning Disabilities, 23*, 298–305.

Bricker, D., Pretti-Frontczak, K., & McComas, N. (1998). *An activity-based approach to early intervention* (2nd ed.). Baltimore: Brookes.

Chard, D. J., & Kameenui, E. J. (2000). Struggling first-grade readers: The frequency and progress of their reading. *Journal of Special Education, 34*, 28–38.

Coyne, M. D., Kame'enui, E. J., & Simmons, D. C. (2001). Prevention and intervention in beginning reading: Two complex systems. *Learning Disabilities, 16*(2), 62–73.

Davis, M. D., Kilgo, J. L., & Gamel-McCormick, M. (1998). *Young children with special needs.* Boston: Allyn & Bacon.

Deshler, D. (1998). Grounding interventions for students with learning disabilities in "powerful ideas." *Learning Disabilities, 13*, 29–34.

Dev, P. C. (1998). Intrinsic motivation and the student with learning disabilities. *Journal of Research and Development in Education, 31*, 98–108.

Erickson, R., Ysseldyke, J., & Thurlow, M. (1997). Neglected numerators, drifting denominators, and fractured fractions: Determining participation rates for students with disabilities. *Diagnostique, 23*, 105–115.

Engelmann, S. (1991). Making connections in mathematics. *Journal of Learning Disabilities, 24*, 292–303.

Fletcher, J. M., Lyon, G. R., Barnes, M., Stuebing, K. K., Francis, D. J., Olson, R. K., Shaywitz, S. E., & Shaywitz, B. A. (2001). *Classification of learning disabilities: An evidence-based evaluation* (http://www.air.org/ldsummit/).

Friend, M., & Bursuck, W. D. (2002). *Including students with special needs: A practical guide for classroom teachers.* Boston: Allyn & Bacon.

Fuchs, D. M., Fuchs, L. S., Mathes, P. G., Lipsey, M. W., & Roberts, P. H. (2001). *Is "learning disabilities" just a fancy term for low achievement: A meta-analysis of reading differences between low achievers with and without the label* (http://www.air.org/ldsummit/).

Gersten, R. (1998). Recent advances in instructional research for students with learning disabilities: An overview. *Learning Disabilities, 13*, 162–170.

Graham, S., Harris, K. R., & Larsen, L. (2001). Prevention and intervention of writing difficulties for students with learning disabilities. *Learning Disabilities, 16*(2), 74–84.

Hallahan, D. P., & Mercer, C. D. (2001). *Learning disabilities: Historical perspectives* (http://www.air.org/ldsummit/).

Hemmeter, M. L., & Grisham-Brown, J. (1997). Teaching language and communication skills in the context of ongoing activities and routines in inclusive preschool classrooms. *Dimensions in Early Childhood Education, 25*, 6–13.

Higgins, K., Boone, R., & Williams, D. L. (2000). Technology trends. *Intervention in School and Clinic, 36*(2), 109–115.

Hock, M. F., Deshler, D. D., & Schumaker, J. B. (1999). Tutoring programs for academically underprepared college students: A review of the literature. *Journal of College Reading and Learning, 29*(2), 101–121.

Kavale, K. A. (2001). *Discrepancy models in the identification of learning disability* (http://www.air.org/ldsummit/).

Kavale, K. A., & Forness, S. R. (1996). Social skills deficits and learning disabilities: A meta-analysis. *Journal of Learning Disabilities, 29*, 226–237.

Kavale, K. A., & Forness, S. R. (2000). What definitions of learning disability say and don't say: A critical analysis. *Journal of Learning Disabilities, 33*, 239–256.

Lenz, B. K., Alley, G. R., & Schumaker, J. B. (1987). Activating the inactive learner: Advance organizers in the secondary content classroom. *Learning Disability Quarterly, 10*, 53–67.

Lerner, J. (2000). *Learning disabilities: Theories, diagnosis, and teaching strategies* (8th ed.). Boston: Houghton Mifflin.

Light, J. G., & Defries, J. C. (1995). Comorbidity of reading and mathematics disabilities: Genetic and environmental etiologies. *Journal of Learning Disabilities, 28*, 96–106.

Meese, R. L. (2001). *Teaching learners with mild disabilities: Integrating research and practice* (2nd ed.). Belmont, CA: Wadsworth.

Mercer, C. D., Jordan, L., Allsopp, D. H., & Mercer, A. R. (1996). Learning disabilities definitions and criteria used by state education departments. *Learning Disabilities Quarterly, 19*, 217–231.

Miller, S. P., Butler, F. M., & Lee, K. (1998). Validated practices for teaching mathematics to students with learning disabilities: A review of literature. *Focus on Exceptional Children, 31*, 1–24.

Murphy-Brennan, M. G., & Oei, P. S. (1999). Is there evidence to show that fetal alcohol syndrome can be prevented? *Journal of Drug Education, 29*(1), 5–24.

National Reading Panel. (2000). *Research-based approaches to reading instruction.* Washington, DC: Author.

O'Shaughnessy, T. E., & Swanson, L. H. (1998). Do immediate memory deficits in students with learning disabilities in reading reflect a developmental lag or deficit? A selective meta-analysis of the literature. *Learning Disability Quarterly, 21*, 123–148.

Price, N., & Youe, S. (2001). The problems of diagnosis and remediation of dyscalculia. *For the Learning of Mathematics, 20*(3), 23–28.

Psychological Corporation. (1992). *Wechsler individual achievement test.* San Antonio, TX: Author.

Psychological Corporation. (1999). *WISC-III.* San Antonio, TX: Author.

Robinson, S. (1999). Meeting the needs of students who are gifted and have learning disabilities. *Intervention in School and Clinic, 34*, 195–204.

Settle, S. A., & Milich, R. (1999). Social persistence following failure in boys and girls with LD. *Journal of Learning Disabilities, 32*, 201–212.

Sewell, T. J., Collins, B. C., & Hemmeter, M. L. (1998). Using simultaneous prompting to teach dressing skills to preschoolers with developmental delays/disabilities. *Journal of Early Intervention, 21*, 132–145.

Shaywitz, S. E., Shaywitz, B. A., Pugh, K. R., Fulbright, R. K., Constable, R. T., Mencel, W. E., Shankweiler, D. P., Liberman, A. M., Skudlarski, P., Fletcher, J. M., Katz, L., Marchione, K. E., Lacadie, C., Gatenby, C., & Gore, J. C. (1998). Functional disruption in the organization of the brain for reading dyslexia. *Neurobiology, 95*, 2636–2641.

Swanson, H. L. (2000). Are working memory deficits in readers with learning disabilities hard to change? *Journal of Learning Disabilities, 33*, 551–566.

Swanson, H. L. (2001). Research on interventions for adolescents with learning disabilities: A meta-analysis of outcomes related to higher-order processing. *Elementary School Journal, 101*, 331–348.

Tarver, S. G. (2000). Direct Instruction: Teaching for generalization, application and integration of knowledge. *Learning Disabilities, 10*, 201–207.

Torgesen, J. K., & Wagner, R. K. (1998). Alternative diagnostic approaches for specific developmental reading disabilities. *Learning Disabilities, 13*, 220–232.

U.S. Department of Education. (2001). *To assure the free appropriate public education of all children with disabilities: Twenty-third annual report to Congress on the implementation of the Individuals with Disabilities Education Act.* Washington, DC: Author.

Woodward, J., & Baxter, J. (1997). The effects of an innovative approach to mathematics on academically low-achieving students in inclusive settings. *Exceptional Children, 63*, 373–388.

Chapter 5

Achenbach, T. M., & Edelbrock, C. S. (1981). Behavioral problems and competencies reported by parents of normal and disturbed children aged four through sixteen. *Monographs of the Society for Research in Child Development, 46*(1), serial no. 188.

Addison, M. M., & Westmoreland, D. A. (2000). Over the net: Encouraging win-win solutions through conflict resolution. *Reaching Today's Youth, 5*(1), 51–54.

American Federation of Teachers & AFL-CIO. (1996). *Full inclusion for special needs students.* Washington, DC: Author.

American Psychiatric Association. (2000). *Diagnostic and statistical manual of mental disorders* (4th ed., revised). Washington, DC: Author.

Bassarath, L. (2001). Conduct disorder: A biopsychosocial review. *Canadian Journal of Psychiatry, 46*(7), 609–617.

Benner, G. J., Nelson, J. R., & Epstein, M. H. (2002). Language skills of children with EBD. *Journal of Emotional and Behavioral Disorders, 10*(1), 43–57.

Bostic, J. Q., Rustuccia, C., & Schlozman, S. C. (2001). The suicidal student. *Educational Leadership, 59*(2), 92–93.

Brendtro, L. K., Brokenleg, M., & Van Bockern, S. (1991). The circle of courage. *Beyond Behavior, 2*(1), 5–12.

Brendtro, L. K., Long, N. J., & Brown, W. K. (2000). Searching for strengths. *Reclaiming Children and Youth, 9*(2), 66–69.

Brownell, M. T., & Walther-Thomas, C. (2001). Stephen W. Smith: Strategies for building a positive classroom environment by preventing behavior problems. *Intervention in School and Clinic, 37*(2), 31–35.

Bryant-Comstock, S., Huff, B., & VanDenBerg, J. (1996). The evolution of the family advocacy movement. In B. A. Stroul (Ed.), *Children's mental health: Creating systems of care in a changing society* (pp. 359–374). Baltimore: Brookes.

Bullock, C., & Foegen, A. (2002). Constructive conflict resolution for students with behavioral disorders. *Behavioral Disorders, 27*(3), 289–295.

Cartledge, G., Kea, C. D., Ida, D. J. (2000). Providing culturally competent services for students with serious emotional disturbance. *Teaching Exceptional Children, 32*(3), 30–37.

Cheney, D., & Muscott, H. S. (1996). Preventing school failure for students with emotional and behavioral disabilities through responsible inclusion. *Preventing School Failure, 40*(3), 109–117.

Costenbader, V., & Buntaine, R. (1999). Diagnostic discrimination between social maladjustment and emotional disturbance: An empirical study. *Journal of Emotional and Behavioral Disorders, 17*(1), 2–11.

Covey, S. R. (2000). *The seven habits of highly effective people.* Philadelphia: Running Press.

Daunic, A. P., Smith, S. W., Robinson, T. W., Miller, M. D., & Landry, K. L. (2000). School-wide conflict resolution and peer mediation programs: Experiences in three middles schools. *Intervention in School and Clinic, 36*(2), 94–100.

Dreikurs, R., Grunwald, B. B., & Pepper, F. C. (1998). *Maintaining sanity in the classroom: Classroom management techniques* (2nd ed.). New York: Taylor & Francis.

Duncan, B. B., Forness, S. R., & Hartsough, C. (1995). Students identified as seriously emotionally disturbed in day treatment: Cognitive, psychiatric, and special education characteristics. *Behavioral Disorders, 29*, 238–252.

DuPaul, G. J., & Hoff, K. E. (1998). Reducing disruptive behavior in general education classrooms: The use of self-management strategies. *School Psychology Review, 27*(2), 290–304.

Eber, L. (1996). Reconstructing schools through the wraparound approach: The LADSE experience. In R. J. Illback & C. M. Nelson (Eds.), *School-based services for students with emotional and behavioral disorders* (pp. 139–154). Binghampton, NY: Haworth.

Eber, L., & Nelson, C. M. (1994). *Compendium digest: Special education and related services for students with serious emotional disturbance.* Unpublished paper.

Eber, L., Nelson, C. M., & Miles, P. (1997). School-based wraparound for students with emotional and behavioral challenges. *Exceptional Children, 63*, 539–555.

Epstein, M. H. (1999). The development and validation of a scale to assess the emotional and behavioral strengths of children and adolescents. *Remedial and Special Education, 20*(5), 258–262.

Epstein, M. H., Cullinan, D., Harniss, M. K., Ryser, G. (1999). The Scale for Assessing Emotional Disturbance: Test-Retest and Interrater Reliability. *Behavioral Disorders, 24*(3), 222–230.

Epstein, M. H., & Sharma, J. (1998). *Behavioral and emotional rating scale: A strength-based approach to assessment.* Austin, TX: PRO-ED.

Faber, A., & Mazlish, E. (1996). *How to talk so kids can learn.* New York: Fireside.

Farner, C. D. (2002). Antidote for zero tolerance: Revisiting a reclaiming school. *Reclaiming Children and Youth, 11*(1), 19–22.

Ford, J. D., Rucusin, R., Ellis, C. G., Daviss, W. B., Reiser, J., Fleischer, A., & Thomas, J. (2000). Child maltreatment, other trauma exposure, and posttraumatic symptomatology among children with oppositional defiant and attention deficit hyperactivity disorders. *Child Maltreatment, 5*(3), 205–218.

Forness, S. R., & Kavale, K. A. (2000). Emotional or behavioral disorders: Background and current status of the E/BD terminology and definition. *Behavioral Disorders, 25*(3), 264–269.

Forness, S. R., & Kavale, K. A. (2001). Reflections on the future of prevention. *Preventing School Failure, 45*(2), 75–82.

Forness, S. R., Kavale, K. A., MacMillan, D. L., Asarnow, J. R., & Duncan, B. B. (1996). Early detection and prevention of emotional or behavioral disorders: Developmental aspects of systems care. *Behavioral Disorders, 21*(3), 226–240.

Franklin, B. (n.d.). *Reaching out to troubled teens* (http://www.handinpaw.org/reachingout.htm). Retrieved February 5, 2003.

Fujiura, G. T., & Yamaki, K. (2000). Trends in demography of childhood poverty and disability. *Exceptional Children, 66*(2), 187–199.

Glassberg, L. A., Hooper, S. R., & Mattison, R. E. (1999). Prevalence of learning disabilities at enrollment in special education: Students with behavioral disorders. *Behavioral Disorders, 25*(1), 9–21.

Goldman, S. K., & Faw, L. (1998). Three wraparound models as promising approaches. In B. J. Burns & S. K. Goldman (Eds.). *Systems of care: Promising practices in children's mental health* (Vol. 4, pp. 17–57). Washington, DC: American Institutes for Research, Center for Effective Collaboration and Practice.

Gresham, F. M., Lane, K. L., MacMillan, D. L., & Bocian, K. M. (1999). Social and academic profiles of externalizing and internalizing groups: Risk factors for emotional and behavioral disorders. *Behavioral Disorders, 24*(3), 231–245.

Hall, N., Williams, J., & Hall, P. S. (2000). Fresh approaches with oppositional students. *Reclaiming Children and Youth, 8*(4), 219–226.

Hallowell, E. M. (1996). *When you worry about the child you love: Emotional and learning problems in children.* New York: Fireside.

Hand-in-Paw. (2002, November 2). *Meeting human needs with animal resources.* Paper presented at the Pawsitive Living workshop, Birmingham, AL.

Hewitt, M. B. (1999). The control game: Exploring oppositional behavior. *Reclaiming Children and Youth, 8*(1), 30–33.

Ialongo, N., Poduska, J., Werthamer, L., & Sheppard, K. (2001). The distal impact of two first-grade preventive interventions on conduct problem and disorder in early adolescence. *Journal of Emotional and Behavioral Disorders, 9*(3), 146–161.

Jablow, M. M. (1992). *A parent's guide to eating disorders and obesity.* New York: Delta.

Jolivette, K. (2000). Improving post-school outcomes for students with emotional and behavioral disorders. *ERIC/OSEP Digest E597*.

Kauffman, J. M. (2000). Future directions with troubled children. *Reclaiming Children and Youth, 9*(2), 119–124.

Kauffman, J. M. (2001). *Characteristics of emotional and behavioral disorders of children and youth* (7th ed.). Upper Saddle River, NJ: Merrill/Prentice Hall.

Keogh, B. K. (2000). Risk, families, and schools. *Focus on Exceptional Children, 33*(4), 1–10.

Kumra, S., Shaw, M., Merka, P., Nakayama, E., & Augustin, R. (2001). Childhood-onset schizophrenia: Research update. *Canadian Journal of Psychiatry, 46,* 923–930.

La Grange Area Department of Special Education. (1993). Making a difference with Project WRAP. *Making a Difference,* pp. 4–5.

Langley, A. K., Bergman, L., & Piacentini, J. C. (2002). Assessment of childhood anxiety. *International Review of Psychiatry, 14,* 102–113.

Laursen, E. K. (2000). Strength-based practice with children in trouble. *Reclaiming Children and Youth, 9*(2), 70–75.

Mandleco, B. L., & Perry, J. C. (2000). An organizational framework for conceptualizing resilience in children. *Journal of Child and Adolescent Psychiatric Nursing, 13*(3), 99–112.

Maslow, A. (1998). *Toward a psychology of being* (3rd ed.). New York: Wiley.

McCoy, K. (1994). *Understanding your teenager's depression.* New York: Perigee.

McIntosh, P. I., & Guest, C. L. (2000). Suicidal behavior: Recognition and response for children and adolescents. *Beyond Behavior, 10*(2), 14–17.

Miklowitz, D. J., & Goldstein, M. J. (1997). *Bipolar disorder. A family-focused treatment approach.* New York: Guilford.

Miller-Johnson, Coie, Maumary-Gremaud, Lochman, & Terry, (1999). Relationship between childhood peer rejection and aggression and adolescent delinquency severity and type among African American Youth. *Journal of Emotional and Behavioral Disorders, 7*(3), 137–147.

Milne, J. M., Edwards, J. K., & Nurchie, J. C. (2001). Family treatment of oppositional defiant disorder: Changing views and strength-based approaches. *Family Journal, 9*(1), 17–28.

Mitchem, K. J. (2001a). Adapting self-management programs for classwide use. *Remedial and Special Education, 22*(2), 75–89.

Mitchem, K. J. (2001b). CWPASM: A classwide peer-assisted self-management program for general education classrooms. *Education and Treatment of Children, 24*(2), 111–141.

Muscott, H. S. (2000). A review and analysis of service-learning programs involving students with emotional/behavioral disorders. *Education and Treatment of Children, 23*(3), 346–368.

Muscott, H. (2001). Fostering learning, fun, and friendship among students with emotional and behavioral disorders and their peers: The SO Prepared for Citizenship program. *Beyond Behavior, 10*(3), 36–47.

National Center for Educational Statistics. (2002). *The condition of education.* Washington, DC: U.S. Department of Education, Office of Educational Research and Improvement.

National Center for Injury Prevention and Control. (2002). *Suicide in the United States.* Atlanta: Centers for Disease Control.

Newton, R. R., Litronik, A. J., & Lansverk, J. A. (2000). Children and youth in foster care: Disentangling the relationship between problem behaviors and number of placements. *Child Abuse and Neglect, 24*(10). 1364–1374.

O'Connor, B. V., & MacDonald, B. J. (1999). A youth-friendly intervention for homeless and street-involved youth. *Reclaiming Children and Youth, 8*(2), 102–106.

Oakwood Solutions. (2002). *Emotional intelligence demonstration programs: Education version.* Oshkosh, WI: Conover Company.

Osseroff, A., Oseroff, C. E., Westling, D., & Gessner, L. J. (1999). Teachers' beliefs about maltreatment of students with emotional/behavioral disorders. *Behavioral Disorders, 24*(3), 197–209.

Oswald, D. P., Cohen, R., Best, A. M., Jenson, C. E., & Lyons, J. S. (2001). Child strengths and the level of care for children with emotional and behavioral disorders. *Journal of Emotional and Behavioral Disorders, 9*(3), 192–000

Panico, A. (1998). Service learning as a community initiation. *Reaching Today's Youth, 3*(1), 37–41.

Peterson, L. D., & Young, K. R. (1999). Effects of student self-management on generalization of student performance to regular classrooms. *Education and Treatment of Children, 22*(3), 357–364.

Pina, V. O., & VanDenBerg, J. (1999). Exercises in a resilient system of care, cultural competency, and the wraparound process. *Reaching Today's Youth, 3*(4), 22–30.

Rubin, K., Chen, X., McDougall, P., Bowker, A., & McKinnon, J. (1995). The Waterloo Longitudinal Project: Predicting internalizing and externalizing problems in adolescence. *Development and Psychopathology, 7,* 751–764.

Rudolph, S. M., & Epstein, M. H. (2000). Empowering children and families through strength-based assessment. *Reclaiming Children and Youth, 8*(4), 207–209, 232.

Saavedra, L. M., & Silverman, W. K. (2002). Classification of anxiety disorders in children: What a difference two decades make. *International Review of Psychiatry, 14,* 87–101.

Sachs, J. J., & Cheney, D. (2000). What do the members of the council for children with behavioral disorders say about inclusion? *Beyond Behavior, 10*(2), 18–23.

Safren, S. A., Gonzalez, R. E., Horner, K. J., Leung, A. W., Heimberg, R. G., & Juster, H. R. (2000). Anxiety in ethnic minority youth. *Behavior Modification, 24*(2), 147–183.

Sargent, J. T. (1999). *The long road back: A survivor's guide to anorexia.* Georgetown, MA: North Star.

Shapiro, E. S., Miller, D. N., Sawka, K., Gardill, M. C., & Handler, M. W. (1999). Facilitating the inclusion of students with EBD into general education classrooms. *Journal of Emotional and Behavioral Disorders, 7*(2), 83–93.

Soulsman, G. (1994, April 4). Anti-depressants: Happy pills. *Gannett News Service.*

Sprague, J. W. H. (2000). Early identification and intervention for youth with antisocial and violent behavior. *Exceptional Children, 66*(3), 14.

Stein, H., Fonagy, P., Berguson, K. S., & Wisman, M. (2000). Lives through time: An ideographic approach to the study of resilience. *Bulletin of the Menninger Clinic, 64*(2), 281–305.

Sternberg, R. J., & Grigorenko, E. L. (1999). Myths in education and psychology regarding the gene-environment debate. *Teachers College Record, 100*(3), 536. U.S. Surgeon General. (2000). *Mental health: A report of the surgeon general* (http://www.mentalhealth.org/specials). Retrieved May 14, 2001.

Sutherland, K. S., Wehby, J. H., & Yoder, P. J. (2002). Examination of the relationship between teacher praise and opportunities for students with EBD to respond to academic requests. *Reclaiming Children and Youth, 10*(1), 6–15.

Townsend, B. L. (2000). The disproportionate discipline of African American learners: Reducing school suspensions and expulsions. *Exceptional Children, 66*(3), 381–392.

U.S. Department of Education. (1998). *To assure the free appropriate public education of all children with disabilities: Twentieth annual report to Congress on the implementation of the Individuals with Disabilities Education Act.* Washington, DC: Author.

U.S. Department of Education. (1999). *To assure the free appropriate public education of all children with disabilities: Twenty-first annual report to Congress on the implementation of the Individuals with Disabilities Education Act.* Washington, DC: Author.

U.S. Department of Education. (2002). *Executive summary: Twenty-third annual report to Congress on the implementation of the Individuals with Disabilities Education Act.* Washington, DC: Author.

U.S. Department of Health and Human Services. (1995). *National data show drop in homicide and increase in youth suicide* (http://www.cdc.gov/ nchswww/releases/95news/95news/ nr43_13.html).

Verdon, R. (2000). Mirror, mirror on the wall, who is thinnest of them all? *Reclaiming Children and Youth, 9*(3), 157–161.

Wagner, M. (1995). Outcomes for youths with serious emotional disturbance in secondary school and early adulthood. *Future of Children, 5*(4), 90–112.

Walker, H. M., Colvin, G., & Ramsey, E. (1995). *Antisocial behavior in school: Strategies and best practices.* New York: Brooks/Cole.

Walker, J. (2002). Building on strengths in community settings. *Focal Point, 16*(1), 3–4.

Walker, H. M., Zeller, R. W., Close, D. W., Webber, J., & Gresham, F. The present unwrapped: Change and challenge in the field of behavioral disorders. *Behavioral Disorders, 24*(4), 293–304.

Webber, J., Coleman, M., & Zionts, P. (1998). Reducing teacher stress with rational emotive behavior therapy. *Beyond Behavior, 9*(1), 20–26.

Wehby, J. H., Symons, F. J., & Canale, A. (1997). Promote appropriate assessment. *Journal of Emotional and Behavioral Disorders, 5*(1), 45–54.

Wehby, J. H., Symons, F. J., & Hollo, A. (1997). Promote appropriate assessment. *Journal of Emotional and Behavioral Disorders, 5*(1), 45–54.

Wehby, J. H., Symons, F. J., & Hollo, J. A. (1998). Teaching students with emotional and behavioral disorders: Discrepancies between research and practice. *Behavioral Disorders, 24*(1), 51–56.

Wood, M., Furlong, M. J., Rosenblatt, J. A., Robertson, L. M., Scozzri, F., & Sosna, T. (1997). Understanding the psychosocial characteristics of gang-involved youths in a system of care: Individual, family, and system correlates. *Education and Treatment of Children, 20*(3), 281–285.

Chapter 6

Agency for Health Care Policy and Research. (1999, August). *Diagnosis of attention-deficit/hyperactivity disorder* Technical Review Summary No. 3 (http://www.ahcpr.gov/clinic/adhdsutr.htm).

Ajibola, O., & Clement, P. (1995). Differential effects of methylphenidate and self-reinforcement on attention-deficit/hyperactivity disorder. *Behavior Modification, 19*, 211–233.

American Academy of Neurology. (1999). Brain abnormalities found in children with ADHD. *CHADD* (http://www.chadd.org/news/press4191999.htm).

American Academy of Pediatrics. (2000). Clinical practice guideline: Diagnosis and evaluation of the child with attention-deficit/hyperactivity disorder. *Pediatrics, 105*(5), 1158–1170.

American Psychiatric Association. (2000). *Diagnostic and statistical manual of mental disorders* (4th ed., rev.). Washington, DC: Author.

Anastapoulos, A. D., Spisto, M. A., & Maher, M. C. (1994). The WISC-III freedom from distractibility factor: Its utility in identifying children with attention deficit hyperactivity disorder. *Psychological Assessment, 6*, 368–371.

Associated Press. (2000, March 28). A cause of hyperactivity? *ABC News* (http://abcnews.go.com/sections/living/DailyNews/hyperactivebrains000328.html).

Auchenbach, T.M. (2000). *Auchenbach system of empirically based assessment* (http://www.aseba.org/index.html).

Aust, P. (1994). When the problem is not the problem: Understanding attention deficit disorder with and without hyperactivity. *Child Welfare, 73*, 215–227.

Baren, M. (1994). *Hyperactivity and attention disorders in children.* San Ramon, CA: Health Information Network.

Barkley, R. A. (1990). *Attention deficit hyperactivity disorder.* New York: Guilford.

Barkley, R. A. (1995). ADHD and IQ. *ADHD Report, 3*(2), 1.

Barkley, R. A. (1996). Research developments and their implications for clinical care of the ADHD child. *Psychiatric Times, 13*(7) (http://www.psychiatrictimes.com/p960738.html).

Barkley, R. A. (1998a). Attention-deficit hyperactivity disorder. *Scientific American, 279*(3), 66–72.

Barkley, R. A. (1998b). *Attention-deficit hyperactivity disorder: A handbook for diagnosis and treatment.* New York: Guilford.

Barkley, R. A. (1998c, February). How should attention deficit disorder be described? *Harvard Mental Health Newsletter, 14*(8), 8.

Barkley, R. A. (2000). *Taking charge of ADHD: The complete, authoritative guide for parents* (rev. ed.). New York: Guilford.

Beach, M. J., Landenberger, J., & Beach, J. (1997). *Take charge and succeed! Coaching* (2nd ed.). Hyannis, MA: Bridges Associates.

Buonomano, L. (1999, September). ADHD: Social problem versus medical disorder. *Brown University Child & Adolescent Behavior Letter, 15*(9), 8.

Bradley, W. (1937). The behavior of children receiving benzedrine. *American Journal of Psychiatry, 94*, 577–585.

Brain Train. (2000). *Software tools to train and test the brain* (http://www.braintrain.com/captains_log/captains_log_home.html).

Brim, S. A., & Whitaker, D. P. (2000). Motivation and students with attention deficit hyperactivity disorder. *Preventing School Failure, 44*(2), 57–61.

Bussing, R., & Zima, B. T. (1998). Children in special education programs: Attention deficit hyperactivity disorder, use of services, and unmet needs. *American Journal of Public Health, 88*(6), 880–887.

Carlso, C. L., Booth, J. E., Shinn, M., & Canu, W. H. (2002). Parent, teacher, and self-rated motivational styles in ADHD subtypes. *Journal of Learning Disabilities, 35*(2), 104–115.

Castellanos, F. X. (1997). Toward a pathophysiology of attention-deficit/hyperactivity disorder. *Clinical Pediatrics, 36*(7), 381–394.

CHADD. (1996). ADD research: A look at today and tomorrow: An interview with Richard D. Todd, Ph.D., M.D. *Attention! 3*(2), 46–47.

CHADD. (1999, June/July). AD/HD project wins at world's largest K–12 science competition. *Inside CHADD,* p. 2.

CHADD. (2002). *The disorder named ADD.* CHADD Fact Sheet No. 1 (http://www.chadd.org/fact1.htm).

Clarke, A. R., Barry, R. J., McCarthy, R., Selikowitz, M., & Brown, C. R. (2002). EEG evidence for a new conceptualization of attention deficit hyperactivity disorder. *Clinical Neurophysiology, 113*(7), 1036–1044.

Council for Exceptional Children, Task Force on Children with AD/HD. (1992). *Children with AD/HD: A shared responsibility.* Reston, VA: Author.

Cramond, B. (1995). The coincidence of attention deficit hyperactivity disorder and creativity. *Attention Deficit Disorder Research-Based Decision Making Series 9508.* Washington, DC: Office of Educational Improvement. (ERIC Document Reproduction Service No. 388016).

Department of Mental Health Services. (1999). *Mental health: A report of the surgeon general.* Pueblo, Co: Author. (http://www.surgeongeneral.gov/library/mentalhealth/index.html).

DuPaul, G. J., Power, T. J., Anastopoulos, A. D., & Reid, R. (1998). *ADHD Rating Scale—IV: Checklists, norms, and clinical interpretation.* New York: Guilford.

Eisenberger, J., Conti-D'Antonio, M., & Bertrando, R. (2000). *Self-efficacy: Raising the bar for students with learning needs.* Larchmont, NY: Eye on Education.

Fischer, S. (2000, April 10). Taking a picture of a mind gone awhirl. *US News and World Report,* p. 48.

Fossey, R., Hosie, T., & Zirkel, P. (1995). Section 504 and "front-line" educators: An expanded obligation to serve students with disabilities. *Preventing School Failure, 39*, 10–14.

Frazier, M. R., & Merrell, K. W. (1997). Issues in behavioral treatment of attention-deficit/hyperactivity disorder. *Education and Treatment of Children, 20*(4), 441–462.

Friss, G. (1998). Research moves fast, but there's no cure yet. *Cape Cod Online* (http://www.capecodonline.com/cctimes/add/day5main.htm).

Goldstein, S. (1991, January). Young children at risk: The early signs of attention-deficit hyperactivity disorder. *CHADDer Box,* pp. 3–4.

Hagmann, M. (2000, March 30). Quiet spot marks hyperactive brain. *Science Now,* p. 3.

Hallowell, E. (1996). *When you worry about the child you love: Emotional and learning problems in children.* New York: Simon & Schuster.

Hallowell, E. M., & Ratey, J. J. (1995). *Driven to distraction.* New York: Simon & Schuster.

Harman, P. L. (2000, May/June). Collaboration instead of litigation. *Attention!* 6(5)27–29.

Harman, P. L., & Barkley, R. (2000). One-on-one with Russell Barkley. *Attention!* 6(4), 12–14.

Henderson, C. W. (1999, November 22). Alcohol use during pregnancy can lead to ADHD. *Women's Health Weekly,* pp. 7–9.

Hoover, D. W., & Milich, R. (1994). Effects of sugar ingestion expectancies on mother-child interactions. *Journal of Abnormal Child Psychology, 22*, 501–515.

Horan, L. (1999). AD/HD coaching: Empowering people to succeed. *Attention!* 6(1), 12–15.

Hynd, G. (1995). *AD/HD and brain activity*. Paper presented at the meeting of the International Council for Exceptional Children, Indianapolis.

Ingersoll, B. (1995). ADD: Not just another fad. *Attention!* 2(2), 17–19.

Lambert, N. M., & Hartsough, C. S. (1998). Prospective study of tobacco smoking and substance dependencies among samples of ADHD and non-ADHD participants. *Journal of Learning Disabilities, 31*(6), 533–545.

Lee, D. L., & Zentall, S. S. (2002). The effects of visual stimulation on the mathematics performance of children with attention-deficit/hyperactivity disorder. *Behavioral Disorders, 27*(3), 272–288.

Mangrum, C. T., & Strichart, S. S. (2000). *Peterson's colleges with programs for students with learning disabilities or attention deficit disorder* (6th ed.). Princeton, NJ: Peterson's.

McBurnett, K. (1995). The new subtype of ADHD: Predominantly hyperactive-impulsive type. *Attention! 1*(3), 10–15.

Medical Tribune. (1999, January 7). Seizures and ADHD. *Pediatrics for Parents*, p. 10.

Merrill, K. W., & Beuter, E. (2001). An investigation of relationships between social behavior and AD/HD in children and youth. *Journal of Emotional and Behavioral Disorders, 9*(4), 260–272.

Moran, M. (1999). Study debunks some fears about drug therapy for kids with AD/HD. *Amednews.com* (http://www.ama-assn.org/sci-pubs/amnews/pick_99/hlta0906.htm).

MTA Cooperative Group. (1999a). A 14-month randomized clinical trial of treatment strategies for attention-deficit/hyperactivity disorder. *Archives of General Psychiatry, 56*, 1073–1086.

MTA Cooperative Group. (1999b). Moderators and mediators of treatment response for children with attention-deficit/hyperactivity disorder. *Archives of General Psychiatry, 56*, 1088–1096.

Murphy, K. (1999). The latest CHADD fact sheet . . . Attention-deficit/hyperactivity disorder in adults. *Attention! 6*(4), 17–21.

Murphy, K. R., Barkley, R. A., & Bush, T. (2002). Young adults with attention deficit hyperactivity disorder: Subtype differences in educational and clinical history. *Journal of Nervous and Mental Disorders, 190*, 147–157.

National Institute of Mental Health. (2002, October 8). Brain shrinkage in AD/HD not caused by medications. *NIH News Release* (http://www.nimh.nih.gov/events/pradhdmri.cfm).

Nolan, E. E., Volpe, R. J., Gadow, K. D., & Sprafkin, J. (1999). Developmental, gender, and comorbidity differences in clinically referred children with ADHD. *Journal of Emotional & Behavioral Disorders, 7*(1), 11–22.

Pineda, D., Ardilia, A., & Rosselli, M. (1999). Neuropsychological and behavioral assessment of ADHD in seven- to twelve-year-old children: Discriminant analysis. *Journal of Learning Disabilities, 32*(2), 159–174.

Play Attention. (2001). *Helping overcome learning difficulties: Play attention* (http://www.playattention.com/playattn.htm).

Reid, R. (1995). Assessment of ADHD with culturally different groups: The use of behavioral scales. *School Psychology Review, 24*, 537–560.

Reid, R., Casat, C. D., Norton, H. J., Anastopoulos, A. D., & Temple, E. P. (2001). Using behavior rating scales for ADHD across ethnic groups: The IOWA Conners. *Journal of Emotional and Behavioral Disorders, 9*(4), 210–220.

Roan, S. (1994, September 28). Square pegs? Being rejected by peers is not only hurtful, it can cause emotional problems and bad behavior. *Los Angeles Times Home Edition*, p. E-1.

Schmidt, C. W. (1999). Poisoning young minds. *Environmental Health Perspectives, 107*(6), A302–A308.

Shank, M. (2002). *Making curriculum sparkle for students with AD/HD*. Unpublished manuscript.

Shapiro, E. S., DuPaul, G. J., Bradley, K. L., & Bailey, L. T. (1996). A school-based consultation program for service delivery to middle school students with attention-deficit/hyperactivity disorder. *Journal of Emotional and Behavioral Disorders, 4*(2), 73–81.

Shapiro, E. S., DuPaul, G. J., & Bradley-Klug, K. L. (1998). Self-management as a strategy to improve the classroom behavior of adolescents with AD/HD. *Journal of Learning Disabilities, 31*(6), 545–556.

Smalley, S. (2000). UCLA genetic study. *Attention! 6*(5), 12–14.

Sohn, E. (2002, August 19). The gene that wouldn't sit still. *US News and World Report, 133*(7), 50–52.

Solanto, M. V. (2002). Overlooked and undertreated? Inattentive AD/HD. *Attention! 9*(1), 28–31.

Sonuga-Barke, E. J. (2002). Psychological heterogeneity in AD/HD—a dual pathway model of behaviour and cognition. *Behavioral Brain Research, 130*(1–2), 29–36.

Still, G. F. (1902). Some abnormal psychical conditions in children. *Lancet, 1*, 1008–1012, 1077–1182, 1163–1148.

Tannock, R., & Martinussen, R. (2001). Reconceptualizing ADHD. *Educational Leadership, 59*(3), 20–25.

Teeter, P. A. (1999). Back to school: Advice for parents of young children with AD/HD. *Attention! 6*(2), 21–27.

Travis, P., Diehl, J., Trickel, K., & Webb, L. (1999, April). *Children with attention deficit disorder: The MDTP early intervention model*. Paper presented at the annual convention of the Council for Exceptional Children, Charlotte, NC.

Volkow, N. D., Fowler, J. S., Wang, G. J., Ding, Y., & Gatley, S. J. (2002). Role of dopamine in the therapeutic and reinforcing effects of methylphenidate in humans: Results from imaging studies. *European Neuropsychopharmacology, 12*(6), 557–566.

Wells, R. D., Dahl, B. B., & Snyder, D. (2000). Coping and compensatory strategies used by adults with attentional problems. *Attention! 6*(5), 22–24.

Williams, L., Lerner, M., Wigal, T., & Swanson, J. (1995). Minority assessment of ADD: Issues in the development of new assessment techniques. *Attention! 2*(1), 9–15.

Zappitelli, M., Pinto, T., & Grizenko, N. (2001). Pre-, peri-, and Postnatal trauma in subjects with attention-deficit hyperactivity disorder. *Canadian Journal of Psychiatry, 46*, 342–348.

Chapter 7

Andrade, H. G. (2000). Using rubrics to promote thinking and learning. *Educational Leadership, 57*(5), 13–18.

Baldwin, A. Y., & Vialle, W. (1999). *The many faces of giftedness: Lifting the masks*. Belmont, CA: Wadsworth.

Berger, S. L. (1989). *College planning for gifted students*. Reston, VA: Council for Exceptional Children.

Bloom, B. S. (Ed.). (1956). *Handbook 1: Cognitive domain*. New York: McKay.

Bruer, J. T. (1999). *The myth of the first three years: A new understanding of early brain development and lifelong learning*. New York: Free Press.

Castellano, J. A. (2003a). The "browning" of American schools: Identifying and educating gifted Hispanic students. In J. A. Castellano (Ed.), *Special populations in gifted education: Working with diverse gifted learners* (pp. 29–44). Boston: Allyn & Bacon.

Castellano, J. A. (2003b). *Special populations in gifted education: Working with diverse gifted learners*. Boston: Allyn & Bacon.

Clark, B. (1997). *Growing up gifted* (5th ed.). Upper Saddle River, NJ: Merrill/Prentice Hall.

Davis, G. A. (2003). Identifying creative students, teaching for creative growth. In N. Colangelo & G. A. Davis (Eds.), *Handbook of gifted education* (3rd ed.). Boston: Allyn & Bacon.

Davis, G. A., & Rimm, S. B. (1998). *Education of the gifted and talented* (4th ed.). Boston: Allyn & Bacon.

Delisle, J. R. (1999). For gifted students, full inclusion is a partial solution. *Educational Leadership, 57*(3), 80–83.

Dickson, K. (2003). Gifted education and African American learners: An equity perspective. In J. A. Castellano (Ed.), *Special populations in gifted education: Working with diverse gifted learners* (pp. 45–64). Boston: Allyn & Bacon.

Doman, G., & Doman, J. (1994). *How to multiply your baby's intelligence* (2nd ed.). New York: Avery.

Elkind, D. (1981). *The hurried child: Growing up too fast, too soon*. Reading, MA: Addison-Wesley.

Elkind, D. (1987). Superbaby syndrome can lead to elementary school burnout. *Young Children, 42*(3), 14.

Elkind, D. (1988). Mental acceleration. *Journal for the Education of the Gifted, 11*(4), 19–31. Ford,

D. Y., & Harris, J. J. (Eds.). (1999). *Multicultural gifted education*. New York: Teachers College Press.

Fishkin, A. S., Cramond, B., & Olszewski-Kubilius, P. (2001). *Investigating creativity in youth: Research and methods*. Cresskill, NJ: Hampton.

Gagne, F. (2003). Transforming gifts into talents: The DGMT as a developmental theory. In N. Colangelo & G. A. Davis (Eds.), *Handbook of gifted education* (pp. 3–10). (3rd ed.). Boston: Allyn & Bacon.

Gallagher, S. A. (2000). Project P-BLISS: An experiment in curriculum for gifted disadvantaged high school students. *NASSP Bulletin, 84*(615), 47–57.

Gardner, H. 1983. *Frames of mind: The theory of multiple intelligences*. New York: Basic Books.

Gardner, H. (1993a). *Creating minds*. New York: Basic Books.

Gardner, H. (1993b). *Multiple intelligences: The theory in practice*. New York: Basic Books.

Gardner, H. (1999). *Intelligence reframed: Multiple intelligences for the 21st century*. New York: Basic Books.

Goleman, D. (1995). *Emotional intelligence*. New York: Bantam.

Goleman, D. (1998). *Working with emotional intelligence*. New York: Bantam.

Haensly, P. A. (1999). The role of cognitive style in transforming preschoolers' gifted potential. *Roeper Review, 21*, 272–280.

Hamilton, D. (1999). *Lawrence School: Empowering bright children to succeed*. Broadview Heights, OH: Lawrence School.

Hebert, T. P., & Neumeister, K. L. S. (2000). University mentors in the elementary classroom: Supporting the intellectual, motivational, and emotional needs of high-ability students. *Journal for the Education of the Gifted, 24*, 122–124.

Henderson, L. M., & Ebner, F. F. (1997). The biological basis for early intervention with gifted children. *Peabody Journal of Education, 72*, 59–80.

Hodge, K. A., & Kemp, C. R. (2000). Exploring the nature of giftedness in preschool children. *Journal for the Education of the Gifted, 24*, 46–73.

Karolyi, C. V., Ramos-Ford, V., & Gardner, H. (2003). Multiple intelligences: A perspective on giftedness. In N. Colangelo & G. A. Davis (Eds.), *Handbook of gifted education* (3rd ed., pp. 100–112). Boston: Allyn & Bacon.

Leal, D., Kearney, K., & Kearney, C. (1995). The world's youngest university graduate: Examining the unusual characteristics of profoundly gifted children. *Gifted Child Today, 18*(5), 26–31, 41.

Lovecky, D. V. (1992). The exceptionally gifted child. *Understanding Our Gifted, 3*(3), 7–9.

Maker, C. J. (1993). Creativity, intelligence and problem solving: A definition and design for cross-cultural research and measurement related to giftedness. *Gifted Education International, 9*, 68–77.

Maker, C. J. (1996). Identification of gifted minority students: A national problem needed changes and a promising solution. *Gifted Child Quarterly, 40*, 41–50.

Maker, C. J., Rogers, J. A., Nielson, A. B., & Bauerle, P. R. (1996). Multiple intelligences, problem solving, and diversity in the general classroom. *Journal for the Education of the Gifted, 19*(4), 437–460.

Nakamura, J., & Csikszentmihalyi, M. (2003). Catalytic creativity: The case of Linus Pauling. *American Psychologist, 56*, 337–341.

Passow, H. A., & Rudnitski, R. A. (1995). *State policies regarding education of the gifted as reflected in legislation and regulation*. Research Monograph. Storrs: University of Connecticut, National Research Center on the Gifted and Talented.

Purcell, J. H., & Leppien, J. H. (1998). Building bridges between general practitioners and educators of the gifted: A study of collaboration. *Gifted Child Quarterly, 42*(3), 172–181.

Piirto, J. (1999). *Talented children and adults: Their development and education* (2nd ed.). Upper Saddle River, NJ: Merrill/Prentice Hall.

Plomin, R., & Price, T. S. (2003). The relationship between genetics and intelligence. In N. Colangelo & G. A. Davis (Eds.), *Handbook of gifted education* (3rd ed., pp. 113–123). Boston: Allyn & Bacon.

Public Law 103-382, Title XIV. (1988). Jacob K. Javits Gifted and Talented Students Education Act.

Renzulli, J. S. (1999a). Reflections, perceptions, and future directions. *Journal for the Education of the Gifted, 23*, 125–146.

Renzulli, J. S. (1999b). What is this thing called giftedness, and how do we develop it? A twenty-five year perspective. *Journal for the Education of the Gifted, 23*, 3–54.

Renzulli, J. S. (2000). *A practical system for identifying gifted and talented students* (http://ww.sp.uconn.edu/~nrcgt/sem/semart04.html).

Renzulli, J. S., & Reis, S. M. (1986). The enrichment triad/revolving door model: A school wide plan for the development of creative productivity. In J. Renzulli (Ed.), *Systems and models for developing programs for the gifted and talented* (pp. 16–66). Mansfield Center, CT: Creative Learning Press.

Renzulli, J. S., & Reis, S. M. (1997). *The schoolwide enrichment model: A how-to guide for educational excellence* (2nd ed.). Mansfield Center, CT: Creative Learning Press.

Renzulli, J. S., & Reis, S. M. (2003). The schoolwide enrichment model: Developing creative and productive giftedness. In N. Colangelo & G. A. Davis (Eds.), *Handbook of gifted education* (3rd ed., pp. 184–203). Boston: Allyn & Bacon.

Seeley, K. (2003). High risk gifted learners. In N. Colangelo & G. A. Davis (Eds.), *Handbook of gifted education* (3rd ed., pp. 444–452). Boston: Allyn & Bacon.

Seraphim, C. K. M. (1997). *Observation of problem solving in multiple intelligences: International assessment of a DISCOVER assessment checklist*. Unpublished doctoral dissertation, University of Arizona.

Silverman, L. K. (1998). Through the lens of giftedness. *Roeper Review, 20*(3), 204–210.

Sony Pictures. (2000). *Finding Forrester*. Culver City, CA: Author.

Sternberg, R. J. (2003). Giftedness according to the theory of successful intelligence. In N. Colangelo & G. A. Davis (Eds.), *Handbook of gifted education* (3rd ed., pp. 88–99). Boston: Allyn & Bacon.

Sternberg, R. J., & Zhang, L. (1995). What do we mean by giftedness? A pentagonal implicit theory. *Gifted Child Quarterly, 39*(2), 88–94.

Torrance, E. P. (1966a). *Thinking creatively with pictures*. Bensenville, IL: Scholastic Testing Service.

Torrance, E. P. (1966b). *Thinking creatively with words*. Bensenville, IL: Scholastic Testing Service.

Torrance, E. P. (1990). *Torrance test of creative thinking: Norms-technical manual figural (streamlined) forms A & B*. Bensenville, IL: Scholastic Testing Service.

Templin, M. A., Engemann, J. F., & Doran, R. L. (1999). A locally based science mentorship program for high achieving students: Unearthing issues that influence affective outcomes. *School Science and Mathematics, 99*, 205–212.

U.S. Department of Education. (1993). *National excellence: A case for developing America's talent*. Washington, DC: Author.

Wallace, M. (1999/2000). Nurturing noncomformists. *Educational Leadership, 57*(4), 44–46.

Ward, S. B., & Landrum, M. S. (1994). Resource consultation: An alternative service delivery model for gifted education. *Roeper Review, 16*(4), 276–279.

Westberg, K. L., Burns, D. E., Gubbins, J. E., Reis, S. M., Park, S., & Maxfield, L. R. (1998). *Professional development practices in gifted education: Results of a national survey*. Storrs, CT: National Research Center on the Gifted and Talented.

White, B. Y., & Fredericksen, J. R. (1998). Inquiry, modeling, and metacognition: Making science accessible to all students. *Cognition and Instruction, 16*(1), 3–118.

Chapter 8

Agran, M., Blanchard, C., & Wehmeyer, M. L. (2000). Promoting transition goals and self-determination through student self-directed learning: The self-determined learning model of instruction. *Education and Training in Mental Retardation and Developmental Disabilities, 35*(4), 351–364.

Agran, M., Snow, K., & Swaner, J. (1999). A survey of secondary level teachers' opinions on community-based instruction and inclusive education. *Journal of the Association for Persons with Severe Handicaps, 24*(1), 58–62.

Alexander, D. (1998). Prevention of mental retardation: Four decades of research. *Mental Retardation and Developmental Disabilities Research Reviews, 4,* 50–58.

Algozzine, B., Browder, D., Karvonen, M., Test, D. W., & Wood, W. M. (2001). Effects of interventions to promote self-determination for individuals with disabilities. *Review of Educational Research, 71*(2), 219–277.

American Association on Mental Retardation (AAMR). (2002). *Mental retardation: Definition, classification, and systems of supports* (10th ed.). Washington, DC: Author.

Bates, P. E., Quvo, T., Miner, C. A., & Korabek, C. A. (2001). Simulated and community-based instruction involving persons with mild and moderate mental retardation. *Research and Developmental Disabilities, 22,* 95–115.

Batshaw, M. L., & Shapiro, B. K. (2002). Mental retardation. In M. L. Batshaw (Ed.), *Children with Disabilities* (5th ed., pp. 287–305). Baltimore: Brookes.

Baumeister, A. A., Kupstas, F. D., & Woodley-Zanthos, P. (1993). *The new morbidity: Recommendations for actions and an updated guide to state planning for the prevention of mental retardation and related disabilities associated with socioeconomic conditions.* Washington, DC: U.S. Department of Health and Human Services.

Bebko, J. M., & Luhaorg, H. (1998). The development of strategy use and metacognitive processing in mental retardation: Some sources of difficulty. In J. A. Burack, R. M. Hodapp, & E. Zigler (Eds.), *Handbook of mental retardation and development* (pp. 382–409). Cambridge: Cambridge University Press.

Bebko, J. M., & McPherson, M. J. (1997). *Teaching mnemonic strategies as a functional skill to cognitively impaired students.* North York, Ontario: York University.

Bellinger, D. C., Stiles, K. M., & Needleman, H. L. (1992). Low-level lead exposure, intelligence, and academic achievement: A long-term follow-up study. *Pediatrics, 90,* 855–861.

Blank, R. M. (2001). An overview of trends in social and economic well-being, by race. In N. J. Smelser, W. J. Wilson, & F. Mitchell, F. (Eds.), *America becoming racial trends and their consequences* (Vol. 1, pp. 21–39). Washington, DC: National Academy Press.

Brantlinger, E. A., & Campbell, Z. R. (2001). Dispelling myths and stereotypes confronting multicultural learners with mild disabilities: Perspectives for school reform. In C. A. Utley & F. E. Obiakor, (Eds.), *Special education, multicultural education, and school reform* (pp. 30–52). Springfield, IL: Thomas.

Bray, N. W., Fletcher, K. L., & Turner, L. A. (1997). Cognitive competencies and strategy use in individuals with mental retardation. In W. E. MacLean, Jr. (Ed.), *Ellis' handbook of mental deficiency, psychological theory, and research* (3rd ed., pp. 197–217). Mahwah, NJ: Erlbaum.

Bryant, B., Campbell, E. M., Craig, E. M., Hughes, C., Rotholz, D. A., Schalock, R. L., Silverman, W., Tassé, M. J., Thompson, J. R., & Wehmeyer, M. L. (2003). *Supports intensity scale.* Washington, DC: AAMR.

Bybee, J., & Ziegler, E. (1998). Outerdirectedness in individuals with and without mental retardation: A review. In J. A. Burack, R. M. Hodapp, & E. Zigler (Eds.), *Handbook of mental retardation* (pp. 434–460). Cambridge: Cambridge University Press.

Centers for Disease Control and Prevention. (1996). Postnatal causes of developmental disabilities in children aged 3–10 years—Atlanta, Georgia 1991. *Morbidity and Mortality Weekly Report, 45,* 130–134.

Chapman, D. A., Scott, K. G., & Mason, C. A. (2002). Early risk factors for mental retardation: Role of maternal age and maternal education. *American Journal on Mental Retardation, 107*(1), 46–59.

Cohen, D. E. (2000). Health promotion and disability prevention: The case for personal responsibility and independence. In M. L. Wehmeyer & R. J. Patton (Eds.), *Mental retardation in the 21st century* (pp. 251–264). Austin, TX: PRO-ED.

Davies, D. K., Stock, S. E., & Wehmeyer, M.L. (2002b). Enhancing independent Internet access for individuals with mental retardation through use of the specialized web browser: A pilot study. *Education and Training in Mental Retardation and Developmental Disabilities, 36*(1), 107–113.

Davis, D. K., Stock, S., & Wehmeyer, M. L. (2002a). Enhancing independent task performance for individuals with mental retardation through use of a handheld self-directed visual and audio prompting system. *Education and Training in Mental Retardation and Developmental Disabilities, 37,* 209–218.

Demchak, M., & Drinkwater, S. (1998). Assessing adaptive behavior. In H. B. Vance (Ed.), *Psychological assessment of children: Best practices for school and clinical settings* (pp. 297–322). New York: Wiley.

Denning, C. B., Chamberlain, J. A., & Polloway, E. A. (2000). An evaluation of state guidelines for mental retardation: Focus on definition and classification practices. *Education and Training in Mental Retardation and Developmental Disabilities, 35*(2), 226–232.

Dietrich, K. M., Berger, O. G., Succop, P. A., et al. (1993). The developmental consequences of low to moderate prenatal and postnatal lead exposure: Intellectual attainment in the Cincinnati Lead Study Cohort following school entry. *Neurotoxicol Teratol, 15,* 37–44.

Duncan, G. J., Brooks-Gunn, J., & Klebanov, P. K. (1994). Economic deprivation and early childhood development. *Child Development, 65,* 196–318.

Ellis, N. R. (1970). Memory processes in retardates and normals. In N. R. Ellis (Ed.), *International review of research in mental retardation* (Vol. 4, pp. 1–32). New York: Academic Press.

Emerson, E., Hatton, C., Bromley, J., & Caine, A. (1998). *Clinical psychology and people with intellectual disabilities.* New York: Wiley.

Feldman, M. A., & Walton-Allen, N. (1997). Effects of maternal mental retardation and poverty on intellectual, academic, and behavioral status of school-age children. *American Journal on Mental Retardation, 101,* 352–364.

Fletcher, K. L., & Bray, N. W. (1995). External and verbal strategies in children with and without mild mental retardation. *American Journal on Mental Retardation, 99,* 363–475.

Ford, A., Davern, L., & Schnorr, R. (2001). Learners with significant disabilities: Curricular relevance in an era of standards-based reform. *Remedial and Special Education, 22*(4), 214–222.

Freeman, S. F. N., & Alkin, M. C. (2000). Academic and social attainments of children with mental retardation in general education and special education settings. *Remedial and Special Education, 21*(1), 3–18.

Fujiura, G. T., & Yamaki, K. (2000). Trends in demography of childhood poverty and disability. *Exceptional Children, 66,* 187–199.

Gordon, B., Saklofske, D. H., & Hildebrand, D. K. (1998). Assessing children with mental retardation. In H. B. Vance (Ed.), *Psychological assessment of children: Best practices for school and clinical settings* (2nd ed., pp. 454–481). New York: Wiley.

Gottlieb, J., Atler, M., Gottlieb, B. W., & Wishner, J. (1994). Special education in urban America: It's not justifiable for many. *Journal of Special Education, 27*(4), 453–465.

Greenspan, S. (1999). A contextualist perspective on adaptive behavior. In R. L. Schalock (Ed.), *Adaptive behavior and its measurement: Implications for the field of mental retardation.* Washington, DC: AAMR.

Guralnick, M. J. (1997). *The effectiveness of early intervention.* Baltimore: Brookes.

Hishinuma, E. (1994). Learning from mentors. *Kamehameha Journal of Education, 5,* 107–114.

Horner, R. H., Dunlap, G., & Koegel, R. L. (Eds.). (1988). *Generalization and maintenance: Life-style changes in applied settings.* Baltimore: Brookes.

Katsiyannis, A., Zhang, D., & Archwamety, T. (2002). Placement and exit patterns for students with mental retardation: An analysis of national trends. *Education and Training in Mental Retardation and Developmental Disabilities, 37*(2), 134–145.

Kesson, K., & Oyler, C. (1999). Integrated curriculum and service learning: Linking school-based knowledge and social action. *English Education, 31,* 135–149.

Kluth, P. (2000). Community-referenced learning and the inclusive classroom [Electronic Version]. *Remedial and Special Education, 21*(1), 19–26.

Krajewski, J. J., & Hyde, M. S. (2000). Comparison of teen attitudes toward individuals with mental retardation between

1987 and 1998: Has inclusion made a difference? *Education and Training in Mental Retardation and Developmental Disabilities, 35*(3), 284–293.

Lambert, N., Nihira, K., & Leland, H. (1993). *AAMR adaptive behavior scale—School* (2nd ed.). Austin, TX: PRO-ED.

Langone, J., Clees, T. J., Oxford, M., Malone, M., & Ross, G. (1995). Acquisition and generalization of social skills by high school students with mild retardation. *Mental Retardation, 33,* 186–196.

Langone, J., Langone, C. A., & McLaughlin, P. J. (2000). Analyzing special educators' views on community-based instruction for students with mental retardation and developmental disabilities: Implications for teacher education. *Journal of Developmental and Physical Disabilities, 12*(1), 17–34.

Luckasson, R., Coulter, D. L., Polloway, E. A., Reiss, S., Schalock, R. L., Snell, M. E., Spitalnik, D. M., & Stark, J. A. (1992). *Mental retardation: Definition, classification, and systems of supports.* Washington, DC: AAMR.

MacMillan, D. L. (1982). *Mental retardation in school and society* (2nd ed.). Glenview, IL: Scott, Foresman.

MacMillan, D. L., Siperstein, G. N., Gresham, F. M., & Bocian, K. M. (1997). Mild mental retardation: A concept that may have outlived its usefulness. *Psychology in Mental Retardation and Developmental Disabilities, 23*(1), 5–12.

Murphy, C. C., Boyle, C., Schendel, D., Decouflé, P., & Yeargin-Allsopp, M. (1998). Epidemiology of mental retardation in children. *Mental Retardation and Developmental Disabilities Research Reviews, 4,* 6–13.

National Research Council. (2002). *Minority students in special and gifted education.* Washington, DC: National Academy Press.

Oswald, D. P., & Coutinho, M. J. (2001). Trends in disproportionate representation in special education: Implications for multicultural education. In C. A. Utley & F. E. Obiakor (Eds.), *Special education, multicultural education, school reform: Components of a quality education for students with mild disabilities* (pp. 53–73). Springfield, IL: Thomas.

Palmer, S., & Wehmeyer, M. L. (2003). Promoting self-determination in early elementary school: Teaching self-regulated problem-solving and goal setting skills. *Remedial and Special Education, 24,* 115–126.

Palmer, S. B., & Wehmeyer, M. L. (2002). *A parent's guide to the self-determined learning model of instruction for early elementary students.* Lawrence, KS: The Beach Center on Disability.

Pasquier, B. (1994). ESL field trips: Bringing the world to the world. *Clearing House, 67,* 192.

Riffel, L. A., Wehmeyer, M. L., Turnbull, A. P., Lattimore, J., Davies, D. K., Stock, S. E., & Fisher, S. (2002). *Promoting independent performance of transition-related tasks using a palmtop PC based self-directed visual and auditory prompting system.* Unpublished manuscript.

Sands, D. J., Spencer, K., Gliner, J., & Swaim, R. (1999). Structural equation modeling of student involvement in transition-related actions: The path of least resistance. *Focus on Autism and Other Developmental Disabilities, 14,* 17–27.

Schonberg, R. L., & Tifft, C. J. (2002). Birth defects, prenatal diagnosis, and fetal therapy. In M. L. Batshaw (Ed.), *Children with disabilities* (5th ed., pp. 27–42). Baltimore: Brookes.

Shilu, T., Baghurst, P., McMichael, A., et al. (1996). Lifetime exposure to environmental lead and children's intelligence at 11–13 years: The Port Pirie cohort study. *British Medical Journal, 312,* 1569–1575.

Shonkoff, J. P., & Phillips, D. (Eds.). (2000). *From neurons to neighborhoods: The science of early childhood development.* Washington, DC: National Research Council, Committee on Integrating the Science of Early Childhood Development, Board on Children, Youth, and Families.

Smith, J. D., & Hilton, A. (1997). The preparation and training of the educational community for the inclusion of students with developmental disabilities: The MRDD position. *Education and Training in Mental Retardation and Developmental Disabilities, 32*(1), 3–10.

Stokes, T. F., & Baer, D. M. (1977). An implicit technology of generalization. *Journal of Applied Behavior Analysis, 10,* 349–367.

Switzky, H. N. (1997a). Individual differences in personality and motivational systems in persons with mental retardation. In W. E. MacLean, Jr. (Ed.), *Ellis' handbook of mental deficiency, psychological theory and research* (pp. 343–378). Mahwah, NJ: Erlbaum.

Switzky, H. N. (1997b). Mental retardation and the neglected construct of motivation. *Education in Mental Retardation and Developmental Disabilities, 32*(3), 194–196.

Thompson, J. R., Bryant, B., Campbell, E. M., Craiq, E. M., Hughes, C., Rotholz, D. A., Schaleck, R. L., Silverman, W., Tasse, M. J., & Wehmeyer, M. L. (2003). *Supports intensity scale.* Washington, DC: AAMR.

Thompson, J. R., McGrew, K. S., & Bruininks, R. H. (1999). Adaptive and mal-adaptive behavior: Functional and structural characteristics. In R. L. Schalock (Ed.), *Adaptive behavior and its measurement: Implications for the field of mental retardation* (pp. 15–42). Washington, DC: AAMR.

U.S. Department of Education. (1997). *To assure the free appropriate public education of all children with disabilities: Nineteenth annual report to Congress on the implementation of the Individuals with Disabilities Education Act.* Washington, DC: Author.

U.S. Department of Education. (2001). *To assure the free appropriate public education of all children with disabilities: Twenty-third annual report to Congress on the implementation of the Individuals with Disabilities Education Act.* Washington, DC: Author.

U.S. Department of Health and Human Services. (2002). *Closing the gap: A national blueprint to improve the health of persons with mental retardation.* Rockville, MD: Author.

Wehmeyer, M. L. (1996). Self-determination as an educational outcome: Why is it important to children, youth, and adults with disabilities? In D. J. Sands & M. L. Wehmeyer (Eds.), *Self-determination across the life span: Independence and choice for people with disabilities.* Baltimore: Brookes.

Wehmeyer, M. L. (2001). Self-determination and mental retardation. In L. M. Glidden (Ed.), *International review of research in mental retardation* (Vol. 24, pp. 1–48). Hillsdale, NJ: Erlbaum.

Wehmeyer, M. L., Agran, M., & Hughes, C. (1998). *Teaching self-determination to students with disabilities: Basic skills for successful transition.* Baltimore: Brookes.

Wehmeyer, M. L., Agran, M., Palmer, S. B., Martin, J. E., & Mithaug, D. E. (2003). The effects of problem-solving instruction on the self-determined learning of secondary students with disabilities. In D. E. Mithaug, M. Agran, J. Martin, & M. L. Wehmeyer (Eds.), *Self-determined learning theory construction, verification, and evaluation.* Mahwah, NJ: Erlbaum.

Wehmeyer, M. L., Agran, M., Palmer, S. B., & Mithaug, D. (1999). *A teacher's guide to implementing the self-determined learning model of instruction (adolescent version).* Lawrence: The University of Kansas, Beach Center on Disability.

Wehmeyer, M. L., & Palmer, S. B. (2000). Promoting the acquisition and development of self-determination in young children with disabilities. *Early Education and Development, 11*(4), 465–481.

Wehmeyer, M. L., Palmer, S. B., Agran, M., Mithaug, D. E., & Martin, J. (2000). Promoting causal agency: The self-determined learning model of instruction. *Exceptional Children, 66*(4), 439–453.

Wehmeyer, M. L., Sands, D. J., Knowlton, H. E., & Kozleski, E. B. (2002). *Providing access to the general curriculum: Teaching students with mental retardation.* Baltimore: Brookes.

Wehmeyer, M. L., & Schwartz, M. (1997). Self-determination and positive adult outcomes: A follow-up study of youth with mental retardation or learning disabilities. *Exceptional Children, 63*(2), 245–255.

Widaman, K. F., & McGrew, K. S. (1996). The structure of adaptive behavior. In J. W. Jacobson & J. A. Mulick (Eds.), *Manual of diagnosis and professional practice in mental retardation* (pp. 97–110). Washington, DC: American Psychological Association.

Yeargin-Allsopp, M., Murphy, C. C., Cordero, C. F., Decouflé, P., & Hollowell, J. G. (1997). Reported biomedical causes and associated medical conditions for mental retardation among 10-year-old children, metropolitan Atlanta, 1985–1987. *Developmental Medicine and Child Neurology, 39,* 142–149.

Chapter 9

Abery, B., & McBride, M. (1998). Look and understand before you leap. *Impact, 11*(2), 2–26.

Batshaw, M. L. (1997a). Heredity: A toss of the dice. In M. L. Batshaw (Ed.), *Children with disabilities* (4th ed., pp. 17–33). Baltmore: Brookes.

Batshaw, M. L. (1997b). PKU and other inborn errors of metabolism. In M. L. Batshaw (Ed.), *Children with disabilities* (4th ed., pp. 389–404). Baltimore: Brookes.

Batshaw, M. L., & Shapiro, B. K. (1997). Mental retardation. In M. L. Batshaw (Ed.), *Children with disabilities* (4th ed., pp. 335–359). Baltimore: Brookes.

Batshaw, M. L., & Tuchman, M. (2002). PKU and other inborn errors of metabolism. In M. L. Batshaw (Ed.), *Children with disabilities* (5th ed., pp. 333–346). Baltimore: Brookes.

Beukelman, D. R., & Mirenda, P. (1998). *Augmentative and alternative communication: Management of severe communication disorders in children and adults*. Baltimore: Brookes.

Browder, D. M., & Snell, M. E. (2000). Teaching functional academics. In M. E. Snell & F. Brown (Eds.), *Instruction of students with severe disabilities* (5th ed., pp. 493–541). Upper Saddle River, NJ: Merrill/Prentice Hall.

Brown, F., & Snell, M. (2000). Meaningful assessment. In M. Snell & F. Brown (Eds.), *Instruction of students with severe disabilities* (5th ed., pp. 67–113). Upper Saddle River, NJ: Merrill/Prentice Hall.

Bui, Y. N., & Turnbull, A. (in press). East meets west: Analysis of person-centered planning in the context of Asian American values. *Education and Training in Mental Retardation and Developmental Disabilities*.

Campbell , P. H. (2000). Promoting participation in natural environments by accommodating motor disabilities. In M. Snell & F. Brown (Eds.), *Instruction of students with severe disabilities* (5th ed., pp. 291–329). Upper Saddle River, NJ: Prentice Hall.

Collins, B. C., Hendricks, T. B., Fetko, K., & Land, L. A. (2002). Student-2-student learning in inclusive classrooms. *Teaching Exceptional Children, 34*(4), 56–61.

Copeland, S. R., McCall, J., Williams, C. R., Guth, C., Carter, E. W., Fowler, S. E., Presley, J. A., & Hughes, C. (2002). High school peer buddies: It's a win-win situation. *Teaching Exceptional Children, 35*(1), 16–21.

Downing, J. E. (2002). *Including students with severe and multiple disabilities in typical classrooms* (2nd ed.). Baltimore: Brookes.

Doyle, M. B. (2002). *The paraprofessional's guide to the inclusive classroom* (2nd ed.). Baltimore: Brookes.

Engleman, M. D., Griffin, H. C., Griffin, L. W., & Maddox, J. I. (1999). A teacher's guide to communicating with students with deaf-blindness. *Teaching Exceptional Children, 31*(5), 64–70.

Eshilian, L., Falvey, M. A., Bove, C., Hibbard, M. J., Laiblin, J., Miller, C., & Rosenberg, R. L. (2000). Restructuring to create a high school community of learners. In R. A. Villa & J. S. Thousand (Eds.), *Restructuring for caring and effective education* (pp. 402–427). Baltimore: Brookes.

Evans, J. R. (1997). The first weeks of life. In M. L. Batshaw (Ed.), *Children with disabilities* (4th ed., pp. 93–114). Baltimore: Brookes.

Falvey, M., Eshilian, L., & Hibbard, J. (2000, April). Collaboration at Whittier High School. *TASH Newsletter, 26*, 8–9.

Falvey, M., Forest, M., Pearpoint, J., & Rosenberg, R. L. (2000). Teaching basic self-care skills. In M. E. Snell & F. Brown (Eds.), *Instruction of students with severe disabilities* (pp. 331–380). Upper Saddle River, NJ: Merrill/Prentice Hall.

Farlow, L., & Snell, M. (2000). Teaching basic self-care skills. In M. Snell & F. Brown (Eds.), *Instruction of students with severe disabilities* (5th ed., pp. 331–379). Upper Saddle River, NJ: Merrill/Prentice Hall.

Giangreco, M. F., Dennis, R., Cloninger, C., Edelman, S., & Schattman, R. (1993). "I've counted Jon": Transformational experiences of teachers educating students with disabilities. *Exceptional Children, 59*, 359–372.

Gierach, J., Obukowicz, M., & Reed, P. (2000). Assistive technology for recreation, leisure, and activities of daily living. In P. Reed (Ed.), *Assessing students' needs for assistive technology: A resource manual for school district teams*. Oshkosh: Wisconsin Assistive Technology Initiative (www.wati.org).

Gilberts, G. H., Agran, M., Hughes, C., & Wehmeyer, M. (2001). The effects of peer delivered self-monitoring strategies on the participation of students with severe disabilities in general education classrooms. *Journal of the Association for Persons with Severe Handicaps, 26*(1), 25–36.

Guess, D., Roberts, S., & Rues, J. (2000). *Longitudinal analysis of state patterns and related variables among infants and children with significant disabilities*. Unpublished manuscript.

Guess, D., & Siegel-Causey, E. (1992). Students with severe and multiple disabilities. In E. L. Meyen & T. M. Skrtic (Eds.), *Exceptional children and youth: An introduction* (4th ed., pp. 293–320). Denver: Love.

Hall, M., Kleinert, H. L., & Kearns, J. F. (2000). Going to college: Postsecondary programs for students with moderate and severe disabilities. *Teaching Exceptional Children, 32*(3), 58–65.

Hamre-Nietupski, S. (1993, September). How much time should be spent on skill instruction and friendship development? Preferences of parents of students with moderate and severe/profound disabilities. *Education and Training in Mental Retardation*, pp. 220–231.

Heller, K. W., Alberto, P. A., Forney, P. E., & Schwartzman, M. N. (1996). *Understanding physical, sensory, and health impairments: Characteristics and educational implications*. Pacific Grove, CA: Brooks/Cole.

Hughes, C., Copeland, S. R., Guth, C., Rung, L. L., Hwang, B., Kleeb, G., & Strong, M. (2001). General education students' perspectives on their involvement in a high school peer buddy program. *Education and Training in Mental Retardation and Developmental Disabilities, 36*(4), 343–356.

Hunt, P., & Goetz, L. (1997). Research on inclusive educational programs, practices, and outcomes for students with severe disabilities. *Journal of Special Education, 31*, 3–29.

Hunt, P., Staub, D., Alwell, M., & Goetz, L. (1994). Achievement by all students within the context of cooperative learning groups. *Journal of the Association for Persons with Severe Handicaps, 19*(4), 290–301.

Iacono, T., Carter, M., & Hook, J. (1998). Identification of intentional communication in students with severe and multiple disabilities. *Augmentative and Alternative Communication, 14*, 102–114.

Jorgensen, C. M. (1996). Designing inclusive curricula right from the start: Practical strategies and examples for the high school classroom. In S. Stainback & W. Stainback (Eds.), *Inclusion: A guide for educators* (pp. 221–236). Baltimore: Brookes.

Kansas State Department of Education. (2001). *Collective wisdom: An anthology of stores and best practices for educating students with severe disabilities and deaf-blindness*. Topeka, KS: Author.

Kennedy, C. H., & Fisher, D. (2001). *Inclusive middle schools*. Baltimore: Brookes.

Kimm, C. H., Falvey, M. A., Bishop, K. D., & Rosenberg, R. L. (1995). Motor and personal care skills. In M. A. Falvey (Ed.), *Inclusive and heterogeneous schooling: Assessment, curriculum, and instruction* (pp. 187–228). Baltimore: Brookes.

Luckasson, R., Coulter, D. L., Polloway, E. A., Reiss, S., Schalock, R. L., Snell, M. E., Spitalnik, D. M., & Stark, J. A. (1992). *Mental retardation: Definition, classification, and systems of supports*. Washington, DC: American Association on Mental Retardation.

Mastropieri, M. A., Spencer, V., Scruggs, T. E., & Talbott, E. (2000). Students with disabilities as tutors: An updated research synthesis. In T. E. Scruggs & M. A. Mastropieri (Eds.), *Advances in learning and behavioral disabilities* (Vol. 14, pp. 247–279). Stamford, CA: JAI.

McDonnell, J. (1998). Instruction for students with severe disabilities in general education settings. *Education and Training in Mental Retardation and Developmental Disabilities, 33*(3), 199–215.

McDonnell, J. M., Mathot-Buckner, C., Thorson, N., & Fister, S. (2001). Supporting the inclusion of students with moderate and severe disabilities in junior high school general education classes: The effects of classwide peer tutoring, multi-element curriculum, and accommodations. *Education and Treatment of Children, 24*(2), 141–160.

McLaren, J., & Bryson, S. E. (1987). Review of recent epidemiological studies of mental retardation: Prevalence, associated disorders, and etiology. *American Journal of Mental Retardation, 92,* 243–254.

Moser, H. (2000). Genetics and gene therapies. In M. L. Wehmeyer & J. R. Patton (Eds.), *Mental retardation in the 21st century* (pp. 235–249). Austin, TX: PRO-ED.

Nickel, R. E. (2000). Developmental delay and mental retardation. In R. E. Nickel & L. W. Desch (Eds.), *The physician's guide to caring for children with disabilities and chronic conditions* (pp. 99–140). Baltimore: Brookes.

Orelove, F. P., & Sobsey, D. (1996). *Educating children with multiple disabilities: A transdisciplinary approach* (3rd ed.). Baltimore: Brookes.

Palmer, D. S., Fuller, K., Arora, T., & Nelson, M. (2001). Taking sides: Parent views on inclusion for their children with severe disabilities. *Council for Exceptional Children, 67*(4), 467–484.

Reichle, J. (1997). Communication intervention with persons who have severe disabilities. *Journal of Special Education, 31,* 110–124.

Salisbury, C. L., Evans, I. M., & Palombaro, M. M. (1997). Collaborative problem solving to promote the inclusion of young children with significant disabilities in primary grades. *Exceptional Children, 63,* 195–210.

Salisbury, C. L., Wilson, L. L., Swartz, T. J., Palombaro, M. M., & Wassel, J. (1997). Using action research to solve instructional challenges in inclusive elementary school settings. *Education and Treatment of Children, 20*(1), 21–39.

Schonberg, R. L., & Tifft, C. F. (2002). Birth defects, prenatal diagnosis, and fetal therapy. In M. L. Batshaw (Ed.), *Children with disabilities* (5th ed., pp. 27–41). Baltimore: Brookes.

Siegel, E., & Wetherby, A. (2000). Nonsymbolic communication. In M. Snell & F. Brown (Eds.), *Instruction of students with severe disabilities* (5th ed., pp. 409–451). Upper Saddle River, NJ: Merrill/Prentice Hall.

Smith, M. G. (2000). Secondary teachers' perceptions toward inclusion of students with severe disabilities. *NASSP Bulletin, 84*(613), 54–60.

Snell, M., & Brown, F. (2000). Development and implementation of educational programs. In M. Snell & F. Brown (Eds.), *Instruction of students with severe disabilities* (5th ed., pp. 115–171). Upper Saddle River, NJ: Merrill/Prentice Hall.

Sobsey, D., & Wolf-Schein, E. G. (1991). Sensory impairments. In F. P. Orelove & D. Sobsey (Eds.), *Educating children with multiple disabilities: A transdisciplinary approach* (2nd ed., pp. 119–154). Baltimore: Brookes.

Spooner, F., & Wood, W. M. (1997). Teaching personal care and hygiene. In P. Wehman & J. Kregel (Eds.), *Functional curriculum for elementary, middle, and secondary age students with special needs* (pp. 251–281). Austin, TX: PRO-ED.

Stephenson, J. R., & Dowrick, M. (2000). Parent priorities in communication intervention for young students with severe disabilities.

Education and Training in Mental Retardation and Developmental Disabilities, 35(1), 25–35.

Thompson, B., Wegner, J. R., Wickham, D., & Ault, M. M. (1993). *Handbook for the inclusion of young children with severe disabilities: Strategies for implementing exemplary full inclusion programs.* Lawrence, KS: Learner Managed Designs.

Thompson, B., Wickham, D., Dhanks, P., Wegner, J. R., Ault, M. M., Reinertson, B., & Guess, D. (1991, Winter). Expanding the circle of inclusion: Integrating young children with severe and profound disabilities into Montessori programs. *Montessori Life,* pp. 11–15.

Thompson, B., Wickham, D., Wegner, J. R., & Ault, M. M. (1996). All children should know joy: Inclusive family-centered services for young children with significant disabilities. In D. H. Lehr & F. Brown (Eds.), *People with disabilities who challenge the system* (pp. 23–56). Baltimore: Brookes.

Thousand, J. S., Villa, R. A., & Nevin, A. I. (2002). *Creativity and collaborative learning: The practical guide to empowering students, teachers, and families* (2nd ed.). Baltimore: Brookes.

Thousand, J., Rosenberg, R. L., Bishop, K. D., & Villa, R. A. (1997). The evolution of secondary inclusion. *Remedial and Special Education, 18*(5), 270–284, 306.

Turnbull, A. P., & Turnbull, H. R. (2001). *Families, professionals, and exceptionality: Collaborating for empowerment* (4th ed.). Upper Saddle River, NJ: Merrill/Prentice Hall.

U.S. Department of Education. (2001). *To assure the free appropriate public education of all children with disabilities: Twenty-third annual report to Congress on the implementation of the Individuals with Disabilities Education Act.* Washington, DC: Author.

Utley, B. L. (1994). Providing support for sensory, postural, and movement needs. In L. Sternberg (Ed.), *Individuals with profound disabilities: Instructional and assistive strategies* (3rd ed., pp. 123–192). Austin, TX: PRO-ED.

Van der Klift, E., & Kunc, N. (1994). Beyond benevolence: Friendship and the politics of help. In J. S. Thousand, R. A. Villa, & A. I. Nevin (Eds.), *Creativity and collaborative learning: A practical guide to empowering students and teachers* (pp. 391–401). Baltimore: Brookes.

Wilson, B. A. (1999). Peer tutoring in the context of cooperative learning: Including middle school students with moderate to severe disabilities in content area classes. *Dissertation Abstracts International Section A: Humanities and Social Sciences, 60* ([1-A]), 98.

Wolfe, P. S., & Harriott, W. A. (1997). Functional academics. In P. Wehman & J. Kregel (Eds.), *Functional curriculum for elementary, middle, and secondary age students with special needs* (pp. 69–95). Austin, TX: PRO-ED.

Chapter 10

Akshoomoff, N. (2000). *Neurological underpinnings of autism* (Vol. 9). Baltimore: Brookes.

American Psychiatric Association. (2000). *Diagnostic and statistical manual of mental disorders* (4th ed.). Washington, DC: Author.

Anzalone, M. E., & Williamson, G. G. (2000). *Sensory processing and motor performance in autism spectrum disorders* (Vol. 9). Baltimore: Brookes.

Apple Computer Inc. (1994). *HyperCard* (Version 2.3.5) [Computer software]. Cupertino, CA: Author.

Barnhill, G., Hagiwara, T., Myles, B. S., & Simpson, R. L. (2000). Asperger syndrome: A study of the cognitive profiles of 37 children and adolescents. *Focus on Autism and Other Developmental Disabilities, 15*(3), 146–153.

Barnhill, G. P. (2001a). Social attribution and depression in adolescents with Asperger Syndrome. *Focus on Autism and Other Developmental Disabilities, 16,* 46–53.

Barnhill, G. P. (2001b). What is Asperger Syndrome? *Intervention in School and Clinic, 36*(5), 259–265.

Barnhill, G. (2001c). What's new in AS research: A synthesis of research conducted by the Asperger Syndrome project. *Intervention in School and Clinic, 36*(5), 300–305.

Barnhill, G. P., & Myles, B. S. (in press). Attributional style and depression in adolescents with Asperger Syndrome. *Journal of Positive Behavioral Interventions.*

Bristol, M., McIlvane, W. J., & Alexander, D. (1998). Autism research: Current context and future direction. *Mental Retardation and Developmental Disabilities Research Reviews, 4*(2), 61–64.

Brownell, M. D. (2000). *The use of musically adapted social stories to modify behaviors in students with autism: Four case studies.* Lawrence: University of Kansas.

Carpenter, M., & Tomasello, M. (2000). *Joint attention, cultural learning, and language acquisition: Implications for children with autism* (Vol. 9). Baltimore: Brookes.

Carr, E. G., Dunlap, G., Horner, R. H., Koegel, R. L., Turnbull, A. P., Sailor, W., Anderson, J. L., Albin, R. W., Koegel, L. K., & Fox, L. (2002). Positive behavior support: Evolution of an applied science. *Journal of Positive Behavior Interventions 4*(1), 4–16, 20.

Carr, E. G., Horner, R. H., Turnbull, A. P., Marquis, J. G., Magito-McLaughlin, D., McAtee, M. L., Smith, C. E., Ryan, K. A., Ruef, M. B., & Doolabh, A. (1999). *Positive behavior support as an approach for dealing with problem behavior in people with developmental disabilities: A research synthesis.* Washington, DC: AAMR.

Carr, E. G., Levin, L., McConnachie, G., Carlson, J. I., Kemp, D. C., & Smith, C. E. (1994). *Communication-based intervention for problem behavior: A user's guide for producing positive change.* Baltimore: Brookes.

Chandler, L. K., & Dahlquist, C. M. (2002). *Functional assessment strategies to prevent and remediate challenging behavior in school settings.* Upper Saddle River, NJ: Merrill/Prentice Hall.

Cheatham, S. K., Smith, J. D., Rucker, H. N., Polloway, E. A., & Lewis, G. W. (1995,

September). (1995). Savant syndrome: Case studies, hypotheses, and implications for special education. *Education and Training in Mental Retardation*, pp. 243–253.

Church, C., Alisanski, S., & Amanullah, S. (2000). The social, behavioral, and academic experiences of children with Asperger Syndrome. *Focus on Autism and Other Developmental Disabilities, 15*(1), 12–20.

Cohen, D. J., & Volkmar, F. R. (1997). *Handbook of autism and pervasive developmental disorders.* New York: Wiley.

Conderman, G., & Katsiyannis, A. (1996). State practices in serving individuals with autism. *Focus on Autism and Other Developmental Disabilities, 11*(1), 29–36.

Cunningham, E., & O'Neill, R. E. (2000). Comparison of results of functional assessment and analysis methods with young children with autism. *Education and training in mental retardation and developmental disabilities, 35*(4), 406–414.

Dalrymple, N. J. (1995). Environmental supports to develop flexibility and independence. In I. K. A. Quill (Ed.), *Teaching children with autism: Strategies to enhance communication and socialization* (pp. 243–264). New York: Delmar.

Dawson, G., & Osterling, J. (1997). Early intervention in autism. In M. J. Guralnick (Ed.), *The effectiveness of early intervention* (pp. 307–325). Baltimore: Brookes.

Dawson, G., & Watling, R. (2000). Interventions to facilitate auditory, visual, and motor integration in autism: A review of the evidence. *Journal of Autism and Developmental Disorders, 30*(5), 415–421.

Derby, K. M., Wacker, D. P., Sasso, G., Steege, M., Northup, J., Cigrand, K., & Asmus, J. (1992). Brief functional assessment techniques to evaluate aberrant behavior in an outpatient setting: A summary of 79 cases. *Journal of Applied Behavior Analysis, 25*, 713–721.

Donnellan, A. M. (1999). Invented knowledge and autism: Highlighting our strengths and expanding the conversation. *Journal of the Association for Persons with Severe Handicaps, 24*(3), 230–236.

Dunlap, G. (1999). Consensus, engagement, and family involvement for young children with autism. *Journal of the Association for Persons with Severe Handicaps, 24*(3), 222–225.

Dunlap, G., & Fox, L. (1999). A demonstration of behavioral support for young children with autism. *Journal of Positive Behavior Interventions, 1*(2), 77–87.

Dunlap, G., Newton, J. S., Fox, L., Benito, N., & Vaughn, B. (2001). Family involvement in functional assessment and positive behavior support. *Focus on autism and other developmental disabilities, 16*(4), 215–221.

Dunn, W., Myles, B. S., & Orr, S. (2002). Sensory processing issues associated with Asperger Syndrome: A preliminary investigation. *American Journal of Occupational Therapy, 56*(1), 97–102.

Earles, T. L., Carlson, J. K., & Bock, S. J. (1998). *Instructional strategies to facilitate successful learning outcomes for students with autism.* Austin, TX: PRO-ED.

Family Connection Staff, DeVault, G., Krug, C., & Fake, S. (1996). Why does Samantha act that way? Positive behavioral support leads to successful inclusion. *Exceptional Parent, 26*(9), 43–53.

Fombonne, E. (1999). The epidemiology of autism: A review. *Psychological Medicine, (29)*, 769–786.

Fox, L., Benito, N., & Dunlap, G. (2002). Early intervention with families of young children. In G. H. S. Singer, A. P. Turnbull, H. R. Turnbull, L. K. Irvin, L. E. Powers (Eds.), *Families and positive behavior support: Addressing problem behavior in family contexts* (pp. 251–270). Baltimore: Brookes.

Fox, L., Dunlap, G., & Philbrick, L. A. (1997). Providing individual supports to young children with autism and their families. *Journal of Early Intervention, 21*(1), 1–14.

Grandin, T. (1997). A personal perspective on autism. In D. J. Cohen & F. R. Volkmar (Eds.), *Handbook of autism and pervasive developmental disorders* (2nd ed., pp. 1032–1042). New York: Wiley.

Gray, C. A. (1998). Social stories and comic strip conversations with students with Asperger Syndrome and high-functioning autism. In E. Schopler, G. B. Mesibov, & L. J. Kunce (Eds.), *Asperger Syndrome or high-functioning autism?* (pp. 167–198). New York: Plenum.

Greenspan, S. I., & Wieder, S. (1999). A functional developmental approach to autism spectrum disorders. *Journal of the Association for Persons with Severe Handicaps, 24*(3), 147–161.

Hagiwara, T., & Myles, B. S. (1999). A multimedia social story intervention: Teaching skills to children with autism. *Focus on Autism and Other Developmental Disabilities, 14*(4), 82–95.

Hawken, L. S., & Horner, R. A. (2001). *Evaluation of a targeted group intervention within a schoolwide system of behavior support.* Unpublished manuscript.

Horner, R. H., Albin, R. W., Sprague, J. R., & Todd, A. W. (2000). Positive behavior support. In M. Snell & F. Brown (Eds.), *Instruction of students with severe disabilities* (5th ed., pp. 207–243). Upper Saddle River, NJ: Prentice Hall.

Howlin, P. (1982). Echolalic and spontaneous phrase speech in autistic children. *Journal of Child Psychology and Psychiatry, 23*, 281–293.

Hwang, B., & Hughes, C. (2000). The effects of social interactive training on early social communicative skills of children with autism. *Journal of Autism and Developmental Disorders, 30*(4), 331–343.

Iwata, B. A., Pace, G. M., Dorsey, M. F., Zarcone, J. R., Vollmer, T. R., Smith, R. G., Rodgers, T. A., Lerman, D. C., Shore, B. A., Mazaleski, J. L., Goh, H., Cowdery, G. E., Kalsher, M. J., McCosh, K. C., & Willis, K. D. (1994). The functions of self-injurious behavior; An experimental-epidemiological analysis. *Journal of Applied Behavior Analysis, 27*, 215–240.

Kelly, S. J., Macaruso, P., & Sokol, S. M. (1997). Mental calculations in an autistic savant: A case study. *Journal of Clinical and Experimental Neuropsychology, 19*(2), 172–184.

Kjelgaard, M. M., & Tager-Flusberg, H. (2001). An investigation of language impairment in autism: Implications for genetic subgroups. *Language and Cognitive Processes, 16*(2/3), 287–308.

Klin, A., Volkmar, F., & Sparrow, S. S. (2000). *Asperger Syndrome.* New Haven, CT: Yale University, Child Study Center.

Koegel, L. K. (2000). Interventions to facilitate communication in autism. *Journal of Autism and Developmental Disorders, 30*(5), 383–391.

Koegel, L. K., Koegel, R. L., Harrower, J. K., & Carter, C. M. (1999). Pivotal response intervention I: Overview of approach. *Journal of the Association for Persons with Severe Handicaps, 24*(3), 174–185.

Koegel, L. K., Koegel, R. L., Shoshan, T., & McNerney, E. (1999). Pivotal response intervention II: Preliminary long-term outcome data. *Journal of the Association for Persons with Severe Disabilities, 24*(3), 186–197.

Kuttler, S., Myles, B. S., & Carlson, J. K. (1998). The use of social stories to reduce precursors to tantrum behavior in a student with autism. *Focus on Autism and Other Developmental Disorders, 13*(3), 176–182.

Leary, M. R., & Hill, D. A. (1996). Moving on: Autism and movement disturbance. *Mental Retardation, 34*(1), 39–53.

Lewis, M. H., & Bodfish, J. W. (1998). Repetitive behavior disorders in autism. *Mental Retardation and Developmental Disabilities Research Reviews, 4*(2), 80–89.

Lord, C. (1997). Diagnostic instruments in autism spectrum disorders. In D. J. Cohen & F. R. Volkman (Eds.), *Handbook of autism and pervasive developmental disorders* (2nd ed., pp. 460–482). New York: Wiley.

Lord, C., Pickles, A., McLennan, J., Rutter, M., Bergman, J., Folstein, S., Fombonne, E., Leboyer, M., & Minshew, N. (1997). Diagnosing autism: Analyses of data from the Autism Diagnostic Interview. *Journal of Autism and Developmental Disorders, 27*(5), 501–517.

Lord, C., & Risi, S. (2000). *Diagnosis of autism spectrum disorders in young children* (Vol. 9). Baltimore: Brookes.

Lord, C., Rutter, M., & Le Couteru, A. (1994). Autism diagnostic interview—revised: A revised version of a diagnostic interview for caregivers of individuals with possible pervasive developmental disorders. *Journal of Autism and Developmental Disorders, 24*(5), 659–685.

Lorimer, P. A., Simpson, R. L., Myles, B. S., & Ganz, J. B. (2002). The use of social stories as a preventative behavioral intervention in a home setting with a child with autism. *Journal of Positive Behavioral Interventions, 4*(1), 53–60.

Lovass, O. I. (1977). *The autistic child: Language development through behavior modification.* New York: Irvington.

Mace, F. C., & Mauk, J. E. (1999). Biobehavioral diagnosis and treatment of self-injury. In A. Repp & R. H. Horner (Eds.), *Functional analysis of problem behavior: From effective assessment to effective support* (pp. 78–96). Belmont, CA: Wadsworth.

Marks, S. U., Schrader, C., Longaker, T., & Levine, M. (2000). Portraits of three adolescent students with Asperger's Syndrome: Personal stories and how they can inform practice. *JASH, 25*(1), 3–17.

McClannahan, L. E., & Krantz, P. J. (1999). *Activity schedules for children with autism: Teaching independent behavior.* Bethesda, MD: Woodbine House.

McGee, G. G., Morrier, M. J., & Daly, T. (1999). An incidental teaching approach to early intervention for toddlers with autism. *Journal of the Association for Persons with Severe Handicaps, 24*(3), 133–146.

Miller, L. K. (1999). The savant syndrome: Intellectual impairment and exceptional skill. *Psychological Bulletin, 125*(1), 31–46.

Myles, B. S., Barnhill, G. P, Hagiwara, T., Griswold, D. E., & Simpson, R. L. (2001). A synthesis of studies on the intellectual, academic, social/emotional and sensory characteristics of children and youth with Asperger Syndrome. *Education and Training in Mental Retardation and Developmental Disabilities, 36*(3), 304–311.

National Research Council. (2001). *Educating children with autism.* Washington, DC: National Academy Press.

Nettelbeck, T., & Young, R. (1996). Intelligence and savant syndrome: Is the whole greater than the sum of the fragments? *Intelligence, 22,* 49–68.

Nickels, R. E.(2000). *Developmental delay and mental retardation.* Baltimore: Brookes.

Perner, J. (1993). The theory of mind deficit in autism: Rethinking the metarepresentation theory. In S. Baron-Cohen, H. Tager-Flusberg, & D. J. Cohen (Eds.), *Understanding other minds* (pp. 112–137). New York: Oxford University Press.

Prizant, B. M. (1983). Language acquisition and communicative behavior in autism: Toward an understanding of the "whole" of it. *Journal of Speech and Hearing Disorders, 48,* 296–307.

Prizant, B. M., & Rubin, E. (1999). Contemporary issues in interventions for autism spectrum disorders: A commentary. *Journal of the Association for Persons with Severe Handicaps, 24*(3), 199–208.

Prizant, B. M., & Rydell, P. J. (1984). Analysis of functions of delayed echolalia in autistic children. *Journal of Speech and Hearing Research, 27,* 183–192.

Prizant, B. M., Schuler, A. L., Wetherby, A., & Rydell, P. (1997). Enhancing language and communication development: Language approaches. In D. J. Cohen & F. R. Volkman (Eds.), *Handbook of autism and pervasive developmental disorders* (2nd ed., pp. 572–604). New York: Wiley.

Prizant, B. M., Wetherby, A. M., & Rydell, P. J. (2000). *Communication intervention issues for young children with autism spectrum disorders* (Vol. 9). Baltimore: Brookes.

Quill, K. A. (1995). *Teaching children with autism: Strategies to enhance communication and socialization.* New York: Delmar.

Rinner, L. (2000). *Asperger Syndrome and autism: Comparing sensory processing in daily life.* Lawrence: University of Kansas.

Rogers, S. J. (1998). Empirically supported comprehensive treatments for young children with autism. *Journal of Clinical Child Psychology, 27*(2), 168–179.

Rogers, S. J. (2000). Interventions that facilitate socialization in children with autism. *Journal of Autism and Developmental Disorders, 30*(5), 399–409.

Rogers, M. F., & Myles, B. S. (2001). Using social stories and comic strip conversations to interpret social situations for an adolescent with Asperger Syndrome. *Intervention in School and Clinic, 36*(5), 310–313.

Ruble, L. A., & Dalrymple, N. J. (1996). An alternative view of outcome in autism. *Focus on Autism and Other Developmental Disabilities, 11*(1), 3–14.

Ruble, L. A., & Dalrymple, N.J. (2002). Compass: A parent-teacher collaborative model for students with autism. *Focus on Autism and Other Developmental Disabilities, 17*(2), 76–83.

Rydell, P. J., & Prizant, B. M. (1995). Assessment and intervention strategies for children who use echolalia. In K. A. Quill (Ed.), *Teaching children with autism: Startegies to enhance communication and socialization* (pp. 105–132). New York: Delmar.

Safran, S. P. (2001). Asperger Syndrome: The emerging challenge to special education. *Council for Exceptional Children, 67*(2), 151–160.

Saloviita, T., Ruusila, L., & Ruusila, U. (2000). Incidence of savant syndrome in Finland. *Perceptual and Motor Skills, 91,* 120–122.

Schwartz, I. S., Boulware, G.-L., McBride, B. J., Sandall, S. R. (2001). Functional assessment strategies for young children with autism. *Focus on Autism and Other Developmental Disabilities, 16*(4), 222–227.

Smith, M. D., Belcher, R. G., & Juhrs, P. D. (1995). *A guide to successful employment for individuals with autism.* Baltimore: Brookes.

Smith, T. (2001). Discrete trial training in the treatment of autism. *Focus on Autism and Other Developmental Disabilities, 16*(2), 86–92.

Smith, T., Green, A. D., & Wynn, J. W. (2000). Randomized trial of intensive early intervention for children with pervasive developmental disorder. *American Journal on Mental Retardation, 105*(4), 269–285.

Sugai, G., Horner, R. H., Dunlap, G., Hieneman, M., Lewis, T. J., Nelson, C. M., Scott, T., Liaupsin, C., Sailor, W., Turnbull, A. P., Turnbull, H. R., Wickham, D., Wilcox, B., Ruef, M. (2000). Applying positive behavior support and functional behavioral assessment in schools. *Journal of Positive Behavior Interventions, 2*(3), 131–143.

Sugai, G., & Lewis, T. J. (1999). *Developing positive behavioral support for students with challenging behavior.* Reston, VA: Council for Children with Behavioral Disorders.

Swaggart, B. L., Gagnon, E., Bock, S. J., Earles, T. L., Quinn, C., Myles, B. S., & Simpson, R. L. (1995). Using social stories to teach social and behavioral skills to children with autism. *Focus on Autistic Behavior, 10*(1), 1–15.

Talay-Ongan, A., & Wood, K. (2000). Unusual sensory sensitivities in autism: A possible crossroads. *International Journal of Disability, Development, and Education, 47*(2), 201–212.

Teitelbaum, P., Teitelbaum, O., Nye, J., Fryman, J., & Maurer, R. (1998). Movement analysis in infancy may be useful for early diagnosis of autism. *Proceedings of the National Academy of Science, 95,* 13982–13987.

Towbin, K. E., Mauk, J. E., & Batshaw, M. L. (2002). Pervasive developmental disorders. In M. L. Batshaw (Ed.), *Children with disabilities* (5th ed., pp. 365–387). Baltimore: Brooks.

Tsai, L. (2000). Children with austim spectrum disorder: Medicine today and in the new millennium. *Focus on Autism and Other Developmental Disabilities, 15*(3), 138–145.

Turnbull, A., Edmonson, H., Griggs, P., Wickham, D., Sailor, W., Freeman, R., Guess, D., Lassen, S., McCart, A., Park, J., Riffel, L., Turnbull, R., & Warren, J. (2002). A blueprint for schoolwide positive behavior support: Implementation of three components. *Council for Exceptional Children, 68*(3), 377–402.

Turnbull, A. P., & Ruef, M. (1996). Family perspectives on problem behavior. *Mental Retardation, 34,* 280–293.

Turnbull, A. P., & Ruef, M. (1997). Family perspectives on inclusive lifestyle issues for individuals with problem behavior. *Exceptional Children, 63,* 211–227.

Twachtman-Cullen, D. (2000). *More able children with autism spectrum disorders: Sociocommunicative challenges and guidelines for enhancing abilities* (Vol. 9). Baltimore: Brookes.

U.S. Department of Education. (2000). *To assure the free appropriate public education of all children with disabilities.* Washington, DC: Author.

U.S. Department of Education. (2001). *To assure the free appropriate public education of all children with disabilities.* Washington, DC: Author.

Volkmar, F. R., Carter, A., Grossman, J., & Klin, A. (1997). Social development in autism. In D. J. Cohen & F. R. Volkmar (Eds.), *Handbook of autism and pervasive developmental disorders* (2nd ed., pp. 173–194). New York: Wiley.

Volkmar, F. R., Klin, A., & Cohen, D. J. (1997). Diagnosis and classification of autism and related conditions: Consensus and issues. In D. J. Cohen & F. R. Volkmar (Eds.), *Handbook of autism and pervasive developmental disorders* (2nd ed., pp. 5–39). New York: Wiley.

Waterhouse, L., & Fein, D. (1997). Perspectives on social impairment. In D. J. Cohen & F. R. Volkman (Eds.), *Handbook of autism and pervasive developmental disorders* (2nd ed., pp. 901–918). New York: Wiley.

Watling, R., Deitz, J., Kanny, E. M., & McLaughlin, J. F. (1999). Current practice of occupational therapy for children with autism. *American Journal of Occupational Therapy, 53,* 498–505.

Weiss, M. J., & Harris, S. L. (2001). *Reaching out, joining in: Teaching social skills to young children with autism.* Bethesda, MD: Woodbine House.

Chapter 11

Agnew, C..M., Nystul, M. S., & Conner, M. C. (1998). Seizure disorders: An alternative explanation for students' inattention. *Professional School Counseling, 2*(1), 54–60.

Amer, K. S. (1999). Children's adaptation to insulin dependent diabetes mellitus: A critical review of the literature. *Pediatric Nursing, 25*(6), 627–639.

American Academy of Allergy, Asthma, and Immunology. (1999, August 2). *Back to school with allergies and asthma* Retrieved May 5, 2002, from (http://www.aaaai.org/media/news_releases/1999/08/990802.html). Retrieved May 5, 2002.

American Academy of Pediatrics. (1999). Disclosure of illness status to children and adolescents with HIV infection. *Policy Statement* (RE9827) Retrieved on May 15, 2002, from (http://www.aap.org/policy/re9827.html).

American Academy of Pediatrics. (2002). Health supervision for children with sickle cell disease. *Pediatrics, 109*(3), 526–535.

American Cancer Society. (2002). *Cancer facts and figures* (http://www3.cancer.org/downloads/STT/CancerFacts&Figures2002TM.pdf). Retrieved May 20, 2002.

American Diabetes Association. (2001). Position statement: Care of children with diabetes in the school and day care setting. *Diabetes Care, 24*(1). (http://www.diabetes.org/diabetescare/FullText/Supplements/DiabetesCare/Supplement101/S108.htm). Retrieved May 16, 2002.

American Diabetes Association. (2002). *Facts and figures* (http://www.diabetes.org/ada/facts.asp). Retrieved May 15, 2002.

American Lung Association. (2002a). *Asthma alert for teachers* (http://www.lungusa.org/school/asthma_alert.html). Retrieved May 5, 2002.

American Lung Association. (2002b, July 26). *Asthma attacks* (http://www.lungusa.org/asthma/astasthmatk.html). Retrieved May 5, 2002.

American Lung Association. (2002c, March). *Asthma medicines* (http://www.lungusa.org/asthma/astasmeds2.html). Retrieved May 5, 2002.

American Medical Association. (1999, May 18). Facts about sickle cell anemia: JAMA patient page. *Journal of the American Medical Association, 281*(18).

Armstrong, F. D., Blumberg, M. J., & Toledano, S. R. (1999). Neurobehavioral issues in childhood cancer. *School Psychology Review, 28*(2), 194–204.

Associated Press. (1999). *Scientists link gene to diabetes* (http://199.97.97.163/IMDS%DIABETES%read%/home/content/users/imds/feeds/associatedpress/2000/09/26/—/0669-2827-Diabetes-Gene). Retrieved November 5, 2000.

Averitt, D. (1998, October). Making treatment decisions in children with HIV. *AIDS Care* (http://www.thebody.com/hivnews/aidscare/oct98/newsline.html). Retrieved on May 15, 2002.

Avert.org. (2002). *HIV and AIDS statistics by age* (http://www.avert.org/usastata.htm). Retrieved May 3, 2002.

Babies who beat AIDS. (1996, June). *Discover,* p. 30.

Barbarin, O. A., & Whitten, C. F. (1994). Sickle cell anemia in children: Psychological aspects. *Health and Social Work, 19*(2), 112–120.

Begley, S. (2000, June 27). A genome milestone. *Newsweek* (http://www.msnbc.com/news/426250.asp). Retrieved June 15, 2002.

Bender, B. G. (1999). Learning disorders associated with asthma and allergies. *School Psychology Review, 28*(2), 204–215.

Bessell, A. G. (2001a). Children surviving cancer: Psychosocial adjustment, quality of life, and school experiences. *Exceptional Children, 67*(3), 345–359.

Bessell, A. G. (2001b, September). Educating children with chronic illness. *Exceptional Parent Magazine, 31*(9), 44.

Beverly, C. L. (1995). Providing a safe environment for children infected with the human immunodeficiency virus. *Topics in Early Childhood Special Education, 15*(1), 100–110.

Bloom, L. A., Perlmutter, J., & Burrell, L. (1999). The general educator: Applying constructivism to inclusive classrooms. *Intervention in School and Clinic, 34*(3), 132–137.

Boice, M. M. (1998). Chronic illness in adolescence. *Adolescence, 33*(132), 927–940.

Bonner, M. J., Schumacher, E., Gustafson, K. E., & Thompson, R. J. (1999). The impact of sickle cell disease on cognitive functioning and learning. *School Psychology Review, 28*(2), 182–193.

Brown, R. T., & DuPaul, G. J. (1999). Introduction to the mini-series: Promoting school success in children with chronic medical conditions. *School Psychology Review, 28*(2), 175–82.

Bruder, M. B. (1995). The challenge of pediatric AIDS: A framework for early childhood special education. *Topics in Early Childhood Special Education, 15*(1), 83–89.

Carta, J. J., Sideridis, G., Rinkel, P., Guimaraes, S., Greenwood, G., Baggett, K., Peterson, P., Atwater, J., McEvoy, M., & McConnell, S. (1994). Behavioral outcomes of young children prenatally exposed to illicit drugs: Review and analysis of experimental literature. *Topics in Early Childhood Special Education, 14*(2), 184–216.

Cassini, K. K., & Rogers, J. L. (1996). *Death in the classroom* (Reprint). Cincinnati: Griefwork.

Centers for Disease Control. (1997, November 27). *Morbidity and Mortality Weekly Report, 46*(46), 1086.

Centers for Disease Control. (1998, December 11). Lead poisoning associated with imported candy and powdered food coloring—California and Michigan. *Morbidity and Mortality Weekly Report, 47*(48), 1041–1043.

Centers for Disease Control. (2001, January 31). *HIV and its transmission* (http://www.cdc.gov/hiv/pubs/facts/transmission.htm). Retrieved May 15, 2002.

Centers for Disease Control. (2002). *Young people at risk: HIV/AIDS among America's youth* (http://www.cdc.gov/hiv/pubs/facts/youth.htm). Retrieved May 15, 2002.

Charkow, W. B. (1998). Inviting children to grieve. *Professional School Counseling, 2*(2), 117–123.

Cleveland Clinic Foundation. (1997). *Frequently asked questions about neurological problems* (http://www.neus.ccf.org/patients/faq.html). Retrieved May 7, 2002.

Committee on Pediatric AIDS. (2000, June). Education of children with human immunodeficiency virus infection (RE9950). *American Academy of Pediatrics, 105*(6), 1358–1360.

Committee on School Health. (2000). Home, hospital, and other non–school-based instruction for children and adolescents who are medically unable to attend school [Electronic version]. *Pediatrics, 106*(5), 1154–1155.

Commonwealth of Massachusetts. (2002). *Childhood lead poisoning prevention program* (http://www.state.ma.us/dph/clppp/clppp.htm). Retrieved June 12, 2002.

Corr, C. A. (1998). Children, adolescents, and death: Myths, realities, and challenges. *Death Studies, 23,* 443–463.

Cosby, B. (1997). *The meanest thing to say.* New York: Scholastic.

Cosden, M., & Peerson, S. (1997). Effects of prenatal drug exposure on birth outcomes and early child development. *Journal of Drug Issues, 27*(3), 525–540.

Crawford, A. (1997). Alcohol, auditory functioning, and deafness. *Addiction Biology, 2*(2), 125–151.

DePaepe, P., Garrison-Kane, L., & Doelling, J. (2002). Supporting students with health needs in schools: An overview of selected health conditions. *Focus on Exceptional Children, 35*(1), 1–24.

DiFranza, J. R., & Lew, R. A. (1996). Morbidity and mortality in children associated with the use of tobacco products by other people. *Pediatrics, 97*(4), 560–69.

Doctor's Guide. (1999, December). Novel drug combination effective in controlling HIV in children. *Global Edition.* (http://www.pslgroup.com/dg/151312.htm). Retrieved on May 16, 2002.

Dowling, C. G. (1997, May). Discovery: An epidemic of sneezing and wheezing. *Life*, pp. 76–93.

Epilepsy Foundation of America. (2001, 2002). *The answer place* (http://www.efa.org/answerplace/teachers/performance.html). Retrieved May 12, 2002.

Fleitas, J. (2002). *Band-Aids and blackboards: When chronic illness or some other medical problem goes to school* (http://funrsc.fairfield.edu/jfleitas/kidsitro.html). Retrieved May 16, 2002.

Getch, Y. Q., & Neuharth-Pritchett, S. (1999). Children with asthma: Strategies for educators. *Teaching Exceptional Children, 31*(3), 30–36.

Grosse, S. J. (1999). Educating children and youth to prevent contagious disease (EDO-SP-1999-8). *ERIC Digest*. Washington, DC: ERIC Clearinghouse on Teaching and Teacher Education (ED437368).

Hayes, J. S. (1999). Practice applications of research. Bibliotherapy: Using fiction in two populations to discuss feelings. *Pediatric Nursing, 25*(1), 91–96.

Helms, J. L. (2002, May 26). The war against asthma. *Mobile Register*, pp. E1, E2.

Henderson, C. W. (1999, November 1). Cancer treatments may cause learning problems in children. *Cancer Weekly Plus*, p. 3.

HIV University. (1995, December 1). *World*, p. 2.

Holmes, C. S., Fox, M. A., Cant, M. C., Lampert, N. L., & Greet, T. (1999). Disease and demographic risk factors for disrupted cognitive functioning in children with insulin-dependent diabetes mellitus (IDDM). *School Psychology Review, 28*(2), 215–243.

Horner, S. D. (1999). Asthma self-care: Just another piece of work. *Pediatric Nursing, 25*(6), 597–603.

Howland, L. C., Gortmaker, S. L, Mofenson, L. M., Spino, C., Gardner, J. D., Gorski, H., Fowler, M. G., & Oleske, J. (2000). Effects of negative life events on immune suppression in children and youth infected with human immunodeficiency virus type 1. *Pediatrics, 106*(3), 540–547.

Hylton Rushton, C., & Catlin, A. (2002) Pediatric palliative care: The time is now! *Pediatric Nursing, 28*(1), 57–59.

Jacobson, J. L., & Jacobson, S. W. (1999). Drinking moderately and pregnancy. *Alcohol Health & Research World, 23*(1), 25–31.

Jacy Group. (1997–2000). *Ed's asthma track for parents of children with asthma.* (http://asthmatrack.org). Retrieved May 5, 2002.

Jakubik, L. D. (2000). Care of the child with sickle cell disease: Acute complications. *Pediatric Nursing, 26*(4), 373–381.

Johnson, G., Johnson, R. L., & Jefferson-Aker, C. R. (2001). HIV/AIDS prevention: Effective instructional strategies for adolescents with mild mental retardation. *Teaching Exceptional Children, 33*(6), 28–33.

Kalwinsky, D. K. (2002). Health care issues as the child with chronic illness transitions to adulthood. *Southern Medical Journal, 95*(9), 966–977.

Kapp-Simon, K., & Simon, D. J. (1991). Meeting the challenge: Social skills training for teens with special needs. *Connections, 2*(2), 1–5.

Katz, S., & Krulik, T. (1999). Fathers of children with chronic illness: Do they differ from fathers of healthy children? *Journal of Family Nursing, 5*(3), 292–316.

Kliebenstein, M. A., & Broome, M. E. (2000). School re-entry for the child with chronic illness: parent and school personnel perceptions. *Pediatric Nursing, 26*(6), 579–583.

Koop, J. E. (1998–2001). *Pediatric AIDS* (http://www.drkoop.com/conditions/AIDS/page_25_128.asp). Retrieved May 15, 2002.

Lavoie, R. (n.d.). *How difficult can this be? F.A.T. City: A learning disabilities workshop* [Video]. Charlotte, NC: PBS Home Video.

Loftus, J., & Block, M. E. (1996). Physical education for students with fetal alcohol syndrome. *Physical Educator, 53*(2), 147–152.

Malik, R., & Hampton, G. (2002). Counseling hospitalized pediatric patients with asthma. *American Journal of Health-System Pharmacy, 59*(19), 1829, 1833.

McGlauflin, H. (1998). Helping children grieve at school. *Professional School Counseling, 1*(5), 46–50.

McNamara, B. E., & McNamara, F. J. (2000). AD/HD and bullies: What you need to know. *Attention! 7*(2), 31–36.

Milton, J. (1999). Loss and grief. *Primary Educator, 5*(3), 10–13.

Naierman, N. (1997). Reaching out to grieving students. *Educational Leadership, 55*(2), 62–66.

National Center for Education Statistics. (2001). *Digest of education statistics, 2001* [Electronic version]. Washington, DC: U.S. Department of Education.

National Center for Education Statistics. (2002). *The condition of education* [Electronic version]. Washington, DC: U.S. Department of Education.

National Environmental Health Association. (1995). Study shows reducing dust, other allergens, could cut kids' asthma. *Journal of Environmental Health, 58*, 38.

National Heart, Lung, and Blood Institute. (1997, July). *Guidelines for the diagnosis and management of asthma: Expert Panel 2.* (http://www.nhlbi.nih.gov/guidelines/asthma/asthgdln.pdf). Retrieved May 5, 2002.

National Heart, Lung, and Blood Institute. (n.d.). *How asthma friendly is your school?* (http://www.nhlbi.nih.gov/health/public/lung/asthma/friendly.htm).

National Institute of Diabetes and Digestive and Kidney Diseases. (2002). *Diabetes.* (http://www.niddk.nih.gov/health/diabetes/pubs/type1-2/index.htm).

National Jewish Center for Immunology and Respiratory Medicine. (2000). What makes asthma worse? Denver, CO: Author.

National Reference Center for Bioethics Literature & the Joseph and Rose Kennedy Institute of Ethics. (2002). *The human genome project* (http://www.georgetown.edu/research/nrcbl/scopenotes/sn17.htm).

National Safety Council. (1997). *Blood borne pathogens* (2nd ed). Sudbury, MA: Jones & Bartlett.

Nidus Information Services. (2001a). *Epilepsy.* New York: Author.

Nidus Information Services. (2001b). *Sickle cell disease.* New York: Author.

Noll, R. B., Garstein, M. A., Vannatta, K., Correll, J., Bukowski, W. M., & Davies, W. H. (1999). Social, emotional, and behavioral functioning of children with cancer. *Pediatrics, 103*(1), 71–79.

O'Donnell, L., Stueve, A., San Doval, A., Duran, R., Haber, D., Atnafou, R., Johnson, N., Grant, U., Murray, H., Juhn, G., Tang, J., & Piessens, P. (1999). The effectiveness of the Reach for Health Community Youth Service Learning Program in reducing early and unprotected sex among urban middle school students. *American Journal of Public Health, 89*(2), 176–182.

P/S/L Consulting Group. (1997). Epilepsy gene found. *Doctor's guide to medical and other news.* (http://www. pslgroup.com/dg/6ec6.htm). Retrieved on June 5, 2000.

Perrin, E. C., & Lewkowicz, C. (2000). Shared vision: Concordance among fathers, mothers, and pediatricians about unmet needs of children with chronic health impairments. *Pediatrician, 205*(1), 277–286.

Perry, B. D. (2000). Children and loss. *Scholastic Parent and Child, 8*(2), 66–69.

Pew Environmental Health Commission. (2000, May 16). *Asthma cases projected to double by 2020; will hit 29 million Americans; 1 in 5 families.* Baltimore: Johns Hopkins School of Public Health.

Podolsky, D. (1997, January 13). Gasping for life. *U.S. News and World Report*, pp. 61–65.

Prater, M. A., & Serna, L. A. (1995). HIV disease. *Remedial and Special Education, 16*, 68–78.

Regan, J. M., & Reeb, R. N. (1998). Neuropsychological functioning in survivors of childhood leukemia. *Child Study Journal, 28*(3), 179–201.

Rosenthal-Malek, A., & Greenspan, J. (1999). (1999). A student with diabetes is in my class. *Teaching Exceptional Children, 31*(3), 37–43.

Shank, M. S. (2002). *Helping students with frequent absences achieve academic standards.* Unpublished manuscript.

Sherman, A. C., & Simonton, S. (2001). Coping with cancer in the family. *Family Journal, 9*(2), 193–200.

Shields, J. D., & Heron, T. E. (1995). The eco-triadic model of educational consultation for students with cancer. *Education & Treatment of Children, 28*(2), 184–201.

Simeonsson, N. (1995). Asthma: New information for the early interventionist. *Topics in Early Childhood Special Education, 15*(1), 32–43.

Spiegel, G. L., Cutler, S. K., & Yetter, C. E. (1996). What every teacher should know about epilepsy. *Intervention in School and Clinic,* 32(1), 34–38.

St. Jude's Children's Research Hospital. (n.d.). *Your child and sickle cell disease.* Memphis, TN: Pediatric Hematologic Division and Biomedical Communications.

STARBRIGHT Foundation. (2002). STARBRIGHT healthcare goals (http://www. starbright.org/about/goals.html). Retrieved June 26, 2002.

Stephens, M. E., Barkey, M. E., & Hall, H. R. (1999). Techniques to comfort children during stressful procedures. *Advances in Mind-Body Medicine,* 15(1), 49–61.

Sullivan, N. A., Fulmer, D. L., & Zigmond, N. (2001). School: The normalizing factor for children with childhood leukemia. *Preventing School Failure,* 46(1), 4–14.

Thies, K. (1999). Identifying the educational implications of chronic illness in school children, *Journal of School Health,* 69(10), 392–398.

Turnbull, H. R., & Turnbull, A. (2000). *Free appropriate education: The law and children with disabilities.* Denver: Love.

Tyler, J. S., & Colson, S. (1994). Common pediatric disabilities: Medical aspects and educational implications. *Focus on Exceptional Children,* 27(4), 1–16.

Wadsworth, D., & Knight, D. (1999). Preparing the inclusion classroom for students with special physical and health needs. *Intervention in School and Clinic,* 34(3), 170–176.

WebMD Health. (1996–2002). *Sickle cell disease* (http://my.webmd.com/content/dmk/dmk_article_40076). Retrieved June 1, 2002.

Wilfert, C. M. (1998, October). 98% sure. *AIDS care: Dedicated to improving the quality of life of all people living with HIV* (http://www.thebody.com/hivnews/aidscare/oct98/newsline.html). Retrieved October 14, 1999.

Young, M., Denny, G., & Speare, C. (1999). Area specific self-esteem and adolescent sexual behavior. *American Journal of Health Studies,* 15(4), 181–189.

Chapter 12

Barnes, K. J., Schoenfeld, H. B., & Pierson, W. P. (1997). Inclusive schools: Implications for public school occupational therapy. *Physical Disabilities,* 15(2), 37–52.

Bigge, J. L., Best, S. J., & Heller, K. W. (2001). *Teaching individuals with physical, health, or multiple disabilities* (4th ed.). Upper Saddle River, NJ: Merrill/Prentice Hall.

Brooke, M. H. (1986). *A clinician's view of neuromuscular diseases* (2nd ed.). Baltimore: Williams & Wilkins.

Bruner, J. P., Tulipan, N. B., Richards, W. O., Walsh, W. F., Boehm, F. H., & Vrabcak, E. K. (2000). In utero repair of myelomeningocele: A comparison of endoscopy and hysterotomy. *Fetal Diagnosis and Therapy,* 2, 83–88.

Bryant, B., & Seay, P. C. (1998). The Technology-Related Assistance to Individuals with Disabilities Act: Relevance to individuals with learning disabilities and their advocates. *Journal of Learning Disabilities,* 31(1), 4–15.

Burstein, J. R., Wright-Drechsel, M. L., & Wood, A. (1998). *Assistive technology.* Baltimore: Brookes.

Centers for Disease Control. (1992). Recommendations for the use of folic acid to reduce the number of cases of spina bifida and other neural tube defects. *Mortality Weekly Reports,* 41(RR-14), 1–7.

Daly, L. E., Kirke, P. N., Malloy, A., Weir, D. G., & Scott, J. M. (1995). Folate levels and neural tube defects: Implications for prevention. *Journal of the American Medical Association,* 274, 1698–1702.

Dormans, J. P., & Pellegrino, L. (1998). *Caring for children with cerebral palsy: A team approach.* Baltimore: Brookes.

Downing, J. E. (2002). *Including students with severe and multiple disabilities in typical classrooms* (2nd ed.). Baltimore: Brookes.

Gimblett, R. J. (2000). *Post-secondary peer support programs: Facilitating transition through peer training and mentoring.* Boston: Association on Higher Education and Disability.

Glennen, S. L., & DeCoste, D. C. (1997). *The handbook of augmentative and alternative communication.* San Diego: Singular Publishing Group.

Heller, K. W., Alberto, P. A., Forney, P. E., & Schwartzman, M. N. (1996). *Understanding physical, sensory, and health impairments: Characteristics and educational implications.* Pacific Grove, CA: Brookes/Cole.

Heller, K. W., D'Andrea, F. M., & Forney, P. E. (1998). Determining reading and writing media for individuals with visual and physical impairments. *Journal of Visual Impairment and Blindness,* 92, 162–175.

Heller, K. W., Forney, P. E., Alberto, P. A., Schwartzman, M. N., & Goeckel, T. M. (2000). *Meeting physical and health needs of children with disabilities: Teaching student participation and management.* Belmont, CA: Wadsworth Thomson Learning.

Honein, M. A., Paulozzi, L. J., Mathews, T. J., Erickson, J. D., & Wong, L. Y. C. (2001). Impact of folic acid fortification of the U.S. food supply on the occurrence of neural tube defects. *JAMA,* 285, 2981–2984.

Horn, L., & Berktold, J. (Ed.). (1999). *Students with disabilities in postsecondary education: A profile of preparation, participation, and outcomes.* Washington, DC: National Center for Education Statistics.

Hostler, S. L., Gressard, R. P., Hassler, C. R., & Linden, P. G. (1989). Adolescent autonomy project: Transition skills for adolescents with physical disability. *Children's Health Care,* 18, 12–18.

Jurasek, G. (2000). A positive spirit. *Exceptional Parent,* 30(5), 40–45.

Kemp, C. E., & Parette, H. P. (2000). Barriers to minority family involvement in assistive technology decision-making processes. *Education and Training in Mental Retardation and Developmental Disabilities,* 35(4), 384–392.

Liptak, G. S. (1997). *Neural tube defects* (4th ed.). Baltimore: Brookes.

Lloyd, L. L., Fuller, D. R., & Arvidson, H. H. (1997). *Augmentative and alternative communication: A handbook of principles and practices.* Needham Heights, MA: Allyn & Bacon.

Lutkenhoff, M., & Oppenheimer S. G. (1997). *Spinabilities: A young person's guide to spina bifida.* Bethesda, MD: Woodbine House.

NCIP. (1998). *NCIP profile: Technology supports inclusion in preschool* (www2.edc.org/NCIP/library/ec/Profile5.htm).

Nickel, R. E. (2000). *Developmental delay and mental retardation.* Baltimore: Brookes.

Pellegrino, L. (1997). *Cerebral palsy* (4th ed.). Baltimore: Brookes.

Powers, L. E., Sowers, J. A., & Stevens, T. (1995). An exploratory, randomized study of the impact of mentoring on the self-efficacy and community-based knowledge of adolescents with severe physical challenges. *Journal of Rehabilitation,* 61(1), 33–41.

Quist, R. W., & Lloyd, L. L. (1997). *Principles and uses of technology, augmentative and alternative communication: A handbook of principals and practices.* Needham Heights, MA: Allyn & Bacon.

Sandler, A. (1997). *Living with spina bifida: A guide for families and professionals.* Chapel Hill: University of North Carolina Press.

Schonberg, R. L., & Tifft, C. F. (2002). Birth defects, prenatal diagnosis, and fetal therapy. In M. L. Batshaw (Eds.), *Children with disabilities* (5th ed., pp. 27–41). Baltimore: Brookes.

Smith, D. (1998). Assistive technology: Funding options and strategies. *Mental and Physical Disability Law Reporter,* 22(1), 115–123.

Szabo, J. L. (2000). Maddie's story: Inclusion through physical and occupational therapy. *Teaching Exceptional Children,* 33(2), 26–32.

U.S. Department of Education. (1995). *To assure the free appropriate public education of all children with disabilities: Seventeenth annual report to Congress on the implementation of the Individuals with Disabilities Education Act.* Washington, DC: Author.

U.S. Department of Education. (2000). *To assure the free appropriate public education of all children with disabilities: Twentieth annual report to Congress.* Washington DC: Author.

U.S. Department of Education. (2001). *To assure the free appropriate public education of all children with disabilities: Twenty-third annual report to Congress on the implementation of the Individuals with Disabilities Education Act.* Washington, DC: Author.

Chapter 13

Advisory Committee on Traumatic Brain Injury in Children. (2000). *Traumatic brain injury in* children and teens: A national guide for families. Washington, DC: Author.

Appleton, R., & Baldwin, T. (1998). Management of brain-injured children. New York: Oxford University Press.

Bergland, M., & Hoffbauer, D. (1996). New opportunities for students with traumatic brain injuries. Teaching Exceptional Children, 28(2), 54–57.

Blake, C., & Fewster, D. (2001). Providing a creative and effective learning environment for students with traumatic brain injury at the middle and high school levels. International Journal of Adolescence and Youth, 10, 117–133.

Buyer, D. M. (1999). Neuropsychological assessment and schools. Brain Injury Source, 3(3), 18–20.

Carney, J., & Porter, P. (2001). The educational needs of children with traumatic brain injury. In L. Schoenbrodt (Ed.), Children with traumatic brain injury: A parent's guide (pp. 293–349). Bethesda, MD: Woodbine House.

Center for Disease Control and Prevention. (2000). National health statistics. Atlanta: Author.

Center for Disease Control and Prevention (2001). National health statistics. Atlanta: Author.

Chapman, S. B., (1998). Bridging the gap between research and education reintegration: Direct instruction on processing connected discourse. Aphasiology, 12, 1081–1088.

DePompei, R. (1999). Run a reverse left: Communication disorders after brain injury. Brain Injury Source, 3(3), 22–25.

Feeney, T. J., Ylvisaker, M., Rosen, B. H., & Greene, P. (2001). Community supports for individuals with challenging behavior after brain injury: An analysis of the New York State Behavioral Resource Project. Journal of Head Trauma Rehabilitation, 16, 61–75.

Hux, K., Marquardt, J., Skinner, S., & Bond, V. (1999). Special education services provided to students with and without parental reports of traumatic brain injury. Brain Injury, 13, 447–455.

Laforce, R., & Martin-MacLeod, L. (2001). Symptom cluster associated with mild traumatic brain injury in university students. Perceptual and Motor Skills, 93, 281–288.

Lash, M. H. (2000). Resource guide: Children, adolescents and young adults with brain injuries. Wake Forest, NC: L & A Publishing/Training.

Lea, P. M. (2001). Traumatic brain injury: Developmental differences in glutamate receptor response and the impact on treatment. Mental Retardation and Developmental-Disabilities Research Reviews, 7, 235–248.

Lees-Haley, P. R., Fox, D. D., & Courtney, J. C. (2001). A comparison of complaints by mild brain injury claimants and other claimants describing subjective experiences immediately following their injury. Archives of Clinical Neuropsychology, 16, 689–695.

LinguiSystems. (2000). Test of problem solving. East Moline, IL: Author.

Mastropieri, M. A., Emerick, K., & Scruggs, T. E. (1988). Mnemonic instruction of science concepts. Behavioral Disorders, 14, 48–56.

Mastropieri, M. A., & Scruggs, T. E. (2001). Promoting inclusion in secondary classrooms. Learning Disability Quarterly, 24, 265–274.

National Institute of Health. (1998). Rehabilitation of persons with traumatic brain injury. National Institute of Health Consensus Statement, 16(1), 1–41

Parente, R., Anderson-Parente, J., & Stapleton, M. (2001). The use of rhymes and mnemonics for teaching cognitive skills to persons with acquired brain injury. Brain Injury Source, 5(1), 16–19.

Ponsford, J., Willmott, C., Rothwell, A., Cameron, P., Ayton, G., Nelms, R., Curran, C., & Ng, K. T. (1999). Cognitive and behavioral outcome following mild traumatic head injury in children. Journal of Head Trauma Rehabilitation, 14, 360–372.

Psychological Corporation. (1998). Wechsler intelligence scale for children—Revised. San Antonio, TX: Harcourt.

Savage, R. C. (1997). Integrating rehabilitation and education services for school-age children with brain injuries. Journal of Head Trauma Rehabilitation, 12(2), 11–20.

Scruggs, T. E., & Mastropieri, M. A. (2000a). The effectiveness of mnemonic instruction for students with learning and behavior problems: An update and research synthesis. Journal of Behavioral Education, 10, 163–173.

Scruggs, T. E., & Mastropieri, M. A. (2000b). Mnemonic strategies improve classroom learning and social behavior. Beyond Behavior, 10(1), 13–17.

Sohlberg, M. M., McLaughlin, K. A., Todis, B., Larsen, J., & Glang, A. S. (2001). What does it take to collaborate with families affected by brain injury? A preliminary model. Journal of Head Trauma Rehabilitation, 16, 498–511.

Swanson, K. (1999). I'll carry the fork! Recovering a life after brain injury. Los Altos, CA: Rising Star.

Tyler, J. S., & Mira, M. P. (1999). Traumatic brain injury in children and adolescents: A sourcebook for teachers and other school personnel. Austin, TX: PRO-ED.

U.S. Department of Education. (2002). To assure the free appropriate public education of all children with disabilities: Twenty-third annual report to Congress on the implementation of the Individuals with Disabilities Education Act. Washington, DC: Author.

Woodcock, R., McGrew, K., & Mather, N. (2003). Woodcock-Johnson III. Itasca, IL: Riverside.

Ylvisaker, M. (1997). Traumatic brain injury rehabilitation: Children and adolescents (2nd ed.). Boston: Butterworth-Heinemann.

Ylvisaker, M., Todis, B., Glang, A., Urbanczyk, B., Franklin, C., DePompei, R., Feeney, T., Maxwell, N. M., Pearson, S., & Tyler, J. S. (2001). Educating students with TBI: Themes and recommendations. Journal of Head Trauma Rehabilitation, 16(1), 76–93.

Chapter 14

Allington, R. L., & Cunningham, P. M. (1996). Schools that work: Where all children read and write. New York: HarperCollins.

American Speech-Language-Hearing Association (ASHA), Committee on Language, Speech, and Hearing Services in the Schools (1980, April). Definitions for communicative disorders and differences, ASHA, 22, pp. 317–318.

American Speech-Language-Hearing Association (ASHA). (1991). Report: Augmentative and alternative communication.

ASHA, 33 (Suppl.), 912.

American Speech-Language-Hearing Association (ASHA). (1993). Definitions of communication disorders and variations. ASHA, 35(Suppl. 10), 40–41.

American Speech-Language-Hearing Association (ASHA). (2002). Communication facts: Incidence and prevalence of communication disorders and hearing loss in children—2002 edition. (http://www.profesional.asha.org/resources/factsheets/children.cfm).

Apel, K., & Swank, L. K. (1999). Second chances: Improving decoding skills in the older student. Language, Speech, and Hearing Services in Schools, 30, 231–242.

Asher, S., & Gazelle, H. (1999). Loneliness, peer relations, and language disorder in childhood. Topics in Language Disorders, 19(2), 16–33.

Battle, D. (1996). Language learning and use by African American children. Topics in Language Disorders, 16, 22–37.

Battle, D. (1998). Communication disorders in multicultural populations (2nd ed.). Boston: Butterworth–Heinemann.

Beukelman, D. R. & Mirenda, P. A., (1998). Augmentative and alternative communication. Baltimore: Brookes.

Bloom, L., & Lahey, M. (1978). Language development and language disorders. New York: Wiley.

Bunce, B. (2003). Children with culturally diverse backgrounds. In L. McCormick, D. F. Loeb, & R. L. Schiefelbusch (Eds.), Supporting children with communication difficulties in inclusive settings School-based language intervention (pp. 347–407). Boston: Allyn & Bacon.

Caruso, A., & Strand, E. (1999). Clinical management of motor speech disorders in children. New York: Thieme.

Chomsky, N. (1957). Syntactic structures. The Hague, The Netherlands: Mouton.

Cirrin, F. (2000). Assessing language in the classroom and curriculum. In J. Tomblin, H. Morris, & D. Spriestersbach (Eds.), Diagnosis in speech language-pathology (pp. 283–314). San Diego: Singular.

Cowley, G. (1997, Spring/Summer). The language explosion. In your child: From birth to three [Special issue]. Newsweek, pp. 16–21.

Cunningham, P. M., & Allington, R. L.,(1999). Classrooms that work: They can all read and write. New York: Addison-Wesley.

Faucheux, S., & Oetting, J. (2001). A clinician-researcher partnership: Working together to improve academic services in middle school. *ASHA Leader Online* (www.asha.org). Retrieved November 18, 2002.

Foley, B. & Staples, A. (2000). *Literature-based language intervention for students who use AAC.* Paper presented at the International Society for Augmentative and Alternative Communication Convention, Washington, DC.

Giangreco, M. (2000). Related services research for students with low-incidence disabilities: Implications for speech-language pathologists in inclusive classrooms. *Language, Speech, and Hearing Services in Schools, 31*(3), 230–239.

Hulit, H. & Howard, M. (2002). *Born to talk: An introduction to speech and language development* (3rd ed). Boston: Allyn & Bacon.

Johnson, J. R., Smith, L. B., & Box, P. (1997). Cognition and communication: Referential strategies used by preschoolers with specific language impairment. *Journal of Speech, Language, and Hearing Research, 40,* 964–974.

Leonard, L. (1987). Is specific language impairment a useful construct? In S. Rosenberg (Ed.), *Applied psycholinguistics* (pp. 1–39). New York: Cambridge University Press.

Loeb, D. (2002a). Diagnostic and descriptive assessment. In L. McCormick, D. Loeb, & D. Schiefelbusch (Eds.), *Supporting children with communication difficulties in inclusive settings: School-based language intervention* (2nd ed., pp. 189–234). Boston: Allyn & Bacon.

Loeb, D. (2002b). Language theory and practice. In L. McCormick, D. Loeb, & D. Schiefelbusch (Eds.), *Supporting children with communication difficulties in Inclusive settings: School-based language intervention* (2nd ed., pp. 43–70). Boston: Allyn & Bacon.

Lombardino, L. J., Riccio, C. A., Hynd, G. W., & Pinheiro, S. B. (1997). Linguistic deficits in children with reading disabilities. *American Journal of Speech–Language Pathology, 6,* 71–78.

MacDonald, J. D., & Rabidoux, P. (1997). *Before your child talks: Practical guides for parents and professionals.* Tallmadge, OH: Family Learning Center.

McCormick, L. (2002a). Introduction to language acquisition. In L. McCormick, D. Loeb, & D. Schiefelbusch (Eds.), *Supporting children with communication difficulties in inclusive settings: School-based language intervention* (2nd ed., pp. 1–42) Boston: Allyn & Bacon.

McCormick, L. (2002b). Policies and practices. In L. McCormick, D. Loeb, & D. Schiefelbusch (Eds.), *Supporting children with communication difficulties in inclusive settings: School-based language intervention* (2nd ed., pp. 155–187). Boston: Allyn & Bacon.

McCormick, L., & Loeb, D. (2002). Characteristics of students with language and communication difficulties. In L. McCormick, D. Loeb, & D. Schiefelbusch (Eds.), *Supporting children with communication difficulties in inclusive settings: School-based language*

intervention (2nd ed., pp. 71–112). Boston: Allyn and Bacon.

McLean, J., & Snyder-McLean, L. (1999). *How children learn language.* San Diego: Singular.

Merritt, D. & Culatta, B. (1998). *Language intervention in the classroom.* San Diego: Singular.

Mervis, C. B., & Bertrand, J. (1997). Developmental relations between cognition and language: Evidence from Williams syndrome. In L. B. Adamson & M. A. Romski (Eds.), *Communication and language acquisition: Discoveries from atypical development* (pp. 75–106). Baltimore: Brookes.

Miranda, A., McCabe, A., & Bliss, L. (1998). Jumping around and leaving things out: A profile of the narrative abilities of children with specific language impairment. *Applied Psycholinguistics, 19,* 647–667.

Ostrosky, M. M., Drasgow, E., & Halle, J. W. (1999). How can I help you get what you want? A communication strategy for students with severe disabilities. *Teaching Exceptional Children, 31*(4), 56–61.

Owens, R. (2001). *Language development: An introduction* (5th ed). Boston: Allyn & Bacon.

Pannbacker, M. (1999). Treatment of vocal nodules: Options and outcomes. *American Journal of Speech-Language Pathology, 8*(3), 209–217.

Sandall, S., & Schwartz, I. (2002. *Building blocks for teaching preschoolers with special needs.* Baltimore: Brookes.

Schneider, P., & Watkins, R. V. (1996). Applying Vygotskian developmental theory to language intervention. *Language, Speech, and Hearing Services in Schools, 27,* 157–167.

Schwartz, S., & Miller, J. E. (1996). *The new language of toys: Teaching communication skills to children with special needs: A guide for parents and teachers.* Bethesda, MD: Woodbine House.

Stuart, S. (2002). Communication: Speech and language. In M. Batshaw (Ed.), *Children with disabilities* (5th ed., pp. 229–241). Baltimore: Brookes.

U.S. Department of Education. (1996). *To assure a free appropriate public education: Eighteenth annual report to Congress on the implementation of the Individuals with Disabilities Education Act.* Washington, DC: Author.

U.S. Department of Education. (2001). *To assure a free appropriate public education: Twenty-third annual report to Congress on the implementation of the individuals with Disabilities Education Act.* Washington, DC: Author.

Verdolini, K. (2000). Voice disorders. In J. Tomblin, H. Morris, & D. Spriestersbach (Eds.), *Diagnosis in speech-language pathology* (2nd ed., pp. 233–280). San Diego: Singular.

Vygotsky, L. S. (1978). *Thought and language.* Cambridge: Harvard University Press.

Vygotsky, L. S. (1987). *The collected works of L. S. Vygotsky* (Vol. 1). New York: Plenum.

Wang, P. P., & Baron, M. A. (1997). Language and communication: Development and disorders. In M. L. Batshaw (Ed.), *Children with disabilities* (4th ed., pp. 275–292). Baltimore: Brookes.

Zebrowski, P. (2000). Stuttering. In J. Tomblin, H. Morris, & D. Spriestersbach (Eds.), *Diagnosis in speech-language pathology* (2nd ed., pp. 199–231). San Diego: Singular.

Chapter 15

Arnos, K. S., Israel, J., & Cunningham, M. (1991). Genetic counseling of the deaf: Medical and cultural considerations. In R. J. Ruben, T. R. Van De Water, & K. P. Steel (Eds.), *Genetics of hearing impairment* (pp. 212–222). New York: New York Academy of Sciences.

Bat-Chava, Y. (2000). Diversity of deaf identities. *American Annals of the Deaf, 145,* 420–428.

Bess, F. H., & Humes, L. E. (1995). *Audiology: The fundamentals* (2nd ed.). Philadelphia: Lippincott Williams & Wilkins.

Bluestone, C. D., & Klein, J. O. (2001). *Otitis media in infants and children* (3rd ed.). Philadelphia: Saunders.

Calvert, D. R. (1986). Speech in perspective. In D. M. Luterman (Ed.), *Deafness in perspective* (pp. 167–191). San Diego: College-Hill.

Carroll, C., & Mather, S. M. (1997). *Movers and shakers: Deaf people who changed the world.* San Diego: Dawn Sign Press.

Cartledge, G., Cochran, L. L., & Paul, P. V. (1996). Social skill self-assessments by adolescents with hearing impairment in residential and public schools. *Remedial and Special Education, 17,* 30–36.

Cazden, C. (1988). *Classroom discourse: The language of teaching and learning.* Portsmouth, NH: Heinemann.

Center for Assessment and Demographic Studies. (1998). *1996–97 Annual survey of deaf and hard of hearing children and youth.* Washington, DC: Gallaudet University.

Cohen, L. G., & Spenciner, L. J. (2002). *Assessment of children and youth* (2nd ed.). Boston: Allyn & Bacon.

Cohen, O. P., Fischgrund, J. E., & Redding, R. (1990). Deaf children from ethnic, linguistic, and racial minority backgrounds: An overview. *American Annals of the Deaf, 135,* 67–73.

Cornett, R. O. (1967). Cued speech. *American Annals of the Deaf, 112,* 3–13.

Coryell, J., & Holcomb, T. K. (1997). The use of sign language and sign systems in facilitating the language acquisition and communication of deaf students. *Language, Speech, and Hearing Services in Schools, 28,* 384–394.

Council for Exceptional Children. (2002). *Performance-based standards for the preparation and licensure of special educators.* Reston, VA: Author.

Diefendorf, A. O. (1999). Screening for hearing loss in infants. *Volta Review, 99*(5), 43–61.

Gallaudet Research Institute. (2002, January). *Regional and national summary report of data from the 2000–2001 annual survey of deaf and hard of hearing children and youth.* Washington, DC: Gallaudet University.

Garton, A., & Pratt, C. (1998). *Learning to be literate: The development of spoken and written language*. Oxford, England: Blackwell.

Hall, C. J. (1998). The association between racelessness and achievement among African American deaf adolescents. *American Annals of the Deaf, 143*, 55–61.

Hilburn, S., Marini, I., & Slate, J. R. (1997). Self-esteem among deaf versus hearing children with deaf versus hearing parents. *JADARA, 30*(2 & 3), 9–12.

Holt, J. (1993). Stanford Achievement Test—8th edition: Reading comprehension subgroups results. *American Annals of the Deaf, 138*, 172–175.

Hyde, M., Power, D., & Cliffe, S. (1992). Teachers' communication with their deaf students: An Australian study. *Sign Language Studies, 75*, 159–166.

Kluwin, T. N. (1993). Cumulative effects of mainstreaming on the achievement of deaf adolescents. *Exceptional Children, 60*, 73–81.

Mayer, P., & Lowenbraun, S. (1990). Total communication use among elementary teachers of hearing-impaired children. *American Annals of the Deaf, 135*, 257–263.

Meadow-Orlans, K. P., Mertens, D. M., Sass-Lehrer, M. A., & Scott-Olson, K. (1997). Support services for parents and their children who are deaf or hard of hearing: A national survey. *American Annals of the Deaf, 142*, 278–288.

Moores, D. F. (2001). *Educating the deaf: Psychology, principles, and practices* (5th ed.). Boston: Houghton Mifflin.

Musselman, C., MacKay, S., Trehub, S. E., & Eagle, R. S. (1996). Communicative competence and psychosocial development in deaf children and adolescents. In J. H. Beitchman, N. J. Cohen, M. M. Konstantareas, & R. Tannock (Eds.), *Language, learning, and behavior disorders* (pp. 555–570). Cambridge, England: Cambridge University Press.

National Center for Education Statistics. (2002a). *The digest of education statistics* (http://nces.ed.gov).

National Center for Health Statistics. (2002b). *Fast stats A to Z/disabilities* (www.cdc.gov/nchs).

Northern, J. L., & Downs, M. P. (2002). *Hearing in children* (5th ed.). Philadelphia: Lippincott Williams & Wilkins.

Perez, B. (1996). Instructional conversations as opportunities for English language acquisition for culturally and linguistically diverse students. *Language Arts, 73*, 173–181.

Salvia, J., & Ysseldyke, J. E. (2001). *Assessment* (78th ed.). Boston: Houghton Mifflin.

Schirmer, B. R. (2000). *Language and literacy development in children who are deaf*. Boston: Allyn & Bacon.

Schirmer, B. R. (2001). *Pyschological, social, and educational dimensions of deafness*. Boston: Allyn & Bacon.

Schoem, S. R. (1997). Update on otitis media in children. *Volta Review, 99*, 97–117.

Schum, R. L. (2000). Developing social skills in elementary school children. *Volta Voices, 7*(5), 14–18.

Snow, C. E. (1986). Conversations with children. In P. Fletcher & M. Garman (Eds.), *Language acquisition: Studies in first language development* (pp. 69–89). Cambridge, England: Cambridge University Press.

Stach, B. A. (1998). *Clinical audiology: An introduction*. San Diego: Singular.

Stephens, M. I. (1988). Pragmatics. In M. A. Nippold (Ed.), *Later language development: Ages nine through nineteen* (pp. 247–262). San Diego: Singular.

Stone, P. (1988). *Blueprint for developing conversational competence: A planning/instruction model with detailed scenarios*. Washington, DC: Alexander Graham Bell Association for the Deaf.

Strauss, M. (1999). Hearing loss and cytomegalovirus. *Volta Review, 99*(5), 71–74.

van Gurp, S. (2001). Self-concept of deaf secondary students in different educational settings. *Journal of Deaf Studies and Deaf Education, 6*, 54–69.

Wolk, S., & Allen, T. E. (1984). A 5-year follow-up of reading comprehension achievement of hearing-impaired students in special education programs. *Journal of Special Education, 18*, 161–176.

Woodward, J., & Allen, T. (1993). Sociolinguistic differences: U.S. teachers in residential schools and non-residential schools. *Sign Language Studies, 81*, 361–374.

Wright, D. (1993). *Deafness: An autobiography*. London: Mandarin.

Chapter 16

American Foundation for the Blind. (1954). *The Pine Brook Report: National work session on the education of the blind with the sighted*. New York: Author.

American Foundation for the Blind. (1957). *Itinerant teaching service for blind children: Proceedings of a national work session held at Bear Mountain, New York, August 20–24, 1956*. New York: Author.

Anthony, T. L. (2000). Performing a functional low vision assessment. In F. M. D'Andrea & C. Farrenkopf (Eds.), *Looking to learn: Promoting literacy for students with low vision* (pp. 32–83). New York: AFB Press.

Barraga, N. C. & Erin, J. N. (2001). *Visual impairments and learning* (4th ed.). Austin, TX: PRO-ED.

Bishop, V. E. (1996). *Teaching visually impaired children* (2nd ed.). Springfield, IL: Thomas.

Bradley-Johnson, S. (1994). Psychoeducational assessment of students who are visually impaired or blind. Austin, TX: PRO-ED.

Caton, H., Pester, E., & Bradley, E. J. (1980). *Patterns: The primary braille reading program*. Louisville, KY: American Printing House for the Blind.

Corn, A. L., & Sacks, S. Z. (1994). The impact of non-driving on adults with visual impairments. *Journal of Visual Impairment and Blindness, 88*(1), 53–68.

Erin, J. (1996). Children with multiple and visual disabilities. In *Children with visual impairments: A parents' guide* (pp. 287–316). Bethesda, MD: Woodbine House.

Erin, J. N., & Paul, B. (1996). Functional vision assessment and instruction of children and youths in academic programs. In A. L. Corn & A. J. Koenig (Eds.), *Foundations of low vision: Clinical and functional perspectives* (pp. 185–220). New York: AFB Press.

Fazzi, D. L., Kirk, S. A., Pearce, R. S., Pogrund, R. L., & Wolfe, S. (1992). Social focus: Developing socioemotional, play, and self-help skills in young blind and visually impaired children. In R. L. Pogrund, D. L. Fazzi, & J. S. Lampert (Eds.), *Early focus: Working with young blind and visually impaired children and their families* (pp. 50–69). New York: American Foundation for the Blind.

Ferrell, K. A. (1996). Your child's development. In M. C. Holbrook (Ed.), *Children with visual impairments: A parent's guide* (pp. 73–96). Bethesda, MD: Woodbine House.

Ferrell, K. A. (2000). Growth and development of young children. In M. C. Holbrook & A. J. Koenig (Eds.), *Foundations of Education* (2nd ed.). Vol. 1: *History and theory of teaching children and youths with visual impairments* (pp. 111–134). New York: AFB Press.

Freeman, R. D., Goetz, E., Richards, D. P., & Groenveld, M. (1991). Defiers of negative prediction: A 14-year follow-up study of legally blind children. *Journal of Visual Impairment and Blindness, 85*(9), 365–370.

Harrell, L. (1992). *Children's vision concerns: Looks beyond the eyes!* Placerville, CA: L. Harrell Productions.

Hatlen, P. H. (1980–1981). Mainstreaming, origin of a concept. *Blindness Annual*, pp. 1–9.

Hatlen, P. H. (1996). The core curriculum for blind and visually impaired students, including those with additional disabilities. *RE:view, 28*(1), 25–32.

Hatlen, P. H., & Curry, S. A. (1987). In support of specialized programs for blind and visually impaired children: The impact of vision loss on learning. *Journal of Visual Impairment and Blindness, 81*(1), 7–13.

Hatlen, P. H., LeDuc, P., & Canter, P. (1975). The blind adolescent life skills center. *New Outlook for the Blind*, pp. 109–115.

Hazekamp, J., & Huebner, K. M. (1989). *Program planning and evaluation for blind and visually impaired students: National guidelines for excellence*. New York: American Foundation for the Blind.

Hoben, M., & Lindstrom, V. (1980). Evidence of isolation in the mainstream. *Journal of Visual Impairment and Blindness, 74*(8), 289–292.

Huebner, K. M. (2000). Visual impairment. In M. C. Holbrook & A. J. Koenig (Eds.), *Foundations of education (2nd ed.). Vol. 1: History and theory of teaching children and youths with visual impairments (pp. 55–76). New York: AFB Press.

Kirchner, C., & Diament, S. (1999). Estimates of the number of visually impaired students, their teachers, and orientation and mobility specialists. Journal of Visual Impairment and Blindness, 93(9), 600–606.

Koenig, A. J., & Farrenkopf, C. (1997). Essential experiences to undergird the early development of literacy. Journal of Visual Impairment and Blindness, 91(1), 14–24.

Koenig, A. J., & Holbrook, M. C. (1993). Learning media assessment of students with visual impairments: A resource guide for teachers. Austin: Texas School for the Blind and Visually Impaired.

Koenig, A. J., & Holbrook, M. C. (2000). Planning instruction in unique skills. In M. C. Holbrook & A. J. Koenig (Eds.), Foundations of education (2nd ed.). Vol. 2: Instructional strategies for teaching children and youths with visual impairments (pp. 196–221). New York: AFB Press.

Kuestler, F. A. (1976). The unseen minority: A social history of blindness in the United States. New York: McKay.

Lewis, S. & Allman, C. B. (2000a). Educational programming. In A. J. Koenig & M. C. Holbrook (Eds.), Foundations of education (2nd ed.). Vol. 1: History and theory of teaching children and youths with visual impairments (pp. 218–259). New York: AFB Press.

Lewis, S. & Allman, C. B. (2000b). Seeing eye to eye: An administrator's guide to students with low vision. New York: AFB Press.

Lewis, S., & Russo, R. (1997). Educational assessment for students who have visual impairments with other disabilities. In S. Z. Sacks & R. K. Silberman (Eds.), Educating students who have visual impairments with other disabilities (pp. 39–71). Baltimore: Brookes.

Lowenfeld, B. (1973). Psychological considerations. In B. Lowenfeld (Ed.), The visually handicapped child in school (pp. 27–60). New York: Day.

Lussenhop, K., & Corn, A. L. (2002). Comparative studies of the reading performance of students with low vision. RE:view, 34(2), 57–69.

Milian, M. (2000). Multicultural issues. In A. J. Koenig & M. C. Holbrook (Eds.), Foundations of education (2nd ed.). Vol. 1: History and theory of teaching children and youths with visual impairments (pp. 197–217). New York: AFB Press.

Nelson, K. A., & Dimitrova. E. (1993). Severe visual impairment in the United States and in each state. Journal of Visual Impairment and Blindness, 87(3), 80–85.

Pugh, G. S., & Erin, J. (Eds.). (1999). Blind and visually impaired students: Educational service guidelines. Watertown, MA: Perkins School for the Blind.

Sacks, S. Z. (1998). Educating students who have visual impairments with other disabilities: An overview. In S. Z. Sacks & R. K. Silberman, Educating students who have visual impairments with other disabilities (pp. 3–38). Baltimore: Brookes.

Sacks, S. Z., & Silberman, R. K. (2000). Social skills. In A. J. Koenig & M. C. Holbrook (Eds.), Foundations of education (2nd ed.). Vol. 2: Instructional strategies for teaching children and youths with visual impairments (pp. 616–652). New York: AFB Press.

Scott, E. P., Jan, J. E., & Freeman, R. D. (1995). Can't your child see? A guide for parents of visually impaired children (3rd ed.). Austin, TX: PRO-ED.

Spungin, S. (Consulting Ed.). (2002). When you have a visually impaired student in your classroom: A guide for teachers. New York: AFB Press.

Stiles, S., & Knox, R. (1996). Medical issues, treatments and professionals. In M. C. Holbrook (Ed.), Children with visual impairments: A parent's guide (pp. 21–48). Bethesda, MD: Woodbine House.

U.S. Department of Education. (2000). Policy guidance on educating blind and visually impaired students. Washington, DC: Author.

U. S. Department of Education. (2001). To assure a free appropriate public education: Twenty-third annual report to Congress on the implementation of the Individuals with Disabilities Education Act. Washington, DC: Author.

Wilkinson, M. E. (1996). Clinical low vision services. In A. L. Corn & A. J. Koenig (Eds.), Foundations of low vision: Clinical and functional perspectives (pp. 143–182). New York: AFB Press.

Wolffe, K. (1996). Career education for students with visual impairments. RE:view 28(2), 89–93.

Wolffe, K. E., Sacks, S. Z., & Thomas, K. L. (2000). Focused on: Importance and need for social skills. New York: AFB Press.

Young, L. (1997). Adding positive experiences with dogs to the curriculum. RE:view, 29(2), 55–61.

Abery, B., 266
Achenbach, T. M., 138
Achilles, C. M., 69
Ackinclose, Matthew, 130–131, 160
ACTBIC, 376
Adams, L., 44
Adams, L. W., 6
Addison, M. M., 149, 150, 151
Adelman, H. S., 6
Advisory Committee on TBI in Children, 374, 379
AFL-CIO, 141
Agency for Health Care Policy and Research, 176
Agnew, C. M., 317
Agran, M., 44, 57, 59, 81, 230, 240, 241, 242–244, 272
Ahlgren, C., 67
Ajibola, O., 185
Akshoomoff, N., 289
Alberston-Sears, JoLynn, 399
Alberto, P. A., 264, 345, 347, 348
Albin, R. W., 287
Alexander, D., 233, 289
Algozzine, B., 241
Alisanski, S., 285
Alkin, M. C., 238
Allen, T., 442
Allen, T. E., 432
Alley, G. R., 119
Allington, Richard, 473
Allington, R. L., 401, 419
Allman, C. B., 459, 469
Allsopp, D. H., 104
Alter, M., 10, 234
Alwell, M., 72, 267
Amanullah, S., 285
Amer, K. S., 322
American Academy of Allergy, Asthma, and Immunology, 317, 318
American Academy of Neurology, 173
American Academy of Pediatrics, 175, 314, 324
American Association on Mental Retardation (AAMR), 226, 227, 229, 230, 231, 235
American Cancer Society, 320

American Diabetes Association, 322, 326
American Federation of Teachers, 44, 141
American Foundation for the Blind, 469
American Humane Society, 138
American Lung Association, 318, 319
American Medical Association, 314
American Psychiatric Association (APA), 134, 135, 137, 165, 166, 175, 176, 284, 285
Anastapoulos, A. D., 178
Anastopoulos, A. D., 178, 179
Anderegg, M. L., 7
Anderson-Parente, J., 395
Andrade, H. G., 208
Andrews, J. E., 68
Anthony, T. L., 465
Anzalone, M. E., 287
Apel, K., 409
Apple Computer, 298
Appleton, R., 379
Aquero, Rae Jean, 43
Archawamety, T., 239
Ardilia, A., 178
Arert.org, 323
Armstrong, F. D., 320, 328
Arnos, K. S., 432
Arora, T., 268
Arvidson, H. H., 356
ASHA, 400, 406, 409, 418
Asher, S., 417
Associated Press, 178, 327
Atler, M., 10, 234
Auchenbach, T. M., 179
Augustin, R., 137
Ault, M. M., 274
Austin, V. L., 90
Averill, Nancy, 420–421
Averitt, D., 326

Bacon, E., 84
Baer, D. M., 228
Baghurst, P., 232
Bahr, M. W., 22
Bailey, Jill, 452
Bailey, L. T., 190
Baldwin, A. Y., 200
Baldwin, T., 379

Bandura, A., 185
Bandy, H., 69
Barbarin, O. A., 314
Baren, M., 172
Barker, K. S., 69
Barkey, M. E., 315
Barkley, R., 164
Barkley, R. A., 191
Barkley, Russell A., 164, 167, 168, 169, 170, 172, 173, 174, 175, 178, 180, 190, 302
Barnes, K. J., 350
Barnett, C., 69
Barnhill, G., 288
Barnhill, G. P., 284, 285, 288
Baron, M. A., 406, 410
Barraga, N. C., 461
Barry, R. J., 174
Bashinksi, Susan, 51–52, 61, 62
Bassarath, L., 141
Bat-Chava, Y., 431
Bates, P. E., 240
Batshaw, M. L., 231, 232, 260, 264, 289
Battle, D., 401, 402
Bauer, A. M., 113
Bauerle, P. R., 207
Baumeister, A. A., 233
Bauwens, J., 88
Baxter, J., 119
Beach, J., 189
Beach, Mary Jane, 189, 190
Bear, G. G., 69
Bebko, J. M., 229
Beethoven, Ludwig van, 445
Begley, S., 326
Behrens, T. R., 436
Belcher, R. G., 302
Bellinger, D. C., 232
Bender, B. G., 318
Bender, W. N., 109
Benito, N., 290, 299
Benner, G. J., 140
Bennett, T., 72
Benz, M. R., 37
Berger, O. G., 232
Berger, S. L., 221
Bergland, M., 394
Bergman, L., 134

Berguson, K. S., 133
Berktold, J., 367
Bertrand, J., 408
Bertrando, R., 185, 186
Bess, F. H., 432
Bessell, Ann G., 320, 321, 330, 331, 335
Bessell, Jonathan, 331
Best, A. M., 144
Best, S. J., 344, 345
Beukelman, D. R., 258, 269
Beuter, E., 180
Beverly, C. L., 325
Beyerck, Chandra, 73
Bigge, J. L., 344, 345, 347, 349, 351, 356
Biklin, D., 6
Bishop, K. D., 88, 269, 270, 277, 357
Bishop, V. E., 466
Blake, C., 378
Blanchard, C., 241
Blank, R. M., 234
Blankenship, Kelsey, 162–163, 191
Bliss, L., 410
Block, M. E., 327
Bloom, B. S., 198
Bloom, L., 84, 408
Bloom, L. A., 332
Blosser, J. L., 374, 380
Bluestone, C. D., 433
Blumberg, M. J., 320
Bocian, K. M., 138, 234
Bock, S. J., 287
Bodfish, J. W., 287
Boice, M. M., 339
Bond, V., 376
Bonner, M. J., 314
Boone, R., 124
Booth, J. E., 183
Bornstein, H., 430
Bostic, J. Q., 135
Boulware, G.-L., 290
Bowker, A., 138
Box, P., 410
Boyd, Karen, 350–351, 360
Boyer, L., 299
Boyer, W. A. R., 69
Boyle, C., 231
Boys, C., 48
Bradley, E. J., 470
Bradley, K. L., 190
Bradley, W., 164
Bradley-Johnson, S., 468
Brady, M. P., 72
BrainTrain, 186
Brantlinger, E. A., 234
Bray, N. W., 228
Brazil, N., 67
Brendtro, L. K., 8, 132, 150, 156–157
Bricker, D., 121
Brim, S. A., 183, 185
Brinckerhoff, L., 115

Bristol, M., 289
Broer, S. M., 85
Brokenleg, Martin, 8, 150, 156–157
Bromley, J., 234
Brooke, M. H., 349
Brooks-Gunn, J., 232
Broome, M. E., 312, 328, 331, 333, 336
Broughton, Debbie, 317
Browder, D., 241
Browder, D. M., 257
Brown, Amala, 424–425, 453
Brown, C. R., 174
Brown, F., 257, 267, 269
Brown, L., 67
Brown, Robyn, 449
Brown, R. T., 328
Brown, W. K., 132
Brownell, M. D., 297
Brownell, M. T., 149
Browning, Jackie, 43
Bruder, M. B., 328
Bruer, J. T., 202
Bruininks, R. H., 229–230
Brumbley, Sarah, 102, 103, 123
Bruner, J. P., 350
Bruns, D., 72
Bryant, B., 34
Bryant-Comstock, S., 142
Bryson, S. E., 260
Bui, Y., 266
Bullis, M., 144
Bullock, C., 150
Bunce, B., 401
Buntaine, R., 133
Buonamano, L., 164
Burrell, L., 332
Burstein, J. R., 356, 359
Bursuck, W. D., 107, 119, 121
Bush, T., 191
Bussing, R., 179–180
Butler, F. M., 107
Buyer, D. M., 375, 378, 381
Bybee, J., 229

Caine, A., 234
Calvert, D. R., 441
Campbell, P. H., 257
Canale, A., 149
Cant, M. C., 323
Canter, P., 469
Canu, W. H., 183
Carlso, C. L., 183
Carlson, J. K., 287, 297
Carney, J., 378, 379
Carpenter, M., 285
Carr, E. G., 286, 287, 294
Carroll, Cathryn, 445
Carroll, D., 85
Carta, J. J., 327
Carter, A., 285

Carter, Alexandra, 456, 457
Carter, C. M., 298
Carter, E. W., 273
Carter, M., 258
Cartledge, G., 144, 431
Caruso, A., 405
Casat, C. D., 179
Cassini, K. K., 337
Castellano, J. A., 204, 207
Castellanos, F. X., 173
Castles, A., 110
Catlin, A., 336
Caton, H., 470
Cazden, C., 442
Center for Assessment and Demographic
    Studies, 432, 433, 434
Centers for Disease Control (CDC), 232,
    323, 324, 325, 327, 339, 347, 381, 391
Chamberlain, J. A., 235
Chambers, A., 72
Chambers, J. G., 32
Chandler, L. K., 287, 290, 292
Chapman, C. D., 37
Chapman, D. A., 232
Chapman, S. B., 378
Chard, D., 107
Charkow, W. B., 336
Cheatham, S. K., 289
Chen, X., 138
Cheney, D., 147
Children and Adults with Attention
    Deficit Disorder (CHADD), 169,
    174, 180, 190
Children's Defense Fund, 10
Chinn, Ginny, 446, 448
Chinn, P. C., 11, 93
Chomsky, N., 409
Church, C., 285
Cirrin, F., 414
Clark, B., 198, 200
Clark, Karen, 450
Clarke, A. R., 174
Clayton, J., 48
Clees, T. J., 229
Clement, P., 185
Cleveland Clinic Foundation, 315
Cliffe, S., 442
Cloninger, C., 267
Close, D. W., 142
Cochran, L. L., 431
Cohen, D. E., 233
Cohen, D. J., 288, 289
Cohen, O. P., 431
Cohen, P., 71
Cohen, R., 144
Coie, 141
Coleman, M., 142
Collins, B. C., 123, 272
Colson, S., 317, 320
Colvin, G., 135

Comford, Margaret, 390, 391–392
Committee on Pediatric AIDS, 325, 326
Committee on School Health, 331
Commonwealth of Massachusetts, 327
Conderman, G., 290
Conner, M. C., 317
Conti-D'Antonio, M., 185, 186
Coopersmith, 156
Copeland, S. R., 273
Cordero, C. F., 231
Corn, A. L., 461, 469
Cornett, R. O., 441
Corr, C. A., 336
Corso, R. M., 95
Coryell, J., 442
Cosby, Bill, 332
Cosden, M., 327
Costenbader, V., 133
Coulter, D. L., 227, 232
Council for Exceptional Children, 7, 179, 427
Council of State Directors for Programs for
        the Gifted, 203
Courtney, J. C., 376
Coutinho, M. J., 234
Covey, S. R., 135
Cowley, G., 406
Coyne, M. D., 107
Coyne, P., 54, 55
Cramond, B., 169, 207
Crawford, A., 327
Csikszentmihalyi, M., 207
Culatta, B., 400
Cummings, Donna, 42, 71
Cunningham, E., 290
Cunningham, M., 432
Cunningham, P. M., 401, 419
Curry, S. A., 459
Cutler, S. K., 315, 316
Cyr, B., 209

Dahl, B. B., 169
Dahlquist, C. M., 287, 290, 292
Daley, T., 298
Dalrymple, N. J., 286, 287, 297
Daly, L. E., 347
D'Andrea, F. M., 356
Datta, H., 110
Daunic, A. P., 149
Davern, L., 47, 241
Davies, D. K., 228
Davis, G. A., 201
Davis, Katie, 188
Davis, L., 67
Davis, M. D., 121
Dawson, G., 287, 298
Deardorff, K., 11
deBettencourt, L. U., 34
DeCoste, D. C., 359
Decouflé, P., 231
Deemer, S. A., 69

Defries, J. C., 110
Deitz, J., 297
Delisle, J. R., 215
DeLorenzo, James, 378
Deluca, D., 72
Demchak, M., 229
Dendy, C. A. Z., 173
Denning, C. B., 235
Dennis, R., 267
Dennis, R. E., 85
Denny, G., 326
DePaepe, P., 314, 319, 328, 330
Department of Mental Health Services, 164
DePompei, R., 374, 378, 380
Derby, K. M., 287
Deshler, D., 115, 116
Deshler, D. D., 115
Dev, P. C., 109
DeVault, G., 300
DeWaard, J., 5
Dickson, K., 205
Diefendorf, A. O., 434
Diehl, J., 189
Dieker, L., 22
Dietrich, K. M., 232
DiFranza, J. R., 327
Dillon, Ann, 301
Dimitrova, E., 463
Doctor's Guide, 323
Doelling, J., 314
Doering, K., 67, 90
Doman, G., 202
Doman, J., 202
Donne, John, 4
Donnellan, A. M., 287
Doran, R. L., 215
Doren, B., 37
Dormans, J. P., 344, 345
Dowling, C. G., 317
Downing, J. E., 264, 351
Dowrick, M., 258
Doyle, M. B., 85, 267
Draper, Becky, 362
Draper, I. L., 49, 53
Drasgow, E., 417
Dreikurs, R., 156
Drinkwater, S., 229
Duff-Mallans, K., 31
Duhaney, L. M. G., 70
Duncan, B. B., 139
Duncan, G. J., 232
Dunlap, G., 228, 299
Dunlap, Glen, 290, 298, 299
Dunn, W., 287
DuPaul, G. J., 149, 178, 190, 328
Durfee, Camille, 344

Eagle, R. S., 431
Earles, T. L., 287
Eber, Lucille, 147, 158

Ebner, F. F., 202
Edelbrock, C. S., 138
Edelman, S., 267
Edelman, S. W., 85
Edison, Thomas Alva, 445
Education, U.S. Department of, 4, 5, 6, 13,
        15, 61, 63, 64, 65, 85, 110, 111, 116,
        132, 133, 142, 144, 147, 205, 226,
        234, 237, 261, 268, 289, 292, 293,
        330, 349, 353, 381, 410, 411, 414,
        415, 439, 463, 468, 469
Edwards, J. K., 135
Edwards, Kyle, 310–311
Ehrle, K., 69
Eisenberger, J., 185, 186
Eldridge, Pam, 42
Elkind, David, 203
Elliott, J. L., 48
Ellis, N. R., 227
Ely, Karen, 2
Emerick, K., 385
Emerson, E., 234
Engelmann, S., 119
Engemann, J. F., 215
Engleman, M. D., 258, 259
Epilepsy Foundation of America, 315, 317, 326
Epstein, M. H., 140, 146
Erickson, J. D., 347
Erickson, R., 47, 113
Erin, J., 459, 466, 469, 479
Erin, J. N., 461, 466
Erwin, E., 70
Eshilian, L., 276, 277
Evans, I. M., 276
Evans, J. R., 264

Faber, A., 140
Fake, S., 300
Falvey, M., 264, 276, 277
Falvey, M. A., 269, 270, 357
Family Connection Staff, 300
Farlow, L., 257
Farner, C. D., 138, 159
Farrenkopf, C., 471
Faucheux, Susan, 421
Faw, L., 159
Fazzi, D. L., 461
Feeney, T. J., 379
Fein, D., 285
Feldman, M. A., 232
Ferguson, D. L., 86
Ferrell, K. A., 459, 460
Fetko, K., 272
Fewster, D., 378
Finn, J. D., 69
Fischer, S., 178
Fischgrund, J. E., 431
Fisher, D., 70, 71, 267
Fisher, S., 228
Fishkin, A. S., 207

Fister, S., 272
Fleitas, J., 331, 332
Fletcher, J. M., 104
Fletcher, K. L., 228
Flumer, D. L., 333
Foegen, A., 150
Foley, B., 419
Fombonne, E., 288, 289
Fonagy, P., 133
Ford, A., 47, 67, 241
Ford, D., 12
Ford, D. Y., 205
Ford, J. D., 141
Forest, M., 264
Forgan, J. W., 71
Forness, S. R., 68, 72, 104, 109, 132, 133, 139
Forney, M. N., 264, 345
Forney, P. E., 347, 348, 356
Fossey, R., 180
Fowler, S. E., 273
Fox, D. D., 376
Fox, Lise, 290, 299
Fox, M. A., 323
Fox, N. E., 69
Frankel, F., 334
Franklin, B., 138
Fraser, Chris, 162–163, 171, 176, 187
Frattura-Kampshroer, 67
Frederiksen, J. R., 209
Freeman, R. D., 459, 462
Freeman, S. F. N., 238
French, N. K., 85
Friedlander, Rhonda, 402
Friend, M., 90, 107, 119, 121
Friss, G., 173, 174
Fryman, J., 288
Fryxell, D., 72
Fuchs, D., 22
Fuchs, D. M., 105, 107, 110
Fuchs, L. S., 22, 105
Fujiura, G. T., 10, 13, 141, 232, 234
Fuller, D. R., 356
Fuller, K., 268

Gadow, K. D., 175
Gagne, F., 197
Gallaudet Research Institute, 432, 433
Gamel-McCormick, M., 121
Ganz, J. B., 297
Gardill, M. C., 147
Gardner, Howard, 197–198, 199, 200, 216
Garner, Jarris, 372–373, 396
Garrison-Kane, L., 314
Gartner, A., 6, 66
Garton, A., 443
Gayan, J., 110
Gazelle, H., 417
Geary, Patricia, 378
Geenen, K., 47

Genochio, Jennifer, 43, 47
Gersten, R., 108
Gessner, L. J., 141
Getch, Y. Q., 318, 319
Giacobbe, A. C., 46, 47, 52
Giangreco, B. F., 85
Giangreco, M., 401, 418
Giangreco, M. F., 85, 267
Gierach, J., 271
Gilberts, G. H., 272
Gillette, Elexis, 456–457, 485
Gimblett, R. J., 369
Glang, A. S., 378
Glassberg, L. A., 140
Glennen, S. L., 359
Gliner, J., 230
Goeckel, T. M., 348
Goetz, E., 462
Goetz, L., 67, 72, 90, 267
Goffman, E., 7
Goldman, S. K., 159
Goldstein, M. J., 135
Goldstein, S., 176
Goleman, Daniel, 198
Gollnick, D. M., 11, 93
Gordon, B., 235
Gordon, Mary, 481–482
Gottlieb, B. W., 10, 234
Gottlieb, J., 10, 234
Goya, Francisco, 445
Gradoudas, Stelios, 9, 10
Graham, S., 107
Grandin, Temple, 287, 288
Gray, C. A., 297
Green, A. D., 298
Green, P., 48
Greene, P., 379
Greenspan, J., 322
Greenspan, S., 229
Greenspan, S. I., 299
Greet, T., 323
Gresham, F., 142
Gresham, F. M., 68, 138, 139, 234
Gressard, R. P., 366
Griffin, H. C., 258, 259
Griffin, L. W., 258, 259
Griffin, S. M., 69
Griffin-Shirley, N., 478
Grigorenko, E. L., 140
Grisham-Brown, J., 121
Griswold, D. E., 284
Grizenko, N., 172, 173
Groenveld, M., 462
Grosenick, J. K., 66
Grosse, S. J., 325
Grossman, H. J., 237
Grossman, J., 285
Grove, K. A., 70
Guess, D., 257
Guest, C. L., 135

Guralnick, M. J., 247
Gustafson, K. E., 314
Guth, C., 273
Gutman, S., 47
Guy, B., 49

Haensly, P. A., 215
Hagiwara, T., 284, 288, 298
Hagmann, M., 178
Hall, C. J., 431
Hall, H. R., 315
Hall, M., 278
Hall, N., 135
Hall, P. S., 135
Hall, Rebecca, 130–131
Hallahan, D. P., 109
Halle, J. W., 417
Hallowell, E. M., 141, 169, 188
Halvorsen, A., 72
Hamburg, Carrie, 43
Hamilton, D., 200
Hampton, G., 317, 318
Hamre-Nietupski, S., 257
Hand-in-Paw, 138
Handler, M. W., 147
Hanson, M. J., 82
Hardman, M., 72
Harman, P. L., 164, 188
Harness, Donald, 80, 98
Harr, J. J., 32
Harrell, L., 459, 461
Harrell, Lois, 481
Harriott, W. A., 257
Harris, H., 205
Harris, K. R., 107
Harris, S. L., 286
Harris, Sweet Alice, 245
Harrower, J. K., 298
Harry, Beth, 82, 94, 96
Hartsough, C., 139
Hartsough, C. S., 172
Hassler, C. R., 366
Hatlen, P. H., 459, 469, 479
Hatton, C., 234
Haupt, Robin, 362
Hawken, L. S., 295
Hayes, J. S., 339
Hazekamp, J., 466
Heal, L. W., 37
Health and Human Services, U.S. Department of, 135, 375
Hebert, T. P., 215
Heins, B., 89
Heller, K. W., 264, 344, 345, 347, 348, 351, 356
Helms, J. L., 318
Hemmeter, M. L., 121, 123
Henderson, C. W., 172, 320
Henderson, L. M., 202
Hendricks, T. B., 272

Heron, T. E., 328
Hewitt, M. B., 135
Hibbard, J., 276, 277
Higgins, K., 124
Hightower, J., 72
Hilburn, S., 431
Hildebrand, D. K., 235
Hill, D. A., 288
Hilton, A., 238
Hirose-Hatae, A., 67, 90
Hishinuma, E., 240
Hitchcock, C., 54
HIV University, 339
Hoben, M., 469
Hock, M. F., 115
Hodge, K. A., 215
Hoerr, T. R., 81
Hoff, K. E., 149
Hoffbauer, D., 394
Holbrook, M. C., 466, 476, 478, 479
Holcomb, T. K., 442
Hollmann, F., 11
Hollowell, J. G., 231
Hollowood, T. M., 72
Holmes, C. S., 323
Holt, J., 431
Honein, M. A., 347
Hook, J., 258
Hooper, S. R., 140
Hoover, D. W., 172
Horan, L., 187, 188
Horn, L., 367
Horner, R. A., 295
Horner, R. H., 228, 287
Horner, S. D., 318, 320
Hosie, T., 180
Hoskins, Briana, 194–195, 222
Hosp, J. L., 14
Hostler, S. L., 366
Hott, Charlotte, 131
Hourcade, J. J., 88
House, A., 48
Howard, M., 400, 406
Howland, L. C., 327
Howlin, P., 285
Hoy, William, 445
Huebner, K. M., 458, 466
Huff, B., 142
Huff, Barbara, 142
Hughes, C., 241, 272, 273, 285
Hulit, H., 400, 406
Humes, L. E., 432
Hunt, P., 67, 72, 90, 267
Hurte, M., 48
Hux, K., 376
Hwang, B., 273, 285
Hyde, M., 442
Hyde, M. S., 238
Hylton Rushton, C., 336
Hynd, G. W., 409

Iacono, T., 258
Ialongo, N., 154, 158
Ida, D. J., 144
Ingersoll, B., 175
Israel, J., 432
Iwata, B. A., 287

Jackson, Carla, 2
Jackson, R., 54
Jacobson, J. L., 327
Jacobson, S. W., 327
Jacy Group, 318, 319
Jakubik, L. D., 314
Jan, J. E., 459
Jannarone, Anne, 452, 453
Jefferson-Aker, C. R., 326
Jenkens, J. R., 72
Jenson, C. E., 144
Johnson, D. R., 81
Johnson, D. W., 90
Johnson, F. P., 90
Johnson, G., 326
Johnson, J. R., 410
Johnson, L. J., 66, 80, 88
Johnson, R. L., 326
Jolivette, K., 140
Jones, Jeremy, 282–283, 306–307
Jordan, L., 104
Jorgensen, C. M., 86, 269
Jorgensen, J., 67
Joseph and Rose Kennedy Institute of
    Ethics, 326
Juhrs, P. D., 302
Jurasek, G., 364

Kalwinsky, D. K., 320
Kalyanpur, Maya, 82, 94, 96
Kame'enui, E. J., 107
Kanny, E. M., 297
Kansas State Department of Education,
    51–52, 269
Kapp-Simon, K., 339
Karasoff, P., 67, 90
Karolyi, C. V., 200
Karp, Naomi, 142
Karvonen, M., 241
Katsiyannis, A., 5, 239, 290
Katz, S., 336
Kauffman, J. M., 68, 140, 153
Kaufman, P., 37
Kavale, K. A., 68, 72, 104, 105, 109, 113,
    132, 133
Kay, K., 209
Kea, C. D., 144
Kearney, C., 201
Kearney, K., 201
Kearns, J. F., 278
Kelly, S. J., 289
Kemp, C. E., 361
Kemp, C. R., 215

Kennedy, C. H., 72, 267
Keogh, B. K., 133
Kercheer, Kelli, 16
Kerns, L. L., 136
Kesson, K., 240
Kiefer-O'Donnell, R., 72
Kiel, Kris, 470
Kiel, Tom, 470
Kilgo, J. L., 121
Kimm, C. H., 269, 270, 357
King-Sears, M. E., 67
Kirchner, C., 463
Kirchner, S., 463
Kirk, S. A., 461
Kirk, Sam, 104
Kirke, P. N., 347
Kjelgaard, M. M., 284
Klebanov, P. K., 232
Kleeb, G., 273
Klein, J., 86
Klein, J. O., 433
Klein, S., 37
Kleinert, H., 48
Kleinert, H. L., 278
Kliebenstein, M. A., 312, 328, 331, 333, 336
Kliewer, C., 6
Klin, A., 284, 285, 288
Klinger, L. G., 6
Klingner, J., 70
Klingner, J. K., 71
Kluth, P., 240, 250
Kluwin, T. N., 431
Knight, D., 333
Knowlton, D., 137
Knox, R., 466
Kocarek, C. E., 22
Koegel, L. K., 284, 298
Koegel, R. L., 228, 298
Koenig, A. J., 466, 471, 476, 478, 479
Kohr, Cheryl, 126
Koop, J. E., 326
Korabek, C. A., 240
Korinek, L., 80
Krajewski, J. J., 238
Krantz, P. J., 287
Krug, C., 300
Krulik, T., 336
Kuestler, F. A., 458
Kumra, S., 137
Kunc, N., 272
Kupstas, F. D., 233
Kuttler, S., 297
Kwon, J. Y., 37

LaForce, R., 381
La Grange Area Department of Special
    Education, 159
Lahey, M., 408
Lambert, N., 235
Lambert, N. M., 172

Lampert, N. L., 323
Lance, G. D., 61, 62
Land, L. A., 272
Landenberger, J., 189
Landrum, M. S., 5, 216
Landry, K. L., 149
Lane, K. L., 138
Langley, A. K., 134
Langone, C. A., 240
Langone, J., 229, 240
Lansverk, J. A., 141
Larsen, J., 378
Larsen, L., 107
Lash, M. H., 375
Latimer, D., 203
Lattimore, J., 228
Lattin, D., 44, 57, 59
Laursen, E. K., 134, 146, 150, 158, 160
Lavender, Tony, 102–103, 128
Lavoie, R., 336
Lea, P. M., 380
Leal, D., 201
Leary, M. R., 288
Le Couteur, A., 290
LeDuc, P., 469
Lee, C., 299
Lee, Christine, 299
Lee, D. L., 183, 185
Lee, K., 107
Lee, S. Y., 49
Lees-Haley, P. R., 376, 381
Lehman, L. R., 70
Leland, H., 235
Lenz, B. K., 119
Leonard, L., 409
Leppien, J. H., 216
Lerner, J., 107, 109
Lerner, M., 179
Levine, M., 285
Lew, R. A., 327
Lewis, G. W., 289
Lewis, M. H., 287
Lewis, S., 459, 466, 469
Lewis, T. J., 294
Lewkowicz, C., 336
Lieberman, A. B., 136
Light, J. G., 110
Linden, P. G., 366
Lindstrom, V., 469
LinguiSystems, 382
Lipsey, M. W., 105
Lipsky, D. K., 6, 66
Liptak, G. S., 347, 348
Litronik, A. J., 141
Livelli, Paul, 303
Livers, A. F., 46
Lloyd, J. W., 144
Lloyd, L. L., 356, 359
Lochman, 141
Loeb, D., 409, 413

Loftus, J., 327
Lombardino, L. J., 409
Long, N. J., 132
Longaker, T., 285
Lord, C., 284, 290
Lorimer, P. A., 297
Los Angeles Unified School District, 465
Lovass, O. I., 285
Lovecky, D. V., 201
Loveland, T., 70
Low, Juliette "Daisy" Gordon, 445
Lowenbraun, S., 442
Lowenfeld, B., 459, 460
Luckasson, R., 227, 235, 260
Luhaorg, H., 229
Lussenhop, K., 469
Lutkenhoff, M., 348
Lynch, E. W., 82
Lyons, J. S., 144

Macaruso, P., 289
MacDonald, B. J., 160
MacDonald, J. D., 418
Mace, F. C., 286
MacKay, S., 431
MacMillan, D. L., 6, 68, 69, 138, 234, 235
Maddox, J. I., 258, 259
Maher, M. C., 178
Maker, C. J., 207
Malik, R., 317, 318
Malloy, A., 347
Malone, M., 229
Maloney, Jean Ann, 42, 43, 47
Mandleco, B. L., 133
Mangrum, C. T., 191
Manson, D., 22
Margus, Brad, 261
Margus, Vicki, 261
Marini, I., 431
Markey, D. J., 80, 96–97, 98, 99
Markey, Ursula, 80, 96–97, 98, 99
Marks, S. U., 285
Marquardt, J., 376
Marshall, L. H., 81
Martin, J., 81, 86, 230
Martin, J. E., 81, 241
Martin-MacLeod, L., 381
Martinussen, R., 174
Maslow, Abraham, 156, 157
Mason, C. A., 232
Mastropieri, Mary A., 69, 269, 385, 387
Mather, Susan M., 445
Mathes, P. G., 105
Mathews, T. J., 347
Mathot-Buckner, C., 272
Mattison, R. E., 140
Mauk, J. E., 286, 289
Maumary-Gremaud, 141
Maurer, R., 288
Mayer, P., 442

May Institute Center for Education and
   Neurorehabilitation, 377
Mazlish, E., 140
McBride, B. J., 290
McBride, M., 266
McBurnett, K., 175
McCabe, A., 410
McCall, J., 273
McCarthy, R., 174
McClannahan, L. E., 287
McComas, N., 121
McCormick, L., 406, 408, 409
McCoy, K., 136
McCrea, L. D., 69
McDiarmid, G. W., 93
McDonnell, J., 72, 272
McDonnell, J. M., 272
McDonnell, L. M., 45, 48
McDougall, D., 72
McGee, G. G., 298
McGlauflin, H., 336
McGregor, G., 66, 72, 88
McGrew, K. S., 229–230
McGuire, J., 115
McIlvane, W. J., 289
McIntosh, P. I., 135
McKinnon, J., 138
McLane, K., 57
McLaren, J., 260
McLaughlin, J. F., 297
McLaughlin, K. A., 378
McLaughlin, M. J., 45, 48
McLaughlin, M. W., 72
McLaughlin, P. J., 240
McLaughlin, V. L., 80
McLean, J., 409, 417
McLeskey, J., 70
McMichael, A., 232
McNamara, B. E., 332
McNamara, F. J., 332
McNear, Donna, 462
McNerney, E., 298
McPherson, M. J., 229
McQuivey, C., 72
Meadow-Orlans, K. P., 434
Medbery, Lucie, 217–220
Medical Tribune, 176
Meese, R. L., 107
Mercer, A. R., 104
Mercer, C. D., 104, 109
Merrill, K. W., 180
Merritt, D., 400
Mervis, C. B., 408
Mesibov, G. B., 6
Meyer, A., 54
Meyers, C. E., 6
Meyers, H., 88
Miklowitz, D. J., 135
Milian, M., 470, 474
Milich, R., 109, 172

Miller, D. N., 147
Miller, J. E., 406
Miller, L. K., 289
Miller, M. D., 149
Miller, S. P., 107
Miller-Johnson, 141
Mills, G. E., 31
Milne, J. M., 135
Milton, J., 336
Miner, C. A., 240
Minke, K. M., 69
Mira, M. P., 375, 376, 381, 384
Miranda, A., 410
Mirenda, A., 418
Mirenda, P., 258, 269
Missouri Head Injury Foundation, 377
Mitchem, K. J., 149
Mithaug, D., 242–244
Mithaug, D. E., 81, 230, 241
Molnar, A., 69
Monda-Amaya, L. E., 69
Montgomery, S. S., 136
Moores, D. F., 432
Moran, M., 176
Morgan, Barbara, 71
Morgan, Heather, 42–43, 74–75
Morgan, Star, 42–43, 74–75
Morison, P., 45, 48
Morrier, M. J., 298
Moser, H., 261
MTA Cooperative Group, 175, 176
Mueller, P. H., 85, 86
Murawski, W. W., 89
Murphy, C. C., 231, 232
Murphy, K., 189, 191
Murphy, K. R., 191
Murphy-Brennan, M. G., 110
Muscott, Howard, 150, 154, 155
Muscott, H. S., 147
Musselman, C., 431
Myles, B. S., 284, 285, 287, 288, 296, 297, 298

Nabors, Karla, 303
Naierman, N., 336
Nakamura, J., 207
Nakayama, E., 137
Nanasca, Rommel, 342–343, 370
National Center for Educational Statistics, 37, 92, 147, 327, 330, 433
National Center for Health Statistics, 433
National Clearinghouse on Child Abuse and Neglect, 143
National Council on Disability, 10, 37, 92
National Environmental Health Association, 319
National Heart, Blood, and Lung Institute, 317, 318
National Institute for Urban Education, 89
National Institute of Diabetes and Digestive and Kidney Diseases, 322

National Institute of Injury and Prevention, 135
National Institute of Mental Health, 164, 176
National Institutes of Health, 381
National Jewish Center for Immunology and Respiratory Medicine, 318
National Organization on Disability, 37, 92
National Reading Panel, 107
National Reference Center for Bioethics Literature, 326
National Research Council, 11, 12, 13, 14, 44, 49, 234, 285, 287, 289
NCIP, 363
Neary, T., 72
Needleman, H. L., 232
Neilson, A. B., 207
Nelson, J. R., 49, 53, 140
Nelson, K. A., 463
Nelson, M., 268
Nettelbeck, T., 289
Neuharth-Pritchett, S., 318, 319
Neumeister, K. L. S., 215
Nevin, A. I., 66, 82, 88, 267
Newton, J. S., 290
Newton, R. R., 141
Nickel, R. E., 264, 284, 344, 347, 348, 350
Nidus Information Services, 314, 315
Nihira, K., 235
Nolan, E. E., 175, 176
Noll, R. B., 320
Norton, H. J., 179
Nurchie, J. C., 135
Nye, J., 288
Nystul, M. S., 317

Oakwood Solutions, 152
Obiakor, F. E., 6, 53
Obukowicz, M., 271
O'Connor, B. V., 160
O'Connor, R. E., 72
O'Donnell, L., 324
Oei, P. S., 110
Oetinger, C., 48
Oetting, J., 421
Olson, R., 110
Olszewski-Kubilius, P., 207
O'Neill, L. M., 47, 49, 52, 55
O'Neill, R. E., 290
Oppenheimer, S. G., 348
Orelove, F. P., 258
Orkwis, R., 57
Orr, S., 287
Oseroff, A., 141
Oseroff, C. E., 141
O'Shaughnessy, T. E., 108
Oster, G. D., 136
Osterling, J., 298
Ostrosky, M. M., 417
Oswald, D. P., 144, 234
Owens, R., 406

Owens, R. E., Jr., 417
Oxford, M., 229
Oyler, C., 240

Palmer, A., 69
Palmer, D. S., 268
Palmer, S. B., 81, 230, 241, 242–244, 248, 249
Palombara, M. M., 276–277
Palombaro, M. M., 72, 276
Palser, Peggy, 43, 65
Panico, A., 150
Pannbacker, M., 405
Parente, R., 395
Parette, H. P., 361
Parker, H. C., 181–182
Parmelee, Judy, 452
Parrish, T. B., 32
Pasquier, B., 240
Passarini, John, 364–365
Passow, H. A., 196
Patton, J. M., 6
Patton, J. R., 34
Paul, B., 466
Paul, P. V., 431
Paulozzi, L. J., 347
Pearce, R. S., 461
Pearpoint, J., 264
Peerson, S., 327
Pellegrino, L., 344, 345, 356
Perez, B., 442
Perlmutter, J., 332
Perner, J., 285
Perrin, E. C., 336
Perry, B. D., 336
Perry, J. C., 133
Pester, E., 470
Peterson, L. D., 149
Pew Environmental Health Commission, 317
Philbrick, L. A., 299
Phillips, D., 247
Piacentini, J. C., 134
Piechura-Couture, K., 89
Pierson, W. P., 350
Piirto, J., 203, 204, 216
Pina, V. O., 148
Pineda, D., 178
Pinheiro, S. B., 409
Pinto, T., 172, 173
Pisha, B., 54, 55
Piuma, C., 72
Play Attention, 186
Plomin, R., 202
Podell, D. M., 70
Podolsky, D., 327
Poduska, J., 154
Pogrund, R. L., 461
Polloway, E. A., 227, 235, 289
Ponsford, J., 378
Porter, P., 378, 379
Power, D., 442

Power, T. J., 178
Powers, L. E., 366
Prater, M. A., 326
Pratt, C., 443
Prelock, P. A., 85
Presley, J. A., 273
Pretti-Frontczak, K., 121
Prevent Blindness America, 463
Price, N., 107
Price, T. S., 202
Prizant, B. M., 284, 285, 298
P/S/L Consulting Group, 327
Psychological Corporation, 111, 113, 382
Public Health Service, U.S., 233
Pugach, M. C., 44, 66, 80, 85, 88
Pugh, G. S., 466, 469, 479
Pumpian, I., 71
Purcell, J. H., 216
Pyle, Dana, 43

Quenemoen, R. F., 48
Quill, K. A., 286
Quist, R. W., 359
Quvo, T., 240

Rabidoux, P., 418
Rainforth, B., 72
Ramirez, Danny, 31
Ramirez, Eloisa, 480
Ramos-Ford, V., 200
Ramsay, E., 135
Ramsey, E., 135
Ratey, J. J., 169, 188
Redding, R., 431
Reeb, R. N., 320
Reed, P., 271
Regan, J. M., 320
Reichle, J., 258
Reid, R., 178, 179
Reid, R. R., 85
Reis, S. M., 203, 210
Reiss, S., 227
Renzulli, J. S., 196, 203, 210, 211, 213
Repp, A. C., 144
Reschly, D. J., 6, 14
Reynolds, M. C., 6, 66
Riccio, C. A., 409
Richards, D. P., 462
Rickard, R., 478
Riffel, L. A., 228
Riggs, C. G., 85, 86
Rimm, S. B., 201
Rinner, L., 287
Risi, S., 284
Roan, S., 180
Roberts, P. H., 105
Roberts, S., 257
Robinson, S., 120
Robinson, T. W., 149
Rodriquez, Luisa, 78, 79, 99

Rogers, J. A., 207
Rogers, J. L., 337
Rogers, Judi, 368
Rogers, M. F., 297
Rogers, S. J., 285, 286, 298
Roof, V., 95
Rose, D., 54, 59
Rosen, B. H., 379
Rosenberg, R. L., 88, 264, 269, 270, 277, 357
Rosenthal-Maleck, A., 322
Ross, G., 229
Rosselli, M., 178
Roy-Campbell, Z. R., 234
Rubin, E., 298
Rubin, K., 138, 139
Ruble, L. A., 286, 297
Rucker, H. N., 289
Rudnitski, R. A., 196
Rudolph, S. M., 146
Ruef, M., 294
Rues, J., 257
Rung, L. L., 273
Rusch, F. R., 37
Russo, R., 466
Rustuccia, C., 135
Rutter, M., 290
Ruusila, L., 289
Ruusila, U., 289
Ryan, A. S., 86
Rydell, P. J., 285

Saavedra, L. M., 134
Sabata, Donna, 399
Sachs, J. J., 147
Sacks, S. Z., 459, 460, 461
Safran, S. P., 284
Safren, S. A., 144
Sailor, W., 66, 68
Saklofske, D. H., 235
Salend, S. J., 70
Salisbury, C., 72
Salisbury, C. L., 72, 88, 276–277
Saloviita, T., 289
Sandall, S., 418
Sandall, S. R., 290
Sander, B., 404
Sandler, A., 346, 351
Sands, D., 44
Sands, D. J., 230
Santos, R. M., 95
Sargent, J. T., 134
Satcher, David, 233
Saulnier, K., 430
Savage, R. C., 392
Sawka, K., 147
Sax, C., 71
Schalock, R. L., 227
Schattman, R., 267
Schendel, D., 231
Schiefelbush, R. L., 408

Schirmer, Barbara R., 427, 432, 435, 442
Schlozman, S. C., 135
Schmidt, C. W., 172
Schmitz, Kathy, 362
Schneider, P., 409
Schnorr, R., 47, 241
Schnorr, R. F., 67
Schoem, S. R., 433
Schoenfeld, H. B., 350
Schonberg, R. L., 231, 261, 350
Schrader, C., 285
Schuler, A. L., 284, 285
Schulz, J. B., 66
Schumacher, E., 314
Schumaker, J. B., 115, 119
Schumm, J. S., 69, 71
Schwartz, I., 418
Schwartz, I. S., 290
Schwartz, M., 230, 241
Schwartz, S., 406
Schwartzman, M. N., 264, 345, 347, 348
Scott, D., 48
Scott, E. P., 459, 463
Scott, J. M., 347
Scott, K. G., 232
Scruggs, Thomas E., 69, 269, 385, 387
Seay, P. C., 34
Seeley, K., 201
Selikowitz, M., 174
Seng, Graziella, 79, 86
Senge, P. M., 90
Seraphim, C. K. M., 207
Serna, L. A., 326
Serventi, Sandy, 483
Settle, S. A., 109
Sewell, T. J., 123
Shank, M., 183, 333, 335–336
Shanks, Pamela, 275
Shapiro, B. K., 231, 232, 264
Shapiro, E. S., 147, 190
Sharma, J., 146
Sharpe, M., 81
Shaw, M., 137
Shaw, S., 115
Shaywitz, S. E., 110
Shea, T. M., 113
Sheppard, K., 154
Sherman, A., 11
Sherman, A. C., 336
Shields, J. D., 328
Shilu, T., 232
Shin, H., 49
Shinn, M., 183
Shoho, A. R., 69
Shonkoff, J. P., 247
Shoshan, T., 298
Shriner, J. G., 48
Shukla, S., 72
Siegel, E., 258
Siegel-Causey, E., 257

Silberman, R. K., 460
Silverman, L. K., 202
Silverman, W. K., 134
Simeonsson, N., 317
Simmons, D. C., 107
Simon, D. J., 339
Simonton, S., 336
Simpson, R. L., 284, 288, 296, 297
Sinclair, M. F., 81
Singh, N. N., 144
Siperstein, G. N., 234
Skinner, S., 376
Slate, J. R., 431
Smalley, S., 174
Smith, Barbara, 363
Smith, D., 34
Smith, Elizabeth, 411
Smith, Fred, 411
Smith, J. D., 238, 289
Smith, J. K., 109
Smith, L. B., 410
Smith, Linda, 188
Smith, M. D., 302
Smith, M. G., 268
Smith, M. J., 86
Smith, Nolan, 2–3, 38–39
Smith, P., 69
Smith, S. W., 149
Smith, T., 298
Smith, T. E., 34
Snell, M., 257, 267, 269
Snell, M. E., 227
Sneve, Virginia Driving Hawk, 156
Snow, C. E., 443
Snow, K., 240
Snyder, D., 169
Snyder-Mclean, L., 409, 417
So, T. H., 70
Sobesy, D., 258
Sobsey, D., 257
Sohlberg, M. M., 378, 384
Sohn, E., 174
Sokol, S. M., 289
Solanto, M. V., 165
Sonuga-Barke, E. J., 174
Soodak, L., 70
Soodak, L. C., 70, 73
Soulsman, G., 141
Sowers, J. A., 366
Sparrow, S. S., 284
Speare, C., 326
Spencer, K., 230
Spencer, V., 269
Spiegel, G. L., 315, 316
Spisto, M. A., 178
Spitalnik, D. M., 227
Spooner, F., 257
Spoor, Joshua, 254–255, 279–280
Sprafkin, J., 175
Sprague, J. R., 287

Sprague, J. W. H., 135
Spungin, S., 468
Stach, B. A., 426
Stapelton, M., 395
Staples, A., 419
STARBRIGHT Foundation, 313
Stark, J. A., 227
Starley, Ellen, 255
Starnes, Waveline, 217
Staub, D., 72, 267
Stein, H., 133
Stephens, M. E., 315
Stephens, M. I., 442
Stephenson, J. R., 258
Sternberg, R. J., 140
Sternberg, Robert J., 196–197, 200
Stevens, T., 366
Stidham, Linda, 392–393
Stiles, K. M., 232
Stiles, S., 466
Still, George, 164
St. Jude's Children's Research Hospital, 314
Stock, S. E., 228
Stokes, T. F., 228
Stone, P., 444
Storm, Sandra, 138
Stout, D., 44
Stover, Linda, 188
Stowe, M., 15, 84
Strand, E., 405
Strauss, M., 432
Strichart, S. S., 191
Strong, M., 273
Stuart, S., 400
Study of Personnel Needs in Special Education, 69
Succop, P. A., 232
Sugai, G., 294
Sullivan, N. A., 333, 335, 339
Sullivan, Rachel, 484
Surgeon General, U.S., 140
Sutherland, K. S., 149
Swaggart, B. L., 297
Swaim, R., 230
Swaner, J., 240
Swank, L. K., 409
Swanson, H. L., 89, 108
Swanson, J., 179
Swanson, K., 70, 376, 379
Swanson, L. H., 108
Swartz, T. J., 276–277
Switzky, H. N., 229
Symons, F. J., 149
Szabo, J. L., 355

Tager-Flusberg, H., 284
Talay-Ongan, A., 287
Talbott, E., 269
Tannock, R., 174
Tarver, S. G., 119

Taylor, John F., 167
Taylor, Ronda, 80, 98
Taylor, S., 67
Teelucksingh, E., 49, 53
Teeter, P. A., 189
Teitelbaum, O., 288
Teitelbaum, P., 288
Temple, E. P., 179
Templin, M. A., 215
Terry, 141
Test, D. W., 241
Thayer-Smith, R., 46
Thies, K., 312, 318, 322, 330
Thomas, K. L., 461
Thomas, T. C., 110
Thompson, B., 235, 274, 276
Thompson, J. R., 229–230
Thompson, R. J., 314
Thompson, S. J., 48
Thorson, N., 72, 272
Thousand, J., 88, 277
Thousand, J. S., 66, 68, 82, 84–85, 88, 90, 267
Thurlow, M., 47, 113
Thurlow, M. L., 44, 47, 48, 49, 52, 53
Tichenor, M. S., 89, 90
Tifft, C. F., 231, 261, 350
Tifft, C. J., 231, 261, 350
Todd, A. W., 287
Todis, B., 378
Toledano, S. R., 320
Tomasello, M., 285
Tootle, Barb, 162, 163
Torgesen, J. K., 108
Torrance, E. P., 207
Towbin, K. E., 289
Townsend, B. L., 144
Travis, P., 189
Trehub, S. E., 431
Trickel, K., 189
Troiano, Peter, 127
Truch, S., 105
Trusty, S., 478
Tsai, L., 284, 289
Tuchman, M., 260
Turnbull, A., 70, 294, 295
Turnbull, A. P., 15, 23, 27, 29, 34, 66, 82, 84, 94, 228, 265, 266, 294, 324
Turnbull, H. R., 15, 19, 23, 27, 29, 30, 34, 82, 84, 94, 265, 324
Turner, David, 188
Turner, L. A., 228
Twachtman-Cullen, D., 285
Tyler, J. S., 317, 320, 375, 376, 381, 384

Udari-Solner, A., 67
University of Kentucky, 139
Urbanczyk, Beth, 392
Utley, B. L., 257
Utley, C. A., 53

Valdez, K., 5
Van Bockern, S., 8, 150, 156–157
Van Deventer, P., 67
VanDenBerg, J., 142, 148
Van der Klift, E., 272
van Gurp, S., 431
Van Reusen, A. K., 69, 81
Vaughn, B., 290
Vaughn, S., 69, 70, 71
Vella, Anne, 311, 315, 335, 338
Verdolini, K., 413
Verdon, R., 134
Vergason, G. A., 7
Vialle, W., 200
Vigra, Helen, 363
Villa, R. A., 66, 82, 88, 90, 267, 277
Vogelsberg, R. T., 66, 72
Vohr, B. R., 436
Volkmar, F., 284
Volkmar, F. R., 285, 288, 289
Volkow, N. D., 176
Volpe, R. J., 175
Voltz, D. L., 67
Vygotsky, L., 409

Wadsworth, D., 333
Wagner, M., 5, 140
Wagner, R. K., 108
Walberg, H. J., 66
Waldron, N. L., 70
Walker, H. M., 135, 138, 142, 144
Walker, J., 133
Wallace, M., 202
Walther-Thomas, C., 46, 67, 80, 85, 88, 149
Walton-Allen, N., 232
Wang, M. C., 66
Wang, P. P., 406, 410
Ward, Nancy, 8
Ward, S. B., 216
Warger, C. L., 44, 85
Warren, S. H., 72
Wassel, J., 276–277
Waterhouse, L., 285
Watkins, R. V., 409
Watling, R., 287, 297
Webb, J. T., 203

Webb, L., 189
Webber, J., 142
WebMD Health, 312, 314
Wedge, George, 398–399, 422
Wegner, J. R., 274
Wehby, J. H., 149
Wehmeyer, M., 272
Wehmeyer, M. L., 44, 57, 59, 61, 62, 68, 81,
    228, 230, 240, 241, 242–244, 248, 249
Weir, D. G., 347
Weiss, M. J., 286
Wells, R. D., 169
Werthamer, L., 154
Westberg, K. L., 216
Westling, D., 141
Westmoreland, D. A., 149, 150, 151
Wetherby, A., 258, 284, 285
Wetherby, A. M., 285
Whitaker, D. P., 183, 185
White, Brenda, 338
White, B. Y., 209
White, K. R., 436
Whitmer, Brian, 456
Whitten, C. F., 314
Whitten, E., 22
Wickham, D., 274
Widaman, K. F., 229, 230
Wieder, S., 299
Wigal, T., 179
Wilcox, B. L., 15, 84
Wilfert, C. M., 323
Wilkes, Debbie, 246
Wilkinson, M. E., 466
Will, M. C., 66
Willams, J., 135
Williams, B. T., 80
Williams, C. R., 273
Williams, L., 179
Williamson, B., 5
Williamson, G. G., 287
Williamson, Katie, 394
Wilson, B. A., 272
Wilson, L. L., 276–277
Winton, P., 70
Wishner, J., 10, 234
Wisman, M., 133

Wolfe, P. S., 257
Wolfe, S., 461
Wolffe, K., 460
Wolffe, K. E., 461
Wolf-Schein, E. G., 257
Wolk, S., 432
Wong, L. Y. C., 347
Wood, A., 356
Wood, K., 287
Wood, M., 133
Wood, W. M., 241, 257
Woodard, Tory, 224–225, 252
Woodley-Zanthos, P., 233
Woodward, J., 119, 442
Wright, David, 431
Wright-Drechsel, M. L., 356
Wynn, J. W., 298

Yamaki, K., 10, 13, 141, 232, 234
Yeargin-Allsopp, M., 231
Yell, M., 15, 23, 34
Yetter, C. E., 315, 316
Ylvisaker, M., 379, 380, 382, 384, 387
Yoder, P. J., 149
Youe, S., 107
Young, K. R., 149
Young, L., 477
Young, M., 326
Young, R., 289
Ysseldyke, J., 47, 48, 113
Ysseldyke, J. E., 48, 69

Zahorick, J., 69
Zappitelli, M., 172, 173
Zebrowski, P., 413
Zeller, R. W., 142
Zentall, S. S., 183, 185
Zhang, D., 239
Zhang, Li-fang, 196–197
Ziegler, E., 229
Zienkewicz, Connie, 29
Zigmond, N., 68, 333
Zima, B. T., 179–180
Zionts, P., 142
Zirkel, P., 180

AAC (augmentative and alternative communication), 356, 358–360, 361, 417, 418

AAMR Adaptive Behavior Scale—School Edition (2nd ed.) (Lambert, Nihira, & Leland), 235

Absence seizures, 315

Academic characteristics. *See* Cognitive/academic characteristics

Accidents, 381

Accommodations. *See also* Instructional augmentation
   and attention deficit/hyperactivity disorder, 180, 181–182, 186
   inclusion through, 66
   and traumatic brain injury, 387

Accountability, 45, 48–49, 52, 53

Acquired communication disorders, 410

Acquired immunodeficiency disease (AIDS), 323. *See also* HIV

Action research, 276–277

Active listening, 140, 151

Activity, 185

Acute conditions, 312

ADA (Americans with Disabilities Act), 34, 35–36, 191, 449, 479

Adaptation. *See* Instructional adaptation

Adaptive skills
   and mental retardation, 229–230, 235
   and severe and multiple disabilities, 257
   and visual loss/impairment, 466, 468, 475–476, 484

ADHD Rating Scale, 178

Advanced organizers, 119

Adventitious visual impairments, 463

African Americans
   asthma, 317, 318
   attention deficit/hyperactivity disorder, 179
   diabetes, 322
   emotional or behavioral disorders, 144
   hearing loss/impairment, 431
   HIV, 323, 324
   mental retardation, 234, 245
   postschool employment, 37
   students with exceptionalities, 12, 13

Age/grade-appropriate placements, 67–68

Age groups, 17, 19

Aggressive behavior, 287

AIDS (acquired immunodeficiency disease), 323

Alerting devices, 450

ALM (autonomous learner model), 217, 218–219

Alteration. *See* Curriculum alteration; Instructional alteration

Alternative assessments, 336

American Sign Language (ASL), 428, 441, 443, 446

Americans with Disabilities Act (ADA), 34, 35–36, 191, 449, 479

Amniocentesis, 261, 262

Anoxia, 374

Anti-inflammatories, 318

Anxiety disorders, 134

Apgar screenings, 264, 350

Aphasia, 379

Applied behavior analysis, 298

Appropriate education, 22–28

Apraxia, 405

Articulation disorders, 404

Artistic ability, 200

Asbury College, 278

Asian Americans, 266

ASL (American Sign Language), 428, 441, 443, 446

Asperger Syndrome, 284, 285, 287, 288, 289

Assessment, 43. *See also* Accountability; Evaluation
   alternative, 336
   curriculum-based, 113–114
   ecological, 290, 351, 353
   emotional intelligence, 152
   functional, 290, 292, 294, 295, 299–300
   functional vision, 465–66
   IDEA on, 23–24
   learning media, 466
   and race/ethnicity, 14
   reflective, 209
   and standards-based reform, 47, 48–49

Assistive listening devices (FM systems), 437

Assistive technology
   augmentative and alternative communication, 356, 358–360, 361, 417, 418

defined, 18
   and physical disabilities, 354, 356, 357, 363–365
   and severe and multiple disabilities, 271
   and visual loss/impairment, 472–473, 475

Asthma, 317–20, 327

Ataxia telangiectasia (AT), 261

Ataxic cerebral palsy, 344

Athens Drive High School, 456–457

Athetoid cerebral palsy, 344

Atrophy, 378

Attention deficit/hyperactivity disorder (AD/HD), 162–193
   case study, 162–163, 191
   causes, 171–175
   characteristics, 165–169
   and collaboration, 185, 187–188
   definitions, 164–165
   diagnostic criteria, 166
   evaluation, 176–180, 181–182
   exemplar programs, 189–191
   and giftedness, 176, 201–202, 203, 209
   impairments, 170
   and inclusion, 180, 184
   legal rights, 35
   positive traits, 169
   prevalence, 175–176
   technology tips, 186
   terminology issues, 7
   types, 165, 167
   and universally designed learning, 183, 185

Audiograms, 426, 429, 436

Audiologists, 18, 435

Audiometer, 435

Augmentation. *See* Curriculum augmentation; Instructional augmentation

Augmentative and alternative communication (AAC), 356, 358–360, 361, 417, 418

Aura, 316

Autism, 282–308
   and attention deficit/hyperactivity disorder, 176
   case study, 282–283, 306–307
   causes, 289
   characteristics, 284–289

Autism, (continued)
and collaboration, 297, 298, 301
and communication impairments, 284–285, 409
definitions, 284
early childhood exemplar programs, 297–300
elementary exemplar programs, 300, 302
evaluation, 289–292
and inclusion, 292, 293
middle/secondary exemplar programs, 302, 304–305
prevalence, 289
technology tips, 298
terminology issues, 7, 284
transitional/postsecondary exemplar programs, 302–303, 306
and universally designed learning, 292, 294–297
Autism Diagnostic Interview—Revised, 290
Autism spectrum disorder, 284
Automatisms, 315
Autonomous learner model (ALM), 217, 218–219

Basic psychological processes, 104
BBF (Blind Babies Foundation), 481
Behavioral and Emotional Rating Scale, 146
Behavioral audiological evaluations, 434–435
Behavioral characteristics
autism, 286–287, 294–296
emotional or behavioral disorders, 138–139
epilepsy, 317
giftedness, 201–202
learning disabilities, 109
traumatic brain injury, 380
Behavioral earthquakes, 138
Behavioral inhibition, 167
Behavior examination, 151
Bidialectal students, 414
Bilingual/bicultural programs. See English as a second language (ESL) learners
Bilingual students, 413
Biomedical factors. See also Genetics/heredity
attention deficit/hyperactivity disorder, 173–174
autism, 289
communication disorders, 410
hearing loss/impairment, 432–433, 434
learning disabilities, 109–110
mental retardation, 231
other health impairments, 326
physical disabilities, 345–346
visual loss/impairment, 462–463
Bipolar disorder, 135
Blind Babies Foundation (BBF), 481
Blue Valley School District, 217–220
Braille, 466, 469–470, 472, 473, 474
Braille embossers, 475
Brain differences

and attention deficit/hyperactivity disorder, 173, 178
and learning disabilities, 109–110
Brainstorming, 265, 266
Brochodilators, 318
Brown v. Board of Education, 15
Bubble effect, 86
Bullying. See Insensitivity

Cancer, 320–321
Captioning, 449–450
Cardiovascular disease, 327
Careers in special education, 15
Case studies, 2–3, 38–39
attention deficit/hyperactivity disorder, 162–163, 191
autism, 282–283, 306–307
communication disorders, 398–399, 422
emotional or behavioral disorders, 130–131, 160
giftedness, 194–195, 222
hearing loss/impairment, 424–425, 453
learning disabilities, 102–103, 128
mental retardation, 42–43, 74–75, 224–225, 252
multicultural responsiveness/collaboration, 78–79, 98–100
other health impairments, 310–311, 340
physical disabilities, 342–343, 370
severe and multiple disabilities, 254–255, 279–280
traumatic brain injury, 372–373, 396
visual loss/impairment, 456–457, 485
CAST (Center for Applied Special Technology), 55
CAT (computerized axial tomography) scans, 109, 382
Categorical element of eligibility, 17, 19
Catholic Charities of New Orleans, 79
Causal agent, 230
Causes
attention deficit/hyperactivity disorder, 171–175
autism, 289
communication disorders, 410
emotional or behavioral disorders, 140–142
giftedness, 202–203
hearing loss/impairment, 432–433, 434
learning disabilities, 109–110
mental retardation, 230–233
other health impairments, 326–327
physical disabilities, 345–346, 347, 349
severe and multiple disabilities, 260–261
traumatic brain injury, 380–381
visual loss/impairment, 462–463
CCTVs (closed circuit televisions), 475
CEC (Council for Exceptional Children), 487–488
Center for Applied Special Technology (CAST), 55

Centers for Independent Living, 366
Central Middle School, 220–221
Central nervous system dysfunctions, 109–110, 320
Cerebral palsy, 344–346
C. Fred Johnson Middle School, 255
CHADD (Children and Adults with Attention Deficit Disorder), 188
Challenge, 185
"Change of placement" rule, 21
Chase Middle School, 125–126
Chemotherapy, 320
Child abuse, 141, 143, 381
Child life specialists, 337, 338
Children and Adults with Attention Deficit Disorder (CHADD), 188
Children's Place, 390–392
Choices, 183
Chorionic villi sampling, 261, 262
Chromosomal disorders, 231
Chromosomes, 231
Chronic conditions, 312
Circle of courage, 153, 156–157
Circle of Inclusion, 274–276
CLAS (Culturally and Linguistically Appropriate Services), 95
CLASS Act, 188, 311, 338
Class size, 69
Classwide, peer-assisted self-management, 149
Clean intermittent catheterization, 348
Cleft palate/lip, 401
Closed captioning, 449
Closed circuit televisions (CCTVs), 475
Closed head injuries, 374–375
Closing the Gap: A National Blueprint to Improve the Health of Persons with Mental Retardation (U.S. Public Health Service), 233
CMV (cytomegalovirus), 432
Coaching, 187–188
Cochlear implants, 437
Cognitive/academic characteristics
autism, 288–289
emotional or behavioral disorders, 139–140
epilepsy, 317
giftedness, 198, 200
learning disabilities, 106–108
mental retardation, 227–229
severe and multiple disabilities, 257
traumatic brain injury, 378
Cognitive retraining, 382
Collaboration, 80–91
administrator roles, 87–88
and attention deficit/hyperactivity disorder, 185, 187–188
and autism, 297, 298, 301
case studies, 78–79, 98–100
and communication disorders, 418, 420–421
co-teaching, 88–90
defined, 80–81

and emotional or behavioral disorders, 83–84, 150, 153–154, 155
and giftedness, 215, 216
and hearing loss/impairment, 446–450
lack of opportunities for, 69
and learning disabilities, 120–121, 122
and mental retardation, 245–246
and other health impairments, 336–337
and paraprofessionals, 85–86
parent roles, 82, 84
and physical disabilities, 360, 362
planning time, 85
process of, 90–91
and related services, 85
and severe and multiple disabilities, 272–273
student roles, 81–82, 83–84
teacher roles, 84–85
and translators/interpreters, 86–87
and traumatic brain injury, 388–390
and visual loss/impairment, 479–480
Collaboration tips, 91
attention deficit/hyperactivity disorder, 188
autism, 301
communication disorders, 421
emotional or behavioral disorders, 155
giftedness, 216
hearing loss/impairment, 447
learning disabilities, 122
mental retardation, 246
other health impairments, 337
physical disabilities, 362
severe and multiple disabilities, 273
traumatic brain injury, 389
visual loss/impairment, 480
Collaborative problem-solving, 276
College Connection Program, 278–279
College planning. *See* Transitional/postsecondary exemplar programs
College Planning for Gifted Students (Berger), 221
College transition. *See* Transitional/postsecondary exemplar programs
Comas, 376
Combined type (CB) of AD/HD, 167, 174, 176
Communication disorders, 398–423
and attention deficit/hyperactivity disorder, 176
case study, 398–399, 422
causes, 410
characteristics, 403–410
and collaboration, 418, 420–421
definitions, 400–402
and emotional or behavioral disorders, 140
evaluation, 411–414
exemplar programs, 419–422
and inclusion, 414–415, 416

prevalence, 410–411
and universally designed learning, 415–418, 419
Communication impairments. *See also* Hearing loss/impairment
and autism, 284–285, 409
and deaf-blindness, 259
and physical disabilities, 356, 358–360
and severe and multiple disabilities, 258
and traumatic brain injury, 378–379
Community involvement
and emotional or behavioral disorders, 150, 153, 154
and giftedness, 215
and mental retardation, 246, 248, 250
Community Parent Resource Centers (CPRCs), 78–79, 84, 97
Community Services for Autistic Adults and Children (CSAAC), 302–303, 306
Comorbidity, 234
Complex partial seizures, 176
Compliance, 135, 137
Computerized axial tomography (CAT) scans, 109, 382
Computerized tomography (CT) scans, 382
Computer software. *See* Educational software; Technology tips
Concussion, 374
Conduct disorder, 135, 137, 176
Conductive hearing loss, 432
Confidentiality, 324–325, 331–332
Conflict resolution, 149–150, 151
Congenital brain injuries, 374
Congenital communication disorders, 410
Congenital visual impairments, 462
Contact signing, 429
Content standards, 45–46, 50–52, 54
Continuum of services, 30, 67–68
Contracts, 183, 185
Conversational scenarios, 442–443, 444–445
Convulsions, 315
Cooperative learning, 81, 185
Co-teaching, 88–90
Council for Exceptional Children (CEC), 487–488
Counseling services, 18
CPRCs (Community Parent Resource Centers), 78–79, 84, 97
Creativity, 169, 198, 200, 207–208
CSAAC (Community Services for Autistic Adults and Children), 302–303, 306
CT (computerized tomography) scans, 382
Cued speech, 441
Culturally and Linguistically Appropriate Services (CLAS), 95
Cultural mediation, 96–97, 99
Cultural reciprocity, 96. *See also* Multicultural considerations
Culture, 92–94. *See also* Multicultural considerations; Race/ethnicity

Curriculum alteration
defined, 54, 56
and giftedness, 213–215
and hearing loss/impairment, 440–442
and mental retardation, 239–240, 241
Curriculum augmentation
and attention deficit/hyperactivity disorder, 183, 185
defined, 54, 56
and giftedness, 210–213
and hearing loss/impairment, 443, 445
and learning disabilities, 119–120
and traumatic brain injury, 387
and visual loss/impairment, 475–479
Curriculum-based assessment, 113–114
Cytomegalovirus (CMV), 432

Daily living skills. *See* Adaptive skills
Dallas (Texas) Regional Day School Program for the Deaf, 450
Dandy Walker syndrome, 398–399
Deaf-blindness, 65, 258, 259
Deaf community, 427, 432, 442, 443, 445
Deaf culture, 443, 445
Deafness. *See* Hearing loss/impairment
Death, 336–337
Decision making, 150, 151
Delayed language, 284–285
Depression, 134–135, 285, 380
Detachment, 461
Diabetes, 322–323, 327
Diagnosis. *See* Evaluation
Diagnostic and Statistical Manual of Mental Disorders (DSM-IV-TR), 134, 166, 284
Dialects, 401–402, 409
DI (Direct Instruction), 119–120, 123
Digital textbooks, 55
Direct Instruction (DI), 119–120, 123
Direct observation, 146
Discipline, 21
DISCOVER assessment, 207
Discrimination, 15, 34, 99
Disinhibition, 380
Documentation, 205
Domain-specific giftedness, 197
Down syndrome, 231
Dropout rates, 37, 140
DSM-IV-TR (*Diagnostic and Statistical Manual of Mental Disorders*), 134, 166, 284
Duchenne's disease, 348
Due process, 27, 31–32
Dyscalculia, 107–108
Dysgraphia, 107
Dyslexia, 7, 107

Ear, 426–427
Early childhood exemplar programs
attention deficit/hyperactivity disorder, 189
autism, 297–300

Early childhood exemplar programs, *(continued)*
  communication disorders, 419–420
  emotional or behavioral disorders, 154,
    157–158
  giftedness, 215–217
  hearing loss/impairment, 450
  learning disabilities, 121, 123
  mental retardation, 247–248
  other health impairments, 337–338
  physical disabilities, 363–364
  severe and multiple disabilities, 274–276
  traumatic brain injury, 390–392
  visual loss/impairment, 481
Early identification, 18
Early intervention services, 4–5. *See also*
    Early childhood exemplar programs
Eating disorders, 134
EBD. *See* Emotional or behavioral disorders
Echolalia, 285
Ecobehavioral analysis approach, 118
Ecological assessment, 290, 351, 353
Economic self-sufficiency, 37
Educability, 21
Educational software. *See also* Technology tips
  and attention deficit/hyperactivity
    disorder, 186
  and autism, 298
  and emotional or behavioral disorders, 152
  and learning disabilities, 124–125
  and other health impairments, 313
Educational Testing Services (ETS), 488–489
Education level, 10
Education of All Handicapped Students Act
    (Public Law 94-142). *See* Individuals
    with Disabilities Education Act
Electroencephalograms (EEGs), 174
Elementary exemplar programs
  attention deficit/hyperactivity disorder,
    189–190
  autism, 300, 302
  communication disorders, 420–421
  emotional or behavioral disorders, 158–159
  giftedness, 217–220
  hearing loss/impairment, 451–452
  learning disabilities, 123–125
  mental retardation, 248–249
  other health impairments, 338
  physical disabilities, 364–365
  severe and multiple disabilities, 276–277
  traumatic brain injury, 392–393
  visual loss/impairment, 481–483
Eligibility, 17
Embedded learning opportunities (ELO),
    121, 123
Emotional characteristics
  emotional or behavioral disorders, 134–137
  giftedness, 201–202
  hearing loss/impairment, 429–431
  learning disabilities, 109
  traumatic brain injury, 379–380

Emotional intelligence (EQ), 152, 198
Emotional or behavioral disorders (EBD),
    130–161
  and attention deficit/hyperactivity
    disorder, 175–176
  case study, 130–131, 160
  causes, 140–142
  characteristics, 133–135, 137–140
  and collaboration, 83–84, 150,
    153–154, 155
  definitions, 132–133
  and dropout rates, 37
  evaluation, 144–146
  exemplar programs, 154–160
  and inclusion, 147–148
  multicultural considerations, 156–157
  and placement, 65, 147
  prevalence, 142, 144
  and race/ethnicity, 12, 144
  technology tips, 152
  terminology issues, 7
  and universally designed learning, 149–150
EMR classrooms, 237
Encephalocele, 254–255
English as a second language (ESL) learners
  and hearing loss/impairment, 441, 442
  and standardized tests, 204–205
  and visual loss/impairment, 470, 474
Enrichment, 203, 210–213
Enrichment triad model, 210, 211, 213
Environmental factors
  attention deficit/hyperactivity disorder,
    171–172
  emotional or behavioral disorders, 141
  giftedness, 202–203
  learning disabilities, 110
  mental retardation, 231–232
  other health impairments, 327
  physical disabilities, 347
Epilepsy, 315–317
EQ (emotional intelligence), 152, 198
Equality, 82
Equality of opportunity, 37
ESL learners. *See* English as a second language
    (ESL) learners
E-texts, 55
Ethnically diverse groups. *See* Race/ethnicity
Etiology, 465. *See also* Causes
ETS (Educational Testing Services), 488–489
European Americans
  asthma, 318
  attention deficit/hyperactivity disorder,
    175, 179
  mental retardation, 234
  other health impairments, 327
  postschool employment, 37
Evaluation
  adaptation, 59, 149
  attention deficit/hyperactivity disorder,
    176–180, 181–182

autism, 289–292
communication disorders, 411–414
emotional or behavioral disorders,
    144–146
giftedness, 204–209, 210
hearing loss/impairment, 433–439
IDEA on, 21–22, 23–24, 25
learning disabilities, 110–114, 115
mental retardation, 235–237
other health impairments, 328–330,
    335–336
physical disabilities, 350–353
severe and multiple disabilities,
    262–265, 266
traumatic brain injury, 382–385
visual loss/impairment, 463–466
Executive functions, 167–169
Exemplar programs. *See* Early childhood
    exemplar programs; Elementary
    exemplar programs; Middle/secondary
    exemplar programs; Transitional/
    postsecondary exemplar programs
Expertise, 198
Expulsion, 21, 138–139
Externalizing behaviors, 138–139, 144
Extracurricular activities, 31, 480

Falls, 381
Families Together, 29
Family training/counseling/home visits, 18
Federation of Families for Children's Mental
    Health, 141, 142
Feedback, 185
Fetal alcohol syndrome, 327
Fetal surgery, 350
Field of vision, 458
Finger spelling, 428, 430
504 plans, 180, 181–182, 328
Fixations, 288
Flexibility, 45, 61
Fluency disorders, 405
FMRI (functional magnetic resonance
    imaging), 110
FM systems (assistive listening devices), 437
Focal motor seizures, 315
Folic acid, 347
Foster care, 141
Frank Lloyd Wright Middle School, 159
Frequency, 426
Full participation, 37
Functional assessment, 290, 292, 294, 295,
    299–300
Functional blindness, 459
Functional communication disorders, 410
Functional element of eligibility, 17, 19
Functional magnetic resonance imaging
    (FMRI), 110
Functional skills, 240, 241, 248
Functional vision assessment (FVA), 465–466
FVA (functional vision assessment), 465–466

Galvez Middle School, 421
Gang membership, 133
Gender
    and asthma, 317
    and attention deficit/hyperactivity
        disorder, 175
    and mood disorders, 135
    and physical disabilities, 348, 349
    of students with disabilities, 5
    and traumatic brain injury, 381
General curriculum, progress in. *See also*
        Collaboration; Inclusion; Multicultural
        considerations; Standards-based reform
    defined, 46–47
    future visions, 74–75
    importance of, 53
    and universally designed learning, 54–61
Generalization, 228–229, 240
Generalized anxiety disorder, 134
Generalized seizures, 315
Generosity, 150
Genetics/heredity
    and attention deficit/hyperactivity
        disorder, 174–175
    and autism, 289
    and emotional or behavioral disorders,
        140–141
    and giftedness, 202
    and hearing loss/impairment, 432
    and learning disabilities, 110
    and other health impairments, 326–327
    and physical disabilities, 347, 349
    and severe and multiple disabilities,
        260–261
Giftedness, 194–223
    and attention deficit/hyperactivity
        disorder, 176, 201–202, 203, 209
    case study, 194–195, 222
    causes, 202–203
    and cerebral palsy, 346
    characteristics, 198, 200–202, 203
    and collaboration, 215, 216
    definitions, 196–198, 199
    evaluation, 204–209, 210
    exemplar programs, 215–217, 219–221
    and inclusion, 209–210, 211
    prevalence, 203–204
    and race/ethnicity, 12, 204–205
    statistics, 5
    and universally designed learning, 210–215
Grade contracts, 183, 185
Granville County Child Development
        Center, 224, 225, 247–248
Graphic organizers, 119, 417, 419
Group awareness, 180
Group behavior support, 295

Handheld prompters, 228
Hard of hearing. *See* Hearing loss/impairment
Headaches, 378

Head injury. *See* Traumatic brain injury
Health care, 233
Health care plans, 328, 330
Health impairments. *See* Other health
        impairments
Health services, 18
Hearing aids, 436
Hearing loss/impairment, 424–454
    case study, 424–425, 453
    causes, 432–433, 434
    characteristics, 427–432
    and collaboration, 446–450
    and communication disorders, 409
    definitions, 426–427, 428
    evaluation, 433–439
    exemplar programs, 450–453
    and inclusion, 431, 439–440
    prevalence, 433
    and residential placement, 65
    and severe and multiple disabilities,
        257–258
    technology tips, 451
    terminology issues, 7, 427
    and traumatic brain injury, 378
    and universally designed learning, 440–445
Hemoglobin, 314
Heredity. *See* Genetics/heredity
Heterogeneity, 134
Hidden curriculum, 296
High-stakes accountability, 49, 52, 53
Hispanic Americans
    asthma, 318
    diabetes, 322
    hearing loss/impairment, 431
    HIV, 323, 324
    postschool employment, 37
HIV, 35, 323–326, 339
HIV University, 339
Homebound services, 321, 330–331
Home-school placement, 66–67
How to Talk So Kids Can Learn (Faber &
        Mazlish), 140
Human Genome Project, 261, 326–327
Human immunodeficiency virus. *See* HIV
Hurried children, 203
Hyperactivity, 165
Hyperfocus, 169, 183
Hyperglycemia, 322
Hypernasality, 405
Hypoactivity, 165
Hypoglycemia, 322–323
Hyponasality, 405

ICC (Inter-Agency Coordinating Council
        for Infants and Toddlers), 398
IDEA. *See* Individuals with Disabilities
        Education Act
IEP. *See* Individualized education program
IFSP (individualized family services plan),
        22–28

Incidental learning
    and hearing loss/impairment, 430–431
    and visual loss/impairment, 459–460,
        468, 476
Incidental teaching, 298
Inclusion, 61–74
    and attention deficit/hyperactivity
        disorder, 180, 184
    and autism, 292, 293
    and communication disorders,
        414–415, 416
    educator perspectives, 68–70
    and emotional or behavioral disorders,
        147–148
    and giftedness, 209–210, 211
    and hearing loss/impairment, 431,
        439–440
    and learning disabilities, 114, 117
    least restrictive environment, 28–31
    and mental retardation, 237–239
    and other health impairments,
        330–333, 334
    outcomes, 72–73
    parent perspectives, 70
    and physical disabilities, 353–354, 355
    placement trends, 61–64
    principles of, 65–68
    and residential settings, 64–65
    and severe and multiple disabilities,
        72–73, 265, 267–268, 269, 274–275
    student perspectives, 70–72
    through accommodations, 66
    through restructuring, 66, 67
    and traumatic brain injury, 385, 386
    and visual loss/impairment, 468–469,
        471, 480
Inclusion tips, 74
    attention deficit/hyperactivity
        disorder, 184
    autism, 293
    communication disorders, 416
    emotional or behavioral disorders, 148
    giftedness, 211
    hearing loss/impairment, 440
    learning disabilities, 117
    mental retardation, 239
    multicultural considerations, 97
    other health impairments, 332
    physical disabilities, 354
    severe and multiple disabilities, 267
    traumatic brain injury, 386
    visual loss/impairment, 471
Independent living, 37
Individual behavior support, 295
Individualized education program (IEP),
        22–28
    conferences, 27–28
    content, 23–24, 26
    other health impairments, 328, 330
    participants, 27

Individualized education program, (continued)
    and personal intervention plan, 384–385
    student participation, 80–81
    and visual loss/impairment, 479
Individualized family services plan (IFSP),
    22–28
Individual Support Program (ISP),
    299–300, 301
Individuals with Disabilities Education Act
        (IDEA) (Public Law 105-17), 17–33
    appropriate education, 22–28
    federal funding, 32–33
    least restrictive environment, 28–31
    nondiscriminatory evaluation, 21–22,
        23–24, 25
    on attention deficit/hyperactivity disorder,
        164–165
    on autism, 284
    on communication disorders, 401
    on emotional or behavioral disorders,
        132–133
    on general curriculum, 46
    on inclusion, 147
    on learning disabilities, 104
    on mental retardation, 226, 229, 240
    on other health impairments, 312
    on physical disabilities, 344
    on positive behavior support, 286, 295
    on related services, 17, 18
    on severe and multiple disabilities, 256, 261
    on traumatic brain injury, 374
    on visual loss/impairment, 458, 466
    outcomes, 36, 37
    parent-student participation, 32
    procedural due process, 31–32
    zero-reject principle, 20–21
Infant hearing screening, 434, 436
Infections, 326
Inner ear, 426
Inner/outer-directedness, 229, 240
Insensitivity, 332–333, 334
Instructional adaptation, 57–59
    and communication disorders, 415–417
    and other health impairments, 333–335
    and physical disabilities, 354, 356–360, 361
    and severe and multiple disabilities,
        268–272
    and visual loss/impairment, 469–475
Instructional alteration, 385–387
Instructional augmentation, 57–59
    and attention deficit/hyperactivity
        disorder, 185
    and autism, 294–297
    and communication disorders, 417–418, 419
    and emotional or behavioral disorders,
        149–150
    and hearing loss/impairment, 442–443, 444
    and learning disabilities, 115–118
    and mental retardation, 240–244
    and traumatic brain injury, 387–388

Instructional conversations, 442–443,
    444–445
INTASC Standards for Teacher Education,
    489–495
Intellectual characteristics. See
        Cognitive/academic characteristics
Intelligence, 227. See also Intelligence tests
Intelligence tests. See also Cognitive/
        academic characteristics
    and attention deficit/hyperactivity
        disorder, 178
    and autism, 288
    and giftedness, 203
    and learning disabilities, 105, 111
    and mental retardation, 227
    and race/ethnicity, 14
    and severe and multiple disabilities, 257
    and traumatic brain injury, 382
Intensity, 426
Inter-Agency Coordinating Council for
        Infants and Toddlers (ICC), 398
Intermittent positive-pressure breathing
        (IPPB) machines, 342
Internalization of speech, 168
Internalizing behaviors, 138, 139, 144, 314.
        See also Depression
Internet resources
    giftedness, 212
    hearing loss/impairment, 450, 451
    physical disabilities, 358
    visual loss/impairment, 473
Interpersonal skills. See Social characteristics
Interpreters. See Translators/interpreters
Interstate New Teacher Assessment and
        Support Consortium (INTASC),
        489–495
IPPB (intermittent positive-pressure
        breathing) machines, 342
ISP (Individual Support Program),
        299–300, 301

Jacob K. Javits Gifted and Talented Students
        Education Act (1988), 196
Jejunum tube, 342
Jessamine Early Learning Village,
        419–420
Job coaches, 34, 303
Johns Hopkins University Prevention
        Intervention Research Center, 154,
        157–158
Journals, 336
Jump Start program, 301

Karyotyping, 231
Kent State University, 452–453
Ketoacidosis, 322
Kids on the Block (KOB), 337–338
Kid watching, 209
KOB (Kids on the Block), 337–338
K-W-L approach, 447

Labels, 6–8
LaGrange (Illinois) Department of Special
        Education (LADSE), 158–159
Language Acquisition Program (LAP),
        372–373
Language development, 284–285, 406–409.
        See also Communication impairments
Language disorders, 400–401. See also
        Communication disorders;
        Communication impairments
LAP (Language Acquisition Program),
        372–373
Latinos/Latinas. See Hispanic Americans
Law, 15–16, 34–36, 354. See also Individuals
        with Disabilities Education Act
Leadership ability, 200
Lead poisoning, 327
Learned helplessness, 109
Learning disabilities, 104–129
    and cancer, 320
    case study, 102–103, 128
    causes, 109–110
    characteristics, 106–109
    classification criteria, 104–105
    and collaboration, 120–121, 122
    definitions, 104
    and dropout rates, 37
    and emotional or behavioral disorders,
        139–140
    evaluation, 110–114, 115
    exemplar programs, 121–128
    and giftedness, 201–202
    and inclusion, 114, 117
    and intelligence tests, 105, 111
    and multicultural considerations, 118
    prevalence, 110, 111
    technology tips, 124–125
    terminology issues, 7
    and universally designed learning,
        114–120
Learning media assessment (LMA), 466
Learning strategies, 115–118, 127
Least restrictive environment (LRE),
        28–31
Legal blindness, 458
Lehigh University Consulting Center for
        Adolescents with Attention-Deficit
        Disorders (LU-CCADD), 190–191
Leukemia, 320
Liberator, 356
Living Skills Center for the Visually
        Impaired, 483–484
LMA (learning media assessment), 466
Low vision, 459
LRE (least restrictive environment), 28–31
LU (CCADD) Lehigh University
        Consulting Center for Adolescents
        with Attention-Deficit Disorders,
        190–191
Luff Elementary School, 42–43

Magnetic resonance imaging (MRI), 109, 382
Mainstreaming, 66
Making Action Plans (MAPs), 264–265, 266, 278
Manic-depression (bipolar disorder), 135
Manifestation determination, 21, 138
Manual alphabet, 428, 430
Manually coded English, 428–429, 442
MAPs (Making Action Plans), 264–465, 266, 278
Mathematics, 107–108
MDTP (University of Florida Multidisciplinary Diagnostic and Training Program), 189
The Meanest Thing to Say (Cosby), 332
Mediation, 31
Medical services, 18
Medication
  for asthma, 318
  for attention deficit/hyperactivity disorder, 176, 178
  for other health impairments, 330
  psychotropic medications, 164, 176, 178
Meeting the Challenge, 339
Melting pot metaphor, 90
Memory
  and learning disabilities, 108, 119
  and mental retardation, 227–228
  nonverbal working memory, 168
Meningitis, 433
Meningocele spina bifida, 346, 347
Mental retardation, 224–253
  and attention deficit/hyperactivity disorder, 176
  case studies, 42–43, 74–75, 224–225, 252
  causes, 230–233
  and cerebral palsy, 346
  characteristics, 227–230
  and collaboration, 245–246
  and communication disorders, 409
  definitions, 226–227
  evaluation, 235–237
  exemplar programs, 247–252
  and inclusion, 237–239
  prevalence, 234
  prevention, 233
  and race/ethnicity, 12, 234
  terminology issues, 7, 235, 237
  and universally designed learning, 239–244
Mentors, 215
Metabolism, 260
Metacognition, 108, 118
Microcultures, 93
Middle ear, 426
Middle/secondary exemplar programs
  attention deficit/hyperactivity disorder, 190–191
  autism, 302, 304–305
  communication disorders, 421
  emotional or behavioral disorders, 159

giftedness, 220–221
  hearing loss/impairment, 452
  learning disabilities, 125–126
  mental retardation, 250
  other health impairments, 338–339
  physical disabilities, 366
  severe and multiple disabilities, 277
  traumatic brain injury, 393–394
  visual loss/impairment, 483
Mild TBI (postconcussional syndrome) (MTBI), 375, 377
Mills v. Washington, DC, Board of Education, 16
Missouri Assessment Program (MAP), 43
Mitchell College, 126–128
Mixed cerebral palsy, 345
Mnemonics, 108, 385–387, 394, 395
Mobility. See Orientation and mobility (O&M) skills
Modifications, 387
Montgomery Knolls Early Childhood Gifted Model Program, 216–217
Mood disorders, 134–135, 136
Morphology, 406, 409
Motivation
  and attention deficit/hyperactivity disorder, 183, 185
  and learning disabilities, 109
  and mental retardation, 229, 240
  and traumatic brain injury, 380
  and visual loss/impairment, 461
Motor development/disorders. See also Physical disabilities
  and autism, 287–288, 297
  and severe and multiple disabilities, 257
Motor neurons, 349
Movement disorders. See Motor development
MRI (magnetic resonance imaging), 109, 382
MTBI (mild TBI) (postconcussional syndrome), 375, 377
Multicultural considerations, 92–99. See also Race/ethnicity
  and attention deficit/hyperactivity disorder, 179
  augmentative and alternative communication, 361
  case studies, 78–79, 98–100
  and communication disorders, 401–402, 413
  and cultural mediation, 96–97, 99
  cultural reciprocity, 96
  and culture, 92–94
  emotional or behavioral disorders, 156–157
  hearing loss/impairment, 442
  HIV, 324
  inclusion tips, 97
  and learning disabilities, 118
  and parent-teacher alliances, 94
  positive behavior support, 296
  and response options, 95–96

and severe and multiple disabilities, 266
  subculture of violence, 391
  technology tips, 95
  visual loss/impairment, 474
Multimodal treatment, 164
Multiple intelligences, 197–198, 199, 207
Muscle tone, 257
Myelomeningocele spina bifida, 346, 347
Myoclonic seizures, 315

National Joint Committee on Learning Disabilities (NJCLD), 104
Native Americans
  circle of courage, 153, 156–157
  communication disorders, 402
  diabetes, 322
Natural proportions, principle of, 67
NCLBA (No Child Left Behind Act) (2002), 36–37
Negotiating, 151
Neurological factors. See Brain differences
Neurologists, 376
Neuropsychologists, 382
NJCLD (National Joint Committee on Learning Disabilities), 104
"No-cessation" rule, 21
No Child Left Behind Act (NCLBA) (2002), 36–37
Nondiscriminatory evaluation, 21–22, 23–24, 25
Nonverbal working memory, 168
Northwest Regional Program, 451–452
Note-taking devices, 475
Novelty, 183
Nursing services, 18
Nutrition services, 18

Obsessions, 286
Obsessive-compulsive disorder, 134
Occupational therapy, 18, 297, 350–351, 355, 376
OCR (Office of Civil Rights), 331
OCRs (optical character readers), 475
Office of Civil Rights (OCR), 331
OHI. See Other health impairments
Open head injuries, 375
Opportunistic infections, 323
Oppositional defiant disorder, 135, 137, 176
Optical character readers (OCRs), 475
Oral/aural communication, 428, 440–441
Oral transliteration, 446, 448
Orientation and mobility (O&M) skills, 18, 477, 478, 483
Orthopedic impairments, 344. See also Physical disabilities
Other health impairments (OHI), 310–341
  asthma, 317–320, 327
  and attention deficit/hyperactivity disorder, 164–165, 179–180
  brain injuries, 374

Other health impairments, *(continued)*
cancer, 320–321
case study, 310–311, 340
causes, 326–327
challenges of, 313
and collaboration, 336–337
definitions, 312
diabetes, 322–323, 327
epilepsy, 315–317
evaluation, 328–330, 335–336
exemplar programs, 337–339
HIV, 323–326
and inclusion, 330–333, 334
prevalence, 327
sickle cell disease, 310–311, 312, 314–315
technology tips, 313
and traumatic brain injury, 381
and universally designed learning, 333–336
Otitis media, 433
Outcomes, 36–37, 72–73
Outer-directedness. *See* Inner/outer-directedness
Outer ear, 426

Pain, 310, 315
Panic disorder, 134
Paraplegia, 349
Paraprofessionals, 85–86
Parents
advocacy centers, 78–79, 84, 97, 245
and collaboration, 82, 84
counseling/training, 18
and emotional or behavioral disorders, 153, 157
IDEA on, 32
and inclusion, 70
and multicultural considerations, 94
Parents of Watts (POW), 245
Part B of the IDEA, 17, 19
Part C of the IDEA, 19
Partial participation, 268–269, 270
Partial seizures, 315
Patterns (Caton, Pester, & Bradley), 470
Pawsitive Living, 138
P-BLISS program, 205
PBL (problem-based learning), 213–215, 217, 219
PDAs (Personal Data Assistants), 388
Peak flow meter, 318
Peer Buddies, 273
Peer relationships. *See also* Inclusion; Peer tutoring; Social characteristics
and attention deficit/hyperactivity disorder, 180
insensitivity, 332–333, 334
and severe and multiple disabilities, 272, 273, 275, 276
Peer tutoring, 81
and physical disabilities, 369

and severe and multiple disabilities, 269, 272, 273
PEGS (Program for Exceptionally Gifted Students), 195, 220–221
Pennsylania Association for Retarded Citizens [PARC] v. Commonwealth of Pennsylvania, 16
Pentagonal implicit theory, 196–197
"People-first" language, 8
Percutaneous umbilical blood sampling, 261, 262
Performance standards, 45–46, 51–52, 54
Perinatal factors, 172, 230–231, 327, 345
Perseveration, 286
Personal Data Assistants (PDAs), 388
Personal intervention plans, 384–385
Personal Skills Map, 152
Pervasive developmental disorders, 284
Pet-assisted programs, 138
Peterson's Colleges with Programs for Students with Learning Disabilities or Attention Deficit Disorder (Mangrum & Strichart), 191
PET (positron emission tomographic) scans, 109, 382
Phenylketonuria (PKU), 260
Phobias, 134
Phonological awareness, 107
Phonology, 406, 409
Physical disabilities, 342–371. *See also* Other health impairments; Severe and multiple disabilities; Traumatic brain injury
case study, 342–343, 370
causes, 345–346, 347, 349
cerebral palsy, 344–346
and collaboration, 360, 362
definitions, 344
evaluation, 350–353
exemplar programs, 363–369
and inclusion, 353–354, 355
muscular dystrophy, 342–343, 348–349
and placement, 65, 353
prevalence, 349
prevention, 350
spina bifida, 346–348, 351
technology tips, 358
terminology issues, 7, 344
and traumatic brain injury, 376, 378
and universally designed learning, 354, 356–360, 361, 362
Physical therapy, 18, 355
Physicians, 176, 388, 389, 463
Pidgin sign language, 429, 442
PKU (phenylketonuria), 260
Placement. *See also* Inclusion
age/grade appropriate, 67–68
and attention deficit/hyperactivity disorder, 180, 183
change of placement rule, 21

and autism, 293
and communication disorders, 415
and emotional or behavioral disorders, 65, 147
and hearing loss/impairment, 439
home-school placement, 67–68
and learning disabilities, 116
and mental retardation, 237, 238–239
and other health impairments, 330
and physical disabilities, 65, 353
residential settings, 64–65, 147, 303
and severe and multiple disabilities, 267–268
trends, 61–64
Pollutants. *See* Environmental factors
Positive behavior support, 283, 286, 287, 294–296, 300, 302
sample plan, 304–306
Positron emission tomographic (PET) scans, 109, 382
Postconcussional syndrome (mild TBI) (MTBI), 375, 377
Postlingual hearing loss, 433
Postnatal factors, 172, 230–231, 327, 345
Postschool employment, 37
Postsecondary/transitional exemplar programs. *See* Transitional/postsecondary exemplar programs
Post-traumatic stress disorder, 134
Poverty, 10, 13. *See also* Socioeconomic status
and emotional or behavioral disorders, 141
and mental retardation, 232, 234, 245
Power of 2, 122
POW (Parents of Watts), 245
Pragmatics, 408, 410
PRAXIS Standards for Special Education, 488–489
Predictability needs, 287
Predominantly hyperactive-impulsive type (HI) of AD/HD, 165, 167, 174
Predominantly inattentive type (IN) of AD/HD, 165, 174
Prelingual hearing loss, 432
Prenatal factors, 172, 230–231, 327, 345, 432
Prenatal testing, 261, 262
Prereferral, 22
Prevalence
attention deficit/hyperactivity disorder, 175–176
autism, 289
communication disorders, 410–411
disabilities, 4–6
emotional or behavioral disorders, 142, 144
giftedness, 203–204
hearing loss/impairment, 433
learning disabilities, 110, 111
mental retardation, 234
other health impairments, 327
physical disabilities, 349
severe and multiple disabilities, 261

traumatic brain injury, 381
  visual loss/impairment, 463
Primary prevention, 233
Privacy, 324–325, 331–332
Problem-based learning (PBL), 213–215, 217, 219
Problem solving, 150, 151, 276, 409
Procedural due process, 27, 31–32
Process evaluation, 208–209
Procrastination, 169
Product evaluation, 208
Professional development, 70, 238, 299
Professional organizers, 187
Professional standards. *See* Standards/topics alignment matrix
Program for Exceptionally Gifted Students (PEGS), 195, 220–221
Project TASSEL, 250–252
Psychological services, 18
Psychomotor (temporal lobe) seizures, 315
Psychotropic medications, 164, 176, 178
Public Law 94-142 (Education of All Handicapped Students Act). *See* Individuals with Disabilities Education Act
Pullout model, 123, 392–393. *See also* Resource rooms
Punishment, 296
Pyramid Parent Training Center, 78–79, 97, 99

Quail Run Elementary School, 420–421
Questioning, 415

Race/ethnicity, 11–14. *See also* Multicultural considerations
  and asthma, 317, 318
  and attention deficit/hyperactivity disorder, 175
  and diabetes, 322
  and discrimination, 15, 99
  and dropout rates, 37
  and emotional or behavioral disorders, 12, 144
  and giftedness, 12, 204–205
  and hearing loss/impairment, 431
  and high-stakes accountability, 53
  and mental retardation, 12, 234
  and placement, 64
  and severe and multiple disabilities, 266
Raintree Montessori School, 275
Reach for Health Community Youth Service Learning Program, 324
Reading
  digital textbooks, 55
  and hearing loss/impairment, 447
  and learning disabilities, 107
  and No Child Left Behind Act, 45
  and visual loss/impairment, 466, 469–470, 471

Reading Mastery curriculum, 119–120
Real-time captioning, 450, 453
Real-time graphic display, 450
Reconstitution, 169
Recreation services, 18
Reentry planning, 335, 392
Referral, 14, 22
Reflective assessment/evaluation, 209
Regular education initiative, 66
Rehabilitation Act, 34, 35, 180. *See also* Section 504 of the Rehabilitation Act
Rehabilitation professionals, 388–389
Rehabilitative counseling services, 18
Related services
  and collaboration, 85
  IDEA on, 17, 18
  and other health impairments, 328, 330
Relaxation techniques, 318–319
Relevance, 183
Repetitive behavior, 286
Residential settings, 64–65, 147, 303
Resiliency, 132, 133, 141
Resonance, 405
Resource reallocation, 69, 88
Resource rooms, 65, 69, 123
Respite care, 330
Response options, 95–96
Restructuring, 66, 67, 88
Role-playing, 422
Routines, 287
Rubella (German measles), 432
Running away, 135

Savant syndrome, 288–289
Scheduling, 89
Schizophrenia, 137
School choice, 45
School factors
  emotional or behavioral disorders, 141–142
  mental retardation, 231–232
School health services, 18
Schoolhouse Palace, 451
School truancy, 135
Schoolwide enrichment model (SEM), 203, 210–213, 217
School year length, 89
Scoliosis, 349
Screen enlargement/navigation systems, 475
Screening, 22
Screen readers, 475
Secondary/middle exemplar programs. *See* Middle/secondary exemplar programs
Secondary prevention, 233
Section 504 of the Rehabilitation Act, 34, 35, 180, 188
Seizures, 176, 315–316
Selective attention, 167
Self-acceptance, 180
Self-advocacy, 477, 479

Self-care skills, 257
Self-concept, 109, 431
Self-determination, 81
  and mental retardation, 230, 240–244, 248–249, 251
  and severe and multiple disabilities, 264–265, 266
Self-determined learning model of instruction, 241–244, 248–249
Self-efficacy, 185, 191, 366
Self-injurious behavior, 286–287
Self-management, 149, 185
Self-questioning strategy, 118
Self-regulation characteristics, 167–169
Self-reinforcement, 185
Semantic mapping, 447
Semantics, 408, 410
SEM (schoolwide enrichment model), 203, 210–213, 217
Sensorineural hearing loss, 432
Sensory disorders, 287, 288, 297
Sensory impairments. *See* Hearing loss/impairment; Visual loss/impairment
Sentence writing strategy, 127
Service coordination services, 18
Service learning, 150, 153–154
Setting events, 300
Severe and multiple disabilities, 254–281
  case study, 254–255, 279–280
  causes, 260–261
  characteristics, 257–259
  and collaboration, 272–273
  definitions, 256
  evaluation, 262–265, 266
  exemplar programs, 274–279
  and inclusion, 72–73, 265, 267–268, 269, 274–275
  prevalence, 261
  prevention, 261, 262
  technology tips, 271
  and traumatic brain injury, 381
  and universally designed learning, 268–272
Severe discrepancies, 105, 111, 113
Sexuality, 368
Shaken-impact syndrome, 381
Short-term memory, 227–228
Siblings, 86
Sickle cell disease, 310–311, 312, 314–315
Silent epidemic, 381
Simultaneous communication, 428–429, 441–442
Social characteristics. *See also* Peer relationships
  attention deficit/hyperactivity disorder, 168, 180
  autism, 285, 296–297
  communication disorders, 417–418
  giftedness, 200, 201–202
  hearing loss/impairment, 429–431
  learning disabilities, 109

Social characteristics. (*continued*)
  traumatic brain injury, 380
  visual loss/impairment, 460
Social factors
  hearing loss/impairment, 429–431
  mental retardation, 231–232
Social interaction theories of language
  development, 409
Social maladjustment, 133, 135, 137
Social stories, 296–297, 298
Social work services in schools, 18
Socioeconomic status, 9–11, 13
  and emotional or behavioral disorders, 141
  and giftedness, 204–205
  and mental retardation, 232, 234, 245
SO Prepared for Citizenship, 153, 154, 155
Spastic cerebral palsy, 344
Special education
  outcomes, 36–37, 72–73
  personnel, 15
  statistics, 4–6
Special education classrooms, 65
Specialized settings, 65. *See also* Placement
Specific language impairments, 409
Speech development, 403
Speech disorders, 400, 404–405. *See also*
  Communication disorders
Speech-language pathologists, 18, 413, 441
Speech reading, 441
Spina bifida, 346–348, 351
Spina bifida occulta, 346, 347
Spinal muscular atrophy, 342–343, 348–349
Sports injuries, 381
Staffing patterns, 89
Standardized tests, 204. *See also* Intelligence
  tests
Standards-based reform, 44–53
  and accountability, 48–49, 52
  and content/performance standards,
    45–46, 50–52
Standards/topics alignment matrix, 487–504
  standards summaries, 487–495
  table, 495–504
STARBRIGHT Foundation, 313
"Stay-put" rule, 21
Strength-based interventions, 132, 133–134,
    147–148, 150, 160
Stress, 318
Student advisory boards, 83–84
Student participation in IEP process, 32
Students with exceptionalities
  race/ethnicity, 11–14
  socioeconomic status, 9–11, 13
  statistics, 4–6
  terminology issues, 6–8
Stuttering, 405
Substance abuse, 135
Suicide, 135, 136, 380
Supplementary aids and support services, 30
Supported employment programs, 34

Supports Intensity Scale, 235
Susceptibility genes, 327
Suspension, 21
Syntax, 406, 408, 409

Tactual/kinesthetic approach, 471–472
Tagging, 135
Take Charge!, 189–190
Talent pool, 203
TBI. *See* Traumatic brain injury
Teasing. *See* Insensitivity
Tech Act. *See* Technology-Related
    Assistance to Individuals with
    Disabilities Act
Technology. *See* Assistive technology;
    Technology tips
Technology-Related Assistance to
    Individuals with Disabilities Act
    (1988), 34, 354
Technology tips
  attention deficit/hyperactivity disorder, 186
  autism, 298
  communication disorders, 418
  emotional or behavioral disorders, 152
  giftedness, 212
  hearing loss/impairment, 451
  learning disabilities, 124–125
  mental retardation, 228
  multicultural considerations, 95
  other health impairments, 313
  physical disabilities, 358
  severe and multiple disabilities, 271
  traumatic brain injury, 388
  universally designed learning, 61, 62
  visual loss/impairment, 475
Temporal lobe (psychomotor) seizures, 315
"Ten-day" rule, 21
Teratogens/pollutants. *See* Environmental
    factors
Terminology issues, 6–8, 235, 237, 427
Tertiary prevention, 233
Test of Problem Solving (TOPS), 382
Text telephones, 449
Thematic organizers, 447
Theme approach, 217
Theory of mind, 285
Thinking Creatively with Pictures (Torrance),
    207, 208
Thinking Creatively with Words (Torrance),
    207–208
Three-ring definition of giftedness, 196
Threshold, 435–436
Tics, 286
Tiffany Park Elementary School, 300, 302
Time perception, 169
Timing factors, 230–231
Tips. *See* Collaboration tips; Inclusion tips;
    Technology tips
Tolerance, 151
Tonic-clonic seizures, 315

Topographical classification systems, 345
TOPS (Test of Problem Solving), 382
T.O. School, 90
Total blindness, 459
Total communication, 441–442
Tracking, 12
Transition-after-graduation plans, 330
Transitional/postsecondary exemplar programs
  attention deficit/hyperactivity
    disorder, 191
  autism, 302–303, 306
  communication disorders, 422
  emotional or behavioral disorders, 159–160
  giftedness, 221
  hearing loss/impairment, 452–453
  learning disabilities, 126–128
  mental retardation, 250–252
  other health impairments, 339
  physical disabilities, 367–369
  severe and multiple disabilities, 278–279
  traumatic brain injury, 394–396
  visual loss/impairment, 483–484
Translators/interpreters, 86–87, 446, 448
Transportation services, 18
Traumatic brain injury (TBI), 372–397
  case study, 372–373, 396
  causes, 380–381
  characteristics, 375–376, 378–380
  and collaboration, 388–390
  definitions, 374
  evaluation, 382–385
  exemplar programs, 390–396
  and inclusion, 385, 386
  and placement, 65
  prevalence, 381
  technology tips, 388
  terminology issues, 7
  types, 374–375
  and universally designed learning, 385–388
Travel, 477, 478
Tunnel vision, 458
Tutoring, 125–126

UCSD (University of California at
    San Diego), 369
Universally designed learning, 54–61. *See
    also* Universally designed learning for
    visual loss/impairment
  and attention deficit/hyperactivity
    disorder, 183, 185
  and autism, 292, 294–297
  and communication disorders,
    415–418, 419
  and curriculum, 54, 56
  defined, 54
  and emotional or behavioral disorders,
    149–150
  and evaluation, 59
  and giftedness, 210–215
  and hearing loss/impairment, 440–445

and instruction, 57–59
and learning disabilities, 114–120
and mental retardation, 239–244
and other health impairments, 333–336
and physical disabilities, 354, 356–360, 361, 362
principles summary, 62
and severe and multiple disabilities, 268–272
technology tips, 61, 62
and traumatic brain injury, 385–388
Universally designed learning for visual loss/impairment, 469–479
curriculum augmentation, 475–479
instructional adaptation, 469–475
Universal precautions, 325
University of California at San Diego (UCSD), 369
University of Florida Multidisciplinary Diagnostic and Training Program (MDTP), 189
University of Virginia Summer Enrichment Program, 202
Utah Extension Consultant Division, 452

Variety, 183
Vassar College, 191
Violence, 381, 391
Virtual reality, 356, 358
Visual acuity, 458
Visual Assistant, 228
Visual disability (including blindness), 458. See also Visual loss/impairment
Visualization, 174
Visual loss/impairment, 456–486. See also Universally designed learning for visual loss/impairment
case study, 456–457, 485
causes, 462–463
characteristics, 459–462
and collaboration, 479–480
evaluation, 463–466
exemplar programs, 481–484
and inclusion, 468–469, 471, 480
prevalence, 463
and residential placement, 65
and severe and multiple disabilities, 257–258
technology tips, 475
and traumatic brain injury, 378

Visual/performing arts, 200
Vocal nodules, 405
Voice disorders, 405

WebQuests, 212
Wechsler Individualized Achievement Test (WIAT), 113
Wechsler Intelligence Scale for Children (WISC), 105, 111, 178, 382
Whittier High School, 277
Whole language, 123
WIAT (Wechsler Individualized Achievement Test), 113
WISC (Wechsler Intelligence Scale for Children), 105, 111, 178, 382
Work to Life program, 150, 153–154
Wraparound model, 147–148, 158–159
Written language, 107

YouthNet/Reseau Ado, 159–160

Zero-reject principle, 20–21
Zero tolerance policies, 138

Photo Credits